INTERNATIONAL POLITICS

International Politics

THE WESTERN STATE SYSTEM
AND THE WORLD COMMUNITY

Frederick L. Schuman

WOODROW WILSON PROFESSOR OF GOVERNMENT

WILLIAMS COLLEGE

Illustrated with Fifty Maps
by George D. Brodsky

SIXTH EDITION

McGRAW-HILL BOOK COMPANY, INC.

New York   Toronto   London

1958

INTERNATIONAL POLITICS

III
55687

To
Karl and Eleanor

PREFACE

A QUARTER of a century ago only one other textbook was available for college courses in World Politics: *International Relations,* by my good friend Raymond Leslie Buell. I nevertheless wrote in the Preface to the First Edition of the present work: "The literature of international relations is already staggering in volume and overwhelming in complexity. This circumstance imposes an imperative obligation upon every author who hurls another tome on top of the pile: that of justifying his conduct to his own conscience and to the decent opinions of mankind."

This obligation is far more imperative in 1958 than in 1933. By now innumerable other texts, flowing endlessly from the fertile pens of eager authors and the busy presses of hopeful publishers, have filled to overflowing a market which at best remains of modest size. Why then add to the torrent with a new version of an old book? Why should not the aging scholars of yesteryear, whatever their illusions of ripeness and wisdom, yield the field to fresh and ardent youth?

My own inclination, I am bound to say, suggests the obvious answers. But my perusal of other texts (may their authors and publishers forgive me!) leads me, alas, to a different conclusion. So mightily have these volumes waxed in numbers that I find it no longer possible even to list them, as I have done in previous editions, much less to attempt a comparative evaluation.

Quantitatively, this output is puzzling. If it reflected a corresponding increase of interest and enrollment in such courses in American colleges and universities, the result would deserve to be hailed with enthusiasm by all toilers in this academic vineyard. But, so far as I am aware, no such increase has taken place, nor does it seem at all likely in the years to come. America's response to the challenge of Russia, even before *sputnik,* was to seek safety not through diplomacy but through armaments. Students are therefore urged not to study the problems of World Politics with a view toward contributing to their nonviolent solution, but to study mathematics, physics, and engineering to the end that Americans may surpass Russians in the art of co-annihilation.

Qualitatively, the deluge of textbooks leaves much to be desired. This circumstance moves me to anguish and guilt, since several of the contributors are my former students. Others have borrowed the title, and sometimes part of the subject matter, of the present work, thus demonstrating anew that mimesis is the sincerest form of adulation. Yet none of these texts, in my possibly prejudiced opinion, meets the needs of American undergraduates engaged in the study of international affairs.

Such students may terminate their academic inquiry into the world community with the completion of such a course as this book is designed for—or may go on to advanced courses with a view toward training themselves for careers in teaching, scholarship, public service, or international business. In either case, as future citizens or future specialists, they require a solid grounding in the antecedents, origins, and development of the State System; in the elements of international law, diplomatic practice, and international organization; in power politics, war, colonialism, and the anti-colonial, nationalist, and racial revolutions of our epoch; in diplomatic history, comparative politics, and the foreign policies of the major Powers; and in political geography and demography. Only through the diligent study of such data can students acquire critical skills in analyzing the alternatives available to policy-makers and interpreting, within a relevant and operationally workable frame of reference, the recent, current, and ever-changing international scene.

My decision to offer a Sixth Edition of the present work is, I hope and believe, less a product of habit than a consequence of the conclusion that no other available text fulfills these requirements. One offers a generalized "theory" of international politics with a minimum of factual information. Another presents a plethora of facts with no hints as to their meaning. Still others, including those advertised as "balanced," stress one or another facet of the phenomena of international relations to the neglect of the rest. Some eschew all judgments in pursuit of a fatuous "objectivity," while others, denying the unity of the human community and the universal fallibility of Man, boldly enlist in the service of Virtue against Vice.

All such efforts should doubtless be welcomed and encouraged. But no adequate education in world affairs can be derived from such sources. To describe the present attempt as "adequate" would be indicative of insufferable conceit. No one is more conscious of its inadequacies than the author. Yet I believe that these pages, if assigned and discussed by imaginative teachers and studied by thoughtful students, will contribute more significantly than other available books to a working knowledge of the origins, forms, forces, and prospects of the World Community in our time of troubles.

This approach to world politics furnishes a method of ordering the multitudinous and confusing data of international relations. It also offers tools of analysis and prediction. And this, pragmatically speaking, is the whole point, since students and other readers will not long remember contemporary factual details but may well retain a method of interpretation and forecasting, applicable to times past, to current happenings, and to the probable shape of things to come.

The utility of the method can best be judged by comparing the speculative prognostications to which it has led over the years with actual subsequent events. The first edition (April, 1933) predicted "world-wide abandonment of the gold standard and world-wide inflation," "the death-knell of German democracy and . . . the 'inevitable' next war between the revisionist States and the *status quo* bloc" (pp. ix–x). It also suggested that current national policies meant "a progressive and accelerated disintegration of the world economy and a relapse of the Western world into international anarchy, war, and suicidal combat between the imperial Powers" (p. 849) ; that Japan would "descend on the Asiatic mainland and wrest the Philippine Islands from the United States" (p. 850) ; and that "Central Europe will be devastated on a scale unknown since the Thirty Years' War. Victors and vanquished alike will be brought to ruin, and out of the wreckage Red revolution will inevitably raise its head" (p. 851).

This grim prognosis was not a product of melancholia but of a conviction, derived from an analysis and interpretation of unpleasant but inescapable facts, that the human community of 1933 had not only failed (despite contemporary illusions to the contrary) to "outlaw war as an instrument of national policy" but had involved itself in schisms among the sovereign manmade monsters of our State System which rendered a second World War almost "inevitable."

The same method of analysis led to forecasts in the second edition (April, 1937) that the "final product of Fascism is imperialist war" (p. 735) ; "the day will come when the dictators will dare to risk new and greater aggressions which will compel their victims, with backs to the wall, to resist by force" (p. 737) ; Germany, Italy, and Japan, "entangled in hopeless inner contradictions leaving them no choice but war, will continue their careers of conquest until halted or crushed by a superior coalition" (p. 740). But the counter-coalition, it was suggested, would materialize too late to avert hostilities. The French bloc would disintegrate. Czechoslovakia would be betrayed, abandoned, and partitioned (p. 741). Should the new war of movement again become a war of attrition, "the Fascist Powers will ultimately prove weak and the USSR will prove strong" and seek to extend Communism by the sword (pp. 742–743).

A Third Edition (April, 1941) postulated the probability of Soviet and American involvement in Britain's war against the Axis and the ultimate defeat of the new world conquerors, to be followed either by a *modus vivendi* between the East and West as a basis for a new world order or by another contest for mastery of the globe. By 1948, when the Fourth Edition was published, the Communist conspiracy and the American resolve to defend the Free World against Red totalitarianism had precipitated "Cold War." But the analytical tools here employed indicated that neither of the Super-Powers could defeat the other in a contest of arms and that World War III was therefore unlikely, regardless of whether contemporary mankind moved, or failed to move, toward the age-old ideal of the Brotherhood of Man and the Federation of the World.

This relatively hopeful estimate of the future, further expounded in a Fifth Edition in 1953, is reinforced by the new analysis essayed in the chapters that follow. World wars require the division of the Powers into hostile coalitions, a prolonged arms race, and "incidents" to precipitate explosion. All these we have once more in abundance. But world wars also require a plausible illusion of military superiority on one side or the other, a plausible strategic plan for "victory," and a resultant willingness by policy-makers to make demands, supported by force, for components or positions of power, deemed decisive for future fighting capacity, which the enemy will resist by force. And these prerequisites of Armageddon are lacking and will continue to be lacking, thanks to the rearmament of the democracies and the industrialization of Russia which, together, promise a global stalemate of indefinite duration.

A few further comments may be in order regarding the methodological presuppositions, the pedagogical assumptions, and the value-preferences implicit in the present work. As for the first of these, I have argued elsewhere (e.g., in July, 1955, at the Ford Foundation Seminar on the Teaching of International Relations at the State University of Iowa, organized by Vernon Van Dyke) that the teaching of World Politics should aim at a systematic application and synthesis of what have come to be called the "behavioral sciences." This I believe, albeit conceding the formidable difficulties of the enterprise. But I do not believe that the time is ripe to essay such a venture in a textbook. Wise teachers can do much in this direction in the classroom. A textbook can suggest inter-relationships and implications. But its primary function, as I see it, is still that of presenting in well ordered and readable fashion the basic factual data of contacts among nations and stimulating new thinking about policy-making in the face of the dilemma of the 20th Century.

Pedagogically speaking, the present text is not designed for "gut" courses imposing few demands on students. Teachers who prefer softness and slackness to rigorous training in disciplined thinking and mastery of facts would do well to avoid this volume. For my own part, I can see little hope for the future unless American students can at least equal, and preferably surpass, their confreres in Western Europe, the USSR, and China in serious concern with the realities of international experience.

As for value-preferences, I do not believe (as one critic alleged of the Fourth Edition of this work) that contemporary Mankind will either achieve World Government or commit suicide. In the long perspective of many tomorrows, I suspect that some facsimile of World Government, at least in atomic matters, will prove essential to save humanity from its age-old propensity, which may no longer be safely indulged in during the thermonuclear era, to engage in mutual slaughter and destruction. In the short run, I believe—more than ever in the spring of 1958 when complex preparations for another

PREFACE

"summit conference" were painfully getting under way—that today's statesmen, if they would serve life rather than death, must subordinate calculations of strategy to the possibilities of diplomacy as a means of resolving the problems of power in a still anarchic world.

I can only hope that this Sixth Edition still possesses some of the qualities which led Charles A. Beard to write of the First Edition: "Professor Schuman is a pioneer in breaking from the solemn formalities of abstract international law and politics and daring to view realistically the moving scene as a whole and to present his interpretation of its choices to the judgment of mankind. I welcome this dynamic, ripping challenge to those who preside with feeble hopes over dust and ashes."

For the rest, I find myself in sympathy with George Frost Kennan's appeals for "disengagement" and "coexistence" (see *Russia, The Atom and The West*, Harper & Brothers, New York, 1958) and with the sentiments voiced by Gen. Douglas MacArthur, speaking in Los Angeles, Jan. 26, 1955:

The agony of the cold war is kept alive by two great illusions. The one a complete belief on the part of the Soviet world that the capitalist countries are preparing to attack them; that sooner or later we intend to strike. And the other a complete belief on the part of the capitalist countries that the Soviets are preparing to attack us; that sooner or later they intend to strike. Both are wrong. Each side, so far as the masses are concerned, is equally desirous of peace. For either side war with the other would mean nothing but disaster. Both equally dread it. But the constant acceleration of preparation may well, without specific intent, ultimately produce a spontaneous combustion. . . .

When will some great figure in power have sufficient imagination and moral courage to translate this universal wish for peace—which is rapidly becoming a necessity—into actuality? It is the leaders who are the laggards. The disease of power seems to confuse and bewilder them. Never do they dare to state the bald truth that the next great advance in the evolution of civilization cannot take place until war is abolished.

Acknowledgments of gratitude for aid in the preparation of the present work are difficult to render with justice. Many have contributed, including my students at Williams, at the University of California (1955), and at the University of Chicago (1956) where in 1932–33 this work was first begun. I owe much to my colleagues, MacAlister Brown and Michael Reagan, who have contributed richly to "Political Science 3–4" at Williams, as did Fred Greene, Dwight Simpson, and their predecessors in earlier years. But my major indebtedness is, as always, to George D. Brodsky of Chicago, who has once more most generously taken time out from a busy life to draft the maps which illustrate the present edition. No textbook in International Relations is any better than the maps which reveal the geographical facts of life. The fifty Brodsky maps in the present work, if carefully perused, will prove to be invaluable guides to past and contemporary issues and problems. I am also

PREFACE

deeply grateful to Grace R. Perez for the faithful and accurate typing of the entire manuscript, and to all who have aided in indexing.

Frederick L. Schuman

Williamstown, Mass.
 February 22, 1958

Postscript in Springtime: At the vernal equinox, 1958, the actors on the stage of world politics played new variations on the themes of earlier months and years. Among many of the world's poor, violence remained the prime mode of political action. Castro's Cuban rebels (perhaps temporarily) failed to overthrow *caudillo* Batista. Sumatra's rebels were crushed (perhaps temporarily) by Indonesian arms. Algeria's rebels continued to harass the French forces arrayed against them. When Gaillard sought to "compromise" the French-Tunisian quarrel through Anglo-American mediation, his Ministry was ousted, April 16, in an Assembly vote of 321 to 255. Ardent Leftists demanding "peace" in Algeria and intransigent Rightists demanding "victory" combined, incongruously, to overthrow the Cabinet. Not soon nor easily would the paradox of a bankrupt French colonialism be resolved.

Among the world's wealthy Super-Powers, overt violence continued to be avoided, albeit precariously. Khrushchev assumed the Soviet Premiership on March 27. Having completed a new series of atomic tests, his government (March 31) announced a unilateral cessation of testing and challenged the USA to follow suit—failing which Soviet experimentation would be resumed. Eisenhower, on the eve of new U.S. tests in search of "clean" bombs and "tactical" thermonuclear weapons, derided the Soviet gesture as a "gimmick" and declined the challenge—despite the certainty that continued tests would make "America" a name of evil all over the globe. Amid involved negotiations for a "summit conference," championed by Moscow and resisted by the Western Powers, Gromyko (April 18) protested "provocative" flights of U.S. bombers over the Arctic toward Soviet frontiers, warned of "accidental" atomic war, and appealed to the UN Security Council—where, obviously, nothing could be done to alleviate East-West tensions so long as neither side would moderate its fear-inspired expectations and demands for the sake of a *detente*.

Mankind in 1958 was more than ever trapped in the dilemma posed by a technology of co-annihilation coupled with the continued practice of power politics in a new era which rendered the age-old game obsolete. The outcome might be the fortuitous immolation of Western civilization and, possibly, the suicide of the human race. Or it might be more "muddling through" and the dawn of a new era of life. The pages which follow offer hope, rather than despair, on a basis of "realism" rather than wishful thinking.

F.L.S., April 20, 1958

CONTENTS

PREFACE vii

MAPS xvii

TREATIES AND OTHER INTERNATIONAL ACTS xix

PROLOGUE: THE HUMAN CONDITION

1. Cosmic Enigma 2
2. How People Think about Politics 6
3. The Ascent of Man 11
4. Culture and Government 14
5. The Mystery of History 18
6. Quo Vadis? 24
   Suggested Readings 28

A BOOK OF ORIGINS

CHAPTER I. EARLY STATES AND STATE SYSTEMS 32

1. Sumeria and Egypt 32
2. The Glory That Was Greece 38
3. The Grandeur That Was Rome 45
4. The Memory of the Great Peace 49
   Suggested Readings 54

CHAPTER II. THE DAWN OF THE WEST 55

1. Europe and Asia 55
2. The Rise of "Realism" 62
3. The European State System 67
4. Europe and the World 72
   Suggested Readings 79

CHAPTER III. FROM MASTERY TO MISERY 80

1. The Magic of Machines 80
2. Patriots and Imperialists 86
3. Europe in the Shadows 90
   Suggested Readings 104

A BOOK OF FORMS

CHAPTER IV. THE QUEST FOR LAW 108

1. The Sources of Justice 108
2. States as Persons 110
3. The Rights of Sovereignties 115

CONTENTS

4. Problems of Ownership 119
5. The Law of Contracts 125
6. The Rules of War 127
7. The Law of Neutrality 133
8. The Puzzle of Enforcement 137
   Suggested Readings 142

CHAPTER V. THE SETTLEMENT OF CONFLICTS 144

1. States as Policemen 144
2. States as Bargainers 148
3. The Role of Arbitrators 152
4. The Task of Courts 157
   Suggested Readings 164

CHAPTER VI. THE PRACTICE OF DIPLOMACY 166

1. The Art of Negotiation 166
2. What Diplomats Do 171
3. The Management of Foreign Affairs 177
4. Around the Green Table 191
   Suggested Readings 201

CHAPTER VII. THE QUEST FOR GOVERNMENT 203

1. Hopes of Order 203
2. Experiment in Geneva 210
3. United Nations 227
4. Formulas for Peace 248
5. Pleas for One World 263
   Suggested Readings 268

A BOOK OF FORCES

CHAPTER VIII. THE GUARDING OF POWER 272

1. The Premise of Violence 272
2. Diplomacy as War 278
3. War as Diplomacy 284
4. Arma Virumque 291
5. The Strategy of Co-annihilation 298
   Suggested Readings 303

CHAPTER IX. THE BUILDING OF EMPIRES 306

1. Colonialism 306
2. The Anti-colonial Revolution 314
3. Recessional 325
   Suggested Readings 335

CHAPTER X. THE MAKING OF NATIONS 336

1. The Religion of Patriotism 336
2. The Cults of Intolerance 341
3. Patriotism and Profits 356
4. The New Nationalisms 370
   Suggested Readings 394

CONTENTS

AN ADDENDA ON THE ANATOMY OF ANARCHY
  A CASE STUDY: SUEZ, SATELLITE, SINAI, 1956–58 396

  1. Comment on Method 396
  2. Two Waterways 399
  3. A Failure of Statesmanship 404
  4. Recourse to Force 415
  5. The Victory of the Vanquished 422
  6. Aftermath 426
     Suggested Readings 431

A BOOK OF PROSPECTS

CHAPTER XI. THE HERITAGE OF FASCISM 434

  1. The New Caesars 434
  2. Japan: From Militarism to Pacifism 437
     Suggested Readings 454
  3. Italy: From Despotism to Democracy 455
     Suggested Readings 467
  4. Germany: From Psychosis to Partition 467
     Suggested Readings 496

CHAPTER XII. THE CHALLENGE OF COMMUNISM 498

  1. USSR: The Endless Mission 498
     Suggested Readings 524
  2. China: The Mandate of Heaven 525
     Suggested Readings 541
  3. The Diplomacy of Coexistence 542
     Suggested Readings 547
  4. Disunity in Marxland 547
     Suggested Readings 553

CHAPTER XIII. THE DEFENSE OF DEMOCRACY 555

  1. France: The Lost Cause 555
     Suggested Readings 574
  2. Britain: Defeat in Victory 575
     Suggested Readings 586
  3. America: The Dilemmas of Power 587
     Suggested Readings 606
  4. Division in Freeland 608
     Suggested Readings 613

CHAPTER XIV. THE PROBLEMS OF THE POOR 614

  1. How Many Worlds? 614
  2. People, Poverty, and the Quest for Plenty 619
  3. The Politics of Penury 628
  4. The New Neutrals 641
     Suggested Readings 649

CHAPTER XV. THE ATOMIC AGE 652

  1. Prometheus and Caliban 652
  2. Physicists and Diplomats 659

CONTENTS

3. The Passing of Power Politics 674
    Suggested Readings 679

APPENDIX I: CHARTER OF THE UNITED NATIONS 681

APPENDIX II: COVENANT OF THE LEAGUE OF NATIONS 703

INDEX 713

MAPS

Early City-States and Kingdoms 35
The Greek State System, *c.* 431 B.C. 41
The Roman World State, A.D. 117 48
The Medieval State System, *c.* A.D. 1360 57
The Saracen Empire, A.D. 750 59
The Ottoman Empire, A.D. 1566 61
Emergence of the Modern State Systems: Europe in 1648 74
Europe in 1740 77
The Napoleonic Empire: Europe in 1810 83
The State System Restored: Europe in 1815 84
Europe in 1914 89
Imperial Germany over Europe, July, 1918 92
Europe after Versailles 94
Europe on Sept. 1, 1939 95
Europe on June 22, 1941 97
Hitler over Europe, Sept. 1, 1941 98
Europe in 1958: Populations 102
The World State System: Populations . . . . f. 105
The Conquest of Manchuria 219
The Conquest of Ethiopia 222
The Conquest of Spain 225
Palestine: The Partition Plan of 1947 239
The Korean War 243
The Caribbean 320
Near East Campaign, 1941 323
Language Groups, Central Europe 354
The Near East: Populations 378
India and Pakistan, 1947 383
Southeast Asia 388
The Mid East, 1956 418
Japan 439
The Expansion of Japan, 1895–1940 442
The Defeat of Japan 447
Italy and the Adriatic, 1919–1939 458
Allied Victory in the Mediterranean, 1942–1945 461
The German Republic 471
The Conquest of Austria and Czechoslovakia 475
The Conquest of Poland, 1939 478
Occupied Germany 484
Russian War Fronts, 1919–1920 500
War in Russia, 1941–1945 510
Soviet Imperialism, 1944–1948 515
Western China 528

MAPS

Eastern China 529
Russia and the Far East 546
The Conquest of France 562
The Western Campaign, 1941–1945 565
The United Kingdom 576
The North Atlantic 593
The New India 634

TREATIES AND OTHER INTERNATIONAL ACTS

(In chronological order of signature; page references are to summaries, excerpts, or full texts; for other references, see Index)

Lagash-Umma, 3000 B.C. 33
Egypt-Hittite, 1280 B.C. . . . . 34f.
Greek, ancient . . . . 41f.
Roman, ancient 47
Westphalia, 1648 74
Anglo-French, April 11, 1713 (Utrecht) 75
Hubertusburg and Paris, 1763 77
French-American, Feb. 6, 1778 589
Paris, May 30, 1814 84
Anglo-American (Ghent), Dec. 24, 1814 85
"Holy Alliance," Sept. 26, 1815 206
Paris, Nov. 20, 1815 85
Paris, March 30, 1856 87
Paris, April 16, 1856 131
Berlin, July 13, 1878 87
Triple Alliance, 1882 89
Constantinople Convention (Suez Canal), Oct. 29, 1888 400
Dual Alliance, 1894 89
Anglo-Japanese, 1902 89
Anglo-Russian, 1907 89
Root-Takahira Agreement, Nov. 30, 1908 327
Lansing-Ishii Agreement, Nov. 3, 1917 327
Covenant of the League of Nations, June 26, 1919 . . . . . . 703f.
Minority Treaties, 1919f. . . . . 347f.
Versailles, June 28, 1919 94
St. Germain, Sept. 10, 1919 94
Neuilly, Nov. 27, 1919 94
Trianon, June 4, 1920 94
Sévres, Aug. 10, 1920 94
Five-Power (Washington Conference), Feb. 6, 1922 253
Nine-Power Pact, Feb. 6, 1922 . . . . 327f.
Rapallo, April 16, 1922 471
Lausanne, July 24, 1923 94
Germany-USA, Dec. 8, 1923 364
Locarno, Aug. 16, 1925 249
Paris, Pact of, Aug. 27, 1928 251
London Naval, April 22, 1930 . . . . 253f.
Anglo-German Naval, June 18, 1935 255
Anglo-French-USA Naval, March 25, 1936 255
Anti-Comintern Pact, Nov. 25, 1936 443

TREATIES AND OTHER INTERNATIONAL ACTS

Munich, Oct. 1, 1938 99
Nazi-Soviet Pact, Aug. 23, 1939 . . . . 476f.
Triplice Pact, Sept. 27, 1940 444
Atlantic Charter, Aug. 14, 1941 193
Triplice Pact, Dec. 11, 1941 481
United Nations Declaration, Jan. 1, 1942 . . . . 193f.
Teheran Agreements, Dec. 1, 1943 194
Yalta Agreements, Feb. 11, 1945 195
Arab League, March 22, 1945 324
Charter of the United Nations, June 26, 1945 . . . . 681f.
Potsdam Agreements, Aug. 2, 1945 . . . . 195f.
Anglo-American Accord on Atomic Energy, Nov. 15, 1945 . . . . 660f.
EDC Accords, May 26–27, 1952 488
Peace Treaties of Feb. 10, 1947 (Italy, Bulgaria, Hungary, Rumania, Finland) . 197f.
U.S. Trusteeship Agreement, April 2, 1947 333
Charter of the Organization of American States, May 2, 1947 . . . . 319f.
Inter-American Treaty of Reciprocal Assistance (Act of Petropolis), Sept. 2, 1947 319
Soviet-Bulgarian Alliance, March 18, 1948 543
North Atlantic Treaty, April 4, 1949 . . . . 595f.
Council of Europe, May 5, 1949 266
Soviet-Chinese Alliance, Feb. 14, 1950 543
Schuman Plan, April 18, 1951 366
USA-Saudi Arabia, June 18, 1951 427
USA-Philippines, Aug. 30, 1951 596
USA-Australia and New Zealand, Sept. 1, 1951 597
Japan, Peace Treaty, Sept. 8, 1951 199
Japanese-American Security Treaty, Sept. 8, 1951 200
Anglo-Egyptian, Feb. 12, 1953 402
Korean Armistice, July 27, 1953 200
Anglo-Egyptian Accord, July, 1954 403
Indochinese Armistice, July 21, 1954 200
Iranian Oil Accord, Aug. 5, 1954 379
SEATO, Sept. 8, 1954 610
Paris Accords, Oct. 23, 1954 490
USA-Formosa, Dec. 2, 1954 . . . . 602f.
Warsaw Pact, May 14, 1955 554
Austria, May 15, 1955 . . . . 200f.
Baghdad Pact, Nov. 22, 1955 405
Suez Canal Accord, Oct. 11, 1956 411
Euromarket, March 25, 1957 366
Euratom, March 25, 1957 366
Morocco-Tunisia, March 30, 1957 373
United Arab Republic, Jan. 27, 1958 431

Naked and alone we came into exile. In her dark womb we did not know our mother's face; from the prison of her flesh have we come into the unspeakable and incommunicable prison of this earth. Which of us has known his brother? Which of us has looked into his father's heart? . . . Which of us has not remained forever a stranger and alone? O waste of loss, in the hot mazes, lost, among bright stars on this most weary unbright cinder, lost! Remembering speechlessly we seek the great forgotten language, the lost lane-end into heaven, a stone, a leaf, an unfound door. Where? When? O lost, and by the wind grieved, ghost, come back again.—THOMAS WOLFE, 1929.

Prologue

THE HUMAN CONDITION

It is possible that our race may be an accident, in a meaningless universe, living its brief life uncared for, on this dark, cooling star; but even so—and all the more—what marvelous creatures we are! What fairy-story, what tale from the Arabian Nights of the jinns, is a hundredth part as wonderful as this true fairy-story of the simians. . . . An amoeba on the beach, blind and helpless, a mere bit of pulp—that amoeba has grandsons today who read Kant and play symphonies. Will those grandsons in turn have descendants who will sail through the void, discover the foci of forces, the means to control them, and learn how to marshal the planets and grapple with space? Would it after all be any more startling than our rise from the slime? . . . Yet, even if we are permitted to have a long reign, and are not laid away with the failures, are we a success? We need so much spiritual insight, and we have so little. Our airships may someday float over the hills of Arcturus, but how will that help us if we cannot find the soul of the world? . . . We have no sure vision. Hopes, guesses, beliefs—that is all. . . . We, who crave so much to know, crave so little but knowing. Some of us wish to know Nature most; these are the scientists. Others, the saints and philosophers, wish to know God. Both are alike in their hearts, yes, in spite of their quarrels. Both seek to assuage, to no end, the old simian thirst.—CLARENCE DAY, *This Simian World*.

PROLOGUE

THE HUMAN CONDITION

1. COSMIC ENIGMA

Who can think of the sun costuming clouds/When all people are shaken/Or of night endazzled, proud/When people awaken/And cry and cry for help?

The craven antiquity of self,/Everyone, grows suddenly cold./The tea is bad, bread sad./How can the world so old be so mad/That the people die?

If, joy shall be without a book,/It lies, themselves within themselves,/If they will look/within themselves/and cry and cry for help

Within as pillars of the sun,/Supports of night. The tea,/The wine is good. The bread,/The meat is sweet./And they will not die.

—WALLACE STEVENS, "A Fading of the Sun," in *Ideas of Order*.[1]

A HUNDRED billion stars are thinly scattered through nothingness in the disk-like shape of a double convex lens. The thickness of the disk is a thousand light-years and its diameter one hundred thousand, with each light-year six trillion miles. The whole system rotates slowly around an axis. Off to one side, perhaps 35,000 light-years from the center, is a dwarf star which completes its circuit once every 200,000,000 years. This star, while not unique, is rare, for its peculiar fate is probably limited by the laws of chance to one star in a million. That fate consists in this—that, by happenstance several billion years ago, another star passed near enough to raise great tides of incandescent matter, some of which tore loose and circled in concentric orbits and then condensed and cooled into nine planets and sundry satellites, planetoids, asteroids, and comets.

The disk thus described, as best we can now discern its size and shape, is our galaxy of the Milky Way. The dwarf star is the sun. Its third planet, beyond Mercury and Venus, is Earth. This tiny globule, a mere mote in the infinities of interplanetary, to say nothing of interstellar space, is also not unique. But it is rare among planets in that its sphere is sheathed by a thin film of soil, water, and air. Within this film, all humans live and move and have their being, along with a bewildering variety of other forms of life—

[1] Reprinted with the permission of Alfred A. Knopf, Inc., from *The Collected Poems of Wallace Stevens*.

out of which human life presumably evolved. Whether any life exists on other planets of our own or other solar systems we do not know.

We know only that beneath the sheath in which we live is a sphere of rock with a core of molten nickel-iron. Beyond the sheath are the black reaches of the endless sky whose secrets many of the earthmen explored further during the International Geophysical Year of 1957–58. Nearby, some 240,000 miles away, the dead orb of the moon circles every month around our earthly home. Far off, 93,000,000 miles from our globe, blazes the blinding radiance of the sun. Here nuclear fusion, transmuting hydrogen into helium, begets huge volumes of light and heat warming the tiny wheeling planets and spreading outward into emptiness. Far beyond our circumambient ribbon of star-dust are other and larger "extra-galactic" nebulae, consisting of other billions of suns, some of which—who knows?—may also have planets; some of which— who knows?—may also sustain life. Beyond these are still other "universes," faintly visible in man's most searching telescopes.

What is the meaning and purpose of the light-spangled spectacle of the cosmos, all aglitter in the night of earth's shadow-side? Only men who fancy they can read the will of God pretend to know the answer. Only Man, among earth's creatures, poses the question. And he alone, and this but recently, is aware of his own insignificance in the scheme of things. Rocks and stars ask no questions. Other earth-animals also ask none, having brains inadequate for such riddles. Only *Homo sapiens,* with his far-ranging vision, his memories and dreams, and his exaggerated talent for thinking, wants to know the purpose and meaning of all he sees about him.

It may well be that his quest is vain, despite the advance of Science. For it is possible that "meaning" and "purpose" are merely puzzling aspects of uniquely human experience. They may have no equivalents or counterparts in nonhuman Nature, which may be purposeless and meaningless, nor even in the divine design of all that is or has been or will ever be.

Yet Man must strive to know and, in our time, to delve into the depths below and penetrate the voids above. Human exploration of space began in 1957 with Russia's *sputniks* circling the planet beyond our film of air. Efforts to reach the moon may one day gain their goal. Farther prospects are doubtful despite the fancies of the science-fiction writers. Venus, when closest, is 26,000,000 miles away. Its surface is forever cloud-covered, thus hiding from prying earthmen's eyes what lies beneath the fog. Mars, when closest, is 35,000,000 miles away. Men may never know whether its thin, cold atmosphere sustains life and, if so, whether any facsimile of human intelligence animates any of its organisms. As for reaching other solar systems, all projects for space travel are speculative. Within our own galaxy, where sunlight takes eight minutes to reach the earth from its source, the next star, Alpha Centauri (often called Proxima Centauri), is four-and-one-half light years away—*i.e.,* twenty-six trillion miles. If our sun, which is

3

332,000 times the mass of the earth, were a dot the size of the period ending this sentence, this nearest star would be a similar dot ten miles away. As for the "universes" beyond the Milky Way, most of those we see are visible by virtue of light emitted millions of years ago, long before mankind had come into being.

All men during most of the human past knew nothing of such matters, despite their insatiable simian curiosity. They "explained" the cosmos by way of anthropomorphic projections of themselves into spirits, demons, angels, heroes, and gods in the starry heavens. The men of today, undaunted either by outer obstacles or by self-ignorance, press on with their quest. They have arrived, in the Atomic Age, at strange results which may render all past human ways obsolete. It is the essence of the modern civilization of the West that its scientists, technicians, entrepreneurs, and statesmen, like Faust bewitched by Mephistopheles, must forever push outward the frontiers of knowledge and power, hoping thereby to enrich human life but risking thereby the damnation and death of the human race itself.

The hope springs from the possibility that humankind may be able so to order its affairs as to make power and knowledge the means of life rather than the instruments of doom. The risk stems from the fact that mankind, thus far, has been incapable of achieving the Brotherhood of Man under the Fatherhood of God and has rejected the ancient vision of One World, now made inescapably real by the victories of Science, in favor of ancestral feuds by violence of clan against clan, tribe against tribe, kingdom against kingdom, empire against empire.

This paradox, which lies at the heart of the contemporary dilemma of "international relations," is part of a larger paradox which few can describe and fewer can resolve. Man is a beast who aspires to be a god. Devils and seraphim struggle incessantly for mastery of his soul. His animal needs for food, drink, shelter, and sex must be satisfied lest he perish prematurely and sans progeny. He knows, as no other creatures know, that his inexorable destiny is from womb to tomb, from sperm to worm, from lust to dust. Yet he must needs strive to make the best of his fortunes between a cradle he did not choose and a grave he cannot escape. What, if anything, lies before birth and after death for each and all of us can, in the nature of things, be a matter of mere guess, hope, or faith, never of certain knowledge. In the words attributed by the Venerable Bede to one of the thegns of King Edwin of Northumbria in a somber time (A.D. 627) when darkness was lighted only by the coming of Christianity to Anglo-Saxon England:

The present life of man, O King, seems to me in comparison of that time which is unknown to us, like to the swift flight of a sparrow through the room wherein you sit at supper in winter with your commanders and ministers, and a good fire in the midst, whilst the storms of rain and snow prevail abroad; the sparrow, flying in at one door and immediately out at another, whilst he is within, is safe from the wintry storm; but after a short space of fair weather, he immediately vanishes from sight into the dark winter from which he had emerged. So this life of man appears for a short space, but of what went before or of what is to follow, we are utterly ignorant. If, therefore, this new doctrine contains something more certain, it seems justly to deserve to be followed.

Meanwhile, here below each must seek food and shelter and a mate. But the brute satisfaction of man's animal needs, unlike those of other "dumb brutes," is forever conditioned by the fact that he is a social animal who must constantly repress his self-seeking and his instinctive legacies of hunger, fear, rage, and carnal desire in order to cooperate with his fellows for the better satisfaction of his wants. The inevitable frustrations imposed by the social condition beget inevitable aggressions. Men are thus moved to fight and kill their fellows to a degree unknown among less socialized and less intelligent animals. But a general war of each against all is intolerable and wholly destructive of the benefits of cooperation. Therefore, from the beginning of human time, men have lumped themselves together in sundry social aggregates in local communities and have, more often than not, sought peace among themselves by waging war on aliens, strangers, and "enemies" beyond the frontiers. Aggressions are thus "harmlessly" discharged against "foreign foes."

More is involved here. Every man and woman, from beginning to end of the mortal adventure, knows, or ought to know, that a life of self-seeking is empty and that the deepest satisfactions of living can only be derived from a sense of "togetherness" with mates, children, parents, and neighbors. Men and women are creatures of appetite, thirst, fright, anger, and erotic passion. But they are also creatures of conscience and morality, of shame, guilt, and repentance, and of a desperate need in their loneliness to be forgiven, respected, and loved by their fellows. Without some conviction of self-respect and dignity, derived from shared experience in the search for truth, beauty, and goodness, life is a mere bestial existence. This need is best fulfilled by solidarity with others in whatever creeds and rituals of State or Church happen to be conveniently at hand. Since men love what is near and dear, and distrust what is far and foreign, local loyalties frequently prevail over general loyalties. Humans have ordinarily organized themselves for the fulfillment of shared purposes in terms of parochial communities rather than in terms of all mankind. The members of each local community have thus found dignity, self-respect, and fellowship through the symbols and practices of local "patriotism" rather than in any sense of allegiance to any concept of humanity as a whole—which, in our time as in many times past, has seemed to most of the sons and daughters of Adam and Eve as meaningless and incomprehensible as the cosmos itself.

But this resolution of the dilemma begets another in our own era when science, technology, and business have made all the world one. A World

Community, if it is to survive and flourish, requires some equivalent of World Government to maintain law, order, and justice among its members. But when the citizens of the parts ignore the whole and cling so loyally to their local loves as to resist all efforts to organize public authority on any basis broader than the sovereign nation-state, then all are threatened with mutual destruction by the persistence of the assumption of violence in the relationships among the "Powers." The efforts of citizens and statesmen to cope, as best they can, with this paradox is the subject-matter, sometimes dismal and sometimes hopeful, of this book.

2. HOW PEOPLE THINK ABOUT POLITICS

"The time has come," the Walrus said, "to talk of many things: of shoes—and ships—and sealing-wax—of cabbages and kings—and why the sea is boiling hot— and whether pigs have wings."—LEWIS CARROLL, *Through the Looking Glass.*

The meaning of life has puzzled men's minds ever since the first appearance on our planet of the puzzle we call the mind of man. The question as usually posed has no answer. The reason has to do with the meaning of "meaning."

Nothing new under the sun—book, picture, or symphony, rock, blossom, or butterfly—has any meaning to any of us unless and until it stirs some feeling or thought derived from past experience. Meaning in the mind, and corresponding action in dealing with the world, is ever a business of defining each day's challenge to our senses and our wits by reference to what has already been built into our organisms through earlier "education," our own and that of our ancestors. Life is like a dictionary: each word means other words; all the words together mean nothing. If each bit of experience is meaningful only in relationship to other bits of experience, then the whole of experience, *i.e.*, the "meaning of life," is literally meaningless save in terms of the connections among the segments or in terms of the mind of God—whose wisdom and will mere mortal men and women can see only dimly.

We shall be concerned in these pages not with all experience (which we leave to the philosophers, the psychologists, and the theologians to ponder upon) but with that fraction of our shared experience known as "politics" and, more particularly, with that area of politics in which nations encounter nations. These contacts are often dramatic. They are also disturbing. Contemporary mankind seems somehow to have so mismanaged the relations among nations as to confront us all with dire peril and often bitter tragedy. But we are unlikely to learn very much that is useful about these matters, or how to act relevantly in the service of our purposes, unless we first try to examine international politics from afar in the widest possible perspective rather than limit our view to this evening's news broadcasts and tomorrow morning's headlines.

People think about, and act upon, each day's events only in terms of what

6

they know about past events and about the things the events remind them of. In politics, as in all of life, what people "know" largely determines what they see, hear, and feel and how they think and act. In looking at world affairs, and at the acts of other men, all men see what is not, and see not what is, because all of us are inevitably prisoners of our past and interpret what we look at in terms of what we want to see or what is easiest to see because we suppose we have seen it before. The difficulties of freeing ourselves from this thralldom were well put 24 centuries ago by an astute psychologist, philosopher, and political scientist (428–348 B.C.) named Plato:

"Behold! human beings living in an underground den . . . here they have been from their childhood, and have their legs and necks chained so that they cannot move, and can only see before them. . . . Above and behind them a fire is blazing at a distance, and between the fire and the prisoners there is a low wall built along the way, like the screen which marionette players have in front of them, over which they show the puppets." "I see." "And do you see men passing along the wall carrying all sorts of vessels, and statues and figures of animals made of wood and stone and various materials, which appear over the wall? Some of them are talking, others silent." "You have shown me a strange image, and they are strange prisoners." "Like ourselves, and they see only their own shadows, or the shadows of one another, which the fire throws on the opposite wall of the cave?" "True. How could they see anything but the shadows if they were never allowed to move their heads?" "And of the objects which are being carried in like manner they would only see the shadows?" "Yes." "And if they were able to converse with one another, would they not suppose that they were naming what was actually before them?" "Very true." "And suppose further that the prison had an echo which came from the other side, would they not be sure to fancy when one of the passers-by spoke that the voice which they heard came from the passing shadow?" "No question." "To them the truth would be literally nothing but the shadows of the images." [*The Republic*, Book VII (Jowett Translation).]

Plato goes on to discuss the wonderment of such bondsmen if suddenly liberated and brought out into the sunshine, and their reluctance to accept the "real truth" in place of what they supposed was the truth. Here undoubtedly is the central difficulty in all life, and most markedly in all politics—as to both its study and its practice. Why it is central was well explained a generation ago by Walter Lippmann in his *Public Opinion* (Harcourt, Brace, 1922), pp. 25, 29, 79:

What each man does is based not on direct and certain knowledge, but on pictures made by himself or given to him. If his atlas tells him that the world is flat he will not sail near what he believes to be the edge of our planet for fear of falling off. If his maps include a fountain of eternal youth, a Ponce de Leon will go in quest of it. It someone digs up yellow dirt that looks like gold, he will for a time act exactly as if he had found gold. The way in which the world is imagined determines at any particular moment what men will do. . . . The world that we have to deal with politically is out of reach, out of sight, out of mind. It has to be explored, reported, and imagined. Man is no Aristotelian god contemplating all existence at one glance. He is the creature of an evolution who can just about span a sufficient portion of reality to manage his survival, and snatch what on the scale of time are but a few moments of insight and happiness. . . . Each of us lives and works on a small part of the earth's surface, moves in a small circle, and of these acquaintances knows only a few intimately. . . . Inevitably our opinions cover a bigger space, a longer reach of time, a greater number of things, than we can directly observe. They have, therefore, to be pieced together out of what others have reported and what we can imagine.

In this process of piecing together, Lippmann points out, we see the world through our "stereotypes"—*i.e.*, through the pictures-in-our-heads that others have called "habits" or "configurations" (*Gestalten*) or "conditioned responses." This way of looking at, and thinking about, and responding to, the world is useful and necessary and is, indeed, the only way we have. But if we are unaware of its nature and its imperatives, we are easily deceived rather than helped to fit our images to reality. For every stereotype has its "blind spot" which closes our eyes to everything which does not fit into the pattern to which we have become accustomed.

Everyone who studies or teaches or writes about world affairs is bound (try as he will to escape) to spend some time considering shadows-on-the-wall as if they were real. And as for politicians, diplomats, strategists, lawmakers, and ordinary citizens who do little studying, their vision is blurred and their judgment twisted, more often than not, by lenses which magnify or minify or otherwise distort. This is chiefly due to the fact that our views of politics, and especially of international politics, are colored not only by our past perceptions but also by our loyalties.

This again is quite inevitable and even necessary and desirable. A man without loyalties is a man without a country, without a faith, without the shared beliefs and hopes which make life livable. But if we would study world politics "objectively" and "scientifically," in the expectation that new wisdom may be acquired thereby, and if we would read printed pages critically (including those you are reading now), then we need to take account of the loyalties of man as a source of prejudice and error as well as of fellowship and faith.

All loyalties are designs for organizing loves and fears and hates. Every human baby responds with "rage" or hate to restraint and deprivation, with "fear" to loud noises and loss of support, and with "love" to food and petting. He soon learns to love mamma and papa and to fear and hate a great variety of things and persons, often including, ambivalently, papa or mamma or both. He later learns, as his universe enlarges, to transfer these feelings to creeds and fatherlands, Churches and States, and the belief systems and value patterns we have come to call "ideologies." In the buzzing, booming world of the Great Society of modern civilization, old loyalties to home and neighborhood, town and province, guild and parish have been merged in newer allegiances to larger communities, and these in turn have been mingled with diverse devotions to symbols of loves and fears and hates transcending physical frontiers—

e.g., Democracy, Fascism, Communism, Atlantic Union, United Europe, the Free World, the Dictatorship of the Proletariat, Free Enterprise, the Brotherhood of Man.

Through such glasses various groups of human beings, or the same groups at different times, observe the passing scene and act upon what they see. Since all thinking is thus conditioned, people think differently and act divergently. Often they act combatively against those labeled as enemies, traitors, heretics, or infidels. Most people unite more readily against what they fear and hate than in dedication to what they love. "Orthodoxy," commented Carlyle, "is my doxy and heterodoxy is your doxy." We each tend to regard our faith as the only faith, our picture of the world as the true picture. Fearing and scoffing and sneering at others is a temptation resisted only by those well skilled in tolerance.

All of the vast literature of international relations bears upon its face the sundry beliefs, values, and hopes of its many authors—with a rigid "line" of political conformism enforced in contemporary totalitarian societies and a fruitful variety of divergent views still permitted in democratic States. Much of this literature is special pleading "for" or "against" specific nations or statesmen or particular creeds or cults. Some of it, including the works commonly regarded as most useful in institutions of higher learning in the Free World, aspires to be "scholarly" and "unprejudiced."

Those publications of the 20th Century that have some claim to be so described may be classified in many ways: price, weight, color, thickness of author's skull, etc. With respect to the problem of how people think about world affairs, two ways of classifying such works are perhaps more illuminating than others—*i.e.*, by the field of learning which each writer has most carefully cultivated, and by the focus of attention of each writer as he tries to interpret the kaleidoscope of international relations.

Historians tell a tale of human events through time. Without accurate and documented accounts of foreign policies, wars, negotiations, and treaties, no knowledge of world politics is possible. Equally indispensable are the contributions of the geographers and geologists who are concerned with relations of space: landways, seaways, gateways, barriers, climates, resources, and other physical aspects of man's earthly home. The economist views the adventure in terms of the production, exchange, and consumption of goods and services and the distribution of wealth and income. The political scientist looks at government—and at the absence of government, approximations to government, and aspirations toward government in the community of nations. His chief concern may be law or administration or political theory or political processes and public opinion, or some combination of these. Psychologists, sociologists, and anthropologists, among other specialists, each supply data and ideas relevant to some phases of the spectacle.

The "science" of international relations is clearly not a single compartment of knowledge but is rather an eclectic or interdepartmental discipline.[2] Each of the social sciences, and the humanities and the biological and physical sciences as well, has gifts to bring to the banquet. But if the diners are not to suffer indigestion or die of a surfeit, the various contributions to the repast must somehow be carefully chosen, skillfully blended, and well cooked and flavored—an arduous but appetizing task which is now only barely begun.

As for the question of what each writer "sees" in what he tries to look at, perceptions are many and varied. Some see the community of nations as an enterprise in law and order. Many of these seers, despite disappointments, envisage a sequence of struggles toward a world in which all sovereignties will ultimately abide by rules of law, settle their disputes peacefully, and build a growing structure of collective security and collaboration. A few see a trend toward World Government, and doubt whether order and law among States are possible without a merging of sovereignties into some supra-national pattern of power. Others see a global arena of power politics in which the "Powers" incessantly compete, by trickery and force, for advantages over their rivals. Still others see in these strivings a combat between Good and Evil. Many other ways of looking at world affairs are available to those still free to choose among differing perspectives.

Since there is no one "correct" way to view the world for those who still enjoy the blessings of liberty, these quarrels are confusing. But they recall the Hindu legend of the blind men who felt the elephant. One described the creature as like a snake (he had grabbed the tail) ; another as like a wall (he had touched the flank) ; a third as like a tree (he had seized the trunk) ; a fourth as like a sword (the tusk) ; etc. All the conclusions were "true." But each was naïve unless balanced by the others. The problem is even more difficult with world affairs, for the elements of international relations are less tangible than elephantine anatomy. Most observers see some aspect of reality. But they see little if they see only that which interests or excites them most.

To see the world truly, one must see it steadily and see it whole. Citizens, teachers, students, and text writers, even in highly literate and free communities, cannot hope to achieve full success in this endeavor. The most learned of savants have not yet turned the trick. But the crises of our era summon each of us to try—and to make whatever contributions we can to insight and foresight through discriminating selections and combinations among the various orientations offered for our guidance. No one can do more. To do less is to betray that faith in human rationality and in the salvation of mankind through wisdom and virtue which we have all alike inherited from the philosophers, prophets, and saints of times gone by.

[2] For a suggestive discussion of the study of international relations as a field of political science, where most academic work in this area of inquiry is done, see pp. 551–603 of *Contemporary Political Science: A Survey of Methods, Research and Teaching* (Paris, UNESCO, 1950).

This then is our enterprise. It is never-ending. All pursuit of truth is a continuing adventure. But understanding is a process, not a destination. It is to be found only in the course of the journey and not at journey's end. Before we set forth on our travels, however, we shall do well to explore where we are and whence we have come—by way of a backward glance at the long and rough route by which humanity has slowly emerged from caves and swamps and savagery into the dangers and opportunities of the thermonuclear era.

3. THE ASCENT OF MAN

I have set thee at the world's center, to observe whatever is in the world. I have made thee neither of heaven nor of earth, neither mortal nor immortal, so that thou mayest with greater freedom of choice and with more honor, as though the maker and moulder of thyself, fashion thyself in whatever shape thou shalt prefer. Thou shalt have the power to degenerate into the lower forms of life, which are animal; thou shalt have the power, out of thy soul's judgment, to be reborn into the higher forms of life, which are divine.—God at the Creation of Man, PICO DELLA MIRANDOLA, *Oratio de hominis dignitate*, 1486.

Some two billion years ago, clouds of star-dust condensed and shrank and blazed and cooled into the third planet outward from the sun. "And the earth was without form, and void; and darkness was upon the face of the deep. And the Spirit of God moved upon the face of the waters." In the film of liquid which covered the surface of this sphere, there finally appeared the strange molecules of an "aperiodic crystal" which is the chief constituent of the granular jelly named (1840) "protoplasm." [3] Each blob possesses the quality of irritability—*i.e.*, it responds to stimuli. Each globule moves, eats, excretes, grows, and reproduces. Each is poised in unstable equilibrium between the deadness of inorganic matter and the promise of dreams beyond the firmament. Through this weird alchemy, life began on earth sometime between 500,000,000 and 300,000,000 years ago.

In the eyes of whatever deities preside over stars and satellites, sea slime and sand, the epic of the ages is the tragicomedy of organic evolution wherein single living cells combine into multicellular creatures which, through reproduction and mutation over endless generations, proliferate into scores of thousands of species. That man should regard himself as the culmination of the process is evidence of human vanity. His life on earth thus far, including the life spans of the semi-men who are long since dust, is but a fraction of the eons during which the planet was successively dominated by trilobites, fish, amphibians, monster reptiles, and giant mammals. If the combined life cycles of prehuman organisms, taken together, were reckoned as one year, man's lifetime to date would be less than a single day. Man's origins, as they are revealed by the record of the rocks, are equally conducive to humility.

[3] See Erwin Schrödinger, *What Is Life? The Physical Aspect of the Living Cell* (New York, Macmillan, 1946).

THE HUMAN CONDITION

In the zoologist's terms, man is an animal belonging to the grade of the Metazoa, or multicellular organisms; to the phylum of the Chordata, or vertebrates; to the subphylum of the Craniata (comprising all fish, birds, reptiles, and mammals); to the class of the Mammalia; to the subclass of the Placentalia; to the order of the Primates (embracing all monkeys, apes, and men); to the family of the Hominidae (including sundry extinct species of ape-men); to the genus *Homo;* and to the species *Homo sapiens.* The living creature which most closely resembles the ultimate ancestor of man (and of all monkeys and apes) is the Tarsius or insect-eating tree shrew of Southeast Asia, with goggle eyes and absurd feet, suggesting nothing so much as a grotesque synthesis of a rat, a bat, a squirrel, and a tiny monkey.

Some 70,000,000 revolutions of the earth around the sun have elapsed between the emergence of the first primates (*i.e.,* the tarsioids) and the most recent commencement exercises on American campuses. The beneficiaries of these rituals bear little resemblance to the timid mammals whose forebears ate insects in the early Eocene period. Yet there is much reason to suppose that today's A.B.'s are biologically related to an age-old tree shrew. From this line branched off the lemurs, the lorises, the Tarsius (only surviving tarsioid, apparently little changed in seventy thousand millennia), the new world monkeys, the old world monkeys, and the living anthropoid apes: gibbon, orangutan, chimpanzee, and gorilla. Along the line of mutation there emerged, perhaps 50,000,000 years ago, an apelike monkey (now extinct) dubbed *Parapithecus* and later (some 35,000,000 years ago) the first true ape, named *Propliopithecus,* a smallish animal whose bones have been found in the Oligocene strata of the upper Nile Valley. Still later, in the Miocene, 20,000,000 years ago, lived such extinct species of larger apes as *Dryopithecus* and its descendants, *Australopithecus* and *Paranthropus.* The first is probably the ancestor of the chimpanzee and gorilla. The other two, whose fossilized remains in South Africa resemble man more closely than any of the living anthropoids, seem nearer to the immediate progenitors of all men.

No biologist would now contend that men are descended from apes, nor did Charles Darwin in *The Descent of Man* (1871) advance any such thesis. But all biologists would hold that in all likelihood the anthropoids have a common simian ancestry with man. All apes and monkeys are vegetarians. All apes, and many monkeys, live in groups which tend to be antagonistic toward one another. Led by older males, each group defends its feeding grounds against out-groups, thus exhibiting the pattern of "international relations" which has reappeared in all the State Systems of *Homo sapiens.*[4]

All apes, save gorillas, are tree dwellers. All have brains weighing about 1 pound, compared with man's 3-pound brain. Man's ancestors evolved into

[4] See Robert Redfield (editor), *Levels of Integration in Biological and Social Systems,* Biological Symposia, Vol. VIII, especially pp. 177–204, "Societies of Monkeys and Apes" by C. R. Carpenter.

the least specialized, and therefore the most adaptable, of mammals, relying for survival on arched feet, upright posture, primate hands, extraordinary sexual drives, and an enlarged brain. The latter made possible the dawn of "intelligence," doubtless best defined as the most exaggerated form of protoplasmic irritability.

But man in the dim past was not of one species. His earliest precursors among the now extinct Hominidae were not even of the genus *Homo*. In 1891, Dr. Eugene Dubois discovered, in early Pleistocene deposits in Java, fragments of an apelike primate that walked erect a million years ago and had a 2-pound brain. He christened it *Pithecanthropus erectus*, after Ernst Haeckel's name for the "missing link." In 1936, Dr. Ralph von Koenigswald unearthed further bits of bone which left no doubt that the Java ape-man belonged to a genus midway between apes and men.[5] In 1908, at the other extremity of Eurasia, Charles Dawson dug up, near Piltdown in Sussex, the bones of *Eoanthropus dawsoni*, with ape's jaw and manlike skull. But this controversial "Piltdown man" was exposed in 1953 as a fraud. In 1927, in a Pleistocene cave near Pekin, Dr. Davidson Black found a tooth, to which Dr. Koenigswald, two years later, was able to add more teeth and sundry skulls and jawbones, comprising parts of 40 skeletons of a species named *Pithecanthropus pekinensis*. In the cave were crude flint instruments, the earliest artifacts of Paleolithic (Old Stone Age) culture, and some evidence of the use of fire. Many skulls and bones were broken and chewed, evidently to get at brains and marrow. The Pekin ape-man was perhaps a cannibal. . . .

These super-apes who were almost men were followed by the first true man, though he clearly was also not of our species. His fossil bones, first found in a Gibraltar cave in 1848, were brought to England in 1862 but aroused no interest. In 1855, parts of a skeleton were found in the Neanderthal cave in the Ruhr Valley. Finally, in 1907, Dr. Otto Schoetensach found a jawbone in a sand pit near Heidelberg. Many more bones have since been dug up throughout Western Europe and a few in Palestine. This "Heidelberg man," or *Homo neanderthalensis*, had a brain of more than 3 pounds, encased in a heavy, low-browed skull. Emerging some 250,000 years ago, he struggled for life with hairy mammoths, saber-toothed tigers, cave bears, and woolly rhinoceroses. He seems to have survived for 200 millennia. He used fire and made crude tools of stone. He lived in caves for protection from other carnivores and from the bitter cold of the third and fourth glacial periods of the Pleistocene era. To the rigors of the fourth age of ice he succumbed some 50,000 years ago.

[5] In 1946, Koenigswald, back from Java and China, brought to the American Museum of Natural History various teeth and bones of three types of still older giant ape-men, which he named *Pithecanthropus robustus, meganthropus*, and *gigantopithecus*. For a lively account of the earlier evidence on man's ancestry, see William Howells, *Mankind So Far*.

Living man is the child of the postglacial epoch—or, if a fifth is to come, of the current interglacial period. His earliest representative, appearing in Europe 35,000 years ago, was Cromagnon man, named for the cave in Dordogne where his remains were first found in 1868. Here was a human being of our own species, tall, sturdy, and with a large brain, but not identifiable with any existing race. He was a hunter, skilled in the arts of the Old Stone Age, and given to painting pictures of animals on cave walls. His numbers declined as changes in climate and vegetation reduced the herds of reindeer and wild horses. About 12,000 years ago, as our earliest immediate ancestors came into Europe from Asia, Cromagnon man passed from the scene. His successors were men of the New Stone (Neolithic) Age, who used polished flints and arrowheads, kept domestic animals, made pottery, practiced simple agriculture, and ultimately learned to smelt bronze and later iron.

All human beings now alive, and all (including Cromagnon man) who have lived since the melting of the last ice sheet, are members of *Homo sapiens*. Harvard men and Hottentots, Teutons and Eskimos, Chileans and Chinese, Slavs and Amerinds, baronets and bushmen, Yale men and Yakuts may, if they choose, interbreed and raise children—a biological fact which is conclusive evidence that all living men are of one species. That species, to be sure, is physically differentiated into "races," which may be classified in various ways, almost all of them unsatisfactory. The mysticism and sadism of modern racial myths have obscured the truth that the only true race is the human race. Yet all the evidence of science supports the central thesis of all the world's higher religions—always more honored in the breach than in the observance— that all men are brothers, all have a common origin, and all are children of God, equal in potential virtue or vice and in capacity for self-realization as human beings.

4. CULTURE AND GOVERNMENT

It is evident that the State is a creation of nature, and that man is by nature a political animal. And he who by nature and not by mere accident is without a State is either above humanity or below it; he is the "tribeless, lawless, heartless one," whom Homer denounces—the outcast who is a lover of war; he may be compared to a bird which flies alone. Now the reason why man is more of a political animal than bees or any other gregarious animals is evident. . . . Man is the only animal with the gift of speech. . . . He alone has any sense of good and evil, of just and unjust; and the association of living beings who have this sense makes a family and a State.—ARISTOTLE, *Politics*, Book I, Chapter 2.

The genealogy of *Homo sapiens* may seem to throw little light on the processes of power politics. The whole fabric of interstate relations is a concomitant of "civilization." None of the early primates, or the ape-men and the sub-men of the Pleistocene, or even the dawn-men of the Paleolithic and Neolithic cultural epochs lived in organized "States" under "governments." It is plain that *Homo sapiens* knew nothing of such matters during the first

14

few tens of thousands of years of his existence. There was apparently no "civilization" whatever among human beings prior to a time which began not much more than 7,000 years ago. If it be true that, on an assumed scale of one year for all life on earth, manlike creatures have thus far enjoyed life for less than a single day, then it is also true, on the same calendar, that within this day only the last hour represents the era of *Homo sapiens* and only the last eight minutes comprise the period of "civilization." How and why did men, living as "animals" among other animals, finally develop "cultures" and at length arrive at the peculiar cultures called "civilizations"? Such queries cannot yet be answered with assurance. But some answers are possible.

The earliest primates suspected of siring man, along with all their forebears, lived as beasts. Their equipment for solving problems consisted primarily of "instinct," or biologically inherited patterns of response to stimuli, built slowly and solidly into nerves, glands, and muscles via the genes, through the mysterious process of organic adaptation over many generations. These early ancestors possessed, as well, some talent for individual learning through trial-and-error "monkeying" or fumbling with strange or dangerous situations. Those who learned best survived. To learn is to change the patterns of response fixed by instinct or previous habit. Capacity for such change grew with the gradual expansion, through species after species, of the cerebral cortex. Such solutions as were stumbled upon, however, could scarcely be transmitted to kinsmen or children through mere grunts and howls.

Ape-men probably hit upon the use of fire and of simple weapons and tools before they arrived at words. The apes of today cannot learn to talk, but they learn to use tools. "Culture" is the totality of *learned* devices for problem solving, as distinct from hereditary equipment. It began at the point at which the sub-men of the dawn successfully transmitted to one another, and to their children, whatever they were able to learn about fire, clubs, flints, caves, fruits, and roots, and the habits of the animals they feared or killed for food. Culture is impossible without effective communication between individuals and between generations. Communication, in turn, creates community, which means the sharing of experiences. To share experience without words to describe it is difficult. But this achievement was doubtless within the capacity of the Java and Pekin ape-men and was certainly accomplished by the Neanderthalers, perhaps with the aid of rudimentary speech.

The invention of words was an immense step forward in the possibility of sharing experience and thus of building up a culture—*i.e.*, a store of transmissible skills, artifacts, beliefs, rules of conduct, and guides to safety, comfort, and success. When, where, and by whom words were first used by human tongues and understood by human ears is unknown. Cromagnon men almost surely used words, though they are forever lost. So with certainty did "modern" man in the Neolithic phase of his artifacts. But the step between words as sounds and words as written symbols is almost as great as the step between

15

the spoken word and no words at all. The culture of Cromagnon and Neolithic man was a "preliterate" culture—*i.e.*, antedating the invention of writing. In this "prehistoric" condition all human beings remained for many more centuries than have elapsed since the first written languages were devised. And in this condition remain the "primitive" or "preliterate" peoples of today, who have somehow never hit upon the art of representing meaningful sounds in equally meaningful visual symbols.

Preliterate "folk" cultures bear little resemblance to Thomas Hobbes's concept of primitive anarchy marked by a "war of each against all" or to Rousseau's idealization of the "noble savage" enjoying freedom. Peoples without writing typically live lives rigidly circumscribed by the folkways and mores of the group, handed down from father to son, surcharged with superstition and magic, and beyond all questioning and willful change. Unity is assured by universal observance of the "rites of passage" (*i.e.*, the beliefs and rituals surrounding the life crises of birth, puberty, marriage, and death), by fear of ancestral ghosts, and by seasonal propitiation of the spirits that bring the seed-time and the harvest, the solstices and the rain, the warmth of the sun, and good luck in the hunt. Government and politics, as we know them, are nonexistent. Relationships of command and obedience are familial or tribal or are temporary arrangements for particular purposes. Blood feuds are often permissible. Punishment of crime is obligatory. But war, as a deliberate organization of the community for violence against other communities, is a rare event. So lived all men 10,000 years ago.

How then did this mode of life change to "civilization" at the so-called "dawn of history"? Men who came to call themselves Sumerians began to live in "civilization" some 7,000 years ago in the then fertile valleys of the Tigris and Euphrates. Other men, later called Egyptians, adopted a similar mode of life along the Nile about the same time. Still later, men became civilized in Crete, in the Indus and Ganges Valleys, in the Tarim Valley of Mongolia, and along the shores of the Hwang Ho (Yellow River) and, presently, along the Yangtze Kiang. Still other men subsequently developed comparable designs for living in what are now Yucatán, Mexico, and Peru, though the respective Maya, Toltec-Aztec, and Inca civilizations never arrived at the use of iron. Nor did the Incas, for all their great empire, planned economy, and elaborate communal life, develop any system of writing other than the use of knotted strings (quipus) to keep accounts and transmit messages.[6]

This emergence of civilization in widely scattered valleys, islands, and plateaus followed upon a slow, thin spread of preliterate peoples over much of the globe. In all likelihood the original center from which the migrants

---

[6] A few cultural anthropologists, following the lead of Elliott Smith, lean to the view that civilization first originated in Egypt and spread elsewhere through cultural diffusion. Most authorities, however, believe that civilization arose in various loci about the same time, independent of any common origin.

fanned out comprised the highlands and plains of north central Asia. Neander-thal man, and after him Cromagnon man, may well have entered Europe by the steppe road out of Asia. From the same source probably came, at the end of the last glacial period, successive waves of wanderers, with the present Negroid peoples moving first and reaching Indonesia, Australasia, and south-ern India and, in the end, occupying most of Africa. Cromagnon man in Europe, or some of his close relatives, may have been Negroid. Next came the Mongoloid peoples, flowing over China and southeastern Asia, with one stream, some 25,000 years ago, crossing Bering Strait into Alaska, and settling the American continents.[7] Most recent of the emigrants were the "white," or "Caucasian," peoples, of whom a small segment (the primitive Ainus of northern Japan) moved eastward, while most, in serried ranks, flowed west-ward over the vast Eurasian prairies and originally peopled all the lands of Europe, North Africa, the Levant, and India.

Although travel is broadening, there is no reason for believing that the excursions of our ancestors promoted the transition from preliteracy to civili-zation. Those who traveled first and farthest have remained preliterate longest. "Civilization" means life in cities. "Politics" stems from the Greek polis, or town. Civilized living is to be distinguished from savage or barbarian lifeways by (1) urbanism; (2) writing; (3) the advent of the territorial State and the practice of politics; (4) the emergence of a priesthood and a church; (5) the institution of private property in land, possessed by a nobility; and (6) the appearance of social classes or castes.

The causal relationships, if any, among these elements of civilization are obscure. Those who think of cultural change in terms of communication will be most impressed by the invention of writing. Early hieroglyphics, cuneiform, and ideographs, all suggest that the advent of picture writing, as the precursor of alphabets, was a major factor in the transition. Written language multiplied greatly the possibility of communicating experience through space and time and thereby made possible the rise of large communities united by shared be-liefs, skills, and traditions. The economic challenge of desiccation, stressed by Arnold J. Toynbee, may well have played a role in causing the peoples of the river valleys to invent irrigation and systematic agriculture as a means of survival.

One hypothesis here merits special mention. This is the war-and-conquest theory of the origin of the State and of private property, slavery, social classes, and "civilized" government. It holds that the crucial event in the shift from barbarism to civilization was the subjugation of primitive farmers by hunters

---

[7] It is now generally agreed that all the Amerindians came originally from Asia by the route here indicated. No fossil remains of sub-men have been found anywhere in the Americas. The so-called "Folsom man," whose Paleolithic artifacts have been unearthed at various points in western United States, apparently flourished some 10,000 years ago and probably represents one of the earliest waves of migration from Asia.

and herdsmen. Nomads somewhere learned that wealth was to be had by war as well as by work. This first lesson of politics led to no State so long as the raiders were content to rob and kill. But some among them learned that more was to be gained by carrying the vanquished off than by putting them all to death. This innovation, well documented in the Old Testament, created the institution of slavery. At a still later stage, *ex hypothesi,* some among the warrior-nomads perceived that maximum benefits were to be derived by settling down upon the lands and necks of the conquered and exploiting them as tillers of the soil.

This third decision, it is argued, gave rise to most of the distinguishing elements of civilization. The victors built strongholds against rebellion and invasion. Around the walls grew towns. The victors asserted rights of property to the lands of the vanquished, who became slaves or serfs. The masters became a hereditary aristocracy, supplemented by a priesthood and claiming a monopoly of arms and of rule-making power within a defined region. All these are typical features of the earliest literate cultures. Writing and religion, no less than the arts of politics and war, enabled the masters to consolidate their mastery by winning the allegiance of their victims. Through the adroit use of force, fraud, and favors, sanctified by magic, the new arrangements were perpetuated and developed into the first urbanized, stratified societies of the first territorial States.[8]

5. THE MYSTERY OF HISTORY

The State, completely in its genesis, essentially and almost completely during the first stages of its existence, is a social institution forced by a victorious group of men on a defeated group, with the sole purpose of regulating the dominion of the victorious group, and securing itself against revolt from within and attacks from abroad. Teleologically, this dominion had no other purpose than the economic exploitation of the vanquished by the victors. . . . From war to peace, from the hostile splitting up of the hordes to the peaceful unity of mankind, from brutality to humanity, from the exploiting state of robbery to the Freeman's citizenship—this has been the path of suffering and of salvation of humanity, its Golgotha and its resurrection into an eternal kingdom.—FRANZ OPPENHEIMER, *The State.*

From the earliest times, men have formed the impression that history repeats itself. Of course, it does not. The dimension of time is not circular, as Nietzsche contended in his doctrine of "eternal recurrence." Cultural events, moreover, exhibit no such similarity or identity as do physical, chemical, astronomical, or biological events. Yet the patterns of change in the annals of

[8] The war-and-conquest theory, expounded by Marx, Engels, and their followers, has also been accepted and set forth by such non-Marxists as Franz Oppenheimer, Lester Ward, Robert H. Lowie, and W. C. MacLeod. For a recent critical evaluation see Robert M. MacIver, *The Web of Government,* pp. 12–38.

various civilizations do reveal a striking conformity to what looks like (or is mistaken for) a master plan of birth, growth, maturity, senescence, and death which may be as much beyond human control as the life cycle of each individual.

Der Untergang des Abendlandes by Oswald Spengler (1880–1936) is the most eloquent recent exposition of the cyclical theory of cultures. Arnold J. Toynbee's *Study of History* is the most learned. England's greatest living historian expressly repudiates Spengler's notion that cultures are organisms. But both treatises contend that the appropriate units of study in perusing the human adventure are not nations or races or languages or religions, but the major literate cultures of mankind. Both reject as absurd the familiar divisions of history into "ancient," "medieval," and "modern." Both present abundant evidence that each distinct culture passes through comparable stages of change, from its entry out of preliterate darkness to its exit into decadence and barbarism. Both writers are persuaded that all phases of each culture—politics, economics, religion, philosophy, science, art—display parallel features of content, style, and direction at "contemporary" periods of evolution. And both are convinced (Spengler more firmly than Toynbee) that our own Western culture has passed its zenith and is on the eve of or in the midst of a decline and potential disintegration similar to that which brought all its predecessors to the grave.

The Spenglerian thesis, in brief, is that a comparative study of the cultures we know most about (the Egyptian, the Babylonian, the Chinese, the Indian, the Classical, or "Apollonian," the Arabian, or "Magian," and the Western, or "Faustian") makes possible a "morphology of history." Each culture is unique in spirit, but all are alike in outer forms and in the broad phases of their development. Each has a life span of a thousand years, unless prematurely destroyed by catastrophe or prolonged beyond senescence and death through empty and "historyless" centuries. The four ages of each cultural organism—"Pre-cultural," "Early Culture," "Late Culture," and "Civilization" (Spengler's special term for the final epoch)—are roughly comparable to Spring, Summer, Autumn, and Winter.

The West, located in this schema, is in its late Autumn, approaching Winter. Its future is, therefore, clear: democracy will decay, dictatorships will flourish, men of money and intellect will lose influence to new groups of ruthless warrior-rulers, global wars of annihilation will succeed one another, and at last will come a world empire as the final political form of a static and increasingly shapeless "civilization" which has lost all creative power. Skeptics should be cautioned that these prophecies, along with others equally striking, were in part written before 1914 and were published in 1918–22.[9] A sample will suggest the flavor of the whole:

[9] The uncanny accuracy of many of Spengler's predictions is pointed out and commented upon by Edwin Franden Dakin in *Today and Destiny*, 1940.

With the formed state, high history also lays itself down weary to sleep. Man becomes a plant again, adhering to the soil, dumb and enduring. The timeless village and the "eternal" peasant reappear, begetting children and burying seed in Mother Earth—a busy, not inadequate swarm, over which the tempest of soldier-emperors passingly blows. In the midst of the land lie the old world-cities, empty receptacles of an extinguished soul, in which a historyless mankind slowly nests itself. Men live from hand to mouth, with petty thrifts and petty fortunes, and endure. Masses are trampled on in the conflicts of the conquerors who contend for the power and the spoil of this world, but the survivors fill up the gaps with a primitive fertility and suffer on. And while in high places there is eternal alternance of victory and defeat, those in the depths pray, pray with that mighty piety of the Second Religiousness that has overcome all doubts forever. . . . Only with the end of grand History does holy, still Being reappear. It is a drama noble in its aimlessness, noble and aimless as the course of the stars, the rotation of the earth, and alternance of land and sea, of ice and virgin forest upon its face. We may marvel at it or we may lament it—but it is there.[10]

Toynbee's "science" of history, elaborated with vastly more erudition than Spengler's, is at once more precise, more mechanical, and more flexible. He identifies no less than 21 distinct civilizations which have developed to maturity, 3 "abortive" civilizations, and 5 "arrested" civilizations.[11] The genesis of each results from response to a challenge, natural or human, severe enough to demand ingenuity for survival, but not so severe as to absorb all energies in meeting it. Growth is marked by differentiation, fruition, and self-fulfillment and then by "breakdown," wherein the original "creative minority" becomes merely a "dominant minority" to which the masses no longer give the obeisance of imitation. This schism leads to disintegration in which the dominant minority, after a "time of troubles," creates a Universal State, while the "internal proletariat" evolves a higher religion and a Universal Church.

But the "Schism in the Soul" of the declining society reflects itself in a Sense of Drift and a Sense of Sin, in promiscuity and vulgarity, in archaism, futurism, and transfiguration. At the close of the drama the Universal State, no longer capable of self-preservation, is destroyed by the "external proletariat"—*i.e.*, barbarian war bands.[12]

. . . The ailing civilization pays the penalty for its failing vitality by being disintegrated into a dominant minority, which rules with increasing oppressiveness but

[10] Oswald Spengler, *The Decline of the West*, Vol. II, p. 435.

[11] The full-grown civilizations, according to Toynbee, are (using his own names for them and in rough order of antiquity) the Egyptiac, the Sumeric, the Minoan, the Hittite, the Sinic, the Babylonic, the Indic, the Syriac, the Hellenic, the Mayan, the Andean, the Yucatec, the Mexic, the Far Eastern (Main Body), the Far Eastern (Japanese Offshoot), the Hindu, the Orthodox Christian (Main Body), the Orthodox Christian (Russian Offshoot), the Iranic, the Arabic, and the Western. The "abortive" civilizations are the Far Western Christian (Celtic), the Far Eastern Christian (Central Asia), and the Scandinavian. The "arrested" civilizations are the Polynesian, the Eskimo, the Nomadic, the Spartan, and the Osmanli.

[12] For a suggestive brief critique of Toynbee, see Paul M. Sweezy, "Signs of the Times," *The Nation*, Oct. 19, 1946.

no longer leads, and a proletariat (internal and external), which responds to this challenge by becoming conscious that it has a soul of its own and by making up its mind to save its soul alive. The dominant minority's will to repress evokes in the proletariat a will to secede; and a conflict between these two wills continues while the declining civilization verges towards its fall, until, when it is in *articulo mortis*, the proletariat at length breaks free from what was once its spiritual home but has now become a prison-house and finally a City of Destruction. In this conflict between a proletariat and a dominant minority, as it works itself out from beginning to end, we can discern one of those dramatic spiritual encounters which renew the work of creation by carrying the life of the Universe out of the stagnation of autumn through the pains of winter into the ferment of spring.[13]

Toynbee's monumental work was brought to completion with the publication in October, 1954, of the final four of its ten volumes. They were preceded by excerpts or paraphrases of sundry themes—*Civilization on Trial* (1948), *War and Civilization* (1950), and *The World and the West* (1953), and followed by *An Historian's Approach to Religion* (1956) and D. C. Somervell's abridgment (1957) of Volumes VII, VIII, IX, and X of the *Study*. Here Toynbee is concerned with Universal States, Universal Churches, heroic ages, contacts between civilizations in space and time, law and freedom in history, the prospects of the Western civilization, and the inspirations of historians. His indictment of nationalism and his bitter attack on Zionism are best reserved for later consideration (see pp. 392–393).

What is here noteworthy and exciting is that Toynbee's *Study* as a whole, spiced with highly controversial judgments and based on the premise that no such thing as "objective" history is possible, is the boldest and most nearly successful attempt to date to achieve a comparative anthropology of the literate cultures of mankind. In the end Toynbee becomes a theologian and sees history as "God revealing Himself in action." Religion is "man's most important pursuit." Therefore, all past civilizations are no longer deemed equals. Those of the "second generation"—the Syriac, the Indic, the Hellenic, and the Sinic—which give rise to the "higher religions" were the most fruitful. Toynbee closes his magnum opus with a moving prayer. He even suggests that Universal Churches may be more significant units of historical study than civilizations as such and that the breakdown of our own Western culture may yet be averted by "a return to God." [14]

Whatever one may make of these views, another quotation from the *Study* (Volume VIII, pp. 148–149) will suggest the style and direction of its concluding volumes:

Communism was proclaiming in a challengingly loud un-Christian voice a commandment of Christ's which, on the Christian Church's lips, had sunk to a discreetly inaudible whisper repeated by churchmen under their breath; and, if

[13] A. J. Toynbee, *A Study of History*, one-volume abridgment of Vols. I–VI by D. C. Somervell, p. 77.
[14] See the author's review in *The Nation*, Nov. 6, 1954: "The Paradoxes of Dr. Toynbee."

Marxism was nevertheless a heresy from a truly Christian point of view, this was because, like most other heresies in their day, it had taken up arms on behalf of one grievously neglected Christian truth to the still more grievous neglect of this one Christian truth's Christian setting. Through the militancy and the animus of its ideological offensive, Communism had deprived itself of any prospect of reconverting a privileged minority in the Western World to the social gospel of Christianity in an anti-Christian dress; but, in the act of thus spiking its own guns, it had reopened for Christianity a prospect of reconverting ex-Christian Western souls to the Christian gospel in its entirety, including its social implications. In 'cold war' which seemed likely to settle the World's fate in the current chapter of the World's history, the decisive weight in the scales would be the sufferings of the vast 'underprivileged' majority of the living generation of Mankind, and this multitude of suffering human beings might be expected to throw in its lot with whichever of the two Powers that were now competing for its allegiance gave practical proof that it was carrying out the social gospel of Christianity *de facto.*

In these circumstances, self-interest would counsel a privileged minority among a dominant Western fraction of Mankind to discard the drill-sergeant's rod and take up Orpheus' lyre. This change of external insignia, however, would be morally sterile so long as the motive for it was one of policy alone; for the Thracian wizard's instrument cannot exert its magic charm unless its music is a genuine expression of the feelings in the player's heart. To achieve its purpose, a calculated policy of philanthropy would have to be caught up and carried away by a spontaneous outburst of love; and if the grace of God were to bring about this miracle in ex-Christian Western hearts genuinely smitten with contrition, and not merely with a self-interested alarm, by the hammer strokes of a Communist challenge, then an encounter between the Modern Western World and Russia, which had already changed the course of Russian history by prolonging the life-span of a time-expired Russian universal state, might change the course of Modern Western history by rejuvenating a body social in which the familiar symptoms of disintegration had already made their appearance. If this encounter were to have this outcome, this might prove to be the opening of a wholly new chapter in the history of Mankind.

No final judgment can yet be rendered on the full sweep of the challenging generalizations offered by Toynbee and Spengler. A more limited and less controversial task is here in order—*viz.,* that of noting that most, if not all, past civilizations in their social structure and political fabric have manifested certain uniformities which are quite beyond debate.

All literate human societies have been pyramidal or hierarchical in the distribution of indulgences and deprivations among their members. The few enjoy maximum individual shares of wealth and influence, usually through ownership and/or control of productive property. The elite (*i.e.,* those who get most of what there is to get) has many shapes. It may consist of nobles, businessmen, plutocrats, or any possible combination. But some elite exists in every civilized society so long as it preserves the attributes of civilization. By the same token, every such society displays at the bottom of the social scale a multitude of the poor: slaves, serfs, peons, sharecroppers, peasants, pariahs, proletarians, or what not. In all ages they have in common their poverty, their humble place, and their relative inability to influence community decisions. Between rich and poor, in many (but by no means in all) societies, is a moderately prosperous middle class of freemen and burghers, looking down upon the masses and imitating the classes above them.

Every civilized society, moreover, displays some form of government and some pattern of politics. Since naked power is always ugly and often ineffective, the processes of rulership are invariably dressed in garments so fashioned as to inspire fear, loyalty, and obedience. Those who act in the name of the State usually have at their disposal a monopoly of coercive power, a legal right to issue orders to all, an arsenal of *credenda* and *miranda* calculated to impress the public, and a variety of means of dispensing rewards and penalties. Politics has been well defined as the science of who gets what, when, and how. It is also the process by which people compete for control of the instrumentalities of favors, fraud, and force that are the essence of all government.

At first, always, the elite consists of nobles and priests, and the masses of slaves or serfs. All live in local city-states, controlling the surrounding countryside and organized to preserve the existing distribution of favors against threats at home or abroad. When a number of such city-states exist in the same region, they create, through their contacts of trade, travel, and war, a miniature State System, marked by leagues, alliances, balance-of-power diplomacy, and an uneasy equilibrium in which each community is the potential enemy of all. Sooner or later one State subdues the rest and establishes a larger kingdom which is "feudal" in form—*i.e.*, land is held by "lords" (originally "loaf-wards") in return for military service to a monarch and is tilled by unfree peasants who receive protection for their labors.

When a number of such kingdoms establish contacts with one another over a broader expanse of land or sea, the result is a larger State System, repeating on a larger stage the original drama of interstate politics. This phase of unstable balance among "Great Powers" often persists for some centuries, during which the growth of trade fosters an urban middle class, promotes the partial displacement of landed aristocrats by businessmen, and frequently engenders the overthrow of ancient dynasties and varying measures of democracy. The terminal phase of international rivalries for power is a series of "world wars," involving all the members of the State System and eventuating typically in the subjugation of all by one.

To insist that all civilizations have traversed this road would do violence to the facts. It would be equally fatuous to argue that the itinerary here outlined represents the "inevitable" course of our own Western culture. Contemporary science and technology, which have no true counterparts in earlier civilizations, have opened out prospects of creation or destruction which are new under the sun. Yet if it can be contended in any sense that all civilizations follow common laws of growth and decay, these laws are at any rate suggested in the preceding formulation.

6. QUO VADIS?

What a piece of work is a man! how noble in reason! how infinite in faculty! in form, in moving; how express and admirable! in action how like an angel! in apprehension how like a god! the beauty of the world! the paragon of animals! And yet, to me, what is this quintessence of dust?—WILLIAM SHAKESPEARE, *Hamlet*, Act II, Scene 2.

The fate of literate man, as it has revealed itself over and again in the course of past civilizations, is a tragic fate. The clue to the mystery as to why, until now, all the great civilizations of mankind have at long last died, even while some of the preliterate cultures have endured for ages, is perhaps to be found in the personality structure of civilized man. That structure first makes possible the creation of vast and fruitful communities and later makes impossible their preservation from self-inflicted dissolution. It may be true, as some psychologists and anthropologists have begun to suggest, that each culture evolves its own unique "basic personality type" and that many patterns of motives and acts are intelligible not in terms of the universal attributes of all men but only in terms of the specific and local experiences which shape particular men.[15] There are nonetheless common motives in all human beings which derive from similar sources and produce similar results.

The deepest roots of motivation spring from our common biological heritage. Men's ancestors were fish for 200,000,000 years. Men's ancestors were small primates for 50,000,000 years before they became anything noticeably different. The earliest multicellular organisms had built into their bodies at the outset a simple repertory of responses to stimuli which has persisted in all their progeny: (1) withdrawal from sources of irritation; and (2) approach for purposes of ingestion, destruction, or impregnation. Such tropisms, at first no more than mechanical reflexes, slowly developed into more subtle devices of survival—*i.e.*, "instincts" to flee before danger, to hunt food, to kill enemies, and to seek erotic joy, each with its "emotion" of fear, hunger, rage, and love.

These are still the major preoccupations of most members of *Homo sapiens* 2,000 years after Christ, 7,000 years after the first civilizations, 50,000 years after the twilight of the Neanderthalers, and 500,000 years and more after the first ape-men. That such motives are dominant in the behavior of all men is not strange. Through tens of thousands of generations all creatures unfit in their capacities for fright, appetite, anger, and lust were displaced in grim competition by others better equipped. Here then are the very bowels of human, as of all animal, motivation. And here, largely suppressed into the "unconscious," is that earliest level of personality, designated by Sigmund

---

[15] See, for example, Abram Kardiner and Associates, *The Psychological Frontiers of Society*, 1945.

Freud as the "Id." This he envisaged as the repository of the Libido—his term for instinctive impulses, governed by the "pleasure principle."

These primitive urgings were in sundry ways refined, modified, and centered on specific stimuli by the long experience of man's progenitors. The young of all mammals depend on their mammas. The duration of dependence increases with the elaboration of mammalian species. Mammals live in families. The first primates to descend from the trees, moreover, took a step of great daring. Fists and teeth avail nothing against the claws and fangs of the larger beasts of prey. Family solidarity, tribal cooperation, slyness, shrewdness, and trickery were needed for survival. Man's huge propensities for fear, rage, and lust and for affection, collaboration, and cleverness are doubtless attributable to the perils of primate life on the ground. When these primates took to meat eating, they had need for weapons and fire and somehow stumbled upon their use. Here are the first rudiments of "culture."

At this point, out of intimate contacts with fellows in families, clans, and hordes, emerging personality developed the elements of a conscious "self," perceptive, adaptable, and self-seeking. This realm of motivation, à la Freud, is the "Ego" governed by the "reality principle." Men's motives are those of beasts, first overlaid and modified (but in no sense expunged) by those of ground-walking and meat-eating anthropoids who learned from "you" and "yours" the meaning of "me" and "mine." They therewith became capable of purposeful social effort—and of attributes of vanity, greed, and cruelty which would put tigers to shame. Forever after, men readily revert, when discouraged or desperate, to mere animalism or egotism. "No beast," wrote Plutarch, wisely, "is more savage than man, when possessed with power answerable to his rage."

But this judgment stems from the most recently acquired component of men's motives, not from the pristine seeds of passion and egotism. That component, clearly, is conscience: Freud's "Super-Ego," ruled by the "morality principle"—into which is built those socially acquired restraints, redirections, and sublimations of impulse without which men are less than human. How did this come about? Concern with virtue is presumably a concomitant of awareness of vice and of a sense of guilt over acts which are "wrong." The first acts judged wrong were doubtless those which threatened the survival of the group. Perhaps primitive cannibalism first begot such sentiments as men dimly saw that the killing and eating of one another was a road to death for all. The mark of Cain is older than Adam. Perhaps, as Freud himself argued, the "original sin" was that reflected ages later in the legend of Oedipus who unwittingly married his mother, slew his father, and took his own life when he learned what he had done.

Freud's thesis here is that in the "primal horde," ruled by an elder male with a plurality of wives and a multiplicity of offspring, the sons as they matured sought to kill the jealous and all-powerful father, to eat his flesh, and to fight to the death among themselves for females. Patricide, incest, and fratricide were thus the first "crimes." Since they spelled ruin to the group, they were at some point renounced and elaborately guarded against through taboos on murder and incest. In many preliterate cultures, men live in clans whose members regard themselves as descendants of a sacred totem animal. They must marry outside the clan, never within it. From time to time, in sacrificial feasts, they kill the totem beast, eat its flesh, drink its blood, and thereby acquire its virtues. The totem symbolizes the original father. The sacrifice and the rules of exogamy are substitutes for murder, cannibalism, and incest. Freud thus derived conscience and primitive religion and indeed the genesis of culture itself from these postulated relationships.[16]

Without exploring the disputes raised by this hypothesis, it may yet be granted that men were truly men, in their psychological as well as in their physical structure, long before the advent of civilization. That is to say, they were (and are) neither brutes nor gods but an unholy mixture of both. Personality is at best a delicately balanced system of motivations, with "instincts," selfishness, and ethical values striving sullenly against one another. When the balance is maintained, the self is integrated. When it breaks down, the result is anxiety, guilt, neurosis, and, in the worst cases, madness. Static and stable cultures develop well-integrated personalities. Dynamic and insecure cultures pose to all personalities hard problems of adjustment. Most preliterate cultures are in the former category. All civilized cultures are in the latter.

Civilized man is neither more nor less brutish, self-seeking, or immoral than preliterate man. But, by virtue of division of labor and the witchery of writing, he lives at length in a great society rather than in a local community. He faces stresses and strains and dilemmas which have few counterparts in preliterate societies. As he grows up, his transfers of fear, rage, and love flow toward abstractions: kings and popes, nobles and priests, castes and classes, sects and factions, provinces and nations, signs and words symbolizing community values. In the process, old gods die, and old ways pass. Fresh learning is called for. All learning is painful. Having crossed the threshold of civilization, man finds his mind by losing his soul. In dread and loneliness, he grasps at feeble symbols of self-assurance. These, invariably, are devices which will recapture some sense of identity with the community and the cosmos. These are, most frequently, the signs and portents of State and Church, of mundane power and divine grace, usually mingled in a unity of belief and action which carries over into a new context much of the comforting magic of the lost days of long ago.

Thus equipped with spiritual armor against the threats and blows of a new, strange life, literate man marches forth to win victories in war and statecraft, art and science, religion and business. But in achieving these triumphs

[16] See Sigmund Freud, *Totem and Taboo,* and Sir James Frazer, *The Golden Bough* and *Totemism and Exogamy.* For a criticism of Freud's thesis, see Bronislaw Malinowski, *Sex and Repression in Savage Society.*

each civilization brings into being, willy-nilly, a larger and more complex community, increasingly divided against itself by internal cleavages of needs and creeds and fraught with growing contradictions in all spheres of life between theory and practice, faith and works, ideals and realities. The uneasy balance of instinct, egotism, and ethics is again lost as the orbit of civilization moves from tribe and kingdom and nation to the complex and confusing imperium of the great society. The acids of rationalism dissolve old loyalties. The injunctions of morality conflict with reason and self-interest. Man is divided against himself. And therefore men become divided against themselves.

This fragmentation of societies, and of most of the personalities that compose them, is at first exhilarating. Many find new solace in frenzied efforts to recapture the past or conquer the future by labeling dissidents as devils and waging war upon them. But this apparent reintegration of motives and morals is a deception. No creative mission is possible in a society so hopelessly split that each embattled group fancies that it has a monopoly of truth and virtue. Fanatics (sometimes defined as those who redouble their efforts as they lose sight of their goal) are men and women who give free rein to the impulses inherited from their past, under the delusion that they are thereby serving the cause of righteousness. This process, even when interrupted by transitory periods of reintegration, is ultimately fatal to the great commonwealth. Human beings incapable of solving their problems, and thus driven toward frustration and aggression, readily revert to greed and violence, to primitive superstition and satanism, and to debauched and vicious forms of brutishness and irresponsibility.

No civilization thus far has found the means of resolving this psychic crisis in any manner conducive to life rather than death. A global civilization, if it is to endure, calls for a transmutation of human nature which no community to date has ever been able to achieve. The children of the ape-men can erect vast and shining mansions of civilized living. But they can save these structures from final ruin only through a reintegration of personality and of society at a still higher level, at which a new morality prevails over the legacy of a violent, ignorant, and bestial past.

In all the great cultures, many philosophers and a few statesmen have seen the need of new morals and new men if civilization is to survive. Never yet has mankind proved capable of achieving the transition. Without it, all adventurers in civilized living stumble at last into the dusk. Man's hope is vanquished. Man's fate remains a tale of ultimate grief. Whether it must always be so is an inquiry best deferred to the end of this volume.

THE HUMAN CONDITION

SUGGESTED READINGS

Barker, Ernest: *Reflections on Government,* New York, Oxford, 1942.
Benedict, Ruth: *Patterns of Culture,* New York, Mentor Books, 1946.
Boas, Franz: *The Mind of Primitive Man,* New York, Macmillan, 1939.
Brinton, Crane, John B. Christopher, and Robert Lee Wolff: *A History of Civilization,* Englewood Cliffs, N.J., Prentice-Hall, 1955.
Burke, Kenneth: *A Grammar of Motives,* Englewood Cliffs, N.J., Prentice-Hall, 1946.
Ceram, C. W.: *Gods, Graves, and Scholars,* New York, Knopf, 1951.
Clough, Shepard B.: *The Rise and Fall of Civilization,* New York, McGraw-Hill, 1951.
Coon, Carleton S.: *The Seven Caves,* New York, Knopf, 1956.
Dakin, E. F.: *Today and Destiny,* New York, Knopf, 1940.
Darwin, Charles: *The Descent of Man,* New York, Appleton-Century-Crofts, 1913.
Ebenstein, William: *Man and the State: Modern Political Ideas,* New York, Rinehart, 1947.
Frankel, Charles: *The Case for Modern Man,* New York, Harper, 1956.
Frazer, Sir James G.: *The Golden Bough,* New York, Macmillan, 1940.
Geyl, Pieter: *Use and Abuse of History,* New Haven, Yale University Press, 1955.
————: *Debates with Historians,* New York, Philosophical Library, 1956.
Haskins, Caryl P.: *Of Societies and Men,* New York, Norton, 1951.
Hooton, Earnest A.: *Up from the Ape,* New York, Macmillan, 1946.
Howells, William: *Mankind So Far,* New York, Doubleday, 1944.
Hughes, H. Stuart: *An Essay for Our Times,* New York, Knopf, 1950.
————: *Oswald Spengler,* New York, Scribner, 1952.
Kahler, Erich: *Man the Measure: A New Approach to History,* Harrisburg, Pa., Stackpole, 1955.
Kardiner, Abram, and Associates: *The Psychological Frontiers of Society,* New York, Columbia University Press, 1945.
Koenigswald, G. H. R. von: *Meeting Prehistoric Man,* New York, Harper, 1957.
Krutch, Joseph Wood: *The Great Chain of Life,* Boston, Houghton Mifflin, 1956.
Lasswell, Harold D.: *World Politics and Personal Insecurity,* New York, McGraw-Hill, 1935.
————, and D. Lerner (eds.): *The Policy Sciences,* Stanford, Calif., Stanford University Press, 1952.
Lips, Julius E.: *The Origin of Things,* New York, Wyn, 1947.
Lowie, R. H.: *The Origins of the State,* New York, Harcourt, Brace, 1927.
MacIver, R. M.: *The Web of Government,* New York, Macmillan, 1947.
————: *Society: An Introductory Analysis,* New York, Rinehart, 1949.
May, Rollo: *Man's Search for Himself,* New York, Norton, 1952.
Merriam, Charles E.: *Systematic Politics,* Chicago, University of Chicago Press, 1945.
Moore, Ruth: *The Earth We Live On,* New York, Knopf, 1956.
Morris, Charles: *Signs, Language and Behavior,* Englewood Cliffs, N.J., Prentice-Hall, 1946.
Muller, Herbert J.: *The Uses of the Past: Profiles of Former Societies,* New York, Oxford, 1952.
Noyes, C. Reinold: *Economic Man in Relation to His Natural Environment* (2 vols.), New York, Columbia University Press, 1948.
Oppenheimer, Franz: *The State,* Indianapolis, Bobbs-Merrill, 1912.
Riencourt, Amaury de: *The Coming Caesars,* New York, Coward-McCann, 1957.
Samuel, Maurice: *The Professor and the Fossil: Some Observations on Arnold J. Toynbee's "A Study of History,"* New York, Knopf, 1956.
Santayana, George: *Dominations and Powers,* New York, Scribner, 1951.
Spengler, Oswald: *The Decline of the West* (2 vols.), New York, Knopf, 1929.
Toynbee, Arnold J.: *A Study of History,* New York, Oxford, 1934, 1939, 1954 (one-volume abridgment of Vols. I–VI, 1947, and one-volume abridgment of Vols. VII–X, 1957, by D. C. Somervell).

SUGGESTED READINGS

Toynbee, Arnold J.: *An Historian's Approach to Religion*, New York, Oxford, 1956.

Voegelin, Eric: *Order and History* (3 vols.), Baton Rouge, La., Louisiana State University Press, 1956, 1957.

Weldon, T. D.: *States and Morals*, New York, McGraw-Hill, 1947.

Wendt, Herbert: *In Search of Adam: The Story of Man's Quest for Truth about His Earliest Ancestors*, Boston, Houghton Mifflin, 1956.

White, Lynn, Jr. (ed.): *Frontiers of Knowledge in the Study of Man*, New York, Harper, 1956.

Wright, Quincy: *The Study of International Relations*, New York, Appleton-Century-Crofts, 1954.

"I will divide all the land of the false god among those who are content with living and have labored with their hands, that they may be happy and bless the name of Aton. I will divide all the land among them, for my heart rejoices at the sight of plump children and laughing women and men who labor in the name of Aton without fear or hatred of any." He said also, "The heart of man is dark; I should not have believed this had I not seen it for myself. For so loosened is my own clarity that I do not comprehend the darkness, and when light pours into my heart, I forget all the hearts that are twisted and shadowy. . . . So near to me then is the darkness! It stands beside me in you, Sinuhe. You cast doubts and obstacles in my path—but truth burns like a fire within me. My eyes pierce all barriers as if they were barriers of pure water, and I behold the world that will come after me. In that world is neither hatred nor fear; men share their toil with one another and there are neither rich nor poor among them—all are equal—all can read what I write to them. No man says to another 'Dirty Syrian' or 'miserable Negro.' All are brothers, and war is banished from the world. And seeing this, I feel my strength increase; so great is my joy that my heart is near to bursting." Once more I was persuaded of his madness. . . . Yet his words were a torment, and my heart felt the sting of them, for there was something in me that had matured to receive his message.—The Pharaoh Ikhnaton to Sinuhe, the physician, in MIKA WALTARI, *The Egyptian.*

A Book of

ORIGINS

The much admired *Republic* of Zeno, the founder of the Stoic sect, may be summed up in this one main principle: that all the inhabitants of this world of ours should not live differentiated by their respective rules of justice into separate cities and communities but that we should consider all men to be of one community and one order common to all. . . . This Zeno wrote, giving shape to a dream . . . but it was Alexander who gave effect to the idea. . . . He believed that he came as a heaven-sent governor to all, and as a mediator for the whole world. . . . He brought together into one body all men everywhere, uniting and mixing in one great loving-cup, as it were, men's lives, their characters, their marriages, their very habits of life. He bade them all consider as their fatherland the whole inhabited earth, as their stronghold and protection his camp, as akin to them all good men, and as foreigners only the wicked.—PLUTARCH, *De fortuna Alexandri.*

CHAPTER I

EARLY STATES AND STATE SYSTEMS

1. SUMERIA AND EGYPT

> Nature, the art whereby God hath made and governs the world, is by the "art" of man, as in many other things, so in this also imitated, that it can make an artificial animal. . . . For by art is created that great "Leviathan" called a "Commonwealth," or "State," in Latin *civitas*, which is but an artificial man; though of greater stature and strength than the natural, for whose protection and defense it was intended; and in which the "sovereignty" is an artificial "soul," as giving life and motion to the whole body.—THOMAS HOBBES, *Leviathan.*

AMONG the first States of which any records remain were those which were cradled in the Tigris-Euphrates Valley about 5000 B.C. These communities were city-states: Eridu, built where the rivers then entered the Persian Gulf; Nippur, in the upper valley; Ur of the Chaldees; Uruk, Assur, Umma, Sumer, Lagash, Kish, and the rest. Their people were Sumerians, speaking a language which they wrote in wedgelike symbols on tablets of clay. Whence they came, and how their culture first began, none can say. Their earliest relics and chronicles are those of people obviously long engaged in irrigation, growing crops, tending herds, and building walls and towers of brick. The first Sumerians also practiced astrology, appeased the seven devils sent by the gods to punish sinners, and paid special reverence in their pantheon to Enlil, the earth-god, Innini (Ishtar), the virgin goddess of heaven, and her brother and/or son, Tammuz, who annually sacrificed his life and was divinely resurrected from the dead.

Just as Sumerian mythology is the source of the Greek cult of Adonis and of the Jewish-Christian drama of the Messiah, so Sumerian "international relations" reveal a design which has repeated itself through the ages. These city-states comprised a true State System. That is to say, power to command obedience was not centralized but dispersed among independent localities. Each magician-prince or god-king represented a ruling elite of landlords and priests, governed his subjects within defined boundaries, and competed with other monarchs for land and power through bargaining and violence—*i.e.*, diplomacy and war. These units traded, conducted hostilities, negotiated peace, and exchanged envoys. War was normal. "Stranger" meant "enemy." But peace could be made by treaty.

The earliest known treaty dates from *c.* 3000 B.C. Many others must have

32

preceded it. Here the Kings of Lagash and Umma agree to submit a frontier dispute to the arbitration of Mesilim, King of Kish, who, calling upon the gods, arrives at a settlement. The actual text of a later treaty between the same States is to be found in the Louvre on the "stele of the vultures." A clay cylinder in Yale's collection contains the text (*c.* 2900 B.C.) of a treaty which Lagash imposed upon Umma after a successful war. Reparations are exacted. Divine wrath is invoked upon the vanquished, should they violate the new boundary. But then, as now, treaties become scraps of paper (in this case, tablets of clay) when political expediency dictates repudiation. A few years after signature, the fighting men of Umma launched a war of *revanche* and defeated Lagash.

In the fullness of time, anarchy gave way to order through the subjection of all by one. The dynasty of Ur-Nina in Lagash, which made extensive conquests, was at length overthrown by the high priest Lugal-zaggisi (*c.* 2677–2653 B.C.), who called himself "King of Kings." At Uruk, he established the first empire, stretching "from the Lower to the Upper Sea." But the Sumerian State System, like many to follow, was destined to attain permanent unification at the hands of alien conquerors rather than from within. Out of the western deserts poured Semitic-speaking barbarians. Among these nomads emerged a leader, Sargon (*c.* 2637–2581 B.C.), of whom legend says that he was born in secrecy and set adrift in a basket of reeds on the Euphrates, whence he was rescued, reared as a gardener, discovered to be of royal lineage, and crowned King of Babylon. This "Sargon of Akkad" founded the Sumerian-Akkadian Empire, extending from the Persian Gulf to the Mediterranean.

Sargon's grandson, Naram-Sin, "King of the Four Spheres," carried on his work, which endured the assaults of the Elamites from Susa. But this imperium finally fell before the blows of the Semitic Amorites, who settled in Babylon and, under a famous lawgiver, Hammurabi (1947–1905 B.C.), established the Babylonian Empire. Be it noted, lest our sense of time be distorted by the rush of tomorrow's headlines, that 32 centuries elapsed between the dawn of urban life in these valleys and the passing of Hammurabi. Of the 38 centuries which have since gone by, only the last 10 span the period of our own civilization.

Meanwhile there had transpired in the valley of the Nile a sequence of experiences not unlike those already reviewed. Here also, about 5000 B.C., possibly earlier, men somehow learned to build cities of wood, brick, and stone, smelt bronze, and use picture writing set down on the first "paper," or strips of papyrus reeds. Here, too, city-states doubtless made war upon one another until they were consolidated by conquest into the two kingdoms of Upper and Lower Egypt, united in turn about 3200 B.C. by Menes. This half-mythical founder of the "First Dynasty" built a kingdom which endured as a Great Power for many more millennia than any other before or since. This amazing civilization is best symbolized by the huge royal sepulchers of the pyramids of Giza, completed in the Fourth Dynasty, by the timeless Sphinx, by the great temples of Karnak and Luxor, and by multitudes of mummified bodies of kings, priests, and nobles. Egypt's quest for immortality was not in vain. Her greatest monuments of stone, built a thousand years before Abraham lived, may well outlast the human race.

In Egypt grew also a rich art and architecture and the beginnings of astronomy, mathematics, engineering, and medicine. Conquest by Semitic nomads, who founded the Sixteenth (Hyksos) Dynasty of the "Shepherd Kings," was followed by revolt and liberation. Under the "New Empire," Egyptian armies carried the power of the Pharaohs from Ethiopia to the Euphrates. One among them, Amenhotep IV (1375–1358 B.C.), established the first monotheistic religion, the worship of Aton, the sun-god (after whom he renamed himself Ikhnaton), only to have his work undone after his passing by the polytheistic priests of Amon Ra, whose will he had defied. This youthful genius triumphed even in death. For he was the first leader of men who caught the vision of all mankind united as brothers in One World and worthy through righteousness of the blessings of One God.

The kings and captains of mighty Egypt had long since reached out to the north and east and encountered other civilizations, whose early States had also been welded together into great feudal kingdoms. For some centuries the major rival Power was the Kingdom of the Hittites in Asia Minor, semi-Sumerian in its culture, whose soldiery sacked Babylon *c.* 1750 B.C. Between the two Powers lay the realm of the Mitannis on the Syrian shore. Egyptian-Hittite wars became chronic after Thothmes III (1480–1450 B.C.) invaded Syria. Clay tablets unearthed in the capital of the Mitannis suggest that *c.* 1400 B.C. the three States concluded a pact of nonaggression, mutual aid, and extradition. But more wars followed until Hattushilish III, King of the Hittites, now under attack by the Assyrians, signed a treaty with Rameses II in 1280 B.C.—notable for the fact that its text has survived in three copies in Egyptian and Hittite, with the lost original apparently written in Babylonian, the diplomatic language of the age.

This agreement, "witnessed by the thousand gods," was a pact of perpetual peace, outlawry of war, and mutual assistance:

There shall be no hostilities between them forever. The great chief of the Hittites shall not pass over into the land of Egypt, forever, to take anything therefrom; Rameses, the great chief of Egypt, shall not pass over into the land of the Hittites to take anything therefrom, forever. . . . If another people (or state) shall come, as an enemy, against the lands of Rameses, the great chief of Egypt, and he shall send to the great chief of the Hittites, saying "Come with me with your army against him," the great chief of the Hittites shall come, and the great King of the Hittites shall slay his enemy. But if it shall not be the desire of the great chief of the Hittites to come, he shall send his infantry and his chariotry, and shall slay his enemy. Or, if Rameses, the great chief of Egypt, be provoked against delinquent subjects, when they have committed some other fault against him, and he shall come to slay them, then the great chief of the Hittites shall act with the lord of Egypt.

These obligations of "collective security" against aggression and revolution were reciprocal, as was also a provision for the extradition of fugitives:

If any of the great men of the land of Egypt shall flee and shall come to the great chief of the Hittites, from either town, or . . . of the lands of Rameses, the great chief of Egypt, and they shall come to the great chief of the Hittites, then the great chief of the Hittites shall not receive them, but the great chief of the Hittites shall cause them to be brought to Rameses, the great chief of Egypt, their lord.

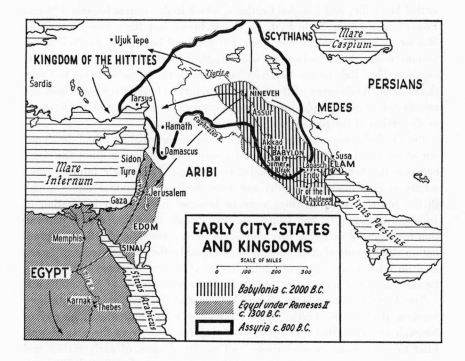

The reference clearly is not to common criminals but to political offenders, who are usually exempted from extradition in modern treaties. In other respects this document of 32 centuries ago reads like a pact of our own time. Then as now, travel and matrimony sometimes serve political purposes; Hattushilish paid a royal visit to the Nile and gave his daughter in marriage to the Pharaoh.

In the late 13th Century B.C., however, the Hittites were overwhelmed by barbarians from the north and west. Egypt fell upon evil days by virtue of Libyan and Ethiopian incursions and rebellions. Under these conditions new opportunities opened for the mid-Levant peoples. Here the original Canaanites had been set upon by Hebrew invaders from Arabia and by Philistine sea raiders and migrants from the Aegean. The Philistines (for whom Palestine is named) achieved no glory and less prestige. The Hebrews founded two kingdoms, Israel and Judah, sometimes united and sometimes independent, which reached a zenith of power and wealth under Solomon (c. 975–935 B.C.). The Phoenicians, probably descendants of the original Canaanites, established themselves at Tyre and Sidon and became notable navigators and traders.

These Syriac peoples left much to later ages. The Phoenicians probably invented alphabetical writing. In their wide-ranging voyages, they "discovered" the Atlantic Ocean; explored the Spanish, French, and African coasts; settled Marseille; and founded Carthage, which in due course became a "Great Power" in a larger State System. The Hebrews lost their independence in 586 B.C., when Jerusalem was taken, pillaged, and burned by the New Babylonians under Nebuchadnezzar, who dragged most of the survivors off as captives. The "Babylonian Captivity" ended with the fall of Babylon to Cyrus the Persian. While many of those liberated returned to the Promised Land and rebuilt Solomon's Temple, others were scattered far and wide. The Diaspora, or dispersion of the Jewish peoples, had already begun.

But the Hebrews, once the "Chosen People" of a tribal god, had developed out of manifold misfortunes, spiritual agony, and an earnest quest for righteousness the first enduring monotheistic religion. From their faith flowered a lofty ideal of human fraternity and an exalted sense of moral values, which in the Jewish sacred writings were to become the common inspiration of Judaism, Christianity, and Islam. No other people has suffered such persecution for its creed or faced, over and again, such systematic efforts at extermination at the hands of others insulted or shamed by the very existence of Israel. And no other people west of China has survived and preserved its identity, its language, and its way to God through the vicissitudes of $3\frac{1}{2}$ millennia.

The Assyrians' story is the antithesis of that of the Jews, though both were Semites. High in the Tigris Valley their early rulers built the stone city of Nineveh and dedicated themselves with singular tenacity to the arts of war. First to use cavalry, war chariots, and sundry devices of early tactics and strategy, they conquered Babylon c. 1100 B.C. in the reign of Tiglath Pileser I. Three and a half centuries later the third monarch of this name began a series of conquests, continued by Sargon II, Sennacherib, and their successors, which have no previous and few later parallels. Philistia, Samaria, Damascus were subjugated. Great Egypt itself was vanquished and precariously held (675–663). Here emerged the first "world empire," extending from the Caspian to the first cataract of the Nile. But the obsession of war-making led inexorably to impoverishment and depopulation. Egypt expelled the Assyrian garrisons in the 650's. Babylon revolted, allied itself with Elam (which the Assyrians demolished), and finally joined the Medes in a counterassault which culminated in the destruction of Nineveh in 612 B.C. Two centuries later, when

Xenophon visited the ruins, all human life was gone, and the very name of Assyria was lost in an empty tomb.

Yet the political pattern of a "World State," bringing order out of the chaos of conflicting sovereignties, persisted in the lands which had given birth to civilization four millennia before Assyria's demise. Another warlike people of the north (Aryan-speaking, or akin in language to the Hittites and to Greeks, Romans, and modern Europeans) presently built a kingdom out of another welter of city-states. These were the Persians, to whose throne in 550 B.C. came Cyrus, reputed to be the grandson of the founder of the royal house, called by the Greeks Achaemenes. After vanquishing Croesus, King of Lydia, Cyrus took Babylon in 538. His son, Cambyses, conquered Egypt. Under Darius I, who took the crown in 521 B.C., the World State of the "Achaemenides" included all the lands from the Danube to the Indus and from the Caucasus and the Aral Sea to Upper Egypt. Having failed to conquer the Scythians in a Balkan expedition, Darius decided to invade Greece. But that is another story.

The design of events recounted above, wherein the small city-states of the first literate cultures finally became municipalities of great kingdoms and later of vast empires, is not peculiar to the regions and peoples whose fortunes have here been reviewed. In the remote world of the Amerindians, other peoples traversed a similar road. In the jungles west of the Caribbean the Mayas developed the arts of urban life sometime before 500 B.C. and, after protracted rivalries among towns and petty kingdoms, arrived at an empire which flourished for four centuries (c. A.D. 300–690). Its successor, the Aztec society and State System, was in process of becoming an empire when it was struck down by Spanish conquerors. To the south, in the high Andes, the Inca Empire of Peru, by the time of its conquest by other Spaniards, had similarly evolved through five centuries from a congeries of rival towns to a far-flung imperium.

In India, the earliest civilization, that of the dark Dravidian peoples, seems to have taken form in the Indus and Ganges Valleys at a time somewhat later than the appearance of the first cities of Sumeria and Egypt. Some scholars perceive evidence of Sumerian influence in the earliest antiquities of northwestern India. Aryan-speaking nomads from the north began invading and conquering these kingdoms before the time of Hammurabi. The cultural fusion which ensued begot a rich new civilization which, in the 6th Century B.C., gave rise to one of the major religions of mankind through the life and teachings of Siddhartha Gautama, the Buddha. The faith of Buddhism spread over most of Asia, although by the 11th Century A.D. it had all but vanished in India itself, where it had never wholly supplanted Brahmanism, or Hinduism.

The civilization that gave Buddhism to posterity remained a chaos of rival States which arrived at no semblance of unity until Chandragupta Maurya conquered the Punjab and the Ganges Valley c. 320 B.C. and fashioned an empire in the northern plains reaching from sea to sea. His successor, Asoka

(264–227 B.C.), was one of the wisest emperors of all time, devoting his energies not to war but to good works and to the propagation of Buddhism in other lands. Confused centuries of invasions, conflicts, and conquests ensued. Apart from the Gupta Empire (*c.* A.D. 400–500) the hundreds of independent Indian States never attained even the shadow of unification until the Islamic Mongols established the "Mogul" Dynasty, whose greatest emperor was Akbar (1556–1605).

Last, but far from least, in this recurring drama of transition from anarchy to unity is the case of China. In the Tarim Valley of Mongolia, and along the shores of the Yellow River and the Yangtze, another great civilization emerged out of primal darkness about 3000 B.C. Here, too, city-states evolved into feudal kingdoms, which at length coalesced into a loose empire under priest-kings or "Sons of Heaven." After a series of semi-legendary rulers, the Shang (*c.* 1766–1122 B.C.) and Chou (1122–250 B.C.) Dynasties consolidated and governed a great realm. But in the first millennium B.C. a multitude of actually independent States, of which Tsi and Ch'in in the north and Chou on the Yangtze were "Great Powers," inflicted chronic anarchy on all the land by their incessant rivalries. The epoch after 500 B.C. is known as *Chan Kuo*— "the Contending States." Leagues of nations, disarmament conferences, and appeals to respect "international law" brought no permanent respite. But Shih-Huang-Ti ("first universal emperor") of the Ch'in Dynasty, who organized the building of the Great Wall against the Huns in the 2d Century B.C. and "burned the books" to break the power of tradition, welded the warring States once more into an effective imperium. His work endured under the Han Dynasty (206 B.C.–A.D. 172) and thereafter, until new "times of troubles," interspersed with periods of unity and order, came to an end through alien conquests. Under the Mongol, Ming, and Manchu Emperors, China remained one polity—until the impact of the West discredited imperial rule, disintegrated the ancient fabric, and initiated a new epoch of revolution and anarchy.

2. THE GLORY THAT WAS GREECE

> There is no hope of a cessation of evils for the States (of Hellas)—and, in my opinion, none for mankind—except through a personal union between political power and philosophy and a forcible disqualification of those common natures that now follow one of these two pursuits to the exclusion of the other. The union may be achieved in either of two ways. Either the philosophers must become kings in our States or else the people who are now called kings and potentates must take—genuinely and thoroughly—to philosophy.—PLATO, *The Republic.*

When Thothmes III ruled Egypt and the Shang Emperors governed China, Aryan-speaking barbarians filtered into the Greek peninsula out of the northern wilderness. In terms of their dialects, the order of their coming was: Ionians, Aeolians, Dorians, Macedonians, and Thracians. All called themselves

"Hellenes." Their earliest epics, set down in the *Iliad* and the *Odyssey* and ascribed to the blind bard Homer, tell of the conquest of Troy and of the later adventures of the victors. Their mythology tells how the hero Theseus went to Knossos, entered the labyrinth with the aid of Ariadne, daughter of Minos, and slew the Minotaur, half bull and half man, who had devoured Athenian youths exacted from Athens by Knossos as tribute and sacrifice. Apart from legend, it is plain that Knossos, capital of Crete and center of the Minoan or Mycenean civilization, was first pillaged and burned *c.* 1400 B.C. and that *c.* 1000 B.C. it was again demolished beyond recovery. Some of the survivors, *e.g.*, the Philistines, found homes elsewhere. Others vanished in the darkness of refugee migration.

The Hellenes adopted the arts and skills of the Cretans. Out of this heritage they evolved a new culture. Here again the creators of a great age first lived in city-states in which the ruling class of citizen-warriors and land-owners consisted of the sons of the conquerors while the vanquished (as in Sparta) were reduced to *helots* (peasant-serfs) or *perioeci* (merchants), who had no political rights. In many Greek communities the concept of "democracy" emerged for the first time as an alternative to monarchy and aristocracy, which in their corrupt form easily became tyranny and oligarchy. All these terms are Greek. Indeed it can be argued, as Sir Henry Maine contended, that everything that moves and lives in modern civilization is Greek in its origin. Yet Athenian democracy at its apogee was still based upon a society in which only "citizens" had voting rights, while all others, including the slaves at the bottom of the social scale, had no voice in community decisions. But the citizens of ancient Hellas, with the Athenians most glorious among them, developed drama, poetry, architecture, and sculpture to an acme of beauty. The subtle, curious, skeptical Hellenic mind, as it emancipated itself from tribalism, arrived at conceptions of scientific inquiry, individual dignity, civic duty, and human freedom which, for 25 centuries throughout the Western world, have been the envy and inspiration of all mankind.

In 490 B.C. Darius the Persian, with the aid of Phoenicia's navy, launched by sea the first assault on Hellas. It brought temporary unity to the rival Greek communities. At Marathon the Athenian infantry crushed the invaders. Ten years later Xerxes led a great army across the Dardanelles and through Thrace, Macedonia, and Thessaly. At Thermopylae (480 B.C.) Leonidas the Spartan held up the foe until all the defenders died at their posts, while the main Greek army retired to the south. With the fall of Athens, Themistocles, long a "big navy" man, persuaded his countrymen to risk a decision at sea. At Salamis the Persian fleet was destroyed before the eyes of Xerxes. In 479 B.C. Persian armies suffered double disaster at Plataea in Thessaly and at Miletus in Asia Minor. Xerxes was later murdered, as his realm decayed. The attempt of the Achaemenides to conquer Greece had failed.

The Golden Age which followed produced deathless masterpieces in all the arts. But the Hellenic States could find no political unity. The familiar process of unification through conquest was here arrested. In each city, rich and poor were ever more divided against one another. Athens became a capitalist plutocracy enamored of "freedom." Sparta embraced a totalitarian Communism dedicated to "discipline" and "planning." The lesser States fell under the influence of the greater. Themistocles built a Delian Confederacy through which Athens dominated its allies and evolved the "Athenian Empire" under Pericles—whose various wars, including a disastrous attempt to wrest Egypt from the Persians (454 B.C.), wasted the strength of his city. Sparta became the leader of the Peloponnesian League, which challenged the ascendancy of Athens.

The uneasy truce between the "Super-Powers" of the Hellenic world was finally broken in 431 B.C. by a life-or-death conflict which brought both contestants to ruin. At the outset Pericles spoke noble words on behalf of "democracy," even though his State was already ruled by rich merchants and ambitious imperialists. Over the graves of those who first fell by Spartan arms, he declared:

There no hearts grew faint because they loved riches more than honor; none shirked the issue in the poor man's dreams of wealth. All these they put aside to strike a blow for the city. Counting the quest to avenge her honor as the most glorious of all ventures, and leaving hope, the uncertain goddess, to send them what she would, they faced the foe as they drew near him in the strength of their own manhood; and when the shock of battle came, they chose rather to suffer the uttermost than to win life by weakness. . . . So they gave their bodies to the commonwealth and received, each for his own memory, praise that will never die.

But this immortal eloquence was the voice less of a future to come than of a past beyond recapture. In 429 B.C. Pericles died in a plague. With his passing the light of Athens slowly faded. Battles, sieges, blockades, and diplomatic moves and countermoves followed in bewildering succession. Athenian fighting power was much reduced by a calamitous attack upon Syracuse, the Sicilian colony of Corinth. Thucydides, in Book III, Chap. 82, of his history of this melancholy conflict, notes the inter-relationship between international and domestic politics in words startlingly suggestive of our own time.

In every country there were struggles between the leaders of the proletariat and the reactionaries in their efforts to procure the intervention of the Athenians and the Spartans respectively. In peace-time they would have had neither the opportunity nor the desire to call in the foreigner; but now there was the war; and it was easy for any revolutionary spirits in either camp to procure an alliance entailing the discomfiture of their opponents and a corresponding reinforcement of their own faction. This access of class-war brought one calamity after another upon the countries of Hellas. . . . War eats away the margins of ordinary life and, in most characters, adjusts the temperament to the new environment by its brutal training.

In the end the armies of Lysander of Sparta won "victory" and forced Athens to yield in 404 B.C. The result was not unity but chaos worse confounded. In a new series of domestic and foreign wars Thebes achieved a transient hegemony over Sparta. But the great days were gone. While the Hellenes were yet to cast their spell over vast regions and many cultures, their chance to win political unity, and therewith to lead the world to a new vision of universalism, had been thrown away in internal strife.

Although the most obvious characteristic of this State System was the in-

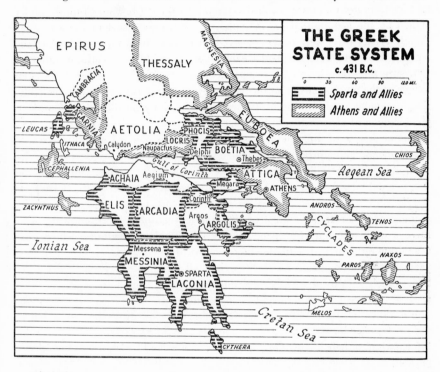

THE GREEK STATE SYSTEM
c. 431 B.C.

Sparta and Allies
Athens and Allies

EPIRUS

THESSALY

MAGNESIA

AMBRACIA

LEUCAS

AETOLIA

PHOCIS

ITHACA

Calydon

LOCRIS

Naupactus

Delphi

BOETIA

CEPHALLENIA

Gulf of Corinth

Thebes

ACHAIA

Aegium

ATTICA

Megara

ATHENS

EUBOEA

CHIOS

Aegean Sea

ZACYNTHUS

ELIS

ARCADIA

Corinth

Argos

ARGOLIS

ANDROS

TENOS

CYCLADES

Ionian Sea

Messena

NAXOS

MESSINIA

PAROS

SPARTA

LACONIA

MELOS

Cretan Sea

CYTHERA

cessant struggle for power among its members, it developed practices and institutions for pacific collaboration which were far in advance of their counterparts in earlier State Systems. The Greeks all acknowledged allegiance to their local State and were jealous of its sovereignty, but they were also aware of themselves as members of one race, with the same gods and a common culture, quite distinct from that of the "barbarians." This circumstance promoted intimate relations between them even when they were not threatened by a common enemy. The network of treaties which the States concluded brought them close to the conception of peace as a normal relationship between them. Treaties were always, in form at least, between equal sovereignties and were sanctioned by Zeus, the guardian of oaths. They established the conditions of peace between the parties, sometimes in perpetuity, sometimes for a term of years. Commercial treaties were common. As early as the remote period of the Homeric epics, ceremonials had developed about the making of treaties which are described in the *Iliad* in the account of the compact between the Trojans and the Achaeans setting forth the conditions of the combat between Menelaus and Alexander for the love of Helen. The divine sanction of treaties was always recognized by solemn oaths.[1] Heralds, ambassadors, secretaries, and a technical terminology became a regular part of the proceedings. Negotiations were usually public, though private conferences and even secret treaties were not unknown. Each party retained a copy in its own dialect, duly signed by the negotiators and stamped with the public seal of the signatory States. Treaty texts were often engraved on marble or bronze and kept in the temples. Hostages were frequently exchanged, especially in treaties of alliance, to ensure the execution of the compact. Treaties might legitimately be broken by one of the parties only if an inconsistency existed between two engagements, if enforcement would lead to hostilities with a friendly third State, or if a complete change of circumstances had taken place.

The exchange of diplomatic representatives also reached a high degree of development. Though permanent embassies were not exchanged, a hierarchy of diplomatic agents developed in terms of rank and prestige. Only fully independent States had the right to send and receive ambassadors. Refusal to receive an envoy was analogous, in modern terms, to nonrecognition of the sending State or to a rupture of diplomatic relations, foreshadowing war. Envoys were received and dispatched by the popular assemblies, which likewise drew up their instructions. Only persons of distinction, wisdom, and ripe years were chosen. From an early period, all diplomatic representatives and their attachés enjoyed inviolability and exemption from local authority and were recognized to have the right to come and go as they pleased in the execution of their duties. A "consular service" likewise grew up in the institution of the *proxenoi*, who were permanent officials appointed to furnish commercial information to their home State and to give advice and assistance to its citizens abroad.

Though Greek scholars, including the prolific Aristotle, never treated in systematic form any body of custom comparable with modern international law, the actual practices of the city-states were based upon general recognition of rules binding on all. There was assumed to exist a universal "law of nature" or of reason to which men were bound. Although there was, in regard to many matters, one law for the Greeks and another for the barbarians, the relations among the Greek States themselves were regulated by principles which closely approximate our "law of nations." They covered such subjects as personal and property rights as affected by conflicting laws of various States ("private international law" in modern terminology), naturalization, status of

---

[1] "Zeus, most glorious, most mighty, and ye other immortal gods! Whosoever shall first commit wrong contrary to their pledges, may their brains and their children's be dispersed on the ground, like this wine, and may their wives prove faithless." See Coleman Phillipson, *The International Law and Custom of Ancient Greece and Rome*, Vol. I, pp. 386–387.

aliens, right of asylum, extradition, alliances, treaties, diplomatic privileges and immunities, and the like. The international law of war was no less developed than that of peace.

Another feature of the Greek State System deserving of special mention was the extensive development of arbitration and of permanent agencies of cooperation, foreshadowing what has come to be described as "international organization" in our Western State System. The pacific settlement of disputes by submission to an impartial third party was a procedure familiar to the Greeks from the earliest times. Controversies were often submitted to the arbitration of the Delphic oracle, the Amphictyonic Council, a third State, or a tribunal of individuals picked by the litigants. Treaties of alliance frequently contained "compromise clauses" providing for the arbitration of such disputes as might arise between the parties. From an alliance to a confederation was but a step. The Greek leagues often served as agencies for the peaceable adjustment of quarels among their members and for the promotion of cooperation in dealing with matters of common interest. The earliest confederations, or amphictyonies, were religious in character and were devoted to the communal celebration of festivals. The antiquity of the Delphian Amphictyony, later called the Amphictyonic League, is attested by the fact that it was an association not of cities but of the 12 kindred tribes of the Greek peoples, each with two votes in the semi-annual councils at Delphi and Thermopylae. This organization has sometimes been described as the Greek prototype of the League of Nations. It promoted religious unity among the Greeks, diminished the barbarities of war, arbitrated disputes, and subsequently became an instrument of Macedonian, and later Roman, hegemony over the peninsula. The other Greek leagues in some cases were approximations of modern federal governments and in others were the means through which a powerful State dominated its weaker allies. Such were the first and second Athenian Leagues, the Peloponnesian League, and the Achaean League.

That the Greek State System never attained stability, unity, and peace and finally collapsed before foreign foes was due to the fact that its members, despite their common heritage, were never capable for long of subordinating the special interests of the local polis to the general interests of the Greeks as a whole. Although the exaltation of city-state patriotism undoubtedly contributed to the rich profusion of Greek civilization, it rendered impossible the development of a type of interstate political organization which could assure permanence to the System. In their days of decadence, when the bright radiance of the great creative period had burned itself out, the city-states fell easy victims to the power of Philip and Alexander of Macedonia, rulers of a younger and more vigorous people to the north. Amid all the political changes of the ensuing centuries in the eastern Mediterranean, they never fully recovered their independence.

If Macedonia succeeded in doing what Persia had failed to do, the cause lay less in superiority of fighting power than in the inner enfeeblement of Greek democracy itself. In 359 B.C. Philip became King of this peasant land of herds-men and fighters north of Thessaly. The court language, however, was Attic Greek. Philip cultivated Euripides and Aristotle—who helped to educate young Prince Alexander. With the aid of disciplined cavalry, a perfected infantry phalanx, and the use of catapults as artillery, Philip extended his realm to include portions of Thrace, Illyria, and Epirus and most of Thessaly. He was tormented by his jealous wife, Olympias, Princess of Epirus, who inflamed Alexander against him. But he became the most potent monarch of his time.

Against "appeasement" of his ambitions Demosthenes (384–322 B.C.) sought in vain to warn the Greeks. The city-states could not act in unison even in the face of this formidable menace. Many among their citizens favored a Pan-Hellenic crusade against Persia under Philip's leadership. In 338 B.C. Philip's army crushed the Athenians and their allies at Chaeronea—and Philip then granted a generous peace with an eye to things to come. Two years later he was murdered. His son, Alexander, aged twenty, inherited the kingdom and devoted himself to a mission.

After destroying rebellious Thebes, he led a great army overland against Persia, conquering Asia Minor in 334–333 B.C. A year later he entered Egypt and liberated it from Persian rule. The time was the Thirty-third Dynasty since Menes. Here he allowed himself to be persuaded by the Oracle of Amon that he was no mere mortal but the son of a god, Amon Ra—or, perchance, of Zeus. Here also he founded the city of Alexandria. In 331 B.C. he destroyed the Persian Army at Arbela, took Babylon and Susa, and then spent seven years subduing and exploring the vast regions of Turkestan and western India, which he entered by the Khyber Pass. He would have pushed on to the Ganges and perhaps to China, but his troops refused. In 323 B.C. after much hard drinking in Babylon, he died of a fever at the age of thirty-three. His last years were marred by cruelty and vanity. His wife, Roxanna, his sons, and finally his mother, Olympias, all died by murder.

The genius of Alexander the Great created the first approximation of a true "world empire" of Eurasia. Through his work much of western Asia was Hellenized, even as Hellas itself fell more and more under cultural influences from the Orient. The imposing political structure which he built dissolved at once into a ferment of secession, disorder, and assassination—until the whole again became an anarchy of separate sovereignties, all of which were now the degenerate remnants of realms in full decay. In life Alexander had caught, and carried to partial realization, the shadowy vision of a united world, em-bracing all men in one great community. In death he became the symbol of a dream.

THE GRANDEUR THAT WAS ROME

3. THE GRANDEUR THAT WAS ROME

Roman history, after the generation of Julius Cæsar, is not the story of political experiments in miniature, such as the brief city states made; nor is it concerned with a balance of power between nations, like so much later European history; nor with the fluctuating strength and weakness of rival Empires, such as forms the background to the history of the Near East in the centuries before Christ. We are justified in saying that the Roman Empire was an experiment in world government. Rome combined in her citizen body almost as many peoples, though not as many races, as the United Nations. She evolved such a flexible system that a native of Spain or Gaul could reach the position of Emperor at Rome by peaceful means. In the best age of her Empire she seemed to have made the *Pax Romana* a working instrument of prosperity, with racial prejudices sinking into oblivion. It was not a world-wide Empire. Other civilizations existed, for example in China and South America, the one known to enterprising Roman traders, the other quite unknown. Nevertheless, it was more than just a neat pun when Roman writers boasted that their *urbs* (city) was being turned into *orbis* (a world), and *vice versa.*—LAWRENCE WADDY, *Pax Romana and World Peace.*

When Alexander died, his imperium did not embrace China, nor the bulk of India, about to attain a measure of unity under the Mauryas. Neither did it extend to the Greek colonies scattered over the shores of the Middle Sea. Midway between the Hellespont and the Pillars of Hercules lay Italy. Here arose slowly a new people and a new Power, destined to complete on a larger stage the work of unification through conquest begun by the Macedonian.

Rome was founded, the Romans believed, in the year we should reckon as 753 B.C. Vergil's *Aeneid* is a late rendering of the legend that its founders were refugees from Troy. Another myth held that Romulus and Remus, sons of Mars and suckled as babies by a wolf, were the first builders of the city. In fact, centuries earlier, barbarians speaking a primitive Latin variant of the Aryan group of languages had filtered into Italy from the north. Later, from the east by sea, came civilized invaders who imposed their rule on the tribes north of the Tiber. These were the Etruscans, who may have been refugees from Crete. At a ford in the Tiber, where Etruscans traded with Latins, a city grew. Its Etruscan Kings were driven out in 510 B.C. Rome became a Latin Republic. Etruscan power was broken by a war with Syracuse and by a devastating invasion of Gauls who plundered Rome itself in 390 B.C. But a century later the Romans were masters of all central Italy.

These early conquerors, whose descendants were to build an imperium the like of which has never since been seen, were farmers. They were divided into "patricians" and "plebeians" (rich and poor) with the two classes originally "castes"—*i.e.*, groups between which intermarriage was forbidden. Slaves and aliens were barred from citizenship. Supreme power was vested in a Senate, whose members were appointed by two elected "consuls." Since the patricians dominated both the Senate and the Consulate, this polity was an aristocracy, mitigated by a Popular Assembly and by a chronic class struggle between nobles and plebs, with the latter represented by the Assembly and its "tribunes." In crises all power was temporarily entrusted to a "dictator." At least in the early centuries, political rivalries were marked by moderation and compromise. In these qualities, coupled with military and administrative skill, lay the secret of the Roman conquest of the Mediterranean world. Allies were conciliated. Conquered peoples were admitted to citizenship. Representative government, as we know it, never developed in Rome. The Senate finally became the tool of a wealthy oligarchy. But the forms of popular participation were never wholly lost.

Across the sea in the Phoenician settlement at Carthage grew another Republic, with a Senate, an Assembly, and two elected "Kings." Its power was naval power. Its elite consisted of wealthy merchants. When Pyrrhus, King of Epirus and a kinsman of the great Alexander, successfully attacked Rome in 280 B.C. with his phalanxes, cavalry, and war elephants, Carthage formed an alliance with Rome and contributed to the defeat of the aggressor. In the apportionment of the spoils of victory Rome took southern Italy, and Carthage, most of Sicily. But with the common threat of a third Great Power removed the victors became rivals. Had the other members of the larger Mediterranean State System perceived that the triumph of either over the other would leave the rest helpless, they would have combined against the stronger in accordance with balance-of-power calculations. But their rulers lacked this wisdom. The results were inexorable and momentous.

"Old, unhappy, far-off things, and battles long ago" can here only be hinted at, since no one unfamiliar with the tale of Rome can pretend to knowledge of the fountainhead of our Western civilization. In the first "Punic War" (264–240 B.C.) the Carthaginians were vanquished and forced to yield Sicily. In the second (218–202) their greatest commander, Hannibal, invaded Italy, destroyed Roman armies at Lake Trasimene and Cannae (216), but finally withdrew and suffered defeat at Zama, near his own capital. In the third (149–146) the Romans besieged and took Carthage, butchered or enslaved the survivors, burned the city, and plowed the site with salt. The legions had already smashed Macedonia's phalanxes at Cynoscephalae (197), beaten Antiochus III, Seleucid King of Asia Minor, and destroyed Corinth in 146 B.C. Rhodes, Pergamum, and the Greek Leagues all passed under Roman rule.

By the time of Julius Caesar, suspected of royal ambitions and assassinated in 44 B.C., the town on the Tiber was already the capital of a World State. Octavian, nephew of Julius, vanquished his rivals in civil war. He refused to be dictator and sought to restore the Republic. But the old times were gone. Senate and people alike called Octavian "Princeps" or First Citizen and gave him the title of *Imperator Caesar Augustus*. When he died in A.D. 14 the Roman State, behind republican forms, had become an imperial monarchy and a Universal Empire.

As an imperium embracing all the civilized world, save for the Parthians and more remote Hindus and Chinese, Rome had no international relations but only a task of defending the frontiers against the barbarians. Yet Roman practices in foreign affairs are not without interest. From early days, decisions of war and peace and the negotiation of treaties were entrusted to the College of Fetials (*collegium fetialium*). All wars were "just wars," declared and conducted in accordance with ceremonial rules and only after efforts at a pacific solution had failed. If the *pater patratus* of the Fetials, acting as negotiator, failed to achieve a peaceful settlement, he so reported to the Senate. In the event of a decision for war, he hurled a bloody spear on the soil of the enemy to the accompaniment of appropriate oaths and invocations to Jupiter and other deities. As Rome expanded, the Fetials were represented by envoys and the ceremony of hurling the spear was performed, in symbolic fashion, on the Campus Martius or, later, before the temple of Bellona. The Fetials were also entrusted with treaty making, but foreign envoys had audiences with the Senate during February in the *Grecostiasis*, an open rostrum near the Capitol. In the imperial period, the Emperor took over these functions. Almost all Roman treaties were unequal and in perpetuity in the sense that they imposed upon the other party a permanent status of dependence. The *jus gentium* of the Romans was not a body of true international law, but a set of legal principles adapted to the problems arising out of the relations of Roman citizens with citizens of other States which were friends or allies of Rome.

Despite their admiration for the Greeks, the Romans never developed any conception of international relations based upon a system of independent States dealing with one another as equals. The vision of world dominion was at all times, consciously or unconsciously, inherent in the attitudes of Rome in dealing with other peoples. The World Empire in its final form rested upon the extinction of the earlier States and State Systems. Though it was a huge international or cosmopolitan structure made up of diverse elements, its whole organization and indeed its very existence precluded the possibility of those customs, procedures, and institutions of international intercourse which inevitably develop within a society of equal and independent political entities.

The rest of Rome's story need not here concern us, save as it created a myth to which all later ages paid homage. Augustus was followed by Tiberius, he by the mad Caligula, and he in turn by his uncle Claudius (A.D. 41–55), raised to "Imperator" by the praetorian or palace guard. Claudius added Mauretania and part of Britain to the Empire and permitted sycophants to make "Caesar" a title of omnipotence and to deify the Emperor. Following the suicide of Nero (A.D. 54–68), four Emperors succeeded one another in a single year until the more secure dynasties of the Flavian and Antonine Caesars restored internal peace and reached their culmination in the reign of the Stoic philosopher, Marcus Aurelius (A.D. 161–180). Under Trajan (A.D. 98–117) the Empire attained its maximum size, with its 44 provinces stretching from

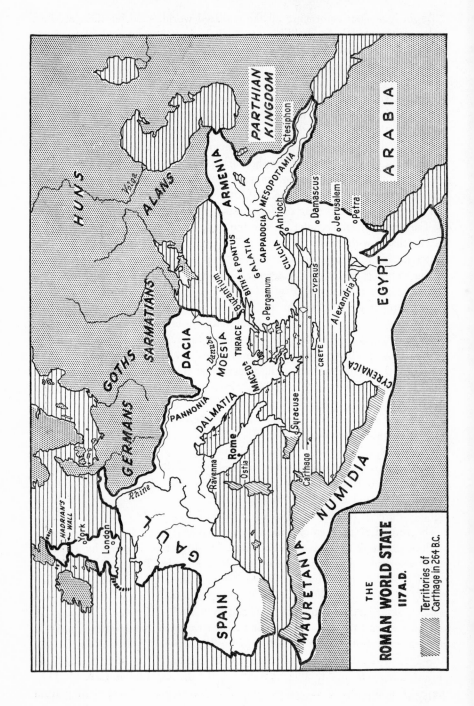

THE
ROMAN WORLD STATE
117 A.D.

Territories of
Carthage in 264 B.C.

mid-Scotland to the Caspian and the Persian Gulf and from the plains of "Romania" to the Sahara. Trajan's successor, Hadrian, abandoned Armenia, Mesopotamia, and southern Scotland, as his successors abandoned Dacia, north of the lower Danube, the better to defend the frontiers by walls and garrisons against the barbarians. In A.D. 395 the Empire was permanently divided into Eastern and Western halves, each with its own Caesar.

In the memory of days to come this Universal State was the most impressive and enduring ever reared by the hand of man. Over 100,000,000 people lived within its far-flung borders. Well-built roads united its parts. Imperial architecture graced its cities. Roman law, first codified in 450 B.C. in the "Twelve Tables," evolved into a magnificent legal system which long afforded justice to all citizens. Races, nations, and cultures were mingled in a cosmopolitan imperium, infused with Hellenic art and learning and with Roman skills in governance. The Roman World State, to be sure, was a military despotism imposed on a corrupt plutocracy. Its masses of slaves, tenant farmers, and urban proletarians were more interested in "bread and circuses" than in any loyalty to a cause or any devotion to a mission. Even by its own standards, its ruling class was dishonest, grasping, and irresponsible. Masses and classes alike relished the cruelties of gladiatorial combats and savage political and religious persecutions to a degree which precluded any real appreciation of individual dignity. Intellectuals and bureaucrats, though able and creative, never caught the vision of science, technology, and industry, nor did they see the need of Romanizing the barbarians before they barbarized Rome. In the end this enterprise of One World failed. But the effort embodied in the Pax Romana was nevertheless the most inspiring in all the annals of the Western peoples.

4. THE MEMORY OF THE GREAT PEACE

But how the world has fared since that "seamless robe" [the Roman Empire] has suffered rending by the talons of ambition, we may read in books; would that we might not see it with our eyes. Oh, race of mankind! What storms must toss thee, what losses must thou endure, what shipwrecks must buffet thee, as long as thou, a beast of many heads, strivest after contrary things! Thou art sick in both thy faculties of understanding; thou art sick in thy affections. Unanswerable reasons fail to heal thy higher understanding; the very sight of experience convinces not thy lower understanding; not even the sweetness of divine persuasion charms thy affections, when it breathes unto thee through the music of the Holy Spirit: "Behold how good and how pleasant it is for brethren to dwell together in unity!"—DANTE, *De monarchia.*

Edward Gibbon in his *Decline and Fall of the Roman Empire* attributed the demise of the World State of the Caesars to the triumph of barbarism and religion. A different formulation is more in accord with current judgments.

Rome was finally overwhelmed by the barbarians because the Roman community itself had already been "barbarized," partly through a slow infiltration of nomads who were never fully assimilated, and partly through an incurable cleavage between elite and masses. The powerful lost effective means of perpetuating their way of life. The poor lost effective interest in whether the *status quo* was preserved or disrupted.

The new religion might have aided its converts to restore unity and strength to a sick society, had they been capable of translating its ethical precepts into social, economic, and political terms. This was beyond their power. But their faith became the means through which something at least of the precious heritage of the old times was rescued from the wreckage and utilized in the coming "Dark Age" to nourish the growth of a new civilization. That new civilization is our own. The religion which helped to give it continuity with the vanished Greco-Roman world is, of course, Christianity—for which Gibbon had small respect.

Diocletian (A.D. 284–305), who converted Roman government from a mockery of republicanism into a burlesque of Oriental despotism, persecuted Christians because they would not admit the divinity of Caesar. But Constantine the Great (306–37), who moved his capital to the new city of Constantinople (Byzantium) on the Bosporus, followed the sign of the Cross and summoned at Nicaea in 325 the first general council of Christian leaders. A creed was written to put an end to doctrinal dissension. Rigid dogma facilitated the organization of a priesthood, regimented in an elaborate hierarchy. The Church was inevitably modeled on the Roman imperial pattern, particularly after Theodosius in 392 made Christianity the State religion. The Bishop-Patriarch of Rome became "Pope" and later adopted the title of *Pontifex Maximus*, earlier claimed by the Caesars. What had first been the humble faith of the poor and lowly was now a Universal ("Catholic") Church, exercising immense power in its own right. St. Augustine's *City of God* was a vision of the Church ruling over all the kings and nations of men. As the barbarians inundated the Empire and embraced the Christian faith, this vision approached realization.

From the time of Marcus Aurelius the Emperors had settled barbarian captives on the land as *coloni* and had taken them into the army. In A.D. 376, the Emperor Valens admitted a great horde of Visigoths who had been driven from their lands by the Huns. But the Visigoths rose in revolt, slew the Emperor and his legionnaires, and ravaged Macedonia and Thrace. Theodosius made peace by settling them south of the Danube. Thirty years later, another Visigothic chieftain, Alaric, led his warriors across the Alps, devastated Italy, and sacked Rome (A.D. 410). The elevation of Alaric's successor, Atolf, to the command of the imperial armies is indicative of the impotence to which the Roman State had been reduced. Britain was evacuated by the legions. The distant frontiers crumbled. Barbarian hosts wandered through the provinces. Out of the east came the dreaded Huns under Attila. After his hordes were beaten at Châlons-sur-Marne in 451, they invaded Italy, only to withdraw again into the eastern wilderness. The Vandals carried fire and sword through Gaul and Spain, occupied North Africa, crossed the sea, and sacked Rome once more in 455. In 476 the little six-year-old Emperor, Romulus Augustulus, was deprived of his throne by Odoacer, chief of the mercenaries. The imperial insignia were sent to Constantinople with the request that the Emperor Zeno permit Odoacer to administer Italy as a province of the Eastern Empire. This final "fall of Rome" was but an incident in a century of turmoil, but it marked the end of the Western Empire as a political entity.

Yet Rome dead was more powerful than Rome alive. The city remained the seat of the Papacy, which asserted its spiritual supremacy over the Christianized barbarian kingdoms. The unity of Christendom was revived by the power of the Church. The memory of the vanished World State lingered in the minds of the barbarians. Catholic Christianity and this vision of order and peace under a Universal Empire were the two great legacies which Classical civilization left to its heirs. The religious and political history of the long springtime of Western civilization—traditionally misnamed the "Middle Ages"—is largely the story of the Church and the "Empire"—the former a living reality of medieval life, the latter the unreal dream of a vanished past which could never be quite recovered. The new State System which rose on the ruins of Roman power was long under the spell of the Popes and the Caesars.

In the "Dark Ages" which followed the fall of Rome, the Eastern Empire was a beacon in the night. The Emperor Justinian (527–65) codified Roman law in its final form and sent his great general, Belisarius, to recover the Mediterranean world from the barbarians. But the rescued provinces were soon inundated once more by hordes from the north. The Byzantine Empire abandoned the enterprise and looked to its own defenses.

In the West the barbarians settled on the land, absorbed the remnants of Roman culture, and embarked upon State building. Conditions were ripe for the development of a new system of independent sovereignties. But the vision of unity persisted. The Kingdom of the Franks, established in what had been Roman Gaul, allied itself with the Papacy and gradually extended its power over its neighbors. It was the Franks who saved Christendom from Moslem conquest by defeating the Saracens at Tours in 732. At the end of the century the greatest of the Frankish kings, Charlemagne, had so widely extended his control over the pagans that his realm reached from northern Spain to the Baltic and from the Atlantic to the Oder. In 799 he restored Leo III to the Holy See by frustrating the schemes of the Pope's enemies. On Christmas Day, A.D. 800, in the Church of St. Peter at Rome, the grateful Leo placed an imperial crown upon the head of the Frankish monarch, while the populace shouted, "To Charles, the Augustus, crowned by God, great and pacific Emperor of the Romans, life and victory!" Thus, with the sanction of the Papacy, the Empire was at length restored by the power of Frankish arms, and one Emperor ruled again over most of Western Christendom.[2]

This restoration was ephemeral, however. The realm of Charles the Great fell to the weakest of his sons, Louis the Pious, in 814 and was promptly divided among the grandsons. Wars and further partitions followed. The eastern, or "German," portion separated itself from the western, or "French," portion. Both halves were set upon during the 9th Century by new invaders. New rulers were crowned "Emperor" by the Popes, but their authority was feeble. The imperial crown was finally transferred to a German King in the person of Charles the Fat in 881. When Henry the Fowler, Duke of the Saxons, was elected King in 919 by the Saxon and Franconian nobles, he renounced imperial ambitions and busied himself with beating back the Magyars and restoring order in his domains. His son, Otto, continued the work with such success that he was able to extend his power into Italy and in 962 was crowned Emperor by the Pope. The compact between the Roman Bishop and the German King laid the basis for what later came to be called the "Holy Roman Empire of the German Nation"—a curious political structure with a double sovereignty, resting upon the notion that the Empire and the Papacy were, respectively, the temporal and spiritual agencies designated by the divine will for the governance of Christendom.

The imperial crown passed to the House of Hohenstaufen and later to the House of Hapsburg, where it remained until the extinction of the Empire in 1806. The theory of the Empire as the successor of the Roman World State was not much modified either by the great conflicts between Popes and Emperors for supremacy or by the fact that the Empire had no effective authority outside of the German States and Italy. Even in these regions the imperial power was constantly flouted by duchies, principalities, and free cities. Such powers as the Emperor wielded he derived less from his imperial office than from the lands and subjects which he controlled as a German King among many kings. It could almost be said of the Empire from the beginning what Voltaire said of it in the 18th Century: that it was neither Holy nor Roman nor

---

[2] David Jayne Hill aptly characterizes the significance of this ceremony as follows: "The two figures before the high altar of St. Peter's on that Christmas Day form a symbolical picture of the whole course of history since the time of the Caesars. The Roman and the German, the overshadowing past and the potential present, the universal and the individual, the majesty of law and the vigor of liberty, the world of the spirit and the world of actuality, imperial right and barbarian energy—all these are present, and all are henceforth to be combined as if swallowed up in one new creation. But it is the German who kneels in pious devotion, the present which humbles itself before the past, the individual who feels the power of the universal, the vigor of liberty which yields to the majesty of law, the actual which seeks strength from the spiritual, and the barbarian who has been conquered by the Empire. It is the Roman who bestows the crown, the Roman who speaks in the name of the divinity, the Roman whose transfigured republic is to profit by Rome's latest conquest; for after centuries of suffering, toil, tragedy, it is the triumph of Rome's work which is before us." (*A History of Diplomacy in the International Development of Europe*, Vol. I, pp. 95–96.)

an Empire. It was the ghost of ancient Rome. Men yearned for peace in a world of endless war. But the structure of Western society doomed that yearning to perpetual frustration. The statesman became a new Tantalus, constantly groping for that which lay beyond his reach, constantly striving to realize an ideal which the conditions of the time put past all realization.

Nowhere in medieval literature is this tragedy more poignantly expressed than in the *De monarchia* of Dante Alighieri, jurist, poet, and author of the immortal *Divine Comedy*. His political essay was described by Lord Bryce as the "epitaph of the Holy Roman Empire." It is indeed a cry of despair, a last plea for unity in a world of inescapable diversity. It represents both the culmination and the close of medieval theorizing on international relations.

De monarchia was written about 1309, twelve years before Dante's death, at the period of the "Babylonian captivity" of the Papacy, when the Popes were residing at Avignon under the surveillance of the French monarchy. No Emperor had visited Italy for over half a century. The Italian city-states were waging chronic war upon one another for power and territory. Great hopes were entertained that the newly elected Emperor, Henry VII, would come to Italy for his coronation and would restore peace to the land. Dante, as a student of law and government who had served on several Florentine embassies, shared this hope and wrote his famous essay as a defense of the Empire and as an appeal for general recognition of its supremacy. In allegorical style, he presented the arguments in favor of his ideal:

Whole heaven is regulated by a single ruler—God. It follows that the human race is at its best state when it is ruled by a single prince and one law. So it is evidently necessary for the welfare of the world that there should be a single monarchy or princedom, which men call the Empire. Whenever disputes arise, there must be judgment. Between any two independent princes controversy may arise and then judgment is necessary. Now an equal cannot rule over his equal, so there must be a third prince of wider jurisdiction who is ruler over both, to decide the dispute. This third ruler must be the monarch or Emperor. And so monarchy is necessary for the world. . . . Moreover, the world is ordered best when justice is most powerful, and justice is most powerful under a monarchy or empire.

Dante cited the age of Augustus as the Golden Age of mankind and concluded with a dramatic exhortation to restore the past. But the hope was vain. Henry came to Italy and was crowned. He brought not peace, but a sword. Rome was torn by the struggles between Guelfs and Ghibellines. Emperor and Pope, whom Dante had envisaged as two facets of a single perfect entity, quarreled violently in words and in arms. Henry was placed under the ban of the Church by Clement V at Avignon, who was supported by the King of France in rendering aid to Robert of Naples and the cities of the north, which resisted the imperial power. Henry laid unsuccessful siege to Florence and died in 1313, carrying with him to the grave all prospects of restoring the prestige of the Empire in Italy. The peninsula, like all Europe, was a welter of warring States, with the Empire but a specter of half-forgotten yesterdays.

Yet the magic which the memory of the Caesars had spun into men's minds has endured through all the centuries since. The Emperors of Byzantium called themselves "Caesars" as long as their realm survived. The Kings of Bulgaria were "Tsars"—*i.e.*, Caesars. Ivan the Terrible, whose Muscovite Empire was already called the "Third Rome," also took the title of Tsar. The Emperor of modern Germany was "Kaiser." The Mongol rulers of India called themselves "Kaisar-i-Hind," the title inherited by British Sovereigns. Not without cause is a new period of despots called an "Age of Caesarism." The work wrought by a vanished Rome lives on in the deeds of posterity. Its ultimate symbol of power and peace will fascinate all rulers and ruled to the end of time.

SUGGESTED READINGS

Aristides, Aelius: *To Rome* (ed. and trans. by Saul Levin), Glencoe, Ill., Free Press, 1953.

Breasted, James H.: *The Dawn of Conscience*, New York, Scribner, 1933.

Bryce, James: *The Holy Roman Empire*, New York, Macmillan, 1914.

Ceram, C. W.: *The Secret of the Hittites*, New York, Knopf, 1955.

Diehl, Charles: *Byzantium: Greatness and Decline*, New Brunswick, N.J., Rutgers University Press, 1957.

Frank, Tenney: *Roman Imperialism*, New York, Macmillan, 1914.

Freud, Sigmund: *Moses and Monotheism*, New York, Knopf, 1939.

Hammond, Mason: *City-State and World State in Greek and Roman Political Theory until Augustus*, Cambridge, Mass., Harvard University Press, 1951.

Hill, D. J.: *A History of Diplomacy in the International Development of Europe* (3 vols.), New York, Longmans, 1924.

Homo, Léon P.: *Roman Political Institutions*, New York, Knopf, 1930.

Hrozny, Bedrich: *Ancient History of Western Asia, India and Crete*, New York, Philosophical Library, 1954.

Lamb, Harold: *Alexander of Macedon: The Journey to World's End*, New York, Doubleday, 1946.

Larsen, J. A. O.: *Representative Government in Greek and Roman History*, Berkeley, Calif., University of California Press, 1954.

Marsh, F. B.: *A History of the Roman World from 146 to 30 B.C.*, New York, Macmillan, 1953.

Numelin, Ragnar: *The Beginnings of Diplomacy*, New York, Philosophical Library, 1950.

Phillipson, Coleman: *The International Law and Custom of Ancient Greece and Rome* (2 vols.), London, Macmillan, 1911.

Rostovtzeff, M.: *The Social and Economic History of the Hellenistic World* (3 vols.), New York, Oxford, 1941.

Runes, Dagobert D. (ed.): *The Hebrew Impact on Western Civilization*, New York, Philosophical Library, 1950.

Scullard, H. H.: *Roman Politics: 220–150 B.C.*, New York, Oxford, 1951.

Tod, Marcus N.: *International Arbitration among the Greeks*, New York, Oxford, 1913.

Turner, Ralph E.: *The Great Cultural Traditions: The Foundations of Civilization*, New York, McGraw-Hill, 1940.

Waddy, Lawrence: *Pax Romana and World Peace*, New York, Norton, 1951.

Walter, Gerard: *Caesar*, New York, Scribner, 1952.

Chapter II

THE DAWN OF THE WEST

1. EUROPE AND ASIA

All nations of the West are of dynastic origin. In the Romanesque and even in Early Gothic architecture the soul of the Carolingian primitives still quivers through. There is no French or German Gothic, but Salian, Rhenish, and Suabian, as there is Visigothic (northern Spain, southern France) and Lombard and Saxon Romanesque. But over it all there spreads soon the minority, composed of men of race, that feels membership in a nation as a great historical vocation. From it proceed the Crusades, and in them there truly were French and German chivalries. It is the hallmark of Faustian peoples that they are conscious of the direction of their history.—OSWALD SPENGLER, *The Decline of the West*, Vol. II.

THE "modern world" in all its aspects, including its State System, has its roots in the culture of Western Christendom, slowly struggling toward the light out of barbaric darkness between the 5th and 10th Centuries of our era. This half millennium, and much that followed, is widely viewed as a time of unprecedented ignorance, squalor, misery, and brutality —so much so as to set the "medieval" age off sharply from "ancient" grandeur and from the wonders wrought by "modern" man.

Despite the glory of the cathedrals and of monastic art and learning, this judgment is not inaccurate. But it stands in need of two corrections. The first is that the conditions of life here noted prevailed only in Europe—which is but a small peninsula of Asia. During this same period Byzantium was the largest and richest city on earth. To the south and east other urban cultures flourished and bred works incomparably superior to anything then done by Europeans. The second flaw in vulgar judgments of the "Middle Ages" is the assumption of an end of the old and a beginning of the new around A.D. 1500. Not only was there no such break, but we and all our works are products of "medieval" civilization.

What tends to blind us to these realities is the fact that the culture of Europe, once equipped with a new science and technology and supplied with increments of power flowing from accumulated wealth, expanding population, and novel weapons of war, spread itself over Asia, Africa, and the Americas with such insistence, tenacity, and invincible might that no other could stand against it. All the peoples of the globe have in varying measure been "Europeanized" in the process. The contemporary State System which covers the planet is, in most of its essentials, European as to origins, practices, and motivations. But its point of departure was early Western Christendom, in whose development the "Dark" and "Middle" Ages were but the sunrise and morning of a day which is now past noon.

The Europe of the dawn (and therefore the world of the afternoon) is unintelligible unless the observer takes note of a unity which has since been lost and of an external threat which is now forgotten. The "unity of Christendom" was more than a phrase in the generations which followed the ascendancy of the Popes of Rome. The Byzantines, to be sure, went their own way. The rift between "Roman" and "Greek" Christianities, already clear in the 5th Century, became a final rupture in 1054. Similarly, the Nestorian and Monophysite Christianities of Central Asia in olden times had little to do with either Byzantium or Rome. But in the West all Christians were Catholics. All were united in a common faith under a common Church.

The Pope was not merely the spiritual head of Christendom but exercised temporal powers as well, both as ruler of the Papal States in central Italy and as the Vicar of Christ upon earth with power over emperors, kings, and princes. As kings were crowned by the bishops of the Church, the Emperor was crowned by the Pope himself. He who gives is superior to him who receives. The Papacy not only asserted its authority over temporal rulers but offered its services as arbitrator to settle disputes between them. Such offers were often coupled with insistence upon acceptance. This arbitral procedure was widely utilized, particularly among the Princes of the Italian States. The national monarchies of the West likewise resorted to it. Among the more famous of the papal arbitrations were those between Philip le Bel and the English King (1298), between Philip le Long and the Flemings (1319), between the Emperor Maximilian and the Doge of Venice in the 15th Century, and between Spain and Portugal regarding their claims in the New World in 1494. Non-ecclesiastical arbitration was also developed as a means of settling disputes by the Swiss cantons, the cities of the Hanseatic League, the German States, and even by the English and French monarchies [1] but the Papacy may properly be regarded as having made the greatest contributions to international arbitration.

The Church likewise played an important part in the development of diplomatic practices and of the rudimentary international law which gradually came to be recognized by the various European States. From early times the Popes had dispatched envoys (*legati*) to attend Church councils and had regularly maintained ambassadors (*apocrisiarii*) at the Byzantine court until relations were severed between Constantinople and the Holy See in consequence of religious differences. Similar representatives were exchanged between the Vatican and the exarch at Ravenna. Later the Popes sent envoys to the Emperor and to

[1] See J. H. Ralston, *International Arbitration from Athens to Locarno*, 1929, pp. 176–178, for types of medieval arbitration treaties.

the courts of England, France, Naples, Hungary, Aragon, Castile, and other States. Ecclesiastical influence was also important in the development of Byzantine diplomacy, which, in turn, influenced the diplomatic practices of the Italian city-states in the 14th Century. As regards international law, the Archbishop of Seville, St. Isidore, was writing as early as the 7th Century, in his *Etymologies,* of the *jus gentium* of the Romans as a body of law having to do with "wars, captivities, enslavements, the recovery of rights of postliminy,

THE MEDIEVAL
STATE SYSTEM
c. 1360 A.D.
Holy Roman Empire
Lands of the Church
Lands of the Hapsburgs
Lands of Edward III

treaties of peace and others, the scruple which protects ambassadors from violence, and prohibition of marriage between persons of different nationality." The efforts of the Church to restrict private warfare and protect noncombatants led to a marked development of what later came to be known as the international law of war and neutrality. In insisting upon the observance of the "Truce of God," the Church forbade fighting on Sunday. In the 11th Century, efforts were made to extend the period of Sabbath peace from Wednesday evening to Monday morning and to apply it to religious holidays and to the whole period of Lent. In 1095, Pope Urban II decreed it for all Christendom in this form. The *Pax Ecclesiae* forbade fighting in the vicinity of Church buildings or against clerics, pilgrims, merchants, women, or peasants, thus neutralizing certain areas and protecting certain categories of persons from the rigors of war.

If ecclesiastical anathemas and excommunications were not always effective in restraining the pugnacity of the embattled baronage, these efforts were nevertheless of great influence on later thought and practice and contributed toward the weaving together of the warp and woof of modern diplomacy. As neighborhood warfare declined under the pressure of clerical persuasion and kingly power, towns grew and waxed prosperous through the wider contacts which peace made possible. The Hanseatic trading cities of the north and the city-states of the Mediterranean maritime leagues built up a flourishing commerce which they fostered by exchanging commercial or consular representatives and by concluding numerous commercial treaties with one another. Political representatives followed on the heels of trading agents, and therewith the modern diplomatic service was established. International maritime law also evolved out of these relationships and received its first clear statement in the *Consolato del Mare* of the 14th Century.

The Crusades to rescue the Holy Land from the infidels united Europe and brought the rough warriors of the West into conflict with Saracen knights who fought like gentlemen. Chivalry was born. War became a science and an art to be practiced in accordance with fixed rules. Travel increased with trading and crusading. Feudal provincialism declined, and governments were brought into closer contact with one another. The dream of imperial unity gradually faded, and the new city-states and national monarchies dealt with one another as equals. Out of these new contacts between larger territorial units emerged a further development of diplomacy, international law, and modern statecraft.

But these are anticipations. Before they are examined, it will be well to review the series of formidable assaults on Christian Europe launched by peoples of other faiths. These incursions had three sources: (1) the Near East; (2) Scandinavia; and (3) the "steppe road" out of Asia, stretching from Mongolia to the Carpathians.

Among the Semitic nomads of Arabia, known to Greeks and Romans as "Saracens," was born in the holy city of Mecca, *c.* A.D. 570, a youth who tended cattle, became servant and then husband of a wealthy widow, and wrestled in the desert with his soul. This Mohammed at length preached a new gospel: God (Allah) is one, not many; after death, hell awaits the wicked and heaven the righteous; Abraham, Moses, Jesus, and other Semites were divine teachers, but the perfection of their work is the message of the Prophet—Mohammed. This founder of the most recent of the world religions fled to Medina in 622 (the Hegira) to escape murder by his foes in Mecca. Interurban and tribal wars ensued. When Mohammed died in 632, he was master of a United Arabia. The faith of Islam is rich in the virtues of generosity, brotherhood, and equality. It is devoid of any professional priesthood and singularly free of theological hairsplitting despite the early and persistent schism between Shiites and Sunnites. Its spread coincided with an astonishing upsurge of military power

58

and of art, literature, and science among the Arab peoples under the Omayyad and Abbasside Caliphs ("successors") of the Prophet.

Mohammed's disciples undertook to conquer the world for Allah. The Saracen armies, infused with holy fervor, struck north, east, and west, taking Palestine and Syria, Egypt and Mesopotamia, conquering all of Armenia and Persia and most of Turkestan, and sweeping like a tempest along the south shore of the Middle Sea. Spain was invaded in 711 and the Kingdom of the Franks soon afterward. The tide receded to the Pyrenees only when the hosts of Islam were beaten near Tours by Charles Martel in 732. In the East the

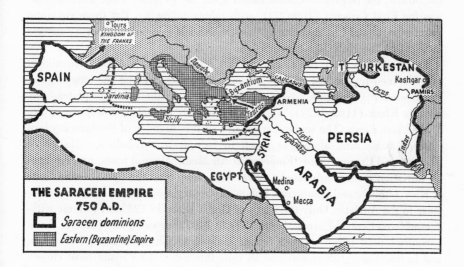

Saracen siege of Byzantium was broken by Leo the Isaurian in 717. The metropolis on the Bosporus was many times assailed but never taken by the Arabs, who likewise failed to break into the Balkans. Under Haroun-al-Raschid (786–809), immortal Caliph of Bagdad, the new Moslem world reached an acme of creative civilization in comparison with which the "Empire" of Charlemagne was a primitive and disorderly community of semi-barbarians. Christendom was saved for a different fate.

But the menace from the south was followed by graver threats from the north. In the 9th Century, swarms of pagan barbarians—variously known as Norsemen, Vikings, and Varangians—poured out of Scandinavia in swift fleets to raid, rob, kill, and at length settle down in England, in northern France (Normandy), and in Novgorod and Kiev, where they founded the first Russian State. Some of the seafarers, after exploring Iceland and Greenland, reached the American continent c. A.D. 1000, but left no settlements. Others took Sicily from the Saracens, attacked Byzantium, conquered England in 1066, and sacked Rome in 1084. But these fierce invaders were absorbed by their victims.

Danes and Normans embraced Roman Catholicism before 900, while the Varangians at Kiev adopted Greek Catholicism from the Byzantines in 989, as did the Bulgarian invaders of the Balkans. Similarly the Magyars, driven out of southern Russia into the Danube plain by the Patzinaks and long busied with destructive raids against the West, embraced the Roman version of Christianity c. A.D. 1000 and founded the Kingdom of Hungary. Against such assailants, the Cross of Christendom finally prevailed even when the sword had failed. When the Seljuk clan of Turks poured out of Turkestan to reunite and energize the now dormant Arab lands, conquering Asia Minor and menacing the Straits, the Byzantine Caesar called upon the Pope for help. The outcome was the First Crusade (1096–99), with others following. But these romantic counterassaults of Christendom against the infidels won only temporary success in wresting the Holy Land from Islam.

Two centuries later the Christian and Moslem worlds alike were almost overwhelmed by the last of the "barbarian invaders" along the steppe road. These were the Mongols, first politically united on their remote plateaus by Jenghis Khan (1162–1227), who established his capital at Karakorum, city of the black sands. The invincible cavalry of this founder of the largest of all empires made him, almost as much in fact as in symbolism, "Master of Thrones and Crowns" and "Emperor of All Men." Mongol hosts, never beaten by Christian arms, subjugated Central Asia, destroyed the first Russian State at Kiev (1240), and conquered Poland, Hungary, and all the lands from the Oder to the Adriatic. Only the death of Ogdai Khan in 1242 led to their withdrawal from Central Europe. From 1240 to 1480 they ruled all of Russia. Even Novgorod paid tribute. Other Khans conquered China, Burma, Indochina, and India. Among all empires of all time this astounding realm most closely approached a truly "World State." But with the passing generations the Eastern Mongols became Chinese, while those in the West embraced the faith of Allah.

One final effort to conquer Christendom and build a Eurasian "World State" on its ruins remains to be noted. The Seljuk Turks were gradually replaced as rulers of Islam by the Osmanli, or Ottoman Turks, under Osman (1288–1326) and Orkhan (1326–59). This new realm was sorely stricken but not crushed by the hideous assaults of the armies of Tamerlane (1369–1405), a Mongol conqueror from Samarkand who sought, with no lasting effect, to restore the Empire of Jenghis Khan by covering southwestern Asia with ashes and piles of skulls. The Ottoman Sultans built a great State and a powerful military machine by the extraordinary device of enslaving the male babies of Christian subjects and training them as Janizaries (professional soldiers), administrators, and statesmen. Unlike the Seljuks, the Osmanlis invaded the Balkans and crushed the Christian Serbs at Kossovo in 1389, thereby establishing a rule over most of Balkania which was to last over four centuries. In 1453, Turkish armies stormed the Roman walls of Byzantium, which had withstood all attacks for a thousand years. The imperial city of the Eastern Caesars, whose last ruler, Constantine Paleologus, fell by the sword of Islam, now became the Ottoman capital.

The victor, Sultan Mohammed II, invaded southern Italy and dreamed of taking Rome. His successors conquered Greece, invaded Poland, subdued Armenia, Mesopotamia, and Egypt, and made themselves Caliphs of all Islam. Under Suleiman the Magnificent (1520–66) the Ottoman realm reached its zenith. His armies defeated the Hungarians at Mohács (1526) and almost

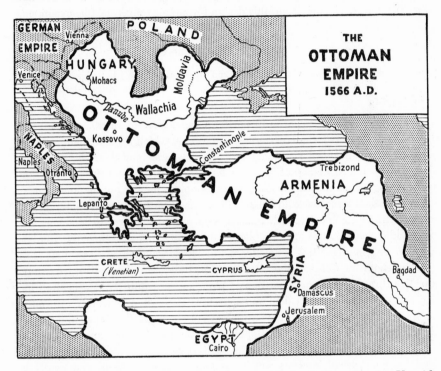

took Vienna in 1529. France made alliances with the Sultan. Charles V paid him tribute. But Christian Europe, although long since disunited, could yet rally against a common foe. At Lepanto (1571) the fleet of the "Christian League," led by the Pope, Venice, Austria, and Spain, destroyed the Ottoman Navy. Here, said Cervantes, who lost an arm in the battle, Christendom "broke the pride of the Osmans and undeceived the world which had regarded the Turkish fleet as invincible." Turkish armies again laid siege to Vienna as late as 1683, but again without success. Thereafter the Turkish wave receded as the imperium of the Sultans slowly decayed. When it died in 1918, it had long ceased to be either a threat to Christendom or even a "Great Power" in the new State System born in Western Europe.

The net result of these age-long efforts to subject Europe to Asia was failure. None of these attempts, and none of the successive endeavors at unification from within, united the Continent. Religious unity perished with the corruption of the Universal Church and the ensuing "Reformation." The memory of Rome, the aspirations of Popes and Emperors, the dream of Dante, and the common hope of those who, through the centuries, abhorred violence and cherished order—all alike came to nothing. Europe, and therefore the larger world community which Europe brought into being, became that which it still remains: a congeries of separate sovereignties, competing with one another for power. The origins of this design for anarchy must next be examined.

2. THE RISE OF "REALISM"

We are much beholden to Machiavel and others, that write what men do, and not what they ought to do.—FRANCIS BACON, *Proficience and Advancement of Learning.*

Modern diplomacy was born in northern Italy. Here there existed from the 12th Century onward a microcosmic State System which became the matrix in which modern statecraft was conceived. Here also emerged the first "modern" societies. Leonardo Pisano of Florence introduced Arabic numerals to Europe in 1202. Half a century later, double-entry bookkeeping made its appearance, along with the Florentine gold florin, which was soon the monetary standard of most of the Continent. Expanding business promoted the growth of a mercantile middle class, alongside the nobles of old. Both groups, in their passion for art, learning, and politics, engendered the "Renaissance."

After the 13th Century the city-states of Italy were free alike from any effective threat of external control and from any possibility of unification by any one of their number. Under these circumstances they inevitably evolved a complex pattern of relationships with one another and developed the art of diplomacy to a high level. The Republic of Venice—"school and touchstone of ambassadors"—perhaps contributed most to this development because of its far-flung commercial interests and its contacts with Byzantium. The Venetian authorities early began the practices of registering treaties, keeping diplomatic archives, and maintaining an elaborate system of commissions, instructions, records, and dispatches. By a law of 1268 a Venetian Ambassador was forbidden to take his wife along, lest she divulge his business, but required to take his cook along, lest he be poisoned. The *Consolato del Mare,* based upon the ancient "Tables of Amalfi," was solemnly approved by the Venetian representatives in Constantinople in 1255 as the basis of maritime international law and was later adopted by Pisa, Genoa, Naples, Aragon, and the States of the north. The ceremonies which the Venetians developed for the reception and dispatch of envoys influenced the practice of other States to a great degree. Agents were carefullly selected from the ranks of the nobility, until Venetian Ambassadors became models of honesty, competence, and *savoir-faire.*

In other States as well, diplomacy attracted the service of distinguished men.

The diplomatic service of Florence during the 13th and 14th Centuries included such illustrious names as Dante, Petrarch, and Boccaccio. These early diplomatic missions were at first limited to a few months' duration and later extended to several years. Not until the middle of the 15th Century did the practice become prevalent of maintaining permanent diplomatic posts at the seats of foreign governments. The first clear instance was the establishment of a permanent embassy at Genoa by Milan in 1455.

This structure of diplomatic practices was based upon the existence of a number of independent territorial States, free from external control and able to pursue their own interests by bargaining and fighting with one another. Here, as always in such a State System, each unit pursued such objectives as best served the interests of its ruling class; these objectives involved in each case a maximum extension of the territory and power of the State at the expense of its rivals. International politics was a competitive struggle for power. Dante might deplore the resulting chaos and plead for unity. Other reflective souls might call for solidarity, as did an obscure priest of Milan:

And thou, Milan, thou seekest to supplant Cremona, to overthrow Pavia, to destroy Novara. Thy hands are raised against all, and the hands of all against thee. . . . Oh, when shall the day dawn in which the inhabitants of Pavia shall say to the Milanese: "Thy people are my people," and the citizen of Novara to the Cremonese: "Thy city is my city." [2]

All in vain. Each prince pursued his own interests. Each community was fired with local patriotism and looked upon its neighbor as a potential enemy or as a possible ally against an enemy still more dangerous. Diplomacy and war were the means to power. War required money and the services of the *condottieri*. Diplomacy required secrecy, espionage, plot and counterplot.

At last a great spokesman emerged who, first among political observers, comprehended the realities of the State System in which he lived. His name has become a symbol. His work may well be regarded as marking the conscious beginning both of modern diplomacy and of political science. Niccolò Machiavelli was born in Florence, May 5, 1469, into an ancient family which had long and faithfully served the State. He reached manhood near the close of the reign of the magnificent Lorenzo de' Medici. He was a republican and gladly entered the service of the Florentine Republic after the French invaders under Charles VIII had brought about the overthrow of the Medici in 1494. While the Florentines rallied to the puritanical Savonarola, then turned against him and put him to death, and engaged in a fierce game of intrigue among rival factions, young Niccolò turned his talents to promoting the power of the Republic through the arts of diplomacy. He went on missions to Caterina Sforza, Cesare Borgia, Louis XII, Pope Julius II, the Emperor Maximilian. Little escaped his shrewd eye in the course of his work and his travels. In

[2] Quoted in D. J. Hill, *History of Diplomacy*, Vol. I, p. 359.

1512 the forces of the Papacy drove the French from Italy. Florence was allied with France. In defeat the Republic perished. The Medici were restored. Thus Machiavelli "found himself at the age of 43 a dejected liberal without a job in a world that had come tumbling down about his ears." [3]

Machiavelli was suspect. An abortive conspiracy of 1513 led to his arrest and torture, though he was innocent. Upon his release from prison, he retired to a small farm near Florence. Since his efforts to return to public life by seeking the favor of the Pope and the Medici were fruitless, he wrote stories, plays, poetry, and several books filled with the distilled wisdom of his own experience: *The Prince, The Art of War, Discourses on Livy, The History of Florence.* His nostalgia and his interests are aptly suggested by a letter to a friend:

> When the evening comes I return to the house and go into my study; and at the door I take off my country clothes, all caked with mud and slime, and put on court dress; and when I am thus decently re-clad I enter into the ancient mansions of the men of ancient days. And there I am received by my hosts with all loving-kindness, and I feast myself on that food which alone is my true nourishment, and which I was born for.

In 1527, soldiers of Charles V defeated the papal armies and sacked Rome. In Florence the Medici were temporarily ousted by the democratic faction. Despite his serious illness, Machiavelli hastened to the city to regain his post. The Council, however, voted against his reappointment. But death came to him before he learned of this last failure of his hopes. And in death he found a place among the immortals not by the public service which he loved but by the writing with which he had relieved the ennui of his idle and lonely years.

The Prince has earned for its author the opprobrium of all right-thinking moralists and has come to be viewed as the most eloquent exhortation to the vices of trickery and dishonesty to which modern diplomacy has fallen heir. In fact, it was nothing more than a realistic account of the behavior of States toward one another, with a wealth of illustrations, coupled with maxims for the guidance of rulers in the type of State System with which Machiavelli was familiar. It contains, in small compass, as he declares in his dedication to Lorenzo, grandson of the Magnificent, "all the experience I have acquired during many years of continual meditation and suffering in the school of adversity." Far from being immoral, it is entirely unconcerned with ethics and regards the State as an end in itself for the service of which all means are legitimate.

Machiavelli opens his most famous work with a description of different types of States and of the problems involved in State building. A prince may establish firm control over newly conquered lands by colonizing his own people on them, by establishing garrisons, and by playing off neighboring

[3] Max Lerner, Introduction, p. xxvii, to *The Prince* and *The Discourses* by Niccolò Machiavelli.

princes against one another. Those who are injured thereby should be disposed of with dispatch, lest they become dangerous enemies—for a man "may revenge a slight injury, but a great one deprives him of his power to avenge." Desire for aggrandizement is normal. "Nothing is so natural or so common as the thirst for conquest, and when men can satisfy it, they deserve praise rather than censure. But when they are not equal to the enterprise, disgrace is the inevitable consequence." And the power for which princes strive is a relative quantity. "The prince who contributes toward the advancement of another power, ruins his own." Monarchies must be conquered by force and then can be easily held, since, once the reigning dynasty is disposed of, none remains to oppose the conqueror. Aristocracies can be conquered by intrigue among the nobles, but once in power the conqueror will encounter "an infinity of difficulty, not only from the conquered, but from those who have assisted in the enterprise." Free States may be subdued only by ruining them, by colonizing them, or by permitting them to remain in the enjoyment of their own laws. The difficulties of rulership which princes encounter vary with the means by which they have acquired power. "The usurper of a State should commit all the cruelties which his safety renders necessary at once, that he may never have cause to repeat them . . . for when time is allowed for resentment, the wound is not so deep; but benefits should be frugally dispensed, and by little at a time, that they may be the better relished." A wise prince will not only make himself a master of warfare but win over his subjects by being liberal, without being prodigal, and merciful without being weak. "It is safer to be feared than be loved, for it may truly be affirmed of mankind in general, that they are ungrateful, fickle, timid, dissembling, and self-interested." But the prince must avoid earning the hatred of his subjects. This can be achieved by respecting his subjects' property and the honor of their wives, "for it is certain that men sooner forget the death of their relations than the loss of their patrimony."

Since force and trickery are twin tools of power, the prince must make the lion and the fox his models. "A prudent prince cannot and ought not to keep his word, except when he can do it without injury to himself, or when the circumstances under which he contracted the engagement still exist." It is unnecessary that a prince should possess many good qualities but indispensable that he should appear to have them, "as men in general judge more from appearances than from reality. . . . The vulgar are ever caught by appearances, and judge only by the event. And as the world is chiefly composed of such as are called the vulgar, the voice of the few is seldom or never heard or regarded."

The long shadow which *The Prince* has cast down the succeeding centuries is attributable less to the influence of the work on the thought of its day or to the pungency of Machiavelli's wisdom than to the fact that his maxims reflected the fundamental nature of the new Western State System which existed in miniature in the Italy of the Renaissance. That System rested upon the un-limited sovereignty of the territorial State and upon the principle of the balance of power through which each checkmated its rivals. The ruler of each unit inevitably strove to protect and further his own interests by force, when force was expedient, by trickery, when force was needless. "To reign is to dissimu-late," declared Louis XI of France. "If they lie to you," he admonished his ambassadors, "lie still more to them." The power of the State justified all means necessary for its enhancement.

The new national monarchies dealt with one another precisely as did the Italian city-states—and neither Pope nor Emperor could say them nay. The Empire was by now a phantom. The Papacy was impotent—in part because the Renaissance Popes were themselves rulers and diplomats who used the same methods for increasing their power as did the lay princes, in part be-cause the forces of revolt against papal Catholicism were already gathering about the person of Martin Luther, in preparation for the schism of the Reformation, which was to shatter the ecclesiastical unity of the Christian world. The great States of the modern age were in process of being born—and the politics which they practiced toward one another were then, and have ever since been, "Machiavellian politics" in the broadest sense of a much-abused phrase. In this fashion *The Prince* symbolized a new dispensation, and the humble servant of the Florentine Republic became the prophet of a new epoch.

3. THE EUROPEAN STATE SYSTEM

With regard to the relations of States among themselves, their sovereignty is the basic principle; they are in that respect in the state of nature in relation to one another, and their rights are not realized in a general rule which is so constituted as to have power over them, but their rights are realized only through their particular wills.—GEORG HEGEL.

The concept of State sovereignty, the principles of international law, and the politics of the balance of power may be regarded as the three cornerstones upon which the Western State System has come to rest. The first has been elevated to the dignity of a political theory and later to that of a juristic idea underlying the whole structure of modern international jurisprudence. The second has evolved into a system of public law in the community of nations. The third has become an avowed principle of foreign policy, accepted and acted upon so consistently by all the great States that it may well be viewed as the central theme about which the web of diplomacy is woven.

It fell to the French scholar, Jean Bodin, to formulate the first systematic presentation of the concept of sovereignty in his *De republica* of 1586—a title which must be literally translated as "Concerning Public Affairs," since its author, far from a republican, was an apologist of the purest absolutism. Bodin, in fact, devised the political theory upon which the French monarchy was to rest its case for unlimited and autocratic central power. Sovereignty he defined as *unlimited power over citizens and subjects, unrestrained by law.* This power, he insisted, is by its nature absolute, unqualified, perpetual, and indivisible and resides not in the whole State but in the body of the citizenry in a democracy, in the estate of the nobility in an aristocracy, and in the person of the king in a monarchy. Rulers rule by divine right but are subject to the laws of God, of nature, and of nations and also to the "laws of the kingdom"—a vague adumbration of constitutionalism. These limitations upon supreme power, however, are ethical rather than legal or political.

Though Bodin's view became prevalent everywhere in Europe among the apologists of absolutism, it was not unchallenged. In fact, two conflicting schools of thought battled for supremacy until their differences were in part reconciled in the formulation of Grotius. The first challenge to absolutism came from that school of political philosophers known as the Monarcho-machs—spokesmen of the persecuted sects of the wars of religion who were anxious to justify resistance to oppression. This group insisted upon the original and inalienable sovereignty of the people and argued that government had come into existence as a result of a written or tacit contract between rulers and ruled as an escape from the anarchy of a precivil state of nature. In the event of a ruler violating the compact, his subjects are *ipso facto* released from the obligation of obedience and may engage in revolution, depose the tyrant, or even assassinate him under extreme provocation."

Johannes Althusius, one of the leading Monarchomachs, defined sovereignty in his *Politics Systematically Considered* (1609) as "the highest and most general power of administering the affairs which generally concern the safety and welfare of the soul and body of the members of the State." This power could be neither absolute nor supreme, since it is limited by the laws of God, the laws of nature, and the terms of the contract with the people, who remain the ultimate source of sovereignty. This conception was sharply at variance with that of Bodin, though Thomas Hobbes in his *Leviathan* (1651) later used the contract theory as the basis for the most imposing intellectual justification of absolutism which has ever been presented.

Grotius resolved the issue, so far as international law and relations are concerned, by defining sovereignty as "that power whose acts are not subject to the control of another, so that they may be made void by the act of any other human will." For the Dutch jurist, sovereignty was not absolute but limited by divine law, by the law of nature, by the law of nations, and also by agreements between rulers and ruled. It is likewise capable of division and resides simultaneously in the government and in the State. Subjects, however, may alienate their portion entirely to their ruler. The important thing to Grotius is the fact that a State is sovereign in relation to other States when it is free from outside control. This idea has become the foundation of the whole structure of modern international law.

This conception grew out of the realities of international contacts in the formative period of modern diplomacy. If carried to its logical extreme, it would result in a situation which can only be described as international anarchy. With the breakdown of the authority of Pope and Emperor, each State pursued its own ends in disregard of the interests of others, redressing its wrongs by self-help, acting as prosecutor, judge, jury, and sheriff combined, and hotly resenting any suggestion of allegiance or responsibility to any superior power. Here, indeed, was a precivil state of nature as Hobbes had described it, in which life was "solitary, poor, nasty, brutish, and short"—in which might makes right—in which power is to the strongest and the devil takes the hindmost. Yet law may restrain the lawless.

International law as a distinct branch of legal science received almost no recognition among lawyers and jurists before the 15th Century, despite the practical development of international usages in the medieval State System. Vittoria (1480–1546) and Ayala (1548–84) made early efforts to integrate these usages into a consistent system of law; and the Spanish Jesuit, Suarez (1548–1617), endeavored to discover the basis for such a system in "natural law," or reason. Gentilis (1552–1608) likewise attempted on a more pretentious scale to set forth the principles governing the relations between States. In this period of groping toward a logical basis for an international jurisprudence, two schools of thought were distinguishable: one looked for guidance to practice and sought to make international law the written customs of States; the other tried to formulate principles on the basis of ethics, theology, and reason. The former school relied much upon the *jus gentium* of Rome, while the latter searched for light in the *jus naturae*, or law of nature, which was the current symbolization of what seemed rational and just.

The task of reconciling the two schools and of erecting an edifice of principles worthy of being called a true "law of nations" was first performed by the same Dutch genius, Huig de Groot, or Hugo Grotius, who contributed to the concept of sovereignty. So profound has been his influence that later generations of jurists conferred upon him the title of "the father of international law." Born at Delft, April 10, 1583, son of the Burgomaster of Leiden, he wrote Latin verses at the age of nine, entered the University at twelve, and was a learned editor at fifteen, when he accompanied a Dutch Embassy to Paris. After winning his LL.D. at the University of Leiden, he devoted himself to writing Latin dramas and poems and practicing law. At twenty he was appointed official historiographer by the States-General, in which capacity he began work on his *De jure praedae* (1604), which was the basis of his later treatise. As advocate of the Dutch East India Company, he defended the capture of a Portuguese galleon in the Strait of Malacca by the Dutch captain, Heemskerk, with the argument that the Portuguese claim to all Eastern waters was contrary to the accepted practice of nations. His part in this early controversy over freedom of the seas won him further fame, and he embarked upon a promising diplomatic career which was rudely cut off in 1619—fortunately, perhaps, for posterity.

Grotius' great treatise, *De jure belli ac pacis* ("Concerning the Law of War and Peace") was in part written in the prison fortress of Louvestein, where the poet-jurist was incarcerated in 1619 on a life sentence because of his unpopular religious views. The Thirty Years' War had just broken out in Bohemia. Young Hugo was a theologian no less than a lawyer; and, like Erasmus a hundred years before, he pleaded for toleration and sought to mediate between the warring sects of Remonstrants and anti-Remonstrants. He was jailed for his pains and had his property confiscated; but prison life was not unbearable, for he was permitted to live with his gifted wife and to continue his studies with the aid of many large chests of books. In 1621 his wife nailed him up in a book chest, and in this guise he escaped and fled to Antwerp and Paris, where Louis XIII granted him a small pension. In 1625 his treatise was completed and published. It brought him no profits but ensured him immortal fame. He subsequently became Swedish Ambassador to France and died at Rostock in 1645.

The *De jure belli ac pacis* was inspired by the author's revulsion at the horrors of the wars of religion. In his Prolegomena he declared:

The civil law, both that of Rome, and that of each nation in particular, has been treated of, with a view either to illustrate it or to present it in a compendious form, by many. But the law of nations, that which regards the mutual relations of several peoples, or rulers of peoples, whether it proceed from nature, or be instituted by divine command, or introduced by custom and tacit compact, has been touched on by few, and has been by no one treated as a whole in an orderly manner. And yet that this be done, concerns the human race. . . .

I, for the reasons which I have stated, holding it to be most certain that there is among nations a common law of rights which is of force with regard to war, and in war, saw many and grave causes why I should write a work on that subject. For I saw prevailing throughout the Christian world a license in making war of which even barbarous nations would have been ashamed; recourse being had to arms for slight reasons or no reason; and when arms were once taken up, all reverence for divine and human law was thrown away, just as if men were thenceforth authorized to commit all crimes without restraint.

He, therefore attempted to compile the rules by which States are, or ought to be, governed, deriving them from the law of nature or dictates of right reason, as set forth by philosophers, historians, poets, and orators, and also from the practices of States and the resulting principles binding upon them by virtue of their having consented to them.

Grotius here laid the foundations upon which subsequent jurists were to build. He combined custom and reason as sources of international law, as did such notable successors as Bynkershoek, Wolff, Vattel, and Wheaton. The Naturalist school, represented by Puffendorf, Thomasius, and Rutherford, continued to give precedence to reason or natural law, while the Positivist school of Selden, Zouch, Bentham, Martens, and others emphasized the actual customs and practices of States as the best possible criteria of their legal rights and obligations. The Grotian view, which was a synthesis of the two, has now come to prevail and has in turn influenced the practice of States and led to the erection of the imposing structure of modern international jurisprudence, the basic principles of which will be reviewed in a later chapter.

If sovereignty is the mast to which the sails of modern statecraft are attached, the precept of the balance of power is the wind which drives the vessel over the stormy seas of international politics. The one has become the central concept of nationhood and of international law. The other has become the most important single pattern of political action in the international arena. Both existed in latent form in early State Systems. Both received their first clear formulation in the 16th Century—tentatively at the hands of Machiavelli and more definitely by his successors.

The principle of the balance has emerged more or less clearly in every system of States in which the units have engaged with one another in a competitive struggle for power. Whenever three States are in contact with one another, the prerequisite conditions for its appearance are present. In a State System composed of three units, it is obvious that an increase in the power of any one involves a decrease in the power of the other two. Should State A conquer State B or deprive it of a portion of its territory, State A might impose its will upon C. If the authorities of State C are wise, therefore, they will attempt to forestall this result by aiding B against A, not because of sympathy for B, but because considerations of self-interest make any enhancement of the power of A dangerous to C itself. In such a situation, B and C have a community of interests in opposing A. By the same token, any attempt by B to increase its power at the expense of C must be resisted by A, and any enhancement of C's power at the expense of either A or B must be resisted by the other. Consequently, each unit in this hypothetical System will inevitably tend to throw its weight into the balance behind either of the other two menaced by the third. If the principle is consistently applied by all, no one will be able to overcome another and all will preserve their independence. The balance-of-power principle is thus designed not to preserve peace, as later rationalizations would have it, but simply to maintain the independence of each unit of a State System by preventing any one unit from so increasing its power as to threaten the rest.

During the 15th and 16th Centuries the States of Europe pursued balance-of-power policies without the principle itself receiving any clear formulation. In the early 1500's Francis I and Cardinal Wolsey, adviser of Henry VIII, both hinted at it in their declarations. But not until the time of Louis XIV does the concept emerge in definite form in the statements of diplomats and the literature of international relations. Lord Bolingbroke, who was responsible for English foreign policy during the last years of the War of the

Spanish Succession (1701–13), was one of the first English Ministers to attempt to build his program with the deliberate purpose of preserving the Continental equilibrium. In the negotiation of the Treaty of Utrecht he was instrumental in arranging the solemn declarations of Philip V and the Dukes of Orléans and Berry by which, in the interest of maintaining a balance between the Powers of Europe, they renounced all ambitions of attempting to unite France and Spain under a single crown. In the words of one of Bolingbroke's friends, these renunciations "lay down the balance of power in Europe as their foundation, expressing that Spain ought not to be united either to France or to the House of Austria." Some years later the French philosopher and political writer, Fénelon, discussed the balance as essential to maintain the liberty, tranquillity, and public safety of Europe. At the opening of the War of the Austrian Succession (1741), Sir Robert Walpole stated the principle with even greater clarity:

The use of alliances . . . has in the last age been too much experienced to be contested; it is by leagues well concerted and strictly observed that the weak are defended against the strong, that bounds are set to the turbulence of ambition, that the torrent of power is restrained, and empires preserved from those inundations of war that, in former times, laid the world in ruins. By alliances . . . the equipoise of power is maintained, and those alarms and apprehensions avoided, which must arise from vicissitudes of empire and the fluctuations of perpetual contest. . . .[4]

Frederick the Great likewise paid lip service to the principle, though his expansionist policies upset the balance and led to new wars to check Prussian power. The English philosopher, David Hume, in his *Political Discourses* (1751), dwells upon the efficacy of Britain's balance-of-power policy in checkmating French efforts to establish hegemony on the Continent. The Swiss jurist, Emeric de Vattel, who based his *Droit de gens* (1758) on the work of Wolff, was one of the first text writers to consider the principle as a problem of international law. He denied that balance-of-power considerations give a State any absolute right of armed action against another, but he conceded that "one is justified in forestalling a danger in direct ratio to the degree of probability attending it and to the seriousness of the evil which is threatened":

If an unknown man takes aim at me in the middle of a forest, I am not yet certain that he wishes to kill me; must I allow him time to fire in order to be sure of his intent? Is there any reasonable casuist who would deny me the right to forestall the act? But presumption becomes almost equal to certitude if the prince who is about to acquire enormous power has already given evidence of an unbridled pride and ambition. In the imaginary case mentioned above, who would have dared counsel the European States to allow Louis XIV to make such a formidable addition to his power?[5]

[4] *Parliamentary History*, Vol. XII, pp. 168–169.
[5] E. de Vattel, *The Law of Nations*, translation of edition of 1758, Washington, D.C., 1916, pp. 248*ff.*

Vattel also sought to present the balance of power as a guarantee of the liberty and independence of States. So it is. The balance may sometimes be preserved, however, by the extinction of a weak State by its stronger neighbors, as happened in the partition of Poland at the end of the 18th Century by Russia, Austria, and Prussia. In any case, the balance-of-power principle has been recognized as an integral feature of the Western State System by Rousseau, Kant, and a host of later writers, as well as by the great majority of diplomats and statesmen.

4. EUROPE AND THE WORLD

Although the medieval Christian world possessed the vision of an ideal unity, the interests of the different States were in actual fact severed by difficulties of communication and backwardness of civilization. A community of interests, or a System of States, were still undeveloped. A war might go on for a hundred years between Germans and Italians, quite distinct from a contemporaneous struggle between English and French, without the remaining Powers having any idea of intervening. The idea of a practical comity of States had not yet penetrated into the flesh and blood of the nations. . . . In the 17th Century the Congress of the Peace of Westphalia offered the astonishing spectacle of a conference of ambassadors from every State, laying down the frontiers for the individual countries. The Peace of Westphalia came to be looked upon like a *ratio scripta* of international law: everyone uttered thanksgiving that some sort of *status quo* had now been established. People began to feel themselves part of an organized European society, and all the sovereign States began, as it were, to form one great family. —TREITSCHKE, *Politik.*

Those aspects of the European State System already reviewed suggest the nature of the paradox which must, perforce, be the central theme of any treatise on modern "international relations." The European (and world) community is a unity and a disunity combined in a contradiction. Unity flows from common Roman-barbarian origins, from common Christianity, from common defense against external enemies, from a common feudalism followed by absolutism and democracy—in short, from a community of shared experiences which are as old as Rome and as new as radar. Disunity stems from diversity of tongues and nationalities, from cleavages of ideologies and social structures, from passionate local loyalties, and, most obviously, from the persistent fragmentation of society into sovereign nation-states. None of these as yet has subjugated the rest. None as yet will either acknowledge the supremacy of another or accept in any effective form any cooperative scheme for uniting all in a single polity.

All efforts by agreement to unite Europe or to unite the later and larger Europeanized world have had only limited and temporary success, since modern men are more devoted to their particularistic allegiances than to any vision of universalism. All efforts by violence to achieve the same result have also failed by virtue of the operation of the balance-of-power principle. The history of modern diplomacy is a tale of these alternative attempts at unity—and of their failure. It is also the story of a compromise which, by its nature, is ephemeral. The essence of the compromise is the conception—as old as the Peace of Westphalia and as new as the UN Charter—of a peaceful family of sovereignties, respecting the law, living as "good neighbors," practicing abstention from ambition and forbearance from violence, and fostering Christian virtues in interstate, no less than in interpersonal, relations. But no such society of sovereigns ever has existed.

Between 1350 and 1650 the unity which European Christendom had enjoyed since its dawn was irreparably sundered by a series of schisms, entangled with one another and eventuating in violence of such scope and intensity as to threaten the very survival of civilization. In passionate pursuit of "truth," "freedom," "unity," "peace," and the eternal salvation of their souls, men tore one another to pieces like wild beasts. Catholics and Protestants, peasants and nobles, tortured and slaughtered in a monstrous saturnalia of cruelty. When German serfs rose up against their masters, Martin Luther, in a mood typical of the times, told the Princes: "Strike with the sword! Kill! Cut their throats! Burn, slay, crush the murderous and rapacious peasants!" In the same spirit Charles V advised the Inquisition to follow his own example in dealing with heretics in the Netherlands, "where all who remained obstinate in their errors were burned alive, and those who were admitted to penitence were beheaded." This orgy of brutality reached its culmination in the Thirty Years' War (1618–48). At its close much of Central Europe was a wilderness of ruins, drenched with the blood of the slain, rent with agonized cries of torment, looted by mercenaries, and traversed by pitiable bands of refugees among whom mass madness and cannibalism were not infrequent.

That the European community somehow survived this self-inflicted paroxysm was scarcely due to belated and reluctant acceptance of peace and toleration through exhaustion. Recovery and new growth were made possible by fresh increments of wealth flowing into the Atlantic communities from overseas and arising from the new science and technology which had gradually undermined feudalism, triumphed over superstition, and laid the basis for that immense expansion of productivity and urban population which characterizes our own age. During the century following the Peace of Westphalia (1648), Europe again attained a semblance of unity, despite the shattering of the Universal Church and the now irrevocable fragmentation of peoples into sovereign nation-states. The dynastic and colonial wars which ensued were limited wars fought for limited objectives by limited professional armies. They were not class conflicts or religious and ideological crusades, which invariably move men to wild outbreaks of self-destructive savagery. Soldiers were hired tradesmen. Officers were gentlemen. Monarchs cherished the ideal of enlightened and benevolent despotism. In the flourishing state of agriculture, industry, and the arts, life was relatively orderly and pleasant—to a far greater degree than is suggested by the chronicles of conflicts among Powers which must here be outlined.

The Peace of Westphalia was the first of the grand settlements which have incorporated the verdict of arms into the public law of Europe after every general war among the Powers. At the close of the prolonged and tedious Peace Conference which opened in 1642, three treaties were concluded: one signed at Münster, Jan. 30, 1648, between Spain and the Dutch; another

signed at Münster, Oct. 24, 1648, between the Empire, France, and the German Princes; and a third of the same date, signed at Osnabrück, between the Empire and Sweden. Mutual toleration between Catholics and Protestants was provided for. The independence of Switzerland and the Netherlands was acknowledged. Brandenburg began that process of expansion which was to lead to the creation of the Kingdom of Prussia. The Empire was reduced to a shadow of its former self. The House of Hapsburg was humbled by the House of Bourbon. An enlarged France stepped forward into the international arena as arbiter of the destinies of Europe.

Following the death in 1661 of Cardinal Mazarin, successor of the great Richelieu, the young Louis XIV (1643–1715)—*le Grand Monarque*—assumed personal direction of policy and became the symbol of an epoch. Absolutism was now the prevalent form of State organization throughout Europe. The period was the great age of French letters. The Court at Versailles was the envy and model of the Western world. The able ministers and generals whom Louis XIV gathered about him—Colbert, Louvois, Vauban, Turenne, and Condé—led the French monarchy forward along the paths of glory in diplomacy and arms. International politics revolved about the attempts of France to impose its will upon the Continent and the counter-efforts of numerous coalitions to thwart this ambition and preserve the established equilibrium. The development of the Western State System since the 17th Century, however, is no longer the story of an isolated Europe. It is constantly complicated by rivalries of the Powers for control of overseas possessions. Competition for the Eastern trade encouraged the search for new sea routes to the Orient. Daring Atlantic captains sailed southward around the Dark Continent and westward toward the setting sun. These first slender filaments were to link Europe to a vast new world. The rounding of Africa by Vasco da Gama in 1497 and the first circumnavigation of the globe by Magellan shortly afterward opened new seaways to southern Asia. Explorers, colonizers, treasure seekers, and empire builders jostled one another in quest of adventure, gold, and power; their respective States were not slow to support claims to territory and to quarrel with one another for new dominions.

This clash of imperial aspirations played a major role in the long duel betweeen the English and French which was about to open in Europe. In the middle period of the 17th Century, when France was crushing the Hapsburgs and extending her frontiers to the Pyrenees, the Alps, the Rhine, and the Meuse, England was torn by the internal disturbances of the Great Rebellion. But when Louis XIV sought to acquire still more territory and to establish French hegemony over the Continent, England actively joined his enemies both to preserve the balance of power in Europe and to challenge French pretensions in Asia and America. A series of far-flung combats culminated in the War of the Spanish Succession (1701–13).

The Peace Conference at Utrecht (1712–13) drew up another great international settlement. Philip of Bourbon, Louis's grandson, was recognized as Spanish King, but it was stipulated that France and Spain were never to unite, since "the most destructive flame of war which is to be extinguished by this peace arose chiefly from hence, that the security and liberties of Europe could by no means bear the union of the Kingdoms of France and Spain under one and the same King" (Art. 6 of the Anglo-French treaty of April 11, 1713). The European equilibrium was preserved through the reshuffling of sundry provinces, islands, and colonies. It should be noted that the contemporaneous Eastern wars between Charles XII of Sweden and Russia, Denmark, and Poland were fought and terminated almost without reference to the relations between the Western States. After Utrecht, however, the State System embraced all Europe.

The next serious disturbance was a result of the rise of a new Power to ascendancy in north Germany—Prussia under the Hohenzollern Dynasty.

In December of 1740, Frederick II, surnamed "the Great," sent his armies into Austrian Silesia to expand Prussian power at Maria Theresa's expense. France, Bavaria, Saxony, and Spain joined Prussia to despoil the young Queen of her possessions. England, supported by the Netherlands, joined Austria to preserve the Continental equilibrium and to continue the struggle against France and Spain in the New World. The War of the Austrian Succession (1740–48), known to the transatlantic colonists as "King George's War," was fought in America and in India as well as in Central Europe. In all arenas it was indecisive. By the Peace of Aix-la-Chapelle of 1748, Frederick managed to retain Silesia. Austria also lost certain Italian dependencies, but Maria Theresa averted the partition of her realm. With Austria determined to check the Prussian menace and with Britain no less bent upon a final reckoning with France, the Peace was but a truce. The Prussian King perceived that Russia might be drawn into the coalition which Maria Theresa was striving to form against him. He therefore devoted himself to preparing for the inevitable, for, to him:

Politics is the science of acting always by convenient means conformably to one's own interests. To act conformably to one's interests, it is necessary to know what they are; and to arrive at this knowledge requires study, research, and application. The politics of sovereigns have two parts: one, which is concerned with internal government, comprises the interests of the State and the maintenance of its system of government; the other, which embraces all the System of Europe, labors to consolidate the safety of the State and to extend as much as is possible by customary and permitted means the number of its possessions, the power and consideration of the prince.[6]

The next general war was to decide whether Austria must permit Prussia to dominate north Germany and whether Britain or France should rule North America and India. In 1754, Anglo-French hostilities broke out in the Ohio Valley in the so-called "French-and-Indian War." In the "diplomatic revolution" of 1756, England became the ally of her erstwhile enemy, Prussia, which was now set upon from all points of the compass by Austria, France, Russia, and Sweden. The military genius of Frederick enabled him to defeat the French and Austrians at Rossbach and Leuthen (1757), but the Russians invaded East Prussia and occupied Berlin in 1760. After initial successes the French cause fared badly outside of Europe. Wolfe wrested Quebec from Montcalm in 1759. In India Clive outwitted Dupleix and seized most of the French strongholds. These failures, coupled with reverses in Brunswick, caused Louis XV to call to his aid the other Bourbon States, Spain, and the Two Sicilies (1762). The Spanish intervention was overbalanced, however, by the accession to the Russian throne of the mad Tsar, Peter III, who deserted Austria, joined Prussia, and restored to Frederick the conquests of his predecessors. He was at once superseded by his wife, Catherine II, who refused to

[6] *Die politischen Testamente der Hohenzollern*, Vol. II, p. 33.

give active assistance to either side. Austria now despaired of recovering Silesia and ruining Prussia.

The Treaty of Hubertusburg (1763) put an end to the Seven Years' War in Europe. With magnificent irony, Frederick placed upon the pinnacle of the New Palace at Potsdam three female figures supporting the Prussian crown—Madame de Pompadour of France, Maria Theresa of Austria, and Catherine of Russia. The combined efforts of these ladies to consummate his

destruction had left his State and his dynasty more powerful than ever. By the Treaty of Paris, also of 1763, Louis XV was compelled to yield to Britain the whole of New France in America, save for a few islands, and all the French holdings in India, save for a few ports.

Between the Seven Years' War and the revolutionary upheaval of 1789–1815, which was temporarily to subvert the European System, two developments took place which produced significant changes in the relationships between the Powers: the American Revolution and the partition of Poland. France concluded an alliance with the American rebels in 1778 and was soon joined in the war against England by Spain and the Netherlands. Britain was at length obliged to sue for peace, and by the Treaties of 1783–84 the United States of America became an independent member of the family of nations. Spain recovered Florida, France reacquired minor possessions in the West Indies and Africa, and Holland lost to Britain a portion of her Asiatic empire.

Meanwhile, Frederick connived with Catherine in 1772 to relieve the weak and disorderly Kingdom of Poland of part of its territory. In order to counterbalance this enhancement of Prussian and Russian power, Austria intervened and annexed Polish Galicia. This bargain at Poland's expense was the means of preventing a general war threatened by Austrian resistance to Russian aggrandizement against the Turks in the Balkans. When Austria later made additional claims to Polish territory, Frederick objected. The balance of power was peaceably preserved by the extinction of the Polish State, Prussia and Russia taking fresh slices in 1792 and all three of the Powers dividing up the remainder in 1795.

By the last quarter of the 18th Century, then, the Western State System comprised five major Powers on the European Continent, a large number of minor Powers, and a new State across the Atlantic, born of European colonialism. Of the States which might have been described as Great Powers in 1648, England, France, and Austria retained their former position. Spain had fallen to the rank of a second-rate Power, in spite of the vast colonies which she still held in the Americas and the East Indies. Holland and Portugal likewise retained extensive overseas possessions, but they had long since passed the halcyon days when they could cope with other Powers as equals. Following the failure of France to establish her supremacy over the Continent, the new State of Prussia, founded on the Mark of Brandenburg, had emerged in Central Europe as the dynastic creation of a line of able kings. In the east, the Tsardom of Muscovy had extended its power over a vast domain. Under Peter the Great (1682–1725), Russia became partly "Westernized" and made itself a member of the European System. Under Catherine the Great (1762–96) it became a Great Power. Its expansion pushed the Swedes from the eastern shores of the Baltic and the Turks from the northern shores of the Black Sea. The Ottoman Empire was already in decay. The end of Poland brought the enlarged States of Russia, Prussia, and Austria into closer relations with one another. The petty States of Italy and Germany remained pawns among their greater neighbors. The first great struggle for overseas empire was ended. The Powers had achieved an equilibrium which seemed reasonably permanent and stable.

Under these circumstances, so astute an observer as Edward Gibbon could write in 1780 of prospects of progress to which today's generation looks back with nostalgia:

Europe is one great republic, whose various inhabitants have attained almost the same level of politeness and cultivation. The balance of power will continue to fluctuate, and the prosperity of our own or the neighboring kingdoms may be alternately exalted or depressed; but these partial events cannot essentially injure our general state of happiness, the system of arts, and laws and manners, which so advantageously distinguish, above the rest of mankind, the Europeans and their colonies. . . . Europe is now divided into twelve powerful, though unequal kingdoms, three respectable commonwealths, and a variety of smaller, though inde-

SUGGESTED READINGS

pendent, States; the chances of royal and ministerial talents are multiplied. . . .
The abuses of tyranny are restrained by the mutual influence of fear and shame;
republics have acquired order and stability; monarchies have imbibed the principles of freedom, or, at least, of moderation; and some sense of honor and justice
is introduced into the most defective constitutions by the general manners of the
times. In peace, the progress of knowledge and industry is accelerated by the
emulation of so many active rivals; in war, the European forces are exercised by
temperate and undecisive contests. . . . The experience of four thousand years
should enlarge our hopes, and diminish our apprehensions; we cannot determine
to what heights the human species may aspire in their advances towards perfection; but it may safely be presumed that no people, unless the face of nature
is changed, will relapse into their original barbarism. . . . We may therefore
acquiesce in the pleasing conclusion that every age of the world has increased,
and still increases, the real wealth, the happiness, the knowledge, and perhaps
the virtue, of the human race.

SUGGESTED READINGS

Artz, Frederick B.: *The Mind of the Middle Ages,* New York, Knopf, 1953.
Bey, Essad: *Mohammed,* New York, Longmans, 1938.
Churchill, Winston S.: *A History of the English-speaking Peoples,* Vol. I. *The Birth of
Britain,* New York, Dodd, Mead, 1956.
Descola, Jean: *The Conquistadors,* New York, Viking, 1956.
Dorn, Walter L.: *Competition for Empire, 1740–1763,* New York, Harper, 1940.
Eyre, Edward (ed.): *European Civilization: Its Origin and Development,* New York,
Oxford, 1936.
Friedrich, Carl J.: *The Age of the Baroque, 1610–1660,* New York, Harper, 1951.
Gilbert, Allan H.: *Machiavelli's Prince and Its Forerunners,* Durham, N.C., Duke Uni-
versity Press, 1939.
Hurewitz, J. C.: *Diplomacy in the Near and Middle East,* Princeton, N.J., Van Nostrand,
1956.
Laski, Harold J.: *The Foundations of Sovereignty,* New York, Harcourt, Brace, 1921.
Machiavelli, Niccolò: *The Prince* and *The Discourses,* New York, Modern Library, 1940.
Oman, C. W.: *A History of the Art of War in the Middle Ages* (2 vols.), London, Methuen,
1924.
Pirenne, Henri: *Mohammed and Charlemagne,* New York, Norton, 1939.
Price, M. Philips: *A History of Turkey,* London, G. Allen, 1956.
Robertson, Priscilla: *Revolutions of 1848: A Social History,* Princeton, N.J., Princeton
University Press, 1952.
Swain, James Edgar: *A History of World Civilization,* New York, McGraw-Hill, 1947.
Webb, Walter Prescott: *The Great Frontier,* Boston, Houghton Mifflin, 1952.

CHAPTER III

FROM MASTERY TO MISERY

1. THE MAGIC OF MACHINES

I have spilt blood? I had to; I shall perhaps shed more, but without anger, and quite simply, because blood-letting is a component of political medicine. . . . It is necessary one should always talk of liberty, equality, justice and disinterestedness, and never grant any liberties whatever. . . . I am not a man like other men and the laws of morality or custom cannot be applied to me.—
NAPOLEON BONAPARTE.

DESPITE the high hopes of the "Enlightenment," the Western State System at the end of the 1700's entered upon another age of violence and disorder, opening with a "world war" and culminating a century later in new "world wars" of annihilation and extermination. A long view suggests that the latest time of troubles, in spite of intermissions, is a single sequence from then to now. The long *Pax Britannica* (1815–1914) was not so much a new epoch as an uneasy interlude between global conflicts for hegemony. These fabulous decades were marked by startling shifts in the distribution of influence among "Great Powers." After a last bid for European and world domination, France gave way to Britain. New Powers emerged in the shape of Italy, Germany, America, and Japan. British ascendancy was questioned by the USA, resisted by Russia, and at length challenged by a new Reich. The "Armed Peace," for all its dreams of universal brotherhood in a wondrous new age, was marked (*e.g.*, Cecil Rhodes, Theodore Roosevelt, Wilhelm II, Poincaré the Lorrainer, and a host of others) by such struttings and posturings and chest thumpings in the name of the tribal gods as presaged blood sacrifices on flaming altars.

The subsequent convulsions and vicissitudes of national fortunes may fairly be regarded as concomitants of a vast revolution in the lives of men—not the work of nobles or priests, captains or kings, plotters or despots, but of humble searchers after truth and of alert entrepreneurs, investors, and traders. Disinterested curiosity about nature and creative quest for gain brought into being a world beyond men's dreams—and possibly beyond their power to control.

Our age differs most markedly from all earlier epochs in being the Age of Science and the Age of the Machine. Its earliest creators were the Greeks before Socrates, who guessed at atoms; Aristotle, who first organized scientific research; Archimedes the inventor, who cried "Eureka!" and imagined a fulcrum with which he could move the earth. These seeds fell on stony soil. Out of Arabia came algebra, spherical trigonometry, and brave beginnings in chemistry, physics, astronomy, and medicine. Amid Europe's darkness of the 14th Century, Roger Bacon preached experimentation and predicted steamships, motorcars, and aircraft. Other men shortly hit upon printing and gunpowder. "Gutenberg carved the alphabet in wood, and ideas dipped their feet in ink and tramped through cities and towns." [1] With the great awakening a mighty procession—Leonardo da Vinci, Copernicus, Kepler, Galileo, Newton, Harvey, and many others—ushered Science into our civilization. James Watt's steam engine (1765) opened a new epoch whose puzzling problems moved by rapid stages through the ages of railroads, steel ships, electricity, internal-combustion engines, aviation, and electronics. These problems will doubtless be mended or ended by the newest and most formidable of powers: atomic energy.

The issue of whether our culture is capable of mastering its artifacts or is doomed, like Frankenstein, to be destroyed by the monsters of its own devising may here be deferred. World politics in our own time is a game with rules and goals as ancient as Thebes and Nineveh. But the stage on which an old play now unfolds is like nothing ever seen before on earth. The impact of invention on European society and politics is a familiar tale. The first result was a swift increase in the numbers, wealth, and influence of town dwellers ("bourgeoisie") who were neither nobles nor serfs. Their initial bids for power found voice in the revolt of the Netherlands against Spain, in the English Civil War and the "Protectorate" of Oliver Cromwell, and in the American Revolution. The explosion of social revolution in France inaugurated half a century of class conflict and ideological warfare throughout the Western world. Further expansion of the new modes of production and distribution led to a growing challenge to the triumphant business classes from the new "proletariat" of wage-workers, culminating in the Russian Revolution and its aftermath—begetting in turn new tyrannies and counter-tyrannies and formidable threats to the survival of freedom and perhaps of civilization itself.

The flaming hatreds, fears, and loves involved in the devastating combats of our time between "Democracy," "Fascism," and "Communism" are but echoes of profound schisms in the body politic of the new world commonwealth. The global society is united as never before by swift travel, swifter communication, and fantastically abundant means of wealth and welfare. But it is also divided as never before by clashes of tribes and classes and creeds which turn all resources to war, all riches to dust, and all dreams of a Golden Age to fire and rubble. Social wars of elites and masses in an epoch of dizzy economic change and rising insecurity are mingled with international

---

[1] Max Otto, *The Human Enterprise* (New York, Appleton-Century-Crofts, 1940), p. 71.

wars of "World Powers," battling one another for control of the minds of men and of the means to mastery over the globe. Many of the chapters to follow will deal with various phases of these contentions and confusions. Here a bare outline must serve to bring to the troubled present this survey of times gone by.

*   *   *   *   *

On the Continent the age of democracy, dictatorship, terrorism, military conscription, total war, and new attempts to unite the world by the sword began abruptly in France after 1789. In the light of the historical evolution of the Western State System, the era of the French Revolution and Napoleon represents the most nearly successful effort prior to the 20th Century at the restoration of universal empire by conquest. The power of earlier aspirants toward ascendancy over Europe—Charles V, Philip II, Louis XIV—was feeble compared with the military might and diplomatic prestige of France under the first Bonaparte. Napoleon had at his back the richest and most populous nation of the Continent, welded into a solid phalanx by the new fire of patriotic fervor. His revolutionary predecessors had already invented military conscription as a means of defending France against Europe. His enemies were likewise obliged to resort to universal conscription, which has ever since been the basis of Continental military organization. But the force and ardor of his soldiery were so effectively supplemented by his own strategic genius and diplomatic astuteness that no State or combination of States could stand against him. The old balance of power was completely disrupted. In 1804, aping ancient Rome, he made himself Emperor—and his Empire seemed likely to include all of Europe within its limits.

The temporary triumph and final failure of this imperial adventure throw further light upon the process of high politics in our State System. From 1792 to 1812, French power rose dizzily in an almost uninterrupted ascent. The origins and course of these wars are best left to the historians. Successive coalitions of all the other Great Powers, aided by lesser States, were defeated and broken. By 1807, when Napoleon met Tsar Alexander at Tilsit to divide Europe between the two Emperors, the Corsican conqueror was ruler of a France that extended from the Pyrenees and the Alps to the North Sea and the Rhine. He was also King of Italy; his relatives, friends, and admirers held the thrones of Naples, Holland, Denmark, Sweden, and other lands. Even England seemed likely to be brought to terms by the Continental System which was to close the European market to British goods and compel the "nation of shopkeepers" to sue for peace. Said the new Caesar: "A new order of things now guides the universe. . . . The present epoch carries us back to the time of Charlemagne."

That Napoleon lived to see the destruction of the whole fabric into which he had woven so much blood and treasure was due primarily to British sea power and to the intense national consciousness which foreign conquest evoked among subject peoples. In 1808, Napoleon deposed the Spanish Bourbons and made his brother Joseph King of Spain. But a popular insurrection broke out almost at once against the usurper. Britain occupied Portugal and sent Wellington to assist the Spanish rebels in harassing the French in the Peninsular War (1808–13). A national uprising took place in Austria in 1809, which Napoleon suppressed with difficulty. The Prussian Government introduced various internal reforms and bided its time. Napoleon was still master of

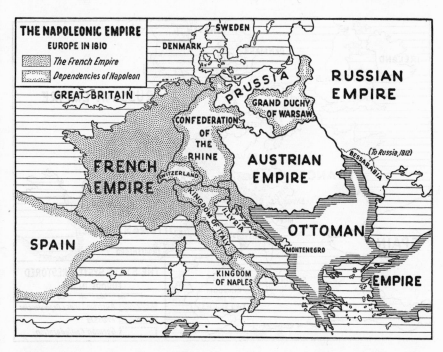

Europe. He might have remained so had he not quarreled with Tsar Alexander and invaded Russia in an effort to enforce the Continental System. By 1812 the French Emperor had gathered together an international army of 600,000 troops for the subjugation of Muscovy. The Russian forces were defeated and withdrew before him. He entered Moscow in September. But the city was burned under his eyes. As the Russian winter descended, enemy soldiers and peasant irregulars assailed the French communications in the rear. The Kremlin was abandoned. The retreat from Moscow became a catastrophe. Only a ragged remnant of the Grand Army recrossed the Niemen in December.

Early in 1813, Alexander, now in alliance with Prussia, England, and Sweden, launched a counterattack which precipitated the German War of Liberation. At the great "Battle of the Nations," fought near Leipzig in October, 1813, the Swedish, Russian, Prussian, and Austrian forces closed in on the French and forced Napoleon to withdraw to the Rhine. His power in Central Europe collapsed. France was invaded from the east by the allies and from the south by Wellington, who had occupied all of Spain. Despite furious resistance, Paris was surrounded in March, 1814. Napoleon was compelled to abdicate and was exiled to Elba. In the spring of 1815, he escaped and returned to power in France to play out the tragic farce of the "Hundred Days" to its dismal end at Waterloo.

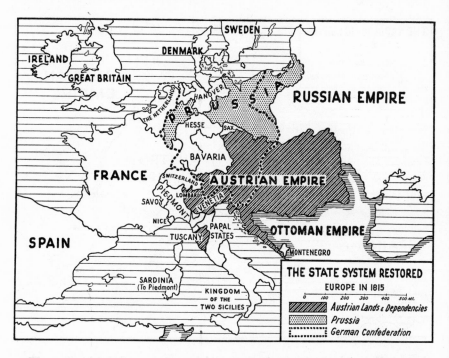

The *ancien régime* thus triumphed over the Revolution. The European State System had proved itself to be more powerful than its most powerful member. In France itself the old order was reestablished, and the Bourbons were restored to the throne in the person of Louis XVIII. At the Congress of Vienna (September, 1814–July, 1815) emperors, kings, princes, and diplomats met in brilliant assemblage to restore dynasties, rebuild the Europe of 1789, and consider "the disposal of the territories given up by his Most Christian Majesty (Louis XVIII) . . . and the relations from whence a real and permanent balance of power is to be derived" (Art. I of the Separate and Secret Articles of the First Treaty of Paris, May 30, 1814).

Under the inspiration of the Austrian statesman, Metternich, the delegates set to work, only to discover that the old Europe had been smashed and that Humpty Dumpty could not, after all, be replaced on the wall. Bargains and compromises were necessary to adjust conflicting interests and ambitions.

France was obliged to renounce her claims over some 32,000,000 people who had been brought under Napoleon's power, but recovered the boundaries of 1792. By the second Treaty of Paris, Nov. 20, 1815, France agreed to cede a number of strategic posts to the allies, to pay an indemnity of 700,000,000 francs, and to submit to the occupation of 18 fortresses for three to five years. Most of the Grand Duchy of Warsaw was given to Russia, which also retained Finland and Bessarabia, conquered, respectively, from the Swedes and the Turks. Prussia received Swedish Pomerania, two-fifths of Saxony, and extensive territories on both banks of the Rhine. In the rest of Germany, it was scarcely feasible to restore either the defunct Holy Roman Empire or the hundreds of petty principalities which Napoleon had abolished. A German Confederation of 38 States was therefore established, with Austria securing the presidency of its Diet. Austria gave up the Austrian Netherlands (Belgium), which were annexed by the Dutch, and also gave up a large part of her territories in Germany proper. In return, she was awarded North Italy (Lombardy-Venetia), Illyria, the Tirol, and Salzburg. The Papal States and the Kingdom of Naples were restored. In the north, Norway was taken from Denmark and joined to Sweden, under whose control it remained until it secured independence in 1905. Britain secured Heligoland, Malta and the Ionian Islands, and other fruits of victory overseas from the remnants of the French and Dutch colonial empires: Cape Colony in South Africa, Ceylon, St. Lucia, Tobago, Trinidad, etc.

A final word regarding events in the American Hemisphere during the Napoleonic epoch: The United States embarked upon its career of expansion by purchasing Louisiana from France in 1803—a region which Bonaparte had reacquired from Spain in 1800 but which he was happy to sell when developments in Europe and the West Indies made a restoration of the French colonial empire impossible. American expansionists next turned their attention to Florida and Canada, but the issue was obscured by long and bitter controversies over blockades, impressments, contraband, and neutral trading rights between the United States on the one hand and Britain and France on the other. In 1812 the USA declared war in the name of "freedom of the seas" and moved at once to occupy Canada and Florida. In spite of Continental preoccupations, England was easily able to defend Canada from American attacks. The United States was invaded, its capital burned, and its commerce swept from the seas. The Treaty of Ghent (1814) restored the *status quo*.

Spain, however, was a weaker rival. A skillful policy of browbeating and bargaining induced Madrid to sell the Floridas in 1819. Meanwhile the Latin American colonies of Spain had secured their independence, and a whole series of new nations was thus added to the Western State System. The USA, no less than Britain, was opposed to any restoration of these States to European control. Canning "called in the New World to redress the balance of the Old," as he put it; the result was the Monroe Doctrine of 1823 by which the USA,

with British approval, expressed its intention to resist any further colonization, interposition, or extension of control by European Powers over the
American continents. At the very outset of Latin-American independence,
therefore, the United States asserted its claim to hegemony over the Western
Hemisphere.

2. PATRIOTS AND IMPERIALISTS

In the social production of the means of life, human beings enter into definite
and necessary relations which are independent of their will—production relations
which correspond to a definite stage of the development of their productive forces.
The totality of these production relations constitutes the economic structure of
society, the real basis upon which a legal and political superstructure arises and
to which definite forms of social consciousness correspond. . . . With the change
in the economic foundation, the whole gigantic superstructure is more or less
rapidly transformed.—KARL MARX.

The century between Waterloo and Sarajevo will probably always remain,
in a peculiar sense, a unique era. The population of the world doubled, and
that of Europe quadrupled. The system of technology which had prevailed
with few changes for many millennia was completely revolutionized. The new
masters of industry, finance, and commerce became a new elite in almost all
the States of the Western world. *Fraternité*, no less than *Liberté* and *Égalité*,
was its battle cry. And as nationalism is always bred of war, the impact of
people upon people in the great Napoleonic conflicts intensified national consciousness at the very time when businessmen were rising to grasp power
from kings and aristocrats. The revolutions of 1830 and 1848 were led and
supported by middle-class patriots for whom the achievements of national
unity and of democratic constitutionalism were but two facets of the same
liberal program. In the era of the triumphant bourgeoisie, nationalism became
a creed and a way of life, shaping the beliefs and acts of millions throughout the world.

The progressive dissolution of the Ottoman Empire presented an opportunity to the Slavic Christians of southeastern Europe to achieve liberation
and statehood. The Serbs gained autonomy in 1815. The revolt of the Greeks
began in 1821 and culminated a decade later in the attainment of Greek
independence through the intervention of Britain, France, and Russia against
the Turks. Belgium rose up against Dutch control in 1830, and nine years
later her independence as a perpetually neutral and inviolate State was recognized. In the 1830's Russia sought to establish a protectorate over Turkey
but was frustrated by Anglo-French opposition. The apprehension of London
and Paris over the extension of Russian power at the expense of "the sick
man of Europe," as Turkey came to be called, led to the Crimean War
(1854–56), in which Britain and France, with the aid of little Sardinia,
fought Russia to a draw in the Black Sea. Russian domination of Constanti-

nople and the Straits was prevented by admitting the Sublime Porte to "the advantages of the public law and system of Europe" (Treaty of Paris, March 30, 1856) and by guaranteeing the independence and integrity of Turkey. In 1877, Russia waged war on Turkey again, now using the Slavic nationalities still under Turkish rule as pawns in her game of expansion. The Powers again intervened. Russia yielded once more, this time without a trial of armed strength. The Treaty of Berlin in 1878 created Bulgaria as an autonomous principality. Serbia, Montenegro, and Rumania were all recognized as independent and granted additional territory at Turkey's expense. In 1912 the Balkan States waged war upon Turkey and further extended their frontiers, only to fall out among themselves to the detriment of Bulgaria, which was set upon by her neighbors in the Second Balkan War (1913) and deprived of many of her conquests. Balkan nationalism thus created six new States (Albania was established by the Powers in 1913) and made the Balkans an arena of the conflicting ambitions of the Great Powers.

Nationalism in Central Europe promoted political union rather than fragmentation. Italians were divided into 7 States and Germans into 39. In both spheres, Austrian power was predominant. Since Vienna refused to yield pacifically, war seemed the only road to unification, particularly after 1848, when the German liberals failed miserably in their efforts to create a German nation by peaceful means. Diplomatic efforts to achieve Italian unity also proved of no avail. In both regions the new nation was forged in the heat of battle, with the Kingdom of Sardinia (Piedmont) under Cavour playing the same role in Italy as the Kingdom of Prussia under Bismarck was to play in Germany. In 1858 the new Bonaparte Emperor at Paris, Napoleon III, formed an alliance with Sardinia against Austria on condition of the return to France of Nice and Savoy, conquered by the first Napoleon but lost in 1815. War followed in 1859. Sardinia was able to annex Lombardy. Nationalist revolutions in central Italy increased the territory of the new State. Garibaldi's filibusters added Naples and Sicily. In 1861, King Victor Emmanuel of Sardinia took the title of King of Italy.

Three years later Prussia under the "Iron Chancellor" joined Austria in war against Denmark and promptly proceeded to quarrel with her ally over the spoils—Schleswig-Holstein. In the Seven Weeks' War of 1866 Prussia defeated Austria and assumed the presidency of the new North German Confederation, while Italy took her chance to wrest Venetia from the control of Vienna. This enhancement of Prussian power was viewed with alarm by Napoleon III, who played into Bismarck's hands by precipitating the Franco-Prussian War of 1870. With the withdrawal of French troops from the Papal States, Italy occupied Rome, and the new Italian nation was complete, save for *Italia Irredenta* ("Italy Unredeemed"), *i.e.*, the provinces of the Tirol and the Trentino, still under Austrian rule.

The French armies were meanwhile crushed by the Prussian military machine. Napoleon III lost his throne. The Third French Republic was compelled to return Alsace-Lorraine to German control. Since the South German States had joined Prussia in the war, the German Empire was proclaimed at Versailles during the siege of Paris, Jan. 18, 1871. Two new Great Powers were thus created at the cost of the defeat and humiliation of France and the exclusion of Austria from German and Italian affairs. Austria and Hungary had already joined themselves together in the Dual Monarchy in 1867; but this political edifice, composed as it was of an incongruous congeries of German, Magyar, Latin, and Slavic peoples, was not a national State but a composite structure which the rising tides of nationalism threatened to engulf.

The mid-century decades of national emancipation and unification, which completely upset the arrangements established by the Congress of Vienna, were followed by a new era of colonial expansion in which almost all the non-European world was seized upon and partitioned by the Great Powers during a short span of 30 years. The impact of European culture upon the older civilizations of the East and upon the primitive peoples of the tropics resulted in almost every instance in the loss of political independence and in social and economic disorganization among the societies which were the victims of imperialism. One exception stood out in sharp contrast. The medieval island empire of Japan was opened to Western influences by an American naval expedition under Admiral Perry in 1854—but, instead of falling prey to the Western Powers as did the other States of Asia, Japan adopted Western ways and emerged 40 years later as a Great Power in her own right.

The course of empire building between 1881 and 1914 was marked by numerous minor wars between the European States and native African and Asiatic communities and by one open conflict between Great Powers: the Russo-Japanese War of 1904–05, in which Japan ousted Russia from South Manchuria and the Liaotung Peninsula. That the Americas did not also become an arena of imperialistic rivalry was due primarily to the preponderant power of the United States in the Western Hemisphere. After the promulgation of the Monroe Doctrine in 1823, no European State made any permanent addition to its American possessions. The USA, on the other hand, annexed Texas in 1845, waged war upon Mexico, took from her almost half her territory in 1846, and purchased Alaska from Russia in 1867. Napoleon III had taken advantage of the Civil War of 1861–65 to attempt to carve out a French Empire in Mexico, but the venture failed dismally. In 1898 the USA resumed its expansion by annexing the Hawaiian Islands and by relieving Spain of Puerto Rico, Cuba, and the Philippines after the Spanish-American War. It subsequently converted Cuba, Panama, Haiti, Santo Domingo, and Nicaragua into protectorates and made the Caribbean an American lake, much to the alarm of the Latin-American Republics, which bitterly resented the hegemony of the "Colossus of the North."

These transformations of the Western State System, which was now literally a World System, did not modify the competitive struggle for power among its members. They rather extended the struggle over the globe and intensified it. The stakes of diplomacy were now larger than ever before. The balance now depended less upon power relationships in Europe than upon developments all over the earth. The "Concert of Europe" operated fitfully to keep the peace in the race for empire, but rapid shifts in the equilibrium as a result of national unification and colonial expansion were constantly threatening new frictions and conflicts.

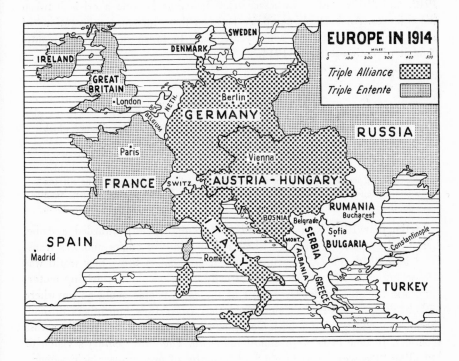

Bismarck's system of alliances to preserve the *status quo* of 1871 was superseded by new arrangements. Italy joined Germany and Austria-Hungary in the Triple Alliance of 1882 out of pique over the French seizure of Tunis, but her ambitions in the Near East and her hope of recovering *Italia Irredenta* made her an unreliable member of the combination. France, bent upon recovering what had been lost in the war with Prussia, won Russia to her side in the Dual Alliance of 1894. After many quarrels over the partition of Africa and Asia, France entered into the Entente Cordiale with England in 1904, which the Anglo-Russian agreements of 1907 converted into the Triple Entente. Through these arrangements and an alliance with Japan (1902), Britain sought security against the growing commercial and naval power of Germany. France dreamed of *revanche*. Russia strove to extend her influence in the Near East and the Balkans in competition with Germany and Austria-Hungary. The Central Powers in turn similarly hoped to achieve security, expansion, and a place in the sun by close cooperation with one another. The two great military coalitions, cemented by common interests and secret treaties, faced one another across the armed frontiers and competed with one another in a race of armaments and a struggle for colonial possessions. Each diplomatic conflict—the Franco-German controversies over Morocco of 1904–05, 1908, and 1911; the Austro-Russian disputes in the Balkans of 1908, 1912, and 1913; and many lesser frictions—thus became a crisis between the alliances. An unstable equipoise between these immense aggregations of power was maintained for some years, only to break down in a gigantic combat of nation-states in 1914.

3. EUROPE IN THE SHADOWS

Ponderous and uncertain is that relation between pressure and resistance which constitutes the balance of power. The arch of peace is mortised by no iron tenons; the monoliths of which it is composed are joined by no cement. A swarm of summer bees upon the architrave, a runnel of April water through some hidden crevice, will cause a millimeter of displacement, will set these monoliths stirring against each other, unheard, unseen—nor can the fragile fingers of man then stay the rush and rumble of destruction.—HAROLD NICOLSON, *Public Faces*, 1932.

In the year 1910 Norman Angell (later knighted and awarded a Nobel Peace Prize) published a book which sold millions of copies and was translated into 20 languages. The time was a happy one. A brave new world was prospering and at peace. Men were already using telephones, driving motorcars, and learning to fly. Over most of the earth people could go anywhere without passports. All currencies were easily convertible into others through the international gold standard. Goods and immigrants moved readily across frontiers. Income taxes were almost unknown. The 19th Century's vision of unending "Progress" was bright with promise of ever greater achievement.

But a shadow lay across the pleasant planet. The home of man was united by a thousand ties of trade and travel, but still divided by the fears and ambitions of the man-made monsters called "Great Powers." An Anglo-German naval race was in full tilt. Teutonic and Slavic envoys intrigued against one another amid the "powder kegs" of the Balkans. To most people another general war was inconceivable. Yet it was possible. To its possibility and its folly Norman Angell addressed himself.

He called his book *The Great Illusion: A Study of the Relation of Military Power to National Advantage*. The essence of its argument is that political and economic frontiers no longer coincide; that under modern circumstances "military power is socially and economically futile; that it is impossible for one nation to seize by force the wealth or trade of another"; and that "war, even when victorious, can no longer achieve those aims for which peoples strive."

Many pondered such warnings, but none knew how to put an end to the ancient game of power. Events were to show that Angell's argument, whatever its "blind spots," was prophetic in asserting that contests in arms among Great Powers would be equally ruinous to victors and vanquished and that the military might of sovereignty against sovereignty could no longer serve any rational purpose. But men and statesmen are seldom wholly rational and are always entangled in old stereotypes. "National interest," "national honor," and tribal pride and righteousness are deemed more important than "peace," even when logic and experience suggest that none of these goals can any longer be well served by war. The "Great Illusion" remains master of men's minds. The Great Society has therefore been plunged anew into recurrent orgies of bloodshed and destruction.

In Sarajevo, capital of Bosnia (a nominally Turkish province annexed by Austria-Hungary in 1908 in defiance of Belgrade's hopes of incorporating it into a Greater Serbia), the heir to the Hapsburg throne, Archduke Francis Ferdinand, and his wife were assassinated on June 28, 1914. The killers were Pan-Serbian terrorists, abetted by Serbian officials. Vienna saw the issue simply: either crush Belgrade or risk the disintegration of the Dual Monarchy under the impact of South Slav conspiracies fostered by Russia. The Cabinet framed an unacceptable ultimatum, rejected the reply, and on July 28 declared war on Serbia. Berlin supported Vienna as its only reliable ally and would put no pressure on Austria-Hungary for negotiations among the Powers until too late. St. Petersburg supported Belgrade rather than risk the loss of all Russian influence in the Balkans. Paris supported St. Petersburg and would put no pressure on France's only reliable ally. Rome hesitated. London, with no firm commitments, sought to mediate.

Russian general mobilization on July 30 evoked a German ultimatum and then a declaration of war on Aug. 1. The French Cabinet, determined to join Russia but anxious to present hostilities to the public and to London as "defensive," was rescued from its dilemma by the strategic imperatives of the "Schlieffen Plan," whereby German armies were to invade France through neutralized Belgium, take Paris in six weeks, and then turn to face the Russian "steam roller." Germany declared war on France on Aug. 3. With the invasion of Belgium, Britain declared war on Germany on Aug. 4, just for "a scrap of paper," sneered Chancellor Bethmann-Hollweg. "The lamps are going out all over Europe," said Sir Edward Grey. "I feel like a man who has wasted his life. . . ."

Ten million lives were to be snuffed out in the fury which followed. Russian invaders of East Prussia were crushed at Tannenberg at August's end. German invaders of France were driven back at the Marne early in September. In the trench warfare which followed massed artillery, poison gas, and the first slow tanks and planes all availed nothing to break the deadlock. On the Somme and Aisne, before Verdun, and elsewhere on long immobile "fronts," defenders with machine guns behind barbed wire slaughtered attackers in a hideous mockery of military science. Changes in the bloody stalemate were chiefly the results of the war at sea, of the successive interventions of neutral States, and finally of the sinister forces of revolution unleashed by the intolerable miseries of a world in chaos.

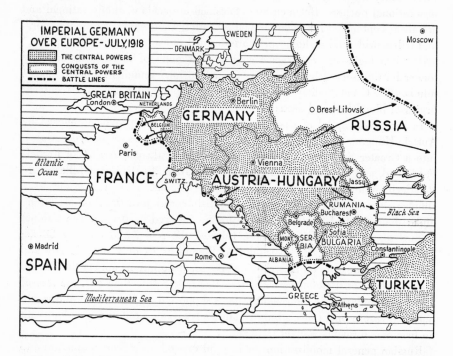

This vortex of death sucked in all the Powers and almost all the lesser States. In the Far East, Japan declared war, seized the German islands in the Pacific and Kiaochow in Shantung, and sought in 1915 to impose a protectorate on China. British forces in Africa took the German colonies. On the Continent, Italy sold her support to the highest bidder and declared war on her erstwhile allies, May 24, 1915. Turkey joined the Central Powers, Nov. 5, 1914, and Bulgaria, Oct. 14, 1915. Allied efforts to take Constantinople via the Dardanelles failed. Outflanked Serbia was overrun. Rumania joined the Entente, Aug. 27, 1916, and was promptly conquered. The defeat and collapse of Russia led to the overthrow of the Tsardom (March, 1917), the breakdown of the efforts of the "Provisional Government" to carry on the war, the triumph of Communism in November, and the separate peace of Brest-Litovsk forced by the victors upon the new Soviet regime and signed March 4, 1918.

Off Jutland, May 31, 1916, the British and German grand fleets fought the only major naval battle of the war. Despite heavier British losses, the German Navy henceforth remained in port and sought to break the British blockade, and counterblockade Britain, by U-boats. The USA, moved by balance-of-power considerations and concern for its lucrative exports of war supplies to the Allies, protested German violations of neutral trading rights and declared war on April 6, 1917. Italy suffered disaster at Caporetto in October. In the following spring the German High Command, enabled by the Russian debacle to move most of its divisions to the Western Front, smashed the British before Amiens and Ypres and drove the French to the Marne once more—only to suffer defeat at Château-Thierry in mid-July and have its hosts rolled back toward Belgium by American, French, and British armies now under the united command of Marshal Foch. Bulgaria and Turkey surrendered in the fall. Austria-Hungary disintegrated. The Hapsburg and Hohenzollern Dynasties went the way of the Romanovs. A new German government sued for peace. An armistice was signed on Nov. 11, 1918. The worst disaster to Western mankind since the Black Death was at an end. But worse was to follow. The "World War" or "Great War" of 1914–18 has long since been renamed "World War I."

"We are the dead," wrote John McCrae. "If ye break faith with us who die, we shall not sleep, though poppies grow in Flanders' fields." Out of the valley of the shadow, men and women everywhere resolved, in Woodrow Wilson's words, that the holocaust was "the War to End War" and to "Make the World Safe for Democracy," to be followed by a "League for Peace" and a new birth of freedom and order in human affairs. That all these hopes were to turn once more to ashes is doubtless due (though many have quarreled violently over "war guilt" and over responsibility for "losing the peace") less to betrayal or malice or stupidity than to the incapacity of citizens and politicians to comprehend or predict or control the fearful forces released by war in a complex and now dangerously sick civilization.

The "peace" which was to prove illusory was largely the work of Wilson, Clemenceau, Lloyd George, Orlando, and their colleagues assembled in Paris. Russia was in the grip of civil war and of Allied blockade and invasion, inspired by a vain effort to liberate her people from the new tyranny of Communism. Soviet regimes in Hungary and Bavaria were smashed. But the Red rulers of Muscovy survived in a ruined land. Russia played no role in the peace making, save to acknowledge the independence of Finland, Estonia, Latvia, and Lithuania and to lose provinces to Rumania and to a revived and expansionist Poland—all constituting a Western *cordon sanitaire* against Bolshevism. Austria-Hungary was no more, having dissolved into a kingless Magyar kingdom, a truncated Austria, a new Czechoslovakia, an enlarged Rumania, and an expanded Serbia (Jugoslavia).

The Treaty of Versailles (June 28, 1919) deprived the German Republic of all prewar colonies, Alsace-Lorraine, the Saar, the Corridor, and Upper Silesia, rigidly limited German armaments, crippled German industry, and contemplated vast "reparations" to the victors on the premise that the war had been due to "the aggression of Germany and her allies." The Treaties of St. Germain (with Austria), Trianon (Hungary), Neuilly (Bulgaria), and Lausanne (1923 with Turkey, following repudiation of the original Treaty of

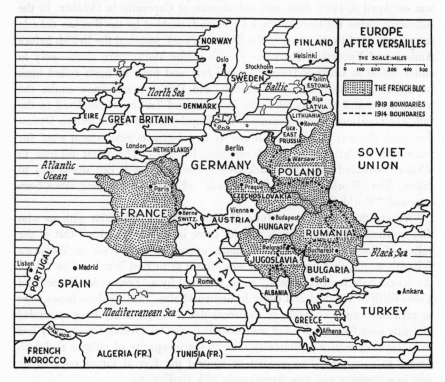

EUROPE AFTER VERSAILLES

THE SCALE: MILES
0   100 200 300 400 500

THE FRENCH BLOC
——— 1919 BOUNDARIES
- - - - 1914 BOUNDARIES

Sèvres and defeat of the Greeks by the new Turkish Nationalists) drew new boundaries in old ways and reflected the traditional injunctions of woe-to-the-vanquished and spoils-to-the-victors. A semblance of order emerged by 1921. The League of Nations was to keep the peace and maintain the new *status quo*. French alliances with Belgium, Poland, and the "Little Entente" (Prague, Belgrade, and Bucharest) were further bulwarks of stability.

Why and how all this crumbled into dust long before the end of the long armistice are questions admitting of many answers. Here we need only note the changing pattern of power which reflected the paralysis of the Western Democracies and the ultimate dedication of embittered peoples and half-mad fanatics to new missions of violence. America, now the greatest of "Great Powers," repudiated Wilson's League and retired into "isolationism." Italy succumbed to Fascism in 1922. The USSR slowly reappeared as a Great

Power, with Western leaders too contemptuous or frightened to assess its
weight correctly. After 1929 the Great Depression reduced scores of millions
to bankruptcy, joblessness, and want all over the earth.

In the sequel Japan evolved a native Fascism, seized Manchuria in 1931,
and undertook to conquer China in 1937. Germany heiled Hitler in 1933,
repudiated Versailles, and armed for glory. Mussolini conquered Ethiopia
and helped Franco to conquer Spain. The democratic leaders embraced

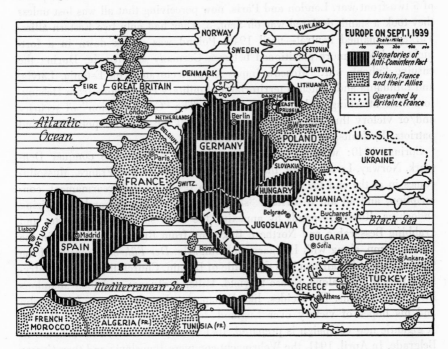

neutrality and acquiesced or connived in Fascist aggression in the hope of
buying peace or of diverting the war makers against Russia in pursuit of
their well-advertised "crusade against Communism." By 1939 the League was
a corpse and the French bloc a memory. The democracies were reduced (apparently) to impotence. Hitler's Reich had refortified the Rhineland, built a
formidable military machine, and seized Austria and Czechoslovakia. Italy
had won two wars and joined Berlin in the "Axis Alliance." Japan was waging
war in China. The three Fascist Powers were united in the Anti-Comintern
Pact of Nov. 25, 1936, and were soon to join forces in the 10-year
alliance treaty of Sept. 27, 1940. Belated Anglo-French efforts to rebuild
an effective coalition against Berlin were doomed by Western refusal to pay
Russia's price for an alliance. Stalin and Hitler then struck a bargain, signed
Aug. 23, 1939, in the form of a neutrality and nonaggression pact coupled
with a secret protocol defining spheres in Poland—which the Nazi leaders had

95

resolved in May to strike down, despite Anglo-French pledges to come to Warsaw's aid.

The new conflict which began on Sept. 1, 1939, with the Nazi blow at Poland, seemed likely to those who unleashed it to be short and cheap. The Wehrmacht had devised a formula of swift tanks, motorized artillery, and dive bombers capable of cracking any static defense and rendering trench warfare impossible. Nazi diplomacy had protected the Reich from the perils of a two-front war. London and Paris, now perceiving that all was lost unless they took a stand, declared war on Sept. 3. They had only two Eastern allies. Turkey remained neutral—until 1945. Poland was struck down in a fortnight and once more partitioned between Germany and Russia. During the ensuing "phony war," Moscow imposed "protectorates" on Estonia, Latvia, and Lithuania and snatched territorial and military concessions from Helsingfors after attacking and defeating Finland. The "Great Illusion" of security and/or victory through martial might was still the creed of politicians and patriots. Its fruits, as before, were deadly.

Spring, 1940: within 10 weeks the German Blitzkriegers conquer Denmark, Norway, Luxembourg, the Netherlands, Belgium, and France. Mussolini comes in at the end for the "kill." America responds with rearmament, conscription, and all aid to Britain "short of war." Japan responds by seizing Indochina. Russia responds by annexing the three smaller Baltic States and grabbing Bessarabia and Northern Bukovina from Rumania—already in the Fascist camp, along with Hungary and Bulgaria. *Der Führer* is master of the Continent. But his airmen lose the Battle of Britain. Churchill and his countrymen, though now alone, refuse to yield. Hitler postpones and then abandons his invasion plans. He decides, like Bonaparte, that the safety of his realm and his hopes of victory over England depend upon his crushing Russia. A gigantic new campaign is prepared. Its execution is delayed by defiance in Belgrade. In April, 1941, the Wehrmacht conquers Jugoslavia and then Greece in a new blitzkrieg.

On June 22, 1941, Hitler invaded Russia. With this fateful decision, the conflict assumed a wholly new shape. Britain and the Soviet Union were now allies, with America extending "lend-lease" aid to both. America was at war in all but name. Roosevelt and Hull demanded Japanese evacuation of Indochina and China as the price of economic concessions. Japan replied at Pearl Harbor, Dec. 7, 1941. Berlin and Rome promptly declared war on the USA. Save for the anomaly that Russia and Japan were still at peace, the struggle for the world was now a global combat of coalitions, with the Triplice and its satellites facing the "United Nations"—*i.e.*, Britain, America, the Soviet Union, China, and their lesser allies. But as Tokyo launched its war against America, Berlin lost its war against Russia. At the gates of Moscow in December, 1941, the Wehrmacht was stopped and then driven back. *Der Führer*, flushed with spectacular early victories, had proclaimed the downfall

of the USSR in October and ordered partial reconversion of German in‧
dustry. His error was to prove fatal.

The horror, misery, grandeur, and disenchantment of the years of blood
cannot here be told. The global tides of war turned against the foe in 1942.
Near MIDWAY in mid-Pacific in early June, in the first naval engagement
fought entirely by carrier-based aircraft, Japan suffered a major defeat at the
hands of American task forces under Admirals Fletcher and Spruance. At

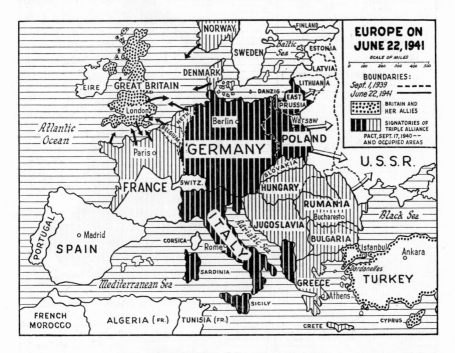

EL ALAMEIN in Egypt in late October, Montgomery's Eighth Army defeated
Rommel and began the long advance westward across the desert to link up
with the Anglo-American expedition under Eisenhower which landed in
Morocco and Algeria in early November. Together they drove Axis forces
from Africa by May of 1943. At STALINGRAD on the Volga, which the Wehrmacht reached in its renewed assault upon Russia in 1942, Paulus's Sixth
Army of 330,000 men was trapped by a Soviet encirclement in late November
and forced to surrender two months later.

These judgments of Mars were decisive, though three more years of
slaughter and devastation were required to seal the verdict. Once more an
effort—the most formidable thus far attempted—to unite Europe and the
world by the sword was undone by the ultimately superior power of victims
and foes. The Roosevelt-Churchill formula of "unconditional surrender" offered no basis for peace short of total victory or total defeat. When Allied

97

forces invaded Sicily in July, 1943, Mussolini was overthrown. But he was rescued by the Germans, who defended Italy so stubbornly that Rome was not taken until June 4, 1944. The failure of the plot to kill Hitler (July 20, 1944) meant that the Reich was condemned to total ruin before the guns stopped

firing. By war's end most German cities were reduced to rubble. Fanatical Japanese resistance brought a similar fate to Nippon.

We must leave the murderous finale to the military historians: how Soviet armies fought their way westward 40 miles a month for 30 months, until they drove the foe from their soil, imposed peace on Rumania, Finland, and Bulgaria in August and September, 1944, helped free Jugoslavia, poured over Poland, stormed Budapest and Vienna, and finally took Berlin (May 2, 1945); how Eisenhower's armies at length swarmed onto the beaches of Normandy (June 6, 1944), defeated the defenders in northern France, liberated Paris, suffered a setback in the Belgian "Battle of the Bulge" (December–January, 1944–45), at last reached the Rhine, trapped 400,000 of the foe in the Ruhr, joined the Russians on the Elbe, overwhelmed Bavaria, reached the Czech frontier, and forced surrender on enemy commanders; how the fighting in Europe ended on May 7–8, 1945, with Hitler and Mussolini both gone; how Burma and the Philippines were taken from the Japanese, after bitter struggles for Guadalcanal, New Guinea, the Solomons, Saipan, Guam, and scores of other islands; how a fanatical enemy fought in vain to hold Iwo Jima and Okinawa; how the USSR entered the Asiatic war; how Hiroshima and Nagasaki were turned into columns of flame and smoke by atomic bombs; and how Tokyo surrendered on Aug. 14, 1945. All this and much else can be read in a thousand books and is burned into the souls of the millions who took part.

* * * * *

That the fruits of common triumph were again to wither, and this time with startling speed, is a portent of our time of troubles. The bright promises of the Atlantic Charter, the "Four Freedoms," and the UN were unfulfilled in the face of the quarrels of the victors and the revolt of Asia. The major victor of 1945 was not Democracy, which thrives ill on war, but the new despotism of Communism, which thrives well on war. In the wake of World War I, Communism conquered Russia. In the wake of World War II, it conquered Eastern Europe, the Balkans, and China and won new converts in Southeast Asia, Italy, and France—thereby compelling America to assume leadership in subsidizing and arming the Free World in the "Cold War" after the war to "contain" the Red Menace.

The "power politics" of this denouement can be simply stated. Past decisions create present issues and future dangers and opportunities. At Munich (Oct. 1, 1938) the Western Powers surrendered all influence in Eastern Europe. Its partition between Germany and Russia was thereby rendered probable if not "inevitable." The subsequent Nazi decision to destroy Russia evoked the Russian decision to make Eastern Europe, in the event of victory, a belt of Soviet satellites or a *cordon sanitaire* in reverse. Communist expansion could have been averted or limited only by a Western invasion of Nazi Europe through the Balkans, as Churchill urged. This was vetoed by America for military reasons, with little thought of the political aftermath. Churchill then sought a "deal" with Moscow on "spheres of influence" in the Balkans. Moscow was agreeable. Washington was opposed. The lateness and locus of the Western "Second Front" gave the Kremlin time to take over Eastern Europe. The partition of Germany, Austria, and the Balkans between the Atlantic Powers and the USSR was implicit in the grand strategy of the war itself.

Stalin at Yalta (February, 1945) promised Roosevelt and Churchill "democracy" in the liberated States, but at once ignored the pledge in the

99

interest of the Politburo's conception of security and its plans of aggrandizement. A naïve and demobilized America, a bankrupt Britain, and a feeble France had no effective power to challenge the results. Challenges without power are futile. Yet acceptance of the result was unthinkable. America was equally impotent to thwart Russian expansion in the Far East, the partition of Korea, and the Communist conquest of China—and equally unwilling to accept the consequences. Hence the American decision in mid-century to build global power for defense against the Red Empire and for effective challenge in the future to its pretensions. The new enemy was no less determined to hold fast to his gains and to expand them at every opportunity in the name of defense against America.

The Cold War of the mid-20th Century hypnotized men's minds in East and West alike and begot an image of a new and super-colossal trial of strength in a now bipolar world community. An age-old pattern of power appeared to reproduce itself on a global stage. The Super-Powers of America and Russia were seemingly destined to re-enact the old drama of Egypt and Assyria, Greece and Persia, Athens and Sparta, Rome and Carthage. The end was mastery of the world, united in a vast imperium under the leadership of the victor. The means were armaments and alliances. The decision, as in ancient days, was to be achieved through ordeal by battle. Most Americans and many West Europeans foresaw the "inevitability" of World War III and envisaged the issue of another "final" struggle between "freedom" and "slavery." Most Russians, all Stalinist Communists, and many Stalinoid sympathizers, while preaching "peace," were no less persuaded of the certainty of war, in which the "progressive" forces of "socialism" would do battle with the "reactionary" hosts of "capitalism" and "imperialism."

Seldom were so many so deluded about so much. This familiar picture of the world, as many have now begun to see, was no photograph of fact. It was at best a blurred image of a small part of reality and at worst an abstract phantasmagoria, compounded of shadows and echoes in a cave far removed from the decisive determinants of destiny in the human community of the middle decades of the 20th Century.

How and why the "Great Illusion" so long persisted, how and why its falsity came slowly and reluctantly to be recognized, and what the moving realities of a new time are will occupy us in many later pages. In this preliminary survey only a few clues to the riddle need be noted. Any new contest in arms between Russia and America would have been fought with atomic weapons. Marxist Muscovy "broke" the American monopoly of such arms in 1949. The new weapons rendered all war, and indeed all traditional power politics, obsolete. Men and statesmen, ever prisoners of the past, could scarcely bring themselves to face the fact and lacked imagination to envisage some alternative way of dealing with problems of power. But in the day-to-day and year-to-year processes of decision-making in the great capitals of the world, power-holders refrained, even under extreme provocation, from "pushing the buttons" which would have unleashed World War III. None could persuade themselves of the military superiority of their own coalition nor devise any plausible strategy of victory, since the new arms race, quite apart from A-bombs and H-bombs, spelled a hopeless stalemate or deadlock. All suspected that an atomic world war would eventuate not in one Rome but in two Carthages.

Armed violence was therefore localized and held to a minimum in the new contest of the giants. As between Marxland and Freeland, wars after the war and in anticipation of more war to come were fought in Korea and Indochina. Both resulted in stalemates, registered in the armistice accords of 1953 and 1954. Elsewhere no trials by arms were risked. Early in 1953 Eisenhower replaced Truman in the White House and a new "collective leadership" replaced Stalin in the Kremlin. Mutual efforts at bargaining replaced threats of violence. The complex consequences included peace in Korea and Indochina, the treaty of May 15, 1955, neutralizing Austria, the "Summit Conference" at Geneva in July, 1955, and subsequent efforts at negotiated settlements—in the course of which opportunities were lost and the two monolithic coalitions almost (but not quite) fell apart in the autumn of 1956 in the face of the abortive Hungarian Revolution and the abortive Anglo-French-Israeli attack on Egypt. After a suitable interval during which all pots called all kettles black, negotiations were resumed in 1957 in the shared hope of achieving some measure of disarmament.

Yet this spectacle of Americans and Russians, reluctantly supported by satellites, allies, and dependencies, quarreling and bargaining over the fate of the world may well be deemed a decade hence a Gargantuan jest, bred of illusions and having little to do with the determinants of human fortunes in days to come. In the One World of our time the immense majority of humankind consists neither of Russians nor of Americans and has little interest in either save as possible sources of aid in realizing new aspirations. Two-thirds of mankind is "colored," not "white." Two-thirds of mankind is not rich, but desperately poor. All these dark and impoverished multitudes are astir with new expectations, whose fulfillment or nonfulfillment may well prove more decisive for the shape of things to come in the World Community than any amount of violence or bargaining between Washington and Moscow.

Thanks to the impact of the West upon the "backward peoples," most of the human race in our time has been brought to the point of a vast and complex revolution against the *status quo*. This "revolution" may be depicted in sundry ways, none of them adequately descriptive of the groping efforts of "the lesser breeds without the law" (in Kipling's phrase) to attain a better life. But mankind as a whole in A.D. 1945–65 was unquestionably in the grip of (1) an anti-colonial revolution, (2) a racial revolution, and (3) a revolution of the poor against the rich. The design of the World Community through many tomorrows is far more likely to be shaped by the course and outcome of these revolts against the past than by any contest between "Capitalism" and "Communism."

The anti-colonial revolutionists demand an end to Western domination and exploitation of subject-peoples. They have already achieved political inde-

EUROPE IN 1958

SCALE OF MILES
0   200   400   600

▤ USSR AND ALLIES
▥ ALLIES OF USA
▢ NEUTRALS
◯ POPULATION IN MILLIONS

Arctic Sea

FINLAND ④⑤
NORWAY ④ SWEDEN ⑦⑤
Oslo   Stockholm   Helsingfors

IRELAND ③ GREAT BRITAIN DENMARK ④⑤
⑤② London
Atlantic NETH. GERMAN ②⓪ GERMAN Berlin
Ocean BELGIUM Bonn DEMOCRATIC Warsaw
⑨ Lux. FEDERAL REPUB. Prague POLAND
Paris REPUBLIC ⑤③ CZECHOSLOVAKIA ⑭
FRANCE SWITZ. ⑤ Vienna ⑦
⑤⓪ AUSTRIA Budapest
PORTUGAL ⑨ ⑤⓪ HUNGARY
Lisbon TRIESTE RUMANIA ⑱⑤
Madrid ③⓪ ⑱ Belgrade Bucharest
SPAIN Rome JUGOSLAVIA BULGARIA
ALBANIA Sofia ⑦⑤
Mediterranean Sea ⑧ GREECE ANKARA ⑦⑤
⑨ Athens TURKEY
MOROCCO ⑩ ALGERIA ④ TUNISIA

Moscow
USSR
②⓪⑥

Black Sea

pendence and the advent of nationhood for many communities long ruled by Western Powers. The racial revolutionists demand abandonment of old convictions that "white" men are somehow superior to men who are black, yellow, or brown in skin-color. The poor demand that the rich bestir themselves to provide plenty for all. The latter demand has little in common with the Marxist call for a revolution of the "proletariat" against the "bourgeoisie." This formula has become meaningless in advanced Western industrial societies and is almost equally so in poor and primitive communities where most of the rich are land-owners and most of the poor are peasants.

102

These three revolutions of our time are closely inter-related. Most colonial subject-peoples are nonwhite and thus easily persuaded that their hopes can best be realized by embracing the symbols and slogans of "anti-white" racialism. All are miserably poor compared with the peoples of Atlantica and even of the Soviet Union. Their interest in the struggle of Freeland vs. Marxland tends to be limited to a single question: which camp is willing and able to contribute most to political independence, racial equality, and the elevation of the world's slum dwellers to some semblance of Western living standards?

Upon the answers to such questions will depend, in the years and decades ahead, the ability of power-holders in the USA and USSR to influence the minds of men. Whatever the answers, it is probable for the longer future that world power will pass from Western Europe, which is already powerless, and even from America and Russia to the multi-millioned masses of China and India and, in lesser measure, to the emergent multitudes of Islam and dark Africa. This almost inevitable "Decline of the West" need not spell ruin for Americans, West Europeans, and Russians if their peoples and leaders display talent for adapting themselves to the inevitable. Whoever shows greater skill in this art will retain greatest respect, prestige, and influence among the world's disinherited, now resolved to recover their place in the sun.

Further speculation on these themes would be presently pointless. Despite efforts at accommodation, policy-makers in Moscow and Washington were still bewitched, as these words were written, by stale illusions of mastery of the globe. In a world of uncertainties, few things are certain. But one is sure: neither America nor Russia will "rule the world" in times to come. All that could come from such efforts, if continued in the late 1950's and early 1960's and accompanied by new threats of violence, would be irreparable disaster for all mankind.

"We may," observed Norman Angell at the close of his autobiography (1951), "learn our lessons too late." In feverish preparations for new tests of force, the still, small voice of old was lost. And the new voice of the scientists, who warned that more war in the Atomic Age meant universal death, was unheeded by politicians and patriots, still dreaming of battles to come, of new "victories" to be gained, of One World to be made by imposing "our" will on "their" will. In the spirit of Richelieu and Machiavelli, in the mood of Cato and Cambyses and Thothmes, with the motives of Neanderthalers or ape-men, statesmen schemed and plotted, sketched out "empires," imagined new and more glorious annihilations, thumped their chests and bellowed their wrath in the worship of the gods and ghosts of their tribes. In these angry bewilderments and frustrations the old, bright vision of "peace on earth, good will to men" seemed all but certain to be betrayed and lost anew.

But our tale, though broken off, is by no means ended. *Homo sapiens,* more apt at learning than all other organisms and yet desperately reluctant to learn new ways, filled with self-destructive fury and yet imbued with an indomitable

FROM MASTERY TO MISERY

will to survive, may yet somehow find the means to avoid an irreparable collapse of his political and social artifacts into the fires of chaos and the gloom of death. He may yet arrive at the vision of a mankind reoriented in its loyalties, reawakened to its dangers and opportunities, and remotivated and reorganized in its politics. Such a race might be capable of using the wonder-working jinni released by the Aladdin's lamp of science to make all the earth a garden and all its children happy dancers in a new dawn of a civilization brighter than any yet known. Perhaps . . . ? The record of the past admits of hope. But man today must pause anew in the stream of time, as he has so often through many yesterdays, before a fateful question having as yet no answer.

SUGGESTED READINGS

Albertini, Luigi: *The Origins of the War of 1914* (3 vols.), New York, Oxford, 1952*f*.
Barr, Stringfellow: *The Pilgrimage of Western Man*, New York, Harcourt, Brace, 1949.
Black, C. E., and E. C. Helmreich: *Twentieth Century Europe*, New York, Knopf, 1953.
Bogart, Ernest Ludlow: *The Economic History of Europe*, 1760–1939, New York, Longmans, 1941.
Churchill, Winston L.: *The Aftermath*, 1918–1928, New York, Scribner, 1929.
Commager, Henry S. (ed.): *The Story of the Second World War*, Boston, Little, Brown, 1945.
Eisenhower, Dwight D.: *Crusade in Europe*, New York, Doubleday, 1948.
Fay, Sidney B.: *The Origins of the First World War* (2 vols.), New York, Macmillan, 1929.
Finer, Herman: *Governments of Great European Powers*, New York, Holt, 1956.
Fuller, Maj. Gen. J. F. C.: *The Second World War: 1939–1945*, New York, Duell, Sloan & Pearce, 1949.
Galbraith, John Kenneth: *The Great Crash*, 1929, Boston, Houghton Mifflin, 1955.
Gottschalk, Louis R.: *The Era of the French Revolution* (1715–1815), Boston, Houghton Mifflin, 1940.
Grey, Edward: *Twenty-five Years* (2 vols.), New York, Stokes, 1925.
Hayes, C. J. H.: *Modern Europe to* 1870 and *Contemporary Europe since* 1870, New York, Macmillan, 1953.
Holborn, Hajo: *The Political Collapse of Europe*, New York, Knopf, 1951.
Howe, Quincy: *The World between the Wars: From the* 1918 *Armistice to the Munich Agreement*, New York, Simon and Schuster, 1953.
Keynes, J. M.: *The Economic Consequences of the Peace*, London, Macmillan, 1920.
Langer, William L.: *The Diplomacy of Imperialism*, 1890–1902, New York, Knopf, 1935.
Lee, Dwight E.: *Ten Years: The World on the Way to War*, 1930–1940, Boston, Houghton Mifflin, 1942.
May, Arthur J.: *The Hapsburg Monarchy*, Cambridge, Mass., Harvard University Press, 1951.
Morse, H. B., and H. F. MacNair: *Far Eastern International Relations*, Boston, Houghton Mifflin, 1931.
Nicolson, Harold: *Peacemaking*, 1919, London, Constable, 1933.
O'Neill, H. C.: *A Short History of the Second World War and Its Social and Political Significance*, New York, Praeger, 1953.
Palmer, Robert R.: *A History of the Modern World*, New York, Knopf, 1953.
Russell, Frank M.: *Theories of International Relations*, New York, Appleton-Century-Crofts, 1936.
Schmitt, Bernadotte E.: *The Coming of the War*—1914 (2 vols.), New York, Scribner, 1930.
Schuman, Frederick L.: *Europe on the Eve*, New York, Knopf, 1939.

SUGGESTED READINGS

Schuman, Frederick L.: *Night over Europe*, New York, Knopf, 1941.
———, and Geo. D. Brodsky: *Design for Power: The Struggle for the World*, New York, Knopf, 1942.
Shugg, Roger W., and Maj. H. A. DeWeerd: *World War II*, Washington, Infantry Journal, 1946.
Taylor, A. J. P.: *The Struggle for Mastery in Europe, 1848–1918*, New York, Oxford, 1955.
Thomson, David: *World History from 1914 to 1950*, New York, Oxford, 1954.
Vinacke, Harold M.: *Far Eastern Politics in the Postwar Period*, New York, Appleton-Century-Crofts, 1956.
Wecter, Dixon: *The Age of the Great Depression: 1929–1941*, New York, Macmillan, 1948.
White, Theodore H.: *Fire in the Ashes*, New York, Sloane, 1953.
Willkie, Wendell: *One World*, New York, Simon and Schuster, 1943.
Wolff, Theodor: *The Eve of 1914*, New York, Knopf, 1936.
Woolbert, Robert Gale: *Foreign Affairs Bibliography*, New York, Harper, 1945.
Zilliacus, Koni: *The Mirror of the Past*, New York, Wyn, 1946.

Current Guides

Foreign Policy Association: *Bulletins* (weekly) and *Headline Books* (semi-annual); Events Publishing Company: *Current History* (monthly); The Council on Foreign Relations: *Political Handbook of the World* (annual); *Foreign Affairs* (quarterly); Chicago Council on Foreign Relations: *Foreign Notes* (biweekly); Carnegie Endowment for International Peace: *International Conciliation Pamphlets* (monthly); Columbia University Press: *The Journal of International Affairs* (quarterly); Funk and Wagnalls: *The New International Year Book* (annual); *The Statesman's Year Book* (annual); Royal Institute of International Affairs: *Survey of International Affairs* (annual), New York, Oxford Press; Princeton Center of International Studies: *World Politics* (quarterly); University of London: *The Year Book of World Affairs* (annual), New York, Praeger.

And it shall come to pass in the last days, that the mountain of the Lord's house shall be established in the top of the mountains, and shall be exalted above the hills; and all nations shall flow unto it. And many people shall go and say, Come ye, and let us go up to the mountain of the Lord, to the house of the God of Jacob; and he will teach us of his ways, and we will walk in his paths: for out of Zion shall go forth the law, and the word of the Lord from Jerusalem. And he shall judge among the nations, and shall rebuke many people: and they shall beat their swords into plow-shares, and their spears into pruninghooks: nation shall not lift up sword against nation, neither shall they learn war any more.—*The Book of Isaiah*, 2:2–4.

A Book of

FORMS

Today men seem politically hypnotized. Yet much of that which is necessary and good for us goes on irrespective of our political strivings—the sunshine, the rain, the blossoming of the flowers, the ripening of the harvests, the passing of the seasons. The hills stand still, friendships remain precious, men and women fall in love, children play and dream, and the stars look down on human life. It has been said that we cannot argue ourselves out of a dilemma, and given many of the values that are commonly held today, there may be no way out of the international dilemma. We can, however, raise ourselves above the dilemma by considering problems from a new level of comprehension, imagination, objectivity, and insight. A deeper appreciation of the totality of life may permit us to have the mental ability and restraint necessary to control the vast forces unleashed by science, which today have revealed the bankruptcy of international political institutions as they are and the insufficiency of man's purpose to channelize them. Dominating all the international problems of today may be the problem whether or not man can control the great things which he has invented, whether or not he has the morality to use what he has created or must succumb to his creations.—LINDEN A. MANDER, *Foundations of Modern World Society*, 1947.

Chapter IV

THE QUEST FOR LAW

1. THE SOURCES OF JUSTICE

Positive (instituted or voluntary) law derives its origin from will and is either human or divine. Human positive law includes civil law, which proceeds from the power of the State, the law of nations, which receives its binding force from the will of all nations or of many, and law which does not emanate from the power of the State though subject to it, such as the commands of a father or a master.
—HUGO GROTIUS, *De jure belli ac pacis*, 1625.

LAWLESSNESS is the son of anarchy and the brother of violence. These unpleasant companions flourish in communities where common purposes, implemented by an effective central power, are insufficient to enforce peace. In an epoch of contending States, with the great aspirants for mastery seeking to crush their rivals, a consideration of "international law" will appear to some to be wholly academic or to have only historical interest. This view, however, is shortsighted. Even in an age of wars of annihilation, the older rules of the law of nations are still widely observed. Here (as elsewhere) respect for law attracts no attention, whereas violations "make the headlines." The painful processes of interstate unification, moreover, whether achieved by the sword of tyranny or by the voluntary federation of those who survive the holocaust, will inevitably continue through the building of the world order of the future on foundations derived from the world public law of the present and the past. That law, therefore, cannot be dismissed as obsolete. So long as men and nations find it useful to act in accordance with established rules, international law will remain a living and growing body of legal principles, honored more in the observance than in the breach.

Attention will here be devoted only to "public," as distinct from "private," international law. The former has to do with States as legal and political entities. It consists of the rules and principles which the whole society of States habitually expects its members to observe in their relations with one another. Private international law, or "conflicts of laws," has to do with the rights and obligations of individuals as they are affected by overlapping jurisdictions and divergencies of national legislation.

Inasmuch as public international law differs in many respects from other types of law, it will be useful to consider at the outset the problem of its "sources." Every statesman, lawyer, and jurist who is confronted with a legal

108

problem must know where to look for the principles, precedents, and established rules and procedures which will indicate the rights and obligations of the parties. In dealing with cases of national, or "municipal," law, as it is sometimes called, this problem is comparatively simple; attorneys can readily "find the law" in written constitutions, in statutes passed by national or local legislatures, or (in Anglo-Saxon countries) in past judicial decisions which furnish precedents for future cases.

The sources of international law are quite different. They may be divided into four categories in order of importance: (1) agreement; (2) custom; (3) reason; (4) authority. In every international law case, the best sources of information regarding the rights of the parties are the written agreements, treaties, conventions, protocols, and the like, which the States involved have concluded with one another. All States have hundreds of treaties with other States, dealing with a vast variety of matters. Their texts are usually published by the signatory parties in a national treaty series and in privately published compilations. Sovereign States are always free to make new law between themselves by treaty, provided that they do not violate the rights of third States. If such agreements cover the case in hand, it is unnecessary to look further for sources of law, for specific agreements supersede all other possible sources.

But if existing pacts do not cover the situation, the established customs, practices, and usages of States in dealing with analogous problems in the past furnish the next best guide. Differences of opinion are obviously more likely to arise regarding rights based exclusively upon custom than is the case where rights are specifically defined in written agreements. When it can be clearly shown, however, that a particular principle or practice has been observed by most States over a long period of time, no question will ordinarily be raised regarding its legal validity. When, for example, the U.S. Supreme Court was obliged to pass upon the legality of the capture of a Spanish fishing smack during the Spanish-American War, it held the capture unlawful on the ground that

at the present day, by the general consent of the civilized nations of the world, and independently of any express treaty or other public act, it is an established rule of international law, founded on considerations of humanity to a poor and industrious order of men, and of the mutual convenience of belligerent States, that coast fishing vessels, with their implements and supplies, cargoes and crews, unarmed, and honestly pursuing their peaceful calling of catching and bringing in fresh fish, are exempt from capture as prize of war. [*The Paquete Habaña*, 175 U.S. 677.]

When appeals to agreements and to customs both fail to indicate the rights and obligations of States, recourse is had to reason and authority, *i.e.*, to logical deductions from established principles, and to arbitral awards, decisions of courts, and opinions of text writers and jurists. Novel cases are constantly arising with regard to which no agreements have been concluded and no customs have developed. These are ordinarily dealt with by seeking to apply to the new facts a line of reasoning resting upon recognized rules accepted as a priori premises. If, by this procedure, a definition of rights and duties can be arrived at which appears to be in harmony with the whole body of international jurisprudence, it is more than likely to be accepted by the parties as a source of law in the novel situation. Similarly, the judgments of courts, national or international, and the views of well-known authorities are constantly relied upon as guides to the law, chiefly to support the conclusions to which a consideration of agreements, customs, and reason has already led. Judicial decisions and arbitral awards are binding only upon the parties to the disputes of which they are settlements, but taken as a whole they indicate to all States the prevalent conception of rights and duties accepted in international society. Agreement and authority are written sources of international law. Custom and reason are unwritten only in the sense that they are not incorporated in treaties or decisions. The precedents, practices, and usages out of which they emerge, however, are to be found in the diplomatic correspondence and State papers maintained in governmental archives.

2. STATES AS PERSONS

"L'État? C'est moi!"—LOUIS XIV

Since States are the persons of public international law, it follows that the law is concerned primarily with such political entities as are generally recognized as "States" within international society. With certain exceptions, no individual or corporation, no community or territorial group can claim rights under international law unless it is regarded by the members of the State System as a State, independent and coequal with other States. It is generally agreed that a State, in order to be worthy of the name, must possess citizens or subjects and a territory. But the question of whether a particular entity does or does not constitute a State in fact (*de facto*) is not, in itself, a problem of law at all. A "State" may exist for a long period of time, but it does not become a State in the legal sense until it has been received into the family of nations as a recognized member. Switzerland and the Netherlands before 1648, the USA between 1776 and 1778, Japan prior to 1854, and Turkey prior to 1856 all constituted *de facto* States without being persons of international law, *i.e.*, without being formally admitted as full-fledged members into the Western State System. States are initiated into the society of States only by the process of diplomatic recognition extended to them by other States.[1]

---

[1] This circumstance renders difficult any accurate reckoning of the number of sovereign States at any given time. Among the communities claiming such status, some will be recognized as such by most or all other States while others, whatever their pretensions to sovereignty, will be denied recognition by some established States. For example, the USA, as of 1958, exchanged diplomatic agents with, and thus recognized as sovereign, 84 countries. These included 3 -Estonia, Latvia, and Lithuania—which had had no existence as

STATES AS PERSONS

The number of sovereign States decreased sharply in the 19th Century with the national unification of hitherto fragmented communities, originally numbering scores of "sovereignties" in Italy and hundreds in Germany, and with the concurrent imposition of colonial rule by European Powers on many previously independent communities in Asia and Africa. With the breakdown and liberation of the colonial empires in the 20th Century, the number of sovereignties once more increased to a total approaching 100 by 1960. During and since World War II the following new States achieved independence, acknowledged by other States: Syria (Jan. 1, 1944); Lebanon (Jan. 1, 1944); Indochina (Sept. 2, 1945), which was divided a decade later into South Vietnam, North Vietnam, Laos, and Cambodia; Jordan (March 22, 1946); Philippines (July 4, 1946); India and Pakistan (Aug. 15, 1947); Burma (Jan. 4, 1948); Ceylon (Feb. 4, 1948); Israel (May 15, 1948); Indonesia (Dec. 27, 1949); Libya (Jan. 1, 1952); Sudan (Jan. 1, 1956); Morocco (March 2, 1956); Tunisia (March 20, 1956); Ghana (March 6, 1957); and Malaya (Aug. 31, 1957). Since claims to "independence" and "sovereignty" in emulation of European models have become universal in our time among non-European peoples long subjected to European rule, the number of sovereign States will continue to increase with consequent additions to the "persons" of public international law—but with no demonstrable increase of actual freedom, order, or stability in the human community.

When and under what circumstances established States shall accord recognition to new States is entirely a matter of policy. It may be granted at once, it may be delayed, or it may be withheld indefinitely for legal reasons, for political reasons, for good, bad, or indifferent reasons. Considerations of convenience and the obvious utility of maintaining diplomatic contacts with a *de facto* State, however, will usually dictate its recognition by other States as soon as its existence and independence are firmly established. New States may be recognized individually or collectively by other States. Greece was recognized collectively by the Powers at the London Conference of 1830. Belgium was likewise recognized collectively in 1831, Montenegro, Serbia, and Rumania in 1878, and Czechoslovakia and Poland in 1918.

Recognition once granted is irrevocable. It dates back, so far as legal rights and obligations are concerned, to the date of the establishment of the new

---

independent States since 1940 when they were annexed by the Soviet Union. The USA continued to recognize the regime of Chiang Kai-shek on Formosa as the "government" of China, although this regime had been driven from the mainland in 1949. Washington, moreover, maintained no diplomatic relations with Bulgaria and Albania and refused to recognize the States of East Germany, Outer Mongolia, North Korea, and North Vietnam —all of which were recognized by many other States. Among the miniscule States and historical curiosities, the USA (1958) recognized Luxembourg (population, 300,000), Iceland (140,000), and Nepal (8,500,000), but exchanged no representatives with other States recognized as such by their neighbors and by some other Powers—*e.g.*, Bhutan (300,000), Monaco (22,000), Liechtenstein (13,000), San Marino (12,000), Andorra (5,000) and Vatican City (1,000).

State. Normally, one State recognizes another by a formal declaration to this effect, followed by an official exchange of diplomatic agents. Either the dispatch or the reception of a diplomat constitutes recognition. The *reception* of the consular agents of a new State through the granting to them of "exequaturs" authorizing them to assume their functions is also equivalent to recognition, though the *sending* of a consular agent to receive an exequatur from the authorities of a new State does not necessarily imply recognition on the part of the sending State. The signature of an international agreement, a salute to the flag, or any other act of like intent authorized by responsible authorities likewise constitutes recognition. In the USA, as in all other countries, the power to recognize new States and governments is vested in the executive, *i.e.*, the President and the Secretary of State. Congress has no power to grant, or to compel the granting of, recognition, and the courts never question executive discretion in such matters.[2] Washington has usually recognized new States by official proclamation of the President or Secretary of State.

If an outside State recognizes the independence of a new State during a period of conflict in which the new State's claim to independence is still being contested by the State formerly having jurisdiction over its territory, the act of recognition takes on the appearance of intervention or unlawful interference in the domestic affairs of another State. The injured party may legitimately regard such premature recognition as a hostile act. France recognized the independence of the United States by signing treaties of alliance and commerce with American representatives at Paris on Feb. 6, 1778. Britain was still making active efforts to subdue her rebellious colonies, and consequently declared war on France. Had the European Powers recognized the independence of the Confederacy during the American Civil War, this action similarly would have been regarded as a *casus belli* on the part of the Union. In every such case, the State whose rights are violated by premature recognition has a valid complaint against the recognizing State, which has thus sanctioned the partition of its territory before the alleged new State has in fact established its independence.

Almost all the foregoing observations are also applicable to the recognition of new governments within States already recognized. A revolution within a State normally terminates its diplomatic relations with other States. The State continues to be a person of international law, but in the absence of the recognition of its new government by other governments it has no means of communicating with outside States. Recognition of revolutionary governments, no less than recognition of new States, is a question of policy on the part of other governments. During the period from 1793 down to the Wilson Administration, the USA usually adhered to the so-called *de facto* theory of recognition, which holds that new governments should be recognized as soon as

[2] See *Williams v. Suffolk Insurance Co.*, 13 Pet. 415; *Jones v. U.S.*, 137 U.S. 202; *Foster v. Neilson*, 2 Pet. 253.

they are in fact in control of the State, in contrast to the *de jure* theory, which denies the right of revolution and holds that only "legitimate" governments are entitled to recognition. When Washington's Cabinet in 1793 granted an official reception to the new French Minister, Citizen Genêt, *i.e.*, extended diplomatic recognition to the revolutionary regime in France, it did so on the basis of Secretary of State Jefferson's view that the only relevant question was whether the new regime was in effective control of France and therefore in a position to represent the French State and discharge its international obligations. The *de facto* theory was followed quite consistently during the 19th Century.

The Wilson Administration (1913–21) reverted to the *de jure* theory in a modified form designed to foster "democracy" in other States, prevent or penalize the revolutionary overthrow of constitutional governments, and express approval or disapproval of new regimes abroad. This use of diplomatic recognition as a weapon of national policy was effective among the lesser States of the Caribbean but fruitless in dealing with major Powers. Washington has since returned in principle, but not always in practice, to the *de facto* theory adhered to by most European States, although the notion that disliked regimes should not be recognized, and if unrecognized will somehow be discredited, still persists. Most jurists and diplomats now accept the Jeffersonian thesis that little is to be gained in time of peace by denying recognition to any functioning government, however abominable, and that many advantages accrue from exchanging agents with all existing governments of sovereign States.[3]

These two divergent "theories" of recognition should not be confused with

---

[3] American practice has been variable. The USA refused for 16 years (until Nov. 16, 1933) to recognize the Soviet Government of Russia on the ground that it repudiated debts, confiscated property, and promoted revolutionary propaganda, thus showing its unwillingness, despite its ability, to discharge its international obligations. From 1917 to 1922, in the name of championing the territorial integrity of Russia, the USA refused to recognize the independence of Estonia, Latvia, and Lithuania, despite recognition of their independence by Moscow. Since 1940 the USA has refused to recognize their reannexation by Russia. On April 19, 1946, Secretary of State Byrnes declared that the USA would henceforth abide by the *de facto* theory, though the Peronista regime in Argentina, established in February, 1944, had not been recognized by Washington until April 3, 1945, following a belated declaration of war on Germany. In subsequent Latin-American revolutions, the USA has usually accorded prompt recognition to new regimes, even when dictatorial and established by violence. Conversely, Washington, once more equating recognition of a Communist government with approval of Communism, refused to recognize the "People's Republic of China," proclaimed Sept. 21, 1949—despite its recognition in 1949–50 by all States of the Soviet bloc and by Britain, India, Pakistan, Burma, Ceylon, Afghanistan, Indonesia, Finland, Sweden, Norway, Denmark, Netherlands, and Switzerland—and continued to deal with the ousted regime of Chiang Kai-shek, established on Formosa, Dec. 8, 1949, as the government of China. On Oct. 20, 1951, President Truman named Gen. Mark Clark as first U.S. Ambassador to the Vatican, which exchanged diplomatic agents with 38 other States. But Congressional and public opposition among Protestants, many of whom equated diplomatic relations with the Holy See with approval of Catholicism, led to the abandonment of the proposal.

the two levels or stages of recognition, *de facto* and *de jure*. The former phrase is applied to recognition of a new State or government not followed at once by an exchange of representatives. Britain, for example, extended *de facto* recognition to the Soviets by the trade agreement of March, 1921. *De jure* recognition was not granted until February, 1924, when diplomatic agents were exchanged.

Premature recognition granted to a pretended revolutionary government when the lawful authorities are still fighting to suppress the uprising is, of course, a violation of the rights of the legitimate government. Examples: U.S. recognition of the "government" of Panama, Nov. 13, 1903; French recognition of the "White" General, Baron Wrangel, as the "government" of Russia, Aug. 11, 1920; Japanese recognition of the "government of Manchukuo" (Henry Pu-yi), Sept. 15, 1932, and of the Nanking regime of Wang Ching-wei as the "government" of China, Nov. 30, 1940; German and Italian recognition of the Franco regime in Spain, Nov. 18, 1936; etc. Ho Chi Minh's "Republic of Vietnam" in Indochina was recognized by China (Jan. 19, 1950), the USSR (Jan. 31), Poland, Rumania, North Korea, Hungary (Feb. 3), and Bulgaria (Feb. 8), while France (Feb. 2), the USA, Britain (Feb. 7), Belgium (Feb. 8, 1950) and other Western States recognized the French-supported regime of Bao Dai. Such acts are "interventions." Whether the government injured thereby can reestablish its authority and collect damages commonly depends on its military power vis-à-vis the rebels and the foreign States supporting them.

We may notice, finally, that there are certain "persons" of international law which are not true States but which enjoy a legal status. Members of confederations and other unions may have their own diplomatic agents abroad and may be granted certain customary rights by outside States. Such is the peculiar position of all the self-governing Dominions of the British Commonwealth and of some of the Republics of the USSR. Neutralized States, protectorates, and suzerainties may be recognized as States by third parties. Insurgents and belligerents, *i.e.*, groups of armed individuals conducting hostilities for public purposes, are also entitled to the usual rights of the international law of war, provided that they observe the reciprocal obligations. When outside States recognize a condition of "insurgency" in a particular State, they take cognizance of hostilities in which they are bound to abstain from, and to restrain their nationals from, any interference which might aid the rebels. The local State is not answerable for the acts of insurgents unless it can be shown to have been negligent in protecting foreign lives and property. When a status of "belligerency" is recognized in a State afflicted with civil strife (*e.g.*, USA, 1861–65), outside States are bound to observe all the rules of neutrality in dealing with both sides. With the exception of such special cases, public international law is concerned only with recognized States and governments.

3. THE RIGHTS OF SOVEREIGNTIES

Nations being free, independent, and equal and having a right to judge according to the dictates of conscience, of what is to be done in order to fulfill its
duties; the effect of all this is, the producing, at least externally, and among men,
a perfect equality of rights between nations, in the administration of their affairs,
and the pursuit of their pretensions, without regard to the intrinsic justice of
their conduct, of which others have no right to form a definite judgment; so that
what is permitted in one, is also permitted in the other, and they ought to be
considered in human society as having an equal right.—EMERIC DE VATTEL, *Droit
des gens.*

The whole structure of law rests upon certain broad concepts inherent in
the idea of the sovereignty of the State. A sovereign is not subject to the will
of another. It exists as an independent entity, coequal with other sovereignties
and with exclusive jurisdiction over its territory. From this elemental fact,
it follows that every State possesses certain fundamental rights and obligations: "existence," or self-preservation; "independence," "equality" with other
States; and a right of exercising its power and enforcing its legislation within
its frontiers, *i.e.*, a right of "jurisdiction." It is sometimes said that States
also possess fundamental rights of property and of intercourse.

The right of existence, or self-preservation, is obviously the most elementary. That every sovereign State is free to take any action which may be
imperative to preserve itself as a political entity, even to the extent of infring-
ing upon the rights of others, has long been recognized as axiomatic. This
right must be strictly construed, however. An attack upon an innocent third
party can never be justified on the plea of self-preservation. The German invasion of Belgium in 1914, in violation of the Treaty of 1839, was defended
on the ground that it was the only procedure available to Germany for attacking France effectively and thus meeting the threat to Germany represented
by the Franco-Russian alliance. But since the existence of Germany was not
conceivably jeopardized by any act of Belgium, the invasion was unlawful.
Chancellor Bethmann-Hollweg recognized this in his address to the Reichstag
of Aug. 4, 1914, in which he declared, "We are in a state of necessity and
necessity knows no law." Ribbentrop sought to justify German destruction of
the independence of Czechoslovakia, Poland, Denmark, Norway, Luxembourg,
Belgium, and the Netherlands in 1939–40 by alleging that German minorities
were persecuted or that the victim of aggression had forfeited his rights by
conniving with France and Britain to attack Germany. Stalin and Molotov
in the same years sought to justify the Soviet extinction of Estonia, Latvia,
and Lithuania and the attack on Finland in the name of "protecting" those
who were assaulted. But a State can lawfully allege self-preservation as a
justification for violating the rights of others only when it is directly and
immediately menaced by some action in the other State which can be thwarted
in no other way.

This principle was laid down in its classic form by Secretary of State Daniel Webster. During the Canadian rebellion of 1838 insurgents gathered on the U.S. side of the Niagara River, seized guns from U.S. arsenals, occupied an island in midstream from which they fired into Canada, and prepared to recross in the American ship *Caroline* to continue hostilities against Canadian forces. In this emergency, British troops invaded New York, broke up the expedition, sent the *Caroline* over Niagara Falls, and withdrew. This violation of U.S. territory evoked a strong protest from Webster in which he demanded an apology and reparation unless the British Government could

show a necessity for self-defense, instant, overwhelming, leaving no choice of means, and no moment for deliberation. It will be for it to show also that the local authorities of Canada, even supposing the necessity of the moment authorized them to enter the territories of the United States at all, did nothing unreasonable or excessive, since the necessity of self-defense must be limited by that necessity and kept clearly within it.[4]

In this instance the British Government had no difficulty in justifying its action, since an instant and overwhelming necessity menacing the existence of the established government in Canada did undeniably exist and the action taken was limited to meeting this threat. Under such circumstances the right of self-preservation renders legitimate any reasonable action to safeguard the existence of the State or of its government.[5]

The right of independence entitles a State to formulate its own foreign policy within the limits of the rights of other States and to conduct its domestic affairs as it sees fit, provided that it does not ignore the obligations which international law imposes upon it. A State is responsible for injury to aliens within its territory, is required to maintain some degree of law and order, and is bound to maintain some authority answerable to foreign governments. A State must exercise "due diligence" in the protection of aliens, who are entitled to at least the same degree of protection as it affords to its own citizens. It is responsible for any obvious miscarriages of justice in its courts. Though the right of independence carries with it the reciprocal obligation of respecting the independence of others, Great Powers have frequently violated the independence of weak States when conditions of domestic disorder have led to damage to foreign lives and property. The extent to which States are justified in taking such action is much disputed, but the general principles indicated are universally accepted.

The right of equality has reference only to legal rights and obligations and not, of course, to territory, population, power, or political influence. The sovereign States of the world differ enormously among themselves in these characteristics. But, before the law, all sovereign States are equal. All have

[4] See W. E. Hall, *A Treatise on International Law*, 1924, pp. 323–324.
[5] See also the case of the *Virginius, Foreign Relations of the United States*, 1894, pp. 922–1117, and Moore's *Digest*, Vol. II, pp. 895ff.

equal opportunities to assert their rights and to demand that others observe their obligations. All have an equal right to make treaties, wage war, maintain or sever diplomatic relations with other States, and the like. From the principle of State equality is deduced the rule of unanimity in international conferences, according to which each State has one vote and no State can be bound without its consent. In practice, however, it has long been conceded that theoretical legal equality is inconsistent with actual political disparity. There appears at times to be one law for the Great Powers and another for the lesser nations. The principle of State equality is, nevertheless, a logical corollary of the concepts of sovereignty and independence, and States always resent hotly any suggestion that they are not the equals of their neighbors.

Any act by one State which infringes upon the sovereignty, the existence, the independence, or the equality of another State is an act of intervention and is *ipso facto* unlawful. Intervention is usually defined as any act of dictatorial interference by a State in the internal or foreign affairs of another State or any effort to coerce another State in its State action. "With the right of independence goes the correlative *obligation* of *nonintervention, i.e.,* of refraining from all acts that would forcibly limit the freedom of another State." [6] By its very nature, intervention is illegal unless it has been authorized by specific treaty agreements, as has sometimes been the case in the relations between the USA and certain Caribbean States. Under peculiar circumstances, however, it may be justified if it is essential to protect the fundamental rights of the intervening State. It is generally agreed that a State may infringe upon the rights of another without incurring liability for paying damages to the victim if its existence or independence is menaced and the act of intervention is limited to meeting the immediate danger. But the burden of proof is always on the side of the intervening State.

In spite of the logic of this principle, interventions have frequently been resorted to on a variety of other grounds. The colonial empires were largely created by intervening in, and extinguishing the independence of, small or weak States. The USA, before the advent of the "Good Neighbor" policy, intervened repeatedly in the affairs of the States of the Caribbean. Interventions, individual and collective, have been embarked upon by States in the name of upholding international law, enforcing treaty rights, preserving the balance of power, maintaining humanitarian principles, ensuring the payment of debts, affording protection to the lives and property of citizens abroad, etc. Since international law rests no less upon custom than upon reason, it might be contended that a general right of intervention had been established by these practices. This is scarcely a tenable position, however, since every act of intervention unauthorized by treaty is clearly a violation of the rights of the victim. No amount of practice can establish it as a principle of law that

[6] G. G. Wilson, *International Law*, 8th ed., 1922, p. 87.

States have a right to violate the rights of other States. The doctrine laid down by Webster would appear to indicate the only legitimate grounds upon which intervention is justifiable. If this principle is not always adhered to, it is because States, in the pursuit of the objectives of high politics, do not always limit themselves to actions permitted by legal principles and because the community of nations cannot yet ensure protection to the rights of States incapable of defending themselves by self-help.[7]

In recent years all statesmen of all schools and blocs—democratic, Communist, and "neutralist" alike—have repeatedly espoused the sanctity of the principle of nonintervention. But all alike have indulged in interventions when the imperatives of power politics have seemed more important than the rules of law. India forcibly conquered and annexed the princely State of Hyderabad in September, 1948, and in 1957 proclaimed the annexation of half of Kashmir, occupied by Indian troops and claimed by Pakistan. The USA in the spring of 1954 resolved to prevent the establishment of a pro-Communist regime near its frontiers and connived with the governments of El Salvador and Honduras to overthrow by force the elected government of President Arbenz in Guatemala in favor of the anti-Communist regime of Castillo Armas—all in violation of customary international law, the UN Charter, and the Charter of the Organization of American States.[8] The USSR, no less determined to forestall the creation of an anti-Communist regime on its borders, crushed the Hungarian Revolution of October–November, 1956, by brutal violence—while Israel, France, and Britain simultaneously attacked Egypt where Col. Nasser's regime, having given ample provocation for forceable counter-measures, was able to garner political victory from military defeat by virtue of American-Soviet-Asian-African support against so-called "colonialism" (see pp. 422–425).

To return to the law, which in such matters is more often a fiction than a fact, a victim of a legally unjustified military intervention is entitled to damages for violation of its rights. But if the intervention is successful, as

[7] Under the "Good Neighbor" policy proclaimed by President Franklin D. Roosevelt the United States renounced its former interventionist policy in Latin America. Article 8 of the Convention on Rights and Duties of States, signed at the Seventh International Conference of American States at Montevideo, Dec. 3–26, 1933, declared, "No State has a right to intervene in the internal or external affairs of another." This principle was reaffirmed at the Inter-American Conference for Maintenance of Peace, held in Buenos Aires in December, 1936. At the Eighth Conference a "Declaration of Lima" (Dec. 24, 1938) asserted that the signatories were resolved to "maintain and defend against all foreign intervention or activity" the principles of continental solidarity, absolute sovereignty, territorial integrity, peace, security, and the "juridical equality" of sovereign States. The "Declaration of American Principles" signed at the same time asserted, "1. The intervention of any State in the internal or external affairs of another is inadmissible." . . . 4. Relations between States should be governed by the precepts of international law."

[8] For details and documentation, see Philip B. Taylor, Jr., "The Guatemalan Affair: A Critique of United States Foreign Policy," *American Political Science Review*, September, 1956, pp. 787–806.

in Hyderabad in 1948, in Guatemala in 1954, and in Hungary in 1956, no one remains to press the claim. When it is unsuccessful, the ability of the victim to collect damages will always depend less on the logic of the law than on the relative power of the litigants. The modern community of nations has thus far devised no means whereby the strong can be compelled to pay damages to the weak after violating their rights. According to one school of jurisprudence there is "no right without a remedy." If the rights of sovereignties, when violated, often admit of no remedy, strict logic might suggest that the "rights" in question are fictitious. But a more hopeful view would hold, more realistically, that the sovereignties of the State System, while all committed to accepted definitions of "rights," "duties," and "remedies," have as yet devised no reliable procedures whereby the rights of the feeble against the powerful can always be adequately safeguarded. This dilemma of international law we must consider further in due course (see p. 142).

4. PROBLEMS OF OWNERSHIP

A thing may become our property by acquisition, original or derivative. Original acquisition formerly, when the human race could meet together and agree, might be made by division; at present it is only made by occupation.—HUGO GROTIUS, *De jure belli ac pacis*, 1625.

Jurisdiction—authority to "say the law"—is the right to exercise State power. It is a corollary of the rights already discussed. States have jurisdiction over the territories in which they are recognized as sovereign and over the persons who are their nationals. Conflicting claims put forward in the name of territorial jurisdiction and in the name of personal jurisdiction have been a fruitful source of controversy in the past; for if States, as was once the case, insist both upon exclusive jurisdiction over their own territory, including all persons within it, and also over all their citizens or subjects, wherever they may be abroad, it is clear that difficulties will result. In the 20th Century the principle of the "territorial" basis of jurisdiction has in almost all countries been granted precedence over the idea of "personal" jurisdiction. A State, therefore, has jurisdiction over all persons within its territory, whether they be nationals or aliens, and possesses no jurisdiction over its nationals who happen to be in the territory of other States. The two bases of jurisdiction, nevertheless, persist.

A State may acquire territorial jurisdiction by "discovery and occupation," by prescription, by accretion, by cession or leasehold, or by conquest. Discovery of hitherto unclaimed land is no longer regarded as conveying valid title unless it is followed by effective occupation. In the 16th Century the maritime States of Europe laid claim to vast regions of the New World on the basis of discovery alone. England granted "sea-to-sea" charters to the

Atlantic seaboard colonists, who occupied only the coastal strip. As late as the 19th Century, Germany sought, unsuccessfully, to lay down the "hinterland doctrine" with respect to Africa, according to which a State occupying a seacoast could claim the interior drained by its rivers. It is now conceded that only continued occupation conveys title. This differs little from "prescription," whereby a State secures title to land by virtue of long occupation acquiesced in by other States. Similarly, if the natural processes of "accretion" build up deposits on a seacoast or otherwise create new soil, the adjacent State has title. The normal method of acquiring territorial jurisdiction is by treaty. Such pacts may take the form of sales or exchanges of territory, with pecuniary or territorial considerations attached; or they may be the result of war, with the victors relieving the vanquished of their possessions.

The only continent not yet partitioned among sovereignties is Antarctica, an uninhabited wasteland of snow and ice around the South Pole. The Byrd expedition of 1946–47, and the further exploration, under various national auspices, of 1956–58, aroused new interest in overlapping claims. While the USA had asserted no formal title, Chile, Argentina, and Britain (long in dispute with Argentina over title to the Falkland Islands) all laid claim to areas of Antarctica between the Pole and Cape Horn. Norway, Australia, France, and New Zealand have claimed other regions on the "sector principle" or on the ground of exploration. In the absence of any occupation, however, none of these claims would appear to have legal validity, nor is it likely that any valid titles will be established in Antarctica save as the result of possible treaties among the claimants.

"Conquest," in the form of military occupation so prolonged as to be permanent, may confer title even when not followed by a treaty of cession, though the League Covenant and the Kellogg-Briand Pact both sought to "outlaw" conquest as a means of acquiring territory. In accordance with the new dispensation, the USA on Jan. 7, 1932, declared to the Chinese and Japanese Governments that "it cannot admit the legality of any situation *de facto* . . . and it does not intend to recognize any situation, treaty, or agreement which may be brought about by means contrary to the covenants and obligations of the Pact of Paris." The Argentine Anti-War Pact of Oct. 10, 1933, pledged its signatories to similar obligations of nonrecognition, as did the Convention on Rights and Duties of States (Art. 11) signed at Montevideo on Dec. 26, 1933. Such efforts to deny recognition to titles secured by force have not thus far been effective in preventing resort to conquest by hungry States. Finally mention may be made of "leaseholds" as a means of acquiring territory. The status of the Panama Canal Zone and (until recently) of certain ports in China is based upon agreements by which the territories in question were leased to an outside State by the State originally having jurisdiction.

As for the extent of jurisdiction, every State has absolute title to the air above its territory and its territorial waters, possibly including extra-atmospheric space.[9] As a matter of comity, however, States are expected to grant a right of innocent passage to foreign aircraft, subject to such reasonable regulations as are necessary to ensure observance of local laws. Jurisdiction over the waters adjacent to a State, on the contrary, does not extend indefinitely but has been historically limited to a zone within 3 miles from the coast line. This limit of territorial waters or maritime jurisdiction, established at a time when it represented the range of coast artillery, is still recognized by many States. The waters beyond are "high seas" and are not subject to the jurisdiction of any State, except for purposes of punishing pirates, who may be proceeded against by all States. In accordance with the so-called "doctrine of hot pursuit," however, coast-guard vessels may pursue foreign ships suspected of violating local laws out into the high seas, provided that the pursuit is begun within territorial waters and is continuous. Within territorial waters, privately owned foreign vessels are subject to local laws, though they are ordinarily granted a right of innocent passage and are exempt from interference by the local authorities except where a violation of local law occurs of such a nature as to "disturb the peace of the port." Foreign public vessels, *i.e.*, war vessels and other ships owned by foreign governments and engaged in public business, are exempt from local jurisdiction and may not be boarded for any purposes by local authorities.

The traditional "3-mile limit" has recently been under attack from several sources. The USSR has claimed a 12-mile limit in the Baltic and shot down foreign planes alleged to be violating Soviet territory. Norway's claim to a 4-mile limit and the right of drawing the line from headland to headland of bays instead of following the sinuosities of the coast was upheld, Dec. 18, 1951, by the International Court of Justice in the face of long-standing British objections. The USA in the 1920's negotiated a score of treaties authorizing jurisdiction over foreign "rumrunners" within an hour's sailing distance from shore. In the Declaration of Panama, Oct. 3, 1939, the American Republics sought to forbid non-American belligerents to commit acts of war within a vast "neutrality zone" or "chastity belt" over the high seas. (All belligerents ignored the ban as unlawful. The first naval battle of World War II—*Admiral Graf Spee* vs. *Achilles, Ajax,* and *Exeter,* Dec. 13, 1939—was fought off Montevideo.) The USA and Mexico in 1945 asserted a right to exploit submarine

[9] The matter is moot. See AJIL, January, 1958, and subsequent issues. The launching of the first sputniks in 1957 was followed by much talk of "conquering space," "manning the moon," etc. Since no State, as yet, can exercise effective authority within extra-atmospheric space above its territory, much could be said for regarding such space as comparable to the "high seas." As of 1958, no State had protested to Moscow that the sputniks were violating its jurisdiction. The fact is that every earth-satellite, once launched, maintains an orbit which is constant. Only the rotation of the earth within the orbit creates the impression that the satellite has a crazy-quilt pattern of transits carrying it over all other States. Both motions (thus far) are beyond human control and would seem to call for new definitions, by international agreement, of spatial jurisdiction.

oil and other resources out to a water depth of 600 feet. In the Act of Petropolis, Sept. 2, 1947, each of the American Republics agreed to regard as an attack upon itself any attack upon another within an area bounded by the North and South Poles and the middle of the Atlantic and Pacific Oceans.

Other water boundaries are usually defined by treaty. In the absence of treaty arrangements to the contrary, river boundaries between States follow the .halweg, or deepest navigation channel. If a boundary river shifts its bed gradually by "accretion," the boundary shifts likewise; but where a sudden change by "avulsion" takes place, the boundary remains as before. Rights of navigation and of water diversion for irrigation or power purposes are always dealt with by treaty provisions. Rivers, lakes, and canals which are entirely surrounded by the territory of one State are completely within its jurisdiction. Straits less than 6 miles in width are within the jurisdiction of the shore State or States, though the vessels of other States have a right of navigation, subject to reasonable local regulations and duties for safety, the upkeep of lighthouses, and the like. Gulfs, bays, and estuaries opening out onto the high seas are within the jurisdiction of the State enclosing them, with the line of maritime jurisdiction parallel to a line drawn from headland to headland, if the mouth is not more than 6 miles wide. Other arrangements have often been made by treaty, however, and more recently a 10-mile limit for width of mouth of territorial bays has been recognized.

These traditional rules of maritime jurisdiction had fallen into sad disorder by the sixth decade of the 20th Century. International law can be changed only by agreement among States or by slow modifications of practice acquiesced in by all. In the swiftly changing world of our time few multilateral agreements were concluded and no new universal code was negotiated to supersede the old rules, although the possibility of such a code was explored at a general conference on maritime law held under UN auspices in 1958. A variety of unilateral claims were meanwhile put forward in the name of extending maritime jurisdiction, all inspired by economic or political aspirations and each protested by other States. In the late 1950's the USA denied the claim of most of the Pacific Coast States of South America to exercise jurisdiction for fishing purposes 200 miles from shore. Egypt sought to close the Gulf of Aqaba and the Suez Canal to Israeli shipping. Egypt, Jordan, and Saudi Arabia claimed a 6-mile limit in the Gulf and asserted that the entire waterway comprised Arab territorial waters. Israel, supported by France and Britain, resorted to force in protest in the autumn of 1956 and was compelled to withdraw by pressure from the USA—whose policy-makers, however, subsequently argued that all States had a right of "innocent passage" through the Canal and through the Gulf of Aqaba, which was deemed "high seas," despite its narrow mouth, because of the multiplicity of States sharing its shores. When the USSR in the summer of 1957 declared the Bay of Vladivostok, 125 miles wide and 50 miles deep, "closed waters," London, Tokyo, and other capitals protested. Indonesia's claim that all waters between its widely scattered islands are "territorial" was also resisted by other States. When disputing States are unwilling to accept old rules and reluctant to negotiate new rules, such controversies cannot be resolved by recourse to the law. All law is effective in promoting order in human relations only when the parties concerned are agreed upon basic rules which are regarded as consonant with their interests. When this condition is lacking, the traditional law is violated and becomes obsolete. This is the central paradox of international law, which depends for its observance not on any global agencies of enforcement but on the willingness of sovereignties to respect old rules or reach agreement on new ones. The alternative is anarchy and threatened violence. Such was the case in mid-century as regards many problems of maritime jurisdiction. The same was true of many vexed questions of jurisdiction over persons.

Such jurisdiction has been claimed by States under two different theories which are still only partly reconciled. Under the rule of *jus soli* (right of the soil), States have claimed as nationals all persons born within their territorial limits. Amendment 14 of the American Federal Constitution declares, "All persons born or naturalized in the United States, and subject to the jurisdiction thereof, are citizens of the United States and the State wherein they reside." Under the rule of *jus sanguinis* (right of the blood), States have claimed that all children of their nationals, wherever born, are their nationals by virtue of parentage. The legislation of States regarding the bases of nationality varies considerably. Because of differences in nationality laws, it is possible for an individual to be a national of two States simultaneously, or to become "Stateless" by taking some action which forfeits his citizenship in one State without entitling him to citizenship in another. No general international agreement has yet been reached regarding these questions. Most States, however, now adhere to the rule of *jus soli*, with certain qualifications. Aliens, in general, are entirely subject to the jurisdiction of the State where they reside. Aliens who are fugitives from justice may be delivered up to the authorities of the State from which they have fled by the process of extradition. This procedure is provided for by treaties which specify the crimes for which extradition shall be granted and the categories of persons subject to extradition. Political crimes, short of attempts at assassination, are normally exempted by specific provisions of such treaties.

Certain common exemptions from local jurisdiction are universally recognized. Sovereigns traveling abroad, diplomatic representatives, and (usually) agents of international organizations are exempt from the jurisdiction of the State in which they reside. The buildings and grounds of embassies and legations are regarded as "extraterritorial," *i.e.*, as part of the territory of the foreign State maintaining them rather than of the local State. They may not be taxed or entered by the local police without permission, and local laws may not be enforced within their precincts. The "extraterritoriality" formerly enjoyed by nationals of Western States in China and other Oriental countries—*i.e.*, the right to trial in foreign consular courts applying foreign law—has now largely lapsed with the denunciation or renegotiation of the original treaties granting this privilege.

These problems assumed their most acute form in the late 1950's in connection with the maintenance of foreign troops by Great Powers in the territories of many dependent or allied States. The USSR felt obliged in 1956–58 to negotiate new accords with Poland, Rumania, Hungary, *et al.*, restricting the rights of Soviet soldiery within the jurisdiction of the satellites. The USA, having entered into "alliances" with no less than 44 States and having negotiated "status-of-forces" agreements for the maintenance of bases and garrisons in many such States, became involved in comparable difficulties. Most such accords specified that offenses committed by U.S. soldiers while "on duty" were to be tried in U.S. military courts (a new form of "extraterritoriality"), while other offenses were to be tried in local courts. Although these arrangements worked well enough in most instances, they led to incidents and in some cases to mob violence and widespread demands of "Yankees, go home!" The legal symbols and the popular psychology of national sovereignty make friction inevitable wherever large numbers of alien nationals are stationed on the territory of other States and accorded sundry exemptions, however carefully defined, from local jurisdiction.[10]

[10] Thousands of such cases were satisfactorily settled without attracting public attention. But when Sgt. Robert G. Reynolds on Formosa shot to death Liu Chi-jin on Jan. 30, 1957, alleging that his victim was a "peeping Tom" spying on Mrs. Reynolds in her bath and had later threatened him in the garden, the results were calamitous. A U.S. court martial found Reynolds "innocent," May 23, 1957, and released him to return home while Americans in the courtroom cheered. A public protest by the victim's widow led to rioting on the next day in the course of which the U.S. Embassy and the U.S. Information Service offices were wrecked and many Americans barely escaped with their lives.

Similar local resentments exploded in Japan when U.S. authorities initially refused to deliver to Japanese courts William S. Girard, who killed a Japanese woman, Mrs. Naka Sakai, while she was gathering empty shell cases on an American firing range. Patriotic Japanese insisted that Girard be tried in a Japanese court. Patriotic Americans insisted he be tried in a U.S. court martial, and introduced legislation in Congress (which Administration spokesmen said would be disastrous) to "protect the constitutional rights" of all American servicemen abroad. On July 11, 1957, the U.S. Supreme Court ruled that Girard was not acting in "line of duty" and must therefore be subjected to Japanese jurisdiction. "A sovereign nation has exclusive jurisdiction to punish offenses against its laws committed within its borders, unless it expressly or impliedly consents to surrender its jurisdiction." Girard was tried, found guilty of manslaughter, and received a 3-year suspended sentence (Nov. 19, 1957).

Similar frictions, albeit less widely publicized, marked the relations between Soviet occupation troops and local civilians in Eastern Europe.

5. THE LAW OF CONTRACTS

In contracts, nature requires equality, and in such a way that, from inequality, he who has the worse share acquires a right. This equality consists partly in the act, partly in the matter concerning which the act is, and in the acts both precedent and principal.—HUGO GROTIUS, *De jure belli ac pacis,* 1625.

It is a convenient, albeit often confusing, fiction of law that sovereign States, like corporations, are "persons" who may enter into contracts with one another. Long before anyone took cognizance of international law, the first States established peace with one another by solemn pacts. International agreements, bilateral and multilateral, now deal with every conceivable subject of common interest.

Any such written accord may loosely be called a "treaty." This term, however, is best reserved for legally binding contracts between States as sovereign entities as distinct from "executive agreements," which are merely promises exchanged between national administrations, not legally binding upon their successors or upon the State as such. Treaties are often given other names, with no particular rhyme or reason in the terminology. Thus multilateral treaties dealing with general principles of law, and bilateral compacts on specific or technical problems, are commonly called "conventions," though occasionally they may be dubbed "protocols" or "declarations." An "armistice" is a treaty or executive agreement for the termination of hostilities. A *"compromis"* is one providing for the submission of a dispute to arbitration. Since all treaty-making would be pointless unless the parties had some expectation that the terms as signed would be observed, the oldest rule of international law (even if often honored more in the breach than in the observance) is *pacta sunt servanda, i.e.,* agreements are to be kept.

In order for a treaty to be legally valid, its preparation must conform to certain standardized rituals. (1) Upon meeting, the agents of each State submit credentials to the agents of the other, "exchange of full powers," showing that they have been regularly authorized to negotiate the contemplated agreement. (2) Next follows the negotiation and signing of the agreement. Prior to the 19th Century, treaty texts usually began with an invocation of the Deity. A preamble may set forth the purposes of the agreement and give the names of the heads of the signatory States and of the negotiators. There follow the numbered articles of the compact, the conditions of ratification, the place and date of signature, and the signatures and seals of the agents. Signatures are usually attached in accordance with the principle of the alternat, whereby each State receives a copy of the treaty signed first by its own delegate. Multilateral treaties are often signed by the delegates in alphabetical order of the names of the States, in French. Many treaties are drawn up in French, long the traditional language of diplomacy, as well as in the languages of the signatory States. (3) The ensuing step is ratification of the signed agreement by the constitutionally designated authorities in the signatory States. Ratification may be withheld, or amendments and reservations may be attached, if irregularities have taken place in the negotiations or if the agreement is regarded as unsatisfactory. In the latter case, however, friction is likely to result, since States normally assume that a treaty which has been negotiated in accordance with instructions ought to be ratified. Amendments and reservations attached by one party are not binding unless accepted by the other. (4) Exchange of ratifications is a formal ceremony whereby the parties indicate to one another that ratification has taken place and guarantee to one another the execution of the terms. Treaties are binding from the date of signature, unless some other time is specified. (5) The execution of the agreement is the final step whereby the terms agreed upon are carried out by the parties. In the USA, execution is preceded by a formal proclamation of the treaty in the name of the President.

In order that an agreement may be legally binding, certain other conditions are essential. The parties must be legally competent; *i.e.,* they must be free under the terms of their constitutions and of earlier treaties to contract the engagement. The plenipotentiaries must have been fully accredited and must have acted within the scope of their authority. There must be freedom of consent, with no hint of fraud, bribery, or coercion. Coercion invalidates a treaty if it is applied against the persons of the negotiators, but not if applied against a State. Treaties of peace are usually accepted under duress; but so long as the coercion is of the State and not of its agents, the agreement is binding. Finally, agreements must conform to international law and must not infringe the rights of third States. If it can be shown that at any step in the proceedings these conditions have not been complied with, the agreement in question can be regarded as void by either party.

States which are not parties to an agreement are, of course, not bound by its terms. Treaties are contracts which specify rights and obligations only for the signatory States. Outside States may protest against a treaty only if it violates their own rights. States not parties to a treaty may express "approbation," by which they indicate approval without becoming a party; or they may announce "adhesion," by which they agree to abide by its principles, also without becoming a party; or, finally, they may announce "accession," in which case they formally become parties to the engagement.

In the interpretation of treaties the real intention of the parties is preferred to grammatical deductions from the words used. Intentions may be ascertained through procès-verbaux, notes, memoranda, and other communications at the time of negotiation. If such documents are accepted by both sides prior to exchange of ratifications, they bind the parties to the interpretation which they set forth. The language of treaties is construed in the ordinary sense of the words employed, unless evidence of a contrary intention is adduced. In conflicts between clauses of a single treaty, special clauses prevail over general clauses, and prohibitory clauses prevail over permissive clauses. Cessions of sovereignty are always strictly construed. As between two conflicting treaties between the same States, the later one prevails. In general, treaties are so construed as to be self-consistent and as not to violate the rights of third States.

Treaties may come to an end by expiration of a time limit, complete fulfillment of terms, an express agreement of the parties, or renunciation of the rights granted. A new treaty, superseding an earlier one, is the most common and satisfactory form of termination. Treaties are likewise terminated by the disappearance of one of the parties. When the independence of a State is extinguished, all its treaties with other States are terminated unless provision to the contrary is made by the new State acquiring its territory. Nonfulfillment of terms by one party, if persisted in despite diplomatic representations, makes it voidable by the other. Treaties cannot ordinarily be denounced by one party without the consent of the other, unless their terms make provision for such a procedure. Under the American Constitution the President or Congress or both may denounce a treaty without the consent of the other party. Under international law, however, it is doubtful whether one party to a treaty ever has a legal right to terminate it without the consent of the other unless the treaty itself provides for this. Under the principle of *rebus sic stantibus* ("conditions remaining the same"), it has been contended that fundamental changes of conditions authorize one party to a treaty to terminate it by unilateral action. Japan, for example, sought in the 1930's to deny the validity of the Nine Power Pact and other obligations to respect the "Open Door" in China on the ground that conditions had been altered fundamentally since ratification. The alteration referred to had been brought about by Japanese aggression in violation of the obligations which were alleged to have been invalidated by the change of conditions. Even when this is not the case the other party almost invariably protests against such a contention. This principle is not part of accepted international law, save when fulfillment has become a physical impossibility.

6. THE RULES OF WAR

Silent enim leges inter arma.—CICERO.

Students and laymen are often puzzled by the apparent paradox presented by that portion of "international law" which deals with organized violence among nations. If law is a device which civilized men have invented as a substitute for the use of force to settle differences, how can any body of law legitimize armed coercion to the extent of prescribing rules for its use? The answer would appear to be that a society of sovereignties is not a true political community in which all agree to abide by established rules for settling legal controversies and to conform, as regards their political controversies, to orderly procedures for modifying the law. The realms of law and politics are not coterminous. Legal principles suffice to adjust differences in which the parties accept as "just" the prevailing distribution of influence and satisfactions. They fail at the point where one side or the other challenges the *status quo* and demands, in the name of "justice," a modification of legal rules. Law is static. Politics is dynamic. Every well-ordered polity provides means, prescribed by law, for changing the law through nonviolent procedures. This is a function of the legislature in every government. The Western State System is not such a polity.

It follows that political controversies among sovereigns are inevitably dealt with through bargaining or violence. Jurists have been forced to take cognizance of the fact of war and have sought, through the elaboration of rules for its conduct, to mitigate its viciousness. This enterprise tends to be self-defeating. In our own time it is increasingly recognized to be futile. Meanwhile the scope and content of the traditional law of war and neutrality deserve examination.

In international law, war is neither "hell," as General Sherman put it, nor is it "justice, nobility and brotherly pity," as Mussolini once insisted. Apart from specific treaties (of which more anon), war as an instrument of national policy is neither permitted nor forbidden. It is merely a fact, however deplorable. In law it is often defined as "a properly conducted contest of armed public forces"—or, better, as a legal status or period of time during which interstate relations are supposed to be governed by the law of war and neutrality rather than by the law of peace.

A state of war involves both an intention to wage war and overt acts of hostility. A legal state of war may exist without hostilities if the parties have expressed an intention to deal with one another as belligerents. But hostilities not treated as war either by the parties or by outsiders do not in themselves create a state of war. They constitute reprisals, retaliation, or intervention; but the rights and obligations of the parties continue to be determined by the law of peace.

In recent wars, it has been customary for States to issue formal declarations of war, making clear their intentions and specifying the time at which a legal state of war shall be regarded as having commenced. The Hague Convention of 1907 with regard to the opening of hostilities forbade the signatory States to commence hostilities without warning through either a declaration or an ultimatum. In 1914 the belligerents specified the exact hour and minute of the commencement of war, a formality useful to prize courts in determining the legality of captures. Germany invaded Poland on Sept. 1, 1939, without a declaration of war and subsequently invaded Denmark, Norway, Luxembourg, Belgium, the Netherlands, Jugoslavia, and the USSR in the same fashion. Britain and France initiated hostilities by formal declarations following ultimata—specifying 11 A.M., and 5 P.M., Sept. 3, respectively, as the time of the commencement of belligerency. Italy entered the war by a formal declaration against France and Britain, effective at 12:01 A.M., June 11, 1940. Declarations of war usually require legislative action under democratic constitutions. In the USA, they require the approval of a majority of both houses of Congress; but such approval has never been withheld when the President has recommended war, nor has Congress ever declared war in opposition to the wishes of the Executive. Federal courts have held that war, in the legal sense, began for the USA in 1941, not with the action of Congress or with the Triplice declarations, but with the Japaneses attack on Pearl Harbor.[11]

War suspends all nonhostile intercourse between belligerent States and their citizens. Diplomatic and consular relations are severed, along with contacts of trade and travel. Political treaties between belligerents are terminated, others are suspended for the duration of the conflict, and agreements on the conduct of hostilities are put into operation. Relations between belligerents are henceforth subject to the law of war, and relations with nonparticipating outside States to the law of neutrality. From the legal point of view, the purpose of war is to bring about the military subjection of the enemy in the shortest time with the least loss of life and property. This conception is shared by the jurist and the strategist, but under modern conditions differences of opinion necessarily arise as to its implications. Mere wanton destruction and slaughter, having no reasonable relation to the military subjection of the enemy, is unlawful. The Continental States of Europe long held that war should, as far as possible, be limited in its effects to armed public forces. Britain long ago regarded it as permissible to attack commercial resources and food supplies through naval blockades. During World War I, Germany developed the theory of *Schrecklichkeit,* or "frightfulness," according to which it is legitimate to attack the entire civilian population of the enemy in order to break its will to resist. This view is the logical corollary of universal military conscription, of the mobilization of industrial resources, and of the decisive importance of civilian morale in a long-drawn-out war of attrition.

These developments tend to break down the old legal distinction between soldiers and civilians. Nevertheless, individuals in wartime are still divided into the two general categories of combatants and noncombatants. Combatants

---

[11] See *N.Y. Life Insurance Company v. Louise C. Bennion,* U.S. Circuit Court of Appeals, 10th Circuit, Nov. 6, 1946, in *American Journal of International Law,* July, 1947, pp. 680*ff.* Mrs. Bennion was the widow of Capt. Mervyn S. Bennion, commander of the U.S.S. *West Virginia,* who was killed at his post. The Company declined to pay double indemnity for accidental death on the ground that the policy excluded "war or any incident thereto." The Court concurred and rejected the claimant's contention that war did not begin until Congress acted. The decision held that any attack by a sovereign State upon another, with intent to wage war and with resistance by the victim, inaugurates war in the legal sense.

may be fired upon and if captured are entitled to be treated as prisoners of war. In this category are members of the regular military, naval, and air forces, officers and crews of merchant vessels resisting capture, and members of levies en masse and of popular civilian uprisings against invaders, provided that they carry arms openly, obey the laws of war, wear emblems or uniforms, and are under a definite command. Noncombatants are all persons not participating in hostilities, not members of fighting forces, and not belonging to any of the special classes mentioned below. Civilian enemy aliens found within a State at the outbreak of war may be expelled, interned, permitted to depart, or permitted to remain unmolested. Since 1914, belligerent States have commonly interned enemy aliens within their jurisdiction, sometimes for their own protection against mob violence. Noncombatants in occupied territory or in the zone of battle are free from violence, constraint, or injury except what is dictated by military necessity or what may befall them through actual hostilities. Officers and crews of merchant vessels taking offensive action against other merchant vessels may be punished by death for piracy since the abolition of privateering by the Declaration of Paris in 1856. Guerrillas, *i.e.*, individuals who engage in military operations without State authorization, may likewise be tried and sentenced for murder, arson, and other crimes which are not individually punishable when committed by soldiers, sailors, or aviators acting under orders. Spies, *i.e.*, individuals who act under false pretenses behind the lines or in occupied territory to secure information for the enemy, are entitled to trial but, if found guilty, are subject to execution.

As regards property in wartime, the general rules are simple, though their application often involves tangled legal problems. Enemy real property owned by a belligerent government within the jurisdiction of another or in a region under hostile military occupation may be administered for the benefit of the State in control but not confiscated. Public movable property, with the exception of works of art, science, or education, is subject to confiscation. Private property of enemy nationals was formerly considered to be subject to confiscation wherever found. This harsh rule has now been modified. Private property of enemy aliens found within a State at the outbreak of war is now usually unmolested or held under bond by the local government for the duration of the war. Private enemy property in occupied territory may no longer be taken by the occupying forces without compensation, though if military necessity requires its destruction no compensation need be paid. The Treaty of Versailles, however, required Germany to pay compensation to the victors for all civilian damages, on the theory that World War I was a result of German aggression. Forces of military occupation may levy taxes for local purposes and may assess penalties on communities where authorities have been negligent in maintaining order and preventing civilian participation in hostilities. In all other cases, as in the levying of money contributions upon the local citizenry, the requisition of food needed by the occupying forces, or the sequestration of vessels, vehicles, and the like, a receipt must be given to the owner as a promise of eventual compensation.

Enemy property at sea is subject to capture and condemnation. Save for ships engaged in humanitarian, educational, or scientific enterprises, there are no exceptions to this rule for public property, *i.e.*, battleships and other vessels and goods owned by the enemy State. With regard to property owned by private individuals, however, various qualifications to the general right of capture have received general acceptance. Enemy merchant vessels in port at the outbreak of hostilities were formerly accorded a specified number of days of grace within which they might escape to sea. Religious, scientific, and philanthropic vessels are exempt from capture, as are hospital ships, fishing vessels, and small coastwise vessels of all types. Under the Declaration of Paris of 1856,[12] it is no longer lawful for belligerents to issue letters of marque and reprisal to private vessels (privateers) authorizing them to capture enemy merchant ships. The Declaration likewise specifies that goods of neutral ownership found on enemy ships shall be exempt from capture and that goods of enemy ownership found on neutral ships shall also be exempt, contraband of war being excepted in both cases. The signatory Powers further declared that a proclamation of a blockade cannot give an indiscriminate right of capture of neutral vessels unless it is, in fact, effectively enforced. Enemy vessels are subject to capture wherever found, even in the absence of a blockade. In the exercise of the right of capture, all vessels are regarded as enemy vessels which fly an enemy flag, which have been transferred to a neutral flag to escape capture, which are under convoy of belligerent war vessels, or which resist search. Captured vessels may be destroyed if there is no means of taking them into port for condemnation, but provision must be made for the safety of passengers and crew.

Well-defined principles have grown up regarding the conduct of hostilities. The more important of these were codified in the Hague Conference Conventions in 1899 and 1907 relating to the laws and customs of war on land. They are for the most part designed to mitigate the cruelties of war. They were formerly well observed, since considerations of expediency dictated compliance on both sides. Wanton destruction of life and property is forbidden, as is the use of poison and dumdum bullets, the refusal of quarter, resort to assassination, deliberate perfidy, and attacks upon undefended towns. Sick and wounded are to be cared for. Prisoners of war must be humanely treated.

---

12 "The plenipotentiaries who signed the Treaty of Paris of the thirteenth of March, one thousand eight hundred and fifty-six, assembled in conference . . . have adopted the following Declaration: (1) privateering is and remains abolished; (2) the neutral flag covers enemy's goods, with the exception of contraband of war; (3) neutral goods, with the exception of contraband of war, are not liable to capture under enemy's flag; (4) blockades, in order to be binding, must be effective—that is to say, maintained by a force sufficient really to prevent access to the coast of the enemy. . . . April 16, 1856."

Civilian populations are, so far as possible, to be spared. Hospitals, churches, schools, museums, public buildings, and the like, are to be safeguarded unless used for military purposes. Naval and aerial bombardment of undefended cities is (or once was) unlawful.

During World War I the established principles dealing with the relations between the armed forces were reasonably well observed, in spite of the introduction of poison gas, liquid fire, and other novel weapons. The rules designed to protect civilians, however, were often ignored, particularly by the Central Powers, which were strategically in a position to strike at enemy centers of population through air raids and long-range artillery. During World War II almost all legal restraints were forgotten in a nightmare of horror which would have appalled Hugo Grotius. Prisoners and noncombatants were slaughtered retail by the Japanese and wholesale by the Nazis. Indiscriminate aerial attacks upon civilians, begun by the Nazis, were completed by British and American "strategic" bombing which leveled most of the cities of the Reich and many of those of Japan. Capture at sea gave way to unrestricted submarine warfare in which enemy vessels were sunk on sight. The Allied coalition lost 4,770 ships totaling 21,140,000 tons. U.S. submarines sank 1,944 Japanese merchant vessels. The rights of neutrals were largely ignored. The concluding atrocities of Hiroshima and Nagasaki, generally condoned in the name of "winning victory," "shortening the war," and "saving lives," were a portent of things to come.

Jurists and humanitarians nevertheless resumed their efforts to "civilize" war by treaty. A Genocide Convention to outlaw mass extermination (sponsored by Dr. Raphael Lemkin and adopted by the UN General Assembly, Dec. 9, 1948) was widely signed and ratified. The International Committee of the Red Cross was instrumental in fostering the negotiation of four new Geneva Conventions (concluded Aug. 12, 1949, and signed by 61 States within the next six months) for the protection of civilians and the amelioration of the treatment of prisoners, sick and wounded in wartime. Yet everyone took it for granted that in the event of World War III all belligerents would use atomic weapons in an effort to exterminate the enemy's population and reduce his land to a desert. The Korean War of 1950–53, with new massacres of prisoners, allegations of germ warfare, and indiscriminate burning and bombing of civilians with napalm and TNT, appeared to validate General MacArthur's judgment: "Convention after convention has been entered into designed to humanize war. Yet each war becomes increasingly savage as the means for mass killing are further developed. You cannot control war; you can only abolish it. Those who shrug this off as idealistic are the real enemies of peace—the real war-mongers." [13]

[13] Address of July 25, 1951. As of 1958 the Genocide Convention had been ratified by most signatory States, but not by the USA which had also failed to ratify the Geneva Convention of 1925 forbidding bacteriological warfare. In denouncing Communist allega-

7. THE LAW OF NEUTRALITY

> The justice or injustice of a war does not affect a common friend. It is not
> for him to place himself as judge between the two belligerents who are the one
> and the other his friends. . . . If I am neither on one side nor the other, I can-
> not aid the one in such a way as will hurt the other.—CORNELIUS VAN BYNKER-
> SHOEK (1673–1743).

In most wars in earlier State Systems and in the early wars in the Western
State System, the notion that an outside State might refrain from participation in a conflict between its neighbors was an unfamiliar one. What is now
known as the international law of neutrality developed slowly. As recently as
the War of the American Revolution, it was regarded as legitimate for a
"neutral" State to rent out its troops to belligerents without violating its obligations. Text writers, from Grotius onward, emphasized the rights of neutral
States to be free from interference by belligerents. Later, after neutral rights
had been more clearly defined, emphasis was shifted to the duty of neutral
States to refrain from participation in hostilities. Still later the great controversies over neutrality again centered in neutral rights as related to trading
privileges. The American Neutrality Code of 1794 was one of the first clear
formulations of the modern conception of neutral obligations.

These may be summarized in terms of abstention, impartiality, and prevention. It is now customary for States to declare their neutrality upon the
outbreak of war by a formal proclamation.[14] A State which has declared itself
neutral has a right to have its neutrality respected by belligerents. It is correspondingly obliged to enforce its neutrality by conducting itself impartially

---

tions of germ warfare in Korea and Communist refusal to agree to an "impartial" investigation, the U.S. delegate on the Security Council in June, 1952, opposed Soviet proposals
for general ratification of the Convention and even declined to commit the USA to non-
resort to germ warfare save in retaliation. This position, coupled with the memory of
Hiroshima and Nagasaki, made the Communist accusations appear plausible to many
Asiatics. Meanwhile the USA (autumn, 1950) had accused the enemy of murdering
thousands of prisoners while the enemy, capitalizing upon widespread disorders on Koje
Island and in other Allied compounds in 1951–52, accused the U.S. and UN of coercing,
torturing, and killing thousands of captives. But Allied motives were humanitarian, as
shown by the "screening" of prisoners and refusal to repatriate those unwilling to return
home—a position which the enemy stubbornly refused to accept, thereby deadlocking the
truce negotiations at Panmunjon and prolonging hostilities. The Hague Convention of
1907 and the Geneva Conventions of 1929 and 1949 all called for repatriation of all prisoners "without delay" on the conclusion of hostilities, but these instruments were obviously
not drafted in anticipation of a situation in which a barbarous belligerent might punish
or liquidate its own returned prisoners for having surrendered while a humane belligerent
might decline to return such prisoners.

[14] On Sept. 5, 1939, President Roosevelt issued a conventional neutrality proclamation
under international law and a second proclamation under the Neutrality Act of 1937 imposing an embargo on the exports of arms, ammunition, and implements of war to Germany, Poland, France, Britain, India, Australia, New Zealand, South Africa (Sept. 5),
and Canada (Sept. 10).

toward belligerents, by abstaining from any part in the conflict, and by preventing its citizens from engaging in certain acts regarded as breaches of neutral obligations. A neutral State may not permit its territory to become a base of hostile operations by either belligerent, or permit its armed forces to be used by either, or officially loan money or sell war supplies to warring governments. It is not obliged, however, to prevent its nationals from lending or selling, provided that they are legally free to sell to both sides on equal terms. Between 1914 and 1917, hundreds of millions of dollars' worth of Allied war bonds were sold in the USA, and billions of dollars' worth of munitions were sold to the Allied Governments by American manufacturers and exporters. Germany complained that this trade was entirely one-sided, since the Allied blockade prevented American munitions from reaching the Central Powers. In law, however, there was no breach of neutral duties since the USA was not responsible for the Allied blockade and Americans were free to sell to both sides on equal terms at their own risk.

A neutral must prevent the enlistment of troops for war purposes on its territory. It must intern belligerent troops and aircraft forced into its jurisdiction. It may grant a right of innocent passage through its territorial waters, however, to belligerent warships. Neutral governments are likewise obliged to prevent their nationals from fitting out, in their ports, vessels designed to take part in the war. The failure of Britain to fulfill this obligation during the Civil War caused the Geneva Arbitration Tribunal, created by the Treaty of Washington of 1871, to award $15,500,000 to the USA for damages committed by the *Alabama,* the *Florida,* and other Confederate cruisers constructed in British ports. A neutral State may not, in the course of a war, modify its neutrality regulations to the advantage of one belligerent. It must use due diligence to ensure observance of its obligations; and it may not extend protection to citizens who engage in "unneutral service," *i.e.,* who commit hostile acts against belligerents and thereby render themselves liable to treatment as enemy nationals.

Acute controversies over neutral rights have arisen as a result of the efforts of belligerent States to cut off commercial contacts between enemies and neutrals. A belligerent has a legal right to intercept such commerce on two grounds. It may proclaim a "blockade" of enemy ports; and if such a blockade is effectively enforced, *i.e.,* if it is not merely a "paper blockade," it entitles blockading war vessels to capture neutral ships seeking to enter or leave the blockaded ports. At the same time, in the absence of any blockade, belligerents may capture neutral goods and ships falling in the category of "contraband of war," *i.e.,* goods of neutral ownership, found on the high seas, of use in war, and destined for the enemy. Neutral vessels may be condemned if more than half the cargo consists of contraband, as measured by volume or by value. All other neutral commerce with States at war is (theoretically) not to be interfered with. Neutral commercial States have usually insisted vehemently upon "freedom of the seas" and neutral trading rights. Belligerents have always been disposed to interpret their rights to intercept neutral commerce as broadly as possible, through the extension of the contraband list and the "doctrine of continuous voyage" or "ultimate destination."

This formula was developed by Britain at the end of the 18th Century, utilized by the Union in the Civil War, and employed by both Powers in World Wars I and II. It holds that neutral vessels going from one neutral port to another may be captured if there is presumption of eventual enemy destination of the cargo.[15] In 1915 and again in 1939 the British Admiralty applied this doctrine both to contraband and to blockade. It went so far as to confiscate neutral cargoes bound for Scandinavian ports in excess of specified quotas, on the ground of presumption that they were destined for transshipment to Germany, either as contraband goods or in violation of the blockade. Belligerents in recent wars have extended the list of contraband to a point where almost all neutral commerce with the enemy is banned. Originally, only war supplies were deemed contraband, but the British lists of 1914–15 and 1939 included almost every conceivable commodity. This procedure was defended on the ground that all the industrial and commercial resources of Germany had been mobilized for war purposes. Neutral ships and cargoes of every nature, destined either for German ports or for neutral ports near Germany, were captured and condemned in wholesale fashion. The USA and other neutrals protested against these practices but resorted to them with even greater enthusiasm after becoming belligerents. Germany's answer was submarine warfare.

On Sept. 3, 1939, the British liner *Athenia* was sunk without warning with heavy loss of life, including 25 Americans. On Oct. 9, 1939, the British-bound American freighter *City of Flint* was captured by the *Deutschland*. The prize crew took the vessel to Norway. On the principle that a neutral may not permit belligerents to bring prizes into its ports except temporarily for fuel, provisions, or repairs,[16] the USA demanded the release of the vessel. Norway complied. Germany protested. German naval forces now began sowing magnetic mines in British waters, in violation of the Hague Convention of 1907, in retaliation for Allied practices which Berlin held unlawful. Early in December the Allies, in counter-retaliation, ordered the seizure of enemy exports in neutral vessels, contrary to the Declaration of Paris. Washington protested to London.

The Allies subsequently contended that Norway was permitting the abuse of its territorial waters. On Feb. 16, 1940, the British destroyer *Cossack* violated

---

15 *Cf. The Maria*, 5 C. Rob. 365, 368; *The Kim*, L. R. 215 (1915); *The Hart*, 3 Wall. 559–560.

16 *Cf.* the case of the *Appam, Berg v. British and African Steam Navigation Company*, 243 U.S. 12 (1917) and Articles 21–23 of the Hague Convention (XIII) concerning the Rights and Duties of Neutral Powers in Naval Warfare (1907).

Norwegian waters by entering Joesing Fiord, boarding the German naval supply ship *Altmark*, and releasing 300 British seamen who had been captured by the *Graf Spee*. Oslo protested to London. Berlin protested to Oslo. On April 5, London threatened action to close Norwegian waters to German shipping on the ground that Norway was permitting abuse of the right of innocent passage. Three days later, British vessels sowed mines along the Norwegian coast to intercept Swedish ore shipments to Germany via Narvik. The Nazi invasion of Norway, launched April 9, had been prepared long in advance but was "justified" by Berlin on the pretext that Norway was not safeguarding its neutrality and was about to be invaded by the Allies and used as a base of operations against the Reich.

The subsequent conduct of neutrals and belligerents in World War II came close to reducing all of the law of war and neutrality to a mockery. Some seekers after peace sought to attain their ends through a new type of neutrality. Others sought peace by abolishing neutrality and universalizing war. The USA had already helped to "make the world safe for aggression" through policies intended to "keep out of other peoples' wars" but eventuating in fact in major assistance to the Triplice Powers in their attacks on Ethiopia, Spain, and China. In 1939, Washington, which had gone to war in 1798, 1805, 1812, and 1917 in the name of "freedom of the seas," forbade Americans to send ships, lend money, or sell arms to belligerents, thus aiding Germany and injuring France and Britain. The new "Neutrality" Act of Nov. 4, 1939, permitted belligerents to buy arms and other goods in the USA and to transport them in their own vessels in the name of "cash and carry," thus aiding the Allies and injuring Germany. By the summer of 1940 the USA was aiding Britain "short of war" by governmental transfers of arms, munitions, and even destroyers—all in clear violation of neutral duties, despite Att. Gen. Robert Jackson's opinion justifying the naval-base–destroyer bargain of Sept. 2, 1940. The Lend-Lease Act of March 11, 1941, carried this policy of "neutral intervention" to its logical conclusion and led to the Triplice attack upon the USA. When considerations of power conflict with principles of law, the latter suffer the fate predicted by Machiavelli. In the Korean War there were neither "belligerents" nor "neutrals," since resistance to aggression was depicted as a UN "police action" against "criminals." War was here waged in the name of peace. Law was ignored in the name of vindicating the "rule of law."

Much of the traditional law of war and neutrality, summarized in the preceding pages, has been rendered meaningless by recent innovations in the arts of violence. The old rules were products of the "limited" wars of the 18th and 19th Centuries in which belligerents sought to defeat their enemies at minimum cost and risk and impose moderate terms of peace, involving modest gains to the victor and acceptable losses to the vanquished. The 20th Century became an era of "unlimited" wars, aiming at the "annihilation" or at least "unconditional surrender" of the vanquished and at "total victory" for the victors.

This irrational pursuit of unlimited objectives through the use of almost any means deemed justified by the end obviously reduced to nonsense many of the customary rules of international law designed in saner times to ensure respect for the rights of noncombatant individuals and neutral States. In the future, "total war" among Great Powers, in the judgment of most observers, means the mutual suicide of the belligerents and the destruction of such "neutral" communities as may lie within the area of nuclear "fall-out." Under such circumstances the old laws of war and neutrality, along with much else, are obsolete. If the international law of a happier epoch is to have any meaning for days to come, it will find its meaning either in a return to the earlier concept of "limited" war or in the renunciation of war itself (see pp. 127–132).

8. THE PUZZLE OF ENFORCEMENT

In the nature of things law cannot be enforced upon sovereign governments or nation-states as units. Power of enforcement must ultimately be exerted upon men individually or collectively. If exerted upon men collectively, that is war. It inevitably involves the destruction of the innocent with the guilty. No matter who wins the contest of force, justice is defeated; not only justice but civilization will be lost, if we do not now establish peace, and peace, as I see it, is a system of order and security under the law which cannot exist without government. . . . Law in the exact sense cannot develop or exist except within the structure of a government of individual citizens.—JUSTICE OWEN I. ROBERTS, 1946.

In all human communities enjoying government, the central principle of criminal justice is that all the power of society, supported by all citizens, shall be brought to bear, within carefully specified safeguards against abuse, upon such erratic individuals as may break the law and violate the peace. The discrepancy of power between the community and the felon is such that peace through law is ordinarily well kept. In the "family of nations," law defines the rights and duties not of individuals but of sovereignties. It is enforced, if at all, by the action of States against States, not by the action of the community against individuals. International society therefore lacks government and consequently lacks the means of enforcing law in the only fashion which has ever been effective in past experience. The problem of government in the Western State System will be explored later in these pages. Here it is fitting to consider the attempts which have recently been made to enforce international law on individuals—without the establishment of any permanent legislative, executive, or judicial authorities in the world community capable of acting on individuals.

Woodrow Wilson in *The State* (1890) argued that international law is really "not law at all," since "it is law without forceful sanction. There is no earthly

power to enforce obedience to rules of conduct as between nation and nation."
Yet most of the rules are most of the time respected. Why? The answer is
that the "sanctions" or guarantees of observance of international law, though
differing from those of municipal law, are nonetheless real and, up to a point,
effective. They may be classified, in order of efficacy, as (1) habit, (2) expediency, (3) good faith, and (4) organized force. Those principles which
have long been habitually observed are obviously most likely to be observed
in the future, since the whole force of inertia lies behind them. The immunity
and inviolability of diplomatic representatives, for example, have been generally observed by States for more than 2,500 years and are almost never
willfully violated at the present time. Considerations of self-interest and political expediency are also important, particularly as regards the international
law of war. At the outbreak of the American Civil War there was some disposition in Union circles to treat captured members of the Confederate armies
not as prisoners, in accordance with the laws of war, but as rebels who might
be punished for treason, arson, murder, and other individual acts. Once it
was realized, however that the Confederacy would promptly retaliate on Federal prisoners, the intention was abandoned. A more farsighted view of self-
interest on the part of the German High Command would similarly have dictated observance of agreements forbidding the use of poison gas in World
War I and might have precluded the Nazi atrocities of World War II.

Good faith as a sanction of international law has been conspicuous by its
absence in the 20th Century. As for "organized force," there is none—for
this term refers, not to violence by State against State, but to coercive authority exercised by the whole community against lawbreakers. Covenants and
Charters, solemnly signed by sovereignties, have provided for collective coercion of international aggressors and criminals. But so long as the culprits
and the "police" are not individuals but States, and so long as diplomats and
patriots act in terms of national self-interest, "collective security" remains at
best an empty dream and at worst a rationalization of *Realpolitik*. Organized
force thus remains the least effective sanction of the law of nations.

Certain categories of individuals have nevertheless always been regarded
as amenable to "international law." Pirates, slave traders, opium peddlers,
spies, and violators of the laws of war have all been proceeded against by
national governments. In their own legislation, moreover, all States prescribe
penalties to be enforced in their own courts against those within their jurisdiction who violate international law. All governments strive to afford diplomatic protection to citizens abroad when jeopardized in their personal or
property rights by local disorders or discriminatory legislation. In 1919 the
Treaty of Versailles (Art. 227) provided for an international tribunal to try
the Kaiser "for a supreme offense against international morality and the sanctity of treaties." Provision was made as well (Arts. 228–230) for the trial
before Allied tribunals of Germans "accused of having committed acts in

violation of the laws and customs of war." A list of over 100 "war criminals" was finally drawn up. But nothing came of these resolves. The Netherlands refused to extradite the former Kaiser. Berlin refused to extradite the other war criminals, of whom a dozen were brought to trial before German courts and either acquitted or given nominal sentences. When one of the "war criminals," Paul von Hindenburg, was elected President of the German Republic in 1925, the Allies made no protest. When Hindenburg appointed Hitler Chancellor in 1933 and the Nazi persecution of Jews began, other governments made diplomatic protests only with respect to victims of their own nationality. Under traditional conceptions, the right of the Nazi regime to rob and murder German citizens of Jewish origin was sacrosanct, since the matter fell within the category of "domestic jurisdiction."

Not until World War II was a systematic effort made to hold individuals, including top political and military figures, accountable for violations of international law. An Inter-Allied Conference in London in January, 1942, resolved to "place among their principal war aims the punishment, through the channel of organized justice, of those guilty of or responsible for these crimes, whether they have ordered them, perpetrated them, or participated in them." At the Moscow Conference of Foreign Ministers in October, 1943, it was agreed, in a statement signed by Roosevelt, Churchill, and Stalin, that "German officers and men and members of the Nazi Party who have been responsible for or have taken a consenting part in atrocities, massacres and executions will be sent back to the countries in which their abominable deeds were done in order that they may be judged and punished. . . . German criminals whose offenses have no particular geographical location will be punished by joint decision of the Governments of the Allies." Even before the end of hostilities, some captured Nazis were locally tried. In December, 1943, for example, three German officers and a Russian traitor were hanged amid the ruins of liberated Kharkov after trial and sentence by a Soviet military court for having killed sick children, beaten women to death, and flogged, hanged, gassed, and butchered war prisoners and civilians during the Nazi occupation. A 16-government United Nations War Crimes Commission, set up in London in October, 1943, advised each participating State to establish a national "war crimes office" to investigate offenses against its own citizens.

The sequel of these decisions was a series of several hundred trials before sundry national and international tribunals in which several thousand suspects were acquitted or sentenced to imprisonment or execution. The two major trials were those held in the War Ministry Building amid the ruins of Tokyo and in the rebuilt Courthouse amid the ruins of Nuremberg. President Truman on Nov. 29, 1945, authorized Joseph B. Keenan "as Chief of Counsel in the preparation and prosecution of charges of war crimes against the major leaders of Japan" to make recommendations for trials. A Charter established an International Military Tribunal, set up April 26, 1946, consisting of prosecutors and judges from the nine States which had formerly accepted the Japanese surrender, plus India and the Philippines. Sir William Webb of Australia was named President by General MacArthur. On April 29, 1946, the 11 associate prosecutors lodged an indictment against 28 accused, charged with "Conventional War Crimes" (*i.e.*, murder, and conspiracy to permit murder, of prisoners and civilians), "Crimes against Peace" (*i.e.*, conspiring to wage aggressive war and plotting to dominate the world), and "Crimes against Humanity" (*i.e.*, atrocities).

Meanwhile another Charter was signed in London, August 8, by representatives of the USA, the USSR, Britain, and France, setting up an International Military Tribunal to try the Nazi leaders. The signatories, respectively, appointed as prosecutors Robert H. Jackson, Gen. R. A. Rudenko, Hartley Shawcross, and François de Menthon and as judges Francis Biddle, Lord Justice Lawrence (President of the Tribunal), Gen. I. T. Nikitchenko, and Prof. Donnedieu de Fabres. On Oct. 18, the prosecutors presented an indictment against 24 individuals and asked a criminal judgment against the Reich Cabinet, the Leadership Corps of the Nazi Party, the SS, the SD, the SA, the Gestapo, and the General Staff and High Command of the Wehrmacht. The indictment contained four counts: (1) the Common Plan or Conspiracy (*i.e.*, a plot to prepare, initiate, and wage wars of aggression); (2) Crimes against Peace (*i.e.*, the actual preparing and waging of such wars); (3) War Crimes (*i.e.*, violations of the laws and customs of war); (4) Crimes against Humanity (*i.e.*, murder, extermination, enslavement, deportation, persecution, etc.).

The course and outcome of these and other trials are well known.[17] Premiers,

---

[17] The quantity of published verbiage flowing from these processes, though by no means complete, is staggering. The judgment alone of the Tokyo Tribunal covers 1,211 pages, with the transcript of proceedings covering 48,412 pages. The Nuremberg verdict, following 403 public sessions in which 33 witnesses for the prosecution and 61 for the defense were heard, covers 300 pages. The State Department published 8 volumes in 1946 entitled *Nazi Conspiracy and Aggression* and, by 1952, had printed and distributed no less than 54 volumes, averaging 1,000 pages per volume, on *Trials of War Criminals before the Nuerenberg (sic) Military Tribunals.*

Gen. Tomoyuki Yamashita, conqueror of Malaya and Singapore, was hanged Feb. 23, 1946, and Gen. Masaharu Homma, commander during the Japanese conquest of the Philippines, was shot April 3, 1946—after conviction by a U.S. Military Commission and a vain appeal to the U.S. Supreme Court (*cf.* 327 U.S. 1). The major Nuremberg trial (Nov. 20, 1945–Oct. 1, 1946) ended with verdicts of "not guilty" for Franz von Papen, Hjalmar Schacht, and Hans Fritzsche; Admiral Karl Doenitz, 10 years; Constantine von Neurath, 15 years; Baldur von Schirach and Albert Speer, 20 years; Rudolph Hess, Walter Funk, and Admiral Erich Raeder, life imprisonment; and Joachim von Ribbentrop, Alfred Rosenberg, Hans Frank, Wilhelm Frick, Julius Streicher, Fritz Sauckel, Arthur Seyss-Inquart, Gen. Alfred Jodl, Gen. Wilhelm Keitel, and Hermann Goering, death. Goering cleverly concealed a vial of potassium cyanide on his person during the trial and took his own life. The rest were hanged Oct. 16, 1946. In later trials, prosecuted by 131 attorneys headed by Brig. Gen. Telford Taylor, 185 defendants in 12 cases received varying sentences or acquittals for military atrocities and mass exterminations of prisoners of war and civilians. (Martin Bormann had disappeared. Robert Ley, Goebbels, and Himmler

Cabinet ministers, ambassadors, admirals, generals, and lesser officials of the defeated governments were imprisoned or put to death by the verdict of international tribunals. There was no novelty in the punishment of individuals who had committed war crimes and atrocities. What was new here was the repudiation of the traditional view that State sovereignty exempts top officials from trial; that superior orders release subordinates from judicial responsibility; and that the planning and waging of aggressive war had been made individual "crimes" by the Pact of Paris of 1928 and other treaties "outlawing" war.

Opinions differed sharply as to the "justice" of the proceedings. "We have taken an important step forward," said Robert Jackson, Aug. 8, 1945, "in fixing individual responsibility for war-mongering, among whatever peoples, as an international crime." "Here," wrote Henry L. Stimson, January, 1947, "is affirmed the simple principle of peace—that the man who makes or plans to make aggressive war is a criminal." Others were doubtful. To some the killing of vanquished by victors was not an advance in civilization but a reversion to barbarism. To others the condemned, other than those who personally perpetrated atrocities, were victims of *ex post facto* legislation, long since renounced as abominable in Western jurisprudence. To still others the major criminals were Hirohito, Victor Emmanuel, Badoglio, Horthy, German "Big Businessmen," and other sundry notables who were either ignored or honored by the governments of the Western Democracies.

Such doubts were increased by the "verdict of history." Within four years after the trials, many prominent Americans, including Cabinet member Francis Matthews, had publicly urged "aggression for peace" to save civilization from Communism—a formula similar to that of the Fascist "war criminals." Mamoru Shigemitsu had returned to an active role in Japanese politics. A memorial was being erected near Nagana to Tojo and his fellow defendants who were hanged. The West German Foreign Office had more Nazis in its employ than had served under Ribbentrop. Lesser war criminals in both Germany and Japan were granted amnesties and often became heroes and leaders. Italy, Japan, and Germany had all become allies of the USA. In the new American view, the only war criminals were Communists, while in the

---

all committed suicide in 1945. Hitler had vanished and was presumed dead.) The major Tokyo trial (May 3, 1946–Nov. 12, 1948) ended with verdicts of guilty for all 25 defendants. (Two others had died during the trial, one went insane, Premier Konoye had committed suicide Dec. 16, 1945, and Premier Hideki Tojo had beeen nursed back to health after shooting himself.) The sentences: 7 years' imprisonment for Mamoru Shigemitsu; 20 years for Shigenori Togo; life for Premiers Kiichiro Hiranuma, Kuniaki Koiso, and 14 ministers, generals, admirals, and ambassadors; and death for Premiers Hideki Tojo and Koki Hirota and Gens. Iwane Matsui, Akira Muto, Kenji Doihara, Heitaro Kimura, and Seishiro Itagaki. Following affirmation of the sentences by General MacArthur and refusal of the U.S. Supreme Court to review the decisions, those condemned to death were hanged Dec. 23, 1948.

THE QUEST FOR LAW

Communist view the only war criminals were Americans. But who, if anyone, would be hanged by whom was not yet clear.

The "law of nations" is here confronted anew with an old and seemingly insoluble dilemma. Law is enforceable on individuals. In major crises and conflicts, it is seldom, if ever, enforceable in any fashion precluding wholesale violence through the action of States against States—whether that action is directed toward whole national communities, as is inevitable in modern war, or against officials of defeated governments after victory has been won. Law and justice are not to be had in the societies of *Homo sapiens* without government among men. Through government, men and women collectively make law, change it in organized deliberation, and enforce it promptly and effectively against individual violators. No such arrangements yet prevail in the family of the sovereign nation-states. Unless or until they are brought into being, it is safe to assume that international law will remain a strangely paradoxical set of rules among sovereignties, establishing doubtfully a fragile and transient reign of law among the lawless.

SUGGESTED READINGS

Appleman, John Alan: *Military Tribunals and International Crimes,* Indianapolis, Bobbs-Merrill, 1954.
Bishop, William W., Jr.: *International Law: Cases and Materials,* Englewood Cliffs, N.J., Prentice-Hall, 1953.
Brierly, J. L.: *The Law of Nations: An Introduction to the International Law of Peace* (4th ed.), New York, Oxford, 1949.
Briggs, Herbert W.: *The Law of Nations,* New York, Appleton-Century-Crofts, 1952.
Chen, T. C.: *The International Law of Recognition,* New York, Praeger, 1951.
Deak, Francis, and Philip C. Jessup (eds.): *Collection of Neutrality Laws, Regulations and Treaties of Various Countries,* New York, Columbia University Press, 1940.
De Visscher, Charles: *Theory and Reality in Public International Law,* Princeton, N.J., Princeton University Press, 1957.
Fenwick, Charles G.: *International Law,* New York, Appleton-Century-Crofts, 1949.
Hackworth, G. H.: *Digest of International Law* (8 vols.), Washington, Government Printing Office, 1940.
Hall, W. E.: *A Treatise on International Law,* New York, Oxford, 1924.
Hershey, A. S.: *Essentials of International Public Law and Organization,* New York, Macmillan, 1927.
Higgins, A. P., and C. John Colombos: *The International Law of the Sea,* London, Longmans, 1943.
Hill, Norman: *Claims to Territory in International Law and Relations,* New York, Oxford, 1945.
Hurst, Sir Cecil: *International Law,* London, Stevens, 1950.
Hyde, Charles Cheney: *International Law Chiefly as Interpreted and Applied by the United States* (2 vols.), Boston, Little, Brown, 1946.
Jackson, Robert H.: *The Nürnberg Case,* New York, Knopf, 1947.
Jessup, Philip C.: *A Modern Law of Nations,* New York, Macmillan, 1948.
———: *Transnational Law,* New Haven, Yale University Press, 1956.
Kelsen, Hans: *Principles of International Law,* New York, Rinehart, 1952.
Lauterpacht, Hersch: *International Law and Human Rights,* New York, Praeger, 1951.
Marek, Krystyna: *Identity and Continuity of States in Public International Law,* Geneva, Droz, 1954.

142

SUGGESTED READINGS

Moore, J. B.: *A Digest of International Law* (8 vols.), Washington, Government Printing Office, 1906.

Nussbaum, Arthur: *A Concise History of the Law of Nations*, New York, Macmillan, 1947.

O'Connell, D. P.: *The Law of State Succession*, New York, Cambridge, 1956.

Oppenheim, L. (ed. by H. Lauterpacht): *International Law*, New York, Longmans, 1937.

Pfankuchen, Llewellyn: *A Documentary Textbook in International Law*, New York, Rinehart, 1940.

Rafuse, Robert W.: *The Extradition of Nationals*, Urbana, Ill., University of Illinois Press, 1939.

Schiffer, Walter: *The Legal Community of Mankind*, New York, Columbia University Press, 1954.

Schwarzenberger, Georg: *International Law* (2d ed.), New York, Praeger, 1952.

Svarlien, Oscar: *An Introduction to the Law of Nations*, New York, McGraw-Hill, 1955.

Weis, P.: *Nationality and Statelessness in International Law*, London, Stevens (for London Institute of World Affairs), 1956.

Westlake, John: *International Law*, London, Cambridge, Vol. I, 1913; Vol. II, 1916.

Wilson, Robert Renbert: *International Law Standard in Treaties of the United States*, Cambridge, Mass., Harvard University Press, 1955.

Wright, Quincy: *Contemporary International Law: A Balance Sheet*, New York, Doubleday, 1954.

Chapter V

THE SETTLEMENT OF CONFLICTS

1. STATES AS POLICEMEN

Fury said to a mouse that he met in the house, "Let us both go to law: *I* will prosecute *you.*—Come, I'll take no denial: we must have a trial; for really this morning I've nothing to do." Said the mouse to the cur, "Such a trial, dear sir, with no jury or judge, would be wasting our breath." "I'll be judge, I'll be jury," said cunning old Fury; "I'll try the whole cause and condemn you to death."—LEWIS CARROLL, *Alice in Wonderland.*

RIGHTS and duties of States were defined long before any procedures for their enforcement existed. It is sometimes argued, as noted above, that there is no right without a remedy. If this notion were applied to international law, it would mean that States have few rights, since "remedies" in international society are often ineffective. It would be more accurate to say, however, that the observance of the rights of States depends upon their power to compel respect on the part of other States. The promptings of ambition, the will-to-power, the lust for conquest, the pursuit of national interests all promote patterns of political behavior among States ill calculated to ensure respect for rights. States seek security and the realization of their aspirations by efforts to impose their will upon one another. Each State must therefore rely upon self-help and its own power, however feeble these devices may be as defenses of rights and interests.

War is obviously the ultimate means of coercion in interstate relations. In war each belligerent acts as policeman, judge, jury, sheriff, and executioner all in one. Questions of legal rights and obligations may be raised on both sides at the beginning of war as excuses, rationalizations, pretexts, or plausible formulations of interests in the pursuit of which war seems preferable to surrender or compromise. War is a means of settling disputes only in the sense that, after an interval of bloodshed and destruction, the weaker party will yield to the stronger or both will fall exhausted and agree to a compromise which seemed unacceptable so long as each felt optimistic about imposing its will on the other. The terms of peace will set up new legal relationships between the disputants, more or less durable, depending upon the wisdom of the victors, the weakness of the vanquished, and subsequent shifts of power relationships. If neither side can impose its will on the other, the terms of the peace may make no reference to the original dispute at all. Such was the

144

case with the Treaty of Ghent in 1814, which terminated the War of 1812. That war is a wholly unsatisfactory method of settling disputes scarcely calls for demonstration. If war were to be judged on such grounds, it would have been banished long ago. But States resort to war because armed coercion is an instrument of State power and a means of protecting and promoting interests, quite apart from questions of legal rights.

There are various methods of hostile redress short of war which also involve coercion. These may be classified as threats of force, acts of retortion, and acts of reprisal. Threats of force may take the form of military, naval, or aerial maneuvers, mobilization, the dispatch of an ultimatum, and the like. None of these is either injurious in fact to the other party or a violation of his legal rights but is a gesture designed to frighten him into a more tractable mood. Most wars break out after threats of force fail to produce the desired result. Acts of retortion are definitely injurious, though not in violation of legal rights. Such measures are always within the bounds of customary international law and are performed entirely within the jurisdiction of the State taking such action. Discriminatory tariff duties or penalties, the suspension of commercial intercourse, and the use of an economic boycott are common examples. In 1808–09 the Jefferson Administration enforced an embargo on American trade with Britain and France in hope of bringing their Governments to terms in the controversies over neutral rights. China's anti-Japanese boycott of 1931–32 was an act of retortion in retaliation for the occupation of Manchuria. Such acts, though not violations of customary legal rights, sometimes involve breaches of treaty obligations and often lead to violent incidents. When the victim retaliates, grave consequences may easily ensue.

The severance of diplomatic relations has been increasingly resorted to in the 20th Century as an expression of displeasure—and, at times, as a device of domestic politics. Whether such an act is materially injurious to the victim depends upon circumstances. Whether it is a legal injury depends upon relevant treaties. Diplomatic ruptures are not per se acts of retortion or reprisal and are scarcely to be regarded any longer as threats of force. The U.S. has often withheld recognition from, or broken relations with, Latin-American Governments which it has disapproved. By so doing it has sometimes promoted their replacement by more acceptable regimes. On May 26, 1927, the Baldwin Cabinet in Britain severed relations with the USSR, which it accused of espionage and anti-British propaganda. They were resumed by the new Labor Government on Oct. 1, 1929. In late October, 1947, President Gabriel Gonzalez Videla of Chile, whose Government was engaged in smashing a strike of miners, found "Communism" a convenient scapegoat. He expelled Jugoslav diplomats, on charges of instigating the strike. Belgrade severed relations with Chile, which in turn broke relations with the Soviet Union and Czechoslovakia. At the same time (Oct. 21, 1947) Brazil, having outlawed its own Communist Party, severed relations with the USSR to avenge "national honor" after the Soviet press asserted that President Dutra had accepted decorations from Hitler. These moves not only had obvious utility in domestic politics but were designed to curry favor with Washington. On Oct. 19, 1957, Bonn severed relations with Belgrade in protest against Jugoslav recognition of the "German Democratic Republic."

Acts of reprisal are in patent violation of the legal rights of the victim. Prior to the abolition of privateering by the Declaration of Paris of 1856, it was common for States to authorize private reprisals by issuing "letters of marque and reprisal" to their nationals with unsatisfied financial claims against a foreign State. Such individuals were then free to plunder the debtor's commerce up to the amount of their claims. Public reprisals are still recognized as a legitimate method of redress, *e.g.*, hostile embargoes, pacific blockades, acts of intervention, and acts of overt hostility indistinguishable from war in everything but name. An embargo is hostile, *i.e.*, a violation of the rights of its victim and therefore an act of reprisal rather than of retortion, when it takes the form of the seizure of the ships or goods of nationals of the other State. This practice is now looked upon with disfavor.

A blockade consists in action by naval forces to intercept commerce. A war blockade may be applied to vessels of all States entering or leaving the blockaded ports. A "pacific" blockade, however, must be limited to the vessels of the parties to the controversy and cannot lawfully be extended to vessels of third States. The first modern instance of this practice was the pacific blockade of Greece by the Powers in 1827. This led to the naval battle of Navarino, in which the Turkish-Egyptian fleet was destroyed; but war was not declared, and the blockade was applied only to Greek and Turkish vessels and to those of the flag of the blockading States. New Granada was subjected to a pacific blockade by Britain in 1836, Mexico by France in 1838, Greece by Britain in 1850, China by France in 1884, Venezuela by Britain, Germany, and Italy in 1902, Soviet Russia by the other Powers in 1918–21, etc. Most pacific blockades are directed by Great Powers against small ones too weak to retaliate effectively. Those directed against strong States usually lead to war.

All acts of intervention are acts of reprisal when they are resorted to as a means of bringing diplomatic pressure to bear upon their victim and when they are unaccompanied by any intention of creating a legal state of war. In 1914 the USA bombarded and occupied Veracruz, and two years later sent a military expedition into northern Mexico, in both instances disclaiming any intention of making war. Interventions in the Caribbean States have been similar in character. The attack of the Powers upon the Shimonoseki forts (Japan) in 1863, the allied expedition against Peiping in 1901, and the Italian bombardment of Corfu in 1923 are other examples. The occupation of the Ruhr in 1923 was likewise an act of reprisal for German nonpayment of reparations, though the French and Belgian Governments insisted that they were authorized to take such action by the Treaty of Versailles. Early in 1932,

Japanese forces, in retaliation against the Chinese boycott, bombarded and occupied Shanghai, after several weeks of severe fighting. In every such case, the victim whose rights are violated may regard the act as a *casus belli* and resort to war. The act itself does not automatically create a state of war, regardless of how much fighting takes place, unless one party or the other expresses an intention to make war. These various forms of pressure may thus be indistinguishable in fact from actual war, but they are "pacific" in the sense that a legal state of war is not inaugurated by them.

More recent instances of States "taking the law into their own hands" are numerous, despite innumerable obeisances to "nonaggression," "nonintervention," and "the rule of law." Egypt thus barred Israeli shipping from the Suez Canal, despite UN resolutions of 1951 and 1953 condemning such action, on the technical ground that the armistice accords of 1948–49 did not establish a legal status of "peace" and that Egypt as a "belligerent" was entitled under the Constantinople Convention of 1888 to close the Canal to "enemy" vessels. Efforts by all the Arab States to blockade Israel constituted not a "pacific blockade" but a "belligerent blockade," coupled with a curious corollary also applied by the Arab Governments to their armed raids into Israeli territory—namely, that Arabs were entitled to wage "war" on Israel, to whose destruction they were pledged, but that the Israelis, pending their liquidation at Arab hands, were somehow bound to observe "peace" toward their Arab neighbors. When Nasser nationalized the Canal on July 26, 1956, those who deemed their "rights" thereby violated could find no "remedy" since the UN was impotent and the USA and USSR were both resolved, for different motives, to acquiesce in the Egyptian action. The result was the abortive armed assault on Egypt (see pp. 416–420), with consequences, as is not unusual in all recourse to force, unanticipated by all.

Meanwhile, to illustrate further the processes of "self-help" in international controversies, Chiang Kai-shek's regime on Formosa sought throughout the 1950's to impose a "blockade" on parts of the coast of Communist China, accompanied by "captures," protests, and intermittent artillery battles between Nationalist and Communist forces. Washington banned all Chinese trade and travel by Americans and sought to induce all its allies to do likewise. By 1957 the allies, including Japan, were resuming trade, while the American press was almost unanimous in condemning Secretary Dulles's refusal to permit reporters to go to China. The Peiping regime was more strengthened than weakened by these manifestations of American hostility, albeit lacking any effective means of protecting its "rights" and redressing the "wrongs" committed against it. Nor did Washington achieve any visible results through such pressures.

Measures of embargo, boycott, and diplomatic nonrecognition, and indeed most threats of force and acts of retortion, reprisal, and intervention, are usually futile in relations among Great Powers. They often lead either to no results whatever, apart from mutual impoverishment and an exacerbation of animosities, or else to armed violence. When each State acts as its own policeman, the outcome is commonly not the settlement of disputes in any durable fashion, but the aggravation of anarchy and disorder. The efforts thus far made—all of them, obviously, of only local and limited efficacy—to ameliorate the consequences of national "self-help" through "international organization" and "collective security" will be explored later in our inquiry.

Here it is enough to note that conflicts among nations as to their rights, interests, and expectations are as inevitable and ubiquitous in the society of sovereignties as are controversies among individuals and groups within national frontiers. In disputes in the latter category, recourse to "self-help" is forbidden by those who act in the name of "government," while accepted procedures of politics, legislation, litigation, and adjudication are available for the orderly resolution of quarrels. In a world community such procedures are still rudimentary and often ineffective, since no international or supranational agencies possess in requisite degree the attributes or powers of "government." Therefore sovereign States, if they are not to fight about their disputes, must bargain over them in efforts to reach agreement by compromise or, at their option, submit them to such procedures of arbitration or adjudication as the members of the State System have developed. These available alternatives to "self-help" are our next concern.

2. STATES AS BARGAINERS

All government, indeed every human benefit and enjoyment, every virtue and every prudent act, is founded on compromise and barter.—EDMUND BURKE, *On Conciliation with America*, March 22, 1775.

If the parties to an international dispute are disposed to discuss their differences rather than to threaten one another or to fight about them, they will resort to negotiation as a means of settlement. Negotiations may be conducted through diplomacy, through conference, or through the services of third States offering good offices or mediation. The conduct of negotiations is a bargaining process. Legal rights will be argued; but considerations of power, equity, and expediency will also be thrown into the scales. Each side will necessarily strive to attain maximum advantages with minimum concessions to the other. In all negotiations the contending States remain judges of their own cases. The time consumed, however, allows an interval for popular passions to cool.

When two States are unable to reach agreement and relations between them become "strained," it is permissible for outside States to offer their services in an effort to facilitate a settlement. If such interposition is dictatorial in character, it constitutes intervention. But if it is purely advisory, it cannot be regarded as an unfriendly act. Neither can the third State take offense if its offer is declined. A "tender of good offices" is a polite inquiry as to whether the third State can be of service in preserving or restoring peace. It is often extended at the request of one of the parties to the controversy and is frequently made after a rupture of diplomatic relations or in the course of a war. If it is accepted on both sides, the third State may transmit suggestions for a settlement between the parties or may make suggestions itself. In the latter case, true "mediation" occurs. Good offices consist in an invitation to resume discussions. Mediation, which normally follows an acceptance of good offices, consists in the actual transmission of suggestions. The mediating State attempts to create the atmosphere and the means necessary for a settlement. In 1813 the Russian Government offered its mediation to Britain and the USA in an effort to terminate the war which had broken out in the preceding year. Washington at once accepted and sent commissioners to St. Petersburg to negotiate, but London declined to reciprocate. Peace negotiations were finally opened by direct conversations between the parties. In 1905 President Roosevelt made a tender of good offices to Russia and Japan, then at war. The offer was accepted on both sides. The USA then acted as mediator and arranged a peace conference at Portsmouth, N.H. Its suggestions were instrumental in enabling the belligerents to come to an agreement and frame a peace treaty.

The first Convention of the first Hague Peace Conference of 1899 contained a number of provisions regarding good offices and mediation. In its revised form, as amended in 1907, it provided that the contracting Powers "agree to have recourse, as far as circumstances allow, to the good offices or mediation of one or more friendly Powers" in cases of serious disputes between them. "The exercise of this right shall never be regarded by one or the other of the parties in conflict as an unfriendly act." The function of a mediator was declared to be that of "reconciling the opposing claims and appeasing the feelings of resentment which may have arisen between the States at variance." It was made clear that mediation is purely advisory and that the function of the would-be mediator is at an end as soon as his suggestions are declined by either party. The Convention likewise made provision for a plan of mediation (never subsequently utilized) whereby disputing States were to refer the controversy to two designated mediating Powers which would have exclusive control over efforts to achieve a settlement for a period of 30 days.

The term "conciliation" is frequently used to refer to the sequel of successful mediation, i.e., to the process whereby an outside party promotes an agreement between contending States. This procedure was institutionalized in the League of Nations Covenant, which made the Council an agency of conciliation. The members of the League agreed by Article 15 to submit to the Council "any dispute likely to lead to a rupture which is not submitted to arbitration or judicial settlement." The Council was authorized to endeavor to settle the dispute. If its report was unanimously agreed to by its members, other than the representatives of the disputing States, the members of the League agreed that they would not go to war with any party to the dispute which complied with the recommendations of the report.

None of these permanent procedures was resorted to in the efforts made in 1939 to avert the outbreak of war. Only in the case of the hostilities between the USSR and Finland did the victim of aggression appeal to the League. In the war crisis of Aug. 4–Sept. 3, 1939, The Hague and Geneva procedures were ignored, but various governments tendered good offices. King Leopold of Belgium, in the name of the Oslo States, broadcast a plea for peace on Aug. 23. Pope Pius XII did likewise on the following day. At the same time, Roosevelt appealed to King Victor Emmanuel to "formulate proposals for a pacific settlement of the present crisis." He also urged Chancellor Hitler and President Moscicki of Poland to refrain from all hostile acts "for a reasonable and stipulated period" and to seek a solution by way of negotiation or arbitration or conciliation through a moderator from one of the American Republics or one of the traditionally neutral European States. Warsaw agreed, but a second message from Washington to Berlin produced no reply until Sept. 1, when Hitler merely said that Poland's attitude had nullified all his efforts to keep the peace. An appeal by the Prime Minister of Canada on Aug. 26 and a tender of good offices by King Leopold and Queen Wilhelmina on Aug. 29 were also without effect.

A last appeal by the Pope was without result. Mussolini offered his mediation on Aug. 31. Even after the German invasion of Poland was launched, Georges Bonnet accepted the Italian proposal for a conference. The British and French notes to Berlin of Sept. 1 were not ultimata but warnings and appeals. Polish Foreign Minister Beck was horrified. "We are in the thick of war, as the result of unprovoked aggression. The question before us is not one of a conference, but of the common action to be taken by the Allies to resist." Halifax would not consent to a conference unless Germany agreed to withdraw her troops and refrain from further attack. Hitler refused. Bonnet was overruled and obliged to phone Ciano Saturday evening that the French Cabinet, also, could not consent to a conference unless German forces would evacuate Polish territory. Rome thereupon informed Berlin that it could do nothing more. Allied ultimata and then declarations of war were delivered to the Reich on Sunday. When one Power is bent upon the destruction of another, there is obviously no possibility of settlement by negotiation, mediation, or conciliation.

To return to the condition (once regarded as "normal") in which compromise is possible: States are sometimes willing to resort to methods of settlement which are in advance of negotiation in the sense that recourse is had to more or less impartial tribunals, but which fall short of arbitration or adjudication in that the disputants are unwilling to bind themselves in advance. In these methods approaching arbitration, the parties remain free to accept or reject the solution proposed. These procedures fall into the categories of mixed commissions, commissions of inquiry, and commissions of conciliation.

A mixed commission is a body of agents chosen by two disputing governments to make recommendations. It consists of an even number of delegates, half chosen by each side—an arrangement which compels the members either to agree, to disagree, or to come to a definite conclusion. The members of mixed commissions are usually technical experts, qualified to ascertain the facts of the controversy. A commission of inquiry differs from a mixed commission in that it usually consists of an odd number of members and limits itself to fact finding. Its findings are again purely recommendations. This method of settlement was first provided for by general international agreement in the Convention for the Pacific Settlement of International Disputes drawn up at the first Hague Conference:

> In differences of an international nature involving neither honor nor vital interests, and arising from a difference of opinion on points of fact, the signatory Powers recommend that the parties who have not been able to come to an agreement by means of diplomacy should, as far as circumstances allow, institute an international commission of inquiry, to facilitate a solution of these differences by elucidating the facts by means of an impartial and conscientious investigation (Art. 9).

A commission of inquiry would make an investigation, hear both sides, call witnesses and experts, and prepare a report limited to a statement of facts, leaving the parties "entire freedom as to the effect to be given to the statement." This procedure was first applied in the Dogger Bank affair of 1904, in which a Russian squadron fired upon British trawlers in the North Sea. London demanded immediate explanations and reparations from Russia. The two States agreed to submit the questions of fact to a Commission of Inquiry of five members, consisting of British, Russian, American, and French naval officers with a fifth member (an officer in the Austro-Hungarian Navy) chosen by the other four. The Commission found the Russian squadron at fault, and the Russian Government paid an indemnity of £65,000. The same procedure was resorted to by Germany and the Netherlands with regard to responsibility for the sinking of a Dutch steamer in 1916. The Commission here found that the vessel was sunk by a torpedo fired by a German submarine, and an indemnity was likewise paid. Resort to the procedure outlined in the Hague Convention was not in any sense obligatory, and the Commissions were not permanent agencies but merely *ad hoc* bodies set up for each controversy.

In an effort to institutionalize this procedure the USA, through Secretary of State Bryan, proposed to other States in 1913 the negotiation of a series of bilateral treaties which should set up permanent boards or Commissions of Conciliation to which all disputes, without exception, should be submitted. They were to consist of five members: two nationals of the parties, two chosen by the parties from among foreign nationals, and the fifth selected by agreement. They were to have a year's time to report, during which period the parties agreed not to resort to hostilities. Thirty of the so-called Bryan "cooling-off" treaties were negotiated, and 21 came into force—9 with European States, 11 with Latin-American States, and 1 with China. Only 10 Commissions were set up. None was ever utilized for the settlement of any dispute. The Saavedra Lamas Anti-War Treaty of Nonaggression and Conciliation, signed at Rio de Janeiro, Oct. 10, 1933, provided for Conciliation Commissions of five members, three of whom should be non-nationals of the disputing States. The signatories undertook to submit disputes to such Commissions, but their reports "shall in no case have the character of a final decision or arbitral award." Again, no recourse was had to this device.

3. THE ROLE OF ARBITRATORS

> It is impossible to attack as a transgressor him who offers to lay his grievance before a tribunal of arbitration.—ARCHIDAMUS, King of Sparta.

> If a difficulty should arise between the aforesaid cities, which cannot easily be settled by themselves, it shall be decided by the arbitration of the Sovereign Pontiff; and if one of the parties violates the treaty, we agree that His Holiness shall excommunicate the offending city.—Treaty between Venice and Genoa, 1235.

Article 37 of the Hague Convention for the Pacific Settlement of International Disputes (1907) defined arbitration as follows: "International arbitration has for its object the settlement of disputes between States by judges of their own choice, and on the basis of respect for law. Recourse to arbitration implies an engagement to submit in good faith to the award."

This definition involves four elements which are the distinguishing features of genuine international arbitration: (1) settlement of disputes between States through their own voluntary action, (2) by judges of their own choice, (3) on the basis of respect for law, and (4) with an obligation to accept the award as binding. The last-named element distinguishes arbitration sharply from the methods dealt with above, in which recommendations are purely advisory. C. C. Hyde defined international arbitration as "an impartial adjudication according to law, and that before a tribunal of which at least a single member, who is commonly a national or a State neutral to the contest, acts as umpire." [1] This suggests that the process of arbitration is identical with that of adjudication except as to the method of choosing judges.

Arbitration as a method of settling international disputes is of great antiquity. Between 1500 and 1800, however, it went out of fashion as a mode of adjusting differences, except for a few 17th-Century English arbitration treaties negotiated by Cromwell. The practice was revived in the Jay Treaty of 1794. By this instrument, four Commissions were set up, to locate the source of the Mississippi, to settle the St. Croix River boundary, to pass upon

---

[1] *International Law Chiefly as Interpreted and Applied by the United States,* Vol. II, pp. 111–112.

the claims of British subjects for confiscated prerevolutionary mercantile debts, and to judge of reciprocal claims arising out of the seizure of American vessels by British cruisers and the capture of British merchantmen by French privateers fitted out in American ports. These Commissions were really arbitral tribunals, with the exception of the first, which might be better described as a commission of inquiry. The first failed in its object. The second located the St. Croix River to the satisfaction of both parties, subject to certain later readjustments of the boundary. The third failed to agree upon an award, but by the Convention of 1802 the British Government agreed to accept $2,664,000 in settlement of the claims in question. The fourth awarded $11,650,000 to the American claimants and $143,428 to the British claimants. Between 1794 and 1900 there were no less than 400 international arbitrations, with more following in our century.

In its simplest form, arbitration involves the negotiation by the parties to the dispute of a bilateral treaty, known as a _compromis,_ in which they state clearly the question to be arbitrated, name the arbitrators or specify the method of their selection, and set forth the rules of procedure and the principles of law to be applied. General rules of arbitral procedure have gradually been developed, however, which now render it unnecessary to specify in detail how a particular tribunal shall act. When a dispute is not submitted to the judgment of a single arbitrator, such as the Sovereign of a third State, a tribunal is set up consisting usually of one or two nationals of each of the disputing States, plus one or more nationals of outside States. These may be named in the _compromis_ or chosen by the other members of the tribunal. One of the outsiders usually acts as umpire. The tribunal—consisting of an odd number of members—meets at a designated place, organizes itself, and proceeds to hear both sides. Each party argues its case through attorneys, who present briefs in the form of cases and countercases. The exchange of written arguments may be followed by oral pleading and the summoning of witnesses, though there is no use of a jury. The tribunal then reaches its decision by a majority vote and submits a written statement of the award, with the reasons therefor, to the respective disputants. Minority opinions may be rendered by the members of the tribunal who differ with the majority, but they are without legal effect.

An arbitral award is binding upon the parties. States sometimes expressly reserve in the _compromis_ the right to demand a reconsideration on the basis of the discovery of some new fact of vital importance, unknown at the time of the award. Arbitral awards may also be rejected on certain other grounds. If the arbitrators exceed their authority under the _compromis_, the award is not binding. In 1827 the USA and Britain submitted to the arbitration of the King of the Netherlands the question of the location of the "highlands" mentioned in the Treaty of 1783 as marking the American-Canadian boundary between Maine and Quebec. The arbitrator drew a compromise line through a valley located between two sets of highlands. Both parties rejected the award on the ground that the arbitrator had exceeded his instructions. The subsequent discovery of fraud, bribery, or coercion in the course of an arbitration also invalidates the award, but such cases are rare. In general, arbitral awards are almost always accepted in good faith and loyally carried out, for States refrain from submitting questions to arbitration unless they are prepared to accept whatever settlement the tribunal may reach.

In the development of arbitral procedure, the next step beyond *ad hoc* agreements providing for the submission of a particular dispute to a particular tribunal was the inclusion in other treaties of provisions for the submission to arbitration of disputes arising thereunder. States also began to negotiate general arbitration treaties, specifying that all future controversies of a designated character betweeen the signatories would be submitted to arbitration. Such treaties provide for what is known as "compulsory," or "obligatory," arbitration. These adjectives are somewhat misleading, since the treaties merely constitute a voluntary pledge that the parties will in future submit to arbitration certain specified types of disputes. They frequently contain such broad qualifications and exceptions as to leave the parties almost complete liberty of action with regard to any particular controversy. Many pre-1914 general arbitration treaties, modeled after the Anglo-French Treaty of Oct. 14, 1903, specified that all cases should be excluded from their operation which involved "national honor, independence, vital interests, or the interests of third parties." Prior to 1917, 36 bilateral treaties had been signed providing for the submission to arbitration of any dispute whatever between the parties, without qualification. The first of these was the Treaty of May 28, 1902, between Argentina and Chile. Nineteen other treaties provided for the arbitration of any dispute not involving constitutional questions. But no general treaty of this kind had been entered into between any two of the Great Powers. Projects of general compulsory arbitration treaties were defeated at both the first and second Hague Conferences of 1899 and 1907. The Hague Convention for the Pacific Settlement of International Disputes bound the parties to resort to arbitration only "in so far as circumstances permit" (Art. 38, Convention of Oct. 18, 1907).

Despite American championship of arbitration, American practice has been measurably behind that of other Powers. This has been due in part to the divergent attitudes of successive administrations and in part to the opposition of the Senate. The American Government has arbitrated numerous controversies, particularly with Britain, through *ad hoc compromis* agreements. It has likewise included arbitration clauses in numerous other treaties but has not always availed itself of the opportunities provided in this fashion. As for general treaties providing for "compulsory" arbitration, so many obstacles have been encountered that the USA has long been in the rear of the procession. In 1896, following the successful arbitration of its boundary dispute with Venezuela, the British Government proposed to Washington a general treaty providing for obligatory arbitration. Secretary of State Olney, who insisted that arbitration should be made "automatic," was even more enthusiastic than Lord Salisbury; and on Jan. 11, 1897, a treaty was signed which went far in the direction of such an arrangement. The Senate, however, rejected it. The USA later signed a number of general treaties for the obligatory arbitration of questions of a legal nature, which, with the exception of controversies involving national honor, independence, vital interests, or the interests of third States, were to be submitted to the Hague Permanent "Court" of Arbitration. Here, as in all such treaties, it was of course contemplated that each *compromis* for the submission of a particular dispute to arbitration would not be a formal treaty requiring ratification but merely an administrative agreement under the terms of the general treaty. But the Senate insisted that each *compromis* must be expressly approved by it as a "treaty" before the arbitration could proceed. President Roosevelt declared that this was "mere nonsense" which made the general treaties "shams." The Administration therefore withdrew the treaties from Senate consideration and abandoned the whole enterprise.

In 1908, Secretary of State Root revived the negotiations and concluded some 25 treaties containing the provisions demanded by the Senate. In fact, as John Bassett Moore pointed out, the treaties represented a step backward since, prior to 1908, pecuniary claims had often been arbitrated without concluding a formal treaty with the foreign government, whereas under the new arrangement a treaty had to be concluded for each arbitration.[2] This feature, added to the exceptions of independence, national honor, and vital interests, made the treaties little more than meaningless gestures. In 1911–12, another group of general arbitration treaties was negotiated by President Taft and Secretary of State Knox. They abandoned the exceptions of vital interests and national honor and pledged the parties to arbitrate all differences "which are justiciable in their nature by reason of being susceptible of decision by the application of the principles of law and equity." These treaties provided for a joint high commission of inquiry to determine whether a particular controversy was "justiciable." The Senate objected to this arrangement, struck it out, and inserted numerous reservations prohibiting the arbitration of a whole series of cases—with the result that President Taft declared of the treaties, after the Senate had finished with them, that "their own father would not recognize them." In disgust, he dropped the whole project.

The post-Versailles arbitration treaties of the USA were for the most part based upon the Treaty of 1928 with France. They omitted the exceptions of national honor and vital interests, but contained exceptions of cases within the domestic jurisdiction of the parties, involving the interests of third parties,

---

[2] See his *Principles of American Diplomacy*, p. 331, and *International Law and Some Current Illusions*, p. 86.

depending upon or involving "the maintenance of the traditional attitude of the United States concerning domestic questions, commonly known as the Monroe Doctrine," or involving the observance of obligations under the Covenant of the League of Nations. Each *compromis*, moreover, had to take the form of a separate treaty which had to be submitted to the Senate. The exceptions were almost as flexible as those in the prewar treaties. Though many other States have entered into general arbitration treaties which really pledge them to arbitrate certain types of disputes, the USA has reserved its liberty of action to such a degree that its general arbitration treaties are little more than empty words.

The most important step thus far taken toward the institutionalization of arbitration was the creation of the Permanent Court of Arbitration by the first Hague Conference of 1899. This agency is neither "permanent" nor a "court," for its members are not required to reside and work at The Hague, nor do they collectively constitute a judicial body. Its name is due to the confusion between arbitration and adjudication which prevailed at the time of its establishment. It came into being through the signature and ratification by a large number of States of the Convention for the Pacific Settlement of International Disputes. This multilateral engagement required each of the signatory Powers to designate for a term of six years "four persons of known competency in questions of international law, of the highest moral reputation, and disposed to accept the duties of arbitrators." The list of arbitrators so compiled is kept at the international bureau of the "Court" at The Hague as a panel from which States may pick an arbitral tribunal for the settlement of particular controversies. A new tribunal is picked for each dispute by means of a *compromis* between the parties. Only the panel is permanent. Resort to this procedure is entirely optional and voluntary. At the second Hague Conference of 1907, it was provided that, of the two arbitrators appointed by each party, "only one can be its national, or chosen from among the persons selected by it as members of the Permanent Court." This ensured a majority of neutral members on each tribunal.

This institution is nothing more than a list of arbitrators and a secretariat. It doubtless received more attention than its practical importance warranted. It did, nevertheless, stimulate general interest in arbitration; and it performed a useful, if limited, function in disposing satisfactorily of a number of disputes submitted to it. Between 1903, when the United States and Mexico established the first tribunal to deal with the "Pious Funds" case, and 1914, 15 cases had been arbitrated in accordance with the procedure outlined in the Convention. After 1922, most of the cases which would have been arbitrated in this fashion were adjudicated by the World Court. From the record of the years, it is clear that arbitration is no substitute for war but merely a convenient device for settling controversies with regard to which the parties are willing to accept the decision of an impartial third party. In recent decades most disputes which the parties would earlier have submitted to arbitration have been "adjudicated"—*i.e.*, submitted to an international judicial tribunal.

Arbitration, like adjudication, is an available method for the settlement of disputes only when the parties, not deeming any "vital national interests" to be involved, are agreeable to such a mode of settlement. This limitation of arbitral and judicial procedure deserves emphasis in view of many popular misconceptions. The limitation is sometimes operative even in disputes over financial claims among States in no way divided by the rivalries of power politics and legally committed to "compulsory" arbitration or adjudication of such controversies. Thus, for example, the USA and Switzerland signed a Treaty of Arbitration and Conciliation on Feb. 16, 1931, specifying that "every dispute arising between the Contracting Parties, of whatever nature it may be, shall, when ordinary diplomatic proceedings have failed, be submitted to arbitration or conciliation . . ." (Art. I), subject to the stipulation that "compulsory arbitration" shall "not be invoked in respect of any difference the subject matter of which is within the domestic jurisdiction of either of the Contracting Parties . . ." (Art. VI). During World War II all the American assets, valued at over $100,000,000, of General Aniline and Film Co., a Delaware corporation, were taken over by the U.S. Alien Property Custodian under the Trading-with-the-Enemy Act on the ground that they were owned or controlled by a German corporation, I. G. Farben. But in law 90% of these assets were owned by Interhandel, a Swiss corporation. On Aug. 9, 1956, following adverse U.S. court decisions and the failure of diplomacy to achieve agreement, Bern requested submission to arbitration of the issue of the return of the properties to their Swiss owners. On Jan. 11, 1957, Washington refused, contending that the question was within U.S. "domestic jurisdiction," despite its obviously international character.[3]

4. THE TASK OF COURTS

Out of the dark years through which we have passed, the light has arisen. The equality of States in law and in justice is now recognized. . . . All existence in this world must be based on order and on harmony, an emanation of the Deity Himself, imposed by Him upon mankind. . . . Justice embodied in human institutions and in the mutual relations between man and man, between people and people, this indeed is the true law.—JUDGE BENJAMIN T. C. LODER, First President of the World Court, February 15, 1922.

Arbitration and adjudication are both modes of settlement whereby disputing States voluntarily submit their differences to an impartial outside agency. In both cases the parties agree in advance to abide by the award or decision. But in arbitration, even under The Hague procedure, the agency of

[3] For details, see Herbert W. Briggs, "Toward the Rule of Law?" in *American Journal of International Law*, July, 1957, pp. 517–529.

settlement is an *ad hoc* tribunal chosen by the parties. In true adjudication the agency of settlement is a permanent judicial body, not chosen by the parties but existing independently of them. A true court proceeds from case to case, builds up precedents, and gradually creates a consistent body of case law. Arbitral tribunals, lacking continuity and corporate existence, are unable to act in this fashion.

Adjudication of disputes is obviously impossible without the prior creation of a court to which they may be submitted. Numerous unofficial proposals were put forward in various States during the 19th Century for the creation of an international judicial tribunal. The principle of State equality seemed to require that all States be represented on any world court—an arrangement which would require a court of impossible size. Regional courts would have only regional utility. There were disputes, moreover, arising from differing national interpretations of certain moot points of international law. What legal principles should such a court apply? How were cases to be brought before it if it were created? What authority, if any, would such a body have to enforce its decisions?

These problems were discussed at the first Hague Conference, but without result. The Permanent Court of Arbitration there established was a court only in name. They were again discussed, more fruitfully but again unsuccessfully, at the second Hague Conference of 1907. Elihu Root instructed the U.S. delegates to work for the "development of the Hague tribunal into a permanent tribunal composed of judges who are judicial officers and nothing else, who are paid adequate salaries, who have no other occupation, and who will devote their entire time to the trial and decision of international causes by judicial methods and under a sense of judicial responsibility." This proposal met with the support of the British and Russian delegates, who likewise presented projects for a world court. A plan was drawn up for the creation of a Permanent Court of Arbitral Justice. But no agreement could be reached regarding the number of the judges and the method of their selection. For all the 44 participating States to be "represented" on the court was out of the question, and the minor Powers were unwilling to establish a court which might be dominated by the Great Powers. The scheme therefore failed, as did the project of an international prize court, also discussed at the second Hague Conference. This tribunal was to consist of 15 judges, the 8 Great Powers to have permanent appointees on the bench and the lesser Powers sharing the remaining seats by rotation. The court was to hear appeals from national prize courts, both States and individuals having a right of recourse to it. The convention for its creation was signed by 33 States, but difficulties developed over the fact that much of the international law of prize is unsettled. The British Government rejected the plan for this reason. The London Naval Conference of 1908–09 sought to codify the law of prize and drew up the Declaration of London. But this in turn was rejected by the House of Lords and failed of ratification. Both these efforts to establish an international court thus failed, in one instance because of disagreement as to the method of choosing judges, in the other because of disagreement over the international law to be applied.

The first genuine international court was the creation of the USA and five Republics of Central America. Under the inspiration of Washington, the Central American Peace Conference of 1907 set up the Central American Court of Justice, consisting of five judges, one each for Costa Rica, Nicaragua, El Salvador, Honduras, and Guatemala. The signatory States agreed to submit all questions to it for decision, without qualifications or reservations. Its jurisdiction was thus "compulsory." This remarkable international agency had an even wider jurisdiction than the U.S. Supreme Court since private citizens might bring suits against States before it. It was established for a 10-year period and went out of existence in 1917, after a decade of useful service, under somewhat peculiar circumstances. Costa Rica and El Salvador had brought suit against Nicaragua, whose puppet Government, supported by U.S. marines, had negotiated the Bryan-Chamorro Treaty of 1916. By this agreement the "Colossus of the North" was given canal rights along the San Juan River, which divides Nicaragua from Costa Rica, and also the right of fortifying the Gulf of Fonseca, which commands the Pacific coasts of Nicaragua, El Salvador, and Honduras. The other States alleged that Nicaragua was legally incompetent to conclude such a treaty without their consent, since it affected their rights adversely. The Court accepted this view and decided the suit against Nicaragua. The latter, however, with the tacit approval of Washington, refused to abide by the decision. The other States then took the view that there was nothing to be gained by maintaining a court if its members were free to ignore its judgments. They accordingly declined to renew the arrangement.

Not until 1919 was it possible to create a permanent international judicial agency of wide jurisdiction. Wilson regarded the creation of a World Court as a necessary feature of the peace settlement. Article 14 of the Covenant of the League entrusted to the Council the task of formulating and submitting to its members plans for the establishment of a "Permanent Court of International Justice," competent to hear and determine any dispute submitted to it by the parties and to give advisory opinions upon any question referred to it by the Council or Assembly of the League. The Council in 1920 appointed a Commission of Jurists, upon which Elihu Root served for the USA. The Commission prepared a "Statute," or constitution, submitted first to the Council and then by the Council to the Assembly and the members of the League. The Statute became effective through ratification by the member States. The first panel of judges was elected in September of 1921. On Feb. 15, 1922, the judges convened at The Hague, and the ceremonies of the official establishment of the Court were performed in the Great Hall of Justice of the Peace Palace, which had been erected by Andrew Carnegie for the Hague tribunal of arbitration created 23 years before. The same strange irony which made Wilson a prophet without honor in his own land made the USA, long an ardent proponent of international adjudication, one of the few States not members of the Court.[4]

The thorny problem of the selection of judges was ingeniously solved. Originally, 11 judges and 4 deputy judges were provided for; but the amendments of 1930 increased the number of judges to 15, and in February, 1936, the deputy judgeships were abolished. All had nine-year terms. Candidates were nominated by the national groups of the Hague Permanent Court of Arbitration, each group having the right to name four, only two of whom might be of its own nationality. The Secretary-General of the League prepared an alphabetical list of the persons so nominated and transmitted it to the Council and Assembly. These bodies, voting independently, elected the judges by majority vote. In the event of disagreement, recourse was had to a conference of six members, three from each, to submit to their respective bodies one name for each vacancy. If agreement was still lacking, the judges already chosen filled vacancies from candidates voted for but not elected. Large and small States thus had an equal voice and the dilemma of 1907 was resolved. At the first election of September, 1921, 89 candidates were nominated. All places were filled by majority vote after three days of balloting. At the second election (1930), 60 candidates were nominated. The Council and Assembly cast 11 ballots for judges and 6 ballots for deputy judges before agreement was reached.[5]

---

[4] The USA became a member of the ILO by a Joint Congressional Resolution of June 19, 1934, authorizing the President to accept membership provided that no obligations were assumed under the League Covenant. Since no formal treaty was necessary, it was impossible for one-third of the Senators to obstruct action. For 12 years, every President and Secretary of State and a large majority in both Houses of Congress favored membership in the Permanent Court of International Justice. But the isolationist Senators, loudly applauded by the Hearst press, the *Chicago Tribune*, Father Coughlin, and sundry superpatriots, attached five reservations to the Protocols in January, 1926. The last of these forbade the Court to "entertain any request for an advisory opinion touching any dispute or question in which the United States has or claims an interest." This proviso, if interpreted broadly, would have given the USA a special veto enjoyed by none of the members of the League Council, whence requests for advisory opinions came. Efforts were made by Elihu Root and others to secure agreement to give America only a position of equality. The "Root formula" of 1929 solved the problem. The isolationists, however, had no desire to see it solved. On Jan. 29, 1935, the final Senate vote showed 52 in favor of ratification and 36 opposed. The Protocols failed to secure the required two-thirds by a margin of 7 votes. Father Coughlin declared, "Our thanks are due to Almighty God that America retains her sovereignty. Congratulations to the aroused people of the United States who, by more than two hundred thousand telegrams containing at least one million names, demanded that the principles established by Washington and Jefferson shall keep us clear from foreign entanglements and European hatreds."

[5] Art. 9 of the Statute provided, "At every election, the electors shall bear in mind that not only should all the persons appointed as members of the Court possess the qualifications required, but the whole body also should represent the main forms of civilization and the principal legal systems of the world." Prof. Manley O. Hudson (U.S.) was a judge of the Court at the time of the outbreak of World War II. John Bassett

The difficult question of jurisdiction was also solved ingeniously. The Commission of Jurists which drafted the Statute recommended compulsory or obligatory jurisdiction with respect to disputes as to (1) the interpretation of a treaty; (2) any question of international law; (3) the existence of any fact which, if established, would constitute a breach of an international obligation; and (4) the nature or extent of the reparation to be made for the breach of an international obligation. This arrangement was rejected by the Council and the Assembly on the ground that Article 14 of the Covenant contemplated a court with voluntary jurisdiction. In general, the Court had jurisdiction only over such disputes as member States were willing to submit to it. Article 36 of the Statute, however, was transformed into an "optional clause" which member States might accept or reject as they wished. Those accepting it recognized the jurisdiction of the Court to be compulsory among themselves, without special agreement, for the four categories of disputes mentioned. States not accepting the clause remained free to submit, or refuse to submit, such disputes to the Court as they chose. Almost 50 States adhered to Article 36 for varying terms of years.

The Permanent Court of International Justice represented the most important and successful effort thus far made to establish an international judicial tribunal for the adjudication of controversies between States. Its record during the 17 years of its existence revealed it to be a body of great value, both as a tribunal to render judgments between States and as an agency to advise the League Council on legal questions. The Court rendered in all 32 judgments, 200 orders, and 27 advisory opinions. All were accepted in good faith, and only rarely, as in the Austro-German customs union opinion of Sept. 5, 1931, were its members criticized for placing national prejudices above impartial logic. If it was not a panacea for war or a means of settling all disputes—and assuredly it was neither—the cause lay in the fact that States do not regard all disputes as justiciable and that the realm of international law is not coterminous with the realm of international politics.

With the collapse of the League, the Permanent Court ceased to function. It came to a formal end with a resolution of the last Assembly of the League in April, 1946. Meanwhile, however, a new World Court emerged phoenixlike from the ashes of the old under the name of the "International Court of Justice." The change of nomenclature perhaps suggests, albeit unintentionally, that "justice" is seldom "international" and that courts among nations are peculiarly impermanent. The new body was described as one of "the principal organs of the United Nations" (Art. 7 of Charter), coordinate in pres-

---

Moore, distinguished American international jurist who died Nov. 13, 1947, at the age of eighty-six, was one of the original judges. Charles Evans Hughes and Frank B. Kellogg also served on the Court. See Manley O. Hudson, *The Permanent Court of International Justice, 1920–1942*. See also the same writer's annual surveys of the Court's work, beginning in 1923, in the *American Journal of International Law.*

tige and authority with the General Assembly and Security Council. On invitation of the Powers sponsoring the San Francisco Conference, an international Committee of Jurists met in Washington in April, 1945, under the chairmanship of Green H. Hackworth, Legal Adviser of the State Department. Its Draft Statute and Report became the basis of the new Statute of the new Court approved at San Francisco.

In reality the "new" tribunal was the old one slightly revised. The provisions of its Statute, even as to the numbering of the articles, were almost identical with the arrangements outlined above. As before, 15 judges are nominated by the groups of the Hague tribunal and elected for nine-year terms by majority vote of the Assembly and Council—one-third of the first panel, however, retiring every three years.[6] The Statute is part of the UN Charter and may be amended in the same fashion. As before, "only States may be parties in cases before the Court" (Art. 34). Advisory opinions may be asked not only by the Assembly and the Council but by the ILO, the Economic and Social Council, UNESCO, the Food and Agriculture Organization, and the Provisional International Civil Aviation Organization. The USA and the USSR are both members of the new Court. Article 36 remains the "optional clause" by which States may accept "compulsory" or "automatic" jurisdiction. In adhering to it, however, the USA—ungraciously and (in the opinion of some jurists) dangerously—asserted that it should not apply to (1) disputes entrusted for settlement to other tribunals; (2) "disputes with regard to matters which are essentially within the domestic jurisdiction of the USA, as determined by the USA"; and (3) disputes under multilateral treaties, unless all signatories are parties to the case or the USA "specially agrees to jurisdiction." [7]

The International Court of Justice met for the first time on April 3, 1946, at The Hague. Judge Guerrero was elected President and Judge Basdevant

[6] For the first election (Feb. 6–9, 1946), no less than 76 candidates were nominated. Among the 15 judges chosen after four ballots, a drawing of lots determined groups of five to serve for nine-, six-, and three-year terms. The General Assembly fixed annual salaries at 54,000 Dutch florins, plus a 15,000-florin allowance for the President and 10,000 florins for the Vice-President. All judges are now elected for a nine-year term.

In 1957 the Court was composed as follows, with the dates in parentheses indicating the expiration of nine-year terms: President, Green H. Hackworth (1961); Members, Abdel Hamid Badawi, Vice-President, Egypt (1958); Enrique C. Armand Ugon, Uruguay (1961); Jules Basdevant, France (1964); Roberto Cordova, Mexico (1964); José Gustavo Guerrero, El Salvador (1964); Helge Klaestad, Norway (1961); Fedor Ivanovich Kozhevnikov, USSR (1961); Hersch Lauterpacht, United Kingdom (1964); Lucio M. Moreno Quintana, Argentina (1964); John E. Read, Canada (1958); Bohdan Winiarski, Poland (1958); Milovan Zoricic, Yugoslavia (1958); Muhammad Zafrulla Khan, Pakistan (1961); V. K. Wellington Koo, China (1958).

[7] The U.S. Declaration of Aug. 14, 1946, Department of State *Bulletin*, 1946, p. 452. Senators Austin, Connally, and Vandenberg and John Foster Dulles favored the qualifications noted above. Interpreted broadly, they virtually leave the USA free to decline to go before the Court, thus establishing an ironic continuity with earlier American policies toward arbitration and adjudication.

Vice-President, and Edvard Hambro was chosen as Registrar. At the Peace Palace on April 18 a public inaugural meeting took place. Revised rules of procedure were adopted. The budget of the Court (part of the UN budget) was $477,208 for 1946 and $638,412 for 1947, the UN paying the Carnegie Foundation at The Hague 48,000 florins a year for the use by the Court of chambers in the Peace Palace.

The first case to come before the Court was the Corfu Channel Case, in which Britain sought reparation from Albania for the blowing up on Oct. 22, 1946, of two destroyers, with the loss of 44 lives, allegedly by mines laid by, or with the knowledge of, Albanian authorities. On April 9, 1949, the Court held, 8 to 6, that British mine-sweeping activities had violated Albanian sovereignty (for which, however, no compensation was due) and that Albania was responsible for the explosions and must pay compensation, which the Court on Dec. 15, 1949, 12 to 2 (the Soviet and the ad hoc Albanian judge dissenting), fixed at $2,363,051. A French-Egyptian case of October, 1949, was dropped in February, 1950, when Paris informed the Court that Cairo had withdrawn its measures discriminating against French nationals. In October, 1950, France brought suit against the USA in connection with insistence by American businessmen in Morocco on special privileges and immunities, based on old treaties, from commercial and foreign exchange restrictions. A complex decision of Aug. 27, 1952, upheld the rights of the American businessmen in most respects but denied that the USA possessed any general exemption from local jurisdiction ("capitulatory rights") in Morocco. In December, 1951, Britain and France asked the Court to rule on the title to the two small Channel Islands of Minquiers and Ecrehou, in dispute for 600 years. In the British suit against Iran arising out of nationalization of the properties of the Anglo-Iranian Oil Company, the Court on July 22, 1952, upheld the Iranian contention that the dispute was not between two States and that it therefore had no jurisdiction.

As for advisory opinions, the Court, up to the time of writing, had ruled that UN members, in voting for the admission of new members, might not attach conditions other than those in the Charter and might not make the admission of one applicant a condition for a favorable vote on another; that the General Assembly could not admit new members whose application had been vetoed in the Security Council; that Israel owed damages to the UN for the death of Count Bernadotte; that the Secretary-General was not authorized to appoint members of treaty commissions to settle disputes arising out of charges of violations of human rights by Bulgaria, Hungary, and Rumania, despite the refusal of these States to do so; and that the Union of South Africa could not modify the status of South-West Africa, as by its attempted annexation, without the consent of the UN.

Subsequent judgments and opinions cannot here be reviewed, but are readily available in the published Court Record and, in summary, in the

THE SETTLEMENT OF CONFLICTS

American Journal of International Law. The record is not encouraging for those who regard adjudication as a panacea for international controversies. Albania refused to pay any reparations to Britain; South Africa ignored the Court; UN members continued to make admission of new members a political, rather than a justiciable question; etc. When States are determined to disagree, recourse to litigation before a Court with no power to enforce its decisions does not invariably promote agreement. The "optional clause," moreover, became progressively attenuated as the States of the Soviet bloc declined to sign it and as more and more of the 33 signatory States (1958) attached reservations making it meaningless, as the USA had done in 1946. Thus in April, 1957, Britain declared that it would continue to accept the "compulsory jurisdiction" of the Court in disputes with other States doing likewise, but only subject to eight categories of exceptions, one of which referred to "any question which, in the opinion of the Government of the United Kingdom, affects the national security of the United Kingdom or any of its dependent territories." Indeed, for these and other reasons, cases submitted to the Court became fewer year by year until some feared that its docket was approaching the vanishing point.[8]

These and subsequent cases, all carefully argued, painstakingly investigated, judiciously considered, and ably reasoned, contributed significantly, nevertheless, to the development of international law and to the practice of adjudication. None of them, however, involved the stakes of diplomacy over which States bargain and do battle in the arena of world politics. These issues are envisaged in terms which make arbitration or adjudication unthinkable to the parties. The original hopes of many jurists and some diplomats, reflected in an astonishing proliferation in the 20th Century of treaties and procedures of pacific settlement, that all disputes could somehow be made justiciable and that litigation might replace violence in international relations are now generally recognized to have been ill founded. The great controversies are questions of power admitting of no settlement through the application of law. They can be resolved only by diplomatic bargaining and compromise or by war, and in no other way whatever.

SUGGESTED READINGS

Borchard, E. M.: *Distinction between Legal and Political Questions*, Washington, Government Printing Office, 1924.

Corbett, P. E.: *Law and Society in the Relations of States*, New York, Harcourt, Brace, 1951.

De Martinie, Raymond: *The Right of Nations to Expand by Conquest*, Washington, Catholic University, 1956.

[8] For a perceptive account of the decline of arbitration and adjudication, and of the reasons therefor, see Lincoln P. Bloomfield, "Law, Politics, and International Disputes," *International Conciliation*, Carnegie Endowment for International Peace, January, 1958.

SUGGESTED READINGS

Fleming, Denna Frank: *The United States and the World Court*, New York, Doubleday, 1945.

Garcia-Mora, Manuel R.: *International Law and Asylum as a Human Right*, Washington, Public Affairs Press, 1956.

Habricht, Max: *Post-war Treaties for the Pacific Settlement of International Disputes*, Cambridge, Mass., Harvard University Press, 1931.

The Hague: *The Permanent Court of International Justice: Ten Years of International Jurisdiction*, Leiden, A. W. Sijthoff, 1932.

Hudson, Manley O.: *International Legislation* (6 vols.), New York, Carnegie Endowment, 1937.

————: *The Permanent Court of International Justice, 1920–1942*, New York, Macmillan, 1943.

Hull, W. I.: *The Two Hague Conferences*, Boston, Ginn, 1908.

Kelsen, Hans: *General Theory of Law and State*, Cambridge, Mass., Harvard University Press, 1945.

Lissitzyn, Oliver J.: *The International Court of Justice*, New York, Carnegie Endowment, 1951.

Ralston, J. H.: *International Arbitration from Athens to Locarno*, Stanford, Calif., Stanford University Press, 1928.

Shea, Donald R.: *The Calvo Clause*, Minneapolis, University of Minnesota Press, 1955.

Thomas, Ann Van Wynen, and A. J. Thomas, Jr.: *Non-intervention*, Dallas, Southern Methodist University Press, 1956.

Wild, P. S., Jr.: *Sanctions and Treaty Enforcement*, Cambridge, Mass., Harvard University Press, 1934.

Wilson, G. G. (ed.) : *The Hague Arbitration Cases*, Boston, Ginn, 1915.

CHAPTER VI

THE PRACTICE OF DIPLOMACY

1. THE ART OF NEGOTIATION

The late Duke of Tuscany, who was a remarkably wise and enlightened prince, once complained to the Venetian Ambassador, who stayed over night with him on his journey to Rome, that the Republic of Venice had sent as resident at his court a person of no value, possessing neither judgment nor knowledge, nor even any attractive personal quality. "I am not surprised," said the Ambassador in reply; "we have many fools in Venice." Whereupon the Grand Duke retorted: "We also have fools in Florence, but we take care not to export them."—M. DE CALLIÈRES, *On the Manner of Negotiating with Princes*, 1716.

"A N AMBASSADOR," wrote Sir Henry Wotton in Christopher Flecka-more's album early in the 17th Century, "is an honest man sent to lie abroad for the good of his country." This conception of the function of diplomats is reminiscent of Machiavelli and Louis XI. Though it is now frowned upon, it suggests the nature of the State System in which modern diplomacy has arisen. In a System of sovereign units, a State may enhance its power at the expense of its rivals through violent coercion or through discussion and bargaining which may well involve trickery and misrepresentation. The end is the same. Which means it is most expedient to use depends upon circumstances. But in any case modern diplomacy, like military might, is a weapon for the enhancement of State power quite as much as a means for the orderly solution of international problems.

In the present chapter, however, attention will be directed to the mechanisms of diplomacy rather than to its purposes. Structure reflects function. But the purposes of diplomacy have become varied and multitudinous as contacts among States have become bewilderingly complicated. Sir Ernest Satow in his *Guide to Diplomatic Practice* defined diplomacy as "the application of intelligence and tact to the conduct of official relations between the governments of independent States." In our time the number of problems which fall within its purview is greater than ever before. A correspondingly complex set of procedures has been developed to meet the needs of international society in the modern era.

Modern diplomacy met its first crucial test as an instrument of collaboration

166

at the Peace Congress of Westphalia, which concluded the Thirty Years' War. The long delay in the conclusion of the peace was due in large part to the absence of rules of diplomatic etiquette and ceremonial. A Venetian offer of mediation was ignored because the Republic had addressed Queen Christina of Sweden as "Sérénissime" and had failed to add "Très-Puissante" to her title. The Venetian Ambassador at Paris apologized for this omission to Grotius, then Swedish Ambassador to France, but the war went on. Not until the close of 1641 were arrangements made for the summoning of a conference. The Swedes then refused to send delegates to Cologne as the Pope suggested or to any place where Sweden's ally, France, might be regarded as having precedence. After much wrangling, it was decided that the Swedes would negotiate with the enemy at Osnabrück and the French at Münster, both cities in Westphalia about 30 miles apart and roughly halfway between Paris and Stockholm. While the war continued, the two towns, as well as the route between them, were neutralized to afford security to the delegates. New controversies arose over the forms of credentials. The Count d'Avaux, representing France, refused to accord the title of Emperor to Ferdinand III; Salvius, the Swedish delegate, would not have the King of France named before his Queen. Finally each delegate in his credentials gave first place to his own rulers. Next the Emperor refused to ratify the preliminary treaty. It recognized the rulers of France and Sweden as his equals, he complained; his own name did not appear first, the neutralization of Westphalia was derogatory to his dignity. . . .

Not until July, 1642, were arrangements for the Congress finally completed. Another 13 months elapsed before any of the delegates arrived. Since the full powers of some were questioned, no business was done till June, 1645. "If," wrote Ogier, friend of the French delegate, Abel Servien, "they create in the substance of the business delays proportioned to those hitherto, I do not know that the unborn child Madame Servien is expecting can hope to see the end of a treaty to which our adversaries create such extraordinary obstacles." [1] Long wrangles ensued over titles, places of honor, and seating arrangements. So numerous were the delegates that one observer declared that "one could not look out the door without seeing ten ambassadors." Each delegate stood upon his dignity. All wanted to be at the head of the conference table. When a round table was at length agreed upon, more quarrels arose over the honor of occupying the place nearest the door. So tedious were the details of the negotiations that the records fill many volumes. Eight years elapsed before the terms of peace were finally settled and embodied in the Treaties of 1648.

Each succeeding European conference has accomplished its work in a progressively shorter period of time. The Congress at Utrecht (1713–14) required 2 years to complete its task. The Congress of Vienna of 1814–15 lasted 14 months. The Paris Peace Conference of 1919 required less than 6 months to

---

[1] D. J. Hill, *History of European Diplomacy*, Vol. II, p. 594.

draw up treaties of peace. Long delays, to be sure, characterized the negotiation of settlements after World War II. The Austrian Treaty of May 15, 1955, was almost ten years in the making. The Korean armistice of 1953 was under discussion for two years. A dozen years and more after 1945 no treaties had been concluded for the unification of Germany or international control of atomic weapons. A decade after the establishment of Israel, no peace treaties had been negotiated with its Arab neighbors. But these instances were due to irreconcilable positions assumed by policy-makers and not to any deficiencies of diplomatic procedures. Where a will to compromise exists, negotiations can now be conducted with ease and dispatch, thanks to the progressive elaboration of rules of precedence, etiquette, and ceremony.

Among these rules are those relating to ranks and titles of diplomatic representatives, formulated at the Congresses of Vienna and Aix-la-Chapelle (1818). Four classes of diplomatic agents are now recognized in order of prestige:

1. Ambassadors extraordinary and plenipotentiary and papal legates or nuncios, accredited to sovereigns or heads of States.

2. Envoys extraordinary and ministers plenipotentiary, also accredited to sovereigns or heads of States.

3. Ministers resident, likewise accredited to sovereigns.

4. "Chargés d'affaires," *ad hoc* when the agent so named is the permanent head of a diplomatic mission, *ad interim* when he is an official left temporarily in charge of an embassy or legation; accredited to the Foreign Minister.

These ranks serve to prevent most of the embarrassments which hampered the work of the Congress of Westphalia. The third rank has lapsed, since States now confer the title of envoy extraordinary and minister plenipotentiary upon their ministers abroad, whether they are sent on special missions or reside permanently at their posts.

Before diplomatic agents are appointed, it is customary to ascertain whether the person about to be chosen is personally acceptable to the Sovereign and Foreign Minister to whom he is sent. All States are free to refuse diplomatic agents of other States on the ground of their being *persona non grata*. No reasons need be given for such refusal; and if trivial or irrelevant reasons are offered, irritation is likely to result. The rule of reciprocity is followed by States in the rank of diplomatic representatives exchanged. Since ambassadors were once regarded as representatives of royalty, the republican government of the USA sent only representatives of lesser rank for over a century after its establishment. Such representatives were literally obliged "to take a back seat" at foreign courts. Congress authorized the President to exchange ambassadors with foreign States in 1893.

The old practice whereby Great Powers exchanged ambassadors with one another and ministers with lesser Powers has lapsed to such a degree in recent years that the lower ranks of diplomats are almost in process of disappearing. By 1958 the USA was exchanging ambassadors with no less than 74 States.

Ministers plenipotentiary and envoys extraordinary were exchanged with only 3 States.[2] No ministers resident or chargés were exchanged.

Every diplomatic agent receives a letter of credence, a special passport, and a set of instructions before starting on his mission. The letter of credence is issued by the head of the State to ambassadors and ministers and by the Foreign Minister to chargés d'affaires. It authorizes the agent to undertake his duties. A diplomatic mission is commenced with the formal ceremony of the presentation and acceptance of the letter. The agent is received by the head of the local State, if he is an ambassador or minister, and by the Foreign Minister if he is a chargé d'affaires. Diplomats of the first and second rank are usually received in a solemn public audience, where they make a short address, to which a formal reply is given.

A diplomatic mission may be terminated by the expiration of the period for which the letter of credence or full power is granted, the change of grade of the representative, or the fulfillment of the purposes of a special mission. In all these conjunctures, as well as in the case of death, resignation, recall, or dismissal for personal reasons, a new letter of credence is required by the new agent. Diplomatic missions are also terminated by war or by recall or dismissal for political reasons in a situation of strained relations leading to a rupture. On Feb. 3, 1917, for example, Count von Bernstorff, German Ambassador, was handed his passports by President Wilson in protest against the resumption of unrestricted submarine warfare. At the same time, James W. Gerard, American Ambassador in Berlin, was recalled to Washington. On Feb. 21, 1950, the USA severed relations with Bulgaria following Sofia's demand for the recall, as *persona non grata*, of Minister Donald R. Heath and its refusal to retract false charges that he had connived in an anti-Communist conspiracy. On Feb. 12, 1953, the USSR severed relations with Israel, alleging official complicity in the bombing of the Soviet Legation in Tel Aviv.

The outbreak of a successful revolution, either in the home State of a diplomat or in the State where he is serving, also terminates his mission under ordinary circumstances. Sometimes, however, this principle is not observed. On March 17, 1917, David R. Francis, U.S. Ambassador to Russia, reported to the State Department the overthrow of the Imperial Government. His request that he be authorized to recognize the new Provisional Government was granted by Secretary of State Lansing two days later. On March 22, Francis called on Miliukov and the new Council of Ministers and presented his new credentials. Shortly afterward, George Bakhmetiev, Tsarist Ambassador in Washington, resigned his post and was replaced by Boris Bakhmetiev (no rela-

---

[2] Hungary, Rumania, and Yemen. In addition, agents for Estonia, Latvia, and Lithuania were still named on the Diplomatic List, though the governments which these agents "represented" had disappeared in 1940. See *Foreign Service List* (quarterly) and *Diplomatic List* (monthly), U.S. Department of State. Myron C. Taylor, appointed by President Roosevelt, Dec. 23, 1939, as his "personal representative" to the Vatican, was given the hitherto unknown rank of "Ambassador without Portfolio."

tion to his predecessor), whose credentials were received by Lansing on June 19. On Nov. 7, 1917, the Provisional Government was overturned by the Bolshevist *coup d'état*, which set up the Soviet regime. Francis received no new credentials, and his mission was presumably terminated, though he remained in Russia and continued to enjoy diplomatic privileges until his departure on July 25, 1918. When, in 1919, Mr. Martens, newly appointed Soviet Ambassador to the USA, sought to present his credentials to the State Department, they were refused and he was arrested and deported. The State Department in Washington continued until 1922 to deal with Boris Bakhmetiev as the accredited representative of Russia, though he represented no existing authority. Bakhmetiev's financial attaché, Serge Ughet, appeared on the rolls of the State Department as Russian representative until 1933. Such situations are anomalous and contrary to general practice.

A diplomatic agent who is officially received is entitled to the usual immunities during his entire mission. He is commonly accorded the same privileges between his departure from his own State and his arrival and likewise, in the event of his return, dismissal, or recall, during the interval between his departure and his safe arrival home. Diplomatic ceremonial has been somewhat simplified as compared with the practice in the 18th Century. No diplomat can claim honors above other diplomats of the same rank. Among those of the same rank, he who has served longest at his post receives precedence. At diplomatic dinners, the host sits at the head of the table. The first place on his right is the place of honor accorded to the ambassador who has served longest; the next ambassador in order of service occupies the first place on the left, the third the second place on the right, and so on. Ministers are next seated in the same order, followed by chargés d'affaires. In processions the place of honor is sometimes the first place and sometimes the last. Diplomats of the first rank are entitled to be addressed as "Your Excellency," to remain covered in the presence of the Sovereign or head of the State, to use a coat of arms over the door of the Embassy, to receive military and naval honors, to be invited to all court functions, and the like. Ambassadors traditionally receive salutes of 19 guns, ministers plenipotentiary 15, ministers resident 13, and chargés d'affaires 11.

Diplomatic privileges comprise inviolability of person, family, suite, and residence, extraterritoriality and exemption from civil and criminal jurisdiction, freedom from taxes, and liberty of worship. Diplomatic premises are seldom invaded by local authorities, even when political refugees seek safety in them. This "right of asylum," comparable to that accorded by the Church in the Middle Ages, is widely recognized and has been insisted upon emphatically by Latin-American States.[3] Every diplomatic representative is entitled

[3] On Jan. 3, 1949, the leader of the "Aprista Party," Victor Raul Haya de la Torre, whose arrest had been ordered following suppression of a rebellion, was granted asylum in the Colombian Embassy in Lima. The Peruvian Government refused safe conduct, held

to bring with him a suite, the members of which share his immunities. The official suite usually comprises a counselor, various secretaries, military, naval, and commercial attachés, interpreters and dragomans, clerks and accountants, a chaplain, a physician, etc. The unofficial suite includes the family, servants, private secretaries, etc., of the head of the mission.

2. WHAT DIPLOMATS DO

> Direct intercourse with the authorities was not particularly difficult, for well-organized as they might be, all they did was to guard the distant and invisible interests of distant and invisible masters, while K. fought for something vitally near to him . . . and . . . for other powers as well which he did not know, but in which, without infringing the regulations of the authorities, he was permitted to believe.—FRANZ KAFKA, *The Castle.*

The broader question of the actual or ideal political functions of diplomats has exercised the fancy of scholars, publicists, and diplomats themselves for many centuries. Among the more exalted definitions is that provided by the U.S. Department of State,[4] which avers that the efficient Foreign Service officer

Creates good will and common understanding, and, with restrained and critical leadership born of mature experience and profound knowledge of men and affairs, uses these as instruments for enhancing international confidence and cooperation among governments and people.

Promotes and protects the interests of the United States and of its citizens.

Negotiates, with tact, sound judgment, and intimate knowledge of conditions at home and abroad, protocols, conventions, and treaties, especially regarding international intercourse, tariffs, shipping, commerce, preservation of peace, etc., in strict conformity to Government instructions.

Establishes and effectively utilizes personal contacts in farsighted ways for the benefit of his Government and of American citizens.

Analyzes and reports on political and economic conditions and trends of significance to the United States.

Exercises skill in following prescribed form and routine procedure when possible; and displays discriminating judgment, as may be necessary in more com-

---

him to be a common criminal, and asked his delivery. Colombia refused. In the complex litigation which ensued, the International Court of Justice held (Nov. 20, 1950) that Peru had no duty to grant a safe conduct unless it requested the departure of the fugitive from its territory and that Colombia had no right, unilaterally and definitively, to qualify the offense as "political," but also (June 13, 1951) had no duty to deliver up Haya de la Torre—who remained in the Embassy. These decisions did not impress laymen or either of the litigants as contributing significantly to a clarification of the law of asylum.

Haya de la Torre was not released until 1957 following a new revolution in Peru. During the Hungarian Revolution of 1956, Imre Nagy took refuge in the Jugoslav Embassy, from which he was released on a promise of "safe conduct" to his home—which promise the Soviet occupation forces promptly violated by deporting him to Rumania. Josef Cardinal Mindszenty took refuge in the U.S. Legation, where he still remained at the time of writing.

⁴ "The American Foreign Service," *Department of State Publication* 235, 1931, pp. 4–6.

plicated situations requiring investigations, careful accumulation of information, or professional understanding of laws, customs, conditions, etc.
Administers an office in a business-like and efficient manner.

Diplomatic agents are no longer called upon to make important decisions of policy as they often did in the days before telegraph, radio, and telephone. Benjamin Franklin in Paris (1777–78) could get no answers to questions sent home in less than three months. His successors, even in the remotest capitals, can secure answers in three hours or less. An ambassador, as Mr. Dooley once put it, has thus become "merely a highly paid messenger boy, and not always a very efficient one at that!" His policy-determining duties have been further reduced by the disposition of Foreign Ministers to confer directly with one another and by the practice of trusting delicate negotiations to special agents.

Ambassadors and ministers, however, are still responsible for gathering and transmitting relevant information, carrying out instructions, and setting the tone of intergovernmental relations. Great Powers typically fill top diplomatic posts with men of independent means who spend most of their time entertaining, and being entertained by, other men of means. This social liaison of elites sometimes promotes solidarity among national aristocracies and plutocracies. In any case the day-to-day business of top-ranking diplomats consists largely of such activities. Walter Hines Page, U.S. Ambassador in London, put the matter sharply in a much-quoted letter of Dec. 22, 1913:

If you think it's all play, you fool yourself; I mean this job. There's no end of the work. It consists of these parts: Receiving people for two hours every day, some on some sort of business, some merely to "pay respects"; attending to a large (and exceedingly miscellaneous) mail; going to the Foreign Office on all sorts of errands; looking up the oddest sort of information that you ever heard of; making reports to Washington on all sorts of things; then the so-called social duties—giving dinners, receptions, etc., and attending them. I hear the most important news I get at so-called social functions. Then the court functions; and the meetings and speeches! The American Ambassador must go all over England and explain every American thing.[5]

That the "social significance" of diplomacy has not much changed in the past generation is suggested by the random comments of other U.S. Ambassadors abroad. William E. Dodd (a professor, a Jeffersonian Democrat, *not* a man of means, and, therefore, *not* a typical ambassador) wrote in Berlin

Feb. 26, 1934: Another dinner! At nine o'clock we sat down in the Herren Klub on the Hermann Goeringstrasse, as guests of Vice-Chancellor and Frau von Papen . . . there were more than fifty people present. My wife sat on von Papen's right, and on both sides of the great semi-quadrilateral table there were counts and countesses, generals, Cabinet officers galore. Of course the conversation could not

[5] See *The Life and Letters of Walter Hines Page* for other interesting comments or the diplomatic function.

be general, just the small talk of each man between two women and each woman between two men. . . . Nov. 13, 1935: I have not talked with Hitler since February 6, 1934, or Goering since June of the same year. Goebbels had us to dinner in early June, 1934. It is rather difficult to remain in my position here and never have any of the triumvirate with us socially. They are the governors of Germany and I represent the United States here. But it is so humiliating for me to shake hands with known and confessed murderers. . . .[6]

Joseph C. Grew, U.S. Ambassador in Tokyo (1932–41), wrote in his diary:

March 23, 1933: Alice, Elsie and I started out in a dismal downpour of rain for the Imperial Duck Hunt. These hunts occur at regular intervals throughout the winter and every embassy and legation is invited to one of them, including the chief of mission, the counselors, and the military, naval and commercial attachés with wives and daughters. One of the Imperial princes also attends, and we were delighted when we found that the Chichibus had chosen to come today because they liked the crowd. . . . The real amusement was in the minor sports which were carried on in front of the lodge—a baby golf course, a clock putting green, ping-pong, quoits, battledore and shuttlecock—and a delicious luncheon. . . . Elsie had a grand time. . . . The Chichibus say that they enjoyed the dinner and movie at our Embassy so much that they want us to ask them soon again; I think the truth is that it is the only way in which they can see a good movie, and we shall arrange it after Easter. . . .[7]

One further example—albeit by no means typical of the routine work of diplomats and consuls, which is clerical, boring, and unadventurous—will suffice to suggest the occasionally bizarre experiences of innocents abroad. A United Press dispatch of Aug. 10, 1957, from Washington read, in part, as follows:

An American ambassador said today he once forsook his diplomatic duties to catch "the biggest frog in the world." Details of the hitherto secret diplomatic mission in 1926 were related by its leader, career diplomat Ellis O. Briggs, now U.S. Ambassador to Brazil. He wrote in the current issue of the *Foreign Service Journal*.
"At Callao, in Peru, I was once a vice consul," Briggs recalled. "I was full of ambition, illusions, and the conviction—convenient to the taxpayers who employed me—that no matter how improbable the project something, somehow, ought to be done about it. A letter had arrived from the United States and from it I shook a crumpled $10 bill. The letter read:
" 'Mr. Consul—I grow the frog for market in New Orleans and . . . they tell of biggest the frog he comes from Peru. Please to send me one dozen those biggest of frogs, six the masculine and six the female. There is no trouble. masculine has larger the ears—like the 50-cent piece.
" 'I send 10 dollars with thanks and respectfully, Mr. Consul. (signed) Alfonse Boucher.' "
Briggs ran into trouble right away. His boss told him, "If you want to chase bull frogs, do it on your own time. . . ."
Briggs on his own then went to museums, read the Encyclopedia Britannica,

[6] *Ambassador Dodd's Diary*, pp. 82, 276.
[7] *Ten Years in Japan* (New York, Simon and Schuster, 1944), pp. 82–83.

interviewed Peruvians, and finally addressed letters to local newspapers suggesting Peru must have the largest frogs in the world. Letters swamped the consular offices at Callao, the consulate general in Lima, and flooded the American embassy. Through the mail many frogs arrived at the consulate—dead.

Finally the President of Peru and the American ambassador became interested. An all-important clue came in—a letter from a priest in the far-off Montaro River area. Father Pierre wrote that "whoppers, the biggest frogs ever" were in that region. The ambassador decided a frog-hunting expedition should be linked with a try at duck hunting. He grandly ordered Briggs to spend the $10 on nets and long poles. The Central Railroad of Peru offered a private Pullman car for the trip.

Briggs continued: "For ten dollars Alfonse in his Louisiana bayou had a private train in Peru consisting of the Pullman car Atahualpa, a caboose for the crew, and a locomotive and tender. For hunters, Alfonse had one American ambassador, one American vice consul, and Father Pierre. For assistant hunters, Alfonse had the train crew, plus uncounted Indians who left off their harvesting and flocked to the river bank in droves." Finally the train stopped.

"The frogs, as the padre had written, were whoppers," Briggs related. "When startled they curved upward in a long leaping parabola, striking the river with the plunk of a stovelid.

"Soon we had 28 frogs, more than enough for Alfonse and his frog farm. The body of the new champion was 11 inches long. . . . Father Pierre christened him Reginald, and when stretched out on a moist board, which Reginald didn't like, he measured almost 2 feet overall, to the tips of his twitching toes. When we deposited him in his box Reginald sat up, looking belligerent, and his ears—those flat discs on either side of his head—were enough like 50-cent pieces to have rung a cash register."

After returning home to Lima "in triumph" Briggs said the 28 frogs plus food ("several bushels of assorted gnats, moths, mosquitoes, ants and beetles") were entrusted to the care of an American ship captain bound for New Orleans.

Alfonse, unfortunately, never received his frogs, for he was meanwhile washed into the Gulf of Mexico by a Mississippi flood. The frogs went to zoos and eating houses. Years later Ambassador Briggs found Reginald's tasty descendants, with ears as big as 50-cent pieces, still being served in Antoine's Restaurant in New Orleans.

Such trivia provide every ambassador with ways of spending his time— and also furnish insight (when the ambassador has vision) into the attitudes and intentions of the elite in the country in which he serves. An able ambassador may even make useful reports on "public opinion" in general, although his necessarily limited contacts and his vocational obtuseness toward disturbing phenomena among the social substrata militate against this possibility. The obverse side of this function has to do with influencing opinion toward his own country among the local populace. Here he competes or cooperates, as best he can, with radiobroadcasters, cultural attachés, press agents, journalists, businessmen, lecturers, etc., in "winning friends and influencing people" through the manipulation of significant social symbols.

Other things being equal, the perfect modern model of diplomatic finesse will strive to inspire love, to elicit respect (sometimes akin to fear), and to minimize hatred toward his own State among those in whose land he works. But other things are seldom equal. If "my" State is the actual or potential ally of "your" State, the problem of influencing attitudes is wholly different from that which arises when "my" State is the rival or prospective enemy of "yours." If its status is doubtful, a just mean between extremes is devoutly to be wished, since ardent affection and violent dislike go ill with diplomatic duties. The astute ambassador will also remember that allies are to be treated as if they might someday be enemies and enemies as if they might someday be allies. Since the qualities of mind and spirit which make for success in this difficult and ambiguous enterprise are rare, the number of truly great diplomats is quite small.

The qualifications of ambassadors and the method of their recruitment have long been unique in the USA. In almost all other States persons named as ambassadors are either able members of the professional Foreign Service or distinguished scholars thoroughly familiar with the language and culture of the country to which they are sent. It is a time-honored American custom for the President, by and with the advice and consent of the Senate, to appoint to the most important ambassadorial posts American millionaires who have contributed generously to the campaign funds of the party currently in power. This practice is not necessarily pernicious even though John W. Foster (grand-father of John Foster Dulles and Secretary of State in the gay '90's) opined in a book titled *The Practice of Diplomacy* (pp. 10–11), that "no man can pass from other pursuits directly into the higher grades of diplomatic and consular service and comprehend clearly the nature and scope of his duties" and also denounced "the baneful influence of political favoritism" on diplomatic appointments. His grandson held (Aug. 6, 1957) that anyone "genuinely devoted to the public service and possessed of integrity of character," and "a sharp and quick intelligence" was a well-qualified ambassador.[8]

This peculiarly American definition of the duties of diplomats was due in part to the refusal of Congress, conforming to American political folkways, to appropriate sufficient funds to support major ambassadorial posts abroad. In 1957–58 career ambassadors received base salaries of $20,000, ministers $17,500, and lesser Foreign Service officers, in eight classes, from $17,000 to $4,300. At the same time two-thirds of ambassadorial posts were filled by

[8] See Hans J. Morgenthau's letter in *The New York Times* of Aug. 13, 1957. On June 18, 1957, in testifying before a House Appropriation Subcommittee in favor of foreign aid, including "soft" loans, Secretary Dulles gave a new twist to the ambassadorial function in his efforts to refute Congressional allegations that gifts and loans abroad make enemies, not friends. "Not for one minute do I think the purpose of the State Department is to make friends. The purpose of the State Department is to look out for the interests of the United States. Whether we make friends I do not care. . . . We try to maintain friendly relations with some foreign countries, not all. . . . If the making of these loans saves a country from Communism, I do not care whether they like us or hate us. We will have accomplished our purpose. . . . [What follows] will be a problem for some other Secretary of State, not me."

career officers, including one woman, Frances E. Willis, transferred in April, 1957, from Ambassador to Switzerland to Ambassador to Norway. But in the major capitals abroad salaries, plus small entertainment allowances, did not begin to cover expenses. For example, the British ambassador in Paris in 1957–58, with a salary of $12,600, received allowances of $72,884 for an annual total of $85,484, while his American counterpart, despite his larger salary, had at his disposal a total of only $54,200 for a post costing $100,000 a year. In London, Paris, Rome, Bonn, Tokyo, and even Moscow, the cost of maintaining the U.S. Embassy was invariably larger than the public funds appropriated for the purpose. Hence the need of millionaires willing to sacrifice part of their private fortunes for the honor of public service by way of campaign contributions and outlays in foreign capitals.

Of sundry and successive noncareer ambassadors named during his two terms by President Eisenhower (whose predecessors of both parties invariably followed the same practice), the following contributed the sums indicated to the G.O.P.: John Hay Whitney (London), $37,500; Maxwell H. Gluck (Ceylon), $21,500; John C. Folger (Brussels), $11,500; Amory Houghton (Paris), $8,500; Jefferson Patterson (Montevideo), $21,000; L. Corrin Strong (Oslo), $20,500; James D. Zellerbach (Rome), $8,500; C. Douglas Dillon (Paris), $27,500; Clare Boothe Luce (Rome), $25,000; Winthrop Aldrich (London), $2,000; etc. Some of these envoys, particularly Mrs. Luce and Mr. Zellerbach, displayed genuine talent for diplomacy. Others did less well.

The current American practice of constantly reshuffling ambassadors produced curious results. George F. Kennan, a brilliant Russian-speaking career-expert on the USSR, after being dismissed as Ambassador by Moscow as *persona non grata* in 1952, was dropped altogether from the Foreign Service. His successor, Charles E. Bohlen, also a Russian-speaking expert, was transferred to Manila in 1957. His successor in turn, Llewellyn E. Thompson, Jr., was the only chief of mission in a Communist country speaking the local language. Only three of the ambassadors to the Arab States spoke Arabic. U.S. ambassadors in 1957–58 in Belgium, the Netherlands, Denmark, Norway, Germany, France, Turkey, Japan, Formosa, Korea, Burma, Thailand, Indonesia, and the Philippines knew nothing of the native languages. Among the professionals David Bruce, who spoke French but no German, was transferred to Germany in 1957, while Amory Houghton, who understood German but knew no French, was sent to Paris.

These confusions almost led to a public scandal in 1957 when Scott McLeod, former F.B.I. agent, and long "hatchet-man" in the State Department against alleged "subversives," was appointed Ambassador to Ireland. Maxwell Gluck, a chain-store owner named Ambassador to Ceylon, conceded before a Congressional Committee that he did not know the name of the Premier of Ceylon and could not pronounce the name of the Premier of India. Other governments, including the USSR, do not commit such mistakes. No doubt the most powerful Power of the world could afford such errors. But they could scarcely be regarded as contributions to the effective conduct of American diplomacy.[9]

3. THE MANAGEMENT OF FOREIGN AFFAIRS

Foreign politics demand scarcely any of those qualities which a democracy possesses; and they require, on the contrary, the perfect use of almost all those faculties in which it is deficient.—ALEXIS DE TOCQUEVILLE, *Democracy in America.*

Every member of the Western State System maintains a small army of officials and employees to spy upon, report about, and talk to all the other sovereignties of the System. The broader purposes of these agents may best be considered below in relationship to the global game of "power politics." Here it will be useful to view these public servants in their capacity as "bureaucrats." This term has become more invidious than honorific, thanks in part to the quasi-anarchistic disposition of most Americans at least to regard all public employees as drones, imbeciles, or thieves, and thanks in larger part to the capacity of all people everywhere to recognize that those who work for the State are often condemned to anonymity, indignity, and dehumanization. Problems of structure, function, recruitment, promotion, tenure, budgeting, auditing, etc., are best left to specialists in public administration. Here a few observations regarding diplomatic and consular bureaucracies must serve to suggest the larger problems of human relations involved in the conduct of foreign affairs.

If diplomats no longer enjoy great discretion and occasional glory they confront problems of administration of ever-increasing complexity. A "Chief of Mission" often has scores of subordinates working under his direction. He must divide the work among them with neatness, dispatch, and economy. He must keep records, make reports, and aid his fellow nationals, who expect his help in getting out of jail, obtaining access to local potentates, securing entry to official functions, acquiring documents needed for travel or business, and the like. Apart from eating, drinking, and indulging in polite discourse, he must spend most of his time in doing favors for fellow citizens with business in the local State and for aliens with business in his own State.

If the role of diplomats has of late become less influential and less glamorous, the work of consuls has become more arduous and more important. States exchanged consular representatives before they exchanged diplomatic agents, for merchants had contacts with one another across political boundaries before governments entered into negotiations. The first consuls of the medieval period were apparently chosen by communities of merchants residing abroad to exercise extraterritorial jurisdiction over them and to represent their interests

[9] See, among many other commentaries on these problems, Vincent M. Barnett, Jr., "Changing Problems of United States Representation Abroad," *Public Administration Review,* Winter Issue, 1957.

in dealing with the State where they resided. The office of consul was fully established by A.D. 1200. The Hanseatic city-states and the Mediterranean trading States exchanged consuls at an early period. The national monarchies of western Europe soon followed their example. The political functions of consuls were gradually diminished, however, with the development of a diplomatic service; and they have lost their extraterritorial jurisdiction except in a few Oriental countries. On the other hand, the growth of commerce has increased the duties of consular officers and led to a great multiplication of their numbers.

The duties of consuls are determined by custom, treaty stipulations, and the provisions of exequaturs, or consular credentials. A consular officer does not act as the spokesman of his government, though he may sometimes exercise quasi-diplomatic functions. He labors primarily to serve business interests and to perform incidental services for his fellow citizens. His concern is with markets. He makes detailed reports to his home government on economic opportunities, tendencies of trade, transportation, navigation, price trends, conditions of competition, etc. These are published for the information of exporters, importers, and investors. The consul seeks to ensure the observance of commercial treaties and to make certain that shipments to his country are properly invoiced and handled in accordance with the laws and regulations of his own State. He also has supervision over merchant vessels of his own State in the port where he is serving. The papers of such ships are deposited in his office. He usually has some jurisdiction over the transportation, wages, relief, and discharge of seamen, the recovery of deserting seamen, the care of the effects of deceased seamen, and sometimes the adjustment of disputes among masters, officers, and crews. The protection of citizens abroad is shared by consular and diplomatic agents. Consuls arbitrate private disputes voluntarily submitted to them, intercede with local authorities on behalf of citizens, administer property of deceased citizens of their own nationality, and assist in the enforcement of immigration laws. In most Oriental States, until recently, consuls also have had extensive jurisdiction in cases involving fellow citizens under treaties providing for extraterritoriality or "capitulations."

Consular agents enter upon their duties when they have been granted an exequatur by the authorities of the local State. When a consul is appointed, his commission or patent is transmitted to the diplomatic representative of the appointing State, who applies to the Foreign Office for an exequatur for the consul. Its issue, usually in the name of the head of the State, may be refused for cause. It may subsequently be revoked, though it is more usual to request the recall of a consul who gives offense. War or a severance of diplomatic relations terminates consular missions. They may likewise be terminated by the recall of the agent or by the revocation of the exequatur. Consular immunities, less extensive than those of diplomatic agents, include the inviolability of archives and other official property, exemption from arrest save on criminal charges, exemption from witness duty, taxation, etc.

To describe the organization of diplomatic and consular services in an epoch of world-wide war and revolution is an impossible task. An outline of the Foreign Service of the United States, however, will prove useful by way of suggesting how a Great Power organizes the work of its agents abroad.

In the late 1950's, the USA was maintaining over 80 embassies and legations and over 250 consular posts, manned by almost 1,500 Foreign Service officers and over 10 times as many reserve officers, staff officers, and employees. A large diplomatic mission in a major foreign capital employs as many as 100 officers and several hundred subordinates, grouped into sections—administrative, political, economic, consular, informational, and cultural. Ambassadors and ministers are appointed by the President and must be confirmed by majority vote of the Senate. Once upon a time all were deserving politicians, spoilsmen, or wealthy contributors to campaign funds, with results more pleasing to the appointees and more serviceable to the party in power than conducive to competence in the conduct of diplomacy. At present most heads of diplomatic missions are men of affairs and two-thirds are "career officers" picked from the lower ranks. A Chief of Mission should obviously be a political appointee in the sense of representing the Administration in office. But his subordinates should be trained and experienced civil servants who know their business.

The desirability, and indeed necessity, of "professionalizing" the Foreign Service was recognized later by the USA than by European States. An executive order of 1906 placed consuls under civil service rules, and another of 1909 did the same for the lower posts of the diplomatic service. The Rogers Act of May 24, 1924, amalgamated the two branches, for purposes of recruitment and promotion, into a single "Foreign Service of the United States." In 1939 the attachés previously sent abroad by the Departments of Agriculture and Commerce were merged with the Foreign Service. The Kee-Connally Act of Aug. 13, 1946, abolished the "Foreign Service Auxiliary" established in 1941 to meet the war emergency and created the category of "reserve officers," the "Director General" and "Board" of the Foreign Service, and the "Foreign Service Institute" for in-service training. The Hoover Commission recommended that the Foreign Service and the State Department staffs be merged. In 1949 the Secretary of State was made administrative head of both and efforts were launched to increase the rotation of officers between Department and overseas missions.

Under these and related regulations, anyone who has been a citizen for at least 10 years, is over twenty-one and under thirty-one years old, and not married to an alien may apply to the Board of Examiners of the Foreign Service to take the written entrance examinations. These are usually given annually in September and often taken by many hundreds of applicants, though annual appointments seldom exceed 100. The four-day examination is no longer highly technical but is rather a test of the applicants' undergraduate "liberal education," including English, foreign languages, mathematics, history, government, and economics. Those who pass are given an oral examination to test appearance, personality, and manners and to eliminate those who are "shy, aggressive, boorish" or who show evidence of "low standards of conduct" or ignorance of the USA. Normally only 10% or less of the original applicants pass both tests. Successful candidates are appointed as Foreign Service Officers at Class 8 grade. Unsuccessful candidates sometimes qualify for the Foreign Service staff, with a lower scale of salaries.

Thanks to these arrangements, the greatest of Great Powers has secured a Foreign Service of first-rate quality. Its personnel has become increasingly representative and democratic, though women and Negroes still have difficulty in securing posts. The hope expressed in 1947 by James F. Byrnes that "it will no longer be necessary to appoint men of wealth as our ambassadors" has not been realized, as we have seen. But American agents abroad are no longer parasites, plutocrats, or "cooky pushers," save in rare and exceptional instances.

Congressional and public criticism has recently shifted to other grounds. In March, 1947, President Truman ordered a "loyalty investigation" of all federal employees. Under Secretary Marshall's order of Oct. 7, authorizing immediate dismissal of "security risks," *i.e.*, subversives, alcoholics, homosexuals, etc., some officers were dishonorably discharged without notice or hearing and with no knowledge of anonymous accusations made against them. Alger Hiss, a high State Department official, was accused by ex-Communist Whittaker Chambers of having given him secret documents in 1938 for transmission to Russia and, having denied the charge, was found guilty of perjury on Jan. 24, 1950, and sentenced to five years in jail. Beginning on Feb. 9, 1950, and continuing for many months to the tune of protracted, partisan, and inconclusive hearings before a Senate Foreign Relations Subcommittee and other investigations, Senator Joseph McCarthy accused the State Department of harboring 205 or 81 or 57 (the number varied with each accusation) Communists or pro-Communists. The imperatives of Cold War obviously required the dismissal and punishment for breach of trust of such enemy agents or sympathizers as had wormed their way into public posts. But in an atmosphere of universal suspicion which bred sweeping and irresponsible allegations, the Foreign Service inevitably suffered. With a premium placed upon conformity and inertia, the qualities of independent thought and creative imagination required for the effective discharge of America's mission of world leadership seemed scarcely likely to be fostered among those entrusted with the conduct of foreign relations.

On the contrary, prior to the waning of "McCarthyism" after 1954, immense damage was done to the morale of all American missions abroad and of the staff of the State Department by indiscriminate witch-hunting, Congressional inquisitions, and the disposition of Secretaries of State, including both Acheson and Dulles, to suspend or dismiss subordinates who ran afoul of Congressional ire. In a frustrated and angry America, furious at the tensions of the Cold War, the costly stalemate in Korea, and what were widely described as the "Yalta betrayal" and the "loss of China," press and public were eager to join in a search for scapegoats. Foreign Service officers were deemed fair game. Under Executive Order 10450 of May 27, 1953, they were required to show that their continued employment was "clearly consistent with national security." Despite repeated "clearings" by the Loyalty Security Board of the State Department, the departmental Loyalty Review Board, and the Civil Service Loyalty Review Board, such able diplomats as John Stewart Service, John Carter Vincent, and John Paton Davies, Jr., were dismissed—rather obviously not because of disloyalty or even indiscretion, but because their views and advice regarding policy toward China were at variance with the prejudices of their superiors and prevailing public opinion.

This trend, which could have reduced the Foreign Service to almost total uselessness for purposes of intelligent policy formulation, was fortunately reversed by a series of decisions of the U.S. Supreme Court on June 17, 1957, reaffirming basic constitutional liberties and sharply curtailing the power of Congress to punish recalcitrant witnesses for "contempt" and the power of the executive branch to send Communists to jail for alleged violation of the Smith Act of 1940. One of these decisions, in this instance unanimous, held that Acheson, in discharging John Stewart Service as a "security risk" in 1951, had acted "wrongfully," *i.e.*, in violation of the Department's own regulations in such matters. In a new time of waning hysteria it seemed probable not only that American faith in freedom would be restored, but that the Foreign Service would again be able to discharge without fear or favor the functions for which it was designed.[10]

---

[10] Congressional ardor to "make headlines" was not limited to accusations against members of the U.S. Foreign Service. In March, 1957, a Subcommittee of the U.S. Senate Committee on Internal Security publicly charged—apparently on the basis of old reports of the Royal Canadian Mounted Police, first transmitted to the F.B.I., then to the State Department, and finally "leaked" to Congressmen—that E. Herbert Norman, Canadian Ambassador to Egypt, had once been a "Communist." Canadian Foreign Minister Lester B. Pearson strongly protested to the State Department, noting that Norman had been completely "cleared" of all such allegations, which should be "treated with the contempt they deserved," and enjoyed the complete confidence of the Canadian Government. The State Department concurred, but the Senate Subcommittee repeated its charge. In April, 1957, Ambassador Norman committed suicide in Cairo. All Canadians of all parties regarded him as a victim of a "smear campaign" by U.S. Senators. In the acrimonious exchange of notes which ensued, Undersecretary of State Christian Herter sought to disclaim responsibility on the ground that the State Department has no control over Congress. Such disclaimers, while valid in U.S. constitutional law, are never persuasive in international law and relations, since every sovereign State must assume collective responsibility for all public acts of all members of its government.

The degree to which other States have similarly debased or improved their Foreign Services cannot here be explored. Britain's top diplomats, even under Labor Governments, tend also to be plutocrats, though every effort is made in the lower ranks to foster intelligence, initiative, and professional skill. The lesser Powers in the American sphere exhibit variants of this pattern. Soviet and Chinese diplomats obviously cannot be men with private fortunes, but all are held to a degree of ideological orthodoxy surpassing anything yet attempted in Washington. Some Soviet agents abroad (*e.g.*, Alexander Barmine and Victor Kravchenko) have turned traitor to their masters out of a devotion to freedom. The Kremlin has as yet found no final solution to this problem—apart from its success in inducing some Western diplomats to "defect" to the USSR. Among instances in the latter category were the defections early in 1948 of Annabal Bucar and James M. McMillan, both of the U.S. Embassy staff in Moscow, and in May, 1951, of Donald Maclean and Guy Burgess, both senior officials of the British Foreign Office, who came out of hiding in Moscow on Feb. 11, 1956.

So long as some semblance remained of the unity of Western civilization, as in the 18th and 19th Centuries, the diplomats and consuls of all Powers, even in an anarchic State System, often could (and sometimes did) give voice in word and deed to the ancient ideal of the unity of mankind. But in an epoch of ideological crusades, unlimited power politics, and total wars, Foreign Service officers tend to become adjuncts of military machines or timid bureaucrats, enjoying little independence of thought or deed.

Consuls and diplomats of all States perform their work under the direction of the department of their own government charged with the administration of foreign affairs. They may be assisted and supplemented by agents maintained abroad by other departments of the national administration. But each State maintains a single department or ministry which is primarily answerable for the conduct of the State's relations with other sovereignties. This agency is under the control of the head of the State—President, Premier, King, or Emperor—and is directed by a Minister or Secretary who always occupies first place in the Cabinet. Into the Foreign Offices, State Departments, or Ministries of Foreign Affairs, as they are variously designated, go all the diplomatic and consular reports from abroad; out of them go the instructions to the hundreds of field agents in scores of foreign cities. Within them are formulated the foreign policies of the States of the world. Between them the great game of international politics is played.

The names commonly given to these nerve-centers of power often, but not always, reflect their locations in the great capitals. In Germany's Second Reich, Weimar Republic, and Third Reich the *Auswärtigen Amt* or Foreign Office was indeed to be found on Berlin's Wilhelmstrasse, by which symbol it was generally known. The French Ministry of Foreign Affairs has long been housed at No. 37 on the Quai d'Orsay between the Chamber of Deputies and the Gare des Invalides. Since 1868 the British Foreign Office has been housed south of the Treasury and west of the Colonial Office on Whitehall in the district of Westminster. It overlooks St. James Park beyond which is Buckingham Palace. It is often dubbed "Whitehall," sometimes "Westminster," and occasionally "Downing Street," site of the residence of the Prime Minister. Since 1951 the Soviet Ministry of Foreign Affairs (Minindel), called until 1946 the Peoples Commissariat of Foreign Affairs (Narkomindel), has had its offices, along with those of the Ministry of Foreign Trade, in Moscow's first skyscraper, a 30-story building on Smolenski Boulevard. But the street name has not yet come into general usage to designate the Ministry. The same is true of the U.S. State Department, which early in 1947 moved from its old quarters in the ornate State, War and Navy Building west of the White House on Pennsylvania Avenue and 17th Street to modern new quarters at Virginia Avenue and 21st Street.

A detailed description and comparison of the organizational structure of these and other Foreign Offices, while of major importance to specialists in public administration, would here be more tedious than fascinating—and would require far more pages than are available. Since the functions of such agencies are identical, their structures, despite variations, exhibit a high degree of uniformity. The customary pattern may be adequately suggested for present purposes by a sketch of the Department of State of the USA.

The Department is headed by the Secretary of State, who is appointed by the President, with the confirmation of the Senate. His political role depends largely on his personal and political relations with the President. Franklin D. Roosevelt, like Woodrow Wilson, was to a great degree his own Secretary of State, despite the fact that Cordell Hull held the post (1933–44) longer than any of his predecessors. Following Hull's resignation for reasons of health, the Secretaryship of State passed through three hands in two years, those of Edward R. Stettinius, Jr. (Dec. 1, 1944–June 27, 1945), James F. Byrnes (July 3, 1945–Jan. 7, 1947), and Gen. George C. Marshall (Jan. 7, 1947–Jan. 7, 1949)—succeeded by Dean G. Acheson, who in turn gave way to John Foster Dulles in January, 1953.

The Department which the Secretary administers has grown in recent years from a small group of amateurs to a vast, sprawling aggregation of specialists, career men, political appointees, and bureaucrats from other agencies—so much so that it is no longer feasible to present any meaningful chart of its structure smaller than a bed sheet. Established by Congress in 1789, the Department long had so many extraneous functions (e.g., census, coinage, territorial records, pardons, patents, and copyrights) that President Jackson asserted in 1829: "I am impressed with the importance of so organizing the Department that its Secretary may devote more of his time to our foreign relations." A reorganization in 1833 established three geographical clerks, one for the major European Powers (then defined as England, France, Russia, and the Netherlands), another for the rest of Europe, and a third for North and South America. By 1870, the Department had 13 bureaus (geographical and functional) and two Assistant Secretaries. By separating the Foreign Service from the Departmental Staff, the Rogers Act of 1924 promoted a cleavage between home officers and agents abroad which has few counterparts in other Foreign Offices. The Department had 8 employees in Washington in 1790, 52 in 1870, 209 in 1909, 631 in 1922, and 963 in 1938. By 1943 it had expanded to 2,750 employees and by 1957, to 23,000, counting 16,500 in foreign posts. The 500 employees of the London Embassy alone outnumbered the total of State Department officialdom in 1914. The more than a third of a billion dollars allotted to the annual upkeep of the Department in recent years exceeds the total annual tax receipts of the federal government prior to the mid-1890's.

The administrative organization of this imposing army of fact gatherers, advisers, and clerks has become so protean and cumbersome in recent years that any effort at detailed description would be baffling rather than illuminating. At the time of writing the Secretary is aided by an Undersecretary and two Deputy Undersecretaries, one charged with departmental administration and the other with coordination of policy. Down one step in the hierarchy are the Assistant Secretaries, one for Public Affairs (including the "Voice of America"), another for Economic Affairs, another for Congressional Relations, and six more in charge of "Bureaus," one of which deals with UN Affairs and five of which are geographical. Other officers on the "staff level" include the Legal Adviser, the Counselor, a Special Assistant for Intelligence, and a Policy Planning Staff designed to achieve perspective for long-range planning. Below the "Bureaus" are "Offices" (formerly called "Divisions"), some functional and some geographical. In 1956 the Office of Africa Affairs, located in the Bureau of Near Eastern, South Asian, and African Affairs, was divided into Offices of Northern Africa and Southern Africa Affairs, both directed by a new Deputy Assistant Secretary for African Affairs. If the constant expansion and recurrent reorganizations of bureaucracies in our time were indices of increased efficiency and wisdom in the conduct of business, then American statesmanship could be expected to reach its zenith in the decade of the 1960's. Unhappily, here, as in other human endeavors, quality of output is sometimes inversely proportional to quantity of personnel, expenditures, and office space.

This general pattern of organization is found in other Foreign Offices. The British Foreign Office is headed by the Secretary of State for Foreign Affairs, who is assisted by a permanent Undersecretary of State, 2 Parliamentary Undersecretaries of State (both members of the House of Commons), a deputy Undersecretary of State, 2 Assistant Undersecretaries of State, 3 Legal Advisers, a Finance Officer, a Press Officer, 12 Counselors, and sundry other high assistants and secretaries. The French Ministry of Foreign Affairs is headed by the Minister who brings into office with him a secretarial staff, or "Cabinet," charged with the direction of the Cabinet Service, the information and press service, the dispatch and receipt of correspondence, and the telegraphic and telephonic service. He always has at his right hand a permanent Secretary-General who supervises the administration of the Ministry. The Ministry of Foreign Affairs of the USSR is set up in similar fashion. In addition to the usual functions of a Foreign Office, it directs and coordinates the activities of such of the Union Republics (*e.g.*, the Ukraine and Byelorussia) as maintain Ministries of Foreign Affairs of their own under the constitutional amendments of February, 1944.

Every Foreign Office, apart from its primary functions of representing the State and conducting negotiations, is in the first place a liaison agency between the executive branch of the government and the diplomatic and consular agents in the field. As such, it dispatches instructions, receives reports, keeps archives, and furnishes the Secretary or Minister with authoritative information and advice. It likewise facilitates communication with agents abroad and acts as a recruiting, examining, and training agency for the Foreign Service. In the second place, it is a liaison agency between the Secretary or Minister, on the one hand, and the public and the press, on the other. Parliamentary undersecretaries, press officers, and sections of current information all function in this capacity. In the third place, it serves as an expert staff through which the Secretary or Minister, and the President or Premier, may secure data and recommendations regarding the conduct of foreign affairs and the formulation of policy. Finally, it performs certain functions for citizens of the State: the issuance of passports, the publication of consular reports, the protection of nationals abroad, and the promotion of the economic interests of citizens in all parts of the world. Practically all the functions of every Foreign Office fall into one or another of these broad categories.[11]

Foreign Offices might be expected (by the naive) to facilitate international travel, which all agree is "broadening" and allegedly conducive to some measure of the "international understanding" that Foreign Offices are presumably

---

[11] The vast efflorescence of public bureaucracies in the 20th Century, particularly in the fields of commerce, propaganda, diplomacy, and war, has imposed strange new tasks on most Foreign Offices and sometimes placed them in competition and confusion, rather than in coordination, with other agencies dealing with international relations. In the USA the State Department, after absorbing the former Office of War Information, undertook the management of the "Voice of America" and other enterprises in the "campaign of truth" against the enemy in the Cold War. Under the direction of the National Security Council, the Department shares responsibility with the Central Intelligence Agency, the Departments of Defense, Treasury, Commerce, and Agriculture, the Mutual Security Agency (established in 1951 as successor to the Economic Cooperation Administration), and sundry other units, some of which maintained separate missions abroad. This latter practice, declared the Hoover Commission, is "confusing to foreign governments, weakens the effectiveness of U.S. representation . . . and is distinctly detrimental to the conduct of foreign affairs."

paid by taxpayers to promote. And indeed in the long, lost, golden years before 1914, when passports were merely certificates of identification and visas were almost unknown, this was in some sense the case. In our time, when policy-makers seek to use travel, no less than trade, as an instrument of power, the reverse is true. Prior to the "thaw" following Stalin's demise, when foreigners were welcome and many Soviet citizens were permitted to go abroad, Moscow and its satellites maintained an "iron curtain" through which very few foreigners and almost no local nationals, save those on official business, were permitted to pass. Forgetting that imitation is the sincerest form of flattery, the world's greatest democracy here aped totalitarianism at its worst during the Cold War. Under the terms of sundry statutes and executive orders aimed at safeguarding American "security," hundreds of foreigners, including Maurice Chevalier, Hewlett Johnson, and many European scientists were denied visas, i.e., permission to enter the USA, while other hundreds of Americans were denied passports, i.e., permission to go abroad, under the formula that such permission would not be in the national interest.

Even in the late 1950's, when Ruth Shipley had been succeeded by Frances Knight as head of the Passport Office and when various decisions of federal courts summoned the State Department to grant hearings and show cause for the denial of passports, the Department still strove not to promote but to impede travel with the "enemy." By the terms of the McCarran-Walter Act, foreigners entering the USA in a private capacity were required, like criminals, to be fingerprinted, a circumstance resented by all, and particularly by Russians, prior to an amendment of the Act in 1957 which made this requirement discretionary with the State Department. As regards American citizens, the State Department banned all trade and travel with Communist China. Its refusal to permit journalists to visit the Marxist Middle Kingdom was denounced by most of the American press. When some 40 young Americans, attending the Moscow "Youth Festival" of early August, 1957, decided to accept an invitation to visit China, Undersecretary Christian Herter, through the Moscow Embassy, warned them (Aug. 13, 1957) against becoming "tools of Communist propaganda," asserted that the USA was in a "quasi state of war" with Red China, and suggested that their visit would be "subversive of U.S. foreign policy," that their passports would be revoked, and that they might be subject to criminal prosecution under the Trading-with-the-Enemy Act. Most of them, defiantly insisting on their "right to travel," went to China regardless.

To return to matters of high policy, most Foreign Ministers in democracies are seldom professional diplomats but usually prominent political leaders. As amateurs they are dependent upon, and often controlled by, the career experts who are, in theory, merely administrators but who are, in fact, frequently the actual makers of policy. In the USA in recent decades most Secretaries of State have been corporation lawyers whose professional background, albeit honorable and lucrative, did not always prove an adequate preparation for the tasks of diplomacy. Secretary Dulles, possessed of phenomenal energy and moral earnestness, discharged his duties during most of his incumbency by flying all over the globe—all in all, over half a million miles—to promote alliances against Communism. The spectacle was dispiriting to many career diplomats but inspiring to press and public, even though some critics contended that "perpetual motion" was no substitute for serious thought regarding the ends and means of foreign policy. But let us at this point revert to the larger aspects of policy formulation and constitutional controls of foreign affairs.

In most democratic States, the national parliament is given some measure of control over foreign relations. In the period of monarchial absolutism, the handling of foreign affairs was a prerogative of the executive, *i.e.*, of the King and his ministers. The American Constitution of 1787 was one of the first to give large powers in this area to the national legislature. Under its provisions, Congress has power over diplomatic appointments, treaties, and declarations of war. The President "shall nominate, and, by and with the advice and consent of the Senate, shall appoint ambassadors, other public ministers, and consuls." Diplomatic and consular appointments are thus subject to the confirmation of a majority of the upper chamber of Congress, except where Congress, by statute, has vested this power in the President alone or in the Secretary of State, as has now been done with regard to all posts except chiefs of missions. The President has power "by and with the advice and consent of the Senate, to make treaties, provided two-thirds of the Senators present concur." In practice, the President and his agents negotiate most treaties without legislative participation, but he may not constitutionally ratify treaties without the approval of two-thirds of the Senators. The President is Commander in Chief of the Army, the Navy, and the Militia; but Congress has power to raise and support armies, to provide and maintain a Navy, and to declare war by a majority vote of both houses. Congress's powers of legislation and appropriation have also been used to influence foreign relations. Congressional resolutions may be ignored by the President; but Congress may grant or withhold money for diplomatic missions and for the enforcement of treaties, and it may, by legislation, carry out treaties, refuse to carry them out, or abrogate them.

It is now well established that all powers over foreign affairs not expressly granted to the legislature by the Constitution are exercised by the executive. The diplomatic recognition of new States or governments and the issuance of neutrality proclamations, for example, are both functions performed by the President and Secretary of State without Congressional participation. Even with regard to those powers which the President must share with Congress, more and more authority has passed to the President. Since 1815, the President has often appointed special agents abroad without consulting the Senate.

Since 1796, treaties have been submitted to the Senate only after they have been signed. Secretary of State Hay observed that they are like bulls going into the arena, with no assurance that they will emerge alive. Friction between President and Senate over treaties has been chronic, for two-thirds of the Senators are seldom of the President's party. But if an international engagement does not require legislation or appropriations, the President can conclude an "executive agreement" which may achieve the same purpose. Similarly, the power of Congress over declarations of war means little in practice, for the President can easily create diplomatic or military situations which leave Congress no choice. American forces have engaged in numerous hostilities abroad without Congressional authorization of any kind.[12]

Much the same situation prevails in parliamentary governments, though the responsibility of the executive to the legislature leaves less room for friction than is possible under the American check-and-balance system. The British Cabinet has full authority over foreign affairs, though Commons may, of course, vote it out of office if it is dissatisfied with its foreign policies. This power is obviously not a very effective or subtle weapon for controlling foreign relations. Diplomatic appointments in Britain are not confirmed by the legislature. Treaties are made and ratified by the Cabinet in the name of the Queen, but important political treaties are sometimes submitted to Parliament for discussion and approval before the act of ratification takes place. Parliamentary objections to the Anglo-Soviet Agreement of 1924 led to the fall of the first Labor Cabinet in the autumn of that year. Decisions of war and peace are also made by the Cabinet. As a matter of well-established convention, Parliament is always consulted before a formal declaration of war is issued, though hostilities are frequently embarked upon in the absence of a formal declaration without parliamentary authorization. The French Constitution of 1875 gave the President of the Republic, i.e., the Cabinet, acting in the President's name, the power to negotiate and ratify treaties, to appoint diplomatic representatives, and to dispose of the armed forces of the State. Certain treaties were valid only when approved by a majority of the Senators and the Deputies: those relating to territory, peace, commerce, finances, and personal and property rights of Frenchmen abroad. Important political engage-

[12] The Supreme Court has held that the Government of the United States is not a government of "limited powers" in the field of foreign affairs and that Congress may confer a large degree of discretion on the executive in this field without unconstitutionally delegating its legislative authority to the President. Thus the familiar "separation of powers" principle and the rule that grants of power to federal authorities are restricted to specific constitutional authorizations do not apply to foreign affairs in the same sense in which they apply to domestic affairs. "Not only . . . is the federal power over external affairs in origin and essential character different from that over internal affairs, but participation in the exercise of the power is significantly limited. In this vast external realm, with its important, complicated, delicate and manifold problems, the President alone has the power to speak or listen as the representative of the nation." *The United States v. Curtiss-Wright Export Corporation*, 299 U.S. 304 (1936).

ments, like treaties of alliance, did not require legislative approval and might be kept secret. These arrangements were not significantly altered by the French Constitution of 1946. The Cabinet was made responsible only to the National Assembly, or lower house, and not to the Council of the Republic, a new upper chamber chosen by indirect election. The new French charter expressed a pious hope of world order: "On condition of reciprocity, France consents to the limitation of sovereignty necessary to the organization and defense of peace."

A word may be added regarding the position of the courts in foreign relations. The U.S. Constitution (Art. VI) declares that all treaties shall be regarded, along with the Constitution itself and laws which shall be made in pursuance thereof, as "the supreme law of the land; and the judges in every state shall be bound thereby, anything in the constitutions or laws of any state to the contrary notwithstanding." In principle, American courts enforce treaties as law. State statutes contrary to treaties are unconstitutional. As between a conflicting federal statute and a treaty, the courts enforce the more recent, since the Constitution places treaties and federal laws in the same category and Congress clearly has the right, under American constitutional law, to abrogate treaties by legislative act. In accordance with the "doctrine of political questions," however, the federal courts accept the interpretation placed upon treaties by the political branch, *i.e.*, the executive branch, of the government. The same applies to the enforcement of customary international law in American courts. In most other States, treaties and international law are likewise enforced in the courts, though sometimes only when they have been enacted into statutory form. In the absence of the judicial review of legislation in most other governments, the executive and the legislature are fully responsible for the observance of the international obligations of the State.[13]

[13] On March 19, 1952, the lower house of the Netherlands Parliament adopted several constitutional amendments abolishing the need of parliamentary approval of treaties implementing previous agreements; providing that all treaties should become effective within 30 days after submission to Parliament unless rejected; authorizing the Cabinet to declare war without legislative approval when it is impossible to convene Parliament; and voiding, by a two-thirds vote of Parliament, Dutch laws contrary to treaties designed to promote "the development of the international legal order." Art. 25 of the Bonn Constitution of 1949 declares: "The general rules of international law shall form part of federal law. They shall take precedence over the laws [in conflict with them] and create rights and duties directly for the inhabitants of the federal territory." *Cf.* Art. 26 of the French Constitution of 1946: "Treaties duly ratified and published shall have the force of law even when they are contrary to internal French legislation."

Meanwhile, comparable problems of the relationship between international law, including treaties, and municipal law, including constitutions, gave rise to a strange controversy in the USA in the 1950's. In *Missouri v. Holland* (252 U.S. 416), the Supreme Court, via Justice Holmes, upheld the constitutionality of a Congressional statute for the protection of migratory birds enacted in enforcement of a Canadian–U.S. treaty, after having previously decided that similar legislation was unconstitutional as an exercise of federal power over interstate commerce. (*Cf. Geer v. Conn.*, 161 U.S. 519; *U.S. v.*

In summary, the constitutional arrangements of most democratic States require some form of legislative participation in diplomacy, but initiative and control still remain for the most part in executive hands. Whatever degree of "democratization" of foreign policy has been attained has been achieved by imposing legislative checks and by making the executive responsible to the legislature, as in European parliamentary regimes, or to the electorate, as in the USA. Direct popular control over foreign affairs is by its nature unworkable. In Switzerland, to be sure, certain treaties must be ratified by popular referendum; and the Utopian French Constitution of June 24, 1793 (which was never put into operation in this respect), required a vote of popular assemblies in the communes for all declarations of war. Popular referenda on questions of foreign policy are, by common consent, impracticable. Such responsibility to the electorate as exists is enforced through legislative action and through the popular election of policy-determining officials. In both cases, such responsibility is vague and intangible, and control continues to reside in executive officials and the diplomatic bureaucracy.

Shauver, 214 Fed. 154; and *U.S. v. McCullagh,* 221 Fed. 288.) In 1951 the State Court of Appeal in Los Angeles held unconstitutional a California law forbidding aliens to own land on the ground that it conflicted with a treaty, *i.e.,* the UN Charter. The State Supreme Court (April 19, 1952) denied that such a non-"self-executing" treaty as the Charter could supersede the Alien Land Law, but held the law void as contrary to the 14th Amendment.

Sundry ex-isolationists expressed alarm over the possibility that the federal government, through the treaty power, might be able to assume functions, in violation of the traditional "division of powers" between Washington and the states of the Union, which would be otherwise "unconstitutional." In 1952 Senator John W. Bricker of Ohio proposed a constitutional amendment stipulating that "a provision of treaty which conflicts with this Constitution shall not be of any force or effect. A treaty shall become effective as internal law in the U.S. only through legislation which would be valid in the absence of a treaty. Congress shall have power to regulate all executive and other agreements with any foreign power or international organization. All such agreements shall be subject to the limitations imposed on treaties by this article." The Bricker Amendment in various versions was periodically debated in the U.S. Senate for many years but, up to the time of writing, had not been passed.

Its purpose, obviously, was to preclude the President (and Senate) from adding anything to the scope of federal powers through the exercise of authority to conclude treaties and executive agreements beyond the limits traditionally established by judicial interpretations of the Constitution in purely domestic matters. But to the extent to which we live in One World, the powers of national government, however constitutionally restricted in federal democracies, must at some points transcend such restrictions in the interests of effective international cooperation (*Cf.* 299 U.S. 304, p. 188*n.*). This imperative of a new era Senator Bricker and his supporters sought, in vain, to deny.

See, on other aspects of U.S. policy-making, Robert R. Bowie, "Analysis of Our Policy Machine," *The New York Times Magazine,* March 9, 1958.

4. AROUND THE GREEN TABLE

A treaty, or, to speak more correctly, a negotiation . . . is a cunning endeavor to obtain by peaceful manoeuvre, and the chicanery of Cabinets, those advantages which a nation would otherwise have wrested by force of arms,—in the same manner as a conscientious highwayman reforms and becomes a quiet and praiseworthy citizen, contenting himself with cheating his neighbor out of that property he would formerly have seized with open violence.—WASHINGTON IRVING.

Ever since the Congress of Westphalia, and indeed before, the sovereignties of the Western State System have supplemented their routine contacts through Foreign Offices and Foreign Services by emergency meetings among heads of States, Foreign Ministers, *ad hoc* delegations, or regular envoys. The Council and Assembly of the League, and the Security Council and General Assembly of UN, along with a large number of affiliated organizations, represent a recent tendency to "institutionalize" the method of conference through periodic or continuous meetings of delegates. These bodies will be discussed in the chapter which follows. Here it is appropriate to notice that despite these permanent arrangements for consultation the number of special meetings of diplomats has increased so phenomenally in the 20th Century as to leave ordinary citizens (and sometimes even statesmen) bewildered and confused.

In the year 1939, for example, the USA took part in 76 international conferences. In 1946 it belonged to no less than 145 international bodies, holding more or less regular meetings, and participated in 250 conferences. Of the 562 days of his incumbency in office, Secretary of State Byrnes spent 350 days attending international conferences, all but one of them outside the USA. In commenting on a single meeting—*i.e.*, the New York session of the Council of Foreign Ministers, held in the Waldorf-Astoria Hotel—he noted that 855,000 pages of data were mimeographed, 143,000 maps were cut, and 44,000 volumes of documents were prepared in the process of completing the five peace treaties signed on Feb. 10, 1947.

A decade later the number and complexity of such conferences had been further compounded. The art of conference is only partially, and with diminishing frequency, a business of chicanery and deception as suggested by Washington Irving. It has been far more a business of propaganda and public relations and, when genuine negotiations are contemplated, a business of research, fact-finding, bargaining, bartering, and compromising. It is fitting that we first consider the procedural mechanics of the conference method of conducting diplomacy.

Apart from periodic sessions of permanent organizations, every international conference meets on the invitation of one or more States. The participants draw up an "agenda" of subjects to be discussed, adopt rules of procedure, and decide whether the discussion shall be public or secret. Ever since Woodrow Wilson popularized the phrase "open covenants, openly arrived at," critics of "secret diplomacy" have demanded public sessions on the assumption that full publicity is "democratic" and promotes honesty, understanding, and agreement. In reality, the reverse is more nearly true. At public gatherings (*e.g.*, UN meetings) national spokesmen invariably talk to the microphones and the gallery instead of talking to one another. Having openly committed themselves to a given position, they cannot recede from it without loss of prestige. Whatever the other evils of private sessions may be, they unquestionably facilitate compromise among divergent views—which is the *sine qua non* of success in every conference.

So much is this the case that ordinary citizens may be safely guided by a simple rule in trying to decide whether any given international conference represents an earnest effort to negotiate agreements or is merely an advertising stunt designed to win friends and influence people. The rule is this: If the conferees admit journalists to their sessions, hand out press releases, and make public speeches carefully distributed through news agencies, radio, and television, then no diplomacy is taking place. If, conversely, they meet in private, say nothing for publication, and otherwise keep their mouths shut except to one another, then it is probable that serious negotiations are proceeding in mutual hopes of accommodation.

If secrecy is essential for successful negotiations, continued secrecy of agreements once reached is scarcely defensible in view of the record. "Secret treaties" played a role which can only be judged pernicious in the processes of power politics which led to World Wars I and II. When pacts are signed and sealed, whether treaties or executive agreements, they are best published so that all may know to what the signatory States have committed themselves. Open covenants are profoundly to be desired, even though few useful covenants can be "openly arrived at."

Conference organization frequently resembles that of a legislature, with a chairman, secretaries, committee meetings, and plenary sessions The analogy is false, however, since legislators represent people, not sovereignties; reach decisions usually by majority vote; and enact law binding on the minority and enforceable on individuals. Diplomats speak for governments, none of which can be bound by any decision which it does not accept. Every conference therefore reaches decisions only by unanimity. Its acts are contracts among States, not statutes to be obeyed by individuals. They take the form of treaties, executive agreements, resolutions, recommendations, joint communiqués, and often agreements to disagree, to adjourn, to reconvene, or to delay, postpone, or ignore the questions at issue. When accords are incorporated into treaties, they are legally binding on the States represented only when ratified by the signatory governments.

Any effort to review, even in outline, all the international conferences of recent years would require many volumes, each much longer than this one. It may nonetheless prove useful to enumerate the more important top-level meetings between diplomats of East and West during and since World War II, ignoring for the present purely regional conferences in these and other areas and periodical sessions of international organizations. The published documents released at the close of most of the wartime gatherings may be found in the fourth edition of the present work (1948, pp. 217–255). Their reproduction here would be pointless, since most of them have since been violated or ignored. Space is lacking for an analysis of the stakes of the game and the moves and countermoves of the players in each instance. Yet a listing of these conferences is the best possible key to the diplomatic genesis of the Cold War, of the conflict of East and West which still plagues the world, and of efforts to end the contest.

NOTE

Atlantic Charter, Aug. 14, 1941. Roosevelt and Churchill meet for the first time off Newfoundland Banks on board U.S.S. *Augusta* and H.M.S. *Prince of Wales* and issue a "Declaration of Principles." [14]

United Nations Declaration, Jan. 1, 1942. Representatives of 26 governments in Washington pledge solidarity against the enemy.[15]

---

[14] Joint declaration: The President of the United States of America and the Prime Minister, Mr. Churchill, representing His Majesty's Government in the United Kingdom, being met together, deem it right to make known certain common principles in the national policies of their respective countries on which they base their hopes for a better future for the world. First, their countries seek no aggrandizement, territorial or other; Second, they desire to see no territorial changes that do not accord with the freely expressed wishes of the peoples concerned; Third, they respect the right of all peoples to choose the form of government under which they will live; and they wish to see sovereign rights and self-government restored to those who have been forcibly deprived of them; Fourth, they will endeavor, with due respect for their existing obligations, to further the enjoyment by all States, great or small, victor or vanquished, of access, on equal terms, to the trade and to the raw materials of the world which are needed for their economic prosperity; Fifth, they desire to bring about the fullest collaboration between all nations in the economic field with the object of securing, for all, improved labor standards, economic advancement and social security; Sixth, after the final destruction of the Nazi tyranny, they hope to see established a peace which will afford to all nations the means of dwelling in safety within their own boundaries, and which will afford assurance that all the men in all the lands may live out their lives in freedom from fear and want; Seventh, such a peace should enable all men to traverse the high seas and oceans without hindrance; Eighth, they believe that all of the nations of the world, for realistic as well as spiritual reasons must come to the abandonment of the use of force. Since no future peace can be maintained if land, sea or air armaments continue to be employed by nations which threaten, or may threaten, aggression outside of their frontiers, they believe, pending the establishment of a wider and permanent system of general security, that the disarmament of such nations is essential. They will likewise aid and encourage all other practicable measures which will lighten for peace-loving peoples the crushing burden of armaments.

[15] A joint declaration by the USA, the U.K. of Great Britain and Northern Ireland, and the USSR, China, Australia, Belgium, Canada, Costa Rica, Cuba, Czechoslovakia, Dominican Republic, El Salvador, Greece, Guatemala, Haiti, Honduras, India, Luxembourg, Netherlands, New Zealand, Nicaragua, Norway, Panama, Poland, South Africa, Jugoslavia. The Governments signatory hereto, Having subscribed to a common program of purposes and principles embodied in the joint declaration of the President of the USA and the Prime Minister of the U.K. of Great Britain and Northern Ireland dated Aug. 14, 1941, known as the Atlantic Charter, being convinced that complete victory over their

LONDON AND WASHINGTON, May 20–June 11, 1942. Molotov confers with Churchill, Eden, Roosevelt, Hull, *et al.* Signs 20-year Anglo-Soviet Treaty of Alliance (May 26) and Lend-Lease Agreement with USA (June 11), together with communiqué declaring that "a full understanding was reached with regard to the urgent tasks of creating a Second Front in Europe in 1942."

WASHINGTON, June 18–25, 1942. Churchill and aides confer with Roosevelt and aides and with Ambassador Litvinov on joint strategy. Secret agreement reached to launch North African campaign, opened November 8.

CASABLANCA, Morocco, Jan. 14–26, 1943. Roosevelt and aides confer with Churchill, Giraud, and De Gaulle on war plans. F.D.R. declares United Nations will make peace only on basis of "unconditional surrender."

MOSCOW, Oct. 19–30, 1943. Hull, Eden, and aides confer with Stalin, Molotov, and aides, plus Ambassador Foo Ping-Sheung, and reach first general Anglo-American-Soviet understanding of the war.

CAIRO, Nov. 22–25, 1943. Roosevelt and Churchill confer with Chiang Kai-shek and pledge restoration to China of all territories seized by Japan since 1914 and independence for Korea "in due course."

TEHERAN, Nov. 28–Dec. 1, 1943. Roosevelt, Churchill, Stalin, and aides confer on war plans, reach secret military accord, pledge independence, sovereignty, and integrity of Iran, and proclaim solidarity to win war and peace.

CAIRO, Dec. 4–6, 1943. Roosevelt and Churchill meet President Ismet Inonu and Foreign Minister Numan Menemencioglu and reaffirm Anglo-Turkish alliance and firm friendship among Turkey, USA, and USSR.

BRETTON WOODS, N.H., July 21, 1944. United Nations Monetary and Financial Conference of 44 States reaches agreement to establish International Bank of Reconstruction and Development, and International Monetary Fund.

DUMBARTON OAKS mansion, Washington, D.C., Aug. 21–Oct. 7, 1944. The U.S., Soviet, British, and Chinese delegations draft a plan for an international security organization.

QUEBEC, Sept. 11–15, 1944. Roosevelt and Churchill confer, along with Eden and representatives of Canada, Australia, and New Zealand. Agree on

---

enemies is essential to defend life, liberty, independence and religious freedom, and to preserve human rights and justice in their own lands as well as in other lands, and that they are now engaged in a common struggle against savage and brutal forces seeking to subjugate the world, declare: (1) Each Government pledges itself to employ its full resources, military or economic, against those members of the Tripartite Pact and its adherents with which such Government is at war. (2) Each Government pledges itself to cooperate with the Governments signatory hereto and not to make a separate armistice or peace with the enemies. The foregoing declaration may be adhered to by other nations which are, or which may be, rendering material assistance and contributions in the struggle for victory over Hitlerism. Done at Washington, January First, 1942. The United States of America, by Franklin D. Roosevelt. The United Kingdom of Great Britain and Northern Ireland, by Winston Churchill. On behalf of the Government of the Union of Soviet Socialist Republics, Maxim Litvinov, Ambassador. National Government of the Republic of China, Tze-Ven Soong, Minister for Foreign Affairs.

occupation zones in Germany. F.D.R. and W.S.C. accept "Morgenthau Plan" for German deindustrialization, which, however, is unacceptable to Hull, is later modified by U.S. Cabinet, and is abandoned by Truman Administration.

MOSCOW, Oct. 9–19, 1944. Churchill and Eden confer with Stalin and Molotov. Agreement reached that USSR is to have "a largely preponderant voice" in Bulgaria and Rumania, with same for Britain in Greece.

YALTA, Feb. 4–11, 1945. Roosevelt, Churchill, Stalin, Stettinius, Eden, Molotov, Marshall, Brooke, Antonov, Hopkins, Cadogan, Vishinsky, *et al.* meet in Crimea. Agree that UN Conference shall meet in USA in April; draft text of Art. 27 of the UN Charter. Peoples liberated from Nazis shall have "democratic institutions of their own choice," sovereign rights, and self-government; joint consultation and assistance contemplated for this purpose. There shall be four occupation zones in Germany. German reparations, in removals, deliveries of goods from current production, and use of German labor, shall "as a basis of discussion" be 20 billion dollars (with Britain dissenting), of which 50% shall go to the USSR. Polish provisional government should be "reorganized on a broader democratic basis with the inclusion of democratic leaders" abroad and then granted Western recognition. Poland's Eastern Frontier shall follow the Curzon Line, with compensation at German expense to the North and West. Jugoslav Parliament, under the Tito-Subasitch agreement, should be enlarged with members of the last prewar Parliament. The USSR will enter the war against Japan "in 2 or 3 months after Germany has surrendered," on condition of preservation of the *status quo* in Outer Mongolia, Soviet annexation of Southern Sakhalin and the Kuril Islands, internationalization of Dairen, a Soviet naval base at Port Arthur, and joint operation of the Manchurian railways by a Sino-Soviet company. "The President will take measures in order to obtain [the] concurrence [of Chiang Kai-shek] on advice from Marshal Stalin."

SAN FRANCISCO, April 25–June 26, 1945 (see pp. 227–228).

POTSDAM, July 17–Aug. 2, 1945. Truman, Byrnes, Churchill, Eden, Attlee, Bevin, Stalin, Molotov, *et al.* meet to consider provisional German settlement, procedures of peacemaking, and other matters. Agree on establishment of a Council of Foreign Ministers "to do the necessary preparatory work for the peace settlements." Germany shall be disarmed, demilitarized, de-Nazified, decartelized, democratized, and "treated as a single economic unit," with reparations, of an amount to be determined within six months, to take the form of German external assets and removals of capital equipment and deliveries of goods from the occupation zones. The USSR "in principle" shall annex northern East Prussia. "Pending the final determination of Poland's western frontier," southern East Prussia and the territories east of the Oder-Neisse line "shall be under the administration of the Polish State," which "has agreed to the holding of free and unfettered elections as soon as possible on the basis of universal suffrage and secret ballot, in which all democratic and anti-Nazi parties shall have the right to take part." "Representatives of the Allied press shall enjoy full freedom to report to the world on developments in Poland before and during the elections." An "orderly and humane" transfer of German populations in Poland, Czechoslovakia, and Hungary is approved. Peace treaties shall be negotiated with Italy, Bulgaria, Finland, Hungary, and Rumania. "The conclusion of peace treaties with recognized democratic governments in these States will also enable the three Governments to support applications from them for membership in the UN" and also from neutrals, but not from the present Spanish Government.

LONDON, Sept. 11–Oct. 3, 1945. Council of Foreign Ministers (Bevin, Byrnes, Molotov, Bidault, Wang Shih Chieh) meets to discuss peace treaties for Italy and Axis satellites. Bevin and Byrnes insist on French and Chinese participation in Balkan treaty drafting, final formulation of treaties by a large general conference, and more democracy in Balkans. Molotov insists on limiting treaty-making to Big Three and Anglo-American recognition of Bulgarian and Rumanian Governments. Deadlock.

MOSCOW, Dec. 16–26, 1945. Three-Power Conference (Bevin, Byrnes, Molotov). Agreed: peace treaty with Italy to be drafted by Foreign Ministers of USA, USSR, U.K., and France; with Rumania, Bulgaria, and Hungary, of USA, USSR, U.K.; and with Finland, of U.K. and the USSR. Council of Foreign Ministers will submit drafts to a Conference of all members of UN which waged war against European enemy States. States signatory to armistice agreements will draw up final texts of treaties. A Far Eastern Commission is established in Washington (USA, U.K., USSR, China, France, Netherlands, Canada, Australia, New Zealand, India, and Philippines) and an Allied Council for Japan in Tokyo to supervise and review decisions of Supreme Commander. An American-Soviet Joint Commission in Korea will "consult with the Korean democratic parties" and make recommendations for a democratic provisional government, national independence, and "a Four Power trusteeship of Korea for a period up to five years." "Need for a unified and democratic China under the National Government" is recognized, along with need for a cessation of civil strife, noninterference in internal affairs, and withdrawal from China of Soviet and U.S. forces "at the earliest practical moment." Rumanian Government is to be broadened by inclusion of one member each of National Peasant Party and Liberal Party and to hold "free and unfettered elections as soon as possible on the basis of universal and secret ballot," with participation of all democratic parties and guarantees of freedom of press, speech, religion, and association. Vishinsky, Harriman, and Clark Kerr will consult with King Michael. USA and U.K. will recognize Rumanian Government when these tasks are accomplished and assurances are received. Same for Bulgaria. Three Powers will recommend to General Assembly establishment of a UN Commission for the Control of Atomic Energy.

AROUND THE GREEN TABLE

LONDON, April 25–May 16, 1946. Council of Foreign Ministers meets to draft five peace treaties.

PARIS, June 15–July 12, 1946. Council of Foreign Ministers completes drafting of five peace treaties.

Paris Peace Conference, July 29–Oct. 15, 1946. Delegates of 21 States meet in Luxembourg Palace to discuss draft treaties. Attlee, Bevin, Mackenzie King, General Smuts, Bidault, Byrnes, Connally, Vandenberg, Molotov, Vishinsky, *et al.* represent Big Four. Total delegates and secretaries 1,385; journalists 2,000; guards 1,040; paper used 5 tons per day on busy days; official languages English, French, Russian. Big Four propose action by two-thirds vote. Small States favor majority vote. Compromise: full "recommendations" to Council of Foreign Ministers to be adopted by two-thirds vote, but "proposals" passed by simple majority may also be forwarded to Council. Conference operates through five commissions (Italy, Finland, Hungary, Rumania, and Bulgaria) and four committees (military, legal, and two economic). Agents of enemy States heard but have no votes.

NEW YORK, Nov. 4–Dec. 12, 1946. Council of Foreign Ministers meets at Waldorf and puts five treaties in final form. Signed at Quai d'Orsay, PARIS, Feb. 10, 1947, by representatives of five enemy States and of Allied States at war with each.

NoTE:

MAJOR TERMS OF PEACE TREATIES OF FEBRUARY 10, 1947

1. Italy and USA, U.K., USSR, France, China, Australia, Belgium, Byelorussia, Brazil, Canada, Czechoslovakia, Ethiopia, Greece, India, the Netherlands, New Zealand, Poland, Ukraine, South Africa, and Jugoslavia. 90 articles. 17 annexes. *Territory:* To France—small districts in the region of Little St. Bernard, Mont Thabor, Chaberton, Mont Cenis, Tenda, and Briga. To Jugoslavia—Zara, Pelagosa, Lagosta and other islands along Dalmatian coast; the Istrian Peninsula and most of the remainder of the Province of Venezia Giulia, with Trieste and environs to become a "Free Territory" to be governed under a statute approved by UN Security Council, which shall also appoint Governor. To Greece—Rhodes and other Dodecanese Islands; sovereignty over African colonies renounced, with their disposition to be determined within one year by USA, U.K., USSR, and France, which, in absence of agreement, will refer issue to UN General Assembly and be bound by its recommendation; independence of Albania and Ethiopia recognized. *Disarmament:* Demilitarization of frontiers with France and Jugoslavia; prohibition of atomic weapons, guided missiles, guns with range over 30 km., manned and noncontact mines and torpedoes, aircraft carriers, submarines, assault craft, and bombing planes; heavy and medium tanks limited to 200, Navy to two battleships, total tonnage of 67,500 tons in all other categories, 25,000 officers and men; Army to 250,000; Air Force to 200 fighter and reconnaissance and 150 transport aircraft. *Reparations:* $100,000,000 to USSR over 7 years out of war-factory equipment, Italian assets in Rumania, Bulgaria, and Hungary, and current industrial production, with USSR furnishing raw materials on commercial terms; $125,000,000 to Jugoslavia, $105,000,000 to Greece, $25,000,000 to Ethiopia and $5,000,000 to Albania over 7 years out of war-factory equipment, current industrial production, and other Italian assets.

197

2. Bulgaria and USSR, U.K., USA, Australia, Byelorussia, Czechoslovakia, Greece, India, New Zealand, Ukraine, South Africa, and Jugoslavia. 38 articles. 6 annexes *Territory:* Frontiers of Jan. 1, 1941, restored. *Disarmament:* Army limited to 55,000, antiaircraft artillery to 1,800 men, Navy to 3,500 men and 7,250 tons, Air Force to 5,200 men and 90 airplanes, of which not more than 70 may be combat types; banned weapons same as for Italy. *Reparations:* $45,000,000 to Greece and $25,000,000 to Jugoslavia in kind over 8 years.

3. Hungary and USSR, U.K., USA, Australia, Byelorussia, Canada, Czechoslovakia, India, New Zealand, Ukraine, South Africa, and Jugoslavia. 42 articles. 6 annexes. *Territory:* Frontiers of Jan. 1, 1938, with Austria and Jugoslavia restored; same as to Czechoslovak frontier, except for cession to Czechoslovakia of three villages west of Danube and south of Bratislava; Vienna award of Nov. 2, 1938,.annulled, with resulting retrocession of Transylvania to Rumania. *Disarmament:* Army limited to 65,000, Air Force to 5,000 and 90 airplanes, of which not more than 70 may be combat types; banned weapons same as for Italy. *Reparations:* $200,000,000 to USSR, $50,000,000 to Jugoslavia, and $50,000,000 to Czechoslovakia in kind over 8 years.

4. Rumania and USSR, U.K., USA, Australia, Byelorussia, Canada, Czechoslovakia, India, New Zealand, Ukraine, and South Africa. 40 articles. 6 annexes. *Territory:* Frontiers of January 1, 1941, restored, except that Hungarian-Rumanian frontier of Jan. 1, 1938, is reestablished along with Soviet-Rumanian frontier fixed by Soviet-Rumanian agreement of June 28, 1940, and Soviet-Czechoslovak agreement of June 29, 1945. *Disarmament:* Army limited to 120,000, antiaircraft artillery to 5,000, Navy to 5,000 men and 15,000 tons, Air Force to 8,000 men and 150 airplanes, of which not more than 100 may be combat types; banned weapons same as for Italy. *Reparations:* $300,000,000 to USSR in kind over 8 years from September 12, 1944.

5. Finland and USSR, U.K., Australia, Byelorussia, Canada, Czechoslovakia, India, New Zealand, Ukraine, and South Africa. 36 articles. 6 annexes. *Territory:* Frontiers of Jan. 1, 1941, restored, except that Province of Petsamo is ceded to USSR. Soviet-Finnish Peace Treaty of March 12, 1940, restored, except that USSR renounces leasehold at Hangö and acquires a 50-year lease, at 5,000,000 Finnish marks per annum, of Porkkala-Udd area, west of Helsingfors, for a Soviet naval base. *Disarmament:* Army limited to 34,400, Navy to 4,500 men and 10,000 tons, Air Force to 3,000 men and 60 airplanes. *Reparations:* $300,000,000 to USSR in kind over 8 years from September 19, 1944.

MOSCOW, March 10–April 24, 1947. Council of Foreign Ministers (Marshall, Bevin, Bidault, and Molotov) meet to consider peace treaties for Austria and Germany. Agree on abolition of State of Prussia. Molotov proposes exchange of views on situation in China. Marshall objects. USSR and Western Powers accuse each other of laxness in demilitarization and de-Nazification of Reich. Molotov protests unification of British and U.S. zones and asks Four-Power administration of Ruhr and $10,000,000,000 in German reparations to USSR, to be paid over 18 years out of current production. Marshall rejects Soviet proposal "categorically" and urges that part of Polish-administered German territory go back to Reich. Deadlock.

LONDON, Nov. 25–Dec. 15, 1947. Council of Foreign Ministers resumes discussion of Austrian and German treaties. Deadlock.

LONDON, Feb. 20–May 6, 1948. Deputies of Foreign Ministers discuss treaty for Austria. Soviet claims on "German assets" in eastern Austria are opposed by Western Powers. Talks suspended when Tito, opposed by West and reluctantly supported by USSR, insists on $150,000,000 in reparations from Austria and Jugoslav annexation of part of southern Carinthia. Subsequent sessions deadlock on other issues.

MOSCOW, July 31–Aug. 30, 1948. Molotov, Stalin, and Ambassadors Walter Bedell Smith, Frank Roberts, and Yves Chataigneau reach a "compromise" formula to end Soviet blockade of western Berlin, but Military Governors in Berlin become deadlocked.

PARIS, May 23–June 29, 1949. Following lifting of Berlin blockade on May 9, Council of Foreign Ministers meets, agrees to facilitate closer economic ties among occupation zones, but admits "inability to reach agreement on the restoration of the economic and political unity of Germany."

PARIS, March 5–June 21, 1951. Deputies of Foreign Ministers in 74 meetings at Palais Rose discuss possibility of a new meeting of Council of Foreign Ministers. USSR insists on inclusion in agenda of North Atlantic Pact and U.S. bases abroad as threats to peace. Western Powers see "no practical utility" in further talk. Deadlock.

SAN FRANCISCO, Sept. 5–8, 1951. General Conference to sign PEACE TREATY WITH JAPAN. Burma, India, and Jugoslavia refuse to attend. China and Korea unrepresented. USSR, Czechoslovakia, and Poland refuse to sign. Treaty of 27 articles signed by 49 States on September 8, with reservations on various items by Australia, Belgium, Egypt, Lebanon, Indonesia, Netherlands, Norway, Philippines, and El Salvador. Treaty specifies that signatories "as sovereign equals" will "cooperate in friendly association to promote their common welfare and to maintain international peace and security." "The Allied Powers recognize the full sovereignty of the people of Japan over Japan and its territorial waters." Japan agrees to support, and apply for membership in, UN; renounces title to Korea, Formosa, Pescadores, Kurils, South Sakhalin, mandated islands, Spratly Islands, Paracel Islands, and Antarctica, and agrees to U.S. trusteeship of Ryukyu, Daito, Bonin, Volcano, etc., islands. Occupation forces to be withdrawn but foreign defense forces to be maintained. For four years, pending new commercial treaties, Japan will accord most-favored-nation treatment to Allied nationals in respect to exports and imports and national treatment (i.e., the same as enjoyed by Japanese) in respect to shipping, navigation, imported goods, taxes, contracts, property, access to courts, etc., on condition of reciprocity subject, however, to an "escape clause" permitting discrimination against Japan (Art. 12). Reparations to be limited to labor, with recipients to supply raw materials, "so as not to throw any foreign exchange burden on Japan." Japan to restore, or make compensation for, property of Allied nationals. Japanese property abroad, with exceptions, may be liquidated. No mention is made of armaments.

Secretary Acheson and Premier Shigeru Yoshida, Sept. 8, 1951, sign JAPANESE-AMERICAN SECURITY TREATY, recognizing that Japan "has the right to enter into collective security arrangements," "possesses an inherent right of . . . self-defense," and will "increasingly assume responsibility for its own defense against direct or indirect aggression, always avoiding any armament which could be an offensive threat." Meanwhile, the USA will maintain armed forces in and about Japan to preserve peace in the Far East, defend Japan against attack, and "put down large-scale internal riots and disturbances in Japan, caused through instigation or intervention by an outside Power or Powers" (Art. 1). Japan agrees (Art. 2) not to grant any rights whatsoever of bases, garrison, transit, etc., to any third Power "without the prior consent of the USA." Japan thus becomes an ally and protectorate of the USA.

During the later 1950's international conferences of all kinds became even more numerous. Our continuing enumeration will be limited to those having direct relevance to problems of power in East-West relations and will exclude all regional and permanently institutionalized gatherings of delegates—e.g., UN, NATO, SEATO, OAS, Council of Europe, other European regional conferences, Cominform, Warsaw Pact, etc. Curiously enough, no such conferences of the type with which we are here concerned took place in 1952. But lost time was regained in the ensuing years.

PANMUNJOM, April 26–July 27, 1953. Negotiations, broken off Oct. 8, 1952, are resumed for an armistice in Korea. Agreement for exchange of prisoners signed June 8. Armistice signed July 27. Exchange of prisoners completed Sept. 6.

BERLIN, Jan. 25–Feb. 18, 1954. Molotov, Eden, Bidault, and Dulles meet to discuss peace terms for Germany and Austria and problems of European security. Renewed deadlock is mitigated by agreement to call a larger conference in Geneva to discuss Korea and Indochina.

GENEVA, April 26–July 21, 1954. Foreign Ministers of the USA, USSR, Britain, France, Communist China, North Korea, South Korea, North Vietnam, South Vietnam, Laos, and Cambodia meet to consider the possibility of the reunification of Korea and peace in Indochina. The Korean discussions end in deadlock June 15. The Indochinese discussions end in an armistice agreement partitioning Vietnam between Communists and anti-Communists at 17°.

MOSCOW, April 11–15, 1955. Austrian Chancellor Julius Raab, Vice-Chancellor Adolf Schaerf, Foreign Minister Leopold Figl, and Deputy Foreign Minister Bruno Kreisky confer with Molotov and Mikoyan and agree on treaty terms.

BANDUNG, April 18–24, 1955. Asian-African Conference (see pp. 641f.).

VIENNA, May 15, 1955. Following a conference of ambassadors, the Foreign Ministers of the USA, USSR, Britain, France, and Austria sign a treaty of 38 articles whereby Austria is evacuated by occupation forces and restored as a sovereign State on the basis of a pledge of neutrality. Signatories agree to "respect the independence and territorial integrity of Austria" within the frontiers of Jan. 1, 1938. *Anschluss* with Germany and any return of the Hapsburgs are forbidden. Austrian armed forces are limited in weapons and in recruitment of ex-Nazis. Austria agrees to deliver one million tons of oil annually for ten years to the USSR, plus industrial and consumers' goods in discharge of a debt of $150,000,000. Last of occupation troops withdraw Oct. 14.

GENEVA, July 18–23, 1955. Eisenhower, Eden, Faure, and Bulganin meet in a "Summit Conference," marked by widely publicized speeches and proposals. No concrete agreements are negotiated, but a new atmosphere of cordiality is evoked: the "Spirit of Geneva."

GENEVA, Oct. 27–Nov. 16, 1955. The U.S., British, French, and Soviet Foreign Ministers meet to discuss Germany and disarmament, cultural exchanges, and the Mid East. They indulge in public reiterations of previously publicized and irreconcilable positions and adjourn without agreement.

The years 1956 and 1957, like 1952, were again barren of any significant East-West conference productive of results, although rich in numerous other conferences, many of them futile, preceding and following the East European and Mid East crises of the autumn (see pp. 396–431). But more would follow in 1958 and beyond.

The end is not yet, for conferences of diplomats, like death and taxes, are with us always. In the series of gatherings reviewed above the science of diplomacy and the art of conference may appear to have failed or to have achieved only limited success. The "peace" settlement after World War II was plainly piecemeal. But it is a "law" of international politics, to which there are no historical exceptions, that every Grand Alliance, once common victory has been won (and sometimes before), splits apart in new rivalries among the victors. Within six years after the joint victory of 1945, the USSR was allied with its European satellites and Red China against the USA, and the USA was allied with Japan, Italy, Western Germany, Britain, France, Australia, New Zealand, etc., against the USSR. On both sides the tasks of diplomacy had thus become not a business of settling the last war but of preventing or preparing for the next. In this there was no novelty, save that in the atomic age the next might literally be the last.

SUGGESTED READINGS

Arnold, R.: *Treaty-making Procedure*, New York, Oxford, 1933.
Bartlett, Ruhl J. (ed.): *The Record of American Diplomacy: Documents and Reading in the History of American Foreign Relations*, New York, Knopf, 1947.
Burdette, Franklin L. (ed.): *Conduct of American Diplomacy*, Princeton, N.J., Van Nostrand, 1951.
Cheever, D. S., and H. F. Haviland, Jr.: *American Foreign Policy and the Separation of Powers*, Cambridge, Mass., Harvard University Press, 1952.
Childs, James R.: *American Foreign Service*, New York, Holt, 1948.

THE PRACTICE OF DIPLOMACY

Cooper, R. M.: *American Consultation in World Affairs*, New York, Macmillan, 1934.

Corwin, E. S.: *The President's Control of Foreign Relations*, Princeton, N.J., Princeton University Press, 1917.

Craig, Gordon A., and Felix Gilbert (eds.): *The Diplomats*, 1919–1939, Princeton, N.J., Princeton University Press, 1953.

Dahl, Robert A.: *Congress and Foreign Policy*, Institute of International Studies, Yale University, 1949.

Dangerfield, R. J.: *In Defense of the Senate*, Norman, Okla., University of Oklahoma Press, 1933.

Dennison, Eleanor E.: *The Senate Foreign Relations Committee*, Stanford, Calif., Stanford University Press, 1942.

Dodd, M., and W. E. Dodd, Jr. (eds.): *Ambassador Dodd's Diary*, New York, Harcourt, Brace, 1941.

Dunn, F. S.: *The Practice and Procedure of International Conferences*, Baltimore, Johns Hopkins Press, 1929.

Elliott, William Y. (Chairman) and Others: *United States Foreign Policy: Its Organization and Control* (report of a study group for the Woodrow Wilson Foundation), New York, Columbia University Press, 1952.

Hale, O. J.: *Publicity and Diplomacy*, 1890–1941, New York, Appleton-Century-Crofts, 1940.

Hendry, James McLeod: *Treaties and Federal Constitutions*, Washington, Public Affairs Press, 1955.

Hill, Norman: *The Public International Conference*, Stanford, Calif., Stanford University Press, 1929.

Leiss, Amelia C. (ed.), in cooperation with Raymond Dennett: *European Peace Treaties after World War II*, Boston, World Peace Foundation, 1947.

London, Kurt: *How Foreign Policy Is Made*, Princeton, N.J., Van Nostrand, 1949.

McCamy, James L.: *The Administration of American Foreign Affairs*, New York, Knopf, 1950.

Macmahon, Arthur W.: *Administration in Foreign Affairs*, University, Ala., University of Alabama Press, 1953.

Nicolson, Harold: *Diplomacy*, New York, Harcourt, Brace, 1939.

Plischke, Elmer: *Conduct of American Diplomacy*, Princeton, N.J., Van Nostrand, 1950.

Rogers, James Grafton: *World Policing and the Constitution*, Boston, World Peace Foundation, 1945.

Satow, Ernest: *A Guide to Diplomatic Practice*, New York, Longmans, 1922.

Seabury, Paul: *The Wilhelmstrasse*, Berkeley, Calif., University of California Press, 1954.

Skilling, H. Gordon: *Canadian Representation Abroad*, Toronto, Ryerson Press, 1946.

Snell, John L., Forrest C. Pogue, Charles F. Delzell, and George F. Lenson (Foreword by Paul H. Clyde): *The Meaning of Yalta*, Baton Rouge, La., Louisiana State University Press, 1956.

Strang, Lord, and Others: *The Foreign Office*, New York, Oxford, 1955.

Stuart, Graham H.: *The Department of State*, New York, Macmillan, 1949.

———: *American Diplomatic and Consular Practice*, New York, Appleton-Century-Crofts, 1952.

U.S. Department of State: *Bulletin* (weekly); *Register* (annual); *Foreign Relations* (annual).

Wright, Quincy: *The Control of American Foreign Relations*, New York, Macmillan, 1922.

Chapter VII

THE QUEST FOR GOVERNMENT

1. HOPES OF ORDER

This is not, of course, to say that the sovereigns will adopt this project . . . but only that they would adopt it if they took counsel of their true interest. . . . All that I do assume in them is understanding enough to see their own interest, and courage enough to act for their own happiness. If in spite of all this, the project remains unrealized, that is not because it is Utopian; it is because men are crazy, and because to be sane in a world of madmen is in itself a kind of madness.— JEAN JACQUES ROUSSEAU.

IN INTERNATIONAL affairs, no less than in other human relations, the patterns of social action which men devise to achieve their purposes embody both Utopian aspirations and the concrete experience of many yesterdays. On the one hand, pacifists and idealists have theorized about the law of nations, the functions of diplomats, and the utility of arbitration and adjudication as a means of promoting peace. On the other hand, the growth of contacts among States has obliged statesmen to face new problems of common interest to all and to invent agencies for their solution. The forms of the Western State System all reflect these two sources of inspiration: theory and practice, spirit and substance, ideal and reality. No community of nations thus far has achieved common government save through the conquest and absorption of its members into a "World State" or through the voluntary federation of its members into a Union. But every community of nations has developed institutions of cooperation. By their nature these scarcely deserve to be called "international government," but may well be labeled, in a more familiar phrase, "international organization."

Practical administrators, as we shall see, have welcomed this development as a means of gearing together public services across frontiers in order better to serve the public. Many political philosophers and humanitarians have seen in these agencies the instruments of peace and justice among nations. With few exceptions until recently, the thinkers and leaders who have presented this thesis have proceeded from a simple premise, flowing from the personification of the State. All of us now know the premise as the principle of "collective security": if all States will agree to wage joint war on any State which breaks the peace, the defeat of the peacebreaker will be certain and peace will be assured, since no State will dare defy the united power of all others leagued

203

against it. The argument is plausible and has been accepted by many of the best minds of the race. The doubts and difficulties to which it gives rise we shall consider in due course. Here it will be helpful to survey the record.

Dante's speculations on world organization were overshadowed by the imperial ideal. His contemporary, Pierre Dubois, was more realistic. His *De recuperatione sanctae terrae*, published in 1305, proposed a temporal union of the princes of Europe with a council and a court, and cooperative action to rescue the Holy Land from the infidel. Three centuries later, as Hugo Grotius was writing his treatise on international law, an obscure monk, Emeric Crucé, issued *Le nouveau Cynée* (1623). He contemplated the formation of a world union of States, including China, Persia, and the Indies, which should strive to promote freedom of trade and keep the peace through an elaborate structure of negotiation and arbitration, embodying a world assembly and a world court.

Another early scheme—the "Grand Design" of Henry IV—is attributed by the Duc de Sully in his memoirs to the French King who assumed the throne in 1593 and died by the dagger of Ravaillac in 1610. It was based upon the assumption that no State of Europe could permanently establish its ascendancy and that all should therefore cooperate to keep the peace. This was to be achieved by dividing Europe into 15 Powers which would have nothing for which to envy one another. These would form a general council, modeled after the Amphictyonic Council of the Greeks, to consist of four commissioners for each of the Great Powers and three for each of the lesser ones, all to be chosen for a three-year term. The commissioners would discuss all problems, pacify all quarrels, and be supplemented by six regional councils, from whose decision appeal could be taken to the general council. The latter would have at its disposal an international army and navy to enforce its decisions. Premiers Tardieu and Herriot of France made this same proposal for the League of Nations at the General Disarmament Conference of 1932. The scheme of King Henry was aimed primarily at reducing the power of the House of Hapsburg. The Tardieu proposal was aimed at preventing any forcible revision of the 1919 peace settlement by Germany, Austria, or Hungary. Both projects failed of adoption.

William Penn, Quaker missionary, theologian, and colonizer, propounded an even more ingenious plan in his *Essay toward the Present and Future Peace of Europe* (1693). He proposed a general diet, estates, or parliament of princes to meet periodically to establish rules of law and settle disputes. "If any of the sovereignties that constitute the imperial States shall refuse to submit their claim or pretensions to them, or to abide and perform the judgment thereof, and seek their remedy by arms, or delay their compliance beyond the time prefixed in their resolutions, all the other sovereignties, united as one strength, shall compel the submission and performance of the sentence, with damages to the suffering party, and charges to the sovereignties that obliged their submission." Since all war, argued Penn, is waged to keep, to recover, or to conquer territory, the imperial diet can keep the peace by adjusting territorial controversies. He suggested that voting strength be based upon national wealth: 12 units for the Holy Roman Empire, 10 each for France and Spain, 8 for Italy, 6 for England, 3 for Portugal, 10 each for Turkey and Muscovy, etc. Peace would be preserved, friendship among princes would be promoted, they would be enabled to marry for love instead of for reasons of State, and, not least important, "the reputation of Christianity will in some degree be recovered in the sight of infidels."

At the time of the Conference of Utrecht the learned Abbé Saint-Pierre published his *Project of Perpetual Peace*, which he communicated to the French Minister, Fleury. The statesman commented dryly: "You have forgotten an essential article, that of dispatching missionaries to touch the hearts of princes and to persuade them to enter into your views." The good Abbé proposed an alliance of all States to guarantee the territory of all its members, suppress revolutions, maintain monarchs on their thrones, and oppose by force of arms any Power which should refuse to give effect to its judgments or make treaties contrary to them. Jean Jacques Rousseau, vagabond philosopher of Geneva, used the Abbé's essay as the basis for his own contribution: *Extrait du projet de paix perpetuelle de M. l'Abbé de Saint-Pierre* (1761). He contended that the imperfections of governments are due less to their constitutions than to their foreign relations. The care which ought to be devoted to internal administration is withheld owing to the need of external security. Men have prevented little wars only to kindle greater ones. The only solution is a union of nations by which States, no less than individuals, are made subject to laws. The confederation must have coercive power to enforce its decisions and must be able to prevent members from seceding. Rousseau accordingly proposed an agreement of five articles for the purpose of achieving "A Lasting Peace through the Federation of Europe." By its terms a perpetual and irrevocable alliance, working through a permanent diet or congress where all disputes would be settled by arbitration or judicial pronouncement, would guarantee to all its members their territorial integrity and present form of government. Any State breaking the treaty would be placed under the ban of Europe and proceeded against in arms.

In his *Principles of International Law* (1786–89) Jeremy Bentham followed in Rousseau's footsteps. He argued that war, which he defined as "mischief on the greatest scale," can be prevented by defensive alliances, general guarantees, disarmament, and the abandonment of colonial imperialism. Conditions must be created for the establishment of a tribunal of peace with power to enforce its decisions on refractory States. Tariff barriers, bounties, and colonies must alike be abolished. Unless governments can be induced to desist from these activities, there can be no hope of peace.

Not least in the list of contributors to the Utopias of international organi-

205

zation was the celibate philosopher of Koenigsberg, Immanuel Kant. In 1795 he published his essay *Zum ewigen Frieden* ("Toward Eternal Peace") which begins with the postulate that the highest of all practical problems for the human race is the establishment of a civil society administering right according to law, *i.e.*, the reconciliation of power and liberty. The external relations of States must be regulated through an international federation. "Every State, even the smallest, may thus rely for its safety and its rights, not on its own power, nor on its own judgment of right, but only on this *foedus amphictionum*—on the combined power of this league of states, and on the decision of the common will according to laws." Kant's articles provided for republican constitutions for all States, world citizenship, national independence, nonintervention, and disarmament.

Since 1800 the number of theoretical plans of international organization has multiplied manifold. Every general war has given rise to a rich crop of schemes for perpetual peace. But international organization was a vision of dreamers rather than a concern of statesmen prior to 1815. Only when the existing European System had been all but demolished did States perceive the necessity of permanent institutions to avert catastrophe. The victors of Leipzig and Waterloo represented triumphant reaction. They were bent upon restoring what had been destroyed and determined to preserve what had been restored. To achieve these objects they banded themselves together into a rudimentary league to maintain the *status quo*, keep the peace, and suppress revolution. The Quadruple Alliance of 1815 became the Quintuple Alliance in 1818 through the admission of a chastened France. At the insistence of the Tsar, the structure was crowned by the Holy Alliance agreement of September 26, 1815, among Alexander of Russia, Francis of Austria, and Frederick William of Prussia. In this romantic document the three Sovereigns, "in the name of the Most Holy and Indivisible Trinity," pledged themselves "to take for their sole guide the precepts of that holy religion, namely, the precepts of justice, Christian charity, and peace," to "remain united by the bonds of a true and indissoluble fraternity," to consider themselves all as "members of one and the same Christian nation," and to receive "with equal ardor and affection into this holy alliance" all other Powers subscribing to its sacred principles.

Behind this façade of mysticism there existed here the first genuine approximation to international organization in the history of the Western State System. It functioned successfully for a time under the leadership of Metternich, its guiding genius. Congresses were summoned at intervals to devise means of keeping the peace and suppressing revolution. At Vienna and Aix-la-Chapelle, European political problems were discussed, and rules of diplomatic precedence were drawn up. At Troppau, 1820, Metternich proposed intervention to put down revolts in Naples and Spain. At Laibach, 1821, Austria was granted a mandate by the Powers to intervene in Italy and sent troops to restore absolutism in Naples and Piedmont. At Verona, 1823, France was given a mandate to suppress the constitutional movement in Spain. Britain withdrew from the organization, however, and joined the USA in opposing any extension of its activities to the Western Hemisphere. The organization failed to act in the Greek insurrection of 1821 and had become moribund by the time of the French and Belgian Revolutions of 1830. The Revolutions of 1848 led to its final collapse.

The disappearance of the Holy Alliance was followed by the development of a habit of consultation among the Powers which came to be referred to as the "Concert of Europe." Here was no organization, but merely a disposition on the part of States to confer with one another at such times as their interests dictated. The Concert of Europe emerged out of the efforts of the Powers to deal with the "Eastern Question." The Powers likewise acted in concert in the recognition and neutralization of Belgium and in the partition of Africa and Asia among the great imperial States. But conflicting interests led to discord. In crises, when its services were most needed, it was nonexistent; for it had no permanent organs or procedures, and each State determined for itself, in each situation, whether it would cooperate or not. In 1870, when Count Beust of Austria failed in his efforts to arrange a conference to prevent the Franco-Prussian War, he exclaimed, "I cannot find Europe!" Whenever the exclusively national interests of the States of Europe reasserted themselves in the face of the general interests of all States, the Concert ceased to function.

If the members of the Western State System were not sufficiently united by political interests to make possible the building of an enduring structure to serve these interests, they were nevertheless constrained by economic developments to cooperate closely for the promotion of lesser interests. This cooperation assumed the form of permanent administrative agencies, usually called "public international unions." In 1856 a number of States established the bases of the European Commission of the Danube, for the purpose of regulating traffic on the great waterway. The Commission was authorized to maintain and improve the navigability of the lower Danube, to fix, collect, and apportion tolls, to enforce navigation rules, and to license tugs, lighters, and pilots. On matters of principle, the Commission acted only by unanimous consent, but on administrative questions it acted by simple majority. The organization has been modified by many subsequent agreements. Many other commissions deal in similar fashion with other waterways.

Telegraphic communication likewise involves numerous problems which can be dealt with effectively only by international action. These problems were first handled through bilateral treaties. Most of the Continental States signed a multilateral convention in 1852. In 1856, at an international conference at Paris at which 20 States were represented, the International Telegraphic Union was established as a permanent regulatory agency. A convention set forth principles, and a *règlement* specified administrative rules to be followed by the signatories and applied by the organization. A conference of diplomatic agents was provided for to discuss common problems and amend the *règlement* by unanimous vote as necessity might require. A permanent bureau was established at Bern to gather and distribute information and to carry out the provisions of the agreement. In 1906, 29 States sent delegates to Berlin, where another convention and *règlement* were signed establishing the International Radiotelegraphic Union, consisting of a conference of plenipotentiaries to revise the convention, an administrative conference to deal with modifications of the *règlement*, and a bureau identical with that of the Telegraphic Union. Its third conference, held in Washington in 1927 and attended by representatives of 79 contracting administrations, drew up a new convention and two sets of regulations, allocating radio wave lengths to various services by international agreement and dealing in detail with various problems of broadcasting and transmission.

The problems of international postal communication led to the creation in 1874 of the best-known of the public international unions—the Universal Postal Union. In 1817, France and the Netherlands signed the first bilateral postal convention. Other treaties followed, but each State sought to place the burden of postal charges on the other. Rates were high and uncertain; and there was no uniformity of national regulations regarding charges, routes, weights, registry, etc. On Aug. 4, 1862, Montgomery Blair, Postmaster General of the U.S., invited other postal administrations to take remedial action. "Many embarrassments to foreign correspondence," he wrote, "exist in this, and probably in other postal departments, which can be remedied only by international concert of action." A meeting was held in Paris in May, 1863, when 31 regulatory articles were agreed upon. Many difficulties remained, however. The Austro-German Postal Union of 1850 was a model of successful cooperation; and in 1868 Herr Stephan, Director-General of Posts of the North German Confederation, proposed the organization of a universal postal union, embracing all civilized States. The Franco-Prussian War interrupted the negotiations, but a few years later the Swiss Government invited the Powers to send delegates to a conference at Bern. In September, 1874, representatives of 22 States assembled and began discussion of various suggestions. Within a few weeks a convention and a *règlement* were drawn up, and the General Postal Union (later renamed the Universal Postal Union) was created.

This remarkably successful organization is based upon the principle that all the member States form a single postal territory for the reciprocal exchange of mail. Under the original arrangements a congress of plenipotentiaries, to meet every five years, was given authority to amend the convention or the *règlement*, and questions of technical detail were to be dealt with by a periodical conference of administrators. A bureau was set up at Bern to collect, publish, and distribute information on postal questions, to issue a journal, and to act as an international clearinghouse for the settlement of accounts. In practice, the conference ceased to exist, and all the work of the organization was done by the congress and the bureau. At the congresses, decisions are really arrived at by majority vote. Members may refuse to sign, but the practical disadvantages of refusal or withdrawal forbid noncooperation. Postal administrations frequently put proposed changes into operation without waiting for formal ratification. The Universal Postal Union has kept postal rates throughout the world at a minimum level and has made possible what could never have been achieved by national action: cheap and rapid postal communication between all parts of the globe under the supervision of a permanent international agency capable of securing uniform regulations and of dealing effectively with all new problems as they arise. By 1957, when the congress met in Ottawa, the Union included 96 postal administrations, although the delegates voted down Soviet efforts to admit East Germany and Communist China to membership.

Problems of health, sanitation, commerce, finance, and humanitarian reform have led to the creation of public international unions no less significant in their respective fields than those dealing with international communication. These organizations are far too numerous to be described here. Reinsch, in his book of 1911 entitled *Public International Unions,* listed 45 such organizations, of which over half had permanent administrative bureaus or commissions. The term should not be applied, however, to international arrangements for cooperation which do not set up permanent central organs, for these differ in no particular from ordinary multilateral conventions. The *Handbook of International Organizations* published by the League of Nations listed some two dozen associations of States, outside of the League itself and its subsidiary agencies, which were true international organizations. All of these were established since 1850, nine of them since 1914. They covered a wide range of interests, as may be suggested by the names of a few: the International Bureau of Weights and Measures, the Bureau of Trade Marks, Copyrights, and Patents, the International Union for the Publication of Customs Tariffs, the International Institute of Agriculture, the International Red Cross, the Union for the Suppression of the African Slave Trade, the International Opium Commission, etc. Many new organizations came into being after 1945, most of them, like the older agencies, loosely affiliated with the United Nations Organization.

Apart from the public international unions, now numbering over a hundred, almost a thousand private international organizations have come into being to serve every imaginable human interest transcending national frontiers. The better to coordinate their activities, they have formed a "Union of International Associations," with headquarters in Brussels. Its Secretary-General, Aake Ording, is firmly convinced, as are the so-called "functionalists" in Britain and on the Continent, that the world order of the future will grow out of such functional organizations rather than out of political agencies and diplomatic conferences.

It is quite true that these activities give more concrete human meaning to "One World" than the Foreign Offices and Embassies have been able or willing to achieve, and that even governmental attitudes and behavior have been curiously modified by the public international unions. In almost every instance the member States, by agreement, have in effect surrendered a portion of their sovereignty and transferred power to an international body over what was once a "domestic question." In the practical operation of the unions, moreover, the obstructive principles of State equality and action by unanimity have been largely abandoned, with decisions reached by majority vote of the member States. Problems which were formerly discussed and quarreled about by diplomats in terms of national honor and prestige are removed from the sphere of "politics" and made problems of "administration," to be considered by administrative experts in terms of efficiency, economy, and the progressive adaptation of means to ends. Organized social intelligence is applied to the fulfillment of human needs. An anarchic and individualistic system of relationships in which each State pursues its own interests, with resulting inconvenience and loss to all, is replaced by organization and planning through which all cooperate to serve the common interests.

It is clear, however, that this form of collaboration is not adaptable to all problems of international concern. The major sources of tension and conflict among States, the great problems of power, prestige, territory, armaments, and markets, cannot readily be transferred from the political sphere to the administrative sphere so long as national attitudes toward these matters remain what they have been in the past. The public international unions have functioned successfully in dealing with concerns of no particular interest to patriots or politicians. States are quite prepared to regard questions of postal service, weights and measures, sanitation, and telegraphy as matters of international action which they can safely and advantageously submit to international regulation. But they are not yet prepared to deal in the same fashion with questions of armaments, colonies, or economic opportunities in "backward" areas; and they are not at all prepared to submit to international control their decisions regarding tariffs, immigration, security, or territorial claims. The problems involving "national honor" and "vital interests" are those which States are unwilling to submit to arbitration or adjudication. They are the same problems which States are reluctant to submit to agencies of international organization and administration.

2. EXPERIMENT IN GENEVA

. . . It would be a master stroke if those Great Powers honestly bent on peace would form a league of peace, not only to keep the peace among themselves, but to prevent, by force, if necessary, its being broken by others. . . . Power to command peace throughout the world could best be assured by some combination between those great nations which sincerely desire peace and have no thought themselves of committing aggressions. The combination might at first be only to secure peace within certain definite limits and certain definite conditions; but the ruler or statesman who should bring about such a combination would have earned his place in history for all time and his title to the gratitude of all mankind.—THEODORE ROOSEVELT, *International Peace*, an address before the Nobel Prize Committee, delivered at Oslo, Norway, May 5, 1910.

Conception. The League of Nations was founded by Woodrow Wilson. Popular interest in the possibilities of a League began to manifest itself in the USA shortly after the outbreak of World War I and grew rapidly during the period of American neutrality. A "League to Enforce Peace" was established by a group of public leaders, including many outstanding Republicans, headed by William Howard Taft. The organization held a conference in Independence Hall, Philadelphia, in June of 1915, and adopted a four-point program which received wide publicity. It called for the submission of all justiciable international disputes to arbitration, the submission of all other disputes to a council of conciliation, the application of economic and military force by all States against any State resorting to war without submitting its disputes to pacific settlement, and the convocation of periodical congresses to codify international law. At another conference in Washington, in late May, 1916, President Wilson declared:

We are participants, whether we would or not, in the life of the world. [Peace] must henceforth depend upon a new and more wholesome diplomacy. . . . The world has a right to be free from every disturbance of its peace that has its origin in aggression and disregard of the rights of peoples and nations. . . . So sincerely do we believe in these things that I am sure that I speak the mind and wish of the people of America when I say that the United States is willing to become a partner in any feasible association of nations formed in order to realize these objects and make them secure against violation.[1]

On Jan. 22, 1917, President Wilson addressed the American Senate on a "World League for Peace." [2]

In every discussion of the peace that must end this war it is taken for granted that that peace must be followed by some definite concert of power, which will make it virtually impossible that any such catastrophe should ever overwhelm us again. Every lover of mankind, every sane and thoughtful man, must take that for granted. . . . It is inconceivable that the people of the United States should play no part in that great enterprise. . . . The right state of mind, the right feeling between nations, is as necessary for a lasting peace as is the just settlement of vexed questions of territory or of racial and national allegiance. . . . I am proposing, as it were, that the nations should with one accord adopt the doctrine of President Monroe as the doctrine of the world: That no nation should seek to extend its policy over any other nation or people, but that every people should be

[1] Full text in "League to Enforce Peace," *Enforced Peace*, 1916, *passim*.
[2] See *Congressional Record*, Senate, Jan. 22, 1917; *International Conciliation, Official Documents Looking toward Peace*, Series 2, p. 111, February, 1917.

left free to determine its own policy, its own way of development, unhindered, unthreatened, unafraid, the little along with the great and powerful.

I am proposing that all nations henceforth avoid entangling alliances which would draw them into competition of power, catch them in a net of intrigue and selfish rivalry, and disturb their own affairs with influences intruded from without. There is no entangling alliance in a concert of power. When all unite to act in the same sense and with the same purpose, all act in the common interest and are free to live their own lives under a common protection.

I am proposing government by the consent of the governed; that freedom of the seas which in international conference after conference representatives of the United States have urged with the eloquence of those who are the convinced disciples of liberty; and that moderation of armaments which makes of armies and navies a power for order merely, not an instrument of aggression and selfish violence.

These are American principles, American policies. We can stand for no others. And they are also the principles and policies of forward-looking men and women everywhere, of every modern nation, of every enlightened community. They are the principles of mankind and must prevail.

Within ten weeks America was at war. In his war message, Wilson again insisted that peace in the future could never be maintained except by a world-wide partnership of democratic nations. "It must be a league of honor, a partnership of opinion." Wilson's facility at phrasemaking made him the chief interpreter of Allied war aims to a weary and blood-sickened world. In response to appeals from London and Petrograd, he issued his famous program of 14 points on January 8, 1918. The last declared: "A general association of nations must be formed under specific covenants for the purpose of affording mutual guarantees of political independence and territorial integrity to great and small States alike."

Birth. By January of 1919 numerous plans for a league had been put forward. In March, 1918, a committee of the British Foreign Office, with Lord Phillimore as chairman, had prepared a draft convention. Three months later, Colonel House, Wilson's confidential adviser, prepared another draft on the basis of Wilson's own ideas. In July of 1918 Wilson typed out his own first draft. In December General Smuts of South Africa proposed a plan containing the germs of the Council and the Mandate System. At the same time Lord Robert Cecil prepared a new draft on the basis of the Phillimore report. Wilson prepared his second draft on Jan. 10, 1919, and his third draft 10 days later to submit to the Peace Conference. Meanwhile, the British delegation to the Conference had combined the Cecil and Smuts drafts into an official British draft of Jan. 20, 1919. Since the third Wilson draft and the British draft diverged at a number of points, they were submitted to Cecil Hurst and David Hunter Miller for revision. The result was the composite Hurst-Miller draft of Feb. 3, 1919, which was used as a basis for discussion by the League of Nations Commission of the Peace Conference.

A Commission of 19 was chosen, with the small Powers in a minority of 1.

Wilson assumed the chairmanship. On Feb. 14 the tentative draft of the Covenant was presented to the Conference as a whole for its consideration. "A living thing is born," asserted the American President. "While it is elastic, while it is general in its terms, it is definite in the one thing we are called upon to make definite. It is a guarantee of peace. It is a definite guarantee by word against aggression. Armed force is in the background in this program, but it *is* in the background, and if the moral force of the world will not suffice, the physical force of the world shall. But that is the last resort, because this is intended as a constitution of peace, not as a league of war. . . . [But] it is not in contemplation that this should be merely a league to secure the peace of the world. It is a league that can be used for cooperation in any international matter."

On April 28, 1919, the revised document was accepted unanimously at a plenary session of the Conference. The other terms of the victors' peace were gradually hammered out, and on June 28 the German delegates were called into the Hall of Mirrors in the great château of Louis XIV and compelled to attach their signatures to the Treaty of Versailles. The first 26 articles of the Treaty contained the Covenant of the League of Nations. The Covenant was likewise incorporated into the Treaty of St. Germain with Austria of Sept. 10, 1919; the Treaty of Neuilly with Bulgaria, Nov. 27, 1919; the Treaty of Trianon with Hungary, June 4, 1920; and the Treaty of Sèvres with Turkey, Aug. 10, 1920. The last-named agreement was repudiated by the Turkish Nationalists. The four other treaties were ratified. On Jan. 10, 1920, the League of Nations came officially into existence with the deposit at the Quai d'Orsay of 18 ratifications of the Treaty of Versailles.

Anatomy. The League was in the first place an agency for the enforcement of certain provisions of the peace treaties and supplementary agreements, *e.g.*, protection of national minorities, the supervision of the Free City of Danzig, the administration of the Saar Valley, and the operation of the Mandate System. In the second place, the League was a means of promoting international cooperation in dealing with problems of health, social questions, finances, transportation, communication, and the like. In this capacity it served to integrate and coordinate the activities of the existing public international unions. In the third place, the League was an agency for the prevention of war and the pacific settlement of disputes. All threats to peace were within its competence; and all controversies among its members were, in theory at least, submitted to the procedures of arbitration, adjudication, or conciliation provided for in the Covenant.

The Covenant, as incorporated in the Treaty of Versailles, was signed by 31 of the 32 States named in the Annex. China became an original member by signing the Treaty of St. Germain. Of these 32 signatories, 3 failed to ratify: Ecuador, the Hejaz, and the USA. By Jan. 10, 1920, 19 ratifications had been deposited at the Quai d'Orsay; and by April of 1920 a total of

42 States had become original members of the League. Subsequently, 21 other States were admitted to membership. Only 6 States of the world never applied for membership: Saudi Arabia, Yemen, Oman, Nepal, Manchukuo, and the United States of America.

The structure of the League can be described in terms of its major organs: Assembly, Council, and Secretariat. The Assembly was the representative and deliberative organ, consisting of all members, with each entitled to one vote. The Assembly met annually every September in Geneva and held several special sessions. Its organization resembled that of a legislative body in that it followed the usual principles of parliamentary procedure and operated through committees. It maintained six regular standing committees—constitutional and legal, technical organizations, reduction of armaments, budgetary, social and humanitarian, and political—and was free to appoint special committees for particular purposes. Article 3 of the Covenant declared that the Assembly "may deal at its meetings with any matter within the sphere of action of the League or affecting the peace of the world." In practice, it exercised three general types of powers: electoral, constituent, and deliberative.

The Assembly elected new members to the League by a two-thirds vote, as occasion arose; it elected annually three of the nine nonpermanent members of the Council by a majority vote; and, in conjunction with the Council, it elected every nine years by majority vote the 15 judges of the World Court. It also approved by majority vote the Council's nominations for the post of Secretary-General. As a constituent body, it amended the Covenant by majority vote, but amendments had to be approved unanimously by the Council and were subject to the ratifications of the member States. As a deliberative body, the Assembly considered general political, economic, and technical questions of international interest, advised the reconsideration of inapplicable treaties under Article 19 (it never exercised this power), supervised the work of the Council and of the technical organizations, and prepared the annual budget of the League, usually totaling about $6,000,000. The Assembly provided for the apportionment of these expenses among the members in accordance with a scale (1937–39) totaling 923 units, on which Britain paid 108 units, the Soviet Union 94, France 80, Italy 60, India 49, China 42, Spain 40, and so on, down to 1 unit each for such small States as Albania, Haiti, Liberia, and Luxembourg.

The Council was designed to be a small body on which the Great Powers should have permanent seats, with the other seats rotated among the lesser Powers. It was originally contemplated that it would consist of 5 permanent seats to be occupied by the USA, Britain, France, Italy, and Japan and 4 nonpermanent seats, assigned temporarily in 1920 to Belgium, Brazil, Spain, and Greece, their successors to be chosen periodically by the Assembly. America's defection reduced the ratio of Great Powers to small Powers to 4:4. In 1922, 2 additional nonpermanent seats were added, making a Council of 10 members. The admission of Germany in 1926 created a "Council crisis" resolved by establishing 9 nonpermanent seats, 3 to be filled annually for three-year terms by the Assembly. In 1933 a tenth nonpermanent seat was provisionally created for three years and was assigned to Portugal (1933–36). In 1936, 2 nonpermanent seats were created for the ensuing three years and assigned to Latvia and China (1936–39). By 1939 the Council consisted of 3 permanent members, Britain, France, and the USSR, and 11 nonpermanent members.

The Council met four times a year, or oftener as occasion required. Like the Assembly, it could deal "with any matter within the sphere of action of the League or affecting the peace of the world" (Art. 4). Its powers could be expanded by treaty. The minorities treaties conferred special powers on the Council in regard to the supervision of the enforcement of their obligations. The Treaty of Lausanne of 1923 similarly gave the Council jurisdiction over the Mosul dispute. In practice, the most important function of the Council was the settlement of disputes. It shared this function with the Assembly, but the latter seldom intervened. The Council also had executive, administrative, and supervisory functions in connection with Danzig, the Saar Valley, the Mandate System, etc. Under Articles 10 to 16 of the Covenant, it had authority to mobilize the sanctions of the League against a Covenant-breaking State. The Council likewise carried out recommendations of the Assembly, prepared plans for disarmament, nominated the Secretary-General, and approved his appointments to subordinate positions in the Secretariat. All other League functions were shared concurrently by the Council and the Assembly.

The Secretariat consisted of an international civil service of almost 600 expert officials and subordinates residing at Geneva. It bore the same relation to the League as a whole as do the bureaus of the public international unions to their respective organizations. The Secretariat was headed by a Secretary-General, appointed by the Council with the approval of the Assembly. Sir Eric Drummond of Great Britain held this office from 1920 to 1933 and was largely responsible for the establishment and organization of the Secretariat. He was succeeded by M. Joseph Avenol of France. His immediate subordinates were two Deputy Secretaries-General and two Undersecretaries. One of each of these higher posts was held by a national of each of the Great Powers in the League. The body of the Secretariat was divided into sections, headed by directors. The officials of the Secretariat were not recruited by civil service examinations but were chosen by the Secretary-General on the basis of professional competence, with a proper regard for the distribution of posts among the various States. The officials were in no sense governmental representatives, however, but were responsible only to the Secretariat itself, to which they made a declaration of loyalty. They were charged with the compilation and publication of information on all the complex problems which came before the League for consideration and with the secretarial work of the Council and

Assembly, which included the preparation of agenda, the translation of speeches into French and English (the two official languages), and the preparation and publication of minutes in the *Official Journal*.

There were organized around the League various technical agencies, commissions, and advisory committees. Two of these—the Permanent Advisory Commission on Armaments and the Mandates Commission—were provided for in the Covenant (Arts. 9 and 22). The others were established by the Council as bodies of experts to supply information and give advice on the problems falling within the sphere of the League's competence. These organizations worked in close cooperation with the corresponding sections of the Secretariat. The four major ones were: the Economic and Financial Organization; the Organization for Communications and Transit; the Health Organization; and the Intellectual Cooperation Organization.

The International Labor Organization (ILO) had its headquarters at Geneva and, though distinct from the League proper, was an integral part of the League system. Its constitution was embodied in Part XIII of the Treaty of Versailles. The Organization consists of three parts. The General Conference comprises four delegates from each State (two representing the participating governments, one chosen by the governments to speak for the most representative employers' organization in their respective countries, and one chosen to speak for the most representative workers' organization). The General Conference assembles annually. The delegates vote individually and draw up, by a two-thirds majority, recommendations or draft conventions on labor legislation. The Governing Body, which meets every three months, consists of 32 members chosen for a three-year term, 16 appointed by the member governments, half representing the States of chief industrial importance and the rest picked by the other government delegates at the Conference, and 16 chosen half by the employers' delegates and half by the workers' delegates. The Governing Body prepares the agenda of the Conferences, appoints the Director of the International Labor Office, and supervises its work. The International Labor Office consists of some 350 experts appointed by the Director and is the secretariat of the Organization. It gathers and publishes information on labor legislation and assists the Governing Body in preparing for the Conferences. M. Albert Thomas was its Director from its establishment until his death in April, 1932. Harold Butler was named his successor, and was succeeded in turn by John G. Winant and Edward J. Phelan. The expenses of the International Labor Organization were met out of the League budget. It is now affiliated with UN, with David A. Morse as Director.

The purpose of the ILO is to promote uniformity of labor legislation throughout the world. National governments are frequently reluctant to enact adequate protective legislation for wage earners because the States granting such protection are alleged to be placed at a competitive disadvantage in world markets in comparison with States where employers are free to exploit labor without legislative hindrances. The problem involved can be dealt with adequately only by international action. But of the 103 ILO conventions drafted thus far, none has been ratified by all the members. Bulgaria has ratified 62, France 52, Britain 49, the USA only 6, and some members none at all. The methods provided for ensuring the execution of such conventions as are ratified do not prevent violations. The Organization provides an international forum for the discussion of labor legislation; it prepares the way for the formulation of international standards of labor legislation and constitutes a useful agency for the collection and publication of labor statistics; it promotes the crystallization of attitudes and policies on the part of governments, employers' associations, and labor unions in the member States. But its actions are purely advisory.

Pathology. The League and its associated agencies never became symbols of human brotherhood eliciting love and loyalty from large numbers of people in all lands and thereby developing the prestige and authority required by an incipient world government. The League remained a method of cooperation among sovereign governments. Their subjects and citizens remained patriots devoted to national interests. In some States, they were bewitched by visions of tribal conquest; in others, frightened into passivity; in still others, befuddled and betrayed. Nowhere were they united in the effective service of common purposes. The League's white palace in Ariana Park, by the shores of Geneva's Lake Leman, therefore became, in the end, a sepulcher.

The outward symptoms of the League's demise are easily described. The rate of withdrawal of States from membership reflected the progress of a fatal disease. The first State to give the required two-year notice of resignation was Costa Rica, Jan. 1, 1925. The reasons were financial. The result was unimportant. But Brazil gave notice on June 12, 1926, for reasons of "prestige." Japan followed (March 27, 1933) and then Germany (Oct. 14, 1933) for reasons of *Realpolitik*. Paraguay did likewise (Feb. 23, 1935); and then, after the destruction of one League member by another, Guatemala (May 15, 1936), Honduras (June 20, 1936), Nicaragua (June 26, 1936), El Salvador (Aug. 10, 1937), Italy (Dec. 11, 1937), Chile (May 13, 1938), Venezuela (July 12, 1938), Peru (April 8, 1939), Albania (April 13, 1939), Spain (May 8, 1939), and Rumania (July 10, 1940).

By the close of 1938, the 62 States that had at one time or another been League members were reduced to 49. Two members, Ethiopia and Austria, had been destroyed and another, Czechoslovakia, half destroyed. In 1939–40, more League members were extinguished by the aggressors. The Soviet Union was "expelled." At the end, only 1 Great Power was left in the League, Britain, and only 31 insecure smaller States. On May 16, 1940, M. Avenol dismissed most of the employees of the Secretariat, and on June 25 he discharged the remainder. He himself resigned. A few "nonpolitical" officials found refuge in Princeton University, over which Woodrow Wilson had once presided. A remnant of the ILO fled to Toronto. The judges of the World Court were scattered to the winds. By summer's end of 1940 the whole League system had become a memory. Even the memory seemed all but lost in a panic flight before the Horsemen of the Apocalypse.

This decease was obviously part of the death of a world. Yet that tragedy was in many of its acts and scenes played at Geneva. Early efforts to cope with aggressors were not reassuring. When Italy bombarded and occupied Corfu in 1923 and Greece appealed to the League, the Italian delegate, Salandra, declared that Article 16 of the Covenant could not be applied, since Italy did not intend to commit an act of war. The Council permitted the Conference of Ambassadors to settle the dispute on terms entirely favorable to Italy. In dealing with small States the League Powers were more resolute and more successful. But in their first great test in dealing with aggression by a Great Power, the League members displayed neither willingness nor ability to restrain the lawbreaker and protect his victim.

Following Japanese occupation of central Manchuria on Sept. 18, 1931, China invoked the Covenant, calling attention by stages to Articles 10, 11, 15, and 16. Sir John Simon, then British Foreign Minister, was determined to thwart any effective action against Japan. In this he was completely successful. A Council resolution of Sept. 21, 1931, calling upon the disputants to withdraw their troops, was ignored by Tokyo. As the fighting spread, the USA, for the first time and the last, authorized a representative (Prentiss B. Gilbert) to sit with the Council in invoking the Pact of Paris. On Oct. 24 the Council called on Japan to withdraw its troops by Nov. 16. By this date Japanese forces were fighting their way into northern Manchuria. On Dec. 10 the Council appointed a Commission of five members, headed by Lord Lytton, to study the situation. When Japan attacked Shanghai, China appealed to the Assembly, which adopted a resolution (March 4, 1932) calling for Japanese evacuation of Shanghai and another (March 11) reiterating the Stimson Doctrine. Tokyo did indeed quit Shanghai under the armistice of May 5 but continued to hold Manchuria—now transmuted into "Manchukuo." After a leisurely visit to the Far East the Lytton Commission issued a report of 100,000 words on Oct. 3, 1932, recommending—much too late—a reasonable compromise. On Feb. 24, 1933, the Assembly adopted a resolution condemning Japan and accepting these recommendations. Tokyo rejected them and left Geneva. The other League Powers did nothing apart from refusing to recognize Manchukuo.

Italians and Germans dreaming of empire were not slow to grasp the lesson of these events. In Europe the paralysis of the Western Powers (and therefore of the League) first manifested itself in the aftermath of the breakdown of the League of Nations Disarmament Conference. When Berlin repudiated the military clauses of Versailles and introduced conscription on March 16, 1935, London and Paris were content to take refuge in a long but wholly innocuous resolution of the League Council (April 17, 1935). When Germany on March 7, 1936, repudiated Locarno and began remilitarizing the Rhineland, the Western Powers avoided any counteraction save another resolution (March 19, 1936) of the League Council. Subsequent German moves of re-

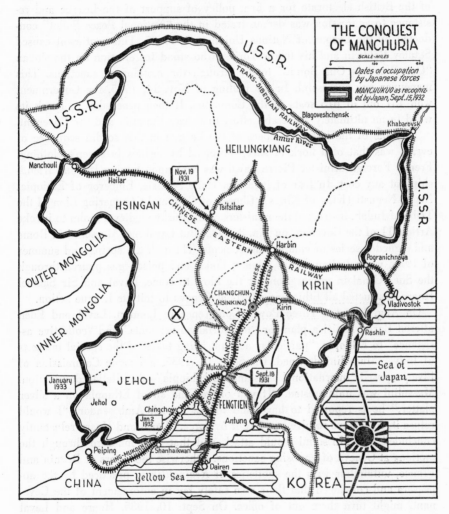

THE CONQUEST OF MANCHURIA

SCALE–MILES

Dates of occupation by Japanese forces

MANCHUKUO as recognized by Japan, Sept.15,1932

armament and aggression produced no echo at Geneva, since London and Paris preferred to act (or not to act) outside of the League.

Crisis. Fascist designs upon Ethiopia put the League Powers to their crucial test. Here as before they were found wanting, despite the imposition for the first time, and the last, of feeble sanctions against the aggressor. This gesture was hypocrisy, for the responsible leaders of France and Britain had agreed not to offer effective opposition to *il Duce's* ambitions. They assumed that

219

Italy could be won as an ally against the Reich by tacit support of Mussolini's African dream. They discovered too late that such tactics made Italy an ally of the Reich against the Western Powers—for the modern Caesars, like those of old, respect strength and despise weakness. The almost unanimous demand of the British electorate for a firm policy of support of the League and resistance to aggression was demonstrated in the "National Peace Ballot" conducted by the League of Nations Union in 1934–35. This sentiment caused Stanley Baldwin and his fellow Tories, who stood for election on the slogan "Our Word Is Our Bond!" to go through the motions of sanctions. This maneuver was successful. In the polling of Nov. 14, 1935, the Government won 431 out of 615 seats in the Commons. It then proceeded to break its word in an ultimately successful effort to betray Ethiopia and the Covenant.

The role of the lesser members of the League in this sordid sequence of events was that of a flock of sheep deceived by jackals in sheep's clothing. French Foreign Minister Pierre Laval was bent upon buying Italian "friendship" at any cost. In fear of invasion, Haile Selassie, Emperor of Ethiopia, Negus Negusti (King of Kings), Chosen of God, and Conquering Lion of the Tribe of Judah, instructed the ministers of his dusky medieval realm to invoke Article 11 of the Covenant on Jan. 3, 1935. But Laval met Mussolini in Rome and signed a series of complex agreements. Through the spring and summer of 1935, while Italian troops, planes, tanks, and poison gas poured through the Suez Canal in preparation for the blow to come, Laval and Sir Samuel Hoare obstructed all Ethiopian efforts at Geneva to initiate League action.

On Aug. 15, at a Three Power Conference in London, Laval and Eden offered Baron Aloisi a plan for "territorial adjustments" and "collective assistance" to Ethiopia, "particular account being taken of the special interests of Italy." Mussolini declined. On Sept. 18, 1935, a League Commission of Five proposed "international assistance to Ethiopia"—i.e., Italian domination. Mussolini was uninterested. "If you offered me all of Ethiopia on a silver platter," he is reported to have said to the French Ambassador, "I would refuse it, for I have resolved to take it by force." Laval and Hoare reluctantly concluded that Mussolini would attack and that they must go through the motions at Geneva of imposing sanctions. Otherwise the voters of Britain and France, unfamiliar with the subtleties of *Realpolitik* as practiced by the appeasers and convinced that their own safety lay in enforcement of the Covenant, might turn them out of office. On Sept. 10, 1935, Hoare and Laval secretly agreed at Geneva to rule out "military sanctions," "naval blockade," "closure of the Suez Canal—in a word everything that might lead to war." On the next day, Hoare declared publicly at Geneva that his Government stood "for the collective maintenance of the Covenant in its entirety, and particularly for steady and collective resistance [meaning "assistance"?] to all acts of unprovoked aggression." Laval asserted, "France is faithful to the Covenant." Both men privately assured Mussolini that he had nothing to fear.

EXPERIMENT IN GENEVA

On Oct. 1, 1935, Mussolini ordered the invasion of Ethiopia. M. Tecla Hawariati for Ethiopia asked for action under Article 16. The Council ruled on Oct. 7 "that the Italian Government has resorted to war in disregard of its covenants under Article 12 of the Covenant of the League of Nations." At the Assembly meeting of Oct. 9, all the members save Italy, Albania, Austria, and Hungary accepted the Council's conclusions and subsequently voted to apply sanctions.

The sanctions themselves were ineffective and indeed aided Mussolini to make an unpopular war popular by pretending that he was successfully defying the British Empire and the world. On Oct. 10, 51 Governments in the League Assembly confirmed the Council's verdict and established a "Committee of Fifty for Coordination of Measures under Article 16." Only Italy and her satellites, Austria and Hungary, voted in the negative, and only 4 other States—Switzerland, Chile, Uruguay, and Venezuela—attached reservations to their acceptance of sanctions. On Oct. 11 the Coordination Committee established a Committee of Eighteen, which drafted five proposals. The first contemplated lifting the earlier arms embargo against Ethiopia and its continued application against Italy. On Oct. 14 the Committee voted to ban all loans and bank credits to Italy. On Oct. 19 the three remaining proposals were adopted, forbidding all imports from Italy, banning the export to Italy of certain raw materials, and providing for mutual assistance among League members to minimize losses entailed by sanctions. The appeal for sanctions met with a surprisingly unanimous response from the League members, many of whom put the arms and loan embargo into effect at once. On Nov. 18, 1935, the "economic siege" of Italy got fully under way.

But on Dec. 8 it became known that Hoare and Laval had agreed to a "peace plan" whereby the aggressor was to be rewarded with control of two-thirds of Ethiopia. The British and French Foreign Ministers did not see fit to communicate their plan to the Council until Dec. 13, exactly a year after Ethiopia had first appealed for protection. Laval requested the Council to express no views until Rome and Addis Ababa had been heard from. The plan failed because of Italian indifference. A storm of British indignation unseated Hoare, but the Council on Dec. 19 thanked the British and French Governments for their suggestions and requested its Committee of Thirteen to examine the situation as a whole.

During January the Council evaded Ethiopian proposals that it undertake an impartial inquiry into Italian bombardments of Red Cross units and that it extend financial aid to Ethiopia. On Jan. 23 the Committee of Thirteen adopted a unanimous report, accepted by the Council, rejecting all inquiry or assistance. During April the Committee considered, discussed, postponed, delayed, and equivocated in a mood of "watchful waiting." On April 20 the Council met. After debate, it expressed regret that conciliation had failed, recalled that both belligerents were bound by the gas convention, and at length,

221

in desperation, addressed to Italy "a supreme appeal that . . . she should bring to the settlement of her dispute with Ethiopia that spirit which the League of Nations is entitled to expect from one of its original members."

Words availed nothing against bombing planes spraying poison from the clouds. Addis Ababa fell to the new barbarians come to save it from barbarism. Haile Selassie fled. From Jerusalem he wired the Secretary-General

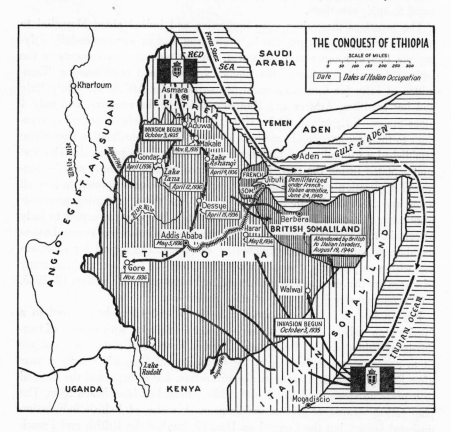

on May 10, 1936, that he had left his capital to "avoid the extermination of the Ethiopian people" and to devote himself to "the preservation of the age-old independence of Ethiopia and the principles of collective security and the sanctity of international obligations, all of which were threatened by Italy." He asked the League not to recognize the conquest and to make full application of Article 16. Among Haile Selassie's last words from Ethiopian territory before his flight was a prophetic utterance:

Do the peoples of the world not yet realize that by fighting on until the bitter end I am not only performing my sacred duty to my people but standing guard in the last citadel of collective security? Are they too blind to see that I have my responsibilities to the whole of humanity to face? I must still hold on until my tardy allies appear. If they never come, then I say prophetically and without bitterness, "The West will perish."

Death Agony. Britain now assumed leadership in destroying the League. On June 5, 1936, as Eden welcomed Haile Selassie to his lonely exile in England, Sir Samuel Hoare reentered the British Cabinet as First Lord of the Admiralty. On June 10 Neville Chamberlain told the Nineteen Hundred Club, "There is no use for us to shut our eyes to realities. . . . If we have retained any vestige of common sense, surely we must admit that we have tried to impose on the League a task which it was beyond its powers to fulfill. . . . Is it not apparent that the policy of sanctions involves a risk of war?" Italy had lost half its gold reserves. Italian imports had been reduced from $14,-650,000 in February, 1935, to $8,239,000 in February, 1936, and exports from $10,775,000 to $5,666,000. A continuation of sanctions might well have undermined the Fascist regime despite its Ethiopian victory. But precisely this was what the Anglo-French appeasers feared most. They now scrambled with indecent haste to betray the victim of banditry and to embrace the bandit.

The Assembly of June 30–July 4, 1936, abandoned Ethiopia to her fate. President Van Zeeland, Premier of Belgium, read a note from Rome: "The Ethiopian populations . . . welcome the Italian troops as champions of freedom, justice, civilization, and order. . . . Italy views the work she has undertaken as a sacred mission of civilization. . . . The Italian Government declares itself ready to give once more its willing and practical cooperation to the League. . . ." Eden had already announced British abandonment of sanctions on June 18. Haile Selassie spoke to an Assembly shamed into silence: "I am here today to claim that justice that is due to my people, and the assistance promised to it eight months ago by fifty-two nations who asserted that an act of aggression had been committed in violation of international treaties. . . . God and history will remember your decision. . . . What answer am I to take back to my people?"

The answer was desertion. Blum spoke of the beauties of peace, disarmament, and collective security. Eden spoke of the failure of sanctions and declared that the Covenant must be amended. Litvinov asserted that sanctions would have stopped aggression had they been vigorously enforced. M. Ter Waters of South Africa declared that the impending decision would "shatter for generations all international confidence and all hope of realizing world peace. . . . Order is losing to chaos: the spectacle of power has hypnotized the world." Ethiopia asked the Assembly to declare that it would recognize no annexation obtained by force and to recommend a loan of £10,000,000 to Ethiopia under conditions to be fixed by the Council. The latter proposal was rejected, 23 to 1, with 25 abstentions. As for the former, the Assembly virtually ignored it and closed its session of July 4 with the adoption of an ignominious resolution expressing "firm attachment to the principles of the

Covenant," soliciting proposals for the reform of the League, and recommending "that its coordination committee shall make all necessary proposals to the Governments in order to bring to an end the measures taken by them in execution of Article 16." Sanctions were abandoned. Ethiopia was abandoned. Collective security was abandoned.

Early in September Secretary-General Avenol went to Rome, like the Emperor Henry IV to Canossa, to beg Fascist forgiveness of the League and to arrange Italy's return to Geneva in exchange for the exclusion of Ethiopia. The last curtain fell in the spring of 1938. London proposed that the League Council, holding its one hundred and first meeting in Geneva, scrap the Stimson Doctrine and approve formal diplomatic recognition of Italian title to Ethiopia on the part of the League members as promised in the Ciano-Perth Accord of April 16, 1938—another tragic milestone along the appeasers' road toward disaster. Washington was silent.

"Nothing is gained and much may be lost by refusal to face facts. Great as is the League of Nations, the ends it exists to serve are greater than itself and the greatest of those ends is peace. . . ." So spoke Lord Halifax, May 12, 1938.

Haile Selassie, small and dark, a ruler of barbarians but every inch a king, replied in words which pronounced the doom of the League and of the Western Powers:

> The Ethiopian people, to whom all assistance was refused, are climbing alone their path to Calvary. No humiliation has been spared the victim of aggression. All resources and procedures have been tried with a view to excluding Ethiopia from the League as the aggressor demands. . . . Will law win as against force? Or force as against law? . . . Many Powers threatened with aggression and feeling their weakness have abandoned Ethiopia. They have uttered the cry of panic and rout: "Everyone for himself." . . . It is a certainty that they would be abandoned as Ethiopia has been, and between the two evils they have chosen one which the fear of aggression led them to consider the lesser. May God forgive them. . . . There are different ways to maintain peace. There is the maintenance of peace through right and there is peace at any price. . . . The League would be committing suicide if after having been created to maintain peace through right it were to abandon that principle and adopt instead the principle of peace at any price, even the price of immolation of a member state at the feet of its aggressor.

The Council chose suicide. Council President Wilhelm Munters of Latvia declared that each member should decide for itself whether to recognize Italian title to Ethiopia. Only four delegations objected: New Zealand, Bolivia, China, and the USSR. Britain and France recognized Italian title to Ethiopia in November. Nineteen months later, Mussolini reciprocated with a declaration of war.

Burial. The League never recovered. On Sept. 13, 1937, the Eighteenth Assembly had celebrated the opening of the magnificent new Assembly Hall. The League Palace cost $15,000,000. The new Council Chamber was decorated with murals by Sert, donated by the Spanish Republic, depicting the liberation of mankind from tyranny, intolerance, and injustice. Aga Khan supplied 2,500 bottles of champagne. But the celebration was a wake. Spain, torn by war and Fascist invasion which the League Powers condoned, failed of reelection to the Council. China, torn by new Japanese invasion which the League Powers condoned, invoked the Covenant. A parley of signatories of

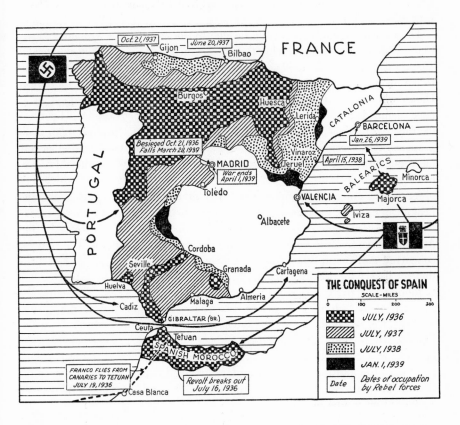

Oct. 21, 1937
Gijon
June 20, 1937
Bilbao
FRANCE
Burgos
Huesca
Lerida
CATALONIA
BARCELONA
Jan. 26, 1939
Besieged Oct. 21, 1936
Falls March 28, 1939
Vinaroz
Teruel
April 15, 1938
MADRID
War ends
April 1, 1939
BALEARICS
Minorca
Toledo
VALENCIA
Majorca
Albacete
Iviza
PORTUGAL
Cordoba
Seville
Granada
Cartagena
Huelva
Almeria
Cadiz
Malaga
GIBRALTAR (BR.)
Ceuta
Tetuan
SPANISH MOROCCO
FRANCO FLIES FROM
CANARIES TO TETUAN
JULY 19, 1936
Revolt breaks out
July 16, 1936
Casa Blanca

THE CONQUEST OF SPAIN
SCALE - MILES
0   100   200   300
JULY, 1936
JULY, 1937
JULY, 1938
JAN. 1, 1939
Date   Dates of occupation
by Rebel forces

the Nine Power Pact met in Brussels on Nov. 3 and adjourned on Nov. 24, 1937, without taking action. In Litvinov's words the conferees said to Japan, "Take your plunder and peace be with you," and to China, "Love your aggressor, resist not evil."

On May 14, 1938, Alvarez del Vayo pleaded with the Council to urge the end of the policy of "nonintervention," as the Assembly had threatened to do in its resolution of Oct. 4, 1937, if foreign troops were not withdrawn from Spain. Halifax and Bonnet voted against his plea. Only Litvinov voted for it. Spain was abandoned. China was abandoned. Austria was already abandoned. Wellington Koo pleaded for the application of Articles 16 and 17

225

against Japan and asked whether the League was "to be no more than an Egyptian mummy dressed up with all the luxuries and splendors of the living but devoid of life." On Sept. 28 the Council held that sanctions were inapplicable to Japan. On Sept. 29, as the Western Powers abandoned Czechoslovakia at Munich, the Assembly passed a resolution expressing hope for European peace. On Sept. 30, it voted to sever the Covenant from the tattered Treaty of Versailles while the Council resolved that sanctions against Japan were discretionary.

The ultimate immolation of the League by its makers was without dignity. Geneva's halls were silent during the crisis which led to war in the summer of 1939. But on Dec. 3, 1939, Joseph Avenol received a note from Finland to the members of the Council invoking Articles 11 and 15 against the Soviet Union whose armies had attacked the Finns four days before. Argentina at once demanded the expulsion of the USSR from the League. The most flagrant aggressions of Japan, Italy, and the Reich had produced no such proposal. But most of the members regarded Communist aggression as far more monstrous than Fascist aggression, despite the fact (or perhaps because of the fact) that up to 1939 the USSR was the only Great Power which had observed its obligations under the Covenant and had striven to make the League an effective instrument of collective security.

Moscow contemptuously declined to discuss the issue. On Dec. 14 the Assembly unanimously voted to approve the Argentine proposal. The Council concurred and found "in virtue of Article 16, paragraph 4 of the Covenant that by its act the USSR has placed itself outside of the League of Nations. It follows that the USSR is no longer a member of the League." Wellington Koo whistled: "China got nothing like that." Nor had any of the earlier victims of aggression. But what Finland got was a hollow gesture. No other sanctions were proposed. Unlike Ethiopia, Finland was granted tangible aid by some of the League members. The aid, however, as Lloyd George put it, was "too little and too late." Helsingfors accepted defeat and made peace on March 12, 1940. The Assembly and the Council were dead. Their futile words against Moscow were a swan song.

The final (Twenty-first) League Assembly, attended by 34 delegations, met in Geneva, April 8, 1946, amid the wreckage of a blasted world. When the Argentine delegation walked out indignantly because of failure to win one of the eight Vice-Presidencies, Sir Hartley Shawcross commented: "But this is a funeral, not a christening." President Carl Hambro reminisced: "We know that we were lacking in moral courage. . . . We know that we were reluctant to show responsibility for great decisions where greatness was needed, and we know we cannot escape history." He dedicated the "funeral" to the success of the United Nations. But a motion to give the USSR a share of the assets of the bankrupt concern was defeated. On April 19 the delegates approved a motion declaring that "with effect from this day, following the close of the present session of the Assembly, the League of Nations shall cease to exist except for the sole purpose of the liquidation of its affairs."

37 1/2 p.

3. UNITED NATIONS

Without an enduring understanding [among the Super-Powers] upon their fundamental purposes, interests and obligations to one another, all organizations to preserve peace are creations on paper and the path is wide open again for the rise of a new aggressor. . . . For these Powers to become divided in their aims, and fail to recognize and harmonize their basic interests, can produce only disaster, and no machinery, as such, can produce this essential harmony and unity.— CORDELL HULL, April 9, 1944.

In biological evolution, species which fail to adapt themselves to environmental change become extinct. In the evolution of the civilizations of *Homo sapiens,* societies which cling to old ways in the face of new challenges experience failure, frustration, and ultimate demise. The peoples and politicians of the Western State System in 1945–46 revived the League of Nations under a new name and resumed the ancient game of power politics under the spell of new symbols, despite the experiences of 1919–39. Those experiences demonstrated that world peace cannot be kept by leagues of sovereignties unless their major members are united in the pursuit of common purposes relevant to the welfare and survival of mankind.

The United Nations Organization is the League in a new guise, despite the several respects in which it differs from its predecessor. The UN was established during, rather than after, a world war. Its Charter, unlike the Covenant, was not devised at a peace conference nor incorporated in peace treaties. Its initial principle, the "sovereign equality of all peace-loving States," was modified to require unanimity of the Great Powers in the Security Council. Its structure was the work, not of any new Woodrow Wilson, but of the American, British, Soviet, and Chinese delegations at Dumbarton Oaks, Aug. 21–Oct. 7, 1944. Its wordy "Constitution" comprised 111 articles as against the 26 articles of the Covenant. The preamble—"We the peoples of the United Nations"—is misleading, since those who drafted it spoke for governments, not peoples, and established not a federation of peoples but a league of States. Fulfillment of the hopes of its founders required continuing cooperation among Great Powers. With the advent of "Cold War," these hopes faded. The genesis and nature of the new league must nevertheless be sketched out, if only to illustrate anew the dilemma in which contemporary mankind is caught.

Deus ex Machina. The Covenant was the work of 19 men who met 15 times in the early months of 1919. The Charter [3] was the work of 50 delegations, toiling mightily in San Francisco, April 25–June 26, 1945, on the invitation of the USA, U.K., USSR, and China. There were present in all 282 delegates, 1,444 assistants, 1,058 members of the International Secretariat, 2,636 jour-

[3] See Appendix for full text.

nalists and radiomen, 2,252 Army and Navy aides, 800 Boy Scouts, 400 Red Cross workers, 188 telephone and telegraph operators, etc. The average output of documents per day was 500,000 pages. On one day 1,700,000 pages were distributed.[4] If the verdict of time on these prodigious labors was already becoming unfavorable a few years after the event, this is not to be attributed to lack of good will, intelligence, or even statesmanship on the part of the founders. Politicians and diplomats by the nature of their functions cannot transcend to any significant degree the cultural context in which they must operate. This privilege is reserved for poets, philosophers, and prophets—who, for the most "realistic" of reasons, are never entrusted with any such task as that of rescuing decadent civilizations from disintegration or saving the human race from suicide. Had the San Francisco Conference known that the atomic age was about to dawn in splendor and terror within three weeks after its adjournment, its members might have come to different conclusions. But such speculation is idle. The past is irreversible. Man's fate, moreover, is to cling always to old solutions in the face of new problems. Like Wilson, Metternich, Kant, Rousseau, Penn, and all their precursors, those who met at the Golden Gate built their hopes for peace on a league of sovereignties.

On Jan. 10, 1946, in the blue-and-gold auditorium of Central Hall, Westminster, the General Assembly of UN met for the first time. The date was the twenty-sixth anniversary of the birth of the League. Dr. Eduardo Zuleta Angel of Colombia, temporary Chairman and President of the Preparatory Commission, gave the opening address. Prime Minister Attlee delivered a speech of welcome and of hope. The first item of business was the election of a permanent President. In the balloting Paul Henri Spaak, Foreign Minister of Belgium, won, 28 to 23, over Trygve Lie, Foreign Minister of Norway. The Assembly next chose six Committees of 51 members each—Political and Security; Economic and Financial; Social, Humanitarian, and Cultural; Trusteeship; Administrative and Budgetary; and Legal—along with a General (or steering) Committee, comprising the chairmen of the six Committees and the seven Vice-Presidents of the Assembly. The delegates next elected the 18 members of the Economic and Social Council: the USA, Colombia, Greece, Ukraine, Jugoslavia, and Lebanon for one year; the U.K., USSR, Cuba, Czechoslovakia, Norway, and India for two years; and France, China, Canada, Chile, Peru, and Belgium for three years.

The Assembly on Jan. 12 designated the six nonpermanent members of the Security Council: Egypt, Mexico, and the Netherlands for one year and Australia, Brazil, and Poland for two years. On Jan. 17, 1946, the Council

[4] See Clyde Eagleton, "The Charter Adopted at San Francisco," *American Political Science Review*, October, 1945; William T. R. Fox, "The Super-Powers at San Francisco," *Review of Politics*, January, 1946; *Documents of the U.N. Conference on International Organization* (15 vols.), (U.N. Information Office, 1946) ; and, for a mere sketch of 992 pages, "The U.N. Conference on International Organization: Selected Documents," *Department of State Publication* 2490, *Conference Series* 83, 1946.

met for the first time and elected Norman J. O. Makin of Australia as its first President, the other members to assume the office by rotation, month by month, in alphabetical order of States. After voting to bar Franco Spain from membership, appointing Trygve Lie (on the recommendation of the Security Council) as Secretary-General for a five-year term, and deciding to establish permanent headquarters in or near New York City, the Assembly adjourned the 1st part of its first session on Feb. 15. The Council followed suit on Feb. 16, agreeing to reconvene in New York and to act, henceforth, as a continuous body. The enterprise thus launched, amid London's winter fogs, was already touched by a malady which boded ill for its future. But hopes were high. If men and statesmen everywhere had made the success of the endeavor the first object of their efforts, hope could have become reality.

The Machinery of Salvation. The vast and sprawling apparatus of UN, when reduced to a neat chart, inspires awe, confusion, and an almost inescapable conviction among the unwary that an effective government of the world community has been brought into being. Since the conviction is false, the chart is here omitted. A brief description of the machine is, nonetheless, in order. The mechanism is elaborate, ingenious, and impressive. Through its cumbersome procedures thousands of earnest and forward-looking men and women, within the UN and in all the member governments, are striving mightily to meet the real needs of millions of human beings and to give substance to their aspirations for a life free from fear and want.

The original members of UN were the 51 States at San Francisco which signed and ratified the Charter. Additional members are admitted (Art. 4)— provided that they are "peace-loving," accept the obligations of the Charter, and are deemed "able and willing" to carry them out—by a two-thirds vote of the General Assembly upon recommendation of the Security Council, which, in such matters, must act with the approval of all five permanent members. When the first eight applications were made in 1946, the USA urged admission of all "to accelerate universality of membership." But the USSR opposed en bloc admissions. When the USA and its supporters on the Council voted against the admission of Albania, Bulgaria, Hungary, and Rumania on grounds of misconduct and violations of treaty guarantees of human rights, and against Mongolia on the ground that it was not independent, the USSR "vetoed" Austria, Italy, Ireland, Portugal, Finland, Jordan, and Ceylon. When the USSR in 1951–52 approved en bloc admission of all applicants, the USA opposed it. But membership had increased to 60 by 1953 with the admission of Afghanistan, Iceland, Sweden (all Nov. 19, 1946), Siam (Dec. 16, 1946), Pakistan and Yemen (both Sept. 30, 1947), Burma (April 19, 1948), Israel (May 11, 1949), and Indonesia (Sept. 28, 1950). American refusal to admit the Soviet satellites led the USSR to cast its fifty-first veto in the Council against the admission of Libya (Sept. 16, 1952) and its fifty-second veto against the admission of Japan (Sept. 18, 1952).

The deadlock over membership was nonetheless finally broken. On Dec. 7, 1955, the Assembly voted 52 to 2 (Cuba and China opposed) to accept a Canadian-sponsored "package deal." But on Dec. 13 in the Security Council Chiang Kai-shek's envoy, Dr. T. S. Tsiang, who held China's seat because of U.S. refusal to see it transferred to Communist China, vetoed the admission of Outer Mongolia in the name of "morality," despite repeated appeals to Chiang from Eisenhower and Dulles to accept all of the proposed applicants. He further moved the admission of South Korea, and South Vietnam, which were not part of the "package deal." Arkady Sobolev for the USSR vetoed both and then vetoed all the other 13 non-Communist applicants, thus casting 15 vetoes in 20 minutes and bringing the total of Soviet vetoes to 74. While the State Department blasted Moscow ("the Soviet Union took the position that the will of the majority be damned . . ."), Sobolev proposed that all 18 applicants be admitted except Outer Mongolia and Japan. After a seventy-fifth Soviet veto of Lodge's proposal to restore Japan to the list, the Council voted the admission of 16 new members: Albania, Austria, Bulgaria, Cambodia, Ceylon, Finland, Hungary, Ireland, Italy, Jordan, Laos, Libya, Nepal, Portugal, Rumania, and Spain. The Assembly approved on Dec. 15, 1955.

Except for Outer Mongolia, Communist China, Switzerland (which refused to join), and the partitioned States of Germany, Korea, and Vietnam, the UN thus achieved virtual universality of membership. Morocco, Tunisia, and the Sudan were admitted Nov. 12, 1956, Japan Dec. 18, 1956, and Ghana March 8, 1957. Members at this juncture numbered 81 and comprised, save for the exceptions noted, all of the self-governing States of the world. Malaya became the eighty-second member on Sept. 17, 1957.

The Charter makes no provision for withdrawal, though such a right is implied in national sovereignty. Members deemed to have violated the Charter may be suspended or expelled by the Assembly on recommendation of the Council (Arts. 5, 6). All members must register their treaties and agreements with the Secretariat for publication and may not invoke any unregistered accord before any UN body (Art. 102).

Like the League, the UN can act only by, through, and on sovereign States. None of its organs is vested with any power of legislation over individuals or with any authority to levy taxes, regulate commerce, or maintain independent armed forces. Like every league or confederation, the UN is dependent for revenues on contributions by members or on philanthropy. Revenues from the UN Postal Administration bring in less than 1% of the budget. With the aid of property gifts valued at $8,500,000 and $2,000,000, respectively, from John D. Rockefeller, Jr., and New York City and an interest-free loan of $65,000,000 from the USA, the UN moved in 1950 from its original headquarters in the reconverted plant of the Sperry Gyroscope Company (later re-reconverted to war production) at Lake Success and Flushing Meadow, Long Island, to the site on the Manhattan side of the East River between 42d and 48th Streets where the 39-story Secretariat Building is flanked by a Conference Building and a General Assembly Hall. The regular budget, as voted and apportioned by the Assembly, rose from $19,390,000 for 1946 to $50,-815,700 for 1957, with the USA contributing 39% of the total, Britain 11.3%, the USSR 7%, China and France 6% each, India 3.4%, etc., down to 1% or less for Bolivia, Costa Rica, Czechoslovakia, Liberia, Luxembourg, and 15 others.

Two-thirds of the budget is devoted to maintenance of the SECRETARIAT, a body of 3,000 international civil servants, of whom two-thirds are U.S. citizens, although more than 60 States have nationals on the staff. The oath of office requires all appointees to exercise their duties "in all loyalty, discretion and conscience" and regulate their conduct "with the interests of the UN only in view, and not to seek or accept instructions in regard to the performance of duties from any government or other authority external to the organization." Salaries range from $1,580 to $11,000 plus reimbursement for payments of national income taxes. The Secretariat is organized into eight Departments—Security Council Affairs, Economic Affairs, Social Affairs, Trusteeship and Information from Non-self-governing Territories, Legal, Conferences and General Services, Administrative and Financial Services, and Public Information—each headed by an Assistant Secretary-General. The Secretary-General receives $20,000, an allowance of like amount, and a furnished residence. The vigorous Trygve Lie contrasted sharply with the two colorless Secretaries-General of the League. He was originally appointed (by majority vote of the Assembly on recommendation of the Council) for a five-year term, which was extended for three years beyond Feb. 1, 1951, by the Assembly in the autumn of 1950 with the Soviet bloc voting in the negative and China (i.e., Formosa) and the Arab States abstaining. On Nov. 10, 1952, Trygve Lie, weary of Soviet enmity and American insistence on "loyalty checks" of UN employees of U.S. nationality, announced his resignation. Dag Hammarskjold of Sweden became his successor on April 10, 1953.

The "policy-making" agencies cannot properly be thought of in terms of legislative and executive organs. These functions, accurately defined, are here nonexistent. Yet the Charter provides elaborately for institutions through which States, if they choose, can settle controversies and undertake joint enterprises. So complex, indeed, is the structure that nothing short of a thick volume could trace out its intricacies. But the broad pattern may be sketched.

The SECURITY COUNCIL, entrusted with "primary responsibility for the maintenance of international peace and security," consists of the USA, U.K., USSR, France, and China as permanent members, plus six nonpermanent members elected for two-year terms by a two-thirds vote of the Assembly.[5]

[5] The First Assembly elected Egypt, Mexico, and the Netherlands for one year and Australia, Brazil, and Poland for two years. In subsequent elections the USSR accused the USA of violating an early "gentleman's agreement" whereby one nonpermanent seat

The Council meets at least once every two weeks. It deals with disputes or situations likely to endanger peace and recommends appropriate methods and/or substance of a settlement. In case of a breach of the peace (Arts. 39 to 54), the Council may call upon member States to sever diplomatic and economic relations with the offender or may resort to demonstrations, blockades, or military operations conducted by contingents supplied by member States and directed by the UN Military Staff Committee—all subject, however, to special agreements (none of which had been concluded by the spring of 1958) and further qualified (Art. 51) by "the inherent right of individual or collective self-defense if an armed attack occurs."

The framers of the Charter thus accepted the theory of "collective security," according to which peace can be kept through the cooperative coercion of peacebreaking States by peace-loving States. But cognizance was taken, as was not the case in the Covenant, of the fact that any collective coercion of a Great Power means not peace but world war. The Charter, therefore, stipulated the unanimity of the Great Powers. The delegates at Dumbarton Oaks were unable to reach agreement on voting procedure. At Yalta a formula was devised and subsequently interpreted at San Francisco, in a Four Power Statement of June 7, 1945, to mean that any permanent member not only could "veto" any proposal to use collective coercion but could veto proposals to investigate or make recommendations (which might initiate a "chain of events" leading to enforcement action) and could even veto a decision as to whether any given question was "substantive" or "procedural" (see Art. 27 of the Charter). This distinction, along with the distinction between "situations" and "disputes," gave rise to endless wrangling and mountains of controversy.

Yet the intent of the framers is clear, however much it may have been distorted or abused. All five permanent members of the Council must agree to coercive measures and to any lesser action which might lead toward such measures. Obviously none of the five would agree to its own coercion by the others. Each may block coercion of a lesser Power if it chooses and may veto inquiries and proposals likely to lead to such a result. Many small States and numerous private critics argued that all this is outrageous, since it means that the Great Powers are "above the law." But, as the framers clearly perceived, the fact is inescapable that any coercion of a Great Power, or of a

---

was always to go to an Eastern European State. In 1955, after 35 ballots had failed to break a deadlock between the Philippines and Jugoslavia, it was agreed that the latter should serve one year and then resign, with the Philippines to be elected for 1957. In December, 1956, the USSR nominated Czechoslovakia for the Jugoslav seat, but the Philippines was elected, 51 to 20. As of 1957 the nonpermanent members consisted of Australia, Cuba, and Philippines (until 1958) and Colombia, Iraq, and Sweden (until 1959). As of 1958 the nonpermanent members consisted of Colombia, Iraq, and Sweden (until 1959) and Japan, Panama, and Canada (until 1960).

small State supported by a Great Power, is a prescription not for law, order, or peace but for wholesale violence. Of this, however, more anon.[6]

The GENERAL ASSEMBLY, often called the "town meeting of the world," functions on the basis of one vote for each member State, important questions requiring a two-thirds vote for action. While the Charter, the delegates, and the press all speak of "decisions" of the Assembly, this term does not mean in law or in fact that the Assembly, by two-thirds vote or any vote, can order any sovereign State to take action it is unwilling to take or refrain from any action it is determined to take. Aside from its budgetary, administrative, and electoral functions, the Assembly merely makes "recommendations" to its members or to other UN organs. It is expressly barred (Art. 12) from making recommendations regarding disputes or situations before the Security Council unless the Council so requests. The Assembly is no more a legislative body than any other conference of diplomats. Its delegates talk, listen, report, study, consider, propose, deliberate, debate, vote, etc. What they do not, and in the nature of the case cannot, do is to make rules of law binding on individuals. Neither can they make rules binding on any government which declines to approve.

The ECONOMIC AND SOCIAL COUNCIL is provided for in Articles 61 to 72 (q.v.) of the Charter. This body of 18 States is also limited to giving advice and making studies and recommendations—a fact which is not altered by the complexity of its organization and by the multiplicity of the specialized agencies with which it consults. The ECOSOC has Commissions on Human Rights (with Subcommissions on Freedom of Information and the Press, Pro-

---

[6] Adlai E. Stevenson on America's Town Meeting of the Air, Nov. 14, 1946, in debate with Norman J. O. Makin over "abolition of the veto," observed: "The veto itself is not the basic course of our difficulties. It is only a reflection of the unfortunate and deep-seated differences with the Russians. If we are to escape from the atmosphere of crisis that surrounds our international relations, we must settle these differences. Merely changing the voting formula will never be enough. . . . The unanimity rule grew out of facts of international political life. . . . If the Big Five disagree on a matter involving their vital interests, the application of force against any of them . . . will produce a major war. That is the very thing the UN was created to prevent. . . . The unanimity rule is the price we have to pay for any effective organization. But the existence of the rule does not put any member of the UN, large or small, above the law, as some people say. All the members are bound equally by the provisions of the Charter. . . . We condemn the attempt to use the veto to circumvent the provisions of the Charter, but to argue from this premise that the rule should therefore be abolished would be, as the French say, 'to throw out the baby with the bath.' "

In view of popular confusion, it should be noted that a "veto" is not simply a negative vote on a motion in the Security Council, but is a "No" vote cast by a permanent member on a motion approved by seven or more other members of the Council. The extraordinary number of Soviet vetoes over the years was attributable not only to Soviet obstructionism but also to the practice of the USA in bringing to a vote numerous proposals unacceptable to the USSR but likely to command a majority of the other delegates. Had the roles been reversed (an obvious impossibility, given the pattern of world power in the 1940's and 1950's), it is likely that the USA would also have cast as many vetoes, if not withdrawn from the UN altogether.

tection of Minorities, and Prevention of Discrimination), Status of Women, Social Questions, Economics and Employment (with Subcommissions on Devastated Areas, Employment, Balance of Payments, Economic Development, etc.), Transport and Communication, Statistics, Narcotic Drugs, etc. The "specialized agencies" include the Educational, Scientific, and Cultural Organization (UNESCO), the Food and Agriculture Organization (FAO), the International Bank for Reconstruction and Development, the International Monetary Fund, the International Civil Aviation Organization (ICAO), the International Labor Organization (ILO), the World Health Organization (WHO), the International Refugee Organization (IRO), abolished in 1951, the Universal Postal Union, and a steadily growing list of similar functional entities far too numerous to be listed.

Mysteries of Thermodynamics. This fantastically elaborate apparatus of international cooperation would have proved puzzling to any sophisticated interplanetary traveler who might have alighted on the UN's skyscraper in the 1950's. He would see many thousands of people busily at work on a great variety of problems. All their tasks, he might perceive, had a common denominator—*i.e.*, a demonstrable relationship to noble purposes: to "save succeeding generations from the scourge of war," "reaffirm faith in fundamental human rights," and promote "justice," "respect for law," "social progress," "better standards of life in larger freedom," "tolerance," "security," and the capacity of men to "live together in peace with one another as good neighbors."

Our mythical man from Mars would doubtless conclude that these objectives are altogether admirable, sensible, and indeed necessary to the collective welfare and even to the survival of *Homo sapiens*. As he watched the men and women of UN working like eager beavers at their manifold tasks, he would get the impression of many wheels and of wheels within wheels, all revolving swiftly amid a maze of motors, pistons, valves, and belts. He would at first conclude that the work in hand was going wonderfully well, that the whole huge locomotive was functioning smoothly, and that the mileage to be traversed would be covered in no time at all.

Then suddenly, to his astonishment, our visitor would see that nothing of the kind was taking place. Amid all the hum and whir and clatter, interspersed with the hiss of steam, the clang of bells, and the blast of whistles, the great machine was standing quite still. Inner wheels appeared unconnected with outer wheels. Some driving wheels were revolving, but these were off the ground. Those on the ground were mired in mud. The tracks originally laid had since been torn up. The entire engine, indeed, was tilting at a crazy angle and seemed likely to slip into the river. The various engineers, firemen, and brakemen, moreover, seemed to be chasing one another madly over the locomotive, shouting imprecations and brandishing monkey wrenches, hot pokers, and sticks of dynamite over each other's heads. The stalled passengers gathered in rival groups to cheer or boo the contestants and seemed rather more than likely to fall into open brawling among themselves, with no further thought of the journey or of their original destination. . . .

How is so great a failure of so inspiring an enterprise in so brief a time to be explained? Two answers suggest themselves: The engine is of faulty construction. The engineers lack will and skill to run it. Both are true. Like the League, the UN rests upon the premise that peace can be kept through the armed coercion of sovereignties by sovereignties. That this premise is demonstrably false will be argued below. But the UN also rests upon the principle of concord and unanimity among Great Powers. So long as that concord was a reality, as at Teheran, Yalta, San Francisco, and Potsdam, it was possible to suppose that the UN, for all its defects, could yet be made to work. But as soon as the giants had fallen out among themselves, the United Nations could no longer function to fulfill the purposes stated in the Charter.

The Great Schism. With the wisdom of hindsight, it is now clear that Washington and Moscow, having decided to wage political war against one another, would each have better served its own cause and the world's hopes had it refrained from carrying the quarrel into the Security Council and General Assembly. The issues at stake had not arisen in UN and plainly could not be settled there. Their settlement depended on willingness by both sides to compromise differences in direct negotiation. Their discord could never be dispelled through UN but might well wreck UN if injected into its counsels. Prudence and foresight would have dictated that the contending colossi should contend outside UN and leave the new organization to develop as best it could in the promotion of such nonpolitical purposes as are common to all men.[7]

---

[7] In *The Cold War* (New York, Harper, 1947), pp. 58–59, Walter Lippmann wrote in the autumn of 1947: "The United Nations cannot deal with disputes that involve the balance of power in the world. The balance of power has to be redressed and settled in the peace treaties by the Great Powers themselves. . . . Until such a settlement is reached, the United Nations has to be protected by its supporters from the strains, the burdens, the discredit, of having to deal with issues that it is not designed to deal with. . . . No good and nothing but harm can come of using the Security Council and the Assembly as an arena of the great dispute, or of acting as if we did not realize the inherent limitations of the Charter and thought that somehow we could by main force and awkwardness use the United Nations Organization to overawe and compel the Russians. All that can come of that is to discredit the United Nations on issues it cannot settle and thus to foreclose the future of the UN, which can begin only if and when these issues have been settled. Judging by the speeches in the Greek affair of the British and the American delegates, Sir Alexander Cadogan and Mr. Herschel Johnson appear to be acting on instructions which treat the UN as expendable in our conflict with Russia. It is a great pity. Nothing is being accomplished to win the conflict, to assuage it, or to settle it. But the UN, which should be preserved as the last best hope of mankind that the conflict can be settled and a peace achieved, is being chewed up. . . . It is implicit in the policy [of the State Department] that the UN has no future as a universal society, and that either the UN will be cast aside like the League of Nations, or it will be transformed into an anti-Soviet coalition. In either event the UN will have been destroyed."

But the temptation on both sides to use UN as an arena and to employ its tangled technicalities as weapons was too strong to be resisted. A brief survey of early disputes brought before the Security Council and General Assembly will serve to suggest how the UN functions in the sphere of world politics and what it became under the pressures of Cold War.

The leitmotiv of the drama appeared *fortissimo* in Scene 1 of Act I. On Jan. 19, 1946, two days after the Security Council first met, Iran accused the USSR of interference in its internal affairs. On March 19 Teheran charged Moscow with maintaining troops in northern Iran beyond March 2 (the date previously agreed upon for withdrawal), invoked Article 35 of the Charter, and asked for "an immediate and just solution of this dispute by the Security Council." Soviet troops had in fact protected a rebel regime in Iranian Azerbaijan and apparently proposed to stay until Teheran should grant Soviet oil concessions in the north to match the Anglo-American concessions in the south. The issue was clearly one between Washington, London, and Moscow, though Byrnes, Bevin, and Molotov had failed to settle it in Moscow in December, 1945. The Kremlin assumed, correctly, that the Iranian accusation was British-inspired. Gromyko and Manuilsky retaliated by complaining to the Council that British troops in Greece and Indonesia were a threat to peace. By early February, Vishinsky and Bevin, supported by Stettinius, were exchanging insults.

The design of things to come was here sharply etched. When the Council met at Hunter College on March 25, 1946, Gromyko's request that the dispute be not placed on the agenda was overruled, 8 to 3. On March 27, he walked out. In the sequel all Soviet troops were evacuated (May 6) after Premier Ghavam had agreed on March 24 to submit to Parliament within seven months a project of a joint Soviet-Iranian company to explore and develop oil resources in northern Iran. (The Premier did not submit the project until October, 1947, when Parliament, with open U.S. encouragement, rejected it.) All through the spring and thereafter, repeated Soviet efforts to remove the item from the agenda, supported at length by Iran itself and by a legal opinion submitted by Trygve Lie, were staunchly resisted by Stettinius and Cadogan.

Thereafter, on more and more issues, the U.S. and U.K. representatives on the Council pushed to a vote proposals which they knew the Soviet delegate would not accept. In each instance the vote went against the USSR, usually 8 to 3 or 9 to 2. And in many cases Gromyko exercised his veto power to prevent action unacceptable to his Government. Anglo-American spokesmen accused the USSR of abusing the veto, "defying the will of the majority" and "paralyzing" the Security Council. Having discovered that they could almost always rally China, France, and the lesser States into an anti-Soviet majority, the State Department and Downing Street pressed their advantage and won victory after victory, to the tune of widespread demands for amending the

Charter to "eliminate the veto" or even for expelling the USSR from the UN.

On Sept. 17, 1947, Marshall told the assembly that voting procedure in the Council should be modified, that a "Little Assembly" (Interim Committee on Peace and Security) should be set up as a continuous body to perform functions which the veto prevented the Council from performing. On Sept. 18, 1947, Andrei Vishinsky retaliated by a slashing indictment of "warmongers" and by submitting a resolution asking the UN to condemn "the criminal propaganda for a new war, carried on in reactionary circles in a number of countries and, in particular, in the USA, Turkey and Greece"; to ask all Governments to impose "criminal penalties" against war propaganda; and to implement swiftly the decisions of Jan. 24 and Dec. 14, 1946, on atomic weapons and reduction of armaments. Despite initial U.S. objections, the Assembly finally passed (unanimously) a diluted resolution (naming no names) in condemnation of warmongering. It also established a weakened version of a "Little Assembly." On Sept. 23, 1947, Trygve Lie vainly appealed for a return to the spirit of Yalta and San Francisco: "The very cornerstone of the UN, Big Power cooperation and understanding, is being shaken. . . . The peoples of the world, and many governments as well, are shocked, frightened and discouraged. . . . Fear breeds hate and hate breeds danger."

A decade later, after many dangers, hatreds, and fears had been traversed, the uses and limitations of the UN were clearer. Dag Hammarskjold, who succeeded Trygve Lie as Secretary-General and was unanimously reelected by the Assembly in 1957 to another five-year term, noted, however, in his annual report for 1957 that some critics of the UN were still unaware of its basic nature. Those who complained of a "double standard" in dealing with small States and Great Powers should remember, he cautioned, that the Assembly "did not have the legal power under the Charter to impose its will on member States by force, but could only recommend action. . . . That this reflected the essential character of the UN as an association of national States in which the sovereign rights of all its members are carefully safeguarded was not sufficiently clear to some critics."

What Price Peace? The puzzling paradox of the UN as an agency to promote peace stems chiefly from the fact that the new league was designed both as a vehicle of global negotiation to prevent, halt, or resolve conflicts between States and as an instrument of collective coercion of aggressors. Both functions presupposed a unanimous concert of Great Powers. The success of negotiations is sometimes facilitated by such devices as an expert secretariat, commissions of inquiry, mediators, and advisory opinions on legal questions. But success in conference is seldom promoted by including in the bargaining a multitude of remote or petty States who have no stake in, and no responsibility for, the outcome. Complete failure is almost invariably guaranteed by publicity.

In this latter respect both Council and Assembly, with microphones, press-men, and public present at every meeting, are the worst agencies imaginable for the conduct of diplomacy, so much so that no diplomacy is possible except behind the scenes. Eloquent oratory about "mobilizing world public opinion" merely reveals that these procedures preclude diplomacy and foster propaganda. Negotiation and coercion, moreover, are often antithetical—and both are impossible or ineffective when the concert of Powers breaks down in discord.

These contradictions and frustrations were in part revealed in the four instances prior to the Korean War in which the UN was summoned to cope with armed hostilities. In July, 1947, Australia and India asked the Council to halt the fighting between Dutch and Indonesians. A resolution of August 1 asked the parties to cease hostilities, have recourse to pacific settlement, and keep the Council informed. A Consular Commission in Batavia and a Com-mittee of Good Offices aided in the signing of a truce in January, 1948, but the Dutch in December resumed their "police action" by attacking the enemy and kidnaping their leaders. The Council issued another cease-fire order, called for the release of the captives, and instructed the Committee of Good Offices (now the UN Commission for Indonesia) to aid negotiations for independence (Jan. 28, 1949). The Netherlands finally yielded and made peace in November, but its decision was due less to UN action than to the hopelessness of trying to restore the old order.

At British request the Assembly in April, 1947, set up a Special Committee on Palestine (UNSCOP) and on Nov. 29 adopted its recommendations for a partition of the Holy Land into separate Jewish and Arab States. Such a "solution" was wholly unacceptable to both sides. Arabs opened hostilities against Jewish settlements. In March, 1948, the USA abandoned the parti-tion plan it had sponsored, insisted that the Council had no obligation to use force to carry out the will of the Assembly, and proposed another special Assembly session to consider a UN trusteeship. The Assembly met on April 16. It could agree on nothing since the Powers had no policy. On May 14, 1948, the day before the day when Britain had announced it would abandon the Mandate, the Zionists declared the independence of Israel. The Arab States promptly invaded Palestine and were promptly defeated, with the Security Council doing nothing except call for a truce and appoint Count Folke Bernadotte as Mediator. With British approval, he finally proposed a return to the partition plan, but with Israel to be reduced from 5,700 square miles to 2,100. On Sept. 17, 1948, he was assassinated by Jewish terrorists. His successor, Dr. Ralph J. Bunche, was successful in effecting a truce on all fronts by July, 1949, though no final boundaries were defined, nor were any peace treaties signed. The "peace" was less a triumph for the UN than a result of Israeli victory in war.

In January, 1948, India brought to the Security Council its conflict with

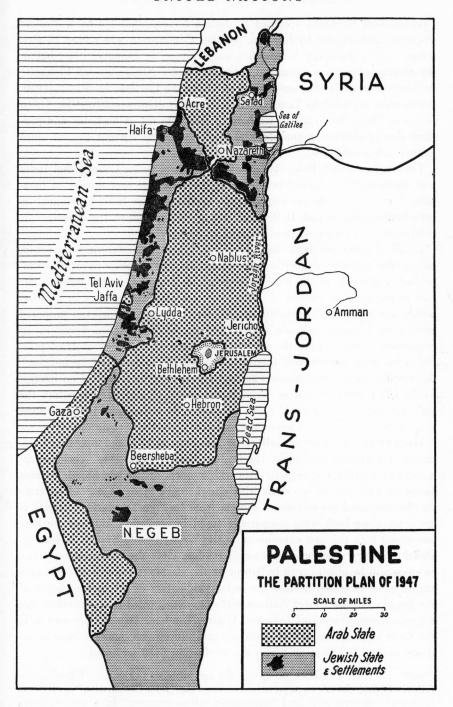

LEBANON

SYRIA

Acre

Safad

Sea of Galilee

Haifa

Nazareth

Mediterranean Sea

Nablus

Jordan River

TRANS-JORDAN

Tel Aviv
Jaffa

Lydda

Jericho

Amman

JERUSALEM

Bethlehem

Gaza

Hebron

Dead Sea

Beersheba

NEGEB

EGYPT

PALESTINE

THE PARTITION PLAN OF 1947

SCALE OF MILES

0   10   20   30

Arab State

Jewish State
& Settlements

Pakistan over Kashmir, occupied by Indian forces, inhabited by a Moslem majority, and claimed by Karachi. Another Commission was named to seek a truce and a plebiscite. A cease-fire was arranged in January, 1949, but in the absence of a truce agreement Admiral Chester Nimitz, named Plebiscite Administrator in March, was unable to undertake his task. In March, 1950, the Council replaced its Commission with a UN Representative—Sir Owen Dixon in 1950, Dr. Frank P. Graham in 1951—to act as mediator and promote demilitarization preparatory to a plebiscite, all without success since neither side would yield.

Finally, in August, 1948, Hyderabad complained to the Council that India was menacing its independence by economic blockade and threats of invasion. A month later, as the Council took up the dispute, India questioned its jurisdiction, denied that Hyderabad was a State, invaded the principality, conquered it in four days, and annexed it. Nobody acted.

In all of these instances the role of the UN as mediator or as a forum of negotiations was of questionable utility. Its role as peacemaker was tangential to the role of the armed forces which prevailed in the fighting. Its role as protector of victims of aggression was nonexistent, even in a moral sense. No "sanctions," economic or military, were applied or even proposed against the "aggressors," nor were any of the States initiating hostilities so condemned. Sovereignties do not risk blood and treasure for abstract principles but only for concrete interests, rationalized in terms of "principles." Aggressions by non-Communists against non-Communists were of no interest to the UN Powers of East or West. In the global rivalry of mid-century the only aggressions which could move the Powers to action were those affecting the balance between the Communist and anti-Communist coalition.

Korea: The Testing of Collective Security. In 1950 and thereafter Communist aggression, resisted by the leading Power of the Free World, swept a faraway peninsula of Eastern Asia with a storm of fire and blood. Various facets of this episode are dealt with elsewhere in these pages. To separate its "international organization" aspects from its "power politics" aspects is artificial, since both were inseparably fused in confusion. But we are here concerned with the first experiment in the Western State System in international "military sanctions" against aggression. Only the chroniclers of days to come will be able to pass judgment on the clashing opinions of contemporaries, some of whom deemed the test a vindication of the highest hopes of the founders of the United Nations while others regarded it as a travesty and a tragic demonstration of folly and failure. The bare facts of UN action, in the form of a chronology of decisions and indecisions, may at least be set down as the basic data on which any evaluation must be based.

SEPT. 17, 1947. The USA refers the Korean problem to the UN, following the failure of Soviet-American negotiations through the "Joint Commission" to establish "national independence" and "democratic self-government" in a united Korea

240

via a Four-Power Trusteeship (see p. 196 above). (This situation is illustrative of two persistent patterns of politics in the era of Cold War: (1) the complete inability or refusal of Soviet policy-makers to define "democracy" or "independence" in any disputed or occupied area in any fashion acceptable to the USA; (2) the disposition of American policy-makers to appeal to the UN in every unresolved controversy with the USSR on the assumption that the mobilization of the pro-American majority would either cause Moscow to yield or at least give Washington a moral victory.) Marshall and Vishinsky exchange accusations at the second General Assembly. Moscow proposes that all occupation troops withdraw and that Korean representatives participate in UN discussions.

NOV. 14, 1947. Assembly adopts, 46 to 0 with 4 abstentions, a U.S. resolution calling for all-Korean elections, under observation of a UN Temporary Commission on Korea (UNTCOK), of a national assembly to establish a security force, dissolve all other military formations, take over administration North and South, and arrange for withdrawal of all occupation forces. UNTCOK, unable to schedule elections because of refusal of Soviet commanders and North Korean authorities to allow it north of 38 degrees, asks further directives from "Little Assembly" which tells it to proceed in South Korea.

MAY 10, 1948. Elections in South with Leftists boycotting balloting, 134 parties participating, and 170 of 200 deputies elected representing Rightist parties supporting Syngman Rhee and Kim Koo, favored by landowners, police force, and USA. UNTCOK declares result "a valid expression of the free will of the electorate." Deputies draft constitution, promulgated July 17, 1948. Syngman Rhee elected President. USSR recognizes North Korean regime of Kim Il-sung in October. U.S. recognizes Rhee regime January 1, 1949.

SEPT. 18, 1948. USSR informs UN it will withdraw troops by end of year and hopes USA will do same. Soviet troops leave by December, except for a military training mission. U.S. troops leave by July, 1949, except for a military training mission.

DEC. 12, 1948. UN General Assembly, 48 to 6, declares that Rhee regime is the "only lawful government" in Korea, and establishes a new UN Commission on Korea (UNCOK) to lend good offices to bring about union of North and South. USSR and North Korea boycott UNCOK. Both Korean Governments apply for admission to UN. Application of North Korea not considered. Application of South Korea (Republic of Korea or ROK) vetoed by USSR in Security Council, April 8, 1949.

OCT. 21, 1949. UN Assembly, 48 to 6 with 3 abstentions, votes to extend life of UNCOK and charges it to observe and report developments "which might lead to or otherwise involve military conflict." Border raids increase. Murder is normal Korean method of political action. Kim Koo assassinated June 26, 1949. (Lyuh Woong Hyung, head of the provisional "Peoples' Republic" of 1945 in Seoul, opposed by USA, had been assassinated July 19, 1947.) Frontier clashes during summer and fall.

MAY 30, 1950. Elections in South for new national assembly. Syngman Rhee and Rightists overwhelmingly defeated. North Korea proposes nationwide elections on August 5 with Rhee, Premier Lee Bum Suk, et al. barred from participation and UNCOK barred from supervision. Radio Pyongyang broadcasts appeal for unification.

JUNE 10, 1950. UNCOK sends a representative across 38° to receive text of plea for peace and unification. June 11, three North Korean representatives cross 38° with copies of plea and are arrested by ROK police. Rhee regime repeatedly threatens to unify Korea by force and is denied heavy weapons by USA lest it carry out the threat.

By summer solstice of 1950, then, there were two "governments" in Korea, one supported by the USSR and the other by the USA, which had induced the UN to sponsor ROK as the "only lawful government." Both claimed sovereignty over the whole country and threatened to achieve unity by violence. Under these circumstances the danger of civil war, and of possible international war, could be averted only by Soviet-American negotiations—which, however, were deadlocked. The impasse was obviously incapable of resolution through any recourse to the UN, since the UN had already irrevocably taken sides in the controversy.

JUNE 25, 1950. North Korean forces invade South Korea, with Kim Il-sung alleging that South Korea has invaded North Korea after rejecting all proposals for peaceful unification. USA calls meeting of UN Security Council same day. UNCOK reports South Korea is victim of "a calculated coordinated attack prepared and launched with secrecy." USA proposes resolution holding attack is "a breach of the peace," calling for "immediate cessation of hostilities" and withdrawal of invaders to 38° and summoning all members "to render every assistance to the UN in the execution of this resolution and to refrain from giving assistance to the North Korean authorities." Jugoslavia abstains. USSR is absent, having boycotted Council since January for its refusal to replace representatives of Chiang Kai-shek by representatives of Red China. Other members vote approval. (For other phases of U.S. decisions, see p. 596 below.)

JUNE 27, 1950. UN Security Council adopts, 7 to 1, U.S. resolution recommending that members furnish ROK "such assistance as may be necessary to repel the armed attack and to restore international peace and security in the area." India and Egypt abstain. Jugoslavia opposed. USSR absent. India "accepts" resolution on June 30.

JULY 7, 1950. Council adopts, 7–0, Anglo-French resolution that military assistance by members be "made available to a unified command under the USA," with a commander to be designated by USA, "to use UN flag at its discretion," and keep Council informed. USSR absent. India, Egypt, Jugoslavia abstain. USSR and allies contend war is result of U.S.-supported ROK aggression, accuse USA of aggression against China and other Asiatic States, and hold UN action illegal because of absence of Soviet and (Red) Chinese representatives. USA and allies refute argument.[8] USSR (Jacob Malik) returns to Council in August and, as President, obstructs further action but fails to secure expulsion of Formosa representative and seating of representatives from Peiping and Pyongyang.

SEPT. 6, 1950. Council resolution condemning North Korea for continued defiance is vetoed by USSR.

SEPT. 11, 1950. USSR proposes Council resolution inviting Red China to send delegate to present complaints against alleged U.S. aerial attacks on Manchuria. Supported by USSR, Britain, France, Norway, Jugoslavia, and India (1 less than a

---

[8] On Nov. 14, 1946, on America's Town Meeting of the Air, Norman J. O. Makin asserted that "if it is a major Power which abstains from voting, it does constitute the equivalent of a veto." But later practice, concurred in by the USSR, established that absence or abstention is not a "veto," as the USA and its supporters cogently argued in 1950.

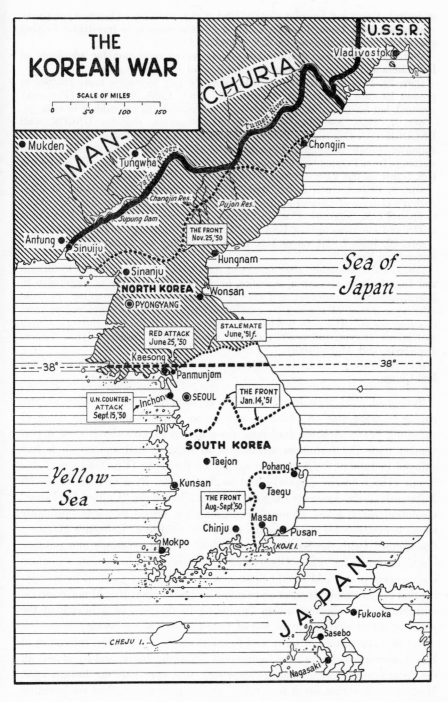

THE
KOREAN WAR

SCALE OF MILES

0   50   100   150

U.S.S.R.

MAN-CHURIA

Vladivostok

Mukden

Tungwha

Yalu River

Tumen River

Chongjin

Changjin Res.

Pujon Res.

Supung Dam

THE FRONT
Nov. 25, '50

Antung

Sinuiju

Hungnam

Sea of
Japan

Sinanju

NORTH KOREA

Wonsan

PYONGYANG

RED ATTACK
June 25, '50

STALEMATE
June, '51 f.

Kaesong

38°

Panmunjom

38°

U.N. COUNTER-
ATTACK
Sept. 15, '50

Inchon

SEOUL

THE FRONT
Jan. 14, '51

SOUTH KOREA

Yellow
Sea

Taejon

Pohang

Kunsan

Taegu

THE FRONT
Aug.-Sept. '50

Chinju

Masan

Mokpo

Pusan

KOJE I.

JAPAN

Fukuoka

CHEJU I.

Sasebo

Nagasaki

majority). Egypt and Ecuador abstain. USA, Cuba, and China (Formosa) opposed.

SEPT. 12, 1950. Council resolution for a UN Commission to investigate Peiping charges of border violations by U.S. vetoed by USSR.

SEPT. 19, 1950. General Assembly rejects Indian resolution for admission of Red China and Soviet resolution for expulsion of Formosa regime.

SEPT. 28, 1950. Council votes 7–3 to invite Peiping to send a representative to present its case against U.S. "aggression." USA, Cuba, and China (Formosa) opposed, but Sir Gladwyn Jebb holds issue procedural and not subject to veto.

OCT. 7, 1950. Assembly, 47–5 with 8 abstentions, replaces UNCOK with UNCURK (UN Commission for the Unification and Rehabilitation of Korea) and authorizes counterinvasion and occupation of all of North Korea, despite repeated warnings from Peiping, confirmed by New Delhi, that Red China will not permit U.S. forces on the Yalu. Chinese military intervention follows.

NOV. 8, 1950. Council invites Red China to participate in discussion of Mac-Arthur's charges of Chinese aggression. Peiping refuses but sends Wu Hsiu-chuan to discuss U.S. "aggression" against China. He demands admission of Red China to UN and sanctions against USA for "aggression" in Korea and Formosa.

NOV. 30, 1950. USSR vetoes U.S. resolution calling for withdrawal of Chinese forces from Korea.

FEB. 1, 1951. Assembly, after failure of Arab-Asian efforts supported by Britain and Jugoslavia to arrange a cease-fire, holds Red China guilty of aggression in Korea, demands withdrawal, and asks "Collective Measures Committee" to "consider as a matter of urgency . . . additional measures to be employed to meet this aggression." The vote is 44–7 (the Soviet bloc, India, and Burma) with 9 abstentions (Egypt, Indonesia, Pakistan, Saudi Arabia, Sweden, Syria, Yemen, Jugoslavia, and Afghanistan).

MAY 18, 1951. Assembly, 47–8, votes an arms embargo against North Korea and Red China.

Spring of 1951 thus found the UN, apparently, in the position of preparing to wage war on China as well as on North Korea in the name of enforcing peace. Acheson had long since moved to give the UN on a permanent basis the fortuitous advantages in fighting Red aggression it had enjoyed in June of 1950—*i.e.*, an agency on the scene (UNCOK); available troops (U.S.) nearby (Japan); and no Soviet veto. By a vote of 52–5 with 2 abstentions, the Assembly on Nov. 3, 1950, adopted the "Uniting for Peace" resolution which asked all members to maintain armed forces to "promptly be made available for service as UN units," established a "Collective Measures Committee" (with the Soviet bloc excluded) to plan economic and military sanctions, created a "Peace Observation Commission" to investigate situations endangering peace, and sought to supersede the Security Council by specifying that the Assembly, to meet on twenty-four-hour notice, should make recommendations for collective action "including in the case of a breach of the peace or act of aggression the use of armed force when necessary."

But this appearance of unity and firmness was deceptive. The resolution of Feb. 1 was opposed by all the Communist States, by India, and by almost all the Asiatic and Moslem States, comprising well over half the human race. Most of those voting for it under U.S. pressure, moreover, had no intention of waging war on China. London firmly opposed "sanctions." The new "sanctions committee" studiously did nothing. The "Good Offices Committee," established Oct. 7, 1950, strove for an exit from the impasse, as did the Asian and Arab States. The dismissal of MacArthur on April 11 was hailed with universal relief outside the USA, since he was committed to war against China as the only means of "victory" in Korea. Truce negotiations began in July, 1951. That they were prolonged over two years was evidence that the war was deadlocked, with each side unable to win and unwilling either to end the stalemated hostilities or extend them to a larger arena.

When all issues were resolved save that of repatriation of prisoners (with the enemy insisting on repatriation of all prisoners and the U.S. insisting that prisoners unwilling to return must not be forcibly repatriated), the negotiations broke down. Not until President-elect Eisenhower visited Korea in December, 1952, and Stalin went to his reward in March, 1953, were serious discussions resumed. The Communists now assented to the repatriation only of those prisoners desiring repatriation. The armistice accord of July 27, 1953, provided for a cease-fire and a line of demarcation following the battle line where the belligerent forces had been stalemated since June of 1951.

Some contended that these events demonstrated the unworkability of collective security through the UN. When Trygve Lie, July 14, 1950, appealed to 50 States to send combat troops to Korea, 35 declined or failed to reply. When the "Collective Measures Committee," April 11, 1951, asked all members to earmark troops for UN service and to reply "as a matter of urgency," the USA delayed a reply until June 8 and then declined to do what was asked, as did all other members. The war was a UN war in name only. Nine-tenths of the non-ROK troops were supplied by, and nine-tenths of their casualties suffered by, the USA which permitted no effective participation by other UN members in military planning, political decisions, or the interminable armistice negotiations.[9] The "UN" armies, moreover, were first defeated in South Korea, then defeated in North Korea, and finally obliged to hold a front near 38° where the war began. When a major Power (China) intervened, the UN members hastily abandoned all thought of unifying Korea by arms and punishing aggression, and agreed to settle for something like the status quo ante bellum. Ergo, argued many, the result was: failure.

On the affirmative side of the debate, it was equally incontestible that 38 States pledged support to the enterprise and 17 made contributions in men and supplies. The Red aggressors were stopped and then driven back. The Communist effort to unify Korea by conquest was thwarted. South Korea

[9] Troops were sent by the U.K., France, Turkey, Australia, Belgium, Luxembourg, Canada, Colombia, Ethiopia, Greece, Netherlands, New Zealand, Philippines, South Africa, and Thailand. (Denmark sent a hospital ship.) These contingents, however, never exceeded a combined total of 26,000 men, over half of them British, or some 10% of the U.S. soldiers, sailors, and airmen dispatched to Korea and 5% of the combined U.S. and ROK forces.

remained "free," albeit ruined and reduced to misery as was the North. Huge casualties and impressive devastation were inflicted on the foe. The plea for peace came from the enemy. Under U.S. leadership the UN States had shown their capacity to bypass the veto and act together in war as in diplomacy. Collective military sanctions were employed for the first time in an international "police action," which ultimately drove the invaders back over the border they had violated. All the Free World was inspired to enlarge and concert efforts for defense elsewhere.[10]

* * * * *

From a broader perspective, it is clear that the UN by the 1950's had become what the League was in the 1930's: an instrument of national policy on the part of the most influential Great Powers among its members. This role is implicit in the very nature of the organization. All such bodies lack independent powers of decision and action and can be no more than a means of collaboration among sovereignties, with the most powerful of them shaping the purposes of collaboration and seeking to enlist the rest in the enterprise. London and Paris used the League as a means of "appeasing" the Fascist aggressors, and ignored it when they saw more effective ways of serving their ends outside of its halls. Washington used the UN as a means of "containing" and resisting the Communist aggressors, and on occasion ignored it (e.g., Truman Doctrine, Marshall Plan, Eisenhower Doctrine) or made alliances in its name (e.g., NATO, OAS, SEATO, and the Pacific Pacts) on the principle, sanctioned in Article 51 of the Charter, of "the inherent right of individual or collective self-defense."

Following the crises of 1956 (see pp. 404f.), the United Nations organization ceased to be even an effective means of mobilizing impressive majorities behind the Free World against Marxland. Many of the 82 members

[10] Said John Foster Dulles (*Advance*, April, 1951): "For the first time in all time a world organization moved with force to halt aggression. The hope of the ages had come true." Dean G. Acheson (June 1, 1951): "The operation in Korea has been a success. Both the North Koreans and the Chinese Communists declared it to be their purpose to drive the UN forces out of Korea and impose Communist rule throughout the entire peninsula. They have been prevented from accomplishing their objective." Trygve Lie (June 25, 1951): "The men who are fighting and dying under their national flags and the flag of the UN serve the noblest of all causes. They are fighting to prevent a third world war. . . . They have won a great victory for the UN and for peace. . . . June 25 should be a day of rededication to the purpose of establishing firm collective security under the UN to prevent armed aggression anywhere in the world." Adlai E. Stevenson (*Foreign Affairs*, April, 1952): "Talk of the 'uselessness' of the Korean War gained currency only when negotiations for an armistice dragged out, and after we had in fact accomplished the primary objective of stopping the aggression and driving the aggressors back from whence they came. . . . The first great collective military effort of the UN to resist aggression demonstrated that the organization is adaptable to the role of enforcement as well as that of conciliation. . . . While Korea has not proved definitely that collective security *will* work, it has prevented the Soviet Union from proving that it *won't* work. . . . We have made historic progress toward the establishment of a viable system of collective security."

were recently emancipated colonial communities disposed to vote on sundry issues not with the Western–Latin American bloc but with the Asian-African bloc or even occasionally with the Soviet bloc. The U.S.-sponsored transfer of "enforcement" functions, moreover, from the Security Council, allegedly paralyzed by the veto, to the veto-less General Assembly, where, said some, the will of the majority could prevail, produced curious results.

The rule of one vote for each State made the Assembly wholly unrepresentative of the distribution of people throughout the world. The Assembly vote of Feb. 1, 1951, holding Red China guilty of aggression in Korea, was 44 to 7 with 9 abstentions. But the "majority" comprised States with total populations of *c.* 900,000,000, while the "minority," including the abstainers and absent Red China, totaled 1,450,000,000 people in their combined populations. Similarly the Assembly vote of Dec. 12, 1956, condemning "the violation of the Charter by the USSR in depriving Hungary of its liberty" and calling upon Moscow to withdraw its troops at once under UN supervision and restore Hungary's independence, was 55 to 8 with 13 abstentions. But the "majority" here represented *c.* 760,000,000, while the "minority," including the abstainers but not including in this instance the population of Communist China, represented *c.* 800,000,000 people. Assembly delegates, to be sure, do not "represent" people, but only governments. All the more meaningless are majorities in conferences of diplomats when most of the delegates speak for States without power or responsibility and when none can be bound in law or fact by any majority, however large.[11]

Widely discussed proposals to amend the Charter, either for the purpose of limiting or abolishing the Security Council veto, or somehow providing for weighted voting in the General Assembly, or with the goal of moving in the direction of federalism, would currently appear to offer no hope of any significant change in the structure or functioning of the organization. Amendments (*cf.* Art. 108) must be adopted by two-thirds of the Assembly and ratified by two-thirds of the members, including all permanent members of the Council. Subject to the same conditions of ratification, a general conference to review the Charter may be called by two-thirds of the Assembly (or, after 1955, by a simple majority) plus any seven members of the Council (*cf.* Art. 109). Since each permanent member of the Council can thus veto

[11] Viscount Cherwell observed to the House of Lords in January, 1957, that in the Assembly "5% of the world's population can carry the day against the other 95%, and 10% could claim a two-thirds majority. . . . Half the population of the world is represented by 4 delegates, the other half by 75." It is "nonsense," he concluded, for States to submit their "vital interests to a body so absurdly constituted." On April 3, 1957, Prime Minister Robert Gordon Menzies of Australia, in criticizing American attitudes, asserted that "it is not a foreign policy to say we will take this to the UN. The UN can help give effect to a policy, but I hope no great nation will ever go to it without knowing first what its own policy is and what it wants to persuade the UN to do. . . . Otherwise we shall have international affairs dominated by numbers. I much prefer to have them dominated by ideas."

any amendment and since there has been so far no consensus among them on the desirability of any proposed change, the question of revision has been indefinitely postponed since 1955.[12]

The UN during a long future seems destined to remain a league of sovereignties which can scarcely be expected to evolve into any semblance of a World Government unless, and until, all the Great Powers are of one mind on the desirability of such a transformation. The contingency is remote. During the decade and a half following the Charter of San Francisco, all the Powers were firmly opposed to any such change. The global utility of the UN in various areas of scientific, educational, humanitarian, economic, and social activity should not be underestimated merely because there is no space to discuss them in a book about politics. The specifically political uses of the UN, as now constituted, are only three, alone or in some combination. The organization can be used by policy-makers (1) to strengthen through propaganda, or rationalize through legalistic-moralistic abstractions of broad appeal, alliances of some States against other States in the traditional pattern of rivalry for power; or (2) to facilitate the pacific solution of problems of power through public debate, private negotiation, factual inquiry, advisory opinions, etc.; or (3) to promote the realization of common purposes based upon a Concert of Powers.

If the United Nations is not to go the way of the League of Nations, its prospects will depend upon the attainment of the third of the possibilities here suggested. The Charter as drafted presupposed that the Great Powers would collaborate in the pursuit of certain minimal shared objectives. The premise was shattered by the Cold War and by more recent rifts and cleavages in both camps of warriors. A politically meaningful and effective UN will be one in which the Powers have achieved a *modus vivendi* and have developed "peaceful coexistence" to a point at which cooperation becomes more important than competition. This prospect, fortunately, seemed likely to be realized in appreciable measure during the 1960's. Under such circumstances, the UN could fulfill the functions its founders intended for it and conceivably develop in the direction of a Parliament of Man and Federation of the World.

4. FORMULAS FOR PEACE

To assert and to show that unilateral national power cannot bring national security without ruining national welfare only proves that, unless the nations of the world can use their power co-operatively and not competitively, disaster will come. It does not of itself prove that the nations will be able or willing to act in accordance with this knowledge. They may or may not be willing to give up their sovereignty, even if one can prove, as I think it can be proved, that adherence to

[12] See *United States Foreign Policy and International Organization*, Proceedings of the 32d Institute of the Norman Wait Harris Memorial Foundation, The University of Chicago, June 26–30, 1956, especially pp. 178*ff.*

national sovereignty threatens ruination all around. For the curious thing is that individuals and nations may misinterpret what their self-interest is and how it can best be achieved. We, therefore, ask the realists whether they have adequately examined the concept of self-interest or whether they have permitted themselves to be hypnotized by a slogan. For national self-interest and national sovereignty and power may well be incompatible. Why, then, do people choose the wrong type of self-interest?—LINDEN A. MANDER, *Foundations of Modern World Society*, 1947.

Contemporary mankind persists in believing that peace can somehow be had by mystic rituals of semantics and statesmanship which are often as relevant to the problem as are the incantations of preliterate sorcerers to the cause and cure of disease. "National preparedness" and "collective security" are currently the most widespread of these illusions. Certain others deserve mention, however, in what must unhappily be a catalogue of follies on the part of politicians, publicists, and patriots. The sad task of enumerating and refuting these errors is justified only by the thought that the discovery of wisdom is impossible without the exposure of fallacy.

Outlawing War. The solution of the problem of peace through international agreements, wherein the signatories pledge themselves to refrain from war, is not distinctive of the post-Versailles and post-Potsdam periods. Early treaties pledging eternal peace and friendship among the parties constituted, by implication, a renunciation of war, as do all treaties providing for the pacific settlement of disputes. The League Covenant was such a treaty, as were the Locarno agreements of 1925.[12a]

The conclusion of the Locarno Pacts was followed by negotiations, initiated by the Soviet Union, for similar pacts in eastern Europe. The USSR supplemented its numerous nonaggression pacts by efforts to define aggres-

---

[12a] On August 16, 1925, representatives of Great Britain, France, Germany, Italy, Belgium, Poland, and Czechoslovakia met at Locarno and agreed to seven historic treaties which were subsequently signed at London, December 1, and ratified by all the parties. The first—a treaty of mutual guarantee—obligated France and Belgium on the one side and Germany on the other to renounce war against one another except in self-defense and under certain treaty provisions, and to settle all their controversies by pacific means, *i.e.*, adjudication, conciliation commissions, or the Council of the League. This agreement guaranteed the inviolability of the frontiers between Germany, France, and Belgium as fixed by the Treaty of Versailles. In the event of unprovoked aggression, as ascertained by the Council, all the signatories, including Great Britain and Italy, were pledged to come to the defense of the victim. Two treaties of mutual guarantee between France and Poland and between France and Czechoslovakia provided for mutual assistance against Germany in the event of her violation of the obligations mentioned above. Four treaties of compulsory arbitration and conciliation completed the series—between Germany on the one side and France, Belgium, Poland, and Czechoslovakia on the other. They obliged the parties to submit all disputes of every kind "with regard to which the parties are in conflict as to their respective rights" to a permanent conciliation commission, arbitration, adjudication, or to settlement by the Council. While the eastern frontiers of Germany were not guaranteed, all the parties were bound to resort only to pacific methods of settling disputes. Germany's entrance into the League of Nations in 1926 followed the conclusion of these agreements.

sion. At the London Economic Conference of 1933, Litvinov signed a multi-lateral convention defining aggression with Afghanistan, Estonia, Latvia, Persia, Poland, Rumania, and Turkey (July 3), another with Czechoslovakia, Rumania, Turkey, and Jugoslavia (July 4), and a third with Lithuania (July 4). Finland adhered later. These agreements were based upon the Politis Report (May 24, 1933) of the Security Committee of the League Disarmament Conference, which in turn was based upon the proposals of the Soviet delegates at Geneva. They declared that the aggressor in an international conflict would be considered that State which first declares war, invades foreign territory, attacks the territory, naval vessels, or aircraft of another State, imposes a naval blockade, or aids armed bands to invade the territory of another State.

These agreements and various others were all regional in character. The Covenant and the Charter were general renunciations of war by world-wide agreement. Following the establishment of the League, a long series of efforts was embarked upon to render more specific and effective the obligations not to resort to war. The first of these was embodied in the Cecil-Requin Draft Treaty of Mutual Assistance of 1923, which declared (Art. 1) that "aggressive war is an international crime and [the contracting parties] severally undertake that no one of them will be guilty of its commission." After the rejection of this arrangement, the Geneva Protocol of 1924 appeared. Its preamble asserted that "a war of aggression constitutes a violation of [the solidarity of the members of the international community] and an international crime." It contemplated the amendment of the Covenant and provided that the signatory States would agree "in no case to resort to war," except in resistance to aggression or with the consent of the Council or Assembly. The signatories also agreed to "abstain from any act which might constitute a threat of aggression against another State." An aggressor State was defined as one going to war after refusing to accept the procedures for pacific settlement provided for or rejecting a decision. In doubtful cases the Council would designate the aggressor and apply sanctions. The British Government failed to ratify the Protocol, and it was abandoned. The Locarno Pacts followed as a regional substitute for general agreement.

The negotiations preceding the Kellogg-Briand Pact (the General Treaty for the Renunciation of War) had been initiated in June, 1927, by a proposal from M. Briand to Secretary of State Kellogg for a bilateral Franco-American treaty solemnly renouncing war as an instrument of national policy. Mr. Kellogg, with the support of peace-seekers everywhere, proposed making the treaty multilateral and general. Briand agreed, provided that it should be restricted to "wars of aggression." Kellogg dissented, and the French Government finally agreed to general renunciation. Britain agreed to become a party on condition of reserving its liberty of action in "certain [undefined] regions of the world, the welfare and integrity of which constitute a special and vital interest for our peace and safety." This British "Monroe Doctrine" was accepted, though the Canadian and Irish Governments and subsequently the Egyptian, Turkish, and Persian Governments declared themselves not bound by it. The Pact was signed at the Quai d'Orsay on Aug. 27, 1928, by representatives of 15 States. By the close of 1930 it had been adhered to by 61 States, Argentina and Brazil being the only important abstinents. After considerable wrangling over ratification and some subsequent interpretations and understandings, President Hoover proclaimed the Pact in force on July 24, 1929. Its essence follows:

1. The high contracting parties solemnly declare in the names of their respective peoples that they condemn recourse to war for the solution of international controversies, and renounce it as an instrument of national policy in their relations with one another.
2. The high contracting parties agree that the settlement or solution of all disputes or conflicts, of whatever nature or of whatever origin they may be, which may arise among them, shall never be sought except by pacific means.
3. The present Treaty shall be ratified by the high contracting parties named in the preamble in accordance with their respective constitutional requirements, and shall take effect as between them as soon as all their several instruments of ratification shall have been deposited at Washington. . . .

The Soviet Union was the first to ratify the Pact, despite the fact that it was denounced in Moscow for its indefiniteness and irrelevance. On Dec. 29, 1928, the Soviet Minister in Warsaw proposed that the two Powers, along with Lithuania, should sign a Protocol (the "Litvinov Protocol") making the Pact effective between them at once without waiting for the general exchange of ratifications. The Soviet note deplored Poland's earlier refusal to sign a nonaggression and neutrality agreement. The Polish Government accepted in principle but made formal objections and counterproposals for the inclusion of Rumania and all the Baltic States. Litvinov accepted these suggestions at once. Lithuania had already accepted the Soviet proposal on Jan. 3, 1929, and suggested to Latvia and Estonia that they should adhere to the Protocol. On Feb. 9, 1929, the Protocol was signed at Moscow by representatives of the USSR, Poland, Latvia, Estonia, and Rumania. Lithuania and Turkey adhered on April 1, Danzig on April 30, and Persia on July 4. Simultaneous efforts to "close the gap in the Covenant" by incorporating the Kellogg Pact into amendments failed.

At French insistence the Pact was understood not to apply to wars of self-defense or to obligations under existing military alliances. At British insistence the Pact was understood not to interfere with a State's liberty of action in areas vital to its interests. In the USA, it was understood (at least by the State Department) that the Pact in no way interfered with the right to enforce the Monroe Doctrine—likewise undefined—in the name of self-defense. It was agreed by all parties that the Pact forbade only "wars of aggression" and did not apply to defensive hostilities, to hostilities against a State violating its obligations under the agreement, or to hostilities required by the League Covenant, the Locarno Treaties, or other engagements of alliance or neutrality.[13]

The Pact, moreover, lacked any effective means of enforcement. It was understood that if one signatory violated the Pact the others were released from it. The Pact was no stronger than its weakest link. But a State resorting to force to protect or promote its interests can always argue that the Pact does not apply, since it is acting in "self-defense." It can also argue that all measures of "settlement" unaccompanied by a declaration of war are "pacific," as indeed they are in a technical, legal sense. Other States may dissent, and "world opinion" may condemn. But a State which is strong and determined will not be restrained by verbal censure. It will be restrained only by superior force.

The efficacy of the Stimson Doctrine as a restraining influence was negligible. The Foreign Office at Tokyo, in its note to the United States of Jan. 16, 1932, commented dryly:

The Government of Japan takes note of the statement by the Government of the United States that the latter cannot admit the legality of matters which might impair the treaty rights of the United States or its citizens or which might be brought about by means contrary to the Treaty of Aug. 27, 1928. It might be the subject of an academic doubt, whether in a given case the impropriety of means necessarily and always voids the ends secured, but as Japan has no intention of adopting improper means, that question does not practically arise.

On Feb. 24, 1933, the League Assembly adopted a report of the Committee of Nineteen which provided that the members of the League would "continue not to recognize this regime [Manchukuo] either de jure or de facto." Washington continued to provoke Japanese resentment by adhering to the Stimson Doctrine in the Far East, but neither the USA nor the League Powers formally applied the Doctrine to the Italian conquest of Ethiopia. Indeed, the Italian decision to annex Ethiopia, rather than to set up a puppet State, was perhaps influenced by the Stimson Doctrine. In May, 1938, the League Council renounced the Doctrine. General recognition of Italian title to Ethiopia followed. The device of the legal boycott did not outlaw war, restrain aggression, or prevent conquest. The revival of the concept of outlawing war in the Nuremberg trials, in the UN Charter (Art. 2), and in various supplementary regional agreements in no way alters the judgment already rendered by logic and by events.

The Dream of Disarmament. For many centuries many seekers after peace have believed that wars are caused by armaments, that arms races

---

[13] Under the Pact and comparable instruments, an aggressor may be legally defined as a State which persists in resorting to force contrary to obligations it has assumed and in violation of procedures it has accepted for implementing such obligations. See Quincy Wright, "The Concept of Aggression in International Law," *American Journal of International Law*, July, 1935, pp. 373–395.

lead to conflict, and that peace can be had by agreement to limit or reduce national military and naval establishments. In reality, the reverse is more nearly true: war machines are reduced only when peace seems probable, the expectation of conflict leads to competition in armaments, and armaments spring from war and from the anticipation of war. Yet men have long sought to put the cart before the horse—since the horse is intractable and best ignored, while the cart can be moved about at will, even if to no effect.

The record of failure between world wars is worth recalling. Following the disarmament of Germany by the Treaty of Versailles, the naval Powers began considering the possibility of putting an end to the new armaments race which had already begun. President Harding invited the other naval Powers—Britain, Japan, France, and Italy—to attended a Conference, which was broadened to include China, the Netherlands, Belgium, and Portugal, for the discussion of Pacific and Far Eastern problems." The measure of success achieved by the Washington Conference, which met on Nov. 12, 1921, has never been equaled by any succeeding disarmament conference." Success was due to the fact that none of the participants at the time had any political purposes to serve by establishing its naval superiority over any of the others and that all of them had both a political and a financial interest in stabilizing armaments at the existing levels."

Britain, the USA, and Japan agreed on a 5:5:3 ratio in capital ships, i.e., battleships and battle cruisers. France and Italy later accepted a ratio of 1.67 each. The Five-Power Treaty Limiting Naval Armament, signed Feb. 6, 1922, provided for the scrapping of 68 ships, built or planned. The USA was left with 18 capital ships of 525,850 tons, Britain with 20 ships (most of them smaller and older than the American) of 558,950 tons, Japan with 10 of 301,320 tons, France with 10 of 221,170 tons, and Italy with 10 of 182,800 tons. The treaty likewise limited aircraft carriers to a total of 135,000 tons each for Britain and the USA, 81,000 for Japan, and 60,000 each for France and Italy. No agreement could be reached on other types of vessels.

On Feb. 10, 1927, President Coolidge invited Britain, Japan, France, and Italy to participate in a conference to limit construction of the types of vessel not covered by the Washington agreement. Britain and Japan accepted. France and Italy refused. The Geneva, or Coolidge, Conference, which met on June 20, 1927, was thus a Three-Power conference, with the participants represented by admirals and naval experts with no great enthusiasm for abolishing their own jobs. On Aug. 4 the Conference broke up in failure. On Feb. 13, 1929, the American Congress authorized the President to construct fifteen 10,000-ton cruisers and one aircraft carrier at a cost of $274,000,000. The London Naval Conference opened on Jan. 21, 1930. It eventuated in a partial, ambiguous treaty for arms limitation, signed April 22, 1930—not worth summarizing since its terms were nullified within a few years.

The General Disarmament Conference of the League of Nations—the culmination of a decade of international efforts to attain disarmament and ensure peace—met at Geneva on Feb. 3, 1932, with Arthur Henderson presiding over 232 delegates, representing 57 States. By an ironic coincidence, open warfare was going on at Shanghai while the delegates deliberated at Geneva. The delegates brought with them no less than 337 separate proposals. But Stresemann was dead (Oct. 3, 1929). Briand died on March 7, 1932. Failure greeted all efforts to prevent the Conference from following him to the grave.

The Nazi revolution of 1933 delivered the *coup de grâce*. On the morning of Oct. 14, 1933, Sir John Simon presented to the Bureau of the Conference a statement, approved by France and the USA, designed to meet German demands for arms equality and French demands for security. The essence of the compromise was a four-year transitional period during which Germany would be content with her inferior status and after which the heavily armed Powers would begin to reduce their armaments. The reply from Berlin came within three hours: Germany announced her withdrawal from the Disarmament Conference and from the League of Nations. Hitler's first venture in the rude diplomacy of the *fait accompli* was a success. The other Powers gasped and did nothing. The German electorate almost unanimously endorsed the policy of defiance in the referendum of Nov. 12. The Conference at Geneva expired.

On March 16, 1935, Germany repudiated Part V of the Treaty of Versailles and reintroduced military conscription. Arthur Henderson died on Oct. 20, 1935. On March 7, 1936, Germany repudiated Articles 42 and 43 of the Treaty of Versailles, denounced Locarno, and sent troops into the demilitarized Rhineland. After 16 years, the circle of frustration was closed. Efforts at world disarmament through the League had begun with the unilateral disarmament of Germany. The efforts ceased with the unilateral rearmament of Germany. The collective intelligence of Europe, having failed to achieve security, turned toward preparations for suicide.

Simultaneously the great sea Powers reached a similar impasse. Naval disarmament had begun in 1921 with the termination of an Anglo-American-Japanese naval race. Naval disarmament ended in 1936 with the resumption of the race. On Dec. 29, 1934, Ambassador Hirosi Saito submitted a communication to Secretary of State Hull:

In accordance with Article 23 of the Treaty concerning the limitation of naval armament signed at Washington on the 6th February 1922, the Government of Japan hereby gives notice to the Government of the United States of America of their intention to terminate the said Treaty, which will accordingly cease to be in force after the 31st December 1936.

The London Treaty of 1930 was scheduled to expire on the same date. Washington moved at once to build its fleet up to full treaty strength by 1942. President Roosevelt expressed his conviction that the United States must keep pace in building with other naval Powers so as to maintain the 5:5:3 ratio. The British Government eyed the new German Navy with some apprehension. On June 18, 1935, in the name of "realism," Sir Samuel Hoare announced a Naval Pact with Joachim von Ribbentrop whereby the Reich was granted a Navy 35% of the strength of the British Navy in all categories of vessels save submarines, which Germany might build up to 45% or even 100% of the British strength. This agreement, so far as Britain was concerned, superseded the naval limitations imposed upon Germany at Versailles. It was negotiated by Downing Street three months after London had protested against German violation of the armaments clauses of the Treaty of Versailles. It was negotiated, moreover, without consultation with France and the USSR, both of which felt that they had been betrayed by Britain and were directly menaced by German sea forces. Moscow and Paris moved to increase their fleets in the face of this threat, just as the USA increased its Navy in the face of Japan's demand for parity.

Despite these inauspicious developments, delegations from the USA, Britain, Japan, France, and Italy met in London on Dec. 9, 1935. Neither the American-Japanese nor the Franco-Italian deadlock over parity had been resolved. An American plea for a 20% reduction in navies, with existing ratios continued, met with no support. The Japanese plea for a "common upper limit" was rejected. On Jan. 15, 1936, the Japanese delegation withdrew from the Conference. Negotiations continued among the four remaining Powers. On March 25, 1936, a new Naval Treaty was signed by Britain, France, and the USA. Japan would have none of it. Italy refused to sign. Its only contribution was an agreement on the tonnage and guns of war vessels. Numerous "safeguarding" and "escape" clauses opened the way for departure from even these limited restrictions.

By the beginning of 1937, all treaties imposing quantitative restrictions on the three great naval Powers were at an end. In March, London announced plans for constructing 238,000 tons of new battleships, including three 35,000-ton dreadnoughts, and for expending over £100,000,000 in the ensuing year on naval armaments. Washington followed suit, and Tokyo struggled desperately to keep pace with her wealthier rivals in a naval race which was far costlier and more dangerous than that which preceded 1914. On April 28, 1939, Hitler denounced the Anglo-German Naval Pact of 1935 on the ground that Britain's alliance with Poland was hostile to the Reich and a violation of the purpose of the agreement. Disarmament had become a memory. On the walls at the feast of Belshazzar, the destruction of his kingdom was foretold by the cryptic words *mene, mene, tekel, upharsin*. The letters of FAILURE, written large over the portals of successive disarmament conferences during the two decades after Versailles, became letters of impending catastrophe for all the Western world.

Since World War II statesmen have resumed the futile activities already surveyed, with no result to date save the temporary disarmament of the vanquished (followed by their rearmament when rival victors sought to use erstwhile enemies against former allies) and the gala opening of the most supercolossal armaments race of all time. If the question be asked as to why governments, under such circumstances, continue to discuss disarmament, several answers are available. Governments, including totalitarian regimes, are responsive to "public opinion." Most publics, being hypnotized by a double fallacy, favor disarmament and/or the most powerful army, navy, and air force in the world as alternative means to "peace." Politicians therefore find it useful to practice preparedness and preach disarmament. Governments find it advantageous, moreover, to put forward proposals which they hope will, if accepted, strengthen their own power and weaken that of potential enemies. This indeed is the sole purpose in *Realpolitik* of all such programs. Finally, governments continually promulgate plans which they know will be rejected on the premise that rejection will put the onus of militarism on the "enemy" and give the proposer a moral or propaganda victory. Since such calculations are the alpha and omega of all diplomacy of "disarmament," the details scarcely merit attention. Yet a résumé is in order.

The UN Charter (see Art. 26) contemplated "a system for the regulation of armament." What came of this with regard to atomic weapons we shall review in the final chapter of our book, since atomic warfare promises a degree of finality never hitherto attained. As for non-nuclear arms, Molotov on Oct. 29, 1946, presented a grandiose plan for disarmament designed to embarrass the Western Powers, as his predecessor, Litvinov, had done at Geneva in November, 1927, in his shocking proposal for the immediate, universal, and total abolition of all armaments and armed forces. On Dec. 14, 1946, the Assembly resolved that the Security Council should formulate "practical measures" for an international system of control, regulation, inspection, and reduction. On Feb. 13, 1947, the Council established a Commission for Conventional Armaments. It met March 24, considered various proposals, and on Aug. 12, 1948, adopted by a vote of 9–2 (the Soviet bloc opposed) a statement of "principles" making disarmament contingent upon agreement on armed forces for the UN (see Art. 43), a system of control of atomic energy, conclusion of peace treaties with Germany and Japan, and agreement for international supervision and effective enforcement against violation. As with atomic arms, the objective was a "foolproof" system of complete security (which is unattainable in an insecure and foolish world) and/or Soviet rejection of the proposals. Moscow replied by proposing to the Assembly in September, 1948, a one-third reduction of all armed forces and prohibition of atomic weapons, both unacceptable to the USA. The Assembly rejected this and called on the Commission to propose methods of obtaining and verifying armament information as the first step toward control—both unacceptable to the USSR which had no intention of supplying any information or submitting to any control. Said Trygve Lie on June 6, 1950: "Up to now there has been virtually a complete failure here."

On Oct. 24, 1950, Truman told the Assembly in a "concession" to the USSR (described by Vishinsky as "skulduggery") that work on reducing and controlling atomic and conventional armaments might profitably be co-ordinated in a consolidated commission. On Nov. 7, 1951, the USA, Britain, and France issued a statement championing "disclosure and verification in successive stages," "effective international inspection," and continued adher-ence to the Baruch Plan (see pp. 664f.). Vishinsky averred that he had been unable to sleep nights for laughing, but on Nov. 16 presented a counterplan which he described as "new . . . momentous . . . tremendous." It proposed a convention for the "unconditional prohibition of atomic weapons and estab-lishment of strict international control," to be followed by a one-third reduc-tion of armaments by the Great Powers within one year, to be followed within one month after acceptance of these commitments by the presentation by all countries of "complete official data" on all armaments, "including data about atomic weapons and military bases on foreign territory," plus a new control body to check on information, reduction, and prohibition. A revised Western plan of Nov. 19 envisaged a combined Disarmament Commission, in place of the Atomic Energy Commission and the Commission for Conventional Arma-ments, to prepare a draft treaty for the "regulation, limitation, and balanced reduction of all armed forces and all armaments" to a level "adequate for defense but not for aggression," with disclosure, verification, "effective inter-national inspection" à la the Baruch Plan, etc. On Dec. 19, 1951, the Political and Security Committee of the Assembly voted approval of the Western plan, 45–5, with 10 abstentions.

The new Disarmament Commission achieved nothing and could achieve nothing so long as the Cold War went on. On April 5, 1952, the USA pro-posed a stage-by-stage world census of arms, with location of atomic plants to come in the first stage and all data to be verified by international inspectors through spot checks and aerial surveys. Malik denounced this as a "smoke screen" and a scheme for "an international spying service to get data for Pentagon and British Intelligence." On May 8 he declared that agreement would be impossible until the USA gave up its insistence, attributed to a "plot by U.S. monopolists," on international ownership of atomic facilities. A low point was reached on May 28, 1952, when the Western Powers pro-posed that the armed forces of the USA, USSR, and China be reduced to 1,500,000, France and Britain to 800,000 each, and other States to a figure not exceeding 1% of their populations, all contingent upon universal ac-ceptance of Western plans for international inspection and control—which the Western Powers knew that the Eastern Powers would never accept. "China" was left undefined. On May 29, the three Western Powers explained that Red China would not be permitted to participate in discussion of the proposal since it was guilty of aggression and not a member of UN. The USSR rejected the Western formula on Aug. 29, 1952, as "hypocritical" and "absurd." Meanwhile, the Congress of the USA had increased annual appropriations for defense from $25,000,000,000 in 1950–51 to $77,202,000,000 in 1951–52, the largest amount ever voted in peacetime, while the Supreme Soviet of the USSR provided 96,376,000,000 rubles for defense in 1951 and 113,800,000,-000 rubles in 1952, the largest amount ever voted in peacetime.

To pursue in detail these chronicles of wasted time would be tedious and unrewarding. For reasons already suggested, almost all attempts, albeit not quite all, to achieve disarmament by international accords negotiated through diplomatic channels, special conferences, or international agencies are fore-doomed to failure by the persistence of the mutual suspicions and rivalries which give rise in the first place to competition in armaments. On May 10, 1955, the USSR publicized an elaborate program of disarming, including partial military evacuation of Germany and reduction of American, Soviet, and Chinese armies to 1,500,000 each and of British and French forces to 650,000 each. At the "Summit Conference" in Geneva, Eisenhower (July 21, 1955) suggested that the USSR and USA exchange blueprints of military bases and arrange reciprocal aerial inspection ("open skies") of each other's territories. (At the time, and until the summer of 1956, Soviet anxiety over enemy espionage was so acute as to forbid publication in any Soviet city of street-plans, guidebooks, or even phone directories.) Faure proposed budgetary limitations on arms. Eden proposed a treaty of mutual defense, a unified Germany, and a demilitarized zone in East Central Europe. Bulganin proposed an exchange of guarantees between the signatories of NATO and the Warsaw Pact.

All in vain. When East pretended to accept Western proposals, West changed its proposals and *vice versa*. New circumstances nevertheless altered prospects slightly. Among them were these: the gigantic new arms race had plainly led to a stalemate in which neither side could hope to achieve any meaningful margin of superiority over the other; Moscow, London, and Washington in 1955–58 all decided on unilateral reductions of armaments for financial and economic reasons; and all three of the atomic Powers feared, with cause, that unless they could somehow agree to halt nuclear tests and the stockpiling of atomic arms, other Powers, and perhaps ultimately all States including the smallest and most irresponsible, would acquire thermonuclear weapons with resulting hazards which even the Super-Powers preferred not to face. In this context disarmament negotiations were somewhat more seriously resumed in 1957. The intricacies need not here be reviewed, the more so as it was clear that if the mountain in labor brought forth anything, the progeny would at best be a mouse. On March 18 in London's Lancaster House the UN Disarmament Subcommittee (USA, USSR, Britain, France, and Canada) began its eighty-seventh session, with the USSR represented by Valerian A.

Zorin and the USA by Harold E. Stassen, President Eisenhower's Special Assistant on disarmament with Cabinet rank, although now subordinated to
directives from Secretary Dulles. Zorin reiterated previous Soviet proposals
with emphasis on suspension of nuclear tests, prohibition of nuclear arms,
and a demilitarized zone in Middle Europe. Stassen, amid much coming and
going, and occasionally obvious lack of coordination with Anglo-French
views, slowly elaborated a complex American program with emphasis on
reduction of conventional arms; international supervision of future production of fissionable materials, to be limited to peaceful uses only; a "foolproof"
system of aerial and ground inspection to preclude surprise attacks and to
include "earth satellites" and "intercontinental missiles"; and a provisional
and conditional suspension of nuclear tests. By the end of April Zorin was
proposing "open skies" to include most of Europe, a western strip of the
USSR, eastern Siberia, Alaska, and all of the western USA. On May 19, Adm.
Arthur W. Radford, Chairman of the U.S. Joint Chiefs of Staff, publicly
opined: "We cannot trust the Russians on this or anything." Eisenhower asserted that America must not be "recalcitrant" or "picayunish."

By June of 1957 Zorin was urging a two- or three-year ban on atomic
testing under an international control system. Dulles strove to make any
moratorium on testing contingent upon a ban on production of atomic materials for military purposes and to make any reduction of conventional
forces contingent upon German unification on terms acceptable to Bonn.
Stassen initially insisted on a ten-month limit to any ban on testing. By
August Dulles was proposing "open skies" for all the territory of the USSR,
all of Canada and the USA, and all of Europe (but not including U.S. bases
in North Africa or the Mid East) or, alternately, all North American and
Eurasian territories within the Arctic circle. He further assented to a possible
two-year ban on atomic testing, but only on condition that production of
atomic materials for weapons be halted under a "foolproof" inspection
system.

The discussions dragged on amid indescribable technical and diplomatic
complexities. The final Western 11-point program was rejected by the USSR
early in September, 1957. Elaborate exchanges of public messages in the
winter of 1957–58 between Bulganin and Eisenhower, coupled with parallel
exchanges between Moscow and other Western capitals, effected no change
in the deadlock. The Soviet objective was to disarm the West—e.g., by
proposals for abolition of atomic weapons, abandonment of overseas bases,
withdrawal of troops from foreign territories, establishment of a Central
European Zone free of nuclear arms (proposed in October, 1957, by Foreign
Minister Adam Rapacki of Poland, endorsed by Khrushchev, and rejected
by Dulles and Eisenhower in February, 1958), etc. The Western objective
was to disarm the USSR via "foolproof" inspection schemes, German unification, "liberation" of Eastern Europe, and agreement to use outer space

only for "peaceful purposes," thus banning as a weapon of war the ICBM, which the USSR had perfected and the USA had not yet perfected. Each side knew that its proposals would be rejected by the other.

Whatever the ultimate outcome (which promised to parallel all previous efforts in this area), the objectives of national policy-makers in negotiations over disarmament are either to prevent agreement, lest "national security" be jeopardized, by presenting clearly unacceptable proposals, all the while persuading their publics that their own solicitude for disarmament is earnest and ardent and would be productive save for the "obstructionism" of the other side, or, less frequently, to negotiate accords which, it is hoped, will strengthen one's own military potential and weaken that of the prospective enemy. Since such calculations of power are the inevitable context of all such discussions and usually the determinants of the result, the noble goal of disarmament through international agreement as a means to peace must, on the record, be relegated either to the category of wishful thinking or, more hopefully, to that of a possibly useful adjunct, concomitant, or sequel to successful efforts to achieve political accommodation and mutual trust through the processes of diplomacy. Clement Attlee told Commons on Nov. 22, 1945: "Where there is no mutual confidence, no system will be effective." His words were true then, are true now, and will be true always.

In Pursuit of Collective Security. One of the oldest convictions of the searchers after peace is the belief that the goal can be gained through arrangements by which all nations will agree to combined coercive action against any nation breaking the law or taking the sword. We have already noted some of the theoretical schemes embodying this idea, its incorporation in the Covenant and Charter, and its testing in the Korean War. The case for collective security has been so often stated and is so universally accepted that it needs no recapitulation.[14] But it may be conducive to sober and possibly creative reflection to mention some of the considerations which may be adduced in support of the view that collective security, as usually defined, offers little hope of the effective enforcement of peace.

States are persons in law, but not persons in fact. States are equal in law, but not equal in fact. States are bound by principles in law, but act to serve their interests in fact—with statesmen and citizens seldom defining "interest" in terms of any duty to risk money and lives in suppressing aggression unless they feel themselves threatened by the aggression or by its foreseeable aftermath if successful. If States were persons, each would doubtless be "deterred" from evil by the prospect of all others acting against it. If States were equal, then a sheriff's posse of 79 against 1, or 75 against 5, or even 60 against 20, could doubtless keep the peace. If States acted on principle, each would gladly give all to the enterprise.

[14] A fuller analysis of these matters is set forth in Chap. 7 of the author's *The Commonwealth of Man: An Inquiry into Power Politics and World Government.*

But the conditions are lacking and the premises are false. Therefore States do not act against aggression unless a Great Power, feeling threatened, decides to act, assumes the burden, and summons others to act with it. In this case, the others will act or fail to act, depending upon how their policy-makers define their interests. The aggressor will seldom be "deterred" by the prospect, since experience demonstrates that inaction is quite as likely as action. If the aggressor is a Great Power, the custodians of collective security will usually be obliged to choose between painful alternatives: diplomatic and economic action which will ordinarily prove ineffective and lead to irresponsibility and acquiescence in aggression; or military action which will lead to a major war in which the outcome will be doubtful but heavy losses will be certain. The "enforcement of peace" by the armed force of States against States, while widely endorsed in principle, is seldom embarked upon in practice by disinterested States. When undertaken, it obviously produces not peace but war. The people of 1984, according to George Orwell, will come to believe that "War is Peace." But the people of the 1950's do not quite accept this paradox. The central difficulty was well put by Walter Lippmann in his column of Jan. 15, 1951:

The trouble with collective security is, if I may reprint something I wrote back in 1946, that "when the issue is less than the survival of the *great* nations, the method of collective security will not be used because it is just as terrifying to the policeman as it is to the lawbreakers. It punishes the law-enforcing states, at least until they have paid the awful price of victory, as much as the law-breaking states. Therefore it cannot be used as a method of ordinary and continuing enforcement, for example, as a means of insuring the inspection of laboratories and plants working with fissionable material. There would be little surgery if the surgeon had to amputate his own arm when he was called upon to amputate the patient's leg. There would be little enforcement of law in our cities if in order to arrest burglars, murderers and violators of the traffic ordinances the police had to start a fight in which the courthouse, the jail, and their own homes were likely to be demolished. Men will not burn down the barn in order to roast a pig: the method of collective security is, I repeat, too crude, too expensive, and too unreliable for general and regular use. It proposes to achieve peace through law by calling upon great masses of innocent people to stand ready to exterminate great masses of innocent people. No world order can be founded upon such a principle; it cannot command the support of civilized men, least of all of democratic men who respect the individual and consider it the very essence of justice to distinguish between the guilty and the innocent, the responsible and the irresponsible."

It is singular that these considerations are now perceived with a minimum of clarity by the very people whose "founding fathers" perceived them with a maximum of clarity. The essence of the fallacy was fully explored and exposed in the Constitutional Convention of 1787. At the outset, many believed that law, order, and peace would be impossible in the then sadly dis-United States unless the new national government were given power to coerce the

States. Both the Virginia and New Jersey Plans originally made provision for this type of collective security. The last clause of the Virginia Plan authorized the United States "to call forth the forces of the Union against any member of the Union failing to do its duty under the Articles thereof."

George Mason of Virginia argued that "punishment could not in the nature of things be executed on the States collectively, and therefore that such a Government was necessary as could directly operate on individuals, and would punish those only whose guilt required it." James Madison opined that "the use of force against a State would look more like a declaration of war than an infliction of punishment, and would probably be considered by the party attacked as a dissolution of all previous compacts by which it might be bound. . . . Any Government for the States formed on the supposed practicability of using force against the unconstitutional proceedings of the States would prove . . . visionary and fallacious." [15]

The New Jersey Plan specified that "if any State, or any body of men in any State, shall oppose or prevent ye carrying into execution such acts or treaties, the federal Executive shall be authorized to call forth ye power of the Confederated States, or so much thereof as may be necessary to enforce and compel obedience to such Acts, or an Observance of such Treaties." Said Mr. Randolph: "There are but two modes, by which the end of Genl. Govt. can be attained; the 1st. is by coercion as proposed by Mr. P's. plan. 2. by real legislation, as propd. by the other plan. Coercion he pronounced to be impracticable, expensive, cruel to individuals. It tended, also to habituate the instruments of it to shed blood & riot in the spoils of their fellow Citizens, and consequently trained them for the service of Ambition. We must resort therefore to a national Legislation over individuals." [16] Alexander Hamilton said that by "force" one might understand "a coercion of laws or coercion of arms. . . . But how can this force be exerted on States collectively? It is impossible. It amounts to a war between the parties. Foreign powers also will not be idle spectators. They will interpose, the confusion will increase and a dissolution of the Union ensue." [17] Added Madison:

The coercion, on which efficacy of the plan depends, can never be exerted but on themselves. The larger States will be impregnable, the smaller only can feel the vengeance of it. He illustrated the position by the history of the Amphictyonic Confederates: and the ban of the German Empire. It was the cobweb which could entangle the weak, but would be the sport of the strong.[18]

Colonel Mason agreed with this view and observed:

[15] Max Farrand (editor), *The Records of the Federal Convention of* 1787 (New Haven, 1923), Vol. I, pp. 34, 54, 164–165. *Cf.* Harrop Freeman and Theodore Paullin, *Coercion of States in Federal Unions* (Philadelphia, 1943), where these and other relevant passages are quoted.
[16] Max Farrand (editor), *The Records of the Federal Convention of* 1787, Vol. I, p. 256.
[17] *Ibid.*, p. 284.
[18] *Ibid.*, p. 320.

It was acknowledged [by Mr. Patterson] that his plan could not be enforced without military coercion. Does he consider the force of this concession? The most jarring elements of nature, fire and water themselves are not more incompatible than such a mixture of civil liberty and military execution. . . . Will not the citizens of the invaded State assist one another till they rise as one Man and shake off the Union altogether.[19]

Before the Virginia Convention, called to pass upon the new Constitution, Madison said of one of the ancient Greek confederacies that "though its powers were more considerable in many respects than those of our present system, yet it had the same radical defect. Its powers were exercised over its individual members in their political capacities. To this capital defect it owed its disorders and final destruction. It was compelled to recur to the sanguinary coercion of war to enforce its decrees." [20] Before the New York Convention, Hamilton put the matter even more strongly:

To coerce the States is one of the maddest projects that was ever devised. A failure of compliance will never be confined to a single State. This being the case, can we suppose it wise to hazard a civil war? . . . The thing is a dream, it is impossible. . . . What is the cure for this great evil? Nothing, but to enable the national laws to operate on individuals, in the same manner as those of the States do.[21]

5. PLEAS FOR ONE WORLD

Experience is the oracle of truth and where its responses are unequivocal they ought to be conclusive and sacred. The important truth, which it unequivocally pronounces in its present case, is that a sovereignty over sovereigns, a government over governments, a legislation for communities as contradistinguished from individuals, as it is a solecism in theory, so in practice it is subversive of the order and ends of civil polity by substituting violence in place of law, or the destructive coercion of the sword in place of the mild and salutary coercion of the magistracy.—*The Federalist*, No. 15.

If peace seems unlikely to be had through the coercion of States by the whole community of States, it is pertinent to inquire what other arrangements, if any, are available. Only two offer substantial promise of attaining the goal. At present, both are unhappily in the realm of the "academic," a term which has come to be synonymous with visionary or impracticable. One is the abolition of a multiplicity of States through the universal dominion of a single Super-State. The other is a union of States through federation. The former development would establish world citizenship in a World State, with no problems of relations among sovereignties remaining. The latter would establish a dual citizenship on a global scale, with all people bound both by a

19 *Ibid.*, pp. 339–340.
20 Freeman and Paullin, *op. cit.*, p. 16, quoting Elliott's *Debates*.
21 *Ibid.*, pp. 13–14. *Cf.* also *The Federalist*, Nos. 15–22.

world federal law within a limited sphere and by State (*i.e.*, national or municipal) law in all other spheres. Both solutions would replace the coercion of States by the enforcement of law on individuals.

Nothing can be clearer in our time than that a single World Imperium to keep the peace is an impossibility. The achievements of the Caesars of ancient Rome and of the Mongol Khans of Tartary in the 13th Century have not been duplicated in the Western State System and will not soon be realized. In the future as in the past, any effort to unite all mankind under one rule can reasonably be expected to encounter the same resistances that defeated the ambitions of Louis XIV, Napoleon I, Wilhelm II, Hitler, and Hirohito. Neither America nor Russia will unite the world by the sword during the next generation. The international community will therefore remain a community of separate sovereignties.

The federation of these sovereignties is a more promising enterprise. Such a union, like every federation, would involve a division of powers between central and local units of government by means of a written constitution which neither alone could change. It would also involve two citizenships and two spheres of law. The global federal law would be enforceable, not on States as States, but on individuals through courts. Within its designated area, it would prevail over national or municipal law in cases of conflict, with a world court not only adjudicating legal controversies among States but also acting in an appellate capacity as a court of last resort for the application and clarification of a body of constitutional principles actually commensurate with the integration and interdependence of the world community. The relations between the two spheres of law would be governed by the principle stated in Section 2 of Article VI of the fundamental charter of the American Union:

This Constitution, and the laws of the United States which shall be made in pursuance thereof; and all treaties made, or which shall be made, under the authority of the United States, shall be the supreme law of the land; and the judges in every State shall be bound thereby, anything in the Constitution or laws of the State to the contrary notwithstanding.

The applicability of these principles to the world problem of uniting effectively a multiplicity of States without subjecting them to the coercion of one another or of a central authority has long been urged by many distinguished Americans. As long ago as 1910, Hamilton Holt wrote: "The United States must become the model for the United Nations." More recently, the same conception has been presented ably and eloquently by many others. All recognize that federalism is no perfect guarantee of peace and that no such guarantee is possible in an imperfect world of imperfect men. One costly civil conflict was required to preserve the United States. A federal United Nations might experience similar crises. But the armed coercion of individuals defying federal authority is a wholly different process from the armed clash of States.

In the difference lies the measure of the progress away from anarchy and toward government which federalism represents.[22]

Despite the fact that the USA, USSR, Brazil, Mexico, Canada, Australia, South Africa, Jugoslavia, etc., all had federal governments, the coalition which won World War II and established the UN never gave serious consideration to creating a global federation rather than a new league of sovereignties. Winston Churchill, to be sure, in his last despairing appeal of June 16, 1940, to Premier Paul Reynaud proposed a genuine Anglo-French federation as a means of keeping France in the war. The offer was not too little, but it was too late. Churchill's later advocacy of federalism was addressed only to the States of the Continent. At Dumbarton Oaks, Soviet spokesmen displayed mild interest in federalism as a basis of world order but later ridiculed and denounced all such projects as bourgeois, "imperialistic," and "anti-Soviet." Aside from the late Wendell Willkie, Henry A. Wallace, and, for a time, Harold Stassen, no prominent American leader raised his voice in favor of federalism during or after the war. Whatever interest President Roosevelt may have had in such a project was effectively stifled by the State Department. Under the Truman-Byrnes-Marshall regime, executive interest in world federation was conspicuous by its absence.

The task of educating public opinion to the merits of federalism fell to private citizens. To do justice to all the individuals and organizations which have participated in the enterprise is quite impossible. By mid-century a bewildering variety of groups, sometimes cooperating and sometimes competitive and hostile toward one another, had emerged on both sides of the Atlantic to promote, in one fashion or another, the federation of local sovereignties into regional or global polities.[23] Apart from differences in approach and method, all fall into two broad categories: those striving for a world federation as the only means toward world order and world peace; and those committed to a federation limited to all or some of the democracies, as a step toward, or a substitute for, a world federation—on the double premise that Communist hostility and Cold War make global federation impossible and that only democracies can federate to form a union based on freedom, the rule of law, and popular government. The list which follows includes only the more influential or representative instances in each group, with the second group illustrated first:

FEDERAL UNION, INC. (FU), founded, 1939, by Clarence K. Streit, author of *Union Now* (1938) and *Union Now with Britain* (1941). Journal: *Freedom and Union*. Program: a federation of democracies with a Union Government, citizen-

[22] This passage and the concluding portions of the preceding section are adapted from "The Dilemma of the Peace-seekers," *American Political Science Review*, February, 1945, by the author.

[23] For a fuller account, with bibliographies and a brief history of each organization, see Chap. 8 of the author's *The Commonwealth of Man: An Inquiry into Power Politics and World Government*.

ship, defense force, currency, customs system, and postal and communications systems, to be granted limited but effective legislative, executive, and judicial powers to protect the rights of its member States and of their individual citizens.

ATLANTIC UNION COMMITTEE (AUC), founded, 1949, by Clarence K. Streit, the late Owen J. Roberts, Will L. Clayton, Hugh Moore, *et al.* Journal: *Atlantic Union News.* Program: a federal union of the sponsors of the North Atlantic Treaty, to meet in federal convention to invite other States to participate with them in an exploration of the possibility of applying among them, within the framework of the UN, the federal principle.

EUROPEAN UNION OF FEDERALISTS (EUF), founded, 1946, at a meeting in Luxembourg of delegates from various federalist groups. Leaders include Henri Frenay, Henri Brugmans, Alexandre Marc, J. Keith Killby, Denis de Rougement. Program: a European Federal Constituent Assembly to frame a Pact of Federal Union.

EUROPEAN MOVEMENT, founded at an unofficial "Congress of Europe" at The Hague, May, 1948. Honorary presidents: Winston Churchill, Léon Blum, Alcide de Gasperi, Paul Henri Spaak. Journal: *Europe Today and Tomorrow.* Its educational and propaganda activities led to the establishment of:

THE COUNCIL OF EUROPE. Statute signed in London, May 5, 1949, by 10 Foreign Ministers. Unlike other groups here listed, this is a public international organization, but is not a European Federation, as some of its supporters hoped it would be, since its organs at Strasbourg have no legislative, executive, or judicial powers. They comprise a Consultative Assembly meeting twice a year and consisting of 127 representatives, almost all members of parliaments: 18 each from Britain, France, Western Germany, Italy; 10 from Turkey; 6 each from Belgium, Greece, Netherlands, Sweden; 4 each from Denmark, Norway, Ireland; 3 each from Iceland, Luxembourg, Saar; a Council of Ministers, consisting of Foreign Ministers or their alternates meeting thrice a year; and a Secretariat of 200 members. Functions are exclusively deliberative and advisory. Austria became a member in 1956.[24]

Advocates of a regional federation of democracies thus achieved a European intergovernmental organization, albeit not a federation. Prospects for an actual federation of Europe, or of the Atlantic Democracies, or of the British Commonwealth, Western Europe, and the Americas were not promising in the 1950's, despite advocacy of European integration by Dwight D. Eisenhower and other distinguished Americans and despite the establishment and growth of NATO, the adoption of the Schuman Plan (see p. 366), and other steps toward unity. Meanwhile, advocates of a global federation, laboring amid many discouragements, won converts. Among the organizations committed to this goal were these:

CITIZENS' COMMITTEE FOR UNITED NATIONS REFORM (CCUNR), founded, 1946, by the late Ely Culbertson, bridge expert and author of *Total Peace* (1943) and supported by Dorothy Thompson, Sidney Hook, Norman Thomas, George S. Counts, *et al.* Program, "with Russia if possible, without Russia if necessary": a "Quota

[24] For a detailed and sympathetic commentary, see the author's "The Council of Europe," *American Political Science Review,* September, 1951; for a negative evaluation, see Karl Loewenstein, "The Union of Europe: Illusion and Reality," *Columbia Law Review,* January–February, 1952. See also the *News Letter* of the American Committee for a United Europe (William J. Donovan, Chairman).

Force Plan" for a UN Police Force, with an international contingent made up of volunteers from small States, to comprise 20% of the world's armed forces; USA, U.K., and USSR each to have 20%; and France and China 10% each, with all thereby, in theory, protected against aggression. Abolition of veto. World Court to determine aggression. Security Council to order punitive action. Despite its verbiage, this is not a proposal for federation, since it still relies on the coercion of States as the means toward peace.

FEDERAL UNION, LTD., founded 1938, and supported by Lionel Curtis, Lord Lothian, Wickham Steed, Barbara Wootton, Lord Beveridge. Secretary: J. Keith Killby. Journal: *Federal News.* Program: European Federation, Atlantic Federation, World Federation, all to be promoted by all effective means.

UNITED WORLD FEDERALISTS (UWF), founded, 1947, by six earlier organizations. President: Cord Meyer, Jr., author of *Peace or Anarchy* (1947); Alan Cranston, 1948*ff.*; Norman Cousins, 1952*ff.* Supporters: Cass Canfield, Grenville Clark, William O. Douglas, W. T. Holliday, Robert E. Sherwood, Raymond Swing, Stringfellow Barr, *et al.* Journal: *The Federalist.* Program: "A world federal government, universal and strong enough to prevent armed conflict between nations, and having direct jurisdiction over individuals in those matters within its authority," to be achieved through amendment of the UN Charter, cooperation and conferences to draft plans, etc. The Rev. Donald Harrington was President in 1958.

PEOPLES' WORLD CONVENTION (PWC), founded, 1948, at Luxembourg Congress of WMWFG (Henry Usborne, first chairman of Steering Committee) on basis of earlier activities of Mary and Georgia Lloyd, Robert Sarrazac's "Mondialization" movement, Garry Davis's "International Registry of World Citizens," British "Crusade for World Government," and Fyke Farmer of Tennessee. Program: a popularly elected global constitutional convention to draft a charter of world government. PWC met in Geneva, Dec. 30, 1950, under chairmanship of Henry Usborne, attended by 500 people from 42 countries, but including only 2 elected delegates, Fyke Farmer and William A. Harwell of Tennessee, with Prof. Eyo Ita of Nigeria accorded same status.

WORLD MOVEMENT FOR WORLD FEDERAL GOVERNMENT (WMWFG), founded, 1946, in Luxembourg as a federation of federalist groups. First President: Lord Boyd Orr. Program: a federal world constitution with a bill of rights, providing for world citizenship, a world legislature, executive, and judiciary, world law enforcement on individuals, and reservation of residual powers to member States. UWF is largest unit.[25]

COMMITTEE TO FRAME A WORLD CONSTITUTION, founded in Chicago, 1945, by Robert M. Hutchins, G. A. Borgese, Mortimer J. Adler, Rexford G. Tugwell, String-

---

[25] At the Fourth Congress in Rome, April 2–9, 1951, Pope Pius XII received the delegates and declared: "What a large amount of moral firmness, intelligent foresight, and supple adaptation this world authority will have to possess, more than ever necessary in critical moments when, in the face of malevolence, people of good will need to be supported by authority! After all our past and present trials, should we dare to say that the resources and methods of government and politics today are adequate? In truth, it is impossible to solve the problem of a world political organization without agreeing to leave the beaten track from time to time, without appealing to the experience of history, and to a sane social philosophy, or even to some kind of vision from creative imagination.

"There, Gentlemen, is a vast field of work, study, and action. You have understood this and looked it squarely in the face; you have the courage to spend yourselves for this cause. We congratulate you. We would express to you our wishes for your entire success and with all our heart we will pray to God to grant you His wisdom and help in the performance of your task."

fellow Barr (President of the Foundation for World Government), Robert Redfield, *et al.* Journal: *Common Cause*, June, 1947–July, 1951. Preliminary Draft of a World Constitution, completed and presented March, 1948, as a "proposal to history." Ingenious solution of the problem of representation through a unicameral World Council, chosen by 9 regional electoral colleges.

These and similar endeavors stirred some to enthusiasm and hope, but the majority of mankind remained unmoved, as did most national policy-makers. The Chicago Committee could say of world government: "It is necessary; therefore it is possible." Chancellor Hutchins wrote in June, 1947: "If we wish to be saved, we shall have to practice justice and love, however humiliating it may be to do so. These practices have long been commended to us by the very highest authority; they now appear to be our only alternative to beggary and annihilation. . . ." Some were persuaded. In Britain and on the Continent, many pronounced themselves "world citizens." Sundry polls and pilot elections were held. Some municipalities declared themselves members of the "world community." In America local referenda and elections indicated widespread popular endorsement of the federalist ideal. Beginning in his native North Carolina in 1941, Robert Lee Humber induced a score of state legislatures to endorse his "Declaration of the Federation of the World." At one time UWF resolutions commanded the support of over a hundred Representatives and a score of Senators.

By 1950, however, the icy hand of Cold War was killing the dream, along with many others. Communists shrieked that all proposals for world government were "Wall Street plots." Anti-Communists, *e.g.*, the D.A.R. and the American Legion, screamed that all world federalists were "subversive." The slogan for 1952 of the Veterans of Foreign Wars was "World Government Means World Communism!" Legislatures and Congressmen hastily withdrew support. Anxious citizens turned back to ancient faith in tribal gods—and to the human sacrifices they demanded.

"We have war," wrote Bartolomeo Vanzetti, "because we are not sufficiently heroic for a life which does not need war." But the alternative to world government is not necessarily world disorder, world war, and world annihilation. If men are wise, the alternative is a new balance of power and a new diplomacy designed to prevent violence and promote order by settling conflicts through bargaining. Yet if men were wise they would perhaps have long since found means of giving political expression to the age-old vision of the unity of mankind. For this today's generation is obviously not yet ready.

SUGGESTED READINGS

Adler, Mortimer: *How to Think about War and Peace*, New York, Simon and Schuster, 1944.

Bartlett, Ruhl J.: *The League to Enforce Peace*, Chapel Hill, N.C., University of North Carolina Press, 1945.

SUGGESTED READINGS

Beckel, Graham: *Workshops for the World: The Specialized Agencies of the United Nations*, New York, Abelard-Schuman, 1954.

Berber, F. J. (ed.): *Locarno: A Collection of Documents*, Edinburgh, Hodge, 1936.

Borgese, G. A.: *Common Cause*, New York, Duell, Sloan & Pearce, 1943.

Bryson, Lyman, *et al.* (eds.): *Foundations of World Organization: A Political and Cultural Appraisal*, New York, Harper, 1952.

Buell, Raymond L.: *The Washington Conference*, New York, Appleton-Century-Crofts, 1922.

Chase, Eugene P.: *The United Nations in Action*, New York, McGraw-Hill, 1950.

Cheever, Daniel S., and H. Field Haviland, Jr.: *Organizing for Peace*, Boston, Houghton Mifflin, 1956.

Chung, Kyung Cho: *Korea Tomorrow*, New York, Macmillan, 1956.

Claude, Inis L., Jr.: *Swords into Plowshares*, New York, Random House, 1956.

Curtis, Lionel: *World Order (Civitas Dei)*, New York, Oxford, 1939.

De Russett, Alan: *Strengthening the Framework of Peace*, London, Royal Institute of International Affairs, 1950.

Dunn, Frederick S.: *War and the Minds of Men* (UNESCO), New York, Harper, 1950.

Eagleton, Clyde: *International Government*, New York, Ronald, 1947.

Ferrell, Robert H.: *Peace in Their Time: The Origins of the Kellogg-Briand Pact*, New Haven, Conn., Yale University Press, 1952.

Finer, Herman: *The United Nations Economic and Social Council*, Boston, World Peace Foundation, 1946.

Fleming, D. F.: *The United States and World Organization*, 1920–1933, New York, Columbia University Press, 1938.

Goodrich, Leland M., and Edvard Hambro: *Charter of the United Nations: Commentary and Documents*, Boston, World Peace Foundation, 1947.

——, and Anne P. Simons: *The United Nations and the Maintenance of International Peace and Security*, Washington, Brookings, 1955.

——: *Korea: A Study of U.S. Policy in the United Nations*, New York, Council on Foreign Relations, 1956.

Gourevitch, Boris: *The Road to Peace and to Moral Democracy: An Encyclopedia of Peace*, New York, International Universities Press, 1954.

Haviland, H. Field, Jr.: *The Political Role of the General Assembly*, New York, Carnegie Endowment, 1951.

Hemleben, Sylvester John: *Plans for World Peace through Six Centuries*, Chicago, University of Chicago Press, 1943.

Hill, Norman: *International Organization*, New York, Harper, 1952.

Hogan, Willard N.: *International Conflict and Collective Security*, Lexington, Ky., University of Kentucky Press, 1955.

Johnson, Julia Emily (comp.): *United Nations: or World Government*, New York, H. W. Wilson, 1947.

Kelsen, Hans: *The Law of the United Nations*, New York, Praeger, 1952.

Leonard, L. Larry: *International Organization*, New York, McGraw-Hill, 1951.

Levi, Werner: *Fundamentals of World Organization*, Minneapolis, University of Minnesota Press, 1950.

Lie, Trygve: *In the Cause of Peace*, New York, Macmillan, 1954.

McCune, George M., and Arthur L. Grey, Jr.: *Korea Today*, Cambridge, Mass., Harvard University Press, 1950.

Maclaurin, John: *The United Nations and Power Politics*, New York, Harper, 1951.

MacMahon, Arthur W. (ed.): *Federalism Mature and Emergent*, New York, Doubleday, 1955.

Mander, L. A.: *Foundations of Modern World Society*, Stanford, Calif., Stanford University Press, 1947.

Mangone, Gerard J.: *The Idea and Practice of World Government*, New York, Columbia University Press, 1951.

——: *A Short History of International Organization*, New York, McGraw-Hill, 1954.

Marburg, Theodore: *Development of the League of Nations Idea* (2 vols.), New York, Macmillan, 1932.

Marriott, Sir John A. R.: *Commonwealth or Anarchy*, New York, Columbia University Press, 1939.

Meyer, Cord, Jr.: *Peace or Anarchy*, Boston, Little, Brown, 1947.

Miller, David H.: *The Drafting of the Covenant*, New York, Putnam, 1928.

Potter, Pitman B.: *An Introduction to the Study of International Organization*, New York, Appleton-Century-Crofts, 1951.

Rappard, William E.: *The Quest for Peace*, Cambridge, Mass., Harvard University Press, 1940.

Reves, Emery: *The Anatomy of Peace*, New York, Harper, 1945.

Reynaud, Paul: *Unite or Perish: A Dynamic Program for a United Europe*, New York, Simon and Schuster, 1951.

Robertson, A. H.: *The Council of Europe*, New York, Praeger, 1956.

Schuman, F. L.: *The Commonwealth of Man: An Inquiry into Power Politics and World Government*, New York, Knopf, 1952.

Schwebel, Stephen M.: *The Secretary-General of the United Nations*, Cambridge, Mass., Harvard University Press, 1952.

Sohn, Louis B.: *World Law: Cases and Materials on U.N.*, Brooklyn, Foundation Press, 1950.

—— (ed.): *Basic Documents of the United Nations*, Brooklyn, Foundation Press, 1956.

—— (ed.): *Cases on United Nations Law*, Brooklyn, Foundation Press, 1956.

Stone, I. F.: *The Hidden History of the Korean War*, New York, Monthly Review Press, 1952.

Streit, Clarence K.: *Freedom against Itself*, New York, Harper, 1954.

Tate, Merze: *The United States and Armaments*, Cambridge, Mass., Harvard University Press, 1948.

The United Nations: *Weekly Bulletin; Handbook; Yearbook; Journal.* (See also *Yearbook of International Organizations;* the World Peace Foundation quarterly, *International Organization;* New York University Press, *Annual Review of U.N. Affairs;* and the unofficial monthly, *United Nations World.*)

Vandenbosch, Amry, and Willard N. Hogan: *The United Nations: Background, Organization, Functions, and Activities*, New York, McGraw-Hill, 1952.

Walters, F. P.: *A History of the League of Nations*, New York, Oxford, 1952.

White, Lyman Cromwell, and Marie Ragonetti Zooca: *International Non-governmental Organizations*, New Brunswick, N.J., Rutgers University Press, 1951.

Whitney, Maj. Gen. Courtney: *MacArthur: His Rendezvous with History*, New York, Knopf, 1956.

Wilcox, F. O., and C. M. Marcy: *Proposals for Changes in the United Nations*, Washington, Brookings, 1955.

Wright, Quincy (ed.): *The World Community*, Chicago, University of Chicago Press, 1948.

Wynner, Edith, and Georgia Lloyd: *Searchlight on Peace Plans*, New York, Dutton, 1944.

York, E.: *Leagues of Nations, Ancient, Medieval, and Modern*, London, Swarthmore Press, 1928.

In all times, kings, and persons of sovereign authority, because of their independency, are in continual jealousies, and in the state and posture of gladiators; having their weapons pointing, and their eyes fixed on one another; that is, their forts, garrisons and guns upon the frontiers of their kingdoms; and continual spies upon their neighbors; which is a posture of war. . . . The notions of right and wrong, justice and injustice, have there no place. Where there is no common power, there is no law: where no law, no injustice. Force and fraud are in war the two cardinal virtues. . . . It is consequent also to the same condition that there be no propriety, no dominion, no "mine" and "thine" distinct; but only that to be every man's that he can get; and for so long as he can keep it.—THOMAS HOBBES, *Leviathan*, 1651.

A Book of

FORCES

O Lord our God, help us to tear their soldiers to bloody shreds with our shells; help us to cover their smiling fields with the pale forms of their patriot dead; help us to drown the thunder of the guns with the cries of the wounded, writhing in pain; help us to lay waste their humble homes with a hurricane of fire; help us to wring the hearts of their unoffending widows with unavailing grief; help us to turn them out roofless with their little children to wander unbefriended through the wastes of their desolated land in rags and hunger and thirst, sport of the sun flames of summer and the icy winds of winter, broken in spirit, worn with travail, imploring Thee for the refuge of the grave and denied it—for our sakes, who adore Thee, Lord, blast their hopes, blight their lives, protract their bitter pilgrimage, make heavy their steps, water their way with their tears, stain the white snow with the blood of their wounded feet! We ask of One who is the spirit of love and who is the ever faithful refuge and friend of all that are sore beset, and seek His aid with humble and contrite hearts. Grant our prayer, O Lord, and Thine shall be the praise and honor and glory, now and ever. Amen.—MARK TWAIN, *War Prayer*.

CHAPTER VIII

THE GUARDING OF POWER

1. THE PREMISE OF VIOLENCE

Statesmen, to be faithful to their duties, must use means that are not permissible to the private citizen.—SIR FRANCIS WALSINGHAM, 1530–90.

> Plenty begets Pride; Pride, Envy, Envy, Warre,
> Warre, Poverty, Poverty humble Care;
> Humility breeds Peace, and Peace breeds Plenty;
> Thus around the World doth rowle alternately.
> —ROBERT HAYMAN, *The World's Whirlegigge*, 1631.

THE INSTITUTION of war has troubled men's minds since the first civilizations. Moralists have denounced it as the greatest of evils. Statesmen have deplored it but often pronounced it salutary or necessary to preserve "independence," "honor," "freedom," and—"peace." Home-front patriots have usually found it good, in so far as it furnished patriotic excitement, vicarious joy of battle without risk, and, more frequently than not, jobs, contracts, profits, and wealth with a minimum of competitive effort. Soldiers and sailors have found it alternately beautiful and hideous, fascinating and boring, heroic and criminal, magnificent and monstrous. Most men and women would doubtless concur in the judgment of Croesus, King of Lydia, in his words of woe to Cyrus the Persian: "No one is so senseless as to choose of his own free will war rather than peace, since in peace the sons bury their fathers, but in the war the fathers bury their sons."

Yet it is only in periods of "World States" or Universal Empires that men have known peace as anything other than an interlude between wars. The anguish of spirit which war brings consciously to many, and unconsciously to all, stems from an inner conflict. All the higher religions of mankind have preached love and brotherhood among the children of God. But all men through the ages have found in war a stimulant to action, an occasion for self-sacrifice, a gaudy escape from tedium and guilt, and a means to the happiness, as Nietzsche put it, of "murder with a good conscience." War has ever been the epitome of the eternal conflict in men's hearts between the bestial and superhuman, the diabolical and the divine. Since men appear incapable of loving one another as members of humanity, they succeed in achieving their most plausible approximation to love, fellowship, solidarity,

272

and collective endeavor for "unselfish" ends through fearing and hating and then butchering one another as members of national communities or religious cults or disciples of ideological creeds. Through war their frustrations, tensions, and aggressions find modes of expression which are not only socially sanctioned but are equated with the highest level of morality and selfless devotion in all the civilized cultures of the species.[1]

War, it will here be argued, is a phenomenon of politics, to be understood within the context of specifically political motives and practices. Love, fear, and hate are as universal as human experience itself. They are the wells of energy and action within all personalities which overflow at the command of the war makers. But men may, and often do, love their wives, their children, their neighbors rather than their country, State, or faith. They may discharge their hates, fears, and frustrations in private rather than public ways by beating their spouses, offspring, or dogs, brawling with their friends, abusing their employers or employees, or losing themselves in alcohol, sex, or gambling— all acts which, however deplorable, are less destructive to society as a whole than organized intergroup violence. War itself is not "instinctive" and is not implicit in "human nature." The collective fixations of rage, fright, or affection on the public symbols of government and fatherland, of "our" side and "their" side, are products of a specific type of civic training and a particular pattern of political activity and purpose.

If it be true that the State itself, as a ubiquitous institution in all literate cultures, most probably had its origins in violence, theft, and exploitation, then it might seem to follow that political man, acting in the name of the State, almost inevitably resorts to exploitation, theft, and violence in dealing with other States. The record of the past, however, scarcely supports any such sweeping conclusion. On the contrary, it suggests almost incontrovertibly that men organized into States are disposed to fight other men organized into States only when the States are fully sovereign and acknowledge no authority superior to themselves. The human communities named Illinois and Wisconsin, Sonora and Chihuahua, Ontario and Quebec, Kazakistan and Kirghizia are also "States." They neither wage war nor assume its possibility among themselves because their citizens acknowledge a loyalty higher than their local allegiance. If such other communities as "France," "Germany," "the United States," and "the Soviet Union" are in a different position toward one another, the difference lies precisely in the circumstance that no higher power stands above them.

The Will to Power. The broader aspects of interstate politics under these conditions admit of simple and precise description. The sovereign members of a community of States lacking common government must inevitably view one

---

[1] For an excellent statement of the problem, see "Tensions Affecting International Understanding" (Paris, UNESCO, May, 1947), A Preliminary Outline of a Study Project in the Social Sciences Section, prepared with the aid of Dr. Edward A. Shils.

another with distrust and anxiety. Since each has no control over the acts of the others, enjoys no participation in any effective merging of local purposes into a larger polity, and accordingly has no assurance as to what others may do, all must suspect the worst of each. Every unit in such a System necessarily seeks safety by relying on its own power and viewing with alarm the power of its neighbors. This being so, the neighbors have no choice but to do likewise.

The "power" which must thus be solicitously guarded in one's own State and looked at askance in others is, in the last analysis, military power or fighting capacity. Power per se is ability to "win friends and influence people," to evoke sympathy, to command obedience, to employ effectively all the devices of coercion, propaganda, and material indulgences and deprivations likely to induce respect and cooperation. But the power which is of prime concern to sovereignties in dealing with other sovereignties is a quality at once simpler, more limited, and more uncertain than the power which concerns politicians, parties, pressure groups, lobbies, and voters acting within the framework of organized government. Here recourse to force is minimized and indeed effectively forbidden (usually) by those entrusted with a monopoly of coercive authority. Fraud and favors—i.e., appeals to prejudice, reason, and avarice—are predominant under conditions regarded as normal. But among independent States these means of influence, while often important, are restricted in their scope and efficacy. The *ultima ratio regum* of sovereigns in dealing with other sovereigns is force.

From all past experience each State must assume that its capacity to protect its interests and defend its existence in the face of other States is contingent upon its ability to employ armed violence persuasively. With some exceptions to be noted presently, no State incapable of waging effective war can reasonably expect other States to meet its demands, heed its wishes, or even acknowledge its right to survival. In the bargaining processes of diplomacy, "prestige" is all-important. Prestige is reputation for power. Diplomacy is thus potential war, just as war is a business of seeking political objectives by military coercion rather than by bargaining. In both cases, ability to use arms with skill and success is rather more than likely to be decisive. The pursuit of power, therefore, tends to become an end in itself rather than a means to other ends. No other ends matter if the State lacks power to serve its ultimate end: self-preservation.

Concern with fighting capacity easily becomes an obsession by virtue of the fact that each State, ideally, can best preserve its power by expanding it and can most surely guarantee its own security by depriving others of theirs. Every sovereignty can best maintain its own independence against all possible threats by extinguishing the independence of its neighbors and rivals. If it possesses sufficient power to do so, and others lack sufficient power to resist the effort, it will, with almost mathematical certainty, proceed to subject them to its authority. This being so, each State which hopes to survive must not

only maintain its own power in a shape adequate for all anticipated contingencies but must seek to thwart any enhancement of the power of others which
might enable them to prevail in a test of force.

Power is thus a relative, not an absolute, quantity. One State's gain is, automatically, another's loss. Each State, moreover, will concern itself not with
power in relationship to all other States, regardless of time or place, but only
with power in relationship to particular States which are envisaged as rivals
and potential foes. Power is local, as well as relative. Its efficacy diminishes
as it is extended through distance, even in periods (like our own) of the most
advanced technology for overcoming mileage and exerting force effectively
at remote points.

The Waltz of the Powers. The Western State System has developed in
such fashion that no one of its members possesses at any time sufficient power
to extend its control over all the others. In the interests of self-defense, the
members tend to combine against any one which is a potential menace to all.
Invariably the pretender to world power is repressed by a coalition of the
prospective victims. Each Power thus retains its independence, and the State
System is preserved. Under these circumstances, an equilibrium, or balance
of power, results. At times it is intangible, imponderable, and in the background of diplomatic action. At other times, it is clearly and sharply defined
in alliances and coalitions. Each member of an alliance has an interest in forestalling any enhancement of the power of the opposing alliance. The two
coalitions are thus held together by a common interest. Conflicts for power
become issues between the alliances as a whole. This pattern of relationships
has characterized the Western State System from its earliest beginnings.

The difficulties involved in the balancing process, and the delicacy and
finesse with which operations must be conducted, were well put by Bolingbroke in the early 18th Century:

The scales of the balance of power will never be exactly poised, nor is the precise
point of equality either desirable or necessary to be discerned. It is sufficient in this
as in other human affairs, that the deviation be not too great. Some there will
always be. A constant attention to these deviations is therefore necessary. When
they are little their increase may be easily prevented by early care and the precautions that good policy suggests. But when they become great for want of this
care and these precautions, or by the force of unforeseen events, more vigor is to
be exerted, and greater efforts to be made. But even in such cases, much reflection
is necessary on all the circumstances that form the conjuncture; lest, by attacking
with ill success, the deviation be confirmed, and the power that is deemed already
exorbitant become more so; and lest, by attacking with good success, whilst one
scale is pillaged, too much weight of power be thrown into the other. In such cases,
he who has considered, in the histories of former ages, the strange revolutions
that time produces, and the perpetual flux and reflux of public as well as private
fortunes, of kingdoms and states as well as of those who govern or are governed
in them, will incline to think, that if the scales can be brought back by a war,
nearly, though not exactly, to the point they were at before this great deviation

from it, the rest may be left to accidents, and to the use that good policy is able to make of them.[2]

The role of small States in this system of relationships is a peculiar one. The very minute States of Europe are historical curiosities and play no part in the game. But such States as Portugal, Belgium, the Netherlands, Denmark, Switzerland, Albania, and the like, are all adjacent to more powerful States which could easily impose their will upon them and extinguish their independence if granted a free hand. But usually this result is rendered impossible by the conflicting interests of the great States themselves. The small States, being impotent, have no power interests of their own save the preservation of their independence; and this they are able to protect, not by their own power, but by fitting themselves into the power relations of their mighty neighbors. The small States are often "buffers." They stand at the focal points of tension between the Great Powers, with the result that each Power prefers the maintenance of the independence of the small State to the extinction of that independence at the hands of a rival. The Low Countries lie between England, France, and Germany, each of which opposes control by either of the others of this strategic area containing the mouths of the Rhine and the Scheldt. Denmark is similarly a buffer between Germany and Britain. Switzerland is most secure of all, for it is surrounded by rival Powers: France, Germany, Italy, and formerly Austria-Hungary. In every case the buffer State is dependent for its security in peacetime upon the diplomatic rivalries of its neighbors. In a general war among the Powers, it may be able to remain neutral, unless it becomes a theater of battle between the belligerents. In the latter case, it must align itself with that coalition which seems least likely to deprive it of independence in the event of victory.

Considerations of a similar character serve to explain the continued independence of small or weak native States in the areas of colonial rivalries between the Powers. Those which survive are located at the tension points between rival imperialisms and can play off the imperialists against one another. Ethiopia was long the vortex of converging drives of British, French, and Italian expansionists, who neutralized one another. Turkey similarly profited by conflicts between Russia, Britain, France, Germany, and Austria-Hungary. Iran and Afghanistan have been buffer States between British and Russian imperialisms. Thailand lay at the focal point of rival imperialisms in southeastern Asia. By the same token, the colonial possessions of minor Powers (e.g., Belgian and Portuguese Africa and the Dutch Indies) are sometimes secure against appropriation by Great Powers, because none of the latter can permit any of the others to acquire them.

The Balance of Indulgences and Deprivations. As regards the complex plays and counterplays of the Great Powers themselves in their constant

[2] *The Works of Lord Bolingbroke*, 1841, Vol. II, p. 291.

efforts to maintain or upset the balance of power, it is useful to recall Bismarck's distinction between "satiated" and "unsatiated" States. At any given time, the existing equilibrium, the prevailing distribution of power, the established ratios of territories, populations, armies, navies, colonies, etc., will appear ideal to the States which are its beneficiaries and inequitable to the States which do not feel that they have received their just due. The satiated, content with the *status quo,* will usually be those which have been victorious in the last armed conflict. The unsatiated will normally be those defeated in the last war and deprived of power by the victors. Rival alliances and coalitions emerge out of these relationships, the satiated combining to protect what they have acquired and the unsatiated combining to acquire what they covet.

A peculiar geographical pattern in the playing of the power game manifests itself in every State System. In 300 B.C. it was described by Kautilya in his *Arthasastra* in commenting on the appropriate rules of political rivalry in ancient India:

> The king, who, being possessed of great character and best-fitted elements of sovereignty, is the fountain of policy, is termed the conqueror. The king who is situated anywhere immediately on the circumference of the conqueror's territory is termed the enemy. The king who is likewise situated close to the enemy, but separated from the conqueror only by the enemy, is termed the friend [of the conqueror]. A neighbouring foe of considerable power is styled an enemy; and when he is involved in calamities or has taken himself to evil ways, he becomes assailable; and when he has little or no help, he becomes destructible; otherwise [*i.e.,* when he is provided with some help], he deserves to be harassed or reduced. Such are the aspects of an enemy. In front of the conqueror and close to his enemy, there happen to be situated kings such as the conqueror's friend, next to him, the enemy's friend, and next to the last, the conqueror's friend's friend. In the rear of the conqueror, there happen to be situated a rearward enemy, a rearward friend, an ally of the rearward enemy, and an ally of the rearward friend.

On the chessboard of power politics, in a multipolar world of many Powers, each Power is typically the potential enemy of its neighbors and the potential ally of its neighbors' neighbors. States which are neighbors are "friends" only when they both fear a third neighbor (as Britain and France vis-à-vis Germany, 1904–40) or when they have by mutual consent renounced the game of power (as the USA and Canada since 1815). Proximity otherwise breeds rivalry for control of border areas which, once controlled, will give the controller superiority of power over his neighbor. Since outflanking and encircling operations are of the essence of war and since diplomacy is potential war, it is advantageous for each Power to have allies on the flanks or in the rear of its foe. Thus France and Britain were aligned with Russia before 1914 and with Poland, Czechoslovakia, Jugoslavia, and Rumania after 1919. In the face of this bloc, Germany, Italy, Hungary, Bulgaria, and the Soviet Union had common interests which found expression in the "Axis" and in the partitions of Poland and Rumania in 1939–40. In the larger arena of the world,

Germany, Italy, and Japan became allies against the USSR and the English-speaking Powers, while the United States, the Soviet Union, and Britain became allies against the opposing coalition.

In the balancing-of-power process, long-festering fears and hatreds lead to periodical explosions of violence because the process operates haltingly and ineffectively. Any increase in the power of unsatiated States, through heavier armaments or alliances, creates new insecurities among the satiated and causes them to seek to redress the balance by still heavier armaments or counter-alliances. But the compensatory policies seldom restore the equilibrium to its old level. They create new insecurities among the "have-nots," driving them to further steps to enhance their ability to overthrow the *status quo* by force. The "haves," moreover, are committed to "peace" and are reluctant to risk conflict or meet a challenge by a war of prevention. They typically procrastinate, make excuses for inaction, and fall victims to depressing anxieties without taking decisive action until it is too late to restore the balance. Imperial Germany after 1871 thus permitted France to rearm and form a coalition against her, without counterattacking until the strategic moment had long since passed. The French bloc and Britain, after 1933, permitted Germany and Italy to increase their power to a point at which they could upset the *status quo* and render any effort to thwart their designs highly dangerous. Counteraction was postponed in proportion as it became more and more difficult. In the bipolar world of mid-century, both the USA and the USSR were determined not to make this mistake in dealing with the other—and resolved to make all their neighbors allies against the enemy, since no potential allies were available at the rear of a foe commanding half the planet. But in every case each equilibrium generates tensions that explode in cataclysmic readjustments because the players of the game are unable or unwilling to achieve smooth and gradual readjustments by other means.

2. DIPLOMACY AS WAR

Even though all high politics tries to be a substitution of more intellectual weapons for the sword and though it is the ambition of the statesman at the culminations of all the cultures to feel able to dispense with war, yet the primary relationship between diplomacy and the war-art endures. The character of battle is common to both, and the tactics and stratagems, and the necessity of material forces in the background to give weight to the operations. The aim too remains the same—namely, the growth of one's own life unit (class or nation) at the cost of the other's.—OSWALD SPENGLER, *The Decline of the West*, II.

In international law the distinction between war and peace is sharp and clear. In political practice the distinction has become less clear for we now "wage peace" and prevent war by "preventive wars" and find ourselves in an age of "phony wars," "cold wars," crusades for peace, and even, as Charles

DIPLOMACY AS WAR

A. Beard once put it, "perpetual war for perpetual peace." Despite semantic confusions, the fact of the matter is that in a State System of competing Powers, the primary objective of foreign policy in peace and in war is neither war nor peace but something common to both: the enhancement of the power of your State to resist the will of others and impose your will upon them, and the diminution of the power of others to resist your will and impose their will upon you. In "war" this goal is pursued by overt violence, and in "peace" by bargaining supported by threats of force.

Means and Ends. Arms and allies are the tools of power. The task of diplomacy is to keep the powder dry and to win friends and influence people. How to succeed in diplomacy is a question simply answered, though the answer is more easily stated than practiced: maintain armed forces larger and heavier than those of your rival and well adapted to the service of your political purposes, and conclude alliances with other Powers against your potential enemy, taking care to keep him isolated. But avoid allies far stronger *note* or far weaker than yourself, for the former will seek to rule you and the latter will bring you to ruin by proving liabilities in war and a constant drain on your resources in peace. One powerful and trustworthy ally is worth a dozen feeble and fickle allies. Therefore, other things being equal, a limited coalition of a few formidable Powers, strategically placed, is preferable to a general aggregation of doubtful States scattered far and wide.

The problem of defining the purposes for which power is to be used is difficult in a Grand Alliance where many must agree on common action. Definition in broad abstractions leaves all uncertain as to who is committed to what in a crisis. Definition in minutely detailed accords is inflexible in unforeseen contingencies. A just mean between these extremes must be sought. And if fortune is to bless the enterprise, every effort must be made to bind allies solidly together through regular consultation, shared advantages and dangers, well-conceived propaganda, and judicious allocation of favors among the nations and the men involved.

As for the broader question of the general orientation of foreign policy, all diplomacy, like all politics, is the art of the possible. Statesmanship consists in perceiving the limits of what is possible, delineating objectives clearly, and organizing power commensurate with commitments. To amass power inadequate to purposes, or excessive for their attainment, is to invite insolvency. An obviously "satiated" State will concern itself with maintaining the *status quo* and resisting all efforts to change it. An "unsatiated" State will strive to take advantage of every opportunity to alter the distribution of satisfactions. Both, if wisely governed, will weigh the consequences of acts less in terms of the "merits" of any given controversy than in terms of the probable effects of alternative solutions on the total balance of power. For in the game of power politics only power can match power, whether it is to be used to preserve or to change the prevailing apportionment of the stakes of diplomacy.

And since power in the final test is military might, the stakes which will be cherished most dearly and pursued most assiduously will be (or ought to be) those things which affect relative fighting capacity.

Here, as in all games of chance and skill, daring players are tempted to risk all in the hope of winning all. Maximum power to rule others and maximum security against being ruled by others are clearly to be had for each State in every State System by the subjugation and annexation of all the rest.[3] Such an "unlimited" goal, pursued by stages from a superiority to a preponderance to a monopoly of power, was achieved in days of old by the Consuls and Caesars of Rome. But experience suggests that this objective is unattainable in the Western State System, since all Powers and combinations of Powers that have striven for it have come to grief and been cast down by a coalition of prospective victims.

Others will doubtless try again, since men must ever relearn what is possible by attempting the impossible. Even in dealing with weak States, every Power discovers that moderate demands supported by superior force will be complied with but that immoderate demands, such as extinction of independence, will often be fought to the death, however hopeless the fight—just as a man set upon by thieves may yield his money to save his life but will offer furious resistance, if only to sell his life dearly, if assaulted by known assassins. Unlimited aggrandizement as a purpose of policy may achieve striking initial successes, even if well advertised in advance (*e.g.*, Hitler's *Mein Kampf*, the Tanaka Memorial, Stalin's *Problems of Leninism*), since few will take such threats seriously. But the terminal point of all such adventures in the Western State System thus far has been so uniform, thanks to balance-of-power policies by others, that responsible statesmanship will eschew such goals.

Moralism vs. Interests. Another form of "unlimited" purpose is the devotion of policy-makers to immutable "principles" of religion, law, or ethics to which all other States are expected to conform as the indispensable condition of national security, peaceful coexistence, and justice in the universe. This is the point of departure in foreign policy of most religious and ideological fanatics. In a world of permanent and inescapable diversity it is more than probable that no single code of conduct will ever be accepted by, or successfully imposed upon, all the communities of the Great Society. Efforts to achieve global unity or the "rule of law" in this fashion lead only to wars of extermination ending in mutual exhaustion. Powers that convert their foreign policies into crusades for righteousness are foredoomed to experience defiance, indignation, and frustration.[4]

---

[3] Cecil Rhodes, having built a vast empire in Africa, said: "I would annex the planets if I could. It makes me sad to see them so clear and so far away."

[4] John Hay once asserted that U.S. foreign policy was based on the Monroe Doctrine and the Golden Rule. Cordell Hull declared on July 16, 1937: "This country constantly and consistently advocates maintenance of peace. We advocate national and international self-restraint. We advocate abstinence by all nations from the use of force in pursuit of policy

DIPLOMACY AS WAR

This is not to say that "national interest" and "moral principles" are of necessity antithetical or incompatible, but only that foreign policies based primarily upon moral precepts which are inapplicable to relationships among sovereignties will in most instances be of no service either to the interests of the Power so afflicted or to the realization of the ethical values thus sought to be served. Judicious *Realpolitik* is a safer guide in diplomacy than universalistic Messianism. Sovereigns are not above morality. But the pursuit and preservation of power in a world of sovereignties lacking common government often require, as the only means of safety and survival, "immoral" or "Machiavellian" policies inconsistent with personal ethics. Wise diplomats, however, will remember the injunction of the Florentine that a Prince must at least appear to be virtuous, and this not for reasons of conscience but for pragmatic reasons of politics. Diplomacy requires bargaining. A Power which repeatedly and flagrantly breaks its word, betrays its allies, and exhibits no decent respect for the opinions of mankind may win many rounds of the contest, but will lose in the end because no others will treat with it or trust it and all will turn their hands against it. Such a fate is likely to prove worse than the fate of a Power with which others find it difficult to negotiate because of its uncompromising adherence to moral abstractions.

Between the Scylla of unrealistic idealism and the Charybdis of unscrupulous ambition, national policy-makers must pick their way as best they can, assessing the plans and power of other States, calculating the consequences of alternative decisions, defining national interest through compromises among the necessary, the desirable, and the possible—and, in democracies at least, always keeping a wary eye on lawmakers, lobbies, pressure groups, the press, and public opinion without whose acquiescence no policy can be carried through. Since survival is the first law of life, the first duty of diplomats is

---

and from interference in the internal affairs of other nations. We advocate faithful observance of international agreements . . ." etc. Such "principles" are unexceptionable but bear little relationship to the facts of the world as it is, are of little service to American interest, and cannot be realized by any practicable pattern of American policy. See the author's "International Ideals and the National Interest" in the *Annals of the American Academy*, March, 1952. For a detailed and trenchant critique of this whole conception of policy, see Hans J. Morgenthau, *In Defense of the National Interest*, and George F. Kennan, *American Diplomacy*, 1900–1950 (University of Chicago Press, 1951). Kennan comments (pp. 95–96): "I see the most serious faults of our past policy formulation to lie in something that I might call the legalistic-moralistic approach to international problems. This approach runs like a red skein through our foreign policy of the last fifty years. . . . It is the belief that it should be possible to suppress the chaotic and dangerous aspirations of governments in the international field by the acceptance of some system of legal rules and restraints. This belief undoubtedly represents in part an attempt to transpose the Anglo-Saxon concept of individual law into the international field and to make it applicable to governments as it is applicable here at home to individuals. . . . It is the essence of this belief that, instead of taking the awkward conflicts of national interest and dealing with them on their merits with a view to finding the solutions least unsettling to the stability of international life, it would be better to find some formal criteria of a juridical nature by which the permissible behavior of states could be defined."

281

the promotion of national security. Its fulfillment demands solicitude for the preservation of the balance of power. When all Powers are evenly balanced, so that none can overwhelm the rest, some may be able to pursue policies of "isolationism" and "neutrality" and others may be able, albeit more dangerously, to adopt the role of *tertius gaudens* or "happy third" while rivals fight one another to a stalemate. But in all times and circumstances security depends upon power, and power is impotent unless translated, when necessary, into terms of armed might. From this truism springs the preoccupation of all Powers with armaments, and from this preoccupation flows a popular fallacy—namely, that armaments ensure peace.

The Quest for Hegemony. Since overwhelming preponderance of power will apparently guarantee its possessor full safety and major opportunities to impose his will on those poor in power, every Power strives to arrive at this coveted position. The ancient cry for "preparedness" stems from this calculation. The Romans, acting on the adage, *"si vis pacem, para bellum"* (if you wish peace, prepare for war), did in fact attain peace by securing a superiority and then a monopoly of armed might through the extinction of the independence of all rivals. But in our own State System, such action inevitably begets a competition in armaments among the Powers in the course of which all security is lost.

"Peace through strength" is as much a delusion as peace through weakness. If weakness invites attack, strength creates temptation to use it and evokes counter-strength which the enemy may use. Yet it is everywhere an article of faith and a principle of policy that armaments ensure peace on the premise that the prospective enemy will be "deterred" from attack if the strength massed to oppose him is so formidable as to make attack fearfully costly or fatal.[5] Such policies are at once fallacious and inevitable in a system of rival sovereignties.

[5] This contention is as old as Athens and Sparta. Before 1914 the catechism of the British Navy League asserted: "Defense consists in being so strong that it will be dangerous for your enemy to attack you." The German Navy League said the same, echoing the English spinster who is alleged to have remarked: "We ought to build our navy up to double the size of theirs if they build theirs up to the point they say they will if we build ours up!" Norman Angell in *The Great Illusion* (pp. 350–351) quotes Sir Edmund C. Cox in *Nineteenth Century*, April, 1910, as saying: "Is there no alternative to this endless yet futile competition in shipbuilding? Yes, there is. . . . It is to say to Germany: 'You must put an end to your warlike preparation. If we are not satisfied that you do so, we shall forthwith sink every battleship and cruiser which you possess. . . . The time shall be of our own choosing and not of yours, and that time shall be now!'" Sir Norman also quotes Admiral Fisher: "If you rub it in, both at home and abroad, that you are ready for instant war, with every unit of your strength in the first line and waiting to be first in, and hit your enemy in the belly and kick him when he is down, and boil your prisoners in oil (if you take any), and torture his women and children, then people will keep clear of you." Sir Norman asks whether Admiral Fisher himself would have been "deterred" by any such threats. "Is it not about time that each nation abandoned the somewhat childish assumption that things which would never frighten or deter it will frighten and deter its rivals?" The answer, half a century later, is clearly: not yet.

DIPLOMACY AS WAR

The fallacy stems from the fact that arms do not deter, save sometimes temporarily, but beget counter-arms. No Power in the Western State System has ever been able to establish enduring superiority over its rivals, and all are finally driven by fear to seek through force what they cannot attain through threats. The inevitability resides in the circumstance that if your enemy is arming against you, you have no choice except to arm against him or risk defeat. So the vicious circle continues to revolve in race after race in armaments, each beginning with weapons in arsenals to preserve peace and ending with weapons on battlefields to win wars. From this tragic destiny modern mankind has as yet found no way of escape. Hence all diplomats and strategists, with the support of all patriots, must continue willy-nilly to play the game.

The end of the game, thus far, has always been the same: a desperate decision to compel a "showdown" rather than endure mounting tensions and burdens which become intolerable. When national policy-makers reach this point their problem is how best to unleash a "preventive war" against the enemy with a show of justification for public consumption, or how best to goad him into attack—with the public then certain to rally to the "defense" of the fatherland.[6]

[6] The first procedure, exemplified in Napoleon's invasion of Russia in 1812, the Austro-Hungarian declaration of war on Serbia in 1914, the Nazi attack on the USSR in 1941, and the Israeli-Anglo-French attack on Egypt in 1956 (see pp. 416–420), appears from the record to be, generally, unwise. The second procedure is often brilliantly successful—e.g., Bismarck's famous "Ems Dispatch" of 1870, Poincaré's policy toward Berlin in 1914, and the diplomacy of the Roosevelt Administration in dealing with Japan in 1941 when Henry L. Stimson, in his diary of November 25, wrote that "the question is how we should manoeuvre them into the position of firing the first shot without allowing too much danger to ourselves." More recent, albeit abortive, instances are represented by U.S. Navy Secretary Francis Matthews's plea in August, 1950, for "aggression for peace," by Maj. Gen. Orville Anderson's appeals for immediate atomic bombing of Russia in 1951, and by Maj. Gen. Robert W. Grow's diary, listing appropriate targets he observed while U.S. Military Attaché in Moscow and declaring: "It seems to me that the time is ripe for a blow this year (1951). . . . This war cannot be conducted by Marquess of Queensbury rules. We must employ every subversive device to undermine the confidence and loyalty of Soviet subjects for their regime. . . . Anything, truth or falsehood, to poison the thoughts of the population! . . . We must understand that this war is total and is fought with all weapons. . . . What should we do to fill out the vacuum after the Soviet regime is destroyed?" Anderson was removed as Commandant of Maxwell Field Airbase. Grow was court-martialed for improper use of secret information and for having failed to safeguard it. (His diary was photostated by a Soviet agent in Frankfurt and published in East Germany by Richard Squires in *On the Path to War*.) On July 30, 1952, Grow was sentenced to a reprimand and suspension from command for six months. The Army explained that Grow was merely predicting a Soviet attack, not advocating an American attack, and that Squires had falsified, distorted, and misinterpreted the diary. On the same day Frank L. Howley, Vice-Chancellor of New York University and former Brigadier General and U.S. Commandant in Berlin, was quoted in Berlin as saying: "Our foreign policy should be based upon the fact that the Russian leaders are thieves and murderers." Wrote William Christian Bullitt in *The Great Globe Itself* (1946, p. 175), anent the possible use of the atomic bomb against Russia: "To execute a murderer is not an immoral act."

THE GUARDING OF POWER

3. WAR AS DIPLOMACY

War is politics continued by other [*i.e.*, forcible] means.—CLAUSEWITZ, *On War.*

When I say that the principal cause of war is war itself, I mean that the aim
for which war is judged worth while is most often something which itself affects
military power. Just as in military operations each side aims at getting anything
which will give it a military advantage, so in diplomacy each side aims at getting
anything which will enhance its power. Diplomacy is potential war. It is permeated
by the struggle for power and when potential breaks out into actual war, that is
usually because irreconcilable claims have been made to some element of power,
and neither side can claim such preponderance as to compel the other to give way
by a mere threat.—R. G. HAWTREY, *Economic Aspects of Sovereignty.*

If experts in sports could predict accurately the outcome of prize fights,
horse races, and football games, there would be no bets, no audiences, and
no contests. If experts in war and diplomacy could forecast correctly the results
of trial by battle, there would be no hostilities between States. Every decision
by national policy-makers to wage war (save in cases of hopeless resistance
to unprovoked attack) flows from an assumption that the forces at their disposal can defeat the enemy. This hypothesis, when tested by experiment, often
proves ludicrously false.[7] The experiment would be unnecessary if the balance
of power could be measured with precision. Since it cannot be, war remains
the sovereign method of ascertaining the relative power of the Powers.

Why States Fight. Wars are fought to secure, retain, or prevent the foe
from acquiring components of power which are deemed decisive for the future
balance of fighting capacity. Moral indignation on both sides is universal,
since men are so constituted that they do not fully enjoy slaughter and devastation unless they convince themselves that they are defending Good against
Evil. The ethical values which are alleged to be in process of defense or vindication are rationalizations—also among those who wage Holy Wars or
crusades against unbelievers in the honest conviction that their souls will be

---

[7] Instances are innumerable—*e.g.*, 1812, 1870, 1914 (on both sides), 1939 (on the Allied
side), 1950 (on the Communist side). When Hitler invaded Russia in June, 1941, British
military authorities opined that "it is possible that the first phase, involving the occupation
of Ukraine and Moscow, might take as little as 3 or as long as 6 weeks." General Marshall,
the U.S. War Department, and the General Staff estimated that Russia would be beaten
in "a minimum of one month and a possible maximum of three months." Well-informed
journalists concurred in these judgments—*e.g.*, George E. Sokolsky: "Soviet Russia has
bluffed the world for a quarter of a century, and the bluff has been called. . . . Soviet
Russia will soon be eliminated from the war altogether." Martin Dies: "Hitler will be in
control of Russia within 30 days." Fletcher Pratt: "It will take a miracle bigger than any
since biblical times to save Russia from a quick and complete defeat." *The New York
Times:* "It seems probable that Hitler will be able to achieve his main military objectives
in Russia within a few weeks." Paul Mallon: "America's diplomats and military men
agree in their expectation of what will be the fate of Russia. They both give the Reds no
more than four to six weeks." Karl von Weygand, Hearst journalist: "Win or lose the war,
the Stalin regime is fairly certain to go. It is doubtful whether the Communist regime can
withstand the shock of such a war."

saved only through the sincere practice of devout ferocity. The "aims" of the war, as elaborated in the course of bloodshed, are relevant to political realities when defined in terms of the elements of power being fought over and are usually relevant to nothing, save the necessity of mobilizing popular enthusiasm, when defined in terms of abstract principles. What wars are about is suggested in the famous answer attributed to Francis I when asked what differences of view involved him in constant hostilities with his royal brother, Charles V: "None whatever. We agree perfectly. We both want control of Italy!"

The persistent and popular idea that democracies are less given to warlike adventures than autocracies or dictatorships has no foundation in fact. Democratic rabble rousers are as much addicted as spell-binding tyrants to embarking upon war abroad as a means of promoting unity and loyalty at home, with the added factor that the free citizens of the democracy, once aroused to bellicose fervor, are less readily restrained from violence than the obedient subjects of a despot. In recent centuries it has been the Atlantic democracies, not the Eastern absolutisms, which have waged war upon and subjugated or dispossessed the native peoples of most of the non-European world. There is no demonstrable historical correlation between devotion to democracy and devotion to peace.[8]

How States Fight. The basic principles of tactics and strategy are also as old as war itself. Timing and placing are of the essence—*i.e.*, "getting there firstest with the mostest"—since victory is most readily won by achieving a decisive superiority over the foe in men and weapons at a decisive point. Since no force of fighters fights well when broken up or obliged to face attack from two or more directions at once, good generalship aims at breaking through enemy lines, splitting enemy forces, and surrounding the remnants. Outflanking, encirclement, and annihilation constitute the eternal triad of successful battle from Arbela to Austerlitz, Cannae to Crete, Salamis to Stalingrad, Trasimene to Trafalgar, Zama to Zeebruge. All the other manifold aspects of belligerent operations are subsidiary to the first and last purpose of so arranging matters that the enemy will cease to resist because the crucial components of his means of fighting are shattered, isolated, and destroyed.

But the practice of the art of war, like that of the science of diplomacy, is more difficult than the theory because of the many imponderable and unpredictable factors entering into the equation. It is always conditioned, and often determined, by the political objective of hostilities, with these ordinarily defined by civilian politicians rather than by professional warriors. The broad objective of enhancing one's own power and reducing that of the enemy

[8] See Quincy Wright's monumental and definitive work, *A Study of War*, especially Vol. 2, pp. 841–844. On the democratic process as an incentive to war, see Walter Millis, *The Martial Spirit* (1931), Thorstein Veblen, *An Inquiry into the Nature of Peace* (1919), and Mark Twain, *The Mysterious Stranger* (1898).

admits of various interpretations and applications. War may be "limited" or "unlimited" in its purposes. In the highly civilized ages of the Baroque and the Enlightenment in western Europe, war as waged by gentlemen was strictly limited in its goals and methods. All belligerents were wise enough to remember what has now long since been forgotten: that enemies should always be treated as if they might presently become allies, and allies as if they might presently become enemies. Victors negotiated amiably as equals with vanquished fellow sovereigns and never asked for more, save under extraordinary temptation or provocation, than the payment of indemnities and the cession of provinces and colonies.

In the 20th Century, however, wars of "annihilation" and demands for "unconditional surrender" have become the order of the day.[9] The announced political objectives of war leaders now range from the mildest to the most extreme form of rendering the foe impotent. The minimum goal always is to compel the enemy governments to capitulate with appropriate humiliation. More extreme and more customary in the world wars of our time is the purpose of bringing about the overthrow of the enemy government and its replacement by a new one which will at least surrender and at most become a "Quisling" or puppet regime through which the victor will rule the vanquished. At the next level of ardor for justice, the objective is the political destruction of the enemy State through partition, annexation, or social revolution. Finally, in righteous reversion to primitive savagery (see Chap. 10 of the Book of Joshua), the end point of "total war" becomes the physical extermination of the enemy population through massacre, starvation, gas chambers, deportation to slave camps or salt mines, and other refinements of the techniques of liquidation, including, more recently, atomic bombs.

Were Machiavelli still alive, he would be horrified at these procedures but would doubtless analyze soberly the problem of which type of political purpose is most appropriate to each set of circumstances. Like assassination, revolution as a weapon of war is often as dangerous to its users as to its victims. Genocide is difficult to practice on a sufficiently large scale to alter the demographic bases of national power. Despite great proficiency in the art, the

[9] In its issue of June 13, 1935, the Nazi journal, *Deutsche Wehr*, forecast the future of wars to come with considerable accuracy: "In such a war there will no longer be victors and vanquished, but survivors and those whose name is stricken from the list of nations. Many an apparently invincible Colossus in reality stands on feet of clay and what one or two generations ago was impossible has today already become possible: with a single powerful blow to break a nation's spiritual backbone, to destroy it forever and trample it in the dust. Just this is the essence, the numbing aspect of the war of annihilation. The elite lies torn to shreds and poisoned on the battlefields. The survivors, a leaderless, demoralized mob of human beings crushed and broken by nameless horrors and sufferings, by unspeakable terror, stand defenceless and without any will before their victors—clay in the potter's hands. . . . Their number does not matter. . . . Fifty million trembling fellaheen are not more difficult to bring into subjection than five; for many million times nought is still nought. A nation will no longer want *something* from its opponent, but will *put an end to its opponent*—make an end of it, once and for all."

Nazis succeeded in murdering only some two million Slavs and other enemy civilians, in addition to six million Jews. The atomic age, however, offers great promise of improved methods. The more extreme are the purposes of belligerent operations, the more desperate and fanatical will be the enemy's resistance and the greater will be the cost in blood and treasure of overcoming it. While politicians and patriots appear to be increasingly unconcerned with costs, a few lonely voices [10] are still raised now and then to suggest the desirability of a return to the more limited objectives of a less brutal epoch. But few give heed.

In contemporary warfare the dictum that the end justifies the means is widely honored, though as always in human affairs men become what they do and frequently find their ends shaped by the means they employ rather than vice versa. If revolution is the goal, then "Trojan Horsemen" and "Fifth Columnists" (so named from two famous incidents of the Trojan War of 1194 B.C. and the Spanish War of A.D. 1936) are often useful. Both Fascists and Communists are much addicted to this technique, though the latter, despite longer experience, have not yet achieved the skill of the former in this art. In all wars, hot or cold, it is frequently helpful to employ the now familiar devices of "governments-in-exile," "committees of liberation," and underground conspiracies of subversives in the enemy camp—subsidized and, if possible, armed for the purpose of organizing sabotage, sedition, secession, or revolution. These activities, however, require great subtlety and adroitness and, if ineffective, often contribute to the strength rather than the enfeeblement of the foe or, at best, produce unforeseen complications and confusions.

The Uses of Horrors and Lies. Atrocities are sometimes valuable in terrorizing enemy soldiers and civilians, but more often provoke counter-atrocities which may prove unpleasant. But men at war are too brave to be deterred by fear of retaliation, and have shown impressive ingenuity and consistency in the systematic torture and butchery of those of wrong colors, inferior races, or heretical creeds. With few exceptions, deemed honorable by those sharing the emotion in question and dishonorable by all others, no national community is ever shocked by the atrocities perpetrated by its own soldiery or sanctioned by its rulers. But all communities are invariably shocked by the atrocities committed by the enemy. Never, since the Mongols, has such shock induced surrender. Always the effect is grim resolve to fight to the death.

[10] George F. Kennan, *op. cit.*, pp. 99*ff.*, comments: "We see that the legalistic approach is closely identified with the concept of total war and total victory, and the manifestations of the one spill over only too easily into the manifestations of the other. And the concept of total war is something we would all do well to think about a little in these troubled times. . . . It is not only a question now of the desirability of this concept; it is a question of its feasibility. . . . In a sense, there is not total victory short of genocide, unless it be a victory over the minds of men. But the total military victories are rarely victories over the minds of men. . . . I am frank to say that I think there is no more dangerous delusion, none that has done us a greater disservice in the past or that threatens to do us a greater disservice in the future than the concept of total victory."

Indeed, the chief value of atrocities in modern war is to imbue all soldiers and citizens with an unshakable belief in the ineffable wickedness of the foe and the moral necessity of destroying him. Intelligence agents must therefore carefully compile data on the enemy's more atrocious deeds from the reports of spies, prisoners, and refugees. The fabrication of such tales is no longer so necessary as it was in earlier wars, since authentic atrocities have now become commonplace. Experts in "psychological warfare" must present such episodes in convincingly grisly form, with suitable documentation, and feed it via press and radio to their own public, allied publics, and enemy publics. At home morale will be visibly improved. At the front eagerness to kill will be enhanced. One's own allies will fight the harder, knowing that the foe is bestial. The enemy's allies may be alienated in effective "wedge driving," even though the enemy himself will almost never be demoralized by a sense of sin. So swift is the modern tempo, however, that the psychological strategists must be prepared on short notice to convert devils into angels and vice versa with shifting diplomatic alignments by keeping in stock a supply of unused atrocity stories or by transferring guilt for past atrocities from one side to the other.[11]

[11] In 1895, 1896, 1915, and at other times, Turkish mobs and troops massacred scores of thousands of Armenians with the connivance of the Turkish Government. The American press was indignant. When Turkish troops occupied Baku in the fall of 1918, they butchered 30,000 Soviet citizens of Armenian origin. The American press was uninterested. Following the promulgation of the Truman Doctrine, Maj. Gen. Lunsford Oliver, head of the U.S. Military Mission to Turkey, announced his discovery, in an address in Chicago, August 28, 1947, that "the massacre of the Armenians after the First World War was really started by the Armenians." The American press approved.

The most impressive single example of the effective propagandistic use of atrocities is unquestionably the Katyn massacre. On April 15, 1943, Paul Joseph Goebbels, via the Nazi press and radio, announced the "accidental" discovery by the Wehrmacht in Katyn forest near Smolensk of a mass grave containing the bodies of 10,000 to 12,000 Polish officers (actually c. 3,000, though the other missing officers were never found), murdered in April, 1940, by the "Jewish executioners of the GPU." When the Polish Government in Exile followed Berlin in asking the International Red Cross to make an "impartial investigation," Moscow severed diplomatic relations with its "ally" (April 25, 1943), thus affording Goebbels his greatest single propaganda triumph of the war. He speedily arranged visits to the dreadful scene by "international experts" who, amid exhumations and autopsies, testified conclusively to Russian guilt. Following Soviet reoccupation of the area, a distinguished Special Commission of the Soviet Extraordinary State Committee on German-Fascist Crimes investigated, amid more exhumations and autopsies, and reported conclusively, Jan. 24, 1944, that the Polish officers had fallen into German hands during the invasion and had been massacred by a Nazi murder organization in the autumn of 1941, with Russian prisoners (subsequently shot) compelled early in 1943 to "prepare" the graves for Goebbels's "revelation." In the spring of 1952 a U.S. Congressional subcommittee, under the Hon. Ray J. Madden, Democrat of Indiana, held hearings in America and Western Europe (though unable to go to the scene for further exhumations and autopsies) and again testified conclusively to Russian guilt. See the author's *Russia Since 1917*, pp. 268–270.

The "truth" of such matters is wholly coincidental to the political purposes of the propaganda. Russian guilt is indicated by the Kremlin's inability or refusal to account for the missing Polish officers and by Soviet failure to press this charge at Nuremberg. German guilt is indicated by the Nazi propaganda handling of the matter, analyzed by this writer at the time while employed in the Foreign Broadcast Intelligence Service of the

Mendacity also has its uses in war propaganda, provided the truth is not too soon discovered. "In wartime," observed Samuel Johnson, "people want to hear only two things: good of themselves and evil of the enemy. And after war, I know not which is to be feared the more, garrets full of scribblers who have learned to lie, or streets full of soldiers who have learned to rob." The doctoring of diplomatic documents to convey a false impression of the rectitude of one's own government and the wickedness of the foe's is an old art. Thus the Quai d'Orsay in the *French Yellow Book of* 1914 made it appear that Russian mobilization was ordered after, instead of before, general mobilization in Germany and Austria-Hungary. The State Department's publication in 1948 of captured German diplomatic documents was so edited as to make it appear that the Nazi decision to attack Poland was reached after the Nazi-Soviet pact of August 23, 1939, instead of in May, and that the Nazi decision to attack Russia was reached in December, 1940, instead of in August.[12]

F.C.C. Goebbels's diary of May 8, 1943, as subsequently published, commented: "Unfortunately German munitions were found in the graves at Katyn. The question of how they got there needs clarification. It is either a case of munitions sold by us during the period of our friendly arrangement with the Soviet Russians, or of the Soviets themselves throwing these munitions into the graves. In any case it is essential that this incident be kept top secret. If it were to come to the knowledge of the enemy the whole Katyn affair would have to be dropped." It may finally be noted that the favorite Soviet method of mass extermination is deliberate starvation, as with the Ukrainian kulaks in 1930–33, and deportation to labor camps where death, for those who survive the journey, is effected by overwork and malnutrition. The favorite Nazi methods were gas chambers and mass shootings. All the Katyn corpses were shot through the head—which procedure, however, is the traditional form of individual execution by the MVD (formerly GPU). But the important point, from the perspective of psychological warfare, is that no patriotic German in 1943 could doubt Russian guilt, no patriotic Russian in 1944 could doubt German guilt, and no patriotic American in 1952 could doubt Russian guilt.

[12] The dispatch of Paléologue, French Ambassador in St. Petersburg, 10:45 A.M., July 31 (sent 16 hours after the event), declared "the mobilization of the Russian Army has been ordered." The falsifiers in the French Foreign Office concocted the following statement in place of the dispatch: "As a result of the general mobilization of Austria and of the measures for mobilization taken secretly, but continuously, by Germany for the last six days, the order for the general mobilization of the Russian Army has been given, Russia not being able, without serious danger, to allow herself to be further outdistanced; really she is only taking military measures corresponding to those taken by Germany. For imperative reasons of strategy the Russian Government, knowing that Germany was arming, could no longer delay the conversion of her partial mobilization into a general mobilization" (*French Yellow Book of* 1914, No. 118). On Jan. 22, 1948, the State Department released a 362-page book of 260 documents on *Nazi-Soviet Relations*, 1939–1941, selected from the captured archives of the German Foreign Office and edited by Raymond James Sontag and James Stuart Beddie. In this instance there were apparently no fabrications, but the false impressions mentioned above were achieved by the omission of other available diplomatic and Wehrmacht documents and, of course, of all non-German sources. Since the falsehoods were pointed out at once by informed American commentators, this volume represented a singularly inept instance of propaganda. The story which it purports to "tell" should be compared with Chester Wilmot's detailed and fully documented account in *The Struggle for Europe* (Harper, 1952). See also my articles, "The Nazi Road to War," in *Current History*, January, April, 1953.

Such petty and old-fashioned tricks, however, are feeble indeed compared to the technique which has come to be known as the "Big Lie." This consists of the adroit fabrication and repetition of falsehoods on the premise that many will believe what is reiterated often and vehemently, provided that it is not susceptible of immediate refutation or convincing denial. Here Nazis and Communists share equal honors in sundry masterpieces of prevarication. Among major Brown lies were allegations that the Communists burned the Reichstag; the Jews betrayed Germany; Communists are Jews; Jews are Communists; Churchill, Roosevelt, and Stalin were controlled by Jews; Hitler's sole purpose was a crusade against Communism; Czechs and Poles tortured and murdered Germans; each annexation was Hitler's "last territorial demand" in Europe; Germany was defending civilization against Bolshevism; etc. Among major Red lies have been allegations that the USSR is a democracy; Chinese Communists were merely "agrarian reformers"; Communists champion peace; America is plotting a war of aggression; "Wall Street" rules the USA; Socialists are tools of American capitalism; freedom exists in Communist countries; the Marshall Plan was an American conspiracy to enslave and exploit Europe; American imperialism threatens the world; South Korea, under U.S. instigation, invaded North Korea; the USA employs bacteriological warfare; etc.

The guiding directives of all propaganda in all wars are extremely simple, though their efficacy depends upon cleverness in execution. Four themes are universal: (1) we are virtuous, the foe is vicious; (2) we are strong, the foe is weak (or, when it is desired to achieve "strength through fear" or "strength through gloom," we are weak, the foe is strong); (3) we are united, the foe is divided; (4) we shall win, the foe will lose. No miracles are possible even through the most masterly propaganda (*e.g.*, à la Goebbels or the Cominform or the Communist-controlled "Partisans of Peace" in 1950*ff.*), because all peoples, including those in totalitarian States, have long been immunized to propaganda by repeated exposure, and because all patriots tend to accept the propaganda of their own leaders, however unpopular they may be, and to reject that of enemy Powers, however envied or admired they may be. Yet a subtle synthesis of symbol manipulation with "propaganda of the deed," and an adroit exploitation of real events and of the actual misdeeds and mistakes of the enemy, can significantly influence attitudes at home and abroad and sometimes contribute to desired military and political results.

The final question in all warfare—what use to make of victory, once it has been won—supplied its own answer in periods of limited war directed toward rational objectives. But no practicable answer is available when Powers wage total war for unattainable purposes. To treat the vanquished harshly is to beget a will to revenge and arouse the suspicions of one's allies. To treat the vanquished leniently is to lose prestige and arouse the suspicions of one's allies. To use the occasion to expand one's territory and power is

290

to win a reputation for cynicism and greed and to rally other Powers against you. To appear self-sacrificing and generous is to invite contempt, sneers of "hypocrisy," suspicion, and possible attack. All victors in both World Wars of our time have "lost the peace." No one can say how peace can be "won" so long as statesmen and patriots pursue heavenly visions derived from Messianism and millennialism by hellish means derived from the application of modern science to the ancient imperatives of the politics of power.

4. ARMA VIRUMQUE

Men, Yron, money, and breade be the strengthe of the warre, but of these fower, the first two be most necessarie; because men and yron fynde money and breade; but breade and money fynde not men and yron.—NICCOLÒ MACHIAVELLI, *The Art of War* (translation of 1586).

Militarism has been by far the commonest cause of the breakdowns of civilizations during the last four or five millennia which have witnessed the score or so of breakdowns that are on record up to the present date. Militarism breaks a civilization down by causing the local States into which the society is articulated to collide with one another in destructive fratricidal conflicts. In this suicidal process the entire social fabric becomes fuel to feed the devouring flame in the brazen bosom of Moloch.—ARNOLD J. TOYNBEE, *A Study of History*.

Liberal illusions about war and peace die hard, particularly the notions that militarism is a military phenomenon and that civilian control of armed forces promotes peace. Even in Imperial Germany and Japan, most "militarists" have been civilians, not soldiers. Decisions for war in 1792, 1812, 1846, 1854, 1861, 1898, 1914, 1939, 1941, and 1950 were in every case decisions of civilian politicians, not of professional military men. Perhaps the only valid generalization which emerges from what we know of the uneasy relationships between politicians and strategists in the formulation of national policies is that the former, in their preoccupation with politics, tend to ignore the costs and risks and limitations of recourse to armed force while the latter, in their preoccupation with military science, often forget that victory is meaningless unless it promotes the achievement of specific and attainable political objectives. Statesmanship consists in knowing what is necessary and what is possible and in combining the uses of arms and of diplomacy in such wise as to obtain maximum advantages at minimum price.

Even in wartime, in democratic and totalitarian States alike, major strategic decisions are more frequently made by civilian leaders than by military specialists. "War," observed Clemenceau sagely, "is far too serious a business to be left to the generals." In postwar periods generals go into diplomacy and politics and gain increasing influence over civilians in the formulation of national policies. George C. Marshall was the first top-ranking general and Chief of Staff to become U.S. Secretary of State. Numerous other executive and diplomatic posts were filled by military career men in the Truman Administration. Government by generals, however, is not inevitably more bellivolent than government by civilians. Statesmen often have a less accurate sense of the limits of what can be achieved by armed force than do soldiers.[13] So determined was Secretary Marshall to come to terms with Communism in Europe and in China in the interest of peace that Senator Joseph R. McCarthy of Wisconsin subsequently declared he had been part of "a conspiracy so immense and an infamy so black as to dwarf any previous such venture in the history of man," while Senator William E. Jenner of Indiana called Marshall a "living lie" and "a front man for traitors."

The menace of militarism to the Great Society of our time does not stem from the greed or conspiracies of vocational specialists in the arts of war but from the transformation of war itself under the impact of the new science and technology, and from the economic, social, and psychological consequences of this transformation. Its character can best be suggested by recalling the progressive elaboration of weapons.

The Sword Forgers. In the evolution of the precursors of *Homo sapiens*, teeth and claws became progressively less formidable as manual dexterity and cortical potentialities increased. While it is uncertain whether ape-men used fists, it is clear that they used sticks and stones and knives of flint against one another as well as against other beasts. In the hunt and in primitive fighting the utility of a knife on the end of a stick, and of missiles hurled by mechanical aids, became obvious long before the invention of writing and the rise of city-states. The former device developed into spear, battle-ax, sword, and bayonet; the latter into sling, catapult, bow and arrow, and gun. The use of fire to discourage the foe is also of respectable antiquity. Since the advent of metallurgy it has been evident to all that the most effective means of inflicting injury is to hurl bits of metal, preferably hot, into the tissues of the victim and that the best way of avoiding injury is to wear metallic garb, acquire speed through the use of horse, wagon, car, or plane, or take refuge behind stone walls, in vehicles of wood or iron, or in holes in the ground. The belated adaptation of gunpowder (long used by heathen Chinese for fireworks) to the arts of war as practiced by Christians did not alter these

---

[13] Hitler in the 1930's was never pushed into military adventures abroad by the General Staff but on the contrary faced the opposition of the military specialists in most of his major moves. He is reported to have said in 1941: "Before I was head of the German Government I thought the German General Staff was like a butcher's dog—something to be held tight by the collar because it threatened to attack all and sundry. Since then I have had to recognize that the General Staff is anything but that. It has consistently tried to impede every action that I have thought necessary. It objected to the military occupation of the Rhineland, to the march into Austria, to the occupation of Czechoslovakia, and finally even to the war against Poland. The General Staff warned me against offensive action in France, and against the war with Russia. It is I who have always had to goad on this 'butcher's dog'" [pp. 34–35 of *They Almost Killed Hitler* (edited by Gero v. S. Gaevernitz). Based on the Personal Account of Fabian von Schlabrendorff (New York, Macmillan, 1947)].

essential characteristics of hostilities, nor did the more recent invention of internal-combustion engines for fast transport by land, sea, or air. The prime objective, even as in the days of Lagash and Ur, is still to put the enemy to flight or render him *hors de combat* by dissecting nerves, muscles, viscera, and bones through the subcutaneous introduction of pieces of metal into his body. All technological progress in warfare has consisted in devising more efficient means of producing and delivering to the ultimate consumer more metal, more swiftly, more cheaply, over greater distances, and at less risk to the producer and the middleman. Not until the invention of the atomic bomb was a truly novel means hit upon to end enemy resistance by ending enemy existence.

The fascinating story of weapons and strategy through the ages cannot here be told.[14] Its leitmotiv, however, is simple. Under the stimulus of war, human ingenuity has ever concentrated on inventing invincible arms and tactics, devising invulnerable armor and fortifications with which they could be countered, and then creating still more lethal tools and schemes of assault whereby to crush the stoutest positions and the toughest battalions. This history of warfare is one of constant oscillation between attack which is superior to defense and defense which is superior to attack. Swords and spears are checkmated by shields and armor. Footmen are smashed by horsemen. Cavalry is cut down by longbows. Castles resist siege and are at length demolished by artillery. Wooden ships are sunk by ironclads. Dreadnoughts are nullified by submarines and bombing planes. Machine guns and barbed wire produce the ghastly futility of trench warfare (1914–18). Tanks, dive bombers, mobile heavy guns, and rockets restore the "war of movement" in 1939–45 and put an end to "impregnable" Maginot Lines and "unassailable" trench systems, with stalemated trench warfare once more restored in Korea in 1951 and thereafter.[15]

---

[14] For a suggestive sketch, elaborated with great erudition in the six-volume work, see Arnold J. Toynbee, *A Study of History*, pp. 194–195 and 331–336 of Somervell's condensation of Vols. I–VI.

[15] Some of the human consequences of this transition are indicated in the two following quotations, one from the early 16th Century, the other from the early 20th.

"In so great a defeat [the Battle of Anghiari, 1439], and in a battle which continued four hours, only one man died and he, not from wounds inflicted by hostile weapons or any honorable means, but, having fallen from his horse, was trampled to death. Combatants then engaged with little danger; being nearly all mounted, covered with armor, and preserved from death whenever they chose to surrender, there was no necessity for risking their lives; while fighting their armor defended them, and when they could resist no longer they yielded and were safe." [Niccolò Machiavelli, *The History of Florence.*]

"Bombardment, barrage, curtain fire, mines, gas, tanks, machine guns, hand-grenades— words, words, but they hold the horror of the world. . . . We see men living with their skulls blown open; we see soldiers run with their two feet cut off, they stagger on their splintered stumps into the next shell hole; a lance-corporal crawls a mile and a half on his hands, dragging his smashed knee after him; another goes to the dressing station and over his clasped hands bulge his intestines; we see men without mouths, without jaws, without faces; we find one man who has held the artery of his arm in his teeth for two

The systematic application of science to war in the 20th Century has produced such a galaxy of death-dealing gadgets as to stagger the imagination. World War I produced heavy siege guns, experimental artillery capable of firing shells 70 miles, poison gas, the first extensive use of submarines and aircraft, improved machine guns, flame throwers, and the first tanks. World War II completely overshadowed its predecessor in the production of new devices of slaughter and devastation. Amphibious warfare (since rendered obsolete by the atomic bomb) became a fine art with the aid of LST's, "ducks," and "weasels." Attack by, and defense against, submarines reached new heights. Radar and loran made it possible to "see" target areas, planes, and ships in the dark. Proximity fuses on shells (first used in antiaircraft guns but employed on land in the Battle of the Bulge and thereafter) enabled death to find its victims almost automatically. Aerial bombardiers acquired "blockbusters," torpedoes, and incendiary bombs of terrible effectiveness. Rocket shells, first successfully employed by the Russians in 1941, evolved into the 14-ton German V-2, carrying a ton of explosives, rising 100 miles above the earth, and hitting targets 200 miles and more away at a speed of 3,800 miles per hour, thus precluding all possibility of interception or local defense by means now available.[16]

Since V-J Day the pace of inventing new weapons and improving old ones has become so rapid that any survey is obsolete before it can be published. Bigger and better atomic bombs replaced the missiles which destroyed Hiroshima and Nagasaki. Atomic war heads in long-range rockets entered into the realm of the possible. Scores of Nazi scientists and technicians were employed by the USA and the USSR to produce improved V-2's. New jet planes surpassed the speed of sound. Various types of robot bombs mushroomed in laboratories and factories. Research in bacteriological warfare made such progress that Dr. Gerald Wendt, speaking September 18, 1946, to a General Electric science forum in Schenectady, N.Y., asserted soberly: "If World War III comes, which we pray will never happen, it will be a war in which most people may die from silent, insidious, anti-human weapons that make no sound, give no warning, destroy no forts or ships or cities, but can wipe out human beings by the millions."

The Markets of Mars. In our own culture, as in others which have preceded it, grave questions have been raised among those given to reflection as to whether the increasing dedication of all energies and resources to the practice of war is compatible with the survival of civilization. The initial

---

hours in order not to bleed to death. The sun goes down, night comes, shells whine, life is at an end. Still the little piece of convulsed earth in which we lie is held. We have yielded no more than a few hundred yards of it as a prize to the enemy. But on every yard there lies a dead man." [Erich Maria Remarque, *All Quiet on the Western Front.*]

[16] The most complete and graphic account of these and many other new weapons is *Scientists against Time* by James Phinney Baxter III.

issue here has to do with the human and material costs of war in an industrialized global society. Universal conscription, economic mobilization, and the concept of the nation in arms, coupled with the size and striking power of modern fighting forces and the deadly effects of modern weapons, make warfare an ever heavier burden. In terms of numbers killed, the French Revolutionary and Napoleonic Wars, continuing intermittently for a quarter of a century and involving all major Powers, cost *c*. 2,000,000 lives. The Crimean War took almost 800,000 lives in two years. The American Civil War killed some 700,000 soldiers. The brief and localized Franco-Prussian and Russo-Japanese Wars each cost less than 200,000 lives, though the Balkan Wars of 1912–13 are estimated to have produced almost 500,000 fatal casualties. The total dead in all wars between 1790 and 1914 was about 4,500,000.

World War I, on the other hand, snuffed out almost 8,600,000 lives in four years, counting only direct casualties. The Allies mobilized 42,190,000 troops, of whom 5,160,000 were slain, 13,000,000 were wounded, and 4,120,000 were prisoners and missing. The Central Powers mobilized 23,000,000 troops, of whom 3,380,000 were killed, 8,400,000 were wounded, and 3,600,000 were prisoners and missing. Of all men in uniform, 6 out of every 10 were casualties. World War II produced *c*. 15,000,000 battle deaths among the Great Powers: USSR 7,500,000; Germany 3,000,000; China 2,200,000; Japan 1,500,000; U.K. 300,000; USA 300,000; Italy 300,000; France 200,000.[17] A Vatican study released November 21, 1945, estimated total military and civilian dead at 22,000,000. This is probably an underestimate. In the USSR apart from military casualties, some 25,000,000 lives were lost through siege, starvation, disease, mass murder, decreased birth rates, and increased death rates. Half a million German civilians perished under aerial bombardment and probably an equal number of Japanese, not counting the victims of the two atomic bombs. The USA, however, suffered almost twice as many deaths from civilian accidents during 1941–45 as from enemy action—a circumstance calculated to impress Americans less than other peoples with the human waste of war.

The material costs of modern war are literally incalculable, since figures of expenditures and damages are no longer meaningful. World War I is estimated to have cost all the belligerent Governments a total of $200,000,000,000, plus an additional $138,000,000,000 for value of lives lost, damage to neutrals, losses of civilian production, relief costs, etc. The combined value of all public-school buildings in the USA in 1913 would have paid total war expenses in 1917 for only one week. With half a dozen exceptions, no university or college in America cost as much to build as a single modern battleship. Aside from China, where no reliable figures are available, World War II is estimated to have cost all the belligerents some $1,154,000,000,000

[17] George C. Marshall in *Ten Eventual Years*, 1937–1947 (Encyclopaedia Britannica, Inc.).

for direct war expenditures and $231,000,000,000 in property losses, with the USA spending $341,000,000,000 (up to 1946), Germany $275,000,000,000, the USSR $200,000,000,000, the U.K. $120,000,000,000, Italy $94,000,000,-000, and Japan $56,000,000,000. All such estimates can be no more than approximations. They nevertheless suggest that the price of total war is astronomical.

It would be naïve to assume, however, that these costs represent sacrifices of goods and services which would otherwise be available for constructive use. In the short run, not only is modern war profitable to all participants (except for the casualties and the veterans whose bonuses and pensions are less than their civilian earning capacity), but it ensures full production, full employment at high wages, and handsome dividends to private investors, manufacturers, and merchants. In both "capitalist" and "socialist" economies, money spent by governments on war flows into the pockets of those who produce the goods to do the job—and is only partly siphoned off in taxes. In 1917, according to the Federal Trade Commission, the leading American steel companies made from 52 to 109% on their investments. World War I created 21,000 new American millionaires and gave workers and farmers higher earnings than they had ever known before. In World War II even larger profits, salaries, and wages were produced by colossal public spending and the very rich became richer and more numerous than ever before.

To contemporary mankind, total war presents the deceptive appearance of a primrose path to plenty. The Nazi regime restored the Reich to prosperity (prior to 1944) through preparing and waging war. In the USA, total national income, estimated at $79,000,000,000 in 1929, did not, amid the doldrums of depression and partial recovery, exceed this level until 1941 ($97,000,000,000), when public expenditures in anticipation of war gave new work to men and machines. The period of American belligerency saw national income doubled—i.e., to almost $200,000,000,000 annually. As America undertook massive rearmament at mid-century to prevent World War III, national income climbed above $400,000,000,000 and productive facilities were vastly expanded, with the output most readily disposed of by pouring it into the maw of Mars.[18] Despite the reduction of actual purchasing power through postwar inflation, the fact is not to be denied that war and preparations for more war gave farmers, workers, some professional people, and almost all businessmen larger real incomes than they had ever known before.

[18] In the Report of the Committee on Foreign Relations on S. 3086 (Mutual Security Act of 1952), published April 30, 1952, it was estimated (p. 22) that U.S. defense expenditures for the fiscal year 1952–53 would total $62,301,000,000, constituting 17.8% of the "gross national product," as compared with 13.7% in 1951–52, 7.1% in 1950–51, 5.1% in 1949–50, and 1.2% in 1938. It was further estimated, hopefully, that all NATO countries would together devote 9.2% of gross national products to defense, with Britain and France leading with 10.8% each, Western Germany 8.5%, etc. Germany in 1936, when the Third Reich was already irrevocably on the road to war, devoted 15.8% of its gross national product to "defense."

The same phenomenon manifested itself in Britain, Germany, Italy, and Japan (until the debacle) and would assuredly have appeared also in "socialist" guise in the Soviet Union except for the staggering human and material losses inflicted by the Axis onslaught.

The conclusions drawn from these experiences of yesterday by many of the immediate beneficiaries of war are at the heart of the world's tragedy of today and tomorrow. War is inexorably a source of destruction, impoverishment, and breakdown. Wealth and welfare cannot possibly be enhanced through systematic waste and ruin. If the reverse appears to be the case, this illusion is attributable to the fact that the nations of the West in the present age have as yet devised no means of assuring full use of labor, capital, and resources save through the vast public spending and planning required by total war. This circumstance suggests that the national communities of modern civilization have become incapable of affording their peoples any assurance of work, well-being, and a sense of salvation except through the exciting imperatives and glittering profits of mutual slaughter. No other definition of social purpose seems capable of arousing comparable energies and inducing comparable acquiescence in political direction and public subsidization of private economic activity.

But, to the degree to which this is in truth the case, the contemporary world society is already far advanced along the road toward suicide. Despite the gaudy achievements of the war makers in stimulating science, technology, industry, and agriculture, only the demented will suppose that prosperity through militarism, plenty through war, and salvation at the hands of the "savior with the sword" are anything other than the hallucinations of mass madness. Productive labor devoted to the tasks of destruction is in the end self-destructive. This conclusion is validated by all past experience from ancient Assyria to the Nazi Reich. If the future of modern man is to be a future of "garrison-states," dedicated wholeheartedly to the work of death, then that future can lead only to the grave. The verdict of time on these dismal prospects is not likely to differ from the judgment of today's greatest living historian:

In the downward course of a broken-down civilization's career there may be truth in the Ionian philosopher Heraclitus's saying that "War is the father of all things." The sinister concentration of the society's dwindling powers upon the absorbing business of fratricidal warfare may generate a military prowess that will place the neighbouring societies at the war-obsessed society's mercy, and may strike out a military technique that will serve as a key to the acquisition of a far-reaching technical mastery over the Material World. Since the vulgar estimates of human prosperity are reckoned in terms of power and wealth, it thus often happens that the opening chapters in the history of a society's tragic decline are popularly hailed as the culminating chapters of a magnificent growth; and this ironic misconception may even persist for centuries. Sooner or later, however, disillusionment is bound to follow; for a society that has become incurably divided against itself is almost certain to "put back into the business" of war the greater part of those additional resources, human and material, which the same business has incidentally brought into its hands. [Arnold J. Toynbee, *A Study of History*.]

5. THE STRATEGY OF CO-ANNIHILATION

When Pyrrhus had retired into Epirus and left Macedonia, he had a fair occasion given him by fortune to enjoy himself in quiet and to govern his kingdom in peace. But he was persuaded that neither to annoy others nor to be annoyed by them was a life insufferably tedious and languishing. His anxiety for fresh employment was relieved by his preparations for war against Rome. A certain Thessalonian named Cineas, one of his trusted advisers and a man of sound sense, perceiving what was afoot, drew Pyrrhus into a conversation. "If it please heaven that we conquer the Romans," he inquired, "what use, Sir, shall we make of our victory?" Pyrrhus explained that the conquest of Rome would open the way to subduing all Italy. Cineas suggested that surely the triumphs were not to stop there. Pyrrhus then allowed his visions of conquest to extend to Sicily, to Carthage, to Libya, to all the other insolent enemies of his kingdom. "But," asked Cineas, "when we have conquered all, what are we to do then?" "Why, then, my friend," said Pyrrhus, laughing, "we will take our ease, and drink and be merry." Cineas, having brought him thus far, replied: "And what hinders us from drinking and taking our ease now, when we have already those things in our hands at which we propose to arrive through seas of blood, through infinite toils and dangers, through innumerable calamities which we must both cause and suffer?" This discourse of Cineas gave Pyrrhus pain, but produced no change in his plans.—PLUTARCH, *Life of Pyrrhus*.

In the perspective of the long centuries during which the Western State System emerged in Europe and evolved into a global constellation of sovereignties, World War II represents another formidable attempt to achieve the political unification of the world community by violence. Here, as before, the Powers aspiring to universal dominion were ultimately crushed by a superior coalition of Powers raised up against them by their own ambitions. The final result was the preservation of the existence and independence of the victors and the restoration of the State System as a congeries of separate sovereignties. And here, as before, the triumphant allies drifted apart and presently became rivals for power among themselves.

Despite the persistence of this antique design for anarchy, some novel features of the new time are noteworthy. One is the schism since 1917 between the new Russia and the Atlantic Powers, the former viewing the latter as a foul matrix of bourgeois decadence, capitalist exploitation, imperialistic sin, and wicked plots to attack and destroy the proletarian paradise; and the latter viewing the former as a hideous citadel of tyranny, slavery, godlessness, and viciously subversive conspiracy to destroy property, piety, and popular rule throughout the world. Another is the subsequent emergence of Fascist totalitarianism in three Great Powers, dedicated in the name of anti-Communism, anti-liberalism, and anti-capitalism to the conquest of the globe—

298

followed by crushing defeat and the reduction of these States to Powers of second or third rank, along with a comparable reduction in the status of the impoverished western European democracies. The result of the victory of the United Nations was to give the USA effective influence over Eurafrica and the Atlantic and Pacific areas and to deliver Eurasia into the hands of the USSR. A new China and a new India were certain to emerge as Great Powers before 1984. But the world of the 1950's was a divided and bipolar world of two colossal Super-Powers, with all others their allies or pensioners.

The fascinating problem of "measuring" the relative power of the giants is scarcely worth pursuing, since now more than ever the decisive elements of imperial power are beyond measurement. Military science is more than ever the wildest guesswork, with each wholly incalculable and irresponsible move in diplomacy and war being dignified and rendered plausible by being called "a calculated risk." We may more usefully conclude our survey of the politics of power by noting some of the efforts, largely futile but occasionally suggestive, on the part of serious students of world affairs to find some key or clue to the confusions and paradoxes of a strange new world.

The focus of professional and public attention has shifted from point to point as each new source of power or weapon of battle has impressed itself most vividly on men's minds. The practices of governmental control of business activity—i.e., mercantilism, neomercantilism, and, more recently, "economic planning"—have led some to develop the thesis that national power rests primarily on wise and masterly regulation of the national economy by the State—e.g., Alexander Hamilton, Friedrich List, Walter Rathenau, and Bernard Baruch, among others. Military writers have argued anew the merits of the swift offensive (e.g., H. von Moltke, Alfred von Schlieffen, Ferdinand Foch, Charles de Gaulle) or the relative impregnability of modern defenses (Maginot, Gamelin, Liddell Hart). The cult of the decisiveness of sea power was first popularized at the turn of the century by Adm. Alfred Thayer Mahan, U.S.N., who was echoed by various British, Continental, and Japanese writers. The more recent contention that contemporary wars are won through air power was first developed in 1921 by Gen. Giulio Douhet of Italy and later propounded in America by Gen. William Mitchell and Alexander de Seversky. The most recent literature on rocket warfare, bacteriological warfare, and atomic warfare is already growing at a rapid rate.

The most impressive single effort thus far to correlate and synthesize these various approaches and to link them with new concepts of global geography is that of the "geopoliticians." This movement, curiously enough, stems in a sense from the "wheel maps" of the Middle Ages, which depicted Jerusalem as the "center" of the world, with the precise spot marked on the floor of the Church of the Holy Sepulcher. This quaint notion is absurd to anyone who pictures the world in terms of the familiar "Mercator's projection," with the American continents in the middle and the northernmost land masses of

the planet vastly inflated by virtue of converting a sphere into a cylinder.[19]
A glance at a globe, however, reveals that the Holy Land does in fact lie near
the mid-point of the great Eurasian-African land mass.

In 1904 the English geographer, Sir Halford J. Mackinder, delivered a
lecture in London on "The Geographical Pivot of History," in which he
pointed out the peculiar role of the "fertile crescent" extending from Palestine to the Persian Gulf. In his *Democratic Ideals and Reality* (1919) he
developed the concepts of the "World Island" (*i.e.*, Asia-Europe-Africa) and
the "Heartland" (*i.e.*, the north central Eurasian plains whose waters drain
into the Arctic or inland seas). He suggested that the holders of the Heartland, while able to threaten peripheral areas, are secure against the sea
power of the Atlantic and Pacific coastal States and that land-based air
power might well prove superior to naval might. His moral was: Never permit
Germany to control eastern Europe. His motto was: "Who rules East Europe
commands the Heartland; who rules the Heartland commands the World
Island; who rules the World Island commands the world."

Meanwhile a German geographer and major general, Karl Haushofer (who
prior to 1914 had visited and written about the Far East and the "Indo-
Pacific sphere"), interested himself in Mackinder's formulations; pursued
the studies suggested by his predecessor at the University of Munich, Friedrich Ratzel (1844–1904); and borrowed the term *Geopolitik* from the writings of the Swedish scholar, Rudolf Kjellen. In 1922, Haushofer founded
in Munich the Institute of Geopolitics, which published the *Zeitschrift für
Geopolitik* and became a large research organization. He predicted approv-
ingly the Japanese program of Greater East Asia and as early as 1923 asserted: "Italy and Japan are the future allies of Germany." He published
Macht und Erde (1927), *Wehrgeopolitik* (1932), *Weltpolitik von Heute*
(1934), and innumerable monographs and articles. His aide-de-camp in
World War I was Rudolf Hess, through whom he first met Hitler in 1924.
Since *der Führer* and his co-conspirators found much of value for their purposes in Haushofer's "new science," they made much of him after 1933, permitting him to keep his Jewish wife, proclaiming his two sons "honorary
Aryans," and expanding the Institute as a center of geopolitical planning for
world conquest.

But this marriage of the new science to the new barbarism came to an
evil ending. Haushofer fully shared the patriotic, Pan-German, expansionist
ambitions of the Nazi leaders and was equally concerned with making the
Reich a "World Power" over the ruins of the British Empire. But he favored
a German-Russian-Japanese bloc and warned that any Japanese frontal attack
on China or any German frontal attack on Russia would bog down in the
vast reaches of Eurasia and end in disaster. When his advice was ignored

---

[19] For a good brief discussion of various map projections and their uses and limitations,
see Nicholas J. Spykman, *The Geography of the Peace*, 1944.

and his predictions were realized, he fell from grace. His eldest son, Albrecht, was arrested for plotting against Hitler, imprisoned, and finally murdered on the eve of the fall of Berlin. Haushofer himself was sent to Dachau concentration camp in 1944. His younger son, Heinz, suffered a like fate. Both were liberated with the end of the war. He returned to Munich, a bitter and broken old man. On March 10, 1946, he and his faithful wife committed suicide.

To extract the wheat of science from the chaff of nonsense and mysticism in the still burgeoning literature of *Geopolitik* is no simple task. There is no past or present evidence to support Sir Halford's original political and strategic generalizations about the Heartland (as he himself conceded in his last days), even though some aspects of Anglo-American policy toward Russia since 1945 suggest acceptance of the error in high places. Haushofer's views of China and Russia have been vindicated by events, along with the emphasis placed on the Near East by all the exponents of this school. The late Nicholas Spykman, outstanding disciple of geopolitics in the USA, applied many of its concepts brilliantly and fruitfully to the problems of the American continents. He reformulated Mackinder's original dictum: If any Power or bloc of Powers brings the "Rimlands," or coastal plains of Eurasia, under unified control, it can command the World Island and threaten the security of both the Heartland Powers (Russia and China) and the Island Powers (Britain and America). Just as Allied victory in World War II was contingent upon effective cooperation among USA, U.K., and USSR, so enduring peace depends upon a stable balance and concert among them to the end that the Rimlands shall not be used by either against the other and shall not again fall under the control of any other Power or coalition.

It is not uncharitable, nor is it a denial of the value of much of the literature in this field, to suggest that these and other valid conclusions can be reached by routes less devious than those taken by the geopoliticians. This discipline or pseudo science views the data of world geography in terms of the struggle for global power among giant sovereignties. Since the outcome of such struggles depends always on unpredictable factors of morale and on incalculable "happenstances" in peace and war, along with consideration of space, position, matériel, and national purpose, a truly "scientific" formula for victory or even for survival is in the nature of the case impossible. Diplomacy and war, like bridge, boxing, chess, and hockey, have their rules, principles, and techniques derived from practice or custom. But none of them makes possible any reliable prediction as to which player will win in any given contest. It is certain, however, that, as long as the struggle continues, the contestants will rationalize their purposes in plausible jargon, seize eagerly upon every new weapon and strategic plan, and grasp always after some principle or hypothesis which promises success. If the effort almost invariably ends in frustration, the cause may lie in the circumstance that the game itself, under the conditions of the 20th Century, is a self-defeating enterprise.

A slowly dawning realization of this fact during the 1950's promoted frustration, confusion, desperation, a reversion to old formulas of warfare, and a groping effort to evolve new ones on the part of the diplomats and strategists of the Powers. All the generalizations and precepts reviewed in the present chapter are applicable to power politics in the Western State System, and in all its precursors, during the long millennia when the art of war advanced from sticks and stones through bows and spears to heavy artillery, tanks, and bombing planes. A new era opened in 1945 (see pp. 655ff.) when scientists gave statesmen and generals a simple device to wipe out whole cities, whole nations, and possibly the human race itself. The advent of atomic and thermonuclear weapons obviously meant that all "total war" among Great Powers, and indeed all "power politics" premised on the assumption of force, was now obsolete if civilization was to avoid suicide. But men are creatures of habit. Statesmen therefore continued the age-old game, hoping that somehow ways could be found to prevent it from eventuating in the self-destruction of the species.

The various formulas designed to reconcile ancient ways with the formidable hazards of a new time need not here be surveyed, for all were futile. Communist power-holders, while secretly fabricating planes, bombs, and rockets capable (they hoped) of annihilating the foe in the "next war," publicly appealed to all mankind, not without effect, to espouse the abolition of atomic weapons. American policy-makers, while engaging less secretly in comparable operations, toyed publicly with the baffling problem of preparing for war under conditions which appeared to mean that any general and total conflict would spell the co-annihilation of the belligerents—not in the sense of total defeat, but in the sense of the physical extermination via blast, fire, and radiation sickness of many or most of the inhabitants of the warring States.

No plausible "solution" had been arrived at when these words were written. The U.S. Strategic Air Command, like its counterpart in the USSR, devoted itself to elaborate plans for the atomic destruction of the foe. American civil defense authorities strove through ceremonial exercises and mock drills against simulated atomic attack to devise ways and means, through planned evacuation of cities and fantastically expensive projects for shelters, to reduce anticipated casualties—with everybody understanding, privately if not publicly, that all such plans were absurd, and that "next war" would spell total chaos and universal death. Russians, Asians, and West Europeans indulged in no such nonsensical rituals. In Washington, "expert" advisers to the Pentagon, the National Security Council, and the State Department struggled vainly to resolve the dilemma with the doubtful aid of sundry unofficial commentators.

None of the formulas propounded in official circles or in the public prints was compatible with common sense. Some contended that the threat of "massive retaliation" via atomic weapons would "deter" any "aggression," forgetting that the suspected "aggressor" had comparable capacity to inflict total destruction and that no war has ever been avoided through prior contemplation of its horrors. Others sought to revive an old concept of "limited war" in which atomic weapons would not be used unless national survival were at stake. Among these, some urged the need of substantial conventional forces to cope with localized or "brush-fire" wars, with atomic attack reserved for all-out global conflicts. Still others strove to develop a new military doctrine whereby "tactical" or small-scale atomic weapons would be used in wars to come only against "military" targets, with great urban centers spared from nuclear annihilation, although no such centers accessible to any belligerent had been so spared from aerial bombardment in World Wars I or II.

It is possible that out of these endeavors there may yet emerge a new "military science" which may facilitate the perpetuation of warfare in the Atomic Age without risking the mutual incineration of the belligerents, the demise of Western civilization, and the prospective doom of the human race. It is far more probable that no such dispensation is obtainable. The strange imperatives of history would seem to be irreversible. In a century of "total wars" in which the antagonists are invariably bent upon the "annihilation" or at least "unconditional surrender" of the enemy, it seems unlikely that any return to the 18th Century practice of "limited war," fought by limited means for limited ends, can be made effective in the minds and motives of national policy-makers or of their highly patriotic constituents.

To the degree to which this prognosis is valid, future war among Great Powers spells suicide and a reversion to barbarism by the miserable survivors, if any. "In the thermonuclear age," said President Eisenhower in the fall of 1954, "there is no alternative to peace." Citizens and statesmen must therefore renounce war or invite irreparable disaster. Their choice as rational human beings would not be in doubt except for the fact that all human beings are prisoners of the past and are often nonrational and sometimes irrational. Mankind is forever called upon to choose between alternatives. The choice now posed is grim and possibly final. There was much reason to hope in the late 1950's that the choice would be conducive to life rather than death. But the time-honored ways of power politics, far older than Western civilization, offered no basis for complacent optimism regarding the future fortunes of mankind.

SUGGESTED READINGS

Baxter, James Phinney, 3d: *Scientists against Time*, Boston, Atlantic–Little, Brown, 1946.
Beard, C. A.: *The Idea of National Interest*, New York, Macmillan, 1934.
Bernardo, Maj. C. Joseph, and Eugene H. Bacon: *American Military Policy*, Harrisburg, Pa., Military Service Publishing Co., 1955.
Clausewitz, Carl von: *Principles of War*, Harrisburg, Pa., Military Service Publishing Co., 1942.
Coblentz, Stanton A.: *From Arrow to Atom Bomb*, New York, Beechhurst Press, 1953.
Cook, Thomas I., and Malcolm Moos: *Power through Purpose: The Realism of Idealism as a Basis for Foreign Policy*, Baltimore, Johns Hopkins Press, 1955.

Earle, Edward Mead (ed.): *Makers of Modern Strategy: Military Thought from Machia-velli to Hitler*, Princeton, N.J., Princeton University Press, 1943.

Ekirch, Arthur A., Jr.: *The Civilian and the Military*, New York, Oxford, 1956.

Fifield, Russell H., and G. E. Pearcy: *Geopolitics in Principle and Practice*, New York, Ginn, 1950.

Finletter, Thomas K.: *Power and Policy*, New York, Harcourt, Brace, 1954.

Fosdick, Dorothy: *Common Sense in World Affairs*, New York, Harcourt, Brace, 1955.

Fox, William T. R.: *The Super-Powers*, New York, Harcourt, Brace, 1944.

Fuller, J. F. C.: *A Military History of the Western World* (3 vols.), New York, Funk & Wagnalls, 1957.

Halle, Louis J.: *Civilization and Foreign Policy*, New York, Harper, 1955.

Hart, B. H. Liddell: *The Revolution in Warfare*, New Haven, Conn., Yale University Press, 1947.

————: *Strategy: The Indirect Approach*, New York, Praeger, 1954.

Hawtrey, R. G.: *Economic Aspects of Sovereignty*, New York, Longmans, 1930.

Huzar, Elias: *The Purse and the Sword: Control of the Army by Congress through Military Appropriations, 1933–1950*, Ithaca, N.Y., Cornell University Press, 1950.

Kaufman, William W.: *Military Policy and National Security*, Princeton, N.J., Princeton University Press, 1956.

Knight, B. W.: *How to Run a War*, New York, Knopf, 1936.

Knorr, Klaus: *The War Potential of Nations*, Princeton, N.J., Princeton University Press, 1956.

Kris, Ernst, and Hans Speier: *German Radio Propaganda*, New York, Oxford, 1944.

Lasswell, Harold D.: *Politics—Who Gets What, When, How*, New York, McGraw-Hill, 1936.

Lerner, Daniel (ed.): *Propaganda in War and Crisis*, New York, Stewart, 1951.

Ludendorff, Gen. Erich von: *The Nation at War*, London, Hutchinson, 1936.

McDonald, John: *Strategy in Poker, Business, and War*, New York, Norton, 1950.

Mackinder, Sir Halford J.: *Democratic Ideals and Reality: A Study in the Politics of Reconstruction*, New York, Holt, 1943.

Marder, Arthur J.: *The Anatomy of British Sea Power* (1880–1905), New York, Knopf, 1940.

Marshall, Charles Burton: *The Limits of Foreign Policy*, New York, Holt, 1954.

Meerloo, Joost A. M.: *The Rape of the Mind: The Psychology of Thought Control, Menti-cide, and Brainwashing*, Cleveland, World Publishing, 1956.

Middleton, Drew: *The Defense of Western Europe*, New York, Appleton-Century-Crofts, 1952.

Millis, Walter: *Arms and Men: A Study in American Military History*, New York, Putnam, 1956.

Montross, Lynn: *War through the Ages*, New York, Harper, 1944.

Morgenthau, Hans J.: *In Defense of the National Interest*, New York, Knopf, 1951.

Nef, John U.: *War and Human Progress*, Cambridge, Mass., Harvard University Press, 1950.

Nickerson, Hoffman: *The Armed Horde, 1793–1939: A Study of the Rise, Survival and Decline of the Mass Army*, New York, Putnam, 1941.

Niebuhr, Reinhold: *Christianity and Power Politics*, New York, Scribner, 1940.

Osgood, Robert Endicott: *Ideals and Self-Interest in America's Foreign Relations*, Chicago, University of Chicago Press, 1953.

Potter, E. B., and J. R. Fredland (eds.): *The United States and World Sea Power*, New York, Prentice-Hall, 1955.

Pratt, Fletcher: *The Battles that Changed History*, Garden City, N.Y., Hanover House, 1956.

Preston, Richard A., and Others: *Men in Arms*, New York, Praeger, 1956.

————, S. F. Wise, and H. O. Werner: *A History of Warfare: Its Interrelationships with Western Society*, New York, Praeger, 1956.

Puleston, Capt. W. D.: *The Influence of Force in Foreign Relations*, Princeton, N.J., Van Nostrand, 1955.

SUGGESTED READINGS

Rockefeller Brothers Fund: *International Security—the Military Aspect*, New York, Doubleday, 1958.

Sargent, William: *Battle for the Mind*, New York, Doubleday, 1957.

Schwarzenberger, George: *Power Politics*, New York, Praeger, 1952.

Scott, John: *Political Warfare: A Guide to Competitive Co-existence*, New York, John Day, 1955.

Slessor, Sir John: *Strategy for the West*, New York, Morrow, 1954.

Smith, Brig. Gen. Dale O.: *U.S. Military Doctrine: A Study and Appraisal*, New York, Duell, Sloan & Pearce, and Boston, Little, Brown, 1955.

Smith, Louis: *American Democracy and Military Power*, Chicago, University of Chicago Press, 1951.

Sprout, Harold, and Margaret Sprout: *The Rise of American Naval Power*, 1776–1918, Princeton, N.J., Princeton University Press, 1939.

——— (eds.): *Foundations of National Power*, Princeton, N.J., Van Nostrand, 1946.

Spykman, Nicholas: *America's Strategy in World Politics: The U.S. and the Balance of Power*, New York, Harcourt, Brace, 1942.

Tannenbaum, Frank: *The American Tradition in Foreign Policy*, Norman, Okla., University of Oklahoma Press, 1955.

Toynbee, Arnold J.: *War and Civilization*, New York, Oxford, 1950.

Vagts, Alfred: *A History of Militarism*, New York, Norton, 1937.

Weigert, Hans W.: *Geopolitics: Myth and Reality*, New York, Oxford, 1942.

Werner, Max: *The Military Strength of the Powers*, London, Gollancz, 1939.

Wright, Quincy: *A Study of War* (2 vols.), Chicago, University of Chicago Press, 1943.

CHAPTER IX

THE BUILDING OF EMPIRES

1. COLONIALISM

Take up the White Man's Burden—
Send forth the best ye breed—
Go bind your sons to exile
To serve your captives' need;
To wait in heavy harness,
On fluttered fold and wild—
Your new-caught, sullen peoples,
Half-devil and half-child.
—RUDYARD KIPLING, 1899.

A new spirit inspired by the policy of the good neighbor was born at Montevideo. It was the spirit of the Golden Rule. . . . We must sell abroad more of our surpluses.—CORDELL HULL, February 10, 1934.

"IMPERIALISM" and "nationalism" are the leitmotivs of "modern" world politics. Both are mouth-filling words which, like other words ending in "ism," have imprecise meanings or so many meanings as sometimes to seem to have no meaning. They may nonetheless serve, providing the user will watch his semantics, as labels for widespread patterns of political attitudes and actions motivating most citizens and statesmen of our epoch. Since, as we shall see, "nationalism" in its contemporary meaning is of quite recent vintage whereas "imperialism" in almost all its meanings is as old as the earliest State Systems, it will be well to examine the latter phenomenon before we consider the former. In so-called "modern times," commonly designated as the period since A.D. 1500, the sovereignties of Europe's Atlantic seaboard, and even some of those of Eastern Europe and Asia, built "empires" long before their subjects constituted "nations" as we now understand the term.

"Imperialism" or "colonialism" or "colonial imperialism" are often mere epithets uttered to discredit the aggrandizements of rival or enemy Powers. During the Cold War Communists and Arab-Asian nationalists and neutralists incessantly denounced the expansion or retention of Anglo-French-American power in far-flung regions of the globe as "colonialism" and "imperialism" (both by definition equated with sin), while many Americans and some West Europeans publicized the same imprecations to refer to Soviet hegemony in Eastern Europe and Central Asia. Conversely, both Marx and Spengler, and

306

Lenin and Toynbee, though each with different developments in mind, used "imperialism" as a name for a specific historical era. In the loose usage of historians, the term often refers to any instance of a state acquiring colonies or building an empire, particularly when the lands involved are overseas and/or the peoples affected are alien in culture and race. The word itself stems from the Latin *imperium*, which originally meant the authority, as defined by law, of a Roman public official. *Imperator* was the name of a military official and, ultimately, of the commander in chief when Augustus Caesar assumed the title. The original meaning—*i.e.*, military rule—is still germane to the modern attitude and policies commonly called "imperialistic."

However defined, imperialism is a phase of the competitive struggle for power among sovereignties. That struggle typically takes the form of efforts to increase power by extending control over new land. In the modern period, it has been easier for the States of Europe—and for the non-European States which have adopted the technology of Europe—to acquire new land at the expense of the small, weak States or politically unorganized natives of the non-European world than to wrest contiguous territory from powerful neighbors. Conquest has followed the paths of least resistance. The political partition and the economic exploitation of America, Asia, Africa, and the islands of the Seven Seas constitute the most grandiose and characteristic expression of the Western will-to-power in recent centuries. It is this process, with all its political, economic, and cultural ramifications, to which the term "imperialism" will be applied in the following pages.

The Old and New Colonialism. In the late 1400's the peoples of Europe invented or adopted a number of devices which enabled their Governments to exercise power overseas much more effectively than had been possible hitherto. The use of gunpowder in warfare, the invention of printing, the construction of more seaworthy sailing vessels, progress in the sciences of navigation, geography, and astronomy, improvements in road building, carriage construction, and fortifications, and the advent of new skills in banking and commerce all played their part in producing those economic and social changes usually associated with the transition from "medieval" to "modern" times. These devices greatly altered the technological differential between the European and non-European world. When competing Mediterranean merchants sought new routes to the Indies in order that they might import more cheaply and sell more profitably the goods of the Orient, they found ships and navigators at their service capable of doing what had not been done before—sailing around Africa, crossing the Atlantic, exploring distant sea routes, and finally circumnavigating the globe.

Statesmen at once perceived possibilities of increasing national power and wealth by assisting merchants in quest of profits, missionaries in quest of converts, navigators and explorers in quest of adventure, fame, and fortune. They accordingly organized companies, fitted out expeditions, and built navies as a means to these ends. And when Negroes, Hindus, Arabs, South Sea Islanders, or Amerindians offered resistance, European Princes sent out men-of-war and men-at-arms to confer upon them the blessings of Christianity, to save them from temptation by relieving them of their riches, or in some cases to exterminate them in order that white men might take their lands. The establishment of political control over newly conquered regions seemed a necessary step to foster colonization, commerce, and economic exploitation. Each State was determined to monopolize for itself and for its subjects as many of the new opportunities as possible. The tools of defense available to the victims of these ambitions were no match for the tools of the conquerors. The bow and arrow, the spear, the lance, the ça̧noe, and the small sailing craft could not cope with the blunderbuss, the cannon, and the galleon. The non-European peoples were consequently vanquished, and great colonial empires were established by the Atlantic seaboard States which possessed navigators, ships, and sea power and had direct access to the ocean highways.

The tale of how the original empires were conquered and governed and partially lost, how even larger domains were carved out of deserts and jungles in the late 19th Century, and what manner of men live where and do what in the remaining colonial territories of today is best told in maps (see pp. 105ff.) and in the detailed data available in yearbooks and other works of reference. The most successful empire-builders in the romantic age of con-quistadores, freebooters, pirates, and pioneers were, *seriatim*, the adventurers of Portugal, Spain, the Netherlands, France, and England, with each newly ascendant Power preying upon its precursors. Between the discovery of Amer-ica and the treaties of 1763 (see p. 76), vast estates were won and lost, with Spain and Britain inheriting the larger shares of the non-European world. During the next century most of the American colonies of Britain, Spain, and Portugal were scenes of successful rebellions and wars of independence. The Romanov Tsardom continued its glacierlike expansion. The young Atlantic giant subdued a continental realm from sea to shining sea. But with the dusk of mercantilism and the dawn of the new industrialism, European Powers displayed less interest than before in overseas possessions.

Then with startling speed the old colonial Powers, joined by Italy, Germany, the USA, and Japan, burst forth anew upon the "lesser breeds." The peoples of preliterate cultures and preindustrialized civilizations were now less capable than ever of opposing empire-builders wielding steamships, ironclads, Gatling guns, machinery, new treasures of capital seeking investment, and new part-nerships of convenience among diplomats, bankers, missionaries, merchants, and naval officers. The French seizure of Tunis (1881) and of Indochina (1884) inaugurated the new imperialism in the course of which the Powers took unto themselves, within three decades, wider and wealthier realms than Columbus and Cortez, Champlain and La Salle, Hudson and Drake had dreamed of. We shall leave it to the historians of empire to recount the politics and diplomacy of this era with its scrambles and quarrels, deals and bargains, "protectorates" and "spheres of influence," annexations and atrocities, and widespread exploitation of colored peoples by the "master race."

By the time the white nations turned their weapons against one another and embarked upon the mutual butcheries of the 20th Century, the British Empire (officially renamed the "Commonwealth of Nations" in 1926) embraced one-fifth of the land area of the globe and one-quarter of its population, with India its most precious jewel and the "Dominions" enjoying independence. France controlled the second largest colonial domain, with Indochina and North and West Africa its largest units. Germany lost its colonies to the victors in World War I, and Italy and Japan all of theirs in World War II. Portugal retained Mozambique and Angola along with scattered ports and islands. The Netherlands clung to Indonesia. King Leopold II of Belgium made millions from the sweat, tears, and blood of Congo natives, forced to supply Western speculators with ivory, rubber, and palm oil. Spain had been relieved of her remaining American and Asiatic possessions by the USA in 1898, but later acquired three strips of African coast by way of costly compensation.

Why Have Colonies? As soon as questions are raised regarding the underlying purposes which are served by the practice of the art of empire-building, complex problems of interpretation and evaluation present themselves for solution. These problems are usually resolved by glib formulas which express half-truths but fail to explain imperialism in its totality. "Over-population," "the need for markets," "the white man's burden," "capital investments," "trade follows the flag," "exploitation of subject peoples," and "the monopolistic stage of capitalism" are among the formulas which have gained wide acceptance. Each emphasizes one element in the process whereby the Western nation-states divided up the world. Each seeks to explain the entire process in terms of this single element, which is regarded at the same time as a clue to motives and purposes and an explanation of results. The validity of each hypothesis can be demonstrated to the satisfaction of its proponents by a careful selection of evidence to prove a case. Each can be as readily disproved by a compilation of negative evidence. As one commentator aptly put it:

The question is too complex, despite its brevity, to be disposed of neatly in a final formula or a facile phrase. The answer can be obtained only by summing up the profit-and-loss account in each of half a dozen departments of activity, and combining the net results. An exhaustive study of each item would require more than one volume and more than a single lifetime. In the end, some of the benefits and evils of imperialism would still be imponderable, and the final judgment would be subjective rather than scientific, for no scientific balance can be devised to weigh ships against schools, raw materials against wars, profits against patriotism, civilization against cannibalism.[1]

[1] P. T. Moon, *Imperialism and World Politics*, p. 526.

The problem of analyzing the purposes and fruits of imperialism is made peculiarly difficult by the fact that prior intentions are usually hopelessly confused with subsequent results, both in official apologies and in public discussions. Results are cited in explanation of original motives with which they have no connection at the time of action. If the American occupation of Haiti leads to the construction of roads, schools, and hospitals, the occupation is defended in terms which suggest that its original purpose was to construct roads, schools, and hospitals. The American annexation of Alaska is justified by gold discoveries, though the existence of gold in the territory was unknown at the time of the purchase. Prior intentions, moreover, are frequently disguised in such ambiguous verbiage that the outside observer may well wonder whether those who framed and executed policies had any clear conception in their own minds of why they were acting. The arts of dissimulation, misrepresentation, and rationalization are so highly developed that the practitioners are deceived by their own cleverness. After naval strategists had dictated the annexation of the Philippine Islands, President McKinley justified the acquisition by solicitude for the little brown brothers "for whom Christ also died." After sugar, investments, and naval policy dictated the conversion of Cuba into an American protectorate, its "emancipation" from Spain was defended in the name of humanity and self-determination. In democratic States, profit motives and power motives must be skillfully concealed in terms of humanitarianism, civilizing missions, religious conversion, and material benefits conferred upon the backward peoples; for, as a distinguished Florentine diplomat once pointed out, "the vulgar are ever caught by appearances and judge solely by the event." The multitudes of patriots and taxpayers are moved to enthusiasm and self-glorification by the tactics of interested minorities, and the shouts of the multitude move statesmen to action as a means of retaining public favor. In this jumble of slogans, catchwords, and appeals to irrationality, it is next to impossible to separate realities and illusions.

The alleged motives may be divided into those which postulate benefits to the home country and those which postulate benefits to the colony. As for the first of these, it is argued that colonies are necessary as outlets for surplus population, as markets for goods, as markets for capital, and as sources for raw materials essential to make the nation self-sufficient and secure. These arguments are at best of the *post hoc, ergo propter hoc* variety. At worst, they are pure rationalizations of quite other purposes, or figments of too vivid imaginations skilled in wish-fulfillment thinking.

The establishment of political control over a backward area works no magic whereby its wealth is appropriated and distributed piecemeal among the citizens of the imperial State. The type of imperialism which involves the seizure of the goods and chattels of the conquered and the distribution of the inhabitants as slaves among the conquerors has, until recently, been regarded as obsolete. When a modern State asserts title to a backward region, the property of the inhabitants remains in the hands of its former owners or is bought up by interested investors of the conquering State for their private profit. In the first case, the total population of the State which has asserted title derives no benefit whatever from the new status; in the second, the general benefit, if any, is entirely incidental. The direction of trade and investment, it is true, may be altered by political means, but it cannot be demonstrated that the masses of voters and taxpayers in the mother country gain anything thereby except additional satisfaction for their patriotic impulses.

The value of colonies to the imperial nation-states as outlets for "surplus population" has been negligible, despite the large role played by this alleged purpose in imperialistic propaganda in Germany, Italy, Japan, and other supposedly "overpopulated" States. Since most of the empires are located in tropical or subtropical areas unsuitable for residence by Europeans and since emigrants prefer to go to congenial lands of easy economic opportunity, there has been no appreciable outflow of population from nation-states to colonies. During the past half century, fewer than 500,000 of the 20,000,000 Europeans who took up permanent residence outside of Europe went to the colonial territories of European Governments. After 30 years of colonialism, only 20,000 Germans lived in Germany's colonies in 1914, compared with over three times this number on Manhattan Island alone. In 1931 all the Italian colonies in Africa contained only 55,000 Europeans, many of whom were not Italians. Twice as many Italians lived in New York City. In 1930 there were only 238,000 Japanese in all Manchuria. By 1935 the number was still under 750,000, though Japan's population had increased almost 5,000,000 in the interval and Manchuria's Chinese population had increased by 4,500,000. In 1933 there were 543,000 Japanese in Korea and 257,000 in Formosa. The "surplus population" argument for imperialism has played its part in convincing patriots of the necessity of expansion. But it can be regarded as an honestly and consciously formulated purpose behind the quest for empire only on the assumption that statesmen are imbeciles or madmen.

It is likewise not difficult to show, despite appearances to the contrary, that most colonies are not acquired by States as markets for goods or for investments, though such motives may influence particular groups of politically influential imperialists and may be regarded as plausible by the citizenry. "Trade follows the flag," cries the imperialist. But trade does *not* follow the flag in most cases; and where it does, the economic results, though profitable for the traders involved, are of little significance to the people of the home State. During the post-Versailles years when "prosperity" still prevailed, the total foreign commerce of the colonies of the world reached an annual figure of about $15,000,000,000, something less than one-quarter of the world's international trade. The British Empire accounted for three-quarters of this colonial trade, the USA enjoyed 10% of it, and the other colonial Powers smaller proportions. Efforts on the part of the imperial States to monopolize such trade for their own nationals in many cases led to an increased percentage of the foreign trade of the colonies being carried on with the mother country. But only two imperial Powers enjoyed over half of the trade of their colonies: the USA and Japan. Even in these cases, colonial trade was a tiny fraction of the State's total foreign trade and an infinitesimal fraction of its total domestic and foreign commerce. The larger part of this fraction would in most cases be enjoyed by the imperial State without political control of the territories with which the trade is carried on. To a few industries in the colonial States colonial markets may be of considerable importance. In the national economy considered as a whole, these markets are of minor significance.

The same statement holds regarding exports of capital. Investment interests have often played a leading role in the process of imperialism. "Dollar diplomacy" suggests empire-building on a grand scale. But most of the foreign investments and loans of the imperial States were made, not in their colonies, but in foreign countries. Between 1931 and 1937, for example, Japan "invested" $682,000,000 in Manchukuo, but $312,000,000 of this sum represented the cost of maintaining armed forces and suppressing "banditry," and only $40,000,000 represented private investments. Each dollar invested by Japanese capitalists thus cost the Japanese taxpayers $17—and the ungrateful capitalists found other markets for investment more attractive.

Finally, we may note that the contention that colonies are acquired as sources of raw materials is also without foundation, either in the political process of empire-building or in the economic results of the process. On the one hand, efforts on the part of imperial States to fix world prices of raw materials exported from their colonies, and thus make profits for their own nationals at the expense of foreign purchasers, have been largely unsuccessful. On the other hand, none of the imperial Powers has ever derived the major portion of its required raw materials from its colonies. Colonial raw materials are sold to purchasers willing to buy them, and such purchasers are quite as likely to be found in foreign States as in the mother country. Purchasers needing raw materials buy them where they are to be had most cheaply, and the sources of supply are quite as likely to be found in foreign States or colonies as in the territories of the State of the purchasers. Self-sufficiency in raw materials is impossible even for Britain, with her vast and variegated Empire, and is quite out of the question for other States. If the empires were acquired to make the imperial States self-sufficient in such goods, the experiment failed miserably. In point of fact, this, too, is not a "purpose" of imperialism, but a phrase employed by profit-seekers and by power-and-prestige politicians to bewilder the uninitiated and win popular approval for policies motivated by considerations of a different character.

If space permitted, it could be demonstrated statistically that the taxpayers of every imperial Power have beeen obliged to pour out blood and treasure for the acquisition and administration of colonies out of all proportion to any economic gains secured by the mother country from colonial areas or to any alleged "benefits" conferred upon the subject peoples. The most that can be said in support of the contention that colonies are "profitable" to the nation holding them is that the progressive fragmentation of the world, coupled with the collapse of the international gold standard, makes it economically advantageous for certain States to have colonies for the disposal of surplus goods and capital and for the purchase of raw materials. In a world of neomercantilism and autarchy, the absence of tariff obstacles, import quotas, and exchange difficulties are welcome features of trade among colonies and the States controlling them. But these "advantages" are themselves by-products of enormous losses accruing to the world economy as a whole from restrictions upon the free flow of goods and services across frontiers. Where all States are alike impoverished, each can relieve its poverty slightly by controlling colonies. Starving men may fight for dry crusts. But the nourishment thus obtained does not demonstrate that dry crusts constitute an adequate diet. In terms of economic welfare, imperialism is almost universally a costly and wasteful luxury.

Each particular purpose, however, plays its role in the total complexity of purposes. The entire process has been so confused, anarchic, and disorderly that no clear, single purpose is discernible. The preceding observations have served their end if they have suggested (1) that no "single-purpose" explanation of imperialism is tenable, whether it be couched in political, economic, religious, or humanitarian terms and (2) that the course of empire-building has been one in which no single directing intelligence has ever played a controlling role, save in a few exceptional instances. Generally speaking, scores of divergent interests in the imperial States, by a more or less blind and uncoordinated pushing and pulling, have contributed to a final result not clearly foreseen at the outset by anyone and certainly not representing any consciously formulated and willfully executed program on the part of any single individual or group. Contemporary colonialism is a phenomenon of Western civilization in the age of private capitalism, bourgeois individualism, planless economy, parliamentary democracy, and demagogic politics. These — note aspects of Western culture suggest one of its dominant characteristics: pluralism, competition among a bewildering multitude of interests and forces, uncontrolled and uncontrollable economic and political drifting under the impact of pressures released by the Industrial Revolution and not yet brought under the control of organized social intelligence. Out of the interaction of interests and forces, certain consequences flow which take on the appearance—which are indeed deliberately given the appearance—of purpose and planning on the part of the whole community of the nation-state. But this is appearance only, for the forces which have produced the consequences are part of a chaotic jumble of interests and groups within each nation. "Imperialism" is such a consequence. Its "purposes" are intelligible only in terms of the nature of the political process within and between the nation-states themselves.

If imperialism is viewed as a facet of the struggle for power between States, its results must be judged in terms of its role in power politics. The most obvious result of the competitive quest for empire is war—war, first between the imperial States and the backward peoples, and then war among the imperial States themselves. Whether investors use Foreign Offices to enhance profits or Foreign Offices use investors to extend State power, the diplomatic influence of the State is placed at the disposal of the empire-builders; and if diplomacy fails to attain the goal, it is supported by coercion and military force. Such force has been used on innumerable occasions against the native States which resist conquest. There is scarcely a single colony of any of the Great Powers which was not won through bloodshed. Such wars are often costly (e.g., the Boer War and the Manchurian hostilities of 1931–33); they are sometimes disastrous to conquerors and conquered alike (e.g., Spain in Morocco, France in Mexico); they almost always involve atrocities, abuses, fierce resentment, and savage repression (e.g., the USA in the Philippines and Haiti, France in Madagascar and Syria, Germany in South-West Africa, Britain in India, Egypt, the Sudan, China, and elsewhere). In general, however, colonial wars do not, in and of themselves, upset the balance of power or bring the conquerors to ruin. They tend rather to increase the power of the imperial States and to enhance the profits of their immediate beneficiaries. The situation is quite different when the imperial States engage in war with one another for mastery of tropical lands or Oriental markets. Prior to 1800, even such wars normally had little effect upon the nation-states themselves, apart from changing titles to territories and bringing about redistributions of power and prestige. In the machine age, however, such conflicts have become enormously costly and destructive of life and property whenever Great Powers have been belligerents on opposite sides. The fruits of empire-building, garnered by the war god, are destruction, death, bankruptcy, and national ruin. Yet these fruits are seldom weighed in the balances of those who tabulate profits and losses.

2. THE ANTI-COLONIAL REVOLUTION

For behold the Lord, the Lord of hosts, doth take away from Jerusalem and from Judah the stay and the staff, the whole stay of bread and the whole stay of water, the mighty man, and the man of war, the judge, and the prophet, and the prudent, and the ancient, the captain of fifty, and the honourable man, and the counsellor, and the cunning artificer, and the eloquent orator. . . . And the people shall be oppressed, every one by another, and every one by his neighbor; . . . For Jerusalem is ruined, and Judah is fallen: . . . Woe unto the wicked! it shall be ill with him: for the reward of his hands shall be given him. . . . What mean ye that ye beat my people to pieces, and grind the faces of the poor? saith the Lord God of hosts.—*The Book of Isaiah*, Chapter 3.

The pattern of world power and world trade which took shape concurrently with the building of the modern colonial empires was by its very nature (as many now perceive with the wisdom of hindsight) a transitory pattern—however durable it appeared to its makers, however long its shadow may persist, and however dubious may be the new pattern destined to replace it. It grew out of the technological, military, and administrative superiority of the North Atlantic communities over those of other continents. It rested upon "terms of trade" between the industrialized States and the agrarian or colonial areas of the earth whereby the former exchanged dear manufactures for cheap foodstuffs, raw materials, and minerals. It found expression in the huge disparity of per capita incomes (see pp. 618–624) between the wealthy third of the world's population dwelling in the "Western" lands and the impoverished two-thirds in the lands of the East and South. It presupposed that the subject peoples for an indefinite period would lack the will or the means to cast off their colonial yoke or would at worst be content, in the course of "tutelage," with small and slow concessions not damaging to imperial interests.

Each of these circumstances was ephemeral. Ideas travel with guns, governors, and goods. Occidental nationalism begets Oriental nationalism. Asians and Africans, as they became aware of Western wealth and their own poverty, demanded "self-determination" and their own "place in the sun." The Western world's colonial "frontier" slowly faded as the fabulous profit-making opportunities of early days waned and the costs of exploiting resources and labor in colonial economies waxed. Once the new intellectuals among "backward" peoples acquired the rudiments of Western skills in science, warfare, and politics, leaders arose among them to demand that they take their destinies into their own hands.

What followed is a vastly complex and confusing chaos of colonial rebellions and civil wars: savage repressions and grudging or gracious concessions; ideological and class conflicts fought with bullets, ballots, and bribery; Great Power rivalries entangled with national struggles among conspirators, assassins, martyrs, and saints; and a huge and baffled yearning for freedom from want and fear and oppression—less often realized than betrayed or buried in empty verbiage. This process cannot be comprehended by being viewed through simple stereotypes, even if each one reflects some phase of reality—*e.g.*, "Minute Men" shooting "redcoats," philanthropists doing natives good, policemen preserving "law and order," sons of liberty mobilizing patriots against alien tyrants, or anti-Communists rallying the virtuous against the godless at the gates. The process might perhaps be adequately analyzed by a detailed survey of the local and international politics of each of the colonial areas during the past century. For such an exploration space and time are

315

here lacking. We must needs content ourselves with generalizations, all of which call for numerous exceptions in time and space, and with illustrative instances which we must hope will call attention to relevant aspects of a world-wide fermentation of grievances and aspirations which, even when unredressed and unfulfilled, have already shattered the colonialism of yesterday.

The Dynamics of Anti-imperialism. Our modest enterprise can scarcely be approached by way of the policy of the imperial Powers. Contrary to the dogma of many Marxists, they have never had any common policy nor has any one of them long pursued a consistent policy in its own domains. Neither would it be helpful to view the anti-colonial revolution in terms of shared ideals of "independence." The slogan is common enough, but it conceals rather than reveals the bewildering multiplicity of differing local circumstances giving rise to differing demands and expectations.

We shall come closer to grasping the moving forces here at work if we bear in mind the social status and the interests (along with the symbols in terms of which "interests" are defined) of four interacting groups of human beings which, in one or another variant, are to be found in all of the colonial, semi-colonial, and recently colonial communities of the world.

The smallest group, usually, consists of the outlanders who have entered the area from the metropole: colonial administrators, missionaries, advisers to native rulers, merchants, agents and managers of foreign corporations (*e.g.*, the United Fruit Company in Central America), and occasionally sizable bodies of permanent settlers (*e.g.*, the 2,600,000 Boers and Britons in South Africa, the million Frenchmen in Algeria, the 150,000 Frenchmen and 90,000 Italians in Tunisia) and sometimes other aliens, or their descendants, who have been brought in as workers or have gone in as businessmen (*e.g.*, the 3,000,000 Chinese and 500,000 Indians in Malaya, comprising 55% of the population, other Chinese throughout Southeast Asia, Hindus in Africa and the West Indies, Negroes in the Caribbean, etc.). Where such outsiders are nationals of the Power asserting sovereignty, they are the vehicles of colonial control and the first targets of indigenous xenophobia, nationalism, and racialism.

Another group, small in size but possessed of wealth and power, consists of the native elite. Where Western industrialism has significantly altered ancient ways, a new plutocracy of native entrepreneurs has emerged. But the colonial lands, including Latin America, are essentially agrarian economies and "feudal" societies in which blue-blooded landlords, often titled and pedigreed, stand at the apex of the social pyramid, as in preindustrial Europe. Of the 41,000 villages of Iran, 40,000 are owned by landlords (most of them absentee), who collect in rents 60% to 80% of the crops raised by the peasant-tenants—to whom they lend money at 200% interest. The *caudillos* or "chiefs" of South America are almost invariably owners of great haciendas. When King Farouk of Egypt was forced from his throne in July, 1952, he owned

316

20,000 acres, netting him $1,160,000 annually, plus shares in other estates netting him half again as much. He was estimated to possess a total fortune of $580,000,000. Of his 20,000,000 subjects, 85% were illiterate, 40% had hookworm, 90% had trachoma, and all but a few thousand landlords were so desperately poor as to beggar description. The private fortunes of the Princes of India and of the spoilsmen of Kuomintang China were fabulous.

Native aristocracies and plutocracies have sometimes been relieved of their wealth by Western fortune-hunters. But in the 20th-Century practice of "imperialism," capitalists, in contrast to Communists, have found it wise to share the wealth with the local elite and sometimes to add to their riches. The vast oil reserves of the Near and Middle East, with new fields being discovered and developed annually, led to the establishment of the Anglo-Persian Oil Company in 1912 and to the acquisition of new concessions in the 1940's by the Bahrein Petroleum Company and the Arabian American Oil Company (Aramco), both formed by Standard of California and the Texas Oil Company. American capital to an amount approaching a billion dollars by the middle 1950's poured into the area through complex arrangements whereby Socony-Vacuum, Standard of New Jersey, and the Gulf Oil Company shared with British, French, and Dutch corporations a variety of lucrative contracts. These agreements resulted in initial royalties (at 22¢ a barrel) of $40,000 per day to King Ibn-Saud and his 40 sons, who received $150,000,000 in 1951—and in 1952 asked for more, and received $300,000,000 annually by 1958. The Anglo-American Kuwait Oil Company agreed in December, 1951, to a new formula of profit sharing with Abdullah el Salim el Sabah, Sheik of Kuwait, whereby he would receive an estimated $140,000,000 a year. Unless blessed with oil, uranium, or other precious materials on their estates, few native rulers or landlords elsewhere could hope to do as well as the Sheiks of Araby. But business arrangements between Western corporations and Eastern and Southern possessors of property and power were usually advantageous to both.

If we descend another step on the ladder of prestige, we encounter something approaching a vacuum in most of the colonial lands. For here in the relative absence of industry, finance, and commerce, there is no equivalent of the "middle class" which is the matrix of democracy in the North Atlantic countries. The nearest approach to this stratum consists of native merchants and a small but unhappy "intelligentsia," consisting chiefly of Western-educated sons of aristocrats, easily attracted to extreme nationalism, Fascism, or Communism. Far from constituting an element of stability, these groups, whether in Bolivia or Burma, Morocco or Madagascar, Nigeria or Nepal, are the breeding grounds of fanatics, assassins, and revolutionaries.

At the bottom of the hierarchy is the teeming horde of the poor, consisting of peasant-tenants, peons, or serfs, along with a relatively few but almost equally miserable "proletarians" in new mines or mills developed by outside capital. Western science has enormously increased their numbers by reducing infant mortality and diminishing famines and plagues, with no proportionate effect on birth rates. (The population of Java grew from 5,000,000 in 1816 to 48,000,000 by 1942; the population of India increased by 51,000,000 souls between 1931 and 1941.) These multitudes are almost wholly illiterate. The French in Indochina and the Dutch in Indonesia kept 90% of the natives from any knowledge of reading or writing in any language, with the proportion of literates scarcely larger throughout most of Africa and South America. Here are hundreds of millions of fellahin living in squalor, dirt, and disease on the narrowest margins of existence, ferociously exploited by their masters (usually more so by native gentries than by Western "imperialists"), and barely able to sustain life by back-breaking labor. So lived their forebears for endless centuries. But contentment with their lot is no longer possible. The glorious vision of the "American way of life" and the specious promises of Communist "Utopia" have penetrated even to the remotest sections of these dark masses. And when discontent fails to generate hope, it fosters violence.

Here then are the elements of the anti-colonial revolution. Red agitators preach anti-imperialism, anti-capitalism, anti-feudalism. Native elites sponsor anti-Western nationalism to thwart Communism and deflect mass unrest away from themselves and against the convenient scapegoats provided by Europeans and Americans. Colonial Powers and their local agents resist the pressures put upon them and thus provoke violent outbreaks of terrorism and rebellion—or yield to pressure and strive for alliances with native feudalists. The latter, ever insecure in the face of mass misery, quarrel over the spoils of office and fall out among themselves in recurrent paroxysms of political murder and palace revolution—from Colombia to Ceylon and from Korea to Cuba. All seek safety in intolerant xenophobia and persecution of pariahs. It is scarcely astounding that policy-makers in Paris, London, and Washington are puzzled by the bubbling of this devil's brew, concocted from timeless evils, some of them far older than modern colonialism. What is surprising is that occasionally sufficient wisdom has been summoned to the task to make possible some moderately hopeful accommodation to the new facts of life in a maladjusted world.

American Dream. The Great Republic of the New World, with its anti-colonialist tradition, has largely freed itself from the incubus of "Yankee Imperialism" in the Americas. But in seeking to adapt its purposes to the exigencies of anti-colonialism elsewhere it has irritated its allies by championing "self-determination" for subject peoples and has alienated potential friends by paradoxically supporting European "imperialists" against native rebels. As regards its own "empire," independence for the Philippines (pledged by the Jones Act of 1916) was championed in the 1930's by trade unionists eager to ban Filipino labor and by businessmen eager to bar from the domestic market sugar and vegetable oils from the islands. In 1934–35 steps were taken toward local self-government. Following liberation from Japan, Philippine independence was proclaimed July 4, 1946, with a sequel: a 99-year Mutual Aid Pact (March 14, 1947), providing for U.S. bases and military missions. Local resentments against American policy toward Tokyo and chronic warfare against the "Hukbalahaps" or Communist-led guerrillas seeking social revolution did not prevent the Philippine Commonwealth from becoming a sovereign member of the family of nations, tightly bound to Washington by the $2,000,000,000 poured into the islands, 1945–49, and by annual subventions of $50,000,000 since 1950.

Meanwhile the pattern of U.S. relations with Latin America was profoundly altered. The J. Reuben Clark Memorandum of March, 1930, reinterpreted the Monroe Doctrine to preclude U.S. intervention. In his first Inaugural Address, Franklin D. Roosevelt espoused the "policy of the good neighbor." In 1934 the USA abandoned its rights of intervention and of military and fiscal control in Cuba. In 1933–35 U.S. Marines were withdrawn from Haiti and Nicaragua, long areas of "dollar diplomacy." Puerto Rico received the boon of an elective Governor in 1948 and was granted a Constitution, confirmed by popular referendum, in 1951, thus achieving a degree of self-rule comparable in fact, if not in form, to that of the states of the American Union.

As for the American hemisphere as a whole, the hated domination of the "Colossus of the North" gave way to a partnership among sovereign equals, though their "equality," as always, was a legal and diplomatic fiction and the 20 Republics south of the Rio Grande remained "colonial" communities in their economic and social structure. The "Pan-American Union," established in Washington in 1889–90, was neither a union nor Pan-American. The key words of the voluminous verbiage which emerged from successive conferences after 1933 suggest the Latin aspirations and the Yankee formulas through which Washington's leadership has since been exercised by methods more subtle and acceptable than those previously employed. Montevideo, 1933: "nonintervention." Buenos Aires, 1936: "neutrality." Lima, 1938: "continental solidarity," "collaboration," and "consultation." Panama, 1939: "neutrality zone." Havana, 1940: "continentalization" of the Monroe Doctrine. Mexico City, 1945: nonintervention, consultation, solidarity, collective security in the "Act of Chapultepec." Rio, 1947: an attack on any American state "shall be considered as an attack against all," but none "shall be required to use force without its consent" (the Inter-American Treaty of Reciprocal Assistance or "Act of Petropolis").

The Ninth International Conference of American States at Bogotá in April, 1948, interrupted by local political assassination and frenzied mob violence, concluded a pact for the "Defense of Democracy" against the Communist menace and drew up the Charter of 112 Articles creating the elaborate "Organization of American States" (OAS), of which the Pan-American Union became the Bureau. This was described as a regional agency for the main-

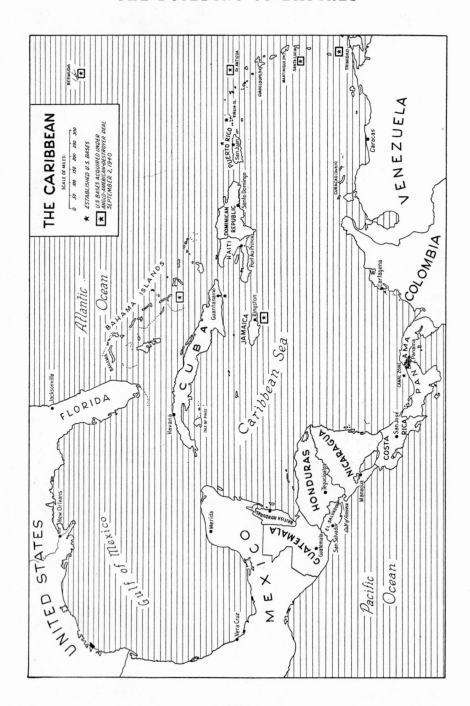

THE CARIBBEAN

SCALE OF MILES:
0 50 100 150 200 250 300

★ ESTABLISHED U.S. BASES

⊠ U.S. BASES ACQUIRED UNDER
ANGLO-AMERICAN DESTROYER DEAL
SEPTEMBER 2, 1940

tenance of peace under Articles 51–52 of the UN Charter and thus became a prototype of NATO. The Ministers of Foreign Affairs, being met for the fourth time in March, 1951, resolved in Washington on "military planning for the common defense" and joint efforts to combat "the subversive activities of international Communism." Throughout Latin America the politicians, intellectuals, landlords, mineowners, and business partners of North American corporations were understandably resentful in mid-century that the USA was more generous in subsidizing allies in Europe and Asia than in the New World. Dictator-demagogues (*e.g.*, Juan Péron in Argentina) still found it good politics to pose as friends of the poor by denouncing Yankee "capitalism" and "imperialism." But in general the elites of the Southlands were content enough with arrangements which afforded them the forms of unrestricted national sovereignty and the tangible benefits of subventions, investments, and other emoluments conducive to the maintenance of the social ·*status quo*.

The mass of the population in most of the American Republics, apart from Canada, the USA, and Argentina, consists of Amerindians and mestizos or half-breeds, with important Negro admixtures in the Caribbean and Brazil. The local elites are predominantly "white" and of Spanish (or, in Brazil, Portuguese) ancestry. Of the 200,000,000 inhabitants of Africa, the larger part consists of native Negroes still living in preliterate tribal communities possessed of no well-defined elite. Until recently, only two of these were possessed of "sovereignty" in our time: the ancient Kingdom of Ethiopia, and Liberia, founded by ex-slaves from the USA and proclaimed independent in 1847. The cultures of black Africa, albeit demoralized by contacts with Western civilization, have only begun to engender articulate demands for emancipation from white rule.

Ferment in Islam. Matters are quite otherwise among the Arab and Berber peoples north of the Sahara. These communities were founded by the Saracens and enjoyed brief independence between the slow breakdown of the Ottoman Empire and the violent advent of the new imperialism. Here are the westernmost of the world's 300,000,000 Moslems (of whom some 50,000,000 speak Arabic), extending from Northwest Africa along the southern shore of the central sea to the Near and Middle East and far beyond to Indonesia. Here rebellion against European colonialism has been chronic, followed, when unsuccessful, by bitter hatreds and, when successful, not by democracy but by the confused and disorderly political life characteristic of most feudal societies.

Moslem efforts to cast off the yoke of the infidel have assumed so many shapes that any generalized account is bound to be misleading. Islam is not a unity, even religiously. Aside from many smaller sects, its devotees are divided into orthodox Sunnites and dissident Shiah-ites (the latter mainly in Iraq and southern Arabia), who refused to recognize the Caliphate at Constantinople—abolished in 1924 with separation of Church and State in the new Turkey. Throughout Arabic and Iranian Islam, rich landowners exploit multitudes of miserable peasants who are illiterate, disease-ridden, half-starved, inarticulate, and live more like beasts than men. The dynasties and aristocracies are slow to act together. They have found it profitable to bargain separately with alien businessmen and diplomats in the interest of enhancing their revenues.

Contemporary imperialism in the Levant and the new clash of Christendom, Judaism, and Islam are unintelligible on any assumption of a simple revolt of united native nationalists against Western rule. The feudal elites have become nationalists because their privileges have lately been jeopardized by dim stirrings among the dark and sodden masses and by voices of protest raised among the still meager but vocal ranks of intellectuals and middle-class liberals. To clamor for "independence," to appeal to native patriotism, to damn European imperialists, to cultivate xenophobia, to assail Jews are all devices whereby insecure ruling classes evoke allegiance from subclasses.

In 1903 the Pan-Islam Society was founded in London. Its efforts to promote Moslem unity met with little success. The Allies of World War I found it expedient to support anti-Turkish Pan-Arabism. By the Treaty of Oct. 24, 1915, Emir Hussein of the Hejaz was promised British aid in creating a united Arab State in exchange for rebellion and war against Turkey. The pledge was broken. Britain and France partitioned the lands north of Arabia between themselves by the secret Sykes-Picot agreement of 1916. Iraq, Syria, and Palestine were made mandates. Local Arab revolts were ruthlessly crushed by British and French troops. In the early 1920's, Hussein's rival, King Abdul Aziz ibn-Saud, defeated him in war, established a united Kingdom of Saudi Arabia, and in 1934 also conquered but then restored the Kingdom of Yemen under the Iman Yahyah. The larger unity of the Arab lands remained remote. Meanwhile, far to the west in Spanish Morocco, Riffian warriors rose in revolt in an effort to throw out the Spanish and French rulers of their country. Under Abd-el Krim, able leader and strategist, they crushed the Spanish forces, fought the French to a standstill, and were not compelled to yield until large European armies under Marshal Pétain drove Krim into the mountains in 1926. At the same time, French battalions drowned in blood a formidable revolt of the Druse tribesmen in Syria, destroying much of Damascus in the process.

This pattern of fierce rebellion, followed by savage suppression, gave way in the fullness of time to new departures. Local uprisings, to be sure, continued far beyond the 1920's. Iraq, Syria, Palestine, Libya, and Egypt were all scenes of sporadic rioting and bloodshed. Hatred of the French seethed in North Africa. In Algeria an insurrection of May, 1945, was put down with the loss of thousands of lives. In 1947 the aging Abd-el Krim, returning from long exile, "escaped" into Egypt from the French ship carrying him through Suez and hinted darkly at new violence in Morocco if independence were not granted. But most Arab leaders seized upon other means of furthering their purposes. Haj Amin el Husseini, Grand Mufti of Jerusalem and head of the Arab Higher Committee of Palestine, took the lead in joining the Axis against the Western Powers.[2] Following the failure of the pro-Nazi revolt in Iraq in 1941, which he helped to organize, he fled to the Reich. After the collapse of the Fascist Powers, he "escaped" from confinement in France (June, 1947),

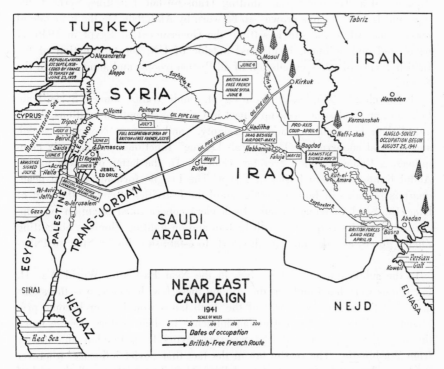

took refuge in Egypt and later in Pakistan, and resumed direction of anti-Jewish and "anti-imperialist" activities. His colleagues among the politicians of Arab nationalism found new opportunities for intrigue, profit, and political success in Britain's postwar debility, in Anglo-American fears of Russia, and in the thirst for oil on the part of American businessmen and strategists.

[2] Nazi anti-Semites were not anti-Arabs, though Arabic, like Hebrew, is of course a Semitic language, just as Yiddish (akin to early German) is an "Aryan" language. For photographic and documentary evidence of the collaboration of the Grand Mufti with Hitlerism, see "The Arab Higher Committee," a report submitted to UN in May, 1947, by The Nation Associates, N.Y. Had the Nazi policy-makers, masters by conquest of Jugoslavia, Greece, and Crete in the spring of 1941, abandoned the decision they had long since reached to attack the USSR, they might well have succeeded, with the aid of Arab sympathizers and Vichy French agents, in penetrating and dominating much of the Near East. Such efforts were peripheral to their main objective and were frustrated by the British and Free French campaign of April–July, 1941, depicted on the accompanying map.

Britain was disposed to yield to blackmail—partly to defend the Near East from the Axis during the war, partly to lubricate postwar oil diplomacy. In the spring of 1945, France was forced by Britain to quit the Levant. Syria and Lebanon became independent States. In May, 1946, London detached Trans-Jordan from Palestine and made it a Kingdom under Emir Abdullah, whose army was commanded by British Brigadier Glubb Pasha. Abdullah dreamed of a "Greater Syria," uniting Trans-Jordan, Palestine, Syria, Lebanon, and Iraq under one crown—to be worn by Abdullah. On the principle of making hay while the sun is setting, the Government of Egypt in 1946–47 negotiated and agitated, inside and outside of UN, for termination of the British Treaty of 1936, evacuation of all British troops, and annexation of the Sudan.

On March 22, 1945, leaders from Egypt, Saudi Arabia, Yemen, Syria, Iraq, Lebanon, and Palestine drew up a pact in Cairo to strengthen relations, "safeguard their independence and sovereignty," and promote economic, social, and cultural cooperation. This "Arab League" functioned through six committees, a Council, and a Secretary-General. To the latter post was named Abdul Rahman Azzam Pasha of Egypt. The League formally opened headquarters in Cairo in January, 1946, amid the festivities attending the visit of King Ibn-Saud to King Farouk. Its leaders concentrated attention on supporting Egypt in its quarrels with Britain and on fighting Zionism, boycotting Zionist goods, and denouncing all efforts to establish a Jewish State in Palestine.[3]

In the subtle interplay of motives in the Near East after World War II, few things were fixed and certain. Among these few, however, was the assurance that the kings and nobles of the Arab lands would never become pro-Soviet or willingly enhance Russian influence in their realms, despite much threatening talk for purposes of wresting favors from London and money from Washington. The reason lay in the fact that Soviet influence, wherever it is extended, spells the end of feudalism. That it may also spell the end of democracy is here irrelevant, since democracy has never existed in the Arab lands. The 30,000,000 Moslems of the USSR have ceased to be serfs and have, in their own eyes, become freemen in enjoying schools, hospitals, factories, and a rich rebirth of native culture.[4] This fact, no less than the existence

[3] See Vernon McKay, "The Arab League in World Politics," *F.P.A. Reports*, Nov. 15, 1946.

[4] After visiting the USSR, Col. C. E. Bonsonby, a Conservative M.P., told the Royal Empire and Royal African Societies on May 30, 1945: "Twenty-one years ago the literacy . . . in Uzbekistan was 7%, practically the only teaching being in the Mohammedan schools, and very few women could write at all. There were one or two small irrigation schemes on the Tsar's estates—there were no factories and no hydroelectric plants. What is the situation after 21 years? Now 98% of the population can read and write; there are 4,000 schools, two universities and several technical institutes; there are large efficient factories; huge irrigation schemes; 20 hydroelectric plants, and, amongst other things, a wonderful ballet and opera."

of a progressive, democratic Jewish Palestine, is a mortal danger to the elites of the nearby Moslem lands, where most of the population still lives in an incredible state of medieval misery. By the same token, the kings and effendis of Islam must cast their lot with the oil corporations and with those Anglo-American diplomats who believe that their own purposes are best served by buttressing reactionary feudalism as a bulwark against Communism. Such a program will be successful so long as the landlords and princes are secure in their positions of privilege and power. Should the dark masses ever catch the vision of a better life and rise in revolt, the strange alliance of American capitalism and Arab feudalism will fail both partners. Such a failure might well enhance Soviet prestige and influence throughout Islam.[5]

Later developments in the communities here dealt with, and their counterparts in other areas once ruled by the empire-builders, are best reserved for subsequent treatment (see pp. 370*f.*, 629*f.*). The tragic tale of colonialism and anti-colonialism is inseparable from the more inspiring, albeit often equally tragic, story of the newer nationalisms which in many respects are carbon copies of the older nationalisms, both of which we shall consider in the following chapter. In fact, all successful rebellions of colonial peoples against their masters are products of a new sense of nationhood among those hitherto innocent of any such sense of collective identity but moved by the impact of the West to imitate the dominant cult of the West and use it to achieve emancipation from the West. Our present survey will be best concluded by noting the decline of the West as a global center of imperial power over colonial subjects.

3. RECESSIONAL

> Far-call'd our navies melt away—
>   On dune and headland sinks the fire—
> Lo, all our pomp of yesterday
>   Is one with Nineveh and Tyre!
> Judge of the Nations, spare us yet,
>   Lest we forget, lest we forget.
>   —RUDYARD KIPLING, 1903

The "white man's burden" in the 20th Century is breaking the back of the bearer. The imperial nation-states have come into disastrous conflict with one another over control of backward regions. The revolt of the colonial peoples has long since doomed the empires to destruction or drastic transformation. The efforts of the empire-builders to meet this double danger have assumed

---

[5] In a letter to *The New York Times*, Nov. 26, 1947, Frank W. Buxton, Bartley C. Crum, S. Ralph Harlow, Walter Clay Lowdermilk, James D. McDonald, and Reinhold Niebuhr asserted: "The United States is today committed to a policy of stopping the spread of Communism in the world. But Communism cannot possibly be stopped by the support of reactionary and backward medieval potentates, who shamelessly exploit the multitudes of their peoples. On the contrary, hungry and starving masses provide the natural breeding ground for revolution and Communism."

a variety of forms, ranging from the grant of complete or partial independence to subject populations to belated attempts on the part of rival Powers to compose their differences and evolve common programs of cooperative action.

Among earlier efforts to diminish frictions were proposals to "internationalize" areas of tension, with economic opportunities open on equal terms to the nationals of all States. The port of Tangier, commanding the western entrance to the Mediterranean, was long a focal point of rivalries. The "Convention Regarding the Organization of the Statute of the Tangier Zone," signed Dec. 18, 1923, left "sovereignty" in the hands of the Sultan of Morocco (controlled by France), but placed the government of the city in the hands of a Committee of Control and an international Legislative Assembly. The Samoan Islands were under a joint Anglo-German-American condominium from 1889 to 1899, when they were partitioned. The Anglo-Egyptian Sudan was under the joint administration of Britain and Egypt. International control of this type is almost always unsatisfactory and is usually unsuccessful in the long run. Either one of the participating States secures a controlling voice in the administration, or the checks and balances provided for lead to endless friction in which the interests of the natives are forgotten.

Open Door Policy. The "Open Door" represented an alternative "solution" of more general application. As an abstraction, it means simply equality of economic opportunity in backward regions. It is to trade and investment in colonial areas what most-favored-nation treatment is to the commerce among the Western States. As a concrete policy, the Open Door was championed most vigorously by States fearing the exclusion of their merchants and investors from some lucrative field of profit-making. In practice, it was ignored by most States in areas where the profits of special privilege and discrimination were large.

The General Act of Berlin of 1885 provided for the maintenance of equality of economic opportunity in the Congo Basin. In 1885 Germany and Britain agreed to observe the Open Door in their possessions on the Gulf of Guinea, and in 1898 Britain and France made a similar agreement for West Africa. The Anglo-German agreement of 1886 guaranteed the Open Door in the Pacific possessions of the two Powers. The Anglo-German-American agreement of 1899 contained a like provision for Samoa. But such arrangements are frequently violated, either openly or through various subtle favors and discriminations contrary to the spirit of the Open Door.

In backward regions still held by native States, the scramble for markets and concessions led to the setting up of "spheres of influence" by the imperial Powers, in order that their nationals may enjoy exclusive opportunities for profit-making in these areas. International agreements for the creation of such spheres usually contemplate the closing of the door to nationals of outside States. The Anglo-Russian compact of 1907 over Persia, the Franco-German agreement of 1914 relating to Turkey, the inter-Allied secret treaties of 1915–17 dealing with the Near East, and sundry agreements concerning Africa and the Pacific were of this character. The pressure of outside States and the interests of the participating States have led, in some of these situations, to treaties for the preservation of the Open Door. The German-Russian agreement of 1910 pledged the parties to observe the Open Door in their respective spheres in Persia and Turkey. The Anglo-Franco-Italian agreement of 1906 over Ethiopia pledged equality of treatment in harbor and railway matters and cooperation in the acquisition of concessions. The Act of Algeciras of 1906 provided for "economic liberty without inequality" in Morocco. The USA was a party to this Act. It has been the most consistent champion of the Open Door everywhere, save in the Caribbean and in its own possessions.

The "Open Door" in China, now only of historical interest, was long a central principle of U.S. foreign policy and a fruitful source of concord and discord among the Powers. When Britain and France wrested trading privileges for their nationals from the Imperial Government in the first and second "Opium Wars" (1839–42 and 1856–60), the USA secured the same advantages for its citizens by concluding most-favored-nation treaties with Peiping—*i.e.*, Caleb Cushing's treaty of 1844 and Anson Burlingame's treaty of 1868. This formula no longer sufficed when the Powers began scrambling in the gay nineties for monopolistic rights and "spheres of influence" within which the Chinese Government was unable to exercise effective jurisdiction and was compelled to grant special privileges. Rather than seek a "sphere" for Americans or abandon altogether the Chinese market, Secretary John Hay (inspired by Lord Beresford and by concern among Anglo-American businessmen over Russian and French intentions) asked the Powers on Sept. 6, 1899, to accept the principle of noninterference with Chinese tariffs, harbor dues, and railway rates. On July 3, 1900, amid the "Boxer Rebellion," he urged the Powers to "preserve Chinese territorial and administrative entity, protect all rights guaranteed by treaty and international law, and safeguard for the world the principle of equal and impartial trade with all parts of the Chinese empire." The objective required what had hitherto seemed safe but was currently in jeopardy: the preservation of the independence, administrative unity, and territorial integrity of the ancient "Middle Kingdom."

The Powers agreed "in principle," meaning, as usual in diplomacy, that their purposes in practice would be quite different. Russian ambitions in Manchuria were checkmated by Japan in 1904–05. Washington induced Tokyo to reaffirm the Open Door in the Root-Takahira agreement of Nov. 30, 1908; reluctantly conceded in the Lansing-Ishii agreement of Nov. 3, 1917, that "territorial propinquity creates special relations"; and secured general acceptance of the Open Door in the Nine Power Pact of Feb. 6, 1922. But observance of "principles" whose violation is profitable depends upon calculations of power. Japan seized Manchuria in 1931, then conquered the China

327

coast, and proceeded to oust non-Japanese traders and investors. U.S. championship of the Open Door and insistence on Japanese evacuation of China and Indochina in 1941 led to war. Japanese defeat in 1945 might have led to a restoration of the Open Door, but the victorious Communists assumed effective control of all China, squeezed out most foreign merchants and investors, and caused the USA to seek to ban all trade between China and the Free World. With all doors closed and the interventions and pressures of the Western Powers thus abruptly ended in China, the problem of the Open Door is unlikely ever to arise again.

The Mandate System. The most interesting international efforts to deal effectively with the double problem of imperialism—that of protecting native interests and that of keeping the peace among the empire-builders—are to be found in the Mandate System, devised at the Paris Peace Conference of 1919 and administered by the League of Nations, and in the Trusteeship System of the United Nations.

Out of a complex background of "self-determination," "rights of small nations," political expediency, and humanitarian sentiments, there emerged the ideas which were subsequently incorporated into Article 22 of the League Covenant and into the mandate agreements. Article 22 in its final form referred to the former enemy territories "which are inhabited by peoples not yet able to stand by themselves under the strenuous conditions of the modern world." To these territories was to be applied the principle "that the well-being and development of such peoples form a sacred trust of civilization and that securities for the performance of this trust should be embodied in this Covenant." The "tutelage" of such peoples was to be entrusted to the "advanced nations" best able to assume this responsibility and was to be "exercised by them as mandatories on behalf of the League."

By Article 119 of the Treaty of Versailles, Germany was compelled to renounce her colonies to the principal Allied and Associated Powers. During the Peace Conference, they were distributed with few departures from the terms of the secret treaties. On May 7, 1919, the Pacific islands were divided among Britain, Australia, New Zealand, and Japan, subject to an informal reservation by President Wilson regarding the island of Yap, which he thought ought to be an internationalized cable center. German South-West Africa was assigned to the Union of South Africa, German East Africa to Britain, and Togoland and Cameroons were partitioned between Britain and France. The French Government originally insisted upon full sovereignty but finally contented itself with annexing that portion of Cameroons ceded to Germany in 1911. France insisted, however, upon her right to recruit troops in her African mandates for general war purposes, in spite of Article 22 of the Covenant. Belgium objected to the transfer of all of East Africa to Britain and on May 30, 1919, was granted Ruanda-Urundi by the British Government. Portugal demanded a mandate but received merely recognition of her sovereignty over Kionga, a small territory adjacent to Mozambique which she had recognized as belonging to Germany in 1894. The Turkish territory was distributed at San Remo on April 25, 1920.

The actual "mandates" in the legal sense were the agreements concluded between the Allied and Associated Powers under the dirction of the Supreme Council. It was here that the A, B, and C classification was made, in conformity with the three categories mentioned in Article 22 of the Covenant. Japan objected to the Closed Door in the British Pacific mandates. The USA objected that British oil interests had been granted exclusive privileges in Palestine and Iraq, reasserted the Open Door principle, and declared that although it was not a member of the League it would not submit to the exclusion of its nationals from the benefits of equality of treatment. Lord Curzon declared that American policy in the Philippines, Haiti, and Costa Rica was not consistent with the Open Door.

In the final arrangements, the original principle of the Mandate System was "mutilated in details and sullied by the spirit of barter." [6] The essential purposes of the secret treaties were carried out. The wishes of the population were ignored and later drowned in blood in Syria, Iraq, and South-West Africa. In Togoland and Cameroons, France was permitted to use native troops for general war purposes outside the territory. The Open Door, formerly maintained by Germany in the C mandates, was closed by the mandatories. It was protected in the A mandates neither by the Covenant nor by the mandate agreements, but only by subsequent treaties, negotiated largely at the insistence of the USA. Only in the B mandates was there a definite obligation laid upon the mandatories to maintain the Open Door. For all practical purposes, the C mandates were treated as annexations, and the B mandate administration was scarcely distinguishable from what would have been established after outright conquest. The A mandates were also under the effective control of the mandatories.

The Mandate System nevertheless represented an adventure in international supervision over backward areas.[7] The whole procedure of League supervision centered in the Permanent Mandates Commission (PMC). It was originally composed of 9 members, with a majority of nationals of nonmandatory Powers. In 1924, M. Rappard, formerly head of the Mandates Section of the Secretariat, was made an "extraordinary member" and provision was also made for an advisory member from the International Labor Office (ILO). In 1927 the number of regular members was increased to 10, in order to provide a place for a German national. The observations of the PMC were purely

[6] Quincy Wright, *Mandates under the League of Nations*, 1930, p. 63.

[7] At the conclusion of an exhaustive discussion of the legal aspects of the Mandate System, Quincy Wright states that "sovereignty of the areas is vested in the League, acting through the Covenant-amending process, and is exercised by the mandatory with consent of the Council for eventual transfer to the mandated communities themselves" (*ibid.*, p. 530).

advisory, but in practice it became the agent of the Council, through which international supervision was exercised. The PMC received its information from the annual reports of the mandatory Powers, from questioning their representatives, and from petitions submitted by the inhabitants of the mandated regions. Such petitions, however, could be submitted only through the mandatory Government, and the Commission refused to consider petitions opposing the mandate itself. In March, 1927, the Council decided that petitioners should not be granted oral hearing. The PMC also received information from other League bodies, but it never visited the mandated areas or dispatched investigators to them.

A survey of the Commission's proceedings leads to the conclusion that it was primarily dependent upon the mandatory Powers for information and that the native populations, in whose interest the whole System was presumably established, had little opportunity for the independent presentation of grievances or for a full and impartial hearing. The Commission did serve to mobilize opinion and, by its suggestions, influenced the conduct of the mandatories to some degree and made a beginning of establishing international standards of colonial administration. Whether international friction in the backward regions was greater or less, whether the natives were better off or worse off than would have been the case under some alternative arrangement, no one can say with any degree of certainty. The collapse of the League and the war of 1939 brought the system to an abrupt end.

The UN Trusteeship System. The replacement of the League by the United Nations in the wake of World War II was accompanied by the substitution of a new international Trusteeship System for the old mandate arrangements. The novelty was more formal than factual. On the basis of the preliminary agreement reached at Yalta, the Charter made provision for trust territories, in which the United Nations would undertake responsibilities of government for the purpose of promoting peace and security, the progress of the inhabitants toward self-government, and respect for human rights, freedom, equality, justice, etc. The new System was to be applied, via trusteeship agreements, to mandated territories, territories detached from enemy States, and other territories voluntarily placed under supervision. The terms of trusteeship, including any subsequent alteration, "shall be agreed upon by the States directly concerned" (Art. 79), subject to approval by the Security Council for "strategic areas" and by the General Assembly for ordinary "trust territories." This new dichotomy replaced the League classification of mandates as A, B, and C. Strategic areas (Art. 82) might be designated in any trusteeship agreement to include part or all of any trust territory. In both the administering authority might make use of local military resources, human and material, for local defense, maintenance of law and order, and fulfillment of obligations toward the Security Council for the "maintenance of international peace and security" (Art. 84).

A Trusteeship Council, consisting of member States administering trust territories, plus those of the Big Five not in this category and an equal number of other States elected for three-year terms by the General Assembly, was empowered to consider reports from the administering States, accept and examine petitions "in consultation with the administering authority," provide for periodic visits "at times agreed upon with the administering authority," and prepare questionnaires on the political, economic, social, and educational advancement of the inhabitants—on the basis of which each trustee would make annual reports to the General Assembly.

These arrangements were supplemented by a general injunction (Chap. XI) that all member States administering non-self-governing territories, whether or not under trusteeship, should "recognize the principle that the interests of the inhabitants of these territories are paramount" and should therefore promote progress, justice, freedom, self-government, peace, security, development, research, cooperation, good-neighborliness, etc.—and should submit data relevant thereto to the Secretary-General, "subject to such limitation as security and constitutional considerations may require" (Art. 73). The new System, judged by the criterion of effective international supervision over the control of subject peoples, was a step backward with respect to local fortifications and recruitment of native troops for overseas service and maintenance of the Open Door, which had been required in the A and B mandates but was not specified in the UN Charter. It was a step forward in that the Trusteeship Council was a body of governmental delegates rather than independent experts, as was the PMC, although some authorities doubted whether this was an improvement. The Trusteeship Council may also arrange local visits of inspection, as the PMC could not. Conversely, the Council's powers with respect to strategic areas are so limited and vague as to be meaningless.

In practice, the changes effected are scarcely calculated to convince colonial peoples or anyone else that any revolutionary reformation has been brought about in the arts of imperialism. Although the Charter made possible the transfer to the new dispensation of nonmandated territories and the establishment of joint trusteeships over other non-self-governing areas, no such steps were taken. The General Assembly created an *ad hoc* Committee (over the opposition of the colonial powers) which met in August–September, 1947, to examine the Secretary-General's summary and analysis of information transmitted under Article 73e of the Charter (*q.v.*). As regards the submission of trusteeship agreements, no proposals were made for territories other than League mandates. Among the former A mandates, Iraq, Syria, Lebanon, and Trans-Jordan were already independent. Most of Palestine was to become Israel. Britain, Belgium, and France submitted agreements on the B mandates: Tanganyika, Ruanda-Urundi, Togoland, and Cameroons. As for the C mandates, Australia and New Zealand submitted agreements for New Guinea and Western Samoa, respectively. Nauru remained in doubt until

Australia, New Zealand, and the U.K. submitted a draft on Sept. 27, 1947, providing for joint administration. The curious instance of the former Japanese mandates will be considered below. The Union of South Africa stubbornly refused to submit South-West Africa to the Trusteeship System and insisted instead on outright annexation.

The General Assembly on Dec. 13, 1946, approved the eight agreements already submitted after 229 proposals for modification had been made and, for the most part, rejected. The USSR voted against the agreements on the ground that they violated the Charter, since "the States directly concerned" had not been consulted, and that the drafts contained provisions indistinguishable from annexation and provided for military bases without the consent of the Security Council. The Trusteeship Council met for the first time March 26, 1947. It consisted of the USA, France, Britain, Belgium, Australia, New Zealand, China, Mexico, and Iraq—the latter two being elected by the Assembly. Francis B. Sayre was elected President and Sir Carl Berendson of New Zealand Vice-President. Its first task was to draw up rules of procedure. It also heard petitions from Tanganyika and Western Samoa, where local demands for self-government were investigated during the summer. The Trusteeship Council held its second session in November, 1947, by which time petitions had arrived from Togoland and Cameroons. The Philippines and Costa Rica were now members, by election in the General Assembly, with Iraq, Argentina, the Dominican Republic, and Thailand serving subsequently. Italy, though not then a member of UN, became a nonvoting member of the Trusteeship Council in 1950 by virtue of being granted a 10-year trusteeship over its former colony of Somaliland. The Council regularly considers hundreds of petitions, sends visiting missions, distributes questionnaires, holds hearings, and makes recommendations to the General Assembly which makes recommendations to the Powers in control—which may or may not pay attention.[8] The "anti-colonial" majority in the Assembly (the Latin-American, Arab-Asian, and Soviet bloc States) often presses for higher standards of education, health, and popular representation in the trust territories than prevail in most of the independent sovereignties comprising the majority—a circumstance naturally resented and resisted by the governments holding trusteeships.

The limitations of these arrangements, as well as the impact upon them

---

[8] The 11 trust territories, comprising about 18,300,000 of the 150,000,000 peoples of the world still living in non-self-governing areas, range in size from Tanganyika, with almost 400,000 square miles and over 7,000,000 inhabitants, to Nauru, with 82 square miles and 3,000 people. The only "strategic areas" are the U.S.-held Pacific islands, currently administered by the Department of the Interior, with the late Senator Elbert Thomas of Utah as first civilian High Commissioner. For fuller accounts of the Trusteeship System, see Amry Vandenbosch and Willard N. Hogan, *The United Nations* (McGraw-Hill, 1952), pp. 169–175, 282–297, and Lawrence S. Finkelstein's three chapters (pp. 477–534) in L. Larry Leonard, *International Organization* (McGraw-Hill, 1951).

of the imperatives of power politics, are illustrated by the case of the former Japanese mandates in the western Pacific—*i.e.*, the Carolines and the Marshall and Marianas Islands (Micronesia) with a total area of less than 1,000 square miles and a population of *c.* 50,000 scattered over an expanse of sea measuring roughly 500 by 2,600 miles. Between January and October, 1944, American forces, at large cost in lives and treasure, captured the major islands from their Japanese defenders. All passed under the administration of the U.S. Navy. On Nov. 6, 1946, President Truman asserted that the USA was prepared to place them under UN trusteeship. A draft agreement was submitted to the Secretary-General on Feb. 17, 1947, with the request that it be placed on the agenda of the Security Council. This procedure was due to the fact that the USA proposed that all the islands should be a "strategic area." New Zealand and India requested, and were granted, participation in the discussion. Australia vainly proposed that the disposition of the islands be confirmed at the final peace conference with Japan. In the subsequent debate the USA, represented by Warren R. Austin, asserted that, if unacceptable amendments were adopted, the agreement would be withdrawn, with American administration of the territories continuing in any case. On April 2, 1947, the Security Council, faced with this "take it or leave it" attitude, confirmed the agreement, which was approved in Washington, July 8, 1947.

The U.S. trusteeship agreement was an instrument of annexation, tempered with expressions of benevolence and thinly disguised by pretenses of "international" administration. The USA as trustee was authorized to apply "such of the laws of the U.S. as it may deem appropriate" (Art. 3) ; to erect fortifications and naval, military, and air bases, station troops in the territory, and use local volunteer forces and facilities (Art. 5) ; to limit most-favored-nation treatment of nationals of States other than the USA (Art. 8) ; to convert the territories, at its option, into a customs, fiscal, or administrative union with the USA (Art. 9) ; and to bar all UN supervision in "areas which may from time to time be specified [by the USA] as closed for security reasons." [9] In short, the USA, long the champion of the Open Door elsewhere and the apostle of international control, disarmament, and eventual self-government for colonial territories, here insisted successfully on the "Closed Door" (*i.e.*, preferential commercial treatment for U.S. nationals), exclusive control, militarization, and unadulterated colonial administration for the territories of which it was trustee. No other trustee dared go quite so far in identifying trusteeship with old-fashioned annexation. Here, as always, hypocrisy was the tribute paid by vice to virtue. This agreement is in itself an adequate commentary on the degree to which the UN Trusteeship System was, or is, capable of effecting any significant change in the old colonial order.

[9] For text, see Department of State *Bulletin*, Nov. 17, 1946; for official explanation, see *ibid.*, March 6 and May 4, 1947. See also *International Conciliation Pamphlet* 435, November, 1947.

Ave atque Vale. The verdict of events makes clear beyond debate that the efforts of the colonial Powers to devise multilateral principles and procedures for the purpose of minimizing international frictions and safeguarding the welfare of subject peoples have, thus far, eventuated in failure, slightly mitigated in particular cases by some small measure of success. The glaring fact of our time is that colonialism is doomed and that the policy-makers of the erstwhile imperial States now have only two choices: to yield graciously to native demands for independence and thereby, in some instances, to retain a modicum of influence; or to fight furiously and suffer ultimate military defeat.

Britain in the 1940's and 1950's pursued the former course most consistently and successfully, thus retaining in the Commonwealth most of the former colonial territories granted sovereignty. The USA did likewise in dealing with Latin America and the Philippines and (with reservations) Puerto Rico, but had not, as of 1958, granted statehood to Alaska or Hawaii. The Netherlands sought to keep Indonesia by force and failed. France, having fought and lost a disastrous colonial war in Indochina (1946–54), granted independence to Morocco and Tunisia and then fought another disastrous colonial war in Algeria (1954*ff.*) which was also certain to be lost. The record elsewhere was mixed.

What was not in doubt on the eve of the 1960's was the twilight of empire and the inevitability of ultimate independence, by violence or agreement, for virtually all of the major colonies of the Western Powers. The new "Soviet empire" seemed certain in the end to experience a like destiny, more probably by orderly devolution rather than by violent revolution, even though Moscow's relations with "subject people," both inside and outside the USSR, displayed few parallels to the colonialism of the Atlantic Powers in Africa and Asia. That the new freedom of yellow men, brown men, and black men from the rule of white men is not an unmixed blessing for those thus liberated is long since obvious. But most men and women in our time, hypnotized by the cult of nationalism, prefer to be badly governed or misgoverned by rulers of their own kith and kin rather than well and wisely governed by aliens.

In this fashion, to the muted music of abdication or the futile thunder of resistance, the great colonial empires, patched together by the daring exploits over the centuries of Western conquistadores, adventurers, missionaries, diplomats, strategists, merchants, and investors, are in process of making their exit from the human stage. In its attempted "conquest of the world" the West met finally with failure. But in failing the West also triumphed. For its proconsuls, with no one planning or anticipating the result, brought willy-nilly to the "lesser breeds without the law" Western concepts of sanitation, public welfare, education, religion, legislation, administration, industrialization, and above all, national Patriotism. All the world was "Westernized" by the very processes which made Western rule of non-Western peoples no longer possible. What the West corrupted or destroyed in non-Western cultures cannot be restored and will soon be forgotten. What the West contributed is irreversible and permanent.

Whether the total result is an addition to, or a diminution from, life, liberty, and the pursuit of happiness for mankind as a whole is a question currently unanswerable. The answer would seem to depend upon the adequacy of Western values in enabling people everywhere to achieve the good life and the good society in a strange new world where new weapons of war threaten mutual suicide and where the groping hopes of the world's poor in their quest for Western living standards may eventuate in common frustration. The verdict will be clearer a decade hence. Meanwhile one of mankind's Great Adventures is ending and another is beginning.

SUGGESTED READINGS

Andrews, F. F.: *The Holy Land under Mandate*, Boston, Houghton Mifflin, 1931.
Chowdhuri, R. N.: *International Mandates and Trusteeship Systems*, The Hague, Nijhoff, 1955.
Clark, Grover: *The Balance Sheets of Imperialism*, New York, Columbia University Press, 1936.
Duncan, Ronald (ed.): *Selected Writings of Mahatma Gandhi*, Boston, Beacon Press, 1951.
Fischer, Louis: *The Life of Mahatma Gandhi*, New York, Harper, 1950.
Furnivall, J. S.: *Netherlands India*, New York, Macmillan, 1945.
Gerig, B.: *The Open Door and the Mandates System*, London, G. Allen, 1930.
Gibb, H. A. R., and Harold Bowen: *Islamic Society and the West*, New York, Oxford, 1950.
Lenin, V. I.: *Imperialism* (rev. ed.), New York, International Publishers, 1947.
McDonald, James G.: *My Mission in Israel, 1948–1951*, New York, Simon and Schuster, 1951.
Main, E.: *Iraq: From Mandate to Independence*, London, G. Allen, 1935.
Mannoni, O.: *Prospero and Caliban: The Psychology of Colonization*, New York, Praeger, 1956.
Menon, V. P.: *The Transfer of Power in India*, Princeton, N.J., Princeton University Press, 1957.
Middleton, L.: *The Rape of Africa*, New York, Random House, 1936.
Moon, P. T.: *Imperialism and World Politics*, New York, Macmillan, 1926.
Nathan, Robert R., Oscar Gass, and Daniel Creamer: *Palestine: Problem and Promise*, Washington, American Council on Public Affairs, 1946.
Nehru, Jawaharlal: *Toward Freedom* (autobiography), New York, John Day, 1941.
————: *Independence and After*, New York, John Day, 1950.
Parkin, Raleigh: *India Today*, New York, John Day, 1946.
Pratt, Julius W.: *America's Colonial Experiment*, Englewood Cliffs, N.J., Prentice-Hall, 1950.
Schumpeter, Joseph A.: *Imperialism and Social Classes*, New York, Kelley, 1951.
Schuster, M.: *The Strangling of Persia*, New York, Appleton-Century-Crofts, 1912.
Spear, T. G.: *India, Pakistan and the West*, New York, Oxford, 1949.
Spiro, Melford E.: *Kibbutz: Venture in Utopia*, Cambridge, Mass., Harvard University Press, 1956.
Winslow, E. M.: *The Pattern of Imperialism: A Study in the Theories of Power*, New York, Columbia University Press, 1948.
Wright, Quincy: *Mandates under the League of Nations*, Chicago, University of Chicago Press, 1930.

Chapter X

THE MAKING OF NATIONS

1. THE RELIGION OF PATRIOTISM

National patriotism is the firm conviction that the best country in the world is the one you happened to be born in.—G. B. SHAW.

Universal conscript military service, with its twin brother universal suffrage, has mastered all Continental Europe—with what promises of massacre and bankruptcy for the 20th Century!—HIPPOLYTE ADOLPHE TAINE, Les Origines de la France contemporaine, 1891.

THE major political trait of the peoples of the Western State System is their devotion to the "nations" into which they have got themselves divided. The Western peoples and their Oriental and African imitators are keenly aware of themselves as "nationals" of particular nation-states, already in existence or striving to be born. Millions are influenced more in their emotions and behavior by a sense of national solidarity and fellow feeling with their fellow nationals than by their racial, religious, economic, esthetic, or recreational interests. This becomes most apparent in wartime, when governments demand and usually receive unswerving and undivided allegiance. But war merely brings to the surface and makes plain through pathological exaggeration what already exists in peace: an almost universal disposition to place the nation before all other human groupings.

Education for Citizenship. The cult and creed of patriotism are instilled into people in every nation by an elaborate process of inculcation. Nationalism is close to the heart of the cultural heritage handed down from generation to generation in every modern society. Upon the eager minds of little children, as upon a blank slate, are written at an early age the large characters of "mother," "home," and "heaven," "flag," "fatherland," and "patriotism." The first impressions of the Great Society outside of the family, the neighborhood, and the kindergarten are associated with national emblems, heroes, and myths. Every child in the Western world, before he has learned how to read and write his national language, has learned how to respond to the gaily colored banner which is the flag of his fatherland, to the stirring rhythm of the song which is his national anthem, to the names and legends of the great nation-builders who are revered as men like gods. Awe, reverence, and enthusiasm toward the nation-state and its symbols are inculcated from infancy.

Next comes the primer, with its quaint little tales of national glory and achievement, and then the elements of national history and geography. In later childhood there is nationalistic history with a vengeance, patriotic exercises, Flag Day celebrations, festivals and fun for Independence Day, or Constitution Day, or Bastille Day, or Guy Fawkes Day. Puberty brings membership in the Boy Scouts or the Girl Scouts, outings and parties and training in citizenship. In adolescence the young citizen becomes acquainted with the alien tongues and customs of enemies and strangers. He studies the national literature, the national history, the national *Kultur*. He becomes politically conscious and emotionally inspired by a fuller appreciation of his identity with his fatherland. *La Patrie* becomes father, mother, mistress, or lover in the heart of the youthful patriot; he (or she) is taught to swear undying allegiance to that which is more sacred even than truth, honor, or life itself. And at length, in early adulthood, comes, in most lands, military service for the young man, romantic attachments to soldier-lovers for the young woman, the right to vote and pay taxes, and a deep sense of loyalty and devotion to that half-real, half-mystical entity which is the nation-state.

The techniques of civic education through which this result is attained have been analyzed in many States by scores of assiduous scholars.[1] The initiation rites of the tribe or clan through which the rising generation is made a participant in the social group are repeated with elaborate variation in the educational processes of every modern nation. Youth is conditioned to allegiance— no longer to the tribe, the clan, the class, the caste, the province, or the city, but to the nation, which demands an allegiance above all other allegiances and a loyalty requiring, if need be, the supreme sacrifice on the altar of patriotism. What youth has been taught, age seldom forgets—and all modern States are nations of patriots whose rulers may ordinarily rely upon the unswerving devotion of the great masses of the citizens to the mighty traditions of the national past. Each State thus develops and enriches its own personality by perpetually recreating itself in its own image. Each State perpetually models its figures of earth and gets them more and more to its liking. Each State becomes symbolized as an anthropomorphic deity to which are attributed the national virtues and vices, the national achievements and frustrations. Each patriot, like a new Narcissus, is enthralled by the beauty of his own image, which he sees reflected in the national mirror; and he feels himself to be one with the nation.

The Genesis of Modern Patriotism. An understanding of the process of manufacturing patriots, however, does not in itself serve to explain why

---

[1] See C. E. Merriam, *The Making of Citizens*, 1931, the concluding volume of the series, which includes Elizabeth Weber, *The Duk-Duks*; C. J. H. Hayes, *France, a Nation of Patriots*; John Gaus, *Great Britain: A Study in Civic Loyalty*; S. N. Harper, *Civic Training in Soviet Russia*; Oscar Jaszi, *The Dissolution of the Hapsburg Monarchy*; and Paul Kosok, *Modern Germany: A Study of Conflicting Loyalties*.

national patriotism has come to occupy such an all-pervading place in Western culture. Hans Kohn, ablest contemporary student of modern nationalism, points out that the new creed "as we understand it, is not older than the second half of the 18th Century." Early tribalism in Israel and Athens gave way to a universalism which has persisted almost (but not quite) to our own times. The great "national" leaders and writers of the Enlightenment, degraded to the stature of tribal patriots by later generations, were nothing of the kind. Frederick the Great made a Frenchman President of the Prussian Royal Academy and declared himself content to have lived in the age of Voltaire. Johann Gottfried Herder denounced Prussia, praised Czechs and Russians, and proclaimed: "The human race is one whole; we work and suffer, sow and harvest, each for all." Hans Kohn concludes:

> Nationalism, taking the place of religion, is as diversified in its manifestations and aspirations, in its form and even its substance as religion itself. . . . Yet in all its diversities it fulfills one great task—giving meaning to man's life and justifying his noble and ignoble passions before himself and history, lifting him above the loneliness and futilities of his days, and endowing the order and power of government, without which no society can exist, with the majesty of true authority. . . . [But] nationalism is only a passing form of integration, beneficial and vitalizing, yet by its own exaggeration and dynamism easily destructive of human liberty. . . . From Jerusalem and Athens shine also the eternal guiding stars which lift the age of nationalism above itself, pointing forward on the road to deeper liberty and to higher forms of integration.[2]

It seems probable that conflicts among culturally divergent populations played a significant role in producing within each community that sense of its own identity, that feeling of solidarity and common interest, that conception of the personality or ego of the group which is of the essence of national patriotism. Contacts of war would seem to be most effective in producing the type of group cohesion which lies behind nationalism. No emotion unifies a group so readily as hatred for a common enemy. International relations in the formative period of nationalism were for the most part those of war. Anglo-Saxon England attained unity for the first time when Alfred the Great rallied his subjects to resist the Danish invasion. Norman England was already an embryonic national State, with a Government of considerable authority and a population increasingly impressed with its "Englishness" by virtue of chronic conflicts with Scots, Irish, and French. In France, provincialism gave way to a common consciousness of "Frenchness" in the course of the Hundred Years' War, when its inhabitants at last organized themselves for effective resistance against English invaders and found a fitting symbol of the cause in the person of Jeanne d'Arc. In Spain, constant warfare against the Moors gave birth to Spanish nationalism and produced that blending of patriotic sentiment and

---

[2] All quotations are from *The Idea of Nationalism*, which deserves to be regarded as the definitive history of the ideological origins of contemporary nationalism.

crusading Catholicism which became its distinctive characteristic. In every case nationalism was born of war against alien groups.

All the later nationalisms between the 15th Century and the 20th were similarly born of conflicts between societies already differing from one another in language, religion, and institutions and made more aware of these differences by increased contacts with aliens. Dutch nationalism attained full flower in the long war against Spanish rule of the Netherlands. Swiss nationalism emerged out of conflicts with Austria. Sweden became a nation through struggles with Russians and Poles and Germans. American nationalism was generated by the War of the Revolution. In the 19th Century, Italian nationalism won unity for Italy as a result of common resistance to foreign invasion and common conflicts with Austria. The German nation became a unified State through battles with Danes, Austrians, and Frenchmen, after the "War of Liberation" earlier in the century converted Prussians, Bavarians, Swabians, and Württembergers into "Germans." The peculiarly intense nationalism of the Balkan peoples was the product of armed revolt against the Turks and of the presence within the Peninsula of many divergent groups, each of which became aware of itself through contact and conflict with neighbors. Irish, Turkish, Japanese, Indian, and Chinese nationalisms were likewise products of conflict against alien rulers, alien invaders, or alien foes across the frontier.

This suggests that the process whereby a community acquires a sense of its own identity and national personality bears a certain resemblance to the process whereby an individual growing up in society acquires a self, or ego, of his own. Social psychologists are generally agreed that an individual growing up to biological maturity in complete isolation from his fellows would not have a human "personality." The individual becomes humanized by social interaction with his fellows. His innate impulses are inhibited, directed, and conditioned through social pressure—until his personality becomes, in the language of the psychoanalyst, a fusion of instinctive biological drives (the "Id"), the conscious thinking and acting self (the "Ego"), and the unconscious controls and repressions of Id and Ego drives (the "Super-Ego").[3] The individual becomes aware of himself and develops distinctive personality traits by "taking the role of the other,"[4] by socialized experience with other persons.

Similarly, a nation acquires its ego by contacts with other nations. It becomes acutely aware of its own identity to the degree to which such contacts are intimate, rich, and varied. Contacts of war would seem to promote national solidarity more effectively than contacts of peace, for war requires cooperation in the interest of self-preservation. It dramatizes the flags, songs, slogans, traditions, and leaders which give unity to the group and distinguish it from other

[3] See Franz Alexander, *Psycho-analysis of the Total Personality*, 1930.
[4] This phrase was frequently used by the late Prof. George H. Mead in his lectures in social psychology at the University of Chicago.

groups. National patriotism is the most complete expression of ethnocentrism. Its devotees are imbued with an intense consciousness of the collective personality of the national community, and this collective personality emerges out of social interaction between divergent groups not dissimilar to those between single human beings which produce and enrich the individual personality. The history of this process remains to be written by social psychologists with historical training or by historians who are also social psychologists.[5]

The Cult of the Tribal Gods. Nationalists everywhere exalt the nation-state as the highest form of social organization. The national community must achieve political independence. It must incorporate within its frontiers all peoples speaking the language and having the culture of the national society. It must compel conformity to the dominant language and culture on the part of alien groups within its frontiers. It must attain unity, uniformity, solidarity. It must assert its rights vigorously and protect its interests energetically in contacts with other national groups. It is the all in all, the *ne plus ultra*, the final and perfect embodiment of social living for all loyal patriots. It is beyond good and evil, right or wrong; for its interests are supreme and paramount, and all means toward its greater glory and power are justified by the end. "A true nationalist places his country above everything; he therefore conceives, treats, and resolves all pending questions in their relation to the national interest." [6] His object is "the exclusive pursuit of national policies, the absolute maintenance of national integrity, and a steady increase of national power—for a nation declines when it loses military might." [7] To the patriot the nation-state is a great goddess to be worshiped, to be loved, to be served— and all sacrifices in her service are noble and heroic. She calls out to her worshipers:

Citizens, it is I (the Great Mother, *la Patrie*) that undertakes to protect your personal safety, your peace, your property: What wilt thou give me in return for constant benefit? If it happens that I am in peril, if unnatural chi dren torment my bosom . . . wouldst thou abandon me in these stormy moments for the price

[5] Lewis A. Dexter ("People, Patriotism and Power Politics" in *Social Studies*, December, 1943) states succinctly the relationship between mass faith and individual personality:

"Nationalism goes back to a basic conflict in the training of the child. On the one hand, he learns that in fact the way to attain rewards is often to be aggressive and assertive. On the other hand, he is taught that the good child is quiet, unselfish, and modest; and he discovers that although being aggressive often pays, it sometimes gets one into more trouble than 'goodness.' Some persons discover a convenient solution for their dilemma: they become selfish, aggressive, pushing in the name of the welfare of the group to which they belong. There is less reason then to fear punishment. The tendency to attack outsiders is re-enforced by the need to hate which some children (especially the ambitious, energetic type) acquire as they grow up. . . . In our society, the foreigner is the easiest person to hate, because there is such a comprehensive documentation, through folklore and tradition, of the thorough-going hatefulness of each different group of foreigners."

[6] Charles Maurras, in *Action Française*, June 10, 1908, p. 969.

[7] Maurras, quoted in C. J. H. Hayes, *The Historical Evolution of Modern Nationalism*, p. 165.

of my invariable protection? . . . No! . . . There are times when I would command the sacrifice . . . even of thy life which I have so steadily protected.[8]

Lord! Let the beautiful ships which are on their way to our Africa arrive safely at their port. Grant that our soldiers on the sunny roads on the other side of the sea have fortune as their guiding star and glory as their goal. Grant that they may crown with fresh laurels the old, glorious flags of Vittorio Veneto, which now wave under the tropic sky. Let the culture of the new Rome of Mussolini fuse with that of Caesar's Rome to a poem of greatness. Let the Italian Empire dreamed of by our great men and our martyrs become reality in the near future. Lord! Let our lives, if Mother Italy demand it, become a joyful sacrifice on the altar of Thy holy and just Will. [Prayer for the Ballila Boys, *L'Azione coloniale*, Rome, 1935.]

The legions which [America] sends forth are armed not with the sword but with the Cross. The higher State to which she seeks the allegiance of all mankind is not of human but of divine origin. She cherishes no purpose save to merit the favors of Almighty God. . . . We extended our domain over distant islands in order to safeguard our own interests and accepted the consequent obligation to bestow opportunity and liberty upon less favored people. [Inaugural Address of Calvin Coolidge, March 4, 1925.]

Finally, as a spokesman of one of the newest (and oldest) nationalisms of our time, Ilya Ehrenburg to the Red Army, 1943:

Together with you marches the frail little girl, Zoya, and the stern marines of Sevastopol. Together with you march your ancestors who welded together this land of Russia—the knights of Prince Igor, the legions of Dmitri. Together with you march the soldiers of 1812 who routed the invincible Napoleon. Together with you march Budenny's troops, Chapayev's volunteers, barefooted, hungry and all conquering. Together with you march your children, your mother, your wife. They bless you! . . . Soldier, together with you marches Russia! She is beside you. Listen to her winged step. In the moment of battle, she will cheer you with a glad word. If you waver, she will uphold you. If you conquer, she will embrace you.

2. THE CULTS OF INTOLERANCE

Our modern Western nationalism has an ecclesiastical tinge; for, while in one aspect it is a reversion to the idolatrous self-worship of the tribe which was the only religion known to Man before the first of the "higher religions" was discovered by an oppressed internal proletariat, this Western neo-tribalism is a tribalism with a difference. The primitive religion has been deformed into an enormity through being power-driven with a misapplied Christian driving-force. The Golden Calf—or Lion or Bear or Eagle, or whatever the tribal totem may happen to be—is being worshipped in our world today with an intensity of feeling and a singleness of mind which ought not to be directed by human souls towards any god but God Himself. And it is not surprising to find that we have been propitiating these blasphemously idolized tribal deities with the human sacrifices which they relish and exact.—ARNOLD J. TOYNBEE, *A Study of History*.

[8] Barrère in *Procès-verbal de l'assemblée nationale*, No. 699, pp. 7–8, cited in Hayes, *op. cit.*, pp. 69–70. This and the preceding quotations all refer to French nationalism, but the values and ideology which they suggest are typical of all nationalisms.

Race and Language. Everywhere, modern nationalism postulates the political independence of a national community as its original goal and its ultimate ideal. To all patriots no truth is more elementary than that the nation must be "free" to govern itself, to work out its own destiny, to formulate its own foreign policy. The nation must therefore attain statehood, *i.e.*, become a sovereign political entity. Nothing engenders patriotic fever among a people more effectively than foreign control. Nothing seems more supremely desirable to the patriot than the political independence of the nation. The cry of "national self-determination" is accordingly the most insistent demand put forward by the nationalists of all countries.

This demand obviously raises questions, as soon as attempts are made to translate it into action, of what *is* the national community. In the contemporary world, two criteria of nationality have received general acceptance: race and language.

The test of race is a wholly unworkable criterion of nationality. But it is frequently emphasized by patriots, largely as a result of their efforts to rationalize designs of aggrandizement or discrimination against disliked minorities. The veriest novice in biology knows that "racial purity" is entirely nonexistent among the nations of the earth and that mankind can be classified into races only in the crudest and most unscientific fashion. Yet men and women *are* white, black, red, yellow, or brown, with various shadings in between; and within each of these groups there are physical differences of stature, body build, hair, skin, and eye color, shape of skull, and the like. These differences are sufficiently marked to enable nationalist doctrinaires to spin finely woven theories of racial virtues and vices, of instinctive racial sympathies and antipathies, and of racial purity as the only proper criterion of nationality. The scientific unsoundness of these theories has not made them less effective in influencing attitudes and behavior. The cult of Aryanism was one of the earliest of the pseudoscientific rationalizations to gain general acceptance. Prof. Max Müller first contributed to the myth of an "Aryan race" on the basis of the resemblances among the various Aryan, or Indo-European, languages. Von Jhering, in his *Evolution of the Aryans,* carried this idea a step farther. Arthur de Gobineau, a Germanized Frenchman, in his *Essai sur l'inégalité des races humaines* (1884), developed the idea of Aryan "superiority" and of racial "purity" as a prerequisite of high civilization. Among the so-called "Aryans," however, were obvious physical differences which led to the familiar divisions of Nordic, Alpine, and Mediterranean. Houston Stewart Chamberlain, a Germanized Englishman, first presented persuasively the notion of "Teutonic" superiority. Teutonism, Gallicism, Anglo-Saxonism were all cut of the same cloth.

These efforts to link nationality with race have intensified racial and national prejudices. They have influenced the immigration legislation and population policies of governments. They have lent popular support to im-

342

perialism and to the subjugation and exploitation of "backward" peoples by the "superior" races. But they have not resulted in any widespread cult of racialism comparable with nationalism. People in most parts of the world continue to regard themselves as Englishmen, Persians, Germans, Japanese, Italians, Bulgarians, etc., rather than as Nordics, Mediterraneans, Alpines, yellow men, black men, or brown men. People identify themselves much more readily with "nations," religious denominations, and economic classes than with largely imaginary racial groups.

Race and language obviously have no necessary connection with one another, since the one is a biological phenomenon and the other is part of the cultural legacy of the past. People are born with skin color, eye color, skull shapes, and the other physical marks of race. But the language they learn depends on their cultural environment. Language, though no indication whatever of race, is everywhere the best index of the cultural group of which one is a member. By the same token, one's mother tongue is everywhere taken as the best criterion of one's nationality. Most of the nations of the earth are "nations" because their peoples use a common speech. Englishmen, Americans, and British colonials, it is true, all speak variants of a single language. Portuguese and Brazilians use a single language. So do Frenchmen and Haitians, and likewise Spaniards, Mexicans, Chileans, Argentines, Peruvians, and the other Spanish-Americans. For these people, varying dialects, rather than language, may indicate nationality. On the other hand, Swiss nationals may speak French, German, or Italian and still be Swiss; and Belgians may speak French or Flemish without ceasing to be Belgians. For the most part, however, distinctions of nationality, in the social and cultural rather than in the legal sense, are coterminous with distinctions of language.

The Demand for "Self-determination." The fact that the national group is so generally regarded as coinciding with the language group has meant that the aspirations of nationalists are usually envisaged in terms of the common "national" interests of all who speak the same tongue. Common language has come to be the test of nationality—so much so that States like Switzerland or Belgium or the old Austria-Hungary, where more than one tongue prevails, are often spoken of as "non-national" or "multi-national" States. Whatever the location of political boundaries may be at any given time, "nations" in the nonpolitical sense are aggregations of people aware of themselves as units by virtue of linguistic and other cultural ties. The national community whose independence is postulated by nationalism is a community whose members employ the same speech. If, having attained independence, it does not include within the nation-state all those who speak the mother tongue, efforts must be made toward their annexation, even at the cost of the dismemberment of neighboring States. If there are those within the State who do not speak the mother tongue, they must be taught, assimilated, and if necessary coerced into abandoning their own language and culture in the name of national unity and power. From these articles of faith of the national patriot flow many of the consequences of nationalism in the realm of international politics.

The most obvious consequence has been the fragmentation of the world into a large number of sovereign nation-states. Each linguistic group, as it has become infected with the nationalist germ (and the malady is extraordinarily contagious), has striven to achieve statehood. The notion that a national language group can live contentedly under the political control of a government representing another and different group is anathema to the national patriot. Frenchmen have resisted English domination, Germans have resisted French domination, Poles have resisted German domination, Lithuanians and Ruthenians have resisted Polish and Russian domination. Each national community has asserted its right to independence as soon as national consciousness has taken root and flourished among its people. In the ancient world and in the Middle Ages, people differing in language and culture were content enough to live together in world empires or in complex feudal State forms. Not so in the modern era of Western civilization. Each distinct linguistic group must build its own State, win its own independence, have its own territory, flag, army, bureaucracy, and all the other trappings of sovereignty.

Demands for national self-determination and independence became peculiarly insistent during World War I. In February, 1918, President Wilson, in an address to Congress, said:

> Peoples and provinces are not to be bartered about from sovereignty to sovereignty as if they were mere chattels and pawns in the game. Peoples may now be dominated and governed only by their own consent. Self-determination is not a mere phrase. It is an imperative principle of action, which statesmen will henceforth ignore at their peril.

At the Paris Peace Conference of 1919 the newly emancipated nationalities insisted that the slogan of self-determination be translated into political reality. The Allied Governments gave effect to these demands wherever they found it politically advantageous to do so. It was clear, however, that in many cases political boundaries could not be made to coincide with language boundaries; for the intermingling of tongues in Central Europe is so confused that this ideal is impossible of attainment. The independence of Poland, Czechoslovakia, Hungary, Austria, Jugoslavia, Albania, and Greater Rumania and later of Finland, Estonia, Latvia, and Lithuania was accepted as a matter of course. But the boundaries which the new States insisted upon and the boundary adjustments which the victors demanded for themselves were dictated quite as much by considerations of economics, strategy, and territorial aggrandizement as by the expressed desire to grant to the populations affected a right of self-determination. When "self-determination" threatened to thwart the territorial ambitions of the victors, it was denied to the peoples in question. But wherever there appeared a possibility of reducing further the territory and power of the defeated States, self-determination was appealed to and the populations in question were given an opportunity to express their wishes through plebiscites.

The Treaties of 1919 provided for nine popular referenda: in Schleswig, Allenstein, Marienwerder, Upper Silesia, Eupen, Malmédy, Klagenfurt, Burgenland, and the Saar Valley. In most of Schleswig the population voted to remain under German, rather than Danish, sovereignty, and in Allenstein and Marienwerder the East Prussians likewise voted for German rather than Polish control. In Upper Silesia 707,000 votes were cast for Germany and 479,000 for Poland (1921). The League Council, however, divided the area, to the great disgust of nationalists in both countries. Eupen and Malmédy, formerly German territories, voted for annexation to Belgium. Klagenfurt, in dispute between Austria and Jugoslavia, voted for Austria. Burgenland voted for Austrian rather than Hungarian rule. The plebiscite of Jan. 13, 1935, restored the Saar to German sovereignty. In a plebiscite of 1947 the Saarlanders voted for France, but in 1955 (Oct. 23) rejected "internationalization" and voted for Germany.

Although the plebiscite method commends itself to idealists, it is fraught with dangers and difficulties. Even when adequate neutral policing is provided and satisfactory suffrage qualifications and electoral procedures are devised, the referendum itself embitters national feeling, creates temptations to bribery, coercion, and terrorism on both sides, and offers no assurance that the voters will record their permanent national preferences rather than their fears, prejudices, and economic interests of the moment. Territories and peoples continue to be transferred from State to State, and to be granted or denied independence, in accordance with the dictates of political expediency and the verdict of force. Whenever the outcome fails to correspond to the demands of the peoples themselves, local dissatisfaction and international tension invariably ensue.

National Irredentism. Another phenomenon of nationalism, which may conveniently be characterized as "irredentism," is closely related to the cry for self-determination and has been an equally fruitful source of conflict. The term is of Italian origin. In 1861, Italian nationalists at length achieved the goal which they had pursued for decades. A United Kingdom of Italy was created through the annexation to Piedmont of the lesser States of the south. Venetia was wrested from Austria in 1867, and Rome was added to the new nation in 1870. But a large Italian-speaking community in Trentino and the Tirol remained under Austrian rule. No Italian patriot could regard the task of national unification as completed until these regions were likewise "liberated." They came to be known as *Italia Irredenta* ("Italy Unredeemed"). Toward them were turned the eyes of all patriots.

Numerous "irredentas" of this character existed in pre-1914 Europe. Alsace-Lorraine under German rule was France irredenta. Bosnia, Herzegovina, and the Dalmatian coast under Austrian rule were Serbia irredenta. Transylvania, under Hungarian rule, and Bessarabia, under Russian rule, were Rumania irredenta. The post-1919 irredentas were even more numerous. Germany now had her own "lost provinces." The eastern provinces of Poland and Rumanian Bessarabia, with their Byelorussian and Ukrainian populations, were a new Russia irredenta. Such attitudes tend to prevail wherever political frontiers fail to follow the boundaries of language, and they are among the most productive causes of tension and conflict among the nations.

Very rarely can these lines be ascertained to the satisfaction of all parties. When they are ascertained, they are often unacceptable for economic or strategic reasons. Italy, for example, recovered *Italia Irredenta* in 1919 but insisted also on acquiring the Brenner Pass and the southern slope of the Tirolean Alps for reasons of defense, with the result that 250,000 German-speaking peoples around Bozen (Bolzano) were placed under Italian rule. Boundaries drawn to conform to considerations of strategy and economics are criticized by patriots as violating the wishes of the population. Boundaries drawn to conform to the wishes of the population are criticized by other patriots (or even by the same ones) for other reasons. In such a situation, no rational basis exists for the demarcation of frontiers. Efforts to minimize tension are frustrated by annexationist ambitions. Each State exerts its power to gain all the territory possible as a means to greater power. Power considerations are rationalized in terms of self-determination or irredentism or, when these are inapplicable, in terms of other catchwords and symbols. "Historic" frontiers are insisted upon. "Natural" boundaries are demanded. "Manifest destiny" is called upon to justify annexation. When the line of linguistic cleavage is gained, then the next river or mountain range becomes the goal; and when that is attained, some line beyond becomes the natural and necessary frontier. Boundaries are fixed by the clash, in peace or war, of the rival wills-to-power of the nation-states. Nationalism spurs the rivalry and furnishes formulas and slogans, in terms of which each national community can reassure itself of the justice and rectitude of its ambitions.

National Minorities. Not only is each nation-state eager, in its quest for territory and power, to extend its control over the peoples beyond its frontier who speak its language, but it is equally anxious to achieve linguistic and cultural homogeneity among the peoples within its frontiers. "Self-determination" is a phrase used by nationalists only with reference to the oppressed subject peoples of other States. Their "liberation" will weaken the power of the State controlling them and thus enhance that of its neighbor. The neighbor is accordingly solicitous over their fate, particularly when they speak his own language and constitute an irredenta. Patriots are concerned in quite a different way, however, with the minority groups in the population of their own State. These groups must under no circumstances be liberated or granted a right of self-determination. They must be assimilated in the name of national unity and patriotic solidarity. They must be induced or compelled to abandon their own identity and their ties with other peoples beyond the frontier. They must learn the prevailing language, adopt the prevailing customs, and make themselves one with their fellow citizens.

In pre-1914 Europe, the prevalent policy pursued by governments toward minorities might be described as one of forcible assimilation. This policy was adopted, with minor variations, by the four Governments of Europe which had the largest minority groups living under their control—those of Russia, Germany, Austria-Hungary, and Turkey. It was, almost without exception, unsuccessful in suppressing the identity of the minorities or in compelling them to adopt the language, culture, creeds, and institutions of the majority group. Indeed, it more frequently intensified to the point of desperation the solidarity of the oppressed groups and thus rendered impossible the achievement of its own purposes.

In 1918–19 the breakup of Austria-Hungary and the partial dissolution of the Russian, Turkish, and German Empires, coupled with the redrawing of frontiers in the name of self-determination, reduced the minorities of Europe from 54,000,000 to about 17,000,000. But 7,500,000 Germans, 3,000,000 Magyars, and about 1,350,000 Bulgarians were placed under alien rule in France, Poland, Czechoslovakia, Jugoslavia, Rumania, Italy, and Greece, along with 500,000 Jugoslavs in Italy; 4,500,000 Ruthenians and Ukrainians in Poland, Czechoslovakia, and Rumania; and several million Russians along Poland's eastern frontier. One-fourth of Jugoslavia's population, one-third of Poland's population, two-fifths of Czechoslovakia's population (not counting the Slovaks as a minority), and over one-tenth of Italy's population consisted of linguistic minorities. To permit a reversion to policies of forcible assimilation on the part of the overenthusiastic patriots of the new States would create widespread domestic disorder and international tension throughout Central Europe.

The Peace Conference of 1919, in considering the broader aspects of the problem, devised a new method of international regulation, involving the incorporation of protective guarantees in treaties between the new States and the Allied Powers and the provision of international machinery through the League of Nations to ensure the observance of these obligations. The first of the minorities treaties was imposed upon Poland and signed June 28, 1919. Other treaties followed, with Czechoslovakia (Sept. 10, 1919), Jugoslavia (Sept. 10, 1919), Rumania (Dec. 9, 1919), Greece (Aug. 10, 1920). The Treaty of St. Germain with Austria, of Sept. 10, 1919 (Arts. 62 to 69), of Trianon with Hungary, of June 4, 1920 (Arts. 54 to 60), of Neuilly with Bulgaria, of Nov. 27, 1919 (Arts. 49 to 57), and of Lausanne with Turkey, of July 24, 1923 (Arts. 37 to 45), likewise contained clauses for the protection of minorities, largely modeled upon the Polish Treaty. The Baltic States and Albania were subsequently induced to accept the same obligations. Fifteen States of Central and southeastern Europe, including Finland, Danzig, and

Greece, were thus obliged to renounce their efforts at forcible assimilation and to protect the rights of minorities living within their frontiers.

In all these arrangements, various general principles were set forth. The States in question must protect the life and liberty of all inhabitants "without distinction of birth, nationality, language, race, or religion" (Polish Treaty, Art. 2). "No restrictions shall be imposed on the free use by any . . . national of any language in private intercourse, in commerce, in religion, in the press or in publications of any kind or at public meetings." The States involved must grant educational facilities for instruction in their own language to minorities in districts where a considerable proportion of the population is of minority speech (Art. 9). Among these items some are essentially guarantees of individual rights, and others protect the minorities as groups by giving them schools and a share of public funds where they constitute a "considerable proportion" (in practice, usually one-fifth) of the population.

Two means were provided for ensuring the observance of these obligations: The guarantees were declared in the treaties to be part of the fundamental law of the States concerned; the minorities were placed under the protection of the League of Nations. The Council of the League, in a series of resolutions, worked out a procedure for dealing with minority problems. The minorities fared better than would have been the case in the absence of such international protection. On the other hand, it could not be said, nor could it be reasonably expected, that all discrimination and persecution were eliminated. States not bound by the minorities treaties were free to treat their minorities as badly as they liked. A Lithuanian proposal of 1925 to make these obligations universal was rejected. Even in treaty States, minorities in which no Government on the Council was particularly interested did not receive a full measure of protection.

In contrast to the ultimately unsuccessful method of protecting minority rights by international guarantees, the USA exhibits on the largest scale the most successful application of still another method of dealing with minorities—one which may be termed "voluntary assimilation." The original American Indian population has been largely confined to reservations. The population groups in the USA whose members are of European ancestry have never been regarded as "minorities" in the European sense. "Americanization" was rapid and amazingly successful because, on the one hand, it was not coercive in character and, on the other, it did not encounter the resistance of national sentiment among those being Americanized. This process is now of only historical interest. By 1940 almost 80% of the population consisted of native-born whites, less than 10% of foreign-born whites, 9% of Negroes, 1% of Mexicans, and less than half of 1% of American Indians, Japanese, and Chinese combined.

The last-named groups, particularly Negroes, continue to be subjected in many parts of America to a variety of social, economic, and political discriminations which still make a mockery of professions of liberty, equality, and fraternity for those who are "off-color." In 1942 most Japanese in the USA, including the Nisei, or native-born American citizens, were uprooted from their homes on the west coast and placed in concentration camps. There was no mob violence against them, however. The lynching of Negroes in the American South, moreover, has declined sharply in recent decades. It is nevertheless true that the America of the mid-20th Century is still a land of widespread anti-Negro, anti-Oriental, anti-Semitic, and anti-foreign sentiment which often reduces a substantial proportion of its citizens to the status of outcasts.

Racial segregation in the USA has a more extreme and explosive counterpart in Africa where small white minorities have long ruled native Negro populations. In apparent deference to Capetown's insistence on *apartheid* (segregation), the British Government in March, 1950, deposed Seretse Khama, chief of the Bamangwato tribe in Bechuanaland, who had married a white woman, and made his exile permanent in March of 1952. In the Union of South Africa, 2,600,000 whites (Britishers and Boers) with full civil rights live in the same land with 1,000,000 half-caste or "colored" peoples, with limited rights, and 8,500,000 blacks, 365,000 Asiatics (largely Indians), and 63,000 Malays, all with no rights whatever. In March, 1952, Premier Daniel F. Malan, defying the Supreme Court, moved to put "colored" voters on separate electoral rolls and to enforce strict segregation on all non-whites, with resultant demonstrations, riots, and threats of worse to come. Here, and in many other areas, the rulers of the Free World are reluctant to grant freedom and equality to those of darker skins, thereby putting themselves at an appreciable disadvantage in seeking to counteract Communist propaganda.

The Communist formula for replacing Tsarist oppression and "Russification" of minorities with equality and fraternity was: autonomy for each group, with its culture to be "national" in form (*e.g.*, as to language) but "proletarian" in content—*i.e.*, conforming to the ideology of Marxism-Leninism-Stalinism and to the dictates of the Party leaders. The Stalin Constitution of 1936, superseding the first federal constitution of 1923, prescribed complete economic, social, and political equality of citizens; outlawed all advocacy of racial or national exclusiveness, hatred, or contempt (Art. 123); and granted to the Union Republics a "right" of secession (Art. 17) and (by the amendments of 1944) a right to maintain their own foreign offices and defense forces. But here as elsewhere in Marxland, shadow and substance were not the same. Minority peoples enjoyed "equality" of a kind and achieved major social and economic gains. But their "freedom" was fictitious under the iron rule of the Party elite. In 1941–42 Crimean Tartars, Volga Germans, and North Caucasians were ruthlessly deported to Siberia on the odious principle of group responsibility for individual disloyalty. "Great Russian" nationalism was revived in World War II. In waging the Cold War, moreover, the Party

oligarchs became fiercely intolerant of all manifestations of minority nationalisms deviating from the "Party Line." And so savagely did they denounce and
harass all alleged agents of Zionism and "Jewish cosmopolitanism" as to
revive anti-Semitism in a new guise.

The Triumph of Hatred. The whole post-Versailles system of protecting minorities broke down in the face of a resurgence of racial and national
intolerance long before 1939. The Polish Government proposed in 1934 that
all the members of the League accept identical obligations to protect minorities. On Sept. 13, 1934, M. Beck told the Fifteenth Assembly that Poland would
refuse all further cooperation in protecting minorities until a general and
uniform system had been accepted. On Sept. 14 the delegates of Britain,
France, and Italy (cosignatories of the Polish Minorities Treaty) declared
that no State could release itself from such obligations by unilateral action.
In the Sixth Committee, it became clear that certain governments were not
willing to accept universal obligations. The Polish proposal was therefore
dropped. The rising tide of anti-Semitism in Poland indicated that minority
rights were no longer being protected with even a semblance of adequacy.
Other States followed the Polish example in ignoring their obligations and
refusing to cooperate with the League.

Germany was not bound by treaty to refrain from persecuting the Jews of
the Reich. No effective action was taken through the League either to halt
Nazi anti-Semitism or to provide a refuge for its victims. Here an old problem
was posed in a new setting. After the "Diaspora," or dispersion of the Jews
over the ancient world, they ceased to be a "nation" and their descendants
have nowhere constituted a "national minority" in the usual sense of the
term. Until the French Revolution they were almost everywhere in the West
discriminated against as a religious minority and confined in ghettos. Religious
anti-Semitism was a characteristic feature of both Catholic and Protestant
Christianity until the 19th Century. As it waned under the impact of liberalism, many Jews lost the age-old religious and cultural heritage which they
had so persistently cherished in the face of persecution. Nationalism made
most Jews loyal and patriotic citizens with no irredentist or self-determination-
ist aspirations. But no sooner had medieval religious anti-Semitism disappeared than modern racial anti-Semitism was born. Jews began to be persecuted once more, not because they were non-Christians, but because they
were falsely alleged to constitute a "race."

Racial anti-Semitism is a product of the insecurities of decaying social
systems. Its sources are to be found, not in the attitudes or behavior of Jews,
but in the fears of power-holders anxious to deflect mass resentments at injustices away from themselves and onto a scapegoat minority. Thus, in Tsarist
Russia, the imperial bureaucracy incited mobs to pogroms in order that impoverished peasants might discharge their aggressions against Jews rather
than landlords and exploited workers might relieve their wrath at the expense

of Israelites instead of employers and officials. In the last decades of the 19th Century, the socially insecure *Kleinbürgertum*, or lower middle class, in Central Europe began to show symptoms of increasing anti-Semitism. This class suffered from a sense of oppression induced by its weak economic position between big business and finance on the one hand and organized labor on the other. In Jew-baiting and racial mysticism, it found a release for its tensions. That the Jews are not a race, that Aryanism is a fiction, that the "Jewish world conspiracy" is a myth were without significance, for these things have no relevance to the social and psychological roots of modern anti-Semitism. Belief in the preposterous is ever the true test of faith.

This resumption of persecution produced its inevitable reaction, the rise of a Jewish counter-nationalism. In 1896, Theodore Herzl published *Der Judenstaat*. "The Jews have but one way of saving themselves—a return to their own people and an emigration to their own land." Herzl's followers held the first Zionist Congress in Basel in 1897. Herzl died in 1904; but political Zionism, aiming at the creation of a Jewish State in Palestine, continued to spread among those who saw no refuge elsewhere. In the Balfour Declaration of Nov. 2, 1917, the British Government yielded to the plea of the Zionist leader, Dr. Chaim Weizmann, and pledged itself to the establishment of a Jewish National Home in Palestine. The mandate indeed became a thriving community and a useful center of Jewish culture. But it was scarcely a substitute for tolerance. Neither did the other Jewish "home" in remote Siberia, Biro-Bidjan, created by the USSR, offer any hope of ultimate salvation to the 16,500,000 Jews of the world.

In the Third Reich of Adolf Hitler, anti-Semitism came to its most appalling contemporary expression. The Jews of Germany had not constituted a minority. They were more indifferent to Zionism and more completely assimilated than most Jews in other countries. They had become good Germans.[9] But anti-Semitism became the basis of the Nazi *Weltanschauung*, the source of the Nazi racial philosophy, the inspiration of the swastika flag, and the alpha and omega of Nazi racial legislation. In the National Socialist dictatorship, *Junkers* and industrialists were protected from the bitterness of peasants, workers, and petty burghers by Jew-baiting. The politicians in power deflected the aggressions of the masses onto Jewish scapegoats. On April 1, 1933,

[9] In 1925 there were 564,379 professing Israelites in Germany, or 0.9% of the population. Extensive intermarriage had created perhaps 2,000,000 more Germans who were partly Jewish by ancestry. During World War I, 12,000 German Jews gave their lives for the Fatherland and three Jewish geniuses helped make possible Germany's long resistance to a world in arms: Fritz Haber, the chemist, who invented the processes of fixing nitrogen from the air in 1915 and thus made Germany independent of foreign nitrates; Erich von Richthofen, greatest of war aces; and Walter Rathenau, organizer of the German war industries. Richthofen was killed in battle and was thus spared the sight of his subordinate, Hermann Goering, becoming a leader of an anti-Semitic movement and Minister of Air in the Nazi Cabinet. Rathenau was assassinated by anti-Semitic nationalists in 1922. Haber, a broken man, died in exile in Switzerland, Jan. 29, 1934.

a one-day boycott of all Jewish businesses and professions initiated the "cold pogrom." There followed a series of laws barring Jews from the civil service, the Army, and a constantly enlarged number of private vocations. As economic and social insecurity in the Nazi State gave rise to increasing popular unrest, the attack upon the Jews was intensified. The "Nuremberg Laws" of September, 1935, deprived the Jews of citizenship, forbade intermarriage between Jews and "Aryans," and barred Jewish children from the public schools. The Jews, having already been driven from the professions in large numbers, were driven from business likewise and became a pariah caste. The nationwide pogrom of November, 1938, shocked all the democratic world.

With their livelihood destroyed and all living made intolerable, thousands of Jews fled Germany. Other governments did little to avert the tragedy. Since no minority treaty protected the Jews, their fate was a German "domestic" matter. But the international problem created by Nazi persecution could not be escaped. On Oct. 26, 1933, the League Council appointed James G. McDonald as High Commissioner for Refugees coming from Germany. McDonald sought to coordinate relief and resettlement activities, but neither he nor the League had any public funds for this purpose. Private contributions were totally inadequate. On Dec. 27, 1935, the High Commissioner resigned. He condemned the Nazi regime for pauperizing hundreds of thousands of its subjects and made a plea for League pressure on Berlin "by all pacific means" to bring the persecutions to an end. But the League neither assumed responsibility for caring for the fugitives nor took any steps to check Nazi anti-Semitism at its source. Thousands of German Jews with means went to Palestine, France, England, America, and other lands. Other thousands faced starvation in exile, and the majority, having no means to go abroad, remained in Germany to face a living death. Meanwhile, other Fascist groups in Poland, Rumania, Hungary, and other countries strove to follow the Nazi example by persecuting Jews and attempting to drive them out into an inhospitable world.

Another heavy blow at Jewish hopes was the British White Paper of May 17, 1939, declaring that His Majesty's Government had no intention of making Palestine a Jewish State and would henceforth appease the Arabs by restricting land sales and limiting Jewish immigration to 10,000 per year for five years, with an additional 25,000 admissible at the discretion of the British High Commissioner. With the coming of war, the last doors were all but closed. Millions of people hitherto free, Jews and non-Jews alike, became victims of Nazi intolerance. With no place to flee, with no one to protect them, they were swallowed in black night with only the faintest echo of their futile lamentations reaching the outer world.

What followed was the most hideous demonstration of our time that "whom the gods would destroy they first make mad"—and that those incapable of solving their problems by acting together in the service of life have no final alternative to acting against one another in the service of death. The conquest of Europe by the Wehrmacht (1939–41) placed scores of millions of defenseless people at the mercy of the sadists who ruled the Reich. So long as prospects of victory were bright, the twisted men of Berlin were content to limit themselves to large-scale deportation and enslavement of alien workers, prolonged detention of war prisoners as a means of reducing birth rates among subjugated populations (*e.g.*, France), looting of conquered lands, and local atrocities and massacres as devices to terrorize unruly subjects. But when the tide of war turned in 1942–43 the Nazi leaders embarked upon a program of systematic extermination of the "inferior races" who dared to defy their will.

This saturnalia of scientifically organized torture and murder became fully known to the world only in the later phases of hostilities. Its scale was so monstrous, its methods so satanic, and its results so revolting that outsiders almost ceased to be shocked. Men's capacity for indignation and sympathy is limited. The wine of violence and brutality, moreover, is a heady wine, which all men like to drink if they dare. The Fascist psychopaths, as they sensed the approach of doom, slew millions of Poles, Czechs, Jugoslavs, and Russians. But here, as always, the first and last victims of the new cannibalism were the Jews. No less than 6,000,000 European Jews were put to death. Almost all were helpless prisoners of their executioners. In only one case behind the Nazi lines were they able to offer resistance: in the spring of 1943 the people of the Warsaw ghetto, facing retail extermination, chose wholesale death in battle as preferable. With fists, knives, stones, and such guns as they could get they fought the Wehrmacht until all their homes were reduced to rubble and ashes and every last man, woman, and child among them was slaughtered.

In the aftermath of Allied victory, all measures of retribution and reparation were of necessity feeble gestures in view of the enormity of enemy crimes. Trials of criminals, denunciations of "genocide," and eloquent reaffirmation of tolerance and brotherhood could not conceal the fact that in a world more broken and insecure than ever (and more addicted than ever to nationalistic megalomania, racial mythology, and ideological fanaticism) the battle for sweetness and light against savagery and black night was by no means permanently won. The breakdown of all devices and formulas between world wars for reconciling justice with nationalism in the treatment of minorities precluded any general revival of plebiscites, treaties, and international guarantees of the rights of outcasts. Surviving Jews on the Continent found almost all doors closed against them. Other refugees, "stateless" individuals, and unrepatriable "displaced persons" included several hundred thousand Poles, Balts, Ukrainians, Jugoslavs, and others who refused to return to their homelands out of hatred of Soviet tyranny or fear of punishment for past collaboration with the foe. They remained dependent on private and public charity. The new International Refugee Organization made only modest progress in finding them new homes and ceased to operate in 1952.

As for the many millions of German-speaking peoples beyond the borders of the Reich, the past role of many as Nazi "Fifth Columnists," exploiters,

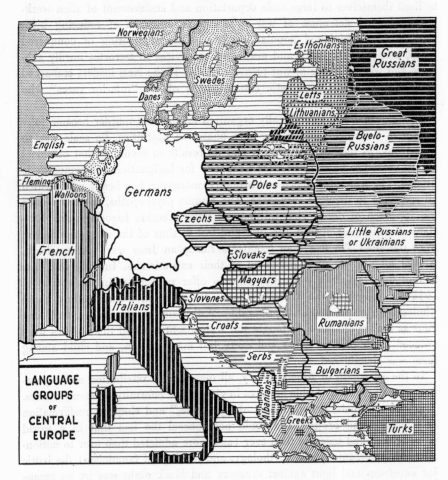

and persecutors led the liberated peoples and their new governments to adopt drastic measures of defense for the future. Warsaw and Moscow expelled many Germans from East Prussia. Poland ousted virtually the entire German population from the territories east of the Oder-Neisse line, which were resettled by Poles from the former eastern provinces. Czechoslovakia deported to the shrunken Reich the majority of the *Sudetendeutsche*. The sufferings of the victims elicited much sympathty in Britain and America, but little elsewhere. The deportees, unlike millions formerly uprooted by the Nazis, were at any rate not converted into slaves, fertilizer, and soap.

On the model of the arrangements of 1919 between Greece and Bulgaria and of 1923 between Turkey and Greece, arrangements were made for the exchange of minorities on either side of the new frontiers between Poland and the USSR and between Hungary and Czechoslovakia. Post-Potsdam Europe had fewer linguistic minorities within national frontiers than ever before. On the other hand, the number of German, Italian, and Magyar "irredentas" was greatly increased. Should the superpatriots of the defeated States ever again have effective military power at their disposal, the new map, like the old, would furnish ample occasion for indignation, incentives for torture and murder, and pretexts for war.

The Prospects of Brotherhood. In the light of the tragic failure of contemporary Christians, bewitched by secular cults of nationalism and racialism, to give human meaning to the egalitarian gospel of the prophets of Israel, the philosophers of Athens, and Jesus of Nazareth, most participant observers, if at all aware of the dilemma here posed, might well despair of any possibility of human beings treating other human beings as human beings in relationships among national and racial groups. Dark portents of fear, hatred, persecution, and revenge still loomed large on the horizons of the late 1950's. Having connived in the most hideous atrocities of all time, some 15,000,000 Germans in Eastern Europe were ruthlessly uprooted, dispossessed, and expelled by the victors of 1945 in Prague, Warsaw, and Moscow. Among the 12,000,000 who survived the ordeal in West Germany, many followed ex-Nazi or neo-Nazi political leaders who preached more hatred of Jews and Slavs and championed a new irredentism, *i.e.*, the recovery of "lost provinces" in the name of *Heimatrecht* or the "right to one's homeland." Among the new nationalists of the Islamic world and of southern Asia, agitators of intolerance often commanded more popular support than preachers of equality and fraternity. The Negro majority peoples of Central and South Africa continued to be dealt with by their white rulers as subhumans. The Negro minority community of the USA continued to be regarded by most of its white neighbors as a pariah caste.

Yet the outlook was by no means altogether bleak. Most human beings everywhere, regardless of creed, and despite frequent lapses in practice, acknowledged in principle that "all men (and women) are created equal" and paid at least lip service, and often much more, to those ideals of equality and dignity common to all the world's "higher religions." The UN Declaration of Human Rights (1949), albeit lacking any force of law and intended as a precursor to a "Covenant of Human Rights," gave eloquent expression to a timeless vision of One World united in fellowship. Most Germans ignored their irredentist and anti-Semitic fellow-citizens. Many voices among the newer nationalists pleaded for love in place of hatred. Following Stalin's demise, the Marxist rulers of Muscovy strove gropingly for equality and justice in dealing with minority peoples at home and dependent peoples abroad.

Under the stimulus of Cold War, the U.S. Supreme Court in the segregation cases on May 17, 1954 (347 U.S. 483), unanimously rejected the "separate but equal" doctrine of *Plessy v. Ferguson* (163 U.S. 537) in favor of the view that the 14th Amendment, as reinterpreted, now forbade racial segregation and discrimination in public education. Subsequent efforts at integration in schools, universities, and public transport, followed by Congressional enactment, for the first time in 80 years, of the "civil rights" legislation of 1957, which was designed to assure Negroes their constitutional access to the ballot, left much to be desired in concrete results but at least demonstrated that large numbers of Americans, both Southerners and Northerners, were at long last seriously concerned with some measure of equality for their colored fellow-citizens.

Which trend in these matters was most likely to prevail during the remainder of the 20th Century would seem to depend upon the capacity of contemporary mankind to so order its common affairs as to promote widespread security and prosperity rather than fear and poverty. Social science is as yet incapable of measuring these relationships among psychological imponderables. But it has demonstrated beyond doubt that hatred, discrimination, and persecution among racial and national groups are products of frustration, deprivation, disillusionment, and resulting aggressiveness. Such attitudes wax amid anarchy, misery, and violence but wane in a context of order, safety, and plenty. Here, as elsewhere, Man's ability to give meaning to his highest ideals is not a product of good will per se but of his collective skills in so governing the affairs of mankind as to reduce anxiety and promote confidence regarding the future.

3. PATRIOTISM AND PROFITS

"Very true," said the Duchess: "flamingoes and mustard both bite. And the moral of that is—'Birds of a feather flock together.'"

"Only mustard isn't a bird," Alice remarked.

"Right, as usual," said the Duchess: "what a clear way you have of putting things!"

"It's a mineral, I *think*," said Alice.

"Of course it is," said the Duchess, who seemed ready to agree to everything that Alice said: "there's a large mustard-mine near here. And the moral of that is—'The more there is of mine, the less there is of yours.'"

"Oh, I know!" exclaimed Alice, who had not attended to this last remark. "It's a vegetable. It doesn't look like one, but it is."

"I quite agree with you," said the Duchess; "and the moral of that is—'Be what you would seem to be'—or, if you'd like it put more simply—'Never imagine yourself not to be otherwise than what it might appear to others that what you were or might have been was not otherwise than what you had been would have appeared to them to be otherwise.'"—LEWIS CARROLL, *Alice's Adventures in Wonderland.*

The past few centuries of the human adventure, traditionally named "modern" history, have witnessed in the communities which cradled Western culture an amazing growth of population and riches under the impact of a new science and technology and of the new pattern of banking, commerce, and industry which we have come to call "capitalism" or the "free enterprise" system. From Europe poured forth over the earth a flood of explorers, missionaries, colonists, fortune hunters, soldiers, and governors who built new empires, expanded the Western State System to global proportions, unknowingly extended the gospel of nationalism to other peoples, and unwittingly wove an intricate web of travel, trade, and finance over all seas and all continents. A Great Society and a World Economy thus came into being— magnificent, productive, and promising beyond the visions of any earlier age.

This planetary community has obviously fallen upon evil days in the 20th Century, albeit still flourishing in the numbers and wealth of its inhabitants despite their earnest efforts at collective impoverishment and suicide. The causes of calamity and their cure, if any, are not as yet matters upon which informed men and women are agreed. Even those phases of the process of growth and breakdown with which we are here concerned give rise to hot disputation as to who or what has been responsible for the frustration of the dreams of many yesterdays. Yet a survey of the changing relations between government and business in the epoch of nationalism and machine industry may stimulate thought on the problem by suggesting at least some of the ways whereby contemporary mankind has entangled itself in a strange labyrinth of paradoxes and has sought, often unsuccessfully, to find or force an exit.

From Mercantilism to Neomercantilism. Two centuries ago, and for two centuries and more before, men took it for granted that business should be elaborately regulated by government for the purpose of enhancing the prosperity and power of the State. These tasks of government came to be called "political economy." The theorists and practitioners known as "Mercantilists" (or "Cameralists") deemed it self-evident that gold was wealth, that a nation exporting more than it imported would be paid in gold for its "favorable" balance of trade, and that one importing more than it exported would lose gold to meet its "unfavorable" balance. Wise public policy should therefore aim at fostering exports through tax exemptions, subsidies, diplomatic protection, grants of monopolistic privileges in shipping and commerce, etc., and hindering imports through embargoes, restrictive or prohibitive taxes or "tariffs" on foreign goods, "protection" of home industries to reduce dependence on alien sources of supply, acquisition and exploitation of colonies, and the like. Government should also fix prices, wages, rents, and interest and determine what branches of agriculture, commerce, and industry should be encouraged and what should be discouraged or forbidden. Despite the fallacy of much of this reasoning, the mercantilist system worked well enough in the age of absolutism—until merchants themselves, perceiving opportunities for good business being closed by bad policies of government, began to resent and resist such restrictions, as many did in the years preceding the American and French Revolutions.

Adam Smith published his *Wealth of Nations* in 1776. He enlarged and improved the doctrines of the French economists known as "physiocrats" and foreshadowed the 19th-Century gospel of "laissez-faire individualism" expounded by Richard Cobden, John Bright, Herbert Spencer, and a host of others in many lands touched by the "Industrial Revolution" which had begun in 18th-Century England. According to the new wisdom, government should let business alone and limit its own activities to protecting private property, defending the nation, and promoting communication and transport. Let each man freely seek his own gain and all would be better off, since the "invisible hand" of a competitive market would bring about the optimum allocation of capital, labor, and resources by the effects upon prices of changing supply and demand. Let international trade be free of all restraints and a worldwide specialization of business would emerge wherein each nation would produce what it could make most cheaply and exchange it for what others could make most cheaply, with all in the global market buying at prices as low as they could find and selling at prices as high as they could get.

These precepts, which are of the essence of the new "economics," came to full expression in public opinion and governmental policies a hundred years ago. They were deemed by optimists to ensure the advent of a mutually interdependent world economy, a global community, and permanent international peace. In 1846 Britain repealed its "Corn Laws" or import duties on grain and embraced "free trade." The Cobden Treaty of 1860 reduced French tariffs. Germany and other States followed suit. Even the USA for a time levied tariff duties "for revenue only." Prospects of prosperity and progress in a bright new time seemed boundless. . . .

If we ask how it came about that within a single century all these hopes faded in a new era of "socialism" (both democratic and totalitarian), marked by governmental ownership of industry, and of "neomercantilism," marked by governmental restriction of imports and promotion of exports, many answers are available. The dynamics of the free enterprise system itself begot more and more limitations, private and public, on the free market and the price mechanism—conceivably self-destructive in the long run, as Marx insisted, or at least calling for governmental intervention, as Lord Keynes contended—to keep saving, spending, and investment in balance as the only alternative to disastrous inflations and depressions. These facets of the transition we shall leave to the economists. If we ask what nationalism has to do with these developments, the answer is simple, though the details of the *modus operandi* are so complex and multitudinous as to admit only of a résumé.

In a world of nations, people inevitably regard the nation as an economic unit, no less than as a political unit, even in the epoch of a "world economy." They look to national governments to protect their interests, which become readily identified with the "national interest." Economic planning, whether equated with the "Welfare State" or with the new "serfdom," was not initiated by Utopian theorists or by power-greedy bureaucrats but by practical businessmen, followed by farmers and workers, seeking to use public power for private advantage through safeguards against the hazards of competition.

In the USA the captains of business in the decades following the Civil War pressed for "protective tariffs" to guard "infant" industries (which somehow seem never to grow up) from competition from abroad. Duties rose steadily, in the name of "national prosperity" and the "full dinner pail," in the tariff acts of 1890, 1897, 1909, 1922, and 1930, when at the outset of the Great Depression national policy-makers sought to restore employment and profits by taxing imports out of the domestic market. Bismarck championed "protectionism" in 1879 and sought to weaken the Socialists by embarking upon a program of "social security" for the underprivileged. In France and elsewhere "social reform" became synonymous with governmental subsidies and other restraints on competition for the benefit of wage-earners, farmers, and small (and even big) businessmen. Tariffs increased constantly to prohibitive heights until finally even Britain abandoned "free trade" in 1931 in favor of "protectionism" and "imperial preference" with the Commonwealth and Empire.

Markets, Merchants, and Machtpolitik. This trend was everywhere equated with the highest patriotism and approved by diplomats and strategists on the ground that national defense required a maximum degree of economic self-sufficiency or "autarchy" lest enemies in wartime cripple the nation by cutting off essential supplies from abroad. Governmental control of business proved profitable to businessmen and useful to politicians in promoting the power of the State. The business to be thus regulated, to the mutual advantage of the controllers and the controlled, presently came to include movements of capital for investment as well as goods for sale. Money flowed out from the industrialized countries to "backward" areas where returns were greater than at home because capital was scarce and resources and/or cheap labor were abundant.[10] Investors and diplomats, supported by the armed forces of the

[10] James W. Angell ("International Investment and Free Enterprise," *Proceedings of the Academy of Political Science*, May, 1947) estimates that British investments abroad totaled 19.5 billions of dollars in 1914, 18.2 in 1929, 22.9 in 1938, and 14.1 in 1946. Dutch investments were 2.0 in 1914, 2.3 in 1929, 4.8 in 1938, but only 1.5 in 1944. French investments declined from 8.6 in 1914 to 1.6 in 1944. World totals were estimated at 41.6 in 1914, 47.5 in 1929, 52.8 in 1938, and 38.7 in 1946. Only U.S. investments increased: 2.5 in 1914, 14.7 in 1929, 11.5 in 1938, 11.4 in 1944, and 20.3 in 1946. The latter figure, however, includes governmental as well as private investment. The trend of the times is toward smaller and smaller investments of private capital across frontiers and ever-larger intergovernmental grants, most of which are in no sense "investments" or even "loans" but gifts or

State, collaborated in the various national equivalents of "dollar diplomacy." [11] Private lending was encouraged by Foreign Offices to strengthen allies, discouraged to weaken prospective enemies, and judiciously manipulated to secure control of undeveloped regions and bar them to rival Powers. In the end bankers became the servants of bureaucrats rather than bureaucrats of bankers.

The imperatives of strategy in an age of global wars, coupled with the exigencies of the Great Depression, accelerated and aggravated all the tendencies here suggested. Faced with mass unemployment and bankruptcy calling for public relief and public works, all governments resorted to taxing and borrowing and spending to restimulate and expand production paralyzed by stagnant private markets. Some governments, and ultimately all, found that inflationary spending on preparing and waging war was the simplest and most popular method of maintaining full employment, increasing profits and wages, and multiplying productive facilities through investment of public funds in private business.

Total war required total mobilization, involving bureaucratic control of all economic activity through currency manipulation, price fixing, rationing, taxation policies, allocation of materials, import and export quotas and embargoes, and scores of other ingenious devices which made free enterprise no longer free or enterprising but the slave of public planners and war lords, albeit a willing slave since the service rendered was a patriotic duty and the returns to entrepreneurs were easy and handsome. Laissez-faire individualism died. Capitalism as a freely competitive system for the private production and exchange of goods and services gave way (where it was not superseded by total socialism) to a mixed economy wherein government came to own and operate many enterprises, to tax and subsidize and regulate most other enterprises, and to supply, directly or indirectly, ever more of the capital and ever more of the market for all enterprises. Apart from other interests and pressures pushing in the same direction, the attitudes and policies commonly known as "economic nationalism," i.e., the use of public power to control private business in the service of power politics, contributed decisively to a new and highly unstable pattern of "political economy" throughout the Western world.

---

subsidies necessitated by considerations of charity, *Realpolitik*, or the need of maintaining export "sales" in order to avert depression at home.

[11] President Taft declared in 1912, "The diplomacy of the present Administration has sought to respond to modern ideas of commercial intercourse. This policy has been characterized as substituting dollars for bullets. It is one that appeals alike to idealistic humanitarian sentiments, to the dictates of sound policy and strategy, and to legitimate commercial aims. It is an effort frankly directed to the increase of American trade upon the axiomatic principle that the Government of the United States shall extend all proper support to every legitimate and beneficial American enterprise abroad" (annual message to Congress, Dec. 3, 1912). See also Herbert Feis, *Europe: The World's Banker*, 1870–1914 (1930).

PATRIOTISM AND PROFITS

The Economic Consequences of War. "Mark well the contrast," wrote Jeremy Bentham in the late 18th Century. "All trade is in its essence advantageous—even to that party to whom it is least so. All war is in its essence ruinous; and yet the great employments of government are to treasure up occasions for war, and to put fetters on trade." Each of these activities at once promotes, and is promoted by, the other, with results that make trade a weapon of war and give war the appearance of a stimulant to trade. Thanks to the strategic and economic position of their country, some Americans may still cherish the belief that war is a primrose path to prosperity. All Europeans and Asiatics know by now, even if they lack wit and will to change old ways, that the way of war is the road to ruin and death.

Among the first casualties was the international gold standard whereby all moneys prior to 1914 were redeemable in gold and therewith exchangeable into other moneys, with the result that the world enjoyed the practical advantages of a single global currency. After World War I governments which had suspended gold payments sought to restore them: at the prewar rate for the pound in 1925, at one-fifth of it for the franc in 1926, and at various levels for other States, following the reduction to waste paper of all Central and Eastern European currencies in the printing-press inflations of the early 1920's. This attempt was abandoned in the Great Depression when all governments sought to recapture the vanishing markets of their exporters by depreciating their media of exchange. London suspended the gold standard on Sept. 21, 1931, with the Dominions, Scandinavia, and much of Latin America following suit and henceforth constituting the "sterling bloc." In March, 1933, with every bank in the country closed, the USA did likewise, with the dollar fixed (Jan. 31, 1934) at 59.6% of its former gold value. France (Sept. 26, 1936) and other States joined the race to depreciate.

The "managed" currencies of the new time have never since attained stable exchange rates because of maladjustments in the world economy which were both causes and results of the instability of moneys. Thanks to a policy inaugurated in 1936 of paying $35 an ounce to anyone who offered to sell gold, the USA by mid-century had accumulated $24,300,000,000 of the yellow metal (80% of all the monetary gold in the world), half of which was buried at Fort Knox, Ky.—somewhat as Fafner guarded the accursed Rheingold in a cave. The pound sterling was again devalued from $4.03 to $2.80 on Sept. 18, 1949. The French franc, worth 20¢ before 1914 and 5¢ in the 1930's, had fallen to less than ⅓¢ by the 1950's. Even the currency of the USA was no longer "sound as a dollar." Total money in circulation increased from 4 billions in 1915 to 51 billions in 1951, with the new "59¢ dollar" losing half its purchasing power after 1939 as inflationary war spending drove prices to ever higher levels.

High finance and high politics effected a strange marriage after Versailles, soon ending in bankruptcy though not in divorce. Apart from credits ex-

361

tended by private banking houses, the U.S. Government during World War I had advanced to the Allied Governments loans which were funded (1923–26) at $22,188,484,000 in principal and interest, to be paid over 62 years. Under the "Dawes Plan" of 1924 and the "Young Plan" of 1930, Germany was to pay to the Allies $26,500,000,000 in reparations in variable annuities extending to 1988. Germany could pay the Allies, and the Allies could pay America, only by huge export surpluses which, by lowering prices in the recipient countries, would have enriched consumers and impoverished competing producers. As always in the politics of economic nationalism, consumers were voiceless and producers clamored for protection. All governments sought to bar imports. The intergovernmental obligations were met in the 1920's through U.S. bankers and bond buyers lending vast sums to Germans, whose government made payments to the Allies, whose governments made payments to the USA, whose government encouraged its citizens to invest their money in Germany. This may appear, in retrospect, the acme of madness in frenzied finance. It was.

The Great Depression left Americans with no more funds for speculative foreign lending. As the stream of private loans dried up, European governments could no longer pay their debts. The "Hoover moratorium" of June 30, 1931, halted all intergovernmental payments on the eve of the collapse of the German banking system. Reparations were abolished at Lausanne in July, 1932. But Washington refused to cancel or even reduce Allied debt payments. Congress in 1934 enacted Hiram Johnson's bill to forbid private American loans to defaulting governments. But all the debtors except Finland ceased all payments in 1934 and thereafter. These particular follies were not reenacted after World War II, since all reparations were collected in equipment and goods while the USA, through "lend-lease" and successive postwar programs of aid, gave away new billions of dollars' worth of goods rather than make "loans" which everyone knew would never be repaid. But other follies followed.

The chief economic consequences of World War II were (1) further industrialization and a rapid recovery of productivity in the socialist economies of the USSR and Eastern Europe,[12] despite fearful devastation suffered during hostilities; (2) a general liquidation of foreign investments and a grave loss of colonial and foreign markets for the highly industrialized economies of Western Europe and Japan, forcing them as the only alternative to a drastic reduction of mass living standards, to become economic dependencies of the USA; and (3) a doubling of the manufacturing facilities of

[12] The *U.N. Economic Survey*, issued in May, 1952, estimated that the indices of industrial production in 1951 (with 1937 as 100) stood at 154 for Denmark; 148, Norway; 141, Netherlands; 133, U.K.; 125, France; 121, Western Germany; and 113, Belgium as compared with 117, Eastern Germany; 160, Rumania; 167, Czechoslovakia; 207, Hungary; 288, Poland; 291, USSR; and 356, Bulgaria.

the USA, "arsenal of democracy" first against Fascism and then against Communism, plus huge increases in agricultural output and in exports, with the deluge of goods from farms and factories beyond the capacity of American consumers to absorb at prevailing incomes and prices, and with vast surpluses therefore devoted to armaments and foreign aid. In the good old days, world trade was balanced by the USA buying more than it sold to Latin America, selling more than it bought from Europe, and buying more than it sold to the rest of the world, while Europe sold more than it bought from Latin America and the rest of the world and bought more than it sold to the USA, all the while enjoying an annual flow of two to three billion dollars a year from overseas investments. In the bad new days, the investments are all but gone and the USA sells everywhere more than it buys, while Western Europe buys everywhere more than it sells.

It is still true in principle that "he who does not buy, neither shall he sell." Americans, as we shall see, could not or would not buy from abroad any equivalent of what they sold abroad. The U.S. Government therefore devoted vast sums from tax revenues to buying goods from American producers and giving them away in a manner which kept them off the American market— *i.e.*, to the armed forces of the USA and its allies, and to foreign governments and their nationals, thereby achieving the mercantilist miracle of a permanent "favorable balance of trade." No one in mid-century could estimate the probable duration of these strange arrangements, which doubtless caused Jeremy Bentham and Adam Smith to turn over in their graves.

In Search of Economic Internationalism. Meanwhile the skills of Western statesmen had long been turned toward efforts to restore some approximation of freedom of trade and commercial balance among nations in the belief that the efforts of each to push exports and ban imports could only impoverish all. The multiplicity and complexity of these efforts would require many large volumes to unravel—an enterprise here to be eschewed, the more so as the efforts themselves have been largely negated by other policies in direct contradiction to them and by new fashions in economic nationalism which altogether preclude any restoration of a freely competitive world market. We need here note only the major devices whereby governments have striven to prevent the complete paralysis of trade across frontiers.

Commercial treaties long consisted of special bargains between two States, whereby each agreed to grant to the other certain shipping and trading privileges and to admit certain imports from the other in exchange for similar favors. Since a growing network of bilateral favors and resultant discriminations against the commerce of third States soon became confusing and burdensome, the practice developed whereby States contracted in such treaties to afford to one another's commerce as favorable treatment as they might grant to any "most favored" outside State. The purpose of this "most-favored-nation" clause is to ensure general equality of commercial treatment among nations, with no special and discriminatory bargains and favors.[13] Beginning with its first commercial treaty (with France, Feb. 6, 1778), the USA sought to evade this purpose by specifying that reciprocal most-favored-nation treatment should be granted "in respect of commerce and navigation . . . freely, if the concession was freely made, or on allowing the same compensation if the concession was conditional." By this "American" or "conditional" form of the clause, Washington could deny to State B concessions it might grant to State A if A had paid a price in reciprocal concessions which B was unwilling to pay or which, if offered, the USA might hold was not "equivalent" compensation. Amid endless controversies, the USA persisted in this attempt to preserve discriminatory tariff treatment until 1923 when it finally embraced the "European" or "unconditional" form of the clause, whereby State B, if a signatory of such a treaty, would be simultaneously and unconditionally entitled to any concessions granted to A.

This formula, it should be noted, has nothing to do with the height of tariff walls but only with their uniformity vis-à-vis all comers entitled to most-favored-nation treatment. If the tariff-makers of State A wish to ban beanbags from B, they are entirely within their treaty rights in so doing providing they do not admit beanbags from C, D, E, etc. Even the goal of nondiscriminatory treatment is often evaded by quotas or foreign-exchange control or minute classifications of goods—e.g., A's tariff on beanbags made of brown burlap and measuring $3\frac{1}{4}$ by $5\frac{1}{2}$ feet (which may happen to be the only kind produced in B) shall be $10 per gross and on all other beanbags 10¢ per gross. By the time of the Great Depression it was clear that other methods would have to be found if barriers to international trade were to be reduced.

The simplest way to lower tariff walls between two or more States (for governments seriously interested in so doing) is to abolish them entirely and prohibit their reimposition. The Constitution of the USA (Art. I, Sec. 10, Par. 2), and the basic law of most other federations, does precisely this among the members of the Federal Union, making all of them a "customs union" with no tariffs between themselves and a common tariff vis-à-vis out-

[13] A typical example is worth careful reading. Art. 7 of the German-American treaty of Dec. 8, 1923, proclaimed in effect Oct. 14, 1925, read as follows:

"Each of the high contracting parties binds itself unconditionally to impose no higher or other duties or conditions and no prohibition on the importation of any article, the growth, produce, or manufacture, of the territories of the other than are or shall be imposed on the importation of any like article, the growth, produce, or manufacture of any other foreign country.

"Each of the high contracting parties also binds itself unconditionally to impose no higher or other charges or other restrictions or prohibitions on goods exported to the territories of the other high contracting parties than are imposed on goods exported to any other foreign country.

"Any advantage of whatsoever kind which either high contracting party may extend to any article, the growth, produce, or manufacture of any other foreign country shall simultaneously and unconditionally, without request and without compensation, be extended to the like article, the growth, produce, or manufacture of the other high contracting party."

side States. Sundry customs unions have also been established by treaty among States not prepared for full federation—*e.g.*, Leichtenstein and Austria-Hungary, Italy and San Marino, France and Monaco, France and the Saar, Luxembourg, Belgium, and the Netherlands (Benelux), Syria and Lebanon, etc. A less extreme step is represented by preferential tariffs among particular States—*i.e.*, lower duties among themselves than are charged outsiders, as in the British imperial preference arrangements adopted in 1932 and adhered to since, and in the post-1945 trade accords among members of the Soviet bloc. In all such schemes, barriers are reduced but discrimination against outsiders is reintroduced.

Since 1934 the USA has sought to promote both equality of treatment and a lowering of tariffs through the Reciprocal Trade Agreement Act (renewed periodically ever since), whereby the President is authorized by Congress to reduce existing duties by as much as 50% in exchange for corresponding concessions by other States, with the reductions thus agreed upon extended to all other States granting and enjoying most-favored-nation treatment. Following the conclusion of more than a score of such pacts, the UN Economic and Social Council called an International Conference on Trade and Employment at Havana in 1947 where, after hard bargaining, agents of 52 States drew up a Charter of an International Trade Organization (ITO) which, however, was never universally ratified, despite its many evasions, equivocations, and "escape clauses." At Geneva, also in 1947, 23 States agreed on bilateral tariff concessions affecting 54,000 commodities and including almost half of all imports in world trade, and also signed a General Agreement on Tariffs and Trade (GATT).

Other devices to liberalize trade appear, to the unwary, impressive: the International Monetary Fund and the International Bank for Reconstruction and Development, both established at Bretton Woods, N.H., in July, 1944, the former (like the European Payments Union) for the purpose of promoting exchange stability by an international pooling of monetary resources to meet temporary national deficits, the latter designed to underwrite foreign investments; the labors of the League of Nations, culminating in a futile World Economic Conference in Geneva in 1927 and another in London in 1933 (killed by U.S. refusal to discuss debts, tariffs, or even currency devaluation); the travail of the United Nations; the resolves of the Council of Europe; etc.

Notable among these efforts, although with ultimate results still dubious in the late 1950's, were various renewed attempts in the weakened and diminished Western Europe which emerged from World War II to establish, somehow, a "United States of Europe." Persisting attitudes and policies of political nationalism precluded any political federation of the ancient States of the Continent. Persisting attitudes and policies of economic nationalism partially frustrated efforts at economic federation—which were nevertheless not wholly unsuccessful. Thus, French Foreign Minister Robert Schuman on May 9, 1950, invited all European States to draft a treaty to merge their coal and steel industries into a single market. A 50-year pact was signed April 18, 1951, by envoys of France, West Germany, Italy, Luxembourg, Belgium, and the Netherlands. The complex machinery of the "Schuman Plan" (actually the work of Jean Monnet), which sought to establish what was simultaneously a super-cartel and a European customs union for coal and steel, included a Council of Ministers, a High Authority, a Common Assembly, a Consultative Committee, and a Court of Justice.

The member States of the Schuman Plan, meeting in Rome, signed on March 25, 1957, two enormously lengthy and elaborate treaties aiming at even more ambitious goals to be served by even more complex international agencies. One established a "European Economic Community" (Euromarket) designed to achieve a full customs union or "common market" through periodical reductions of tariffs over a span of 15 years. The overseas territories of the signatories were to be "associated" with the common market. Numerous exceptions, qualifications, and "escape clauses" render the prospect of the scheme obscure. The other pact created a "European Atomic Authority" (Euratom), contemplating common international ownership and development —through sharing of research, materials, facilities, and a common nuclear market—of a "powerful nuclear industry" for peaceful purposes in Western Europe. Plans were announced on May 7, 1957, for the cooperative creation of a nuclear-powered network of electric stations capable of supplying 15,000,000 kilowatts by 1967.

Economic Illusions and Political Realities. Such endeavors seemed likely to eventuate in appreciable reductions in trade barriers and fruitful forms of international economic cooperation in Western Europe and possibly in other regions of the globe. They appeared quite unlikely to lead to any approximation of world-wide "free trade" or any global abandonment of economic nationalism in favor of a "common market" coterminous with the World Community. Why this is so can best be suggested by surveying the current economic position and policies of the wealthiest economy on earth in our century—the United States of America, whose Senators, as of 1958, had persistently refused, despite Presidential prodding, to ratify GATT or make America a member of ITO.

The USA at mid-century was (almost) consuming more raw materials of all kinds and producing more manufactures of all kinds than all the rest of the world put together. Its economy could not only afford to import, and pay for, more than it exported but would stand to gain greatly thereby and confer comparable gains on friends abroad who begged for "trade not aid." But its businessmen, farmers, and workers who were most influential in Congress and before the Tariff Commission were often in favor of competitive enterprise only in principle and not in practice. As American diplomats sought absolute security against the power of others, American entrepreneurs sought absolute protection against the goods of others. Most of the painfully negotiated tariff reductions of the previous 20 years affected commodities which were noncompetitive and had no mass market in the USA.

When British bicycles, French motorcars, Dutch and Danish cheeses, Belgian felts, Swiss watch movements, and even Italian garlic threatened to compete in the domestic market with like commodities produced at home, action was taken at once to raise duties to prohibitive heights under the new "escape clause" of the Reciprocal Trade Agreements Act of 1951. Foreign governments protested and retaliated, but to little effect. The President in his discretion rejected Tariff Commission recommendations for higher duties on garlic and watches but granted them on dates and figs and other goods. When Japan in July, 1952, asked to join GATT and thereby obtain most-favored-nation treatment, there was consternation in Washington, London, and capitals of other lands in whose markets Japanese exports might profitably compete if not discriminated against. So paradoxical had this situation become that President Truman, in proposing a broad inquiry into U.S. foreign-trade policies (also in July, 1952), referred to the "cheese amendment" to the Defense Production Act as an example of "an increasing body of restrictive laws attempting to further the interests of particular American producers," which "poses a very real dilemma for our whole foreign policy," since it works "at cross purposes with the basic objectives of the Mutual Security Program to achieve economic strength and solvency among the free nations."

At the same time that the USA continued to "buy American" and to bar many possible imports from its allies, it banned virtually all American exports to its enemies in the Cold War. It further sought, in waging economic warfare against the foe, to deprive Western Europe, West Germany, and Japan of their natural and alternative markets in Eastern Europe, the USSR, and China —even threatening, as in the "Battle Act" amendment to the Mutual Security Act of 1952, to cut off U.S. aid from countries permitting the export of "strategic" materials to the Soviet bloc. The premise of this policy was that the East would somehow gain more from East-West trade in the way of components of national prosperity and power than would the West, despite the fact that the West's need for Eastern markets was greater than the East's need for Western markets. But here, as so often, the logic of economic nationalism passes understanding.

The nature of the result may be suggested by a few eloquent statistics as a fitting close to our survey. The USA roughly doubled its industrial capacity in World War I and repeated the process in World War II. Between 1940 and 1951, inclusive, the USA exported 182.9 billions of dollars' worth of goods and imported only 103.7 billions, with the "favorable" balance largely paid for through 72.6 billions in grants and "loans" from the U.S. Government.[14] Between July 1, 1945, and Dec. 31, 1951, the gross expenditures of U.S. foreign aid programs were 35.6 billion dollars, with almost 17 billions available for such expenditures for 1953.[15] Total annual U.S. exports rose from 9.8 billion dollars in 1945 to 15 billions in 1952 and 16 billions in 1953, while total imports for the same years were 4.1, 11, and 10.9 billions. UN statisticians calculated that total world imports and exports, excluding intra-Soviet-bloc trade, amounted in 1951 to $76 billion, "occasioned mainly by new and large defense requirements." U.S. exports totaled $19 billion and U.S. imports $15 billion, of which one-third came from Latin America, one-fifth from Canada, one-fifth from the sterling area, and only one-seventh from Western Europe, which exported $22 billion and imported $24 billion. By 1958, before trade was reduced by the American recession, U.S. imports were coming in at a rate of $14 billion annually while U.S. exports were going out at a rate of almost $24 billion. It is true in world affairs, as elsewhere, that who pays the piper may call the tune. It is even more emphatically true that nations which insist upon selling without buying must give away the difference if they wish the buyers to continue to buy in order that the sellers may continue to sell.

If we may put the business even more bluntly (although it is seldom so put, since businessmen and policy-makers prefer other formulas more palatable to the public), the gargantuan productivity and prosperity of the USA in the 1950's were in large part maintained by governmental policies of restricting imports, subsidizing exports, pouring billions of dollars of public funds abroad in military and economic aid, and spending scores of billions of dollars of public funds at home for "defense," thereby maintaining full employment, high wages, and fabulous corporation profits through "creeping inflation." America was not quite a "Garrison State," nor was its economy wholly dependent upon gifts abroad or arms spending at home. But the "power elite" in the USA of mid-century consisted of corporation directors, military specialists, and civilian politicians, all overlapping and interlocking, most of whom were persuaded that national power and prosperity could best be served by the devices here noted, all of which were rationalized and rendered popular in terms of "anti-Communism."

Thus, U.S. exports and imports in the 1950's increased from 25 to 45 billion dollars, with exports exceeding imports by almost 5 billion dollars each year. "Foreign aid," under various guises, came close to the same amount each year, albeit declining in the late 1950's as Congress kept reducing Executive requests under pressure from disgruntled taxpayers. At the same time

[14] *Hearings before the Committee on Foreign Relations on the Mutual Security Act of 1952*, U.S. Senate, 82d Cong., 2d Sess. (1952), pp. 534ff.

[15] U.S. Department of Commerce Reports, summarized in Report of the Committee on Foreign Relations on the Mutual Security Act of 1952, U.S. Senate, 82d Cong., 2d Sess., pp. 14, 52–53.

the U.S. military budget varied between 30 and 40 billion dollars, comprising one-tenth of the gross national product and contributing decisively to high corporate profits and high wages for industrial workers. During the first seven years of NATO, its member States spent over 300 billion dollars for defense, of which the USA contributed 252 billions. Even this sacrosanct category of federal appropriations was somewhat reduced by Congress in 1957 and thereafter, for consumers and taxpayers were dissatisfied with ever higher levies and prices and often failed to comprehend the new formula for plenty. The formula required constant crises, "brinkmanship," and threats of war to induce Congressmen and their constituents to approve vast outlays of public funds at home and abroad in the name of "national security." To the degree to which successive Administrations in Washington were seriously concerned with negotiating peace via nonviolent coexistence, the formula of the Cold War became increasingly difficult to apply.[16]

The ultimate resolution, if any, of this dilemma was invisible in the early 1960's. Most politicians, publicists, and citizens who, if sufficiently frightened, gladly approved the spending of billions for defense were quite unwilling, if unfrightened, to condone any comparable public expenditures for schools, hospitals, roads, or other services which, if comparably supported by federal appropriations, might come to be a constructive substitute for spending on armaments and foreign aid. It is enough to note for the problem here in hand that in mid-century the world's wealthiest nation was in goodly measure pursuing riches not through any program of "economic internationalism," as understood through many yesterdays, but through a program of militarized "economic Nationalism" which promised to persist through many tomorrows.

[16] In a summer address of 1957 (cf. The Nation, Aug. 17, 1957), Gen. Douglas MacArthur, speaking to the Sperry-Rand stockholders on the evils of high taxation, observed: "Our government has kept us in a perpetual state of fear—kept us in a continuous stampede of patriotic fervor—with the cry of grave national emergency. Always there has been some terrible evil at home or some monstrous foreign power that was going to gobble us up if we did not blindly rally behind it by furnishing the exorbitant funds demanded. Yet, in retrospect, these disasters seem never to have happened, seem never to have been quite real." At the same time (cf. The New York Times, June 19, 1957) Donald A. Quarles, Deputy Secretary of Defense, echoing Adm. Arthur W. Radford and Adm. Felix B. Stump in appeals to the House Foreign Affairs Committee for "foreign aid," commented: "The threat to the future of American peace and prosperity which is posed by militant international Communism was never greater than it is today. It is a threat which a rapidly advancing and war-oriented technology of the Soviet Union has mounted in unprecedented power and diversity. They have maintained massive forces and have developed modern weapons of terrible potency with delivery systems capable of spanning the continents and seas which formerly were barriers between us. The consequence has been that, for the first time in history, the United States is exposed to the possibility of an instantaneous and widespread attack of the most violent and destructive sort." For a lively running account of continuing developments in the application of the formula, see Lawrence Dennis's fortnightly analysis, entitled The Appeal to Reason, West Springfield, Mass.

THE MAKING OF NATIONS

4. THE NEW NATIONALISMS

"Cheshire-Puss," Alice began . . . "would you tell me please which way I ought to go from here?" "That depends a good deal on where you want to get," said the Cat. "I don't much care where—" said Alice. "Then it doesn't matter much which way you go," said the Cat. "—so long as I get *somewhere*," Alice added as an explanation. "Oh, you're sure to do that," said the Cat, "if only you walk long enough. . . . In *that* direction lives a Hatter; and in *that* direction lives a March Hare. Visit either you like: they're both mad." "But I don't want to go among mad people," Alice remarked. "Oh, you can't help that," said the Cat, "we're all mad here. I'm mad, you're mad." "How do you know I am mad?" said Alice. "You must be," said the Cat, "or you wouldn't have come here."—LEWIS CARROLL, *Alice in Wonderland.*

Imitation, someone observed once upon a time, is the sincerest form of flattery. The national patriots of the North Atlantic communities painfully discovered in the middle years of the 20th Century that their prolonged and highly successful efforts to impose their power upon the "lesser breeds" were no longer successful in the face of the revolt of the victims. These, in turn, found no better way to resist their erstwhile masters than the way of copying Western nationalism and adapting it to their own purposes. In this wise, the Western cult of the nation-state has become in our time the universal faith of all mankind, with all of its glories, frustrations, and aberrations, plus some unique features of achievement and failure in the making of nations attributable to the legacy of colonialism and to the special circumstances of the human condition among those long disinherited and still impoverished.

Take a world map (see pp. 105*f.*) or, better, a globe, and trace a long line eastward and southeastward from the coast of Africa south of Gilbraltar to the equatorial islands northwest of Australia. Along this line, if we exclude China, dwell almost 800,000,000 people, or nearly one-third of the human race—thinly scattered in the deserts and coastal plains of North Africa and the Levant, and densely crowded in the lush plains of southern and southeastern Asia and in what Westerners once called the "Spice Islands." Among these peoples African and Asian nationalisms, faithfully imitating earlier European prototypes, have come to full flower in our era. The peoples of the region thus delineated have nothing in common, linguistically, culturally, or religiously—and nothing in common politically save a common rebellion against Western rule. The followers of the faith of Islam, to be sure, are to be found along the line all the way from Morocco to Indonesia. But Islam was never a unity nor is it now. Its disciples are interspersed along our perimeter of demarcation with millions of Christians and Jews and with many millions of Hindus and Buddhists.

Yet all the inhabitants of this vast expanse, intercepted by 20° north latitude, have more in common than they know. They know, indeed, very little beyond their local problems, fears, and hopes, for almost all of them are illiterate, ignorant, poor, and miserable as were all their ancestors for ages past. Many among them are peasants, still exploited by landlords in the ancient "feudal" pattern of human relations. In our time all are animated, dimly or brightly, with new dreams of a better life begotten by Western example. Whether their dreams are capable of fulfillment is a problem best deferred (see pp. 619–640). Here it is in order to note that all these peoples have been moved by misery — *note* and resentment to adopt Western nationalism as a weapon against the West.

A full account of these new ventures in nation-making would require far more pages than are here available. Each local community in these far-flung homes of humankind has sought its way toward "freedom" in ways which its leaders deemed appropriate to immediate circumstances of time and place. A bare outline of politics may nonetheless suggest the troubles and puzzles, and the puzzling and troubling role, of the African and Asian peoples of 20° north latitude in the world politics of our years.

* * * * *

The Maghreb. All across North Africa, confronting Europe over the Middle Sea and reaching to the Atlantic, stretches the western arm of Islam, the common faith of almost all the Arab and Berber peoples of the Maghreb or "West." At its extremity lies MOROCCO, a fertile land of valleys and coastal plains wherein dwell almost 10,000,000 people. Long partitioned into Spanish and French Protectorates, the "Sherifian Empire," or country of the "Moors," at last achieved unity and independence in 1956, after long and bitter struggles against alien rule (see pp. 321*f*.). In a vain effort to retain what was untenable, French authorities in 1953 exiled Sultan Mohammed (V) ben Youssef to Madagascar and sought to rule through pro-French followers of the new Sultan Sidi Mohammed ben Arafa and Thami el Glaoui, Berber Pasha of Marrakech. When el Glaoui (who died Jan. 23, 1956, aged 78), Sidi, and the Istaqlil, the leading nationalist party, all demanded the return of Mohammed V, Paris permitted him to resume the throne in November, 1955. A month later the first all-Moroccan Cabinet was appointed and called for an end of the Protectorate and a constitutional monarchy. In the face of mob violence and acts of terrorism, Paris recognized Moroccan independence on March 2, 1956. Following conferences in Madrid between the Sultan and Gen. Franco, Spain did likewise on April 7, 1956, with Moroccan authority extended in October to the formerly internationalized zone of Tangier while the USA renounced its extraterritorial rights.

The new nation, led by Premier Si Bekkai and Mohammed V (who changed his title from Sultan to King in midsummer of 1957) grappled as best it could with problems of mass poverty and illiteracy, internal disorders, and urgent need of foreign technical and financial aid. On Nov. 12, 1956, the ruler opened the first session of an appointive National Consultative Assembly designed to pave the way for representative government. Morocco's foreign relations were painfully complicated by the Algerian war and by hopes, which led to border clashes, of annexing the Spanish enclave of Ifni and French Mauretania to the south.

Here, as in the lands to the east, the new nationalism was a mingling of local loyalties and vague visions of pan-Arab unity with a bitter, irrational, albeit understandable, "anti-colonialism." The sources of such attitudes were well exemplified in neighboring ALGERIA. Here is an area of 852,000 square miles, four times the size of France—of which, however, only the coastal plain and the mountains beyond are fit for human habitation. Seven-eighths of the land is Sahara Desert, lifeless and worthless apart from recently discovered oil deposits. Algeria, seized by France in the 1830's, now supports 10,000,000 people, of whom 9,000,000 are Arabs and Berbers and 1,000,000 are French *colons* or settlers. The latter long owned much of the best land, monopolized public service, and often lived by the labor of the former, most of whom were wretchedly poor farm or factory workers. Under the statute of 1947 all Algerians became French citizens and the four northern departments of Oran, Alger, Constantine, and Bône were made "part of France," but under electoral arrangements which made one million Frenchmen equal to nine million natives.

Rebellion broke out in the fall of 1954, under the leadership of the "Algerian National Liberation Front," in the form of guerrilla activities in the mountains and terroristic attacks in cities. Minister of the Interior François Mitterand in the Mendès-France Cabinet declared: "Algeria is France. The only negotiation possible is with bullets." The rebels also acquired bullets. The horrors which ensued involved murder raids against French settlers, assassinations, bomb outrages, mutual tortures and atrocities, and indiscriminate killing of the innocent on both sides. Here, as earlier with regard to Morocco and Tunisia, the USA, although championing in principle the independence of colonial peoples, supported in practice its French ally with money and arms in the hope of continued commercial privileges and retention of the elaborate network of air bases throughout North Africa. Washington consistently opposed any consideration of these conflicts by the UN.

By 1958 Paris was maintaining over half a million troops in Algeria and spending a billion dollars a year in attempts to crush the rebellion. Premier Guy Mollet named Georges Catroux as Governor General. Since he favored compromise, the French *colons* demonstrated and rioted against him. On Feb. 10, 1956, Mollet yielded and appointed Robert Lacoste, who regularly promised imminent victory over the rebels and found himself faced with an endless war which took thousands of lives. The ultimate shape of Algerian nationhood could not be delineated in 1958 since independence had not yet been won. All that was certain was that the French cause would ultimately be lost.

In neighboring TUNISIA, seized by France in 1881, the path to independence was less painful. Here live almost 4,000,000 people, almost all of whom are native Arabs. Here in the postwar years the Neo-Destour Party, led by Habib Bourguiba, first collaborated with the French in hope of more posts for natives in the civil service and then in 1951, with the support of Bey Sidi Mohammed al-Amin, demanded a representative Assembly and control of the Cabinet. French resistance found expression in "state of siege" laws, suppression of the nationalist press, shootings of rioters, and arrests of Bourguiba and his collaborators in January, 1952, followed by the arrest of the Premier and other Ministers in March. Counter-resistance took the form of strikes, murder, arson, and riots. In early spring of 1952 Paris browbeat the Bey into yielding and appointing a Cabinet of French puppets headed by Salahaddine Baccouche.

As usual in such matters, such devices prove vain. Baccouche was soon discredited. Rigged "elections" in 1953, boycotted by most nationalists, were followed in 1954–55 by more violence and complex negotiations for "autonomy." All in vain. As lovers are satisfied with nothing short of love, nationalists are satisfied with nothing short of nationhood. Yielding to the inevitable, Paris granted independence March 20, 1956. Meanwhile, Salah ben Youssef, former Secretary General of the Neo-Destour Party, "declared war" on Bourguiba in January and provoked much violence before fleeing the country. Bourguiba's "National Front" won overwhelming victory in the elections of March 25, 1956. He became Premier April 14, 1956, and initiated a program of constitution-making and social reform.

Relations with France were gravely strained by the French seizure through deceit, Oct. 22, 1956, of five Algerian rebel leaders en route from Morocco where they were guests of the Sultan, to Tunisia where sympathy for the Algerian nationalists was no less ardent. On March 30, 1957, Bourguiba, at the close of a visit to Rabat, signed a treaty of alliance and friendship between Morocco and Tunisia, meanwhile conferring with leaders of the Algerian rebellion. In his subsequent visit to Libya, he further espoused the rebel cause. In midsummer of 1957 the monarchy was peacefully abolished and Tunisia became a republic.

Paris subsequently charged that Tunisia was a base for rebel operations in Algeria. French acts of "retaliation" and "hot pursuit" culminated in a savage bombing raid (with U.S. planes), Feb. 8, 1958, on the border village of Sakiet-Sidi-Youssef. Many women and children were among the 79 killed and the several hundred wounded. Bourguiba's "pro-Westernism" was discredited. He recalled his ambassador to Paris, demanded the immediate evacuation of all French troops still in Tunisia, and appealed to the UN against "aggression." Washington and London offered "good offices" to avoid an embarrassing UN debate. The aftermath indicated that France would be obliged either to grant Algerian independence or face war with all the Arab nationalists of North Africa.

LIBYA, east of Tunisia, became the first of the communities of the Maghreb to attain independence, although less fitted for self-government than its neighbors. Here in the three provinces of Cyrenaica, Tripolitania, and Fezzan live a million Arabs, of whom at the time of independence only 14 were university graduates and only 5,000 had had more than five years of school. Libya became "independent" on Dec. 24, 1951, by virtue of a UN decision of 1949 reflecting the inability of the Powers to agree upon any other disposition of the territory. Seized by Italy from Turkey in 1911, the land was one of the three units of Italy's prewar African empire. Eritrea was federated with Ethiopia by a UN Assembly resolution of Dec. 2, 1950. Somaliland became a UN trust territory under Italian administration on April 1, 1950, and was slated to become independent after 10 years. Emir Sayed Idris el Senussi, as King Idris I of the federated United Kingdom of Libya, presided over elections to a bicameral parliament in 1952. The USA retained its large air base at Wheelus Field near Tripoli. Libya remained dependent for economic and political viability on subventions from America, Britain, and Italy.

EGYPT, by far the most populous and potentially the most powerful of all the Arab States, despite the desperate poverty of most of its 23,000,000 people, became under Nasser the focal point of widespread intrigue, propaganda, and agitation for Arab unity against Zionism and Western "imperialism." Since the problems of Egypt are dealt with *in extenso* elsewhere in these pages (see pp. 399–426), we will here move on to Egypt's southern neighbor on the upper reaches of the Nile.

In the SUDAN dwell 9,000,000 people in an area of almost a million square miles, producing and exporting gum arabic, cotton, senna, peanuts, dates, hides, and a little gold. The people comprise a ruling Arab minority in the north and a Negroid majority in the south. Long an Anglo-Egyptian condominium, the Sudan attained independence as a republic on Jan. 1, 1956, with Abdullah Kahlil succeeding Ismael el Azhri as Premier on July 5, 1956. As a member of the Arab League, the Sudan was committed to Arab solidarity against Israel and Western colonialism, but was involved in complex problems with Cairo regarding Egyptian ambitions and questions of allocating the waters of the great river.

The LEVANT. East of Suez extends the "fertile crescent" from the Mediterranean shore to the Persian Gulf, half circling the desert lands to the south. In the great rectangle between Egypt, Turkey, Iran, and the Arabian Sea live some 25,000,000 people, all of them (save for a million Christians in Lebanon and almost two million Jews in Israel) Arabic in language and culture and Moslem in religion. But these elements of unity, along with a shared Arab nationalism uniting all in common hatred of Israel and the West, were insufficient to overcome parochial and dynastic rivalries and to merge separate sovereignties in a common polity.

The politics of palace revolution, military *Putsch*, and mob violence became "normal" in the Near East as the feudal elites sought security against mass misery in internecine quarrels and calculated hatred of the Western Powers.

In the 1950's SAUDI ARABIA remained an absolute monarchy, enriched by
Aramco and bound by a five-year Mutual Defense Assistance Pact (June 18,
1951) by which the USA continued to lease and operate the huge air base
at Dhahram on the Persian Gulf, within easy striking distance of the trans-
Caucasian Soviet oil fields. Ibn Saud continued to oppose any union of JORDAN
and IRAQ, both ruled by dynasties of the Hashemite family. In the former
kingdom Abdullah ibn Hussein was assassinated in July, 1951, and succeeded
by his eldest son, King Talal who, being of unsound mind, was succeeded by
his son in turn, King Hussein, who took the throne on May 2, 1953, his
eighteenth birthday.

In Iraq King Feisal II and Regent Emir Abdul Illah won new royalties
from the oil companies in 1951 and beyond. The Republic of LEBANON lost its
Premier, Read el-Sulh, by assassination in Jordan in July, 1951. The Republic
of SYRIA, despite an admirable Constitution of 1951 and the election to the
Presidency of the venerable Hassan al-Atassi, also conducted its politics by
coup d'état, with Col. Adib Shishakly in November, 1951, arresting the Cabinet,
dismissing Parliament, proclaiming himself President, and making new threats
against Israel.

The turbulent course of Arab politics at home and abroad in more recent
years is touched on below (see pp. 426*f*.).

The Resurrection of Israel. Except for Lebanon to the north, Palestine is
the smallest of the Near Eastern countries, having an area of only 10,000
square miles (about the size of Vermont), much of which is desert. This
ancient land was the matrix of Judaism and Christianity and is almost equally
sacred to Mohammedans. All these faiths are religions of love and brotherhood. But in the 20th Century their holy birthland has been a scene of hatred
and violence on a scale unknown since the Crusades.

This paradox is one of many. The residents of Palestine have been under
foreign rule for the better part of 25 centuries. They were predominantly
Jewish after 1400 B.C. For 30 centuries a large part of the inhabitants, though
seldom a majority, has been Jewish. Alien rulers during the past 1,500 years
have included Romans, Byzantines, Saracens, Crusaders, Turks, and Britons—
who conquered Palestine from the Turks in 1918 when the population numbered *c.* 750,000, of whom 84,000 were Jews, 77,000 Christians, and 589,000
Moslems. During the ensuing 25 years the population increased to 1,765,000
as prosperous farms and thriving cities blossomed out of the wastelands. This
miracle was due to Jewish immigration and to Jewish capital, industry, and
enterprise, inspired by Theodore Herzl's vision of a new Zion in which Jewry
would again find refuge, nationhood, and a haven of salvation. The Jewish
population increased from 84,000 to almost 600,000. The Arabs, sharing in the
new prosperity, increased from 600,000 to more than 1,000,000.

By the Balfour Declaration of Nov. 2, 1917, the British Government
promised to Dr. Chaim Weizmann, leader of the Zionist Movement, the

"establishment in Palestine of a national home for the Jewish people, it being clearly understood that nothing should be done which might prejudice the civil and religious rights of existing non-Jewish communities in Palestine, or the rights and political status enjoyed by Jews in any other country." This language was repeated in the mandate agreement. All went well until the threat of war caused London to yield to Arab demands, supported by terrorism and rioting, for the abandonment of efforts to fulfill the purposes of the mandate. Arab nationalists contended with reason that Palestine had been predominantly an Arab land for 1,300 years and (with less reason) that a Jewish State or "national home" would be an intolerable affront to Arabs everywhere.

By the White Paper of May, 1939, Jewish immigration was limited to 75,000 during the ensuing five years and was to be suspended entirely thereafter unless Arab authorities should consent to its resumption. Acquisition of land by Jews was also restricted. These steps, along with the creation of Trans-Jordan as a separate Kingdom, appeared to many a violation of the mandate and of the Anglo-American accord of 1924, since no consent was secured from the League members, the League Council, or the USA. The Permanent Mandates Commission (PMC) declared the White Paper a violation of the mandate. Churchill called it a "breach and a refutation of the Balfour Declaration." Herbert Morrison described it as "a cynical breach of pledges given to the Jews and the world." The Labor Party Conference of 1939 said it "violates the solemn pledges contained in the Balfour Declaration and in the mandate"—a position reiterated in April, 1945.

But the Labor Party, after its victory of July, 1945, swallowed its words and continued without change the policy of its predecessors. This result was due to calculations of political expediency, in which Zionist hopes and the ghastly tragedy of European Jewry received little consideration. Meanwhile, American political leaders consistently supported the policies which their British counterparts had rejected. Cynics held that these statements merely demonstrated that Arab votes were negligible while Jewish votes were locally significant in American elections. Others interpreted them as a solemn enunciation of an American national purpose.

The sequel is too complex to be narrated here in full. Downing Street was trapped between old and contradictory pledges to Jews and Arabs, worried about British defenses in the Near East, anxious over oil supplies, and eager to avoid offense to the Arab League. *Divida et impera* still seemed a safe guide to British colonial administrators. In Washington the high strategists of the State Department were moved by similar considerations, while the White House and Congress were influenced, ambivalently, by humanitarianism and domestic politics. The result was a continuation into the postwar period of the British policy of 1939, despite the desperation of Europe's surviving Jews, most of whom saw no hope save in Palestine. Commissions, committees, and boards of inquiry met, deliberated, and recommended endlessly. Violence in Palestine began in October of the year of victory, with 100,000 British troops striving to halt the flow of Jewish refugees whose transit from Europe was carefully planned and financed by Zionists and their sympathizers throughout the world. Jewish terrorists, convinced that only force would produce results, blew up railroads, pipe lines, and public buildings.

We have already noted (see p. 238) how the issue was finally referred to the UN; how partition was proposed and rejected; how the Arab States waged war and were defeated by the Jews in a striking demonstration of the incompetence and corruption of their feudal regimes; and how Israel was reborn as a nation (May 14, 1948). The armistice frontiers gave it an area of only 8,000 square miles (the size of New Jersey) with the balance of Palestine, including the Old City in Jerusalem, occupied by Jordan and the remaining Arab population of Israel reduced, largely by the flight of refugees, to 175,000. With all bars to immigration now removed, many wanderers returned "home" in the *kibbutz galuyoth* or "ingathering of exiles," boosting the Jewish population to almost 1,500,000 by 1953, including scores of thousands of quite primitive settlers from Yemen, Iraq, and the ghettos of North Africa. Dr. Weizmann was elected President and David Ben-Gurion chosen Premier by the Knesset (Assembly) in February, 1949. When the revered Dr. Weizmann died in December, 1952, he was succeeded as President of Israel by Itzhak Ben-Zvi. In the face of incredible difficulties in this tiny and half-desert land, a democratic and semi-collectivist Zion became a new monument to ancient ideals—and a dreaded symbol of social change to the princes and effendis of the surrounding Arab states.

The New Achaemenides. In IRAN, as in Egypt, the ruling class of landlords sought to buttress the social *status quo* by mobilizing popular unrest against the West. The forms of constitutional democracy, under Shah Mohammed Riza Pahlavi, scarcely concealed the realities of oligarchy. On March 7, 1951, Premier Ali Razmara, who had been denounced by mobs and by deputies in the Majlis or lower house of Parliament for failing to nationalize the oil industry, was assassinated by a religious fanatic, Khalil Tahmassebi—who was pardoned, praised, and liberated by the Majlis in August of 1952. Meanwhile, in the face of British warnings and protests, the deputies voted nationalization in mid-March of 1951, with the aged and erratic Dr. Mohammed Mossadegh assuming the Premiership in April. Following involved negotiation, litigation, and unsuccessful U.S. mediation through Averell Harriman, the Iranian Government in June and July took over the properties of the Anglo-Iranian Oil Company, including the vast refineries at Abadan. When British technicians were forced out, all production ceased, with the sale of stocks on hand made impossible by British counter-measures.

Mossadegh's autumn visit to Washington in quest of "justice" from the UN and a "loan" of $120,000,000 from the USA produced no solution. With its

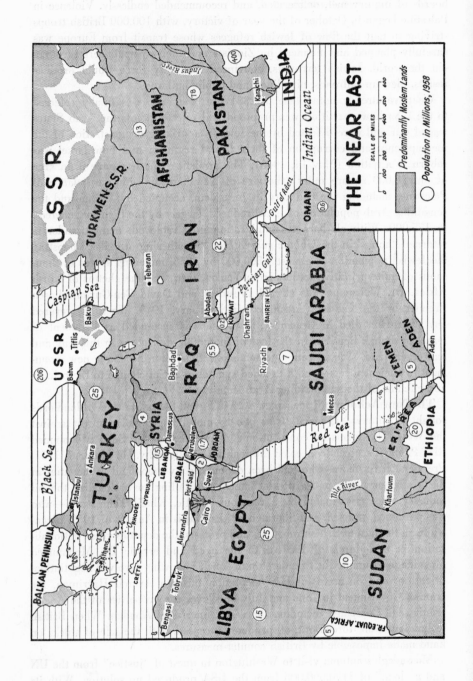

THE NEAR EAST

SCALE OF MILES

0 100 200 300 400 500 600

Predominantly Moslem Lands

◯ Population in Millions, 1958

major industry paralyzed and its government facing bankruptcy, Iran's public life relapsed into mob rule and dictatorship. On July 17, 1952, Mossadegh resigned and was replaced by the conciliatory Ahmed Ghavam. But when Mossadegh's partisans and supporters of the Communist-led Tudeh Party rioted against the new Premier, he was ousted as a "traitor" and replaced on July 22 by Mossadegh once more—now entrusted with dictatorial powers by Parliament amid much talk of "land reform" and a national frenzy of anti-British and anti-American agitation.

In July of 1953 President Eisenhower rejected a personal plea for aid from Mossadegh. When the Shah sought to dismiss his histrionic and hysterical Premier, only to be defied, he fled the country in August—to return within a few days and, with the support of the army and of loyal street mobs, to oust Mossadegh, who was subsequently tried and sentenced to three years in prison. The Shah and his new Premier, Marshal Fazollah Zahedi (saved from imminent bankruptcy by a U.S. grant of $45,000,000), resumed negotiations over oil while Herbert Hoover, Jr., the State Department's petroleum expert, played a major role in discussions among Washington, London, and Teheran. After a rigged and coerced election of a new Majlis, Zahedi's Cabinet secured a firm majority. An oil accord was signed Aug. 5, 1954, and pushed through the Majlis in October—with petroleum production and export resumed in November.

The incredibly complex bargain here arrived at can justly be described as a victory for the U.S. oil companies and for Washington, which now made Iran for all practical purposes an American protectorate, and a qualified defeat for London and for the more extreme Iranian nationalists. The Anglo-Iranian Oil Company gained compensation but lost its monopoly and, in form though not in fact, lost its properties. Teheran in fact, though not in form, abandoned Mossadegh's ill-fated attempt at nationalization in exchange for U.S. subsidies and larger oil royalties.

The agreement, to run for 25 years with the right of renewal for another 15, was made with a consortium, incorporated in the Netherlands, of 8 oil companies, with Anglo-Iranian holding 40% of the stock, Royal Dutch Shell 14%, Compagnie Française de Petrole 6%, and Socony-Vacuum, Standard of New Jersey, Standard of California, Texas, and Gulf each 8%. The Iranian National Oil Company was limited to the Kermanshah fields and refinery, which serve only the local market. Iran agreed to pay Anglo-Iranian $70,000,000 over 10 years, beginning in 1957, while the other members of the consortium agreed to pay Anglo-Iranian another $500,000,000. The associated companies, now in effective control of Iran's oil industry, agreed to pay Teheran, in addition to other sums, a 50% income tax, which some Iranian leaders hoped to use for economic development. Many Iranians may in fact gain riches from these arrangements, although any alleviation of the miserable lot of the peasant masses appeared unlikely. In this instance, if not in many others, a new and stream-lined "dollar diplomacy" scored an impressive triumph over anti-colonial nationalist fanaticism.[17]

India and Pakistan. To the east of Iran lies the vast subcontinent of Hindustan, politically united by Mongol invaders in the 15th Century. The land remained united under the British Raj, whose emissaries conquered India in the 18th Century and long governed it through the curious device of a private trading company. This home of one-sixth of the human race has long been the largest single exhibit on earth of modern colonial imperialism at its worst and best and of native rebellion, at its best and worst, against the white man's rule. India is also a vast museum of races and cultures, its peoples embracing all types of all epochs and places, from the primitive savages of the hill tribes, the 40,000,000 outcasts, or untouchables, of the Hindu caste system, and the multi-millioned masses of abysmally poor and ignorant peasants to graduates of Oxford and Cambridge, native magnates in textiles and steel, and medieval princes of fantastic wealth.

The Census of 1941 revealed a total population of 389,000,000, of whom, in terms of religion, 255,000,000 were Hindus, 94,000,000 Moslems, 6,300,-000 Christians, 5,700,000 Sikhs, 230,000 Buddhists, and the balance pagans or worshipers of less-well-known gods. Over 200 languages are spoken, but the major tongues in the north—Hindi, Bengali, Marathi, Gujarati, etc.—are all derived from Sanskrit, while the Dravidian languages of the south—Tamil, Telugu, Malayalam, Kanarese, etc.—have a comparable kinship. In terms of race, all is unclear save that the present population of India is a mixture of stocks (like all other populations) and that most of the remote ancestors of today's children, despite dark skins, were Caucasians rather than Negroids or Mongoloids. In terms of literacy, only 12.2% of India's people could read and write any language in 1941, compared with 6.9% in 1931. In terms of income, the average yearly earnings of each Indian was about $23.

This appalling spectacle of human degradation is further documented by the fact that the annual birth rate on the eve of World War II was 33 per thousand people (compared with 18 in the USA), the death rate was 22 per thousand (compared with 11 in the USA), infant mortality was 160 per thousand live births (compared with 47 in the USA), and the life expectancy of Indians was 27 years (compared with 61 years for the white population of

[17] At the time of writing the bargain here summarized seemed to be working out to the satisfaction of all concerned—with the obvious exceptions of an illiterate peasantry still exploited by native landlords, the followers of Mossadegh and of the outlawed Tudeh or Communist Party which had supported Mossadegh, and of the USSR. Moscow, however, acquiesced and cultivated "good relations" with Teheran, apart from warnings against the possible consequences of the Baghdad Pact. The resignation of Premier Hussein Ala in favor of Dr. Manouchehr Eghbal, April 3, 1957, was not an indication of a new period of political instability in Iran, but only further proof of Iran's dependence upon the USA. The shift was occasioned by the murder, at the hands of local bandits in a desert region near the Pakistan frontier, of two U.S. aid officials, Brewster A. Wilson and Kevin M. Carroll, and of Mrs. Carroll.

the USA). Life for the impoverished, debt-ridden, and ever-expanding peasant masses was a nightmare of exploitation, misery, hunger, and early death— alleviated only by the fact that most of its victims knew no other life and were too deeply immersed in illiteracy, superstition, and black ignorance to have any inkling of any other design for living.[18]

The pursuit of these themes, although of the essence of "Mother India" in all her dignity, squalor, beauty, ugliness, and frustration, must be left to other commentators. All politics is meaningless without reference to economic and social structure. But the present account must be limited to the surface phenomena of public affairs. In 1858, British rule of India through a private trading company gave way to British rule of India through agents of the Crown, after the crushing of the great Sepoy Rebellion. Slowly and painfully the literati imbibed Western ideas of nationalism and put forward demands for *swaraj* (self-government) with increasing frequency and urgency. The first "India National Congress" met in 1885 as a gathering of upper-class Hindus to criticize British rule and agitate for larger native participation in the government. In 1912 the Moslem League was established for a similar purpose. By 1918 both groups were cooperating in pushing a program of self-rule.

The long and painful story of repressions and concessions, and of resistance and liberation, we shall leave to the historians of British colonialism and Indian nationalism. Only a few scenes need here be recalled. In the face of a British-granted "Constitution" of 1919, the apostles of *swaraj* found new inspiration in a new leader, Mohandas Gandhi, presently to be known as Mahatma or "Holy Man," who preached a strange gospel derived from David Thoreau, Leo Tolstoy, and Jesus of Nazareth. His message came to this: love your enemies, resist not evil, eschew all force, oppose your oppressors with nonviolent civil disobedience. Against this weapon, so alien to Western civilization, the greatest imperial Power of the world finally found itself defenseless. Force is effective only against those who oppose it with lesser force. Against those who meet it with nonresistance, if they are numbered in millions and dedicated to a cause, force is helpless. Gandhi cheerfully went in and out of prison, fasting and praying and advising his followers to boycott British goods, return to the spinning wheel and village handicrafts, practice asceticism, evade taxes, disobey laws, and submit meekly but proudly to beating, jail, or death.

In the fall of 1931 this grotesque little figure, clad only in a sheet and loincloth, appeared in London at a Round Table Conference, which he described as a "complete failure." Another "Constitution" of 1935 established a federation of 11 provinces with considerable autonomy for the units and a semidemocratic central regime. Pandit Jawaharlal Nehru, elected President

[18] See *India Today* by Raleigh Parkin, probably the most objective and informative single book of recent vintage on Indian society and politics.

of the Congress Party in May, 1936, declared, "We must fight, not spin." Gandhi wept but continued to hope. The Congress had 5,000,000 members by 1939, when London made India a "belligerent" by action of the Viceroy. Nehru and many others were jailed. Only the American offensive against Japan and the Russian defense of Stalingrad saved India from invasion and possible conquest.

The mission of Sir Stafford Cripps in the spring of 1942 offered Dominion status and conceivably independence—after the war. Both the Congress and the Moslem League rejected the offer. When a new campaign of civil disobedience was threatened, London outlawed the Congress Party in August, 1942, and jailed Gandhi, Nehru, and other leaders. Widespread disorders did not quite create the revolutionary situation which Britons feared and the Congress hoped for. U.S. "mediation" failed. Churchill asserted that he "had not become the King's First Minister to preside over the liquidation of the British Empire." Mohammed Ali Jinnah, President of the Moslem League, declared (September 13, 1942) that his supporters would join no provisional government with the Congress unless their demands were met for "Pakistan"—i.e., an independent Moslem State. Mrs. Gandhi died in jail, February 22, 1944. Gandhi was released but could reach no accord with Jinnah.

By 1945 it was clear from murderous "communal" rioting that religious fanaticism had made Hindu nationalism more anti-Moslem than anti-British, and Moslem nationalism more anti-Hindu than anti-British. Yet the ancient imperial principle of "divide and rule" could no longer be made to work. In 1946–47 Prime Minister Attlee moved toward granting freedom—to a united India if possible, to a divided India if necessary. A White Paper of June 2, 1947, asserted that power would be transferred during the current year to Indian authorities in two separate States, if need be, with each entitled to Dominion status or, if they chose, complete independence outside the Commonwealth.

Commons voted the new India Bill on July 10, 1947. Lord Louis Mountbatten became Governor General of the Dominion of India with Nehru as Prime Minister. Jinnah became Governor General of the Dominion of Pakistan with Nawabzada Liaquat Ali Khan as Prime Minister. The new order was formally inaugurated at New Delhi on August 15. Long and agonizing negotiations followed over frontiers, since no definition of boundaries could place all Moslems in Pakistan and all Hindus in India. Exchanges of population uprooted no less than 8,000,000 people. Throughout these painful discussions and migrations, during most of the year 1947, mobs of fanatics, both Hindu and Moslem, looted, burned, murdered, and massacred in an orgy of violence in major cities and throughout the countryside which had no modern counterparts save in the wholesale crimes of the German Hitlerites. In both cases, despite vast differences in the ideological contexts of

atrocities, men hated and slaughtered their fellows because of their fears, bred
of desperate insecurities. How many hundreds of thousands of Indians perished in this frightful bloodletting may never be known. It stained with shame
and grief the beginnings of the new Dominions.

Both India and bifurcated Pakistan, like Ceylon to the south and unlike

Burma to the east, chose to remain within the Commonwealth as "democratic
republics"—a decision which was striking testimony to the wisdom of British
moderation. Both initially adopted a "neutralist" attitude toward the Cold
War, refusing to take the Soviet menace seriously, recognizing Red China, and
often joining other Asian and Moslem states in words and acts highly critical
of Western "imperialism" and U.S. foreign policy. Both quarreled bitterly over
Jammu and Kashmir (see pp. 240, 634), and armed against one another,
particularly after Pakistan joined the Baghdad Pact and SEATO and, as
America's ally, began receiving U.S. military aid. Since the village masses in
both states were illiterate peasants, afflicted with chronic hunger and disease

and often exploited by landlords and money-lenders, the human prerequisites of effective democracy could not soon or easily be achieved. Violence remained a common political recourse of the frustrated, while the siren song of Communism beguiled some intellectuals and a few workers and peasants.

On Jan. 30, 1948, as he left Birla House to go to prayer, Mohandas Gandhi was shot to death by a young Hindu fanatic. Said Nehru in a broken voice: "The light has gone out of our lives. . . ." Under the Constitution adopted Nov. 26, 1949, India became a Federal Republic with an elected President (Rajendra Prasad); a bicameral five-year Parliament consisting of a Council of States, chosen by the state legislatures, and a popularly elected House of the People; and a Prime Minister (Nehru, who was also Foreign Minister) and Cabinet responsible to Parliament. In the first national election, spread over the winter of 1951–52, 107 million voters, out of 176 million eligible, elected 364 Congress Party deputies out of a total of 489, with the Communists and their allies making significant gains and electing 27 deputies as the largest opposition group. Nehru's passion for democracy and social justice was viewed without enthusiasm by the propertied elite and the religious conservatives in the Congress, neither of whom he could afford to alienate. American aid in 1951–52, in the form of famine relief, technical assistance, and the tact and wisdom of genial Ambassador Chester Bowles, evoked gratitude but no disposition to align the new India, potentially a "Great Power" in its own right, with the USA against China and the USSR.

In Pakistan, most populous of Moslem States next to Indonesia, Jinnah died on Sept. 11, 1948. Prime Minister Liaquat Ali Khan was assassinated, Oct. 16, 1951. He was succeeded by Governor General Khwaja Nazimuddin, whose previous post went to Ghulam Mohammed. At the UN, Foreign Minister Sir Mohammed Zafrullah Khan repeatedly denounced Indian "aggression" in Kashmir. The new republic, preoccupied by its conflict with its giant neighbor, often gave diplomatic support to other Moslem States, but was in no position to render effective aid to its brothers in Islam.

Southeastern Asia. Between the Bay of Bengal and the wilds of New Guinea, 3,500 miles beyond, and between the China Sea and the easternmost waters of the Indian Ocean, washing the north coast of Australia, lie lush lands of coastal plains, high mountains, teeming jungles, rich river valleys, and tropical islands where live almost 300,000,000 human beings. These peoples are all predominantly of Mongoloid race, but exhibit a bewildering diversity and semifusion of various cultures: Indian, Chinese, Malay, and European. Prevailing religious faiths are no less diverse: Buddhism in Burma and Thailand; Christianity in the Philippines; Islam in Malaya and Indonesia; Confucianism among the Annamites of Indochina and the Chinese settlers elsewhere. For half a century this area has been the world's largest single source of tin and natural rubber and an important source of sugar, coconut oil, hemp, petroleum, and quinine.

THE NEW NATIONALISMS

These widely scattered and disunited communities have these things in common: (1) all have been ruled by Western "imperialists"—British, French, Spanish, Dutch, or American; (2) all were more or less willingly conquered by Japan in 1941–43 in the name of "Asia for the Asiatics"; (3) all have rebelled against white colonialism; and (4) all have lately achieved some measure of independence, with the symbols of sovereignty supplying no magic to alleviate old evils of exploitation and new woes of overpopulation and mass poverty. A hasty survey of recent developments will suggest uniformities, diversities, and common problems.

BURMA, rice bowl of Asia, achieved independence on Jan. 4, 1948, followed by years of politics by assassination and chronic civil strife precipitated by several varieties of Communists, at war among themselves, by refugee Kuomintang troops continuing hostilities on the northern frontier, and by rebellions of the Karen peoples aspiring to independence from Burma. Premier Thakin Nu pursued a policy of nationalizing foreign enterprises (with compensation to the owners from borrowed funds) and accepting U.S. and UN economic aid, but followed the Indian and Indonesian policy of "neutralism" in the Cold War. Neighboring THAILAND (renamed Siam in 1945 and re-renamed Thailand in 1948) is the only State of the region which never wholly succumbed to Western conquest, thanks to its becoming a "buffer" between British and French pressures. Following Japanese withdrawal, Phumiphon Adundet became constitutional monarch, after the death of his brother, Ananda Mahidol, in 1946. Premier Pibul Songgram (twice deposed by military *coups* and twice restored in 1951) accepted U.S. economic and military aid and gave token support to Washington in the Korean War. In mid-September, 1957, Army Chief Sarit Thanarat deposed Songgram in a bloodless *coup*, with Pote Sarasin, Secretary-General of SEATO, named premier by the king on September 21.

INDOCHINA, long the richest and most populous unit of the French colonial empire, became a major theater of warfare following Japanese withdrawal. On September 7, 1945, the Nationalist Party issued a declaration of independence and established a regime at Hanoi under Communist Ho Chi Minh. French troops arrived in U.S. transports to restore the *status quo*. In March of 1946, however, an agreement signed in Paris recognized the Republic as "a free state within the Indochinese Federation and the French Union." But discord over its application led to open warfare in December. Léon Blum's emissary, Marius Moutet, asserted early in 1947: "Before there is any negotiation it will be necessary to get a military decision. There is nothing left but military action." The war which ensued soon became a bloody and costly stalemate. Ho—supported by native Communists, many non-Communists, and ultimately given material aid by Red China—championed independence, land reform, literacy, and expulsion of the French. His supporters taught eager peasants new techniques of terrorism, arson, sabotage, and guerrilla warfare which frustrated all French efforts to restore order. Paris sought to checkmate Ho by reestablishing in Vietnam the playboy Emperor Bao Dai in June, 1949, and by setting up in 1950 other puppet monarchies in Cambodia and Laos, all recognized by the USA on February 7, 1950, but bitterly resented and resisted by most native nationalists regardless of their attitude toward the Stalinist ideology of Comrade Ho.

A French-controlled Vietnamese national army took form slowly because of French fears that it would strengthen demands within the Bao Dai regime for full independence. In mid-century 150,000 French troops, maintained at a cost of a billion dollars a year and supported by U.S. subventions and U.S. guns, tanks, planes, and bombs to the amount of a hundred thousand tons by 1952, were waging indecisive warfare against Ho's fighters. Most of those killed in the service of France were Algerians, Tunisians, Senegalese, and Foreign Legionnaires, but Jean Monnet declared in April, 1952, that "France has lost more officers than are graduated annually from her military academies." The French held the coast, Saigon, and, precariously, Hanoi and the Red River delta. The rebels held most of the countryside. Successive French Cabinets, unable or unwilling to recognize that the old colonialism could never be restored by violence, were unable to end or win the war. American policy-makers, terrified at the prospect of a Communist conquest of Indochina, had no choice but to support French colonialists and their puppets. The Indochinese peasantry had no choice but to support Ho in holy war against white imperialism.

The denouement of 1954 was dramatic. With aid from China in weapons and other supplies, Ho's fighters succeeded in occupying the entire hinterland of Tonkin, leaving the French hemmed in around the delta of the Red River. In desperation, French paratroopers were landed at Dienbienphu in a remote western valley in the hope that they might somehow be able to smash, or at least counteract, enemy guerrillas. They found themselves instead closely besieged by General Giap's Vietminh troops who gradually pressed the defenders into an ever smaller circle and finally, after two months, stormed the stronghold and captured its entire garrison of 15,000 men on May 7, 1954. During the siege Paris appealed to Washington for aid. Washington proposed joint military intervention to London, which refused to participate. Admiral Radford urged unilateral American action, amid talk of using atomic weapons. Eisenhower finally opted for a peace of compromise as preferable to the hazards of enlarging a war already lost.

Meanwhile on April 26 at Geneva the largest and longest international conference of 1954 (see p. 200) had met in the old League Palace under the chairmanship of Prince Wan Waithayakon, Foreign Minister of Thailand, in an attempt to enable the assembled Foreign Ministers of the USA, USSR, Britain, France, China, North Korea, South Korea, North Vietnam, South Vietnam, Laos, Cambodia, et al. to try their hands at bringing order out of chaos. Bidault was authorized to seek peace. The Vietminh armies were now capable in time of taking all of Indochina. But Chou En-lai and Molotov urged moderation on Ho Chi Minh. The fall of the Laniel Cabinet on June 12 on a vote of confidence in its Indochina policy brought to the Premiership and the Quai d'Orsay Pierre Mendès-France who pledged peace by July 20 or "my government will hand in its resignation." He conferred with Chou En-lai in Bern on June 23 and went to Geneva on July 10.

The Geneva Conference closed July 21, 1954, with the signature of an armistice. Indochina was partitioned at 17°. The new nationalism here effected no national unification, thanks to the stalemate of the Super-Powers in the global game of politics and the division of native nationalists between pro-Communist followers of Ho Chi Minh in Hanoi and anti-Communist followers of Roman Catholic Ngo Dinh Diem in Saigon. But the vanquished French abandoned North Vietnam and its 14,000,000 people—among whom Ho consolidated his "Democratic Republic" via land reform, systematic indoctrination, and material aid from China and the USSR—and soon abandoned South Vietnam as well, with its 11,000,000 people, and conceded the full independence of Vietnam, Laos, and Cambodia.

A national election for unification, scheduled at Geneva for July, 1956, never took place because of Diem's refusal to have any dealings with the Communists. (He had refused to sign the Geneva accord.) The prospects of his regime were dismal in view of French obstructionism, the rebellions of bandit groups known as Binh Xuyen, Cao Dai, and Hoa Hoa, and the corruption and indolence of Bao Dai. But with U.S. encouragement and material support, Ngo Dinh Diem succeeded in restoring order, ousting Bao Dai in 1955, making himself President and Chief of State in the new Republic, and concocting a quasi-democratic, quasi-authoritarian Constitution in 1956. While South Vietnam became, in effect, a U.S. protectorate, the independent anti-Communist governments of Laos and Cambodia chose a course of "neutralism."

MALAYA, long ruled by warring local sultans, passed under British control in 1909 and soon became the world's chief source of tin and natural rubber. So large was the influx of Chinese settlers and businessmen that by 1947 seven-ninths of Singapore's population of 938,000 were Chinese, while, on the mainland, Chinese numbered 1,900,000 to 2,400,000 Malays. Japanese conquest in 1942 shattered British prestige, but the ultimate victors were welcomed back in 1945. A British-protected Federation of nine States was proclaimed on Feb. 1, 1948. Communist terrorists, largely Chinese but tacitly aided by much of the Malay peasantry and operating effectively out of jungle strongholds, crippled rubber production on the plantations and made life miserable for those engaged in seeking to maintain law and order. As in Indochina, napalm bombs, the burning of villages, and the rounding up of suspects in concentration camps were all of no avail in ending the war. On Oct. 6, 1951,

INDIA
Imphal

E. PAK.

Mandalay

BURMA

Akyab

Irrawaddy R.

Sittang R.

Salween R.

Prome

Bay of
Bengal

Rangoon

Moulmein

Mouths of the
Irrawaddy R.

THAILAND

Andaman

Andaman Is.

Sea

ISTHMUS OF KRA

Nicobar Is.

SOUTHEAST ASIA

SCALE MILES
0   100   200

CHINA

Cao Bang
TONKIN
Dien Bien Phu
Hanoi   Haiphong
Nam Dinh   Gulf of Tonkin
Luang Prabang   Ninh Binh
NORTH VIET
NAM   HAINAN
Vinh

LAOS

Vientiane

Partition Line
July 22, 1954

Hue

Ubon

Surin

ANNAM

Mekong R.

SOUTH

Binh Dinh

VIET

Bangkok   Poipet

Battambang

CAMBODIA

NAM

Phnom Penh

Kampot   Saigon

COCHIN CHINA

Gulf of Siam

Long Xuyen

Mouths of the
Mekong R.

Surat Thani

Songkhla

South

China

Sea

Malacca Strait

PERLIS

KEDAH

PENANG   Taiping

Kota Bharu

KELANTIN

TRENGGANU

MALAYAN

PERAK   Ipoh

SELANGOR

Kuala Lumpur

MALACCA

Malacca

PAHANG   FEDERATION

NEGRI-SEMBILAN

JOHORE

Johore Bharu

Singapore
(BR.)

SUMATRA

British High Commissioner Sir Henry Gurney was ambushed and slain near the capital, Kuala Lumpur. A U.S. mission in November, seeking lower tin prices, toured the mines in armored cars, with automatics kept handy. British property owners, when not murdered, still made fortunes from the rising price of rubber and tin under the impact of the global arms race. But 40,000 British troops were long unable to suppress the "bandits."

Despite jungle warfare, Communist intrigue and terrorism, and friction among Malays, Chinese, and Indians (each, respectively, comprising one-half, three-eighths, and one-eighth of the total population of 6,500,000—with the Malays Moslems, the Chinese Confucians or Buddhists, and the Indians Hindus or Moslems), Kuala Lumpur on Aug. 31, 1957, celebrated the independence of the Federation of Malaya as a self-governing Dominion of the British Commonwealth. Prime Minister Tengku Abdul Rahman indicated that the new State would abstain from membership in SEATO and steer clear of all military blocs. Whether sufficient internal unity could be achieved to make nationhood viable and effective remained to be seen. Singapore, with its Chinese majority, was excluded from the new Federation and remained a British Crown Colony. Meanwhile, Sir Abdul Rahman (no relation to the Prime Minister of the same name), ruler of Negri Sembilan, was elected King of Malaya for a five-year term by a conference of the nine Princes of the Federated States.

INDONESIA, granted independence by the reluctant Dutch on Dec. 27, 1949, after four years of warfare (see p. 238), displayed a picture of relative order, despite 80% illiteracy, mass poverty, and the highest concentration of population per square mile in the world on the central island of Java. The original federation of 16 states became a unitary government in 1950. President Achmed Sukarno and successive coalition cabinets were plagued by strikes, Communist terrorism, other local rebellions, and disaffections among the Chinese minorities. Jakarta claimed title to Western New Guinea (Irian), which the Netherlands refused to yield. The Republic of Indonesia accepted U.S. aid, but its foreign policy was well summarized by Sukarno on UN Day of 1951: "Our position is in the no-man's-land which lies between the opposing blocs, hoping thereby to act as a buffer between the antagonists."

Here, on a dozen large islands and hundreds of lesser isles scattered over the 3,000 miles of tropic seas between Malaya and Australia, live 82,000,000 people, comprising the most populous of Moslem States and the sixth most populous State of the contemporary State System after China, India, the USSR, the USA, and Japan. The internal politics and economics of Indonesia, its problems of foreign policy, and its probable future role in world affairs are therefore worthy of careful study, even though space is here lacking for a full inquiry.

Indonesia's first decade of independence was marked by a discouraging record of corruption, confusion, violence, and semi-anarchy in public affairs.

Outlying islanders, seeking local autonomy, keenly resented "Javanese imperialism." The tenuous Netherlands-Indonesian "Union" was dissolved in 1954 when The Hague resisted Indonesian attempts to modify the 1949 guarantees to Dutch property-owners. Jakarta in 1956 held the guarantees void. Party politics in what was designed to be a parliamentary democracy were chaotic. Nationalists and Masjumi (Moslems) alternated (1949–52) in control of the Cabinet. A pro-Western Masjumi Cabinet was voted out in 1952 for accepting U.S. aid under the Mutual Security Program, this decision being denounced by the Nationalists as a betrayal of "neutralism." A Nationalist Cabinet under Ali Sastroamidjojo, blessed by President Sukarno and dependent for parliamentary support on the Communists, championed neutrality and the annexation of Irian. Army opposition brought to power in 1955 another Masjumi Cabinet under anti-Communist Bernanuddin Harahap. In the parliamentary elections of Sept. 29, 1955, 80% of 60,000,000 eligible voters cast ballots for candidates of 20 parties. The Nationalists (with 8,434,-653 votes) balanced the Masjumi (7,903,886) with each winning 57 seats. The new Moslem Teachers Party won 6,955,141 and 45 seats. The Communists, with 6,176,914 votes, elected 39 deputies. President Sukarno favored Communist participation in the Cabinet. Both Moslem parties objected but agreed to enter a new coalition Cabinet with the Nationalists under Ali Sastroamidjojo, formed March 26, 1956.

By October, 1956, Sukarno was opining that the creation of political parties had been "a great mistake. . . . Let us dream away the existence of so many parties." To the new Constituent Assembly he said in November: "We cannot copy the liberal democracy of the West; neither can we import the concept of dictatorship from another range of ideas. . . . For the time being our democracy must be a guided democracy." Vice President Mohammed Hatta resigned in protest. In the face of widespread Army revolts in outlying islands, Ali's cabinet left office on March 14, 1957, while President Sukarno proclaimed martial law, appealed for unity, and asked Nationalist leader Suwirjo to form a new cabinet. When he failed, Sukarno, on April 8, 1957, named economist Djuanda as head of an extra-parliamentary Cabinet of "experts." Communists cheered. Masjumi and other critics questioned the constitutionality of this procedure. Djuanda pledged responsibility to Parliament. In June Sukarno appointed his controversial "National Council" to "advise" the Cabinet. A fourth of its members were Communist sympathizers. Local rebellions in Sumatra, Borneo, and the Celebes continued against central rule.

Although Indonesians were skillful during their first decade of independence in surmounting all crises, their political disunity threatened civil war early in 1958. Sukarno's regime strove to promote internal unity by an intensive anti-Dutch campaign for annexation of Irian, to the tune of expropriations and expulsions of Dutch nationals in Indonesia. Sukarno departed in January on a "vacation" tour abroad. In his absence, anti-Communist military leaders in

Sumatra issued a five-day "ultimatum" to Jakarta, demanding the resignation of the Djuanda Cabinet. When the demand was ignored, the Sumatra rebels set up a rival "government," headed by Sjafruddin Prawiranegara (Feb. 15, 1958). Sukarno returned from Japan, ordered the arrest of the members of the rebel regime for "treason," and appealed for unity "with the help of God" in solving the "manifold problems" of the new republic.

Whether these evidences of disunion were merely the "growing pains" of a vigorous Indonesian democracy or signalized fatal schisms in the body politic was unclear a decade after independence. The emotional, intellectual, and civic foundations of a workable Indonesian nationalism were still in process of construction and perhaps could not attain solidity without a return to federalism. Meanwhile, most Indonesians were at least agreed that they should look with suspicion on the USA and the European colonial powers, learn what they could from Red China and the USSR, and pursue an undeviating course of "neutralism" in world politics.

*   *   *   *   *

The story of the new nationalisms, here briefly recounted, is too recent and too tentative to permit of any definitive conclusions regarding consequences for the new local patriots or for the larger fortunes of mankind. Insofar as these fumbling aspirations toward self-rule on the part of peoples hitherto governed by "colonial imperialists" represent an effective quest for "freedom" and "self-determination," they constitute an endeavor deemed praiseworthy in public utterance (often with tongue in cheek) by all Communists and by most erstwhile Western "colonialists." Insofar as they represent, as unquestionably they do, an aggravation of international anarchy through the constant multiplication of the number of independent sovereignties in a World Community still lacking World Government, they constitute future sources of disorder and violence in human affairs.

While we suspend judgment, waiting for the evidence of events to come, it may be well to recall a common view among the literati of the West, and also of Asia and Africa, which holds that nationalism itself in all its forms is a "false religion" which, on balance, is productive of more harm than good— even though, obviously, no true nationalists anywhere can be expected to share this view.

Since the view in question has been most eloquently expressed, most elaborately documented, and most persuasively argued by the Western world's greatest living philosopher of history, sample quotations from his voluminous writings will serve to make the point. Arnold J. Toynbee in his *Study of History*, Volume IX, pp. 441–442, observes:

In studying the breakdowns of civilizations, we found that the cause was, in every case, some failure of self-determination, and that, when human beings thus lost control over their own destinies, this social disaster usually turned out to have been the consequence of a moral aberration. A broken-down society, community, or individual would prove to have forfeited a salutary freedom of choice through having fallen into bondage to some idol of its own making. Midway through the twentieth century of the Christian Era the Western Society was manifestly given over to the worship of a number of idols that had been the bane of other civilizations in the past; but, among these, one stood out above all the rest, and this was the cult of the institution of Parochial Sovereignty embodied in parochial states that were being worshipped by their respective subjects as very gods and that were demonstrating their demonic power over their devotees by exacting from them human sacrifices of ever greater enormity in cycles of fratricidal wars of a violence that was increasing in a geometrical progression.

This grimly prominent feature of post-Modern Western Life was a terrifying portent on two accounts: first because this idolization of belligerent parochial sovereign states was the true, though unavowed, religion of a great majority of the inhabitants of the Westernizing World of the day and, secondly, because this false and maleficent religion had been the death of no less than fourteen civilizations for certain, and perhaps of no less than sixteen, out of the twenty-one civilizations that had come into existence during the currency of this species of Society up to date.

Fratricidal warfare of ever increasing violence between parochial sovereign states had been by far the commonest cause of mortality among civilizations of all three generations.

In an earlier passage of the *Study* (Volume VII, p. 510), Toynbee, in a more religious mood, sees all nationalism as a barrier to the brotherhood of man:

The truth is that the unity of Mankind cannot be achieved either by stitching together local communities into a pantheon of tribal deities presiding over a terrestrial conglomeration of parochial states, on the pattern of Cyrus's 'Kingdom of the Lands,' or by purging Society of its primitive divine participants and making Humanity itself the Absolute, as had been attempted by Humanists of a Modern Western school. In another context we have already taken note of the paradoxical but profound truth that the most likely way to reach a goal is to be aiming not at that goal itself but at some more ambitious goal beyond it. The unity of Mankind can be achieved only as an incidental result of acting on a belief in the unity of God, and by seeing this unitary terrestrial society *sub specie aeternitatis* as a province of a Commonwealth of God which must be singular, not plural, *ex hypothesi.*

This is the necessary condition because, without a harmony of wills, Society cannot maintain itself even on the most narrowly restricted tribal range, not to speak of its becoming world-wide, and the only society in which there can be a harmony of wills is one in which two or three—or two or three thousand million— are gathered together in God's name with God Himself in the midst of them. In a society including the One True God as well as His human creatures, God plays a unique part. He is a party to the relation between each human member and Himself; but in virtue of this He is also a party to the relation between each human member and every other human member, and through this participation of God, breathing His own divine love into human souls, human wills can be reconciled.

Be it noted, lest even the best of us be beguiled into the fallacy of imputing infallibility to an eloquent disciple of universalism, that Toynbee himself has stumbled in overstating his case. All nationalism, he argues, is evil. The Jews

long ago, he contends, renounced nationalism and all secular political ambitions in favor of a quest for spiritual vision and moral righteousness. Therefore—since Jews should know better while ignorant Gentiles have no insight
into the eternal verities—Zionism or neo-Judaic nationalism is the most repre-
hensible of all nationalisms and is a base betrayal of the highest values of
Judaism. From this it follows in Toynbee's strange logic that the crimes of
unenlightened Nazis against the Jews—namely, the planned and systematic
extermination of six million human beings—are somehow less monstrous than
alleged Zionist "crime" against the Palestinian Arabs, of whom some hundreds
died by violence and three-quarters of a million fled, or were expelled, from
Palestine during the Arab-Israeli War of 1948–49. So determined is Toynbee
to "prove" his anti-Zionist case that he distorts the facts of this tragic episode
and thus comes close to discrediting his entire argument.[19]

Quite apart from such manifestations of fanatical detestation of fanaticism,
it is probable that future generations of mankind (if mankind survives its
own brutalities and irrationalities) may well regard the Afro-Asian imitations
of Western nationalism in the middle years of the 20th Century as deplorable
rather than salutary. In a World Community which is One World, all efforts
to cultivate the worship of tribal gods spell failure, frustration, and potential
disaster. But the people of the West have no moral or rational basis for
criticizing Asian or African imitations of their own folly, since they inaugurated the folly and used it for centuries as a rationalization for the conquest
and exploitation of hundreds of millions of subject peoples. Those coerced
into servitude are scarcely to be blamed if they ultimately copy the ways of
their masters.

The people of the new nations of our time in the regions we have traversed
will either find ways and means of converting nationalism into a creative
faith, conducive to human welfare, or will use its symbols and values to foster
hatred and conflict among human groups. In this respect the "problem" of
nationalism is no different in Asia and Africa than in Europe and America.
The choice here posed is common to all mankind. What choice men make
will determine whether the human race will realize its human potentialities
or descend once more into barbarism and savagery. The choice may likewise
determine quite conceivably whether the species itself will live or die. Despite
confusions, discouragements, and dangers, it seemed probable at the dawn
of the 1960's that the option chosen might be for life rather than death. If
so, the new nationalisms may yet be welcomed as harbingers of a new era of
freedom.

[19] See George Kirk, *Survey of International Affairs: The Middle East, 1945–1950,* edited
by Arnold J. Toynbee, The Royal Institute of International Affairs (Chatham House),
London, Oxford, 1951; Marie Syrkin, "Mr. Toynbee and the Jews," in *Jewish Frontier,*
December, 1954; Maurice Samuel, *The Professor and the Fossil,* New York, Knopf,
1956; and the author's article, "Toynbee and Zionism," in *Hadassah Newsletter,* February,
1955, reprinted in *Land Reborn,* February–March, 1955.

THE MAKING OF NATIONS

SUGGESTED READINGS

Adorno, T. W., and Others: *The Authoritarian Personality*, New York, Harper, 1950.
Barghoorn, Frederick C.: *Soviet Russian Nationalism*, New York, Oxford, 1956.
Benedict, Ruth: *Race: Science and Politics*, New York, Modern Age, 1940.
Biddle, Francis: *The Fear of Freedom*, New York, Doubleday, 1951.
Bidwell, Percy W.: *What the Tariff Means to American Industries*, New York, Harper, 1956.
Bolitho, Hector: *Jinnah: Creator of Pakistan*, New York, Macmillan, 1955.
Brown, Delmer M.: *Nationalism in Japan*, Berkeley, Calif., University of California Press, 1955.
Cassel, G.: *The Downfall of the Gold Standard*, New York, Oxford, 1936.
Chadwick, H. Munro: *The Nationalities of Europe and the Growth of National Ideologies*, New York, Macmillan, 1945.
Chalmers, Henry: *World Trade Policies*, Berkeley, Calif., University of California Press, 1953.
Claude, Inis L., Jr.: *National Minorities: An International Problem,* Cambridge, Mass., Harvard University Press, 1955.
Cobban, Alfred: *National Self-Determination*, New York, Oxford, 1945.
Condliffe, J. B.: *The Commerce of Nations*, New York, Norton, 1950.
Coupland, R.: *The Cripps Mission*, New York, Oxford, 1943.
Deutsch, Karl W.: *Nationalism and Social Communication*, New York, Wiley, 1953.
Einzig, Paul: *World Finance, 1914–1935*, New York, Macmillan, 1935.
Ellis, Howard S.: *Economics of Freedom: The Progress and Future of Aid to Europe*, New York, Harper, 1950.
Ellsworth, P. T.: *The International Economy*, New York, Macmillan, 1950.
Fall, Bernard B.: *The Vietminh Regime: Government and Administration in the Democratic Republic of Vietnam*, Ithaca, N.Y., Dept. of Far Eastern Studies, Cornell University (issued jointly with the Institute of Pacific Relations), 1954.
Ford, Alan W.: *The Anglo-Iranian Oil Dispute of 1951–1952*, Berkeley, Calif., University of California Press, 1954.
Grodzins, Morton: *The Loyal and the Disloyal: Social Boundaries of Patriotism and Treason*, Chicago, University of Chicago Press, 1956.
Hammer, Ellen J.: *The Struggle for Indochina*, Stanford, Calif., Stanford University Press, 1954.
Handlin, Oscar: *Race and Nationality in American Life*, Boston, Atlantic–Little, Brown, 1956.
Hayes, C. J. H.: *The Historical Evolution of Modern Nationalism*, New York, Richard R. Smith, 1931.
Heilperin, Michael A.: *The Trade of Nations*, New York, Knopf, 1947.
Hertz, Frederick: *Nationality in History and Politics*, New York, Oxford, 1944.
Hexner, Ervin: *International Cartels*, Chapel Hill, N.C., University of North Carolina Press, 1945.
Higham, John: *Strangers in the Land: Patterns of American Nativism, 1860–1925*, New Brunswick, N.J., Rutgers University Press, 1955.
Hodgkin, Thomas: *Nationalism in Colonial Africa*, London, Muller, 1956.
Hodgson, J. G. (ed.): *Economic Nationalism*, New York, Richard R. Smith, 1931.
Janowsky, Oscar I.: *Nationalities and National Minorities*, New York, Macmillan, 1946.
Jennings, Sir Ivor: *Constitutional Problems in Pakistan*, New York, Cambridge, 1957.
Kahin, George McTurnan: *Nationalism and Revolution in Indonesia*, Ithaca, N.Y., Cornell University Press, 1952.
Karunakaran, K. P.: *India in World Affairs, August, 1947–January, 1950*, New York, Oxford, 1953.
Kindleberger, Charles P.: *The Terms of Trade: A European Case Study*, New York, Wiley, 1956.

SUGGESTED READINGS

Kohn, Hans: *The Idea of Nationalism: A Study of Its Origins and Background,* New York, Macmillan, 1945.

———: *Nationalism: Its Meaning and History,* Princeton, N.J., Van Nostrand, 1956.

———: *Making of the Modern French Mind,* Princeton, N.J., Van Nostrand, 1956.

———: *American Nationalism: An Interpretative Essay,* New York, Macmillan, 1957.

Landau, Rom: *Moroccan Drama,* 1900–1955, San Francisco, American Academy of Asian Studies, 1956.

Lawrence, T. E.: *Seven Pillars of Wisdom,* New York, Doubleday, 1935.

Loucks, William N., and J. Weldon Hoot: *Comparative Economic Systems: Capitalism, Socialism, Communism, Fascism, Cooperation,* New York, Harper, 1952.

Lumby, E. W. R.: *The Transfer of Power in India,* 1945–7, New York, Praeger, 1954.

Mason, Edward S.: *Controlling World Trade: Cartels and Commodity Agreements,* New York, McGraw-Hill, 1946.

Meade, J. E.: *The Balance of Payments,* New York, Oxford, 1951.

———: *The Theory of International Economic Policy.* Vol. 2: *Trade and Welfare,* New York, Oxford, 1955.

Mitchell, Kate L.: *India without Fable,* New York, Knopf, 1942.

Myrdal, Gunnar: *An American Dilemma,* New York, Harper, 1947.

———: *An International Economy,* New York, Harper, 1956.

Playne, Carolyn E.: *The Neuroses of the Nations,* New York, Boni, 1925.

Sachar, Abram Leon: *Sufferance Is the Badge,* New York, Knopf, 1940.

Schattschneider, E. E.: *Politics, Pressures, and the Tariff,* Englewood Cliffs, N.J., Prentice-Hall, 1956.

Schiller, A. Arthur: *The Formation of Federal Indonesia,* 1945–1949, The Hague, Van Hoeve, 1955.

Schumpeter, Joseph A.: *Capitalism, Socialism and Democracy* (3d ed.), New York, Harper, 1950.

Shafer, Boyd C.: *Nationalism: Myth and Reality,* New York, Harcourt, Brace, 1955.

Snyder, Louis L.: *The Meaning of Nationalism,* New Brunswick, N.J., Rutgers University Press, 1954.

———: *German Nationalism: The Tragedy of a People,* Harrisburg, Pa., Stackpole, 1955.

Snyder, Richard Carlton: *The Most-Favored-Nation Clause,* New York, King's Crown Press, 1948.

Staley, Eugene: *World Economy in Transition,* New York, Council on Foreign Relations, 1939.

Stevens, Edmund: *North African Powder Keg,* New York, Coward-McCann, 1955.

Towle, Lawrence W.: *International Trade and Commercial Policy,* New York, Harper, 1947.

Villard, Henry Serrano: *Libya: The New Arab Kingdom of North Africa,* Ithaca, N.Y., Cornell University Press, 1956.

Wambaugh, Sarah: *Plebiscites since the World War,* New York, Carnegie Endowment, 1933.

Wertheim, W. F.: *Indonesian Society in Transition,* The Hague, Van Hoeve, 1956.

Woodman, Dorothy: *The Republic of Indonesia,* New York, Philosophical Library, 1956.

Woytinsky, W. S., and E. S. Woytinsky: *World Commerce and Governments: Trends and Outlook,* New York, Twentieth Century Fund, 1955.

AN ADDENDA ON THE ANATOMY OF ANARCHY

A CASE STUDY

SUEZ, SATELLITE, AND SINAI, 1956–58

> The world is a stupendous machine, composed of innumerable parts, each of
> which being a free agent, has a volition and action of its own; and on this
> ground arises the difficulty of assuring success in any enterprise depending on
> the volition of numerous agents. We may set the machine in motion, and dispose
> every wheel to one certain end; but when it depends on the volition of any one
> wheel, and the correspondent action of every wheel, the result is uncertain.—
> NICCOLÒ MACHIAVELLI, *On Fortune, Chance. . . .*

1. COMMENT ON METHOD

WHETHER any science of international politics is possible is in part'
a semantic question and therefore in part an unreal question. For
words at best are distorting symbols of human experience and never
the equivalents of the experience itself. The semantic question hinges on our
definition of "science." If the term means merely a systematic ordering of
knowledge (*i.e.*, of representations of things seen, heard, felt, or believed—
often by others remote in time or space whose experience is transmitted to us
through writing), then every well-ordered scholarly discipline is a "science,"
including international politics. But Science means more than this in the
"modern" period of Western civilization. It involves a successful search for
uniformities, repetitions, or cycles in the phenomena under study rather than
concern for unique facts and nonrecurring events; the formulation of ex-
planatory hypotheses regarding causal relationships; the constant testing of
such hypotheses through observation and experiment with a view toward
their validation, invalidation, or correction; and the practical application of
verified hypotheses for purposes of controlling and/or predicting the sundry
components of our environment.

The first steps in this sequence were taken long ago by the ancient Egyptians, Greeks, Indians, and Chinese, though none among them went very
far with the later steps. Only the practitioners of the "modern science" of
the West have found ways and means of completing the sequence and therewith giving to contemporary mankind a measure of mastery over the ma-

396

terial universe far beyond the dreams of the alchemists and astrologers of old. The sequence itself may fairly be deemed the conceptual framework within which astronomers, geologists, physicists, chemists, and biologists have wrought their wonders. Accuracy of prediction, as in cosmology and meteorology, often admits of no "control," since man cannot yet command the weather or the movements of heavenly bodies. A maximum degree of control, as in the physical sciences, often goes along with a minimum capacity for prediction in any given instance, with forecasts based only on statistical averages. Yet it is reasonable to say that Science, as we now know it, is basically a business of discovering repetitive patterns among phenomena for purposes of prediction and control.

How can the method of science be applied to international relations or to human relations in general? Can "political science" and the other "social sciences" be made worthy of their names? The quest may be vain, albeit vigorously pursued by many investigators. Those who study nonhuman Nature can usually conduct "controlled experiments" in laboratories. Even when they cannot, they can and do make mathematically precise observations. Social scientists can conduct experiments only rarely and within narrow limits. Their efforts at quantification are always provisional and conditional. When Man studies Nature, moreover, he studies things outside of himself. When Man studies Man, the objects of his study are willy-nilly inside himself. Self-knowledge is ever the most difficult and elusive sort of knowledge to come by.

Chemists, physicists, and, occasionally, biologists, furthermore, can reduce the results of years of observation and experiment to concise equations which can be tested, verified, and used by their colleagues. Despite the valiant efforts of some economists and sociologists and political scientists, and even some students of international relations, social scientists are usually unable to imitate this procedure effectively. No mathematically exact "science" of world politics has yet emerged in any form admitting of accurate prediction or adequate control of the phenomena under observation. The same is true of other "humanistic" studies.

Perhaps we should not wish it otherwise, despite our quest for "scientific truth" in all areas of inquiry. We like to believe, and indeed for all practical purposes we must believe, that men and statesmen are in some sense "free" to make choices among available alternatives. To the extent to which this is so, no exact science of Man is possible. The impossible would be possible only if human beings were robots. But robots would lack the simian curiosity which has led us to science. Despite their vanity, men are not "masters of their souls and captains of their fate." But neither are they similar to electrons, atoms, molecules, or single living cells which lack volition or choice and behave as they do by virtue of mechanistically determined and mathematically determinable properties inherent in their natures.

We must conclude that no science of international politics is possible in terms comparable to the stocks in trade of the physical and biological scientists and of the mathematicians. Such a science is feasible only in the more limited sense of taking cognizance of recurring patterns in the inter-relationships among sovereignties and of generalizing about the uniformities—with limited prospects of "prediction" and little possibility of "control." This is what Machiavelli sought to do four centuries ago. Few, if any, have improved upon his effort. Effective statesmanship involves the capacity to recognize the nature of available choices; to practice the art of the possible; to avoid illusion and self-deception; to forecast the acts of others; and to choose attainable ends and devise workable means toward their attainment. Sound scholarship in world affairs requires similar talents, even though the scholar, unless he becomes statesman, is observer rather than actor.

In our time abstractions about "power politics," "imperialism," and "nationalism" throw little light on what statesmen and citizens believe and do in concrete situations even though these generalizations in fact represent recurring uniformities of political behavior in the Western State System. If our purpose is to understand why and how people act as they do in *Weltpolitik,* then one concrete case is worth a thousand generalities. If adequately analyzed, any such case would serve. Cases of "crises" are most illuminating, given the persistent predisposition of men to violence in international relations.

Among available crises, the images of 1914 and 1939 come at once to mind along with the vicissitudes of the Cold War following upon World War II in anticipation of World War III. Each of these crises has given rise to immense libraries of books, monographs, articles, and documentations, all of which must be perused by anyone seriously interested in how and why decision-makers did what they did in each situation. The same is true (since social scientists and diplomatic historians have as yet devised no mathematical "shorthand" to record their findings) of the crisis about to be offered as an illustration of the complex inter-relationships among national power-holders, variously and ambivalently motivated by the directives of international law, international organization, power politics, imperialism, and nationalism.

Each of these words, let us never forget, is but a label for a particular configuration of hopes, fears, loves, hates, ambitions, and expectations, in the heads and hearts of human beings—each moved to attitudes and deeds by his beliefs and loyalties but each, even the humblest, having some degree of freedom of choice and action. Such freedom is strictly limited even for the policy-makers of "Great Powers" or "Super-Powers," as we have repeatedly seen, and shall see again. Not even the most formidable and fully sovereign of Powers is free to do what it likes, despite the anarchic nature of the game of power. Acts beget counter-acts and always have consequences. Results seldom conform to expectations. Such conformity was at a minimum in the sequence of decisions about to be considered.

The crisis here to be discussed has to do with the Israeli-Anglo-French attack on Egypt in the autumn of 1956, the simultaneous Russian suppression of the Hungarian Revolution, and the immediate sequel of both events. In years to come new mountains of documentation will inevitably throw further light on these matters and make possible some approximation of the "inside story" of policy-making in full and rich detail. The present account, like most accounts of most international events, is therefore tentative, with "ultimate truth" far in the future and perhaps never attainable. Such a provisional account, based upon what was known within a year after the events in question, may nevertheless illuminate the ways in which contemporary citizens, diplomats, and strategists respond to the dangers, challenges, and opportunities of our Time of Troubles—which, unhappily, promises to be of long duration.

2. TWO WATERWAYS

The River Danube (which, despite Johann Strauss, is not blue but brown) rises in the Black Forest and empties into the Black Sea 1,750 miles from its source. Next to the Volga, it is the longest and broadest river of Europe, draining an area of over 300,000 square miles. On its banks men built long ago the famous German cities of Ulm, Ingolstadt, Regensburg, Passau, and Linz; the Slovak city of Bratislava (Pressburg); the great capitals of Vienna, Budapest, and Belgrade; and sundry Jugoslav, Bulgarian, and Rumanian towns along its lower reaches. In the mid-Danube plain the Magyar or Hungarian migrants from the steppe road out of Asia settled a thousand years ago.

The Suez Canal is a man-made channel, 101 miles long, 300 to 500 feet wide, and 46 feet deep as dredged and broadened in recent years, extending from Port Said and Port Fuad on the Mediterranean by way of Ismailia, Lake Timso, and the Bitter Lakes to Suez and Port Tewfik on the Red Sea. On Nov. 30, 1854, Ferdinand de Lesseps, a French diplomat, obtained from his friend, Said Pasha, Khedive or Viceroy of Egypt and a suzerain of the Ottoman Sultan, a concession authorizing him to found the "Universal Company of the Maritime Canal of Suez" for the purpose of constructing a ship channel across the isthmus. A second agreement of Jan. 5, 1856, specified that the concession was to last for 99 years from the opening of the canal, after which the waterway would become the property of the Egyptian Government. Although De Lesseps did not secure the Sultan's assent until 1866, he began selling shares in the company in 1858 to the amount of 400,000 shares of 500 francs each, more than half of which were purchased by Frenchmen.

Digging began in April, 1859. In 1863 Khedive Ismail, supported by the Sultan, demanded that the Company cease employing forced labor and restore the lands outside the Canal Zone granted to it in 1856. The dispute was submitted to the arbitration of Napoleon III. His award of July, 1864, granted the Company an indemnity of 84,000,000 francs for complying with these demands. In November, 1869, the Canal was formally opened with the Empress Eugénie on board the first vessel to make the transit. The first performance of Verdi's "Aïda" in Cairo in December, 1871, was a slightly belated celebration of the occasion.[1]

The Danube has never been permanently under the control of a single sovereignty since the demise of the Roman Empire. Its valley was a major route of the Ottoman invasions of Europe in 1529 and 1683, both halted at the gates of Vienna. Most of the waterway in the late 19th Century was within the territory of the Dual Monarchy of Austria-Hungary, although traffic through the delta was regulated by the European Commission of the Danube, comprising eight States and established by the Treaty of Paris of 1856. By the Treaty of Versailles of 1919, the Commission was limited to Britain, France, Italy, and Rumania. A convention of 1921 declared the Danube open from Ulm to the Black Sea to vessels of all States, with a new international commission, including the members of the previous one plus all the riparian States, administering the watercourse.

The Suez Canal was from the outset entirely within Egyptian territory, but as an international waterway built and owned by an international company it was also subject to international regulation and administration by agreement with Egypt and Turkey. By the terms of the Suez Canal Convention signed at Constantinople, Oct. 29, 1888, by agents of Britain, France, Spain, Italy, Germany, Austria-Hungary, Russia, the Netherlands, and Turkey, the Canal was "always to be free and open, in time of war as in time of peace, to every vessel of commerce or of war, without distinction of flag" (Art. I) —an obligation honored more in the breach than in the observance by Britain in World Wars I and II vis-à-vis the Central Powers and by Egypt vis-à-vis Israel after 1948 by the device of intercepting "enemy" ships approaching the Canal before they could enter the waterway. By Article X, which even the most subtle of lawyers would have difficulty in reconciling with Article I, this obligation "shall not interfere with the measures which" the Khedive or Sultan "might find it necessary to take for securing by their own forces the defense of Egypt and the maintenance of public order." Yet such measures, said Article XI, were not to interfere with freedom of transit.

Since nothing is permanent in human affairs except change, it is not astonishing that control of the Danube and of the Suez Canal passed through sundry vicissitudes in the course of a century. Khedive Ismail, facing bankruptcy, sold his shares in the Canal Company, then constituting 44% of all shares, to the British Government in 1875, when Benjamin Disraeli perceived that the profits and power to be derived from a shrewd imperial bargain were

---

[1] The allegation of official Egyptian propagandists in 1956 that 120,000 forced workers died during the construction of the Canal would appear to be a daring transposition of the statement of Herodotus that 120,000 workers died in the construction of another canal, never completed but begun by the Pharaoh Necho in 609 B.C.

too tempting to be scorned. The Sultan ousted Ismail as being of "unsound mind," but too late. Egypt's European creditors in effect took over the government of the country in 1876, thereby provoking a revolt suppressed by British arms in 1882. This "temporary" British occupation of Egypt lasted until 1922 when Cairo achieved independence. British control of the Canal, in various forms, was to endure until 1956.

As for the Danube, the whole course of the river passed under the brief control of power-holders in Berlin during World Wars I and II, thanks to Germanic conquests of Danubia and Balkania. In 1945, in the wake of the Nazi military debacle, all of the Danube as far north as Vienna was occupied by the Red Army or Communist partisans. The masters of the waterway were henceforth the men of Moscow who, between 1945 and 1948, negotiated new conventions with their new "allies" excluding the Western Powers, despite their protests, from any participation in the international commission. As for Hungary, Churchill and Stalin agreed in Moscow in October, 1944, that Britain and the USSR should share influence 50–50 in both Jugoslavia and the land of the Magyars. The Hungarian peace treaty signed in Paris, Feb. 10, 1947, was regarded in the West as an assurance of "independence," "sovereignty," and even "democracy" in Budapest. The Kremlin tolerated a semi-democratic coalition regime on the mid-Danube between 1945 and 1947. But with the advent of Cold War, Muscovite Communists forced Premier Ferenc Nagy into exile in May, 1947, jailed or shot many anti-Communist leaders, and made Matyas Rakosi Stalin's "boss" in Budapest. He was a Soviet citizen and long a Magyar Communist in Muscovite exile.

What ensued is well known. Despite innumerable Western protests and UN resolutions, Josef Cardinal Mindszenty, accused of "treason," was sentenced to life imprisonment on Feb. 7, 1949. Rakosi's "Peoples Front" won 95.6% of the votes in the "election" (Soviet-style) of May 15, 1949, and, through a new Constitution, made Hungary a "Peoples Republic." In a drive against alleged "Titoists"—Stalin having broken with Tito in June, 1948—Lazlo Raijk and sundry colleagues were expelled from the Party, tried as "imperialist spies" and "Trotskyite agents," and hanged on Oct. 15, 1949. Janos Kadar, another Cabinet member, was arrested, jailed, and tortured. Despite Stalin's decease in 1953, Hungary in 1956 remained a Stalinist totalitarian police-state whose rulers, because of their intolerance and their mismanaged efforts at collectivization and industrialization, were detested by large numbers of their subjects.

Politics in Egypt, while conducted in a wholly different context, were no less explosive. Here a new nationalism struggled obscurely for total emancipation from "colonialism" in a milieu in which property and power were monopolized by a feudal aristocracy of a few thousand wealthy land-owners ruling 20,000,000 subjects—mostly miserably poor fellahin, of whom 85% were illiterate, 40% had hookworm, and 90% had trachoma. Fat and fatuous

401

King Farouk owned 20,000,000 acres, collected millions of dollars annually from his estates, and had an estimated personal fortune of $580,000,000.

Egypt had agreed in a 20-year treaty of 1936 to British defense of the Suez Canal and joint dominion in the Sudan. Following the failure of earlier efforts to remove these humiliations, the Egyptian Parliament (dominated by great estate owners and nationalist politicians) abrogated the treaty in October, 1951, and rejected an invitation to participate in an Anglo-American-French-Turkish "Middle East Command" to defend the whole area against Communism. London, supported by Washington, reaffirmed its treaty rights and reinforced its Suez garrison—which fired upon Egyptian police and rioters in the "Battle of Ismailia" in mid-November. In late January, 1952, anti-British rioters in Cairo killed, burned, and looted in an orgy of violence which led King Farouk to dismiss Premier Mustafa Nahas Pasha, leader of the Wafd Party, and appoint Aly Maher Pasha—who was replaced on March 1 by Hilaili Pasha. He suspended Parliament, postponed elections, and resigned in late June in favor of Sirry Pasha. In July, 1952, Gen. Mohammed Naguib led an army *coup* and made himself military dictator, following the overthrow of the Cabinet and the exile of the King. Naguib's campaign against "corruption," his pleas for American aid, and his plans for "land reform" offered little hope of alleviating the lot of the peasantry or of imposing Egyptian demands on Britain. His suppression of all political parties (January, 1953) promised despotism tempered by anarchy. A treaty signed in Cairo, Feb. 12, 1953, provided for self-government, international supervision, and eventual self-determination for the Sudan, thus promising a partial solution of the Anglo-Egyptian quarrel.

Having abolished the monarchy and proclaimed himself President, Naguib, agent of a military junta led by Col. Gamal Abdel Nasser, was himself ousted from the Presidency in October, 1954, amid much political confusion, by Nasser and his fellow officers who established another dictatorship, vaguely committed to "democracy" and "social reform." Between January and June of 1956, Nasser promulgated a "republican" constitution and got himself unanimously elected President. The dynamism of the Nasser regime rested less upon anti-monarchism and anti-feudalism (both themes were popular among the miserable masses of all the Arab States) than upon grandiose dreams of pan-Arab or even pan-Islamic unity and power in the name of defying the West, denouncing "colonialism," embracing "neutralism," and vowing the destruction of Israel. Escaped Nazi war criminals and Soviet agents became Nasser's advisers. All were welcome who might further the anti-Israel, anti-British, and anti-"imperialist" orientation of a regime still representing the interests of the feudal aristocracy and thus constrained to deflect popular unrest with the *status quo* onto "foreign foes."

Meanwhile, policy-makers in London were persuaded, partly by American advice, to sign an accord in July, 1954, for the phased withdrawal over 20 months of the 80,000 British troops in the Canal Zone. The last contingents departed in mid-June of 1956. Weeks later Nasser "nationalized" the Canal, thus precipitating the crisis to come.

What was to follow is comprehensible only if we keep in mind the fact that the Suez Canal, unlike the Danube, is a major artery of world trade and indeed *the* major artery, through which, during the 1950's, tonnage of goods shipped was more than double the cargoes going through the Panama Canal. The Company, though officially registered as an Egyptian joint stock corporation, maintained its chief office in Paris. Receipts in 1955 were c. 35 billion francs, expenditures 18 billions, and profits over 16 billions, of which 11 billions (c. $39,000,000) went to shareholders. Most of the shares were held by the British Government and by French private investors. Revenues were largely derived from tolls on ships passing through the waterway, numbering on the average 40 a day in 1955–56. Total cargoes each year in recent years (30,000,000 tons in 1938 and 156,000,000 tons in 1955) comprised one-seventh of all cargoes in world-wide international trade.

By 1955 two-thirds of all cargoes consisted of oil or oil products moving from south to north from the fabulously rich and recently developed oil fields of Iran and Arabia to Britain, France, and other Western European countries. Other major cargoes for Western Europe included minerals from China, India, East Africa, and Australia, wheat and meat from Australia and New Zealand, and rubber from Malaya and Indonesia. North-south traffic included cement from Western Europe to East Africa, India, and Pakistan; fertilizers for China and Japan; and manufactures, machinery, and railway equipment for African and Asian markets. In 1955 the percentages of total national supply shipped through the Suez Canal were: for Britain, 56% of oil, 85% of rubber, 95% of jute, and 70% of wool; for France, for the same commodities, 47%, 76%, 97%, and 70%; and for the Netherlands, 63%, 62%, 91%, and 23%. The USA, conversely, acquired only 15% of its imported oil and only 10% of its imported wool through the Canal, and almost no rubber or jute. Soviet trade through the Canal was negligible.

In short, Suez had become the principal supply route of Western Europe for indispensable shipments of Mid-Eastern oil and other Asian and East African goods, without which Western European industry would stagnate and starve. The long and expensive alternative voyage around Africa for the 15,000 ships a year traversing the Canal would add half a billion annually to transport costs—a burden which the Western European economies could scarcely bear. "Economic determinism" is seldom a safe guide to human conduct or national policies. But it is well to note, in considering national decision-making in 1956–57, that freedom of transit through the Suez Canal was of no importance to the Soviet economy, of little importance to the Ameri-

—note

403

can economy, and of life or death importance to Britain, France, and most of Western Europe.[2]

3. A FAILURE OF STATESMANSHIP

National policy-makers usually act as they do in pursuit of the protection or promotion of what they conceive to be the "national interests" of their States. Altruism, self-sacrifice, and abnegation here play no such role as is often possible in interpersonal relations, for all statesmen by definition are answerable less to their consciences than to their constituents. They are thus bound to act, or at least to pretend to act, not in the service of private purposes but of public interests—which are commonly defined in our age in terms of the sovereign nation-state. Such definitions invariably involve disputes, conflicts, and clashes among the man-made monsters into which mankind is divided, for reasons already explored in previous pages and abundantly illustrated in pages to come.

How then, amid the confusions of 1956, did power-holders in various capitals envisage the "interests" they were sworn to protect and promote and how did they define the "stakes of diplomacy" in the game of power? Eisenhower and Dulles in Washington were dedicated, like their predecessors, to "anti-Communism"; earnestly concerned with "peace"; devoted to Anglo-French-American solidarity; sympathetic toward "anti-colonialism"; well disposed toward Israel; and inclined to "appease" Arab nationalism in the hope of protecting the huge investments of U.S. oil companies in the Mid East and America's strategic bomber bases in the Islamic lands. These ambivalences were paralleled in Moscow where the ruling oligarchs simultaneously strove for the global triumph of Communism; "peaceful coexistence" with the West; promotion of Asian and African anti-Western nationalism; and a non-Stalinist pattern of relations with Muscovy's European "satellites," particularly Poland and Hungary, where unrest was most obvious. Eden and Selwyn Lloyd in London, and Mollet and Pineau in Paris, sought solidarity with America, peace with Russia, defense of Anglo-French interests in the Mid East and Africa, and security against the more extreme form of Asian-African anti-colonialism. Ben-Gurion in Tel Aviv sought survival for Israel; a cessation of Arab boycotts, blockades, and murder raids; and a tolerable peace with Israel's neighbors. Nasser in Cairo strove for hegemony over the Arab world; the destruction of Israel; the liquidation of all vestiges of Western "impe-

---

[2] I am deeply indebted for much of the data here presented to one of my students in "Political Economy 20," Mr. Joel Robinson of the Williams College Class of 1957, for a superbly analytical study, unfortunately unpublished, of "The Economics and Politics of the Suez Canal." As regards Hungary and the USSR in 1956–57, a fuller account will be found in the author's *Russia Since 1917* (New York, Knopf, 1957), from which some paragraphs from pp. 461–470 are reproduced in the following two sections by permission of the publisher.

rialism"; and pan-Arab "neutralism" as between the USA and the USSR.

The catalogue need not be continued. It is enough to note that when national policy-makers are able to devise, each within their sovereign domain, a self-consistent program of policy, the problem of achieving without violence a viable accommodation of inevitably conflicting purposes is at best extraordinarily difficult. When national policy-makers pursue mutually contradictory purposes, among which they are unable to choose, the result is chaos.

Statesmanship in the relations among nations is the art of accommodating through compromise the divergent interests, expectations, and demands of rival sovereignties. Problems of power can be resolved only by bargaining or by force. In our time resort to force is almost invariably self-defeating. Yet bargaining is futile when the would-be bargainers regard all bargaining as immoral because they are fanatical disciples of faiths admitting of no compromise—whether Islam, Christianity, Zionism, nationalism, colonialism, anti-colonialism, Communism, anti-Communism, or what not. Thus the statesmanship of the 20th Century has repeatedly suffered bankruptcy and led to disaster.

The tragedies of these years, and of years past and years to come, could have been averted if the policy-makers of the Great Powers had been able to agree on some minimum definition of common purposes. Weak States must, willy-nilly, concur when strong States are in accord. But when the Powers are in discord, the mice will play while the cats are away, with consequences often dismal for cats and mice alike. An East-West accord regarding Eastern Europe, faintly foreshadowed by the top-level consultations of 1955, could have averted the tragedy of Hungary in 1956. An East-West accord regarding the Mid East could have averted the tragedy of Egypt and Israel in 1956 and thereafter. Statesmen in West and East alike were incapable of any such accommodation. Therefore thousands of human beings (happily not millions, as in the aftermath of the insolvency of statesmanship in 1914 and 1939) were condemned to die by violence in 1956–57. How and why this came to pass is our next concern.

*　　*　　*　　*　　*

The miscalculations of American policy-makers played a major role in the sequence of events to come. Having visited the Levant in the spring of 1953, Secretary Dulles sought to cultivate Arab favor by denying arms to Israel, acquiescing in the Egyptian blockade and the murder raids across the frontier from the Sinai Peninsula and the Gaza Strip, and pressing London to abandon its bases and garrisons in the Canal Zone. Although Moscow was relatively inactive in the area and without significant influence, Dulles was persuaded that here, as elsewhere, salvation from Communism was to be had through military alliances. On Nov. 22, 1955, envoys of Britain, Turkey, Iran, Iraq, and Pakistan signed the Baghdad Pact for mutual defense against aggression or subversion. Since all the Arab States save Iraq were committed to "neutralism," the USA declined to sign for fear of offending them, although Washington had initiated the policy of trying to arm and align all the Mid-East countries against the USSR.

Egypt and Syria in their counter-measures at once began cultivating Moscow and buying arms from the Soviet bloc. The Muscovites, unable to resist so tempting an opportunity to extend Communist power, championed Arab "independence," denounced Anglo-American-Israeli "imperialism," and boldly leapfrogged over the "northern tier" by sending Soviet weapons and missions to Damascus and Cairo. New possibilities loomed when young King Hussein of Jordan dismissed Lieut. Gen. John Bagot Glubb as Commander of the Arab Legion (March 2, 1956), insisted upon the withdrawal of all British troops and advisers, signed a military accord with Syria (May 31), and named pro-Nasser Suleiman Nabulsi as Premier (Oct. 29).

Much Mid-East diplomacy during the early months of 1956 revolved around Nasser's project of a High Aswan Dam, designed to increase Egypt's arable land area by 2,000,000 acres (25%) and thereby improve the miserably low living standards of the peasantry or at least prevent further impoverishment in view of an annual population increase of 350,000. The dam would require 15 years to complete and cost $1,300,000,000. Early in February Cairo came tentatively to terms with the International Bank for Reconstruction and Development for a loan of $200,000,000. In later negotiations Nasser claimed that he could secure funds for the dam from the USSR if the West declined to help. Thanks to mutual suspicions, and lack of imagination and initiative in both Washington and Moscow, no consideration was given to the possibility of joint American-Soviet aid to Egypt. In mid-April some thought was devoted in Washington to the desirability of enlisting Soviet cooperation, inside or outside the UN, to put an end to incessant bloody raids and reprisals along Israel's frontiers, but this opportunity was also lost—despite a Soviet proposal of April 17 for joint action to achieve Arab-Israeli peace. Dag Hammarskjold's efforts on the scene, culminating on April 19 in another Israeli-Egyptian cease-fire agreement, and subsequent debates and resolutions at the UN, effected no change in the fanatical determination of Arab nationalists to destroy Israel and the fanatical determination of the new Zion to survive and to retaliate for each act of Arab violence.

Between April and July, 1956, Nasser concluded military alliances with Yemen and Saudi Arabia; rejoiced that the Bulganin-Khrushchev visit to Britain eventuated in no meaningful Anglo-Soviet accord; continued to accumulate Soviet arms for the conquest of Israel; recognized Red China (May 15) to Dulles's "regret"; celebrated final British evacuation of the Canal Zone; received new Foreign Minister Shepilov in June and hinted at Soviet willingness (later denied in Moscow) to lend Egypt $1,200,000,000 for 20 years at 2% interest; sought to woo Iraq and Libya away from the West;

sent aid to anti-British terrorists on Cyprus and anti-French rebels in Algeria; and otherwise so conducted himself as to merit, at least in part, the French appellation of "the Hitler of the Nile." Premier Ben-Gurion warned of war and purchased planes from France. Premier Mollet (June 30) denounced Nasser's "megalomania." "He hopes to line up behind himself not only the Arab world, but the entire Moslem world. One would think oneself back in the Middle Ages. Today Pan-Islamism is a threat to peace."

Washington and London long remained complacent. Dulles continued to ban American arms to Israel and to ship American arms to Saudi Arabia. Both London and Washington jointly, from December, 1955, continued to dangle before Nasser an offer of an initial grant of $70,000,000 ($56,000,000 from the USA and $14,000,000 from Britain) in addition to the proposed $200,000,000 from the International Bank for the Aswan Dam. Not until July was the Anglo-American course reversed—for the strangest of motives and with the most astonishing of results. Shepilov had allegedly warned Nasser against war on Israel. U.S. Ambassador Henry A. Byeroade, transferred to South Africa and replaced by Raymond A. Hare, hinted in Cairo before his departure that Nasser's anti-Western policies might cause Washington to withdraw its offer of aid. Assistant Secretary of State George V. Allen, in Cairo on a special mission, was believed by Nasser to be the bearer of a "threatening" message. "If your emissary utters one word," declared the Egyptian President-Dictator, "I will kick him out of my office!"

On July 19, 1956, the State Department publicly declared, vis-à-vis the Aswan Dam, that

. . . developments within the succeeding seven months have not been favorable to the success of the project, and the U.S. Government has concluded that it is not feasible in present circumstances to participate in the project. Agreement by the riparian States (the Sudan and Ethiopia) has not been achieved, and the ability of Egypt to devote adequate resources to assure the project's success has become more uncertain than at the time the offer was made. This decision in no way reflects or involves any alteration in the friendly relations of the Government and people of the U.S. and the Government and people of Egypt. . . .

London and the International Bank followed suit. Nasser, returning from a State visit to Jugoslavia, thus found himself "slapped in the face" by the West. Shepilov now denied that the USSR had ever offered aid for the dam. The U.S. decision was evidently reached, as Senator Fulbright later alleged, by the Secretary of State and his advisers with no consultation with the President, the Cabinet, or the National Security Council.

The miscalculation behind this decision was first revealed in April, 1957, with the publication of a eulogistic semi-official biography of the Secretary of State by John R. Beal of *Time* Magazine:

For Dulles, a moment of cold-war climax had come. It was necessary to call Russia's hand in the game of economic competition. It was necessary to make the demonstration on a grand scale. Nasser combined the right timing, the right geography and the right order of magnitude for a truly major gambit in the cold war. Why did (Dulles) turn down Nasser so brutally, without a chance to save face? Since the issue involved more than simply denying Nasser money for a dam, a polite and concealed rebuff would fail to make the really important point. It had to be forthright, carrying its own built-in moral for neutrals in a way that the formula of applied propaganda would not cheapen. . . . As a calculated risk the decision was on a grand scale, comparable in the sphere of diplomacy to the calculated risks of war taken in Korea and Formosa. But his experience at sailing in diplomatic waters convinced him that the breeze would be better if he took a new and independent tack.

When questioned in press conferences about the accuracy of this version, Dulles neither affirmed nor denied it. If, in fact, the object of the decision was to "punish" an anti-Western "neutral" and embarrass Moscow, the result was the antithesis of the anticipation. Policy-makers in Washington and London had it within their power to make financial aid for the dam contingent upon moderation in Cairo and a cessation of fedayeen murder raids across the Israeli frontiers. Given the will, they could undoubtedly have negotiated a bargain with Moscow for joint aid to Egypt on conditions acceptable to all parties and conducive to peace and stability in the Mid East. Anti-Communism, which is often even more the Nemesis of our time than the evils of Communism itself, precluded any such rational arrangements. The Anglo-American decision was to lead inexorably to war, to a fateful disruption of Atlantic solidarity, to successful American efforts in November to rescue from disaster the Cairo dictator whom Washington had sought to discredit in July, and to a further vast enhancement of Soviet prestige and influence throughout the Mid East. The "moral" of the tale about to be told is, obviously and sadly, the old moral expressed to his son by Count Axel Oxenstierna (1583–1654), Chancellor of Sweden: *"Quintilla prudentia regitur orbis!—*With how little wisdom is the world ruled!"

Nasser's riposte to the Western rebuff was swift and startling. On July 26, 1956, he proclaimed the "nationalization" of the Suez Canal and the seizure of all the accessible assets of the Company, with compensation promised and with Egypt pledged (except as regards Israel) to abide by the Constantinople Convention of 1888. "They are punishing Egypt because it refused to side with military blocs. . . . The Americans have been stalling us for many years while promising aid all the time. . . . They were addressing themselves to the Egyptian people to overthrow me. I answer back: 'Let your hate choke you to death . . . Egypt will not yield to any foreign ultimatum.' " The Aswan Dam, he declared, would yet be built from the profits of the Canal. "The Suez Canal Company's annual income is $100,000,000. . . . We don't have to seek American or British aid for building the High Dam. We will build it ourselves and with our own money."

In what followed, Anglo-French policy-makers were determined to prevent

Nasser's exclusive control of a waterway indispensable to the economic life of Western Europe; American policy-makers were determined, by the mixed imperative of oil profits, strategic bases, and "legalistic-moralistic abstractions," to prevent any violence against Nasser; Israeli policy-makers were determined, in one of the few authentic instances of a "preventive war," to ensure Israel's survival; Egyptian policy-makers were determined to defy the West and destroy Israel; and Soviet policy-makers were determined to capitalize to the maximum from the crisis, after their own efforts to come to terms with the Western Powers on a common program were rejected.

London and Paris at once protested to Cairo against an "arbitrary action," constituting "a serious threat to the freedom of navigation on a waterway of vital international importance," "reserved all their rights," and declared that "responsibility for the consequences must rest entirely upon the Egyptian Government." In Paris the Cabinet favored immediate military occupation of the Canal Zone, provided Britain would join in the enterprise. On July 28 the British Treasury blocked all Egyptian accounts in the United Kingdom, the French Cabinet discussed plans for international control of the Canal, Washington sent Robert Murphy to London, and Nasser, almost mobbed by hysterically patriotic crowds, declaimed: "We shall meet force with force and will fight to the last drop of blood. . . . I warn the imperialist countries that any interference on their part will cause obstruction of navigation in the Suez Canal." On the next day Dulles deplored the nationalization as "a grievous blow to international confidence."

But any prospect of Western solidarity soon waned. Dulles strove for "peace" and appeared indifferent to the interests of France, Britain, and Israel. Selwyn Lloyd, Pineau, and Mrs. Golda Meir, Israel's Foreign Minister, strove for "justice," which they defined in terms of "cutting Nasser down to size." After hectic and complex negotiations, with Dulles in London early in August, it was agreed by the three Western Powers that the Suez Canal should be administered by an international authority to be discussed at a 24-nation conference, including Egypt and the USSR, to be convened in London on Aug. 16. But the "agreement" proved illusory. Dulles and Eisenhower forbade any resort to force, while Britain ordered partial mobilization and the dispatch of naval and air units to Cyprus. France did likewise. The French Assembly on Aug. 2 resolved, 422 to 150 (with only the Communists in opposition), that Nasser was "a permanent menace to peace." On the next day Mollet spoke of the possible need of force to "impose" international control, while Dulles in a nationwide broadcast from the White House declared that Nasser's action "was an angry act of retaliation against fancied grievances" and that it was "inadmissible" for the Suez Canal to be "exploited by one country for highly selfish purposes."

London rejected Soviet proposals for a larger and later conference. Egypt and Greece refused to attend, with Nasser calling the meeting "a conspiracy of collective colonialism." On Aug. 16, 1956, delegates of 22 nations met in Lancaster House. As the Canal Company tried to prevent Nasser from keeping the Canal open by withdrawing Western pilots, Dulles, amid much talk, urged international operation. India, supported by the USSR, Indonesia, and Ceylon, argued for acceptance of Egyptian control of the waterway, subject to an international board with advisory functions. When the conference closed on Aug. 23, eighteen States agreed to ask Egypt to negotiate for international operation of the Canal, on the basis of an amended U.S. plan, through a committee representing the USA (Loy W. Henderson), Sweden, Iran, Ethiopia, and Australia—whose Prime Minister, Robert Gordon Menzies, was named chairman.

Neither Downing Street nor the Quai d'Orsay had any confidence in Dulles's firmness against Nasser nor any hope that the Cairo dictator could be induced, short of force, to back down. By August's end, French troops were proceeding to Cyprus, Cairo was alleging a British "plot" to overthrow Nasser, and London, Paris, and Tel Aviv (according to *Figaro*, March 27, 1957) were already secretly concocting plans to attack Egypt, with Israel to move first and Anglo-French forces subsequently to occupy the Canal Zone. Such plans were carefully concealed from Washington, whose diplomats and intelligence agents evidently remained in ignorance. The Menzies mission arrived in Egypt on Sept. 2, and departed on the 9th, having failed to persuade Nasser to assent to any form of "internationalization" of the Canal. Cairo's proposal for another conference was abruptly rejected by Britain and France. Eden and Mollet in London concerted measures of economic pressure on Egypt and *pro forma* appealed (Sept. 12) to the UN Security Council to discuss the Egyptian attitude as "a manifest danger to peace and security."

At the same time, as new violence flared on Israel's borders, plans were announced on Dulles's initiative for a "Suez Canal Users Association" to employ its own pilots, collect tolls, and manage the waterway in disregard of Egyptian claims of ownership and control. Cairo cried "war." Dulles denied that the USA would "shoot its way" through the Canal and toyed with plans of American oil aid to Western Europe and a boycott of Suez via shipments around Africa. As Soviet pilots enabled Egypt to continue operating the Canal, Dulles on Sept. 17 took off again for London where the Cabinet had summoned a new conference of the 18 States supporting the proposals of Aug. 23. On the same day Cairo appealed to the UN Security Council to take cognizance of Anglo-French threats and to regard "the proposed users association as being incompatible with the dignity and sovereign rights of Egypt" and a "flagrant violation of the UN Charter and the 1888 Convention." All such appeals were vain, since the UN is politically paralyzed, save as a forum for propaganda, when the Great Powers are at odds. London and Paris assumed that Washington would cooperate in using the "users association" to compel Nasser to "internationalize" the Canal. Dulles had no such intention.

A FAILURE OF STATESMANSHIP

The second London conference closed on Sept. 21 with a vague and tentative draft plan for a SCUA involving "consultation," no threats of force, and reliance on the UN. The conference, said Dulles, "registered solid gains. . . . There was a splendid spirit of fellowship. . . . The door to a peaceful and fair solution is kept widely open, if only the Government of Egypt will choose that way." On Sept. 23 London and Paris appealed anew to the UN Security Council, with Cairo filing a counter-protest on Sept. 24.

The SCUA was formally inaugurated in London on Oct. 1, with 15 States participating, with Eyvina Bartels (Danish Consul General in New York) named as administrator, and with its functions, if any, in doubt. Anglo-French journalists commented acidly on Dulles's "disassociation" from Anglo-French "colonialism" in a press conference. Projects for transferring control of the Canal to a consortium of U.S. oil and shipping companies came to nothing. Verbose debates at the UN also came to nothing. Egypt and the USSR rejected all proposals for international control of the waterway. Eisenhower opined (Oct. 11) that American policy had been "clear and firm" and that neither he nor Dulles had ever heard "any intimation from anyone in British officialdom" that London was "dissatisfied with our stand in this thing." In the Security Council the USSR vetoed a resolution in support of the SCUA. On Oct. 11 all members of the Council, including Dr. Mahmoud Fawzi, Egyptian Foreign Minister, reached agreement on six principles—which, however, left unresolved the issue of whether the Canal was to remain under exclusive Egyptian control.[3] Selwyn Lloyd and Pineau reiterated their support of the 18-nation plan for internationalization.

Israelis killed fifty Jordanians in a reprisal raid of Sept. 26 and threatened war if Iraqi troops moved into Jordan. Dulles in mid-October reiterated American resolve to aid any victim of aggression in the Mid East. Ben-Gurion warned the Knesset (Parliament) against "the Egyptian fascist dictator" who "rules Egypt by force, suppresses by violence all who oppose him, aspires to dominate by force all the Arab countries, and who does not conceal his intention to liquidate the State of Israel." While official Washington exuded

---

[3] The six principles were as follows:

"Arrangements made should meet the following requirements:

"1. There shall be free and open transit through the canal without discrimination, overt and covert. [By way of clarification: this principle covers the same ground as the corresponding principle of the Constantinople Convention of 1888; that is, it covers the technical as well as the political aspects with which Point 3, below, is also concerned.]

"2. Egypt's sovereignty shall be respected.

"3. The operation of the canal shall be insulated from the politics of any country.

"4. The manner of fixing tolls and charges shall be decided by agreement between Egypt and the users.

"5. A fair proportion of the dues shall be allotted to development.

"6. In case of dispute unresolved affairs between the Suez Canal Company and the Egyptian Government shall be settled by arbitration with suitable terms of reference and suitable provisions for the payment of sums found to be due."

411

ignorant optimism on the eve of war, the men of Moscow, who knew what was impending, sought in vain to avert violence.

As revealed in London on April 22, 1957, Bulganin on Sept. 11, 1956, addressed Prime Minister Eden, warning that any use of force unauthorized by the Security Council would be a violation of the Charter.

Presumably the British and French Governments intend to seize the Suez Canal. . . . It can scarcely be doubted that such action would result in tremendous destruction of the Canal itself. . . . Oil deliveries to Europe would become completely disrupted. . . . Such action would arouse the profound hatred of the peoples of Africa and Asia. . . . It is no longer possible to threaten and brandish weapons. Nowadays one can no longer act in the same way as in the age of colonial oppression. Military measures can only end in failure. . . . We wish to warn you in a friendly way as to the dangerous developments of events which might follow if necessary prudence is not shown.

Eden's reply of Sept. 16 espoused "peace" and accused Nasser of "militarism." Bulganin's rejoinder of Sept. 28 contended that the SCUA, supported by threats of force, "would mean a gross violation of the Convention of 1888 and defiance of the sovereign rights of Egypt" and urged further efforts for a peaceful solution. Eden's retort of Oct. 6 repeated his indictment of Nasser and denied that Egypt's "sovereignty" was at issue. Bulganin's final message of Oct. 23 bespoke confidence in the UN and hopes of peace. Comparable warnings were addressed by Bulganin to Mollet on Sept. 11, with Mollet's reply bespeaking friendship but condemning Egypt and evading the question of violence.

By a curious paradox, typical of many quests for power and peace in a context of *Machtpolitik*, the men of Moscow were soon obliged to resort to force in Hungary on a scale no less brutal, albeit more successful, than the impending use of violence by Israel, France, and Britain against Egypt. The double outbreaks of bloodshed on the Danube and the Nile in late October, 1956, were apparently unrelated. But in One World all things are of a piece. The attack against Egypt almost certainly would have been deferred except for the fact that Egypt's giant sponsor became involved in unexpected conflict with its Polish and Magyar subjects during late October and was therefore presumably unable to act in the Mid East. Conversely, Moscow's savage suppression of the Hungarian Revolution was the sequel, begotten of ancient fears, of the outbreak of war on the Nile.[4]

Menace from without begets unity within. The waning of the "Cold War" and the relaxation of Stalinist techniques of terror fed a rising yeast of discontent in all the satellites, as already shown by the East German riots of June 17, 1953. Even in the USSR the processes of de-Stalinization begot violence in Tiflis on March 9, 1956, with a loss of life of uncertain proportions. In late June and early

---

[4] The fourteen paragraphs which follow originally appeared in *Russia Since 1917* and are here reprinted with the permission of Alfred A. Knopf, Inc., copyright 1957 by Frederick L. Schuman.

July, Polish workers, long weary of alien domination and exploitation and now hopeful of achieving a new dispensation, fought Communist police and troops in Poznan and other Polish cities and yielded only to *force majeure* after many casualties. In what followed, Rumanians, Bulgarians, and Albanians remained quiescent while, in a current Warsaw witticism, "Hungarians acted like Poles, Poles acted like Czechs, and Czechs acted like pigs." The surging tide of revolution in Poland, restrained from futile mass violence by the wisdom of the Polish Communist leaders and by Stefan Cardinal Wyszynski's pleas for order and moderation, led the Party Central Committee on Oct. 20 to restore to membership Wladyslav Gomulka, ousted in 1947 and jailed as a "Titoist" in 1951.

On the same day Khrushchev, Zhukov, Molotov, Mikoyan, and Kaganovich arrived in Warsaw as Soviet troops maneuvered in an apparent effort to forestall any triumph of "National Communism." Precisely what was said and done is still unknown. Jozef Cyrankiewicz remained Premier. But Gomulka's admission to, and Rokossovsky's exclusion from, the new Politburo was a portent, emphasized by Gomulka's restoration to the decisive post of First Secretary of the Party. The Muscovites, whatever threats they may have made, finally accepted a new order in Poland. Rokossovsky, symbol of Soviet domination, returned to Russia on Oct. 28 and was replaced as Polish Minister of Defense on Nov. 13 by Gomulka's colleague in earlier disgrace, Gen. Marian Spychalski. In later negotiations Moscow came to terms with the new "Titoist" Polish regime, still Communist-ruled but liberalized and no longer controlled from the USSR. Debts were remitted. Credits and grants of grain were extended. Soviet troops in Poland were restricted. In short, a new and viable pattern of Soviet-satellite relationships seemed in process of emerging from the Polish crisis.

The shape of things to come was quite otherwise in Hungary, where local patriots —some of them deluded over the years by promises or implications of "liberation" broadcast by the Voice of America and Radio Free Europe, operated from Munich by the "Crusade for Freedom"—vainly essayed a total revolution by violence against Communist rule. What transpired in the land of the Magyars is inseparable from earlier Muscovite efforts to achieve a *modus vivendi* with Tito, symbol of "National Communism" independent of Moscow.

On April 17, 1956, the Central Committees of the Communist Parties of the USSR, Poland, Czechoslovakia, Hungary, Rumania, Bulgaria, Italy, and France jointly decreed the dissolution of the Cominform as having "exhausted its uses" under changed conditions. This regional Comintern, which had "expelled" Tito as a schismatic in 1948 under Stalin's delusion that Tito could readily be disposed of, thus readmitted him to the fold and dissolved itself in proof of repentance and in hope of reconciliation. Tito had meanwhile obtained almost a billion dollars from America, while Moscow had extended long-term credits to other Communist countries, chiefly for industrialization, to the amount of 21 billion rubles. The policy-makers of both the Super-Powers, all "materialists" in their divergent ways, were evidently persuaded that every man has his price. Many do. But fanatics never do. Such devoted souls always put "principle" above advantage and sometimes above life itself. Eastern Europe and the Mid East were both seething in 1956 with the fanaticism of nationalism.

Tito arrived in Moscow on June 1, enjoyed a gala performance in his honor at the Bolshoi, and departed on June 20, 1956, after a trip to Stalingrad. His joy in the journey was enhanced by Molotov's resignation as Foreign Minister on the day of Tito's arrival in favor of 51-year-old Dmitri Trofimovich Shepilov. The new incumbent, son of a Don metal worker and a 1926 graduate of Moscow State University, was tall, burly, handsome, and charming. After serving as a local prosecutor and agricultural student, editor, teacher, and Major General (Deputy Chief of Agitation and Propaganda for the Armed Forces in World War II), he became chief editor of *Pravda* in 1952. This representative of the "new man" among the Soviet elite was without previous diplomatic experience, aside from having joined Bulganin and Khrushchev on various missions abroad in 1954-5 while the veteran Molotov was ignored. (Molotov was named Minister of State Control, Nov. 22, 1956; the import of the appointment was uncertain because of the ambiguities of its duties.) Shepilov's promotion in the context of Tito's advent suggested that he was believed by the top Party leaders to possess some special talent for coming to terms with schismatics, heretics, and dissidents within the Red Empire. No such talent was displayed in his activities, as publicly recorded, during 1956.

At the close of the Tito-Kardelj visit a joint communiqué of June 20 bespoke friendship, "common aims" and "mutual understanding," and espoused peace, disarmament, coexistence, Red China's entry into the UN, and German unity only through negotiations between the two German States. Economic and cultural contacts would be enlarged. Cooperation between the Soviet and Jugoslav parties would henceforth be based on "complete freedom of will and equality, on friendly criticism, and on the comradely character" of controversies, all on the premise that "the roads and conditions of socialist development are different in different countries."

In a further effort to reorder relations among the faithful and resolve confusions among the comrades abroad, the Central Committee of the CPSU drafted in late June, and released on July 2, a lengthy "Marxist-Leninist" exposition of the new orientation. Khrushchev's indictment of Stalin was reiterated. The abuses of the "cult of personality" were attributed to "conditions of enemy encirclement and a constant threat of attack from without." This menace, coupled with "the successes of socialist construction," had made any action against Stalin impossible, since it "would not have been understood by the people." Yet the view that Stalin's crimes were attributable to the Soviet social order or to its "degeneration," as alleged by Togliatti, was "absolutely wrong." "The 20th Congress indicated that the most important feature of our era is the conversion of socialism into a world system. The most difficult period is behind us." The resolution ended with a new attack upon American "cold warriors" and "imperialists" and an expression of confidence in Communist solidarity and the inevitable global triumph of Marxism-Leninism.

The most difficult period lay ahead. Such verbalizations, while not unimpressive to "hard-shelled" Communist converts imbued with a will to believe, had little effect upon doubters within the ranks and none upon the non-Communists and anti-Communists whose hopes of freedom, particularly in Hungary, rose week by week with each new piece of evidence that their Marxist masters were quarreling among themselves. Khrushchev appeared mysteriously in Jugoslavia, "on vacation," on Sept. 18. Ten days later Tito conferred at Yalta with Khrushchev, Bulganin, and Erno Gero from Budapest. At month's end Belgrade revealed that the Central Committee of the CPSU had again warned other Eastern parties against "Titoism" and that the recent parleys concerned "ideological differences" not unrelated, we may assume, to growing tensions in Hungary.

The sequel was interpreted by most Americans and many West Europeans as a heroic struggle against "tyranny" and for "democracy" by the Hungarian people. All Communists still faithful to Moscow interpreted it as an abortive effort by "Fascists" and "subversive" agents of "Western imperialism" to destroy the Danubian "People's Democracy" by force. The truth lay somewhere between—if

414

truth can ever be arrived at in efforts to comprehend the irrationalities and brutalities of men. Magyar patriotic traditions included fanatical revolt against alien rule, best exemplified by Louis Kossuth's ill-fated revolutionary "Republic" of 1849, also suppressed by Russian troops. They included no legacy of democracy. The thousand-year-old feudal kingdom of Hungary, united with Austria in the Dual Monarchy of 1867–1918, suffered the Communist dictatorship of Bela Kun in 1919 and then passively acquiesced for decades in the Fascist dictatorship of Regent Nicholas Horthy (in 1956 an 88-year-old exile in Portugal), who came to power amid the "White Terror" of 1920 and delivered Hungary to Hitler during World War II. During the past several centuries Hungary had enjoyed democratic government not longer than a total of five years and this only during spasmodic and ephemeral interludes between various types of despotism. In the middle decades of the 20th Century Hungary, no less than Poland and the Balkan States, was condemned by the balance of forces within, and by implacable pressures from without, to choose between Fascism and Communism as alternative forms of dictatorship. Western and Soviet preferences between these options could scarcely be expected to coincide.

The immediate background of the disaster to come is worth noting, if only as illustrative of the dilemmas confronting Communist power-holders in the era of de-Stalinization and "peaceful coexistence." Premier Imry Nagy's "new course" had been denounced as "Titoism" and "Right Deviationism" by veteran Party boss, Matyas Rakosi. Nagy had been ousted from the Premiership in favor of Andres Hegedus on April 18, 1955, and later expelled from the Party. Stalinist Rakosi nonetheless felt obliged in March 1956 to "rehabilitate" Lazlo Rajk, Andras Szalai, Tibor Szoenyi, and Gyorgy Pallfy (all hanged for "treason" and "Titoism" on October 15, 1949, on Rakosi's orders), along with Bela Kun, purged in Russia in the 1930's. Early in October 200,000 people marched by the coffins in Budapest's central cemetery in a ritual designed to demonstrate the Cabinet's concern for "justice" but having the effect of discrediting the regime. Meanwhile, Rakosi made sundry "concessions," all too little and too late, and, under popular pressure, finally resigned as First Secretary of the Party on July 18, 1956, in favor of Erno Gero, who bespoke reconciliation with Tito and "no Poznans here."

On the advice of Mikoyan, on his way to Jugoslavia, the Politburo presently released from jail and readmitted to its ranks several former "Titoists," including Janos Kadar. Other concessions and reshuffles proved vain. Between Oct. 15 and 23 Gero, Hegedus, Kadar, and other leaders were in Belgrade, where they espoused "cooperation" and "friendly relations" with Tito's regime. During their absence Hungarian students organized mass demonstrations to demand freedom of the press, abolition of capital punishment, and, finally, the restoration of Imry Nagy as Premier, the punishment of Rakosi, the freeing of Cardinal Mindszenty, and the withdrawal of Soviet troops. The young intellectuals, whom the Communists had flattered, pampered, and regimented, and the workers, in whose name the Communists purported to rule, were in the forefront of rebellion, thereby demonstrating anew that the "dictatorship of the proletariat" as a façade for the rule of an intellectual elite was often deemed abominable by intellectuals and proletarians alike.

4. RECOURSE TO FORCE

On Oct. 23 mobs in Budapest demolished Stalin's statue, tore down the red star atop the parliament building, and in the evening sought to storm the radio station from which Gero had just spoken. First blood was shed when the Security Police (AVO) opened fire. There ensued a popular uprising, apparently without central leadership, direction, or purpose, marked by book-burning, the murder of many of the hated Security Policemen, the defection to the rebels of many units of the Hungarian Army, and the indiscriminate killing of Jews and Communists by hooligans and mobsters. In the early morning hours of Oct. 24 the panic-stricken "rulers" of Hungary promised concessions and named Imry Nagy as Premier. He and Gero summoned Soviet troops to crush the rebels. On Oct. 25 Suslov and Mikoyan arrived from Moscow as Russian forces mowed down demonstrators and bombarded factories and apartment buildings. Gero, later reported killed, gave way to Kadar as First Secretary of the Party. Kadar promised to negotiate for the withdrawal of Soviet forces as soon as order should be restored.

The men of Moscow, faced with anarchy on the Danube, were evidently prepared (unless their gestures be interpreted as hypocrisy) to swallow, as the lesser evil, a drastic alteration of their relations with Hungary, including acceptance of a non-Communist coalition and perhaps an anti-Communist regime. On Oct. 29–30 they announced their willingness to withdraw Soviet troops from Hungary and the other Warsaw Pact States. What course of belated concessions they were ready to pursue may never be known, thanks to new events in Budapest and in Egypt which led them, in new fear, to a wholly different decision.

The events in Budapest were these: while Bishop Groesz appealed for peace, Cardinal Mindszenty, freed by rebels on Oct. 31, lauded the insurgents, appealed for Western aid, and hinted at his availability as head of an anti-Communist regime. The frantic Nagy, in hope of causing the rebels to lay down their arms, told the Soviet Ambassador on Nov. 1 that the new Hungary was denouncing the Warsaw Pact, asking Western help, soliciting intervention by the UN, and demanding the immediate evacuation of all Soviet troops. As for Egypt, the Israeli Army on October 29 launched a massive invasion of the Sinai Peninsula in obvious connivance (despite denials) with Anglo-French policy-makers, who, following rejection of an ultimatum, began bombarding Egyptian airports on Nov. 1 and prepared to seize the Suez Canal. Faced with the prospect of an anti-Soviet regime in Hungary and of open warfare in the Mid East, the policy-makers of Moscow decided to crush the Hungarian revolution by force.

The details of planning the attack upon Egypt were still unknown when this account was written. But a few features of the conspiracy are reasonably clear. The Israeli leaders, having no more confidence in "Perfidious Albion" than in Eisenhower and Dulles, limited their liaison work to the French. It was agreed that Israel should strike first. It is probable, although not currently provable, that the action was originally planned for mid-November. Anglo-French preparations on Cyprus were obviously not complete. With the outbreak of revolution in Hungary, the date was advanced. New provocations were available in late October in further frontier raids, Egyptian naval maneuvers off the Israeli coast, and a new Syrian-Jordanian-Egyptian accord for a joint military command to be led by Egypt.

Having struck the first blow and being in no position to wage a protracted war of attrition, Israel asked immediate Anglo-French intervention lest Nasser use his new Soviet planes to bomb Tel Aviv while his Arab allies prepared to invade Israel. All the "plotters" told Washington nothing. On the very eve of invasion Ben-Gurion, Golda Meir, and Ambassador Abba Eban were declaring that "Israel will never start a war." All assumed, correctly, that the slogan of the USA, in effect, was: "Come weal, come woe, my status is quo!" Eisenhower and Dulles had abundantly demonstrated their disposition to ignore the security of Israel and the vital interests of France and Britain, to support Egypt and the other Arab States in resisting retaliation against their own provocations and outrages, and to equate all military counter-moves as "illegal" and "immoral" aggression which must at all costs be thwarted in the name of rectitude and the "rule of law."

The enterprise plainly had to be conceived and executed in defiance of both of the Super-Powers. The USSR was preoccupied with violence on the Danube. The USA was immersed in an election campaign. Whether tiny Israel, co-operating with the two erstwhile "Great Powers" of France and Britain, could under any circumstances have carried to conclusive victory its "preventive war" in defiance of both Washington and Moscow was from the outset doubtful, even though the giants were in process of resuming their interrupted Cold War. Yet there was a gambler's chance. Men and statesmen reduced to desperation are seldom unwilling to gamble. The failure of the gamble was attributable primarily to Anglo-French mismanagement and weakness of will. If left unimpeded by its allies or effectively supported by them, the Israeli Army might well have occupied all of the Canal before Nasser wrecked it and conceivably have reached Cairo and toppled a disgraced Nasser into oblivion. But these are speculations. Let us note what in fact took place.

On Sunday, Oct. 28, Tel Aviv announced mobilization. Reserves were sent to their posts while all motor vehicles from the *kibbutzim* or cooperative farms were assembled for the task at hand. Eisenhower twice warned Ben-Gurion against force and referred to the Anglo-French-American declaration of May 25, 1950, against any aggression in the Mid East—obviously ignorant of Anglo-French-Israeli plans. On Monday, the 29th, Israeli troops under the command of Maj. Gen. Moshe Dayan, Chief of Staff, poured into the Sinai Peninsula from the Negev, sweeping all before them, and approached the Suez Canal within hours. A Foreign Ministry statement at Tel Aviv declared:

Israel has taken the necessary measures to destroy Egyptian fedayeen bases in the Sinai Peninsula. . . . Col. Nasser has persistently declared that despite the explicit provisions of the Egyptian-Israel (Armistice) Agreement, his country remained in a state of war with Israel. He has carried on a war of limited liability. . . . It is not Israel which has sent murder gangs into Egypt. . . . It is not Israel which has sought to strangle Egypt's economy. . . . It is not Israel which has sought to encompass Egypt with a ring of steel with the announced and flouted purpose of annihilating her at the appropriate moment. . . . Col. Nasser has ignored his international obligations under the Charter of the UN, has flouted his duty under the Constantinople Convention of 1888 and the Security Council resolution of Sept. 1, 1951, to permit free passage through the Suez Canal for the vessels of all nations at all times. . . . Israel has done everything in her

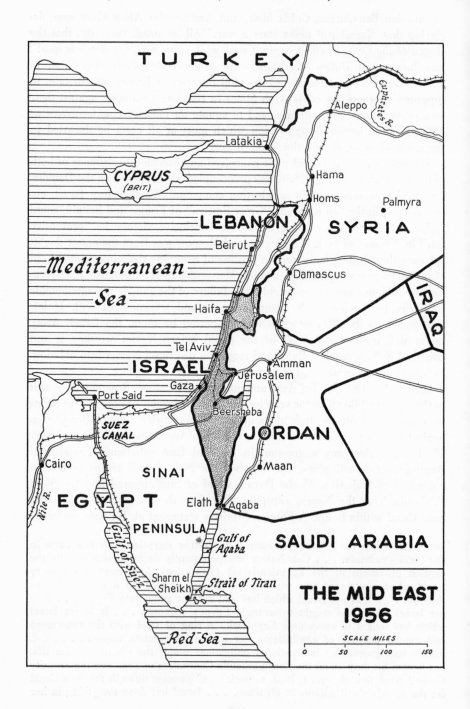

TURKEY

Aleppo

Latakia

CYPRUS
(BRIT.)

Hama

Homs

Palmyra

LEBANON

SYRIA

Beirut

Mediterranean

Damascus

IRAQ

Sea

Haifa

Tel Aviv

ISRAEL

Amman

Jerusalem

Gaza

Port Said

Beersheba

SUEZ
CANAL

JORDAN

Cairo

SINAI

Maan

Nile R.

EGYPT

Elath

Aqaba

PENINSULA

Gulf of
Aqaba

SAUDI ARABIA

Gulf of Suez

Sharm el
Sheikh

Strait of Tiran

THE MID EAST
1956

Red Sea

SCALE MILES

0   50   100   150

power to achieve peace with Egypt. . . . Israel seeks a relationship with the people of Egypt based upon mutual respect of rights, free from the threat of attack on her citizens, blockade, or interference with her communications, whether by land or sea.

Still unaware that Paris and London, no less than Tel Aviv, had repudiated American "leadership," Dulles conferred with the Anglo-French *chargés d'affaires* on "the applicability of the tripartite declaration of 1950 to the present situation," while the White House announced that "the President recalled that the U.S. has pledged itself to assist the victim of any aggression in the Middle East. We shall honor our pledge. The U.S. is in consultation with the British and French Governments, parties with us to the tripartite declaration of 1950, and the U.S. plans, as contemplated by that declaration, that the situation shall be taken to the UN Security Council tomorrow morning. . . ."

Great was Eisenhower's anger and Dulles's indignation when they discovered on Tuesday that they had been deceived. At the Security Council Ambassador Lodge introduced a resolution calling upon Israel "immediately to withdraw its armed forces behind the established armistice lines" and asking all members "to refrain from the use of force or the threat of force" and "to refrain from giving any military, economic, or financial assistance to Israel." In a vote of 7 to 2, with Australia and Belgium abstaining, the French and British envoys vetoed the resolution.

Also on Tuesday, Oct. 30, 1956, Ben-Gurion ignored pleas from Eisenhower and the UN as did Eden and Mollet. Downing Street and the Quai d'Orsay dispatched a 12-hour ultimatum to Tel Aviv and Cairo, demanding under threat of military action a cessation of fighting, withdrawal of all forces 10 miles from the Canal, and Egyptian consent, in the interests of freedom of transit by ships of all nations, to temporary Anglo-French occupation of Port Said, Ismailia, and Suez. Tel Aviv agreed on condition that Cairo would concur. Nasser at once rejected the ultimatum. Secretary Dulles became acutely ill and soon underwent surgery for cancer.

On Wednesday, Oct. 31, British bombers began attacking Egyptian air fields while Israeli forces damaged and captured the Egyptian destroyer *Ibrahim Awal* off Haifa. The Security Council voted 7 to 2 (Britain and France) with Australia and Belgium abstaining, to call an emergency session of the General Assembly on Thursday. As Anglo-French naval and landing forces under Gen. Sir Charles Keightly and Vice Admiral Pierre Barojot moved from Cyprus toward the Canal, which the defenders were soon to block completely with sunken ships, Dayan's Zionist troops scored a brilliant victory in Sinai over the soldiery of Nasser, none of whose Arab allies came to his aid. Almost 6,000 Egyptian prisoners were taken and later exchanged for 4 Israelis. Half of Nasser's new Soviet tanks and guns were destroyed or captured. The Gaza Strip and Sharm el Sheik, commanding the Strait of Tiran to the Gulf of Aqaba, were seized by Israeli forces, with all the Sinai desert.

On Nov. 5 British and French parachute troops occupied Port Said and then took Port Fuad and pushed 30 miles southward along the Canal with every prospect of occupying the entire waterway. But this objective was abandoned when Eden and Mollet capitulated and agreed to a cease-fire as of midnight, Nov. 6. The nine-day war of 1956 was ended, with the victors defeated and the defeated soon to be victorious.

Before considering why and how this came to pass, let us notice the effects of violence on the Nile on the course of violence on the Danube. Any disposition of the Soviet policy-makers to come to terms with the Hungarian rebels was ended by the outbreak of war in the Levant. Fear is contagious, as violence is contagious. If France and Britain were prepared to assault Egypt by force, the men of Moscow concluded that they could not afford to abandon Hungary to a non-Communist or anti-Communist regime. They knew that what they were about to do would sacrifice all or most of the good will they had been so carefully cultivating in the West since 1953 and would sow further confusion and dissension in the ranks of all Communists everywhere. But here, as usual, strategic interests of "security" in the global game of power, whether rightly or wrongly defined, took precedence over all "ideological" desiderata and over all concern for winning friends and influencing people.

At dawn of Sunday morning, Nov. 4, 1956, thousands of Soviet tanks moved into Budapest and other Magyar cities. All opposition was pitilessly smashed. Pathetic rebel appeals for Western aid elicited no response save sympathy and shouts of "Murder!" The Nagy Cabinet was suppressed. The luckless Premier, long a fugitive in the Jugoslav Legation, was ultimately deported to Rumania despite protests from Belgrade at violation of a promise of "safe-conduct" to his home. The Cardinal sought safety in the U.S. Legation. A new "Revolutionary Workers' and Peasants' Government" headed by Kadar acquiesced in the flight of 175,000 refugees to Austria and thence to other lands (with a conscience-striken America generously supporting the escapees) and strove to restore order by a combination of concessions and repressions, while rejecting all proposals for UN "observers."

How many perished is uncertain. Budapest acknowledged 2,000 dead. Nehru, relying on reports by Ambassador K. P. S. Menon, who shuttled between Moscow and Budapest during the rebellion, calculated that 25,000 Magyars and 7,000 Russians had been slain. This estimate was undoubtedly exaggerated, perhaps by a factor of ten. The abortive attack upon Egypt probably sacrificed more lives than were lost in Hungary. And the French war in Algeria was far more costly in blood. The French Army boasted of killing 18,000 rebels in 1956 alone. The Hungarian martyrs aroused fierce anti-Soviet indignation throughout the Western world and evoked few echoes elsewhere. The Algerian victims of French arms elicited only mild regret in the West, but stirred millions to indignation throughout the Arab-Asian lands. Here, as always, moral indignation at man's inhumanity to man is a matter of whose ox is gored.[5]

[5] This and the preceding paragraph originally appeared in *Russia Since 1917* and are here reprinted with the permission of Alfred A. Knopf, Inc., copyright 1957 by Frederick L. Schuman.

Why was Moscow, in the face of world-wide indignation, able to drown the Hungarian Revolution in blood while Tel Aviv, Paris and London, in the face of world-wide indignation, were obliged to confess failure in their attempt to dethrone the contumacious dictator of Cairo? The answer can *note* scarcely be found in "world opinion." In November of 1956 thousands demonstrated against Anglo-French-Israeli wickedness throughout Eastern Europe, Asia, and Africa, while other thousands demonstrated against Soviet wickedness throughout Western Europe and the Americas. When all pots call all kettles black, "world opinion" is nonexistent. Neither is the answer to be found in the UN where, apparently, the USSR successfully defied the world organization while Israel, France, and Britain yielded to its resolves. But this too is illusory. London and Paris vetoed Council resolutions and voted against Assembly resolutions condemning their "aggression" on the Nile. Moscow vetoed Council resolutions and voted against Assembly resolutions condemning Soviet aggression on the Danube. Any persuasive answer to our question must be sought on another plane.

In the pattern of power prevailing in our time, America can, if it chooses, impose its will anywhere in the world, whenever American policy-makers are agreed upon their goals, except in areas dominated by the USSR and China. By the same logic, Moscow and Peiping can, if they choose, impose their will anywhere in the world save in regions controlled by the Atlantic allies. Lesser Powers are helpless to defy either of the Super-Powers unless supported by one against the other. In 1956 Israel, France, and Britain were "pressured" from both Washington and Moscow and from all the "neutralist" Asian-African world, to abandon their assault on Egypt. The pressure proved irresistible. Pressure from Washington on the USSR to abandon its assault on Hungary was supported only feebly by the States of Western Europe and scarcely at all by Asians and Africans, most of whom, whatever their doubts regarding Muscovite mistakes and crimes, viewed American championship of "freedom" with suspicion and Soviet championship of "anti-colonialism" with sympathy. Washington could thwart Israel, France, and Britain in Egypt with no risk whatever of precipitating a world war. Washington could not thwart the USSR in Hungary without risking a world war. These divergent outcomes of the two crises were thus foreordained by the facts of power.

The Anglo-French capitulation was not the result of Soviet threats, nor yet of American threats. Soviet threats were fictitious. No overt American threats were necessary, since all three of the "aggressors" against Egypt were dependent upon American good will and economic aid. Muscovite gestures, designed to distract attention from bloodshed in Hungary and to capitalize upon Asian-African attitudes, were bluffs. On Nov. 4, Moscow publicly rebuked France and Britain for "aggression" as Muscovites "demonstrated" outside the French, British, and Israeli Embassies. On Nov. 5, the USSR asked the Security Council to approve joint American-Soviet military aid to

Egypt. The motion was rejected 4 to 3, with 3 abstentions. Eisenhower repudiated the idea as "unthinkable" and hinted at American resistance to any introduction of Soviet forces in the Mid East. On Nov. 6 in messages to Eden, Mollet, and Ben-Gurion, the USSR indicated willingness to use force to "crush the aggressors and restore peace" and began recruiting "volunteers" to aid Egypt, while Eisenhower denounced Soviet deeds in Hungary. A passage in Bulganin's note to Eden of Nov. 5 read: "In what position would Britain have found herself if she herself had been attacked by more powerful States possessing every kind of modern destructive weapon? . . . If rocket weapons had been used against Britain and France, they would probably have called this a barbarous act. Yet in what way does the inhuman attack on the nearly disarmed Egypt differ from this?" This passage was later interpreted as a Soviet threat of atomic warfare against the Western Powers.

In fact all Soviet blusterings were empty verbiage, designed for purposes of propaganda, and were correctly so interpreted in Paris and in London, if not always in Washington. To maintain Soviet power on the Danube, the men of Moscow might have risked global war. Nasser was a peripheral and ephemeral asset, worth no such risk even if his doom were pending. No Soviet "volunteers" could get to Egypt without violating by air the neutrality of intervening States or forcing passage by sea through waterways controlled by hostile States. Under no circumstances would Muscovite policy-makers risk hostilities with Western Powers in pursuit of such a purpose. As for alleged threats of war via atomic rockets, the questions were rhetorical.

The Mid-East "aggressors" surrendered not to Moscow but to Washington. The wisdom, ethics, and expediency of the American course will long be debated. To desert allies in the name of "morality" and to inflict upon them a humiliating capitulation is seldom conducive to long-range national interests.[6] To evade pressing problems and to insist on the *status quo*, however intolerable to its victims, is seldom good statesmanship. Conversely, to oppose "aggression," to champion "peace," and to defend the weak against the strong, particularly when millions of Asians and Africans will cheer, is always good propaganda, as was realized in Washington as well as in Moscow. How the trick was turned is our next concern.

5. THE VICTORY OF THE VANQUISHED

Nasser's Egypt, defeated in the contest of arms it had provoked with Israel, France, and Britain, emerged triumphant from its trial, thanks to U.S. solicitude for "morality" and widespread abhorrence, shared by the British Labor Party and by a few French critics of the Mollet Cabinet, of any recourse to

[6] See Hans J. Morgenthau, "The Decline and Fall of American Foreign Policy," *The New Republic*, Dec. 7 and Dec. 13, 1956; Louis Halle, "A Touch of Nausea," *ibid.*, Jan. 21, 1957; and the author's letter in *The Nation*, Dec. 22, 1956.

force, whatever the provocation. On Nov. 1, 1956, Dulles presented a resolution to the UN Assembly calling for a cease-fire and the withdrawal of Israel's troops. Following overwhelming approval, Paris and London, although rejecting an immediate cease-fire, offered to give way in their tasks of occupation to a UN force designed to keep the peace, as proposed by Canadian Foreign Minister Lester Pearson. Dulles and Lodge bespoke the need of "final settlements" of the Arab-Israeli feud and of the status of the Canal. No such settlements emerged. Innumerable UN resolutions and endless debates led to an Assembly vote on Nov. 7 (65 to 1 with only Israel in the negative and with ten abstentions, including Britain and France) calling on Israel, France, and Britain to evacuate all Egyptian territory. Ben-Gurion breathed defiance, contending that the 1949 armistice lines were "dead and buried" and that Israel would not withdraw from Sinai or consent to the stationing of UN forces on its territory until Egypt agreed to a peace and a cessation of boycotts, blockades, and murder raids.

What followed was a slow and painful process of restoring the *status quo* on American initiative with UN aid, resulting in acquiescence in Nasser's *fait accompli* in seizing the Canal and in a resumption of Israel's precarious position among its Arab enemies. Maj. Gen. E. L. M. Burns of Canada commanded the new UN Emergency Force of Danes, Norwegians, and other nationals of lesser States, designed to maintain order in areas which the "aggressors" had agreed to quit. The first tiny contingents arrived in the Canal Zone in mid-November, as Nasser's agents began expropriating and expelling Jews residing in Egypt. The wrecked Canal was again opened to traffic, thanks to UN clearance operations, on March 29, 1957, with Western Europe meanwhile surviving its oil shortage through U.S. aid.

The last British and French forces left Egyptian soil Dec. 22, 1956. The Israelis refused to follow suit, pending guarantees of security. Central Sinai was evacuated in January, but Tel Aviv declined to quit Sharm el Sheik and the Gaza Strip without assurances against renewed fedayeen raids and against continued closure of the Canal and Gulf to Israeli shipping. Dulles would give no assurances, denounced Israeli efforts to "profit from aggression," and insisted that Israeli must comply in full with the UN resolution of Nov. 2 demanding withdrawal behind the 1949 armistice lines. The Assembly reiterated its resolve on Jan. 19 by a vote of 74 to 2 (Israel and France) with two abstentions (Cuba and Costa Rica). The Atlantic bloc (except for France), the British Commonwealth, the Soviet bloc, and the neutralist bloc were thus united in insisting that the *status quo* be restored. Israeli reluctance to yield soon evoked Egyptian threats to halt the clearing of the Canal and Asian-African demands for UN sanctions.

Washington proposed in mid-January that the UN Emergency Force should be deployed in the Gaza Strip and at the entrance to the Gulf of Aqaba in the wake of Israeli withdrawal. When Hammarskjold on Jan. 26 urged unconditional withdrawal with no guarantees, the Israeli Foreign Ministry declared his report a "masterpiece of obscurity," "negative and unconstructive," and "worthless." Repeated Israeli rejection of U.S. and UN appeals for prompt and unconditional evacuation led Washington policy-makers to contemplate sanctions against Israel—a proposal which aroused bitter opposition in many quarters in view of the fact that no such measures had been applied against the USSR in its comparable defiance of UN resolutions. In an extraordinary broadcast to the nation on Feb. 20, 1957, President Eisenhower declared:

The United Nations must not fail. I believe that—in the interests of peace—the United Nations has no choice but to exert pressure upon Israel to comply with the withdrawal resolutions. Of course, we still hope that the Government of Israel will see that its best immediate and long-term interests lie in compliance with the United Nations and in placing its trust in the resolutions of the United Nations and in the declaration of the United States with reference to the future.

I do not believe Israel's default should be ignored because the United Nations has not been able effectively to carry out its resolutions condemning the Soviet Union for its armed suppression of the people of Hungary. Perhaps this is a case where the proverb applies that two wrongs do not make a right.

No one deplores more than I the fact that the Soviet Union ignores the resolutions of the United Nations. Also no nation is more vigorous than is the United States in seeking to exert moral pressure against the Soviet Union, which by reason of its size and power and by reason of its veto in the United Nations Security Council, is relatively impervious to other types of sanction.

The United States and other free nations are making clear by every means at their command the evil of Soviet conduct in Hungary. It would indeed be a sad day if the United States ever felt that it had to subject Israel to the same type of moral pressure as is being applied to the Soviet Union.

There can, of course, be no equating of a nation like Israel with that of the Soviet Union. The people of Israel, like those of the United States, are imbued with a religious faith and a sense of moral values. We are entitled to expect, and do expect, from such peoples of the free world a contribution to world order which unhappily we cannot expect from a nation controlled by atheistic despots.

Since Israel was not a Super-Power ruled by immoral and despotic atheists but a tiny democracy of God-fearing people, it was, by the President's logic, an appropriate target for economic and physical coercion to compel compliance. Ben-Gurion demanded "justice." On Feb. 22 Charles Malik of Lebanon presented a UN resolution, co-sponsored by Iraq, Pakistan, Afghanistan, Indonesia, and the Sudan, proposing economic sanctions. After complex negotiations Golda Meir told the Assembly on March 1 that Israel would yield. Dulles assured Arab envoys in Washington that Israel had obtained "no promises or concessions whatsoever" from the USA. When Tel Aviv hesitated and sought a "clarification" of American policy, Eisenhower urged upon Ben-Gurion withdrawal "with the utmost speed." On March 4 the Israeli Premier ordered withdrawal on the basis of certain "assumptions," which were promptly denounced at the UN by Indian and Soviet spokesmen. UN troops occupied the

Gaza Strip on March 6 and Sharm el Sheik on March 8. On the basis of Hammarskjold's instructions that both military and civilian administration in Gaza would be "exclusively by the UNEF in the first instance," Maj. Gen. Burns named Col. Carl Engholm of Denmark as Governor.

After provoking pro-Egyptian rioting in Gaza, Nasser on March 11, 1957, adroitly accused the UN force of exceeding its authority, named Gen. Hassan Abdel Latif as Governor of Gaza, and proclaimed full Egyptian control of the Strip, with the UN soldiery limited to guarding the Israeli frontier. On March 15 he announced that Israeli shipping would continue to be barred from the Canal. Nasser's triumph was all but complete. Shipping, to be sure, proceeded during the spring of 1957 up the Gulf of Aqaba to the Israeli port of Elath since the invaders had demolished the Egyptian batteries on the Strait of Tiran. But Jordan and Saudi Arabia—both now in effect, as we shall see, U.S. protectorates—were sworn to keep the Gulf closed to Israel. With King Saud about to acquire a navy, with Washington's help, it seemed probable that the Gulf would again be closed and the *status quo* of Arab-Israeli "belligerency" fully restored.[7]

As regards the Canal, Nasser's victory was unqualified. Washington "in principle" continued to champion some form of international control as it championed "innocent passage" for ships of all nations through both the Canal and the Gulf. But Washington in practice virtuously opposed any coercion of any of the Arab States. Since Nasser would yield only to force, the result was total triumph snatched incongruously from military defeat with the help of the USA and the UN. Protracted negotiations during 1957 over administration of the Canal got nowhere. America compelled Western Europe to acquiesce in Egyptian control of the waterway as it compelled Israel to acquiesce in the *status quo ante bellum*, threatening Israel's ultimate extinction. Thus American diplomacy in 1956–57, dedicated to "anti-Communism" and "peace," wrought strange wonders in strange ways, eventuating in jeopardy for America's friends and allies and in the aggrandizement of America's enemies.

No comparable verdict can be rendered on Soviet diplomacy in 1956–57, since the men of Moscow succeeded in doing in Hungary what the men of Tel Aviv, Paris, and London failed to do in Egypt—*i.e.*, crushing their enemies —and emerged from the crisis with a net gain of power and prestige, despite disgrace, world-wide condemnation, and consternation everywhere among the Communist faithful. The Marxist Muscovites were able to depict their role in Egypt, quite plausibly to much of the world, as a victory over "Anglo-French imperialism" and their role in Hungary, half plausibly to part of the world, as a victory over "Fascism" and "American imperialism."

[7] For a detailed and documented analysis of these issues, with conclusions adverse to the Arab case, see Leo Gross, "Passage through the Suez Canal of Israel-bound Cargo and Israel Ships," *American Journal of International Law*, July, 1957, pp. 530–568.

Only in a tenuous sense could it be said that the "vanquished" in Eastern Europe in 1956 became the "victors" in 1957. Resistance on the Vistula and revolt on the Danube at least convinced the Soviet oligarchs that they must somehow strive for fresh formulas in dealing with their satellites in place of Stalinist despotism and terrorism. To the extent to which the Red Empire in 1958 and beyond might conceivably evolve into a commonwealth of free and independent members, each seeking its "way to socialism" by its own devices, the martyrs of Budapest might yet come to be regarded as contributors to a new birth of freedom.

6. AFTERMATH

During the year of confusion and frustration which followed the autumn crises of 1956, America's policy-makers, while never openly conceding that their championship of the Baghdad Pact and of the "liberation" of the Soviet satellites had contributed to violence and tragedy, nevertheless displayed some symptoms of awareness that their previous course fell somewhat short of the standards of successful statesmanship. In their efforts to arrive at a more promising dispensation, they strove hopefully for new negotiations with the USSR over disarmament (see pp. 258–260 and pp. 672–674), for a reconstruction of the shattered Atlantic alliance, for enhanced influence in Araby, and for measures, never fully acknowledged as to purpose, to "contain" the ambitions of the Egyptian dictator whom they had rescued from disaster. But the major result of an "agonizing reappraisal" was, as we shall see, a reversion to the stale formulas of the Cold War against Communism, from which few, if any, creative contributions to statesmanship could any longer be expected.

A résumé of decisions and indecisions will suggest some of the multiple dilemmas confronting Washington in the wake of the international anarchy of 1956. Having forbidden Israel, France, and Britain to "cut Nasser down to size" by force, the USA sought to achieve the same end through favors and fraud early in 1957 by cultivating Nasser's potential rivals for Pan-Arab leadership. Early in January, the White House invited King Saud of Saudi Arabia—a fabulously rich monarch with innumerable wives, 40 sons, incredible oil royalties, and golden Cadillacs—to a State visit to Washington. He arrived in New York on Jan. 29, 1957, where, despite U.S. and UN amenities, Mayor Wagner denounced him as "pro-slavery, anti-Jewish, and anti-Catholic" and condoned boycotts and picket lines protesting his reception. The King bespoke peace to the UN Assembly and was warmly welcomed by President Eisenhower on Jan. 30. Consultations and negotiations, with Crown Prince Abdul Illah of Iraq simultaneously in the U.S. capital, eventuated in a joint Eisenhower-Saud communiqué on Feb. 8 full of amiable generalities about "friendship," "cordiality," "cooperation," "independence," "self-determination," and opposition to all aggression, plus a pledge of more American arms to Saudi Arabia in return for a further five-year extension of the accord of June 18, 1951, for American use of the Dhahran Air Base, designed, in case of war, for bombing the Soviet oil fields of Trans-Caucasia.

An accord to this effect was announced in Washington April 8, 1957, in the form of an exchange of letters between Robert Murphy, Undersecretary of State, and Sheik Abdullah Al-Khayyal, Ambassador, providing for U.S. military, naval, and economic aid to defend "the independence and territorial integrity of Saudi Arabia and for the maintenance of internal security." What use in fact the King would make of the aid was clearly beyond Washington's control. Since the accord, like its predecessor, barred American citizens of Jewish faith from Saudi Arabia, Senator Jacob K. Javits, among others, protested that its terms were "intolerable"—with no result apart from explanations by the State Department that the base was indispensable. During his conference in Cairo in late February, 1957, with Nasser, President Shukri al-Kuwatly of Syria, and King Hussein of Jordan, the Arabian monarch had assured his colleagues, in effect, that Washington was now anti-Israeli as well as anti-Communist, but he declined, amid expressions of renewed Arab solidarity, to endorse the American anti-Communist orientation toward Mid-East issues.

Meanwhile, Eisenhower, Dulles, and aides conferred in Tuckers Town, Bermuda, March 20–23, with Harold Macmillan (who succeeded the discredited and ailing Eden as Prime Minister on Jan. 10), Selwyn Lloyd, and sundry advisers. This effort to restore the Anglo-American alliance ended in "general satisfaction" and in a communiqué of March 24, 1957, reaffirming faith in NATO, European unity, American willingness to participate in the Military Committee of the Baghdad Pact, German unification, sympathy for Hungary, American supply of guided missiles to Britain, continued nuclear tests pending a disarmament accord, and willingness to "permit limited international observation of such tests if the Soviet Union would do the same." Quite clearly, amid these generalities, no effective restoration of Anglo-American concord was achieved nor was any such result possible, despite British dependence on America, after Washington had made plain that it deemed "appeasement" of Arab nationalism more important than the defense of British interests in the Mid East.

The ultimate American remedy for the apparently insoluble problems of clashing ambitions and expectations in the Levant was, as elsewhere, new alliances against Communism on the model of the Baghdad Pact, despite the demonstrated fact that such alliances were not only irrelevant to the actual problems of the area but were certain to enhance, rather than diminish, Communist prestige.

On Jan. 5, 1957, in a new version of the Truman Doctrine of March 12, 1947, and the Formosa Resolution of Jan. 24, 1955, the President asked Congress for authorization to "undertake, in the general area of the Middle

427

East, military assistance programs with any nation or group of nations of that area desiring such assistance. Furthermore, he is authorized to employ the armed forces of the United States as he deems necessary to secure and protect the territorial integrity and political independence of any such nation or group of nations requesting such aid against overt armed aggression from any nation controlled by international Communism. . . ." Expenditures of $200,000,000 a year for military and economic aid to such Mid-East nations were contemplated.

The problems and conflicts of the area had little relationship to any threat of Communist aggression. Acheson ridiculed the doctrine: "To fight an enemy that is not going to attack with forces that do not exist to carry out a policy you have not yet decided upon." Moscow's response to this new challenge in the renewed "Cold War" was adroit. On Feb. 11, 1957, Shepilov delivered notes (at once made public) to the U.S., British, and French Ambassadors, proposing a "six-point program" for peace in the Levant. The four Great Powers should pledge themselves to a settlement by way of (1) "exclusively peaceful means on the basis of the method of negotiation"; (2) "non-interference in internal affairs" and "respect for the sovereignty and independence" of all Near and Middle Eastern countries; (3) "refusal to undertake any attempts to draw these countries into military alignments with the participation of the Great Powers"; (4) "the liquidation of foreign bases and the withdrawal of foreign troops"; (5) "joint refusal to supply arms to countries of the Near and Middle East"; and (6) "assistance in economic development . . . without putting forward any political, military, or other conditions incompatible with the dignity or sovereignty of these countries." Three days later Moscow asked the UN Assembly to consider U.S. "aggressive acts constituting a threat to security and peace"—e.g., the Eisenhower Doctrine, new atomic bases abroad, enlarged appropriations for arms, the "militarization" of West Germany, etc.

The appeal to the UN, as expected, was rejected. The "six-point program" was at once dismissed by Washington officialdom as "propaganda," and formally rejected on March 11. So it was. Yet it was shrewdly calculated to make a powerful appeal, as in fact it did, to all Arab-Asian "neutralist" leaders, and to embarrass an America which, early in 1957, had no policy for dealing with the issues of the hour except more military alliances against a non-existent threat of Communist armed assault.

The "Eisenhower Doctrine" was, after much debate, approved by the House, 355 to 61, Jan. 30, and by the Senate, 72 to 19, March 3, after slight modifications had been reconciled. The President signed the Congressional Joint Resolution, March 9, 1957, in the name of "friendship," "peace," "freedom," and reduction of "the Communist danger in the Middle East" and strengthening "the general stability of the area." Ex-Congressman James P. Richards was dispatched to the Levant to promote "cooperation" and "the greatest

possible measure of understanding and recognition of common interests."
Although spurned by Syria, Jordan, and Egypt, and received with reserve in
Israel, he succeeded by the end of his mission in committing American taxpayers to pay $175,000,000 to various Mid-East governments in the name of
economic and military aid against Communism.

Since the conflicts of competing nationalisms and imperialisms in the Mid
East had nothing to do with "Communism," it is not strange that the first
application, if the term is permissible, of the Eisenhower Doctrine should
have had a confused context and a confused result. The locus was the Hashemite Kingdom of Jordan, a ramshackle, unviable "sovereignty," long dependent on British subsidies. Of Jordan's 1,500,000 inhabitants, almost half
were Arab refugees from Palestine residing miserably in the areas east of
Israel which passed to Jordan under the armistice accord of 1949. Here, as
in Iraq and Saudi Arabia, medieval kings sought to perpetuate feudalism while
young intellectuals, bureaucrats, army officers, and desperate peasants saw
hope in Nasser's anti-monarchism and promises of social reform. Jordan's
King Abdullah ibn Hussein had been assassinated in July, 1951. His eldest
son and successor, King Talal, was *non compos mentis* and was replaced in
turn by a young grandson, King Hussein.

Hussein's Premier, Suleiman Nabulsi, was pro-Nasser and anti-West. He
was dismissed by the King on April 10, 1957. What followed was total confusion, with Jordan threatened with intervention and possible partition by
Syria, Iraq, and Egypt, and Israel resolved to strike if Iraqi troops should
enter Jordan. On April 14 King Hussein executed a military *coup* against
allegedly pro-Nasser elements, eventuating in the arrest of Nabulsi and the
deportation to Syria of Maj. Gen. Ali Abu Nuwar, Chief of Staff, replaced by
Maj. Gen. Ali Hayari. Dr. Hussein Fakhri Khalidi, a bitterly anti-Zionist and
"pro-Western" Palestinian Arab, was named Premier while Washington
warned Israel against any intervention. On April 20 Hayari joined his
predecessor in exile in Damascus and accused "certain foreign military attachés" in Amman of "conspiring." The White House announced on April
24 that "the independence and integrity of Jordan is vital," apparently on
the assumption, which was wholly problematical, that Jordanian politicians
were somehow engaged in choosing between a pro-Western orientation and a
pro-Nasser, neutralist, and presumably pro-Communist orientation.

King Hussein, being much in need of cash, gladly embraced "anti-Communism," alleging an Egyptian-Syrian-Soviet plot to overthrow the monarchy
and accusing his foes at home of being "brothers and collaborators of Communist Jews" and of taking orders from Tel Aviv, "the center of Communism
in the Middle East." On April 25, 1957, he dismissed Khalidi, named octo-
genarian Ibrahim Hashem Premier, proclaimed martial law, outlawed all
political parties and trade unions, and ordered all suspected "subversives"
jailed. The USA rushed its Sixth Fleet to the Eastern Mediterranean, ap-

parently to prevent any Israeli, Syrian, or Egyptian intervention, and granted Hussein $10,000,000, with more to follow, to help save his kingdom from "international Communism." Thus Jordan became an American protectorate and Washington celebrated victory, although no one could say with certainty who had triumphed over whom about what.

Amid other confusions, British forces were engaged in two frontier wars by midsummer of 1957. One was fought against Yemen to protect the Aden Protectorate against Yemeni incursions or, so the Yemeni alleged, to enlarge it at Yemen's expense. The other was waged in support of Said bin Taimor, Sultan of Muscat and Oman, against rebels led by the Iman of Oman, Ghalib bin Ali and his brother, Talib bin Ali. Both the Oman rebels and the Yemeni received aid and encouragement, including American arms, from Saudi Arabia and Egypt. Both accused Britain of "aggression" and appealed to the USA, the USSR, and the UN for help. Meanwhile both Syria and Egypt, in public treason trials of scapegoats, accused agents of the USA of seeking to overthrow their governments through bribery and intrigue. . . .

The next crisis, in a series which promised to be of long duration, was precipitated on Aug. 18, 1957, when President al-Kuwatly of Syria, on the eve of a week's visit with Nasser in Cairo, dismissed Gen. Tewfik Nizamudden as Chief of Staff and appointed to his post Col. (now Gen.) Afif Bizri, a pro-Soviet "Leftist" like his friend, Lt. Col. Abdul Hamid Serraj, director of Syria's Army Intelligence. Bizri accused Washington of having conspired to murder him. Washington, having been accused by President al-Kuwatly of trying to overthrow the Syrian Government, expelled the Syrian Ambassador and voiced alarm that Syria was about to become a "Soviet satellite." Loy Henderson was rushed to Turkey to confer with Premier Adnan Menderes and Kings Hussein and Feisal.

The alarm was unwarranted. In any case the Eisenhower Doctrine was inapplicable, since the power-holders in Damascus welcomed Soviet aid and arms and, while reiterating their devotion to "neutralism," scorned U.S. "help" and bitterly denounced American meddling. In such a devil's brew the policy-makers of Washington, having long since alienated their friends and assisted their foes in the Mid East, were incapable, for the present at least, of formulating any policy having any relevance to real problems or even to American objectives—which continued to lack definition save in terms of perpetuating an untenable *status quo.*

The American dilemma was aggravated in the fall and winter of 1957–58. In September Moscow warned of "Western aggression" against Syria. By October Khrushchev was accusing Henderson and Dulles of plotting a Turkish attack and declaring that the USSR would come to Syria's defense. Washington cried "lies" and warned that the USA would defend Turkey against any Soviet assault. This "war scare" waned with Zhukov's ouster. Moscow claimed credit for averting hostilities and saving Syria. On Jan. 27, 1958, as Dulles

arrived in Ankara as "observer" at a Baghdad Pact conference, Syria negotiated union with Egypt, approved Feb. 21, by a 99% vote in a plebiscite in
both countries ratifying the formation of a "United Arab Republic" with
Nasser as President. Iraq and Jordan promptly formed a monarchical counter-
federation. Yemen federated with the Egyptian-Syrian Union. Saudi Arabia
and Lebanon hesitated. Arab unity was still remote. But Nasser had become
the central symbol of age-old Arab aspirations, whose partial realization
threatened new perils for Israel, new opportunities for the USSR, and new
embarrassments for the USA—whose policies had facilitated Nasser's experiment in Caesarism.

If we may paraphrase Goethe, who once observed that "against stupidity
even the gods are helpless," we may note that against outbreaks of anarchy
even the boldest of "doctrines" and the most virtuous of UN resolutions are
futile. Violence is endemic in places of hatred in times of trouble. It threatened
to continue in the Mid East so long as outside Powers sought to use against
one another the new fanaticisms of the peoples of the Levant. Some measure
of order and stability, some hope of peace, some promise of ultimate plenty
throughout the area could perhaps be had if—but only if—decision-makers
in Washington, London, Paris, and Moscow should come to terms regarding
their respective interests and their common purposes in the region. Such a
consummation may be finally inevitable, since the alternative is intolerable.
But it was not yet in sight in 1958.

SUGGESTED READINGS

Anshen, Ruth Nanda (ed.), in collaboration with Ernest Jackh: *Mid-East: World-Center*,
  New York, Harper, 1956.
Beal, John Robinson: *John Foster Dulles: A Biography*, New York, Harper, 1957.
Beatty, Charles: *De Lesseps of Suez: The Man and His Times*, New York, Harper,
  1957.
Ben-Gurion, David: *Rebirth and Destiny of Israel*, New York, Philosophical Library, 1957.
Black, C. E. (ed.): *Challenge in Eastern Europe*, New Brunswick, N.J., Rutgers Univer-
  sity Press, 1954.
Davis, Helen Miller (ed.): *Constitutions, Electoral Laws, Treaties of States in the Near
  and Middle East*, Durham, N.C., Duke University Press, 1947.
Eban, Abba: *Voice of Israel*, New York, Horizon Press, 1957.
Fernau, Friedrich Wilhelm: *Moslems on the March*, New York, Knopf, 1954.
Foot, Michael, and Mervyn Jones: *Guilty Men, 1957: Suez & Cyprus*, New York, Rine-
  hart, 1957.
Frank, Waldo: *Bridgehead: The Drama of Israel*, New York, George Braziller, 1957.
Goitein, S. D.: *Jews and Arabs*, New York, Schocken, 1955.
Haines, C. Grove (ed.): *The Threat of Soviet Imperialism*, Baltimore, The Johns Hop-
  kins Press, 1954.
Henriques, Robert: *A Hundred Hours to Suez: An Account of Israel's Campaign in the
  Sinai Peninsula*, New York, Viking, 1957.
Izzeddin, Nejla: *The Arab World*, Chicago, Regnery, 1953.
Jarvis, H. Wood: *Pharaoh to Farouk*, New York, Macmillan, 1956.
Kertesz, Stephen D. (ed.): *The Fate of East Central Europe*, Notre Dame, Ind., Uni-
  versity of Notre Dame Press, 1956.

Kirk, George: *The Middle East, 1945–1950*, New York, Oxford, 1954.
Laqueur, Walter Z.: *Communism and Nationalism in the Middle East*, New York, Praeger, 1956.
Lasky, Melvin J. (ed.): *The Hungarian Revolution: The Story of the October Uprising*, New York, Praeger, 1957.
Lenczowski, George: *The Middle East in World Affairs*, Ithaca, N.Y., Cornell University Press, 1956.
Litvinoff, Barnet: *Ben-Gurion of Israel*, New York, Praeger, 1954.
Lukacs, John A.: *The Great Powers in Eastern Europe*, New York, American Book, 1953.
Michener, James A.: *The Bridge at Andau*, New York, Random House, 1957.
The Middle East: A Political and Economic Survey, New York, Royal Institute of International Affairs, 1954.
Nuseibeh, Hazem Zaki: *The Ideas of Arab Nationalism*, Ithaca, N.Y., Cornell University Press, 1956.
Philby, H. St. John: *Sa'udi Arabia*, New York, Praeger, 1955.
Sanger, Richard H.: *The Arabian Peninsula*, Ithaca, N.Y., Cornell University Press, 1956.
Shwadran, Benjamin: *The Middle East, Oil and the Great Powers*, New York, Praeger, 1955.
Sulzberger, C. L.: *The Big Thaw: A Personal Exploration of the "New" Russia and the Orbit Countries*, New York, Harper, 1956.
Ulam, Adam B.: *Titoism and the Cominform*, Cambridge, Mass., Harvard University Press, 1955.
United Nations: *Report of the Special Committee on the Problem of Hungary*, New York, General Assembly, 1957.
Zinner, Paul E. (ed.): *National Communism and Popular Revolt in Eastern Europe*, New York, Columbia University Press, 1956.

As I walked through the wilderness of this world . . . I saw a man clothed with rags, standing in a certain place, with his face from his own house, a book in his hand, and a great burden on his back. I looked, and saw him open the book, and read therein; and, as he read, he broke out with a lamentable cry, saying . . . "I am for certain informed that this our city will be burned with fire from heaven; in which fearful overthrow, both myself, with thee my wife, and you my sweet babes, shall miserably come to ruin, except (the which yet I see not) some way of escape can be found, whereby we may be delivered. . . ." And as he read, he burst out crying: "What shall I do to be saved?"—JOHN BUNYAN, *Pilgrim's Progress*, 1678.

A Book of

PROSPECTS

In times like the present, men should utter nothing for which they would not willingly be responsible through time and in eternity. . . . The dogmas of the quiet past are inadequate to the stormy present. The occasion is piled high with difficulty, and we must rise with the occasion. As our case is new, so we must think anew and act anew. We must disenthrall ourselves. . . . Fellow-citizens, we cannot escape history. . . . No personal significance or insignificance can spare one or another of us. The fiery trial through which we pass will light us down, in honor or dishonor, to the latest generation. We shall nobly save or meanly lose the last best hope of earth.—ABRAHAM LINCOLN, 1862.

CHAPTER XI

THE HERITAGE OF FASCISM

1. THE NEW CAESARS

Tyranny naturally arises out of democracy, and the most aggravated form of tyranny and slavery out of the most extreme form of liberty. . . . The leaders of the poor deprive the rich of their estates and distribute them among the people, at the same time taking care to reserve the larger part for themselves. And the persons whose property is taken from them are compelled to defend themselves before the people as best they can. And then, although they may have no desire of change, the others charge them with plotting against the people and being friends of oligarchy. And the end is that when they see the people, not of their own accord, but through ignorance, and because they are deceived by informers, seeking to do them wrong, then at last they are forced to become oligarchs in reality. . . . This, and no other, is the root from which a tyrant springs. . . . Having a mob entirely at his disposal, he is not restrained from shedding the blood of kinsmen. . . . Some he kills and others he banishes, at the same time hinting at the abolition of debts and the partition of lands. . . . Then comes the famous request for a bodyguard, which is a device of all those who have got thus far in their tyrannical career. . . . Then he is always stirring up some war or other, in order that the people may require a leader. . . . He must look about him and see who is valiant, who is high-minded, who is wise, who is wealthy . . . and must seek occasion against them whether he will or no, until he has made a purge of the state. . . . And the more detestable his actions are to the citizens the more satellites and the greater devotion in them will he require. . . . This is real tyranny, about which there can no longer be a mistake: as the saying is, the people who would escape the smoke which is the slavery of freemen, have fallen into the fire which is the tyranny of slaves.—PLATO, *The Republic.*

WORLD politics in the 20th Century resembles world politics in other centuries (save for the ages of the Universal Empires) in that it revolves around the efforts of sovereign nation-states to get the better of one another in the game of power—and therefore around the efforts of particular Powers to conquer all and the counter-efforts, thus far successful, of others to preserve their sovereignty. But the process differs from most historical antecedents in this: that some contemporary Powers in their domestic political arrangements are democracies, while others are despotisms, autocracies, oligarchies, or "dictatorships," with the latter aspiring most assiduously to domination of the world and being successively checkmated and vanquished by the former.

This distinction, which may not long endure, does not demonstrate that non-

434

democratic governments are *ipso facto* more addicted to efforts at world mastery than democratic governments. It perhaps suggests that the insecure and "marginal" nation-states of our time, in their quest for a "place in the sun," are more given to despotism and aggression than the wealthy and "satiated" Atlantic democracies. What is striking in the ensuing conflicts is that each military triumph of democracy over autocracy has eventuated in an ultimate diminution of democracy and an extension of autocracy. The triumphant democracies of 1918 shortly found themselves in a world in which there was less democracy than in the world of 1914. The victorious freemen of 1945 found themselves by 1950 in a world in which there was less freedom than in the world of 1939.

Cautious scholars will be scholarly and cautious in drawing general conclusions from these facts. The conclusion which might seem justified by the evidence perhaps comes to something like the following. Democracy in its modern form, as a pattern of government and a way of life, flourishes best where most people have been taught to read and write, where living standards are high, and where a growing middle class looks forward to an ever more abundant life. These conditions of existence in our era have come to prevail in years of prosperity in most of Western Europe and North America, in Australia, New Zealand, Japan, and a few other areas on the edge of vast slums full of illiterate and impoverished people among whom "democracy" has little meaning. Even among the favored "Western" peoples, want and worry, if sufficiently acute, beget desperation productive of despotism. Effective democracy presupposes full stomachs, high hopes, general tolerance, and peace of mind. These goals of "progress" have been periodically wiped out for millions of human beings by the impact of great wars and great depressions. Widespread anxiety and misery, even in literate and once wealthy communities, engender fanatical demands for salvation and mass support for demagogues and dictators who promise it. The promise can most readily be fulfilled through the magic of militarism which in turn promotes war which produces more poverty and fear. Given these circumstances, it is scarcely strange that successive world wars should produce a constant diminution of the areas where democracy prospers and a constant expansion of the areas where autocracies prevail, regardless of the verdict of battle.

The "totalitarians" of our time, despite their fruity rhetoric, represent a reversion to ancient forms of enslavement of body and mind. Most of mankind in most past ages has been hungry and fearful and ignorant and therefore ruled by despots or oligarchs. The expectation, conceived by the Industrial Revolution, of universal abundance and general security and literacy has come to birth only in a few happy Western societies and even here has been often crippled in childhood by the business cycle and by armed struggles among the Powers. The first "totalitarian State" of the 20th Century, with its apparatus of mass propaganda, secret police, political terrorism, and suppression of human dignity, personal freedom, and representative government, emerged out of the Russian Revolution. The democratic aspirations of the short-lived "Provisional Government" of 1917 were betrayed by conspirators promising the millennium and supported by a people traditionally committed to autocracy by their historical experience—and now reduced to beggary, anarchy, and despair by war, defeat, and social breakdown. Other adventurers, copying the techniques of the new oligarchs of Muscovy, later established other "totalitarian States" on the ruins of democracy in Italy, Japan, Germany, Portugal, Spain, and elsewhere amid the miseries of inflation, depression, and economic paralysis.

The disciples of liberty have as yet no message which is very meaningful to the dark and dismal multitudes of Asia, Africa, and South America. The message rings hollow even to the most sophisticated Western peoples when men have no jobs, no hope, and no peace. Those who are desperate demand desperate measures and desperate leaders. Democracy presupposes the absence of mass despair which, once rampant, breeds dictatorship. The mass woes which drove Russians (and, a generation later, Chinese) to Communism, and drove Italians, Japanese, and Germans to Fascism also won converts to socialism in Western Europe and Britain and produced the "New Deal" in America. Even in the richest land on earth, however, full prosperity was not recaptured until public spending for total war provided abundance for all.

Since it is true in mathematics that things equal to the same thing are equal to each other, we easily assume that the same theorem holds true in politics and that Communism and Fascism as ideologies and State forms are therefore identical, with the latter equivalent to "Brown" or "Black Bolshevism" and the former equivalent to "Red Fascism." This stereotype among the Atlantic peoples, happily unafflicted by either type of despotism, is wholly understandable since both forms of contemporary totalitarianism have much in common. The analogy is nevertheless false in at least one respect. Communist dictators, without exception, are committed in theory and practice to "socialism," meaning the collectivization of agriculture and the planned promotion under public ownership of industrialization in hitherto "backward" communities. Fascist dictators, without exception, are committed in theory and practice to preserving the privileges of agrarian and industrial elites against mass unrest and popular demands for "equality" and "social justice." Both use the weapons of the Police State to secure obedience, but employ their "monopoly of legality" for quite different purposes.

Communists in power, while conspiratorially concerned with "saving the world," are not dependent upon militarism and war as a means to economic, social, and political stability. But Fascists in power, at least in industrialized States, are invariably dependent upon militarism and war as a means to economic, social, and political stability. As the proof of the pudding is in the eating, so the proof of the proposition here advanced lies in the fact that

436

World War II was unleashed by Fascists, not by Communists, and in the probability that World War III, if men permit it to come, will be unleashed by Fascists, not by Communists.

Contemporary Communism is a totalitarian system of governance dedicated, in the name of achieving a "classless society," to replacing the traditional social hierarchy of nobles-plutocrats-middle-class-workers-peasants with the new hierarchy of rulers (Party bosses)-intelligentsia-workers-peasants, and maintaining the authority of a political oligarchy through socialist industrialization and through the systematic persecution of scapegoats—*e.g.*, "class enemies," kulaks, businessmen, ideological and political dissidents, and any other potentially heterodox group against which mass aggressions can be mobilized. Contemporary Fascism is a totalitarian system of governance, dedicated, in the name of the "Corporative State," to preserving the traditional social hierarchy of nobles-plutocrats-middle-class-workers-peasants and maintaining the authority of a political oligarchy through mass militarism and through the systematic persecution of scapegoats—*e.g.*, liberals, pacifists, Marxists, Masons, Jews, and any other potentially heterodox group against which mass aggressions can be mobilized. Communist oligarchs are upstarts and traitors to their class and country who dispossess and destroy the old elites by violence and make themselves a new elite of manipulators and managers of "backward" societies pulling themselves up by their bootstraps, with infinite agony, toward industrialized and urbanized economies based on socialism. Fascist oligarchs are adventurers who make deals with the old elites and become directors of "advanced" societies by a program of deflecting middle-class and lower-class resentments away from elites and against pariahs and of promoting prosperity via public spending through an alliance of Big Business and Big Brass for armaments, conquest, and total war.

These similarities and differences between the two major types of totalitarians in our time will be illustrated in the surveys of the recent foreign policies of the Powers which follow. Although Communism is the older form of the new tyranny, with Fascism the extreme form of counter-revolution against it, we shall first examine the diplomacy and strategy of the erstwhile Fascist Powers, since the decisions of their rulers (rather than those of policy-makers in democratic or Communist States) precipitated World War II and unwittingly built the global arena in which the Communist Powers and the Democracies were later to be pitted against one another.

2. JAPAN: FROM MILITARISM TO PACIFISM

Japan cannot remove the difficulties in Eastern Asia unless she adopts a policy of "blood and iron." . . . If we want to control China, we must first crush the United States. . . . But in order to conquer China, we must first conquer Manchuria and Mongolia. In order to conquer the world, we must first conquer China.

. . . Having China's entire resources at our disposal, we shall proceed to conquer India, Asia Minor, Central Asia, and even Europe. But to get control of Manchuria and Mongolia is the first step if the Yamato race wishes to distinguish themselves.—PREMIER BARON TANAKA, in a memorial to the Emperor, July 25, 1927.

In the summer of the year 1945 the people and government of the newest of the world's "Great Powers" found themselves reduced to a parlous pass. Almost all of a once proud Navy and a mighty merchant marine was far-scattered wreckage resting on sands and corals at the bottom of the sea. A great Army, despite suicidal heroism, had lost battle after battle and island after island, with its reserves bogged down on a continent which none, since the Mongols, had ever conquered. Most cities were wastelands of ruin, seared with fire bombs and high explosives. Millions were dead. Living millions were sick unto death of suffering and dying to no purpose.

At Yalta the USSR secretly agreed to declare war on Japan three months after the capitulation of the Reich. On April 5, 1945, Molotov informed Ambassador Naotake Sato that the Soviet Government was denouncing the Neutrality Pact of 1941 because Japan had aided Germany against the USSR and "is fighting the USA and Britain, which are allies of the Soviet Union." Koiso at once resigned and gave way to a new Cabinet headed by Adm. Kantoro Suzuki. Tokyo vainly offered to make a bargain with Moscow, involving the evacuation of Manchuria and North China. Tokyo put out peace feelers in various capitals, hoping, again in vain, to use Moscow as a mediator.

On July 26, 1945, Truman, Churchill, and Attlee, with the approval of Chiang Kai-shek and in the presence of Stalin, proposed a program for ending the war. They threatened "the inevitable and complete destruction of the Japanese armed forces and just as inevitably the utter devastation of the Japanese homeland" unless Japan, "brought to the threshold of annihilation," would "follow the path of reason." The terms demanded the elimination "for all time" of the "authority and influence of those who have deceived and misled the people of Japan into embarking on world conquest. . . . Points in Japanese territory to be designated by the Allies shall be occupied to secure the achievement of the basic objective we are here setting forth. . . . We do not intend that the Japanese shall be enslaved as a race or destroyed as a nation, but stern justice shall be meted out to all war criminals [and] just reparations [will be exacted]." Under the Cairo Declaration Japanese sovereignty would be limited to Honshu, Hokkaido, Kyushu, Shikoku, "and such minor islands as we determine." Japanese forces would be disarmed. Civil liberties and democracy must be established. Allied troops would be withdrawn with the attainment of these objectives and the establishment, "in accordance with the freely expressed wish of the Japanese people, of a peacefully inclined and responsible Government. We call upon the Government of Japan to proclaim now the unconditional surrender of all Japanese armed forces, and to

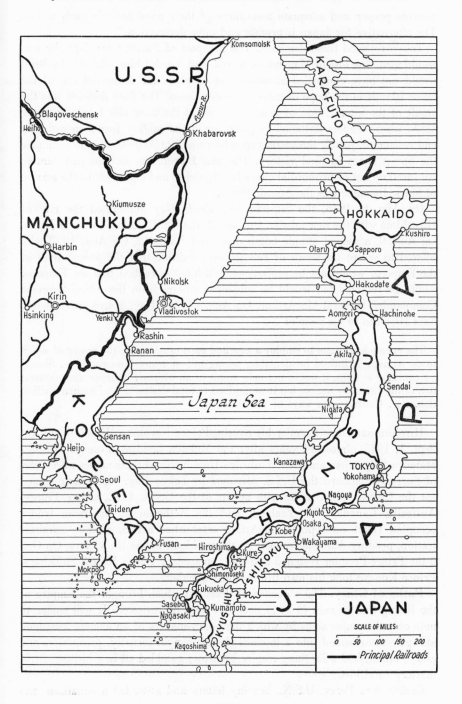

provide proper and adequate assurances of their good faith in such action. The alternative for Japan is prompt and utter destruction."

Tokyo rejected these demands. The prospect of Soviet entry into the war would mean the loss of Manchuria, Korea, and North China. But this by itself would not have compelled abandonment of plans for fierce defense of the home islands in the hope of more favorable terms. The final decision was the result of the intervention of a new Power—at the time allied only with the USA, whose leaders hastened to make use of its mighty forces in order to end resistance, justify the secret expenditure of $2,000,000,000, and minimize the Soviet share in final victory. The new Power was an inhuman demon, conjured up out of primordial chaos by physicists and engineers in the service of Mars. Its name was the Atomic Bomb.

On Aug. 6, 1945, the Superfortress *Enola Gay* obliterated the city of Hiroshima with the new missile. On Aug. 8, the USSR declared war on Japan. On Aug. 9, a second atomic bomb destroyed Nagasaki. On Aug. 10, Toyko offered to accept the terms of July 26 on condition that the prerogatives of the Emperor would not be prejudiced. Washington replied that the Emperor would be retained but would be subject to orders from the Allied Supreme Commander, General MacArthur. On Aug. 14, V-J Day, Tokyo surrendered. Said Hirohito to his people:

> The enemy has begun to employ a new and most cruel bomb, the power of which to do damage is indeed incalculable, taking toll of many innocent lives. Should we continue to fight, it would not only result in an ultimate collapse and obliteration of the Japanese nation, but it would lead to total destruction of human civilization. . . . Cultivate the ways of rectitude.

Hirohito named as Premier his cousin, Prince Naruhiko Higashi-Kuni. On Sept. 1, 1945, almost 14 years after the Mukden incident, Foreign Minister Mamoru Shigemitsu and Gen. Yoshijiro Umezh signed their names to Articles of Surrender aboard the U.S.S. *Missouri* in Tokyo Bay. MacArthur signed for the United States, along with agents of the USSR, U.K., China, France, Australia, Canada, New Zealand, and the Netherlands. American troops occupied Tokyo on Sept. 8. MacArthur established a U.S. military administration, pending Allied agreement on the problems facing the victors. On Oct. 5 the Prince-Premier resigned and was replaced by Baron Kijuro Shidehara. Prince Konoye took his own life in mid-December.

Paths of Glory. The sequence of decisions which brought the Empire of the Rising Sun to ruin in 1945 need not here be reviewed. It will suffice to note only the major steps by which the policy-makers of an ancient kingdom, abruptly transformed into a modern Power, sought security, prosperity, and glory; established a far-flung empire by arms; gambled all in a bid for world mastery; and lost.

Commodore Perry, U.S.N., bearing letters and gifts, led a squadron into

JAPAN: FROM MILITARISM TO PACIFISM

Tokyo Bay in 1853 on a mission to "open" to Western commerce a long-isolated land whose rulers and people wanted no contacts with aliens. This instance of Western dynamism was to have the curious result that the land thus opened was to become 6 decades later the ally of the USA against Germany, 9 decades later the mortal enemy of America in the Pacific, and 10 decades later the ally of the USA against Russia. Contact with the West led the feudal nobles of Japan to overthrow the Shogun or Regent in 1867, grant full power to the young Emperor Mutsu Hito, and embark upon a program of "Westernization"—*i.e.*, railways, steamships, machines, factories, banks, and the modernized Army and Navy.

Once possessed of Western components of power, Japan's elite, now a fusion of nobles, businessmen, and militarists, proceeded to employ them in Western ways. In 1894 Japan invaded Korea, long a dependency of the Chinese Empire. War with China followed. The year 1895 brought victory and the annexation of Formosa, the Pescadores, and the Liaotung Peninsula—with Russia, Germany, and France intervening to compel the victors to give up Liaotung. The conclusion in Tokyo was to isolate and challenge Russia. In 1902 Japan made an alliance with Britain. In 1904 Japan attacked and defeated Russia, acquiring in the Treaty of Portsmouth (Sept. 5, 1905) Southern Sakhalin (Karafuto), Russia's leaseholds in Port Arthur and elsewhere on the Liaotung Peninsula, and Russian railway and mining rights in South Manchuria. "Teddy" Roosevelt obligingly agreed in July, 1905, that Tokyo might do what it liked in Korea on condition of abandoning any designs on the Philippines. Japan annexed Korea in 1910 and four years later took Kiaochow from Germany and sought in the "21 demands" of 1915 to impose a protectorate on China. The year 1918 found Japan in occupation of Shantung, Manchuria, Inner Mongolia, Northern Sakhalin, and Eastern Siberia.

But an alarmed America now made clear that the Tokyo expansionists had overreached themselves. In the settlements of 1922–25 Japan was compelled to accept naval inferiority to the USA and Britain; abandon the Chinese and Russian territories it had seized; and agree to respect the Open Door and the *status quo* in the Pacific.

The Way of Fascism. The rulers of Japan had already demonstrated that they had learned Western ways all too well. Capitalism, nationalism, imperialism, militarism were faithfully copied. A new society of teeming poor and worried rich had somehow to find means of promoting patriotism and prosperity. The new businessmen dominated the Minseito Party. Eight *Zaibatsu* families—Mitsui, Mitsubishi, Asano, Sumitoma, Shibusawa, Yasuda, Okura, and Suzuki—controlled industry and banking. The old aristocrats and the Army dominated the Seiyukai Party. Both paid lip service to democracy. Government was in form a constitutional monarchy. In a world of expanding markets the rulers of this land of flourishing industry and rapidly growing population might have found the means to security and stability without vio-

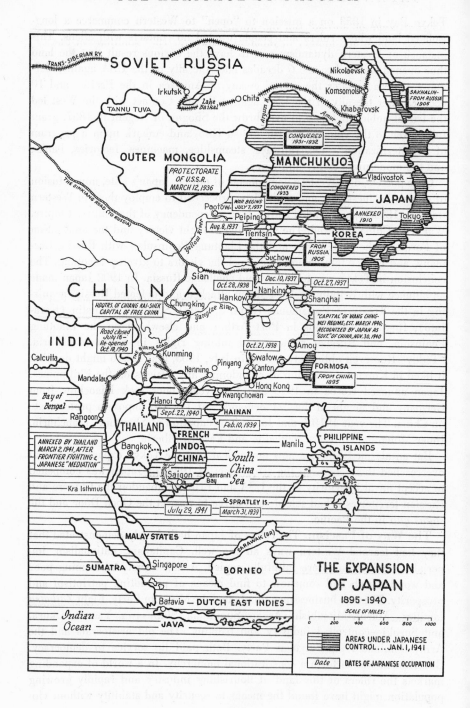

THE EXPANSION
OF JAPAN
1895-1940

SCALE OF MILES:

0   200   400   600   800   1000

AREAS UNDER JAPANESE
CONTROL...JAN.1,1941

Date   DATES OF JAPANESE OCCUPATION

lence at home or abroad. But the world economy collapsed in 1929, leaving millions jobless and hungry in Japan as elsewhere. The "solution" of Fascism was embraced with fervor by those responsible for Japanese destinies.

On Nov. 14, 1930, Premier Hamaguchi was assassinated. Premier Inukai was next slain by patriotic terrorists, inspired by the Army. On Feb. 26, 1936, in an attempted *coup*, military terrorists killed Saito, Keeper of the Privy Seal, Finance Minister Takahashi, and General Watanobe. Premier Okada, who barely escaped death, resigned his post to Koki Hirota. Government by murder became, as usual, government by secret police and "thought control." But the ultra-patriots and militarists supplemented violence at home with violence abroad as the sovereign means of enlisting popular support of their purposes and finding an "answer" to the desperate problems of Japan's impoverishment.

Tokyo's war lords seized Manchuria in September, 1931. They discovered that China was helpless and that the Western Powers were indisposed to say them nay. When it became clear that anti-Communism was a useful symbol for arousing patriotism and befuddling the Western Democracies, Japan's policy-makers joined the Nazi Reich in signing the Anti-Comintern Pact of Nov. 25, 1936,[1] waged border warfare in Manchuria and Mongolia against the Russians (with signal lack of success), and finally sought to solve their prob-

---

[1] "The German Government and the Japanese Government, recognizing that the aim of the Communist International known as the Comintern is directed at disrupting and violating existing States with all means at its command and convinced that to tolerate the Communist International's interference with the internal affairs of nations not only endangers their internal peace and social well-being but threatens world peace at large, animated by a desire to work in common against Communist disruptive influences, have arrived at the following agreement: 1. The high contracting parties agree to mutually inform each other concerning the activities of the Communist International, to consult with each other concerning measures to combat this activity, and to execute these measures in close cooperation with each other. 2. The two high contracting States will jointly invite third parties whose domestic peace is endangered by the disruptive activities of the Communist International to embark upon measures for warding these off in accordance with the spirit of this agreement or to join in it. 3. For this agreement, both the German and Japanese texts are regarded as original versions. It becomes effective the day of signing and is in force for a period of five years. The high contracting States will, at the proper time before expiration of this period, arrive at an understanding with each other concerning the form this cooperation is to take." SUPPLEMENTARY PROTOCOL:
"A. The competent authorities of both high contracting parties will cooperate most closely in connection with the exchange of information concerning the activities of the Communist International, as well as in connection with publicity and defense measures against the Communist International. B. The competent authorities of both high contracting parties will, within the framework of existing laws, take strict measures against those who, at home or abroad, directly or indirectly, are active in the service of the Communist International or lend a helping hand to its disruptive work. With a view to facilitating the cooperation of the competent authorities of both high contracting parties, specified in (A), a Permanent Commission will be created. In this Commission the further defensive measures necessary for combatting the disruptive work of the Communist International will be considered and deliberated upon. Berlin, Nov. 25, 1936; that is, the Nov. 25 of the eleventh year of the Showa Period. RIBBENTROP, MUSHAKOJI."

443

lem in July, 1937, by launching an all-out effort to conquer China. The ensuing war proved endless and hopeless, despite vast slaughter and devastation—verbally deplored but tacitly connived in by Western statesmen who were favorably impressed with Japan's "anti-Communist" crusade.

The outbreak of war in Europe confronted Tokyo's Fascist warrior-politicians with new opportunities and difficult choices. The Nazi conquest of France enabled them to impose a protectorate on Indochina. Prince Konoye returned to the Premiership in July, 1940, as head of a purely militarist Cabinet in which Yosuke Matsuoka was Foreign Minister. Political parties were dissolved in the name of undiluted totalitarianism. The continued neutrality of the USA and the USSR was essential for the achievement of Japanese purposes in Asia and of Axis objectives in Europe. Washington, like Moscow, was granting small-scale aid to China and preparing (unlike Moscow) to give large-scale aid to Britain, as by the naval base–destroyer exchange of Sept. 2. Konoye finally yielded to Nazi pleas for a full alliance. On Sept. 27, 1940, in Berlin, Ribbentrop, Ciano, and Ambassador Saburo Kurusu signed a 10-year treaty of "cooperation," by the terms of which Japan and the Axis Powers reciprocally "recognized and respected" one another's "leadership" in establishing "a New Order in Europe" and "a New Order in Greater East Asia" and agreed (Art. 3) to "assist one another with all political, economic, and military means when one of the three Contracting Powers is attacked by a Power at present not involved in the European war or in the Chinese-Japanese conflict." This joint menace failed to deter the USA from increasing aid to Britain and China. Tokyo voiced threats—and waited.

The Year of Decision. The war lords of Nippon at first moved cautiously through the vicissitudes of the strange year 1941. As early as August of 1940 Hitler had come to his decision to attack Russia and begun preparing "Operation Barbarossa." He ordered his plan to be kept secret from the Japanese whom he desired to attack Britain in Southeast Asia on the assumption that the Wehrmacht alone could speedily crush the USSR. Konoye suspected the truth, doubted the success of the enterprise, and determined to keep clear of it. In the spring of 1941 he sent Matsuoka on tour. In Berlin and Rome the Nipponese envoy was evasive. In Moscow on April 13, he concluded a five-year Japanese-Soviet nonaggression pact by which each Power pledged itself to neutrality if the other should become involved in hostilities with a third. So anxious was Tokyo not to become entangled in the impending Nazi-Soviet war that Matsuoka, as later became known, agreed to the cancellation of Japanese coal and oil concessions in Northern Sakhalin as the price of the neutrality accord with the Kremlin.

Comparable caution and judicious duplicity in the face of *der Führer's* folly might yet have saved Nippon from disaster to come. But in the Cabinet changes in Tokyo which followed the German assault on Muscovy, Matsuoka resigned, commenting, "Now that I am a free man, I shall devote myself to reading."

JAPAN: FROM MILITARISM TO PACIFISM

Gen. Hideki Tojo replaced Konoye as Premier on Oct. 18 and named Shigenori Togo as Foreign Minister. Lt. Gen. Teiishi Suzuki opined, "The essence of total war is to live and die for the State. . . . Let us live with a conviction of race and elevate ourselves to a more glorious history with a light heart." Kurusu joined Ambassador Nomura in Washington for the crucial negotiations of the autumn. All of Indochina was now in Japanese hands. Washington, London, and the Dutch Government in Exile were taking counter-measures and applying economic pressures.

What choices were available to Japan's policy-makers in 1941? A policy of restoring and maintaining peace was not among them, for the Fascist combine of Big Business and Big Brass had brought into being an economy and a polity dependent for viability on armaments, war, and conquest. Within these limits, Tokyo still had choices: to make an all-out effort to complete the conquest of China; to join Hitler in attacking Russia; to attack the British and Dutch empires of Southeast Asia; or to force a showdown with the USA. The first course might have succeeded, but the view prevailed among the military planners that the attempt would fail unless America were induced or coerced into abandoning its support of Chinese resistance. The second course was never seriously considered since Japanese experts, unlike their German counterparts, had learned the hard way that those who grab a bear by the tail, without being able to kill it, can never let go. The third course would undoubtedly have "worked" and, given the state of American opinion, might not have precipitated open U.S. intervention. But the final conclusion was that everything hinged on relations with the major "enemy Power" and that the attainment of all other objectives depended upon bribing, blackmailing, or beating the USA into accepting the "New Order" in the Orient. The conclusion was correct if the trick could be turned. But it was mad if it could not be, for it is always irresponsible for a Great Power to force another into a position where it must either surrender or accept the hazards of total victory or total defeat in total war.

Up to a point, to be sure, Tojo and Togo had no such intention but were prepared to bargain—forgetting, if they ever knew, that the Roosevelt Administration was unprepared to bargain because it was already casting about for plausible means of making the USA a full belligerent against the Fascist Triplice. Nomura and Kurusu were authorized to offer evacuation of southern Indochina and a reciprocal pledge of no further troop movements to any areas of Southeast Asia and the southern Pacific in exchange for the lifting of U.S. trade restrictions, assurance of oil supplies, and approval of "peace" with China on Japanese terms. Hull offered commercial concessions in exchange for multilateral pacts of nonaggression, Japanese abandonment of its Chinese puppet regime, and Japanese withdrawal of "all military, naval, air and police forces from China and Indochina" (final U.S. note of November 26). What Tokyo was asking seemed to Tokyo within the limits of what the

USA might be prepared to grant. What Washington was asking—*i.e.*, abandonment of all the conquests of a decade and restoration of the *status quo* of 1931—Washington knew that Tokyo could never grant. Roosevelt, Hull, Stimson, and Marshall also knew that Japan would risk war rather than yield. But they assumed that the first blow would fall on Malaya, the Dutch Indies, or, at worst, the Philippines.

Blitz out of Asia. This calculation proved false. Tokyo's calculation was to prove suicidal. But it appeared reasonable at the time. Every new device of warfare seems certain to its inventors to ensure victory. The strategists convinced the diplomats that they possessed the means of rendering the USA helpless throughout the Pacific area. On Nov. 27 Vice-Adm. Chuichi Nagumo led a task force of cruisers and half a dozen small aircraft carriers out of the waters of Etorofu Island and across the mid-Pacific. At 2:30 P.M., E.S.T., Sunday, Dec. 7, 1941, Kurusu and Nomura delivered their final message to Hull, rejecting his proposals and accusing America of conspiring with Britain against the New Order in East Asia.

The time was early morning in Hawaii. Nagumo's undetected task force, 200 miles to the north, launched 105 planes against Pearl Harbor. In two hours they put out of action half the capital ships of the U.S. Navy: the *Arizona, Oklahoma, California, Nevada, West Virginia, Pennslyvania, Maryland,* and *Tennessee,* plus the *Utah,* three cruisers, three destroyers, sundry smaller vessels, and most of the Army and Navy planes on the Island. General Marshall was taking his usual morning horseback ride in Washington. Admiral Kimmel and General Short, on the scene, were taken completely by surprise. U.S. casualties were 2,343 dead, 1,272 wounded, and 960 missing.

Tojo's calculation appeared correct. Two days later land-based bombers sank H.M.S. *Prince of Wales* and *Repulse* off Malaya. War was declared on the USA, Britain, and the Netherlands. Hitler and Mussolini declared war on the USA on Dec. 11, though the USSR and Japan, by mutual design, remained "at peace." With China and Russia now, in intent, to be cut off from Anglo-American aid, both could be crushed, it was assumed, with America and Britain left helpless to alter the result. There were only three errors in this calculus of relative fighting power: Russia could not be beaten; China could not be conquered; and American industry, safe from attack and gigantic in productivity, would ultimately build weapons against which the aggressors could not stand.

From Victory to Catastrophe. Within a few months Hirohito's war machine swept over Hong Kong, Guam, the Philippines, Siam, Burma, Malaya, Singapore, the Dutch Indies, and even the western Aleutians. A vast realm of sea and land, comprising well over 500,000,000 people, passed under the flag of the Rising Sun. Not until the Battle of Midway (June 3–6, 1942) did the tide begin to turn, and then only slowly. The Anglo-American decision to defeat Germany first gave Tokyo respite. But in spite of, and in part because

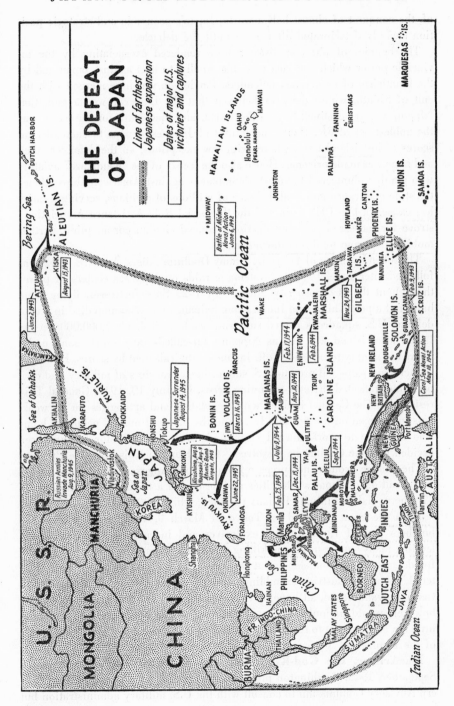

THE DEFEAT OF JAPAN

Line of farthest Japanese expansion

Dates of major U.S. victories and captures

of, the conquest of almost half a world, Japan's economic and strategic position steadily deteriorated after 1943 until the debacle.

The agonies of ultimate disaster were rendered excruciating by the invincible power which America was able, finally, to hurl against Japan and by the fanaticism of its doomed defenders. Patriotism was here merged with the cult of Shinto, whose devotees believed that the Emperor was a god, that Nippon was yet destined to rule the world, and that death for the cause was the noblest act of life. Hence the refusal of Japanese troops to surrender on scores of lost island bases where, with few exceptions, all the defenders died and none was made prisoner. Hence also the frenzy of the "Kamikaze" aviators who gladly volunteered to smash their planes against American ships. Hence the stoic endurance and mad defiance of millions of civilians, serving a hopeless cause. In late 1943 Tojo and the "Imperial Rule Assistance Association" strove for increased plane production, reduced civilian consumption, further mobilization, and total totalitarianism.

The token bombing of Tokyo by Jimmy Doolittle's fliers, April 18, 1942, was followed after June, 1944, by systematic raids on Japanese centers of power throughout the "Coprosperity Sphere" by B-29 Superfortresses, flying from bases in Saipan, China, and India. From Saipan, where Nagumo died in a vain defense, U.S. squadrons rained ruin and death on Tokyo's 7,000,000 people. Island after island was lost as Nippon's far-called Navy slowly sank under blows too mighty to be fended off. Japanese admirals died by scores. Hundreds of merchant ships fell prey to U.S. submarines. Transfers of military and civil personnel reflected the ever-mounting crisis. On July 19, 1944, General Tojo resigned: "The Cabinet is filled with trepidation and apologizes for its weakness to the men on the fighting front and the hundred million people at home who continue to work toward certain victory. . . . Therefore it has been decided that the Cabinet be dissolved." Gen. Kuniaki Koiso became Premier.

The change brought no surcease from sorrow. American Superforts all but wiped out 44 of Japan's 206 cities and destroyed a third of the buildings in 37 others. Half a million civilians perished, while 9,000,000 were left homeless. In the great fire raid on Tokyo of March 9, 1945, no less than 279 bombers poured 1,667 tons of explosives and incendiaries on the capital, leveling many square miles and killing thousands. Japan still had a large Army for defense of the homeland. But its Navy was lost, its merchant fleet shattered, its war industries crumbling, and its defeat certain. With Italy and Germany vanquished, all hope of victory was gone. Leaders and people alike, however, would undoubtedly have continued a war of desperation, resisting invasion at great cost to the invaders, except for the weird and terrifying events of the summer of 1945 with which this account began.

MacArthur, the God-King, and the Ways of Righteousness. In September, 1945, Washington proposed the creation of a 10-nation Far Eastern Advisory Commission to consult with the U.S. military administration but to have no powers of decision. Australia, China, and the USSR objected. In December, at Moscow, agreement was reached to set up an Allied Council for Japan, consisting of representatives of the USA, U.K., USSR, and China, under the chairmanship of the Supreme Commander of the Allied Powers (SCAP)—*i.e.*, General MacArthur. It was further decided to establish in Washington a Far Eastern Commission of 11 States—*i.e.*, the 4 above, plus France, the Netherlands, Canada, Australia, New Zealand, India, and the Philippines— to formulate policies on the fulfillment of surrender terms, review directives, offer advice, etc. MacArthur complained that he had not been consulted. "[The Allied Council is] in my opinion not acceptable . . . but it is my firm intent to try to make it work." In practice, it worked well. The Far Eastern Commission, having no power, modestly contented itself with quiet approbation of the policies of SCAP. The Allied Council was often the scene of noisy disputes between Soviet and American spokesmen, and occasionally between others. But here, too, SCAP had its way. Its way was the American way.

In terms of public statements of purpose, the American occupation was designed to disarm Japan, to foster a democratic State in a democratic society, and to promote a viable Japanese economy, stripped of war industries and monopolistic controls. These objectives were to be achieved through minimum disturbances of the political and social *status quo* and maximum use of the Emperor, the established machinery of government, and the traditional ruling classes. War criminals were brought to trial and sentenced. Notorious fire-eaters in political circles were barred from office. The emancipation of women and the emergence of an independent trade union movement were encouraged. The *Zaibatsu* were broken up into smaller units. Limited agrarian reform was introduced. Shinto was disestablished as the State religion. These changes, while sweeping, effected no revolutionary transformation in the economy, society, or polity of Japan. In carrying them out the occupation authorities encountered no resistance and much obsequious cooperation from their hosts. The war lords were discredited and deposed. Fascism as a doctrine and habit of governance was displaced by the forms of democracy. But the elites of land and money remained largely intact. The total balance of indulgences and deprivations in the social hierarchy remained much as it had been before.

The retention of Hirohito facilitated the tasks of administration. An Imperial Rescript of New Year's Day, 1946, explained to the masses that the divinity of the Emperor was "a false conception," as was the notion that "the Japanese people are superior to other races and fated to rule the world." On Feb. 19, MacArthur restored extraterritoriality for UN nationals. He and Hirohito approved the draft of a new Constitution, carefully prepared in consultation with Allied authorities, which the Shidehara Cabinet made public on March 6, 1946. The proposed charter stripped the Emperor of all governmental power, aside from his role as constitutional monarch and "symbol of the State and of the unity of the people." Responsible parliamentary government was provided for. The old House of Peers was converted into an elective House of Councilors which was made subordinate to the Diet. The elaborate Bill of Rights was based on the American model. The most novel feature of the document was the provision that "war, as the sovereign right of the nation, and the threat or use of force, is forever renounced as a means of dealing with other nations. The maintenance of land, sea and air forces, as well as other war potential, will never be authorized. The right of belligerency of the State will never be recognized. . . . We have determined to rely for our security and survival on the justice and good-will of the peace-loving peoples of the world. . . ."

Politics under SCAP. The relationship between the verbal symbols of government and the social realities of power, always a fascinating problem in all the cultures and communities of men, was here a peculiarly elusive issue because of the balance of forces within Japan and throughout the entire arena of world politics. The first election under the occupation was held on April 10, 1946, after MacArthur had rejected proposals for delay from the Far Eastern Commissions, whose members felt that Japanese reactionaries were still in the ascendancy. The results of the polling confirmed this view. Out of 466 seats in the Diet, including subsequent shifts and by-elections, Shidehara's "Progressives" (*i.e.*, ultraconservatives) won 110; Ichiro Hatoyama's "Liberals" (reactionaries) 148; the Social Democrats (liberal and faintly socialist) 96; the Cooperative Democrats 45; and the Communists 6, the balance going to "Independents" and minor groups. One-third of the votes cast were women's; 38 women were elected. The semantic confusion of Japanese public life was not alleviated when the extreme conservatives calling themselves "Progressives" changed their name within a year to "Democrats."

Shidehara proposed to remain in office, since no party had won a majority. Outcries of opposition forced his resignation on April 22. Hatoyama was about to succeed when MacArthur barred him from the Diet under the purge directives, since his record was that of a Fascist. When Tetsu Katayama, Christian leader of the Social Democrats, failed to secure Progressive and Liberal support for a coalition Cabinet, Foreign Minister Shigeru Yoshida assumed leadership of the Liberals and formed a conservative Ministry on May 15.

The new Constitution was debated and approved by the Diet in August, confirmed in October and officially promulgated on Nov. 3, 1946, in an Imperial Rescript. Inflation and food shortages bred popular discontent. In view of labor unrest, SCAP on August 29 told the Government that "strikes, walkouts, or other work-stoppages which are inimical to the objectives of the military occupation are prohibited." Yoshida charged that the strikes were the result of "leftist plots" to oust the Cabinet.

The political pendulum during 1947 swung slightly leftward—a movement which SCAP viewed with mixed feelings. "If we can bring democracy to Japan and make it work," declared MacArthur, "all of Asia will look toward this *Ha!* land. History shows that democratic nations do not wage wars of aggression." In the election of April 25, 1947, the Social Democrats won 143 seats, the Liberals 132, the Democrats (consisting in the main of the old "Progressives") 122, the Cooperatives 31, and the Communists only 4. Despite the Socialist victory, the two conservative parties still dominated the Diet. MacArthur hailed the defeat of Communism. After a long Cabinet crisis, Tetsu Katayama became Premier May 23 in a Cabinet consisting of Socialists, Democrats, and Cooperatives. Yoshida's Liberals held aloof, alleging that the left-wing Socialists had "Communist ties."

Since subsequent political changes have all been in one direction, they admit of brevity in summary. "The pattern has been etched," declared General MacArthur's New Year message of 1948. "The path has been laid. The development lies largely in your own hands." The Katayama Cabinet gave way in February, 1948, to a Cabinet headed by Democrat Hitoshi Ashida, which fell in October amid charges of corruption, with the Premier himself arrested. Yoshida, now leader of the reorganized "Democratic Liberal" (meaning ultraconservative) Party, became Premier once more in October, 1948, and retained his post for years to come. In Diet elections on Jan. 23, 1949, Yoshida's supporters won a majority and were backed by the "new capitalist" Democrats. The Communists, led by Tokuda, polled three million votes and raised their Diet representation from 3 to 35 seats. Liberals and Democrats united under Yoshida in a vigorous anti-Communist program, approved by SCAP. In the spring of 1950, with MacArthur's blessing, the Communist Party was outlawed (as between 1937 and 1945) by the methods of indirection employed in the USA, its press abolished, and its leaders purged and jailed, save for those who went "underground." Gen. Matthew Ridgway replaced MacArthur in April, 1951, and was succeeded by Gen. Mark Clark in June of 1952. In the election of Oct. 1, 1952, Yoshida's "Liberals" won 240 seats, the "Progressives" 67, Independents 30, Right Socialists 57, Left Socialists 64, and Communists 0.

Within half a decade after 1945 the Rising Sun had turned full circle with regard to all issues and attitudes of domestic politics. Fascists and war criminals were "depurged" and restored to respectability, including Hatoyama. The anti-monopoly program of decartelization was "revised." Press laws were tightened to forbid "dangerous thoughts," searched out by an "Un-Japanese Activities Committee." Disarmament gave way to rearmament with the National Police Force of 75,000 becoming the nucleus of a new army—which, said John Foster Dulles, the new Japan now had a "moral obligation" to establish. On May Day of 1952 and thereafter, Red rioters clashed with police. But the forces of conservatism, if not of reaction, were firmly entrenched in power beyond all likelihood of early displacement, since they enjoyed American favor and protection.

The political spectrum in the late 1950's began to assume the form, however tentatively, of a two-party system of the Anglo-American type, though no one could be certain, in view of widespread habits of corruption, factionalism, violence, and irresponsibility, that parliamentary democracy was securely established as the enduring pattern of Japanese politics. Revolutionary extremists of Right and Left were discredited. Ex-Fascist totalitarians, while not without influence in conservative circles, evolved no party or other popular organization of their own. Communist votes, almost 10% of the total in the election of January, 1949, declined to 2% in the election of February, 1955. The only effective opposition to triumphant conservatism was furnished by the Socialist Party whose sundered factions reunited in October, 1955, on a platform of "neutralism," resistance to American pressure, and opposition to large-scale rearmament. Many Socialists were pacifists. Almost all, in fear of revived militarism, resented the re-creation of an army of 160,000 (1956), with a goal of 180,000 by 1960, and resisted U.S. pleas for a much larger force. In November, 1955, the two conservative groups of "Democrats" and "Liberals" united in a single Liberal-Democratic Party, commanding 297 seats out of the total of 466 in the Diet elected in February, 1955.

As for the Premiership, the adroit Yoshida, having held the office in successive Cabinets from October, 1948, until December, 1954, gave way to the aged Ichiro Hatoyama who, in turn, was briefly succeeded in December, 1956, by Tanzan Ishibashi, who fell ill, and in February, 1957, by Nobusuke Kishi. In May, 1957, Kishi visited Formosa, India, Pakistan, Ceylon, Burma, and Thailand, and in June came to Washington, played golf with Eisenhower, and secured a pledge of the withdrawal of U.S. troops from Japan. This decision symbolized the vastly changed, albeit still problematical, international status of Tokyo a dozen years after total defeat.

Nipponese Dilemma. The rapid and remarkable progress of vanquished Nippon toward respectability was primarily an achievement of American statesmanship, determined to make a free Japan an ally and bulwark of the Free World against the menace of Communist aggression. After long delay and deadlock, Washington decided to proceed with the negotiation of a peace treaty (with John Foster Dulles as negotiator) regardless of Soviet views. A draft was circulated among friendly governments in March, 1951, followed by an Anglo-American draft and a final draft, signed at San Francisco, Sept. 8, 1951, by envoys of 49 States. By the terms of this settlement (see p. 199), Japan recovered sovereignty, subject to the conditions implicit in becoming an ally and protectorate of the USA. The security and peace pacts were both ratified in Tokyo, after parliamentary approval, on Nov. 19, 1951. The U.S. Senate, 66 to 10, approved ratification on March 20, 1952, with President Truman formally ratifying both accords, along with the new security treaties with Australia and New Zealand, on April 15, 1952. In the face of Soviet protest, both pacts were declared in effect on April 28. On the same day Japan signed a separate peace treaty with "China"—*i.e.*, on U.S. insistence, the Nationalist Government on Formosa.

The framework of the peace thus formally restored was a product of Cold War between the giants. Japan's status within it, though subordinate, was honorable and capable of development toward a new position of significant influence in the Orient. Of the segments of the old empire, the Kurils, Northern Sakhalin, North Korea, Manchuria, and all the Chinese mainland were now lost to the new enemy—though Washington, seconded by Tokyo, was hopeful of somehow achieving their eventual liberation from Communism. The other major segments, save for "neutral" Indonesia and Burma, were all American allies or protectorates. But Nippon remained the most populous, most productive, and potentially most powerful community in the new security zone of the western Pacific which the USA had fashioned. Japanese leaders and patriots could therefore look forward, not unreasonably, to an ultimately independent role once more as a Power.

This hope promised to be qualified, however, by a number of circumstances beyond Japanese control at mid-century. The sources of economic and social instability which had delivered Japan to Fascism were not alleviated by the new dispensation. The livelihood of Japan's millions depended upon the markets of the mainland unless alternative markets, not yet in sight, could be found. To conquer such markets by the sword, as the war lords and *Zaibatsu* had sought to do in the 1930's, was no longer possible, since Red China was now a major Power and allied with the USSR. Even a heavily rearmed Japan fully supported by the USA in a new war to liberate Asia from Communism could only anticipate destruction because of its locus and its peculiar vulnerability to atomic bombing. Peaceful recapture of mainland markets was forbidden by Washington in the interest of depriving the enemy of trade.

Japan would therefore be obliged to rely indefinitely on U.S. subsidies and thus remain an American dependency—unless and until some future cabinet might risk a break with America by concluding economic and political bargains with Peiping and Moscow. Since dependency is resented, and the process of playing off rivals against one another is the sovereign road to maximum advantage at minimum cost in all *Realpolitik*, it could be taken as certain that Japanese statesmen would sooner or later contemplate such a course.

In the late 1950's, however, all was provisional and tentative. In dealing with Red China to the west, Tokyo dared not defy Washington by extending recognition and seeking a political entente, although restrictions on trade were relaxed in 1957, following the example of Britain and other States, despite Washington's preference for a total embargo. In dealing with the USSR to the north, Tokyo entertained overly ambitious hopes of recovering Southern Sakhalin and the Kurils. Negotiations with Soviet envoys in London early in 1956 were broken off when Moscow made clear that it would grant no such concessions. Foreign Minister Mamoru Shigemitsu came to Moscow in August. Bulganin exchanged letters with Premier Hatoyama. In September Sunichi Matsumoto arrived in the Soviet capital as Special Ambassador. He was followed by Hatoyama. On Oct. 19, 1956, a "Peace Declaration" was signed in Moscow, ending the state of war, resuming diplomatic and consular relations, pledging Soviet support for Japanese membership in the UN, providing for repatriation of Japanese nationals in the USSR, and renouncing all claims for war damages. A "Trade Protocol" established reciprocal most-favored-nation treatment. The small islands of Habomoi and Shikotan, south of the Kurils, would be transferred to Japan "after the conclusion of a peace treaty."

A formal Japanese-Soviet peace treaty was still pending in 1958. Faced with the certainty of total destruction in any atomic war and confronted with the industrialization of Russia and the projected industrialization of China, both giant Powers against which Japan was powerless, the policy-makers of Tokyo—whether conservative or socialist, and despite prodding from an anti-Communist USA—seemed likely, sooner or later, to opt for some formula of "neutralism" as a last best hope for peace and trade, without which Japan's millions could not live. Reliance on subventions from Washington and alliance with America offered little ultimate promise of either trade or peace or of any sense of Japanese national self-respect. A different role, more in harmony with the preferences of most other free Asian peoples, offered brighter prospects for the people of Japan and could well contribute to hopes of disengagement and enduring peace between the Super-Powers.

SUGGESTED READINGS

Benedict, Ruth: *The Chrysanthemum and the Sword*, Boston, Houghton Mifflin, 1946.
Bisson, T. A.: *Zaibatsu Dissolution in Japan*, Berkeley, Calif., University of California Press, 1955.
Borton, Hugh: *Japan's Modern Century*, New York, Ronald, 1955.
Byas, Hugh: *Government by Assassination*, New York, Knopf, 1942.
Cameron, Meredith E., Thomas H. D. Mahoney, and George E. McReynolds: *China, Japan, and the Powers*, New York, Ronald, 1951.
Embree, John P.: *The Japanese Nation: A Social Survey*, New York, Rinehart, 1945.
Fearey, Robert A.: *The Occupation of Japan*, New York, Macmillan, 1950.
Feis, Herbert: *The Road to Pearl Harbor*, Princeton, N.J., Princeton University Press, 1950.
Gayn, Mark: *Japan Diary*, New York, Sloane, 1948.
Grew, Joseph C.: *Ten Years in Japan*, New York, Simon and Schuster, 1944.
Haring, Douglas G. (ed.): *Japan's Prospect*, Cambridge, Mass., Harvard University Press, 1946.
Ike, Nobutaka: *Japanese Politics: An Introductory Survey*, New York, Knopf, 1957.
James, David H.: *The Rise and Fall of the Japanese Empire*, New York, Macmillan, 1951.
Jones, F. C.: *Japan's New Order in East Asia: Its Rise and Fall*, 1937–45, New York, Oxford, 1954.
Kato, Masuo: *The Lost War*, New York, Knopf, 1946.
Latourette, Kenneth Scott: *The History of Japan*, New York, Macmillan, 1947.
Lattimore, Owen: *Manchuria, Cradle of Conflict*, New York, Macmillan, 1935.

ITALY: FROM DESPOTISM TO DEMOCRACY

Lockwood, William W.: *The Economic Development of Japan: Growth and Structural Change*, 1868–1938, Princeton, N.J., Princeton University Press, 1954.

Maki, John M.: *Japanese Militarism: Its Cause and Cure*, New York, Knopf, 1945.

Quigley, Harold S., and John E. Turner: *The New Japan: Government and Politics*, Minneapolis, University of Minnesota Press, 1956.

Reischauer, Edwin O.: *The United States and Japan*, Cambridge, Mass., Harvard University Press, 1950.

Sansom, G. B.: *The Western World and Japan: A Study in the Interaction of European and Asiatic Cultures*, New York, Knopf, 1950.

Scalapino, Robert A.: *Democracy and the Party Movement in Prewar Japan*, Berkeley, Calif., University of California Press, 1953.

Shigenori, Togo: *Diplomacy and the Pacific War*, New York, Simon and Schuster, 1956.

Stimson, H. L.: *The Far Eastern Crisis*, New York, Harper, 1936.

Swearingen, Rodger, and Paul Langer: *Red Flag in Japan: International Communism in Action*, 1919–1951, Cambridge, Mass., Harvard University Press, 1952.

Takeuchi, Sterling: *War and Diplomacy in the Japanese Empire*, New York, Doubleday, 1935.

Togo, Shigenori: *The Cause of Japan*, New York, Simon and Schuster, 1956.

Vinacke, Harold M.: *History of the Far East in Modern Times*, New York, Appleton-Century-Crofts, 1936.

ITALY: FROM DESPOTISM TO DEMOCRACY

Insatiable Italy, with furtive glances, roves restlessly hither and thither, instinctively drawn on by the odor of corruption and calamity—always ready to attack anybody from the rear and make off with a bit of plunder. It is outrageous that these Italians, still unsatisfied, should continue to make preparations and to conspire in every direction.—CHANCELLOR OTTO VON BISMARCK.

I could not help being charmed by Signor Mussolini's gentle and simple bearing and by his calm, detached poise in spite of so many burdens and dangers. . . . If I had been an Italian I am sure that I should have been whole-heartedly with you from the start to the finish in your triumphant struggle against the bestial appetites and passions of Leninism. . . . Your movement has rendered a service to the whole world. . . . Italy has shown that there is a way of fighting the subversive forces which can rally the masses of the people, properly led, to value and wish to defend the honor and stability of civilized society. She has provided the necessary antidote to the Russian poison. Hereafter no great nation will go unprovided with an ultimate means of protection against the cancerous growth of Bolshevism.—WINSTON S. CHURCHILL, in Rome, January 20, 1927.

On the 29th of April of the year 1945 a man, accompanied by a woman, returned to Milan. The city had just been entered by Allied troops. The man knew the city well. This time he traveled, strangely, on the floor of a moving van. He saw nothing because he was dead, as was his mistress. Both had been caught by partisans and shot two days previously near lovely Lake Como as they sought to flee. The bodies were manhandled by a mob, strung up by the feet in the Piazza Loretta, spat upon, and then buried in the paupers' section of the Cimitero Maggiore. A year later secret sympathizers dug up the man's corpse and spirited it away. It was found in August in a monastery and secretly hidden for the next eleven years in a crate among the Capuchin monks of Cerro Maggiore near Milan. The woman's name was Clara Petacci. The man's name was Benito Mussolini.

This name was a symbol to the world, over a whole generation, of glorious and immortal Italy. Most of those who later deemed the symbol shameful had hailed it with ecstasy when its bearer first demolished a decadent Italian democracy by fraud and force and proclaimed himself Caesar. His career was the epitome of an epoch by no means ended, despite his demise.

Demagogue. Benito Mussolini was born in the village of Dovia in the commune of Predappio, near Forli, July 29, 1882. His mother was a country schoolteacher. His father was a poor farmer and blacksmith who, like many of Italy's poor, had embraced revolutionary Marxism. In the same year King Umberto's ministers in Rome, piqued at French seizure of Tunisia, made Italy the ally of Austria-Hungary and Germany. The belatedly united Kingdom ruled by the House of Savoy was the poorest and weakest of the Great Powers. Its elite consisted of nobles, businessmen, and priests, enjoying the fruits of an old feudalism, a new capitalism, and a timeless clericalism. Its middle class was small and poor. Its peasants and workers were illiterate and impoverished and much given, as they awakened to awareness of the larger world, to emigrating to America or embracing cults of social radicalism. Its politicians, with few exceptions, tended to be spoilsmen manipulating a pliant electorate through the forms of democracy and soliciting money from the rich and votes from the poor on the pretext of protecting each from the other.

By the year 1900, when Umberto died and was succeeded by Victor Emmanuel II, young Benito had become a schoolteacher. But two years later he went to Switzerland to evade military service and took a miserable job as a hod carrier. "I chafed with the terrible rage of the powerless." He quit, begged, starved, became a vagrant, a labor agitator, a Socialist orator, and a dangerous radical. By 1910, when his father died, he was living in sin at Forli with Rachele Guidi, whom he married in 1914. Their first child was Edda, who was destined to marry Count Galeazzo Ciano, who was destined to become Foreign Minister under his father-in-law, to betray him in defeat, and to be ordered shot for treason (Jan. 11, 1944) by the man who was the son of the blacksmith.

But this man, amid many amours, had no true love save his love for the applause of crowds. He founded a paper, *The Class Struggle*, and got himself arrested for agitating against Italy's war on Turkey. He proclaimed that God was a fraud, the Pope a charlatan, the King a fake, the ruling class a gang of thieves, and the flag "a rag to be planted on a dunghill." By 1912 he was editor of *Avanti* and a national leader of the Socialists, whose revolutionary rhetoric he found fascinating and a tonic to his own self-importance. "I am possessed by this mania. It inflames, gnaws and consumes me, like a physical malady. I want to make a mark on history with my will, like a lion with his claws. . . ."

456

Such maladies were chronic among the insecure, including Italy's states-men. In their maneuverings for national and imperial prestige, they were obliged by weakness to rely more upon perfidy than upon violence. The first effort to conquer Ethiopia met with crushing defeat in 1896. In 1902 they secretly agreed to remain neutral in any French-German war, hoping for French acquiescence in their designs upon Libya. In 1909 they secretly agreed to support Russian designs on the Straits in exchange for Russian support of their designs on Libya. In 1911–12 they seized the territory from Turkey, along with the Island of Rhodes. When the Powers fell furiously on one another in 1914, Rome remained neutral, offered favors to the highest bidder in a spirit of *sacro egoismo*, concluded the secret Treaty of London, and finally declared war on Austria-Hungary and Germany in May of 1915 on the promise of *Italia Irredenta* and colonial compensations in the event of Entente victory.

Mussolini, advocating military intervention, broke with his Socialist com-rades in 1914 and was expelled from the Party as a renegade. With French funds he founded a new paper, *Il Popolo d'Italia*, to urge war as the only revolutionary heroism. "It is blood which gives movement to the wheels of history." He joined the Army and in January, 1917, was hit in the rear by 40 fragments when a shrapnel shell exploded in trench-mortar practice. On recovery, he resumed the war as an editor preaching patriotic glory—while millions were slain and Anglo-French divisions had to be sent to hold the Italian front after the disaster of Caporetto.

Despot. For Italy the fruits of victory in 1918 were sour. Annexations were won in the north in the face of Wilsonian resistance and Jugoslav resent-ment, but little was gained in Africa and nothing in the Near East save the Dodecanese Islands near Rhodes. Patriots felt that the peace was lost. The land was more than ever plagued with poverty, exploitation, and corruption. Socialists and Communists preached revolution. Lockouts, strikes, and riots became chronic. Aging boss Giolitti, once more in the Premiership, knew that the specter of "Red Revolution" was a myth and let nature take its course. But frightened factory owners and landlords sought to buy protection. Among the political groups of disgruntled war veterans was the Fasci di Combatti-mento, founded in Milan on March 23, 1919. Its *Duce* or leader was Benito Mussolini, whose program was nothing save a poetry of violence, but whose followers donned black shirts, gave Roman salutes, and equipped themselves with brass knuckles, castor oil, knives, and guns to use against their critics.

Not until November of 1921 did the Fascisti become a "party." Never in a free election did they win anything approaching a majority. "Our program is simple," said Mussolini. "We wish to govern Italy." How this came to pass is not more mysterious than the social dynamics of all later Fascisms. Musso-lini was subsidized by anxious nobles and industrialists to save them from "Bolshevism." He appealed to middle-class nationalism and, with the connivance of the Cabinet and the police, turned loose his gangsters to beat, burn, and kill. The victims were Socialists, Communists, liberals, trade union leaders, officers of cooperatives, editors of Leftist newspapers—in short, all whose shouts for "reform" or "revolution" were feared by Mussolini's new paymasters.

ITALY
AND THE ADRIATIC
1919 — 1939
SCALE OF MILES:
0   50   100   150   200
■ ■ ■ ■ 1914 BOUNDARIES
FRANCE AND ALLIES

In late October of 1922 he ordered his "legions" to "march on Rome" as a means of inducing the King to appoint him Premier. A vacillating Cabinet hesitated between resigning and resisting. The King was quite willing to abandon democracy and experiment with a dictatorship committed to monarchism. The Army looked favorably upon a movement dedicated to militarism. The Church was benign toward the champions of religion. Big business and the estate owners were delighted with "blackshirts" who smashed unions and disciplined land-hungry peasants. Liberals and radicals were paralyzed. No one else cared. The "legions" marched. Mussolini waited safely in Milan and then crossed the Rubicon in a sleeping car when the King called him to Rome. On Oct. 30 he formed a Cabinet. Through murder, propaganda, and bluster, his Fascists destroyed the trade unions, cowed the peasants, suppressed all other political parties by 1925, copied the devices of the Communist Police State, made the trains run on time, "saved Italy from Bolshevism," and won the praise of all right-thinking people of property and piety throughout the Western world.

To retell the history of the "Fascist era" is no part of our task. It is enough to note that the new tyranny, up to a point, was highly profitable to the businessmen, aristocrats, churchmen, and army officers who put it in power; that it "solved" all problems of class conflict, proletarian unrest, agrarian discontent, and cries for freedom by suppressing dissent and preaching a creed of "believe, obey, fight" and "*il Duce* is always right"; and that it sought unity and prosperity at home by public spending for armaments and warlike adventures abroad on the correct assumption that all true patriots (save eccentrics, cranks, and exiles) must approve and applaud, since not to do so would be unpatriotic.

Disaster. *Fascismo* came to ruin, after two decades of power, by virtue of its foreign policy. Churchill and others have argued that even at the end Mussolini could have saved himself by betraying Germany and joining the Allies at the right moment as his predecessors had done in 1915. But the imperatives of Fascism required unreserved adventurism abroad as the price of peace at home, with little possibility of prudent self-restraint, the more so as the Anglo-French "appeasers" gave *il Duce* every possible encouragement as Hoare, Halifax, Laval, and Bonnet sacrificed everything and everybody to Mussolini's ambitions out of their sincere admiration for Fascism and their hopes for an alliance with Italy against the resurgent Reich.

Modest and successful beginnings led step by step to irrevocable and disastrous endings. In 1923 the Greek island of Corfu was bombarded and seized, and then evacuated under British pressure. In 1926 a protectorate was imposed on Albania. In 1934–35 Mussolini cultivated Anglo-French favor by championing Austrian "independence" and buttressing the Fascist-clericalist regime of Dollfuss and Schuschnigg against Hitler. This maneuver "paid off" in Anglo-French acquiescence in the Fascist conquest of Ethiopia (see pp. 219–224) and in the Fascist intervention in Spain.[2] But the prospective glories of making common cause with Hitler against the "decadent" democracies appeared more tempting than the advantages of playing off Berlin against London and Paris. Machiavelli had warned against such a course, but the infallible Mussolini failed to perceive that if he irrevocably allied himself with a stronger Power, particularly one ruled by a madman, he himself would become a vassal, would win little from a common victory, and would lose all in a common defeat.

---

[2] The politics, diplomacy, and strategy of the Spanish Civil War are outlined in the 4th edition of the present work, pp. 660–665, and discussed in detail in *Europe on the Eve* (Knopf, 1939).

Edda's husband, Count Ciano, who had won his laurels by bombing Ethiopians, struck a bargain with Berlin on Oct. 25, 1936, whereby Austria was to become a buffer and bridge between the two Fascist Powers. "We can mobilize 8,000,000 men," shouted *il Duce.* "We reject the absurdity of eternal peace. . . . We must be always stronger. . . . We raise the banner of anti-Bolshevism." Three years later: "Our enemies are too stupid to be dangerous." Mussolini had no choice but to acquiesce in the Nazi seizure of Austria in March, 1938, and the partition of Czechoslovakia at Munich. He seized Albania, April 7–8, 1939. On May 22 Ciano and Ribbentrop in Milan signed the 10-year "Pact of Steel," pledging each signatory, in the event of the other becoming involved in hostilities, to "immediately rally to his side as ally and support him with all his military resources on land, at sea, and in the air." The Pact in fact was putty, since Rome told Berlin that it could not risk general war for another three years. *Il Duce* remained "neutral" in September, 1939, but, despite British and American pleas and offers, declared war on France and Britain (June 10, 1940) when he believed that the Wehrmacht had rendered the enemy helpless. "The hand that held the dagger," said Roosevelt at Charlottesville on the same day, "has struck it into the back of its neighbor."

Il Duce, poorly rewarded by *der Führer* for his belated aid, nevertheless joined Berlin and Tokyo in the Triplice Pact of Sept. 27, 1940, and sought glory by invading British Somaliland, Kenya, the Sudan, Egypt, and Greece. Each campaign ended in disaster or required German aid to postpone disaster. Mussolini obediently followed Hitler in declaring war on Russia in June, 1941, and on America in December. But when Allied forces invaded Sicily in June, 1943, those who had brought Mussolini to power concluded they had more to gain by ousting him than by keeping him, particularly after Allied airmen bombed Naples and the outskirts of Rome. On July 24 the Fascist Grand Council, in a stormy session in which Ciano, Grandi, and other Fascist veterans turned against *il Duce,* voted "lack of confidence" in a quaint imitation of the parliamentary procedures all had long since ridiculed. On July 25, 1943, King Victor Emmanuel dismissed Mussolini, ordered his arrest, and named a new Cabinet under Marshal Pietro Badoglio. The dissolution of the Fascist Party was decreed on July 28.

The sequel unfolded in the best Italian manner. Badoglio declared that the war would go on, persuaded Berlin to agree to defend all of Italy, and opened secret negotiations in Lisbon eventuating in the signature of an armistice with the Allies on Sept. 3. But the Wehrmacht took Rome on Sept. 10, as King and Marshal fled south, and two days later effected Mussolini's rescue from jail by a well-planned *coup* of parachute troops and SS men. In the north *il Duce* established a "Republican Fascist State" and threatened death to the Sovereign, the Premier, and all "cowards and traitors." The Allied invasion was long delayed by stubborn Nazi resistance. Naples held out until

460

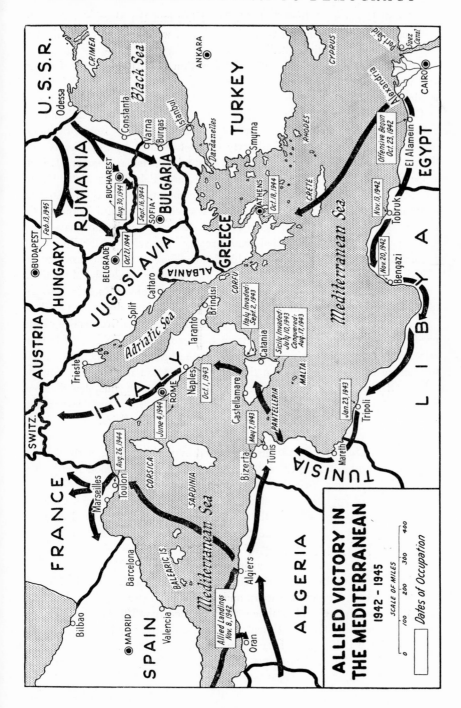

ALLIED VICTORY IN
THE MEDITERRANEAN
1942 – 1945

SCALE OF MILES

0   100   200   300   400

☐ Dates of Occupation

Oct. 1 and Rome until June 5, 1944. The King and the Marshal obligingly declared war on Germany on Oct. 13, 1943, and were hailed by Washington and London as "cobelligerents."

But the new Committee of National Liberation (CNL), made up of exiled and underground anti-Fascists, demanded an end of the House of Savoy (which Churchill ardently championed) and described the King, in the words of Count Carlo Sforza, as "a stupid, vile, abject, criminal monarch" and his government as "a putrid little corpse." With the liberation of Rome, Badoglio was forced to give way to an all-party Cabinet, headed by Socialist Ivanoe Bonomi and including Sforza, Alcide de Gasperi (Christian Democrat), Giuseppe Saragat and Pietro Nenni (Socialists), and Palmiro Togliatti (Communist). Churchill forced Sforza out in December while the CNL began to break up as a portent of new alignments. Meanwhile, Mussolini in the north, now a Nazi puppet, wrought vengeance on "traitors" and scapegoats—and finally perished in 1945 as Allied armies reached the valley of the Po.

On Aug. 29, 1957, 12 years after his death, 35 years after his assumption of the mantle of a pseudo-Caesar, and 75 years after his birth, Mussolini's body was turned over by a new officialdom to his widow, Rachele, and interred in the family vault in the cemetery of San Cassiano di Predappio. This final burial of *il Duce* may or may not symbolize the definitive demise of the neo-Caesarism of our century. Nations unable to solve their problems of human relations and international relations may, in the future, as in the past, revert to Caesarism under the delusion that all problems can thereby somehow be solved. Disillusionment in one generation is no guarantee against new illusions in the next. But the Italy which Mussolini bequeathed to his successors moved toward a different and more hopeful pattern of public affairs.

Democracy. By December of 1945 the astute Alcide de Gasperi had become Premier. His Christian Democrats, supported by various allies, controlled the national government long thereafter. He and his followers stood for democracy and Christianity, meaning in practice support of liberalism, capitalism, clericalism, and feudalism and staunch opposition to Socialism and Communism. This orientation ensured the continued ascendancy of the old elites of land, money, and religion and the defeat of all attempts, by election or revolution, to establish a new tyranny of the Left in the name of social reform. Victor Emmanuel abdicated in favor of son Umberto on May 9, 1946—and died in Alexandria, Dec. 28, 1947. In the voting of June 2, 1946, 10,718,000 ballots were cast for the Monarchy and 12,719,000 for a republic. Umberto went to Spain. The Italian Republic was proclaimed June 10, 1946, with Enrico di Nicola elected by the Constituent Assembly as Provisional President—succeeded in May, 1948, by Christian Democrat Luigi Einaudi.

The Christian Democrats elected 207 deputies, the Socialists 115, and the Communists 104. A new Constitution, in force Jan. 1, 1948, provided for a unitary parliamentary regime based on universal suffrage with Catholicism the state religion (the Communists approving) and with Mussolini's Vatican Concordat of 1929 continued in effect. The coalition of Right and Left endured until the Cold War became acute. Washington supported De Gasperi and poured floods of dollars into the country in the name of "saving Italy from Communism." The Socialists split into a Right party, headed by Saragat and supporting the Cabinet, and a Left party headed by Nenni and collaborating with Togliatti's Communists in opposition. The Peace Treaty of Feb. 10, 1947 (see pp. 196–197) was not a party issue. The new Cabinet of May 31, 1947, for the first time excluded the Left Socialists and Communists— who continued to command a large popular following by virtue of inflation, unemployment, land hunger, and continued misery for the mass of a poor and crowded populace.

In preparation for the elections of April 18, 1948, the Communists and Left Socialists formed a "Popular Front" while the Vatican and the USA spared no effort to strengthen the Christian Democrats. London and Washington promised a restoration of Trieste to Italy, though Tito's break with Stalin in June left the pledge unfulfilled. Ambassador James C. Dunn and the Catholic clergy campaigned vigorously in favor of "Christianity" and "democracy" against "totalitarianism" and "atheism." The Left bloc won 31% of the popular vote and 182 deputies. The Christian Democrats gained 49% of the ballots and 307 (a majority) of the seats in the Assembly, but continued to maintain a coalition Cabinet with the Right Socialists and minor parties.

Defense. By virtue of the benefits of the Marshall Plan and adherence to the North Atlantic Treaty (see pp. 595–597), the new Italy became a member of the American–West European coalition against Soviet aggression. The Left Socialists and Communists bitterly denounced U.S. "imperialism" and even threatened to welcome Soviet armies should they be obliged to pursue "aggressors" into Italy. The Christian Democrats, assured of American support by virtue of their staunch anti-Communism, tended to resist U.S. pressures for land reform and a more equitable system of taxation. Of Italy's 9½ million private land-owners, 46,000 or ½ of 1% owned 36% of all land, while three-fifths of Italy's 10 million farmers owned no land at all.

The Left retained control of the General Confederation of Labor, made converts among the southern peasants, and appeared little affected by the Vatican's threat of July, 1949, to excommunicate all Catholics supporting Communism. Red-sponsored strikes, seizures of rural estates, and demonstrations in favor of "peace" and against rearmament continued to meet with appreciable popular support. "Titoism" raised its head among Italian Communists but made few converts. In 1950–51 the Right Socialists split, reunited, and quit the Cabinet. The Christian Democrats were increasingly divided into conservatives and reactionaries but avoided any open rupture. On the extreme right a variety of neo-Fascist groups made dubious progress: Guglielmo Gianninni's *l'Uomo Qualunque* or "common man" movement, Gioacchino

Cipola's "Anti-Communist Front," and Giovanni Tonelli's "Italian Social Movement" or MSI, dedicated to a one-party "Corporative State," outlawry of strikes, ultranationalism, and imperialism—and subsidized, despite its anti-Americanism, by a few aristocrats and industrialists. Such movements proved to be ineffective and ephemeral.

The balance of political groups was reflected in municipal and provincial elections in June of 1951. Under new electoral laws whereby two-thirds of the seats in local councils went to any party or coalition winning a plurality of votes, the Left lost many posts. But in popular votes the strength of the Christian Democrats declined to 38% of the total, while the MSI won 13% in Sicily and the Communists–Left Socialists 30% in the south and 38% in the north. The Vatican organ, *l'Osservatore Romano*, commented that $1,300,000,000 of U.S. aid since 1948 had not sufficed to overcome Communist exploitation of the poverty of Italian workers and peasants. In provincial elections in the center and south in May, 1952, the MSI won 11% of the popular votes, the Monarchists 10%, the Left bloc 30%, and the Christian Democrats 30%.

De Gasperi's Italy conducted diplomacy vigorously, but the limits of its possible achievements were circumscribed by its dependent relationship to the Atlantic Powers and their problems. Generous subventions flowed from the USA, but barely equaled Italy's "dollar deficit." Industrial production by May of 1951 was 140% of the prewar level, but a million and a half workers were chronically jobless. The living standards of the rest were the lowest in Western Europe outside of Portugal and Spain. Rearmament, spurred by Eisenhower in 1951, brought gains to some businesses but seemed irreconcilable with national economic self-support in the absence of larger U.S. subsidies. "Revisionism" attained only what the Western Powers were able and willing to grant.

Politics and Diplomacy. In the course of Italian public affairs in the later 1950's successive Cabinets in Rome maintained the ascendancy of the Christian Democrats, sometimes precariously, in an era of growing prosperity and relative internal stability, and succeeded in attaining abroad many objectives of the Republic's foreign policy. De Gasperi, in the seventh year of his Premiership, pushed through Parliament early in 1953 the "Scelba Law" for "electoral reform," modeled on the French statute of 1951, whereby 65% of the seats in the Chamber (380 out of 590) would go to any party or coalition winning over 50% of the popular vote. This search for a stable majority was disappointed in the polling of June 7–8, 1953, in spite of active support of the candidates of the Christian Democrat–Liberal–Right Socialist–Republican coalition by the Vatican, Cardinal Spellman, and new U.S. Ambassador Clare Boothe Luce, bearing new American subsidies. The Christian Democrats won 40.09% of the vote, the Right Socialists 4.5%, the Liberals 3.0%, and the Republicans 1.6%. With 49.19% of the total, the coalition thus fell short of its coveted 50%. The Communists won 22.6%, the Left Socialists 12.7%, the Monarchists 6.9%, and the Social Movement 5.8%. Togliatti celebrated victory. Nenni's Left Socialists offered to join the Cabinet providing EDC and the Atlantic Pact were "revised."

De Gasperi presented his eighth and all-Christian Democratic Cabinet to the Chamber in late July, 1953, and was defeated. In mid-August Giuseppe Pella formed a temporary Christian Democratic Ministry of "experts," which survived with Monarchist support despite numerous strikes for higher wages inspired by rising prices. The crisis of January, 1954, eventuated in February in a Right coalition Ministry headed by Mario Scelba. On Aug. 19 the 73-year-old de Gasperi died of a heart attack. On Oct. 5, 1954, a vexed question productive of stormy scenes, reciprocal threats, and complex negotiations, was finally settled: by the terms of an Anglo-American-Italian-Jugoslav memorandum signed in London, Zone A of the Trieste territory, including the city, was annexed by Italy, and Zone B by Jugoslavia, which also acquired two border towns as compensation. The Anglo-American occupation of the disputed frontier region was brought to an end.

President Einaudi's seven-year term having expired, Chamber and Senate jointly elected left-wing Christian Democrat Giovanni Gronchi to the Presidency on April 28, 1955. Premier Scelba, who had made a State visit to the USA in late March, resigned on June 26 amid parliamentary confusion. The new Cabinet of Christian Democrat Antonio Segni, formed on July 6, was the old with a few changes. It was Italy's seventeenth Cabinet since 1945. Foreign Minister Gaetano Martino, benefiting from the "Spirit of Geneva" which enabled Italy to pursue a more independent role, concluded accords with Warsaw and Moscow on peaceful uses of atomic energy, opened trade talks with Peiping, received Dulles in October, visited Thailand and Japan in November, and was host to Nasser in Rome. He and Segni declined an invitation to visit Moscow and went instead in February, 1956, to Bonn, where they championed German unification and voiced complete agreement with Adenauer on all international issues. Martino and Gronchi made a State visit to Washington in late February and received Chancellor Konrad Adenauer in Rome in July.

The violence of autumn, 1956 (see pp. 416–426), reduced, rather than enhanced, Italy's weight in the scales of power and had curious domestic repercussions. Having failed to "mediate" between Cairo and the West, Martino succeeded by diverse proposals in alienating London, Paris, and Cairo alike. Christian Democrats reiterated their adherence to an "Atlantic policy" and their opposition in Parliament to any "opening to the Right" (*i.e.*, the Monarchists) or any "opening to the Left" (*i.e.*, the Left Socialists). The weird politics of de-Stalinization discredited and confused the Communists and led Nenni to open negotiations with Saragat for a reunion of the two Socialist parties. But the discussions failed in 1957 as Nenni, despite reservations, continued to collaborate with Togliatti, who retained his leadership over a weakened but still formidable Communist Party.

When President Gronchi, in late March, 1957, penned a message to Eisenhower criticizing Dulles, condemning the Eisenhower Doctrine, deploring Italy's minor role in NATO, and advocating a Central European "neutral zone," the Foreign Ministry declined to send it. Gronchi demanded Martino's resignation. The Cabinet refused. A reconciliation was effected. But when Saragat, inspired by obscure political calculations relating to foreign policy and his fruitless talks with Nenni, withdrew from the Cabinet, Premier Segni resigned, May 6, 1957. On May 19 left-wing Christian Democrat Adone Zoli formed an all-Christian Democratic Cabinet. He championed "neo-Atlanticism" —i.e., adherence to the Western alliance but with revisions according Italy a more equal and influential role—and survived parliamentary votes in early June, only to resign when a recount revealed that the Cabinet's majority depended upon neo-Fascist votes. When Amintore Fanfani failed in efforts to form a new Cabinet, Gronchi in late June prevailed upon Zoli to reconsider his resignation and to carry on with the Cabinet of May.

Italia Minor. In the new Italian Republic, as in successive French Republics through many decades, Cabinets come and Cabinets go while bureaucrats carry on public services and kaleidoscopic parliamentary majorities shift now leftward, now rightward, with little enduring effect upon the balance of political forces or upon the daily lives of the populace. This unstable and seemingly meaningless pattern of politics evokes contempt among Communists and derision among many Anglo-Americans. Yet it might be judged in a long perspective to be an unsought and unplanned blessing. If it be true that "happy is the land whose annals are brief," it may be true as well that fortunate are the people whose politicians, although apparently engaged in ardent contests over "principles," are preoccupied in parliamentary and ministerial maneuverings having little ultimate effect on the destinies of their constituents.

Such a land was the Italy of the 1950's and 1960's. Changing Presidents, Premiers, and parties in Parliament commanded much public attention, but had little effect upon public well-being. To be sure, the programs of land reform and education in the poor and illiterate southland or *Mezzogiorna*, and of electrification and further industrialization in the wealthier northland, were not without results for the economy and society of the nation. Businessmen, land-owners, and the middle-class masses, if hopeful of continued prosperity, were unlikely to repeat the disastrous experiment of Fascism, even in the face of peasant and proletarian mass unemployment and unrest, reflected during a decade of Cold War in one-third of the electorate giving its support to Communists and Left Socialists. These "revolutionists," in turn, were wholly unlikely to attempt revolution, for their leaders, now become party bureaucrats, had nothing to gain and everything to lose by new social and political convulsions. Peace at home therefore seemed likely to be of long duration. Peace abroad depended upon circumstances beyond Italian control. Despite a population of 50,000,000 by 1958, Italy's role as a Great Power was forever ended by the weakness of Western Europe as a whole in world affairs and the emergence of America and Russia, and prospectively of China and India, as Super-Powers. Rome henceforth might perform a modest function as moderator, but could play no role as an equal in the global game of power. No other function was possible unless both of the great coalitions should disintegrate completely or should inadvertently precipitate World War III. In the former event Italy, as Machiavelli once hoped, might again play an independent role. In the latter event Italy would suffer revolution and civil war and share in common ruin. Meanwhile, in times of peace, the Republic could reasonably be expected to survive indefinitely as the old Kingdom had done between the *Resorgimento* and 1914.

SUGGESTED READINGS

Alfieri, Dino: *Dictators Face to Face*, New York, New York University Press, 1955.
Borgese, G. A.: *Goliath: The March of Fascism*, New York, Viking, 1937.
De Bono, Emilio: *Anno XIIII: The Conquest of an Empire*, London, Cresset, 1937.
Dombrowski, Roman: *Mussolini: Twilight and Fall*, New York, Roy, 1956.
Finer, Herman: *Mussolini's Italy*, New York, Holt, 1935.
Gibson, Hugh (ed.): *The Ciano Diaries, 1939–1943*, New York, Doubleday, 1946.
Grindrod, Muriel: *Rebuilding of Italy: Politics and Economics, 1945–1955*, New York, The Royal Institute of International Affairs, 1956.
Halperin, S. William: *The Separation of Church and State in Italian Thought from Cavour to Mussolini*, Chicago, University of Chicago Press, 1939.
Hughes, H. Stuart: *The United States and Italy*, Cambridge, Mass., Harvard University Press, 1953.
Kogan, Norman: *Italy and the Allies*, Cambridge, Mass., Harvard University Press, 1956.
Macartney, M. H. H., and P. Cremona: *Italy's Foreign and Colonial Policy, 1914–1937*, New York, Oxford, 1938.
McKnight, John P.: *The Papacy: A New Appraisal*, New York, Rinehart, 1952.
Megaro, G.: *Mussolini in the Making*, Boston, Houghton Mifflin, 1938.
Naughton, James W.: *Pius XII on World Problems*, New York, America Press, 1943.
Pichon, Charles: *The Vatican and Its Role in World Affairs*, New York, Dutton, 1950.
Salvemini, Gaetano: *Under the Axe of Fascism*, New York, Viking Press, 1936.
———: *Prelude to World War II*, New York, Doubleday, 1954.
Sforza, Count Carlo: *Contemporary Italy: Its Intellectual and Moral Origins*, New York, Dutton, 1944.
Villari, Luigi: *Italian Foreign Policy under Mussolini*, New York, Devin-Adair, 1956.

4. GERMANY: FROM PSYCHOSIS TO PARTITION

It is heartbreaking to see the weakness of the older cultural group in face of this barbarism; its bewildered, confused retreat. Dazed and abashed, with an embarrassed smile, it abandons one position after another, seeming to concede that in very truth it no longer understands the world. It stoops to the foe's mental and moral level, adopts his idiotic terminology, adjusts itself to its pathetic categories, his stupid, spiteful and capricious propaganda—and does not even see what it is doing. Perhaps it is already lost.—THOMAS MANN, 1938.

The problem of "Bolshevism" is once more brought to the fore in all severity and today all of civilized humanity faces anxiously the question whether or not it will be possible, once more, to save Western civilization from being flooded from the Eastern steppes.—DR. PAUL JOSEPH GOEBBELS in *Das Reich*, "The Great Venture," May, 1943.

On May 7, 1945, at 2:41 A.M. in a schoolhouse in Rheims, General Jodl for the German High Command signed a simple document of unconditional surrender. On May 8 an identical document was signed in Berlin by Keitel, Friedeburg, and Stumpf for the Army, Navy, and Luftwaffe and by Zhukov, Tedder, and Spaatz for the victors. Within another week the last German forces still fighting were cut to pieces west of Prague. *Der Führer's* Reich, which was to have lasted a thousand years, was at an end.

Himmler had left Hitler in his bunker below the Chancellery building in Berlin and, from his northern headquarters, had offered through a Swedish intermediary to surrender to the Western Powers while continuing the war with Russia. The offer was ignored. He sought safety in flight but finally took poison to avoid capture. Martin Bormann vanished. Goebbels, who remained with Hitler, committed suicide. On April 29, Hitler, who refused to leave the bunker, was married to Eva Braun, allegedly his mistress. Exploding Soviet shells supplied the wedding music. On April 30, he shot himself as his bride took poison. The bodies were burned in the courtyard. No remains were ever found.

Hitler still lives as a portent of the infamy and dementia to which the human psyche can be reduced by the breakdown of an acquisitive culture, dedicated to national tribalism and the cult of violence. He also lives as a sign of times to come. For his predictions of new conflict between "Bolshevism" and the "plutodemocracies" came to pass—not in time to save the Third Reich but perhaps in time to build the Fourth, and assuredly in time to give Fascism in many lands a new lease on life and, it may be, new opportunities for "wedge driving," conspiracy, war plans, and another saturnalia of fear-driven, hate-crazed massacre and annihilation. . . .

Furor Teutonicus. The inner life of nations is often revealed by their symbols of leadership. The history of Germany began with a man symbol, continued with three successive dynasty symbols, and ended with a man symbol: Hermann, the Hohenstauffens, the Hapsburgs, the Hohenzollerns, Hitler. The first of these leaders, called by the Romans Arminius, was the chieftain of the Cherusci who led his followers out of the darkness of barbarism to butcher the legions of Varus in Teutoburger Wald (A.D. 9), thereby compelling Imperial Rome to abandon the dream of a frontier on the Elbe. The early dynasties typified the "First," or Holy Roman, Reich, established in its initial form eight centuries after Hermann by Karl der Grosse (Charlemagne) when the Germanic tribes had long since learned to revere and imitate the great world of ancient Rome which their ancestors had destroyed. Under Hohenstauffen and Hapsburg Emperors, this curious realm endured as a living polity for eight centuries more, symbolizing the catholic universality of medieval Christendom and the common culture of Frenchmen, Germans, Czechs, Poles, Italians, and others. The life span of the Hohenzollern Dynasty was the life span of the modern cult of the nation-state in Germany—from the Mark of Brandenburg through the Kingdom of Prussia to the German Empire (the "Second Reich") of 1871–1918. Hitler, the little man of Austria who became tyrant over Europe, symbolized the twilight time of nationalism and Christianity when Germans returned to a debased cult of imperial power, reverted to barbarism and paganism, dreamed of a World State conquered by the sword of a "Third Reich," and surrendered themselves in their political and social relations to utter formlessness—violent, empty, and touched with the shadow of darkness.

But Hitler, like Mussolini, is less significant as a mad genius than as a symptom of a sick civilization. He mirrored in his life the anxieties of an insecure *Kleinbürgertum*, finally driven to frenzy by its fears and used by frightened elites of money and land to protect themselves by methods which reduced civilized men to savages, beasts, and devils. Like Stalin, he was son of a shoemaker. This shoemaker was the illegitimate son of Maria Schikl-gruber. Not until he was forty did he change his name to Hitler, after his Austrian peasant father who married his mother when he was five. This Alois Hitler secured a post in the Austrian customs service at Braunau-am-Inn, northeast of Salzburg, where his third wife on April 20, 1889, bore the son they named Adolf. This boy, like millions of others in lower middle-class families, hated his father, who died when Adolf was fourteen—and quarreled with his mother who died when he was seventeen. They wanted him to be-come a respectable petty official, like papa. He wanted to be an artist. He sought to study art in Vienna and got nowhere. Poverty forced him to become a laborer. In resentment he learned to hate Socialists and Jews and Slavs. In his early twenties he lived miserably in Munich, painting postcards and dreaming of being a hero. The year 1914 brought him the joy of war, and then a corporalship and an Iron Cross and poison gas in 1918. The defeat left him in despair. Still in uniform, he returned to Munich, dabbled with the political agitators who harangued disgruntled veterans in beer halls, and, on a June evening of 1919, joined, as Member No. 7, a tiny group called the "German Labor Party." A year later he was orating against Jews, Com-munists, and capitalists in the name of his party, now renamed the "National Socialist German Labor Party" (NSDAP). A platform of anti-Semitism, Pan-Germanism, pseudosocialism, militarism, and vengeance was adopted at the Hofbrauhaus on Feb. 24, 1920. Other misfits joined: Goering, Hess, Röhm, Rosenberg. By 1923, when the French seized the Ruhr and the flood of marks from the printing presses declined to worthlessness, the Party had 70,000 members and money from men of wealth and influence.

On Nov. 8, 1923, these spinners of nightmares sought to overthrow the government by force and violence through a theatrical *Putsch* in the *Bürgerbrau*. The police shot down the paraders and suppressed the Party. On trial for treason, Hitler orated, "The future of Germany means the annihilation of Marxism. Who is born to be a dictator will not be halted. I wish to be the drummer of the 'Third Reich.' " Since what he had said and done was "patriotic" (the man, though queer, was obviously anti-Communist), he was sentenced to only five years in prison, where he began writing *Mein Kampf.* He was actually released in December, 1924. All this was absurd and unimportant, even after Hitler revived his "Party" and got nowhere with it during the years of German prosperity in the 1920's.

Wisdom and Woe in Weimar. What happened to the most populous, prosperous, and civilized community of Western Europe to make the Nazi madmen its masters is the story of a schizoid and paranoid culture whose people in the end could find no better way to regain a lost prosperity and restore their unity and pride. Imperial Germany between 1870 and 1914 became the envy and emulation of mankind and, next to America, the most shining citadel of science and industry in all the world. But within the web of folkways and motives we call nationalism, capitalism, and the politics of power, the very forces of technology and business which made for a richly abundant life were used by men of influence in the service of greed and ambition, private and public. Hard problems of social engineering for the general wealth and welfare were evaded by industrialists and aristocrats through militarism, adventurous diplomacy, and dreams of global hegemony. Even this course, though primitive and dangerous, need not have led to disaster if the foresight of Bismarck had continued to prevail. This master politician of Germany's unification understood the logic of Germany's position in the Western State System: however powerful Germany might become on the Continent, the Reich must never embark upon policies which might involve war with Britain or Russia or America; German-Russian cooperation is the prerequisite of German security in Europe.

The last Kaiser and his ministers ignored this advice and finally involved their country in war with Russia, Britain, and America, leading to inevitable defeat. The new Republic born of the debacle, with its Constitution framed in Weimar, had a hard row to hoe in foreign affairs. Its life span of 15 years (1918–33) was brief and not productive of any burning devotion by very many Germans to the liberal way of life. The feudal *Junkers* of Prussia and the great industrialists of the Ruhr and Rhineland continued to rule the roost, despite the socialist hopes in the early years of the Social Democrats—who crushed all efforts at Communist revolution in 1918–20 and then gave way in the seats of power to the conservative and clericalist beneficiaries of their

470

work. But the men of Weimar understood Bismarck's wisdom. In 1922, at Rapallo near Genoa in the course of an otherwise fruitless international conference, they struck an economic and political bargain with Red Moscow, signed by Walter Rathenau and George Chicherin.[3] The bargain ended the diplomatic isolation of the two outcast Powers. It reflected a German conviction that any restoration of the Reich vis-à-vis the West required German-

THE GERMAN REPUBLIC
SCALE: MILES
0   50   100   150
FRONTIERS 1871-1914 -------
FRONTIERS 1919-1938 ———

Russian understanding, regardless of what type of regime prevailed in Muscovy.

[3] The Genoa gathering was an economic and financial conference called to promote "the economic reconstruction of Central and Eastern Europe." The USSR attended. The USA refused. No settlement was achieved of the German reparations problem nor of the financial claims of the Allies and the Soviet Union against one another, though peaceful coexistence of differing economic systems was endorsed. Lloyd George, for the Allies, claimed $13,000,000,000 for confiscated properties and repudiated debts. Chicherin advanced counterclaim of $60,000,000,000 for damages done in the "illegal" allied intervention of 1918–21, though offering to settle for a tiny fraction of the total and to acknowledge Allied claims on condition of a substantial new loan for reconstruction. In the midst of this deadlock, Rathenau and Chicherin signed the Treaty of Rapallo, April 16, 1922, whereby Germany and Russia canceled all claims against one another, provided for full diplomatic and consular relations, and laid the basis for promoting trade on the most-favored-nation principle and for surreptitious military collaboration. For a full account see Louis Fischer, *The Soviets in World Affairs* (Cape & Smith, 1930), Vol. I, pp. 318–354.

What the ultimate fruits of this German-Russian entente might have been we can never know, since Germany was abruptly plunged into economic ruin by the Great Depression which descended upon all the Western lands in 1929. The disaster begot 6,000,000 unemployed and general bankruptcy and impoverishment. Jobless workers flocked to the Communist Party. Desperate burghers and peasants joined the NSDAP or Nazis, whose hysterical *Führer* promised prosperity, pride, and power through the overthrow of the "Weimar Jew Republic" and the establishment of a glorious "Third Reich" to be based upon anti-Marxism, anti-Semitism, anti-capitalism, and a misty "National Socialism." Industrialists and *Junkers* subsidized the brown-shirted Nazi Stormtroopers, hoping to make use of them against Communists, Socialists, the trade unions, and other threats, real or imaginary, to property and privilege. In the Reichstag election of Sept. 14, 1930, the Nazis won 6,400,000 votes. In the Presidential election of April 10, 1932, Hindenburg was re-elected by a slim margin, with 13,400,000 votes cast for Hitler. The Nazi voters rose to 13,745,000 or 37% of the total in the Reichstag election of July 31, 1932, and then declined in the last free election, Nov. 6, 1932, to 11,737,000 as business conditions registered a slight improvement. Far from winning a majority of voters, the Party appeared on the verge of bankruptcy and disintegration by midwinter.

The Nazi Road to Totalitarianism. The Reich was delivered to Fascism not by an electoral victory but by a conspiracy, entered into against the last Republican Chancellor, Kurt von Schleicher, whose old friend, Franz von Papen, resolved to use Hitler to put himself back in power. Papen had been head of the "Baron's Cabinet" which Hindenburg had appointed after ousting Chancellor Heinrich Brüning in May, 1932. In January, 1933, Papen spun his plot. His tools, so he thought, were Hitler, mob hypnotist; Hugenberg, ultranationalist publisher; Fritz Thyssen, steel magnate; the *Reichsverband der Industrie*; and the *Junker Landbund*. On Jan. 4, 1933, with champagne salesman Joachim von Ribbentrop as intermediary, Papen invited Hitler to a secret "love feast" in Cologne at the home of Thyssen's friend, the banker Baron Kurt von Schroeder. The plot was woven. Rhineland industrialists gave 4,000,000 marks to the Nazi treasury.

Hindenburg, who had been reelected to the Presidency nine months previously by the support of Brüning and of all the Liberals and Socialists in order that he might save the Reich from Hitler, was persuaded to "save agriculture" (*i.e.*, the *Junkers*) from "agrarian Bolshevism" (*i.e.*, an exposure of the use to which they had put State subsidies) by dismissing Schleicher on Jan. 30, 1933, and appointing Hitler Chancellor, Papen Vice-Chancellor, Hugenberg Minister of Economics, and other reactionaries to the remaining posts. Hitler dissolved the Reichstag and ordered an election on March 5, 1933.

Six days before the balloting Nazi secret agents burned the Reichstag building. Hitler at once accused the Communists of arson and bloody revolution. He posed as savior from the "Red menace," ordered the arrest of thousands of Communists and Social Democrats, suppressed the campaign activities of the anti-Nazi parties, induced Hindenburg to abolish civil liberties in the name of defense against the Communist peril, and threw the electorate into a panic. His followers polled 44% of the vote. They promptly secured a majority in the new Reichstag by excluding and arresting all the Communist deputies. An "Enabling Act" transferred dictatorial powers to the Cabinet. Only the Social Democrats voted in opposition.

Within three months Hitler and his colleagues succeeded in achieving what it had taken Mussolini three years to do in Italy: smash all organized opposition, outlaw all other parties, and establish a "total" State as absolute and intolerant as that of the Communists in Russia, but dedicated to purposes even more dangerous to the Free World. German radicals, liberals, and conservatives set the example in 1933 of complete paralysis, incomprehension, and suicide. The German Communist Party, the largest and most formidable in the world outside the USSR, had spent the years of crisis fighting the Socialists as "Social Fascists" and assuming fatuously that Nazi victory would lead to Communist revolution. Hitler's suppression of the Communists was approved by all anti-Communists, including the Socialists—for who but a pro-Communist could question the wisdom of suppressing the Communists? May Day of 1933 was proclaimed by the Nazis a "Day of National Labor." Huge demonstrations of the solicitude of the new Cabinet for the interests of the workers were an unqualified success. On the next day, with no resistance, Stormtroopers suppressed all German labor unions, arrested their leaders, banned their press, seized their funds, abolished the right to strike, and "coordinated" organized labor into Robert Ley's Nazi *Arbeitsfront*. On May 17 the Social Democrats in the Reichstag joined all other parties in voting "confidence" in Hitler's proclaimed foreign policy of "peace." On June 22 the Cabinet decreed the suppression of the Social Democratic Party. All anti-Socialists approved, for who but a pro-Socialist could question the wisdom and necessity of suppressing the Socialists?

Hugenberg was forced out of the Cabinet on June 29 and his Nationalist Party "voluntarily" dissolved. All anti-reactionaries approved. By July the Nazis had a majority of Cabinet posts. On July 3 the regime signed a Concordat with the Vatican. On July 4 it suppressed the Catholic Center Party and the Bavarian Peoples' Party. A Cabinet decree declared: "The NSDAP is the only political party in Germany," and threatened dire penalties for any who might establish or support any other. Under the new "leadership principle," Goering asserted correctly on Sept. 15, 1933: *"Der Führer* carries final responsibility. His will is law." The men of money and land who had put Hitler into power under the delusion that they could control him were now at the mercy of a dictatorship ruled by madmen. But they saw new

473

prospects of profit and privilege in the new order and gave willing support.

Whatever doubts remained regarding the social structure and economic program of the new regime were soon resolved. On "Bloody Saturday," June 30, 1934, the radicals and Stormtroop leaders within the Party who challenged the old military caste and took national "socialism" seriously were all shot for "treason"—Ernst Röhm, Gregor Strasser, Karl Ernst, and scores of others, along with Schleicher and his wife, Erich Klausener, and the aides of Papen who barely escaped with his own life and was bundled off to Vienna as ambassador. Hitler assumed the powers of the Presidency on Hindenburg's death, Aug. 2, 1934.

The program was one of restoring prosperity through a "planned economy" based on private monopoly and operating on public spending for massive rearmament which provided jobs for workers, incomes for farmers, profits for industrialists, army commissions for *Junkers,* pride for patriots, and happiness for everybody save the new pariahs. The neurotic *Kleinbürgertum* was enabled to resume its upward social climb toward the status of its superiors and to discharge its aggressions against inferiors—*i.e.,* foreign "enemies" and domestic scapegoats, above all the Jews who were insulted, robbed, beaten, and ultimately exterminated. These surgical operations on the society and economy of Germany were completely successful in replacing the miseries of depression with the prosperity of militarism—though the patient, to be sure, went insane and finally died in convulsions.

The Nazi Road to War. "To forge a mighty sword," wrote Hitler in *Mein Kampf,* "is the task of internal political leadership; to protect the forging and seek allies in arms is the task of foreign policy." *Der Führer* had outlined his program clearly: rearmament, alliances with Italy, Japan, and, if possible, Britain; the destruction of France; and the conquest of Russia in the name of anti-Communism and the old Germanic *Drang nach Osten* against the Slavs. Western statesmen were most favorably impressed with the anti-Communism and the prospect of a German-Russian war.

The inner dynamics of German Fascism made war abroad a necessity for peace and prosperity at home. But choices were still possible with regard to victims. Loud talk about a "crusade against Communism" was popular among Germans and effective in befuddling Frenchmen, Britishers, and Americans. Yet the precepts of Bismarck and Rathenau need not have been forgotten. Neither Hitler nor Stalin, as events were to demonstrate, was so far gone in folly as to regard ideological fanaticism as a proper basis of foreign policy. Nazi "anti-Communism," like Communist "anti-Fascism," did not preclude a mutually advantageous bargain. Karl Haushofer and the new General Staff were certain that any attack upon Russia would prove disastrous, should therefore be avoided, and could in fact be avoided without danger to the Reich and with vast benefits accruing from a Berlin-Moscow entente.

The problem of Germany's role between Russia and the Western Powers

was the most crucial single problem of European politics in the time of
Frederick the Great and in the Napoleonic era of the "War of Liberation."
It became the most crucial single problem of world politics in the periods of
Bismarck and of Wilhelm II. It was the core problem for the diplomats of
the Weimar Republic and of the Nazi Reich. It is now more than ever, and
will long remain, the decisive problem of power for the destinies of Germany,
of Europe, and of all the world, both West and East, and therefore deserves
to be the leitmotiv of our survey of the foreign policy of the Reich during

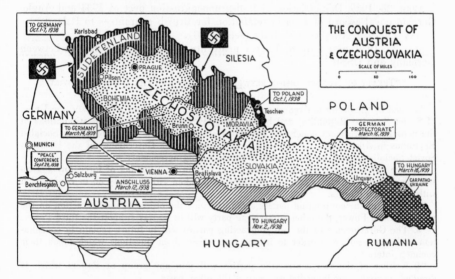

and since the epoch of Hitler. Experience gives appreciable support to the
hypothesis that German and Russian interests, though obviously not Western
interests, are best served under most circumstances by a German-Russian
entente. Nothing is more obvious, however, than that policy-makers are often
unwise and that the "lessons of history" are as often forgotten as remembered.
Hitler's program of aggrandizement was pursued with rare skill and phenomenal success during the first eight years of the Third Reich. This fascinating
sequence of perfidy and conquest, accepted or even welcomed by the Western
"Munichmen," is an oft-told tale. Here we need note only the timetable of
successive triumphs:

OCT. 14, 1933. Withdrawal from the League of Nations and the Disarmament
Conference.

JAN. 26, 1934. Signature of 10-year nonaggression pact with Poland.

MARCH 1, 1935. Recovery of the Saar.

MARCH 16, 1935. Reintroduction of conscription and repudiation of Part V of
the Treaty of Versailles.

JUNE 18, 1935. Signature of Anglo-German naval pact sanctioning German rearmament.

THE HERITAGE OF FASCISM

MARCH 7, 1936. Remilitarization of the Rhineland and abrogation of the Locarno Treaties.

OCT. 25, 1936. Berlin-Rome accord to cooperate in Spain and the Danube area.

NOV. 25, 1936. Berlin-Tokyo Anti-Comintern Pact (see p. 443).

MARCH 12, 1938. Invasion and occupation of Austria.

OCT. 1, 1938. The "Peace" of Munich, following Nazi campaign of terror and threats, Chamberlain's flights to the Reich, and Anglo-French ultimatum to Prague, Sept. 19, demanding surrender of Sudetenland to Hitler. Anglo-German non-aggression pact, Oct. 1. French-German nonaggression pact, Dec. 6.

MARCH 15, 1939. Invasion and occupation of Czechoslovakia.

APRIL 28, 1939. Denunciation of Polish nonaggression pact of 1934 and Anglo-German naval accord of 1935 in retaliation for British guarantees to Poland.

MAY 22, 1939. Alliance with Italy (see p. 460).

AUG. 23, 1939. Signature of 10-year neutrality and nonaggression pact between Germany and USSR.[4]

[4] "TREATY OF NONAGGRESSION BETWEEN GERMANY AND THE UNION OF SOVIET SOCIALIST REPUBLICS, AUG. 23, 1939

"Guided by the desire to strengthen the cause of peace between Germany and the Union of Soviet Socialist Republics, and basing themselves on the fundamental stipulations of the neutrality agreement concluded between Germany and the Union of Soviet Socialist Republics in April, 1926, the German Government and the Government of the Union of Soviet Socialist Republics have come to the following agreement:

"1. The two contracting parties undertake to refrain from any act of force, any aggressive act and any attacks against each other undertaken either singly or in conjunction with any other Powers.

"2. If one of the contracting parties should become the object of warlike action on the part of a third Power, the other contracting party will in no way support the third Power.

"3. The Governments of the two contracting parties will in future remain in consultation with one another in order to inform each other about questions which touch their common interests.

"4. Neither of the two contracting parties will join any group of Powers which is directed, mediately or immediately, against the other party.

"5. In case disputes or conflicts on questions of any kind should arise between the two contracting parties, the two partners will solve these disputes or conflicts exclusively by friendly exchange of views or if necessary by arbitration commissions.

"6. The present agreement is concluded for the duration of ten years with the stipulation that unless one of the contracting partners denounces it one year before its expiration, it will automatically be prolonged by five years.

"7. The present agreement shall be ratified in the shortest possible time. The instruments of ratification are to be exchanged in Berlin. The treaty comes into force immediately it has been signed." SECRET ADDITIONAL PROTOCOL:

"On the occasion of the signature of the Nonaggression Pact between the German Reich and the Union of Soviet Socialist Republics the undersigned plenipotentiaries of each of the two parties discussed in strictly confidential conversations the question of the boundary of their respective spheres of influence in Eastern Europe. These conversations led to the following conclusions:

"1. In the event of a territorial and political rearrangement in the areas belonging to the Baltic States (Finland, Estonia, Latvia, Lithuania), the northern boundary of Lithuania shall represent the boundary of the spheres of influence of Germany and the USSR. In this connection the interest of Lithuania in the Vilna area is recognized by each party.

"2. In the event of a territorial and political rearrangement of the areas belonging to the Polish state the spheres of influence of Germany and the USSR shall be bounded approximately by the line of the rivers Narew, Vistula, and San.

"The question of whether the interests of both parties make desirable the maintenance

With this bargain, Hitler abruptly abandoned his "crusade against Communism" in favor of a return to the logic of Rapallo and Bismarck. How rich were the dividends of this course in the Nazi career of conquest is clear from the sequel:

SEPT. 1–28, 1939. Invasion and conquest of Poland, followed by German-Soviet partition of the territory of the former Polish State.
APRIL 9, 1940. Invasion and conquest of Denmark and Norway.
MAY 10, 1940. Invasion of Luxembourg, Belgium, the Netherlands, and France. British evacuation of Dunkirk, June 3. Fall of Paris, June 14. French capitulation and armistice, June 22.
SEPT. 27, 1940. Signature of Triplice Alliance (see p. 444).
OCT. 8, 1940. Occupation of Rumania.
APRIL 6–27, 1941. Invasion and conquest of Jugoslavia and Greece.

Nemesis. Why did the Nazi leaders, undisputed rulers of all Europe west of Russia and masters of an invincible Wehrmacht against which no Western army could stand, risk ruin by abandoning the wisdom of 1939 for the madness of 1941? The answer suggested by the U.S. State Department (*e.g.*, James Byrnes's *Speaking Frankly*, pp. 288*ff.*, and *Nazi-Soviet Relations, 1939–1941*) —namely, that the Nazi decision was a product of Molotov's "demands" in Berlin in November, 1940—is, as we shall see, in error. At no time did the Nazi leaders expect to be attacked by the USSR, and in this expectation they were correct. Some, though by no means all, German authorities (like most Western "experts") were certain that the USSR could be conquered in six weeks. The temptation presented by this conviction was difficult to resist. But the facts, as we now know them, are worth reviewing, since the fatal error here committed had been committed before and may be committed again.

Der Führer's problem in mid-1940 was to conquer or make peace with Britain. He put out feelers in late June, asking only the return of the German colonies and British acceptance of his dominion over Western Europe. There was no response. But the notion of a "compromise" and of British approbation of a German attack on Russia was long in dying. As late as May 10, 1941, Rudolf Hess, Nazi No. 2, flew to Scotland (where he was captured) in what he seemed to regard as a "peace mission." The problem of preparing an

---

of an independent Polish state and how such a state should be bounded can only be definitely determined in the course of further political developments.

"In any event both Governments will resolve this question by means of a friendly agreement.

"3. With regard to Southeastern Europe attention is called by the Soviet side to its interest in Bessarabia. The German side declares its complete political disinterestedness in these areas.

"4. This protocol shall be treated by both parties as strictly secret.

"Moscow, Aug. 23, 1939.

For the Government	Plenipotentiary of the
of the German Reich:	Government of the USSR:
v. RIBBENTROP	V. MOLOTOV"

invasion of England ("Operation Sea Lion") proved insoluble. German sea power was inadequate. German land power could launch a cross-Channel attack only if Goering's Luftwaffe wrested control of the air from the RAF. Elaborate preparations were made, but the Luftwaffe lost the Battle of Britain in September, 1940. Invasion was indefinitely deferred.

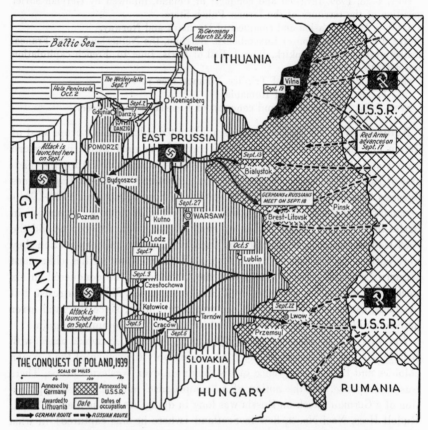

THE CONQUEST OF POLAND, 1939

   The decision to crush Russia before seeking a final reckoning with Britain was reached in secret in August of 1940. Plans for an invasion in the autumn were abandoned for logistic reasons, but preparations were pushed forward energetically through the winter and spring with a view toward an assault in May—finally deferred to June because of the Jugoslav-Greek campaign. Ribbentrop's invitation to Molotov, like his "negotiations" with Poland in August, 1939, was no more than a device to allay suspicion and gain time.[5]

[5] See appropriate index entries in *Trial of the Major War Criminals before the International Military Tribunal* (Nuremberg, 1947) for documentary proof that the Nazi decision to invade Poland on Sept. 1, 1939, was reached on May 23, 1939, and that the Nazi decision to invade the USSR was reached in August, 1940. For excerpts and evaluation, see "The Nazi Road to War," in *Current History*, January, April, 1953.

The spirit of the new crusade is suggested by Hitler's words to his Generals, Nov. 23, 1939: "I shall strike and not capitulate. . . . Every hope of compromise is childish. It is Victory or Defeat. The question is not the fate of Nazi Germany, but who is to dominate Europe in the future. . . . I am staking all my achievement on a gamble. . . . I shall shrink from nothing and shall destroy everyone who is opposed to me. I shall stand or fall in this struggle. I shall never survive the defeat of my people. There will be no capitulation to the Powers outside, no revolution by the forces within." Seven years before he had said to Hermann Rauschning at Berchtesgaden, "We may be destroyed, but, if we are, we shall drag a world with us—a world in flames!"

Ribbentrop and Hitler told Molotov in Berlin, Nov. 12–14, 1940, that Britain was beaten and that Russia should join the Triplice Pact, seek southward access to the sea, and participate with Italy, Germany, and Japan in the dismemberment of the British Empire. "Which sea?" asked Molotov, displaying more interest in the Straits and the Mediterranean than in his host's suggestion of the Persian Gulf. The Russians asked the withdrawal of German troops from Finland, protested at the German "guarantee" to Rumania, and suggested a Soviet "guarantee" of Bulgaria. When they met again at night, Ribbentrop submitted a draft of a Four-Power Alliance with a secret protocol assigning the territories "in the direction of the Indian Ocean" as the projected Soviet sphere. Molotov stubbornly wanted to know about German intentions in Sweden, Poland, Hungary, Rumania, Jugoslavia, and Greece. Ribbentrop complained he was being "interrogated too closely," and pleaded that Russia should join Germany in liquidating the British Empire. Molotov asked, "If England is in fact defeated, why are we conducting this discussion in your air-raid shelter?"

A fortnight later Moscow said it would sign the draft on condition that Germany quit Finland immediately, accept a Soviet-Bulgarian mutual-aid pact, agree to Soviet bases on the Dardanelles, recognize the area between the Caucasus and the Persian Gulf as a Soviet sphere, and arrange for Japanese renunciation of coal and oil concessions on Northern Sakhalin. Stalin was seeking to protect Soviet interests and now knew whence they were threatened. Hitler called Stalin a "cold-blooded blackmailer." He had already decided on his course: conquer Russia before Britain, aided by America, could challenge his position and then wage war for years, if need be, against an Anglo-American bloc which would be difficult to beat down but would be helpless to assail Nazi Eurasia.

Before dawn on Sunday, June 22, 1941, Nazi bombers struck at Soviet airfields while three gigantic armies, filled with the fervor of invincibility, poured over the frontier, one aiming at Leningrad, another at Moscow, and a third at Kharkov, Rostov, and the Caucasus. Hitler and Ribbentrop denounced Bolshevism and accused the victim of aggressive intent. Britain and America at once rallied to Russia's defense, though their means of extending aid were as yet insignificant. Italy, Slovakia, Croatia, Hungary, Rumania, and Finland, along with Vichy France and Franco's Spain (which sent a "Blue Legion" to fight Bolshevism), joined *der Führer* in his holy war. All across the steppes there was reenacted on an immense scale what Churchill had described a year previously in Flanders and Picardy: "The German eruption swept like a sharp scythe to the rear of the armies of the north. Behind this armored and mechanized onslaught came a number of divisions in lorries, and behind them again plodded comparatively slowly the dull brute mass of the ordinary German Army and German people, always ready to be led in the trampling down in other lands of liberties and comforts they have never known in their own." Berlin reported the slaughter or capture of millions of Soviet troops. The assault indeed seemed irresistible as German armor pushed onward over incredible distances, destroying all in its path. "This enemy," proclaimed *der Führer* on Oct. 3, "is broken and will never rise again." Almost everyone in the Atlantic communities agreed. To crush Russia was to win the world. This vision was within Hitler's grasp by midautumn of 1941.

The vision crumpled before the guns of the defenders of Leningrad and Sevastopol, who chose starvation and death in preference to surrender. The vision died under the shells of the defenders of Moscow, who in a series of savage battles during October and November halted the Wehrmacht—for the first time in World War II—and then slowly pushed it back. Nazi spokesmen complained that Soviet soldiers were too "brutalized" by Communism to fight fairly, too demoralized by Marxism to be intimidated, and too stupid to know when they were hopelessly defeated. At November's end the first general counteroffensive by the Red Army was launched with the recapture of Rostov and the destruction of Von Bock's divisions, almost within sight of the Kremlin.

"I go my way," said *der Führer* once upon a time, "with the assurance of a sleep-walker, the way which Providence has sent me." Hitlerian intuition had led the Reich to the conquest of all Europe and then to the same enterprise which had brought Bonaparte to ruin. The Corsican had won the capital of Muscovy, to no avail. The Austrian corporal was never to win it. If Russia could not be crushed by blitz, Russia must be bled to death in a war of attrition. And, in this case, supplies from America (still a trickle, but destined to become a flood) must be cut off. If Japan could decimate U.S. naval power and seize all of Greater East Asia, Nazi U-boats in the Atlantic could, it was hoped, close the sea lanes between America and Britain and sink such supply ships as might get through to the northern routes to Murmansk. Then Russia could be conquered. Then Britain. . . . Then America . . . ?

Pearl Harbor marked the realization of part of the dream. On Dec. 11, 1941, the Reich declared war on the USA. "A historic revenge has been entrusted to us by the Creator," said Hitler to the Nazi Reichstag, "and we are now obliged to carry it out. There is a world-wide gulf between the outlook of

President Roosevelt and myself. It does not impress me very much if Roosevelt sees fit to call me a gangster. I cannot be insulted by Roosevelt, because, just as with President Wilson, I consider Roosevelt to be insane. We know of course that the Eternal Jew is behind all this. Our patience has come to the breaking point."

On the same day a new pact was signed as a supplement to the Tripartite accord of Sept. 27, 1940. It pledged Rome, Berlin, and Tokyo to conduct war jointly against Britain and America, abstain from any separate armistice or peace, and collaborate after victory "in order to realize and establish an equitable new order in the world." By midsummer of 1942, Japan was master of East Asia, and the Wehrmacht, in its second all-out attempt to conquer Russia, had reached the Volga. All might yet be won. . . .

Götterdämmerung. Russian valor, American war production, British fortitude, and the secret war of the Underground in the conquered lands denied to the rulers of the Reich their chance of global victory. The RAF was able to bomb Berlin with 400 planes on Nov. 7, 1941. On May 30, 1942, a thousand planes dropped 3,000 tons of bombs on Cologne. On the next day, another thousand blasted the Krupp Works in Essen. By the summer of 1943, hundreds of American bombers were leveling German cities by day while the RAF continued its work by night. Despite death and ruin from the skies the German war lords succeeded in maintaining and even increasing production in 1943, while the Luftwaffe, though unable to defend the Reich, kept its active strength unimpaired and took a heavy toll from the enemy. Early in 1944, Allied bombing was concentrated on aircraft plants. On March 8, 1944, over 2,000 American planes smashed Berlin—which by war's end was a hollow shell with all its central area reduced to rubble.

But the Nazi monster was to suffer its mortal wound from other blows. Events to come were forecast by the surrender on Feb. 1, 1943, of Paulus's Sixth Army, trapped at Stalingrad by the second major Soviet counteroffensive. In an all-out propaganda campaign of "heroization" and "strength through gloom," Goebbels strove, not without success, to stir a desperate people to new miracles of work, fanaticism, and savagery in defense of "Fortress Europe." The Nazi leaders preached and prayed for a schism between the USSR and the Atlantic Powers. Their prayers were to be answered, but too late to save their cause. The failure of the U-boat campaign, the loss of North Africa, the defection of Italy, the Normandy invasion in June, 1944, the remorseless advance of Soviet forces toward the Dnieper, the Vistula, the Oder, the sweep of Anglo-American armies to the Rhine and beyond, all heralded a grim finale.

That there was no yielding short of complete collapse was due less to the Allied policy of "unconditional surrender" than to the fact that all efforts within the Reich to depose the Nazi leadership proved futile. On July 20, 1944, Radio Berlin canceled a scheduled program on "The Extermination of Rats" to announce that *der Führer* had been the target of assassins. Col. Count Claus von Stauffenberg had placed a brief case near Hitler's chair during a staff conference at headquarters in the east. The time bomb which it contained killed several officers, wounded a dozen, but inflicted only slight burns and bruises on Hitler. He rushed to the microphone to deny reports of his death, as the plotters sought to seize public buildings in Berlin. "In sacred anger and unbounded fury," said Grand Adm. Karl Doenitz, "we will get even with these traitors" and destroy this "mad, small clique of generals." The conspiracy included such diplomats as Ulrich von Hassell and Count Friedrich Werner von der Schulenberg, last Ambassador in Moscow, and such industrialists as Karl Goerdeler.

A new "blood purge" followed. Among those who died by suicide, hanging, or shooting were Gens. Friedrich Olbricht and Ernst Hoepner, the alleged leaders; Gens. Ludwig von Bock and Kurt Zeitzler, both former Chiefs of the General Staff; Rommel, Helldorf, Hassell, Schulenberg, Goerdeler, Witzleben, Albrecht Haushofer, and scores of lesser figures. This outcome meant war to the end, waged with insane frenzy by a Wehrmacht now retreating on all fronts toward the German frontiers and by a new Volkssturm, or Home Army. George H. Earle, U.S. naval attaché in Istanbul, was approached by Nazi agents with an offer to surrender on condition that the Russians be kept "out of Europe" with the aid of the Wehrmacht under Allied command. Favorably impressed, Earle sent the proposal to Roosevelt, who made no reply except to transfer Earle to Samoa. In his message of November on the anniversary of the Beer Hall *Putsch,* Hitler said: "Sovietism, supported by the democracies, is endeavoring to destroy the Reich and exterminate our people. The Jew is the wire-puller of democracy as he is the creator and inciter of the Bolshevik world-beast. . . . Our people have been hit by treachery after treachery. . . . [But] as long as I am alive, Germany will not suffer the fate of European States that have been overrun by Bolshevism."

In its last agonies the doomed Wehrmacht in December, 1944, struck back at the Russians in Hungary and broke through American lines in Belgium and Luxembourg. The former blow failed to lift the siege of Budapest. Rundstedt's surprise offensive in the Ardennes smashed the American First Army and almost reached the Meuse. But by mid-January the "Battle of the Bulge" was lost, as the Red Army launched its final offensive in central Poland. As the invaders closed in, the Nazi leaders stormed, exhorted, and threatened. At the death of Roosevelt, Hitler rejoiced that "fate has taken the greatest war criminal of all times from this earth." Plans were made for a defense of an "Alpine Redoubt," for an organization of "Werewolves" behind Allied lines to kill collaborators, for such final paroxysms of violence as can only be guessed at.

All of this was of no avail. Vienna fell to the Russians on April 13, Munich to the Americans on April 30. Zhukov's armies opened their final assault on Berlin on April 22 to the relentless thunder of thousands of guns, tanks, and planes. Three days later Russians and Americans met joyfully on the Elbe at Torgau. In the doomed capital the Reichstag building was burned once more— this time actually by Communists, who had fought their way from the Volga to taste this day of triumph. On April 29, at Caserta, a million German troops in Italy and Austria laid down their arms. Berlin fell on May 2. On May 4 the Wehrmacht units in Holland, Denmark, and North Germany yielded to Montgomery. To capitulate to the Russians was unthinkable, but this, too, was not to be avoided.

Occupation. In early May of the year of debacle, Doenitz at Flensburg sought without success to set up a "government" to make peace with the Western Powers and continue the war against Russia. But the major "United Nations" supposed that they had reached agreement at Yalta on a joint solution of the "German problem." Germany was divided into four occupation zones. The wreckage of Berlin, jointly governed by the victors, was divided into four sectors. A military Allied Control Council (Eisenhower, Montgomery, Zhukov, and De Lattre) first met in Berlin on June 5, 1945, to deal jointly with matters affecting Germany as a whole. The "Morgenthau Plan" for de-industrialization was never seriously considered, since it would have deprived 25,000,000 Germans of all means of livelihood. At Potsdam (see p. 195) it was agreed that the Council of Foreign Ministers should ultimately prepare "a peace settlement for Germany to be accepted by the government of Germany when a government adequate for the purpose is established." The joint objectives of the occupation were (1) de-Nazification, (2) demilitarization, (3) de-cartelization, and (4) democratization.

All of this soon came to be reconsidered by virtue of "Cold War" among the victors. This circumstance likewise enabled German nationalists, with Nazis increasingly influential among them, to achieve in record time, albeit in a bifurcated Reich, the substance of recartelization, remilitarization, and re-Nazification. As in Italy and Japan, defeat and occupation begot no social revolution save in the East where Russians and Poles dispossessed the *Junkers* who had been the landed aristocracy and politico-military elite of Prussia for many centuries. Since social revolution would obviously serve the purposes of Communist aggrandizement, the Western Powers in their zones effected few changes in the traditional status of the landed gentry and the industrial and commercial magnates who had been the bulwarks of the Second and Third Reichs.[6]

[6] For a detailed account of what happened to "decartelization," see James Stewart Martin, *All Honorable Men* (Little, Brown, 1951). A symbol of the process is provided by Alfred Krupp von Bohlen und Halbach, whose family had owned most of the armories which equipped German forces in both World Wars. He served 6 years of a 12-year sentence as a "war criminal," for having employed and mistreated slave labor. U.S. High Commissioner John J. McCloy reduced the sentence and canceled that portion of it which provided for the confiscation of the Krupp properties, though still leaving them subject to decartelization measures. In cooperation with Allied authorities, Krupp agreed

Allied agreement faded rapidly. All four zones were to have been treated as an economic unit. Paris withheld cooperation unless the Ruhr and Rhineland should be separated from the Reich. Washington and London refused. Moscow withheld cooperation unless the Ruhr should be subjected to Four-Power control and $10,000,000,000 in reparations should be pledged to the USSR. Washington and London refused. In the hope of allaying French and Soviet

fears, Byrnes proposed (April 29, 1946) a 25-year, or 40-year, Four-Power Pact to keep Germany disarmed. Paris and Moscow were unimpressed. Moscow was able to extract reparations from its agrarian and self-supporting eastern zone. But Washington and London, in order to prevent starvation and promote economic recovery, were obliged to pour a billion dollars a year into the highly industrialized and urbanized western zones, further afflicted by millions of fugitives expelled by Poland and Czechoslovakia or refugees from Communist terror in the east. Under these conditions Moscow delayed, Paris haggled, and London and Washington moved to merge their areas into

in August, 1952, to sell or lease his steel and coal enterprises and some other businesses in Essen but retained his locomotive and truck works, hotel chains, other real estate, various other industrial establishments, and a controlling interest in the huge Blohm and Voss shipyards of Hamburg.

"Bizonia" and to press for a settlement which might make the broken land an asset instead of a liability.

The vanquished "master race" had meanwhile resumed political activity on a local level. Four major parties emerged: Christian Democrats, Free Democrats, Social Democrats, and Communists. The latter were impotent save in the Russian zone where they served as tools of Russian rule. Here, under Soviet pressure, Social Democrat Otto Grotewohl and Communists Wilhelm Pieck and Walter Ulbricht effected a merger in April, 1946, of the two Marxist parties into a "Socialist Unity Party" or SED. The western Social Democrats denounced Grotewohl as a traitor. The SED was barred in the western zone. The Social Democrats as an independent party were barred in the eastern zone.

Local elections in 1946 established a pattern which persisted through later years. In the east, Soviet-style "elections" gave the SED large majorities. In the west, where elections were free, the Christian Democrats, led by conservative Konrad Adenauer, commonly secured almost half of the votes cast and the Social Democrats, led by fiery Kurt Schumacher, well over a third—and a majority in the western sectors of Berlin. The Free Democrats usually commanded not more than 10% of the electorate and the Communists seldom over 5%. Openly Nazi groups were outlawed, though it was clear that many Germans were nostalgic for the gay days of Jew-baiting, Red-hunting, and conquest and blamed Hitler not for starting the war but only for losing it. Such neo-Nazi and crypto-Nazi splinter groups as the German Reich Party (Karl Schaefer) and the Socialist Reich Party (Fritz Dorls) did no better than the NSDAP in the early 1920's, but cherished similar dreams for days to come.

The Super-Powers curried German favor in the hope of using Germans against one another. Molotov championed German recovery, disarmament, neutrality, anti-Fascism, "socialism," and "unity" within the new frontiers. Byrnes, at Stuttgart (Sept. 6, 1946) and elsewhere, echoed by Gen. Lucius Clay and William H. Draper, Jr., championed German sovereignty, capitalism, anti-Communism, revision of the Oder-Neisse line in Germany's favor, and "unity" to be achieved, if need be, by a separate peace treaty with West Germany under which steps should be taken to rescue Prussia from the Russians. All of this within two years after allied victory brought new hope to German hearts, for it was "just what the doctor ordered"—*i.e.*, the late Dr. Goebbels.

Duel for Deutschland. In the struggle for Germany in mid-century the USA feared that the Reich might be reunited and rearmed as the satellite of the USSR, thereby making impossible any effective counterweight to Russia on the Continent and facilitating possible Red conquest of all Europe. The USA hoped that all of Germany, or at least West Germany, might be won to the West against the East. The USSR feared that Germany might be united and rearmed as an ally of the USA, thereby threatening the hegemony

THE HERITAGE OF FASCISM

over Eastern Europe won by the Kremlin in 1945 and frustrating all dreams of "Sovietizing" Western Europe. Moscow hoped that a united Germany, if it could not be allied with the USSR, might be kept disarmed and neutralized or, barring this, that East Germany might be brought into the Soviet bloc and rearmed as a counterweight to the West.

Neither Super-Power dared to resort to force against the other to allay its fears and realize its hopes, since neither could figure out how the resulting global war could be "won." Both were therefore reduced to political and diplomatic maneuvering. But since successful diplomacy presupposes bargaining, and since neither side would compromise "vital" interests and "sacred" principles, the result of the maneuvering was not a bargain but a stalemate eventuating in a partition of the Reich along the lines of the original occupation zones.

Following a Soviet walkout, the Allied Control Council in Berlin ceased to function in March, 1948. The Western Powers moved toward the establishment of a West German State in "Trizonia." In June a new currency was introduced in the West, with 1 *Deutsche Mark* exchangeable for 10 old *Reichsmarks*. On June 24 Soviet authorities blocked all land and water transport and travel between West Berlin and the western zones on the pretext of "technical difficulties" and the necessities of preventing the introduction of the new Western currency. The "Berlin Blockade" was in fact a test to see whether the Western Powers could be pushed out of Berlin or at least be coerced into abandoning their plans for a West German State. General Clay contemplated an attempt to reopen the highways by armed force, but was overruled. Washington, London, and Paris replied with a spectacular "airlift" whereby huge cargoes of food and fuel were flown to the beleaguered West Berliners. If any Soviet official contemplated shooting down the Allied planes, he was overruled, though Communist purposes were obviously frustrated by the enterprise.

Complex and protracted negotiations outside and inside the UN (see p. 199) produced repeated deadlocks. But the Jessup-Malik parleys in New York in January, 1949, made it clear that Moscow was now prepared to forget the currency question and lift the blockade if the Western Powers would lift their counterblockade and consent to a new meeting of the Council of Foreign Ministers. On these terms, constituting a victory of the eagle over the bear, the blockade was ended on May 11, 1949, albeit no resolution of the larger issue was effected at the Council meeting in May.

A House Divided. The Western Powers meanwhile pressed forward with their plans. The USA overcame British doubts and French fears and yielded increasingly to German demands—in the name first of economic recovery, then of political unity, and finally of rearmament for the sake of a German contribution to the defense of the West. An International Ruhr Authority, with the USSR excluded, was created in 1949 and later superseded by restoration of the Ruhr to German sovereignty. After much wrangling an Assembly

486

in Bonn drafted a Basic Law (Constitution) which went into force on May 20, 1949, establishing the *Bundesrepublik Deutschland* or "German Federal Republic." Military government gave way to an "Occupation Statute" and an Allied High Commission, with Clay replaced by McCloy. In elections for the new lower house or Bundestag on Aug. 14, 1949, the Christian Democrats won 139 seats, the Social Democrats 131, the Free Democrats 52, the Bavarian Party and German Party 17 each, and the Communists 15. In the new regime in the Beethoven city of Bonn Theodore Heuss (Free Democrat) became President and Konrad Adenauer Chancellor. Moscow countered by setting up in its own zone through the SED a "German Democratic Republic," with Berlin its capital, Wilhelm Pieck its President, Otto Grotewohl its Premier, and Walter Ulbricht its Vice-Premier (Oct. 11, 1949).

The Republic of the West, prodded by Schumacher's Social Democrats, denounced French control of the Saar, demanded restoration of the German frontiers of 1937, insisted that the Reich should be defended on the Vistula, condemned the treaties with Warsaw and Prague by which the Republic of the East acknowledged the territorial *status quo,* and jumped at the chance of obtaining new concessions implicit in American demands in 1950 (advanced before the outbreak of the Korean War and vigorously pressed thereafter) for German rearmament. The Social Democrats and many others bitterly opposed rearmament, as did all Frenchmen and many Britishers. Despite phenomenal economic recovery, most German cities were still in ruins with the slogan *"Ohne mich!"* (Count me out!) scribbled or posted on many piles of rubble. But Adenauer would have been lacking in all sense of patriotism and *Realpolitik* had he not capitalized upon American insistence. Washington and Bonn were obliged to pay for French cooperation by assenting to the Schuman Plan, signed April 18, 1951, whereby the German coal, iron, and steel industries would be merged with those of France, Benelux, and Italy, and to the Pleven Plan whereby German armed forces would be merely units in a "European Army." At Washington in September, 1951, the Western Foreign Ministers agreed to full independence for the Federal Republic, the transformation of the occupation forces into security troops for defense against Soviet aggression, and the replacement of the Occupation Statute with a "Contractual Agreement"—*i.e.,* a separate peace treaty, though the men of Bonn did not want it so named lest they should seem to be approving a partitioning of Germany.

In the course of labyrinthine negotiations, the Republic of the West bargained astutely for every conceivable advantage. Since Washington was not generously granting to Bonn a "right" to rearm but desperately pleading with Bonn to assume a duty to rearm (subject only to the necessity of obtaining French and British acquiescence), Adenauer could impose conditions for consenting to do what otherwise he might have been begging to do. The outcome was the signature in Bonn on May 26, 1952, of a complicated American-

Anglo-French-German "Convention on Relations," a "Convention on Matters Arising out of the War and Occupation," a "Convention on the Rights and Obligations of Foreign Forces and their Members in the Federal Republic," a "Finance Convention," and various exchanges of letters forming part of the "Contractual Arrangement." On the next day in Paris representatives of Bonn, Paris, Rome, and the Benelux States signed a supplementary 50-year treaty establishing the "European Defense Community" (EDC), with a General Staff, a Commissariat, Council of Ministers, Assembly, and Court of Justice—the latter two being the same as the organs provided in the Schuman Plan—plus a British treaty of guarantee to EDC, a protocol to the North Atlantic Treaty extending its guarantees to EDC, and an annex contemplating within three years a European Army of 55 divisions, 40 in being, of which 14 would be French, 12 German, 11 Italian, and 3 Benelux, and 15 in reserve. West Germany was thus to be rearmed to support the "European Army" and to become an equal and sovereign co-ally of the North Atlantic coalition. West German acceptance of this formula was facilitated by the death on Aug. 20, 1952, of its most bitter enemy, Kurt Schumacher, but ratification had become doubtful by 1953, despite pressure from President Eisenhower and Secretary Dulles.

The Republic of the East, meanwhile, went willy-nilly the Soviet way. In the face of Western protests, it organized a "People's Police" in 1950 and concluded accords with other "People's Democracies." A Soviet-style election of Oct. 15, 1950, chose a "People's Chamber" in which the SED and its affiliates automatically secured 70% of the seats and the Christian Democrats and Free Democrats 30%. Grotewohl appealed to Bonn for German "unity" and rejection of American demands. He offered "free all-German elections," but displayed no enthusiasm for Bonn's prerequisite conditions of political rights, personal freedoms, and release of political prisoners.

Comedy of Make-believe. The partition of Germany achieved in 1949 did not prevent the Super-Powers from going through the motions of renewed "negotiation" for German unity, since both sought to capitalize upon German hopes for unification. That the "negotiations" were exercises in propaganda and not attempts at diplomacy is shown by the fact that they took the form not of private discussions but of published "notes"—endlessly repeated for years.

These exchanges presented an appearance of "bargaining" which is worth recapitulation as an illumination of American and Soviet techniques of Cold War and as a further clue to the "German problem" of mid-century. In genuine diplomacy each side, in striving to get the other to meet its wishes, offers inducements of advantages which it hopes may be found attractive and threats of penalties which it hopes may be deemed painful. Adroit use of "carrots" and "sticks" makes even mules move—and, among diplomats, often leads to "horse trades" pleasing to all.

In the present case the USA offered Germans, as an inducement to rearm, full sovereignty, an alliance, German unity, and frontier revision in the East. America could deliver on the first two items but not on the second two, since unification and border changes were both impossible without an American-Russian accord. The USA could make no threats beyond a perpetuation of the *status quo*. As an inducement to resist the wiles of Washington, the USSR offered Germans unification, a national army, withdrawal of occupation forces, and new markets—all on condition of "neutrality," *i.e.*, no alliance with the West, and all coupled with threats, in the event of noncompliance, of indefinite partition and possible civil war.

As for American inducements to the USSR, none was offered—in conformity with the Acheson conception of "total diplomacy." Washington expressed willingness to resume negotiations for a joint treaty with a unified and rearmed Germany on condition of international supervision of free all-German elections and on further condition that all of Germany should be enlarged by revision of the Oder-Neisse frontier and should then become America's ally against Russia. Washington could not threaten to rearm West Germany (being already committed to doing so) nor to cut off East-West trade (having already done so) and had no other stick with which to beat the bear. As for Soviet inducements to the USA, Moscow offered German unification, rearmament, "free" elections, a peace treaty, and, inferentially, an abandonment of the Grotewohl-Pieck regime—all of which Washington had declared it desired—but all contingent on German neutrality which Washington held to be impossible. Moscow threatened permanent partition, rearmament of East Germany, and a possible resumption of the Berlin blockade.

In this three-dimensional chess game, the two major players were merely pretending to play since the USA was resolved not to accept the "neutrality" of a united Germany at any price, lest a neutral Germany later join the USSR against the USA, while the USSR was resolved not to accept the "democracy" of a united Germany at any price, lest a democratic Germany later join the USA against the USSR. But Germans would ultimately decide what Germany's role should be. Full freedom to decide was most easily to be had not by joining either East or West against the other but by playing them off against one another.

The Riddle of Rearmament.[7] If the problem of unification remained unsolved for years for reasons already indicated, the problem of rearmament was "solved," at least on paper, but by way of a solution which in Germany, as in Japan, had no relevance to the tasks of defense in the Atomic Age. The Paris scheme of May 26, 1952, for German units in an international army under a "European Defense Community" came to nothing. Despite heavy pressure from Dean Acheson and even heavier pressure from his successor,

[7] The four paragraphs which follow originally appeared in a slightly altered version in *Russia Since 1917* and are here reprinted with the permission of Alfred A. Knopf, Inc., copyright 1957 by Frederick L. Schuman.

John Foster Dulles—who in January, 1953, threatened an "agonizing reappraisal" of U.S. defense policy in the event of West European rejection of the American formula—the French Assembly, after long and anxious debate, repudiated the EDC treaties in August, 1954. Premier Pierre Mendès-France felt obliged, however, to yield to demands from Washington for a new formula for German rearmament: a new *Wehrmacht* (rechristened *Bundesheer*) as a contingent of a "Western Union" Army, with West Germany to enter NATO and be subject to sundry restrictions and controls on its armaments, all of which were demonstrably meaningless by all past experience. These complex arrangements were embodied in treaties signed in Paris on Oct. 23, 1954, and ratified by large majorities in Commons and Congress. Mendès-France, still hoping against hope to forestall German rearmament, urged upon London and Washington an inter-allied arms pool, West European Federation, and a Big Four conference—all in vain. On Dec. 24, 1954, the French Assembly rejected the pact for German rearmament, 281 to 257, despite the Premier's appeal for overwhelming endorsement. When Mendès-France posed the issue of "confidence," the deputies, sullenly and reluctantly, accepted the pact, 287 to 260, on Dec. 30 with many abstentions. Then, after Washington, London, and Bonn had turned down all the Premier's safeguarding proposals, the Assembly voted his Cabinet out of office, 319 to 273, on his North African policy, Feb. 5, 1955, but with no reversal of French endorsement of the rearming of the Reich.

Western hopes and Soviet fears regarding German rearmament were both unwarranted by the new facts of power. The projected German force of 12 divisions, including 6 motorized divisions, 2 mechanized divisions, and 4 *Panzer* divisions, would constitute, to be sure, the most formidable army in Western Europe. But it promised to be wholly useless, either defensively or offensively, against the Communist bloc (now including a rearmed East Germany), which could easily, if need be, match the *Bundesheer*, tank for tank, gun for gun, division for division, in a ratio of 2 or 3 to 1. The industrialization of Russia may well be deemed to have ended forever Germany's role as a "Great Power."

In December, 1954, the NATO Council decided to compensate for the obvious and irreversible preponderance of Soviet land and air forces on the Continent by using tactical atomic bombs at the outset of any new war. The *Frankfurter Allgemeine Zeitung* in February, 1955, published two articles by Liddell Hart, contending that any such strategy would be suicidal. In March, Col. Bogislaw von Bonin was dismissed from his post in Bonn by Defense Minister Theodore Blank for saying in public, and contrary to orders, that Germany could not be expected to raise an army in the service of a strategy which would make the total destruction of the Reich inevitable in the event of hostilities. NATO air maneuvers of June, 1955, code-named "Carte Blanche," indicated that 335 small atom bombs dropped between Hamburg and Munich would kill 1,700,000 and wound 3,500,000 Germans, not counting casualties from radiation.

It is self-evident, from the reported results of other tests, that ten hydrogen bombs, properly placed, could annihilate all of West Germany and all of its inhabitants. Given these facts, the new *Bundesheer* could play no military role against the USSR. Its only possible role, quite unintended by its Anglo-American sponsors, might be to dominate Western Europe—with possible Soviet connivance. This prospect was not changed by the appointment (announced by U.S. Gen. Lauris Norstad, Feb. 6, 1957) of Nazi Gen. Hans Speidel as commander of NATO land forces in Central Europe as of April 1, 1957.

The Era of Adenauer. During the 1950's Western Germany, in rags and ruins only a few years before, became the most prosperous community in Europe. This "economic miracle" was attributable only in part to some three billion dollars of U.S. subsidies and to governmental policies in Bonn identified with Economics Minister Ludwig Erhard and Finance Minister Fritz Schaeffer. Even the most astute of political economists have no means of measuring precisely what causes produce what results in a "capitalistic" or "free enterprise" economy. But it is clear that West German prosperity was also due to recartelization; to the hard work and ingenuity of industrialists and bankers; to the docility and discipline of a "proletariat" which, albeit ostensibly Marxist, was staunchly anti-Communist and addicted to intensive and skillful labor as a means of sharing in plenty; and to the energy and enterprise of a *Kleinbürgertum* and peasantry whose members, having experienced ruin through an opposite course, preferred apathy to fanaticism in politics and devoted themselves to money-making. In this happy context, politics was little more than an incidental footnote to the prosperous business of Business. Let us nevertheless trace its course.

On Sept. 6, 1953, the electorate chose a new Bonn Bundestag of 484 deputies under a complex electoral law which compromised between proportional representation and majority vote in the hope of eliminating "splinter parties." These could win no seats unless they gained a majority in one constituency or polled 5% of the total vote. Konrad Adenauer's Christian Democrats won a sweeping victory with 12,440,799 votes and 244 seats. The Social Democrats, with 7,939,774 votes and 150 seats, were a poor second. The Free Democrats got 2,628,146 votes and 48 seats; the German Party 897,952 votes and 48 seats; and the Refugee Party (BHE) 1,614,474 votes and 27 seats. Communists and neo-Nazis won no seats.

Adenauer's new Cabinet, in which he initially retained the Foreign Ministry along with the Chancellorship, was a coalition of Christian Democrats, Free Democrats, German Party, and Refugees. By December industrial production reached 266% of the 1948 level, exports were booming, and the Central Bank was accumulating ever larger reserves of foreign currencies. Upon his return from a good-will tour to the Balkans and Turkey, Adenauer in April,

1954, was delighted with a unanimous parliamentary resolution in which the Social Democrats concurred: "The German Bundestag declares that the German people will never tolerate the division of Germany nor accept the existence of two German States. The Bundestag reiterates that the Communist regime in the Soviet occupation zone exists only through force and is not representative of the German people."

But pressures mounted against Adenauer's "West orientation" and in favor of negotiations with the East—from conservative business and press circles no less than from the Social Democrats. Early in June, ex-Chancellors Brüning and Luther, speaking before the industrialists of Düsseldorf, espoused a policy of "independence" between West and East. In the North Rhine–Westphalia election of June 27, 1954, votes for the Christian Democrats declined from 49% to 41%. The overwhelming reelection (July 17, 1954) for another five-year term of President Theodore Heuss—by the combined West German parliamentarians assembled for the purpose in West Berlin—bespoke a large measure of unity which, however, seemed to be belied in late July by the defection to the Communist East of West Germany's top security officer, Dr. Otto John. He explained his act in terms of fear that the policies of Bonn and Washington were leading to re-Nazification and war. (He returned in December, 1955, was tried for treason, and was sentenced to four years' hard labor in December, 1956.) Adenauer visited Washington and New York in late October, but by year's end found his party ousted from power in local elections in Bavaria and Hesse, where the Social Democrats scored victories by opposing rearmament and championing "neutralism" as the road to reunification.

On Feb. 27, 1955, the Bundestag ratified the Paris accords for rearmament despite widespread opposition and sharp criticism of Adenauer's "compromise" formula regarding the Saar. Ratification meant the end of the Occupation Statute and the High Commission and a full restoration of West German sovereignty. Adenauer pressed for rearmament in the face of opposition among his own followers, but accepted a Soviet invitation (after once more visiting Washington) to go in mid-September to Moscow where he negotiated a resumption of diplomatic and trade relations between West Germany and the USSR, but got nowhere on the issue of reunification. The midsummer "Summit Conference" at Geneva also registered no progress on the issue, since East and West continued to adhere to the irreconcilable views previously enunciated. Despite pressures for a new departure, Adenauer and his Foreign Minister, Heinrich von Brentano, continued to envisage the problem of unity in terms of the Western alliance and negotiation from "strength." In December, 1955, the Bonn Government declared its determination to break off relations with any State extending recognition to the East German regime.

Amid these vicissitudes and confusions, the new Reich regained the Saar. In the local referendum of Oct. 23, 1955, contemplated by the Paris accords, the Saarlanders rejected "Europeanization" of the territory, 2 to 1, in favor of a return to Germany, finally achieved Jan. 1, 1957. In spite of this success Adenauer's allies, the Free Democrats, increasingly shared the view of the Social Democrats that the Chancellor was indifferent to reunification and that the goal could be approached only through negotiations with the East. Subse- quent political controversies, aggravated by consistent Christian Democratic losses in local elections, led the Chancellor, in October, 1956, to reshape his Cabinet, with Franz Josef Strauss replacing Theodore Blank as Defense Min- ister, and to retard sharply the planned pace of German rearmament (notably by limiting draft service to 12 months), amid new frictions with Moscow and the outlawry of the insignificant West German Communist Party. In March, 1957, Brentano visited Washington and reaffirmed Bonn's support of U.S. policies. When Bonn proposed to cut back its military plans and equip a smaller army with atomic weapons, 18 German physicists, including 4 Nobel prize winners, proclaimed their resolve (April 12, 1957) to refuse all coopera- tion in the production, testing, or use of nuclear arms. Dulles and Macmillan in Bonn in mid-May, and Adenauer in Washington and Gettysburg in late May, effected no resolution of problems of rearmament and unification, for these problems were rendered insoluble by the context of policies, in West and East alike, in which they were posed.

Thanks to phenomenal prosperity, Adenauer's Christian Democrats scored another victory in the Bundestag elections of Sept. 15, 1957, winning 14,998,- 754 (51.8%) of the popular votes and 270 seats out of 497, while the Social Democrats won only 9,490,726 (31.7%) of the popular votes and 169 seats. The Free Democrats emerged with 2,304,846 ballots (7.7%) and 41 deputies. The Communists, being outlawed, had no candidates. All the neo-Nazi Rightist groups—the Refugee Party, the German Party, and the German Reich Party— failed to win a majority in any district or to poll 5% of the total vote and thus elected no deputies. The West celebrated, and the East deplored, Adenauer's striking triumph.

But the doughty and venerable Chancellor was now in his eighty-second year, with no equally adroit and vigorous successor in sight. His feckless formula for unification had succeeded in keeping Germany divided, a result not wholly unwelcome to some of his followers since a united Germany would have a Protestant majority in religion and possibly a Social Democratic ma- jority in politics. In 1958 it was uncertain as to whether his successors could carry on indefinitely with the program that spelled continued frustration of national aspirations for unity, an ever-present menace of the annihilation of the Reich in the event of atomic war, and complacent acquiescence in parti- tion and in an uneasy peace between the Super-Powers.

Beyond the Elbe. Meanwhile matters went far less well in the "German Democratic Republic," despite the alleged economic magic of Marxism (Soviet- style), where President Wilhelm Pieck and Premier Otto Grotewohl governed with the aid of an "elected" *Volkskammer* or People's Assembly of 400 members. Public policies were made in Moscow rather than in East Berlin and therefore often had little relevance to the needs and hopes of East Germany's 17,000,000 people. Successive "purges" of allegedly delinquent officials, including the arrest of Foreign Minister Georg Dertinger, Jan. 15, 1953, effected little change. In the spring of 1953 Moscow reduced military control of its satellite while Grotewohl made sweeping concessions in economic policies to alleviate unrest. But on June 16, 1953, strikers in East Berlin rioted against the regime. On the next day mobs in many cities attacked Communist Party headquarters. Soviet troops "restored order" after scores (perhaps hundreds) were killed and much property destroyed.

Another widespread purge ensued, followed by a mission to Moscow by Grotewohl and Ulbricht—after which the Kremlin, hoping to bolster the East German regime, announced economic concessions and released some thousands of war prisoners, including Marshal Paulus. On March 25, 1954, Moscow granted full "sovereignty" to its East German ally, although Soviet troops still remained. In another Soviet-style "election" of Oct. 17, 1954, the "National Front" won 99.3% of the votes. In Grotewohl's new Cabinet, 18 of the 27 members were Communists. Ulbricht and Grotewohl trailed Adenauer to Moscow in September, 1954, and returned with a new treaty amplifying the "full sovereignty" already accorded.

By January, 1956, the "German Democratic Republic" as a member of the Warsaw Pact was converting its People's Police into an army, with Willi Stoph as Minister of Defense. Its leaders followed the Moscow line in the weird politics of de-Stalinization (see pp. 412–415), viewed events in Poland and Hungary with alarm, and strove to appease popular dissatisfaction by sundry measures of economic and social reform.

East Germany remained poor in comparison with the West. During the 1950's tens of thousands of its people went west each year in search of freedom and a better life. Despite material aid from Moscow and grandiose programs of economic growth, no "worker's paradise" emerged east of the Elbe. Yet this artificial satellite police-state seemed likely to have a long life. Soviet military might precluded successful revolution. Caution in Bonn, London, Paris, and Washington precluded any Western effort to "liberate" the East. Western insistence on German rearmament and alliance with the West, and Soviet insistence on German "neutrality" as the price of unity, precluded any East-West bargain for German unification. The "Republic" of the East therefore carried on as best it could, grappling with painful economic and social problems, suppressing dissent by force, and adhering to the Muscovite position that German unity could be promoted only by negotiations between the two German States—a position which the men of Bonn, despite some questioners, were wholly unprepared to accept.

The Puzzle of the Reich. The subtleties and imponderables in the complex equation of Germany in the 1950's admit of no such sure prognosis as was possible at points in the past when German policy-makers, for better or worse, had made irrevocable decisions. Wise statesmen do not make decisions which are irrevocable. Divided statesmen can make no decisions. The Germans of the 1950's were not only divided into two Germanys but were split within each area between friends and foes of the regime in power and between various schools of thought as to how German interests could best be served. The past record of German wisdom in estimating the power and intentions of Russia and America was such as to make forecasts of future wisdom or folly altogether hazardous.

A few factors relevant to the problem may yet be worth recalling. Since the age of nationalism is still with us, a Germany divided is inevitably a Germany striving for reunion, though the striving may long be thwarted. Since the era of power politics is *in medias res*, a Germany united is inevitably a Germany striving for the promotion of the power of Germany, not of other Powers. German reunion was possible only through an American-Soviet accord or through the defeat of Russia by America or America by Russia in World War III. An American-Soviet accord was precluded by Washington's refusal to permit the neutralization of Germany and by Moscow's refusal to permit the alliance of Germany with the West. An American-Soviet war, whatever its ultimate outcome, would mean the final annihilation of the German community. German survival therefore required acceptance for years to come of German partition—with the Republic of the West allied with the Western Powers and the Republic of the East allied with the Eastern Powers.

Ultimately German political leaders might perhaps find means of capitalizing sufficiently upon East-West rivalry to achieve unity and full freedom of foreign policy. This goal, both as to the means toward it and as to the fruits to be garnered from it, could doubtless better be served by assuming the role of an independent "third force," as practical calculations of *Realpolitik* would prescribe, than by enduring commitments to either Super-Power against the other, as "ideological" considerations might dictate. Permanent commitments preclude further bargaining. If and when German statesmen are in a position to bargain, they may be expected to take cognizance, if they remain sane, of the old wisdom of Frederick, Bismarck, and Rathenau. And they may note the fact that under the new pattern of world politics in the second half of the 20th Century, America can offer little save subsidies, defense of the *status quo*, and the prospect of annihilation in World War III, while Russia can offer markets, possible restoration of lost provinces, and partnership in the domination of Europe. Neo-Fascism may drive Germans, whose capacity for sanity is limited, to a repetition of Hitler's aberration. But rationality, if it survives among Germans, will suggest a different course which may conceivably prove to be more conducive to the survival of Germany, of Europe, and of the global Great Society of our time.

THE HERITAGE OF FASCISM

SUGGESTED READINGS

Almond, Gabriel A. (ed.): *The Struggle for Democracy in Germany*, Chapel Hill, N.C., University of North Carolina Press, 1949.

Bathurst, M. E., and J. L. Simpson: *Germany and the North Atlantic Community*, New York, Praeger, 1956.

Baumont, Marice, John H. E. Fried, and Edmond Vermeil (eds.): *The Third Reich*, New York, Praeger, 1955.

Baynes, Norman H. (ed.): *The Speeches of Adolf Hitler: April, 1922–August, 1939*, New York, Oxford, 1942.

Brady, Robert A.: *The Spirit and Structure of German Fascism*, New York, Viking, 1937.

Bullock, Alan: *Hitler: A Study in Tyranny*, New York, Harper, 1953.

Clay, Gen. Lucius D.: *Decision in Germany*, New York, Doubleday, 1950.

Craig, Gordon A.: *The Politics of the Prussian Army, 1640–1945*, New York, Oxford, 1955.

Dirksen, Herbert von: *Moscow, Tokyo, London*, Norman, Okla., University of Oklahoma Press, 1952.

Ebenstein, William: *The German Record: A Political Portrait*, New York, Farrar, Straus, 1945.

Freidin, Seymour, and William Richardson (eds.): *The Fatal Decisions*, New York, Sloane, 1956.

Frischauer, Willi: *The Rise and Fall of Hermann Goering*, Boston, Houghton Mifflin, 1951.

Gatzke, Hans W.: *Germany's Drive to the West (Drang Nach Westen)*, Baltimore, Johns Hopkins Press, 1950.

Gerschenkron, Alexander: *Bread and Democracy in Germany*, Berkeley, Calif., University of California Press, 1943.

Goerlitz, Walter: *History of the German General Staff, 1657 to 1945*, New York, Praeger, 1955.

Guderian, Gen. Heinz: *Panzer Leader*, New York, Dutton, 1952.

Hilger, Gustav, and Alfred G. Meyer: *The Incompatible Allies*, New York, Macmillan, 1953.

Hill, Russell: *The Struggle for Germany*, New York, Harper, 1947.

Hitler, A.: *Mein Kampf*, New York, Reynal & Hitchcock, 1939.

Holborn, Hajo: *History of Modern Germany*, New York, Knopf, 1957.

Horne, Alistair: *Return to Power: A Report on the New Germany*, New York, Praeger, 1956.

Jarman, T. L.: *The Rise and Fall of Nazi Germany*, New York, New York University Press, 1956.

Kolnai, Aurel: *The War against the West*, London, Gollancz, 1938.

Krieger, Seymour (ed.): *Nazi Germany's War against the Jews*, New York, American Jewish Conference, 1947.

Kurenberg, Joachim von: *The Kaiser*, New York, Simon and Schuster, 1955.

Litchfield, Edward H., and Associates: *Governing Postwar Germany*, Ithaca, N.Y., Cornell University Press, 1953.

McGovern, William M.: *From Luther to Hitler: The History of Fascist-Nazi Political Philosophy*, Boston, Houghton Mifflin, 1941.

Nathan, Otto, in collaboration with Milton Fried: *The Nazi Economic System: Germany's Mobilization for War*, Durham, N.C., Duke University Press, 1944.

Neumann, Franz: *Behemoth: The Structure and Practice of National Socialism, 1933*, New York, Oxford, 1944.

Oppen, Beata van (ed.): *Documents on the Occupation of Germany, 1945–1954*, New York, Oxford, 1955.

Padover, Saul K.: *Experiment in Germany*, New York, Duell, Sloan & Pearce, 1946.

Papen, Franz von: *Memoirs*, New York, Dutton, 1953.

Pinson, Koppel S.: *Modern Germany: Its History and Civilization*, New York, Macmillan, 1954.

SUGGESTED READINGS

Pollock, J. K., and Homer Thomas: *Germany in Power and Eclipse*, Princeton, N.J., Van Nostrand, 1952.

——, and Others: *German Democracy at Work*, Ann Arbor, Mich., University of Michigan Press, 1955.

Rauschning, Hermann: *The Revolution of Nihilism: Warning to the West*, New York, Longmans, 1939.

Rossi, A.: *The Russo-German Alliance, August, 1939–June, 1941*, Boston, Beacon Press, 1951.

Russell, Lord, of Liverpool: *The Scourge of the Swastika*, New York, Philosophical Library, 1954.

Salomon, Ernst von: *Fragebogen (The Questionnaire)*, New York, Doubleday, 1955.

Schuman, F. L.: *The Nazi Dictatorship: A Study in Social Pathology and the Politics of Fascism*, New York, Knopf, 1936.

Schuschnigg, Kurt: *My Austria*, New York, Knopf, 1938.

Schwarz, Paul: *This Man Ribbentrop: His Life and Times*, New York, Messner, 1943.

Shirer, William L.: *End of a Berlin Diary*, New York, Knopf, 1947.

Snyder, Louis L.: *German Nationalism: The Tragedy of a People*, Harrisburg, Pa., Stackpole, 1954.

Taylor, Telford: *Sword and Swastika*, New York, Simon and Schuster, 1952.

Thayer, Charles W.: *The Unquiet Germans*, New York, Harper, 1957.

Trevor-Roper, H. R.: *The Last Days of Hitler*, New York, Macmillan, 1947.

Valentin, Veit: *The German People*, New York, Knopf, 1946.

Warburg, James P.: *Germany: Lost Key to Peace*, Cambridge, Mass., Harvard University Press, 1953.

Weymar, Paul: *Adenauer*, New York, Dutton, 1957.

Wheeler-Bennett, J. W.: *Wooden Titan: Hindenburg in Twenty Years of German History, 1914–1934*, New York, Morrow, 1936.

——: *The Nemesis of Power: The German Army in Politics, 1918–1945*, New York, St. Martin's, 1953.

Wiskemann, Elizabeth: *Germany's Eastern Neighbours*, New York, Oxford, 1956.

CHAPTER XII

THE CHALLENGE OF COMMUNISM

1. USSR: THE ENDLESS MISSION

A spectre is haunting Europe—the spectre of Communism. . . . Where is the party in opposition that has not been decried as Communistic by its opponents in power? . . . It is high time that Communists should openly, in the face of the whole world, publish their views, their aims, their tendencies, and meet this nursery tale of the spectre of Communism with a manifesto of the party itself. . . . The Communists disdain to conceal their views and aims. They openly declare that their ends can be attained only by the forcible overthrow of all existing social conditions. Let the ruling classes tremble at a Communist revolution. The proletarians have nothing to lose but their chains. They have a world to win. Workingmen of all countries, unite!—KARL MARX, FRIEDRICH ENGELS, *The Communist Manifesto*, 1848.

RUSSIA has long been the most populous and most extensive of the European Powers. It has also been, until recently, the most backward industrially, thanks to a severe climate, a primitive peasantry, a reactionary nobility, a benighted autocracy, and a national disposition to alternate fearfully between "Westernization" and retreats into Oriental isolation. These attributes, in part at least, are explicable by a harsh past. A thousand years ago the first "Russians," who called the Vikings to Kiev to be their rulers, derived their religion and other contacts with the West from Byzantium—and were constantly assailed by barbarian invaders along the steppe road out of Asia. They were conquered and long subjugated (1240–1480) by the last and most formidable of these invaders: the Mongols. Emancipation under the leadership of the Dukes of Muscovy called for ruthless despotism as the only available defense against internal anarchy and external attack. The stimulating Western experiences of the Renaissance and Reformation had here no counterparts. Subsequent conflicts with stronger Powers reinforced the imperatives of tyranny under the Romanov Tsardom (1613–1917). By the 19th Century this community had expanded over Eurasia until it covered one-sixth of the land surface of the planet. And in belated awakening, it was producing works of fiction, poetry, drama, music, and science among the most exciting in the history of cultures.

Russia in 1917 fell into the political control of a tiny group of revolutionary fanatics. Revolution had long been endemic in this land of arbitrary autocrats, insecure aristocrats, land-hungry peasants, and, more recently, impoverished urban workers. Whenever the State suffered defeat in war abroad, the forces of revolution boiled up at home. Defeat in the Crimea (1854–56) was followed by "reform"—*i.e.*, the abolition of serfdom and the beginnings of local self-government. Defeat in the Far East was followed by the abortive revolution of 1905–06 and the establishment of the first Parliament or Duma. Defeat in World War I was followed by the collapse of the autocracy and by social revolution in which soldiers deserted, peasants seized estates, and workmen took over factories, mills, and mines in a nebulous and anarchic aspiration toward "socialism." Nicholas II abdicated March 15, 1917. At Ekaterinburg (Sverdlovsk) on July 17, 1918, amid civil strife and growing chaos, he and his wife, children, and servants were all shot to death by Red guards.

Brandishing the slogans "Peace, Land, Bread," and "All Power to the Soviets!" a little band of returned exiles and underground conspirators, led by Vladimir Ilych Ulianov (1870–1924), who signed his writings "Lenin," rose to leadership of these revolutionary multitudes. On Nov. 7, 1917 (Oct. 25 by the old Russian calendar), these dedicated adventurers overthrew the "Provisional Government" headed by Kerensky and established a "Soviet Government" which they insisted upon identifying with the Marxist concept of "the dictatorship of the proletariat." This regime, faced in 1918 with Allied intervention, blockade, and civil war, became a one-party polity, a "police-state," and the first "totalitarian" government of our time. Its rulers were members of the extremist majority (Bolshevik) faction, sharply at odds with the moderate minority (Menshevik) faction, of the Russian Social Democratic Labor Party. They resumed the original Marxist name, "Communist," in 1918. They rallied sufficient support to defeat their foes, domestic and foreign, in 1919–21 and undertook, from the very outset of their power, the conquest of the globe in the name of "World Revolution" to overthrow "capitalism" (*i.e.*, to confiscate and socialize private property in the means of production) and "liberate" (*i.e.*, subject to Communist rule) the allegedly oppressed workers, peasants, and colonial natives of other lands.

Hopes and Facts. Ever since the "October Revolution," Westerners have debated, often to little purpose, two questions: (1) Are the Communist rulers of Muscovy chiefly interested in World Revolution or in Russian national interest? (2) Is peaceful coexistence possible or impossible with the Red masters of the Kremlin? The answer to the first question is: both in equal measure, with the power of the USSR to be used to promote World Revolution whenever and wherever possible without excessive risk, and with Communist Parties elsewhere to be used to serve the purposes of Soviet foreign policy. The answer to the second question can perhaps be found in the fact that the Soviet regime by 1958 had coexisted with the Western Powers for 41 years, of which only 9 (1918–21 and 1939–45) were years of war and 32 were years of, more or less, peace. The years of war, moreover (save for the localized Winter War with Finland of 1939–40, precipitated by Soviet aggression

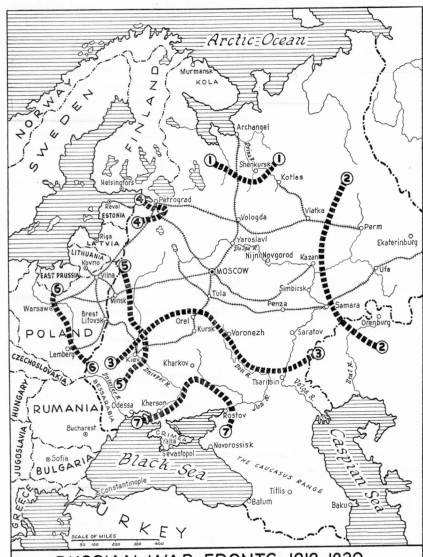

RUSSIAN WAR FRONTS: 1919-1920

① *Farthest Southern Advance of Allied Troops in North Russia, January 1919*
② *Farthest Westward Advance of White Army of Kolchak, May 1919*
③ *Farthest Northward Advance of White Army of Denikin, October 1919*
④ *Farthest Eastward Advance of White Army of Yudenitch, October 1919*
⑤ *Farthest Eastward Advance of Polish Army, June 1920*
⑥ *Farthest Westward Advance of Red Army into Poland, August 1920*
⑦ *Farthest Northward Advance of White Army of Wrangel, November 1920*

and Finnish resistance), were not the consequence of Communist military attacks upon the Western Powers but of anti-Communist military attacks upon the USSR.

Lenin learned through the defeat of the Red Army before Warsaw in the summer of 1920 (in a war launched in the spring by the new Poland of Pilsudski in an attempt to conquer the Ukraine) that reliance upon military force to extend Communism was a "mistake." The lesson was learned again in Finland in 1939 and in Korea in 1950. Communist aggrandizement, unlike Fascist aggrandizement, relies more upon conspiracy than upon invasion, though it is doubtless all the more puzzling and dangerous to the Free World for this very reason. Nowhere, however, has conspiracy alone thus far established any enduring Communist regime, outside of Russia, nor has any Communist Party (except in San Marino and Kerala) ever won a majority in any free and honest national election. Conspiracy and counter-invasion together in 1944–48, to be sure, delivered most of Eastern Europe to Communist rule, albeit in the aftermath of a Soviet war of defense against unprovoked attack aimed at the annihilation of the Soviet State.

We may take it as a "constant" of Soviet foreign policy that the Red rulers in the Kremlin believe in, and seek to promote, the eventual collapse of "capitalism" and the Messianic universalization of the gospel of Marxism-Leninism-Stalinism—and therefore expect to be attacked by the Powers threatened thereby. They also declare on Mondays, Wednesdays, and Fridays that war between the "two systems" is inevitable and, on Tuesdays, Thursdays, and Saturdays, that peaceful coexistence is possible and desirable. Which postulate do they believe and act upon? Again: both. Westerners unfamiliar with the higher dialectic are naturally unable to grasp such ambivalences.

We may also take it as a "constant" in the tangled East-West relations of the 20th Century that Western policy-makers in self-defense cherish the perennial hope of overthrowing and destroying the Soviet State, while Soviet policy-makers, also in "self-defense" by their own Byzantine-Mongoloid-Marxist logic, likewise cherish the perennial hope of overthrowing and destroying the Western Powers. Such hopes in simple form are implicit in all power politics among all Powers in all State Systems. They are here powerfully reinforced by "ideological" considerations—i.e., Communist fears of "inevitable" attack by "capitalistic imperialism"; Kremlin visions of "liberating" all the "oppressed"; Western fears of Communist enslavement with its adjuncts of the knock-on-the-door at 2 A.M., salt mines and slave camps, and the bullet-in-the-back-of-the-head for dissenters; and Western hopes of freeing enslaved peoples from Red tyranny. But among power-holders who are sane, action to dispel fears and realize hopes is always moderated, and often inhibited, by calculations of cost, risk, and advantage. The rulers of Red Muscovy, while obviously dastards, have never thus far acted like lunatics in world affairs, nor do they govern a community so constituted that internal tensions can be resolved only by external military aggression. The policy-makers of the Western Powers have also exhibited, thus far, persistent symptoms of sanity in calculating the probable consequences of wish-fulfilling action—save for the Fascist madmen who ruled Italy, Japan, and Germany in the 1930's.

The historical results of the considerations here adduced come to this: the Russian Revolution brought to power obscure converts of a suspect cult who proceeded forthwith to abrogate treaties, repudiate debts, confiscate property, and summon everybody everywhere to rebellion. The Western Powers, dimly but rightly sensing a mortal threat in such outrageous behavior, sought by force and violence to strangle the new regime at birth. Comrade Lenin & Co. raised revolutionary hosts which defeated the invaders and the "White Armies," and in March of 1919 established the "Communist International" as the "General Staff of the World Revolution" in the hope of carrying Bolshevism westward. Hope rose when co-conspirators established "Soviet" regimes in Munich and Budapest in the spring of 1919. Hope fell when these regimes were suppressed by the forces of law and order. Hope rose again when the Red Army reached the gates of Warsaw in July of 1920—and fell again when it was beaten back. The Soviet State survived, but failed to expand the revolution beyond the confines of Russia. The Western Powers beat down the "World Revolution" but failed to destroy the Soviet State. The risks and costs for each side from any attempt to continue the enterprise were disproportionate to anything that could conceivably be gained thereby.

The "truce" of 1921 and beyond was, for both antagonists, a compromise between expectations and realities. Moscow recognized the independence of Finland, Estonia, Latvia, and Lithuania; accepted the incorporation of Western Byelorussia and Western Ukraine into the new Poland, and of Bessarabia into Rumania; acquiesced in the loss of Kars and Ardahan to Turkey; achieved a substantial restoration of Russia's previous position in the Far East; and cultivated peace and trade with "capitalist enemies" in the Western Powers. These in turn (except for the USA, which refused to compromise with sin) recognized the Soviet Government and concluded such commercial and political pacts as interest dictated. This *modus vivendi* was of long duration. It might have endured indefinitely but for the Great Depression and the triumph of Fascism in Japan and Germany.

New Power. Western contempt for benighted Muscovy, coupled with persistent underestimation of Russian capacities, is an old habit. The wrecked and ruined Russia of the 1920's was neither a threat nor a factor of power which anyone needed to consider seriously. Yet there emerged, out of appalling suffering, a new Russia which Western statesmen did ill to ignore or minimize. Lenin retreated from Marxist dogma in the "New Economic Policy" of 1921–28. When prewar production was restored, Stalin embarked upon socialist industrialization and collectivization of agriculture in the first "Five Year Plan" (1928–32) and its successors. Millions died in famine and slavery. Other millions worked themselves to death in devotion to an ideal. Trotsky championed "World Revolution," denied that "Socialism in one country" was possible, and fought Stalin's leadership of the Party. He was demoted, exiled, deported, and finally died by murder in Mexico (Aug. 21, 1940). Stalin's bureaucrats, mouthing Marxist phrases and promulgating a "democratic" Federal Constitution in 1936, built a polity which was a modern synthesis of the methods of governance developed by Jenghis Khan, Ivan the Terrible, and Peter the Great.

The methods were exemplified in ideological intolerance, sycophancy, the liquidation of millions of kulaks or well-to-do peasants in 1929–33, the bloody purge of all dissenters in 1935–38, the restoration of slavery in "correctional labor camps," and the complete subordination of each to all and all to one. By the use of these methods, however, this monstrous leviathan, so alien and hideous to the West, won masses of people to enthusiasm and self-sacrifice and somehow succeeded, entirely out of resources squeezed from the poor, in establishing a prosperous collectivized agriculture and a productive socialist industry. This transformation of Russian society from a backward, agrarian, primitive culture to an urbanized civilization deserves to be regarded (next to the implications for the future of the Chinese Revolution) as the most decisive new fact of world politics in the 20th Century.

The fact was grasped feebly, or not at all, by Western governments and peoples in the 1930's. The democracies, belatedly frightened by Fascist aggression, looked dubiously to the USSR for support. The Soviet Union, on Western invitation, joined the League of Nations (Sept. 18, 1934) and concluded alliances with France (May 2, 1935) and Czechoslovakia (May 16, 1935). The men of the Kremlin, alarmed by Japanese and German ambitions, now sponsored "collective security" through the eloquent voice of Litvinov and championed, through Communist Parties elsewhere, "Popular Fronts" of all Communists, Socialists, and liberals against Fascism.

But, for good reason, there was no mutual trust in this uneasy entente. Policy-makers in Paris and London remained more fearful of Communism than of Fascism. Their "appeasement" of the Caesars, culminating in the "Peace" of Munich, suggested to Moscow that other means would have to be devised to protect the USSR from becoming an isolated victim of Fascist assaults while the democracies stood aside. At Congress XVIII of the Communist Party of the USSR, Stalin (March 10, 1939) hinted at other possibilities:

The majority of the non-aggressive countries, particularly England and France, have rejected the policy of collective security, the policy of collective resistance to the aggressors, and have taken up a position of non-intervention, a position of "neutrality." . . . The policy of non-intervention reveals an eagerness, a desire, not to hinder the aggressors in their nefarious work: not to hinder Japan, say, from embroiling herself in a war with China, or, better still, with the Soviet Union;

not to hinder Germany, say, from enmeshing herself in European affairs, from embroiling herself in a war with the Soviet Union. . . . Cheap and easy! . . . Take Germany, for instance. They let her have Austria, despite the undertaking to defend her independence; they let her have the Sudeten region; they abandoned Czechoslovakia to her fate, thereby violating all their obligations; and then they began to lie vociferously in the press about "the weakness of the Russian Army," "the demoralization of the Russian Air Force," and "riots" in the Soviet Union, egging the Germans on to march farther east, promising them easy pickings, and prompting them: "Just start war on the Bolsheviks, and everything will be all right." . . .

Far be it from me to moralize on the policy of non-intervention, to talk of treason, treachery, and so on. It would be naïve to preach morals to people who recognize no human morality. Politics is politics, as the old, case-hardened bourgeois diplomats say. It must be remarked, however, that the big and dangerous political game started by the supporters of the policy of non-intervention may end in a serious fiasco for them. . . .

1. We stand for peace and the strengthening of business relations with all countries. That is our position; and we shall adhere to this position as long as these countries maintain like relations with the Soviet Union, and as long as they make no attempt to trespass on the interests of our country.

2. We stand for peaceful, close, and friendly relations with all the neighbouring countries which have common frontiers with the USSR. That is our position; and we shall adhere to this position as long as these countries maintain like relations with the Soviet Union, and as long as they make no attempt to trespass, directly or indirectly, on the integrity and inviolability of the frontiers of the Soviet state.

3. We stand for the support of nations which are the victims of aggression and are fighting for the independence of their country.

4. We are not afraid of the threats of aggressors, and are ready to deal two blows for every blow delivered by instigators of war who attempt to violate the Soviet borders.

"Neutrality" and "Defense." Within a week, Hitler liquidated Czechoslovakia, gave Carpatho-Ukraine to Hungary, and finally convinced the Western Munichmen that their States, rather than the USSR, were "on the list and would never be missed" after the Reich should strike. They accordingly sought to rebuild a coalition against Germany. The enterprise required Soviet collaboration. In the absence of mutual respect and of an equal sense of common danger, however, the obvious logic of *Realpolitik* led nowhere. British willingness to guarantee Poland and even Rumania and Greece before coming to terms with the USSR evoked contempt in Moscow. *Pravda's* cartoon of April 4, 1939, showed a silk-hatted British lion in a boat extending a rock-loaded life belt to small nations struggling in a stormy sea swarming with sharks.

When Anglo-Soviet negotiations were initiated in mid-April, Moscow asked a binding alliance. London refused, preferring some more "flexible" formula. On May 3, Litvinov resigned his post as Commissar for Foreign Affairs in favor of Premier Vyacheslav Molotov. Chamberlain drew no conclusions, although four days later the French Ambassador in Berlin began a series of ominous reports on the possibility of a Soviet-Nazi *rapprochement* to be fol-

lowed by a new partition of Poland (*French Yellow Book of* 1939, No. 123*ff.*).
British counter-proposals of May 8 contemplated Soviet aid to Britain and
France should they be obliged to fight in defense of Poland or Rumania.
Moscow asked Anglo-French aid to the USSR should it be attacked or be
obliged to fight in defense of the Baltic States. All three Powers should agree
to defend one another and should guarantee all the border States between
the Reich and the Soviet Union, as well as the border States (Switzerland,
Belgium, and the Netherlands) between the Reich and the Western Powers.
Churchill and Lloyd George urged acceptance of Molotov's terms. Chamberlain and Halifax refused. The Baltic States worshiped "neutrality" and desired no international guarantee participated in by the USSR. Downing Street
would not guarantee States unwilling to be guaranteed. It proposed "consultation" in the event of any Nazi aggression in the Baltic. But Moscow
knew that this was only a formula Britain proposed to evade any commit-
ment.

At the end of May, Molotov publicly declared that Moscow would make
no pact save on the basis of "reciprocity and equality of obligations" and
that this required (1) a binding alliance, (2) a joint guarantee of all European countries bordering the USSR, and (3) a concrete agreement for mutual
aid and defense of the guaranteed States in the event of attack by aggressors.
London and Paris now accepted (1) but balked at (2) and (3). The negotiations dragged on inconclusively. At the end of June, Andrei Zhdanov, Leningrad Party leader, wrote in *Pravda* that he did not believe that the British
and French Governments desired an equal treaty with the USSR. At the end
of July, Chamberlain announced that Anglo-French military missions would
go to Moscow to initiate staff talks, pending conclusion of a definitive agreement which had been held up by differences of views on the proper definition
of "indirect aggression." The missions were of wholly undistinguished personnel. They made a leisurely trip to the Soviet capital. Molotov, Voroshilov,
and Stalin expected that they would have authority to sign a pact giving the
USSR the right to decide when the Baltic States were threatened, to act to
meet the threat, to have necessary military access to the Baltic States and
Poland, and to summon Britain and France to its support. They had no such
authority Hitler had already reached a secret decision in April to invade
Poland in September.

A complete revolution in Soviet diplomacy followed the failure of these
discussions. Ribbentrop came to Moscow on August 23 and signed a German-
Soviet Nonaggression Pact. Voroshilov declared that the USSR could not
defend Poland unless the Red Army were permitted to enter Polish territory.
Neither Warsaw, Paris, nor London had been willing to grant such permission.
Molotov told the Supreme Soviet on Aug. 31, when the Pact with Hitler was
ratified, that the Western Powers had "plotted to involve us in war" without
being willing to see the Soviet Union strengthened. Germany had dropped its
anti-Soviet policy. The USSR had no need to join either side. It would

505

remain at peace. After several weeks of confusion, due to obvious ignorance of the Kremlin's new decision, the Communist Parties of France, Britain, and America dropped all slogans of "People's Front," "Unity against Fascist Aggression," and the like; denounced as an "imperialist war" the new conflict which Hitler unleashed by his invasion of Poland; and developed a line of "revolutionary defeatism" which admirably served the purposes of Stalin— and of Hitler.

The Kremlin's policy after the outbreak of hostilities was strict neutrality, tempered by a firm determination to sell neutrality to Hitler at a price which would strengthen the defenses of the USSR against the Reich. The first step was to seize the former Russian territories of Poland and to reach new agreements with Berlin on the division of the carcass of the victim of the blitzkrieg. On Sept. 17, 1939, Moscow declared that the Polish State had "virtually ceased to exist" and that the Red Army must undertake the protection of its abandoned "blood brothers," the Ukrainians and Byelorussians. Soviet troops were already on the march. They rapidly occupied all eastern Poland not yet in the hands of the Wehrmacht. Ribbentrop flew again to Moscow. On Sept. 28 a new German-Soviet accord partitioned Poland along the ethnographic frontier, the Reich taking the Polish areas and the USSR the Byelorussian and Ukrainian areas, including western Galicia, which had been part of Austria-Hungary before 1914. Details of the frontier were defined more precisely by accords of Oct. 5, 1939, and Jan. 10, 1941. This extension of Bolshevism 250 miles westward was but the first of Stalin's victories and the initial installment of the price paid to Moscow by Berlin for "reinsurance" in the East.

The Kremlin's next step was the imposition of protectorates on the Baltic States. Hitler acquiesced not only in Soviet military control of the ancient realm of the Teutonic Knights but in the "voluntary" evacuation to the Reich of the Germans who had lived on the Baltic shore for seven centuries. By a combination of trumped-up accusations, invitations, and threats of invasion, Moscow induced Estonia (Sept. 28), Latvia (Oct. 5), and Lithuania (Oct. 10) to sign Mutual Assistance Pacts pledging common defense "in the event of a direct aggression or threat of aggression on the part of any European Great Power" against the Baltic frontiers of the signatories. Moscow acquired the right to establish garrisons on Baltic territory and to maintain naval and air bases at Paltiski, Oesel, Hiiumaa, Libau, and Ventspils. The Baltic Republics secured in return a short-lived "protection" of their "integrity" and their "sovereign" rights. Lithuania was granted the long-coveted city and region of Vilna.

Moscow now gave moral support to Berlin's bid for "peace" in October, 1939. This attitude, far from being indicative of the Soviet desire to see the Reich win the war, was inspired by the conviction that a "negotiated" settlement on the basis of the new *status quo* would leave the USSR secure in its new outposts. Such a development would also save the Western Powers from possible destruction and compel their discredited leaders to seek a new *rapprochement* with the USSR on Moscow's terms as the only means of future protection against the victorious Reich. These strictly *Realpolitik* desiderata were rationalized by Communists everywhere in terms of stereotyped eulogies of peace and denunciations of Anglo-French "imperialism." But London and Paris were committed to restoring the *status quo ante bellum* and would neither recognize Moscow's title to the new Soviet territories nor consider peace with Hitler. Stalin therefore considered what further measures he should take to strengthen his State against the bourgeois Powers.

The Agony of Victory. In the autumn of 1939 Turkey rejected Soviet proposals of a pact of mutual aid, preferring the doubtful blessing of a Western alliance to the certain discomfort of "protection" by the bear. Moscow acquiesced. When Finland also rejected Soviet proposals, the Kremlin went to war (Nov. 30, 1939) on the fatuous assumption that Soviet support of a puppet regime of exiled Finnish Communists, headed by Otto Kuusinen, would evoke capitulation in Helsingfors. When the Finns, led by Marshal Gustav Mannerheim, offered heroic resistance, the Kremlin was obliged to mass heavy forces to defeat them. Great losses and slow progress contributed to the Western illusion that the USSR was negligible as a military Power. Since the West could give no effective aid, Helsingfors yielded. By the peace of March 12, 1940, Finland gave up the Karelian Isthmus and the shores of Lake Ladoga, a strip of northern territory near Petsamo, most of the Gulf Islands, and a Soviet leasehold and naval base at Hangö. The "security" which Moscow thus achieved in the north proved ephemeral.

Having rejected an alliance with the Western Powers because they would not pay the Kremlin's price, Moscow found itself dangerously isolated when the Wehrmacht conquered the Continent in the spring of 1940. Moscow took local measures of defense: military occupation of the Baltic States, June 15–17, and their incorporation into the USSR after local "elections" and the seizure of Bessarabia and Northern Bukovina on June 28. Nazi occupation of the rest of Rumania in October brought no comfort to the Kremlin. The Nazi decision to attack Russia, as we have seen, was reached in August, not in consequence of these or later Soviet acts but because of the *Führer's* mad conviction that he could and must annihilate the USSR before he could hope to conquer Britain. Moscow, warned of what was to come, sought to do what it could in the spring of 1941 to thwart Nazi domination of the Balkans and to ensure Japanese neutrality. It was successful in the latter endeavor and unsuccessful in the former.

The USSR was assaulted in June, 1941, by all of Fascist Europe, with a population of over 300,000,000 people, compared with the Soviet's 200,-000,000; a combined steel production of almost 50,000,000 tons, compared with Russia's 18,000,000; a 3:2 advantage over the victim of attack in available military man power; and a 5:2 advantage in weapons and war machines.

The blow of the hitherto invincible Wehrmacht and its sundry allies was the most formidable and lethal onslaught ever hurled against any nation-state in modern times. That the Soviet armies and people stood up against it was a demonstration that the Soviet polity and economy were capable of bearing burdens heavier than those ever faced by any other modern community. The cost in death and ruin was appalling. By paying it, the Soviet peoples purchased national survival—and ultimately victory for their cause and for all the United Nations.

Churchill at once proclaimed solidarity with Russia against Hitler—"this bloodthirsty guttersnipe" who "is a monster of wickedness, insatiable in his lust for blood and plunder." Through Sumner Welles, Roosevelt did likewise. Cripps and Molotov signed an accord on July 12, which led later to the Anglo-Soviet alliance of May 26, 1942. Harry Hopkins went to Moscow in August, Harriman and Beaverbrook in October. The New York State Convention of the American Legion accused Stalin of "ruthless murder," while Martin Dies protested "in the name of tens of thousands of voiceless Christian martyrs who have been murdered by the Soviets." But, on Nov. 7, F.D.R. sent greetings to Kalinin and revealed that he had pledged $1,000,000,000 to the USSR in lend-lease aid. Ultimate American shipments were impressive, amounting to some $11,000,000,000, out of total lend-lease appropriations of $50,000,000,000, of which half went to the British Commonwealth. The USSR received from the USA 6,800 tanks, 13,300 planes, 1,000 locomotives, 406,000 motorcars, 2,000,000 tons of steel, 11,000,000 pairs of shoes, etc. But this flood was the merest trickle in 1941 and was still negligible in 1942 and early 1943. No effective "second front" was established until three years after the Russian war began. Soviet armies bore almost the entire brunt of the struggle against the Reich and, until 1944, fought almost entirely with Soviet-made arms and transport.

On July 1, 1941, a "State Committee of Defense" was set up, with Stalin as Chairman, Molotov as Vice-Chairman, and Voroshilov, Beria, and Malenkov as members. The Commissariats of Internal Affairs and National Security were merged into a united NKVD under Beria. The "Second Patriotic War," so named by way of recalling victory over Napoleon in 1812, was the most gigantic, destructive, and murderous combat in the history of warfare. The new borderlands were lost in a fortnight, since the Red Army's High Command had decided that only "defense in depth" could avert defeat. In the north the armies of Mannerheim and Falkenhorst struck at Leningrad. In the south, Antonescu's forces invaded the Ukraine. Between them, huge Nazi armies under Leeb, Bock, and Rundstedt aimed at Leningrad, Moscow, and Rostov. Smolensk was lost in mid-July, though Timoshenko temporarily checked the invaders east of the city. Kiev, Odessa, and Kharkov were lost in October.

Early in October, as Nazi spokesmen announced that Russia was finished, the Wehrmacht moved on Moscow. Many Commissariats and the Diplomatic Corps were moved to Kuibyshev (Samara) on the Volga, but Stalin remained in the Kremlin. On the anniversary of the Revolution, he preached staunch resistance to the foe and embraced a moderation of despair which was to be wholly reversed when brighter fortunes brought new opportunities:

No mercy for the German invaders! Death to the German invaders! . . . [But] we have not and cannot have such war aims as the seizure of foreign territories and the subjugation of foreign peoples—whether it be peoples and territories of Europe or peoples and territories of Asia, including Iran. Our first aim is to liberate our territories and our people from the German-Fascist yoke. We have not and cannot have such war aims as the imposition of our will and our regime on the Slavs and other enslaved peoples of Europe who are awaiting our aid. Our aid consists in assisting these peoples in their struggle for liberation from Hitler's tyranny, and then setting them free to rule their own land as they desire. No intervention whatever in the internal affairs of other nations! But to realize these aims it is necessary to crush the military might of the German invaders. . . . This is now our task. We can and must fulfill this task. Only by fulfilling this task and routing the German invaders can we achieve a lasting and just peace.

By late November, the Wehrmacht was within 13 miles of Moscow. When all seemed lost Gen. (later Marshal) Georgi K. Zhukov ordered and led the first major counterattack. Early in December, as Litvinov arrived in America and Japan blitzed Pearl Harbor, the Battle of Moscow was won by its defenders. The enemy reeled back, shivered in the Russian winter, and clung tenaciously to "hedgehog" positions from which the assault was to be renewed.

In the summer of 1942, the Fascist hosts, far larger and more formidably armed than they had been a year before, struck anew and in overwhelming force at the defenders of Sovietland. A crushing assault in the south aimed at reaching the Volga, seizing the Caucasian oil fields, and outflanking Moscow from the east. By late August the invaders were in Stalingrad. Here half a million troops, commanded by Gen. Friedrich von Paulus and abundantly supplied with all possible weapons, poured into a metropolis only a few miles wide and strung out over 50 miles along the high western bank of a broad river with no bridges. Reason dictated the withdrawal of Soviet forces to the eastern shore. But the defenders strove to resist the foe block by block, street by street, house by house, room by room in what soon became the most savage single combat of World War II.

By September's end Hitler could announce, not inaccurately: "We have taken Stalingrad." Most of the city was in Nazi hands. All of it was in ruins. But the defenders refused to accept defeat. From piles of rubble and crumbling factories and apartments, they struck back to decimate the enemy in ferocious man hunts with rifles, grenades, machine guns, flame throwers, rockets, artillery—and knives. In New York, 20,000 Americans gathered on

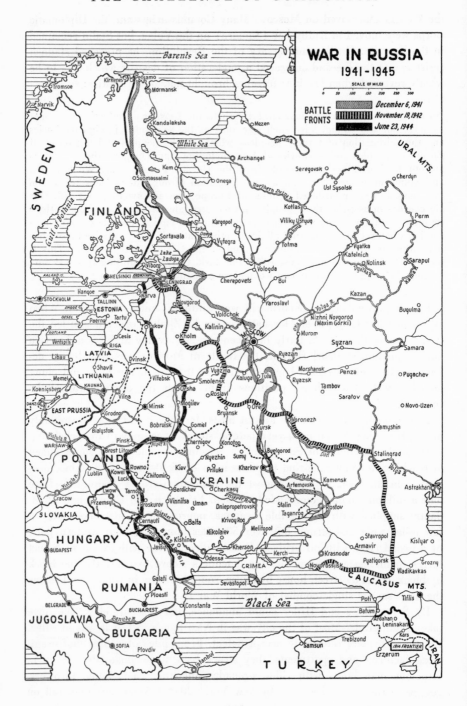

"Stalingrad Day" (Nov. 8, 1942) to receive greetings from Roosevelt and Eisenhower, to hear Litvinov, and to applaud Henry A. Wallace's plea for a new democracy. In the shadow of death, Americans and Russians were comrades in arms. Three years later they would be suspicious strangers. Four years later they would be potential enemies. But, in 1942, all people everywhere throughout the United States and the United Nations paid humble tribute to the warriors of Stalingrad, who, more than any other single group of Allied fighters, denied to the common foe his chance for victory.

On Nov. 19, 1942, Stalin, Zhukov, Vatutin, Voronov, Yeremenko, and Rokossovsky, after meticulous planning, released the springs of a huge trap. New Soviet armies attacked north and south of Stalingrad, met at Kalach on Nov. 23, and encircled the German Sixth Army west of the Volga. Hitler insisted that Paulus hold out, but all efforts to break the ring failed. After desperate resistance, 330,000 Nazi troops were cut to pieces. Paulus yielded on Feb. 1, 1943, along with 24 other generals, 2,400 officers, 91,000 surviving soldiers, 750 planes, 1,550 tanks, 6,700 guns, 61,000 motor vehicles, and other equipment.

The Wehrmacht was never again able to mount an offensive promising total victory. Soviet forces drove 400 miles westward in the winter of 1942–43, liberated 200,000 square miles of Russian earth, captured a third of a million enemy troops, and slew almost 1,000,000. Along a front of 2,000 miles, Soviet forces fought their way forward, at a rate of 40 miles a month, from the Volga to the Elbe. When the Wehrmacht opened its third summer offensive in July, 1943, around Kursk, Orel, and Belgorod, it lost 1,000 guns, 3,000 tanks, and 70,000 men in a few days of fierce fighting against a foe that now had superiority in arms, men, and generalship. Much of the Ukraine was liberated by autumn. In January the agony of Leningrad was ended with the smashing of the Nazi siege lines around the city. By summer, Soviet forces were invading Finland, Poland, and Rumania.

The Soviet drive timed to assist the Anglo-American invaders of France liberated Byelorussia and more of Poland. "It is the Russian Army," said Churchill, Aug. 2, 1944, "that has done the main work of tearing the guts out of the German Army." Rumania, Finland, and Bulgaria capitulated in the autumn. After liberating the Baltic and reaching Budapest, the victors opened their final offensive in central Poland in mid-January, 1945. It ended in Berlin and on the Elbe, with the demise of the Nazi Reich. On Moscow's V-E Day, Stalin declared:

. . . The age-long struggle of the Slav peoples for their existence and their independence has ended in victory over the German invaders and the German tyranny. Henceforth the great banner of freedom of nations and peace among nations will fly over Europe. . . . Eternal glory to the heroes who fell in the battles against the enemy and gave their lives for the freedom and happiness of our people!

The cost of victory was staggering. Among the citizens of the USSR, 38,000,000 were driven from their homes; 7,000,000 soldiers, sailors, airmen, partisans, and civilians died in battle, succumbed from wounds, or perished from starvation, forced labor, torture, or mass extermination behind enemy lines; increased death rates and decreased birth rates attributable to the war probably meant the loss of another 8,000,000 lives at least. Soviet casualties were ten times those of all the other Western United Nations combined. Property damage was estimated at 679,000,000,000 rubles. The destruction included 6,000,000 buildings in 1,700 devastated cities and 70,000 ruined villages, including 84,000 schools, 43,000 libraries, 31,000 factories, 13,000 bridges, and 40,000 miles of railway track. Also lost were 7,000,000 horses, 17,000,000 cattle, 20,000,000 pigs, 27,000,000 sheep and goats, etc. The USA would have suffered a comparable disaster if 9,000,000 Americans had been slain, with 27,000,000 homeless and most of the area east of the Mississippi occupied and devastated. . . .

Victory Harvest: The New Imperialism. By mid-century Western governments and peoples were no longer interested in the horror and heroism of Russia's years of blood. Kremlin conduct, flowing from and at the same time reinforcing the long-standing anxieties of the West, had convinced most Westerners that Communist victory over Nazism was as menacing to Western safety as Nazi victory over Communism might have been. Neither were Westerners interested in, or, thanks to the "Iron Curtain," much informed about the impact and aftermath of the war on the Soviet polity, economy, and society, though these developments and Western responses to them were clearly to be decisive for the lives and fortunes of all mankind during the balance of the century.

The Kremlin oligarchy, during the war and the "Cold War" after the war, grappled with its problems of ensuring obedience, mobilizing enthusiasm, and maintaining, restoring, and expanding production by a variety of measures—many of them muddled and all of them touched with the Mongoloid-Muscovite tradition of arbitrary power, but most of them successful in achieving their purposes. Minority peoples sympathetic with the enemy were ruthlessly uprooted and deported to Asia. The Union Republics were granted larger "autonomy" by a constitutional amendment of Feb. 1, 1944, authorizing them to maintain their own armed forces and to enter into diplomatic relations with other States. Membership in the Communist Party was almost doubled, to *c.* 6,000,000 by 1947, but there was no resumption of the forms or fictions of intra-Party democracy until the convening of Congress XIX in October, 1952. The top leadership remained constant and self-perpetuating. A fierce new Soviet patriotism, glorifying the heroes of the Great Russian past, replaced the revolutionary internationalism of earlier years. The "League of the Godless" was dissolved and the Orthodox Church restored to respectability, though Communists remained atheists. National elections of the Supreme

Soviet (Feb. 10, 1946, March 12, 1950, March 14, 1954, and March 16, 1958) remained ceremonial exercises in unanimity in the name of the "Bloc of Party and Nonparty People," without rival parties or multiple candidacies. Ideological orthodoxy was enforced in literature, science, and the arts.

Socialist economic planning not only withstood the test of war but demonstrated marked capacity to restore and expand production. Wartime rationing was abolished Dec. 14, 1947, while a "currency reform" disposed of excess purchasing power in the hands of consumers flowing from wartime inflation. Annual price reductions thereafter, adjusted to increased output, slowly raised living standards and avoided the discouraging postwar experiences of Western Europeans and Americans of an endless race between rising prices and rising wages. Capital accumulation through the devices of totalitarian socialism, whereby consumption was always kept below production, made possible vast new investment in productive facilities in industry and agriculture with resultant increases in production larger than increases in consumption, with the process endlessly repeated. With no aid from abroad, the business managers of the USSR and its satellites were able by their own devices to increase industrial output at a rate more rapid than that achieved in Western Europe or even in America. Ambitious projects of canals, dams, irrigation enterprises, hydroelectric stations, and new industrial units, particularly in the Volga Valley, Siberia, and Central Asia, promised fulfillment of the goals and a probable doubling of Soviet industrial production by 1970.

On the eve of Congress XIX of the Party (Oct. 5–15, 1952), Stalin declared that the basic economic "law" of socialism was "uninterrupted growth of production"; that the Communist bloc was self-sufficient and would soon have export surpluses; and that a new "crisis of capitalism," due to the end of the world market, made future war between bourgeois States more likely than any war of "capitalism" against "socialism." The Congress adopted new Party rules, chose a new Central Committee of 125 members and 110 alternates and replaced the old Politburo with a new "Presidium" of 25 members and 11 alternates—all without changing the character of the top leadership as a self-perpetuating oligarchy, in which Georgi M. Malenkov was Stalin's heir-apparent.

The Kremlin oligarchy abroad made a pretense of collaboration with its Western allies, under the cover of which it strove for maximum aggrandizement of Soviet power, thereby driving the West to "Cold War" as the only apparent means of protection against the Red bid for world mastery. From the perspective of 1984 this decision may be judged to have been shrewd and masterly in view of Western hostility, weakness, and befuddlement. It may equally be judged to have been suicidal, since its ultimate result was the dedication of America to implacable hostility toward the Soviet Union. In the 1950's judgments (among the judicious) must remain tentative. Yet the process is worth outlining.

Moscow dissolved the Communist International on May 22, 1943, to assuage Western fears of renewed Russian dedication to World Revolution. But Moscow revived the demon on Oct. 5, 1947, in the form of the anti-American "Communist Information Bureau" or Cominform. At Teheran, Yalta, and Potsdam (see pp. 194–196), Moscow agreed to "democracy" in the liberated lands and then proceeded to impose Communist despotisms upon them in pursuit of a carefully calculated policy of incorporating Eastern Europe into the Soviet sphere of power in the wake of Nazi defeat. In the planning of grand strategy in World War II, Churchill sought to avoid this result first by concentrating Anglo-American effort in Southern Europe and the Balkans and then, when this was vetoed in Washington (where policy-makers seemed interested only in "victory," regardless of political consequences), by striking a bargain with Stalin in October, 1944, for a division of southeastern Europe into "spheres." Washington again objected. Roosevelt sought to avoid this result by establishing cordial personal relations with "Uncle Joe" and assuring the Kremlin that all its "reasonable" aspirations could be met in a context of enduring East-West collaboration. In defining the adjective, Moscow gave lip service to every "principle" the West proposed and then did what it liked, while Western policy-makers soon came to regard any Soviet proposal on any issue as *ipso facto* "unreasonable" and further evidence of unbridled ambition.

Western statesmen did not at first object to Soviet demands for extensions of frontiers beyond the borders of 1939—*i.e.*, the "Curzon Line" as the new Russo-Polish frontier, Bessarabia and Northern Bukovina, even Carpatho-Ukraine (ceded by Prague, June 29, 1945), northern East Prussia, Tannu Tuva in Mongolia, Southern Sakhalin, the Kurils, and Port Arthur. Conflict arose over the status of the Balkans and Eastern Europe. The use of British troops in Greece in the winter of 1944–45 to crush the attempt of the Greek Communists to destroy the Athens government provoked Anglo-American friction and thus helped to persuade Stalin (though he kept his bargain with Churchill whereby Greece was to be in the British sphere) that the rude diplomacy of the *fait accompli* would induce Anglo-American acquiescence. At Yalta, he won major victories under an appearance of yielding to Anglo-American appeals and then proceeded at once to impose Soviet power on Eastern Europe.

On Feb. 27, 1945, Churchill told Commons that "the Soviet leaders wish to live in honorable friendship and equality with the Western Democracies. Their word is their bond." That night Vishinsky in Bucharest compelled King Michael to dismiss Premier Radescu. Four days later Roosevelt told Congress: "I am sure that under the agreements reached at Yalta there will be a more stable political Europe than ever before." The same night Vishinsky compelled Michael to appoint as Premier Petru Groza, leader of the Rumanian Communists.

SOVIET
IMPERIALISM
1944-1948

SCALE OF MILES
0   100   200   300

The Front, Jan. 12, 1945
Soviet Republics
Soviet Allies
Soviet Occupation Zones
NATO Members

NORWAY
Oslo
Stockholm
SWEDEN
Bornholm
Kaliningrad
Stettin
Berlin
Warsaw
POLAND
Prague
CZECHO-
Munich
SLOVAKIA
Vienna
AUSTRIA
Trieste
HUNGARY

SOVIET ALLY, 1945
BREAK WITH MOSCOW,
JUNE 1948
Belgrade
JUGOSLAVIA

ITALY
Naples

Petsamo
FINLAND
Helsinki   Viipuri
KARELO
FINNISH
S.S.R.
Leningrad
Tallin
EST. S.S.R.
LATVIAN
Riga   S.S.R.
LITH. S.S.R.
Kaunas
Minsk
BYELORUSSIAN
S.S.R.

R.S.F.S.R.
MOSCOW

Kiev
UKRAINIAN S.S.R.
C-U
MOLDAV
IAN
S.S.R.   Odessa
RUMANIA
Budapest
Bucharest
Sofia
BULGARIA

U.S. PROTECTORATES
UNDER TRUMAN
DOCTRINE
MARCH 1947

ALB.
GREECE
Istanbul
TURKEY

This pattern of deception and aggrandizement was to be repeated in Poland, Hungary, Jugoslavia, Albania, Bulgaria, Czechoslovakia, and East Germany. On the eve of his death (April 12, 1945) Roosevelt was involved in hot controversy with Stalin—and with Churchill who had long known what the results of Anglo-American strategy in World War II would probably be. The Western Powers, having originally renounced at Munich all interest in Eastern Europe and the Balkans, had gone to war a year later to prevent Nazi control of these areas—and now found themselves confronted with the specter of their control by Communism.

Cold War. The "battle for the world" between the Super-Powers after 1945 seemed to many participants and observers to involve an effort by the Kremlin to conquer the world and a counter-effort by America to checkmate and "contain" this ambition, to "roll back" the tide of Soviet expansion and, if possible, to breach the Muscovite citadel of the Red Conspiracy and liberate its slaves. This picture-in-the-mind bore some relation to reality, for many influential Russians and Americans talked and acted in the fashion here suggested. The initial issue, however, was more limited: who should control Eastern Europe and the Balkans? Washington and London assumed in 1944–45 that Soviet assent to "democracy" in these areas meant that they would not pass under Russian domination. Moscow assumed that the only true democracy was Communism and brought them all under Soviet control. This fateful decision may have been motivated less by the Kremlin's resolve to use these marchlands as a base for the subjugation of all the Continent (though Communist propaganda and conduct often justified this suspicion) than by a desire to establish a *cordon sanitaire* in reverse against the West. Had they been less distrustful of ultimate Soviet intentions, the Western Powers might have acquiesced in Soviet hegemony over Eastern Europe. But they could not acquiesce in what their policy-makers came to believe was a deliberate design by the Kremlin to take over all of Europe.

In the ensuing conflict, the rulers of the USSR, as well as their enemies, experienced the usual vicissitudes of success and failure. Jugoslavia was lost in 1948, not because of Western artistry in the game of power but because Moscow defeated its own purposes by seeking to impose, as elsewhere within its sphere, undeviating obedience and slavish subservience upon a native Communist regime which was here able and willing to defy the Kremlin's will. With Jugoslavia lost, all hope of communizing Greece disappeared, though Albania was retained in the Soviet orbit. The other marchlands were likewise held, despite Western diplomatic challenges and propaganda campaigns designed to bring about their emancipation. Sweden remained "neutral." Finland was spared the blessings of a "People's Democracy" in order to maintain Swedish neutrality. Germany and Austria remained split. Jugoslavia, Greece, Turkey, and Iran passed into the American camp, along with all of Western Europe. But American influence was precarious in the Arab lands, negligible in India,

Burma, and Indonesia, and of debatable ultimate efficacy in Southeast Asia and the Far East.

The men of the Kremlin were convinced by their dogma that all mankind must inevitably arrive at Communism and that it was their duty to promote the inevitable. But since they had no fixed "timetable" and were neither psychopaths nor victims of a social system so oddly contrived that it left its leaders no alternative to wars of conquest, they could afford to watch and wait in the hope that America would make a mess of its global responsibilities, suffer discouragement and depression at home, or yield to the fatal temptation of launching a "preventive war" against Russia or China or both. The Muscovite course in mid-century was one of waiting and watching, all the while insulting and provoking the USA and seeking to entangle its resources and power in hopeless local wars on the periphery of Marxland, driving its leaders and people into anti-Communist hysteria, and ultimately capitalizing upon American incapacity to face and meet effectively in the long run the strange and monstrous challenge which the Red Empire presented.

From Stalin to Khrushchev. These long-standing scripts of Soviet foreign policy were much modified after 1953 by virtue of new hopes, fears, aspirations, and opportunities, flowing in part from significant shifts of scenery on the world's stage, and in part from internal changes in the USSR which brought new actors into the play. The subsequent direction and course of Soviet diplomacy will be discussed later in the chapter. Since it is no less true in totalitarian oligarchies than in democracies that domestic and foreign politics are inseparable, let us here review in outline the major internal transformations in the USSR in the later years of the fourth decade of the Soviet regime.[1]

In mid-January, 1953, the Soviet press publicized the alleged discovery of a monstrous conspiracy wherein top Kremlin physicians, mainly Jewish, had "confessed" to collaborating with "imperialist and Zionist spies" in killing Shcherbakov (d. 1945) and Zhdanov (d. 1948) through wrong diagnosis and treatment and in plotting the death of sundry high military leaders. Anti-Semitism became a leitmotiv of Soviet journalism. When terrorists bombed the Soviet legation in Tel Aviv, Moscow (Feb. 12) severed diplomatic relations with Israel. This final political maneuver of Stalin, who became progressively more paranoid and vindictive in his senescence, clearly foreshadowed a new "blood purge" of unpredictable scope.

But even nightmares have an end. On March 4, the Central Committee of the Party and the Council of Ministers jointly announced that Stalin had

---

[1] For fuller accounts of all these matters see the books listed at the close of this section of the present chapter, the author's annual articles on the USSR in Funk and Wagnalls' *New International Year Book*, and *Russia Since 1917: Four Decades of Soviet Politics* (Knopf, 1957), from which a few further passages are paraphrased in the following pages.

suffered a stroke during the night of March 1–2. Further medical bulletins ended with word that Stalin died at 9:50 P.M., March 5, 1953. The eulogies at the State funeral were delivered by Malenkov, Molotov, and Beria. So passed from the scene in his seventy-fourth year Josef Vissarionovich Djugashvili, son of a Georgian cobbler, theology student in Tiflis, professional revolutionist, and Marxist autocrat over Russia for three decades.

On March 6, 1953, the Party Central Committee, the Council of Ministers, and the Presidium of the Supreme Soviet jointly named Georgi Maximilianovich Malenkov, aged 51, as Premier; and Beria, Molotov, Bulganin, and Kaganovich as Vice Premiers. The Party Presidium (Politburo) was reduced from 25 to 10 members. The slogans of the day were "Unity," "Calm," "Vigilance," "Civil Liberties," "Peace," "Collective Leadership," and no more "Hero-worship." Malenkov retired as Secretary of the Central Committee in favor of Nikita S. Khrushchev. An amnesty released many prisoners from jails and labor camps. The "Jewish Doctors" were freed and the "Plot" denounced as a fraud.

In what ensued, we may infer from events that most, although not all, of the new "collective leaders" were persuaded by the irreversible facts of the massive industrialization, urbanization, and education of Russia that Stalin's demise posed an opportunity, and indeed a necessity, for putting an end through various legal reforms and measures of decentralization to Stalin's obsolete police-state in favor, somehow, of a more liberalized and humanized pattern of power. Groping efforts toward the goal raised many problems of extraordinary difficulty and complexity at home and abroad, as is always the case in periods of transition from one *status quo* which is dead to another still struggling to be born. In the USSR which Stalin bequeathed to his successors most workers, collective farmers, soldiers, intellectuals, and members of the new managerial middle class welcomed with relief the efforts of the new leadership to liquidate the darker phases of Stalin's legacy. Some bureaucrats and Party *apparatchiks* resisted the process. The result was a series of crises in which, through the peculiar processes of Soviet politics, the resisters were ultimately vanquished and the new anti-Stalinist "liberals" prevailed.

Summer calm was broken on July 10, 1953, with the announcement that Beria had sought to make his MVD or political police "superior to Party and Government," had become "an agent of international imperialism," had been dismissed and arrested on June 26 as "an enemy of the people," and would be tried for treason. In the name of "socialist legality" and the "rule of law," the MVD was subsequently downgraded and deprived of its powers of arbitrary arrest, imprisonment, and execution of "subversives." After a secret trial before a military tribunal, in the best Stalinist manner, Beria and his accomplices were reported to have been executed in December, 1953. Others were demoted, tried, jailed, or executed later. Under such bizarre circumstances the MVD ceased to be a "State within a State" in the Soviet polity and largely lost its time-honored function as a totalitarian instrument of terror.

Other issues of power and policy among Stalin's successors were more complex. The complexities admit of no brief review, for they were compounded of involved calculations of probable profit or loss to the rulers of the USSR in choices among alternative courses in both domestic and foreign affairs. Despite much talk in the Western press of questions of emphasis or preference in Soviet economic planning between consumers' goods and further industrialization, the shift of power in 1955 was almost certainly a response to final Western ratification of German rearmament. This prospect, in the view of Soviet policy-makers, demanded a closer liaison of Party and Army and a new diplomatic offensive to be conducted dramatically by top leaders rather than by professional diplomats. On Feb. 8, 1955, Malenkov resigned as Premier, pleading insufficient experience and responsibility for the unsatisfactory state of agriculture, in favor of Marshal Nikolai A. Bulganin. Malenkov became Vice Premier and Minister of Electric Power Stations. Zhukov became Minister of Defense.

Khrushchev emerged as the new *Vozhd* or "boss," although disclaiming personal power and espousing "collective leadership." At Party Congress XX, 1,355 delegates representing 7,215,505 Party members met (Feb. 14–25, 1956) in St. Andrew's Hall of the Great Kremlin Palace. Amid much talk of "democratization" and "peaceful coexistence" and little evidence of free debate and decision-making as known in the West, Khrushchev closed the Congress with a lengthy indictment of Stalin's crimes—unpublished in the USSR but read to millions of citizens in thousands of meetings by local Party leaders. The apparent purpose of this performance was to shock Party and public into abandoning the long-established cult of Party infallibility and developing new habits of criticism, self-criticism, and initiative as means of promoting more popular participation in policy-making. Many were shocked. After a generation of totalitarian tyranny, few were inspired to reorient their habitual political attitudes of uncritical acceptance of the decisions of the oligarchs. To subvert a democracy into a dictatorship is, under suitable circumstances, simple. To convert a dictatorship into a democracy is difficult.

This remained the domestic goal, however ambiguously defined, of Khrushchev and his supporters in the late 1950's. Totalitarian controls were progressively relaxed and limited freedom of expression was encouraged in the spirit of the post-Stalin "thaw." Yet a two-party or multi-party system of politics was still inconceivable to the Communist rulers, who strove to "liberalize" the police-state by fostering democratization of the Party hierarchy and humanizing the relations between rulers and ruled in the complex and ubiquitous bureaucracy of the USSR. The popular results of these endeavors were still obscure when the Soviet regime entered upon its fifth decade in

1957. The official results were reflected in further shifts of leadership during the fortieth year of Communist rule.

On June 1, 1956, as Tito arrived in Moscow, the veteran Molotov was replaced as Foreign Minister by Dmitri Shepilov, editor of *Pravda*, whose tenure, however, was brief. On Feb. 15, 1957, he was succeeded by Andrei Gromyko, long a professional Soviet diplomat. During the spring of 1957 Khrushchev pushed through a massive decentralization of industrial management, with most of the industrial Ministries in Moscow giving way to some 90 regional administrations of industry. He further espoused an economic program which was designed to give Soviet consumers as much meat and dairy products per capita as were enjoyed by consumers in the USA and to abolish compulsory deliveries of produce from the family garden plots of collective farmers. These policy directives encountered opposition among colleagues who regarded them as fantastic or hazardous.

The result of this conflict of judgments was announced on July 4, 1957. Khrushchev's critics, seeking his ouster, evidently won a majority of the Party Presidium to their views in late June. He insisted on carrying the issue to the Party Central Committee where the Khrushchev "line" prevailed. Molotov, Malenkov, Kaganovich, and Shepilov, under accusation of "anti-Party" activity, were ousted from the Presidium and from the Party Central Committee, deprived of their governmental posts, and subsequently charged with direct complicity in Stalin's blood purges of the 1930's and in the fabrication of the "Leningrad case" of 1949 which led to the purge and execution of Voznesensky. On July 5 Pervukhin and Saburov were dismissed as First Deputy Premiers and dropped from the Party Presidium.[2]

Despite ominous accusations against them in public speeches and the press, the losers did not suffer the fate of prominent dissenters under Stalin—*i.e.*, expulsion from the Party, arrest, and a bullet in the head with or without benefit of extorted "confessions" and stage-managed public trials. On the contrary, Malenkov was named manager of a hydroelectric station in Ust-

---

[2] From what became known in the immediate aftermath of these events, it appeared that the decisions reached were not a result of arbitrary dictation by the "boss," as in the days of Stalin, but of genuine debates and votes in both the Party Presidium and Central Committee. In the previous 11-member Presidium, many of Khrushchev's innovations were opposed by Malenkov, Molotov, and Kaganovich, partially opposed by Saburov and Pervukhin, and supported by Bulganin, Mikoyan, Voroshilov, Suslov, and Kirichenko. Upon the return of Khrushchev and Bulganin from Finland, June 14, 1957, he was voted down in the Presidium, but only because Voroshilov, Suslov, and Kirichenko were initially absent from Moscow during the discussions. He was supported by Zhukov, who spoke powerfully for the Army even though he was then only an alternate (nonvoting) member of the Presidium. The new 15-member Presidium comprised six men of the "old guard" (Bulganin, Khrushchev, Mikoyan, Shvernik, Voroshilov, and Kirichenko); another "old Bolshevik," Otto Kuusinen, a Finnish Communist long in Muscovite exile; technician Suslov; the Army incarnate in the person of Marshal Zhukov; an outstanding woman leader, Ekaterina Furtseva; and five relative newcomers about whom less was known: F. R. Kozlov, Leningrad Party leader; Leonid I. Brezhnev, Party leader in Kazakistan; N. G. Ignatiev, Aristov, and Belyayev.

Kaminogorsk in the Kazak Republic, Molotov Ambassador to Outer Mongolia, and Kaganovich executive of a cement plant somewhere in Central Asia. The new duties of Shepilov, Saburov, and Pervukhin were not at once revealed. In late October, 1957, Zhukov was replaced as Minister of Defense by Marshal Rodion V. Malinovsky. On Nov. 2 the Party Central Committee announced Zhukov's expulsion from the Party Presidium and Central Committee on charges of promoting his own "cult of personality," resisting Party control of the Army, and "political unsoundness, inclining to adventurism" in foreign policy. The Soviet war hero was assigned to "new duties." Humiliating as were these demotions of men once mighty among rulers of Russia, they represented a marked change in methods of dealing with opponents. In his visit to Prague in mid-July, 1957, Khrushchev opined that the "black sheep" had been appropriately disposed of and that "it is not bad if, in improving the theory of Marx, one throws in also a piece of bacon and a piece of butter. . . . Nothing can stop the birth of a new social order. . . . We are the world's second industrial power and we will catch up with the USA. We will catch up in milk and butter soon."

New Horizons. Many Westerners remained skeptical, despite their sense of shocked surprise at the news that the USSR broke the U.S. monopoly of atomic weapons in September, 1949, acquired the H-bomb in August, 1953, and in the summer of 1957, before the USA had turned the trick, made the first successful tests of a Soviet Intercontinental Ballistic Missile (ICBM) — all the while graduating annually more engineers and scientists than America and Western Europe combined. The overtaking of America in industrial productivity and living standards was far off and might never be achieved. But in the muscle, bone, and sinew of national power, Marxist Muscovy was approaching rough parity with the American colossus by 1960.

The fascinating but futile problem of the "balance of power" between Marxland and the Free World is quite beyond solution in material terms, since here more than ever the nonmaterial components of power are decisive. Yet a comparison of physical elements of national strength available to each of the Super-Powers is worthy of study as a key to trends of change and a partial index of relative force. Soviet heavy industry by 1955 had attained a level of over-all output roughly half of that of the USA in 1951 (though plainly much less than half on a per capita basis), as compared with less than one-third in 1945 and one-tenth or less in 1925 before industrialization began. Average Soviet living standards in the 1950's would represent perhaps a third of their American counterpart. Moscow possessed the largest standing army in the world, the largest submarine fleet, and probably the largest air force. Washington possessed a navy larger than that of all other States combined and total industrial capacity almost half of that of all the rest of the world together. To American components of power were added, so long as they could be held by reliable allies, all the peoples and products of Western Europe,

521

Africa, Latin America, Japan, and Southeast Asia, giving the Western bloc (on paper) an overwhelming preponderance over the USSR. But to Soviet components of power were added, so long as they could be held by reliable allies, all the peoples and products of Eastern Europe and of gigantic China, poor in industry but teeming in population, giving Marxland a rough parity with the USA.

As the 1950's closed, the USSR with some 208,000,000 inhabitants scattered over 8,400,000 square miles confronted a USA with some 175,000,000 inhabitants in 3,000,000 square miles. Soviet coal production was approaching equality with American output at figures close to 500,000,000 tons a year. Soviet oil production was still less than a fifth of its American counterpart while Soviet motorcar production totaled 600,000 units per year to America's 7,000,000 or more. Soviet output of electrical power was climbing toward 200,000,000 thousand kilowatt hours per year compared to America's 500,-000,000 thousand. Soviet steel output was approaching 70,000,000 tons per annum as against America's 110,000,000-ton capacity. Soviet power in terms of naval tonnage, aircraft, and atomic weapons was second to the USA. The annual rate of Soviet economic growth, although beginning to decline slightly, was about 8% against America's 4%, prior to the 1958 recession.

But all such comparisons, if devoted to deciding as a popular parlor game "who will win the next war," are pointless. No one will win the next war. The more hopeful problem of establishing a global equilibrium in the name of preventing the next war or winning the Cold War is equally elusive, for success in the global struggle of the Super-Powers is less a problem of translating human and material resources into terms of military might than a matter of effective propaganda, far-sighted calculations, and judicious diplomacy in winning and keeping allies, while undermining the enemy coalition, and striking bargains with the enemy, if he could be induced to bargain, which might prove ultimately advantageous in their future effects on the total balance of potential fighting capacity.

The masters of the Red Empire, thanks to their fanaticism, immoderation, and stubborn insistence on all-or-nothing, were inept in dealing with allies, and self-defeating in negotiating with foes or even friends, as shown by their genius in arousing universal suspicion, fear, and hatred. But they had demonstrated the capacity of their economic and social arrangements to lift "backward" peoples by their bootstraps to positions of great power and pride and to some semblance or promise of plenty as compared with previous penury. Despite all betrayals, oppressions, and horrors, they had also demonstrated the enormous and continued appeal of their dogma to warped intellectuals, debt-ridden farmers, unhappy workers, and the dark and discontented masses of Eurasia and Africa—and the ability of their elite to play politics, conduct diplomacy, and wage war with subtlety and skill. The major market for their wares would continue to be the backward and impoverished multitudes of the earth, aspiring toward Western living standards and ignorant or skeptical of American values and American ability to serve their needs.

By exploiting these markets and capitalizing upon Western mistakes, the rulers of the new realm of Kubla Khan might yet extend Marxland to even more impressive dimensions. They could not "conquer the world," nor were they likely to try, since any such attempt would inevitably spell total war and total defeat at the hands of the USA. And since, in the absence of such provocation, America could not destroy them or seriously weaken their power without destroying itself in the process, they would continue to remain far into the future a constant irritant, challenge, and menace to the Free World. To try to remove this menace by violence rather than endure contumacious insolence and bear heavy burdens indefinitely would remain a constant temptation. To yield to this temptation would be to shatter irrevocably the whole fabric of the Great Society. The Western peoples could hope for security only through vigilance, wisdom, and patience, through keeping their own houses in order, and through calm acceptance of responsibility over decades to come for looking to their defenses and vindicating the values by which they live in the face of threatening challenge posed by the most formidable would-be conquerors of the world since the Mongols.

* * * * *

In the long perspective of times to come, it may transpire that the most important consequence for mankind as a whole of the industrialization, urbanization, and education of Russia wrought by Stalin, by methods most monstrous, was not a consequence to be measured in the scales of power in international politics. Without these transformations, to be sure, the new Muscovy could not have defeated Hitler in the 1940's or defied America in the 1950's. But Russia's new era had implications of a different and more hopeful import. A Soviet Union of great cities, big industry, and mass literacy could not possibly be ruled by the methods of Stalinism which were viable only in the primitive, poor, backward, and rural USSR of a generation ago. A "reformed," "liberalized," and "democratized" regime was imperative and inevitable if the new collective leaders, as they well understood, were to avoid breakdown and a new revolution. What final form the new order would take was still unclear when these words were written. But the direction of the change was obvious.

By virtue of these circumstances, Russia's future role in world affairs seemed likely to be defined by its rulers in terms of a progressive de-emphasizing of "World Revolution" and of the ancestral Messianic "mission" of the Slavs to save all the world from sin, whether "capitalistic" or otherwise. A new and ever larger and more prosperous "ruling class" of executives, technicians, engineers, professional specialists, and skilled workers had acquired a vested interest in the *status quo*. To jeopardize these privileges by rash foreign adventures, risking war in which all would be lost, would be a course of mad-

THE CHALLENGE OF COMMUNISM

ness. The rulers of Marxist Muscovy were not madmen, nor were they driven by domestic problems and tensions to seek unity at home through conflict abroad. Hopes of the "collapse of capitalism" and of the universal triumph of Communism, to be sure, were deathless among the orthodox disciples of Marxism. But deeds promised to be tempered to the advantages of survival amid prospects of ever-growing wealth for the elite, and even for the masses, of the USSR.

SUGGESTED READINGS

Baykov, Alexander: *The Development of the Soviet Economic System*, New York, Macmillan, 1946.
Carr, Edward Hallett: *The Bolshevik Revolution, 1917–1923* (Vols. I, II, III), New York, Macmillan, 1951–1953.
Crankshaw, Edward: *Russia and the Russians*, New York, Viking, 1948.
Curtiss, John Shelton: *The Russian Revolutions of 1917*, Princeton, N.J., Van Nostrand, 1957.
Dean, Vera Micheles: *The United States and Russia*, Cambridge, Mass., Harvard University Press, 1947.
Dennett, Raymond, and Joseph E. Johnson: *Negotiating with the Russians*, Boston, World Peace Foundation, 1951.
Deutscher, Isaac: *Stalin: A Political Biography*, New York, Oxford, 1949.
———: *The Prophet Armed: Trotsky, 1879–1921*, New York, Oxford, 1954.
Dobb, Maurice: *Soviet Economic Development since 1917*, New York, International Publishers, 1949.
Fainsod, Merle: *How Russia Is Ruled*, Cambridge, Mass., Harvard University Press, 1953.
Fischer, Louis: *The Soviets in World Affairs* (2 vols.), New York, Cape & Smith, 1930.
Fisher, Harold H.: *The Communist Revolution: An Outline of Strategy and Tactics*, Stanford, Calif., Stanford University Press, 1955.
Foster, William Z.: *History of the Three Internationals*, New York, International Publishers, 1955.
Harper, Samuel N., and Ronald Thompson: *Government of the Soviet Union*, Princeton, N.J., Van Nostrand, 1949.
Hart, B. H. Liddell (ed.): *The Red Army*, New York, Harcourt, Brace, 1956.
Kennan, George F.: *Russia Leaves the War* and *The Decision to Intervene* (Vols. I, II of *Soviet-American Relations, 1917–1920*), Princeton, N.J., Princeton University Press, 1956 and 1958.
Kulski, W. W.: *The Soviet Regime: Communism in Practice*, Syracuse, N.Y., Syracuse University Press, 1954.
Martin, John Stuart (ed.): *A Picture History of Russia*, Crown, 1956.
Masaryk, Thomas Garrigue: *The Spirit of Russia: Studies in History, Literature, and Philosophy*, London, G. Allen and New York, Macmillan, 1919.
Maynard, Sir John: *Russia in Flux*, New York, Macmillan, 1948.
Mazour, Anatole G.: *Finland between East and West*, Princeton, N.J., Van Nostrand, 1956.
Ministry of Foreign Affairs of the U.S.S.R.: *Documents and Materials Relating to the Eve of the Second World War* (2 vols.), New York, International Publishers, 1949.
Pares, Sir Bernard: *A History of Russia*, New York, Knopf, 1944.
Pope, Arthur Upham: *Maxim Litvinov*, New York, Fisher, 1943.
Reshetar, John S., Jr.: *The Ukrainian Revolution, 1917–1920*, Princeton, N.J., Princeton University Press, 1952.
Roberts, Henry L.: *Russia and America: Dangers and Prospects*, New York, Harper, 1956.
Rostow, W. W., in collaboration with Alfred Levin: *The Dynamics of Soviet Society*, New York, Norton, 1953.
Schuman, Frederick L.: *Soviet Politics at Home and Abroad*, New York, Knopf, 1946.
———: *Russia Since 1917: Four Decades of Soviet Politics*, New York, Knopf, 1957.

CHINA: THE MANDATE OF HEAVEN

Schwartz, Harry: *Russia's Soviet Economy*, Englewood Cliffs, N.J., Prentice-Hall, 1950.
Scott, John: *Behind the Urals*, Boston, Houghton Mifflin, 1942.
Shub, David: *Lenin: A Biography*, New York, Doubleday, 1948.
Simmons, Ernest J. (ed.): *Continuity and Change in Russian and Soviet Thought*, Cambridge, Mass., Harvard University Press, 1955.
Towster, Julian: *Political Power in the U.S.S.R., 1917–1947*, New York, Oxford, 1948.
Trotsky, Leon: *The History of the Russian Revolution* (3 vols.), New York, Simon and Schuster, 1937.
Vernadsky, George: *A History of Russia*, New Haven, Conn., Yale University Press, 1954.
Williams, W. A.: *American-Russian Relations: 1781–1947*, New York, Rinehart, 1952.
Wolfe, Bertram D.: *Three Who Made a Revolution: Lenin-Trotsky-Stalin*, New York, Dial Press, 1948.

2. CHINA: THE MANDATE OF HEAVEN

Of the best rulers, the people know only that they exist. The next best they love and praise. The next they fear. And the next they revile. When they do not command the people's faith, some will lose faith in them. And then they resort to oaths! But, of the best, when their task is accomplished, their work done, the people all remark, "We have done it ourselves."—LAO-TSE, *The Book of Tao*, c. 540 B.C., translation by Lin Yutang.

Tzu-chang asked about government. The Master said, "The requisites of government are that there be a sufficiency of food, sufficiency of military equipment, and the confidence of the people in their ruler." Tzu-chang said, "If it cannot be helped, and one of these must be dispensed with, which of the three should be foregone first?" "The military equipment," said the Master. Tzu-chang again asked, "If it cannot be helped, and one of the remaining two must be dispensed with, which of them should be foregone?" The Master answered, "Part with the food. From of old, death has been the lot of all men; but a people that has no faith in their rulers is lost indeed."—CONFUCIUS, *Analects*, c. 490 B.C.

The ruin and destruction of World War I, coupled with the follies of allies and enemies, delivered Russia to Communism. The destruction and ruin of World War II, coupled with the follies of enemies and allies, delivered China to Communism. Both developments were so shocking to the USA as to cause many Americans in 1917–18 to explain the Russian Revolution as a "German plot" and, in 1949–50, to explain the Chinese Revolution as a "Russian plot" or the consequence, somehow, of a conspiracy of "traitors" in Washington.[3]

[3] In 1949–50 and thereafter, Secretary Acheson and his aides repeatedly made public pronouncements denying that the Chinese Communists were "Chinese" and depicting them as tools of the Kremlin, serving their Muscovite masters for the purposes of promoting Soviet annexation of Manchuria, Mongolia, Sinkiang, etc., and Soviet enslavement of the rest of China. Senator Joseph McCarthy repeatedly argued in the same period that what had happened in China was the result of the "treasonable" activities of Gen. George C. Marshall, Owen Lattimore, *et al.* Senator Pat McCarran, in releasing in July, 1952, the voluminous report of the subcommittee which he headed to investigate the Institute of Pacific Relations asserted: "Twenty-five years ago a small group of men interested in the Far East made a deal with Russia. . . . But for the machinations of the small group that controlled and activated that organization (IPR), China today would be free and a bulwark against the further advance of the Red hordes into the Far East." The *Washington Post* (July 4, 1952) described this interpretation as "extravagant nonsense," a

Since these explanations are unworthy of serious consideration, they need not be dwelt upon here. Red conquest of Russia was the work of Russians. Red conquest of China, albeit Russia's greatest victory and America's greatest defeat in the 20th Century, was the work neither of Americans nor of Russians, but of Chinese.

How this evil came to pass, and to be mistaken for good by many Chinese, cannot yet be told in full. What can be told within these pages is best told by recalling at the outset that today's China is a million square miles larger than the USA, half the size of the USSR, and by far the most populous of the national mansions of mankind with its more than half a billion souls comprising one-quarter of the human race. China is also the oldest living civilization of *Homo sapiens,* since its people began writing and reading and living in cities 5,000 years ago, only 20 centuries after the Sumerians and Egyptians, both long since dust, first arrived at these inventions. The China of 2,000 years ago, when Greece was still glorious and Rome was young, was a community dedicated to the ideal of a universal empire of all men, to a rigid orthodoxy of beliefs regulating all aspects of life (Confucianism), to authoritarianism and despotism in government (exercised by an absolute Emperor or "Son of Heaven"), and to the rule of an elite of carefully indoctrinated intellectuals. In these respects at least the new Marxism is less an innovation than a return and fulfillment of ancient ways in modern form. What is new is the adoption of Western science and technology to change the face of a long-static and stagnant rural economy, and the adoption of Western totalitarianism as a means toward social revolution and economic transformation.

From Celestial Empire to Kuomintang. The vast human sea of China has always engulfed all rivers of doctrine flowing into it and all tempests of conquest beating upon it. The tides and storms of the past century will prove no exception to the rule. The bright years of the Sung Dynasty (960–1280) ended with the Mongol conquest and the Mongol dynasty (1280–1368). But the new rulers became Chinese. The Ming Dynasty (1368–1644) was overthrown by the Manchus, but in the course of the Manchu Dynasty (1644–1911) these invaders too became Chinese. The traditional Chinese response to the challenge of nomad barbarians or "foreign devils" was to absorb them. Only the sharp impact of the Western Powers in the middle 1800's seemed to admit of no such answer. The ancient Chinese arts of handicraft industry and old-fashioned warfare were no match for the power of the West. Nor could the Imperial Government cope with external aggression and internal upheavals engendered by Western pressures upon the "Middle Kingdom."

China's long disorders, ever since the first lost war with the West (1839–42) and the destructive frenzy of the Taiping rebellion (1848–64), may fairly

---

"despicable abuse of Congressional immunity," and "a revision of history, compounded out of McCarthian bigotry, McCarranesque spleen, and MacArthurian legend. It is an attempt to perpetrate another fraud and hoax on the American people."

be regarded as a confused quest for the political, military, and technical means of resisting attempts at conquest or partition by the European Powers and later Japan. The quest, long thwarted, begot a new nationalism, a new form of State, and in the end widespread peasant revolt against feudal oppression by the rural gentry. The confusions may be pursued in any history of modern China. The results and the prospects in their consequences for world politics are here our main concern.

Sun Yat-sen (1866–1924) became the spiritual father and the political organizer of the Chinese Revolution. The Nationalist Revolutionary Movement was at first directed against the corrupt and decrepit Manchu Dynasty. It later aspired to the political and social regeneration of China. In 1911 the Manchus were overthrown—but the Presidency of the new Republic passed, not to Sun Yat-sen, who retired to Canton, but to the opportunist adventurer, Yuan Shih Kai, who aspired to become Emperor. Followers of Sun, organized into the Kuomintang, or National People's Party, were committed to a Western program of parliamentary democracy, tinctured with socialist elements. Yuan's subservience to foreign bankers, his surrender to Japan in 1915, and his assumption of royal honors in the following year led to a new revolution and to the commencement of an epoch of prolonged civil war. This state of affairs was due to the impotence of the central government, the uncontrolled greed of the semi-independent provincial *tuchuns*, or "war lords," the emergence of a mass of undisciplined mercenary soldiery, and the progressive disintegration of all the social and economic bases of political unity and cohesion.

In June, 1916, Yuan Shih Kai died amid a ferment of revolutionary disturbances. There followed years of turmoil, marked by chronic struggles for the control of the central government among the war lords: Wu-Pei-fu of the Chihli clique, Chang Tso Lin of Manchuria, Feng Yu-hsiang, the "Christian general" of Shansi, and other lesser feudal chieftains. Chang's sphere of power was Manchuria, and he was at all times dependent upon the whim of Japan for the continued rulership of his satrapy. Feng centered his power in Mongolia and looked toward Moscow. While the north was torn by these internecine conflicts, the Kuomintang followers of Sun Yat-sen remained in power at Canton and prepared themselves for the mission of unifying China on the basis of Sun's "three principles": people's nationalism, people's democracy, people's livelihood. In 1921, Sun was "elected" President of the Republic by a group of 1913 rump parliamentarians at Canton, but he encountered constant resistance from the militarists and led a precarious existence. In his search for foreign aid, Sun received much sympathy from the rulers of Communist Russia.

In September, 1923, Michael Borodin arrived from Moscow as chief adviser of the Kuomintang. His leadership, strengthened by a naval demonstration on the part of the Western Powers against Sun's threat to seize the Canton customs receipts, initiated a four-year period of successful Soviet-Kuomintang coopera-

TO U.S.S.R.
1945

Kyzl

SIBERIA

TANNU TUVA

Sergiopol

RUSSIAN PROTECTORATE, 1913
SOVIET ALLY SINCE 1934

L. Balkash

Chuguchak

MONGOL

Alma Ata

DZUNGARIA

PEOPLES' REP

Tihwah
(Urumchi)

GOBI

Kashgar

SINKIANG

KANSU

NINGSI

TARIM BASIN

Nin

Yarkand

Cherchen

Khotan

TSINGHAI

Sining

Lan

PAK.

TIBET

SZEC

BRITISH
PROTECTORATE
1914

NEPAL

Lhasa

SIKANG

Kangting

CHUNG

BHUTAN

INDIA

PAK.

TO BRITAIN, 1886
INDEPENDENT, 1947

Kunming

Calcutta

BURMA

YUNNAN

Lashio

Mandalay

WESTERN CHINA

SCALE OF MILES

10   100   200   300   400   500

Rangoon

LAOS

THAILAND

528

Irkutsk
L. Baikal
Chita
Ulan Ude

TO RUSSIA, 1858-1860

Blagoveshchensk
Amur R.
Khabarovsk

SO. SAKHALIN
TO JAPAN, 1905
TO U.S.S.R., 1945

HEILUNGKIANG

Tsitsihar

Harbin

Ulan Bator

I A N
UBLIC
DESERT

CHAHAR

M A N C H U R I A
KIRIN

Hsinking

Vladivostok

SUIYUAN

Kweisui
Kalgan
Peiping

JEHOL
Mukden
Jehol

LIAOTUNG
LIAONING

SOVIET
ZONE, 1945

TO JAPAN, 1910

A
Piatow

gsia

Tientsin
Port Arthur

TO RUSSIA, 1897
TO JAPAN, 1905
TO U.S.S.R., 1945

Seoul

K O R E A

U.S. ZONE
1945

J A P A N

HOPEH

Wei Hei Wei

TO BRITAIN, 1898

Yenan
Yangku

Kiaochow

ALLIANCE
WITH U.S.A.
Sept.8, 1951

chow

SHANSI

Tsinan

Yellow R.

SHANTUNG

TO GERMANY, 1897-
TO JAPAN, 1914-
EVACUATED, 1922

Sian
Kafeng

KIANGSU

SHENSI
HONAN

Chinkiang

HWAN

Hankow
Wuchang

Yangtze R.

Nanking
Hwaining

Shanghai
Hangchow

KING

HUPEH

ANWHEI

CHEKIANG

LIU-KIU ISLANDS

HUNAN
Changsha

Nanchang

KIANGSI

OKINAWA

KWEICHOW

Kweiyang

FUKIEN

Foochow

Taipei

KWANGSI

Nanning

KWANGTUNG

Amoy

PESCADORES

FORMOSA

HQ. OF CHINESE
NATIONALIST GOVT.
Dec. 19, 1949 f.
U.S. PROTECTORATE
June 27, 1950

Swatow
Canton
Kowloon
Hong Kong

TO JAPAN, 1895
TO CHINA, 1945

TO BRITAIN, 1842, 1860

Kwangchowan

TO FRANCE, 1898

HAINAN

VIET NAM

PHILIPPINE ISLANDS

Manila

EASTERN CHINA

SCALE OF MILES

0   100   200   300   400   500

Mid-Century
Protectorates
of the U.S.A.

529

tion. Russian military officers trained the new Nationalist Army. The Kuomintang was reorganized on the model of the Russian Communist Party as a rigidly disciplined brotherhood designed to assume dictatorial power. In 1924 the Chinese Communists, who were increasing in numbers, were admitted to the Party. With this, there began the internal struggle between the bourgeois elements and the peasant-proletarian elements, which was later to lead to disaster. For the moment, however, the movement was greatly strengthened by its alliance with Soviet advisers and native Communists. It launched upon a career which offered a brief hope of uniting China.

Despite Sun's death in April, 1924, Chiang Kai-shek, with the assistance of Borodin, assumed control in Canton after a period of disorder. A campaign was now launched to convert and unite the entire nation. By March, 1927, the Yangtze Valley and Shanghai had fallen to the southerners. But success brought the inevitable break between Chiang and Borodin, each of whom had sought to use the other for his own ends. While Chiang now summoned anti-Communist, bourgeois, and militarist elements to his aid, the Communistic left wing of the Kuomintang occupied Nanking and began a general assault upon foreign interests which led to the bombardment of part of the city by American and British war vessels. Chiang now allied himself with the merchants and bankers of Shanghai. In April, 1927, he purged Shanghai and Canton of Russians and Communists by wholesale arrests and executions. Feng Yu-hsiang now joined the right-wing Nationalists.

In July Borodin retired to Russia, after thousands of labor leaders, peasants, students, and radicals had been put to death by the now thoroughly bourgeois Kuomintang under Chiang's military domination. Borodin's Chinese followers, including Mme Sun Yat-sen, denounced Chiang as a renegade and a betrayer of the revolution. Chiang set up a personal dictatorship at Nanking, while the closing of Soviet consulates and the slaughter of Communists continued in the cities of the south. The Nationalist armies now moved on Peiping, controlled by Chang Tso-lin; but they were delayed by an armed clash with Japanese troops at Tsinan. In June the Manchurian war lord, under Kuomintang pressure and on the advice of the Japanese Minister, left Peiping for Mukden. He was killed by a bomb explosion during the journey and was succeeded by his son, Chang Hsueh-liang. At the same time Yen Hsi-shan's troops occupied Peiping in the name of the Kuomintang, and all of China was seemingly united under the Nationalist Government of Chiang Kai-shek at Nanking.

Chaos in Cathay. This unity, however, was illusory. The Party program of abrogating the unequal treaties, abolishing extraterritoriality, occupying the foreign concessions, and ousting foreign interests was soon paralyzed by new dissensions. In October, 1928, an Organic Law of the National Government of the Republic of China was promulgated, providing for the indefinite perpetuation of the one-party dictatorship of the Kuomintang. But all efforts to demobilize the predatory armies of the *tuchuns* failed. In February, 1929, civil strife broke out in Shantung and Hunan. Chiang waged war on the Wuhan-Kwangsi faction and sent a punitive expedition against the now rebellious Feng, who "resigned" shortly afterward. In July, 1929, young Marshal Chang seized the Chinese Eastern Railway, with the result that Soviet forces under General Blücher, formerly Borodin's colleague and military adviser at Canton, entered Manchuria and compelled the war lord to observe established treaties. This incident led to the final rupture of diplomatic relations between Moscow and Nanking.

The unstable balance of power among independent war lords, self-seeking provincial governors, and rival Kuomintang factions could not long be maintained. Mutinies, riots, and *coups d'état* brought the Nanking Government to the verge of destruction. Early in 1930 civil war broke out between Chiang and Feng and Yen Hsi-shan. By October, Chiang was again victorious, after tens of thousands of lives had been lost, much property destroyed, and the country reduced to bankruptcy. Chang Hsueh-liang cooperated with Chiang in crushing Feng and Yen, but was removed from the scene by the Japanese occupation of Manchuria in 1931. The Sino-Japanese hostilities which accompanied these events brought no unity to the country. Though Japanese trade was ruined by a nationwide boycott, the Chinese Government was helpless against Japanese military power. Chiang was more interested in keeping himself in power than in organizing the nation for resistance. Diplomatic relations with the Soviet Union were resumed, but the days of Soviet-Kuomintang collaboration had long since passed. Chiang's passivity in the face of new Japanese aggression generated a widespread demand among patriots, students, and intellectuals for war against Tokyo in the spring of 1936. Chiang's annual crusades against the Communists, whose local Soviets ruled some 50,000,000 people in scattered provinces, were costly and futile enterprises that precluded any possibility of national unity in the face of Japanese aggression. In 1934-35 the Red chieftains led the more fanatical of their followers on the incredible "long march" from Kiangsi to Shensi (see p. 529), where they established a new "capital" at Yenan.

When he visited Sianfu in Shensi, Chiang Kai-shek found himself "kidnaped" (Dec. 12-24, 1936) by followers of Chang Hsueh-liang, who released him only on condition that he cease his wars against Red China, work for an anti-Japanese "United Front," and cooperate with the Communists and the northern military leaders against Japan. When it appeared that genuine unity might develop on this basis, the Japanese Army leaders launched a new and murderous assault upon China in July, 1937. The resulting conflict dragged on through dark and bloody years and finally became part of World War II. The new aggression not only brought death to hundreds of thousands and left millions homeless but resulted in a new Kuomintang-Communist coalition, in the emergence of a People's Army, in the growth of cooperative industry and agriculture in the interior provinces, and in a genuine national regeneration of the Chinese masses. Despite the seizure of the coastal cities and the Yangtze Valley, the invaders were balked by peasant partisans and by the ill-clad and ill-armed divisions which Chiang's Government at Chungking was able to muster.

Subsequent revelations indicated that China at war was not quite what it seemed to be. On the face of things the Japanese invaders controlled Manchuria, the northern provinces, the coastal cities, and most of the Yangtze Valley under the puppet regime of Wang Ching-wei (d. Nov. 10, 1944), while the Kuomintang regime of Chiang Kai-shek at Chungking, allied with the Communist partisans of the north, offered staunch resistance in the rest of the land. In fact, matters were different. Most of the "Japanese-occupied" provinces were held by the Chinese Communists. In the south the shape of reality is suggested by family relationships among the holders of power. Sun Yat-sen and Chiang Kai-shek had married sisters, both daughters of "Charlie" Soong, Americanized Methodist, who begat three girls and three boys and made a fortune selling Bibles. The eldest daughter, Ai-ling Soong, married "Yaleman" H. H. Kung, who devoted himself to amassing riches. The second daughter, Ching-ling Soong, became the wife of Sun Yat-sen. The youngest daughter, Mei-ling Soong, wed Chiang Kai-shek in 1927. The first was devoted to wealth, the second to liberty, and the third to power. Chiang's first loyalty was to power and privilege, as was that of his brother-in-law, T. V. Soong, who was made Foreign Minister in December, 1941. The ambitions of the Kungs and Soongs symbolized the corruption and nepotism of the Kuomintang, which consisted for the most part of a venal bureaucracy of civil and military spoilsmen, interested only in "squeeze"—i.e., graft.

During the decade following 1937 the Chinese Communists, led by Chou En-lai and Mao Tse-tung, extended their authority from a few million peasants in the north to a population of 100,000,000 souls and their armed forces from 100,000 to 1,000,000 regular troops and 2,000,000 peasant partisans. This miracle was not a product of Soviet aid but was due almost entirely to the fact that in the eyes of the masses of Chinese peasants, workers, and even many businessmen the Communists, for all their sins, represented a hopeful alternative to the graft, despotism, and terrorism of the Kuomintang. The Communists' economic program was one not of Communism or even of socialism, save in the far future. It was, above all, one of dividing up large estates into individual peasant holdings, reducing rents, preventing exploitation, and assessing and collecting taxes honestly. It was also one of promoting mass literacy and education, fostering cooperatives, encouraging better methods of cultivation, and treating peasants as human beings. At no time did the Japanese invaders succeed in crushing the will or ability of the Communist forces to resist. But the enemy campaigns of 1942 isolated Chiang Kai-shek's China from America and Britain and raised the question as to how Chungking could be kept in the war at all, even in a formal sense.

CHINA: THE MANDATE OF HEAVEN

The American Intervention. Between 1942 and 1949 in China, as between 1917 and 1921 in Russia, the USA did what it could to aid an ally against a common enemy and to defeat the disciples of Communism and buttress the cause of law and order. Both efforts failed not for lack of trying nor by virtue of "treason" in high places, but through mistakes of judgment and miscalculations of the forces at work. Since most men are xenophobes and patriots, those who accept foreign aid in civil wars are more commonly defeated than victorious. Since all power is limited, the power of the greatest of Super-Powers is still inadequate to control human destinies among the multi-millioned masses dwelling in the vast expanses of Eurasia. The sequence of hard decisions and indecisions can here only be outlined, with the hot hatreds and bitter accusations bred of defeat left to the "verdict of history."

In February, 1942, the late Lt. Gen. Joseph W. Stilwell was dispatched to China and soon made Commander in Chief in the China-Burma-India theater and Chief of Staff of Chiang's armies. His task, in the face of wholly inadequate resources, was to save what could be saved and organize effective Chinese resistance to Japan. Burma was lost. "I claim," said "Vinegar Joe," "that we took a hell of a beating." The USA extended help to Chiang's Government at Chungking and, along with Britain, gave up extraterritoriality by the treaties of Jan. 11, 1943. Mme Chiang came to Washington in February, addressed Congress, and charmed all with eloquent talk of democracy, freedom, and justice. Stilwell in his efforts to train Chinese troops and retake Burma found Chiang uncooperative and his regime incompetent and corrupt. He urged "reforms" and came to despise the Generalissimo, whom he called "the Peanut." Chiang in turn pressed for Stilwell's removal. In the spring of 1944 Vice-President Wallace was sent to China to see what could be done to promote Communist-Nationalist collaboration in the war effort. In the presence of, and with the approval of, Owen Lattimore and John Carter Vincent, Wallace recommended to Roosevelt that Stilwell be replaced by Wedemeyer and that the Kuomintang regime be liberalized. On Oct. 19, 1944, Stilwell was recalled. Gen. Albert Wedemeyer soon established cordial relations with Chiang. Maj. Gen. Patrick Hurley, already Roosevelt's special agent in China, became Ambassador in January, 1945.

Hurley became the first architect of American postwar policy. His expert advisers, John Davies, John Stewart Service, *et al.*, warned that Russian ambitions were aggressive, that the Kuomintang was disintegrating, that the Communists would win any civil war, and that the USA should seek to promote a Communist-Nationalist compromise. Hurley in Moscow, in August, 1944, and again in April, 1945, was told by Molotov and Stalin that the Chinese Communists were not "real Communists" and that the USSR supported the American policy of promoting Chinese unity under Chiang Kai-shek. Kennan warned Harriman that Hurley was too optimistic about Soviet intentions. Hurley later asserted that the Chinese Communists were about the same as

533

"Oklahoma Republicans with guns." He participated in November, 1944, in inconclusive Communist-Nationalist negotiations for a coalition government. Hurley won Roosevelt's support for his view (opposed by his own advisers) that no United States military aid should be dispatched to the Chinese Communists.

The Yalta bargain was dictated, like all other U.S. moves at the time, by an overwhelming desire to promote the speedy defeat of Japan at minimum cost in American lives. Wedemeyer, MacArthur, Marshall, Eisenhower, and the Joint Chiefs of Staff were all insistent on the need of bringing Russia into the war against Japan. The result was the accord of Feb. 11 and the Sino-Soviet treaty of Aug. 14, 1945, which, while pledging Soviet support to the National Government, gave the Russians military control and political privileges in Manchuria which they used after the Japanese surrender to strip the area of industrial equipment and to enable the Chinese Communists to secure Japanese arms and supplies and establish their control of much of the territory. The U.S. sought to counter these results by airlifting half a million Nationalist troops to North China. Hurley resigned in high dudgeon on Nov. 26, 1945, accusing his advisers and "subversives" in the State Department of siding with "Communists" and "imperialists" in opposition to American interests in China.

General Marshall was named the next day as Presidential Special Envoy with instructions to prevent civil war by promoting a Communist-Nationalist coalition and thus fostering a unified and democratic China—under threat of withholding economic aid to the National Government if it refused to come to terms. Since this policy was to fail, millions of words were to be devoted to assessing blame, with a minimum of analysis of the alternatives actually available. Some—e.g., Walter Judd, Freda Utley, William C. Bullitt, and the amorphous group around Alfred Kohlberg which later came to be known as the "China Lobby"—urged all-out military aid to Chiang to crush the Chinese Communists and hinted at pro-Communism in high places in Washington as the cause of the debacle. Others, e.g., Senators McCarthy and Jenner, accused Marshall himself of treason. No neat formula fits all the facts or the fluctuating shadows-on-the-wall which often pass for facts. Far from "abandoning" Chiang Kai-shek, the USA granted him economic and military aid (largely used against the Communists or wasted in colossal graft) which amounted at official estimates to $2,254,000,000 between V-J Day and the end of 1949 and was worth thrice this amount or more in terms of replacement cost. Marshall's mission was initially successful, and finally failed because of irreconcilable conflict between Communists and Nationalists. The irreconcilability was due to innumerable factors other than U.S. policy. But America could not overcome it so long as Chiang, profoundly suspicious of his enemies and certain of continued U.S. support in the name of anti-Communism, was unwilling to meet the Communists halfway—and so long as the Communists, profoundly suspicious of Chiang and deeply resentful of U.S. aid to their foe, were equally unwilling to meet the Nationalists halfway.

Failure of a Mission. Marshall as "mediator" arranged a truce on Jan. 10, 1946. Complex formulas for constitutional government and a unified National Army moved him to optimism, tempered by the hope that the outcome would not be "soiled by a small group of irreconcilables who, for a selfish purpose, would defeat the Chinese people in their overwhelming desire for peace and prosperity." The truce broke down over the struggle for Manchuria. The Communists objected to a U.S. military mission to the Nationalists and began condemning Marshall as a "tool of American imperialism." With a 3-to-1 military superiority over the Communists, the Generalissimo, despite the warnings of Marshall and Ambassador J. Leighton Stuart, launched a military campaign to crush the Reds in North China. Truman publicly appealed to Chiang on Aug. 10, 1946, to offer "convincing proof" of "genuine progress" toward "peaceful settlement," and deplored the "selfish interests of extremist groups" and of "militarists and politicial reactionaries who are obstructing the advancement of the general good of the nation by failing to understand the liberal trend of the times. The people of the U.S. view with violent repugnance this state of affairs."

What ensued was due to Chiang's overconfidence, strengthened by U.S. military aid, in his ability to dispose of the Communists by force. Leaders of the Democratic League, the only liberal group in China, were assassinated in July, 1946, and the League suppressed in October, 1947. Meanwhile the USA in 1946–47 embargoed shipments of arms to China for almost a year, but during the same period transferred almost $1,000,000,000 of "surplus" military equipment in China and the Western Pacific to Chiang and concluded a treaty of friendship and commerce (Nov. 4, 1946). The problem of how to "mediate" successfully in a civil war while subsidizing and supplying one side and giving no aid to the other was never solved. American pleas for peace, and criticisms of corruption and reaction, fell on deaf ears so long as Chiang could rely on U.S. aid. Both the Democratic League and the Communists boycotted the "National Assembly" convoked in Nanking in mid-November, 1946, to draw up a "democratic" constitution. Chou En-lai broke off negotiations. Truman recalled Marshall Jan. 7, 1947, and made him Secretary of State. In his carefully balanced concluding statement, Marshall spoke of "overwhelming suspicion" between the contestants, the "devastating" obstructionism of "a dominant group of reactionaries" in the Kuomintang, and the "vicious propaganda" and destructive acts of the "dyed-in-the-wool Communists" whose suspicion that Chiang sought only to destroy them seemed justified by Chiang's conduct. He expressed hope for "leadership by the liberals . . . under the leadership of Chiang Kai-shek."

As the Kuomintang now waged all-out war on the Reds, UNRRA granted Chiang's China half a billion dollars in goods while other aid, civil and military, flowed from the USA, including 271 U.S. Navy vessels, guns, munitions, planes, and other war supplies. Some 6,000 U.S. troops remained in China to advise the National Government. Many Americans later convinced themselves that Chiang could have beaten the Communists had the USA doubled or tripled its aid or sent armies of its own to fight the foe. This hypothesis is beyond proof or disproof. What is beyond dispute is that the Kuomintang lost the war less because of lack of troops and arms than because its behavior completely alienated the intellectuals and the peasants of China. Thousands of Formosans were butchered by Chiang's soldiery in January, 1947, for resisting Kuomintang corruption and oppression. His police hunted down all liberals. His troops crushed all peasant appeals for agrarian reform. His spoilsmen and carpetbaggers made fortunes through exploitation, theft, inflation, speculation, and even the sale of American arms to the enemy. His fliers, in U.S. planes carrying U.S. bombs, rained death on helpless civilians. China's scholars, farmers, workers, and soldiers, faced with the choice of evils, chose that which seemed to them the lesser.

The Way of Mao. Washington meanwhile sent General Wedemeyer on a "fact-finding" mission in July, 1947. His report of Sept. 19 (kept secret until August of 1949) urged all-out resistance to Communism, praised the Kuomintang regime for its staunch anti-Communism although sharply condemning incompetence and graft, and urged a UN trusteeship over Manchuria. He recommended moral, material, and military support to Chiang on condition that the Generalissimo agree to UN action to restore peace in Manchuria and accept U.S. advisers to "assist China in utilizing U.S. aid in the manner for which it is intended." The Communists should be regarded as "tools of Soviet foreign policy." Washington policy-makers concurred and continued their support to Chiang, but they could evolve no formula for victory in alliance with an ally who, like the Bourbons, learned nothing, forgot nothing, and seemed bent on political suicide.

Government forces took Yenan, the Communist "capital," in March, 1947, and won other "victories" in Manchuria and Shantung. But by year's end most Kuomintang troops in Manchuria were surrounded in Hsingking and Mukden—which fell Oct. 5 and Nov. 1, 1948. Red forces retook Yenan in April, 1948, and reoccupied Shantung. By January, 1949, Gen. Li Tsung-jen, Acting President after another of Chiang's many "resignations," was seeking to make a deal with Moscow, secure increased U.S. aid, and resume negotiations with the Communists—who demanded, however, as the price of peace that Chiang and other top Kuomintang officials be arrested as "war criminals." The Kuomintang regime now collapsed as most of its supporters joined the enemy. The Government fled to Nanking in February. Red forces took Nanking on April 20 and Shanghai on May 25, 1949. The "People's Republic of China" was proclaimed at Peiping on Sept. 21, 1949. Canton fell Oct. 15. By December all was lost, with the remnants of the Kuomintang regime, again headed by Chiang, fleeing to Formosa where they enjoyed the blessing and, after June 27, 1950, the military protection of the USA against the conquerors of the mainland. In commenting on the disaster, Secretary Acheson declared:

> The unfortunate but inescapable fact is that the ominous result of the civil war in China was beyond the control of the Government of the United States. Nothing that this country did or could have done within the reasonable limits of its capabilities could have changed that result; nothing that was left undone by this country contributed to it. It was the product of internal Chinese forces which this country tried to influence but could not.[4]

The triumph of the "People's Liberation Army" delivered all of the ancient territories of the Celestial Empire (save Formosa and the "People's Republic of Outer Mongolia," long a Soviet protectorate) into the hands of a totalitarian party, committed to Marxism and looking to the Kremlin for guidance —though Moscow was as much surprised by the triumph as Washington was chagrined. The internal program of the new regime sought to solve the problem of 20th Century China by laying the basis for an industrial economy and providing a structure of power through which Red China could deal as a "Great Power" with other Powers. The means employed were so shocking to the West as to nourish the perennial American hope that eternal China must sooner or later repudiate its Red masters. As in the USSR, the ruling party, controlling a government which was in form a coalition of the Communists, the Democratic League, the "Revolutionary Committee of the Kuomintang," and lesser groups, consisted of some 6,000,000 members, with the Muscovite apparatus of a Party Congress, a Central Committee, and sundry "mass organizations." The Politburo included Mao Tse-tung, Chief of State; Liu Shao-chi, Secretary-General of the Party; Chou En-lai, Premier and Foreign Minister; Chu Teh, Commander in Chief of the armed forces; Chen Yun, Chairman of the Financial and Economic Commission; Kao Kang, Lin Piao, Kang Sheng, Chang Wen-tien, *et al.*, with Mme Sun Yat-sen playing an active role in the new government.

The goal, as expounded in Mao Tse-tung's "new democracy," was advance via socialism toward communism, to be prepared during the 1950's by a Chinese equivalent of Russia's "New Economic Policy" of 1921–29, involving partition of large farms among small peasants pending future collectivization; toleration of private business for profit pending future socialization; mass education; mass propaganda; and the beginnings of national economic planning and industrialization through the accumulation of capital by mass sacri-

[4] P. xvi of the 1054-page "White Paper" of August, 1949, "United States Relations with China, 1944–1949," *Department of State Publication* 3573, designed through elaborate documentation to justify the course of American policy. This volume must be the point of departure for all future research into this period, along with the voluminous *Hearings on the Military Situation in the Far East*, U.S. Senate, Committee on Armed Services and Committee on Foreign Relations, 82d Cong., 1st Sess., May and June, 1951.

fices. The means were political despotism; ideological intolerance; "brain-washing" and "thought control"; crusades against grafters and profiteers; forced labor for dissidents, suspects, and "class enemies"; and ferocious blood purges of "enemies of the people," involving the execution of scores of thousands in 1949–52.

The foreign policy of Red China was in most respects a simple expression of anti-Americanism, since the USA had armed the enemies of the new regime, refused to grant it recognition, repeatedly called for its overthrow, protected the Nationalist Government on Formosa, and granted new aid to Chiang with a view toward eventual liberation of the mainland. Peiping's response *ipso facto* involved close collaboration with the USSR and support of "anti-imperialist" (*i.e.*, anti-Western) Red rebels in Indochina, Malaya, and elsewhere. What role, if any, Peiping played in the Red aggression of North Korea against ROK in 1950 is unclear. But Peiping's resolve to prevent U.S. forces from reaching the Yalu was made abundantly clear long before the massive military intervention of Chinese "volunteers" in the Korean War. What was ominous was the ability of these forces to defeat and then "contain" Western troops, an experience unknown in Asia for the preceding century and foreshadowing the re-emergence of a China possessed of military might and political prestige commensurate with its size and population.

Marxist Middle Kingdom. China's Communist rulers, having achieved power by the support of the peasantry (contrary to all orthodox Marxist prescriptions), did not re-enact the Russian tragedy of the 1930's of "class war in the villages." Large landlords, to be sure, were expropriated, rural debts were canceled, and tenants were granted holdings, all initially in the name of ending ancient evils and equalizing ownership of land. When steps were later taken toward "collectivizing" agriculture through uniquely Chinese forms of cooperative farming, there was little persecution of well-to-do farmers and little coercion of the poor to join the cooperatives. By persuasion and example, most of China's half a billion peasants had joined cooperatives of one kind or another by the early 1950's because they perceived the advantages of collective endeavor. Honest collection of taxes (a novelty in China's history), plus widespread rural education in better methods of cultivation, replaced the exactions of the landlords who, while discriminated against tax-wise and deprived of former privileges, were not liquidated. The result was a steady rise in farm output, a fruitful liaison between the new State and the old peasantry, and a slow improvement in rural living standards.

As regards the urban economy—still minor in a predominately peasant population—the new rulers checked inflation, stabilized prices, balanced the State budget by 1951, and pushed the construction of new railways and roads. New problems occasioned by the costs of the Korean War and subsequent floods and poor harvests were surmounted by 1953–54. Massive industrialization, as elsewhere in Marxland, was the golden goal. The method, as in Russia, was public economic planning, financed by sundry devices of forced saving and investment to keep consumption below production. Private business was not outlawed as in the USSR, but in many ways encouraged. Yet by 1952 the State controlled 67% of all industrial production, including all railways, 80% of heavy industry, 60% of light industry, 90% of all banking, half of all wholesale, and a third of all retail, trade.

Athough accumulation of capital proceeded slowly among a people miserably poor, the Communist techniques of saving, planning, and investing proved effective in furthering industrialization with no foreign help save loans, technical aid, and imports of machinery from the USSR. The modest goals of a First Five Year Plan (1953–57) were enlarged in a Second (1958–62). Almost 12% of gross national product by 1955 was devoted to investment, almost half of it in industry. Peiping aimed, not unreasonably in view of the record, at annual outputs by 1957 of 113,000,000 tons of coal, 5,500,000 tons of steel, and 18 billion kilowatt hours of electrical power. Planned industrial production was to be doubled by 1962. The gravest problem was growth of population. China's more than 600,000,000 people were increasing at the rate of at least 12,000,000 a year in the late 1950's. To maintain, much less to increase, living standards, agricultural production must rise by 25% between 1952 and 1962. Peiping aimed at 35%. Western experts estimated a probable increase of 20%. The State pressed the masses to practice birth control and scientific agriculture. Despite formidable difficulties looming ahead, the record of Red China's economic achievements was impressive.[5]

The Marxist State which effected these results was in principle a complex and cumbersome coalition and in practice a set of devices whereby the leaders of the Communist Party carried out their decisions. The original arrangements of 1949 included a Chinese People's Political Consultative Conference, with a non-Communist majority; a Central People's Government Council, with Mao as Chairman; a State Administrative Council, with Chou En-lai as Premier; a People's Revolutionary Military Council, with Mao as Chairman and Chu Teh as Vice Chairman; etc. The new Constitution of Sept. 1, 1954, as adopted by the first National People's Congress, made this body the "highest organ of State power." But it bore little resemblance to Western parliaments or even to the Supreme Soviet of the USSR. Its 1,226 members were indirectly elected by provincial congresses. On paper it controlled the Chairman of the Chinese People's Republic (Mao), the Vice Chairman (Chu Teh, 1954f.), and the State Council in which Chou En-lai remained Premier and Foreign Minister. A new "State Supreme Conference," composed of leaders of these and other agencies, may "advise" other governmental organs on pol-

[5] For some of the foregoing and following data I am indebted to my colleague, Dr. Fred Greene, for his admirable text, *The Far East* (New York, Rinehart, 1957) and for much enlightenment in other ways regarding contemporary economics and politics in the Orient.

icy. Local government is organized in provinces, regions, districts (*chou*), counties, and municipalities, with each unit ruled by a People's Council and a People's Congress indirectly elected by deputies at the next lower level, as was the pattern in the USSR, 1917–36.

Real power rests with the leadership of the Communist Party, which had 12,000,000 members by 1957. As in Russia, the Party structure culminates in a Congress which chooses a Central Committee which chooses a Politburo and a Central Secretariat. Authority in fact flows from the top down, not from the bottom up. Mao from the outset was chairman of Congress, Politburo, and Secretariat. Local units, down to each village, city block, and factory, carry out party policy throughout the nation. By means of vast popular organizations the Party has striven to indoctrinate and educate the masses— aided by a secret police, early mass trials and executions of "subversives," and constant campaigns against grafters and corrupt bureaucrats, "cheating" among private businessmen, and "deviations from socialism" among Party leaders. These procedures for inducing obedience and conformity, while involving in the early years the liquidation of hundreds of thousands and possibly millions of alleged "enemies" of the new police-state, have relied more in recent years on criticism, self-criticism, confessions, repentance, and "brain-washing."

The new China collaborated closely with Moscow, but emerged as a "Great Power" with aspirations of its own. Sino-Soviet solidarity was less a result of identity of interests and views than of common fear and hatred of the USA, whose policy-makers, bewitched by illusions and trapped by a misinformed public opinion, were incapable of exploiting potential Chinese-Russian cleavages. Mao and Chou, in the name of "unity," negotiated an end of Soviet privileges in China and obtained substantial Soviet aid for industrialization. Moscow yielded to Peiping, Dec. 31, 1953, its partnership and property rights in the Manchurian railways. Following further negotiations, it was agreed, Oct. 11, 1954, that the USSR would grant credits and machinery to the value of almost a billion rubles; yield to China all Soviet shares in "mixed companies"; promote cooperation in railway construction and scientific and technical activities; and evacuate Port Arthur by Jan. 1, 1955.

Mao and Chou thus restored full Chinese sovereignty over Manchuria. They also secured effective control over Sinkiang and in 1951 occupied Tibet, which had long enjoyed autonomy and where Britain had transferred its "protectorate" to India in 1947. New Delhi finally conceded Peiping's sovereignty over Tibet in April, 1954, and agreed to withdraw its garrisons in exchange for trading rights. Elsewhere on the periphery of the new China, the power-holders in Peiping were long obliged by American might to forego the "liberation" of Formosa, but were able to fight the USA to a standstill in Korea and to make both North Korea and North Vietnam, in effect, Chinese protectorates. In the late 1950's Chinese prestige was high throughout neutralist

SUGGESTED READINGS

Asia and Africa. Red China would continue its efforts to extend its influence and to discredit the USA, though not by acts which could provoke open warfare unless Washington should seriously embark on the "liberation" of the mainland or endeavor, as in 1950 in Korea, to send troops to China's frontiers. Whether other areas of Asia would "go Communist" or remain "neutral" or join the American coalition seemed likely to depend in the end on the capacity of other Asians, with U.S. aid, to equal or surpass Peiping's accomplishments in lifting the poor to some hope of plenty.

SUGGESTED READINGS

Adler, Solomon: *The Chinese Economy*, New York, Monthly Review, 1957.

Belden, Jack: *China Shakes the World*, New York, Harper, 1949.

Chen, Stephen, and Robert Payne: *Sun Yat-Sen: A Portrait*, New York, John Day, 1946.

Cressey, George B.: *Asia's Lands and Peoples* (2d ed.), New York, McGraw-Hill, 1951.

———: *Land of the 500 Million: A Geography of China*, New York, McGraw-Hill, 1955.

Fairbank, John King: *The United States and China*, Cambridge, Mass., Harvard University Press, 1948.

Feis, Herbert: *The China Tangle*, Princeton, N.J., Princeton University Press, 1953.

Hahn, Emily: *Chiang Kai-shek: An Unauthorized Biography*, New York, Doubleday, 1955.

Hunter, Edward: *Brain-Washing in Red China: The Calculated Destruction of Men's Minds*, New York, Vanguard, 1952.

Hutheesing, Raja: *The Great Peace*, New York, Harper, 1953.

Isaacs, Harold R.: *Tragedy of the Chinese Revolution*, Stanford, Calif., Stanford University Press, 1952.

Kai-shek, Chiang: *Soviet Russia in China: A Summing-up at Seventy*, New York, Farrar, Straus, 1957.

Keeton, George W.: *China, The Far East and the Future*, London, Stevens, 1949.

Lattimore, Owen: *Inner Asian Frontiers of China*, New York, American Geographical Society, 1940.

Li Chien-nung: *The Political History of China, 1840–1928*, Princeton, N.J., Van Nostrand, 1956.

Linebarger, Paul M. A.: *The China of Chiang K'Ai Shek*, Boston, World Peace Foundation, 1942.

———, Djang Chu, and Ardath W. Burks; Franklin L. Burdette (gen. ed.): *Far Eastern Governments and Politics: China and Japan*, Princeton, N.J., Van Nostrand, 1956.

Liu, F. F.: *A Military History of Modern China: 1924–1949*, Princeton, N.J., Princeton University Press, 1956.

Payne, Robert: *Mao Tse-tung: Ruler of Red China*, New York, Schuman, 1950.

Rostow, W. W., and Others: *The Prospects for Communist China*, New York, Wiley, 1954.

Rowe, David Nelson: *China among the Powers*, New York, Harcourt, Brace, 1945.

Schwartz, Benjamin I.: *Chinese Communism and the Rise of Mao*, Cambridge, Mass., Harvard University Press, 1955.

Snow, Edgar: *Red Star over China*, New York, Random House, 1938.

Stuart, John Leighton: *Fifty Years in China*, New York, Random House, 1954.

Tse-tung, Mao: *Selected Works*, New York, International Publishers, 1954.

Utley, Freda: *The China Story*, Chicago, Regnery, 1951.

Vinacke, Harold M.: *The United States and the Far East, 1945–1951*, Stanford, Calif., Stanford University Press, 1952.

Wales, Nym: *Red Dust: Autobiographies of Chinese Communists*, Stanford, Calif., Stanford University Press, 1951.

Walker, Richard L.: *China under Communism: The First Five Years*, New Haven, Conn., Yale University Press, 1955.

THE CHALLENGE OF COMMUNISM

White, Theodore H., and Annalee Jacoby: *Thunder out of China*, New York, Sloane, 1946.
Wilbur, C. Martin, and Julie Lien-ying How: *Documents on Communism, Nationalism, and Soviet Advisers in China*, 1918–1927, New York, Columbia University Press, 1956.
Winfield, Gerald F.: *China: The Land and the People*, New York, Sloane, 1948.
Wittfogel, Karl A.: *Oriental Despotism: A Comparative Study of Total Power*, New Haven, Conn., Yale University Press, 1957.
Wu, Aitchen K.: *China and the Soviet Union*, New York, John Day, 1950.
Wu, Yuan-li: *An Economic Survey of Communist China*, New York, Bookman Associates, 1956.

3. THE DIPLOMACY OF COEXISTENCE

We are living not merely in a State, but in a *system of States;* and it is inconceivable that the Soviet republic should continue to exist for a long period side by side with imperialist States. Ultimately one or the other must conquer. Until this end occurs a number of terrible clashes between the Soviet Republics and bourgeois States is inevitable.—LENIN, *Sochineniya*, XXIV, 122, March, 1919.

If our capitalistic partners abstain from counter-revolutionary activities in Russia, the Soviet Government will abstain from carrying on revolutionary activities in capitalist countries; but we shall determine if they are carrying on counter-revolutionary agitation. There was a time when a feudal State existed alongside capitalist States. In those days liberal England did not fight continuously against serf-owning Russia. We think that now capitalist countries can exist alongside a proletarian State. We consider that the interests of both parties lie in concluding peace and the establishment of the exchange of goods, and we are therefore ready to conclude peace with every country which up to the present has fought against us, but in future is prepared to give us in exchange for our raw materials and grain, locomotives and machinery. The guarantees which our enemies are demanding from us lie in the interests of both parties.—KARL RADEK, *Wireless News*, Moscow, March 3, 1920.

Peace *per se* is never the objective of foreign policy in the traditional pre-atomic pattern of the Western State System. The goal of policy is national power—to be preserved against threats, to be maintained against contingencies, and to be enlarged and extended when opportunities present themselves for so doing without unreasonable risk. By the time of Stalin's demise, and indeed before, the policy-makers of Red Russia and Red China had come to the conclusion that the risks of continuing the Cold War were no longer reasonable. In the interest of preserving, maintaining, and if possible, extending their power, they therefore sought "peace."

So long as Stalin lived, the quest was pursued, both in Moscow and Peiping, primarily through elaborate propaganda campaigns and sundry world-wide "front organizations" designed to embarrass and put pressure upon the Western Powers and the "American imperialists"—with results largely self-defeating. With Stalin dead, his successors had recourse, more realistically, to the time-tried methods of diplomacy, here utilized in the name of "peaceful coexistence" to effect a *modus vivendi* with the Atlantic coalition. The Muscovite attempt, albeit dramatic, was, as we shall see, only partially successful. Its less impressive Chinese counterpart need not here concern us.

While incessantly ridiculing and reviling the prevailing American conception that effective diplomacy must be conducted from "positions of strength," the policy-makers of Moscow and Peiping conducted their "diplomatic offensive" at all times on precisely the same premise. In the ancient game of power, "strength" is equated with armaments and alliances. The Communist power-holders, like their foes, thus strove to build formidable military forces and impressive coalitions to overawe their antagonists and persuade the "neutrals" of their might.

The two giant units of this imperium, in a 30-year treaty of friendship, alliance, and mutual aid signed by Chou En-lai and Vishinsky in Moscow, Feb. 14, 1950, pledged the parties to immediate military support of one another in the event of renewed aggression by Japan or "any other State which, directly or indirectly, would unite with Japan in acts of aggression." In supplementary accords, Moscow assumed obligations of extending 10-year credits to China, sixty million dollars annually for 5 years at 1% interest, for the purchase of Soviet machinery and railway equipment; restoring to China all Manchurian properties acquired from Japanese owners; and returning Port Arthur, Darien, and the Manchurian Changchun Railway to Chinese control not later than the end of 1952. In the course of Chou's visit to Moscow in the summer of 1952, it was announced (Sept. 16) that the Changchun Railway would forthwith be returned to China, but that Port Arthur, at Peiping's request, would remain a Soviet base, pending a Japanese peace treaty with China and Russia. As we have seen, the base was yielded to China early in 1955.

The European satellites of Red Muscovy enjoyed fictitious "sovereignty" and were bound to one another and to the USSR by treaties which in every case provided, as in the typical article of the Bulgarian-Soviet pact of March 18, 1948:

In the event that one of the High Contracting Parties shall become involved in military operations against Germany, attempting to revive its aggressive policy, or with any other State whatsoever which may directly or in any other manner whatsoever join Germany in its policy of aggression, then the other High Contracting Party will give promptly to the Contracting Party involved in military operations all military and other assistance with all the means at its disposal.

But actual power was exercised through local control of cabinets and "parliaments" by national Communist Parties, with these in turn rigidly controlled from the Kremlin. Those addicted to independence, even when faithful servants of the cause over many years, were ruthlessly demoted, jailed, or shot as deviationists or "traitors"—e.g., Nikola Petkov in Bulgaria, Lazlo Rajk in Hungary, Rudolf Slansky in Czechoslovakia, Ana Pauker in Rumania, and scores of other dissident leaders, along with scores of thousands of humble men and women suspected of disloyalty to the vision of a new heaven and a new earth or, more simply, of resistance to tyranny.

Such devices as the Cominform and the "Comecon" (aimed at economic coordination among Communist States) were supplemented by a larger scheme of alliance. On May 14, 1955, Bulganin and Molotov, meeting in Warsaw with envoys of Poland, Czechoslovakia, Hungary, Rumania, Bulgaria, Albania, and East Germany, signed an 8-power, 11-article, 20-year Treaty of Friendship, Cooperation, and Mutual Aid, designed as a counterpart of NATO, with Marshal Ivan S. Konev as Chief of a Common Command. This "Warsaw Pact" created at least an appearance of strength, on the basis of which the Muscovites felt free to embark on an ambitious program of winning friends and influencing people.

The campaign got under way slowly and gathered momentum as it continued. In the summer of 1953 Moscow resumed diplomatic relations with Jugoslavia, Greece, and Israel and assured Turkey that it had abandoned its claims for the retrocession of Kars, Ardahan, and Artvin and for participation in defense of the Straits. The armistice in Korea (see pp. 245f.) was unquestionably a result of new directives from Moscow and Peiping. Malenkov appealed for peace and friendship with the USA on New Year's Day of 1954 and, on March 31, conceded that an atomic war would not merely destroy "capitalism" but "world civilization." Meanwhile, for the first time in five years, the Council of Foreign Ministers (sans China) reassembled in Berlin on Jan. 25, 1954, and on Feb. 18 agreed to call a conference in Geneva to deal with Korea and Indochina. The Geneva Conference (see pp. 200f.) of April 26–July 21, 1954, put an end to hot warfare in southeastern Asia through armistice accords and the grant of independence to Laos, Cambodia, and a partitioned Vietnam.

Moscow's proposal of March 31, 1954, for ending the Cold War through a new European security scheme and Soviet membership in NATO was rejected by Washington on May 7. Sundry other Muscovite overtures were rebuffed. On May 7, 1955, the Presidium of the Supreme Soviet abrogated the alliance treaties of 1942 and 1944 with Britain and France (see pp. 581 and 567), holding that Anglo-French approval of German rearmament had rendered them meaningless. But on May 15, 1955, in Vienna—thanks to an abrupt reversal of previous Soviet policies—Molotov, Dulles, Pinay, Macmillan, and Figl signed a treaty of 38 articles recognizing Austria as a "sovereign, independent and democratic state" and putting an end to the military occupation on the basis of a pledge of Austrian neutrality (see pp. 200–201).

The ensuing "Summit Conference" at Geneva, July 18–23, 1955, of Eisenhower, Bulganin, Faure, and Eden was animated by the spirit of two comments on its eve—by Bulganin: "Even a bad peace is better than a good quarrel," and by Eisenhower: "The free people of the world hate war and want peace." Amid much cordiality and many constructive proposals, no concrete accords emerged, thanks to the maintenance of irreconcilable positions on the terms of disarmament and German unification. The subsequent meeting of the four foreign ministers in Geneva (Oct. 27–Nov. 16, 1955) ended in a deadlock of wasted opportunities for negotiating accords regarding the Mid East and Eastern Europe—which, if negotiated, might have averted the tragedies of 1956.

Having failed to achieve any solid results in their campaign for "coexistence" beyond the Austrian Treaty and the "Spirit of Geneva," Soviet policy-makers reverted to bilateral bargains and spectacular journeys of "friendship." Khrushchev and Bulganin welcomed Nehru in June and Ho Chi Minh in July, 1955; visited East Germany in late July; received Adenauer and Brentano in Moscow in early September, followed forthwith by Grotewohl; welcomed in late September the leaders of Finland, to which the Porkkala Naval Base was restored in exchange for a 20-year renewal of the mutual defense pact of 1948; played hosts in October to the Foreign Minister of Canada and the Premiers of Norway and Burma; and, between Nov. 17 and Dec. 22, 1955, made a triumphal tour of India, Burma, and Afghanistan, bespeaking peace and friendship and negotiating loans and exchanges of goods.

Prospects darkened during 1956. Malenkov visited Britain in late March and April and was followed by Khrushchev and Bulganin (April 18–27). Their reception was chilly, the more so as Gen. Ivan A. Serov of the MVD had arrived in London in an alarming new Soviet jet transport, the TU-104, to discuss security arrangements with Scotland Yard and had been denounced in the British press as a "thug," a "jackal," and a "Himmler." Again no concrete accords emerged. Mikoyan visited India in March. Mollet and Pineau were welcomed in Moscow, May 15–19. As the Shah of Iran toured the USSR, Shepilov went to Cairo and Athens in June while Ekaterina Furtseva visited Britain in July and Italy in November. In September, as Mikoyan went to Peiping, Sukarno came to Moscow and returned with a $100,000,000 Soviet loan to Indonesia. President Kuwatly of Syria followed in November and went home with pledges of Soviet arms and aid. But these comings and goings had few tangible consequences in the way of contributions toward an East-West settlement—apart from the "Peace Declaration" with Japan of Oct. 19, 1956 (see p. 454 above), whereby Moscow resumed diplomatic and commercial relations with Tokyo, reaffirmed its retention of Southern Sakhalin and the Kurils, and promised to restore to Japan the small islands of Shikotan and Habomoi when a formal peace treaty should be concluded.

With the keen vision of hindsight, it is easy to see that all the Powers, and above all the USSR and the USA, should have striven more seriously in 1955 for a Concert of Powers as a means of avoiding the violence to come on the Danube and the Nile (see pp. 397–431). Both coalitions were gravely weakened by these failures of statesmanship. Prospects of accommodation between them were diminished. Western good will toward the USSR, laboriously cul-

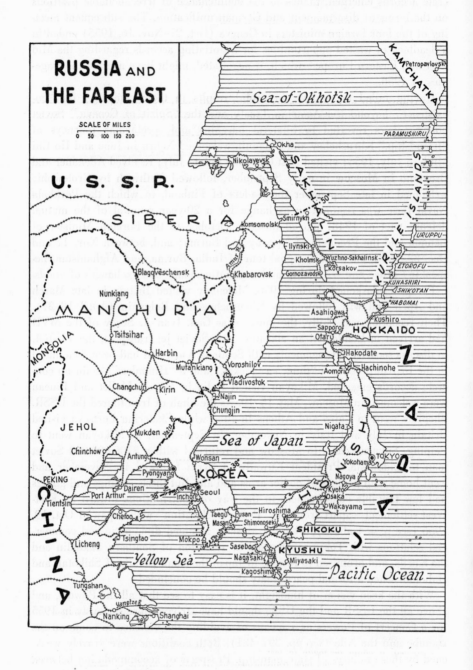

RUSSIA AND THE FAR EAST

SCALE OF MILES
0 50 100 150 200

tivated during the preceding three years, was dissipated by brutal Soviet suppression of the Hungarian Revolution and by Soviet support of Egypt, Syria, and Yemen against the West.

Yet the imperatives of each persisting pattern of power in world politics can seldom be successfully resisted or defied by any of the participants. In the late 1950's it was obvious to all that neither the USA nor the USSR could conceivably win any meaningful "victory" through war against one another, and that the Communist bloc and the Atlantic coalition were mutually checkmated through the efforts of each to gain superiority of power over the other. When force is futile or suicidal as a means of solving problems of power, no alternative is available save bargaining. Therefore the years to come will see new efforts by Communist and Western diplomats alike to achieve, somehow, an accommodation as the only ultimate alternative to co-annihilation. Such efforts will be only moderately successful. They will assuredly not end the competition between Marxland and Freeland for control of the minds of men. But such competition, if not pursued by violence, may prove creative, rather than destructive, for the hopes of most of mankind during the balance of the 20th Century.

SUGGESTED READINGS

Arnold, G. L.: *The Pattern of World Conflict*, New York, Dial, 1955.
Feis, Herbert: *Churchill-Roosevelt-Stalin: The War They Waged and the Peace They Sought*, Princeton, N.J., Princeton University Press, 1957.
Fischer, Louis: *This Is Our World*, New York, Harper, 1956.
Gaitskell, Hugh: *The Challenge of Coexistence*, Cambridge, Mass., Harvard University Press, 1957.
Ingram, Kenneth: *The History of the Cold War*, New York, Philosophical Library, 1955.
Jackson, J. Hampden: *The World in the Postwar Decade: 1945–1955*, Boston, Houghton Mifflin, 1956.
McNeill, William Hardy: *Survey of International Affairs*, 1939–1946. *America, Britain, and Russia: Their Cooperation and Conflict*, 1941–1946, New York, Oxford, 1953.
Posnack, Emanuel R.: *World without Barriers*, New York, Morrow, 1956.
Shepherd, Gordon: *The Austrian Odyssey*, New York, St. Martin's, 1957.
Smith, Howard K.: *The State of Europe*, New York, Knopf, 1949.
Toynbee, Arnold, and Veronica M. Toynbee (eds.): *The Realignment of Europe*, New York, Oxford, 1955.
Wilmot, Chester: *The Struggle for Europe*, New York, Harper, 1952.

4. DISUNITY IN MARXLAND

Panslavism is a movement which endeavors to undo what a thousand year old history has created. It cannot achieve its aim without sweeping Turkey, Hungary, and half of Germany off the map of Europe. Should this result ever be accomplished, it could be made to last by no other means than the subjugation of Europe. Panslavism has now transformed itself from an article of faith into a political program. By now, it is no longer only Russia, but the whole Panslavistic plot which threatens to found its realm on the ruins of Europe. This leaves Europe only one alternative—subjugation through slavery or the lasting destruction of the center of its offensive strength.—KARL MARX, *Neu Oderzeitung*, April, 1855.

We wanted freedom and not a good comfortable life. Even though we might lack bread and other necessities of life, we wanted freedom. We, the young people, were particularly hampered because we were brought up amidst lies. We continually had to lie. We could not have a healthy idea, because everything was choked in us. We wanted freedom of thought. . . . —An 18-year-old girl student and Hungarian rebel of 1956, to the UN Special Committee on the Problem of Hungary, 1957.

The totalitarians of the 20th Century, both Fascist and Communist, are addicted to interpreting the course of human destinies in terms of conspiracies, with the former fond of "Jewish plots," "Masonic plots," "capitalist plots," and "Marxist plots," and the latter fond of "Fascist plots," "capitalist plots," "Wall Street plots," and "imperialist plots." This habit is due to the circumstance that Fascists and Communists are both conspirators and plotters, attributing to others their own techniques by way of justifying to themselves their methods of acquiring and retaining power. Those who believe in and practice the democratic way of life, while taking due precautions against actual plotters, Left or Right, in their midst, will hesitate, if they are wise, to attribute mass movements in major communities to the machinations of conspirators, even when the conspiracy is a reality and revolutionary leaders are without doubt conspirators. Such hesitation is justified by the consideration that in all the processes of politics men do not command from other men that measure of support or devotion sufficient to bring them to power and keep them in power, by whatever conspiratorial or despotic means they may use, unless they have hit upon some semblance or pretense of fulfilling human needs and satisfying, if only symbolically, human aspirations.

Foolish men are often dupes of knaves, for knavery and folly are widely distributed among all men everywhere. But the "conspiracy theory of history" assumes that all men or most men are knaves or fools, a postulate easily shown to be false by elementary observation. Most people always, and all people often, are moved to behave as they do in politics by some definition, however mistaken, of their interests and by some foiled yearning, however fatuous or mad, for the good life in the good society. They give allegiance to those they suppose will serve their interests or bring to life their dreams. That both hopes are commonly betrayed, more often by unforeseen vicissitudes than by deliberate deception, need not move us to cynicism nor yet blind us to the fact that even the worst of men, including Fascists and Communists, usually strive to live by their hopes, not by their greeds and fears and hates.

The Communist world conspiracy is a fact, not a myth. All men have been duly warned, ever since 1848. But this conspiracy cannot be comprehended in the scope of its triumphs to date, and therefore cannot be effectively opposed, on any simple assumption that scoundrels have won knaves to their cause and bewitched fools to their own enslavement or destruction in some wild phantasmagoria of mass madness. It is true that collective paranoia, though ill understood as yet, plays a political role in maladjusted societies in fostering the rise and spread of Communism and Fascism and even in engendering the occasional demagoguery of democratic politics. But great mass movements never become "mass" or "great," unless they cause millions of unhappy men and women, perhaps perversely twisted by despair, to feel that here somehow is a road to happiness, whatever sacrifices it may demand, and a formula for human salvation.

The Red Conspiracy of our time flows from the conversion of befuddled multitudes to a secular faith founded by the words and acts of four men. One, almost 100 years ago, pored bleary-eyed over books in the British Museum. Another ran a factory in Manchester and enjoyed wine, women, and song. The third, a half-century past, lived miserably in Switzerland, scribbled articles, and presently found himself leader of a revolution. The fourth organized bank robberies and moved in and out of sundry jails. Marx, Engels, Lenin, and Stalin founded a creed whose disciples in mid-20th Century ruled 14,000,000 square miles of earth, from the Elbe to the China Sea, inhabited by almost 800,000,000 people, comprising one-third of the human species— with other millions *in partibus infidelium* slavishly following the guidance of the high priests and giving their prime loyalty not to their own countries but to the so-called "Workers' Fatherland" of the USSR.

This new image of a Universal State, to be achieved by world-wide "proletarian revolution" and to eventuate in a World Soviet Republic in which Communists will rule the globe, has enjoyed widespread support among much of humankind in our time. Many have seen in its contours a glorious vision of the oneness of mankind, at long last united in brotherhood and dedicated to "social justice." Such visions in practice usually prove fatuous, even when noble in purpose and pure in inspiration. The Marxist vision, as applied by its disciples in Russia and China, begot totalitarian tyranny, monstrous oppression and persecution, and a negation of all the human values which moved Marx and the original Marxists. Yet the faithful, in desperate need of faith, remained faithful, for lack of any other faith, to a cause which in most respects had betrayed the faith of its followers.

Our present concern is with the elements of unity and strength in a new Red Empire and with the sources and course of cleavages and schisms between its parts and among its Communist supporters beyond its frontiers. As regards the origin of the Empire, it is well, in the interests of truth, to dispose at the outset of a widely accepted American myth (shared by Chiang Kai-shek) which holds that China, as well as Eastern Europe, was "Communized" through the wily machinations of the men of Moscow who allegedly consum-

549

mated a "Russian Conquest" of much of Eurasia by force and fraud. This facile formula has the advantages of simplicity and of the capacity to frighten out of their wits all those who accept it as they contemplate, appalled, the diabolical might of the Muscovite anti-Christ. It has the disadvantage of bearing no resemblance to the facts.

Stalin told Mao in 1945 that the Chinese Revolution "has no prospect," and that the Chinese Communists should dissolve their army, cooperate with the Kuomintang, and support Chiang Kai-shek. Stalin later conceded that he had been "mistaken," but as late as 1948 was advising Mao to limit his campaigns to guerrilla warfare and avoid any attempt to take China's major cities. Mao and his colleagues smiled politely and did what they thought best. Thanks to American policies based in part on delusions, Red China and the USSR became firm allies. But the power-holders in Peiping are not, and never were, stooges of the Kremlin nor is their regime in any sense a Soviet satellite. On the contrary, as noted in previous pages, Stalin and his successors found it expedient and necessary, whatever their reluctance, to abandon to Peiping all of their rights and privileges in Manchuria, including Port Arthur and Dairen, and, far from exploiting China to Soviet advantage, to extend loans and material and technical aid to their new ally at appreciable sacrifice to the Soviet economy.

As for Eastern Europe, the portrait of a monstrous Muscovite colossus coercing and exploiting the hapless victims of Soviet imperialism bears somewhat more resemblance to reality. But even here the sequence of events was not quite what many Westerners supposed. In 1944–46 the men of Moscow envisaged the extension of their power to the Elbe and the Adriatic in terms of semi-democratic, "bourgeois" coalition regimes in the new marchlands. This relatively tolerant conception was abandoned only when Bevin, Byrnes, Churchill, and Truman made clear their resolve to challenge the whole Soviet position in Eastern Europe, to roll back the "Iron Curtain," if possible, to the old frontiers, and to embark on the economic rehabilitation and military rearmament of Western Europe against the Red Menace. Moscow's response to the Truman Doctrine and the Marshall Plan was to organize the Cominform (September, 1947) and to proceed in the marchlands to exile or liquidate all non-Communist leaders, to crush or coordinate their followers, and to impose 100% Communist regimes—with the process culminating in the Czechoslovak coup of February, 1948. After Tito was "excommunicated" by the Cominform in June, 1948, for daring to insist on national autonomy, all the satellite regimes, under Stalin's savage guidance, embarked upon a wholesale blood purge of suspected "Titoists," "Trotskyites," and "imperialist agents"—almost all of whom were later acknowledged to have been victims of frame-ups and to have been guilty of nothing more than a desire for national self-determination. Again Czechoslovakia was last in the procession. In December, 1952, only three months before Stalin's death, Rudolf Slansky, ex-Secretary General of the C.P., Vladimir Clementis, ex-Foreign Minister, and sundry "confederates" were hanged in Prague.[6]

With Stalin's decease and the determination of Khrushchev to put an end to his policies of terrorism at home and abroad, the monstrously monolithic Marxland he had fashioned began to come apart at the seams. Such dramatic events as the East German riots of June, 1953, the Poznan riots of June, 1956, the Polish crisis, and the Hungarian Revolution (see pp. 412–420) were surface manifestations of a vast ferment throughout the satellites and among all Communists everywhere. The tale of "de-Stalinization" is too long and confused to admit of brief review. But we may note the major consequences throughout Marxland of repeated denunciations of the "cult of personality" at Party Congress XX and Khrushchev's concluding address on Stalin's crimes, first published by the U.S. State Department on June 4, 1956.

In Italy, Togliatti opined that Russia's new rulers had participated in crime and were ignoring "the real problem—how and why Soviet society could and did depart from the self-chosen path of democracy and legality to the point of degeneration." Nenni gave up his Stalin Peace Prize, sought to negotiate a reunion with Italy's Right Socialists, and declared that "The social crisis concerns not only the so-called errors of Stalin, but the Soviet system." In America's microscopic Communist movement, Howard Fast (who later broke with the cause) asserted that the Khrushchev speech "itemizes a record of barbarism and paranoid blood-lust that will be a lasting and shameful memory to civilized man" and avowed that he would never again condone intolerance and injustice in the name of socialism. Eugene Dennis (reprinted in *Pravda*, June 27, 1956) added his *mea culpa*, while *The Daily Worker* condemned the CPSU for not releasing and publicizing the speech. In Paris *L'Humanité*, organ of the French Communist Party, said the same and denounced Khrushchev on other grounds.

In Poland anti-Stalinism and "National Communism" swept the Party, whose Secretary, Wladyslaw Gomulka (arrested as a "Titoist" in 1951) was freed, restored to his post, and enabled by mass support to effect a peaceful revolution in Polish relations with the USSR. Hungary's tragedy enhanced, rather than reduced, demands among Communists elsewhere for a new departure. Tito, the original symbol of "National Communism" and now courted by Moscow, judged the first Soviet military intervention in Hungary to have been a mistake and the second a painful necessity. He espoused the now prevailing "polycentrist" view among non-Russian Communists that each Marxist State should be free to seek its own "way to Socialism" in its own fashion

---

[6] For details of these procedures, see references at end of section and pp. 347–410 of *Russia Since 1917* (Knopf, 1957). For some of what follows, I am much indebted to my former student, Stuart Auerbach, of the Williams College Class of 1957 and currently on the staff of the *Berkshire Eagle* of Pittsfield, Mass., for a brilliant study, unhappily unpublished, of "The Twentieth Party Congress and Anti-Stalinism."

without dictation from, or slavish imitation of, the USSR. The new Muscovite oligarchs quibbled and quarreled but in general concurred as they strove, by trial and error, for a new, more viable, and non-Stalinist pattern of relations between Mother Russia and her unhappy adopted children in Eastern Europe. Gomulka, on a state visit to Belgrade in mid-September, 1957, announced agreement with Tito on cordial cooperation among all the States of Marxland on the basis of autonomy and national independence, and joint support of the major goals of Soviet foreign policy.

Peiping's role in these matters was ambiguous, but portentous of things to come. Red China's leaders, while assiduously winning friends and influencing people by numerous good-will journeys to other Asian States, alternately criticized and praised "Titoism," condemned the Hungarian Revolution as a "crazy subversive movement" (Chou En-lai in Warsaw, Jan. 12, 1957), and championed "equality" among all Communist States—all of whose differences should be adjusted in friendly conferences, since all had a common aim. In a major address on "the correct solution of contradictions" in late February, 1957, to the State Supreme Conference in Peiping, Mao criticized Soviet conduct in Hungary and contended that all conflicts within the Red Empire should be resolved by "patient persuasion and re-education" and not by "crude administrative methods." Stalin's "rule by terror" was condemned. Even strikes and demonstrations should be tolerated, for they reveal "mistakes." Bad things can be turned into good things. Enemies must be opposed but critics among the people should be heeded and conciliated. Distinctions must be made between fragrant flowers and poisonous weeds. But wisdom and justice are best served by freedom of discussion, not by the forcible imposition of any orthodoxy. "Let a hundred flowers blossom and a hundred schools of thought contend." (See full text in *The New York Times*, June 19, 1957.)

This appeal for "liberalism" in the governance of Marxland was warmly welcomed in Poland, which Mao visited in October, 1957, after traversing the USSR and conferring with Soviet leaders in Moscow. In China, meanwhile, the flood of criticism released by Mao's new line soon exceeded the limits deemed permissible by the Party oligarchs, who replied with a new campaign of condemnation against "Rightists." In Warsaw Mao nonetheless reiterated his plea for tolerance, with ultimate results not immediately apparent but obviously calculated to discourage any Muscovite efforts to reimpose totalitarian controls on the satellites.

The Khrushchev regime, despite ambivalences, had no such intent. Within the unhelpful and confusing confines of the Marxist dialectic, it continued to struggle toward a more hopeful design for power in dealing with the marchlands. The problem was as difficult as the related task of striving to "democratize" the Soviet State after decades of Stalinist autocracy. Western hopes that it would prove insoluble and that the whole edifice of the Red Empire

SUGGESTED READINGS

would disintegrate and collapse into chaos seemed, in the late 1950's, unwarranted by past achievements and future prospects. The new, tough, and
flexible managerial elite of the USSR had, by hard experience, acquired skills
in solving seemingly impossible problems. Marxland was unlikely to evolve
into a cooperative commonwealth of free nations, on the British model, or to
conform in the foreseeable future to other Western conceptions of liberty,
democracy, and international cooperation among sovereign equals. Neither was
it likely to develop into a true federation. The theory of federalism, written
into the Constitutions of both the USSR and Jugoslavia, bore little relationship to the realities of power, in sharp contrast to Western federal governments. But in ways not yet predictable it was probable that the masters of
Marxland would invent means of their own devising to hold together their
new imperium without a reversion to Stalin's techniques of terror which, if
repeated, would almost certainly lead to revolution and disintegration. In the
longer perspective of the years ahead effective power throughout the Red
Empire would almost inevitably pass, sooner or later, from Moscow to
Peiping. China's emergence as a major industrial power is still in the far
future. But China has thrice the population of the USSR. Its Marxist rulers,
moreover, enjoy immense prestige throughout Asia. Their fanaticism in the
service of what was originally a Western creed, unlike that of Lenin, Stalin,
and even Khrushchev, is tempered by the moderating wisdom of Confucianism
and by the humanistic tradition of the oldest living civilization on earth. No
Westerner should be astonished if, by A.D. 1984 or 2000, the directing center
of the Marxist imperium has subtly shifted from Muscovy to Cathay.

[note]

SUGGESTED READINGS

Boorman, Howard L., Alexander Eckstein, Philip E. Mosely, and Benjamin Schwartz: *Moscow-Peking Axis: Strengths and Strains*, New York, Harper, 1957.
Crankshaw, Edward: *Russia without Stalin: The Emerging Pattern*, New York, Viking, 1956.
Cretzianu, Alexandre (ed.): *Captive Rumania: A Decade of Soviet Rule*, New York, Praeger, 1956.
Dallin, David J.: *The Changing World of Soviet Russia*, New Haven, Conn., Yale University Press, 1956.
Deutscher, Isaac: *Russia: What Next?*, New York, Oxford, 1953.
Djilas, Milovan: *The New Class: An Analysis of the Communist System*, New York, Praeger, 1957.
Draper, Theodore: *The Roots of American Communism*, New York, Viking, 1957.
Gruliow, Leo: *Current Soviet Policies*, New York, Praeger, 1953.
——— (ed.): *Current Soviet Policies: II*, New York, Praeger, 1957.
Hazard, John N.: *Law and Social Change in the U.S.S.R.*, Toronto, The Carswell Co. Ltd., 1953.
———: *The Soviet System of Government*, Chicago, University of Chicago Press, 1957.
Kennedy, Malcolm: *A History of Communism in East Asia*, New York, Praeger, 1957.
Ripka, Hubert: *Czechoslovakia Enslaved: The Story of the Communist Coup d'État*, New York, Macmillan, 1951.
Roberts, Henry R.: *Rumania*, New Haven, Conn., Yale University Press, 1951.

Russian Institute (eds.) : *The Anti-Stalin Campaign and International Communism,* New York, Columbia University Press, 1957.

Stipp, John L. (ed.) : *Soviet Russia Today: Patterns and Prospects,* New York, Harper, 1956.

Sulzberger, C. L.: *The Big Thaw,* New York, Harper, 1956.

USSR, Ministry of Foreign Affairs: *Correspondence between the Chairman of the Council of Ministers of the USSR and the Presidents of the USA and the Prime Ministers of Great Britain during the Great Patriotic War of 1941–45* (2 vols.), Foreign Language Publishing House, Moscow, 1957 (in English).

Wolfe, Bertram D.: *Khrushchev and Stalin's Ghost,* New York, Praeger, 1956.

Wolfe, Robert Lee: *The Balkans in Our Time,* Cambridge, Mass., Harvard University Press, 1956.

Addenda: The Communist Bloc, as of 1958, had no such multifarious institutional structure as the "Free World" with its NATO, SEATO, ANZUS, Baghdad Pact, and other alliances. The Comintern was dissolved May 22, 1943. The Cominform of Oct. 5, 1947, was dissolved April 17, 1956, as a contribution to reconciliation with Tito. The conference of leaders of Communist Parties in Moscow, November, 1957, eventuated in no new organization. Apart from the Sino-Soviet alliance of Feb. 14, 1950, and the Warsaw Pact of May 14, 1955, collaboration among Communist regimes (and among the Parties controlling such regimes) remained "informal."

Chapter XIII

THE DEFENSE OF DEMOCRACY

1. FRANCE: THE LOST CAUSE

Sad tidings bring I to you out of France, Of loss, of slaughter, and discomfiture; Guienne, Champagne, Rheims, Orleans, Paris, Guysors, Poictiers, are all quite lost. . . . "How were they lost? What treachery was us'd?" No treachery but want of men and money. Amongst the soldiers this is muttered—That here you maintain several factions, And whilst a field should be dispatch'd and fought, You are disputing of your generals. One would have lingering wars with little cost; Another would fly swift, but wanteth wings; A third thinks, without expense at all, By guileful fair words peace may be obtain'd. . . . Cropp'd are the flower-de-luces in your arms; Of England's coat one half is cut away.—WILLIAM SHAKESPEARE, *King Henry* VI, Part I, Act I, Scene 1.

WINSTON CHURCHILL once commented that democracy was the worst form of government in the world, except for all the others that had been tried. The verdict of events on the policies of the democratic Great Powers during the 40 years following 1917 is a testament of valor and of freemen's will to life but is scarcely a demonstration of prudent statesmanship or of the capacity of "government by the people" to safeguard national interests and vindicate the democratic way of life in the face of successive totalitarian challengers. Yet it may prove true now, as in the past, that free peoples always somehow "muddle through," despite incredible confusion, hideous blunders, disastrous and preventable wars, and wasted victories. "Tyranny, like hell," wrote Tom Paine in 1776, "is not easily conquered." Yet tyrannies would seem to fail and fall more frequently than democracies. A survey of the failures, successes, and continuing problems of the major democracies in a dangerous world may suggest some sources of weakness and strength possibly relevant to the challenges of times to come. France, the earliest and oldest of the modern nation-states, was long the richest, most populous, and most powerful of the European "Great Powers." In the Great Revolution and thereafter, it became the second fatherland of all liberals and the prime source of inspiration for freemen throughout Europe and the world. During the past century French power has been successively overshadowed by the greater power of Britain, Germany, America, and Russia, while French democracy has been weakened by inner conflicts of class and creed. How the citizens and statesmen of France adapted themselves, or often

555

failed to adapt themselves, to these difficult circumstances is here our initial theme.

Lost Fruits of Victory. In 1918, after four years and three months of ghastly bloodshed and destruction, France achieved the goal which her diplomats and soldiers had pursued since 1871. Only a world in arms against the Central Powers enabled France to achieve victory. The Republic's Russian ally had been ground to pieces. Britain, Italy, the USA, and a host of lesser allies stood in the way of a purely French peace. They opposed French annexation of the Rhineland. They opposed outright annexation of the German colonies. They refused to conclude an alliance against Germany for the future. But much had been gained despite these obstacles. If Poincaré and other extreme nationalists were bitter over the "leniency" of the Peace Settlement, at least the new Europe offered ample opportunities for the permanent humiliation of Germany and the perpetuation of French ascendancy.

Post-Versailles French foreign policy was directed almost exclusively toward this end, although differences of opinion developed as to the best means thereto. The attainment of security, *i.e.*, the maintenance of hegemony over the Continent, required that Germany be kept weak and that France be kept strong. To achieve this goal, Paris strove to keep the Reich disarmed, poor, and isolated, and to find allies against any future Germanic resurgence. Belgium and Poland became French allies. The Little Entente—Czechoslovakia, Jugoslavia, and Rumania—was no less resolved to maintain the *status quo*. All its members became allies of France and, under French guidance and with the aid of French loans, resolved to oppose all efforts to modify the existing distribution of territory and power, whether from Germany to the north, from Hungary or Austria within their midst, from Italy to the west, or from Russia to the east. These common interests stretched a broad cordon of French power around Germany's frontiers. For 15 years, no aggregation of power emerged which could hope to challenge French ascendancy. But this "security" was as uneasy as that of the proverbial head that wears a crown.

The year 1933 inaugurated a new and disastrous epoch in French diplomacy. Refusal to make larger concessions to the German Republic contributed to the collapse of liberalism across the Rhine and to Hitler's rise to power. As German truculence increased and German might grew, French willingness to resort to force to maintain the *status quo* diminished. French opinion was so firmly attached to peace that it would no longer approve recourse to preventive violence to meet the menace of the new militarism now dominant in the Reich. French refusal to act against the Third Reich drove Pilsudski into his Nonaggression Pact with Hitler in January, 1934.

An unstable balance between political extremes in Parliament rendered difficult the development of any consistent policy. A desire to secure British and Italian support against Germany inhibited action likely to alienate London or Rome. The rise of Fascism in France, represented in the *Croix de Feu* of François de la Rocque, in the followers of the renegade Communist Jacques Doriot, and in a variety of other groups, was a further source of confusion, as was the delayed but nevertheless damaging impact of the Great Depression on French economy. The great issue before the Republic was no longer that of keeping a weak Germany in subjection but that of preserving the remnants of security and checkmating a strong, rearmed, and defiant Reich. Could liberal France prevent the establishment of Nazi hegemony over the Continent? Could liberal France protect itself from domestic Fascism? Upon answers to these questions depended the future of the French position in the game of power politics and the future of the Republic itself as a democratic State form.

La grande nation moved hesitantly and without clear guidance amid its new difficulties. Some positive steps were taken toward an affirmative answer to the questions posed. The "Maginot Line"—a wall of steel and concrete, dotted with subterranean batteries and machine-gun nests—was rushed to completion along the German frontier. The Fascist riots in Paris of Feb. 6, 1934, drew the powerful Socialist and Communist Parties together into an anti-Fascist coalition, joined in January, 1936, by the Radical Socialists. This "People's Front" frustrated the internal Fascist danger, at least temporarily. In the diplomatic field, Foreign Minister Louis Barthou had moved earlier to counter-balance the possible defection of Poland and the new might of Germany by a *rapprochement* with the USSR. In May, 1935, Franco-Soviet and Czech-Soviet Mutual Assistance Pacts were signed. In the elections of April and May, 1936, the People's Front Parties won a sweeping victory and put in power a Left Cabinet headed by the Socialist leader, Léon Blum. French democracy was apparently saved. French security was apparently assured. In August, 1936, General Gamelin, Chief of the French General Staff, visited Warsaw. In September, Gen. Edward Rydz-Smigly, who had succeeded Marshal Pilsudski (*d.* May 12, 1935) as dictator of Poland, visited Paris. The alliance was reaffirmed in the face of Polish fears of Nazi militarism and French promises of new loans. Perhaps Poland was to be saved for the French bloc. The USSR was a new ally. Belgium and the Little Entente seemingly remained bulwarks of French power.

Counter-balancing these favorable developments was a series of blunders which were ultimately to prove fatal. On Oct. 9, 1934, Barthou and King Alexander of Jugoslavia were assassinated at Marseille by a Croatian terrorist. This tragedy left France's ally on the Adriatic with a boy king, Peter II, and removed from the scene the only French Foreign Minister of great ability during the period of crisis. Barthou's successor, Pierre Laval, hesitated to ratify the Soviet Pact until Germany's *démarche* in March, 1936, compelled such action. Laval sought to conciliate Britain and Italy on the assumption that these Powers could be counted upon for support against Berlin. In order to placate Downing Street and "preserve peace," he acquiesced in German rearmament and supported Britain in imposing sanctions on Italy. In order to placate Rome and "preserve peace," he acquiesced in Italian designs on Ethiopia and undermined the League system of collective security. In the execution of this devious course, Paris fell between two stools.

Toward the Abyss. When on March 7, 1936, Hitler repudiated Locarno and remilitarized the Rhineland, the French General Staff perceived that effective military aid to Czechoslovakia or the USSR in the event of Nazi aggression would be rendered impossible if Berlin were allowed to fortify the Rhine frontier. It urged French military occupation of the Rhineland, as was permitted by the Treaty of Versailles. But such a step would require expensive mobilization and would seem to threaten war. It would be highly unpopular in France and might lead to an open break with London. Gamelin did not insist. The Sarraut Cabinet took no action but limited itself to protests in accordance with the example set a year previously, when Paris acquiesced in Hitler's repudiation of the military clauses of the Treaty. The Blum Cabinet continued the same policy, hoping that French inaction in the Rhineland and French support of British initiative in deserting Ethiopia and abandoning sanctions against Italy would at least preserve an Anglo-French-Italian common front against Germany. Again the hope was vain. Britain refused to accept any commitments in Central or Eastern Europe. Mussolini at once reached an understanding with Hitler. The Quai d'Orsay was again betrayed by its own illusions.

If Laval epitomized the blindness of the conservative French plutocracy in the face of mortal danger from the Caesars, Blum epitomized the paralysis of French liberals and radicals. The Right would do nothing to halt the aggressors because it feared the Left more. It hoped to make appeasement the means of protecting the class interests it represented. The Left would do nothing to halt the aggressors because its spokesmen were pacifists more interested in "social reforms" than in national security. The Right, moreover, was not above threatening civil war if the Left ventured either to attack the privileges of the wealthy "200 families" or to translate its anti-Fascist convictions into diplomatic and military action. On June 4, 1936, Léon Blum became Premier in a "People's Front" Cabinet of Radical Socialists and Socialists, supported in Parliament by these parties plus their Communist allies against Fascism. When the Spanish "Popular Front" was violently attacked by the generals and the propertied classes, aided by the Axis, the Socialist deputies in the French Chamber declared their solidarity with the Loyalists on July 24. On the next day, however, Blum and Foreign Minister Yvon Delbos persuaded the Cabinet in the name of "peace" and "nonintervention" to forbid all arms shipments to Spain. In deference to Tory Britain and the pro-Franco parties of the Right, Blum appealed to the Powers on Aug. 1 to adopt "common rules of nonintervention." On Aug. 15, Britain and France put an arms embargo into effect. Other States adhered with a variety of qualifications. The farcical

London "Non-intervention" Committee was set up. The betrayal of the Spanish Republic was launched. Blum's own followers protested bitterly and demanded, "Planes for Spain!" But Blum was imperturbable.

This decision was fatal not only to the Spanish Republic but to the French Republic. France was to fall, not because of the People's Front "reforms," but because the diplomacy of the People's Front was identical with that of the extreme Right. The ensuing collaboration with the Axis in conquering Spain drove more nails into the coffin of France's eastern alliances and left *la grande nation* discredited and weakened. It also strengthened enormously the pro-Fascist element within France, whose slogan was: "Better Hitler than Blum!" In the autumn of 1937 a series of outrages revealed the existence of a "Secret Committee of Revolutionary Action," popularly known as the "Cagoulards" ("Hooded Men"), who were securing arms and money from Berlin and Rome to set up a Fascist Directory—to be headed by Jacques Doriot, Jean Chiappe, Pierre Laval, Maxime Weygand, and Henri Philippe Pétain. Exposure of the plot was hastily hushed up. Too many "respectable" personages in the Army and in high finance were implicated. Blum had been succeeded in the Premiership in June, 1937, by Camille Chautemps (Radical Socialist). To the Finance Ministry went the sly and sinister figure of Georges Bonnet. The Chautemps Cabinet fell on March 10, 1938. Blum tried in vain to form a new Ministry. On March 12, Hitler took Austria. Blum formed a Cabinet on March 13—and did nothing. On April 8, he resigned once more. He was succeeded by Edouard Daladier, who, like many French politicians, began public life as a radical (he was a baker's son) and finally acquired wealth and "wisdom" and therewith became first a conservative and later a reactionary. Daladier was to remain Premier of France until March, 1940. Although brought to power by the People's Front, he kept power with the support of the Right. His Foreign Minister (April 8, 1938–Sept. 13, 1939) was Georges Bonnet. The two men were destined to bring France and the Republic to destruction.

Descent into Night. Munich was the symbol of their folly. They made the Quai d'Orsay completely subservient to Chamberlain's designs. They dreaded war or threats of war to save Czechoslovakia because any such war would have to be fought against Fascism in the name of democracy and the People's Front and, *horribile dictu,* in alliance with Moscow. Bonnet publicly pledged support of Prague and privately worked for an entente with Hitler at Prague's expense. He denied (falsely) that France could rely on British support. He exaggerated the weakness of the French Army to London. He alleged (falsely) that Litvinov was abandoning Beneš. He cooperated with Pierre-Etienne Flandin (who sent Hitler a congratulatory telegram after the "peace") and with the defeatist press of the Right, much of it in the pay of the Axis. Bribed journalists denounced Prague and Moscow and shouted over and again to a befuddled public, "No war for Czechoslovakia." On his return from Munich,

Daladier feared that the crowd at the airport might denounce him for betraying France. But it had come to cheer the "savior of peace." He was joined by Bonnet and Gamelin. All were praised as heroes for having thrown away the victory of 1918 for which 1,500,000 Frenchmen had died. Gamelin was silent when a visitor remarked, "General, you have just lost 35 divisions!"—*i.e.*, the Czech Army. "I accept my popularity," declared Daladier, "with the modesty that is only one of the forms my duty takes." Blum, in a mood he admitted was "cowardly relief," rejoiced that "peace was saved." Winston Churchill's judgment was more accurate: "France and Britain had to choose between war and dishonor. They chose dishonor. They will have war."

Bonnet and Daladier moved after Munich to surrender the Continent to Hitler's *Drang nach Osten*, to wage war at home against "Communism," and to undermine the social reforms of the French "New Deal." Labor resisted and ordered a one-day general strike on Nov. 30. It was broken. Daladier declared he had saved France from Bolshevism. On Dec. 6, 1938, Bonnet signed with Ribbentrop a declaration of "pacific and good neighborly relations." "It is the struggle against Bolshevism," wrote Bonnet a week later, "which is essentially at the basis of the common German and Italian political conception and, without saying so formally, Ribbentrop perhaps wished to give us to understand that there is no other objective to be attributed to it. . . . In regard to Spain, it is again the struggle against Bolshevism which alone has inspired the German effort from the beginning." Ambassador Robert Coulondre in Berlin agreed: "To secure mastery over Central Europe by reducing Czecho-Slovakia and Hungary to a state of vassalage and then to create a Great Ukraine under German control—this is what essentially appears to be the leading idea now accepted by the Nazi leaders" (*French Yellow Book of* 1939, No. 33). Bonnet and Daladier were willing.

When Hitler yielded Carpatho-Ukraine to Hungary on March 16, 1939, immediately after the occupation of Prague, the last leaders of a doomed nation awakened belatedly to their error. "Will the *Führer*," asked Coulondre on March 19, "be tempted to return to the idea expressed by the author of *Mein Kampf* which, be it said, is identical with the classic doctrine held by the German General Staff, according to which Germany cannot accomplish her high destiny in the East until France has been crushed and, as a consequence, Britain reduced to impotence on the Continent? . . . The Reich will first turn against the Western Powers" (*ibid.*, No. 80). Paris joined London in belated efforts to reconstruct the coalition which had been thrown away. The result was reaffirmation of the Polish alliance, support of Britain in guaranteeing Rumania and Greece, and the conclusion on June 23, 1939, of a French-Turkish alliance, paid for by the cession of Hatay to Ankara. But many of the Rightists were furious at such moves. "Danzig," wrote Flandin on May 7, "is merely an episode of the revision of the Peace Treaty. . . . If there were a new world war, in which Germany would doubtless be defeated, the German people would probably become Communist. . . . If the present crisis continues, revolution will come." The Quai d'Orsay, no less than Downing Street, was unwilling to pay Stalin's price for a new alliance against the Reich. The result was the collapse of the "peace front," the Nazi-Soviet Pact, the coming of war.

At the end, Bonnet made one last effort to arrange another Munich. On Sept. 1–2, 1939, he accepted Italian proposals for "peace" through a conference, with German troops remaining where they were on Polish soil. Halifax insisted that there could be no conference without a cessation of the blitzkrieg and German evacuation of Poland. The French Cabinet agreed. Bonnet reluctantly assented. Ciano replied that, since Hitler was unwilling to accept the condition, no further action could be taken. At 10:20, Sunday morning, Bonnet wired Coulondre of "the decision of the French Government" and instructed him to prevent an ultimatum at noon and to inform the Wilhelmstrasse in the event of a negative reply that Paris would be "compelled to fulfill as from today Sept. 3 at 5 P.M. the engagements France entered into towards Poland." The British ultimatum was delivered at 9 and was followed by war at 11 A.M. At 11:20, Ribbentrop submitted a contemptuous note of rejection to Henderson. At 12:30 the Nazi Foreign Minister received Coulondre and told him that if France attacked the Reich "this would be on her part a war of aggression." At 5 P.M., Sept. 3, 1939, war began between France and Germany. Bonnet had failed. He was obliged to yield the Quai d'Orsay to Daladier 10 days later and content himself with the Ministry of Justice.

Debacle. The Third French Republic entered upon its last war under leaders who were utterly inept. Its citizens were confused, baffled, and hopelessly divided against themselves. "Passive defense" was thought to be cheap in money and lives and was expected to save the State. No one was enthusiastic for war against the foe across the Rhine. Daladier, however, developed much enthusiasm for war against radicalism at home. On Sept. 26, he decreed the dissolution of the Communist Party. Bonnet schemed with Laval and Adrien Marquet to end the war and resume appeasement. After the outbreak of fighting in Finland, Daladier, Gamelin, and Weygand laid plans for war —not against Germany, but against the USSR. The failure of Allied policy in Finland, however, led to a parliamentary vote of nonconfidence on March 19, 1940. Daladier resigned but retained the Defense Ministry in the new Cabinet of Paul Reynaud. Bonnet was out. Reynaud had long been an anti-Munichois and therefore anathema to the Right and to many of the Radical Socialists. "I have come too early," he remarked. He secured a majority of only one vote in his first test in the Chamber on March 21.

In reality, Reynaud had come too late. He realized Gamelin's incompetence but was obliged by political considerations to keep Daladier in the Cabinet— and Daladier insisted on Gamelin's retention. His friend, the Countess Hélène de Portes, moreover, was a defeatist and a friend of Munichman Paul Baudouin. Reynaud and Daladier quarreled violently during the Nazi conquest of the northlands and the Low Countries. Gamelin had no plan for meeting the blitzkrieg save "Win or die." All his calculations were based on the belief

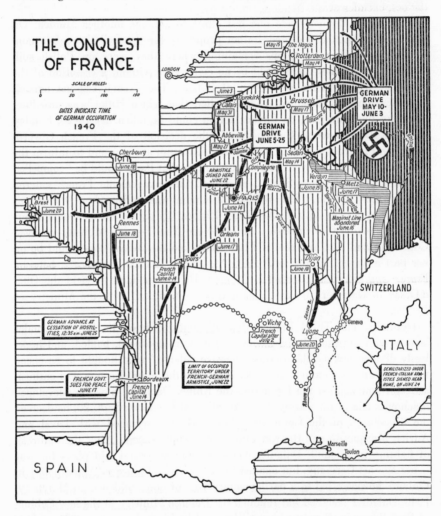

THE CONQUEST OF FRANCE

SCALE OF MILES:
0   50   100   130

DATES INDICATE TIME
OF GERMAN OCCUPATION
1940

that the Maginot Line was impregnable. Years before, Reynaud had urged in vain the thesis of Charles de Gaulle, an obscure officer who had been denied promotion by the conservative General Staff, that German tanks and planes could break through the line near Sedan and that France must have armored divisions and a powerful air force to meet the threat. They were not available. On May 18, Reynaud formed a new Cabinet, putting Daladier at the Quai d'Orsay and appointing as Vice-Premier Marshal Henri Philippe Pétain, aged eighty-four. He also took into the Cabinet the ultra-Rightists Louis Marin and Jean Ybarnégary, Vice-President of the Fascist *Croix de Feu*. On May 19, he dismissed Gamelin and made Gen. Maxime Weygand (aged seventy-three) Commander in Chief. These men were all clerical reactionaries, Anglophobes, enemies of the Republic, and warm admirers of Franco and Mussolini if not of Hitler.

France was now beyond saving. On June 5, as the full force of the invaders struck south from the Somme, Reynaud dropped Daladier and named Charles de Gaulle as Undersecretary at the War Ministry. Hélène persuaded him to name Baudouin as Undersecretary at the Quai d'Orsay. Weygand was baffled. His armies were overwhelmed. "A modern retreat," he observed, "has no limits." The Cabinet fled to Tours (June 11–14) and then to Bordeaux. Weygand alleged (falsely) that Communists were "rioting" in abandoned Paris prior to the German occupation and that the Cabinet must surrender to "save France from Bolshevism." Pétain, Chautemps, Baudouin agreed, as did Bonnet, Laval, and Flandin. To move to London or to North Africa, to carry on the war with the fleet and the colonies and the unbroken might of the British Empire would have been quite feasible. But the Munichmen gave Britain up for lost and preferred surrender for reasons of class interest. Reynaud appealed in vain for immediate American aid and asked Churchill to release France from the engagement of March 28 not to make a separate peace. Churchill asked that the French fleet should first be dispatched to British ports. On June 16, he offered "Union Now" to Reynaud. But the capitulators won a majority in the Cabinet at Bordeaux the same evening. Reynaud resigned. He was later injured and Hélène killed in a motor accident. In August, he was arrested and imprisoned, along with Daladier, Gamelin, Blum, Mandel, and others, to be tried for "treason" by those who had betrayed France. Meanwhile, President Albert Lebrun named Pétain Premier, Baudouin Foreign Minister, and Laval Minister of Justice. They sued for peace at once through Franco.

Death and Resurrection. The liberation of France, after four years of Nazi occupation, was the work of Britishers, Americans, and Russians. Among the Frenchmen who contributed, the leading figures were distrusted by London and Washington and by all French conservatives. They comprised Charles de Gaulle, a man of the Right who became a hero of the Left by leading the "Free French" abroad and becoming the head of a "Committee of National Liberation" (CNL) in the summer of 1943. They also included many Communists (who became fanatical anti-Nazis after the Nazi invasion of Russia) in the internal resistance movement, organized locally as "Le Maquis" or "Underbrush." The old French Right rallied to the puppet regime at Vichy, where Pétain and Laval preached and practiced Fascism, clericalism, and anti-Semitism and sought, without quite daring to act, to make their shamefaced "France" the ally of the Reich against Britain.

THE DEFENSE OF DEMOCRACY

In the wake of the Normandy invasion, De Gaulle returned to France on June 14, 1944. With Paris liberated, the CNL proclaimed a "Provisional Government" on Aug. 30, 1944, with De Gaulle as President, in combination with the Resistance and as a coalition of the Center and Left. Pétain was sentenced to death for treason, with the sentence commuted to life imprisonment. He died, unhonored save by a few neo-Fascists, on July 23, 1951. Laval fell before a firing squad, Oct. 14, 1945. Other "collaborators" were brought to trial. A new France rose from the ashes and was graciously granted the status of a "Great Power" by its allies.

On Oct. 13, 1946, the electorate approved a second draft of a new Constitution, not dissimilar to the old in its provision for an honorary President and a Cabinet responsible to a bicameral Parliament—in which, however, the indirectly elected Council of the Republic could neither oust the Ministry nor veto legislation, and the National Assembly was the controlling chamber. De Gaulle, defeated in his championship of a strong executive, had resigned Jan. 20, 1946, and organized a political party proclaiming its enmity to political parties: the "Rally of the French People" (RPF), founded in Strasbourg, April 8, 1947, and committed to authoritarianism and a vague "corporativism." The Assembly elected Socialist Vincent Auriol first President of the Fourth Republic, Jan. 14, 1947. Since government, as in the old days, was a business of short-lived coalition Cabinets, a recital of successive Premiers would be tedious and meaningless. The broad trends can be easily outlined.

Three major parties emerged in the first elections (Oct. 21, 1945, June 2 and Nov. 10, 1946): the liberal Catholic "Popular Republicans" (MRP) of Georges Bidault and Robert Schuman; the Socialists of Léon Blum (who died March 30, 1950) and Paul Ramadier, theoretically committed to Marxism; and the Communists of Maurice Thorez and Jacques Duclos, wholly committed to Stalinism. All participated in early Cabinets in a hopeful spirit of national rebirth and unity well expressed by the venerable Édouard Herriot, President of the Assembly, in January, 1947, when he recalled that the martyrs of the occupation often went before Nazi firing squads singing *La Marseillaise*. "They went to their death united, the unbeliever and the priest, the civilian and the soldier, the bourgeois and the worker, the city dweller and the peasant. It is that *Marseillaise* that they sang on the way to their sacrifice that speaks to us now, and that we must apply in the work before us. It is that *Marseillaise* that says to us now: '*Allons, enfants de la Patrie!*'"

This unity soon waned in the face of inflation, governmental deficits, unbalanced foreign trade, the poverty of the poor, the tax evasion of the rich, and, above all, the exigencies of the Cold War. The Communists, albeit the largest party in the Assembly, were dropped from the Cabinet in May, 1947. They devoted themselves in opposition to serving Soviet foreign policy by denouncing the Marshall Plan and the Atlantic Pact, championing "peace," condemning the war in Indochina, and exploiting the grievances of French

564

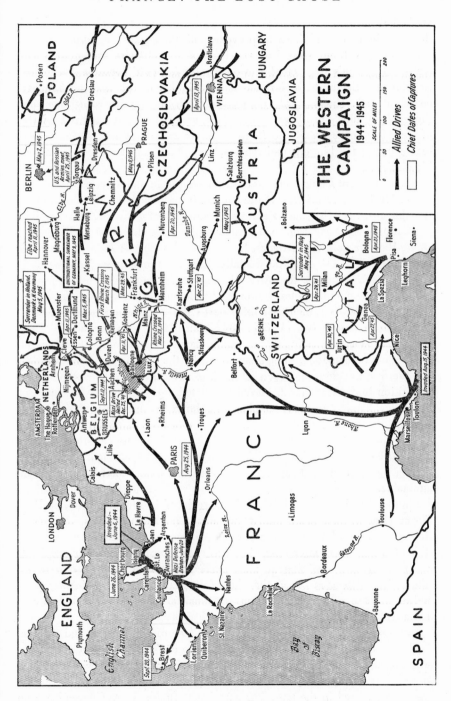

THE WESTERN
CAMPAIGN
1944-1945

SCALE OF MILES

Allied Drives

Chief Dates of Captures

workers through their control of the General Confederation of Labor—which they sought to use at times to provoke political strikes and promote, if a favorable opportunity should present itself, a revolutionary seizure of power. Robert Schuman's Cabinet of November, 1947, was a coalition of Popular Republicans, Socialists, and Radicals (*i.e.*, in French political terminology, conservatives). The political drift toward the Right was henceforth constant, though De Gaulle's neo-Fascists were long unable to profit from it by virtue of the refusal of *le grand Charlie* to share power with others, his inability to secure power for himself, and the resultant development of schisms among his disciples.

Amid incessant Cabinet crises, the Premiership in 1948 passed to Radicals André Marie and Henri Queuille in constantly reshuffled coalitions of Popular Republicans, Socialists, and Radicals. A new electoral law of 1951 modified proportional representation in the interest of cutting down the parliamentary strength of the political extremes. In the Assembly chosen June 17, 1951, the De Gaullists won 118 seats, the Socialists 104, the Communists 103, the Radicals and their allies 94, the MRP 81, and sundry conservative and peasant groups 99. In popular votes, however, the Communists remained the largest single party (26.5%), the De Gaullists next (21.7%), and the Socialists, MRP, and Radicals (respectively 14.5%, 12.2%, and 11.5%) in decline. A "Third Force" or "Center" majority was still difficult to maintain. René Pleven's Cabinet of August, 1951, though supported by the Socialists in the Assembly, was the first to contain no Socialist ministers. When the Socialists joined the opposition in January, 1952, Pleven was voted out of office, to be succeeded by Radical Edgar Faure, to be replaced in March by conservative businessman Antoine Pinay as head of a Right-Center Cabinet—which strove, with small ultimate success, to balance the budget, halt inflation, cut prices, and achieve a measure of economic and social stability which the persistent cleavages in French society and the troubles of a disordered world seemed to render unattainable.

Pinay fell in December, 1952, and was replaced in January, 1953, by René Mayer (Radical) as head of a Cabinet dependent upon De Gaullist support. Robert Schuman, for four years Foreign Minister, was succeeded by Georges Bidault. Eight years after liberation, *la belle France* was ruled by Rightists and reactionaries, dedicated to a sterile neo-nationalism and an obsolescent colonialism, dependent upon the USA (albeit increasingly anti-American), and headed toward further inflation, tax evasion, social crises, and class conflict auguring ill for the fortunes of French democracy.

The Diplomacy of Impotence. In the face of the internal and external conditions confronting the Fourth Republic, no one lacking omniscience could have prescribed with any assurance a pattern of foreign policy well calculated to serve French interests, or at least avoid worse disasters in the future than had been suffered in the past. The actual pattern was one of dependence on stronger Powers, grim resolve to cling to a colonial empire already in dissolution, fear of Russia coupled with greater fear of Germany and grave doubts regarding the course of the USA, and brilliant, albeit seldom successful, improvisation.

The Quai d'Orsay, presided over by Bidault, Robert Schuman, and again Bidault in the years of mid-century, was ever confronted with a series of contradictions which no French wisdom could quite resolve. On Dec. 10, 1944, Bidault and Molotov signed a 20-year French-Soviet alliance, pledging the parties to adopt "all measures necessary to eliminate any new threat on the part of Germany," to give each other "all the help and assistance in its power" in the event that either should be involved in "hostilities with Germany" as a result of future German aggression or of French or Russian steps to prevent such aggression, and "not to conclude alliances and not to participate in any coalition directed against either of them." This pact became waste paper as soon as policy-makers in Washington, seconded in London and Paris, concluded in 1946–47 that Western Europe was now threatened not by German but by Russian aggression.

The new France, despite the ultra-patriotic outcries of De Gaulle, the subversive propaganda of the Communists, and pleas for "independence" by the "neutralists," found itself wholly dependent for even a semblance of solvency and security on the USA. Here, as always, who pays the piper may call the tune. On March 4, 1947, Britain and France signed at Dunkirk a 50-year alliance pledging mutual support in the event of future hostilities with Germany arising out of "armed attack" or international action "for the purpose of preventing any infringement by Germany of her obligations with regard to disarmament and demilitarization and generally of insuring that Germany shall not again become a menace to peace." On March 17, 1948, France joined Britain and the Benelux States in the 50-year Brussels alliance treaty, pledging mutual aid under Article 51 of the UN Charter against any "armed attack in Europe" (origin now unspecified) and abstention from participation in any alliance or coalition "against any other of the high contracting parties." The North Atlantic Treaty of April 4, 1949 (see pp. 595–597), seemed to represent a further extension of this formula and thus an additional bulwark of French security.

But the fat was in the fire as soon as the USA decided that European defense against Soviet aggression required the rearmament of Germany. The tortured course of the Quai d'Orsay in the face of this dilemma was at once pathetic, tragic, and hopeful. Paris had once more seized the Saar as a means of strengthening France against the Boche and was determined never to give it up again. All patriotic Germans were equally determined never to renounce their claims to the Saar or rest until they, were met. Paris was resolved not to be dragged into war with Russia by German efforts to reconquer the lost Eastern Provinces. Bonn was equally resolved that they must be recovered, while most Americans seemed convinced that Eastern Europe must ultimately be liberated from Communist slavery.

The official Parisian response to this painful paradox in the early 1950's was the Schuman Plan to pool the steel, iron, and coal industries of Western Europe into a joint cartel in the hope that France, rather than Germany, could control its policies; the Pleven Plan for the incorporation of small German units into a European Army in the hope that France, rather than Germany, could control the purposes for which it was to be used; repeated appeals for increased U.S. aid to finance the French economy, French rearmament, and the war in Indochina; and vague support of American championship of a West European federation in the hope that France, rather than Germany, could shape its structure and program. Reactionary De Gaullists, liberal "neutralists," and pro-Muscovite Communists, representing among them a large segment of the people of France, were all agreed that this pattern of policy was detestable and disastrous. But since they were in complete disagreement regarding any alternative, and since French Cabinets could see no alternative, this became the schema of a French foreign policy in which everyone reposed hope but no one had faith.

What was sadly obvious was that France, now reduced to a lesser Power, was no longer master of its destiny. In war between the Super-Powers, France would be occupied by Russia, since no local defenses of Western Europe against the Red behemoth were any longer possible, with or without German participation. One Frenchman out of four was a Communist and might well welcome the invader and serve as "Fifth Columnist," "Trojan horseman," and "collaborator." The prospect of ultimate "liberation" by an American army, wielding atomic bombs, seemed to most Frenchmen a formula for national suicide. In peace, Frenchmen feared a new German hegemony over Europe, sponsored by the USA. An "independent" foreign policy which might offer other possibilities was precluded by the continued refusal of Frenchmen to subordinate class and group interests to the national interest and to bring order out of chaos in the French economy and in French politics. This pattern of public life had produced catastrophe in the past. It might do so again in the future.

Yet immortal France, while fearing the worst, might yet hope for the best on the not unreasonable assumption that Divine Providence would never permit the annihilation of the most beautiful and the most civilized of all the contemporary communities of mankind.

Plus Ça Change. . . During the middle and late 1950's the scenery and the actors shifted slightly at the Palais Bourbon and the Quai d'Orsay in accordance with the usual vicissitudes of politics and foreign policy without effecting any significant change in the play at home and abroad. The French mission, if any, in Europe was no longer within French control. The French mission in Asia and Africa was a foredoomed enterprise of seeking to perpetuate by force a colonial empire which could be preserved, if at all, only by granting independence to its native peoples. Indochina was lost in July, 1954, after eight years of costly and futile warfare. The error was avoided in Morocco and Tunisia, but repeated in Algeria where more years of costly and futile warfare began in November, 1954. A sketch of events will suggest the libretto of a pathetic *opéra bouffe* in which the music was the cacophony of parliamentary politics and the leitmotivs were the apathy or *incivisme* of the French electorate and the successive failures of French statesmanship.

The Rightist experiment of 1952 in deflation, budget-balancing, and monetary stability ended in December with the resignation of Pinay (head of France's seventeenth Cabinet since 1944) and his replacement in January by a Ministry headed by René Mayer, pledged to modifications of EDC and to fiscal and constitutional "reforms"—all of which came to nothing. Proposed budget cuts precipitated the Cabinet's fall on May 21, 1953. After weeks of vain maneuvers to achieve a majority in the Assembly, Joseph Laniel, a conservative businessman and a leader of Reynaud's Independent Party, put together a "stop-gap" Ministry which survived in Parliament by postponing all issues. Since most of the poor were persuaded that all appeals for austerity and economy were merely devices to enrich the rich, the Republic was paralyzed in August, 1953, by nationwide strikes of more than 2,000,000 workers demanding higher wages. The strikes, while exploited by the Communists, were launched by the Catholic unions and the anti-Communist *Force Ouvrière*. The Government made concessions. Workers returned to work. But no victory was won. All problems were deferred.

The year 1954 brought new leadership, new hopes, new decisions, and promises of a "new deal"—all of which, however, were to prove ephemeral. Laniel sought the Presidency of the Republic in the parliamentary balloting at Versailles, but withdrew on the 12th ballot. On the 13th (Dec. 22, 1953), the 71-year-old René Coty, a hitherto obscure reactionary, won a majority and in January succeeded Auriol at the Palais d'Élysée. Communist appeals to Socialists for a new "Popular Front" were rejected, but the Left gained popular support because of widespread discontent with inflation, EDC, and the hopeless war in Indochina. Laniel postponed all decisions, including a response to constantly mounting U.S. pressure to ratify EDC. Foreign Minister Bidault was rebuffed by Eisenhower in his appeals for massive American military intervention in Indochina. The Cabinet would neither negotiate with Ho Chi Minh nor grant independence to Vietnam. The fall of Dienbienphu (see p. 386) during the Geneva Conference led to the fall of the Cabinet on June 12.

Laniel's successor was a Leftist, an economist, a Jew, a lukewarm advocate of EDC, and a firm champion of ending the lost war: 47-year-old Radical, Pierre Mendès-France, who assumed the Foreign Ministry as well as the Premiership. His paradoxically Rightist Cabinet, so constituted because of

Socialist refusal to participate and an MRP decision to abstain, won an extraordinary majority of 419 to 47. He pledged peace in Indochina by July 20 or resignation. At Geneva he signed the cease-fire agreements on July 21. "The texts are sometimes cruel," he told the Assembly, "because they consecrate facts which are cruel." His vote of confidence on July 23 was 471 to 14. He further won from the deputies "special powers" to modernize industry and agriculture and expand output in a projected "economic revolution."

As regards German rearmament, he was less successful. His proposed amendments to EDC were rejected at a six-Power conference in Brussels in August. Despite pleas from Eisenhower, Dulles, and even Adlai Stevenson, he decided to submit the EDC accords to the Assembly without urging ratification. On Aug. 30, 1954, the Deputies rejected them, 319 to 264. But Anglo-American pressure now proved irresistible. At a nine-Power conference in London (Sept. 28–Oct. 3), agreement was reached on a new formula: West Germany would join NATO and the Brussels Treaty Organization (BRUTO), rechristened "Western European Union," and raise 12 divisions, but would accept the continued maintenance of Anglo-American armies in Germany; place its forces under NATO command; abstain from force to achieve unification; renounce heavy armaments, missiles, and biological, chemical, and atomic weapons; and agree to possible "Europeanization" of the Saar. On Oct. 23, 1954, at the Quai d'Orsay, diplomats of 15 States signed incredibly complex accords designed to accomplish these and related purposes. Since fear of German rearmament was far keener among most Frenchmen than fear of Soviet aggression, the Deputies in a preliminary vote rejected the accords on Dec. 24, 281 to 257, despite Mendès-France's plea for overwhelming endorsement. When he posed the question of confidence, the treaties were approved, Dec. 30, 287 to 260, with many Deputies abstaining.

From Mendès-France to Faure. The "victories" of Mendès-France in foreign affairs were all French defeats, rendered palatable in the name of "realism." Peace in Southeast Asia was achieved by acknowledging the loss of Indochina. Peace in Morocco and Tunisia (see pp. 371, 373) was had at the same price. Peace in Algeria was unattainable because Paris would not pay the price. Unlike the Portuguese possessors of Goa, France yielded to India, Oct. 21, 1954, the small coastal enclaves of Pondichéry, Karikal, Mahé, and Yanaon, comprising 193 square miles and 320,000 inhabitants. The Saar was to be lost (see p. 345). The hope of preventing German rearmament was lost. A France hungry for peace but also fearful for its security and loathe to abandon its ancient glories soon turned against its most popular and promising Premier of a decade.

Mendès-France, early in 1955, visited Italy and Germany, following his triumphal reception in the USA and Canada in November, 1954, and urged upon France's allies a European "arms pool," further steps toward European federation, and a Big Four Conference with the USSR in a last hope of averting German rearmament. All in vain. When, in his striving for peace in Algeria through compromise with nationalist aspirations, he asked the Assembly to approve his North African policies, he was defeated, 319 to 273, on Feb. 5. The new Cabinet of Feb. 23, 1955, in which Antoine Pinay became Foreign Minister, was headed by Radical Edgar Faure (soon to become a bitter political foe of Mendès-France), but was the most Rightist Ministry since World War II.

The Faure Ministry could afford to ignore Soviet abrogation of the alliance treaty of 1944 (see pp. 567 and 544), but was troubled by the rise of Pierre Poujade's neo-Fascist "Union for the Defense of Tradesmen," which he directed with demagogic skill in a "tax strike" by small businessmen and farmers. Pinay visited London in April, Washington and San Francisco in June, the Big Four Conferences in Geneva in July and October, and delayed his acceptance of an invitation to visit Moscow. But the fortunes of French diplomacy did not mend. When Faure proposed new parliamentary elections in December, rather than in June, 1956, when the mandates of the Deputies would expire, Mendès-France accused him of political trickery to weaken the Left and strengthen the Right. Amid an involved wrangle over proposed changes in the electoral system, the Deputies, 318 to 218, voted the Faure Cabinet out of office, Nov. 30, 1955. Under Arts. 49 and 51 of the Constitution, the Cabinet may ask the President to dissolve the Assembly and order new elections if two Cabinet crises within 18 months reveal more than an absolute majority (314) of the Deputies in opposition. The condition was fulfilled by the Assembly votes of Feb. 5 and Nov. 30, 1955. The Cabinet, for the first time since 1877, decreed dissolution and ordered elections on Jan. 2, 1956. Mendès-France accused Faure of a *coup de force*, consolidated his own leadership of the Radicals, and engineered Faure's expulsion from the party.

From Faure to Mollet and Beyond. The results of the polling of Jan. 2, 1956, were even more confused and bewildering than those of the election of 1951. They were more disturbing, since a full third of the voters of France, embittered by grievances and disgusted at the unending spectacle of a meaningless political vaudeville, cast protest votes for candidates of extremist parties which were anti-parliamentary and anti-democratic. The Communists won 145 seats, the Poujadists 51, and the Gaullists 16. The Socialists emerged with 88 Deputies, the MRP with 70, and the Independents, 94. The divided Radicals elected only 71, with Mendès-France triumphing over Faure in a common Radical defeat. In popular votes the Communists won 25% of the total, the Poujadists 12%, and the Socialists, MRP, Independents, and Radicals each, roughly, 15%. The new Assembly was more hopelessly split than the old.

Communist pleas for a new "Popular Front" were again spurned by Socialists and Radicals alike, though no stable Parliamentary majority was possible without Communist or Poujadist support. Socialist Guy Mollet, a 50-year-old former high school teacher, struck a bargain with Mendès-France in January and concocted a Ministry of Socialists and Radicals, with Mollet as Premier, Mendès-France as "Minister of State without Portfolio," and Socialist Christian Pineau as Foreign Minister. Although in terms of party composition this Cabinet could not hope to command a parliamentary majority, it was nevertheless approved by the Assembly, 420 to 71, on Feb. 1, 1956, and was ironically to be the longest-lived to date of the Fourth Republic because no alternative was available and because it was supported for many months not only by the Center but by the Communists on some issues and by the Poujadists on others.

Under such circumstances the safest course for the Ministry was to do nothing which might disintegrate its precarious parliamentary support and thus to delay or equivocate on all controversial public issues. By converting this sensible, even if unheroic and unproductive, procedure into a fine art, Mollet survived as Premier until May 21, 1957. It was the unhappy fate of this Socialist leader, like that of Léon Blum a decade earlier, to direct a "dirty" and hopeless colonial war against native demands for independence, contrary to all "Socialist" principles—thereby suggesting that Socialists, like Bourbons, learn nothing and forget nothing. But the comparison is unfair, for the Mollet Ministry had no choice in the light of the balance of forces in Parliament. Morocco and Tunisia were granted independence, March 2 and 20, 1956. Mollet and Pineau visited Moscow in May and received Nehru in Paris in July, but all with no results in promoting either an East-West settlement or some formula of accommodation between France and the new nationalists of Western Asia and North Africa. Mendès-France quit the Cabinet May 23, 1956, in protest against Mollet's refusal to seek a political, rather than a military, solution in Algeria—and subsequently lost his leadership, perhaps temporarily, of the Radical Party.

Any remaining doubts as to whether France was still a "Great Power" were resolved by the muddles and miseries of the mismanaged attack on Egypt, in connivance with Israel and Britain, in the fall of 1956 (see pp. 415–422), in feeble and short-lived defiance of the USA, the USSR, the UN, and all the Asian-African governments and peoples. Mollet, unlike Eden, survived the débâcle. Most French Socialists, unlike British Laborites, approved this feckless resort to violence and only deplored its failure. Pineau complained that it was "not just" that the USA should give its aid to Nasser. "Whatever our bitterness, we cannot renounce American friendship and the Atlantic Alliance, which is our only safeguard against sharing the fate of Hungary. But this does not mean that we should always give way to American desires. . . ." Dulles's visit to Paris in mid-December, 1956, reaffirmed "solidarity." But it was clear to all save the blind that Anglo-French-American solidarity had suffered damage which was irreparable in the sense of precluding any return to the patterns of mutual confidence and cooperation prevailing before 1956. It was even more clear that any hope of an independent role for France as a "Great Power" was visionary and fatuous unless both of the Grand Coalitions should disintegrate altogether, a contingency not yet on the horizon of the late 1950's.

Pineau in Washington in January, 1957, achieved no change in these hard realities, nor did Mollet's visit in late February—when he reaffirmed "solidarity" with Eisenhower in the customary clichés of such meetings, while publicly espousing the Israeli position on issues in dispute between Washington and Tel Aviv. Golda Meir, on her way to Washington, conferred in Paris in mid-March with Mollet and Maurice Bourgès-Maunoury, Minister of Defense, and declared, "I believe there is no difference of opinion between our two governments." French policy-makers deplored France's absence at the Anglo-American Bermuda Conference in March. Édouard Herriot, for decades the veteran and venerable leader of the French Radicals, went to his final rest, aged 84, on March 26, 1957, leaving in doubt the succession to leadership in the Radical Party. Queen Elizabeth II was hailed on a State visit to Paris in April. Meanwhile men killed men, and often women and children, in the unending horror of the Algerian war which the Mollet Cabinet was unable to win or to end.

On May 21, 1957, the Deputies, 250 to 213, defeated the Ministry on its thirty-fourth vote of confidence. The technical issue was a bill to increase taxes. The actual issue was the inability of the Cabinet to make peace in Algeria or to make the voice of France heard in world affairs. No voice remained save nostalgic echoes of lost prestige and power. After Pierre Pflimlin (MRP) failed at Cabinet-making, 42-year-old Radical Maurice Bourgès-Maunoury contrived a Socialist-Radical Ministry which won lukewarm parliamentary approval, 240 to 194, on June 13, 1957—again because no alternatives seemed available. The new Cabinet gained reluctant approval for new taxes. But the Deputies on Sept. 30, 1957, rejected the Cabinet's lukewarm Algerian "reform bill" and thereby precipitated the most prolonged ministerial crisis to date in the Fourth Republic. Not until the end of October did the party leaders agree to support a Cabinet headed by the brilliant Radical economist, Félix Gaillard, the youngest (37) of French Premiers. Yet youth and brilliance were alike helpless to remedy the political paralysis of France, which precluded any effective economic or political reforms at home and condemned the nation abroad to helpless warfare in North Africa and to impotence in world affairs.

The French economy, while enjoying inflationary prosperity in the late 1950's, was suffering from a chronic deficit in international payments, due to a constant excess of imports over exports, and from a chronic excess of governmental expenditures over receipts of public revenues (despite yearly subsidies from the USA), thanks to the costs of the Algerian war and to the ingenuity of Frenchmen in evading taxes. The devaluation of the franc (which before 1914 was exchanged at 5 to the dollar) from 350 to the dollar to 420 in August, 1957, promised only a temporary alleviation of the difficulty. In all States citizens pay taxes willingly, if seldom gladly, only to governments which they believe have some minimal desire and capacity to cope with domestic and foreign problems. Few Frenchmen had any such confidence in the political pattern of the Fourth Republic in its second decade.

Yet they lived the good life, despite bitterness between rich and poor, and perhaps enjoyed as of old the best life possible in the human condition—not in material terms, even if French cuisine and the arts of luxury remained incomparable, but in aesthetic, spiritual, and intellectual adventures and experiences. No other national community in the contemporary world, save possibly West Germany, was so dedicated to the proposition that politics and diplomacy are unimportant so long as disaster at home and abroad are not imminent. This salubrious rejection of the apparent paramountcy of the political process is a happy omen in an era of totalitarian police-states—unless it should transpire once more, as in the France of 1914 and 1939, that neglect of politics is the prelude to catastrophe and that informed political concern may prove more hopeful and constructive than most cynical citizens of France supposed, from long and painful experience, that it could ever possibly be.

SUGGESTED READINGS

Blum, Léon: *For All Mankind*, New York, Viking, 1946.

Brogan, D. W.: *France under the Republic*, New York, Harper, 1940.

Cot, Pierre: *Triumph of Treason*, Chicago, Ziff-Davis, 1944.

Daladier, Édouard: *In Defense of France*, New York, Doubleday, 1939.

De Gaulle, Charles: *The Call to Honour: 1940–1942*, New York, Viking, 1955.

Draper, Theodore: *The Six Weeks' War: France, May 10–June 25, 1940*, New York, Viking, 1944.

Earle, Edward Meade (ed.): *Modern France: Problems of the Third and Fourth Republics*, Princeton, N.J., Princeton University Press, 1951.

Ehrenburg, Ilya: *The Fall of Paris*, New York, Knopf, 1943.

Ehrmann, Henry W.: *French Labor from Popular Front to Liberation*, New York, Oxford, 1947.

Furniss, Edgar S., Jr.: *France: Keystone of Western Defense*, New York, Doubleday, 1954.

Godfrey, E. Drexel, Jr.: *The Political Fate of the Non-Communist Left in Postwar France*, New York, Doubleday, 1954.

Jellinek, Frank: *The Civil War in Spain*, London, Gollancz, 1938.

Lorwin, Val R.: *The French Labor Movement*, Cambridge, Mass., Harvard University Press, 1955.

Luethy, Herbert: *France against Herself*, New York, Praeger, 1955.

McKay, Donald D.: *The United States and France*, Cambridge, Mass., Harvard University Press, 1951.

Manuel, Frank E.: *The Politics of Modern Spain*, New York, McGraw-Hill, 1938.

Martel, Francis: *Pétain: Verdun to Vichy*, New York, Dutton, 1943.

Matthews, Ronald: *The Death of the Fourth Republic*, New York, Praeger, 1955.

Mendès-France, Pierre: *Economics and Action*, New York, Columbia University Press, 1955.

Micaud, Charles A.: *The French Right and Nazi Germany, 1933–1939; A Study in Public Opinion*, Durham, N.C., Duke University Press, 1943.

BRITAIN: DEFEAT IN VICTORY

Pertinax: *The Gravediggers of France*, New York, Doubleday, 1944.
Pickles, Dorothy: *France: The Fourth Republic*, London, Methuen, 1955.
Russell, Frank M.: *The Saar: Battleground and Pawn*, Stanford, Calif., Stanford University Press, 1951.
Schoenbrun, David: *As France Goes*, New York, Harper, 1957.
Taylor, O. R.: *The Fourth Republic of France*, London, Royal Institute of International Affairs, 1951.
Thomson, David: *Democracy in France—The Third Republic*, New York, Oxford, 1947.
Werth, Alexander: *France and Munich*, New York, Harper, 1939.
———: *France, 1940–1955*, New York, Holt, 1956.
Williams, Philip: *Politics in Post War France*, New York, Longmans, 1954.

2. BRITAIN: DEFEAT IN VICTORY

This royal throne of kings, this sceptred isle, This earth of majesty, this seat of Mars, This other Eden, demi-paradise, This fortress built by Nature for herself Against infection and the hand of war, This happy breed of men, this little world, This precious stone set in the silver sea, Which serves it in the office of a wall Or as a moat defensive to a house, Against the envy of less happier lands,—This blessed plot, this earth, this realm, this England, This nurse, this teeming womb of royal kings, Fear'd by their breed, and famous by their birth, Renowned for their deeds as far from home, For Christian service and true chivalry, As is the sepulchre in stubborn Jewry Of the world's ransom, blessed Mary's Son: This land of such dear souls, this dear dear land, Dear for her reputation through the world, Is now leas'd out—I die pronouncing it—Like to a tenement or pelting farm. England, bound in with the triumphant sea, Whose rocky shore beats back the envious siege Of watery Neptune, is now bound in with shame, With inky blots and rotten parchment bonds; That England, that was wont to conquer others, Hath made a shameful conquest of itself. Ah, would the scandal vanish with my life, How happy then were my ensuing death!—WILLIAM SHAKESPEARE, *King Richard the Second*, Act II, Scene 1.

On a fair June day of 1953, with appropriate pageantry, Queen Elizabeth II of the House of Windsor was formally crowned, "by the Grace of God, Queen of Great Britain, Ireland, and the British Dominions beyond the Seas, Defender of the Faith." On Feb. 6, 1952, while in Kenya in the course of an imperial tour with her husband, Philip Mountbatten, Prince of Greece and Duke of Edinburgh, she learned of the death of her father, King George VI, and flew back to London to take the oath of accession. He in turn had been crowned King-Emperor on May 12, 1937, following the death on Jan. 20, 1936, of his father, George V, and the enforced abdication (Dec. 11, 1936) of his older brother, Edward VIII, who gave up the crown to marry "the woman I love." The new Queen, like Elizabeth I, took the throne at the age of twenty-five and doubtless hoped for a long reign as worthy of happy remembrance, despite the austere conditions confronting Britons in the 20th Century, as the original Elizabethan Age.

This magic of monarchy, incomprehensible but exciting to many beyond the sceptred isle, was a symbol of the unity of all Britishers throughout the world and of their unfailing sense of historical continuity and perspective. It recalled the noble glories of times of old when their ancestors established the "Mother of Parliaments," built the greatest of empires, initiated the In-

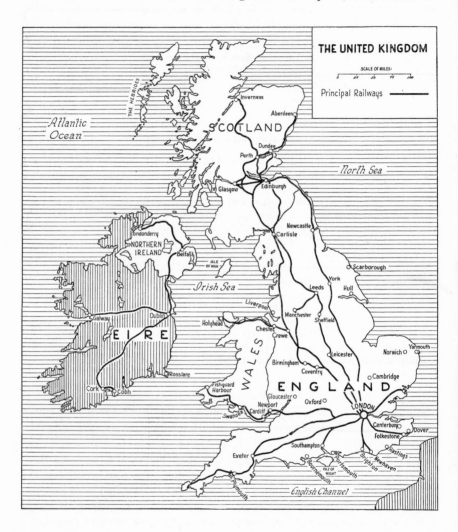

dustrial Revolution, and served all men well through the *Pax Britannica*. The "United Kingdom" of England, Wales, Scotland, and Ireland (limited since the Free State Act of 1921 to the six northeastern counties, with the rest independent and unreconciled to the loss) was no longer in mid-century the greatest of Powers, but a poor third—or fourth, if Red China be counted among the new giants. This decline of British fortunes was in part a result of developments quite beyond British control—*e.g.*, the industrialization of Germany,

America, and Russia. It was also in part a consequence of British difficulties and failures in meeting effectively the successive challenges posed by younger Powers competing for mastery of the world. Unless utter madness overtakes mankind, a contingency almost realized in the 1930's and still possible in the 1960's, "there will always be an England" with its rich contributions to the wealth, health, and happiness of all the human race. Our task is to survey the decisions and indecisions of those who made British foreign policy in an unhappy time of recurrent troubles.

How the "Balance of Power" Was Lost. British security against aggression from the Continent, and British prosperity through world-wide trade and investment, have depended for centuries on a simple policy of preventing any single Power from dominating Europe. In pursuit of this purpose alliances and arms were built, and war (when need be) was waged, against Philip II, Louis XIV, Napoleon I, and Wilhelm II to the end of preserving an equipoise. The goal required aid from Russia against France in the Napoleonic era, from Russia and America against Germany in World War I, and from both once more against the Fascist Triplice in World War II. But the objective was apparently forgotten in the 1930's and thereby rendered impossible of restoration in the 1950's. How and why this came to pass is the necessary point of departure for any consideration of British diplomacy in our time.

Victory over Germany in 1918 restored a balance on the Continent. The hegemony of the French bloc, though often thwarted by Downing Street, was rightly regarded as no threat to British interests. But when France was in dire need of British support and commitments to maintain its hegemony, London's policy-makers, both Laborite and Conservative, held aloof—on the premise, unspoken but obvious, that Britain could afford "isolationism" so long as no one Power seemed likely to control the Continent. The premise was correct so long as the condition was real. When Hitler's Reich dedicated itself to dominating Europe, Downing Street under the Tory Governments of the 1930's lost contact with reality. Every major decision served to facilitate German-Italian aggrandizement and to weaken France and her Eastern allies. This policy of "appeasement" of the Caesars, so diligently pursued by Prime Ministers Stanley Baldwin (1935-37) and Neville Chamberlain (1937-40), made sense in terms of British interests only on the assumption that Germany and Russia would "balance" one another or would fight one another to mutual exhaustion with France and Britain remaining neutral and secure. Should the assumption prove false (as it did), the policy in retrospect assumed a quality of suicidal folly by no means characteristic of the great days of England, the Commonwealth, and the Empire.

How did the wisest of contemporary statesmen, diplomats, and strategists come to embrace a nonsensical, and therefore disastrous, policy? Disputation over the answer has gone on for years and will go on for years to come, since British leaders, even *in extremis*, seldom forget the age-old injunction of *Real-*

THE DEFENSE OF DEMOCRACY

politik to use words to conceal meaning. The simplest answer, and the most nearly correct answer, is that in the 1930's the Tory aristocrats and businessmen who shaped British policy honestly admired Fascism in Italy, Germany, and Spain as a "protection" against Communism and assumed, if worst came to worst, that Nazi aggression could be deflected eastward and away from the Western Powers. Public support for this policy was readily mobilized by presenting it as essential for "peace." [1]

In the game of power politics, the test of policy is not intentions or hopes

---

[1] This view was put forward as early as 1921 by Viscount D'Abernon, post-Versailles British Ambassador in Berlin. *Cf. The Diary of an Ambassador: Versailles to Rapallo,* 1920–1922 (New York, Doubleday, 1929), pp. 21*ff.* The reasoning behind this view may be suggested by the following quotations:

In 1934 Mr. L. Lawton wrote in the *Fortnightly Review:* "Whereas formerly German statesmen looked both to the East and to the West, Hitler at present looks to the East only. . . . No one who studies the map of eastern Europe can doubt that there are immense possibilities of a German-Polish compromise at the expense of others. The idea of including Ukraine within the Western European System, and moving Russia on towards the East is certainly tempting. . . . With Ukraine as part of a democratic federated system there would, it is hoped, come into existence a grouping of States with which Great Britain could be on friendly terms. The moment is long overdue for the creation of some such grouping in eastern Europe."

Mr. L. S. Amery, former Colonial Minister, wrote in *The Forward View* (1935) : "The first condition of European peace today is the frank acknowledgment that Germany's armaments are now her own affair and nobody else's [p. 71]. . . . The time has come for such a revision of the Covenant as will get rid of all those clauses (more particularly 10 and 16) which give an encouragement to the Super-State theory of the League [p. 272]. . . . The doctrine of the inevitable contagion of war is, of course, pure nonsense [p. 283]. . . . We do not regard ourselves as one of the nations of Europe [p. 285]. . . . It would be no concern of ours . . . to prevent Japanese expansion in eastern Siberia [p. 288]."

The Marquess of Londonderry, owner of many mines and large estates, differed from most of his collaborators in a somewhat naïve prospensity to state his convictions in print, with the aid of Lady Desborough and Mr. G. Ward Price. Thus:

"Our Foreign Office appears to condone the associations with Communism and Bolshevism through our affiliation with France, while paying but little regard to the robust attitude of Germany, Italy, and Japan which wholeheartedly condemn Communism and Bolshevism. Bolshevism is a world-wide doctrine which aims at the internal disruption of all modern systems of government with the ultimate object of what is termed World Revolution. That Germany, Italy, and Japan condemn Bolshevism is an attitude of mind which is not properly appreciated in this country. . . . We fail to recognize that the present condition of Spain is mainly the result of Red machinations. We console ourselves with the reflection that, owing to the conservatism of the French peasant, Bolshevism will not prevail to any serious extent among the urban industrial population of France, although the Communist representation in the Chamber has increased to the number which Herr Hitler personally prophesied to me over two years ago. Belgium is showing signs of Bolshevism. And Germany sees herself surrounded by Bolshevist countries and militarily and economically hemmed in with what may well be disastrous consequences. We watch this movement with strange equanimity. We throw in our weight under 'non-intervention' on the side of the Reds in Spain. Belgium and France do the same. And we wonder why Germany and Italy appear more truculent and challenging as their strength and prestige increase [pp. 21–22]. I was at a loss to understand why we could not make common ground in some form or other with Germany in opposition to Communism. . . . The anti-Communist platform was (and still is) invaluable [p. 129]" (*Ourselves and Germany,* 1938).

but results. The result of the policies of Baldwin, Chamberlain, Simon, Halifax, and Hoare in the 1930's was to enable the Third Reich to conquer Europe and confront Britain with the gravest peril to national survival it had ever known since the Norman conquest. The peril could probably have been averted *note* by coming to terms with Russia for a Grand Alliance to checkmate the Axis. This the Tory leaders of the wasted years were never willing to do, since they seemed to regard any extension of Soviet power as more dangerous to Britain than any extension of German power. This view was in the long run theoretically sound. In the short run it led to the German-Russian bargain and to a war which initially threatened Britain with German invasion and ended with Russia in control of most of Europe. Chamberlain was forced to resign on May 10, 1940, as the Wehrmacht poured into the Low Countries and France. He died on Nov. 9, 1940. Churchill had for years cautioned his countrymen in vain against these dangers. Under his inspiring leadership after 1940 the dangers were met with "blood, tears, toil, and sweat." All men said indeed of Britishers, in Churchill's words: "This was their finest hour." But the ultimate victory, of which he was prime architect, was made possible only by Hitler's folly in attacking Russia and by massive American aid. Churchill's warning of 1940 was fully realized but his high hopes were fulfilled only in part: "Death and sorrow will be our companions on the journey, hardship our garment, constancy and valor our only shield. We must be reunited, we must be undaunted, we must be inflexible. Our qualities and deeds must burn and glow through the gloom of Europe until they become the veritable beacons of its salvation."

The Politics of Poverty. The central fact of Britain's position in world affairs after 1945, inexorably controlling all others and shaping all public attitudes and policies, was a simple economic fact. It was, put bluntly, that Britain was bankrupt. Unlike its counterparts in Paris and Rome, the Exchequer, to be sure, was able to collect sufficient taxes to defray public expenditures (up to a point) and most British firms and families remained able somehow to pay their bills. Insolvency consisted in a self-evident circumstance—which to many was confused rather than clarified when it was called an "export deficit," an" import surplus," a "dollar gap," an "exchange imbalance," or even a "wabe" at "brillig" full of "slithy toves." The circumstance was this: what the British economy as a whole was able to produce and sell abroad no longer sufficed to buy the foodstuffs and raw materials needed to maintain the living standards which the people of Britain had attained and hoped to improve. The available answers to the problem, all easy in theory and extraordinarily difficult in practice, were to sell more, to buy less, to accept lower living standards, to maintain them as they were through foreign charity, or to arrive at some combination of these solutions which would restore solvency.

The sources of bankruptcy were not obscure. World War II reduced British exports to 30% of their prewar volume and liquidated four-fifths of British investments abroad. During hostilities British debts owed abroad increased from 760 to 3,335 million pounds. When the abrupt end of Lend-Lease in August, 1945, threatened catastrophe, the USA in December extended a loan of $3,750,000,000 to be repaid by A.D. 2001 with interest at 2% to begin in 1951. This reversion to the fiscal follies of the 1920's was soon seen to be irrelevant. The USA now began giving, instead of lending, dollars to Britain to an amount approaching a billion a year under the Marshall Plan and its successor, the Mutual Security Agency. Britishers grappled courageously with all the devices of solution suggested above, plus a 30.5% devaluation of the pound on Sept. 19, 1949. Inspiring accomplishments were registered. But the fact remained during the mid-century years, despite the ups and downs of the economic fever chart, that the British economy was unable to attain solvency in the kind of world created by the Russian-American Cold War.

British politics at home and abroad was a business of wrestling with the specter of bankruptcy and finding (to date) no permanent means of laying the ghost. On July 5, 1945, the voters, electing a new Parliament for the first time in 10 years, gave 12,000,000 ballots to the Labor Party, 9,000,000 to the Tories, and 2,330,000 to the Liberals. Since Britain, for better or worse, lacks proportional representation, Labor won 393 seats in Commons, the Conservatives 198, and the Liberals only 24. Col. Clement R. Attlee became Prime Minister and trade unionist Ernest Bevin Foreign Minister in a Cabinet dedicated to democratic socialism. The Bank of England was nationalized in February, 1946, and then *seriatim* the coal industry, civil aviation, railroads, other transport, and the iron and steel industries. "Key" segments of the economy were socialized with others left in private ownership, while incomes were drastically leveled in the name of "fair shares" and social services were vastly extended to include free medical and dental facilities for all and complete security from cradle to grave.

Socialism was deplored by the old elites of land and money and generally welcomed by the "lower classes" which gained much thereby. But the painful dilemma of the British economy in its precarious relationship to the outer world could not be resolved by either "socialism" or "capitalism" at home. The imperatives posed thereby required governmental exchange controls, allocation of resources and labor, price-fixing, rationing, export subsidies, import restrictions, and public "economic planning" regardless of the ideology or class preferences of the majority in the House of Commons.

Labor "went to the country" on Feb. 23, 1950, and won 315 seats; the Conservatives won 297 and the Liberals 10. The slimness of this majority led Attlee to appeal to the electorate once more on Oct. 25, 1951. Labor polled 48.7% of the popular vote and the Conservatives 48%, but the latter won 321 seats in Commons to Labor's 295 and the Liberal's 6. Churchill again became Prime Minister and Eden Foreign Minister. But their Government clearly did not command a majority of an almost evenly divided electorate.

The British Diplomatic Dilemma. Under the economic circumstances already noted, British policy-makers, whether Labor or Tory, felt that they had no alternative to aligning their foreign policy with that of the USA, since the USSR had neither any desire nor any means to subsidize the British economy. Churchill had argued in vain during the war for a strategy which he hoped would prevent or limit Soviet control of Eastern Europe. Failing in this, he had striven for a bargain with Moscow—with which Washington again would have nothing to do. On May 26, 1942, long before these issues became acute, Eden and Molotov signed a 20-year alliance pledging mutual support against Germany and similar support in the postwar period in the event of the involvement of either signatory in hostilities "with Germany or any of the states . . . associated with her in acts of aggression in Europe."

The parties further pledged themselves to "the two principles of not seeking territorial aggrandizement for themselves and of non-interference in the internal affairs of other States" and agreed "not to conclude any alliance and not to take part in any coalition against the other high contracting party."

Thanks to Soviet policy in Eastern Europe and the American reaction to it, these pledges came to nothing. Bevin joined Byrnes in August, 1945, in protesting Soviet violations of solemn commitments and challenging Soviet control of Eastern Europe. "We must prevent the substitution of one form of totalitarianism for another." Left-wing Laborite rebels criticized what seemed to them the Cabinet's "Tory" foreign policy, but with no immediate results. On March 5, 1946, at Fulton, Mo., in the presence of President Truman, Churchill, borrowing without acknowledgment a favorite phrase of Goebbels, denounced the Soviet "Iron Curtain" across Europe and argued for an Anglo-American alliance to champion freedom and protect Christian civilization. There followed, a year later, the "Truman Doctrine" (see p. 595) and then the Marshall Plan, the Dunkirk and Brussels treaties, the North Atlantic Pact . . . and the Korean War. Britain thus became the ally of the USA and of the States of Western Europe against Soviet aggression.

This formula "solved" British problems in the sense of ensuring continued American subsidies and affording the support of the American leviathan against any Russian effort to subjugate all of Europe. But it raised grave questions as soon as the USA engendered doubts as to the ultimate objectives of its policy of "peace through strength" and began insisting on the massive rearmament of Britain and Western Europe. Few Britons accepted the American view that the Continent was imminently menaced with Soviet military aggression and occupation. Fewer believed that the security of the Atlantic communities required the "liberation" of Eastern Europe from Communist domination. Many became increasingly skeptical of the responsibility and rationality of American policy. All were opposed to any Western war against Red China. And almost all were convinced that if the U.S. program should eventuate not in peace but in open warfare between the Super-Powers, Western

Europe would be overwhelmed and Britain would be helpless and exposed to destruction. "In an alliance with America," declared Prof. N. F. Mott, British atomic physicist, on Sept. 17, 1947, "nothing that this country could do would save us if war should break out against a Power capable of occupying the Channel ports and equipped with atomic bombs. . . . Fifty of these missiles, launched with V-2 weapons in the present stage of development, could kill a quarter of the population of London and make the city uninhabitable. . . ."

Such grim considerations begot a growth of "neutralism" in Britain, despite abhorrence of Red totalitarianism and economic dependence on America. They also begot Cabinet warnings to Washington and parliamentary warnings to the Cabinet. Thus Churchill:

JUNE 5, 1946. "We should not again let the years slip by while we are pushed and slide down the slippery slope. . . . It is better to have a world united than a world divided; but it is also better to have a world divided than a world destroyed."

JAN. 23, 1948. "The best chance of preventing a war is to bring matters to a head and come to a settlement with the Soviet Government before it is too late. . . . There are very grave dangers in letting everything run on and pile up until something happens, and it passes, all of a sudden, out of your control. . . . The best chance is, by formal diplomatic processes with all their privacy and gravity, to arrive at a lasting settlement."

MARCH 28, 1950. "Another world war would begin by . . . fearful cataclysms. . . . Moralists may find it a melancholy thought that peace can find no nobler foundations than mutual terror. But for my part I shall be content if these foundations are solid, because they will give us the extra time and the new breathing space for the supreme effort which has to be made for a world settlement."

These sentiments, echoed in Arnold J. Toynbee's slogan, "No annihilation without representation!" came to most vigorous expression within the ranks of the Labor Party. In early December of 1950 Attlee flew to Washington to tell Truman to abandon any notion he may have entertained that Britain would approve the atomic bombing of China or join the USA in war against Peiping. Under American pressure he nevertheless announced on Jan. 29, 1951, a program for spending £4,700,000,000 ($13,160,000,000) on British rearmament during the ensuing three years. He also supported the U.S. resolution in the UN condemning China as an aggressor. In the Foreign Office (March 9, 1951) Herbert Morrison replaced ailing Ernest Bevin, who died on April 14. MacArthur's dismissal was hailed with universal British relief. On April 22, 1951, Aneurin Bevan, Minister of Labor, joined by Harold Wilson, President of the Board of Trade, resigned from the Cabinet in protest against the Government's resolve to put rearmament above social services. He denounced "hysteria, intolerance, hatred, and witch-hunting," condemned British dependence on "American capitalism, unable to restrain itself at all," and asserted that "we have allowed ourselves to be dragged too far behind the wheels of American diplomacy." The proposed arms budget he pronounced "fantastically wrong" and "already dead." The Attlee Cabinet survived this new revolt on the Left, but the Laborites were increasingly torn by factional feuds with Bevan bidding for leadership on an anti-American program of socialism and peace. On Dec. 6, 1951, Churchill, once more in power, conceded that Bevan had been right "by accident" about the arms budget which would have to be sharply reduced—a decision perpetuated by sheer necessity in 1952, despite increased U.S. aid.

The degree of confusion and division over such issues was indicated in late February, 1952, when Churchill, after visiting Washington, was assailed by the Laborite opposition for having told Congress that British support of the USA would be "prompt, resolute, and effective" in case a Korean armistice should be signed and later violated by the enemy. His answer was to reveal that Attlee and Morrison in May, 1951, had agreed to the bombing of Manchuria in the event of heavy aerial attack from Chinese bases on UN forces in Korea and had agreed in September, 1951, to "more limited action" against China if the truce negotiations should break down.

The Britain of mid-century had no option but to support the USA against Soviet aggression or face possible destruction, certain bankruptcy, or both. But the Britain of mid-century could not conceivably, by any rational definition of national interests, give willing support to American policies which paralyzed East-West trade, made Western Europe and the Commonwealth forever dependent on U.S. subsidies, insisted on rearmament on a scale and at a tempo spelling mass impoverishment to the peoples to be thus defended, jeopardized British imperial interests in the Near and Middle East, and appeared (to many Britishers) bent upon "strength" not as a means to a settlement but as a means to Holy War against Russia and China to liberate all victims of Red Sin from Communist tyranny. Such a war, with Britain as America's "Air Strip No. 1" and the base for another reconquest of Europe, would mean, whatever its ultimate outcome, the reduction of the people of the British Isles to irreparable ruin and beggary.

With the balance of power on the Continent gone forever, despite American efforts to rearm Germany, British security and eventual prosperity were to be had only by a global equilibrium between America and Russia so contrived and maintained as to preclude the possibility of World War III. Britain's contribution to such an outcome admitted of no easy prescription, for it appeared to require a course which would convince Moscow that Britain and America would stand together in any war precipitated by Red aggression and convince Washington that Britain would have no choice but neutrality in any conflict unleashed by an American anti-Communist "crusade" or "preventive war." British statesmanship, albeit disastrous in the 1930's, had displayed talent for comparably difficult tasks in the 19th and 18th Centuries. If a great tradition could be translated into 20th-Century terms and made effective in its influence on Moscow and Washington alike, Downing Street could yet play a decisive role in assuring the survival of Britain, of Europe, and of contemporary civilization.

From Bermuda to Suez. The rulers of Britain—*i.e.*, the leaders of the majority party in the House of Commons—were highly successful in the mid-1950's in furthering the continued devolution of the Empire into a voluntary Commonwealth of independent States, united by such symbols as Queen Elizabeth's round-the-world tour of British lands, November, 1953–May, 1954, from Bermuda and Jamaica to Malta and Gibraltar by way of New Zealand, Australia, Aden, and Uganda. They were moderately successful in restoring British prosperity and in winning most Britons, socialists and anti-socialists alike, to the "Welfare State" in which social security and public economic planning made old issues of "free enterprise" vs. "nationalization" less and less meaningful. They were unsuccessful, at least temporarily, in "mediating" between Washington on the one hand and Moscow and Peiping on the other or in arriving at a viable pattern of relationships with their giant transatlantic ally.

Churchill, now in his eightieth year, was host at Bermuda in December, 1953, to Eisenhower and Laniel and saw his long-standing appeals for top-level negotiations with the USSR come to partial fruition in 1954 and 1955. Aside from the Austrian treaty (see p. 200) and the "Spirit of Geneva" (see p. 201), the results were nebulous and fell short of any comprehensive East-West *modus vivendi*. Other British diplomatic "successes"—*e.g.*, the accords with Iran (see p. 379) and Egypt (see p. 403), membership in SEATO (see p. 609), and sponsorship of the new formula of 1954 for German rearmament (see p. 490)—all turned out in retrospect to have been American "victories" of doubtful import for British interests, even though Foreign Secretary Anthony Eden was honored for his triumphs by being awarded the Knighthood of the Garter, Oct. 20, 1954. He and Churchill had visited Washington in July in an attempt to reconcile Anglo-American differences.

On April 5, 1955, Churchill retired and yielded the Prime Ministership to Eden, who named Harold Macmillan Foreign Secretary and Selwyn Lloyd Minister of Defense. (The former presently became Chancellor of the Exchequer and the latter Foreign Secretary.) In December Clement Attlee, aged 73, also retired, with Hugh Gaitskell becoming leader of the Parliamentary Labor Party. Meanwhile, Eden called for a general election on May 26, 1955. After a desultory campaign, the Conservatives increased their seats in Commons from 321 to 344 and reduced Laborite strength from 295 to 277. During the 18 months which followed, complex diplomatic exchanges with Washington and Moscow and sundry gestures of Anglo-American solidarity and of Anglo-Soviet friendship (culminating in the Khrushchev-Bulganin visit to Britain of April, 1956) achieved no enduring results. Whether a more vigorous and imaginative British diplomacy could have averted the tragedies to come through more determined efforts to reach accords with Washington and

Moscow can never be known with any assurance. American and Soviet prejudices, no less than British, contributed to common frustration.

The outcome was violence in Sinai, Suez, and Hungary in the autumn of 1956. Since we have already reviewed these events in detail (see pp. 396–431), no recapitulation is here needed. Suffice it to say that British policy-makers, like their French colleagues, sought to resume the traditionally sovereign and independent role of "Great Powers," able and willing, if need be, to resort to force to protect "national interests." Under American, Asian-African, and Soviet pressure, the venture was ignominiously abandoned on the eve of success.

Doubtful Prospect. Tory connivance with Paris and Tel Aviv in the abortive attack on Egypt led Anthony Nutting, Sir Edward Boyle, and a few other Conservatives to quit their public posts in protest and evoked a storm in the Laborite opposition. Gasoline rationing was ordered Dec. 17, and later rescinded only when American petroleum supplies began arriving in abundance after London had agreed to evacuate Egypt. Mounting anti-American sentiment came to full expression when more than 100 Conservative M.P.'s, Nov. 27, 1956, signed a manifesto declaring that Washington's policies were gravely endangering the Atlantic Alliance. In December London was obliged to ask the USA and Canada to waive interest payments on the 1946 loans, simultaneously borrowing $1,300,000,000 from the International Monetary Fund and $500,-000,000 from the Export-Import Bank in Washington.

According to an ancient adage, beggars cannot be choosers. The Britain of the late 1950's was in no sense reduced to beggary, but on the contrary was enjoying a phenomenal inflationary prosperity. Britain, moreover, had become the third Power possessed of A-bombs and H-bombs. But the holy goal of an "independent" foreign policy, scarcely available any longer even to the Super-Powers of America and Russia, was wholly unattainable for a "tight little island" whose people were dependent for their livelihood on world-wide foreign trade and who were foredoomed to annihilation in the event of atomic war. British capacity to influence the course of world politics would henceforth depend less on the traditional components of "national power" than on more subtle means of winning friends and influencing people. The same was true, to be sure, of all the erstwhile "Powers." But people and policy-makers in the USA and the USSR were understandably less aware than Britishers of the painful necessities of the new time.

How the problems thus posed were to be grappled with, apart from the traditional and pragmatic British methods of trial-and-error fumbling and "muddling through," was clear to no one in 1957–58. These methods were perhaps the best to be had under the circumstances, since no others seemed available. On Jan. 9, 1957, it was announced from Buckingham Palace that "the Right Honorable Sir Anthony Eden, M.P., had an audience of the Queen this evening and tendered his resignation as Prime Minister and First Lord of the Treasury, which Her Majesty was pleased to accept." On Jan. 10 "the Queen received the Right Honorable Harold Macmillan, M.P., in audience this afternoon and offered him the post of Prime Minister and First Lord of the Treasury. Mr. Macmillan accepted Her Majesty's offer and kissed hands upon his appointment."

By such quaint formulas, the Conservative Party accepted the ailing Eden's retirement and effected a reshuffle of the Cabinet under Macmillan, with Selwyn Lloyd carrying on as Foreign Secretary. "Britain," he told the nation on Jan. 17, "has been great, is great, and will stay great, providing we close our ranks and get on with the job." He called off a projected visit to Moscow but insisted that Britain must be an "equal ally," not a "satellite," of the USA. On April 4, 1957, a Cabinet "White Paper," prepared by Duncan Sandys, Minister of Defense, announced a drastic reform of military policy. "It must be frankly recognized that there is at present no means of providing adequate protection for the people of this country against the consequences of an attack with nuclear weapons." The Government therefore would henceforth rely on the "deterrent" effect of bombers and rockets with nuclear warheads and would cut down the Navy, Army, and Air Force from 690,000 to 375,000 by the end of 1962, scrap battleships, reduce garrisons throughout the Empire and in Germany, end conscription, and cut Britain's annual $4,000,000,000 defense bill to some more modest figure compatible with the solvency of the British economy.

This radical innovation, decried as "defeatism" in Washington, was a graphic manifestation of British inability to continue to play the game of power politics. But it may also be judged in the perspective of tomorrow as another instance of British leadership in pointing the way to the future for all mankind, as the England of old had repeatedly done in founding parliamentary government, inaugurating the Industrial Revolution, and granting independence to subject peoples. In the thermonuclear age "national defense" cannot be attained by arms alone nor, ultimately, by arms at all. This truth was not yet clear in Washington and Moscow (nor in Peiping, Paris, Bonn, or Rome) by 1958. It was wholly clear to most Britons of all parties. Here, as in times past, a new England, vanquished by victory and enfeebled in the now obsolete components of power, might yet achieve global prestige and leadership by pointing the way to the imperatives of a new age.

SUGGESTED READINGS

Allen, H. C.: *Great Britain and the United States*, New York, St. Martin's, 1955.
Bardens, Dennis: *Portrait of a Statesman: The Personal Life Story of Sir Anthony Eden*, New York, Philosophical Library, 1956.
Bell, Philip W.: *The Sterling Area in the Postwar World*, New York, Oxford, 1956.
Bevan, Aneurin: *In Place of Fear*, New York, Simon and Schuster, 1952.
Brady, Robert A.: *Crisis in Britain*, Berkeley, Calif., University of California Press, 1950.

AMERICA: THE DILEMMAS OF POWER

Chamberlain, Neville: *In Search of Peace*, New York, Putnam, 1939.
Churchill, Winston S.: *War Memoirs* (5 vols.), Boston, Houghton Mifflin, 1951*ff*.
Cole, G. D. H., and Raymond Postgate: *The British People*, 1746–1946, New York, Knopf, 1947.
———: *The Post-war Condition of Britain*, New York, Praeger, 1957.
Cowles, Virginia: *Winston Churchill: The Era and the Man*, New York, Harper, 1953.
Elliott, William Yandell, and H. Duncan Hall (eds.): *The British Commonwealth at War*, New York, Knopf, 1943.
Europa Publications: *The British Commonwealth*, London, 1956.
Evans, Trevor: *Bevan of Britain*, New York, Norton, 1946.
Feiling, Keith: *The Life of Neville Chamberlain*, New York, Macmillan, 1947.
Gardner, Richard N.: *Sterling-Dollar Diplomacy*, New York, Oxford, 1956.
Gedye, G. E. R.: *Betrayal in Central Europe*, New York, Oxford, 1939.
Halifax, Lord: *Speeches on Foreign Policy*, 1934–1939, New York, Oxford, 1940.
Henderson, Sir Nevile: *Failure of a Mission*, New York, Putnam, 1940.
Hutchinson, Keith: *The Decline and Fall of British Capitalism*, New York, Scribner, 1950.
Johnson, Alan Campbell: *Anthony Eden*, New York, Ives Washburn, 1939.
Somervell, D. C., and Heather Harvey: *The British Empire and Commonwealth*, London, Christophers, 1954.
Taylor, Robert Lewis: *Winston Churchill: An Informal Study of Greatness*, New York, Doubleday, 1952.
Walker, Eric A.: *The British Empire: Its Structure and Spirit*, 1497–1953, Cambridge, Mass., Harvard University Press, 1956.
Willcox, William B.: *Star of Empire: A Study of Britain as a World Power*, 1485–1945, New York, Knopf, 1950.
Williams, Francis: *Socialist Britain*, New York, Viking, 1949.
Windrich, Elaine: *British Labour's Foreign Policy*, Stanford, Calif., Stanford University Press, 1951.
Wolfers, Arnold: *Britain and France between Two Wars*, New York, Harcourt, Brace, 1940.

3. AMERICA: THE DILEMMAS OF POWER

It is very difficult to ascertain, at present, what degree of sagacity the American democracy will display in the conduct of the foreign policy of the country; and upon this point its adversaries, as well as its advocates, must suspend their judgment.—ALEXIS DE TOCQUEVILLE, *Democracy in America*, 1839.

The Meaning of America. In the mid-20th Century the most populous member of the World State System was China. The most extensive, in contiguous territory, was the Soviet Union. The largest in overseas lands and peoples was the British Commonwealth. But the richest, most productive, most powerful, most gigantic, stupendous, titanic, and supercolossal was, beyond all question, the United States of North America.

The ultimate import of America to its own people and to the world can be defined only by those who are naïvely dogmatic or innocently ignorant. For America is in its essence protean, flexible, and all things to all men. This judgment has been validated anew by tortured efforts to devise "loyalty tests" and to formulate an orthodox definition of "Americanism." Among sensitive observers, aware of their lack of omniscience, America has long been and will long remain a pluralistic land of paradoxes. For here, cheek by jowl, are revolutionary radicalism and reactionary conservatism; political democracy and economic oligarchy; a melting pot of nations and a cesspool of racial hatred; a fortress of freedom and an arena of witch-burning; a dream of liberty and a stronghold of privilege. In the USA have flourished, successively and often simultaneously, universal education and mass illiteracy; tiled bathrooms and tar-paper shacks; wholesale immigration and deportation delirium; charitable foundations and the "robber barons"; Christian tolerance and the "Christian Front"; Walt Whitman and Edgar Guest; the I.W.W. and Rotary International; Thomas Paine and Calvin Coolidge; New Harmony and the New York Stock Exchange; trust-makers and trust-busters; Eugene Debs and Joseph Pew; fervent pacifism and 100% Americanism; Andrew Volstead and John Barleycorn; soap operas along with new symphonies; Justice Holmes and Martin Dies; burlesque shows and clerical puritanism; Jack London and Adolphe Menjou; fantastic greed and incredible generosity; Paul Bunyan and George F. Babbitt; Joseph McCarthy and Earl Warren; lynching mobs and community chests; etc., ad infinitum.

To resolve or explain this bewildering and ever-shifting kaleidoscope is, happily, no part of the present task. It is enough to emphasize that America, seldom defined by Americans save in the slogans of hucksters, is still indefinable. Its world mission, belatedly perceived, may yet bring to its people, and to all their neighbors over the earth, infinite weal or endless woe. American politics, flowing from English models, French inspiration, and native experience, has ever been an exalted epic of debate among free men in search of truth and a petty comedy of provincial prejudice and greedy self-seeking. Foreign critics are wholly right in asserting that Americans worship at the altar of Mammon and are devotees of games of chance, unearned income, pecuniary emulation, and conspicuous waste. Foreign admirers are equally right in affirming that Americans cherish liberty and justice above all other values. As judged by the timeless standards of the Jewish-Greek-Christian tradition, inherited by America, along with all the West, from a remote past, the American dream is at times a nightmare of ignorant avarice and at others a vision beyond the stars, summoning all mankind to climb a stairway into heaven.

Foreign policy, like all policy, is a mirror of these competing purposes and pressures, conditioned by the fixed facts of geography and the fluid facts of power relationships in an unstable State System. The definition of American national purposes in dealing with other sovereignties has, through half a dozen generations, reflected the interests and cherished symbols of successive elite groups: the wealthy and the wellborn, the slavocracy, the merchant princes, the factory owners, the bankers, the industrial monopolists, the stockbrokers, the brain trusters, and the brass hats. It has also reflected the aspirations, usually more vaguely defined, of sub-elite groups challenging the current elite: pioneers and artisans, frontiersmen and farmers, workers and consumers, small businessmen and sharecroppers, "economic royalists" and seekers after peace. Only the results can be noted here, not the baffling processes of democracy by which they were reached.

Those results, viewed in retrospect, reveal a loom of popular preferences and public policies in coping with the outer world over which experience has woven a pattern of "principles," slowly embroidered into almost sacred symbols. Three became major guides to future action: (1) Americans should do business with Europeans but should abstain from involvement in European power politics. (2) Europeans should do business with Americans but should abstain from power politics in the Americas. (3) Americans and Europeans alike should do business with Asiatics but should jointly abstain from power politics in Asia. The first injunction received classic expression in Washington's Farewell Address and Jefferson's Inaugural, the second in the Monroe Doctrine, and the third in the Open Door policy. All three served American interests well in the 19th Century. All three failed of their purposes in the 20th, since the world changed more rapidly than did American formulas for dealing with it. In consequence, America was pushed or dragged into extensive interventions, by diplomacy and by arms, in Europe, Africa, and Asia, and compelled, willy-nilly, by considerations of security, prosperity, and self-interest and by the sheer fact of its own overwhelming power, to assume a role of "world leadership." At the time of writing, the final character of that role was still unclear.

Isolationism and *Realpolitik*. All people possess some capacity to learn from experience. But when lessons once learned are embalmed in magic phrases which stir emotions deeply and thereby inhibit rational adjustment to new problems, then the products of experience are obstacles rather than aids to new learning. They render more difficult the task of facing emergencies and achieving that progressive adaptation to environmental change which is the prerequisite of survival for all living things. Still more is this the case when the magic phrases are not only irrelevant today and dangerous tomorrow but false as descriptions of yesterday.

American foreign policy is commonly envisaged by Americans and non-Americans in terms of an alternation in the past, and a choice in the present, between "isolationism" and "internationalism." This formula, while superficially plausible, is a product of echoes-in-the-cave which tell us nothing as to what American foreign policy is about. What it is about (even when Americans themselves seem to be innocents abroad) can best be grasped by recalling the elementary imperatives of power politics which every member of the Western State System must observe if it wishes to avoid political extinction.

The USA established its independent existence as a member of the State System through a treaty of military alliance with France, signed in Paris Feb. 6, 1778—the first, last, and only military alliance of the USA prior to the North Atlantic Treaty of April 4, 1949. The engagements with "allies"

589

in World Wars I and II were in no case treaties of alliance. The original alliance was not a product of mutual ideological admiration between French monarchists and American revolutionists. It was the outgrowth of a shared desire to defeat and weaken England, an objective achieved in 1783 when London made peace and acknowledged American independence.

The new "Power" was safe as long as a balance of power among the older Powers was assured. The new "Power" was unsafe whenever any of the older Powers might subdue the rest and thereby confront America with a combination of power it could not resist. When revolutionary France went to war in 1792, young America was confronted with a difficult choice. Treaty obligations and ideological sympathy appeared to require that America join France against England and the Continental monarchies. National interest dictated neutrality. The U.S. proclaimed its neutrality in 1793 and, by act of Congress, abrogated the treaty of alliance in 1798. So embarrassing were these commitments that Washington's Farewell Address of 1796 (written by Alexander Hamilton) urged abstention from permanent alliances with any portion of the foreign world, and Jefferson's Inaugural of 1801 championed "peace, commerce, and honest friendship with all nations, entangling alliances with none."

The American aberration of 1812 made the USA the ally in fact, if not in form, of France against Britain— *i.e.*, cobelligerent of the most powerful of the Powers against the Power fighting to restore the balance. The defeat which followed was far more conducive to American security than would have been a victory over Britain coupled with Bonaparte's triumph in Russia. For in this event the State System would have been permanently subverted to the ultimate peril of the USA. As Jefferson put it in 1814: "None of us wishes to see Bonaparte conquer Russia, and lay thus at his feet the whole Continent of Europe. This done, England would be but a breakfast . . . and he might spare such a force to be sent in British ships as I would as leave not have to encounter."

For a century after 1815 the whole design of U.S. foreign policy, with its precepts of neutrality, Monroe Doctrine, and Open Door, rested upon and presupposed, though few Americans were consciously aware of the fact, an enduring balance among other Powers in Europe and Asia. "Isolationism" was but the shadow on the wall of a global equipoise. Whenever the equilibrium was threatened the shadow vanished. Thus America went to war in 1917 to prevent the unification of Europe by imperial Germany. With the balance restored, America could pretend in the 1920's and 1930's to be unconcerned with European and Asiatic "power politics" and even pledge itself to "keep out of other people's wars" through the so-called "Neutrality" Acts of 1935–37 which forbade Americans to sell arms or make loans to foreign belligerents or to travel on belligerent vessels—all on the irrelevant assumption that abandonment of "freedom of the seas" and of munitions exports would ensure American noninvolvement in conflicts abroad.

America and the Balance of Power. As soon as the balance was once more jeopardized by the Nazi plan for mastery of Europe and the Japanese program for conquest of Asia, all these follies were promptly abandoned to the tune of repeated protestations that they were unalterable expressions of eternal wisdom. A new "Neutrality" Act of Nov. 4, 1939, once more forbade Americans to loan money to, travel in, or trade with belligerents and barred American ships from belligerent waters, but repealed the arms embargo (and this is what mattered) and in the name of "cash-and-carry" allowed belligerents (*i.e.*, France and Britain) to buy munitions and ship them in their own vessels. When it became clear in the spring of 1940 that the Triplice bid for global dominion was well on its way to victory, an alarmed America took further steps. William Allen White's "Committee to Defend America by Aiding the Allies" competed successfully for public support against Gen. Robert Wood's "America First Committee," committed to "neutrality." Congress voted $12,000,000,000 for arms by year's end. Guns and planes were rushed to England in the summer. On Sept. 2 Roosevelt announced an executive agreement whereby the USA transferred 50 destroyers to Britain in return for 99-year leaseholds on naval and air bases in the western Atlantic.

These and later decisions were all gross violations of the traditional legal definition of neutral duties (despite casuistry to the contrary) and a wholesale repudiation of the "isolationist" view that the USA should abstain from aid or injury to either side in wars among other Powers. The "revisionist" scholars of the 1950's, like their predecessors in the 1920's, argued that the Roosevelt Administration, like the Wilson Administration, deliberately plunged America into war by its unneutral course. So indeed it did. The premise of the argument, however, was either that a European "negotiated peace" by stalemate would have materialized in 1917 and in 1941, thus preserving the balance, or that the destruction of the balance of power in Europe and Asia constituted no danger to America. The latter position, while theoretically. arguable, has never been accepted by Americans, despite their perennial delusions and befuddlements. The key to American foreign policy, whatever words of rationalization may be employed, is as simple as the key to British foreign policy in earlier centuries: never permit any single Power or coalition of Powers to gain undisputed control of Europe and Asia, for the most basic national interest of America, *i.e.*, political survival as an independent sovereignty, will then be threatened; oppose all such efforts by diplomacy and by arms and, if need be, by all the weapons of total war.

What is fearfully confusing to Americans and non-Americans alike is that Americans are invariably incapable of stating and acting upon their national interests as they actually exist, and must ever persuade themselves and others that their foreign policy is not concerned with problems of power (which are the only problems with which a rational foreign policy can ever be concerned) but with questions of ethics (which clearly have nothing to do with power politics, save as a basis of propaganda). Thus in 1917–18 the rational objective of thwarting a German conquest of Europe was couched in terms of moral indignation over the Black Sins of the Kaiser and of "Militarism" and "Autocracy" and of crusading to annihilate "Prussianism," to "make the world safe for democracy," and to win "the war to end war." Thus in 1940–45 the rational objective of thwarting a German-Japanese conquest of Europe and Asia was couched in terms of moral indignation over the Brown Sins of Hitler and the viciousness of Fascism and of crusading to annihilate the dictatorships and establish the "four freedoms" (F.D.R., Jan. 6, 1941) "everywhere in the world." And thus in the 1950's, the rational objective of thwarting a Russian-Chinese conquest of Europe and Asia was couched in terms of moral indignation over the Red Sins of Stalin and Mao and the wickedness of Communism, and of crusading to annihilate Red tyranny and liberate all mankind from Marxist slavery.

What is striking and heartening is that behind these façades of semantic obfuscation and romantic nonsense the USA does nevertheless pursue a simple, consistent, and logical course in world affairs and may reasonably be expected to continue to do so unless its policy-makers should lose their minds or its people should come to mistake ethical irrelevancies for political realities. The direction of the course is a matter of record and, behind the fog of self-righteous verbiage, is readily comprehensible and predictable. The "Lend-Lease" Act of March 11, 1941, authorized the President to transfer arms to "any country whose defense the President deems vital to the defense of the USA." Such a policy in 1936 might, conceivably, have averted World War II. In 1941 it provoked Triplice attack. "A stitch in time saves nine." But in American foreign policy, whatever its virtues, other proverbs usually prevail —e.g., penny wise, pound foolish; always lock the barn door after the horse is stolen; never cross bridges until you've burned them behind you; never do today what should have been done the day before yesterday if you can postpone it until the day after tomorrow; a penny wasted is a penny saved; etc.

By August of 1941, when the mouth-filling precepts of the Atlantic Charter were enunciated (see p. 193), America was granting all-out aid (albeit still small in amount) "short of war" to Britain, Russia, and China against Germany, Italy, and Japan, with the Administration wholly committed to the defeat of the Triplice and determined to provoke enemy attack so that Congress and the public would be equally committed. Two days after Pearl Harbor F.D.R. told the nation:

It will not only be a long war, it will be a hard war. The U.S. can accept no result save victory, final and complete. . . . We are going to win the war, and we are going to win the peace that follows. . . . The vast majority of the members of the human race are on our side. . . . We represent our hope and their hope for liberty under God.

The war, as usual, was won, with America growing rich in the process and the would-be conquerors of Europe and Asia smashed. The peace, as usual, was lost, since Americans, while skilled in waging wars engendered by the

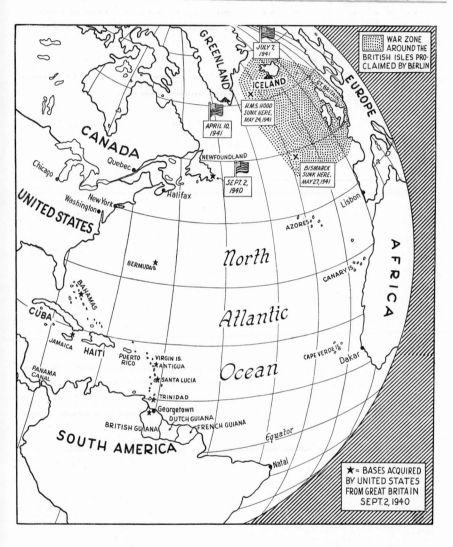

politics of power (though never in preventing them), have few skills in practicing the politics of peace—largely because they suppose that the only objective of war is military victory and that the new problems of power posed by victory are not really problems of power, to be dealt with by diplomatic bargaining supported by effective force, but are problems of ethics to be dealt with by proclaiming "principles" and then denouncing as unprincipled sinners all who act on different principles. America could safely afford "isolationism" after 1920, for the defeat of the Central Powers was followed by a new balance of power in Europe and Asia. America could not safely afford "isolationism" after 1945, for the defeat of the Triplice was followed (thanks in part to the American strategy of victory) by a new hegemony of the Communist Powers over Europe and Asia.

New Challenge and New Response. In the tangled sequel, and this time with less tardiness and reluctance than usual, Americans did once more what they have always done when faced with such a challenge: amass arms, support allies, and prepare, if need be, to threaten the new aspirants to hegemony with total war. They also did once more, more quickly and eagerly than usual, what they have always done: identify their national interests with Virtue and those of the foe with Vice. From the bleak perspectives of the 1950's, the result might again be what it had been twice before: the smashing of the would-be conquerors in victorious war, the rise of new conquerors out of a lost peace, and so on forever. But the result, conversely, might be nothing of the kind. The new challenge was more formidable and more sinister than any previous challenge and, beyond a point, could not be effectively met by the conventional means of armaments and alliances. In war, moreover, the new challengers invariably gained new power rather than losing old power. And in atomic war there might well be no victors but only a few barbarized survivors. These circumstances made the American task of preserving the balance of power in Europe and Asia, assumed for the third time in half a century, one of novel and extraordinary difficulty. But the task was assumed with eagerness and energy, if not always with wisdom.

The major steps in the enterprise were not items of any "Grand Design" but improvisations in the face of challenge, begetting counterchallenge, and producing new improvisations. Yet a logic emerged from successive decisions in successive crises, for behind the verbiage the goal was clear—*i.e.*, prevention of the conquest of Europe and Asia, while the means (alliances and armaments) were as old as politics among nations. What the "peace" might have been had Franklin D. Roosevelt lived beyond April 12, 1945, is as interesting and futile a subject of speculation as the problem of what another peace might have been had Abraham Lincoln lived beyond April 14, 1865, fourscore years before. The Truman Administration will be judged by history to have been a regime of brass, braid, and business, shot through with demagogery and corruption, inspired by a vision of social justice and defense of freedom, and shaped by the almost pathological fear of Communism which gripped most Americans of mid-century. A chronology of major decisions will suggest the emergent pattern of global policy whereby America tried to meet the Communist threat.

AUG. 18, 1945. Byrnes, seconded two days later by Bevin, challenges the adequacy of democracy in the provisional Bulgarian Government. Months and years follow of Anglo-American indictments of Moscow for violating the Yalta pledges of "democracy" and "free elections" in Eastern Europe. Western efforts are unsuccessful in undermining the puppet regimes of the "Peoples' Democracies" whereby the USSR assumed control of the areas conquered from the Nazis by Soviet forces in 1944–45.

MARCH 5, 1946. Winston Churchill in Fulton, Mo., urges an Anglo-American alliance to protect Christian civilization from the Soviet menace, to break the "Iron Curtain," and ultimately to liberate the peoples enslaved by Communist tyranny.

SEPT. 20, 1946. Truman, on Byrnes's demand, asks for the resignation of former Vice-President and Secretary of Commerce, Henry A. Wallace, who in New York on Sept. 12 had publicly appealed for a Soviet-American entente: "We should recognize that we have no more business in the political affairs of Eastern Europe than Russia has in the political affairs of Latin America, Western Europe, and the USA."

MARCH 12, 1947. Truman asks Congress for $400,000,000 to aid Greece and Turkey in the name of help to "free people to maintain their free institutions and their national integrity against aggressive movements that seek to impose upon them totalitarian regimes." The "Truman Doctrine" is envisaged as part of a broader policy of "containment" of Soviet expansion (see George F. Kennan or "X," on "The Sources of Soviet Conduct," *Foreign Affairs*, July, 1947) on the premise that such containment would lead to the ultimate "mellowing" or disintegration of the Soviet Power.

JUNE 5, 1947. Marshall at Harvard espouses U.S. aid to Europe to combat "hunger, poverty, desperation, and chaos." The "Marshall Plan" or European Recovery Program (E.R.P.) follows, with the USA granting almost 20 billion dollars to Western Europe in the ensuing four years in the name of economic recovery and anti-Communism, while the USSR and its satellites refuse to participate and denounce the program as "American imperialism."

JUNE 11, 1948. The U.S. Senate approves the Vandenberg resolution, based on the Pan-American "Act of Petropolis," reaffirming the hope of "international peace and security through the UN" and urging "progressive development of regional and other collective arrangements for individual and collective self-defense . . . based on continuous and effective self-help and mutual aid" under Article 51 of the UN Charter (*q.v.*).

JAN. 4, 1949. Truman promulgates the "Point Four" program (see p. 625f. above).

APRIL 4, 1949. The USA signs the 20-year North Atlantic Treaty with Canada and 10 States of Western Europe pledging mutual defense against Soviet aggression. The formula is the Vandenberg formula of 1947–48. Greece and Turkey are admitted to the coalition by the time of the Lisbon Conference of NATO (February, 1952) where swift and massive rearmament of Western Europe is pledged but proves impossible of achievement on the scale and at the tempo contemplated.[2]

---

[2] PREAMBLE: The parties to this treaty reaffirm their faith in the purposes and principles of the Charter of the United Nations and their desire to live in peace with all peoples and all governments.

They are determined to safeguard the freedom, common heritage and civilization of their peoples, founded on the principles of democracy, individual liberty and the rule of law.

They seek to promote stability and well-being in the North Atlantic area.

They are resolved to unite their efforts for collective defense and for the preservation of peace and security.

They therefore agree to this North Atlantic Treaty:

THE DEFENSE OF DEMOCRACY

JUNE 27, 1950. The USA comes to the military defense of South Korea against Communist aggression, assumes a protectorate over Formosa and other areas threatened by Red aggression in Asia, and embarks upon massive rearmament on the premise that Communism is now prepared to seek world domination through military conquest.

APRIL 11, 1951. Truman dismisses MacArthur for insubordination after his repeated public advocacy of all-out war with China following Chinese defeat of U.S. forces in North Korea in the fall of 1950. USA, enjoying the highest levels of prosperity in its history, replaces Marshall Plan with the Mutual Security Agency (MSA) for continued economic and military aid to Europe and all the Free World. Washington champions the rearmament of Germany, Italy, and Japan as necessary to effective mutual defense.

SEPT. 8, 1951. USA signs treaties of peace and alliance with Japan (see p. 200). In the course of related negotiations, the USA signs a mutual defense pact with the Philippine Republic (Aug. 30, 1951) and a tripartite defense pact with

---

ARTICLE 1: The parties undertake, as set forth in the Charter of the United Nations, to settle any international disputes in which they may be involved by peaceful means in such a manner that international peace and security, and justice, are not endangered, and to refrain in their international relations from the threat or use of force in any manner inconsistent with the purpose of the United Nations.

ARTICLE 2: The parties will contribute toward the further development of peaceful and friendly international relations by strengthening their free institutions, by bringing about a better understanding of the principles upon which these institutions are founded, and by promoting conditions of stability and well-being. They will seek to eliminate conflict in their international economic policies and will encourage economic collaboration between any or all of them.

ARTICLE 3: In order more effectively to achieve the objectives of this treaty, the parties, separately and jointly, by means of continuous and effective self-help and mutual aid, will maintain and develop their individual and collective capacity to resist armed attack.

ARTICLE 4: The parties will consult together whenever, in the opinion of any of them, the territorial integrity, political independence or security of any of the parties is threatened.

ARTICLE 5: The parties agree that an armed attack against one or more of them in Europe or North America shall be considered an attack against them all; and consequently they agree that, if such an armed attack occurs, each of them, in exercise of the right of individual or collective self-defense recognized by Article 51 of the Charter of the United Nations, will assist the party or parties so attacked by taking forthwith, individually and in concert with the other parties, such action as it deems necessary, including the use of armed force, to restore and maintain the security of the North Atlantic area.

Any such armed attack and all measures taken as a result thereof shall immediately be reported to the Security Council. Such measures shall be terminated when the Security Council has taken the measures necessary to restore and maintain international peace and security.

ARTICLE 6: For the purpose of Article 5 an armed attack on one or more of the parties is deemed to include an armed attack on the territory of any of the parties in Europe or North America, on the Algerian departments of France, on the occupation forces of any party in Europe, on the islands under the jurisdiction of any party in the North Atlantic area north of the Tropic of Cancer or on the vessels or aircraft in this area of any of the parties.

ARTICLE 7: This treaty does not affect, and shall not be interpreted as affecting, in any way the rights and obligations under the Charter of the parties which are members of the United Nations, or the primary responsibility of the Security Council for the maintenance of international peace and security.

ARTICLE 8: Each party declares that none of the international engagements now in

596

Australia and New Zealand (Sept. 1, 1951), all to "remain in force indefinitely." Key provisions are substantially identical in both instruments: "Art. 2. In order more effectively to achieve the objective of this Treaty the Parties separately and jointly by means of continuous and effective self-help and mutual aid will develop their individual and collective capacity to resist armed attack. Art. 3. The Parties will consult together whenever in the opinion of any of them the territorial integrity, political independence, or security of any of the Parties is threatened in the Pacific. Art. 4. Each Party recognizes that an armed attack in the Pacific area on any of the Parties would be dangerous to its own peace and safety and declares that it would act to meet the common danger in accord with its constitutional processes. Any such armed attack and all measures taken as a result thereof shall be immediately reported to the Security Council of the UN. Such measures shall be terminated when the Security Council has taken the measures necessary to restore and maintain international peace and security. Art. 5. For the purpose of Art. 4, an armed attack on any of the Parties is deemed to include an armed

---

force between it and any other of the parties or any third state is in conflict with the provisions of this treaty, and undertakes not to enter into any international engagement in conflict with this treaty.

ARTICLE 9: The parties hereby establish a council, on which each of them shall be represented, to consider matters concerning the implementation of this treaty. The council shall be so organized as to be able to meet promptly at any time. The council shall set up such subsidiary bodies as may be necessary; in particular it shall establish immediately a defense committee which shall recommend measures for the implementation of Articles 3 and 5.

ARTICLE 10: The parties may, by unanimous agreement, invite any other European state in a position to further the principles of this treaty and to contribute to the security of the North Atlantic area to accede to this treaty. Any state so invited may become a party to the treaty by depositing its instrument of accession with the Government of the United States of America. The Government of the United States of America will inform each of the parties of the deposit of each such instrument of accession.

ARTICLE 11: This treaty shall be ratified and its provisions carried out by the parties in accordance with their respective constitutional processes. The instruments of ratification shall be deposited as soon as possible with the Government of the United States of America, which will notify all the other signatories of each deposit. The treaty shall enter into force between the states which have ratified it as soon as the ratifications of the majority of the signatories, including the ratifications of Belgium, Canada, France, Luxembourg, the Netherlands, the United Kingdom and the United States, have been deposited and shall come into effect with respect to other states on the date of the deposit of their ratifications.

ARTICLE 12: After the treaty has been in force for ten years, or at any time thereafter, the parties shall, if any of them so requests, consult together for the purpose of reviewing the treaty, having regard for the factors then affecting peace and security in the North Atlantic area, including the development of universal as well as regional arrangements under the Charter of the United Nations for the maintenance of international peace and security.

ARTICLE 13: After the treaty has been in force for twenty years, any party may cease to be a party one year after its notice of denunciation has been given to the Government of the United States of America, which will inform the Governments of the other parties of the deposit of each notice of denunciation.

ARTICLE 14: This treaty, of which the English and French texts are equally authentic, shall be deposited in the archives of the Government of the United States of America. Duly certified copies thereof will be transmitted by that Government to the Governments of the other signatories.

IN WITNESS WHEREOF, the undersigned plenipotentiaries have signed this treaty.

attack on the metropolitan territory of any of the Parties, or on the island territories under its jurisdiction in the Pacific, or on its armed forces, public vessels,
or aircraft in the Pacific."

MAY 26, 1952. The USA signs treaties of peace and alliance with West Germany (see p. 487).

1952–53. Numerous American public figures declare that "containment" is
"negative" and "inadequate," that no compromise settlement with the enemy is
possible in Europe or Asia, and that the USA and its allies must evolve and
apply a program of "liberating" enslaved peoples, if possible by methods other
than war.

Twenty years of Democratic rule meanwhile ended with Republican victory
in November, 1952. Yet Governor Stevenson's defeat and General Eisenhower's
inauguration as President meant no sharp break with the past. Likable "Ike"
was committed to the broad pattern of foreign policy already developed. As
for the domestic "balance of power," the shift of influence away from organized labor, the farm bloc, and the civil bureaucracy toward "Big Business"
and professional military specialists was already far advanced in the Truman
Administration. Its consummation effected a close fusion of economic and
political power in the American society of the mid-century—a condition long
ago deemed the prerequisite of stability by such political philosophers as Harrington, Montesquieu, and Madison. Thanks to popular conviction that the
"time for a change" had come, corporate industry and finance, long under a
cloud during the "New Deal" and "Fair Deal" epoch, here achieved a new
opportunity to serve the Great Republic and the Free World, and a new responsibility to face creatively the challenge of the future.

The new era began with the President-elect's journey to Korea in December,
1952, and with Winston Churchill's journey to America in January, 1953.
The Prime Minister opined that stalemate was preferable to checkmate or
global war. Secretary of State John Foster Dulles, champion of "liberation"
in place of "containment," [3] was at once confronted with formidable obstacles

[3] Mr. Dulles's hopes were well expressed in his address in Buffalo of June 21, 1952:
"Today one-third of the human race is subject to the despotic terrorism of a new dark
age. It is morally impossible for us to reconcile ourselves to that as a permanent condition
or to buy security for ourselves by some 'deal' which would confirm that servitude. We
cannot settle for a containment which contains 800,000,000 captive souls." George F.
Kennan, chief architect of the original "containment" policy, continued to argue that
moral values should be applied to foreign policy only as negative restraints upon action,
not as affirmative goals to be implemented through diplomacy or war. See p. 281n. above.
Kennan became U.S. Ambassador to the USSR on May 14, 1952. Unlike his predecessors, he knew Russians and Russia and regarded "national interest," prudently defined,
as a better guide to policy than legal or ethical abstractions. In spite of, or possibly because of, these qualities, the USSR declared him *persona non grata* on Oct. 3, 1952,
and forced his recall, allegedly because of a press interview in Berlin on Sept. 19 in
which he told reporters, recalling his internment in Germany in 1941, that "had the Nazis
permitted us to walk the streets without any right to talk to any Germans, that would
be precisely how we have to live today" in Moscow. This characterization of the status
of foreign diplomats in Muscovy, reminiscent of many similar comments in earlier
centuries, was denounced by the Kremlin as a "slander," "libel," and "lie."

in the way of realizing American hopes of rearming and unifying Western Europe, promoting the solvency of the British and Continental economies, taking the offensive against Russia, and finding effective means, through "deneutralizing" Chiang Kai-shek or blockading or bombing Red China, of compelling the foe to yield. Inconclusive "Cold War"—unaccompanied by any global or total hot war because of the impossibility of either antagonist entertaining serious expectations of defeating the other—thus promised to remain an enduring *motif* of U.S. foreign policy and of world politics.

American Destiny. Judgments varied as to the successes and failures of America's response in mid-century to the most recent threat of world conquest by totalitarian Powers. In one sense the response was a failure since the new enemy during these years conquered all of China, save Formosa, and retained his grip on all of Eastern Europe and the Balkans, save Jugoslavia. In another sense the response was successful since the enemy made no new conquests in Southeast Asia, the Near and Middle East, or Western Europe. The response promoted inflationary prosperity and met with almost unanimous and bipartisan public approbation. Its implications and ultimate consequences appeared to depend on whether American policy-makers would continue to be content with "containing" and balancing the power of Marxland with a view toward an ultimate *modus vivendi* from a "situation of strength," or would be tempted by strength and by the political imperatives of an armaments economy to undertake the emancipation of the enslaved peoples and the military annihilation of the enemy. The former course was attainable without war and was compatible with the traditional and necessary objective of maintaining a global equilibrium. The latter course threatened a new Holy War or Crusade in which, as always, there can be no victors. In terms of these alternatives, the crucial questions of American foreign policy in the 1950's were these:

1. Should America "balance" Communist power in global terms by major reliance on American industry, arms, and guarantees to allies or seek to build up local equivalents of Communist military strength in Western Europe and Eastern Asia? The USA committed itself to the latter course in 1950*f.*, but found that the enterprise was difficult to reconcile with the solvency and the economic, social, and political stability of its European and Asian allies.

2. Should America seek indefinitely to subsidize Western Europe and Eastern Asia or permit these economies to sell enough to America and to the "enemy" to make them self-supporting? The USA committed itself to the former course in 1950*f.*, but found that it was unacceptable to most of its allies, who increasingly demanded "trade, not aid."

3. Should America seek prosperity indefinitely by gigantic spending for armaments and foreign aid (a course to which the USA committed itself after 1950) or strive to find other markets, at home and abroad, for the colossal output of its industry and agriculture?

4. Should America seek to win the Cold War, without the necessity of

waging a global hot war, by instigating and organizing revolution among the enslaved peoples in the enemy camp, or acquiesce in the division of the world into rival spheres in the hope of an ultimate equipoise and *modus vivendi?* The USA committed itself to the former course in 1951, amid much discussion of the inadequacies of mere "containment" and the necessity of "liberation," but achieved no triumphs in its liberating endeavors.[4]

5. Should America launch a new armed crusade against sin, directed toward liberating the victims of tyranny, or come to terms with the powers of evil on the basis of a partition of the world and a new global balance of power? The latter course appeared unacceptable to most Americans in mid-century as a dishonorable compromise with wickedness and a betrayal of American ideals of freedom. The former course ensured World War III, with no one knowing who would "win" or whether anyone would be left alive to be liberated.

All these questions were hard questions. Those who supposed they had easy answers were victims of wishful thinking. The basic American objective would remain, behind moralistic verbiage, what it had always been: to prevent the conquest of Europe and Asia by any rival Power. Whether the American decisions of 1945–55 were well calculated to attain the objective or threatened

[4] Through an amendment, offered by the Hon. Charles J. Kersten of Wisconsin, to the Mutual Security Act of 1951 (and continued in subsequent enactments), Congress authorized official efforts to foster revolution in the enemy camp by voting $100,000,000 "for any selected persons who are residing in or escapees from the Soviet Union, Czechoslovakia, Hungary, Rumania, Bulgaria, Albania, Lithuania, Latvia, and Estonia, or the Communist-dominated or occupied areas of Germany and Austria, or any other countries absorbed by the Soviet Union to form such persons into elements of the military forces supporting NATO or for other purposes." The men of Moscow had specialized in such activities for a third of a century but apparently did not regard imitation as the sincerest form of flattery, since they protested bitterly at this American attempt at emulation. An interesting analysis of the problem of promoting revolution and liberation among the peoples of the Communist Empire, with texts of statements by Mr. Kersten, Prof. James Burnham, and Prof. Lev E. Dobriansky of Georgetown University and President of the Ukrainian Congress Committee of America (who urged that a billion dollars be devoted to the enterprise) is to be found on pages 501–521 of *Hearings before the Committee on Foreign Relations on the Mutual Security Act of 1952*, U.S. Senate, 82d Cong., 2d Sess. (1952).

On Aug. 14, 1952, Admiral Alan G. Kirk, former U.S. Ambassador in Moscow and subsequently Chairman of the "American Committee for the Liberation of the Peoples of Russia," was appointed by President Truman as Director of the Psychological Strategy Board, previously headed by Dr. Raymond B. Allen, President of the University of Washington. That Admiral Kirk was well qualified for his new post was shown by his success in reconciling various groups of anti-Soviet Russians, Ukrainians, etc., previously hostile, and uniting them in concerted efforts to destroy the Soviet regime. On the same day Mr. Kersten was quoted as saying that the present "negative policy of containment and negotiated co-existence" was "immoral and un-Christian," since it implied "agreement with forces which by every religious creed and moral precept are evil. It abandons nearly one-half of humanity . . . to enslavement of the Communist police state. It is un-American because it violates the principles of the Declaration of Independence. It will lead to all-out World War III . . . is uneconomic and will lead to national bankruptcy." Dwight D. Eisenhower commented: "A true program of peace for the U.S. must include as one of its peaceful aims the restoration of the captive nations of Europe and Asia."

to bring about that which America was bound to try to prevent depended upon innumerable factors, incalculable and imponderable, which could scarcely be grasped by the wisdom of Solomon—and upon the response to be made to the American enterprise by the men of Moscow and Peiping. The response, up to now, was hysterical in rhetoric but prudent in action, thus vindicating the sagacity of American statesmanship in the conduct of the Cold War. Things to come would plainly hinge upon continued prudence, or the lack thereof, in Washington, Moscow, and Peiping. Rational *Realpolitik* on both sides would lead to balance and to the uneasy peace which the balance always provides. Messianism on either side might lead to a war of annihilation, inspired by, but certain to betray, the hope expressed in an old American hymn: "From Greenland's icy mountains, From India's coral strands, Where Afric's sunny fountains Roll down their golden sands, From many an ancient river, From many a palmy plain, They call us to deliver Their lands from error's chain. . . ."

From Liberation to Accommodation. Soup, says an old Russian proverb, is never eaten as hot as it is cooked. The spokesmen of the Eisenhower Administrations (1953–61) began by breathing fire in foreign policy but ended by seeking peace. Dulles's initial appeals for "liberation" were echoed by the President: "We shall never acquiesce in the enslavement of any people in order to purchase fancied gains for ourselves. . . . The freedom we cherish and defend in Europe and in the Americas is no different from the freedom that is imperiled in Asia." On Feb. 2, 1953, the "new and positive" foreign policy came to its first expression when Eisenhower "deneutralized" Formosa by removing the U.S. Seventh Fleet and thus authorizing Chiang Kai-shek to carry out his endlessly reiterated resolve to "return to the mainland" and "liberate China from Communism." Nothing happened. Following Stalin's demise and Communist capitulation on the issue of repatriation of prisoners, the stalemated fighting in Korea was ended by the armistice accords of July 26, 1953, after 25,604 Americans had been killed, 108,718 wounded, and 7,955 reported as missing. A year later Eisenhower rejected the advice of his Joint Chiefs of Staff for U.S. military intervention in Indochina and acquiesced in, without becoming a party to, a comparable peace by checkmate and partition negotiated at the Geneva Conference of 1954 (see p. 200).

American prestige abroad was reduced almost to the vanishing point during the first Eisenhower administration by the vagaries of "McCarthyism"—a pathological *reductio ad absurdum* of anti-Communism to which President, Cabinet, State Department, Congress, press, and public yielded for months and years or equated, despite doubts, with the highest patriotism. Anti-Communist hysteria reached an early climax with the electrocution on June 19, 1953, of Julius and Ethel Rosenberg as "atomic spies." Their guilt was questionable. Their offense, if any, was transmission of "secrets" to the USSR when the USSR was a wartime ally of the USA. Their punishment did not fit the crime. In consequence, millions of liberals throughout the Free World and the neutralist world were shocked, while Communists everywhere were enabled to obscure the infinitely worse atrocities their own high priests had perpetrated by capitalizing on the Rosenberg case in the name of "anti-Americanism." During 1954 and 1955 the junior Senator from Wisconsin, Joseph McCarthy, became a global symbol of demagogery, irresponsibility, persecution of the innocent, witch-hunting, book-burning, and calculated irrationality—until the new Grand Inquisitor overreached himself, fell from grace and public favor, was censured by the Senate, and finally died discredited (May 2, 1957, aged 47) when America had returned to some semblance of sanity in its search for "subversives." Meanwhile thousands of other victims of McCarthyism, almost none of whom were Communists, suffered dismissal from their jobs, social ostracism, or imprisonment. In 1954 in the Federal Penitentiary in Lewisburg, Pa., William Remington, convicted of perjury for denying that he had been a Communist, was murdered by fellow inmates while Alger Hiss, similarly convicted for denying he had transmitted secrets to Communist spies, was released upon the expiration of his sentence.[5]

The policy-makers of the USA, like those of the USSR—and, earlier, of Mussolini's Italy and Hitler's Reich—belatedly discovered that a nation committed to intolerance and injustice in the name of "security" cannot hope to win friends or influence people abroad save by force or favors. The crimes of the totalitarian pseudo-Caesars, to be sure, were far more monstrous than those of the McCarthyites in the USA. But it was the North American Republic, not the despots of Rome, Berlin, and Moscow, which was posing in the mid-20th Century as the world-wide center of democracy, freedom, and justice. And it was in America that millions of colored Americans continued to be subjected to ostracism, discrimination, and segregation as members of a pariah caste. Millions abroad drew their own conclusions.

Under these conditions it was astonishing that Washington was still able, thanks to American might and money and to universal detestation throughout the Free World of the far greater evils of Communist totalitarianism, to exercise some limited control over the preferences and decisions of other peoples and governments. Official moods in Washington in 1955 and thereafter oscillated between renewed defiance of the Communist foe and efforts at compromise.

Alleged crises continued to center in the Far East. On Dec. 2, 1954, the USA and Nationalist China signed a treaty of mutual defense aimed at reciprocal support against "armed attack and Communist subversive activities directed from without against their territorial integrity and political stability"

[5] The voluminous literature regarding these matters cannot here be cited. But see Owen Lattimore, *Ordeal by Slander* (Boston, Little, Brown, 1950); William A. Reuben, *The Atom Spy Hoax* (New York, Action Books, 1955); Harvey Matusow, *False Witness* (New York, Cameron and Kahn, 1955); Alger Hiss, *In the Court of Public Opinion* (New York, Knopf, 1957); and Fred J. Cook, "Hiss," *The Nation*, Sept. 21, 1957.

and formally authorizing the USA to "dispose such land, air, and sea forces in and about Taiwan (Formosa) and the Pescadores as may be required for their defense, as determined by mutual agreement." When Red assaults compelled the Nationalists to quit the Tachen Islands and appeared to threaten Quemoy and Matsu, off the South China coast, and possibly Formosa itself, the President on Jan. 24, 1955, asked Congress to approve a resolution (voted by the House, 409 to 3, Jan. 25, and by the Senate, 85 to 3, Jan. 28) authorizing him "to employ the armed forces of the U.S. as he deems necessary for the specific purpose of securing and protecting Formosa and the Pescadores against armed attack, this authority to include the securing and protection of such related positions and territories now in friendly hands and the taking of such other measures as he judges to be required or appropriate in assuring the defense of Formosa and the Pescadores."

This highly dramatized threat of war soon dissolved. Dulles deliberately left vague the question of whether the USA would defend Quemoy and Matsu, both more than 100 miles from Taiwan across the Straits of Formosa, declaring that Washington would defend them if an attack upon them seemed preparatory to an attack upon Formosa. No attack materialized, since the power-holders in Peiping had no desire to provoke war with the USA and were convinced that, sooner or later, Formosa would be theirs, whatever Washington might do or threaten to do.

Here again the inescapable fact of stalemate was reaffirmed, with neither side in the contest of the giants able or willing to challenge the other to trial by battle. The year 1955 thus became a year of earnest search for a *modus vivendi,* reflected in the "Summit Conference" at Geneva and the subsequent Geneva gathering of Foreign Ministers (see p. 201 above). Apart from the Austrian treaty of May 15, 1955, the search led to no concrete results and was followed by the mutual meddling and muddling amid the lost opportunities of 1956 which provoked local violence in the Mid East and Hungary in a harvest of wasted time (see pp. 396*f.* above).

The Enigma of American Foreign Policy. In spite of, or perhaps because of, the demonstrated failure of U.S. diplomacy to keep the peace and "contain" Communism, Dwight D. Eisenhower was reelected President, Nov. 6, 1956, by the largest majority ever recorded—9,553,349 more than Adlai E. Stevenson's 26,028,887—with "Ike" winning 457 electoral votes by sweeping 41 states to Adlai's 74 electoral votes from 7 states. At the same time, paradoxically, the Democrats won, and the Republicans lost, control of both Houses of Congress. Foreign policy, being allegedly "bipartisan," presumably played no role in the choice of the American electorate, despite Stevenson's belated pleas for a cessation of atomic bomb testing (seconded by Bulganin) and Eisenhower's repudiation of any such folly.

With few exceptions, "Ike" left foreign policy to "Foster." The Dulles dispensation in the late 1950's offered little hope of either winning a war or negotiating a peace with the Communist bloc. The former possibility was pre-cluded by the obvious facts of power. "The sole use of armed forces," declared Eisenhower in his press conference of May 23, 1956, "so far as war between two great countries possessing atom and hydrogen bombs today is this: their deterrent value." The latter possibility was precluded by the unwillingness of American policy-makers to negotiate any settlements with Moscow or Peiping (save on terms of "unconditional surrender") as regards Germany, China, disarmament, or the tangled problems of the Mid East.

The foreign policy of the USA, mightiest of Super-Powers, was thus con-demned to a frustrating pattern of expediency, improvisation, and opportun-ism, with no common denominator save "anti-Communism." This negative directive, it must be granted, was a new version of the age-old injunction of opposition to any domination of Eurasia by a rival Power. But most of the Free World and all of the neutral world wanted desperately to know not what America was against, but what America was for—and to this question an America championing Chiang Kai-shek and Tito, Syngman Rhee and Gomulka, Adenauer and Franco, Fascist dictatorship and democracy, Israel and Arab nationalism, colonialism and anti-colonialism, militarism and disarmament, anti-Communism and the "Welfare State," racial segregation and racial equality, feudalism and anti-feudalism, etc.—could, alas, give no consistent answer which "made sense" to other people.

American "defense policy" was equally baffling. In various public statements Dulles began his tenure of office by threatening "massive retaliation" (atomic) against any Communist aggression anywhere in the world. Three years later (cf. Life Magazine, Jan. 11, 1956) he was explaining that the "necessary art" of statesmanship consisted, as he alleged was the case in Korea, Indochina, and Formosa, in going to the "brink" of war. "We walked to the brink and looked it in the face. We took strong action." Few people abroad could recon-cile this exegesis of U.S. high policy with the known facts or comprehend how peace could be promoted by "brinkmanship." By autumn of 1957 (see Foreign Affairs, October, 1957), the Secretary of State was contending that atomic bomb tests must be continued to develop "clean," small-size, and tactical thermonuclear weapons whereby attacking Red hordes could be stopped and destroyed without risking the incineration of civilization. This formulation likewise appeared to many people abroad to bear no relationship to reality.

American policy-makers meanwhile persisted in building up bombing bases all around the periphery of the Red Empire; exporting military hardware to allies with a constantly declining minimum of economic aid; championing disarmament by international agreement; insisting on "foolproof" inspection schemes which made any disarmament accord impossible; and progressively reducing U.S. armed forces in the name of "economy" to a point at which some Democratic critics contended that "security" was jeopardized. America's friends and foes abroad were both puzzled by the resultant riddle of American "world leadership" and in 1956–57 (see pp. 396–431) were reduced to desperation and defiance.

Many Americans were no less puzzled by their failure to win friends and influence people abroad, after giving away $62,000,000,000, or $324 per capita, in foreign aid between July 1, 1945, and July 1, 1957. The puzzlement on both sides cannot here be resolved. Yet some of its sources may be suggested. The sprawling and expensive federal bureaucracy of the USA was not so organized as to promote consistency of ends or means in foreign policy. Conflicts and confusions were worse confounded by Congressional "investigators" bent upon headlines and votes. Only vigorous Executive leadership, seldom conspicuous in 1953–61, could bring order out of chaos. Political leaders who strive to be liked by everybody often end by being liked by nobody. Who seeks friends through the bounty of his charity often discovers that those he aids resent his generosity, suspect his motives, and easily yield to the temptation to demand more and more as a "right," often to the point of blackmail. Other elements relevant to the paradox will occur to discerning observers of the recent and contemporary American scene.

The central dilemma of U.S. foreign policy in the late 1950's can nevertheless be reduced, not inaccurately, to a relatively simple equation. Washington was striving, quite rightly by all the imperatives of national interest and power politics, to preserve a global balance of power by thwarting the pretensions to hegemony of the latest would-be aspirants to world dominion. The enterprise required respect for the interests of allies and equal respect for those who preferred "neutralism." But Washington repeatedly ignored or negated the purposes of its major allies and constantly pressed unwilling neutrals to join the Grand Alliance against Communism. As regards the "enemy," he could not possibly be disposed of, as his predecessors had been dispatched in 1918 and 1945, by total victory in global war, since his power was too great and any such effort to destroy it threatened the atomic suicide of civilization.

When problems of power cannot be solved by force, they can only be resolved by diplomacy—i.e., by bargaining and bartering in earnest search of a *modus vivendi*. But Americans, while sincerely desirous of "peace," are reluctant to compromise with Sin and are easily persuaded that "justice" and "freedom" (as defined in America) are more important than peace and that inability to vindicate these values throughout the world is not only "immoral" but is a confession of "failure," deemed intolerable by a people who worship success. The America of mid-century, while prudently retreating from total catastrophe in crisis after crisis, continued to hope that somehow Virtue could be made to prevail over Vice in a new crusade against the wicked, waged in the name of what the late Charles A. Beard once called "perpetual war for perpetual peace."

Peace, obviously, is never to be had on such terms. Another World War is

THE DEFENSE OF DEMOCRACY

now impossible and unthinkable. The alternative is compromise with the forces of Evil as a means of avoiding infinitely greater evil. The incomparable popularity of President Eisenhower, who partially comprehended this necessity, enabled him in 1955 to approach the brink of compromise with Marxland. His ensuing illness and subsequent vacillation among alternative courses reduced later negotiations to sterility. To refuse in self-righteous rectitude to acknowledge Communist control of China and to pretend to "negotiate" with the USSR over disarmament, German unity, and the Mid East on terms which all knew could never be accepted by the men of Moscow was to foredoom diplomacy to futility.[6] Yet the failure was temporary. In the end, however long deferred, Washington, Moscow, and Peiping would be obliged to "come to terms," since no tolerable alternative was available.

SUGGESTED READINGS

Almond, Gabriel A.: *The American People and Foreign Policy*, New York, Harcourt, Brace, 1950.

Bailey, T. A.: *A Diplomatic History of the American People*, New York, Appleton-Century-Crofts, 1939.

Bartlett, Ruhl J.: *The Record of American Diplomacy: Documents and Readings in the History of American Foreign Relations*, New York, Knopf, 1954.

Beale, Howard K.: *Theodore Roosevelt and the Rise of America to World Power*, Baltimore, Johns Hopkins Press, 1956.

Beard, Charles A.: *President Roosevelt and the Coming of the War, 1941*, New Haven, Conn., Yale University Press, 1948.

Bemis, S. F.: *A Diplomatic History of the United States*, New York, Holt, 1950.

Berle, Adolf A., Jr.: *Tides of Crisis: A Primer of Foreign Relations*, New York, Reynal & Hitchcock, 1957.

Brookings Institution: *Major Problems of United States Foreign Policy* (annual), Washington, D.C.

Brown, William Adams, Jr., and Redvers Opie: *American Foreign Assistance*, Washington, Brookings, 1953.

Brown, W. Norman: *The United States and India and Pakistan*, Cambridge, Mass., Harvard University Press, 1953.

Buehrig, Edward H.: *Woodrow Wilson and the Balance of Power*, Bloomington, Ind., Indiana University Press, 1955.

Burns, James MacGregor: *Roosevelt: The Lion and the Fox*, New York, Harcourt, Brace, 1956.

Campbell, John C.: *The United States in World Affairs, 1947–1948*, New York, Harper, 1948.

[6] The attitudes here referred to were manifested in official U.S. rejection of repeated proposals from Moscow during 1957 (Feb. 11, April 19, and Sept. 3) for top-level negotiations over conflicts and rivalries in the Mid East (see pp. 428f.). The apparent premise of American policy-makers was that all U.S. interventions and arms shipments to the area were virtuous and that all Soviet counterparts were wicked. The further premise was the hope that the entire region, which was 6,000 miles away from the USA and on the doorstep of the USSR, could be effectively controlled from Washington, with all Soviet interests ignored and Muscovite aspirations negated. Since the course of events demonstrated conclusively the impossibility of realizing any such hope, ultimate negotiations were certain to be embarked upon, despite (or because of) the "crisis" of October, 1957, when Moscow and Washington, the former defending Syria and the latter Turkey, publicly warned one another against war in the Mid East.

SUGGESTED READINGS

Chamberlain, Lawrence H., and Richard C. Snyder: *American Foreign Policy*, New York, Rinehart, 1948.
Council on Foreign Relations: *The United States in World Affairs* (annual), New York.
Dean, Vera Micheles: *Foreign Policy without Fear*, New York, McGraw-Hill, 1953.
Dennis, Lawrence: *The Coming American Fascism*, New York, Harper, 1936.
———: *The Dynamics of War and Revolution*, New York, The Weekly Foreign Letter, 1940.
Donovan, Robert J.: *Eisenhower: The Inside Story*, New York, Harper, 1956.
Drummond, Donald F.: *The Passing of American Neutrality*, 1937–1941, Ann Arbor, Mich., University of Michigan Press, 1955.
Dulles, Foster Rhea: *America's Rise to World Power*, 1898–1954, New York, Harper, 1955.
Elliott, W. Y.: *The Political Economy of American Foreign Policy*, New York, Holt, 1955.
Ellis, L. Ethan: *A Short History of American Diplomacy*, New York, Harper, 1951.
Fischer, John: *Master Plan: U.S.A.*, New York, Harper, 1951.
Gerson, Louis L.: *Woodrow Wilson and the Rebirth of Poland*, 1914–1920, New Haven, Conn., Yale University Press, 1953.
Goldman, Eric F.: *The Crucial Decade: America*, 1945–1955, New York, Knopf, 1956.
Gordon, Morton, and Kenneth N. Vines: *Theory and Practice of American Foreign Policy*, New York, Crowell, 1955.
Hull, Cordell: *The Memoirs of Cordell Hull*, New York, Macmillan, 1948.
Jones, Joseph M.: *The Fifteen Weeks* (1947), New York, Viking, 1955.
Kelly, Alfred H. (ed.): *American Foreign Policy and American Democracy*, Detroit, Wayne University Press, 1954.
Kennan, George F.: *American Diplomacy*, 1900–1950, Chicago, University of Chicago Press, 1951.
———: *Realities of American Foreign Policy*, Princeton, N.J., Princeton University Press, 1954.
Knappen, Marshall: *An Introduction to American Foreign Policy*, New York, Harper, 1956.
Koenig, Louis W. (ed.): *The Truman Administration: Its Principles and Practice*, New York, New York University Press, 1956.
Langer, William L., and D. Everett Gleason: *The Challenge to Isolation*, 1937–1940, New York, Harper, 1952.
———: *The Undeclared War*, 1940–1941, New York, Harper, 1953.
Leonard, L. Larry: *Elements of American Foreign Policy*, New York, McGraw-Hill, 1954.
Lerner, Max: *America As A Civilization*, New York, Simon and Schuster, 1957.
Lippmann, Walter: *U.S. Foreign Policy*, Boston, Little, Brown, 1943.
———: *U.S. War Aims*, Boston, Little, Brown, 1944.
Mikesell, Raymond F.: *United States Economic Policy and International Relations*, New York, McGraw-Hill, 1955.
Millis, Walter, with the collaboration of E. S. Duffield: *The Forrestal Diaries*, New York, Viking, 1951.
Mills, C. Wright: *The Power Elite*, New York, Oxford, 1956.
Pratt, Julius W.: *History of United States Foreign Policy*, Englewood Cliffs, N.J., Prentice-Hall, 1955.
Reischauer, Edwin O.: *Wanted: An Asian Policy*, New York, Knopf, 1955.
Reitzel, William, Morton A. Kaplan, and Constance G. Coblenz: *United States Foreign Policy*, 1945–1955, Washington, Brookings, 1956.
Rovere, Richard H.: *Affairs of State: The Eisenhower Years*, New York, Farrar, Straus, 1956.
———, and Arthur M. Schlesinger: *The General and the President*, New York, Farrar, Straus, 1951.
Royal Institute of International Affairs: *Atlantic Alliance*, New York, 1952.
Sherwood, Robert: *Roosevelt and Hopkins*, New York, Harper, 1948.
Smith, Louis: *American Democracy and Military Power*, Chicago, University of Chicago Press, 1951.
Synder, Richard C., and Edgar S. Furniss: *American Foreign Policy: Formulation, Principles and Programs*, New York, Rinehart, 1954.
———: *Introduction to American Foreign Policy*, New York, Rinehart, 1955.

THE DEFENSE OF DEMOCRACY

Stettinius, E. R., Jr.: *Lend-Lease, Weapon for Victory,* New York, Macmillan, 1944.
Stevenson, Adlai E.: *Call to Greatness,* New York, Harper, 1954.
Stimson, Henry L., and McGeorge Bundy: *On Active Service in Peace and War,* New York, Harper, 1948.
Tansill, C. C.: *America Goes to War* (1917), Boston, Little, Brown, 1938.
———: *Back Door to War: The Roosevelt Foreign Policy,* 1933–1941, Chicago, Regnery, 1952.
Truman, Harry S.: *Memoirs. Volume I: Year of Decisions,* New York, Doubleday, 1955.
———: *Memoirs. Volume II: Years of Trial and Hope,* New York, Doubleday, 1956.
Van Alstyne, Richard W.: *American Diplomacy in Action,* Stanford, Calif., Stanford University Press, 1947.
Warburg, James P.: *The United States in a Changing World,* New York, Putnam, 1954.
Westerfield, H. Bradford: *Foreign Policy and Party Politics: Pearl Harbor to Korea,* New Haven, Conn., Yale University Press, 1955.
Wilcox, Francis O., and Thorsten V. Kalijarvi (eds.): *Recent American Foreign Policy,* New York, Appleton-Century-Crofts, 1952.

4. DIVISION IN FREELAND

In a single battle the Peloponnesians and their allies may be able to defy all Hellas, but they are incapacitated from carrying on a war against a Power different in character from their own by the want of the single council-chamber requisite to prompt and vigorous action, and the substitution of a diet composed of various races, in which every state possesses an equal vote, and each presses its own ends, a condition of things which generally results in no action at all. The great wish of some is to avenge themselves on some particular enemy, the great wish of others is to save their own pocket. Slow in assembling, they devote a very small fraction of the time to the consideration of any public object, most of it to the prosecution of their own objects. Meanwhile each fancies that no harm would come of his neglect, that it is the business of somebody else to look after this or that for him; and so, by the same notion being entertained by all separately, the common cause imperceptibly decays.—THUCYDIDES, *The Peloponnesian War* (Crawley translation, The Modern Library), quoting Pericles.

If we seek to assess the solidity and the weaknesses of the Grand Alliance organized by the USA in the 1940's and the 1950's, as we have already sought to do for the counter-coalition of Marxland (see pp. 547–553), we are confronted at the outset with the vast dispersal and heterogeneity of the "allies," comprising as of 1958 no less than 44 States, with most of which the USA had concluded "status-of-forces" accords as well as treaties of alliance—and with the infinite complexities of interallied relationships through time and space. These very qualities of the anti-Communist coalition were, as we shall see, the major sources of confusion and friction among members. What was designed as a global bloc of united sovereignties, dedicated to success in diplomacy or victory in war through "positions of strength," turned out to be, at least in part, a façade of pretended solidarity, scarcely concealing profound internal cleavages and schisms. Had the threat of Communist military aggression been more real than imaginary, the coalition would doubtless have exhibited a measure of unity customary among allies waging or contemplating

608

total war to the death against mortal foes with whom no compromise is deemed possible. But the condition was lacking. Therefore the Grand Alliance was more productive of disunity than unity.

The semantics of the enterprise are worthy of initial notice. It is no longer feasible to concoct old-fashioned military alliances among some States against other States. These time-honored devices are discredited. All statesmen must pay lip service to the ideals of the UN Charter, which postulates a global system of "collective security" in a world community of "peace-loving" States. The premises are false and unworkable. But millions of men and women hope and believe they are true. Therefore diplomats must couch their schemes of alliances in language compatible with the premises. America's Great Design for global coalition against Communism thus began with the Act of Petropolis and the Vandenberg Resolution of 1948 (see p. 595), in which the key words were "regional and other collective arrangements for individual and collective self-defense . . . based on continuous and effective self-help and mutual aid" under Article 51 of the Charter. This formula proved palatable to Western publics in subsequent endeavors and was incorporated into the North Atlantic Treaty of April 4, 1949 (see pp. 596f.), and in many later pacts designed to extend and consolidate the coalition of Freeland.

If the successive expansions of the Grand Alliance failed to fulfill the hopes of American policy-makers, the cause lay less in the logical defects of verbal formulas (for in such matters any formula will serve if the populace approves) than in a misguided departure from an ancient rule regarding all alliances, as old as all the State Systems of mankind. The rule is this: a few alliances with powerful allies, bound together by a mutuality of interests, are always preferable, because operationally more effective, than many alliances with a congeries of impotent States, most of which will prove liabilities rather than assets.

Secretary Dulles's passion for "pactomania" (to use the term once applied to his diplomacy by Cyrus L. Sulzberger of *The New York Times*) led to innumerable compacts, some of which had no operational utility and others of which alienated "neutrals" and aided "enemies" more than they strengthened ties with "friends." The ultimate verdict of events may well vindicate such a judgment regarding U.S. alliances with Germany (see p. 490), Japan (see p. 200), Formosa (see p. 602), and Franco's Spain. Immediate consequences wholly justify such a judgment regarding the Baghdad Pact (see pp. 405f.), the results of which negated its purpose. A mixed judgment is warranted, thus far, regarding SEATO or the Southeast Asia Treaty Organization.

In 1949 Britain, Australia, South Korea, and the Philippines began urging a counterpart of NATO in Asia. Washington was unresponsive until Red China's intervention in the Korean War and Chinese aid to the rebels in Indochina threatened a dangerous expansion of Communist power. Anglo-American friction in the spring of 1954 delayed action. After the conclusion of the

Indochinese Armistice at Geneva (see p. 200), the USA pressed for a conference. British hopes were dashed when India, Burma, Ceylon, and Indonesia made clear that they would have no part in any such military bloc. Nehru asserted that any such pact would do more harm than good. Delegates nevertheless met at Baguio near Manila on Sept. 6, 1954, with Dulles accompanied by Senators Alexander Smith and Mike Mansfield, and refused to be deterred by Radio Peiping's denunciation of the project as "an aggressive alliance hostile to the peoples of China and of various Asian countries."

The "Southeast Asia Collective Defense Treaty" represented compromises among divergent views among the participants and was formally signed on Sept. 8, 1954, by agents of the USA, Britain, France, Australia, New Zealand, Pakistan, Thailand, and the Philippines. They championed "sovereign equality" and "equal rights and self-determination of peoples," settlement of disputes by "peaceful means," and abstention "from the threat or use of force in any manner inconsistent with the purposes of the UN." They pledged themselves "separately and jointly, by means of continuous and effective self-help and mutual aid" to "maintain and develop their individual and collective capacity to resist armed attack and to prevent and counter subversive activities directed from without against their territorial integrity and political stability [Art. 2]." "Aggression by means of armed attack in the treaty area" was to be met (Art. 4) by each party "in accordance with its constitutional processes." Other threats would be a subject of consultation, but with no action to be taken "except at the invitation or with the consent of the government concerned." The "treaty area" was so defined as to exclude Formosa. A Protocol extended "protection" to Laos, Cambodia, and South Vietnam, none of which was a party to the pact. A U.S. statement limited American obligations to "Communist aggression." An appended "Pacific Charter" championed peace, security, liberty, justice, self-determination, etc.

SEATO, proclaimed in effect Feb. 19, 1955, lacked the binding commitments and the formal organization of NATO. It included, moreover, only three Asian States, and these poor and weak, and evoked condemnation in Jakarta, Rangoon, and New Delhi, as well as in Peiping and Moscow. The SEATO Council of Foreign Ministers, under the Chairmanship of Prince Wan Waithayokon of Thailand, met in Bangkok, Feb. 23–25, 1955, and agreed to set up a Secretariat in Bangkok, but arrived at no effective formula for making SEATO a viable alliance. "War games" in Thailand in February, 1956, designed to counteract "creeping neutralism" in Southeast Asia and to convince Peiping that the new coalition was more than a "paper tiger," evoked skepticism in Japan and nonparticipation by Pakistan. London urged a shift of emphasis from military to economic cooperation. Early in March the SEATO Council met in Karachi, with Dulles and Selwyn Lloyd publicly warning of the continued danger of Communist aggression and privately differing as to the proper functions of the alliance. Dulles in New Delhi and Jakarta sought in vain to reassure India and Indonesia, with no result save Dutch indignation over his "anti-colonial" utterances.

The vicissitudes of SEATO in 1957 illustrated the difficulties and frustrations of military alliances without power directed against dangers which could not be met by military means. Early in March, following rigged elections in which Premier Pibul Songgram won a narrow majority, a Thai Army spokesman alleged a "plot" to overthrow the Thai government from "abroad" (source unspecified), which SEATO had revealed to Bangkok, presumably in the nick of time. By mid-March Dulles was in Canberra, telling the SEATO Council that the pact had promoted "increased stability, unity, and strength" and that international Communism was "a passing and not a permanent phase." A lengthy communiqué of March 13 bespoke optimism regarding SEATO's contribution to peace and reiterated abhorrence of Communism. On Sept. 17, 1957, an Army *coup* ousted Pibul Songgram, who fled to Cambodia. Marshal Sarit Thanarat pledged a continued pro-Western policy and persuaded King Phumiphon Adundet to dissolve parliament, order new elections, and name as provisional Premier Pote Sarasin, former Ambassador to Washington and Secretary General of SEATO. This reassurance could not conceal the fact of political instability among the Siamese and a steady growth of "neutralist" sentiment.

On the larger stage of *Weltpolitik*, American policy-makers, in their ceaseless efforts to maintain and expand the anti-Communist coalition, encountered even more difficulties and dilemmas. A full catalogue would be endless and doubtless misleading if it implied that the Grand Alliance was in process of dissolution, as assuredly it was not—as yet. But a survey will suggest the nature of the hard problems confronting Washington.

Latin Americans complained bitterly and repeatedly that the USA, by its generosity in military and economic aid to European and Asian allies and its relative miserliness in dealing with the Republics of the South, was neglecting and alienating its nearest and closest friends. Canadians, on June 11, 1957, elected 110 Conservatives and 103 Liberals to the House of Commons, thus ending 22 years of Liberal rule and replacing Louis St. Laurent in the Prime Ministership by John Diefenbaker, who subsequently criticized U.S. investment and tariff policies as a threat to Canadian independence and prosperity. The story of how Washington unwittingly provoked Paris, London, and Tel Aviv to violence in 1956 and how American policy-makers involved themselves in insoluble dilemmas in the Mid East we have already reviewed (see pp. 397–431), along with the paradox of rearming Germany and Japan in the face of fears by all their neighbors.

These problems were simple, even if insoluble, compared to others far more complex and even more insoluble. A few examples must suffice. America was allied with Britain, Greece, and Turkey. The island of Cyprus was a British colony (seized from the Ottoman Empire in 1878) and a major naval, military, and air base. Its 500,000 people were 80% Christian Greeks and 20% Moslem Turks. In 1954–55 Greek nationalists, in Greece and on Cyprus, decided that "justice" required *Enosis*—i.e., an end of British rule and the union of the island with Greece. British and Turkish opposition led to widespread terrorism, marked by retail and wholesale murder, robbery, and destruction, while "allied" Britain and Greece and "allied" Greece and Turkey became mortal foes. The USA, sponsor of the alliances, was unable to formulate any policy acceptable to the embittered contestants. London leaned toward qualified independence, Athens toward annexation, and Ankara toward partition. On March 9, 1956, British authorities accused Archbishop Makarios of the Greek Orthodox Church in Cyprus of cooperation with the terrorists and deported him to the Seychelles Islands in the Indian Ocean. Strikes and riots followed in Cyprus and in Greece and Turkey with many slain (including some Americans) in an orgy of murder. On March 28, 1957, London released Makarios, when he agreed to urge an end of violence, on condition that he could not return to Cyprus. He went to Greece. Mutual recriminations on all sides and reciprocal appeals to the UN had effected no solution by 1958, nor were statesmen in Washington able to restore unity among the sundered allies. Comparable frustrations confronted American policy-makers in dealing, or failing to deal, with violence in North Africa (see pp. 372*f*.) and in grappling with conflicting expectations, fears, and ambitions in southern Asia. Pakistan was a member of both the Baghdad Pact and SEATO and thus a recipient of substantial military aid from the USA. Neighboring Afghanistan, cherishing annexationist hopes of access to the sea through the creation of "Pushtunistan" at Pakistan's expense, became anti-American and turned to Moscow for support. Neighboring India, deadlocked with Pakistan over disputed Kashmir, complained bitterly that U.S. military aid to Karachi was negating U.S. economic aid to India by compelling New Delhi to engage in an arms race which the Indian economy could ill afford.

Other instances need not be multiplied. All had a common denominator, as was also the case in Marxland. Muscovite efforts to control all Communist-ruled States in common opposition to "American imperialism" failed of their purpose when it became clear that Moscow's "allies" were more concerned with local independence than with common subjection to the Kremlin in defense against an imaginary threat. American efforts to unite all anti-Communist States in defense against "Communist imperialism" foundered when it became clear that Washington's allies all had interests of their own to serve and were no longer impressed with the "Red Menace."

America's Grand Alliance would doubtless endure in some form as long as Muscovy's Great Coalition. But both were bound to prove ephemeral and feckless in the 1960's if it turned out, as seemed highly probable, that the issues of the Cold War should come to be regarded by more and more of mankind as irrelevant or tangential to the actual problems and to the con-

SUGGESTED READINGS

fused and conflicting aspirations of statesmen and patriots in all or most of the sovereign societies of the world community. Apologists for American foreign policy in the 1940's and the 1950's would argue to the end of time that Washington's course had prevented a Communist "conquest of the world" and thus preserved a "balance of power" indispensable for American security. Critics would argue that the threat of Communist military aggression was largely imaginary or exaggerated; that the actual danger of Communist competition for influence over the minds of men called for a wholly different conception of "defense"; and that emphasis on alliances and military aid did more harm than good in furthering American interests. The "verdict of history" promised to remain forever inconclusive. But it was evident before 1960 that America was faced with the inescapable necessity of an "agonizing reappraisal" of the course in foreign affairs it had pursued during the preceding two decades.

SUGGESTED READINGS

Battistini, Lawrence H.: *The United States and Asia*, New York, Praeger, 1956.
Bowles, Chester: *Ambassador's Report*, New York, Harper, 1954.
———: *Africa's Challenge to America*, Berkeley, Calif., University of California Press, 1956.
———: *American Politics in a Revolutionary World*, Cambridge, Mass., Harvard University Press, 1956.
Brecher, Michael: *The Struggle for Kashmir*, Toronto, Ryerson Press, 1953.
Brown, W. A., Jr., and Redvers Opie: *American Foreign Assistance*, Washington, Brookings, 1953.
Brown, W. Norman: *The United States and India and Pakistan*, Cambridge, Mass., Harvard University Press, 1953.
Castle, Eugene W.: *Billions, Blunders and Baloney*, New York, Devin-Adair, 1955.
———: *The Great Giveaway*, Chicago, Regnery, 1957.
Douglas, William O.: *Strange Lands and Friendly People*, New York, Harper, 1951.
Ellis, Howard S.: *The Economics of Freedom*, New York, Harper, 1950.
Emerson, Rupert: *Representative Government in Southeast Asia*, Cambridge, Mass., Harvard University Press, 1955.
Korbel, Josef: *Danger in Kashmir*, Princeton, N.J., Princeton University Press, 1954.
Lippmann, Walter: *The Public Philosophy*, Boston, Atlantic–Little, Brown, 1955.
Mende, Tibor: *Southeast Asia between Two Worlds*, London, Turnstile Press, 1955.
Panikkar, K. M.: *Asia and Western Dominance*, New York, John Day, 1954.
Strausz-Hupé, Robert, and Others: *American-Asian Tensions*, New York, Praeger, 1956.
Ward, Barbara: *Policy for the West*, New York, Norton, 1951.

Total = 6399.

Chapter XIV

THE PROBLEMS OF THE POOR

1. HOW MANY WORLDS?

You ought to speak of other States in the plural number; none of them is a city, but many cities. . . . For indeed any city, however small, is in fact divided into two, one the city of the poor, the other of the rich; these are at war with one another; and in either there are many smaller divisions, and you would be altogether beside the mark if you treated them all as a single state.—PLATO, *The Republic.*

IN CONTEMPLATING the stirrings and strivings of the masses of humanity in the world community of the 20th Century, most Americans and many West Europeans, along with most Russians and some Chinese, were disposed on the basis of their experiences in the middle decades to envisage the future in terms of continued divergencies, antagonisms, and rivalries between Freeland and Marxland, each seeking to thwart the aspirations of the other for global hegemony and to win "world leadership" for itself. Through such lenses as these, the home of mankind was seen from the West as divided into three "worlds": the world of misguided neutrals, to be sooner or later won over or taken over into the rival camps of the Super-Powers; the world of Soviet-style Socialism and political totalitarianism, aiming at the subversion, conquest, and enslavement of all peoples everywhere; and the world of free enterprise, capitalism, and democracy, showing all men the golden road toward liberty and riches. The same lenses, when focused from the East, revealed Communism as the creative "wave of the future," capitalism as a decadent and doomed system of domestic exploitation and foreign imperialism, and the neutralist nations as predestined ultimately to embrace and to share in the Red millennium of a new epoch.

This persisting image of the mansions of men bore less and less resemblance to reality with the passing years and by the late 1950's was already a false guide to the probable shape of things to come. The familiar portrait of Cold War for mastery of the globe was increasingly falsified not only by the diplomacy of coexistence but, more significantly in the longer view, by an ever greater degree of "cultural convergence" (to borrow a useful concept of anthropology) between the mass industrial societies of the USSR and the Atlantic communities and by the "revolution of expectations" among the multimillioned masses of the vast "backward" or "economically undeveloped" regions of the earth. An adequate grasp of the moving forces which are

614

troubling the present and promise to be decisive for the future of the world community requires that we take full cognizance of these trends of change.

The New "Capitalism." The historic mission of Marxism, contrary to the hopes of Marx and the beliefs of Marxists, turns out in retrospect to have little relevance to the "evils" of capitalism or to its long anticipated "collapse." What relevance it has had has been paradoxically negative and ironically constructive. The challenge of Marxism, with its century-old appeals for "proletarian revolution" to "overthrow the bourgeoisie," has been a powerful incentive for "capitalists" and for "bourgeois States" to mend their ways and outbid the challengers. By such devices Bismarck fought Marxism, not unsuccessfully, in the Second Reich. During ensuing decades—despite the havoc of recurring world wars and indeed as part of the task of waging them—the Atlantic communities have transformed "capitalism" into something which Marx himself, were he still alive, would never recognize as identical with, or even comparable to, his own description and analysis of the laissez-faire economies in the mid-19th Century.

On the one hand legislators, moved by the pressures of social reformers and organized labor, and corporate entrepreneurs, moved by the need of dealing with trade unions and by the imperatives of efficiency in ever larger-scale production, have provided protection in ever greater measure to the "proletariat" against the hazards and injustices of early industrialism. In every highly industrialized State, without exception, workers now enjoy shorter hours, higher wages, protection for women workers, prohibition of child labor, and comprehensive "social security" against accidents, sickness, unemployment, and old age on a scale undreamed of a few generations ago. On the other hand, and this more recently, public policy-makers, inspired by the economics of Keynes rather than of Marx, Ricardo, or Adam Smith, have invented devices of monetary and fiscal controls, taxation, regulation, public spending and planning, and sundry ways of keeping savings, investments, production, and consumption in a dynamic balance of economic growth in which the "business cycle" in its old form has vanished and major "panics" and "depressions" are no longer possible.

To assert that "capitalists" have become "socialists," or that capitalism, as a means of protecting itself against socialism, has "gone socialist," is to play upon words which have lost their meaning. Yet the fact is inescapable, whether we welcome it or deplore it, that the economies of the USA, Canada, and Western Europe now live and move and have their being in a context in which cut-throat competition and the fluctuations of the "free market" have long since given way to public regulation and planning, "administered prices," minimum wages, collective bargaining, and massively decisive intervention by government in the affairs of business.[1] The result may be described, as one

[1] From the data available from the U.S. Department of Commerce and the *Federal Reserve Bulletin*, the new dynamics of the American economy are self-evident. In a

chooses, as "People's Capitalism" or the "Welfare State" or "creeping social-ism" or "the road to serfdom." Here we are concerned only with the fact, not with judgments of it. And the fact is plain for all with eyes to see.

The New "Socialism." Conversely the industrialization, urbanization, and education of Russia have wrought transformations in Soviet society which are equally irreversible and tend to make the daily lives and community problems of the people of Moscow, Leningrad, Kiev, and Stalingrad more and more comparable to those of Hamburg, Munich, and Rome; Paris, London, and Manchester; New York, Detroit, and Chicago. Persisting ideo-logical and institutional differences, to be sure, should not be ignored. In politics Soviet oligarchy has not yet evolved into democracy and may never do so. Yet the progressive liberalization and democratization of the Com-munist regime is rendered quite inevitable by the social and economic trans-mutation of the Soviet community, which can plainly no longer be ruled by the methods of Stalinism. In the USSR all productive property is "national-ized" or publicly owned, whereas most such property in the West is still "privately" owned. Yet the divorce between "ownership" and "management" is no less striking in contemporary Russia than in America. The new "power elite" of the USSR, comprising the managerial bureaucracy, machine politi-cians, and the "big brass," strangely resembles its American counterpart. In one respect, and an important one for world politics, the Soviet economy still differs markedly from its Western analogues: through sundry "socialist" devices of forced savings and planned investments, the USSR for many years has attained an annual rate of economic growth (*c.* 8%) roughly double that usually prevailing in Western Europe and America.

In all else that matters the two systems, supposedly so incompatible and irreconcilably antagonistic, are swiftly becoming as alike as two peas in a pod. The "Welfare State" is common to both. "People's Capitalism" and "People's Socialism," despite differences in nominal ownership of the means of pro-duction, share common achievements and common problems. The "capital-istic" devices of sharp differentials in wages and salaries, bonuses, prizes,

---

gross national product in 1929 of $104 billions, personal consumption accounted for $78 billions, private investment for 16, and government purchases of goods and services for 8. By 1933, at the nadir of the Depression, these items *seriatim* stood at 46, 1, and 8 in a gross national product of $55 billions. After two decades of pre-war, war-time, and post-war boom, the same items in 1955 constituted 255, 59, and 75 billions in a gross national product of $387 billions. The "government sector" of the economy thus repre-sented less than 8% of all transactions in 1929 and 20% in 1955. Advance estimates for 1957 postulated a gross national product of $425 billions, of which purchases of goods and services for private investment would represent 15% of the total and government purchases over 20%. In President Eisenhower's projected federal budget of almost $72 billions for 1957-58, 75% of the items, directly or indirectly, represented costs of past, present, and future wars. For a perceptive running analysis of the American transition to "socialism" via military spending and creeping inflation, see Lawrence Dennis's bi-monthly bulletin, *The Appeal to Reason* (West Springfield, Mass.). See also the present writer's article, "How Many Worlds?" in *The New Republic*, Feb. 3, 1958.

and other rewards for "profit-making" make the distribution of national income in the USSR not dissimilar to the prevailing pattern in the USA. The disturbing phenomena of *anomie* or loss of conviction, juvenile delinquency, depersonalization, conformism, anti-intellectualism, bureaucratism, traffic jams, alcoholism, "feather-bedding" and "moonshining" among workers, and stomach ulcers and hypertension among executives are common to both societies.

All these and a thousand other facets of daily life, quite regardless of "social systems," are inevitable concomitants of Big Industry, Big Business, Big Cities, Big Government, and Big Labor, whether "Capitalist" or "Socialist." In short, Marxland, in its efforts to equal American industrial output, and Freeland, in its efforts to achieve "defense against Communism," have become more and more alike and have given a new content to De Tocqueville's famous forecast of 1839: "There are, at the present time, two great nations in the world which seem to tend towards the same end, although they started from different points: I allude to the Russians and the Americans."

These processes of assimilation in all industrial societies should not be naïvely equated with any assurance of "peace" between them. Peace is always precarious in a State System lacking any semblance of World Government. The two World Wars of our time are ample evidence that highly industrialized nation-states are quite as likely to embark upon their mutual destruction as to harmonize their policies by virtue of common purposes and problems in their economic and social life. But the "Great Powers" which clashed in arms in 1914 and 1939 were all "Powers" because they were already far advanced on the road to industrialization. They had therefore long enjoyed the luxury of competing with one another for ascendancy over the passive agrarian masses of most of Asia and Africa, few of whose people had yet imagined the possibility that they too might embark upon industrialization and thus conceivably put an end to ancient misery by attaining Western standards of living.

All this is now gone. The more recent achievements of Western science, technology, and industry have widened, not narrowed, the gap between wealthy nations and poor nations. But "colonialism" is now obsolete. The erstwhile "natives" have caught the Western vision, embraced Western nationalism, borrowed Western guns, insisted on Western "sovereignty," and dedicated themselves to determined efforts to emulate the West in industrialization.

The New "Proletariat." Such are the considerations, among others, which lend weight to the view that the future fortunes of the world community are likely to be shaped more decisively by the relations between rich and poor than by the relations between "capitalists" and "Communists," both of whom are fabulously wealthy with the fruits of modern industry in comparison with *les misérables* of most of Asia, Africa, and Latin America. So much is this the case that it is already self-evident from the course of events that whatever advantages Marxland or Freeland may gain over the other in the course of nonviolent global competition in winning friends and influencing people will depend almost exclusively on their relative capacities to aid the poor to realize their yearnings for a richer life.

The formidable difficulties in the way of success for either side in this competitive endeavor to achieve economic miracles will be suggested below in due course. The magnitude of the problem can best be indicated by noting at the outset the appalling disparity in living standards between the well-to-do nations and the impoverished nations of the contemporary world community.

UN economists and statisticians, on the basis of the most accurate available data, estimated that in 1949 (*National and Per Capita Income*, 1949, Statistical Office of the UN, October, 1950) average per capita annual income in U.S. dollars of 1949 value came to more than $400 per head for the peoples of 15 national communities, comprising 300,000,000 out of the 2,400,000,000 people then in the world—*i.e.*, USA, $1,453; Canada, $870; New Zealand, $856; Switzerland, $849; Sweden, $780; U.K., $773; Denmark, $689; Australia, $679; Norway, $587; Belgium, $582; Luxembourg, $553; Netherlands, $502; France, $482; Iceland, $476; and Ireland, $420.

The peoples with per capita annual incomes between $100 and $400 comprised another 500,000,000—*e.g.*, Israel, $389; Czechoslovakia, $371; Finland, $348; Argentina, $346; West Germany, $320; USSR, $308; Hungary, $269; Italy, $235; Turkey, $125; Mexico, $121; Brazil, $112; etc.

The desperately poor—*i.e.*, those with per capita incomes below $100 a year—comprised two-thirds of the human race: much of Latin America; most of Africa and the Middle East; Iran, $85; Ceylon, $67; India, $57; Pakistan, $51; Philippines, $44; Burma and Thailand, $36; Korea, $35; China, $27; and Indonesia, $25.[2]

Be it noted, lest we forget, that the poorest of human beings are "dark-skinned" in contrast to the wealthy "whites" of the Atlantic world, even as most of the 15,000,000 Negroes of the USA, thanks to economic discrimination, are among the poorest of the poor in the world's richest country. The "revolution of expectations" among the impoverished is inseparable from the colonial and racial revolutions of our time. These upheavals have already elicited new respect, mingled with fear, among "white" men for "black,"

[2] These figures, unfortunately, cannot be brought up to date, since neither the UN statisticians, nor anyone else so far as I can discover, have undertaken any comparable world-wide estimate since 1949. The U.S. Census Bureau calculated that personal incomes of U.S. citizens in 1956 averaged $1,940 per capita, before taxes, with the citizens of Delaware ($2,858) far above the average and those of Mississippi ($964) far below. Comparable figures, if available, would undoubtedly raise substantially the estimate of per capita national income in 1956-60 for the USSR, West Germany, most other States of Western Europe, possibly China, perhaps India (slightly), etc. But the broad pattern indicated by the UN survey of 1949 still stands as evidence that two-thirds of mankind is still desperately poor in comparison with the far wealthier communities of North America and Northern Europe.

"brown," "yellow," and "red" men, few of whom are any longer willing to acquiesce in a status of permanent inferiority. Whether poverty among the poor can be replaced by plenty, or even by some approach thereto, is dubious, for reasons next to be explored.

2. PEOPLE, POVERTY, AND THE QUEST FOR PLENTY

Come, Malthus, and in Ciceronian prose, show how a rutting population grows, until all the produce of the soil is spent, and brats expire for lack of aliment.— Popular British version of Malthusianism.

Economics became known as "the dismal science" early in the 19th Century when the new entrepreneurs of the Industrial Revolution, particularly in England where the process began, strove for profits by herding workers into factories at bare subsistence wages, employing women in coal mines, and hiring even little children at a pittance to toil in the "dark, Satanic mills"— all, more often than not, for 12 or 14 hours per day. Humanitarians and social reformers slowly became aware of the frightful miseries inflicted upon the new working class by the masters of the burgeoning laissez-faire capitalism of the early machine age and began insisting upon "factory legislation" and other forms of governmental action to end the new evils. Few could find persuasive evidence of Adam Smith's "invisible hand" whereby each, through pursuing his own gain, would allegedly contribute to the good of all.

These abuses, which inspired Karl Marx and Friedrich Engels to indict capitalism as a monstrous and self-destructive system of exploitation, are now unhappy memories in the mature capitalism of the highly industrialized nations. But they remind us that the beginnings of industrialization are almost invariably painful for large masses of people who must somehow be induced or coerced into producing more than they consume. No other means have been thus far devised for accumulating capital for investment, expansion, and economic growth in hitherto poor agrarian societies. Even more shocking abuses characterized the earlier phases of capital accumulation in the "socialist" industrialization of the USSR before any prospect of plenty loomed on the horizon. Comparable problems and dilemmas confront all the world's poor in their efforts to outgrow their poverty.

The most dismal of the earlier economists was undoubtedly Thomas Malthus (1776–1834), who posed a paradox which once seemed fictitious but is now recognized as being woefully real for much of contemporary mankind. His melancholy meditations on the human condition led him to a grim conclusion which events have proved wrong for the industrialized West but all too right for much of Asia and Africa. He postulated a constant growth of population in geometric ratio as against an increase of means of subsistence in arithmetic ratio. Improvement of living standards was thus impossible, since the pressure

619

of ever-expanding numbers of people upon resources would keep the poor as poor as ever.

The Puzzle of Population. Malthus was in error in overlooking the effects of industrialization on living standards and rates of population increase. Urban populations seldom reproduce themselves. The restriction and planning of parenthood through contraception is now quite general in the Western nations, despite Catholic ecclesiastical disapproval. Population growth is determined, not by any simple relationship between reproduction and resources, but by (1) birth rates, affected by the number and fecundity of childbearing mothers, by birth control, and by social habits and customs; (2) death rates, affected by longevity, war, and the control of disease; (3) the natural resources at the command of a given population, which influence both the birth rate and the death rate; and (4) the level of technology, which has a bearing upon all the three other factors.

Such glib phrases as "overpopulation," "underpopulation," or "surplus population" have no meaning except as they are related to these factors. Overpopulation in a given area has nothing to do with the size, density, or resources of the population but can refer only to a situation in which there is sufficient pressure of population on resources to cause a reduction of living standards or to retard their improvement. Underpopulation can mean only a situation in which the number of people available to exploit natural resources is too few for the most profitable exploitation possible. Overpopulation—or underconsumption, or underdeveloped technology (these are all the same thing)—has long existed in large parts of Asia, where the level of technology has been constant for centuries, where contraception has never been generally practiced, and where living standards have been kept down to a bare subsistence level. Famines, pestilences, unemployment, and extensive emigration are typical symptoms of overpopulation of this kind. But an improvement in technology may make it possible for a given area to sustain an enormously greater population on a higher standard of living than was possible at a lower technological level. The present territory of the USA sustained only a million or so impoverished Indians in pre-Columbian days, because hunting and fishing and primitive agriculture were the only means of livelihood. It now sustains 175,000,000 people, with the highest living standard on earth, through intensive agriculture, industry, and commerce. Germany, with 30,000,000 in the mid-19th Century, was overpopulated, as shown by low living standards and wholesale emigration. Germany, with 60,000,000 people in the early 20th Century, was no longer overpopulated, for the industrialization of the country had intervened. It was long alleged that Japan and Italy were overpopulated, but no deterioration of living standards had taken place in either country prior to the Great Depression. Density of population per square mile is also no index to overpopulation. Before World War II the Netherlands had 669 people to the square mile, Belgium 755, Britain 500, Germany 371, Italy 350, and Japan

476. On the other hand, the USA had 34 people to the square mile, the USSR 21, Brazil 9, Argentina 7, Canada 2, and Australia less than 2. These figures by themselves do not in the least prove that the first group of States is overpopulated or that the second group is underpopulated, if one measures these conditions by living standards. One can properly speak of overpopulation only in relation to numbers, resources, technology, and standards of living. This phrase is more frequently a rationalization of expansionist ambitions than a statement of economic and social facts.

A rational and scientific population policy would be one aimed at securing an economic optimum population, *i.e.*, a population of such size in relation to resources and technology that all its members could enjoy the highest possible standard of living. Such a policy might call for a larger population in such States as Russia, Australia, and Argentina, and a smaller population in highly developed industrial States. Though expert opinion is not unanimous on this point, it is probable that, if economic well-being were the sole test of wisdom in such matters, it would follow that a substantial reduction of population in most of the great States of the world would be advantageous to succeeding generations. Such reductions, however, are traditionally viewed with alarm by governments.

Patriotism and People. Military power, rather than social well-being, is a prime objective of the economic nationalists who so largely dictate governmental policies. The patriot favors all measures, except unrestricted immigration, that seem likely to increase population. He condemns all that threaten to limit the unchecked growth of population. He is joined in condemnation by many churchmen who are opposed to birth control for theological reasons. He is also joined by moralists and reformers to whom liberty means license and to whom compulsions, inhibitions, and prohibitions are preferable to organized intelligence and freedom of choice as roads to the good life. He is joined by many others: the employer of labor who wants labor to be cheap and who knows that it can be cheap only when it is abundant; the military expert who feels that men rather than machines win wars; the physician who would keep the laity in ignorance; the timeserving politician; and, until recently, a few sincere sociologists and economists who viewed what looked like an impending decline of population with apprehension for reasons not directly connected with the economic welfare of the next generation. This combination is usually overwhelming and decisive.

The USA was established by immigrants and built into the wealthiest and mightiest power on earth by the toil and dreams of later immigrants. On its Statue of Liberty is inscribed: "Give me your tired, your poor, your huddled masses, yearning to breathe free, the wretched refuse of your teeming shore; send these, the homeless, tempest-tossed, to me. I lift my lamp beside the Golden Door." For a decade before 1914 European immigrants averaged a million a year, though Orientals were barred in 1882. But after 1920 America admitted only 150,000 immigrants annually, and these selectively on a quota system discriminating against southern and eastern Europeans in favor of northern and western Europeans.

Like other nation-states under the spell of an increasingly fear-ridden, suspicious, and "protectionist" nationalism, America no longer regards all men as having been created equal and no longer bids welcome to those who come to seek work and homes. The McCarran-Walter Immigration Act of 1952, codifying all previous legislation, retained the "national origin" quota system of 1924 whereby the percentage of the American population in 1920 represented by each alien group determines its present proportion of the 154,658 aliens admissible annually. Orientals, including the 85,000 Japanese in the USA, were for the first time made admissible to citizenship, but new immigrants from Asia are restricted to minute numbers—e.g., 185 a year from Japan and 100 each for other Asiatic countries. Irish, British, and Germans were favored. Latins, Slavs, and all persons of even partial Oriental ancestry, wherever born or residing, were discriminated against. Aliens already in America and found to be "subversive to the national security" or "prejudicial to the public interest," even though the beliefs or acts complained of were legal when committed, were made subject to deportation. The slogan of the new time, by no means restricted to America, was not "Welcome!" but "Keep Out! Trespassers will be prosecuted." [3]

Boom in Babies. Changing trends of population growth in the mid-20th Century confounded the prognostications of earlier "experts" and came close to vindicating the gloom of Malthus in the slumlands of the world. The Great Depression of the 1930's led to a marked decline in rates of population growth, particularly in the Atlantic communities. Western peoples who are without work usually find means of limiting their families. During the same years the Communist oligarchs of the USSR abandoned previous "freedom" of divorce, contraception, and abortion, and began offering numerous incentives for matrimonial stability and large families. These were continued after World War II, in which the human losses of the Soviet community were so appalling

---

[3] Although the McCarran Act had been endorsed by the State and Justice Departments, the F.B.I., CIA, and the Immigration and Naturalization Service, President Truman vetoed the bill in a message of June 25, 1952, describing it as inhumane, undemocratic, aimed at "thought control," and "worse than the infamous Alien Act of 1798." Senator Pat McCarran declared that the veto was "one of the most un-American acts I have witnessed in my public career" and based on "the doctrine promulgated by *The Daily Worker*." Congress overrode the veto. The Act, which became law on June 27, 1952, reenacted and extended some of the provisions of the (McCarran) Internal Security Act, also passed over the President's veto Sept. 23, 1950, requiring the registration of Communist-action and Communist-front organizations, denying passports to Communists, and specifying that subversive aliens who cannot prove they were "dupes" are barred from admission and naturalization and, if here, are to be denaturalized and deported. Contrary to the hopes and proposals of President Eisenhower, Congress in 1957 "liberalized" the Act only slightly to relieve certain categories of "hardship cases" without altering its restrictive, exclusive, and discriminatory character.

that a total population of 191,700,000 in 1940 had increased to only 200,-200,000 by April, 1956 (far less than most Western estimates), according to figures released by the Central Statistical Board of the Council of Ministers in July, 1956. The Ukraine and Byelorussia still had fewer inhabitants in 1956 than in 1940. Voluntary abortions without cost were nevertheless legalized once more in 1955.

These and other indications of a coming era of relatively stationary populations were abruptly reversed, even in Russia and most strikingly in Communist China, in a veritable "population explosion" during the 1950's. UN estimates put the world's total population at 1,810,000,000 in 1920; 2,013,000,000 in 1930; 2,504,000,000 in 1950; 2,652,000,000 in 1954; 2,750,000,000 in 1957; with a minimum prospect of 3,500,000,000 earth-dwellers by 1975 at the 1956 rate of growth, i.e., 40,000,000 per year. But the annual increment was climbing toward 50,000,000 by 1958.

This vast expansion in the numbers of the human denizens of the planet was in some industrialized communities a concomitant of inflationary prosperity. In the USA the annual death rate per thousand of population declined only slightly between 1935 and 1955 (from 11 to 9), but the birth rate increased from 17 to 25, thus adding over 2,500,000 people annually to the population. Americans, swimming in plenty (albeit on the installment plan) and unfrightened by threats of atomic war, found pride and joy in having more and more children.

Russia's experience was more typical of the rest of the world. In Marxist Muscovy birth rates per thousand declined from 32 in 1940 to 26 in 1955, but death rates diminished from 18 to 8 during the same interval. Among the slumlands of the colonial, or recently colonial, dwelling places of the world's poor, the gradual diffusion of Western techniques of hygiene, sanitation, and medicine effected a drastic fall in death rates with no corresponding decline in birth rates. Ceylon, with the aid of WHO, reduced its death rate from 20 to 10 between 1945 and 1955, with the birth rate remaining at 40 and the population thus promising to double within 25 years. The same was true in Malaya, Mexico, Puerto Rico, Colombia, Turkey, Syria, etc. In Eastern Asia, where 5,000,000 people were being added annually to India's population in the late 1950's and 12,000,000 to China's, humans were breeding three times faster than the peoples of Northwestern Europe. The Latin American rate of multiplication was four times that of Europe. While death control became general in most of the nonindustrialized regions of the world, birth rates remained almost double those prevailing in the North Atlantic nations.

The Dilemma of the "Backward" Areas. This enormous proliferation of *Homo sapiens* in our time threatened, if continued, to negate all efforts, national or international, to raise the living standards of that two-thirds of mankind which was predominantly "colored" and universally poor, often to the point of penury. By all past experience, industrialization, once achieved, will reduce birth rates from 40 to 20 or less. But the effective industrialization of the world's slumlands is still far off and may in many cases be precluded altogether by the avalanche of babies which means, among other things, that such populations become progressively "younger" in their composition, with more and more minor dependents relying on working adults for sustenance and with young mothers living longer and bearing ever more babies.

What governments can do about such problems is seldom decisive even when (as is often not the case) public policy-makers are persuaded of the necessity of halting the skyrocketing of population. Yet the possibilities of public control need not be minimized. Japan's people increased from 56,000,000 in 1920 to 91,000,000 in 1957. In 1948, when a birth rate of 34 and a death rate of 12 threatened to double the population in 32 years, the Diet legalized abortion and sterilization and set up a nation-wide system of birth control clinics. By 1955 the birth rate had dropped to 19. The governments of China and India have embarked upon similar programs, with results which may be equally hopeful. If, as, and when a cheap and effective oral contraceptive is made widely available, the "population explosion" may be brought under control, despite outcries in some church groups against "immorality." Even the poorest and most ignorant of men and women may be expected to prefer to rear a few children who can be educated toward a better life than many children condemned to never-ending illiteracy and poverty.

Even if the oversupply of babies can be reduced, the hard problems of lifting the world's poor to some promise of plenty will still remain enormously difficult. These masses live on the land. They till the soil by primitive methods and raise barely enough to feed themselves with little surplus left for sale in urban markets. In much of Islam and Latin America they are still exploited by feudal landlords and thieving politicians. Communists everywhere offer them hope in a challenge not yet met by the West. The hope is a promise of higher living standards through expropriation of landlords, liquidation of politicians, collectivization of agriculture, and public economic planning of industrialization. Such devices have wrought wonders in Russia and are achieving much in China. Yet China's half-billion peasants are still producing barely enough to keep themselves alive and provide a small surplus for industrialization. And in the USSR, even under the Sixth Five Year Plan, 50,-000,000 collectivized peasants were producing less in the way of marketable foodstuffs and raw materials for the new industries in the new cities than were produced by 6,000,000 farmers in the USA.

The vicious circle of poverty is not broken easily even by the most drastic and revolutionary reforms. The poor, being poor, save little above what they need for subsistence. They are ignorant because they cannot afford schooling. Being ignorant, they cannot learn the skills of more efficient agriculture. Lacking a more efficient agriculture, they can neither raise their own living standards nor contribute much to the necessary capital for industrialization.

Throughout Asia and Africa, moreover, they are often trapped in ancestral patterns of family structure, community life, caste distinctions, and feudal relationships which place a premium upon conformity to ancient ways and discourage the initiative and independence without which no significant economic growth is possible. Not soon nor easily can these human obstacles athwart the way to a better life be transcended.

Operation Rescue. Meanwhile Freeland and more recently Marxland have been reaching out in rivalry for the allegiance of *les misérables* in sundry programs of grants, loans, investments, technical aid, etc., ostensibly designed to help the poor become rich, or at least less poor. The size and scope of such efforts, despite much eloquence, remain at present negligible and almost inconsequential. The USA, wealthiest of nations, has thus far refused to support SUNFED (Special United Nations Fund for Economic Development) on the ground that indispensable expenditures for armaments preclude any such global enterprise to alleviate poverty. Most recent and current programs of economic aid from the industrialized States to raise living standards in the slumlands are unilateral and small-scale gambits in the Cold War, all of them thus far indecisive and almost insignificant. Yet the bare bones of the record is worth reviewing.

In his Inaugural Address of Jan. 20, 1949, President Truman asserted that

in the coming years, our program for peace and freedom will emphasize four major courses of action—(1) unfaltering support to the United Nations; (2) continuation of our programs for world economic recovery; (3) strengthening of freedom-loving nations against the dangers of aggression; and (4) we must embark upon a bold new program for making the benefits of our scientific advances and industrial progress available for the improvement and growth of under-developed areas. More than half the people of the world are living in conditions approaching misery. Their food is inadequate. They are victims of disease. Their economic life is primitive and stagnant. Their poverty is a handicap and a threat both to them and to more prosperous areas. For the first time in history, humanity possesses the knowledge and the skill to relieve the suffering of these people. . . . I believe that we should make available to peace-loving peoples the benefits of our store of technical knowledge in order to help them realize their aspirations for a better life. And, in cooperation with other nations, we should foster capital investment in areas needing development. Our aim should be to help the free peoples of the world, through their own efforts, to produce more food, more clothing, more materials for housing, and more mechanical power to lighten their burdens. . . . This should be a co-operative enterprise in which all nations work together through the United Nations and its specialized agencies wherever practicable. It must be a world-wide effort for the achievement of peace, plenty, and freedom. . . . Guarantees to the investor must be balanced by guarantees in the interest of the people whose resources and whose labor go into these developments. The old imperialism—exploitation for foreign profit—has no place in our plans. What we envisage is a program of development based on the concepts of democratic fair-dealing.

The American Congress voted appropriations that were microscopic in comparison with funds approved for arms. The UN launched a technical-

assistance program. At the Colombo (Ceylon) Conference of Foreign Ministers of the British Commonwealth in January, 1950, Mr. Spender of Australia
proposed, and secured approval of, a program for devoting almost £2,000,-
000,000 over a six-year period to the development of agriculture, industry,
transport, and health and educational services in South and Southeastern Asia.
President Truman's "International Development Advisory Board," of which
Nelson Rockefeller was chairman, made public on March 11, 1951, a report
entitled "Partners in Progress," based on the premise that free peoples were
faced with "two main threats. One is military aggression and subversion. The
other is hunger, poverty, disease, and illiteracy." The Board made proposals
designed to increase American private investment abroad from one billion to
two billion dollars annually by way of "tax incentives," new treaties, an insurance program, an "International Finance Corporation" as an affiliate of the
International Bank for Reconstruction and Development, and the creation of
an office of "Assistant Overseas Economic Adviser" to "encourage the maximum and most effective use of private enterprise." President Truman expressed appreciation: "The Point Four concept, properly carried out, is essential to the successful defense of the free world. . . ."

What was called for, if the "bold new program" was to have any appreciable effect, was the type of boldness urged by Stringfellow Barr, James P.
Warburg, Henry A. Wallace, Walter Reuther, Senator McMahon, and others
who perceived that nothing significant could be achieved without some type
of World Development Authority, possessed of vast funds for investment, and
wholeheartedly supported by the governments and peoples of the wealthy
Atlantic communities. Even such an agency might well flounder and fail unless
its direction were dedicated to two revolutionary goals: channeling capital
away from the traditional enterprises devoted to private profit and national
power into projects of development having no connection with the armament
industries and unlikely to pay dividends for many years; and fostering such
changes in the social and economic structure of "backward" areas as would
make investments productive without "exploitation" of native workers, bribery
of native landlords and bureaucrats, and alien infringements on local sovereignty. Quite apart from the arms race, which made the whole issue academic, these conditions seemed unlikely to be met by the rulers of America,
the only important source of investment capital. Private capital was no longer
flowing freely to backward areas in a time when nationalistic regimes (e.g.,
Indonesia, Egypt, Bolivia, Iran, Thailand), reacting against old abuses, were
nationalizing or confiscating foreign investments and imposing restrictions of
all kinds on the conduct of foreign-owned business. For a Great Power to
guarantee the profits of its private investors and to burden its taxpayers with
their losses, or to pour public funds in "socialist" fashion into the development of backward economies overseas rather than into its own depressed areas,
seemed unlikely to arouse public enthusiasm at home. Any such arrangement,

moreover, would inevitably have attached to it political or military "strings" which in the end would prove unacceptable to the recipients.

But the crucial obstacle was this: in most of the backward areas, no effective use appeared likely to be made of "Point Four" funds and goods without some means of putting an end to feudal exploitation and bureaucratic corruption and oppression. Since the beneficiaries of these ancient practices had everything to lose and nothing to gain by embracing the new vision, they rejected it, made feeble pretenses of meeting it, or sought to distort it to their own purposes. The USA in turn was everywhere committed to the subsidization and support, as bulwarks against Communism, of the very elites whose property and power made effective land reform, popular education, industrialization, and improved living standards impossible. In the face of this dilemma, Justice William O. Douglas in 1951–52 urged a "Point Five"—*i.e.*, encouragement of social revolution in backward areas. But such advice seemed naïve, if not irresponsible, to those who understood political and economic realities.

These obstacles to the raising of living standards among the world's poor are not, under all imaginable conditions, insuperable. They are merely of such character and magnitude that they can scarcely be overcome within the social, political, and ideological context of American foreign policy and the Atlantic alliance in their mid-century patterns. The "Point Four" program is envisaged by most of its proponents as an alternative to social revolution, not a means toward it—and as an antithesis, rather than an imitation, of Communism. Posed in these terms, the problem may reasonably be deemed insoluble per se, and quite irrelevant to the issue of war and peace—unless it should somehow, in ways not now foreseeable, furnish a means whereby American assembly lines, swiftly geared to the tasks of anticipated war, could find outlets for their vast production in markets less lethal than those of Mars. Meanwhile, most of the miserable masses of mankind in the slums of Asia and Africa seemed likely to be left to their own devices or to alien example, inspiration, or leadership in their yearning for a more abundant life.

The ultimate loyalties of the dark millions of Asia, Africa, and other colonial areas would depend less on the semantic magic practiced by the policy-makers of the great States than on their own dim guesses as to whether their deepest aspirations toward justice and a decent life could better be served by Western democracy and capitalism or by Soviet totalitarianism and socialism. The choice was still in doubt at mid-century. In the end there could be no finale save in One World, so ordered and governed as to afford some semblance of liberty and justice to all. Such a world could scarcely be a Soviet world or an American world. Only the ideal of the United Nations, cleansed of hypocrisy and fashioned into an effective tool of action, offered promise and hope. That ideal was far from realization as these words were written. That it might somehow find rebirth and new life was the prayer of all the spokesmen of the oppressed and the miserably poor of the earth who knew what their people had suffered and who knew also that salvation and liberation were not to be found in the replacement of selfish alien colonialisms by narrow native nationalisms or by the new "imperialism" of the Cold War.

3. THE POLITICS OF PENURY

> All mankinde is of one Author, and is one volume. . . . No man is an Iland, intire of it selfe; every man is a peece of the Continent, a part of the maine. . . . Any man's death diminishes me, because I am involved in Mankinde; And therefore never send to know for whom the bell tolls; It tolls for thee.—JOHN DONNE.

Whoever travels through the lands of the world's impoverished people must inevitably be impressed by the bewildering variety of races, religions, languages, customs, and social structures to be found among them. Indeed they appear to have so little in common, apart from all being poor and almost all being colored, that any effort to generalize further about their problems and politics may seem futile. Yet certain similar features of public life, varying from region to region, are observable in all such areas. And since these shared characteristics are of prime importance not only for the peoples concerned but for the world community *in toto* it is well to enumerate them and to consider at least a few illustrative instances.

In most such communities the preconditions of effective democracy are lacking, even when formal constitutions and prevailing ideologies are "democratic." Here one commonly discovers a small and insecure elite of land-owners and merchants; a disgruntled intelligentsia whose members can find few opportunities for respected careers aside from the civil service; a corps of army officers seldom "above politics" but more often immersed in politics; a body of professional politicians, for most of whom public office is not a service to the community but a means of personal enrichment through "squeeze," graft, and spoils; a negligible middle class quite incapable of lending continuity and stability to the conduct of public affairs; and a vast mass of illiterate, debt-ridden peasants living on the bare margins of subsistence. Under such conditions, democracy is always more shadow than substance, whatever the forms of the State may be.

Political instability in such communities is both a cause and a consequence of recurrent recourse to dictatorship by military juntas or civilian demagogues, with or without the benefit of rigged or bought elections. Orderly transfers of authority alternate with despotisms tempered by assassination or revolution. Dictators exploit their subjects and seek, when resentment becomes irresistible, to flee abroad with their mistresses and the public treasury. The gentle arts of earnest campaigning and the subtle skills of legislation, administration, and adjudication are in short supply where the requirements of the political market put a premium on the techniques of the *coup d'état*, of secret police, of espionage and slander, and of the systematic intimidation of critics and opponents. Classes, fearful for their privileges, are tempted to embrace the theory and practice of Fascism. Masses, despairing of any amelioration of their lot, are tempted to lend willing ears to the agitators of Communism, promising "reforms" of millennial scope. That Communist victory spells the end of democracy and civil liberties means nothing to people who have never had any civil liberties and to whom democracy is a mockery.

Hatred and violence are major components of political behavior wherever widespread frustrations breed widespread aggressions. Hungry and ragged multitudes are ever ready to applaud leaders who find scapegoats for mass misery. To alleviate the misery is difficult, particularly where a landlord class fears a loss of its privileges. But nothing is easier than to denounce foreign "colonialists" and "imperialists"; to vent mass rage against members of minority races or religions; to preach and practice intolerance; to manipulate mobs to rob, burn, and murder; and to provoke armed conflict with neighboring States.

Such has been the melancholy course, during the recent years and decades, of the practice of politics in most of the poor, backward, and nonindustrialized communities of mankind. Westerners have no occasion to feel superior in such matters, for many Western peoples—Russians, Italians, Germans, Spaniards, Austrians, Hungarians, etc.—"solved" their political problems in much the same way amid the mass frustrations engendered by World War I and the Great Depression of a decade later. This pattern of politics, "abnormal" in the major industrialized societies of our time, but quite "normal" among the poor, is nevertheless worthy of review and illustration if we would comprehend the politics of poverty. Its consequences and implications have already been suggested for the Mid East (see pp. 321*f.* and 371*f.*). Counterparts in other areas of the world's slumlands are our next concern.

Latin America: The *Caudillos*. In the vast expanses of high plateaus, coastal plains, sunswept islands, tropical jungles, lush valleys, and broad pampas lying between the Rio Grande and the southern tip of South America live (as of 1958) almost 200,000,000 people, divided into 20 sovereign States, interspersed in the Caribbean and in Guiana with a few vestiges of European colonialism. These nearest southern neighbors of the USA are racially Amerindian, Caucasoid, Negroid, and mestizo or mixed as to ancestry. Negroes predominate in many of the Caribbean lands and constitute a significant part of the population of Brazil (11%, with mulattoes 26%), where all people of partially white ancestry are deemed "white," in contrast to the USA where all people of partially Negroid ancestry are deemed "Negro." Amerindians and mestizos predominate in Mexico, Colombia, Ecuador, Peru, and Bolivia. The descendants of Hispanic conquistadores and of later European immigrants comprise most of the population of Argentina, Chile, Paraguay, and Uruguay. Religiously, almost all of these people are Roman Catholics. Linguistically, they are Spanish (or Portuguese in Brazil) with many of the Amerindians speaking only their pre-Columbian tongues. The vast majority of the masses in most of Latin America is still illiterate, *i.e.*, incapable of reading or writing any language.

No account of the tangled and turbulent politics, national and international, of Latin America can here be attempted. Detailed analyses of these matters are fortunately available elsewhere. The all-embracing pattern, ever since independence, has been one of recurrent struggles, frequently frustrated, for stable and orderly democracy, alternating with periods of dictatorship by *caudillos* or "chiefs." Latin America's second most populous State, Mexico, now with over 30,000,000 people, has achieved a high degree of political stability following the upheavals of the social revolution of 1910–17, during which land was nationalized and widely distributed among the peons in their *ejidos* or village communities—and after which the oil industry, largely owned by U.S. companies, was also nationalized and a semi-socialist "Welfare State" was painfully established. The recent Presidents of the Federal Republic, elected for a six-year term and ineligible for reelection under the Constitution of 1917, have been Miguel Aleman (1946–52) and Adolfo Ruiz Cortines (1952–58).

The United States of Brazil, largest and most populous Republic of the South, embracing a third of the area and people of South America, has enjoyed less stability and less impressive progress in economic development. Of its 60,000,000 inhabitants (1958), 40,000,000 have never seen a doctor, worn shoes, slept in a bed, or gone to school. Under the impact of the Great Depression the forms of democracy gave way to rule by a military junta in 1930, with Getulio Vargas assuming the Presidency and holding it intermittently until Aug. 24, 1954, when he committed suicide after being forced to retire by the Army. The Constitution of 1946 champions democracy and social justice but bans "anti-democratic" parties, including the widespread pro-Communist movement long led by Carlo Luis Prestes. Dr. Juscelino Kubitschek was elected President in October, 1955, and inaugurated Jan. 31, 1956. He promised a program of economic growth, obtained small-scale U.S. loans, censored the press, and suppressed local rebellions.

Argentina's 20,000,000 people have been even less fortunate in their public affairs, despite the largest per capita income among the major Latin American communities, a greater degree of industrialization and literacy, and a population which is over 80% of European origin. After sundry earlier alternations between despotism and democracy, Argentina during World War II came under the control of the semi-Fascist, quasi-totalitarian dictatorship of Juan Perón. Rebellion began in 1951 and culminated on Sept. 16, 1955, in Perón's overthrow and flight into exile. The "liberal" Constitution of 1853 was restored May 1, 1956. Five years after its expropriation by Perón and its conversion into an official organ of the Peronista Confederation of Labor, *La Prensa* of Buenos Aires resumed publication in February, 1956, as an independent journal under its former owner and publisher, Dr. Alberto Gainza Paz, in a notable victory for freedom of the press. The new regime of President Pedro Eugenio Aramburu (1955*f.*) revived democratic patterns of politics, but continued to be menaced by armed rebellion, allegedly of Peronista inspiration.

Among the lesser Republics, politics remained a chaotic struggle for power among rival politicians and Army officers, often closely linked with local landlords and merchants and foreign investors. "Liberals" and "radicals," striving for a reformation of age-old patterns of semi-feudal and semi-colonial economies, were more often frustrated than successful in their endeavors. Under the Presidency of Gen. Carlos Ibanez (1952–58), Chile experienced a fantastic currency inflation, strikes in the copper mines, and sporadic political riots instigated by Leftists. Elsewhere a random sample from the long calendar of political acts of violence will suggest the remoteness of an orderly pattern of public life, rendered impossible by the miseries endemic to societies cursed by poverty and riven by endless wars of rich and poor and by wars among the rich for the privilege of exploiting the poor.

JAN. 3, 1955. President José Antonio Ramon of Panama is assassinated. Ex-President Arnolfo Arias is arrested. The National Assembly proclaims a state of siege. New President José Ramon Guizado is impeached and indicted. Following a transitional regime, Ernesto de la Guardia, Jr., is elected to the Presidency, May 13, 1956.

JAN. 9, 1955. President José Figueres of Costa Rica charges before the OAS a threat of invasion from Nicaragua, whose dictator, Anastasio Somoza, had previously charged a Costa Rican plot to assassinate him. Somoza challenges Figueres to a duel while rebels, allegedly supported from Nicaragua, raid Costa Rican towns. USA sends four fighter planes to defend Costa Rica. Rebels are routed and a buffer zone along the border agreed upon.

FEB. 19, 1955. Somoza shows U.S. Vice President Richard M. Nixon, in Nicaragua on a "good-will" tour, the weapons allegedly sent by Figueres to kill him and asks the USA to "tie the hands of that crazy man," whom he alleges has Communist affiliations.

SEPT. 19, 1955. Joint investigation of border conditions by attachés of the USA, Argentina, Brazil, and Chile avert a clash between Ecuador and Peru in their long-standing frontier dispute, in which each accuses the other of planning invasion.

DEC. 10, 1956. A general strike in Port-au-Prince leads the Army of Haiti to oust President Paul E. Magloire, dictator since 1950. Gen. Leon Cantave succeeds to the Presidency in May, 1957, after three intervening Presidents are arrested. He imposes Army rule, May 21, 1957. Following extensive mob violence, Pierre Eustache Daniel Fignole is sworn in as provisional President in a "coalition" regime May 26, 1957. Army ousts Fignole on June 14.

MAR. 13, 1957. Forty students in Havana, attempting to overthrow the dictatorial regime of President Fulgencio Batista in Cuba, are killed at the Presidential palace. Rebels under Fidel Castro are accused by Batista of being "Communists." Further attempts at revolution ensue.

MAY 10, 1957. Dictator Gustavo Rojas Pinilla of Colombia, President since 1933, is ousted by a military junta after widespread rioting.

MAY 29, 1957. U.S. State Department charges that the disappearance of Gerald

THE PROBLEMS OF THE POOR

Lester Murphy, co-pilot on the Dominican Airlines, on Dec. 3, 1956, is linked with the disappearance on March 12, 1956, of Dr. Jesus de Galindez, a Columbia University professor and long-time foe of Gen. Rafael L. Trujillo, dictator of the Dominican Republic since 1930.

AUG. 10, 1957. President Carlos Castillo Armas (who in 1954, with aid from El Salvador, Honduras, and the USA, "saved Guatemala from Communism" by ousting, via invasion and revolution, the Leftist regime of President Jacobo Arbenz Guzmán in June, 1954) is assassinated.

JAN. 23, 1958. In oil-rich Venezuela, where $3,000,000,000 of U.S. capital is invested, Gen. Marcos Pérez Jiménez, dictator since 1948, is ousted after bloody rioting and replaced by a junta headed by Rear Admiral Wolfgang Larrazabal.

Our catalogue, if continued for other Latin American Republics or for those mentioned as to subsequent political events, would be tedious and monotonous. A similar catalogue of 50 years or 100 years ago would reveal a comparable pattern of disorder. It may well be that another catalogue of 50 years hence will reveal little change, although all people of good will must hope otherwise. The "moral" of such chronicles is not that Latin Americans are incapable of democratic self-government. Innumerable Latin American citizens and statesmen have contributed richly to the theory and practice of democracy. Many of their fellows among Latin American intellectuals have made invaluable contributions to the literature, art, and science which are the common heritage of all mankind. The moral is rather that political stability and orderly government are difficult to achieve in communities afflicted with mass misery and illiteracy—which are as widespread in Latin America as in most of Asia and Africa.

Such hopes as many Latins have long entertained, despite their traditional suspicion of "Yankee imperialism," that the fabulously wealthy "Colossus of the North" would somehow decide to alleviate these conditions, and find effective means for so doing, have thus far been disappointed. Latin America is not only a slumland, but is peripheral to the major rivalries which the statesmen of the "Great Powers" suppose, perhaps mistakenly, will prove decisive for the destinies of the world community. Aside from innumerable other conferences and diplomatic exchanges, President Eisenhower met with the Latin American Presidents in Panama in July, 1956. On the occasion of the signing of another "Declaration of Panama," reiterating the customary platitudes, he proposed an inter-American commission to "hasten the beneficial use of nuclear forces" throughout the Western hemisphere. All cheered. But results, if any, in alleviating Latin American poverty would be long deferred. Meanwhile, Washington took vigorous action, as in Guatemala in 1954, only when it appeared possible that "international Communism" might gain a foothold somewhere in the Americas.

For the rest, U.S. economic and technical aid to Latin America during the 1940's and 1950's was almost microscopic in comparison with the vast military subventions and appreciable economic grants extended to the allies of

Washington in Europe and Asia. The premises of such policies were that Latin America could safely be neglected and that Latin hopes of escape from poverty were in any case perhaps foredoomed in any foreseeable future. The validity of the premises could be tested only by events to come.

India: The Planners. When Christopher Columbus, faring into the unknown, first touched land in the Caribbean, Oct. 12, 1492, he did not know that he had come upon a "New World"—to be named, unjustly, after his mendacious contemporary and acquaintance, Amerigo Vespucci, whose widely publicized voyage of 1497 was fictitious. Columbus, in westward search of "the Indies" and of India, was doubtless responsible, by bringing Carib natives back to Spain for conversion, for the error of all Europeans in dubbing these strange people "Indians." They were Mongoloid nomads who had filtered into the New World out of Asia 20,000 years ago by way of the Bering Strait, possibly mingling with eastward-sailing South Sea Islanders of Malay origin who may have reached the west coast of South America. We can do no better than call them "Amerindians," even though both parts of the name are, historically and geographically, false.

The original India, halfway across the world from the Americas and home of one of the most ancient literate cultures of mankind, had become by the mid-20th Century the second most populous State of the world, with almost 400,000,000 people crowding its rich valleys, coastal plains, and broad highlands and, much more sparsely, eking meager livings in its tropical jungles and snow-peaked northern plateaus rimming, athwart Tibet and China, the highest mountains on earth. The people of India have little in common, save a common humanity, with the predominantly "Indian" people of much of Latin America. Racially, linguistically, and religiously they are half a world removed. Yet Indians share abundantly with Amerindians one quality which is equally painful to both. That quality is poverty.

The Republic of India was conceived in liberty and dedicated to the proposition that all men are created equal. Its struggle against poverty was for all the world a test as to whether a State so conceived and so dedicated could equal or surpass the accomplishments of totalitarian police-state methods in the Soviet Union and China in inaugurating the vast processes of industrialization, urbanization, and education without which no escape from poverty was possible. In the late 1950's the verdict of events was still unclear on the Indian venture in "democratic planning." But the enterprise itself merits close attention.

The context of the enterprise must first be noted, lest any doubts remain regarding the reality of Indian democracy. Apart from the frightful mass murders attending the Hindu-Moslem riots of 1947 at the time of partition (see pp. 380–382), India—and even Pakistan, albeit less fully—has succeeded in avoiding, thus far, most of the usual political concomitants of mass poverty and illiteracy. In an effort to prevent or reduce frictions among communities of diverse cultural and racial backgrounds, state boundaries were redrawn in 1955–56, largely on linguistic lines, with the former princely states absorbed into the 16 members of the Federation. The proceses was not

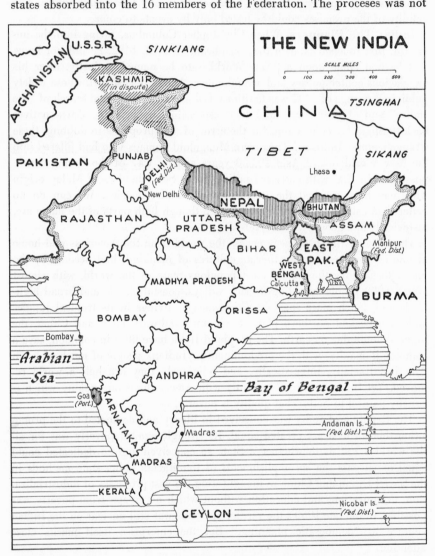

without violence. The initial attempt to divide the Bombay region into Gujarati-speaking and Marathi-speaking states envisaged Bombay itself (with its Gujarati upper class and Marathi lower-class majority) as a Federal District. These arrangements provoked Marathi rioting, until it was decided to establish one large state of Bombay, embracing both language groups. Other inevitable dissatisfactions were kept below the threshold of public disorder, with English remaining the common language of the educated minority, and British traditions of moderation, plus the Gandhi legacy of nonviolence, perhaps contributing to domestic tranquillity. The five north central states were Hindi-speaking. Each of the new southern states embraced most of the speakers of the major Dravidian languages: Andhra (Telegu), Madras (Tamil), Karnataka (Konnada), Kerala (Malayali).

Within this federal structure the dominant Congress Party, under Nehru's leadership, made appreciable, if not as yet decisive, progress in overcoming ancient evils standing in the way of economic growth. By 1955 five of the sixteen Indian states had abolished the *zamindar* system of absentee land ownership. Although tenancy was still widespread and one in seven peasant families was still landless (1958), many other peasants obtained title to land, paying its price in annual installments over a period of years to the government which compensated the former owners. Gandhi's dream of a small-scale, self-sufficient handicraft and family farm economy is mingled in the Indian quest for equality, stability, and prosperity with Western concepts of social security, the Welfare State, and democratic socialism. To assure equality to women (without which economic progress is difficult) is a long-range task requiring the transformation of traditional attitudes. To break down the caste system and achieve full emancipation and equality for the outcasts or "untouchables" (without which economic progress is almost impossible) is even more difficult. Yet legislative measures and public pressures all pointed in the same hopeful direction.

These processes all moved forward within the framework of government provided by the enormously lengthy Indian Constitution of 1950. The Republic is a Federal Union, but residual powers are reserved to the nation, as in Canada, not to the states, as in the USA. The federal government is headed by a President and Vice President elected for five-year terms by both houses of the federal parliament and the elected members of the state legislatures. The President names the Prime Minister and other Cabinet members who must, in order to remain in office, command majority support in the House of the People, consisting of 500 deputies elected for five-year terms by universal suffrage. The upper chamber or Council of States has 250 members chosen by the state legislatures.

In the elections of 1951–52, contested by 8 major and 40 minor parties— all represented on ballots by symbols intelligible to an illiterate electorate— the Congress Party won 45% of the popular vote and 367 seats in the House of the People; the Communists, 27 seats; the Socialists, 12; the anti-Communist People's Party, 10; the conservative Hindu Party, Mahasabha, now called Jan Sangh, 3; etc. In the second national elections (Feb.–March, 1957), over half of the 193,000,000 eligible voters cast ballots. Congress candidates again won a handsome victory, now polling over 50% of the popular vote, while the Socialists declined and the Communists increased their popular vote

THE PROBLEMS OF THE POOR

from 5% to 10% and won control of the state of Kerala. Here in the miserable southland Communist Elamkulam Manakai Sankaran Namboodiripad, an intellectual of impeccably Brahmin or top-caste background, became Premier on April 5, 1957, and pledged agrarian reform, despite the curious Communist slogan: "We are not going to do anything wonderful!"

Amid such electoral successes, reverses, and challenges, the Congress Party and the federal government set up a Planning Commission of Ministers and economists, all of Cabinet rank, which devised the First Five Year Plan (1951–56). The major objectives were to raise grain and cotton production, develop electric power, expand transportation and irrigation, and foster the textile industry. A public investment of $4,500,000,000 was contemplated, over half of it to be devoted to transportation, communication, irrigation, and power, to which it was hoped that $1,250,000,000 in private investments would be added. *In toto* the Plan was to absorb 5 or 6% of the national income (estimated at less than $20 billion in 1951) and to achieve by 1956 a small rise (11%) in national income. Thanks to good weather, the planned goals of grain production for 1956 (61.6 million tons) were exceeded in 1954 (65.4 million tons). Total industrial production rose by 40% over 1950, but electric power output attained only 42% of its target and steel expansion less than 15%.

The more ambitious Second Five Year Plan (1956–61) envisaged an 18% rise in per capita national income, to be achieved by an investment of $11.7 billions. Half would go to transport, communication, education, and electric power; one quarter to industry; and only one-sixth to agriculture and village industry, although these segments of the economy were expected to provide almost half the increase of national income. By the end of the Plan, it was hoped that grain output would be expanded by 15%, cotton by 31%, jute by 25%, sugar cane by 28%, and oil seeds by 27%.[4]

By mid-1957 it was evident that the Planners were in serious difficulties. Public dissatisfaction with the pitiably slow progress from poverty toward plenty under the First Plan prompted the more ambitious goals of the Second —the more so as Communist China, committed to "socialist" planning by totalitarian methods, appeared to be doing appreciably better. The goals were not immoderate. If all targets were met, Indian per capita national income, estimated by the UN at $57 in 1949, would still be only $69.5 in 1961. But even these modest objectives were based on assumptions which proved questionable. One was that foreign aid would double. Despite U.S. economic grants and Soviet loans, including arrangements for Russian construction of a $100,-000,000 Indian steel mill, foreign aid in 1957 seemed in process of declining. It was also assumed that prices would remain stable and that savings available for investment would increase. In fact world prices continued to climb,

[4] For fuller details on the matters dealt with above, see the excellent account by Fred Greene, *The Far East* (New York, Rinehart, 1957), pp. 367–394.

thus raising the prospective cost of the plan by $2,000,000,000. Indian private savings diminished. Finance Minister T. T. Krishnamashari came to the USA in September, 1957, hoping to obtain $500,000,000 for the next 18 months and almost $2,000,000,000 in all. When scandals in his Ministry forced his resignation early in 1958, no such sums were in prospect.

India's planners thus faced problems which left open the question as to whether "democratic planning" in a desperately poor community could in fact initiate effective industrialization and increase agricultural surpluses without resorting to nondemocratic methods of forced savings and coerced collectivization of farms. Indians comprise one-seventh of the human race. India was the only major democracy among the world's poor striving by democratic means to conquer poverty. Upon the outcome of the effort much hinged, not only for India but for mankind.

Africa: The Terrorists. The politics of poverty in Africa are well exemplified in their less hopeful aspects at two extremities of the Dark Continent. In Algeria (see pp. 372 and 573), 1,250,000 white French *colons* confront 8,000,000 natives, largely Arabs and Berbers. Their relationships in the 1950's have been relationships of arson, robbery, torture, murder, and massacre. In South Africa some 3,000,000 Dutch and English white settlers confront 300,000 Indians and other Asians, 1,000,000 "colored" or mulattoes, and over 9,000,-000 Negro natives. Their relationships have been relationships of carefully organized segregation and discrimination by the white minority against the nonwhite majority—almost certainly productive of violence in years to come.

Between Algiers and Cape Town from north to south, and between Dakar and the Gulf of Aden from west to east, dwell some 200,000,000 people, all of them (except for white land-owners, merchants, colonial officials, and a few native rulers) miserably poor, most of them illiterate in any language, and many of them still living in preliterate tribal cultures scarcely touched, save deleteriously, by contacts with white civilization. To survey their trials and tribulations and their hopes and opportunities, region by region, is beyond the scope of our inquiry. But a few key pieces of the complex mosaic may usefully be sketched.

Where white settlers are few and native experience in self-government is considerable, independence from alien rule is quite inevitable in our time. Thus, in the British colony of the Gold Coast, Kwame Nkrumah (educated at Lincoln University, Oxford, Pa., and at the University of Pennsylvania), was released from Jamestown Prison in Accra in February, 1951, to become the first African Prime Minister of an African colony. On March 6, 1957, this territory of 5,000,000 natives, producing a third of the world's cocoa, became fully independent under the name of Ghana in a colorful ceremony attended by envoys of many States. Whitehall was simultaneously preparing Nigeria to the east, home of 32,000,000 natives and largest all-Negro country in the world, for increased self-government and ultimate independence. The policy-makers

637

of France, Belgium, and Portugal, each possessed of vast central African lands, moved much more hesitantly, if at all, in the direction of native self-rule. Here natives continued to be kept in ignorance and deprived of participation even in local administration. In Angola and Mozambique Portuguese authorities still imposed a system of forced labor (which had become an open scandal in the Belgian Congo early in the century) and laid plans, equally ill-calculated to promote future peace, for large-scale white settlement in the colonies.

In British East Africa, the picture was mixed and the prospects doubtful. The 5,000,000 natives of Uganda, split into a dozen districts each with local self-government and a keen sense of local loyalties, were not yet animated by any widespread nationalist demand for independence, despite the activities since 1952 of the Uganda National Congress Party. The largest unit is the kingdom of Buganda, whose monarch, the Kabaka of Buganda, was deported to London and then restored to his throne in Kampala in October, 1955, as a constitutional ruler in deference to popular protest and demands. Whether the complex federal structure of the Protectorate would promote national unity and an orderly transition to independence remained to be seen.[5]

In neighboring Kenya some 30,000 white people live among 150,000 Hindus and Pakistanis and 6,000,000 natives, among whom the million-strong Kikuyu tribe is the largest. A third of the whites took unto themselves the best farm lands of the Kikuyus and condemned the tribesmen to landlessness or to a wretched sustenance-living on poor farms where the growing of cash crops (cotton, coffee, and sisal) was forbidden lest they compete with the European-owned plantations of the "White Highlands." The result was a peculiarly atrocious and abortive attempt at social revolution wherein the Kikuyus, originally led by Jomo Kenyatta, sought to recover their lost lands and drive all the whites from Kenya. The secret society of the rebels was Mau Mau. Their weapon was terrorism.

Between 1952, when the "Mau Mau Emergency" was declared, and October–November, 1956, when the Dedan Kimathi, last major Mau Mau leader, was captured and shot and British military operations were ended, man's inhumanity to man was king of Kenya. Terrorists killed some scores of Europeans and Asians, 1,500 Africans, and 600 members of the "security forces," which in turn herded 70,000 natives into jails and concentration camps, hanged 700, and slew 8,000 in battle, amid an orgy of murder, pillage, and fiendish torture of suspects on both sides. Given this dark legacy, the grant of limited voting rights to natives in 1957–58 seemed unlikely to end unrest in a tragic land where white men live by despoiling, oppressing, and exploiting black men— who had access to only one high school in all the country and to no higher education whatever.[6]

[5] See David E. Apter, "Political Developments in Uganda," *Current History*, May, 1956, pp. 269–278.

[6] See John V. Murra, "Kenya in the Emergency," *ibid.*, pp. 279–284.

To the south a veritable devil's brew boiled and bubbled in the 1950's with ominous threats of explosions to come. South Africa's white nationalists, having virtually annexed South-West Africa in defiance of the UN, aspired to expand their power over Bechuanaland and Rhodesia and to extend *apartheid* to these areas. In order to avoid any such development, British policy-makers, despite native opposition, created the Central African Federation of Southern and Northern Rhodesia and Nyasaland, inaugurated by an Order in Council signed by Queen Elizabeth II on Aug. 1, 1953. But segregation and discrimination are here as much the rule as in South Africa, with fewer than 300,000 whites dominating 7,000,000 natives, only a handful of whom have any voting rights. The giant Kariba Dam on the Zambesi, to be completed in 1961, will doubtless further economic development and improve living standards. Meanwhile the economy of the Federation is dominated by the North Rhodesian copper industry, half owned by the Anglo-American Corporation of the late Sir Ernest Oppenheimer, a South African magnate, and half by the American Metal Company. Among underground workers in copper mines, whites in the early 1950's averaged over $6,000 per year and Africans less than $400. When African workers in 1955 staged a two-month strike for higher wages, they lost and found themselves worse off than before. In housing, health services, and schooling, whites get much and natives get little. Self-government is remote, lest it jeopardize the privileges of the European elite.

This sinister pattern of racial relations has reached its logical culmination in the Union of South Africa, where a "free people" in a "free" and independent Dominion exercises its "freedom" by limiting freedom to the white minority and denying all freedom to the native majority. While the USA struggled painfully to reduce racial segregation and discrimination in the hope that its Negro minority might enjoy some minimum measure of civil rights and equality of opportunity, South Africa strove with equal energy to increase and enlarge discrimination and segregation (*apartheid*) in the hope that its dominant white ruling caste might perpetuate its advantages in the face of the rising tide of color.

In Pretoria Johannes G. Strydom, leader No. 2 in Prime Minister Daniel F. Malan's Afrikaner Nationalist Party, appealed on Aug. 17, 1954, for French, Belgian, Portuguese, and British support for policies of "white supremacy." "White rule must be maintained; otherwise they, as well as we, are doomed to disappear. The white man who does not view with fear conditions throughout Asia and Africa is an irresponsible fool." On Nov. 30, 1954, Strydom succeeded Malan as Prime Minister. The opposition United Party, led by J. G. N. Strauss, was no less committed to *apartheid*. The Liberal Party, seeking a multi-racial egalitarian democracy, won no mass support whatever during the 1950's among either the Afrikaner or English elements of the white population.

The meaning of *apartheid* as practiced in South Africa would doubtless astonish even the most ardent segregationists of the American South. Separate trains, separate buses, separate schools, separate neighborhoods, no votes for Negroes, and legal bans on intermarriage were, until recently, all of a piece in both citadels of "white supremacy." But more is involved. As early as 1913 Africans in South Africa were permitted to own land only in special "reserves," constituting 12.5% of the land area of the Union. As early as 1936 Africans were removed from the voting lists and allowed to elect only a handful of white "representatives" to the two houses of the Parliament. Every African, when not on reservation, must carry a pass to prove his right to visit a city or a white-owned farm or to seek a job or live on "location" in an urban area or stay out at night after curfew. So stringent are these controls that it has not been uncommon in recent years for a million natives to be arrested annually for "violations" and for 200,000 per year to be jailed.

Under the Group Areas Act of 1950, scores of thousands of natives in Johannesburg and elsewhere were evicted from their homes. Under the Bantu Education Act of 1950, Africans are to be trained only as unskilled workers, farm laborers, and domestic servants. When the Appeals Court held unconstitutional the "Separate Representation of Voters Act" disfranchising all non-whites, on the ground that such legislation required a two-thirds vote of both houses of Parliament, the Nationalists enlarged the chambers in 1952 and thus acquired the requisite majority. Under the "Suppression of Communism Act" (1950), all outstanding leaders of the African National Congress and the South African Indian Congress are barred from organization activity as "subversives." When Africans, Indians, and Colored united in a six-month campaign of nonviolent violation of the pass laws, a Public Safety Act and a Criminal Laws Amendment Act of 1953 made possible the suspension of civil liberties, the arrest of 9,000 volunteers, and the punishment of many by 5 years in jail, a £300 fine, and 15 lashes with the whip.

Such policies are favored by the frightened white rulers of the land, despite repeated protests from India and other Asian States, condemnation in the UN, British and American pleas for a different course, and world-wide denunciation, shrewdly exploited in Communist propaganda. South Africa's Africans, thus far, have resorted neither to terrorism nor to attempted revolution to alleviate their lot. But if South Africa's Europeans can find no better way to achieve security against the Africans of South Africa, then sooner or later an attempted racial and social revolt will burst forth in insane violence with consequences incalculable. Its prospective horrors will contribute nothing (quite the contrary) to raising the living standards of Africans. But it may well put an end in blood to white rule of darker peoples—unless white men display some capacity to act upon the Christian and democratic creeds of charity and equality among all human beings in which they profess to believe.

4. THE NEW NEUTRALS

The great rule of conduct for us in regard to foreign nations is, in extending our commercial relations, to have with them as little _political_ connection as possible. So far as we have already formed engagements let them be fulfilled with perfect good faith. Here let us stop.

Europe has a set of primary interests which to us have none or a very remote relation. Hence she must be engaged in frequent controversies, the causes of which are essentially foreign to our concerns. Hence, therefore, it must be unwise in us to implicate ourselves by artificial ties in the ordinary vicissitudes of her politics or the ordinary combinations and collisions of her friendships or enmities. . . .

It is our true policy to steer clear of permanent alliances with any portion of the foreign world, so far, I mean, as we are now at liberty to do it. . . .

Taking care always to keep ourselves by suitable establishments on a respectable defensive posture, we may safely trust to temporary alliances for extraordinary emergencies. . . .

There can be no greater error than to expect or calculate upon real favors from nation to nation. It is an illusion which experience must cure, which a just pride ought to discard. . . .—GEORGE WASHINGTON, Sept. 17, 1796.

The two-thirds of the human race still living in poverty and ignorance were, by virtue of ignorance and poverty, quite incapable of arriving at any common formula or program for knowledge and plenty. Some embraced, or acquiesced in, Communism as the road toward the goal—in North Korea, North Vietnam, and many-millioned China. Others, as in India and Pakistan, sought prosperity through democratic and semi-socialist economic planning. Still others resorted to terrorism and violent rebellion against white "colonialism." Some remained passive, watching, waiting, and hoping. Others, _e.g._, Turkey, Iran, Iraq, Pakistan, Thailand, the Philippines, and the Latin American republics, allied themselves with the West against the East in hope of military protection and economic aid. But the overwhelming majority of the world's poor were at least of one mind in common opposition to racialism and colonialism and in a quest for solidarity and collaboration among the States of Africa and Asia. And many among them were hostile to all military coalitions and were committed to a new "neutralism" in a strange new world, echoing the traditional neutrality of Sweden and Switzerland and the recently adopted neutral roles of Austria and Jugoslavia. Before seeking to assess the significance and prospects of the new neutral bloc, it would be well to notice the first major attempt to promote joint action toward common goals among the African and Asian nations.

Conference at Bandung. Between April 18 and April 24, 1955, the political leaders of 29 Asian and African nations met in the Indonesian mountain city of Bandung, 75 miles southeast of Jakarta, in an effort to formulate common aspirations. The meeting did not eventuate, nor was it intended to, in any new bloc, alliance, or coalition. But it furnished an occasion for important contacts and new departures in world affairs and for an enhanced sense of solidarity among peoples recently liberated from colonial rule.[7]

At Bogor, near Jakarta, the Premiers of the "Colombo Plan" Powers (Mohammed Ali of Pakistan, Jawaharlal Nehru of India, U Nu of Burma, Sir John Kotelawala of Ceylon, and Ali Sastroamidjojo of Indonesia) conferred, Dec. 28–29, 1954, and decided to act upon a suggestion first made at their previous meeting in April. They agreed to invite 25 other countries to send their Premiers or Foreign Ministers to Indonesia in late April, 1955, "to promote goodwill and cooperation among the nations of Asia and Africa . . . to consider social, economic, and cultural problems . . . to consider problems of special interest to Asian and African peoples, e.g., problems affecting national sovereignty and racialism and colonialism [and] to view the position of Asia and Africa and their peoples in the world today and the contribution they can make to the promotion to world peace and cooperation." Of the States invited, the Central African Federation did not attend. All others sent delegations: Afghanistan, Cambodia, Communist China, Egypt, Ethiopia, the Gold Coast, Iran, Iraq, Japan, Jordan, Laos, Lebanon, Liberia, Libya, Nepal, the Philippines, Saudi Arabia, the Sudan, Syria, Thailand, Turkey, North Vietnam, South Vietnam, and Yemen. Japan was included to meet Ceylonese and Pakistani objections to Communist China, sponsored by India and Burma. Israel was excluded lest the Arab States refuse to attend. Formosa, South Africa, and the colonial Powers were excluded by common consent.

On April 11 an Air India Constellation, flying from Hong Kong to Jakarta with 8 crewmen, 2 European journalists, a Vietnamese, and 8 minor representatives of Communist China, exploded and fell into the sea in Indonesian waters off Borneo, with only 3 crew members surviving. Peiping at once accused "secret agents" of the USA and Chiang Kai-shek of sabotage and held the Hong Kong authorities, who had been allegedly forewarned, guilty of negligence. On April 17 London rejected the charge and enumerated the safety precautions that had been taken. Three days later Hong Kong reported that an inquiry had revealed no sabotage at the airport. On May 26 New Delhi and Jakarta released the report of an Indonesian investigation which concluded that the crash was caused by a planted time bomb. On June 12 Hong Kong police offered a reward of 100,000 H.K. dollars ($17,200) for information leading to the discovery of the saboteurs. A score of arrests ensued. Formosa in September rejected a British request for the extradition of a Chinese airport worker who had fled from Hong Kong in May.

In mid-April, 1955, four Premiers, on their way to Bandung, conferred in Rangoon: Chou En-lai, Nehru, U Nu, and Abdel Gamel Nasser of Egypt. The 29 delegations which gathered in the former Dutch Club on April 18

---

[7] The section which follows is reprinted, with minor changes, from the author's article on the "Asian-African Conference" in *The New International Year Book, Events of 1955,* with the permission of Funk and Wagnalls Company, Publishers.

represented over half of the population of the world. President Sukarno said in welcome: "I hope this Conference will give guidance to mankind. I hope it will give evidence that Asia and Africa have been reborn. The life of man today is corroded and made bitter by fear." A seven-point agenda was proposed: economic cooperation, cultural cooperation, self-determination and human rights, peaceful use of nuclear energy, world peace, destructive use of nuclear weapons, and problems of dependent peoples. Nehru's leadership was challenged at the outset by Iraqi and Iranian attacks on Zionism and Soviet imperialism, and by Carlos Romulo's warning of the new tyranny of Communism. On April 20 Chou En-lai mildly urged unity, peace, nonintervention, and coexistence. Two days later Ceylon's Prime Minister assailed Soviet colonialism anew. While the State Department rejoiced at the trend of the proceedings, Congressman Adam Clayton Powell, in Bandung as an unofficial observer, warned that the Conference was anti-American and could become anti-white if the USA did not bestir itself against colonialism and racial discrimination.

On April 23 Chou En-lai created a sensation by declaring: "The Chinese people are friendly to the American people. The Chinese people do not want to have a war with the USA. The Chinese Government is willing to sit down and enter into negotiations with the U.S. Government to discuss the question of relaxing tension in the Formosa area." When the State Department replied that Nationalist China must participate as an equal in any talks, Chou, on April 24, reiterated Peiping's "right" to "liberate" Formosa, though again championing a negotiated settlement.

The final communiqué of April 24 sponsored economic development of the Asian-African area through foreign aid, a UN fund, exchanges of technicians, multilateral trade, and diversification of exports; urged "the speedy establishment of an international atomic energy agency which should provide for adequate representation of the Asian-African countries"; condemned racialism and colonialism "in whatever form it may be," especially in North and South Africa, as a denial of human dignity; declared "its support of the rights of the Arab people in Palestine" and called for the implementation of the UN resolution and for "the peaceful settlement of the Palestine question"; endorsed Indonesian claims to West Irian; asked for enlargement of membership in the UN and more adequate Asian-African representation; demanded disarmament, prohibition of nuclear weapons under effective international control, and suspension of tests of such weapons; and espoused freedom, peace, and tolerance through respect for human rights, the sovereignty and integrity of all States, the equality of all races and nations, nonintervention, respect for the right of self-defense "singly or collectively in conformity with the Charter of the UN," abstention from power politics, pressure, and aggression, and pacific settlement of disputes.

Apart from the platitudes typical of all such conferences, the Bandung meeting had various concrete results, among them these: the evacuation of 40,000 pro-Communist Vietnamese refugees from Thailand; negotiations at Geneva between the USA and Red China; enhanced prestige for the Peiping regime; new problems for American policy-makers posed by Soviet exploitation of anti-racialism and anti-colonialism; and the emergence of an Asian-African bloc in the UN. Bandung was the mirror, however clouded, of the clamant demand of that majority of the human race which is not white in epidermal pigmentation but yellow, brown, or black for a fair share of the future. At a subsequent nongovernmental "Asian-African Peoples' Solidarity Conference" in Cairo in December, 1957, Soviet spokesmen championed all anti-colonial independence movements and offered economic aid to all Africans and Asians "as brother helps brother."

Trialogue. During the late 1950's a large part of all diplomatic exchanges among Foreign Offices, of propaganda activities by governments, and of world-wide journeys by Foreign Ministers and Heads of States consisted of a kind of three-cornered conversation among spokesmen of Freeland, Marxland, and the new neutrals. Washington, London, and Paris sought to convert the neutrals to their cause. Moscow and Peiping, unable to entertain so ambitious a hope, strove to confirm the neutrals in their neutrality and to persuade others of the blessings of neutralism. The neutrals themselves, by no means inactive in the discussion, attempted to vindicate and justify their own preference for nonalignment and preached to both Grand Alliances regarding the wages of sin, the rewards of virtue, and the need of repentance and reformation. Since most of the neutrals had painful memories of Western colonialism and no experience with Soviet imperialism, their exhortations and strictures were more often addressed to the West than to the East.

Thus, when he came to Washington in mid-May of 1956 to address Congress, confer with Eisenhower, meet the press, and deliver sundry speeches, President Sukarno of Indonesia condemned colonialism, asserted that "a larger freedom for mankind" was more important than "the defeat of Communism," and appealed for U.S. support of Indonesian claims to West Irian (Netherlands New Guinea). He toured the capital in an open car with Vice President Nixon; fraternized with children and passers-by; eulogized Washington, Jefferson, and Lincoln; and charmed all. He decried U.S. military aid abroad and appealed for economic help and greater American understanding of the new nationalism, without which, he told Congress, "no amount of thinking, no torrent of words, and no Niagara of dollars will produce anything but bitterness and disillusionment."

Nehru's message was similar. In March, 1956, following visits to New Delhi by Selwyn Lloyd and Dulles, who sought in vain to persuade him that SEATO was no threat to India, the Prime Minister declared that all military alliances were a menace to peace in general and to India in particular. In July he consulted with Nasser and Tito in Jugoslavia and, after conferring with Adenauer in Bonn, rejected the Chancellor's view of German unification, denounced Soviet domination of Eastern Europe, and blamed Moscow and Washington alike for the Cold War. Mid-November, 1956, found the Premiers of Burma, Ceylon, and Indonesia meeting with Nehru in New Delhi and jointly condemning violence against Hungary and Egypt. Chou En-lai arrived in late November and was warmly welcomed, the more so as he acted with decorum and spoke softly. By mid-December, 1956, Nehru was in Washington, conferring with Eisenhower and Dulles. Via television and radio, he told the American public on Dec. 18:

> The preservation of peace forms the central aim of India's policy. It is in the pursuit of this policy that we have chosen the path of nonalignment. This does not mean passivity of mind or action, lack of faith or conviction. It does not mean submission to what we consider evil. It is a positive and dynamic approach to such problems as confront us. We believe that each country has not only the right to freedom, but to decide its own policy and way of life. . . . We believe, therefore, in non-aggression and non-interference by one country in the affairs of another, and the growth of tolerance between them and the capacity for peaceful coexistence.

Nehru's Western critics deemed his neutralism "pro-Soviet" and "anti-Western" and considered his moderation conspicuous by its absence in the Indian dispute with Pakistan over Kashmir. Two-thirds of the area and four-fifths of the population (c. 4,000,000) of this predominately Moslem region were under the control of Indian military forces by the terms of the cease-fire accord of July, 1949, including Srinagar, the capital, and the lush and lovely Vale of Kashmir. After years of equivocating, Krishna Menon told the UN Security Council on Jan. 23, 1957, that India had no intention of consenting to a plebiscite. The Council, 10 to 0 with the USSR abstaining, reiterated its appeal for a plebiscite on Jan. 24. New Delhi ignored the resolution and formally and "irrevocably" incorporated the Indian-held segment of Kashmir into the Indian Union. Subsequent efforts to negotiate a settlement acceptable to Pakistan proved fruitless. In its determination to hold most of Kashmir, and ultimately to oust the Portuguese from Goa, neutral India was as much moved by national interests and territorial ambitions as was neutral Indonesia, equally determined to acquire West Irian and to ignore the Dutch-sponsored "Republic of the South Moluccas," which maintained a kind of "government-in-exile" in the Netherlands.

The tale of rival American and Soviet efforts to "woo the neutrals" is too long and complex for brief review. Muscovite propaganda and politics in Asia and Africa have already been reviewed (see pp. 412f. and 545f.). Soviet appeals were weakened by overly emphatic denunciations of the West, often embarrassing to the Asian hosts of Russian visitors, and by Russian suppression of the Hungarian Revolution of 1956. They were strengthened by Moscow's ability and willingness to achieve "trade not aid," to purchase surplus commodities (*e.g.*, rice and cotton), to make long-term loans at low interest rates, to refrain from imposing political conditions or seeking military bases, and to supply technical aid via trained personnel lacking in color-consciousness or race prejudice.[8] Conversely, American incapacity or reluctance to do these things, coupled with a program of gifts and grants more productive of resentment than of gratitude, and with constant preoccupation with anti-Communism and an incessant quest for military allies, weakened the ability of the USA to compete successfully with the USSR for influence among the world's poor, despite the vastly greater resources at America's disposal.[9]

The American dilemma in such matters was well exemplified in 1957. On Feb. 28 Vice President Richard M. Nixon embarked upon a 19,000-mile State journey to Africa where, after visiting Morocco, he represented President Eisenhower at the ceremonies celebrating the independence of Ghana. In Accra he and Mrs. Nixon lunched at the home of Finance Minister Kimla Agbell Gbedemah and presented gifts, including a 2,000-volume technical library, to Premier Kwame Nkrumah. In Liberia, Nixon presented two Coast Guard cutters to the Negro Republic, visited the rubber plantation of the Firestone Company, and conferred on economic aid with President William V. S. Tubman—who indicated that he would turn down a Polish proposal to send an economic mission and a Soviet invitation to visit Moscow. After stopping in Uganda, the Vice President conferred with Emperor Haile Selassie in Addis Ababa and sought a U.S. Air Force center and anchorage privileges at Massawa on the Red Sea—a proposal which the Emperor declared himself willing to consider but only on the basis of "equality," which he defined as more U.S. military aid to Ethiopia. After visiting the Sudan (which also asked more U.S. aid), Libya, Tunisia, and Italy, where he was received by Pope Pius XII, Nixon returned to Washington on March 21. In his public report of April 6 he urged increased American attention to, and help for, Africa—"a priority target for the international Communist movement"— and sagely observed: "We cannot talk [racial] equality to the peoples of Africa and Asia and practice inequality in the United States. In the national interest, as well as for the moral issues involved, we must support the neces-

[8] See Klaus E. Knorr, *Ruble Diplomacy: Challenge to American Foreign Aid*, Center of International Studies, Princeton University, 1956.

[9] The frequently constructive role of U.S. private companies in fostering economic development and public welfare in connection with investments and enterprises in "backward" areas should not be ignored by the reflective student of world affairs in our time, even though the total impact of such activities has thus far been small and space is here lacking for an account of them. But see the pamphlet series of case studies of "United States Business Performance Abroad" published by the National Planning Association, 1606 New Hampshire Avenue, NW, Washington 9, D.C., which comprised at press time *Sears, Roebuck de Mexico* (1953), *Casa Grace in Peru* (1954), *The Philippine-American Life Insurance Company*, (1955), *The Creole Petroleum Corporation in Venezuela* (1955), *The Firestone Operations in Liberia* (1956), and *Stanvac in Indonesia* (1957).

sary steps which will assure orderly progress toward the elimination of discrimination in the United States."

The wisdom of these words and the difficulty of giving them content came to dramatic expression in the autumn of 1957. When Gov. Orval Faubus in the name of preserving "law and order" against mob violence ordered the Arkansas National Guard to keep nine Negro students out of Little Rock's Central High School, which they were scheduled to attend as part of a gradual program of racial desegregation in public education, American prestige fell to a new low throughout Africa and Asia—from which it was raised only slightly by President Eisenhower's belated dispatch of federal troops to Little Rock to protect the right of the Negro pupils to attend classes. Hard upon this deflation of American claims to moral superiority over the USSR and Red China came the deflation of claims to scientific and technological superiority with the advent of the Soviet ICBM and earth-satellite before the USA had developed either device. On Oct. 9, Finance Minister Gbedemah of Ghana was barred from a Howard Johnson restaurant in Dover, Delaware, and told, "Colored people are not allowed to eat here." President Eisenhower at once invited Gbedemah to breakfast at the White House. But again, as in all such incidents, the fat was in the fire and America's claim to "world leadership" was in jeopardy in a world community in which two-thirds of all human beings were "colored."

Whither Neutralism? Many troubling tensions and complex problems afflicted the world's poor in the 1950's and beyond by virtue of racial prejudice, fanatical local nationalisms, vestiges of "colonialism" and "white supremacy," and the vastly difficult task, even under the most favorable of conditions, of transmuting poverty into plenty. None of these problems admitted of easy or simple solutions. For their sources lay not in money or arms or technology, or the lack thereof, but in the minds and hearts of human beings committed to traditional attitudes and ancient ways in a new era in which many such commitments, among rich and poor alike, were almost insuperable barriers to progress toward the good life in the good society.

Let us conclude our survey by considering only one of these problems, albeit one by no means limited to the world's poor and one crucial to the present and future alignment of sovereignties in the endless game of world politics. The problem, posed simply, is this: May we expect the States pledged to "neutralism" to increase in number and influence, or is it more likely that more and more will see the "error of their ways" (as defined in Washington and Moscow) and join one or the other of the Grand Alliances?

Amid obscure prospects on clouded horizons, no certainties were visible in such matters. The outcome depended on the impact upon citizens and policymakers in many capitals of emotional attractions and repulsions and the interplay of calculations of advantage, nonrational stereotypes, memories of past experiences, and anticipations of future fortune. In Europe, Switzerland

and Sweden were incurably committed to neutrality, since the formula was popularly and officially credited with sparing both nations from involvement in both the World Wars of the 20th Century. Tito's Jugoslavia adopted a similar stance after 1948, as did Austria in 1955 as the necessary price of ending foreign occupation and achieving independence. Many political leaders, Communist and non-Communist alike, aspired toward a similar status for Czechoslovakia, Poland, Hungary, Rumania, and even Bulgaria and little Albania. Moscow, understandably, resented and resisted such aspirations but championed the "neutralization" of Germany as a condition of German re-unification. Bonn and Washington, dubiously supported by London, Paris, and Rome, insisted upon the impossibility of German neutrality and labored to achieve a unified Reich allied with the West against the East—a formula foredoomed by the obvious circumstance that the Western Powers were wholly incapable of imposing it upon the Soviet bloc and, by persisting in it, could only perpetuate the partition of the Germans.[10]

If alignment with West against East or East against West was, in the 1950's, deemed disadvantageous by many critics of the long-established policies of sundry European governments, the same was true in far greater measure in the newer nations of Asia and Africa. Moscow and Peiping offered a revolutionary formula for rapid industrialization through the liquidation of the old elites of land and money and the adoption of totalitarian methods of collectivization and economic planning. Among the dark masses, those few capable of comprehending the formula often responded favorably to its enticing appeal, while all people of property and privilege understandably opposed it tooth and nail. Washington offered military alliances against Communism, massive armed aid, modest economic aid, and complex (and sometimes self-defeating) programs for economic development.

Under these circumstances it seemed obvious to many of the spokesmen of the new nationalisms of Asia and Africa that maximum advantages and minimum risks were to be derived by abstaining from political and military commitments and playing off East and West against one another in bargaining for favors. States which rejected this course in favor of alignment with Freeland against Marxland gained little thereby save arms, subventions, and guarantees of military security, none of which contributed significantly to the conquest of poverty. States which embraced "neutralism" and accepted economic aid from both of the Great Coalitions gained much by virtue of their ability to solicit favors from both sides, each fearful lest the other should prove more persuasive.

So long as this pattern prevailed, and it promised to persist for long, the incentives for "neutralism" among the newer nations appeared likely to outweigh such fears or hopes as might dictate alliances with one or the other

[10] See Frederick L. Schuman, "The Soviet Union and German Rearmament," *Annals of the American Academy of Political and Social Science*, July, 1957, pp. 77–83.

of the Super-Powers. Such considerations were reinforced by the self-evident circumstance that the titans, already stalemated by 1950 in their rivalry for global hegemony, were a decade later hopelessly deadlocked in a military checkmate which neither could afford to try to break without risking co-annihilation and the possible extermination of the human race. *Les misérables* of the world community had everything to gain and nothing to lose by re-fusing to support either of the giants and by fostering disengagement and a negotiated *modus vivendi*. For this reason among others (see pp. 547*f*. and 645*f*.), the prospects of the Grand Alliances were darkening toward the end of the 1950's while the prospects of "neutralism" were bright.

Few if any areas under Communist control seemed likely to be lost to Marxland. But the uncommitted neutrals were all but certain to remain neutral, while some Asian and African, and even European, States aligned with Washington against Moscow might be expected to reconsider their course. Should such a development eventuate in a broad band of neutral States in Central Europe and southern Eurasia, such a "neutral bloc," if acting to-gether out of common interests and purposes, might wield sufficiently decisive power to preclude forever any remaining possibility, however remote, of the Super-Powers resorting to arms to resolve their quarrels. Beyond this prospect, further projection of future trends would be futile.

Needless to say, "neutralism" is no formula to lift the poor to wealth. It is merely a protective device to reduce the danger of a new Armageddon in which all may lose all. Given a viable pattern of nonviolent coexistence and the transformation of the rivalry between the coalitions from a struggle for power into a competition for prestige among the people of the slumlands, possibilities will loom on tomorrow's horizons for cooperative endeavors on the part of the industrialized societies of both "Capitalism" and "Communism" to help the world's impoverished peoples to achieve some prospect of plenty. Since their problems are such that few among them can achieve this transition without external aid, their last best hope may well reside in days to come in the promise of joint programs to conquer poverty throughout the world community.

SUGGESTED READINGS

Alexander, Robert J.: *Communism in Latin America*, New Brunswick, N.J., Rutgers University Press, 1957.
Arcinegas, German: *The State of Latin America*, New York, Knopf, 1952.
————: *America and the New World*, New York, Knopf, 1955.
Barr, Stringfellow: *Citizens of the World*, New York, Doubleday, 1952.
Bartlett, Vernon: *Struggle for Africa*, New York, Praeger, 1953.
Bate, H. MacLear: *South Africa without Prejudice*, London, Laurie, 1956.
Belshaw, Horace: *Population Growth and Levels of Consumption*, New York, Institute of Pacific Relations, 1956.
Bemis, Samuel Flagg: *The Latin American Policy of the United States*, New York, Harcourt, Brace, 1949.

Brown, Harrison: *The Challenge of Man's Future*, New York, Viking, 1954.
Buell, Raymond L.: *The Native Problem in Africa*, New York, Macmillan, 1928.
Butland, Gilbert J.: *Chile*, London, Royal Institute of International Affairs, 1952.
Capital Formation and Economic Growth, Princeton, N.J., Princeton University Press, 1955.
Chandrasekhar, S.: *Hungry People and Empty Lands*, London, G. Allen, 1954.
Cook, Robert C.: *Human Fertility: The Modern Dilemma*, New York, Sloane, 1951.
Crow, John A.: *The Epic of Latin America*, New York, Doubleday, 1946.
Cumberland, C. C.: *Mexican Revolution*, Austin, Tex., University of Texas Press, 1952.
Du Bois, W. E. Burghardt: *The World and Africa*, New York, Viking, 1947.
Gunther, John: *Inside Africa*, New York, Harper, 1955.
Haines, C. Grove: *Africa Today*, Baltimore, Johns Hopkins Press, 1955.
Herring, Hubert: *A History of Latin America: From the Beginnings to the Present*, New York, Knopf, 1955.
Hertzler, J. C.: *The Crisis in World Population*, Lincoln, Neb., University of Nebraska Press, 1956.
Houston, John A.: *Latin America in the United Nations*, New York, Columbia University Press, 1956.
Jorrin, Miguel: *Governments of Latin America*, Princeton, N.J., Van Nostrand, 1953.
Kahin, George McTurnan: *The Asian-African Conference: Bandung, Indonesia, April, 1955*, Ithaca, N.Y., Cornell University Press, 1956.
King, John Kerry: *Southeast Asia in Perspective*, New York, Macmillan, 1956.
Kundra, J. C.: *Indian Foreign Policy, 1947–1954*, Groningen, Wolters; Bombay, Vora, 1955.
Kuznets, Simon, and Others: *Economic Growth: Brazil, India, Japan*, Durham, N.C., Duke University Press, 1955.
Lasker, Bruno: *The Peoples of Southeast Asia*, New York, Knopf, 1944.
Lorimer, Frank, and Others: *Culture and Human Fertility*, Paris, UNESCO, 1954.
MacDonald, Austin F.: *Government of the Argentine Republic*, New York, Crowell, 1942.
———: *Latin American Politics and Government*, New York, Crowell, 1954.
Meade, J. E.: *Trade and Welfare*, New York, Oxford, 1955.
Moraes, Frank: *Jawaharlal Nehru: A Biography*, New York, Macmillan, 1956.
Nkrumah, Kwame: *Ghana: The Autobiography of Kwame Nkrumah*, New York, Nelson, 1957.
Romulo, Carlos P.: *The Meaning of Bandung*, Chapel Hill, N.C., University of North Carolina Press, 1956.
Rosinger, Lawrence K., and Associates: *The State of Asia: A Contemporary Survey*, New York, Knopf, 1951.
Russell, Sir E. John: *World Population and World Food Supplies*, New York, Macmillan, 1955.
Schechtman, Joseph B.: *European Population Transfers, 1939–1945*, New York, Oxford, 1946.
Smith, T. Lynn: *Brazil*, Baton Rouge, La., Louisiana State University Press, 1956.
Staley, Eugene, *The Future of Underdeveloped Countries*, New York, Harper, 1954.
Stillman, Calvin W. (ed.): *Africa in the Modern World*, Chicago, University of Chicago Press, 1955.
Stuart, Graham H.: *Latin America and the United States*, New York, Appleton-Century-Crofts, 1956.
Taft, Ronald R., and Richard Robbins: *International Migrations: The Immigrant in the Modern World*, New York, Ronald, 1955.
Thayer, Philip W.: *Southeast Asia in the Coming World*, Baltimore, Johns Hopkins Press, 1955.
Thompson, Warren S.: *Population Problems*, New York, McGraw-Hill, 1953.
Warne, William E.: *Mission for Peace: Point 4 in Iran*, Indianapolis, Bobbs-Merrill, 1956.
Whitaker, Arthur P.: *The Western Hemisphere Idea: Its Rise and Decline*, Ithaca, N.Y., Cornell University Press, 1954.
Wilgus, A. Curtis: *The Caribbean: Peoples, Problems, and Prospects*, Gainesville, Fla., University of Florida Press, 1952.

SUGGESTED READINGS

Williamson, Harold F., and John A. Buttrick (eds.): *Economic Development: Principles and Patterns*, Englewood Cliffs, N.J., Prentice-Hall, 1954.
Woytinsky, W. S.: *India: The Awakening Giant*, New York, Harper, 1957.
Woytinsky, W. S., and E. D. Woytinsky: *World Population and Production: Trends and Outlook*, New York, Twentieth Century Fund, 1953.
Wright, Richard: *The Color Curtain: A Report on the Bandung Conference*, Cleveland, World Publishing, 1956.

Chapter XV

THE ATOMIC AGE

1. PROMETHEUS AND CALIBAN

Retaliation is the only way of gaining the decision over our opponent. . . . The [first] attack will come . . . across the North Polar Basin. . . . The result may be a casualty list of 25,000,000 men, women and children in the first 24 hours. . . . To stop our enemy from continuing his assault, we must be prepared to carry the war to him. . . . Accordingly, the long-range striking force composed of long-range, heavy-load-carrying bombers and long-range fighters to protect them is a must item [in national defense] . . . for it furnishes the best guarantee that the battle for the air will be won and that the final phase, the actual invasion and occupation of the enemy country by our surface forces can get under way.—GEN. GEORGE C. KENNEY, U.S. Strategic Air Command, to the 21st Women's Patriotic Conference on National Defense, Washington, D.C., Jan. 26, 1947.

Planes, whether bombers or fighters, are now in their decline. . . . We now have all the rockets we need, long-range rockets, intermediate-range rockets, and close-range rockets. . . . We can launch satellites because we have a carrier for them, namely the ballistic missile. . . . You will have it too. . . . We must not deceive ourselves and other people. As statesmen we must do everything possible to prevent wars and to reach agreement on major international problems, including the problem of disarmament.—NIKITA S. KHRUSHCHEV to James Reston, Oct. 7, 1957.

ONE peculiarity of this age," writes a famous British essayist, "is the sudden acquisition of much physical knowledge. There is scarcely a department of science or art which is the same, or at all the same, as it was 50 years ago. A new world of inventions . . . has grown up around us which we cannot help seeing; a new world of ideas is in the air and affects us, though we do not see it. . . . If we wanted to describe one of the most marked results—perhaps the most marked result—of late thought, we should say that by it everything is made 'an antiquity.' . . . Man himself to the eye of science has become 'an antiquity.' "

Thus begins a well-known book entitled *Physics and Politics* by Walter Bagehot, written, strangely enough, not in 1945 but in 1869. Its author perceived the early impact, since multiplied a thousandfold, of the new science on modern civilization. He hoped that scientific method, applied to the study of human relations, would give mankind a new measure of self-understanding and self-control. During the ensuing century it has become clear that science alone is not enough. Death rather than life for contemporary culture may be

652

the most probable consequence of man's mastery of the powers of heaven and the fires of hell, snatched from nature's gods and devils by modern Fausts, whose new alchemy makes mockery of the old.

The roots of this paradox may lie, as Spengler and Toynbee suggest, in the very character of civilization itself. In a more immediate sense, the curious consequences of science for our own civilization are intelligible in terms of Plato's ancient lament. The great decisions in human communities are made not by philosophers or scientists but by power-holders who, usually, are neither scientists nor philosophers. The social purposes to which new knowledge is put are defined not by scholars and technicians, most of whom would shrink from the task, but by the blind and confused interplay of nations, classes, and interest groups and by traditional conceptions of the good, the true, and the beautiful.

In most of the Western nation-states, effective influence over social decisions has rested for centuries with priesthoods, nobilities, and plutocracies whose rule has been tempered by conflicts between competing elites and by pressures from the substrata. Clergymen, as custodians of the Christian gospel, have suffered a diminution of prestige in an increasingly secular world and have, more often than not, been indifferent or hostile toward science. Men of title and men of money, conversely, have for the most part been eager to employ scientific knowledge, but they have largely been disciples of the peculiarly Western or Faustian cults of power and wealth. Science, like art, has had its private or public patrons. By them its uses have been largely shaped. Science has thus served modern mankind most conspicuously by aiding entrepreneurs in their quest for profits and by assisting patriots, diplomats, and strategists in their search for new increments of national fighting capacity.

If, as many now suspect, the ultimate effects of this process appear to be divisive and destructive of the Great Society, the immediate effects have been of a different order. "World trade" and "world politics" both became possible by virtue of the revolutions in production, distribution, travel, transport, and communication wrought by the application of science to business and to government. The Great Society itself is the product of an emerging global economy and a nascent global polity. If the rich became richer, the poor became less poor, contrary to the Marxist prognosis. Vast populations flourished on both shores of the Atlantic and came to enjoy higher standards of health and comfort than any dreamed of in olden times. Colonial multitudes suffered conquest and exploitation but, in due course, also came to share in a modest way in the material benefits flowing from the new dispensation. Wars became more murderous and destructive, but the vastly enhanced productivity and reproductivity of the populations of the great Powers more than compensated (until recently) for the high cost of conflict. All the peoples of the planet were, willy-nilly, knit ever more closely together into a fabric of many hues and patterns which, for all its diversity, was yet a unity, woven ever more tightly into one grand design with each passing generation.

It has long since become a truism, among philosophers if not among kings, that the continued political fragmentation of humanity into rival sovereignties is incompatible with the new unity of the world fashioned by science, technology, and business. Man's fate seldom poses sharp alternatives of "either," "or"—for cultural opposites often mingle and blur and emerge anew in strange shapes not foreseen by earlier commentators on initial contradictions. Yet there is much reason to believe that the Western State System and the global civilization of which it is a part have reached, or are about to reach, an irrevocable parting of the ways.

Men may preserve and improve further the fruits of a world economy and a world community, made one by the labors of scientists, engineers, and vendors of goods and services in a world market. Or men may return to their ancient ways of international anarchy, power politics, economic nationalism, and war—which, indeed, they have never abandoned. It is scarcely probable that they can long succeed in doing both. An effective choice of either would seem to involve, somehow, the sacrifice of the other. To pursue both at once is to invite failure and frustration, begetting aggression and promoting such paroxysms of mass madness and violence as seem likely to be fatal to civilization itself.

The circumstances which might appear to pessimists to warrant a dismal conclusion regarding the resolution of this dilemma include the fact that the Great Society is not, after all, a united global community. All peoples everywhere on earth, to be sure, now share in one way or another the fashions, habits, or vices bred of the cultural borrowings several centuries ago among the European civilization of the West and the civilizations of the Amerindians and the peoples of Asia—e.g., tobacco, alcohol, coffee, tea, chewing gum, narcotics, maize, potatoes, rubber, chinaware, cutlery, cosmetics, perfumes. All of these world-wide articles of consumption sustain or enrich or debase life and help to unite mankind in common activities of producing and selling and buying. But they do not unify humanity in any common devotion to symbols of shared purposes and ideals. It is no less true that almost all men and women everywhere on the planet have been blessed or cursed with the newer products of Western science and technology—e.g., printing, steam engines, telegraphy, electricity, internal-combustion engines, jet engines, movies, radio, television. But again these means of communication and sources of industrial power do not in fact unite mankind so long as men are divided against one another by cleavages of creed and class and economic status reflected in competing nationalisms, imperialisms, and ideologies. The choice between unity and ruin has been most starkly posed by man's most important invention since he first learned to use fire.

*   *   *   *   *

PROMETHEUS AND CALIBAN

On Dec. 2, 1942, a notable nonathletic event occurred in the squash courts at the west end of Stagg Field at the University of Chicago. It marked a halfway point in an ultrasecret project which began in the fall of 1939 when Alexander Sachs, bearing a letter from Einstein, persuaded President Roosevelt to encourage a strange quest. The enterprise was disguised as "Development of Substitute Materials," operating through the "Manhattan District" of the U.S. Army Corps of Engineers. Its cost was $2,000,000,000. Its director was Brig. Gen. Leslie R. Groves. Its personnel consisted at first of nuclear physicists and chemists and later of engineers, corporation executives, and thousands of workers, all sworn to secrecy and (save for a few) all ignorant of the import of their endeavor.

The event at Stagg Field, arranged by Enrico Fermi of the "Metallurgical Laboratory," took place in an oblate spheroid, or "pile," of graphite, interspersed with a lattice of uranium and movable strips of cadmium as "controls." When the pile reached the requisite size through the addition of further units, it produced heat—and slowly converted uranium into a new element, named "plutonium," with the process continuing at a steady rate. This weird realization of ancient hopes of transmuting elements was the result of the successful attainment, for the first time on earth, of a self-sustaining nuclear chain reaction. Its aftermath promised to carry mankind into a wholly new age—which might resemble (depending on men's wishes) either a Paradise or an Inferno.

In mastering fire, *Homo sapiens* learned to use the power released through the rearrangement of molecules in organic compounds, effected through rapid oxidation or combustion. In discovering electricity, he learned to use the power released through the transposition of the electrons surrounding the nuclei of atoms. In achieving nuclear fission, he learned to use the powers locked in the core of the atom itself. That this power should be vastly greater than all other powers combined is at once the brightest hope and the most deadly danger of our time.

The natural phenomenon of nuclear disintegration was first recognized in the 1890's by H. Becquerel and Pierre and Marie Curie in their studies of the rare metal, radium. The mind which first perceived that matter and energy were but different forms of a basic unity, and first stated the relationship between them, was that of Albert Einstein. Working purely in terms of mathematical deduction, he wrote in 1905 that when matter is converted into energy the result can be expressed in the equation $E = mc^2$, in which E means energy, m mass, and c the velocity of light (187,000 miles per second).

The burning of 1 kilogram (2.2 pounds) of coal produces 8.5 kilowatt-hours of heat energy. If 1 kilogram of coal could be converted *in toto* into energy in accordance with Einstein's formula, the resulting heat energy would approximate 25,000,000,000 kilowatt-hours—*i.e.*, 2 months' output of the entire electric power industry of the USA. In fact, no such complete transformation or "annihilation reaction" ever occurs. In the sun and stars the atomic disintegration of elements low in the periodic scale (*e.g.*, hydrogen) into other elements (*e.g.*, helium) leaves a fraction of the mass (1%) unconverted into different matter and changed by the reaction into heat and light. In an atomic-fission chain reaction of elements high in the periodic scale (*e.g.*, uranium 235 or 233, thorium, or plutonium), a heavy nucleus, bombarded with neutrons, splits into two parts of roughly equal mass, with an accompanying release of other neutrons, which in turn split other nuclei, the neutrons of which repeat the process in geometrical progression—provided that the neutrons are prevented from escaping or from being absorbed beyond their reproduction rate by impurities or by isotopes not producing a chain reaction, *e.g.*, uranium 238. The resulting fission products weigh slightly less than the original mass. Only 1/1100 of the mass is converted into energy. But so tremendous is the energy in relationship to the mass, that the complete fission of 1 pound of U-235 or plutonium produces an effect equivalent to the combustion of 1,800,000 pounds of gasoline or 2,800,000 pounds of coal or to the explosion of 26,000,000 pounds of TNT.

A small piece of pure U-235 or plutonium will not produce a chain reaction, since the neutrons lost through the surface of the metal exceed the number produced through the fission of nuclei. A large piece—*i.e.*, one beyond the "critical size" and having no "retarders" or "controls" enmeshed in the mass—will produce a quick and massive chain reaction. But the energy released will shatter the piece into small bits, in which the reaction abruptly stops. If two or more small pieces of optimum shape are fired into one another at great velocity within a heavy covering ("tamper") of material which reduces absorption or escape of neutrons to a minimum, the resulting chain reaction will penetrate much of the combined lump before the remainder is blown apart into nonfissionable pieces. The reaction, it is estimated, will be over in one-millionth of a second. The fission fragments have speeds corresponding to 1 trillion degrees of temperature. Thirty new elements are produced, many of them radioactive, along with sundry radiations of varying speeds and intensities. In the quantity and quality of the energies liberated, the "explosion" thus effected is so far beyond all other combustions or explosions produced by man on earth as to bear no resemblance to any previous accomplishments in the arts of destruction.

Despite widespread illusions to the contrary, the "secret" of the atomic bomb became common knowledge among nuclear physicists everywhere as soon as experiment in the USA demonstrated that a nuclear chain reaction could be produced in explosive form. Such "secrets" as existed after August, 1945, had to do, not with the mechanics of the bomb, but with the complex industrial processes for mass production of fissionable material from uranium ore. In natural uranium, the isotope U-235 exists in only 1 part in 140 of the isotope U-238. The latter in a slow reactor is transformed into plutonium, but the rate of transformation is so slow as to make bomb production by this method quite impossible. The problem of 1942–43 was to find means of separating U-235 from U-238 in sufficient quantities to make a uranium bomb. While plutonium can be separated from uranium by chemical means, no such means are available to separate U-235 and U-238, for both are different forms of the same element. The problem was finally solved in the gigantic plants at Oak Ridge, Tenn., and Hanford, Wash.

These processes are described in general terms in the official report by Henry deWolf Smyth. When metallic uranium is chemically combined with fluorine into the gas, uranium hexafluoride, the isotopes of uranium can be separated and concentrated through gaseous diffusion, centrifugation, or thermodiffusion. Through these fantastically elaborate and difficult procedures, enough U-235 was obtained to make several uranium bombs. But the process itself made possible the production of ever-larger amounts of plutonium from U-238—so that, so far as is now known, all atomic bombs beyond the first two exploded have been plutonium bombs.

A new industry was herewith born—first in the USA, and everywhere socialized since private enterprise could neither supply the required capital nor be expected to assume responsibility for producing products which were long to remain, in a business sense, unprofitable. Through an ultimate investment of almost a billion and a half dollars, the Government of the USA in 1943 began manufacturing U-235 from U-238 in the plant at Oak Ridge, Tenn. Through another investment of over a billion dollars, the manufacture of plutonium from uranium began in the same year at Hanford, Wash. Through an investment of a further billion and a half dollars, a new plant was announced on the Georgia–South Carolina border in November, 1950, with another at Paducah, Ky., at a cost of almost a billion dollars, to produce U-235 by gaseous diffusion as at Oak Ridge. In August, 1952, another U-235 plant was projected in Pike County, Ohio, at a cost of a billion and a quarter dollars. More followed. The location and cost of Soviet atomic plants are not matters of public knowledge.

The chronology of the bomb in brief résumé was as follows during the first seven years of the Atomic Age:

1. JULY 16, 1945, Alamagordo Air Base, 120 miles southeast of Albuquerque, N.M. First test of a uranium bomb, mounted on a steel tower. Operation directed by Dr. J. R. Oppenheimer. A flash brighter than the sun is followed by a tremendous blast and pressure. A globe of fire dissolves into a multicolored, mushrooming column of boiling fumes, ascending 40,000 feet into the substratosphere. Tower vaporized. Desert floor of vast crater fused into radioactive volcanic glass.

2. AUG. 6, 1945, Hiroshima, Japan, population c. 300,000. Superfortress *Enola Gay*, flying at 30,000 feet, releases over the city, 8:15 A.M., the first atomic bomb used in warfare, weighing 4,000 pounds and containing 125 pounds of U-235. Explosion estimated to equal 20,000 tons of TNT. A blinding flash several hundred feet above the center of the city is followed by a vast cloud of smoke, ascending

40,000 feet. Flash burns, blast, falling debris, and conflagrations kill 78,150 people, with 13,983 missing, 37,425 injured, of whom many die later of radiation sickness, and 176,987 rendered ill, homeless, hungry, or indigent. Almost 5 square miles of the city are leveled by blast and by the subsequent "fire storm." Out of 90,000 buildings, 62,000 are destroyed and 6,000 severely damaged. All transport and power lines paralyzed. Of 200 doctors in the city, 180 are casualties. Of 1,780 nurses, 1,654 are killed or injured. Of 45 hospitals, only 3 remain usable. Flight of survivors and death of victims reduces population to 137,000 by November 1, 1945.''

3. AUG. 9, 1945, Nagasaki, Japan, population *c.* 253,000. Superfortress *Grande Artiste* releases over the city at 11:02 A.M. a bomb weighing 11,000 pounds, containing 12 pounds of plutonium. Effects comparable to Hiroshima. Explosion more powerful, though configuration of city amid hills reduces casualties. Results: 35,000 killed, 40,000 injured, 14,000 out of 52,000 buildings destroyed, and 80 per cent of the city's hospitals demolished.

4. JULY 1, 1946, Bikini Atoll, Marshall Islands. U.S. Navy test ("Operation Crossroads"), under Vice-Adm. William H. E. Blandy. A bomb is dropped over a concentrated target fleet of 73 ships, of which 5 are sunk, 9 severely damaged, and 45 damaged in lesser degree, although only 1 ship was within 1,000 feet of the point over which the bomb exploded. Measurements of heat, blast, gamma rays, and neutrons indicate that all personnel aboard ships within a mile of the explosion would have suffered heavy casualties. All within a radius of half a mile would have been killed or fatally injured.

5. JULY 25, 1946, Bikini Atoll. A bomb is exploded under water at moderate depth amid the remainder of the target fleet. In a column half a mile wide and a mile high, 10,000,000 tons of water are hurled into the air and fall back into the lagoon, producing waves 30 to 100 feet high and spraying all the target vessels. Sunk: battleships *Arkansas* and *Nagato*, carrier *Saratoga*, a landing ship, a landing craft, an oiler, several submarines. Numerous other vessels severely damaged. Almost all vessels drenched with radioactive sea water, sufficiently poisonous to be ultimately fatal to all personnel. Lagoon waters and salvaged vessels, despite decontamination measures, remain dangerously radioactive for many months.

6. APRIL 7–8, 1948, Eniwetok, Marshall Islands. Three "atomic weapons" are tested, under conditions of strictest secrecy. Purposes and effects unannounced, but results are described as "successful" and "highly encouraging."

7. FEB. 10, 1949. President Truman rejects proposals by the USSR and by Senator Brian McMahon that the USA reveal the size of its "atomic stock pile."

8. SEPT. 23, 1949. Truman announces: "We have evidence that within recent weeks an atomic explosion occurred in the USSR. . . . This probability has always been taken into account." Senator McMahon: "We must avoid hysteria or panic. We must appreciate that the U.S. faces the most crucial dilemma of its history." Vishinsky says, Nov. 10, that the USSR is using atomic energy to raze mountains, build canals, irrigate deserts, cut through jungles and tundra, etc. (amid general Western skepticism) and indicts U.S. "atomic diplomacy" and "mad plans for world domination."

9. JAN. 31, 1950. Truman orders the Atomic Energy Commission to continue its work on a hydrogen "Super-Bomb," aimed at using the energy of a conventional atomic explosion to convert tritium, an isotope of hydrogen, into helium through a thermonuclear reaction (as in the sun) with a destructive release of power theoretically 1,000 times that of the plutonium bomb. *New York Times* headline, reporting on views of various physicists, Feb. 7, 1950: "Ending of all life on earth by hydrogen bomb held a possibility."

10. JAN. 27, 1951. U.S. Atomic Energy Commission begins a series of tests near Las Vegas, Nev., resumed in late October and on April 22, 1952, the latter constituting the twenty-seventh announced U.S. atomic bomb explosion.

11. MAY, 1951. New tests of atomic explosives at Eniwetok, with progress reported on H-bomb, on tactical use of atomic weapons, and on atomic artillery shells.

12. AUG. 12, 1951. U.S. Navy awards first contract for a nuclear-powered submarine to Electric Boat Company of Groton, Conn., with contracts for atomic war vessels and planes following.

13. OCT. 4, 1951. White House announcement: "Another atomic bomb has recently been exploded within the Soviet Union." Stalin in *Pravda* (Oct. 6) asserts that atomic bombs of "various calibers" will be tested in the future and assails U.S. proposals for control of atomic energy as devices for their "legalization and legitimization. . . . The Soviet Union does not dream at any time of attacking the U.S. or any other country."

14. OCT. 22, 1951. The White House announces a third "atomic explosion" in the USSR.

15. OCT. 3, 1952. The first experimental explosion of a British atomic bomb is successfully consummated near the Monte Belle Islands, off Australia.

16. NOV. 1, 1952. At Eniwetok, U.S. authorities conduct what is officially described as "successful" experiments "contributing to thermonuclear weapons research." "We are being hurried forward," asserts the Presidential statement, "toward yet unforeseeable peaks of destructive power." Fission bombs are for the first time used to produce "fusion" reactions of hydrogen isotopes, creating the theoretical possibility of a hydrogen bomb equivalent to 20,000,000 tons of TNT and capable of devastating 300 square miles by blast and 1,200 square miles by fire, thereby demolishing in one blow any of the great cities of the world and exterminating all their inhabitants. No "civil defense" measures could significantly mitigate this result—save two: prior flight from the target area, and prevention of the explosion. The former solution threatened the end of urban civilization. The latter solution was not so much a problem of technology or strategy as a problem of diplomacy.

2. PHYSICISTS AND DIPLOMATS

We in America are living among madmen. . . . These madmen have a comet by the tail, but they think to prove their sanity by treating it as if it were a child's sky-rocket. They play with it; they experiment with it; they dream of swifter and bigger comets. Their teachers have handed them down no rules for controlling comets; so they take only the usual precautions of children permitted to set off fire crackers. . . . Why do we let the madmen go on with their game without raising our voices? . . . There is a reason: we are madmen, too. We view the madness of our leaders as if it expressed a traditional wisdom and a common sense; we view them placidly, as a doped policeman might view with a blank, tolerant leer the robbery of a bank or the bare-handed killing of a child or the setting of an infernal machine in a railroad station. Our failure to act is the measure of our madness. . . . When atomic war finally breaks out, the planet will become our extermination camp, and the cities will be our incinerators. This will be the madmen's final homage to the Mad Leader of all Madmen, who, dying, has scattered about this dust of madness which blinds our eyes and numbs our senses.—LEWIS MUMFORD, "Gentlemen: You Are Mad!" *Saturday Review of Literature*, March 2, 1946.

On Aug. 6, 1945, Anglo-American officialdom announced the destruction of Hiroshima, the result of the test of July 16, and the advent of the atomic epoch. President Truman's statement spoke of "a harnessing of the basic power of the universe." Secretary Stimson reviewed the history of the enterprise. Churchill reported to Commons. All emphasized, in the interests of "security," the need of secrecy regarding details of production and use. Chancellor Hutchins opined that world government was now essential and that fear of the bomb might move mankind into taking steps toward the goal. General Groves, however, insisted (Sept. 21) that "this weapon must be kept under the control of the U.S. until all the other nations of the world are as anxious for peace as we are." Press reports that Secretary of Commerce Henry A. Wallace had urged the "sharing of the secret" with Russia were denied by President Truman, who said that he alone would decide what Administration policy should be. In mid-October Dr. J. R. Oppenheimer, supported by Drs. Robert Wilson and H. J. Curtis, warned that the "secret" was "no secret at all"; that no nation could "win" an atomic-arms race, since only a few bombs would be necessary to put an enemy "out of action," regardless of the size of his own stock pile; and that nothing short of effective international control could meet the issue. Einstein urged (Oct. 26) that America and Britain invite Russia to join them in establishing a World Government, to which all possible information regarding the bomb should be transmitted. . . .

"Not until mid-November, 1945, were any steps taken at top level to evolve an international program for coping with the menace of the bomb." On Nov. 10, Prime Ministers Attlee and Mackenzie King began a series of conferences with President Truman in Washington. Attlee was reported to have urged the "sharing of the secret" (subject to satisfactory assurances of good intent from Russia) with the members of the Security Council, which should devise and administer a system of controls. The Joint Declaration issued on Nov. 15 recognized that the bomb constituted "a means of destruction hitherto unknown, against which there can be no adequate military defense, and in the employment of which no single nation can in fact have a monopoly. . . . We are aware that the only complete protection for the civilized world from the destructive use of scientific knowledge lies in the prevention of war." Exchange of scientific information "for peaceful purposes" was espoused, but "the spreading of specialized information regarding the practical application of atomic energy, before it is possible to devise effective, reciprocal, and enforceable safeguards acceptable to all nations," was eschewed as not constituting a contribution "to a constructive solution of the problem of the atomic bomb." A reciprocal exchange of information "concerning the practical industrial application of atomic energy" was favored "just as soon as effective, enforceable safeguards against its use for destructive purposes can be devised." Despite this ambiguous and evasive phraseology, the declaration concluded hopefully with a proposal that the UN should set up a Commission to make recommendations:

The Commission should be instructed to proceed with the utmost dispatch and should be authorized to submit recommendations from time to time dealing with separate phases of its work.

In particular the Commission should make specific proposals:

(*a*) For extending between all nations the exchange of basic scientific information for peaceful ends,

(*b*) For control of atomic energy to the extent necessary to insure its use only for peaceful purposes,

(*c*) For the elimination from national armaments of atomic weapons and of all other major weapons adaptable to mass destruction,

(*d*) For effective safeguards by way of inspection and other means to protect complying states against the hazards of violations and evasions.

The work of the Commission should proceed by separate stages, the successful completion of each one of which will develop the necessary confidence of the world before the next stage is undertaken. Specifically it is considered that the Commission might well devote its attention first to the wide exchange of scientists and scientific information, and as a second stage to the development of full knowledge concerning natural resources of raw materials.

Faced with the terrible realities of the application of science to destruction, every nation will realize more urgently than before the overwhelming need to maintain the rule of law among nations and to banish the scourge of war from the earth. This can only be brought about by giving whole-hearted support to the United Nations Organization, and by consolidating and extending its authority, thus creating conditions of mutual trust in which all peoples will be free to devote themselves to the arts of peace. It is our firm resolve to work without reservation to achieve these ends.

This formula solved no problems but opened a way toward a solution. That no solution had been arrived at more than a decade later was a consequence of circumstances generally deemed extraneous to the problem but actually inseparable from it. Prospects were not unfavorable in the fall of 1945. In his Charleston address of Nov. 16, Byrnes was forthright: "The civilized world cannot survive an atomic war. This is the challenge to our generation. To meet it we must let our minds be bold." In Commons (Nov. 22) Attlee sagely observed that "where there is no mutual confidence, no system will be effective. . . . We wish to establish between all nations just such confidence." Commented Eden: "For the life of me, I am unable to see any final solution that will make the world safe from atomic power other than that we all abate our present ideas of sovereignty."

At Moscow in December, 1945, the Foreign Ministers of the "Big Three" achieved agreement on preparation of peace treaties with Italy and the lesser enemy States; on the administration of Japan; on Korea, China, Rumania, and Bulgaria; and, as a result, on a procedure for dealing with atomic energy. The communiqué of Dec. 26 proposed a resolution, to be submitted to the General Assembly, for the establishment of a UN Commission on Atomic

Energy to make proposals for the four purposes quoted above. It was stipulated that the Commission should consist of delegates of the States on the Security Council, plus Canada, and should "submit its reports and recommendations to," and "be accountable for its work to," the Security Council, which should "issue directives to the Commission in matters affecting security." [1]

Truman and Byrnes were obliged to assure Vandenberg and other worried members of Congress that no "secrets" would be revealed to Russia until Congress was satisfied regarding the efficacy of a system of inspection and control. On Jan. 24, the Assembly adopted a resolution reiterating the language of the Moscow declaration. Despite the UN injunction to "proceed with the utmost urgency," the Commission did not meet for another six months. On March 18, 1946, President Truman named multi-millionaire Bernard M. Baruch as U.S. representative, to be assisted by John Hancock (Wall Street banker), Ferdinand Eberstadt (Wall Street banker), Herbert Bayard Swope (publisher), and Fred Searles (mining engineer and businessman). Whether a group so constituted was best calculated to promote a viable Soviet-American accord and to deal boldly with a challenge having no precedents in the vocational experience of bankers and stock speculators remained to be demonstrated.[2]

A bright hope dawned on March 16, 1946, with the release of the Lilienthal-Acheson proposals: "A Report on the International Control of Atomic Energy" (*Department of State Document* 2498), prepared by Chester I. Barnard, J. R. Oppenheimer, Charles A. Thomas, Harry A. Winne, and David E. Lilienthal (Chairman), as consultants to the Secretary of State's Committee on Atomic Energy, consisting of Undersecretary Dean Acheson, Vannevar Bush, James B. Conant, Leslie R. Groves, and John D. McCloy.

---

[1] Department of State *Bulletin*, Dec. 30, 1945, pp. 1027–1032.

[2] Bernard Baruch, born in 1870 in a family of modest means, symbolized in his career one version of the "American dream"—*i.e.*, poor boy makes good by shrewdness and hard work, amasses millions, and lives happily ever afterward on unearned income. Before a Congressional committee on one occasion, he answered candidly a question as to his profession: "Speculator." Early in the century he accumulated a vast fortune from speculation in securities, making profit in every panic and depression as well as in boom periods. In a single day (Dec. 18, 1916) he netted half a million dollars through short selling amid a sharp decline in the market resulting from rumors of peace negotiations in Europe. His annual income in 1916 was $2,301,000. Baruch's later interests were horse racing, philanthropy, sitting on park benches, enjoying his 23,000-acre estate, "Hobcaw Barony," in South Carolina, and cultivating a reputation as "elder statesman." He served as chairman of the War Industries Board in World War I and acted as adviser to Presidents Wilson, Hoover, Roosevelt, and Truman. See his "profile" by John Hersey, *The New Yorker*, Jan. 3, 1948ff., and Carter Field, *Bernard Baruch, Park Bench Statesman* (McGraw-Hill, 1944). His role in the UN Atomic Energy Commission won him numerous honors, medals, prizes, academic degrees, and all but universal praise in top business and political circles in the USA. The ultimate verdict of history may very well be a different one as the consequences of Baruch's policies become more clearly apparent. But see Bernard M. Baruch, *Baruch: My Own Story*, New York, Henry Holt, 1957.

This masterpiece of unanswerable logic admits of no brief summary. It should be read and reread by all who are seriously concerned with the fate of civilization. It distinguishes between "safe" and "dangerous" operations in the use of atomic power. The mining of uranium and thorium, the maintenance of reactors for making and separating plutonium, and all research and production in atomic explosives are designated as "dangerous" under all conditions when left to exclusively national exploitation. The "solution" proposed is a UN Atomic Development Authority, which, under the direction of the Security Council, will own and operate all uranium and thorium mines throughout the world, as well as all laboratories and plants using fissionable materials in their dangerous form, and will conduct all activities all over the earth in atomic research, inspection, licensing, and leasing— for the double purpose of making impossible the production of atomic bombs and making available atomic power and its by-products for the good of mankind.

This program was modeled, wisely, on the Tennessee Valley Authority. It contemplated an international public corporation (the ADA), which would possess the minimum power needed to fulfill its function without unduly restricting local autonomy and national sovereignty. What the Report did not make clear, but what was implicit in its reasoning, was that the ADA would, of necessity, become a limited "world government" within the sphere of its delegated powers. It would operate on the federal principle of enforcing law (here, atomic law) on individuals through investigation, local police action, indictment, and adjudication. It would not operate (since, plainly, it could not in the nature of its duties) on the unworkable principle of the coercion of States by other States or by any international agency. There are no solid grounds for supposing that the problem could have been solved, or can ever be solved, in any other way. It could be solved in this way only if the Great Powers in UN were willing and eager to establish an ADA with requisite authority. Such a decision, in turn, presupposed that Washington, London, and Moscow were united in the pursuit of common objectives rather than divided as rivals and potential enemies in a new struggle for global hegemony.

The tragic fact was that the presupposition was already in process of destruction before the enterprise of reaching a joint decision regarding atomic energy was actually launched. The mounting enmity between the Super-Powers was less a consequence than a cause of failure to agree about the bomb. Assessment of responsibility for lack of concord is almost academic in the light of the appalling fact of discord. Soviet policy in Iran and in the Balkans in the winter of 1945–46 evoked fear in London and Washington. The Byrnes-Bevin Doctrine evoked fear in Moscow. The USSR and its satellites had already been placed in the position of an obnoxious minority in UN. On March 5, 1946, in Fulton, Mo., Churchill, applauded by Truman, called for an Anglo-American alliance against Russia. President Truman, apparently astonished that this spectacle should have provoked anger in the Soviet Union, sought to mend matters (April 5) by inviting Stalin to cross the sea aboard the U.S.S. *Missouri* and to deliver an address, in Truman's presence, in Columbia, Mo. Stalin politely declined, as any Chief Executive of a Great Power would necessarily have declined so naïve and humiliating a proposal.[3]

In this context, all hope of an accord was foredoomed. The USA continued to produce atomic bombs at the wartime rate. Moscow accused America of "brandishing the atomic weapon for purposes which have little in common with the peace and security of nations" (*New Times*, Moscow, March 20, 1946). The result, willfully or unwittingly, was that the USA proposed a plan for control of atomic energy which its leaders knew the USSR would never accept, while the USSR proposed a plan which its leaders knew the USA would never accept. When the UN Atomic Energy Commission finally met on June 14, 1946, Bernard Baruch put forward the American proposals:

> We are here to make a choice between the quick and the dead. That is our business. Behind the black portent of the new atomic age lies a hope which, seized upon with faith, can work our salvation. If we fail, then we have damned every man to be the slave of fear. Let us not deceive ourselves: We must elect world peace or world destruction. . . .

Mr. Baruch went on to endorse the goal of a global ADA. But he offered no assurance that his Government would discontinue the manufacture and stock-piling of atomic bombs or share relevant information with others, until it should be satisfied, at some remote and unspecified date, that the successive stages of international control were operating effectively—during which indeterminate interval other nations (*i.e.*, the USSR) would, by implication, be precluded from producing atomic bombs. His major motif, however, was a reversion to an irrelevant conception of sanctions. Despite his comment (later negated) that "our solution lies in the elimination of war," he proposed that atomic obligations should be enforced through the threat of war—*i.e.*, the coercion of States by States. He demanded that in all atomic matters the Great Powers must renounce the central principle of the UN Charter and agree to abolition of the "veto" on coercion, thereby presumably agreeing in advance that others might legitimately wage war upon them if a simple majority in the Security Council should hold an accused State guilty of violating its obligations.

> We must provide immediate, swift and sure punishment of those who violate the agreements that are reached by the nations. Penalization is essential. . . . Condign punishments [must be] set up for violations of the rules of control, which are to be stigmatized as international crimes. . . . It would be a deception, to which I am unwilling to lend myself, were I not to say to you, and to all peoples, that the

[3] See Barnet Nover in the *Chicago Daily News* and the *Denver Post*, Feb. 2, 1948. White House Press Secretary Charles G. Ross confirmed this exposé on Feb. 5, 1948.

matter of punishment lies at the very heart of our present security system. It might as well be admitted, here and now, that the subject goes straight to the veto power contained in the Charter of the UN so far as it relates to the field of atomic energy. . . . There must be no veto to protect those who violate their solemn agreements.[4]

On June 19, 1946, without referring to Baruch's proposal, Andrei Gromyko for the USSR proposed a wholly different procedure: All States should agree by treaty to forbid the production and use of atomic weapons and to destroy all stock piles within three months. They should further agree to set up a UN committee for the exchange of scientific information and another committee to propose measures of inspection and control. "Efforts made to undermine the activity of the Security Council, including efforts directed toward undermining the unanimity of the members upon questions of substance, are incompatible with the interests of the United Nations. . . . Such attempts should be resisted." Gromyko later indicated that the USSR would never accept the Baruch proposal in whole or in part.

The deadlock recorded in June, 1946, in the first sessions of the UN Atomic Energy Commission was never broken. The Soviet proposal for "outlawing the bomb" could not reasonably be expected to meet the exigencies of the problem unless accompanied by a program for global legislation in the field of atomic energy capable of being enforced effectively on individuals. Without this the treaty urged by Moscow would become another scrap of paper. Since Washington also rejected any federalist solution and relied for safety upon arrangements for war by States against States, the American proposals were also tragically irrelevant to the needs of a new time. Each Government, moreover, knew that its program had no chance of acceptance by the other. In both capitals, therefore, some policy-makers may be presumed to have reconciled themselves from the outset to an atomic-arms race, doubtless on the assumption that "our" side could win. "I pray God," said Senator Mac-Kellar on Feb. 17, 1947, "we will never have an agreement."

Prior to his statement of June 14, 1946, Bernard Baruch was vainly urged by David E. Lilienthal and Chester I. Barnard not to introduce the "veto" question on the ground that it was meaningless and would lead into a "blind alley." [5] After the predicted impasse was reached, Secretary of Commerce Henry A. Wallace, in a letter to the President of July 23 and in his public address of September 12, declared the veto question to be "entirely irrele-

---

[4] See Walter Lippmann's comments in the *Washington Post*, June 20, 1946, pointing out that the Charter, like the U.S. Constitution, does not "protect" States violating agreements but is silent on the point "for the very good reason that the only thing that can be done is to make war. . . . I cannot see what Mr. Baruch thinks he can gain by binding the U.S. now to fight, not necessarily with its own consent, in the future. What is more, I do not think that he and our Senate today can under our Constitution legally commit a future Congress to war. . . ."

[5] See the *Dartmouth Alumni Magazine*, quoted in the *New York Herald Tribune*, March 28, 1948.

vant" and accused Baruch of promoting an atomic-armament race by ignoring the legitimate anxieties and security needs of the USSR. The ensuing exchange of public recriminations early in October produced more heat than light.

In this context, the diplomacy of nuclear fission stumbled dolefully toward its doom.[6] Within the USA, control of bomb making was taken out of military hands and placed in those of a civilian Atomic Energy Commission headed by Lilienthal—in the face of stout and almost successful Senatorial opposition. But in the UN the principles championed by the USA and the USSR admitted of no compromise. On Dec. 27, Baruch asserted: "It has been said that . . . if a great nation does not have the right to release itself from its obligations by veto the result will be war. I agree. I believe that a clear realization of this would be the greatest step toward peace that has been taken in history. . . . Gentlemen, it is either . . . or." On Dec. 30, the UNAEC voted approval of a program based on the Baruch approach. Poland and the USSR abstained. Baruch resigned on Jan. 4, 1947. Warren R. Austin and Frederick H. Osborn carried on, with no change of U.S. policy. Gromyko continued to restate Soviet policy, also without change.

By June, 1947, Osborn was calling the Soviet proposals "a fraud on the people of the world," while Gromyko insisted anew on outlawry of atomic weapons and immediate establishment of a limited inspection and control system on this premise. At June's end the Emergency Committee of Atomic Scientists issued a solemn warning: "The American people should understand that . . . the creation of a supra-national government, with powers adequate to the responsibility of maintaining the peace, is necessary. Is this realistic? We believe that nothing less is realistic. . . . Men must understand that the times demand a higher realism."

All in vain. By August, Osborn was declaring new Soviet proposals "wholly unacceptable." Gromyko replied that the American proposals were designed to secure for the USA "a position of monopoly in the field of atomic energy. The Soviet Union cannot agree to accept such proposals." Efforts by other governments (most of which, for obvious reasons, sided with the USA) to promote a change in the American or Soviet position, or to achieve a compromise between them, all failed. Efforts by physicists and other anxious observers to impress politicians and public opinion with the desperate urgency of solution were also without result. On April 5, 1948, the Working Committee of the UNAEC reported that the Soviet proposals for limited international control were inadequate, unworkable, and unacceptable. In May, 1948, the Commission announced that it had "reached an impasse" and, on

[6] For details, see *Records of the U.N. Atomic Energy Commission; International Conciliation Pamphlet* 430, April, 1947; William T. R. Fox, "The Struggle for Atomic Control," *Public Affairs Pamphlet* 129, 1947; Second Report of the U.N. Atomic Energy Commission to the Security Council, Sept. 11, 1947; and draft of Third Report, May 7, 1948.

the initiative of the USA, Britain, and France, suspended further discussion in an admission of complete failure.

The rest of the tale is all of a piece. Its intricacies were meaningless, since neither side at any time had any intention of compromising. Moscow, determined to acquire atomic energy for its own purposes, adhered to its proposals for outlawry of atomic weapons by treaty, knowing that the USA would never agree. Washington—equally determined to prolong the American monopoly, to seek absolute safety (which can never be had in the world of men), and, if possible, to prevent any other Power from acquiring the bomb—adhered to its proposals for "international" ownership and management and for abolition of the "veto," knowing that the USSR would never agree. The UNAEC voted to suspend its work on July 29, 1949. Subsequent "negotiations" led to a report of continued deadlock on Oct. 24, 1949. Moscow conceded that a convention for control of atomic energy should be signed simultaneously with a convention for outlawry and destruction of stock piles and that the veto should not apply to the day-to-day operations of any ADA or international control commission. Washington conceded that national quotas of atomic facilities should be written into the control treaty. But these "concessions" were empty gestures. Trygve Lie asserted correctly in January, 1950: "There has been no real negotiation."

The advent of the Soviet bomb [7] effected no modifications in the positions already taken. Acheson: "This event makes no change in our policy." Tass: "The Soviet Government adopts, and intends adopting in the future, its former position." In fact the Soviet bomb had prospective strategic consequences of the utmost importance. Churchill's view that Soviet seizure of Western Europe had been prevented only by the American monopoly of the bomb was now invalidated, if it ever had validity. American policy-makers hastened to project the rearmament of Germany and of Western Europe as a whole as a kind of counterweight to the Soviet bomb. But since the crowded urban centers of the Continent and of the British Isles were far more vulnerable to atomic bombing than any areas of Marxland, the Soviet bomb may well be regarded as having reduced to doubtful efficacy the concept of building locally in Western Europe a structure of military power commensurate with that of the USSR and its allies—just as the comparable vulnerability of Japan rendered doubtful the similar American project in the Far East.

---

[7] The extent to which Soviet development of atomic energy was the result of the work of "atomic spies" rather than of Soviet scientists and engineers admits of no judgment on the basis of available evidence. The trial records of convicted spies are inconclusive on this point, though worth studying for other reasons—e.g., Allan May Nunn; Klaus Fuchs, sentenced to 14 years by a British court, March 1, 1950; Harry Gold, sentenced Dec. 9, 1950, by a U.S. court to 30 years as an accomplice of Fuchs; Martin Sobell (30 years), David Greenglass (15 years), and Julius and Ethel Rosenberg (death) sentenced by Federal Judge Irving R. Kaufman in April, 1951; Bruno Pontecorvo, who fled from Britain to Russia; et al.

But it is of the essence of the issue we are considering that modern mankind is here, more than ever, a victim of "cultural lag." The bomb renders all power politics obsolete, since the "victors" in an atomic war will in all probability be as miserable and barbarized as the "vanquished." Nuclear fission therefore calls, by all reason and logic among men who prefer life to death, for radical new departures in political thought and action, looking either toward world government or toward a new diplomacy dedicated irrevocably to peace. But statesmen, strategists, and patriots continue to deal with every new weapon as they have always in the past dealt with every new weapon.

*   *   *   *   *

Before considering the more recent efforts (unsuccessful up to the time these pages went to press) of national policy-makers to apply the methods of diplomacy to the solution of a problem which, left unsolved, threatened the survival of mankind, it is quite literally a matter of life or death to note the new wonders wrought by the physicists, engineers, and military planners in their quest for "national security" in the face of the new menace. These achievements were products of the continued annual testing of nuclear weapons by the USA, the USSR, and Great Britain. The tests themselves continued to pollute the atmosphere all around the globe with radioactive fission products which, drifting earthward, were absorbed by plants and animals and entered increasingly into human diet amid heated debate among "authorities" as to what was to be regarded as a "safe" dose of radiation. All conceded that any dose, however small, was harmful.

Many physicists and geneticists warned that continued tests, quite apart from the appalling consequences of anticipated atomic war, were jeopardizing the human future. Strontium 90, a fission product with a half-life of 25 years, is, like calcium, deposited in bone tissue and is productive of bone cancer and leukemia. All fission products are poisonous. Most of them, in ways still ill understood, speed up the rate of "mutations" in germ plasm, with most of such mutations likely to impair the faculties and shorten the lives of successive generations. On the basis of such considerations, thousands of scientists and intellectual leaders made vain appeals for a cessation of nuclear tests, including Nehru, Bertrand Russell, and Dr. Albert Schweitzer—whose worldwide broadcast of April 23, 1957, warned that nuclear explosions were threatening the future of the human race. Other experts, particularly those employed by the U.S. Atomic Energy Commission, minimized the danger and insisted on the need of continued testing to assure "national security." Most laymen, unable to judge between the quarreling "experts," reconciled themselves to the inevitable, without the slightest notion of what it held in store.

To review the tests would be tedious. It is enough to note that the USSR, having broken the American monopoly of the A-bomb in September, 1949, and of the H-bomb in August, 1953, continued its testing with faithful regularity but with little publicity. Washington announced most of the Soviet tests—all of which can readily be detected anywhere in the Northern Hemisphere by sampling the atmosphere for new fission products. Britain, the third nuclear Power of mid-century, did its best with far more limited resources. The first British A-bomb cost "well over £100,000,000," said Churchill, and would "lead to a much closer American interchange of information" with Britain. This hope was vain. The U.S. Congress, frantically seeking safety, forbade any exchange of "classified" nuclear information even with America's closest ally—and had not lifted such restrictions by 1958. On Oct. 15, 1953, the second British A-bomb was tested at Woomera Range in South Australia. On May 15, 1957, the first British H-bomb was exploded over Christmas Island, 1,200 miles south of Hawaii, and, on May 31, the second. The USA, year after year, continued elaborate series of annual tests, some in Yucca Flats, Nevada (northeast of Death Valley), and others at Bikini or Eniwetok in the Marshall Islands in the South Pacific, each with its colorful "code name"—from Trinity, Crossroads, Sandstone, Ranger, Greenhouse, Buster, and Jangler (1945–51) to Castle, Teapot, Wigwam, Redwing, Plumbob (1954–57).

What was "discovered" by the tests—and how public officials, moved by fear, hope, despair, or wishful thinking, responded in all-too-human fashion to the discoveries—can best be indicated by reviewing the American record. In 1952–53 the USA developed nuclear artillery shells and soon proposed to equip NATO forces in Europe with atomic artillery on the assumption that the USSR was lacking in such weapons and that their "tactical" use (*i.e.*, against enemy armies) as distinct from their "strategic" use (*i.e.*, against enemy cities) would afford Freeland security against the superior man power and tank power of Marxland. But such "small-scale" devices and fanciful conceptions of "limited" atomic warfare were overshadowed by other developments promising unlimited nuclear warfare of total destruction. These involved the discovery that the intense heat of an A-bomb, generated through nuclear fission of heavy elements, *e.g.*, plutonium, could be made to trigger a reaction of nuclear fusion of light elements, *e.g.*, hydrogen, in an H-bomb, thus reproducing on earth a miniature replica of the processes of conversion of matter into energy operative in the sun and all the stars. Possibilities of destructions herewith became "unlimited" in terrestial terms, since the kilotons of explosive force (thousands of tons of TNT) were now transmuted into megatons (millions of tons), with no limit imposed save by the mechanics of bombmaking and available methods of delivery.

On Nov. 1, 1952, "Mike-shot" of "Operation Ivy" at Eniwetok produced a fireball 3¼ miles in diameter which destroyed the island of Elugelab, leaving a crater 175 feet deep and one mile across under an atomic cloud 20 miles high and 100 miles wide. According to Congressman W. Sterling Cole (Feb.

17, 1953) such a bomb would destroy everything within a circle six miles in diameter and inflict heavy damage within a ten-mile circle, encompassing 300 square miles. On his departure from office, President Truman confirmed this estimate but hopefully opined (Jan. 27, 1953): "I am not convinced Russia has the bomb. . . . I am not convinced that the Russians have achieved the know-how to put the complicated mechanism together to make the A-bomb work." Dissent was voiced by Gordon Dean and President Eisenhower—who, on June 23, 1953, named Adm. Lewis L. Strauss (pronounced Straws) as Chairman of the U.S. Atomic Energy Commission. The new Chairman had earlier joined Gordon Dean, against the advice of Dr. J. Robert Oppenheimer, in urging all-out efforts to develop the H-bomb.

When Malenkov implied on Aug. 8, 1953, that the USSR had acquired the H-bomb, Secretary Dulles asserted: "There is no evidence to support the correctness of the allegation." In October Val Peterson, head of the U.S. Civil Defense Administration, declared that atomic war was "inevitable," since he doubted that "mankind will be sensible enough soon enough to escape this sort of disaster. The weight of human nature and human experience run contrary to the hope of a peaceful settlement of our problems."

Late in 1953, in an ambivalent reconsideration of the possible uses of atomic energy, Washington announced plans to build the first American power station, with a projected capacity of 60,000 kilowatts; and President Eisenhower (Dec. 8, 1953) boldly proposed to the UN an international agreement to establish a world-wide "pool" of atomic materials and "know-how" for peaceful purposes. After much discussion this hopeful initiative was unanimously endorsed by the UN Assembly on Dec. 4, 1954, and eventuated in a multilateral accord to create an International Atomic Energy Agency, first ratified by the USSR in April, 1957, and subsequently by many other States. The Agency was formally inaugurated in Vienna in October, 1957, with W. Sterling Cole chosen as its first Director-General. This enterprise offered high hope for the health, welfare, and prosperity of mankind, particularly in "backward" regions where other sources of power were sparse—but only if public attention and public policy in the three nuclear Powers and elsewhere should be concentrated on "atoms-for-peace" instead of on "atoms-for-war."

No such shift of goals was visible in what followed, despite the waning of the Cold War and the "Summit Conference" in Geneva in 1955. On Jan. 21, 1954, at Groton, Conn., the USA launched the *Nautilus*, first of a series of atomic-powered submarines. On March 1, 1954, at Eniwetok, American H-bomb No. 2 was tested. The results were disturbing. Amid much reticence, the U.S. Atomic Energy Commission conceded on March 11 that 28 Americans and 236 natives had been "unexpectedly" exposed to "some radiation," but all were recovering. On March 31 Admiral Strauss revealed that the tests had led to "a stupendous blast in the megaton range . . . double that of the calculated estimate," now enabling the USA to destroy totally any city in the world. The test also led, as revealed in February, 1955, to an unanticipated lethal "fall-out" covering 7,000 square miles, slightly less than the total area of New Jersey or Massachusetts. Within this area the 23 crewmen of the Japanese fishing boat, *Fortunate Dragon,* were dusted with radioactive poisons. One died. All were ill. Poisoned fish were destroyed. To appease Japanese indignation, the USA paid $2,000,000 in damages. The Marshall Islanders petitioned the UN Trusteeship Council for an end of bomb tests. Despite supporting pleas from the spokesmen of India and the USSR, the Council rejected the appeal.

Any assumption that any such appalling demonstration of man's capacity for self-destruction might lead statesmen to reconsider their course was soon belied by things to come. On April 12, 1954, the U.S. Atomic Energy Commission, with the prior approval of President Eisenhower, took action against J. Robert Oppenheimer who had directed the construction of America's first A-bomb. He was suspended from access to all "classified" data on the ground that he had opposed the development of the H-bomb and had "associated with Communists" in the early 1940's. A year later, on April 18, 1955, Einstein died. More than any other genius of the 20th Century, he had inaugurated the Atomic Age. He died defeated in his hopes that atomic energy might be used for the welfare, rather than for the ruin, of mankind. On June 15, 1955, Americans elaborately tested their "defenses" against H-bombs by "Operation Alert," wherein the government left Washington, streets were cleared in all major cities, and America officially "survived" a mock attack with only 8,200,000 "killed" and 6,550,000 "injured." Atomic physicist Ralph E. Lapp opined that the entire operation was meaningless, since each megaton bomb would through "fall-out" render uninhabitable for two weeks an area of 100,000 square miles and kill all the residents therein.

What followed was a new demonstration (if we may use Arnold J. Toynbee's leitmotivs of the history of civilizations) of the futility of *hybris* or pride and of the inevitability of Nemesis or retribution. On July 29, 1955, authorities in Washington announced that the USA would launch an earth-satellite or moonlet in 1957 or 1958. At December's end the same authorities expressed doubt of Bulganin's claim that the USSR had developed an effective Intercontinental Ballistic Missile (ICBM). Adlai Stevenson's appeal, late in the presidential campaign of 1956, for a halting of nuclear tests was denounced by some Republicans as "subversive," particularly after Bulganin had expressed approval. American superiority in atomic warfare was taken for granted by almost all Americans.

This assumption was plausible if certain premises could be taken as established. One was the scientific backwardness of the USSR—envisaged by many Americans as still a primitive community of miserable slaves ruled by wicked and stupid tyrants. Another was the capacity of the U.S. Strategic Air Command, operating from hundreds of overseas bases, to consummate

671

note

the atomic annihilation of the Soviet Union in the event of war, with America and Western Europe not exposed to any comparably devastating attack thanks to alleged Soviet inferiority in aviation and atomic weapons. Still another was the premise that the USA led the world in the development of rocket engines and missiles capable of carrying nuclear warheads thousands of miles across the globe for the swift and accurate incineration of enemy cities. Here, as always, pride goeth before a fall.

"In the "disarmament" negotiations of 1956–57, as in those of 1946–47, each side adhered to proposals it knew were unacceptable to the other, since each assumed that it stood to gain military advantages by preventing any accord." Washington continued to insist upon "foolproof" schemes of aerial and ground inspection, allegedly to minimize the dangers of surprise attack, as a condition of any cessation of atomic tests or any renunciation of nuclear weapons—all the while knowing that Moscow would never consent to any such formula for Western espionage throughout the USSR. Moscow, while paying lip-service to inspection, continued to insist on an unconditional ending of tests and banning of the bomb, knowing full well that Washington would never agree. In this dangerous game of mutual pretense and obfuscation, Moscow had "won" in 1946–49. Moscow was to "win" again in 1957, even if sane people might question the meaning of "victory" between wrestlers grappling on the brink of Inferno."

By 1957 the USA had spent over $4,000,000,000 on its missile program. But when on June 11, 1957, at Cape Canaveral, Florida, the first test was made of the Atlas ICBM, the rocket weapon exploded soon after its take-off and fell into the sea—a circumstance which did not inhibit Gen. Lauris Norstad from telling Congress the next day that NATO had the "absolute capacity" to "destroy everything of significance" in the USSR. Much was said in official quarters in Washington in the summer of 1957 regarding the need for continued nuclear tests in search of a "clean" H-bomb, *i.e.*, one with a minimum of widespread lethal "fall-out" and thus likely to kill people only by the hundreds of thousands instead of by the millions. Given such a weapon, the security of America and of the Free World, it was assumed, would be assured, thanks to the imagined global supremacy of the U.S. Strategic Air Command.

Russians, no less fearful of "enemy" intentions, thought otherwise and acted otherwise. They developed, to be sure, a long-range Air Force capable of carrying A-bombs and H-bombs to American targets. But they suspected that the atomic war of the future, if it could not be averted by diplomacy, would be waged by other weapons rendering bombing planes obsolete, precisely as bombing planes had made battleships obsolete. The new weapons would be rockets. American military planners were equally aware of this possibility, but somehow lagged in the rocket race. On Aug. 26, 1957, Moscow announced the perfection of an ICBM capable of launching atomic warheads on targets many thousands of miles away. The customary expressions of skepticism followed in Washington.

But on Friday, Oct. 4, 1957—a date which will be forever memorable in human annals—the USSR launched the first earth-satellite or Sputnik, allegedly weighing 184 pounds. It circled the planet, some 500 miles above the earth, at 18,000 miles per hour for many weeks thereafter before losing speed and altitude and finally burning up as it fell back into the earth's atmosphere. The scientific significance of this achievement was unhappily overshadowed by its military significance. The launching of Sputnik, with more to follow, meant that the USSR had developed rocket engines of tremendous thrust and therefore unquestionably possessed an ICBM capable of rendering all air forces and all civil defense measures obsolescent. As of 1957–58 the USA possessed no comparable capacity, although the acquisition of such capacity was imminent, as Khrushchev cheerfully conceded.[8]

—note

We are here in the presence of the ultimate *reductio ad absurdum* of power politics. When each Super-Power has the means of annihilating the other, then war is obviously not a method of solving problems of power but only an instrument of mutual suicide. In the long past of the Western State System, and of its predecessors in earlier civilizations, war has been a more or less rational procedure for protecting "national interests" or pursuing purposes of aggrandizement. Since 1957, if not since 1945, war among Great Powers is a formula for universal death. Precisely for this reason (see the Preface), the final atomic war for mastery of the globe is wholly unlikely ever to be fought, since statesmen, with rare exceptions, are not madmen. Policy-makers in both of the Grand Alliances of the mid-20th Century, insofar as they were aware of their responsibilities to their constituents and to the future of the human race, could therefore be reasonably expected to eschew a course of co-annihilation and to negotiate, by the ancient and honorable methods of diplomacy, some viable pattern of coexistence between the great antagonists of our time.

But the time available for the enterprise was swiftly approaching zero. America's DEW-line of radar stations (Distant Early Warning), and Russia's counterpart, could, as of 1957, give several hours' notice to HQ of the ap-

[8] Sputnik I, a 23-inch sphere weighing 184 pounds and carrying two radio transmitters and batteries, traveled 35,000,000 miles as it circled the earth 1,370 times in 92 days. It lost altitude and burned, Jan. 4, 1958. Sputnik II, fired into orbit Nov. 3, 1957, to circle the earth at a maximum height of 1,050 miles, was a cylinder weighing 1,120 pounds and carrying the dog *Laika*, who survived in good health for a week. The satellite was still orbiting early in 1958. American humiliation was acute when the U.S. Navy Vanguard, carrying a small satellite, blew up at Cape Canaveral, Florida, Dec. 6, 1957, but was relieved on Jan. 31, 1958, when the Army's Jupiter-C missile put into orbit a cylinder-shaped satellite, "Explorer," 6 feet 8 inches long and 6 inches in diameter, weighing 29 pounds, 11 ounces, and traveling at a maximum height of 1,700 miles. On March 17, 1958, at Cape Canaveral, the U.S. Navy Vanguard put into orbit (maximum height 2,500 miles) a 6.4-inch, 3¼-pound sphere. Other and larger satellites, both Soviet and American, were scheduled for launching later in 1958.

proach of enemy bombers and thus make possible, albeit with difficulty, a verification of signals and a hasty decision by national policy-makers regarding counter-measures or acts of retaliation. But warning time in 1958 and beyond for an ICBM (or for a meteorite or other unidentified flying object mistaken for an ICBM) would never be more than 15 minutes. Under these conditions the "pushing of the buttons" to unleash nuclear war would, of necessity, have to be entrusted to jittery pilots on guard in the skies, nervous intelligence officers and engineers manning the missile bases, or electronic computing machines—with decision-making rapidly passing out of human control. By 1960, moreover, or soon thereafter, more and more States would come to possess atomic weapons and rockets—France, China, Italy, Germany, and ultimately, perhaps, sundry irresponsible dictators in the world's slumlands where frustration begets aggression and ready resort to violence. Should Western diplomacy prove so bankrupt as to fail to prevent such an eventuality, all mankind—trapped by its own scientific ingenuity and by its political stupidity and moral myopia—would have passed beyond the point of no return. . . .

3. THE PASSING OF POWER POLITICS

We have defiled our intellect by the creation of such scientific instruments of destruction that we are now in desperate danger of destroying ourselves. Our plight is critical and with each effort we have made to relieve it by further scientific advances, we have succeeded only in aggravating our peril. As a result, we are now speeding inexorably toward a day when even the ingenuity of our scientists may be unable to save us from the consequences of a single rash act or a lone reckless hand upon the switch of an uninterceptible missile. For twelve years we've sought to stave off this ultimate threat of disaster by devising arms which would be both ultimate and disastrous. In short, we have attempted to avoid global suicide by making suicide quicker, easier, and more certain. . . .—GENERAL OF THE ARMY OMAR N. BRADLEY, at St. Alban's, Washington, D.C., Nov. 5, 1957.

The crowded events reviewed in the preceding pages will soon be lost in the torrent of events to come. Their content and contour are certain to be blurred and presently erased from memory, save among archivists, bibliophiles, historiographers, and keepers of accounts. This is a surety, for human recollection of things past is always evanescent, except when they are vividly known from immediate personal experience. "Times of troubles" in all cultures, moreover, are so rich in recurring crises of all kinds—wars and rumors of war, revolutions, fanaticisms, reformations, and flaming paroxysms of fear and hate—that last week's headlines are almost as dull and meaningless as last year's almanac or a past-century chronicle.

But those who flee from the task of trying to comprehend the fortunes of yesterday out of a conviction that today is more urgent and tomorrow more significant are self-defeated. Time is a river, not a chain of lakes and ponds. The research magnificent of human self-fulfillment flows through it in a constant stream from a remote source to a distant delta, regardless of the vicissitudes of storm and tide, the ever-changing configuration of the stream bed, and the influence of many tributaries on the moving waters. If human destiny be pictured not as the waterway itself but as a vessel moving over its waves, then the pilot, while controlling the course of his craft, can succeed in completing the voyage without shipwreck only as he knows the rocks and shoals and eddies both upstream and downstream and is familiar with landing places, channels, and reports of expected weather.

Contemporary mankind in its long voyage from early Israel, Athens, and Rome toward a future which may be one of world unity or world chaos finds itself beset by violent tempests, menaced by hidden dangers, and tossed wildly about among rapids and whirlpools. Given the obvious incompetence of the pilots, the reluctance of the crew to obey orders, and the manifold uncertainties of the course, all analyses and prognoses of the destiny of the Western State System, and of the world community which has grown up within its confines, deserve to be approached with doubt and humility. Yet the question is inescapable: what can be said concerning the prospects of men during the second half of the 20th Century after Christ?

From the perspective of generations dead and generations yet unborn, the most striking fact regarding the Great Society in our time is that its members are united in their professions of purpose but are divided among themselves in apparently irreconcilable cleavages in their diverse conceptions of means toward the ends which all alike say they accept. All men everywhere of almost all faiths proclaim the brotherhood of man under the fatherhood of God. Almost all men preach liberty, equality, fraternity, personal dignity, social justice, freedom under law, and the desirability and necessity of One World. But the same men are so entangled in the loves and hates of particular nationalisms, ideologies, and sectarian solidarities that they seem quite unable to practice what they assert they believe. In a maladjusted global economy and an anarchic world polity, moreover, recurrent experiences of frustration, fear, and misery so shape motives that many men are moved to serve the interests of all men, as they see them, by directing their worry and rage against other men who are odious because their ways are different, disturbing, or heretical.

Most of those emotionally involved in the larger controversies of our years are disposed to envisage these schisms in simple terms of black and white. On the lowest level of response to socially significant symbols, the issue tends to be viewed as one of good vs. evil, virtue vs. vice, truth vs. falsehood. At the next level of awareness, crises are comprehended in sharp and conflicting dichotomies of beliefs and acts. Each of the major patterns of dualism is for the most part restricted to definable geographical areas. One such area em-

675

braced the Rimlands of Eurasia, the adjacent islands, and the Continents of the Americas. Here most of those most influential in forming public attitudes and policies envisaged the current choices of mankind in terms of freedom vs. despotism, liberty vs. totalitarianism, capitalism vs. collectivism (with local variants of social democracy vs. economic or political monopoly), liberalism vs. Communism, a world of peace-loving and cooperating sovereignties vs. a world of police-states subservient to a central autocracy. Another major area embraced the Heartlands of Eurasia, along with a fringe of dependencies and marchlands. Here those most influential in shaping policies and attitudes pictured the choices of men in terms of egalitarianism vs. discrimination, social justice vs. exploitation, collectivism vs. capitalism, Communism vs. reaction, a world of "democratic" sovereignties vs. a world of "bourgeois imperialism" and renascent Fascism. Although these two patterns of symbols and preferences tended to impinge upon all people everywhere throughout the Great Society, many millions in lower Asia and throughout Africa, other millions in the Levant, and still others in significant numbers within each of the major camps were unwilling or unable to accept either set of alternatives and were clinging to older creeds or groping blindly for some new formula for the good life.

A hasty view of man's hope and man's fate might suggest that the form of the future is to be found in the conversion of the doubtful to one or the other of the great competing faiths, and in the ultimate and definitive triumph of one over the other, with victors converting penitent survivors among the vanquished to the ways of rectitude. Such an anticipation is reinforced by a backward glance at the destiny of earlier State Systems, in most of which one Power finally subdued all rivals and, by diplomacy and by arms, built a Universal State. By this logic, either the USA or the USSR is inexorably fated to overthrow the other and to unify all mankind and refashion the world in its own image.

But this prognosis is of dubious validity by virtue of two sets of considerations seldom publicized on either side of the line of conflict: (1) In each Super-Power, with its allies, puppets, and satellites, the discrepancies between verbal statements of purpose and living realities of experience are so wide as to raise grave doubts as to the eagerness or capacity of masses of men to risk their fortunes and their lives to effective purpose in any global crusade to crush the foe. (2) Because of the inescapable facts of geography, strategy, and geopolitics, neither coalition can reasonably be expected, under any presently imaginable circumstances, to "conquer" the other.

The strategic problem confronting both Muscovy and America in a world headed toward a war for global hegemony is, in military terms, an insoluble problem. For another generation at least, the USA will remain the wealthier, more productive, and more formidable of the antagonists in many of the physical components of fighting capacity. In the event of hostilities in the near years to come, American air forces can probably destroy most of the larger cities of the USSR and China and bring death to scores of millions. But the facts of space are such that the armed hosts of America, however mobilized and directed in the game of war, cannot conceivably prevent the subjugation of all of Continental Europe and most of Asia by enemy armies. In the atomic era a protracted campaign of "liberation" as a means toward establishing adequate bastions from which to invade and strike down the foe can have no result other than the reduction of all Eurasian Rimlands to utter ruin and barbarism. That such a condition of affairs would permit of the mounting of a successful assault on the Heartland Powers is altogether implausible. Should this miracle nevertheless be achieved, it is still inconceivable that American forces could actually occupy and administer the "liberated" regions, presumably embracing most of Europe and Asia, in the face of social dissolution, economic prostration, famine, pestilence, demoralization, and savage guerrilla resistance on the part of the desperate and demented survivors among the vanquished. Failure or prolonged reverses at any stage of the endeavor would mean, almost certainly, the atomic vaporization of many American cities and the cremation of millions of American citizens through long-range raiders and rockets by air and sea, aided by *saboteurs,* enemy agents, and native traitors.

The problem of unifying the world via Soviet-Communist conquest also admits of no solution. Marxland constitutes an impressive power bloc, rich in territory, resources, and military man power, and possibly superior to Freeland in many of the political and psychological components of fighting capacity. In the event of open war, Communist armies could and would occupy most of Europe and Asia, thereby compelling British and Japanese neutrality. Yet this "victory," facilitated by indigenous Communists in all the areas thus subjugated, could not prevent the atomic annihilation of most centers of population and industry in the Red Empire, nor could it conceivably furnish any adequate bases for a successful invasion and occupation of the Americas.

These calculations of grand strategy and *Realpolitik* offer no assurance whatever that the Super-Powers will not, in fact, arrive at a clash in arms in the years to come. Despite democracy, the rulers of America have need of foreign devils to serve their own purposes. Because of totalitarianism, the rulers of Russia and China have need of foreign devils to perpetuate themselves in power. Such needs may well spell war. Men always act together, not in terms of what is rationally best in the end, but in terms of what is emotionally most satisfying at the moment in a context of immediate economic and political expectations. If World War III is permitted to come, and if it is waged as a "total war" of atomic annihilation (as will almost inevitably be the case), there will be no victors. Much of the human community will in the end experience doom and death, followed by a condition of human fortunes indistinguishable from primitive savagery for many of those so unfortunate as to survive. This prospect has been vividly depicted, with the anguish of guilt and the urgency of despair, by most atomic physicists since 1945. It was anticipated by others before the dawn of the atomic age.[9] But such forecasts have made little impression on public opinion or politicians. They do not in any sense preclude the possible advent of a final and fatal catastrophe for Western culture.

A conceivable alternative to this dismal prospect is the voluntary establishment of a World Federal Republic, brought into being through agreement among governments and peoples regarding the minimal essentials of central power to serve the common defense and general welfare of all peoples everywhere—or, if this is beyond the creative imagination of contemporary mankind, a return to the attitudes and policies of the 18th Century when war and diplomacy were recreations of gentlemen, conducted by limited and rational means for limited and rational ends, with little effect upon people in the mass and with no thought of crusading against wickedness, saving the world, or annihilating sinners.

It may well be that those most successful in winning friends and influencing people in the national segments of the Great Society of our time will be unable or unwilling to move toward either of these goals—since ethnocentrism and immoderation appear thus far to evoke more popular applause than appeals to sanity. In this event the decline of the West must proceed inexorably toward the ultimate immolation of our common civilization in the fires of hell and the gloom of night.

It is equally possible that the children of the ape-men, now possessed of fire from heaven, will find ways to live together in peace (or at least to keep their wars limited and local) and ultimately build together in constructive competition a worthy Mansion of Man. Here the children of God can find the means, if they will, to use the new magic which science has given them to conquer fear and want; to put an end at long last to the cult of the tribal deities and to the politics of power; to make all the earth a garden of beauty and creative toil; and, it may be in days to come, to reach out to other planets in an endless adventure in quest of new frontiers and new triumphs of the human spirit.

But *Homo sapiens* is a contrary creature who has less knowledge of himself than of atoms and galaxies and has less control over his own motives

---

[9] See H. G. Wells, *The Shape of Things to Come,* and James Hilton, *Lost Horizon.* From the latter novel, President Roosevelt, in his Chicago address of Oct. 5, 1937, quoted the following passage which is far more relevant now than then: "Men, exultant in the technique of homicide, will rage so hotly over the world that every precious thing will be in danger, every book and picture and harmony, every treasure garnered through two millenniums, the small, the delicate, the defenseless—all will be lost or wrecked or utterly destroyed. . . . There will be no safety by arms, no help from authority, no answer in science. The storm will rage until every flower of culture is trampled and all human beings are leveled in a vast chaos." More probably, a thermonuclear World War will put an end to the human race. See Nevile Shute's novel of 1957, *On the Beach.*

and destinies than over the animals, vegetables, and minerals he has used for his purposes. Neither of the alternatives suggested may ever be realized. The race may somehow "muddle through" to a doubtful future as dismal and hopeful, as reassuring and dangerous, as most of the long past. Future generations may still fear the end of the world and still hope for the Millennium, but experience in their daily lives nothing very different from the half-fulfilled dreams and quiet desperations of all their ancestors.

In all probability, this is the shape of the future we face together, on the basis of such forecasts as flow from the type of analysis attempted in the preceding pages and in the previous editions of this work. Neither "World Government" nor a return to the "Age of Reason" is likely in the years to come. Muddle and drift and fear will long be with us. But they may not this time eventuate in the fatal folly of World War III—and this for a simple reason. World wars are unleashed only when policy-makers on one side or the other are persuaded that "victory" is possible. No such conviction can now be entertained, or can prospectively be entertained, by any group of policy-makers in Marxland or Freeland possessed of even a suspicion of sanity. So long as this is true (and it bids fair to remain true indefinitely) power-holders on both sides will draw back in each crisis from the final, irrevocable step of global hostilities. Endless friction and conflict lie ahead, but not global war. And out of an endless stalemate may ultimately come some mutually tolerable pattern of accommodation.

Such an outcome will, in turn, offer for men's choices alternative courses of great danger or of great promise. Man's very humanity here offers hope. Men have wills and are not mere playthings of chance. If they will to go on in their ancient ways in an epoch in which the new powers at their disposal render these ways a recipe for anarchy, violence, and death, they cannot reasonably expect the Great Society to survive the effects of their folly. If they will to use their new powers to build a new heaven and a new earth, this is now within the range of their capabilities. For man, now more than ever, has a choice between the alternatives posed almost five centuries ago by Pico della Mirandola: "Thou shalt have the power to degenerate into the lower forms of life, which are animal; thou shalt have the power, out of thy soul's judgment, to be reborn into the higher forms of life, which are divine."

SUGGESTED READINGS

Agar, Herbert: *A Declaration of Faith*, Boston, Houghton Mifflin, 1952.
Blackett, P. M. S.: *Fear, War and the Bomb*, New York, McGraw-Hill, 1948.
———: *Atomic Weapons and East-West Relations*, New York, Cambridge, 1956.
Brinton, Crane: *Ideas and Men: The Story of Western Thought*, Englewood Cliffs, N.J., Prentice-Hall, 1950.
Brodie, Bernard (ed.): *The Absolute Weapon: Atomic Power and World Order*, New York, Harcourt, Brace, 1946.

THE ATOMIC AGE

Burchard, John Ely (ed.): *Mid-century: The Social Implications of Scientific Progress,* Cambridge, Mass., Technology Press, and New York, Wiley, 1950.

Clarke, Arthur C.: *The Exploration of Space,* New York, Harper, 1952.

Compton, Arthur Holly: *Atomic Quest,* New York, Oxford, 1956.

Cousins, Norman: *Who Speaks for Man?,* New York, Macmillan, 1953.

Dean, Gordon: *Report on the Atom,* New York, Knopf, 1957.

Hachiya, Michihiko: *Hiroshima Diary,* Chapel Hill, N.C., University of North Carolina Press, 1955.

Hersey, John: *Hiroshima,* New York, Knopf, 1946.

Isard, Walter, and Vincent Whitney: *Atomic Power,* New York, McGraw-Hill, 1955.

Kissinger, Henry A.: *Nuclear Weapons and Foreign Policy,* New York, Harper, 1957.

Laurence, William L.: *The Hell Bomb,* New York, Knopf, 1951.

Leyson, Burr W.: *Atomic Energy in War and Peace,* New York, Dutton, 1951.

Master, Dexter, and Katharine Way (eds.): *One World or None,* New York, McGraw-Hill, 1946.

Miksche, Lieut. Col. F. O.: *Atomic Weapons and Armies,* New York, Praeger, 1955.

Oberth, Hermann: *Man into Space: New Projects for Rocket and Space Travel,* New York, Harper, 1957.

Parson, Nels A., Jr.: *Guided Missiles in War and Peace,* Cambridge, Mass., Harvard University Press, 1956.

Pennock, J. Roland: *Liberal Democracy: Its Merits and Prospects,* New York, Rinehart, 1950.

Rapoport, Anatol: *Science and the Goals of Man: A Study in Semantic Orientation,* New York, Harper, 1950.

Rosebury, Theodor: *Peace or Pestilence?,* New York, McGraw-Hill, 1949.

Schubert, Jack, and Ralph E. Lapp: *Radiation: What It Is and How It Affects You,* New York, Viking, 1957.

Schurr, Sam. H., and Jacob Marschak: *Economic Aspects of Atomic Power,* Princeton, N.J., Princeton University Press, 1950.

Smith, Wilbur M.: *This Atomic Age and the Word of God,* Boston, Wilde, 1948.

Smyth, Henry deWolf: *Atomic Energy for Military Purposes,* Princeton, N.J., Princeton University Press, 1945.

Strausz-Hupé, Robert (ed.): *Air Power in the Nuclear Age,* New York, Praeger, 1956.

Thomson, George: *The Foreseeable Future,* New York, Cambridge, 1955.

U.S. Atomic Energy Commission: *The Effects of Nuclear Weapons* (Samuel Glasstone, ed.), prepared by the U.S. Department of Defense, Washington, Government Printing Office, 1957.

Wendt, Gerald: *Atomic Energy and the Hydrogen Bomb,* New York, McBride, 1950.

Wright, Quincy: *Problems of Stability and Progress in International Relations,* Berkeley, Calif., University of California Press, 1955.

APPENDIX I

CHARTER OF THE UNITED NATIONS [1]

We, the peoples of the United Nations, determined to save succeeding generations from the scourge of war, which twice in our lifetime has brought untold sorrow to mankind, and

to reaffirm faith in fundamental human rights, in the dignity and worth of the human person, in the equal rights of men and women and of nations large and small, and

to establish conditions under which justice and respect for the obligations arising from treaties and other sources of international law can be maintained, and

to promote social progress and better standards of life in larger freedom,

and for these ends to practice tolerance and live together in peace with one another as good neighbors, and

to unite our strength to maintain international peace and security, and

to ensure, by the acceptance of principles and the institution of methods, that armed force shall not be used, save in the common interest, and

to employ international machinery for the promotion of the economic and social advancement of all peoples,

have resolved to combine our efforts to accomplish these aims.

Accordingly, our respective Governments, through representatives assembled in the City of San Francisco, who have exhibited their full powers found to be in good and due form, have agreed to the present Charter of the United Nations and do hereby establish an international organization to be known as the United Nations.

CHAPTER I: PURPOSES AND PRINCIPLES

Article 1

The purposes of the United Nations are:
1. To maintain international peace and security, and to that end: to take effective collective measures for the prevention and removal of threats to the peace, and for the suppression of acts of aggression or other breaches of the peace, and to bring about by peaceful means, and in conformity with the principles of justice and international law, adjustment or settlement of international disputes or situations which might lead to a breach of the peace;
2. To develop friendly relations among nations based on respect for the principle of equal rights and self-determination of peoples, and to take other appropriate measures to strengthen universal peace;

[1] *Department of State Publication 2353, Conference Series 74.*

3. To achieve international cooperation in solving international problems of an economic, social, cultural, or humanitarian character, and in promoting and encouraging respect for human rights and for fundamental freedoms for all without distinction as to race, sex, language, or religion; and

4. To be a center for harmonizing the actions of nations in the attainment of these common ends.

Article 2

The Organization and its Members, in pursuit of the Purposes stated in Article 1, shall act in accordance with the following Principles.

1. The Organization is based on the principle of the sovereign equality of all its Members.

2. All Members, in order to ensure to all of them the rights and benefits resulting from membership, shall fulfill in good faith the obligations assumed by them in accordance with the present Charter.

3. All Members shall settle their international disputes by peaceful means in such a manner that international peace and security, and justice, are not endangered.

4. All Members shall refrain in their international relations from the threat or use of force against the territorial integrity or political independence of any state, or in any other manner inconsistent with the Purposes of the United Nations.

5. All Members shall give the United Nations every assistance in any action it takes in accordance with the present Charter, and shall refrain from giving assistance to any state against which the United Nations is taking preventive or enforcement action.

6. The Organization shall ensure that states which are not Members of the United Nations act in accordance with these Principles so far as may be necessary for the maintenance of international peace and security.

7. Nothing contained in the present Charter shall authorize the United Nations to intervene in matters which are essentially within the domestic jurisdiction of any state or shall require the Members to submit such matters to settlement under the present Charter; but this principle shall not prejudice the application of enforcement measures under Chapter VII.

CHAPTER II: MEMBERSHIP

Article 3

The original Members of the United Nations shall be the states which, having participated in the United Nations Conference on International Organization at San Francisco, or having previously signed the Declaration by United Nations of January 1, 1942, sign the present Charter and ratify it in accordance with Article 110.

Article 4

1. Membership in the United Nations is open to all other peace-loving states which accept the obligations contained in the present Charter, and, in the judgment of the Organization, are able and willing to carry out these obligations.

2. The admission of any such state to membership in the United Nations will be effected by a decision of the General Assembly upon the recommendation of the Security Council.

Article 5

A Member of the United Nations against which preventive or enforcement action has been taken by the Security Council may be suspended from the exercise of the rights and privileges of membership by the General Assembly upon the recommendation of the Security Council. The exercise of these rights and privileges may be restored by the Security Council.

Article 6

A Member of the United Nations which has persistently violated the Principles contained in the present Charter may be expelled from the Organization by the General Assembly upon the recommendation of the Security Council.

CHAPTER III: ORGANS

Article 7

1. There are established as the principal organs of the United Nations: a General Assembly, a Security Council, an Economic and Social Council, a Trusteeship Council, an International Court of Justice, and a Secretariat.
2. Such subsidiary organs as may be found necessary may be established in accordance with the present Charter.

Article 8

The United Nations shall place no restrictions on the eligibility of men and women to participate in any capacity and under conditions of equality in its principal and subsidiary organs.

CHAPTER IV: THE GENERAL ASSEMBLY

Composition

Article 9

1. The General Assembly shall consist of all the Members of the United Nations.
2. Each Member shall have not more than five representatives in the General Assembly.

Functions and Powers

Article 10

The General Assembly may discuss any questions or any matters within the scope of the present Charter or relating to the powers and functions of any organs provided for in the present Charter, and, except as provided in Article 12, may make recommendations to the Members of the United Nations or to the Security Council or to both on any such questions or matters.

Article 11

1. The General Assembly may consider the general principles of cooperation in the maintenance of international peace and security, including the principles governing disarmament and the regulation of armaments, and may make recommendations with regard to such principles to the Members or to the Security Council or to both.
2. The General Assembly may discuss any questions relating to the maintenance of international peace and security brought before it by any Member of the United Nations,

or by the Security Council, or by a state which is not a Member of the United Nations in accordance with Article 35, paragraph 2, and, except as provided in Article 12, may make recommendations with regard to any such questions to the state or states concerned or to the Security Council or to both. Any such question on which action is necessary shall be referred to the Security Council by the General Assembly either before or after discussion.

3. The General Assembly may call the attention of the Security Council to situations which are likely to endanger international peace and security.

4. The powers of the General Assembly set forth in this Article shall not limit the general scope of Article 10.

Article 12

1. While the Security Council is exercising in respect of any dispute or situation the functions assigned to it in the present Charter, the General Assembly shall not make any recommendations with regard to that dispute or situation unless the Security Council so requests.

2. The Secretary-General, with the consent of the Security Council, shall notify the General Assembly at each session of any matters relative to the maintenance of international peace and security which are being dealt with by the Security Council and shall similarly notify the General Assembly, or the Members of the United Nations if the General Assembly is not in session, immediately the Security Council ceases to deal with such matters.

Article 13

1. The General Assembly shall initiate studies and make recommendations for the purpose of:

a. promoting international cooperation in the political field and encouraging the progressive development of international law and its codification;

b. promoting international cooperation in the economic, social, cultural, educational, and health fields, and assisting in the realization of human rights and fundamental freedoms for all without distinction as to race, sex, language, or religion.

2. The further responsibilities, functions, and powers of the General Assembly with respect to matters mentioned in paragraph 1 (b) above are set forth in Chapters IX and X.

Article 14

Subject to the provisions of Article 12, the General Assembly may recommend measures for the peaceful adjustment of any situation, regardless of origin, which it deems likely to impair the general welfare or friendly relations among nations, including situations resulting from a violation of the provisions of the present Charter setting forth the Purposes and Principles of the United Nations.

Article 15

1. The General Assembly shall receive and consider annual and special reports from the Security Council; these reports shall include an account of the measures that the Security Council has decided upon or taken to maintain international peace and security.

2. The General Assembly shall receive and consider reports from the other organs of the United Nations.

APPENDIX I

Article 16

The General Assembly shall perform such functions with respect to the international trusteeship system as are assigned to it under Chapters XII and XIII, including the approval of the trusteeship agreements for areas not designated as strategic.

Article 17

1. The General Assembly shall consider and approve the budget of the Organization.
2. The expenses of the Organization shall be borne by the Members as apportioned by the General Assembly.
3. The General Assembly shall consider and approve any financial and budgetary arrangements with specialized agencies referred to in Article 57 and shall examine the administrative budgets of such specialized agencies with a view to making recommendations to the agencies concerned.

Voting

Article 18

1. Each member of the General Assembly shall have one vote.
2. Decisions of the General Assembly on important questions shall be made by a two-thirds majority of the members present and voting. These questions shall include: recommendations with respect to the maintenance of international peace and security, the election of the non-permanent members of the Security Council, the election of the members of the Economic and Social Council, the election of members of the Trusteeship Council in accordance with paragraph 1 (c) of Article 86, the admission of new Members to the United Nations, the suspension of the rights and privileges of membership, the expulsion of Members, questions relating to the operation of the trusteeship system, and budgetary questions.
3. Decisions on other questions, including the determination of additional categories of questions to be decided by a two-thirds majority, shall be made by a majority of the members present and voting.

Article 19

A member of the United Nations which is in arrears in the payment of its financial contributions to the Organization shall not vote in the General Assembly if the amount of its arrears equals or exceeds the amount of the contribution due from it for the preceding two full years. The General Assembly may, nevertheless, permit such a Member to vote if it is satisfied that the failure to pay is due to conditions beyond the control of the Member.

Procedure

Article 20

The General Assembly shall meet in regular annual sessions and in such special sessions as occasion may require. Special sessions shall be convoked by the Secretary-General at the request of the Security Council or of a majority of the Members of the United Nations.

Article 21

The General Assembly shall adopt its own rules of procedure. It shall elect its President for each session.

APPENDIX I

Article 22

The General Assembly may establish such subsidiary organs as it deems necessary for the performance of its functions.

CHAPTER V: THE SECURITY COUNCIL

Composition

Article 23

1. The Security Council shall consist of eleven Members of the United Nations. The Republic of China, France, the Union of Soviet Socialist Republics, the United Kingdom of Great Britain and Northern Ireland, and the United States of America shall be permanent members of the Security Council. The General Assembly shall elect six other Members of the United Nations to be non-permanent members of the Security Council, due regard being specially paid, in the first instance to the contribution of Members of the United Nations to the maintenance of international peace and security and to the other purposes of the Organization, and also to equitable geographical distribution.

2. The non-permanent members of the Security Council shall be elected for a term of two years. In the first election of the non-permanent members, however, three shall be chosen for a term of one year. A retiring member shall not be eligible for immediate re-election.

3. Each member of the Security Council shall have one representative.

Functions and Powers

Article 24

1. In order to ensure prompt and effective action by the United Nations, its Members confer on the Security Council primary responsibility for the maintenance of international peace and security, and agree that in carrying out its duties under this responsibility the Security Council acts on their behalf.

2. In discharging these duties the Security Council shall act in accordance with the Purposes and Principles of the United Nations. The specific powers granted to the Security Council for the discharge of these duties are laid down in Chapters VI, VII, VIII, and XII.

3. The Security Council shall submit annual and, when necessary, special reports to the General Assembly for its consideration.

Article 25

The Members of the United Nations agree to accept and carry out the decisions of the Security Council in accordance with the present Charter.

Article 26

In order to promote the establishment and maintenance of international peace and security with the least diversion for armaments of the world's human and economic resources, the Security Council shall be responsible for formulating, with the assistance of the Military Staff Committee referred to in Article 47, plans to be submitted to the Members of the United Nations for the establishment of a system for the regulation of armaments.

APPENDIX I

Voting

Article 27

1. Each member of the Security Council shall have one vote.
2. Decisions of the Security Council on procedural matters shall be made by an affirmative vote of seven members.
3. Decisions of the Security Council on all other matters shall be made by an affirmative vote of seven members including the concurring votes of the permanent members; provided that, in decisions under Chapter VI, and under paragraph 3 of Article 52, a party to a dispute shall abstain from voting.

Procedure

Article 28

1. The Security Council shall be so organized as to be able to function continuously. Each member of the Security Council shall for this purpose be represented at all times at the seat of the Organization.
2. The Security Council shall hold periodic meetings at which each of its members may, if it so desires, be represented by a member of the government or by some other specially designated representative.
3. The Security Council may hold meetings at such places other than the seat of the Organization as in its judgment will best facilitate its work.

Article 29

The Security Council may establish such subsidiary organs as it deems necessary for the performance of its functions.

Article 30

The Security Council shall adopt its own rules of procedure, including the method of selecting its President.

Article 31

Any Member of the United Nations which is not a member of the Security Council may participate, without vote, in the discussion of any question brought before the Security Council whenever the latter considers that the interests of that Member are specially affected.

Article 32

Any Member of the United Nations which is not a member of the Security Council or any state which is not a Member of the United Nations, if it is a party to a dispute under consideration by the Security Council, shall be invited to participate, without vote, in the discussion relating to the dispute. The Security Council shall lay down such conditions as it deems just for the participation of a state which is not a Member of the United Nations.

APPENDIX I

Article 33

1. The parties to any dispute, the continuance of which is likely to endanger the maintenance of international peace and security, shall, first of all, seek a solution by negotiation, enquiry, mediation, conciliation, arbitration, judicial settlement, resort to regional agencies or arrangements, or other peaceful means of their own choice.

2. The Security Council shall, when it deems necessary, call upon the parties to settle their dispute by such means.

Article 34

The Security Council may investigate any dispute, or any situation which might lead to international friction or give rise to a dispute, in order to determine whether the continuance of the dispute or situation is likely to endanger the maintenance of international peace and security.

Article 35

1. Any Member of the United Nations may bring any dispute, or any situation of the nature referred to in Article 34, to the attention of the Security Council or of the General Assembly.

2. A state which is not a Member of the United Nations may bring to the attention of the Security Council or of the General Assembly any dispute to which it is a party if it accepts in advance, for the purposes of the dispute, the obligations of pacific settlement provided in the present Charter.

3. The proceedings of the General Assembly in respect of matters brought to its attention under this Article will be subject to the provisions of Articles 11 and 12.

Article 36

1. The Security Council may, at any stage of a dispute of the nature referred to in Article 33 or of a situation of like nature, recommend appropriate procedures or methods of adjustment.

2. The Security Council should take into consideration any procedures for the settlement of the dispute which have already been adopted by the parties.

3. In making recommendations under this Article the Security Council should also take into consideration that legal disputes should as a general rule be referred by the parties to the International Court of Justice in accordance with the provisions of the Statute of the Court.

Article 37

1. Should the parties to a dispute of the nature referred to in Article 33 fail to settle it by the means indicated in that Article, they shall refer it to the Security Council.

2. If the Security Council deems that the continuance of the dispute is in fact likely to endanger the maintenance of international peace and security, it shall decide whether to take action under Article 36 or to recommend such terms of settlement as it may consider appropriate.

688

APPENDIX I

Article 38

Without prejudice to the provisions of Articles 33 to 37, the Security Council may, if all the parties to any dispute so request, make recommendations to the parties, with a view to a pacific settlement of the dispute.

CHAPTER VII: ACTION WITH RESPECT TO THREATS TO THE PEACE, BREACHES OF THE PEACE
AND ACTS OF AGGRESSION

Article 39

The Security Council shall determine the existence of any threat to the peace, breach of the peace, or act of aggression and shall make recommendations, or decide what measures shall be taken in accordance with Articles 41 and 42, to maintain or restore international peace and security.

Article 40

In order to prevent an aggravation of the situation, the Security Council may, before making the recommendations or deciding upon the measures provided for in Article 39, call upon the parties concerned to comply with such provisional measures as it deems necessary or desirable. Such provisional measures shall be without prejudice to the rights, claims, or position of the parties concerned. The Security Council shall duly take account of failure to comply with such provisional measures.

Article 41

The Security Council may decide what measures not involving the use of armed force are to be employed to give effect to its decisions, and it may call upon the Members of the United Nations to apply such measures. These may include complete or partial interruption of economic relations and of rail, sea, air, postal, telegraphic, radio, and other means of communication, and the severance of diplomatic relations.

Article 42

Should the Security Council consider that measures provided for in Article 41 would be inadequate or have proved to be inadequate, it may take such action by air, sea, or land forces as may be necessary to maintain or restore international peace and security. Such action may include demonstrations, blockade, and other operations by air, sea, or land forces of Members of the United Nations.

Article 43

1. All Members of the United Nations, in order to contribute to the maintenance of international peace and security, undertake to make available to the Security Council, on its call and in accordance with a special agreement or agreements, armed forces, assistance, and facilities, including rights of passage, necessary for the purpose of maintaining international peace and security.

2. Such agreement or agreements shall govern the numbers and types of forces, their degree of readiness and general location, and the nature of the facilities and assistance to be provided.

3. The agreement or agreements shall be negotiated as soon as possible on the initiative of the Security Council. They shall be concluded between the Security Council and Members or between the Security Council and groups of Members and shall be subject to ratification by the signatory states in accordance with their respective constitutional processes.

Article 44

When the Security Council has decided to use force it shall, before calling upon a Member not represented on it to provide armed forces in fulfillment of the obligations assumed under Article 43, invite that Member, if the Member so desires, to participate in the decisions of the Security Council concerning the employment of contingents of that Member's armed forces.

Article 45

In order to enable the United Nations to take urgent military measures, Members shall hold immediately available national air-force contingents for combined international enforcement action. The strength and degree of readiness of these contingents and plans for their combined action shall be determined, within the limits laid down in the special agreement or agreements referred to in Article 43, by the Security Council with the assistance of the Military Staff Committee.

Article 46

Plans for the application of armed force shall be made by the Security Council with the assistance of the Military Staff Committee.

Article 47

1. There shall be established a Military Staff Committee to advise and assist the Security Council on all questions relating to the Security Council's military requirements for the maintenance of international peace and security, the employment and command of forces placed at its disposal, the regulation of armaments, and possible disarmament.

2. The Military Staff Committee shall consist of the Chiefs of Staff of the permanent members of the Security Council or their representatives. Any Member of the United Nations not permanently represented on the Committee shall be invited by the Committee to be associated with it when the efficient discharge of the Committee's responsibilities requires the participation of that Member in its work.

3. The Military Staff Committee shall be responsible under the Security Council for the strategic direction of any armed forces placed at the disposal of the Security Council. Questions relating to the command of such forces shall be worked out subsequently.

4. The Military Staff Committee, with the authorization of the Security Council and after consultation with appropriate regional agencies, may establish regional subcommittees.

Article 48

1. The action required to carry out the decisions of the Security Council for the maintenance of international peace and security shall be taken by all the Members of the United Nations or by some of them, as the Security Council may determine.

2. Such decisions shall be carried out by the Members of the United Nations directly and through their action in the appropriate international agencies of which they are members.

Article 49

The Members of the United Nations shall join in affording mutual assistance in carrying out the measures decided upon by the Security Council.

Article 50

If preventive or enforcement measures against any state are taken by the Security Council, any other state, whether a Member of the United Nations or not, which finds itself confronted with special economic problems arising from the carrying out of those measures shall have the right to consult the Security Council with regard to a solution of those problems.

Article 51

Nothing in the present Charter shall impair the inherent right of individual or collective self-defense if an armed attack occurs against a Member of the United Nations, until the Security Council has taken the measures necessary to maintain international peace and security. Measures taken by Members in the exercise of this right of self-defense shall be immediately reported to the Security Council and shall not in any way affect the authority and responsibility of the Security Council under the present Charter to take at any time such action as it deems necessary in order to maintain or restore international peace and security.

CHAPTER VIII: REGIONAL ARRANGEMENTS

Article 52

1. Nothing in the present Charter precludes the existence of regional arrangements or agencies for dealing with such matters relating to the maintenance of international peace and security as are appropriate for regional action, provided that such arrangements or agencies and their activities are consistent with the Purposes and Principles of the United Nations.
2. The Members of the United Nations entering into such arrangements or constituting such agencies shall make every effort to achieve pacific settlement of local disputes through such regional arrangements or by such regional agencies before referring them to the Security Council.
3. The Security Council shall encourage the development of pacific settlement of local disputes through such regional arrangements or by such regional agencies either on the initiative of the states concerned or by reference from the Security Council.
4. This Article in no way impairs the application of Articles 34 and 35.

Article 53

1. The Security Council shall, where appropriate, utilize such regional arrangements or agencies for enforcement action under its authority. But no enforcement action shall be taken under regional arrangements or by regional agencies without the authorization of the Security Council, with the exception of measures against any enemy state, as defined in paragraph 2 of this Article, provided for pursuant to Article 107 or in

regional arrangements directed against renewal of aggressive policy on the part of any such state, until such time as the Organization may, on request of the Governments concerned, be charged with the responsibility for preventing further aggression by such a state.

2. The term enemy state as used in paragraph 1 of this Article applies to any state which during the Second World War has been an enemy of any signatory of the present Charter.

Article 54

The Security Council shall at all times be kept fully informed of activities undertaken or in contemplation under regional arrangements or by regional agencies for the maintenance of international peace and security.

CHAPTER IX: INTERNATIONAL ECONOMIC AND SOCIAL COOPERATION

Article 55

With a view to the creation of conditions of stability and well-being which are necessary for peaceful and friendly relations among nations based on respect for the principle of equal rights and self-determination of peoples, the United Nations shall promote:

a. higher standards of living, full employment, and conditions of economic and social progress and development;

b. solutions of international economic, social, health, and related problems; and international cultural and educational cooperation; and

c. universal respect for, and observance of, human rights and fundamental freedoms for all without distinction as to race, sex, language, or religion.

Article 56

All Members pledge themselves to take joint and separate action in cooperation with the Organization for the achievement of the purposes set forth in Article 55.

Article 57

1. The various specialized agencies, established by intergovernmental agreement and having wide international responsibilities, as defined in their basic instruments, in economic, social, cultural, educational, health, and related fields, shall be brought into relationship with the United Nations in accordance with the provisions of Article 63.

2. Such agencies thus brought into relationship with the United Nations are hereinafter referred to as specialized agencies.

Article 58

The Organization shall make recommendations for the coordination of the policies and activities of the specialized agencies.

Article 59

The Organization shall, where appropriate, initiate negotiations among the states concerned for the creation of any new specialized agencies required for the accomplishment of the purposes set forth in Article 55.

APPENDIX I

Article 60

Responsibility for the discharge of the functions of the Organization set forth in this Chapter shall be vested in the General Assembly and, under the authority of the General Assembly, in the Economic and Social Council, which shall have for this purpose the power set forth in Chapter X.

CHAPTER X: THE ECONOMIC AND SOCIAL COUNCIL

Composition

Article 61

1. The Economic and Social Council shall consist of eighteen Members of the United Nations elected by the General Assembly.
2. Subject to the provisions of paragraph 3, six members of the Economic and Social Council shall be elected each year for a term of three years. A retiring member shall be eligible for immediate re-election.
3. At the first election, eighteen members of the Economic and Social Council shall be chosen. The term of office of six members so chosen shall expire at the end of one year, and six other members at the end of two years, in accordance with arrangements made by the General Assembly.
4. Each member of the Economic and Social Council shall have one representative.

Functions and Powers

Article 62

1. The Economic and Social Council may make or initiate studies and reports with respect to international economic, social, cultural, educational, health, and related matters and may make recommendations with respect to any such matters to the General Assembly, to the Members of the United Nations, and to the specialized agencies concerned.
2. It may make recommendations for the purpose of promoting respect for, and observance of, human rights and fundamental freedoms for all.
3. It may prepare draft conventions for submission to the General Assembly, with respect to matters falling within its competence.
4. It may call, in accordance with the rules prescribed by the United Nations, international conferences on matters falling within its competence.

Article 63

1. The Economic and Social Council may enter into agreements with any of the agencies referred to in Article 57, defining the terms on which the agency concerned shall be brought into relationship with the United Nations. Such agreements shall be subject to approval by the General Assembly.
2. It may coordinate the activities of the specialized agencies through consultation with and recommendations to such agencies and through recommendations to the General Assembly and to the Members of the United Nations.

Article 64

1. The Economic and Social Council may take appropriate steps to obtain regular reports from the specialized agencies. It may make arrangements with the Members of

693

APPENDIX I

the United Nations and with the specialized agencies to obtain reports on the steps taken to give effect to its own recommendations and to recommendations on matters falling within its competence made by the General Assembly.

2. It may communicate its observations on these reports to the General Assembly.

Article 65

The Economic and Social Council may furnish information to the Security Council and shall assist the Security Council upon its request.

Article 66

1. The Economic and Social Council shall perform such functions as fall within its competence in connection with the carrying out of the recommendations of the General Assembly.

2. It may, with the approval of the General Assembly, perform services at the request of Members of the United Nations and at the request of specialized agencies.

3. It shall perform such other functions as are specified elsewhere in the present Charter or as may be assigned to it by the General Assembly.

Voting

Article 67

1. Each member of the Economic and Social Council shall have one vote.

2. Decisions of the Economic and Social Council shall be made by a majority of the members present and voting.

Procedure

Article 68

The Economic and Social Council shall set up commissions in economic and social fields and for the promotion of human rights, and such other commissions as may be required for the performance of its functions.

Article 69

The Economic and Social Council shall invite any Member of the United Nations to participate, without vote, in its deliberations on any matter of particular concern to that Member.

Article 70

The Economic and Social Council may make arrangements for representatives of the specialized agencies to participate, without vote, in its deliberations and in those of the commissions established by it, and for its representatives to participate in the deliberations of the specialized agencies.

Article 71

The Economic and Social Council may make suitable arrangements for consultation with non-governmental organizations which are concerned with matters within its competence. Such arrangements may be made with international organizations and, where appropriate, with national organizations after consultation with the Member of the United Nations concerned.

Article 72

1. The Economic and Social Council shall adopt its own rules of procedure, including the method of selecting its President.
2. The Economic and Social Council shall meet as required in accordance with its rules, which shall include provision for the convening of meetings on the request of a majority of its members.

CHAPTER XI: DECLARATION REGARDING NON-SELF-GOVERNING TERRITORIES

Article 73

Members of the United Nations which have or assume responsibilities for the administration of territories whose peoples have not yet attained a full measure of self-government recognize the principle that the interests of the inhabitants of these territories are paramount, and accept as a sacred trust the obligation to promote to the utmost, within the system of international peace and security established by the present Charter, the well-being of the inhabitants of these territories, and, to this end:

a. to ensure, with due respect for the culture of the peoples concerned, their political, economic, social, and educational advancement, their just treatment, and their protection against abuses;

b. to develop self-government, to take due account of the political aspirations of the peoples, and to assist them in the progressive development of their free political institutions, according to the particular circumstances of each territory and its peoples and their varying stages of advancement;

c. to further international peace and security;

d. to promote constructive measures of development, to encourage research, and to cooperate with one another and, when and where appropriate, with specialized international bodies with a view to the practical achievement of the social, economic, and scientific purposes set forth in this Article; and

e. to transmit regularly to the Secretary-General for information purposes, subject to such limitation as security and constitutional considerations may require, statistical and other information of a technical nature relating to economic, social, and educational conditions in the territories for which they are respectively responsible other than those territories to which Chapters XII and XIII apply.

Article 74

Members of the United Nations also agree that their policy in respect of the territories to which this Chapter applies, no less than in respect of their metropolitan areas, must be based on the general principle of good-neighborliness, due account being taken of the interests and well-being of the rest of the world, in social, economic, and commercial matters.

CHAPTER XII: INTERNATIONAL TRUSTEESHIP SYSTEM

Article 75

The United Nations shall establish under its authority an international trusteeship system for the administration and supervision of such territories as may be placed thereunder by subsequent individual agreements. These territories are hereinafter referred to as trust territories.

Article 76

The basic objectives of the trusteeship system, in accordance with the Purposes of the United Nations laid down in Article 1 of the present Charter, shall be:

a. to further international peace and security;

b. to promote the political, economic, social and educational advancement of the inhabitants of the trust territories, and their progressive development towards self-government or independence as may be appropriate to the particular circumstances of each territory and its peoples and the freely expressed wishes of the peoples concerned, and as may be provided by the terms of each trusteeship agreement;

c. to encourage respect for human rights and for fundamental freedoms for all without distinction as to race, sex, language, or religion, and to encourage recognition of the interdependence of the peoples of the world; and

d. to ensure equal treatment in social, economic, and commercial matters for all Members of the United Nations and their nationals, and also equal treatment for the latter in the administration of justice, without prejudice to the attainment of the foregoing objectives and subject to the provisions of Article 80.

Article 77

1. The trusteeship system shall apply to such territories in the following categories as may be placed thereunder by means of trusteeship agreements:

a. territories now held under mandate;

b. territories which may be detached from enemy states as a result of the Second World War; and

c. territories voluntarily placed under the system by states responsible for their administration.

2. It will be a matter for subsequent agreement as to which territories in the foregoing categories will be brought under the trusteeship system and upon what terms.

Article 78

The trusteeship system shall not apply to territories which have become Members of the United Nations, relationship among which shall be based on respect for the principle of sovereign equality.

Article 79

The terms of trusteeship for each territory to be placed under the trusteeship system, including any alteration or amendment, shall be agreed upon by the states directly concerned, including the mandatory power in the case of territories held under mandate by a Member of the United Nations, and shall be approved as provided for in Articles 83 and 85.

Article 80

1. Except as may be agreed upon in individual trusteeship agreements, made under Articles 77, 79, and 81, placing each territory under the trusteeship system, and until such agreements have been concluded, nothing in this Chapter shall be construed in or of itself to alter in any manner the rights whatsoever of any states or any peoples

or the terms of existing international instruments to which Members of the United Nations may respectively be parties.

2. Paragraph 1 of this Article shall not be interpreted as giving grounds for delay or postponement of the negotiation and conclusion of agreements for placing mandated and other territories under the trusteeship system as provided for in Article 77.

Article 81

The trusteeship agreement shall in each case include the terms under which the trust territory will be administered and designate the authority which will exercise the administration of the trust territory. Such authority, hereinafter called the administering authority, may be one or more states or the Organization itself.

Article 82

There may be designated, in any trusteeship agreement, a strategic area or areas which may include part or all of the trust territory to which the agreement applies, without prejudice to any special agreement or agreements made under Article 43.

Article 83

1. All functions of the United Nations relating to strategic areas, including the approval of the terms of the trusteeship agreements and of their alteration or amendment, shall be exercised by the Security Council.

2. The basic objectives set forth in Article 76 shall be applicable to the people of each strategic area.

3. The Security Council shall, subject to the provisions of the trusteeship agreements and without prejudice to security considerations, avail itself of the assistance of the Trusteeship Council to perform those functions of the United Nations under the trusteeship system relating to political, economic, social, and educational matters in the strategic areas.

Article 84

It shall be the duty of the administering authority to ensure that the trust territory shall play its part in the maintenance of international peace and security. To this end the administering authority may make use of volunteer forces, facilities, and assistance from the trust territory in carrying out the obligations towards the Security Council undertaken in this regard by the administering authority, as well as for local defense and the maintenance of law and order within the trust territory.

Article 85

1. The functions of the United Nations with regard to trusteeship agreements for all areas not designated as strategic, including the approval of the terms of the trusteeship agreements and of their alteration or amendment, shall be exercised by the General Assembly.

2. The Trusteeship Council, operating under the authority of the General Assembly, shall assist the General Assembly in carrying out these functions.

APPENDIX I

Composition

Article 86

1. The Trusteeship Council shall consist of the following Members of the United Nations:

    a. those Members administering trust territories;

    b. such of those Members mentioned by name in Article 23 as are not administering trust territories; and

    c. as many other Members elected for three-year terms by the General Assembly as may be necessary to ensure that the total number of members of the Trusteeship Council is equally divided between those Members of the United Nations which administer trust territories and those which do not.

2. Each member of the Trusteeship Council shall designate one specially qualified person to represent it therein.

Functions and Powers

Article 87

The General Assembly and, under its authority, the Trusteeship Council, in carrying out their functions, may:

    a. consider reports submitted by the administering authority;

    b. accept petitions and examine them in consultation with the administering authority;

    c. provide for periodic visits to the respective trust territories at times agreed upon with the administering authority; and

    d. take these and other actions in conformity with the terms of the trusteeship agreements.

Article 88

The Trusteeship Council shall formulate a questionnaire on the political, economic, social, and educational advancement of the inhabitants of each trust territory, and the administering authority for each trust territory within the competence of the General Assembly shall make an annual report to the General Assembly upon the basis of such questionnaire.

Voting

Article 89

1. Each member of the Trusteeship Council shall have one vote.

2. Decisions of the Trusteeship Council shall be made by a majority of the members present and voting.

Procedure

Article 90

1. The Trusteeship Council shall adopt its own rules of procedure, including the method of selecting its President.

2. The Trusteeship Council shall meet as required in accordance with its rules, which shall include provision for the convening of meetings on the request of a majority of its members.

APPENDIX I

Article 91

The Trusteeship Council shall, when appropriate, avail itself of the assistance of the Economic and Social Council and of the specialized agencies in regard to matters with which they are respectively concerned.

CHAPTER XIV: THE INTERNATIONAL COURT OF JUSTICE

Article 92

The International Court of Justice shall be the principal judicial organ of the United Nations. It shall function in accordance with the annexed Statute, which is based upon the Statute of the Permanent Court of International Justice and forms an integral part of the present Charter.

Article 93

1. All Members of the United Nations are *ipso facto* parties to the Statute of the International Court of Justice.
2. A state which is not a Member of the United Nations may become a party to the Statute of the International Court of Justice on conditions to be determined in each case by the General Assembly upon the recommendation of the Security Council.

Article 94

1. Each Member of the United Nations undertakes to comply with the decision of the International Court of Justice in any case to which it is a party.
2. If any party to a case fails to perform the obligations incumbent upon it under a judgment rendered by the Court, the other party may have recourse to the Security Council, which may, if it deems necessary, make recommendations or decide upon measures to be taken to give effect to the judgment.

Article 95

Nothing in the present Charter shall prevent Members of the United Nations from entrusting the solution of their differences to other tribunals by virtue of agreements already in existence or which may be concluded in the future.

Article 96

1. The General Assembly or the Security Council may request the International Court of Justice to give an advisory opinion on any legal question.
2. Other organs of the United Nations and specialized agencies, which may at any time be so authorized by the General Assembly, may also request advisory opinions of the Court on legal questions arising within the scope of their activities.

APPENDIX I

Article 97

The Secretariat shall comprise a Secretary-General and such staff as the Organization may require. The Secretary-General shall be appointed by the General Assembly upon the recommendation of the Security Council. He shall be the chief administrative officer of the Organization.

Article 98

The Secretary-General shall act in that capacity in all meetings of the General Assembly, of the Security Council, of the Economic and Social Council, and of the Trusteeship Council, and shall perform such other functions as are entrusted to him by these organs. The Secretary-General shall make an annual report to the General Assembly on the work of the Organization.

Article 99

The Secretary-General may bring to the attention of the Security Council any matter which in his opinion may threaten the maintenance of international peace and security.

Article 100

1. In the performance of their duties the Secretary-General and the staff shall not seek or receive instructions from any government or from any other authority external to the Organization. They shall refrain from any action which might reflect on their position as international officials responsible only to the Organization.

2. Each Member of the United Nations undertakes to respect the exclusively international character of the responsibilities of the Secretary-General and the staff and not to seek to influence them in the discharge of their responsibilities.

Article 101

1. The staff shall be appointed by the Secretary-General under regulations established by the General Assembly.

2. Appropriate staffs shall be permanently assigned to the Economic and Social Council, the Trusteeship Council, and, as required, to other organs of the United Nations. These staffs shall form a part of the Secretariat.

3. The paramount consideration in the employment of the staff and in the determination of the conditions of service shall be the necessity of securing the highest standards of efficiency, competence, and integrity. Due regard shall be paid to the importance of recruiting the staff on as wide a geographical basis as possible.

CHAPTER XVI: MISCELLANEOUS PROVISIONS

Article 102

1. Every treaty and every international agreement entered into by any Member of the United Nations after the present Charter comes into force shall as soon as possible be registered with the Secretariat and published by it.

2. No party to any such treaty or international agreement which has not been regis-

tered in accordance with the provisions of paragraph 1 of this Article may invoke that treaty or agreement before any organ of the United Nations.

Article 103

In the event of a conflict between the obligations of the Members of the United Nations under the present Charter and their obligations under any other international agreement, their obligations under the present Charter shall prevail.

Article 104

The Organization shall enjoy in the territory of each of its Members such legal capacity as may be necessary for the exercise of its functions and the fulfillment of its purposes.

Article 105

1. The Organization shall enjoy in the territory of each of its Members such privileges and immunities as are necessary for the fulfillment of its purposes.

2. Representatives of the Members of the United Nations and officials of the Organization shall similarly enjoy such privileges and immunities as are necessary for the independent exercise of their functions in connection with the Organization.

3. The General Assembly may make recommendations with a view to determining the details of the application of paragraphs 1 and 2 of this Article or may propose conventions to the Members of the United Nations for this purpose.

CHAPTER XVII: TRANSITIONAL SECURITY ARRANGEMENTS

Article 106

Pending the coming into force of such special agreements referred to in Article 43 as in the opinion of the Security Council enable it to begin the exercise of its responsibilities under Article 42, the parties to the Four-Nation Declaration, signed at Moscow, October 30, 1943, and France, shall, in accordance with the provisions of paragraph 5 of that Declaration, consult with one another and as occasion requires with other Members of the United Nations with a view to such joint action on behalf of the Organization as may be necessary for the purpose of maintaining international peace and security.

Article 107

Nothing in the present Charter shall invalidate or preclude action, in relation to any state which during the Second World War has been an enemy of any signatory to the present Charter, taken or authorized as a result of that war by the Governments having responsibility for such action.

CHAPTER XVIII: AMENDMENTS

Article 108

Amendments to the present Charter shall come into force for all Members of the United Nations when they have been adopted by a vote of two-thirds of the members of the General Assembly and ratified in accordance with their respective constitutional

701

processes by two-thirds of the Members of the United Nations, including all the permanent members of the Security Council.

Article 109

1. A General Conference of the Members of the United Nations for the purpose of reviewing the present Charter may be held at a date and place to be fixed by a two-thirds vote of the members of the General Assembly and by a vote of any seven members of the Security Council. Each Member of the United Nations shall have one vote in the conference.

2. Any alteration of the present Charter recommended by a two-thirds vote of the conference shall take effect when ratified in accordance with their respective constitutional processes by two-thirds of the Members of the United Nations including all the permanent members of the Security Council.

3. If such a conference has not been held before the tenth annual session of the General Assembly following the coming into force of the present Charter, the proposal to call such a conference shall be placed on the agenda of that session of the General Assembly, and the conference shall be held if so decided by a majority vote of the members of the General Assembly and by a vote of any seven members of the Security Council.

CHAPTER XIX: RATIFICATION AND SIGNATURE

Article 110

1. The present Charter shall be ratified by the signatory states in accordance with their respective constitutional processes.

2. The ratifications shall be deposited with the Government of the United States of America, which shall notify all the signatory states of each deposit as well as the Secretary-General of the Organization when he has been appointed.

3. The present Charter shall come into force upon the deposit of ratifications by the Republic of China, France, the Union of Soviet Socialist Republics, the United Kingdom of Great Britian and Northern Ireland, and the United States of America, and by a majority of the other signatory states. A protocol of the ratifications deposited shall thereupon be drawn up by the Government of the United States of America which shall communicate copies thereof to all the signatory states.

4. The states signatory to the present Charter which ratify it after it has come into force will become original Members of the United Nations on the date of the deposit of their respective ratifications.

Article 111

The present Charter, of which the Chinese, French, Russian, English, and Spanish texts are equally authentic, shall remain deposited in the archives of the Government of the United States of America. Duly certified copies thereof shall be transmitted by that Government to the Governments of the other signatory states.

IN FAITH WHEREOF the representatives of the Governments of the United Nations have signed the present Charter.

DONE at the City of San Francisco the twenty-sixth day of June, one thousand nine hundred and forty-five.

APPENDIX II

COVENANT OF THE LEAGUE OF NATIONS [1]

With Amendments in Force, June 26, 1945

THE HIGH CONTRACTING PARTIES,

In order to promote international cooperation and to achieve international peace and security

by the acceptance of obligations not to resort to war,

by the prescription of open, just and honorable relations between nations,

by the firm establishment of the understandings of international law as the actual rule of conduct among Governments, and

by the maintenance of justice and a scrupulous respect for all treaty obligations in the dealings of organized peoples with one another,

agree to this Covenant of the League of Nations.

Article 1

Membership and Withdrawal

1. The original members of the League of Nations shall be those of the Signatories which are named in the Annex to this Covenant and also such of those other States named in the Annex as shall accede without reservation to this Covenant. Such accessions shall be effected by a declaration deposited with the Secretariat within two months of the coming into force of the Covenant. Notice thereof shall be sent to all other Members of the League.

2. Any fully self-governing State, Dominion or Colony not named in the Annex may become a Member of the League if its admission is agreed to by two-thirds of the Assembly, provided that it shall give effective guaranties of its sincere intention to observe its international obligations, and shall accept such regulations as may be prescribed by the League in regard to its military, naval and air forces and armaments.

3. Any Member of the League may, after two years' notice of its intention so to do, withdraw from the League, provided that all its international obligations and all its obligations under this Covenant shall have been fulfilled at the time of its withdrawal.

---

[1] Entered into force on January 10, 1920. The texts printed in italics indicate the amendments. Article 6 as amended has been in force since August 13, 1924, Articles 12, 13, and 15 as amended since September 26, 1924, and Article 4 as amended since July 29, 1926.

APPENDIX II

Article 2

Executive Organs

The action of the League under this Covenant shall be effected through the instrumentality of an Assembly and of a Council, with a permanent Secretariat.

Article 3

Assembly

1. The Assembly shall consist of representatives of the Members of the League.
2. The Assembly shall meet at stated intervals and from time to time, as occasion may require, at the Seat of the League or at such other place as may be decided upon.
3. The Assembly may deal at its meetings with any matter within the sphere of action of the League or affecting the peace of the world.
4. At meetings of the Assembly each Member of the League shall have one vote and may have not more than three Representatives.

Article 4

Council

1. The Council shall consist of representatives of the Principal Allied and Associated Powers [the United States of America, the British Empire, France, Italy, and Japan], together with Representatives of four other Members of the League. These four Members of the League shall be selected by the Assembly from time to time in its discretion. Until the appointment of the Representatives of the four Members of the League first selected by the Assembly, Representatives of Belgium, Brazil, Greece and Spain shall be Members of the Council.
2. With the approval of the majority of the Assembly, the Council may name additional Members of the League, whose Representatives shall always be Members of the Council; the Council with like approval may increase the number of Members of the League to be selected by the Assembly for representation on the Council.
2. *bis. The Assembly shall fix by a two-thirds' majority the rules dealing with the election of the non-permanent Members of the Council, and particularly such regulations as relate to their term of office and the conditions of re-eligibility.*
3. The Council shall meet from time to time as occasion may require, and at least once a year, at the Seat of the League, or at such other place as may be decided upon.
4. The Council may deal at its meetings with any matter within the sphere of action of the League or affecting the peace of the world.
5. Any Member of the League not represented on the Council shall be invited to send a Representative to sit as a member at any meeting of the Council during the consideration of matters specially affecting the interests of that Member of the League.
6. At meetings of the Council, each Member of the League represented on the Council shall have one vote, and may have not more than one Representative.

Article 5

Voting and Procedure

1. Except where otherwise expressly provided in this Covenant or by the terms of the present Treaty, decisions at any meeting of the Assembly or of the Council shall require the agreement of all the Members of the League represented at the meeting.

704

APPENDIX II

2. All matters of procedure at meetings of the Assembly or of the Council, including the appointment of Committees to investigate particular matters, shall be regulated by the Assembly or by the Council and may be decided by a majority of the Members of the League represented at the meeting.

3. The first meeting of the Assembly and the first meeting of the Council shall be summoned by the President of the United States of America.

Article 6

Secretariat and Expenses

1. The permanent Secretariat shall be established at the Seat of the League. The Secretariat shall comprise a Secretary-General and such secretaries and staff as may be required.

2. The first Secretary-General shall be the person named in the Annex; thereafter the Secretary-General shall be appointed by the Council with the approval of the majority of the Assembly.

3. The secretaries and the staff of the Secretariat shall be appointed by the Secretary-General with the approval of the Council.

4. The Secretary-General shall act in that capacity at all meetings of the Assembly and of the Council.

5. *The expenses of the League shall be borne by the Members of the League in the proportion decided by the Assembly.*

Article 7

Seat, Qualifications of Officials, Immunities

1. The Seat of the League is established at Geneva.

2. The Council may at any time decide that the Seat of the League shall be established elsewhere.

3. All positions under or in connection with the League, including the Secretariat, shall be open equally to men and women.

4. Representatives of the Members of the League and officials of the League when engaged on the business of the League shall enjoy diplomatic privileges and immunities.

5. The buildings and other property occupied by the League or its officials or by Representatives attending its meetings shall be inviolable.

Article 8

Reduction of Armaments

1. The Members of the League recognize that the maintenance of peace requires the reduction of national armaments to the lowest point consistent with national safety and the enforcement by common action of international obligations.

2. The Council, taking account of the geographical situation and circumstances of each State, shall formulate plans for such reduction for the consideration and action of the several Governments.

3. Such plans shall be subject to reconsideration and revision at least every 10 years.

4. After these plans shall have been adopted by the several Governments, the limits of armaments therein fixed shall not be exceeded without the concurrence of the Council.

5. The Members of the League agree that the manufacture by private enterprise of munitions and implements of war is open to grave objections. The Council shall advise how the evil effects attendant upon such manufacture can be prevented, due regard being had to the necessities of those Members of the League which are not able to manufacture the munitions and implements of war necessary for their safety.

705

6. The Members of the League undertake to interchange full and frank information as to the scale of their armaments, their military, naval and air programs and the condition of such of their industries as are adaptable to warlike purposes.

Article 9

Permanent Military, Naval and Air Commission

A permanent Commission shall be constituted to advise the Council on the execution of the provisions of Articles 1 and 8 and on military, naval and air questions generally.

Article 10

Guaranties against Aggression

The Members of the League undertake to respect and preserve as against external aggression the territorial integrity and existing political independence of all Members of the League. In case of any such aggression or in case of any threat or danger of such aggression the Council shall advise upon the means by which this obligation shall be fulfilled.

Article 11

Action in Case of War or Threat of War

1. Any war or threat of war, whether immediately affecting any of the Members of the League or not, is hereby declared a matter of concern to the whole League, and the League shall take any action that may be deemed wise and effectual to safeguard the peace of nations. In case any such emergency should arise the Secretary-General shall on the request of any Member of the League forthwith summon a meeting of the Council.

2. It is also declared to be the friendly right of each Member of the League to bring to the attention of the Assembly or of the Council any circumstance whatever affecting international relations which threatens to disturb international peace or the good understanding between nations upon which peace depends.

Article 12

Disputes to Be Submitted for Settlement

1. The Members of the League agree that, if there should arise between them any dispute likely to lead to a rupture, they will submit the matter either to arbitration *or judicial settlement* or to inquiry by the Council, and they agree in no case to resort to war until three months after the award by the arbitrators *or the judicial decision*, or the report by the Council.

2. In any case under this Article the award of the arbitrators *or the judicial decision* shall be made within a reasonable time, and the report of the Council shall be made within six months after the submission of the dispute.

Article 13

Arbitration or Judicial Settlement

1. The Members of the League agree that, whenever any dispute shall arise between them which they recognize to be suitable for submission to arbitration *or judicial settle-*

ment, and which cannot be satisfactorily settled by diplomacy, they will submit the whole subject-matter to arbitration *or judicial settlement.*

2. Disputes as to the interpretation of a treaty, as to any question of international law, as to the existence of any fact which, if established, would constitute a breach of any international obligation, or as to the extent and nature of the reparation to be made for any such breach, are declared to be among those which are generally suitable for submission to arbitration *or judicial settlement.*

3. *For the consideration of any such dispute, the court to which the case is referred shall be the Permanent Court of International Justice, established in accordance with Article 14, or any tribunal agreed on by the parties to the dispute or stipulated in any convention existing between them.*

4. The Members of the League agree that they will carry out in full good faith any award *or decision* that may be rendered, and that they will not resort to war against a Member of the League which complies therewith. In the event of any failure to carry out such an award *or decision,* the Council shall propose what steps should be taken to give effect thereto.

Article 14

Permanent Court of International Justice

The Council shall formulate and submit to the Members of the League for adoption plans for the establishment of a Permanent Court of International Justice. The Court shall be competent to hear and determine any dispute of an international character which the parties thereto submit to it. The Court may also give an advisory opinion upon any dispute or question referred to it by the Council or by the Assembly.

Article 15

Disputes Not Submitted to Arbitration or Judicial Settlement

1. If there should arise between Members of the League any dispute likely to lead to a rupture, which is not submitted to arbitration *or judicial settlement* in accordance with Article 13, the Members of the League agree that they will submit the matter to the Council. Any party to the dispute may effect such submission by giving notice of the existence of the dispute to the Secretary-General, who will make all necessary arrangements for a full investigation and consideration thereof.

2. For this purpose the parties to the dispute will communicate to the Secretary-General, as promptly as possible, statements of their case with all the relevant facts and papers, and the Council may forthwith direct the publication thereof.

3. The Council shall endeavor to effect a settlement of the dispute, and, if such efforts are successful, a statement shall be made public giving such facts and explanations regarding the dispute and the terms of settlement thereof as the Council may deem appropriate.

4. If the dispute is not thus settled, the Council either unanimously or by a majority vote shall make and publish a report containing a statement of the facts of the dispute and the recommendations which are deemed just and proper in regard thereto.

5. Any Member of the League represented on the Council may make public a statement of the facts of the dispute and of its conclusions regarding the same.

6. If a report by the Council is unanimously agreed to by the Members thereof other than the Representatives of one or more of the parties to the dispute, the Members of the League agree that they will not go to war with any party to the dispute which complies with the recommendations of the report.

7. If the Council fails to reach a report which is unanimously agreed to by the members thereof, other than the Representatives of one or more of the parties to the dis-

pute, the Members of the League reserve to themselves the right to take such action as they shall consider necessary for the maintenance of right and justice.

8. If the dispute between the parties is claimed by one of them, and is found by the Council, to arise out of a matter which by international law is solely within the domestic jurisdiction of that party, the Council shall so report, and shall make no recommendation as to its settlement.

9. The Council may in any case under this Article refer the dispute to the Assembly. The dispute shall be so referred at the request of either party to the dispute, provided that such request be made within 14 days after the submission of the dispute to the Council.

10. In any case referred to the Assembly, all the provisions of this Article and of Article 12 relating to the action and powers of the Council shall apply to the action and powers of the Assembly, provided that a report made by the Assembly, if concurred in by the Representatives of those Members of the League represented on the Council and of a majority of the other Members of the League, exclusive in each case of the Representatives of the parties to the dispute, shall have the same force as a report by the Council concurred in by all the members thereof other than the Representatives of one or more of the parties to the dispute.

Article 16

Sanctions of Pacific Settlement

1. Should any Member of the League resort to war in disregard of its covenants under Articles 12, 13 or 15, it shall *ipso facto* be deemed to have committed an act of war against all other Members of the League, which hereby undertake immediately to subject it to the severance of all trade or financial relations, the prohibition of all intercourse between their nationals and the nationals of the covenant-breaking State, and the prevention of all financial, commercial or personal intercourse between the nationals of the covenant-breaking State and the nationals of any other State, whether a Member of the League or not.

2. It shall be the duty of the Council in such case to recommend to the several Governments concerned what effective military, naval or air force the Members of the League shall severally contribute to the armed forces to be used to protect the covenants of the League.

3. The Members of the League agree, further, that they will mutually support one another in the financial and economic measures which are taken under this Article, in order to minimize the loss and inconvenience resulting from the above measures, and that they will mutually support one another in resisting any special measures aimed at one of their number by the covenant-breaking State, and that they will take the necessary steps to afford passage through their territory to the forces of any of the Members of the League which are cooperating to protect the covenants of the League.

4. Any Member of the League which has violated any covenant of the League may be declared to be no longer a Member of the League by a vote of the Council concurred in by the Representatives of all the other Members of the League represented thereon.

Article 17

Disputes Involving Non-members

1. In the event of a dispute between a Member of the League and a State which is not a Member of the League, or between States not Members of the League, the State or States not Members of the League shall be invited to accept the obligations of membership in the League for the purposes of such dispute, upon such conditions as the Council may deem just. If such invitation is accepted, the provisions of Articles 12

to 16, inclusive, shall be applied with such modifications as may be deemed necessary by the Council.

2. Upon such invitation being given, the Council shall immediately institute an inquiry into the circumstances of the dispute and recommend such action as may seem best and most effectual in the circumstances.

3. If a State so invited shall refuse to accept the obligations of membership in the League for the purposes of such dispute, and shall resort to war against a Member of the League, the provisions of Article 16 shall be applicable as against the State taking such action.

4. If both parties to the dispute when so invited refuse to accept the obligations of membership in the League for the purposes of such dispute, the Council may take such measures and make such recommendations as will prevent hostilities and will result in the settlement of the dispute.

Article 18

Registration and Publication of Treaties

Every treaty or international engagement entered into hereafter by any Member of the League shall be forthwith registered with the Secretariat and shall as soon as possible be published by it. No such treaty or international engagement shall be binding until so registered.

Article 19

Review of Treaties

The Assembly may from time to time advise the reconsideration by Members of the League of treaties which have become inapplicable, and the consideration of international conditions whose continuance might endanger the peace of the world.

Article 20

Abrogation of Inconsistent Obligations

1. The Members of the League severally agree that this Covenant is accepted as abrogating all obligations or understandings *inter se* which are inconsistent with the terms thereof, and solemnly undertake that they will not hereafter enter into any engagements inconsistent with the terms thereof.

2. In case any Member of the League shall, before becoming a Member of the League, have undertaken any obligations inconsistent with the terms of this Covenant, it shall be the duty of such Member to take immediate steps to procure its release from such obligations.

Article 21

Engagements that Remain Valid

Nothing in this Covenant shall be deemed to affect the validity of international engagements, such as treaties of arbitration or regional understandings like the Monroe Doctrine, for securing the maintenance of peace.

APPENDIX II

Article 22

Mandatory System

1. To those colonies and territories which as a consequence of the late war have ceased to be under the sovereignty of the States which formerly governed them and which are inhabited by peoples not yet able to stand by themselves under the strenuous conditions of the modern world, there should be applied the principle that the well-being and development of such peoples form a sacred trust of civilization and that securities for the performance of this trust should be embodied in this Covenant.

2. The best method of giving practical effect to this principle is that the tutelage of such peoples should be entrusted to advanced nations who by reason of their re-sources, their experience or their geopraphical position can best undertake this respon-sibility, and are willing to accept it, and that this tutelage should be exercised by them as Mandatories on behalf of the League.

3. The character of the mandate must differ according to the stage of the develop-ment of the people, the geographical situation of the territory, its economic conditions and other similar circumstances.

4. Certain communities formerly belonging to the Turkish Empire have reached a stage of development where their existence as independent nations can be provisionally recognized subject to the rendering of administrative advice and assistance by a Manda-tory until such time as they are able to stand alone. The wishes of these communities must be a principal consideration in the selection of the Mandatory.

5. Other peoples, especially those of Central Africa, are at such a stage that the Mandatory must be responsible for the administration of the territory under conditions which will guarantee freedom of conscience and religion, subject only to the mainte-nance of public order and morals, the prohibition of abuses such as the slave trade, the arms traffic and the liquor traffic, and the prevention of the establishment of fortifi-cations of military and naval bases and of military training of the natives for other than police purposes and the defense of territory, and will also secure equal oppor-tunities for the trade and commerce of other Members of the League.

6. There are territories, such as Southwest Africa and certain of the South Pacific islands, which, owing to the sparseness of their population, or their small size, or their remoteness from the centers of civilization, or their geographical contiguity to the terri-tory of the Mandatory, and other circumstances, can be best administered under the laws of the Mandatory as integral portions of its territory, subject to the safeguards above mentioned in the interests of the indigenous population.

7. In every case of mandate, the Mandatory shall render to the Council an annual report in reference to the territory committed to its charge.

8. The degree of authority, control or administration to be exercised by the Mandatory shall, if not previously agreed upon by the Members of the League, be explicitly defined in each case by the Council.

9. A permanent Commission shall be constituted to receive and examine the annual reports of the Mandatories and to advise the Council on all matters relating to the observance of the mandates.

Article 23

Social and Other Activities

Subject to and in accordance with the provisions of international conventions exist-ing or hereafter to be agreed upon, the Members of the League:

a. will endeavor to secure and maintain fair and humane conditions of labor for men, women and children, both in their own countries and in all countries to which their commercial and industrial relations extend, and for that purpose will establish and maintain the necessary international organizations;

b. undertake to secure just treatment of the native inhabitants of territories under their control;

c. will entrust the League with the general supervision over the execution of agreements with regard to traffic in women and children, and the traffic in opium and other dangerous drugs;

d. will entrust the League with the general supervision of the trade in arms and ammunition with the countries in which the control of this traffic is necessary in the common interest;

e. will make provision to secure and maintain freedom of communications and of transit and equitable treatment for the commerce of all Members of the League. In this connection, the special necessities of the regions devastated during the war of 1914–1918 shall be borne in mind;

f. will endeavor to take steps in matters of international concern for the prevention and control of disease.

Article 24

International Bureaus

1. There shall be placed under the direction of the League all international bureaus already established by general treaties if the parties to such treaties consent. All such international bureaus and all commissions for the regulation of matters of international interest hereafter constituted shall be placed under the direction of the League.

2. In all matters of international interest which are regulated by general conventions but which are not placed under the control of international bureaus or commissions, the Secretariat of the League shall, subject to the consent of the Council and if desired by the parties, collect and distribute all relevant information and shall render any other assistance which may be necessary or desirable.

3. The Council may include as part of the expenses of the Secretariat the expenses of any bureau or commission which is placed under the direction of the League.

Article 25

Promotion of Red Cross and Health

The Members of the League agree to encourage and promote the establishment and cooperation of duly authorized voluntary national Red Cross organizations having as purposes the improvement of health, the prevention of disease and the mitigation of suffering throughout the world.

Article 26

Amendments

1. Amendments to this Covenant will take effect when ratified by the Members of the League whose Representatives compose the Council and by a majority of the Members of the League whose Representatives compose the Assembly.

2. No such amendment shall bind any Member of the League which signifies its dissent therefrom, but in that case it shall cease to be a Member of the League.

INDEX

A Word to the Wise: All entries have been listed by F.L.S.; painstakingly carded, alphabetized, and consolidated by my wife, Lily Caroline Abell, my niece, Marcia Armstrong Sweet, and my neighbor, Barbara Carlton; and accurately typed by Bessie Wright. To all these good people the author is (and all readers ought to be) deeply grateful.

This is a complete index of persons, including all writers mentioned, quoted, or cited, and all the dramatis personae of our story—which is as it should be, since politics is meaningless apart from the people who play the game, who record and judge the moves, or who are led to weal or woe by the outcome. This is a good index of subjects, concepts, events, places, and problems. But see also the chronology of Treaties and the list of maps by George Brodsky—to whom the author and (I hope) all readers are profoundly indebted for historical and geographical guidance—following the Contents.

The abbreviations employed have the following meanings: $B.$ = battle; $C.$ = conference or congress; $c.$ = cited; $d.$ = death of; $f.$ = and page or year following; $ff.$ = and pages or years following; $n.$ = footnote; $q.$ = quoted; $T.$ = treaty or other international pact; $W.$ = war. Names of ships, court cases, and terms in languages other than English are italicized.

Alphabetical shorthand, in the Index as in the text, is to be transcribed as follows:

EDC	European Defense Community
FAO	Food and Agriculture Organization
GATT	General Agreement on Trade and Tariffs
ICBM	Intercontinental Ballistic Missile
ILO	International Labor Organization
ITO	International Trade Organization
IWW	Industrial Workers of the World
L. of N.	League of Nations
M-F-N	most-favored-nation
NATO	North Atlantic Treaty Organization
NSDLP	National Socialist German Workers' Party (Nazi)
OAS	Organization of American States
PMC	Permanent Mandates Commission (L. of N.)
SCAP	Supreme Command, Allied Powers (Japan)
SEATO	Southeast Asia Treaty Organization
SUNFED	Special United Nations Fund for Economic Development
U.K.	United Kingdom of Great Britain and Northern Ireland
UN	United Nations
UNAEC	United Nations Atomic Energy Commission
UNCOK	United Nations Commission on Korea
UNCURK	United Nations Commission for the Unification and Rehabilitation of Korea
UNESCO	United Nations Educational, Scientific, and Cultural Organization
USA	United States of (North) America
USSR	Union of Soviet Socialist Republics
WHO	World Health Organization

Abadan, 337
Abd-el Krim, 322
Abdul Aziz ibn-Saud, 322
Abdul Illah, 375, 426
Abdul Rahman, 389
Abdul Rahman Azzam Pasha, 324
Abdullah, Emir, 324
Abdullah Al-Khayyal, 427
Abdullah el Salimel Sabah, 317
Abdullah ibn Hussein, 375, 429
Abdullah Kahlel, 374
Abortion, 622ff.
Abu Nuwar, 429
Accession, 126
Accretion, 120, 122
Achaean League, 43
Achaemenes, 37
Acheson, Dean, 181, 183, 244, 525n., 662; q.246n., 428, 537, 667
Addis Ababa, 222
Adenauer, Konrad, 465, 485, 487, 491ff., 545, 604, 645
Adhesion, 126
Adjudication, 157f.
Adler, Mortimer J., 267, c. 268
Adler, Solomon, c.541
Adorno, T. W., c.394
Adundet, Phumiphon, 385, 611
Advisory opinions, 161ff.
Afghanistan, 612
Africa, 321f., 637ff.
African National Congress, 640
Agar, Herbert, c.679
Aggressor, definition, 250
Aisne, B., 92
Aix-la-Chapelle, C., 168, 206; Peace of, 76
Akbar, 38
Alamogordo, 657
Alaric, 50
Alaska, 88, 310, 334
Albania, 87, 164, 459, 460
Albertini, Luigi, c.104
Aldrich, Winthrop, 176
Aleman, Miguel, 630
Aleutians, 446
Alexander the Great, 30, 43f.
Alexander, King of Jugoslavia, 557
Alexander I of Russia, 82f., 206
Alexander, Franz, c.339n.
Alexander, Robert J., c.649
Alexandrine Empire, 44
Alfieri, Dino, c.467
Algeciras, Act of (1906), 327
Algeria, 322, 334, 372, 407, 569ff., 572f., 612, 637
Algerian National Liberation Front, 372
Ali Khan, Liaquat, 382, d.384

Allen, George V., 407
Allen, H. C., c.586
Allen, Raymond B., 600n.
Allenstein, 345
Aliens, 123; enemy, 130
Allied Council for Japan, 196, 449
Almond, Gabriel A., c.496, 606
Aloisi, Pompeo, 199
Alpha Centauri, 3
Alsace-Lorraine, 94, 345
Althusius, Johannes, 67
Altmark, 136
Aly Maher Pasha, 402
Ambassadors, 168ff. (See also specific names)
Amenhotep IV, 34
American Legion, 268
American Metal Company, 639
American Revolution, 77f., 133
Americanism, 587
Amerindians, 17, 633
Amery, L. S., c.578n.
Amorites, 33
Amphictyonic Council, 43
Ananda Mahidol, 385
Anderson, Orville, q.283n.
Andhra, 635
Andorra, 111n.
Andrews, F. F., c.335
Angel, Eduardo Zuleta, 228
Angell, James W., c.359n.
Angell, Norman, q.90, 103, 282n.
Anglo-Iranian Oil Company, 317, 377, 379
Angola, 309, 638
Anshen, Ruth Nanda, c.431
Antarctica, 120, 199
Anthropoid apes, 12f.
Anti-Comintern Pact, 95, 476; q.443
Antiochus III, 46
Anti-Semitism, 469ff.; German, 350ff.; USSR, 517
Antonescu, Ion, 508
Antonov, Alexei, 195
Apartheid, 349, 639f.
Appam, 135n.
Appeasement, 577ff.
Appleman, John Alan, c.142
Approbation, 126
Apter, David E., c.638n.
Aqaba, Gulf of, 122
Arab-Israeli W. (1948), 238
Arab League, 324, 374
Arabian American Oil Company, 317, 375
Aramburu, Pedro Eugenio, 631
Aramco, 317, 375
Arbela, B., 44
Arbenz, Guzman (see Guzman)

Arbitration: 152*f.*; ancient Greek, 43; arbitration treaties, general, 154*f.*; Geneva Tribunal, 134; Papacy, 56*f.*; Permanent Court of, 156, 158, 160
Archidamus, King of Sparta, *q.*152
Archimedes, 81
Arcinegas, German, *c.*649
Ardahan, 502, 544
Argentina, 154, 630; Anti-war Pact (1933), 120; recognition, 113*n.*
Arias, Arnolfo, 631
Aristides, Aelius, *c.*54
Aristotle, 42, 44; *q.*14
Aristov, Averky B., 520*n.*
Armaments, 293*ff.*
Armand Ugon, Enrique C., 162*n.*
Armas, Carlos Castillo, 118, 632
Armenian massacres, 288*n.*
Arminius, 468
Armistice, 125 (*See also* names of States for specific armistice agreements)
Arnold, G. L., 547
Arnold, R., *c.*201
Artvin, 544
Artz, Frederick B., *c.*79
Aryanism, 342, 351
Ashida, Hitoshi, 451
Asian-African Peoples' Solidarity Conference, 644
Asoka, 37*f.*
Assyrians, 36
Aswan Dam, 406*ff.*
Athenia, 135
Athens, ancient, 39*ff.*
Atlantic Charter, *q.*193
Atlantic Union Committee, 266
Atomic bomb, 440, 490, 657*ff.*, 669*ff.*
Atomic energy, 652*ff.*, 662
Atomic Energy Commission (USA), 666*f.*
Atomic spies, 667*n.*
Atrocities, 287*ff.*
Attila, 51
Attlee, Clement, 195, 228, 382, 438, 580–583, 660; *q.*260, 661
Auerbach, Stuart, *c.*551*n.*
Auriol, Vincent, 564, 569
Austin, Warren R., 162*n.*, 333, 666
Australia, 597, 610, 626
Australopithecus, 12
Austria: 74*ff.*, 198*f.*, 208, 225, 459*f.*, 544, 648; *T.* of 1955, 101, 168, 200, 603; *T.* of St. Germain, 213
Austria-Hungary, 88, 91*ff.*
Avenol, Joseph, 215, 217, 224, 226
Avulsion, 122
Ayala, Lopez de, 68
Aztecs, 37

Babbitt, George F., 588
Babylonian Empire, 33
Baccouche, Salahaddine, 373
Bacon, Eugene H., *c.*303
Bacon, Francis, *q.*62
Bacon, Roger, 81
Bacteriological warfare, 294
Badawi, Abdel Hamid, 162*n.*
Badoglio, Pietro, 460*f.*
Bagehot, Walter, *q.*652
Baghdad Pact, 383, 405*ff.*, 426*f.*, 431, 609
Bahrein Petroleum Company, 317
Bailey, T. A., *c.*606
Bakhmetiev, Boris, 169*f.*
Bakhmetiev, George, 169
Balance of power: 275*f.*, 577*ff.*; origins of, 70; USA, 591*ff.*; USA and USSR, 521*f.*
Baldwin, Stanley, 220, 577*ff.*
Balfour Declaration, 351; *q.*375*f.*
Balkan Wars (1912*f.*), 87
Bandung, C. (1955), 641*ff.*
Bao Dai, 114, 386*f.*
Bardens, Dennis, *c.*586
Barghoorn, Frederick C., *c.*394
Barker, Ernest, *c.*28
Barleycorn, John, 588
Barmine, Alexander, 182
Barnard, Chester I., 662, 665
Barnett, Vincent M., *c.*177*n.*
Barojot, Pierre, 419
Barr, Stringfellow, 268, 626; *c.*104, 649
Barrère, M., *q.*341
Bartels, Eyrina, 411
Barthou, Louis, 557
Bartlett, Ruhl J., *c.*201, 268, 606
Bartlett, Vernon, *c.*649
Baruch, Bernard, 257, 299, 662*f.*, 665; *q.*664, 666; *c.*662*n.*
Baruch Plan, 257, 662*f.*
Basdevant, Jules, 162
Bate, H. MacLean, *c.*649
Bathurst, M. E., *c.*496
Batista, Fulgencio, 631
Battistini, Lawrence H., *c.*613
Battle Act, 367
Battles: Aisne, 92; Arbela, 44; Berlin (1945), 482; Britain, 478; Bulge, 99, 482; Cannae, 46; Caporetto, 93; Chaeronea, 44; Châlons-sur-Marne, 51; Château-Thierry, 93; Dienbienphu, 386, 569; El Alamein, 97; Jutland, 93; Leipzig, 83; Leningrad, 480, 511; Lepanto, 61; Leuthen, 76; Marathon, 39; Marne, 91, 93; Midway, 97, 446; Miletus, 39; Mohács, 61; Moscow, 96, 480, 509; Navarino, 146; Okinawa, 99; Pearl Harbor, 446, 480; Plataea, 39;

Rossbach, 76; Salamis, 39; Sevastopol, 480; Somme, 92; Stalingrad, 97, 481, 509*f.*; Tannenberg, 91; Thermopylae, 39; Tours, 51, 59; Trasimene, 46; Verdun, 92; Warsaw, 502; Waterloo, 84; Zama, 46
Baudouin, Paul, 562*f.*
Baumont, Maurice, *c.*496
Baxter, James Phinney, III, *c.*294*n.*, *c.*303
Baykov, Alexander, *c.*524
Baynes, Norman H., *c.*496
Beal, John R., *q.*407*f.*; *c.*431
Beale, Howard K., *c.*606
Beard, Charles A., *q.*xi, 279, 605; *c.*303, 606
Beatty, Charles, *c.*431
Beaverbrook, Lord, 508
Bechuanaland, 349, 639
Beck, Joseph, 350; *q.*150
Beck, Ludwig von, 482
Beckel, Graham, *c.*269
Becquerel, H., 655
Beddie, James Stuart, *c.*289*n.*
Bede, the Venerable, *q.*4*f.*
Belden, Jack, *c.*541
Belgian Congo, 638
Belgium, 85*f.*, 91, 96*f.*, 114, 115, 477
Belgorod, *B.*, 511
Belisarius, 51
Bell, Philip W., *c.*586
Belligerents, 114, 128*f.*
Belshaw, Horace, *c.*649
Belshazzar, 255
Belyayev, Nikolai I., 520*n.*
Bemis, Samuel Flagg, *c.*606, 649
Benedict, Ruth, *c.*28, 394, 454
Beneš, Eduard, 559
Ben-Gurion, David, 377, 404*ff.*, 407*ff.*, 417, 419, 424; *q.*411, 423; *c.*431
Bennion, Mervin S., 129*n.*
Bentham, Jeremy, *q.*205, 361
Ben-Zvi, Itzhak, 377
Berber, F. J., *c.*269
Berendson, Carl, 332
Berg v. British and African Steam Navigation Company, 135*n.*
Beria, Lavrenti, 508, *d.*518
Berle, Adolf A., Jr., *c.*606
Berlin, *T.*, 87; Act of, 544; *B.* 482; blockade, 199, 486; *C.*, 200, 544
Bermuda, *C.*, 1953, 584
Bernadotte, Folke von, 163, 238
Bernardo, C. Joseph, *c.*303
Bernstorff, Johann von, 169
Bessarabia, 85, 96, 346, 502, 507, 514
Bethmann-Hollweg, M. A. von, *q.*91, 115
Beust, Count, *q.*207

Bevan, Aneurin, *q.*582, *c.*586
Beveridge, Lord, 267
Bevin, Ernest, 195*f.*, 236, 550, 580, *d.*582, 594, 663; *q.*581
Bey, Essad, *c.*79
Bhutan, 111*n.*
Bidault, Georges, 196, 387, 564, 566*f.*, 569
Biddle, Francis, 140, *c.*394
Bidwell, Percy, *c.*394
"Big Lie," 290
Bikini Atoll, 658
Binh Xuyen, 387
Biro-Bidjan, 351
Birth control, 624
Bishop, William W., Jr., *c.*142
Bismarck, Otto von, 87, 89, 470*f.*, 474, 477, 495, 615; *q.*277, 455
Bisson, T. A., *c.*454
Bizri, Afif, 430
Black, C. E., *c.*104, 431
Black, Davidson, 13
Blackett, P. M. S., *c.*679
Blair, Montgomery, *q.*208
Blandy, William H. E., 658
Blank, Theodore, 490, 493
Blockade, 13?, 134, 346*f.*
Bloomfield, Lincoln P., *c.*164*n.*
Blucher, V. K., 531
Blum, Léon, 223, 266, 557*ff.*, 563, *d.*564, 572; *q.*560; *c.*574
Boas, Franz, *c.*28
Bock, Ludwig von, 480, 508
Bodin, Jean, 66*f.*
Bogart, Ernest Ludlow, *c.*104
Bohlen, Charles E., 176
Bolingbroke, Lord, 70; *q.*275*f.*
Bolitho, Hector, *c.*394
Bolzano, 346
Bonaparte, Napoleon, 82*ff.*, 508, 577; *q.*80, 82
Bonin, Bogislaw von, 490
Bonnet, Georges, 150, 225, 459, 559*ff.*, 561, 563; *q.*560
Bonomi, Ivanoe, 462
Bonsonby, C. E., *q.*324*n.*
Boorman, Howard L., *c.*553
Borchard, E. M., *c.*164
Borgese, G. A., 267; *c.*269, 467
Borgia, Cesare, 63
Bormann, Martin, 140*n.*, 468
Borodin, Michael, 527, 530
Borton, Hugh, *c.*454
Bosnia-Herzegovina, 345
Bourgès-Maunoury, Maurice, 573*f.*
Bourguiba, Habib, 373
Bowles, Chester, 384; *c.*613
Boxer Rebellion, 327

Bradley, Omar N., *q*.674
Brady, Robert A., *c*.496, 586
Brain washing, 538*ff*.
Brandenburg, 74
Braun, Eva, 468
Brazil, 145*f*., 629*f*.
Breasted, James H., *c*.54
Brecher, Michael, *c*.613
Brentano, Heinrich von, 492*f*., 545
Brest-Litovsk, *T*., 92
Bretton Woods, *C*., 1943, 194, 365
Brezhnev, Leonid I., 520
Briand, Aristide, 250, 254
Bricker, John W., 190*n*.
Bricker Amendment, 190*n*.
Brierly, J. L., *c*.142
Briggs, Ellis O., 173
Briggs, Herbert W., *c*.142, 157*n*.
Bright, John, 358
"Brinkmanship," 604
Brinton, Crane, *c*.28, 679
Britain (*see* United Kingdom)
British Navy League, *q*.282*n*.
British White Paper of May 17, 1939, 352, 376
Brodie, Bernard, *c*.679
Brogan, D. W., *c*.574
Brooke, Alan, 195
Brookings Institution, *c*.606
Brown, Delmer M., *c*.394
Brown, Harrison, *c*.650
Brown, W. Norman, *c*.606, 613
Brown, William Adams, Jr., *c*.606, 613
Bruce, David, 176
Brugmans, Henri, 266
Brüning, Heinrich, 472, 492
Brussels Alliance Treaty, 567
Brussels Treaty Organization (BRUTO), 570
Bryan, William J., 151*f*.
Bryan-Chamorro, *T*. (1916), 159
Bryce, James, *c*.54
Bryson, Lyman, *c*.269
Bucar, Annabel, 182
Buddha, Gautama, 37
Buddhism, 37
Buehrig, Edward H., *c*.606
Buell, Raymond L., *c*.vii, 269, 650
Buffer states, 276
Buganda, 638
Bukovina, 507, 514
Bulganin, Nikolai A., 201, 258*f*., 414, 454, 518*ff*., 520*n*., 544*f*., 671; *q*.412, 422, 544
Bulgaria: 169; 1939, 96*f*.; Peace *T*. (1947), 198; *T*. of Neuilly, 213; *T*. with USSR (1948), 543

Bulge, *B*., 99
Bullitt, William C., 534; *q*.283*n*.
Bullock, Alan, *c*.496
Bunche, Ralph J., 238
Bundy, McGeorge, *c*.608
Bunyan, John, *q*.433
Bunyan, Paul, 588
Burchard, John Ely, *c*.680
Burdette, Franklin L., *c*.201
Bureau of Trade Marks, Copyrights and Patents, 209
Burgenland, 345
Burgess, Guy, 182
Burke, Edmund, *q*.148
Burke, Kenneth, *c*.28
Burks, Ardath W., *c*.541
Burlingame, Anson, 327
Burma, 111, 383, 385, 533
Burnham, James, 600*n*.
Burns, E. L. M., 423*f*.
Burns, James MacGregor, *c*.606
Bush, Vannevar, 662
Butland, Gilbert J., *c*.650
Butler, Harold, 216
Buttrick, John A., *c*.651
Buxton, Frank W., *q*.325*n*.
Byas, Hugh, *c*.454
Byelorussia, 185
Byeroade, Henry A., 407
Bynkershoek, Cornelius van, *q*.133
Byrnes, James F., 113*n*., 183, 191, 195*f*., 236, 484*f*., 550, 581, 594, 662*f*.; *q*.180, 661; *c*.477
Byzantium, 51*ff*., 55, 59*f*.

Cadogan, Alexander, 195
Caesar, Julius, 46
Caesar Augustus, 46*f*., 307
Cagoulards, 559
Cairo, *C*., 1943, 194
Cairo Declaration, 438
Caligula, 47
Callières, M. de, *q*.166
Cambodia, 111, 200, 386*f*., 544, 610
Cambyses, 37
Cameron, Meredith E., *c*.454
Cameroons, 328*f*., 331*f*.
Campbell, John C., *c*.606
Canaanites, 35*f*.
Canada, 181*n*., 611
Canfield, Cass, 267
Cannae, *B*., 46
Cannibalism, 25
Canning, Lord, *q*.85
Cantave, Léon, 631
Cao Dai, 387

INDEX

Capitulations, 178
Caporetto, *B.*, 93, 457
Carinthia, 199
Carlyle, Thomas, *q.*9
Carnegie, Andrew, 159
Caroline, 116
Carolines, 333
Carpatho-Ukraine, 504, 514, 560
Carpenter, C. R., *c.*12*n.*
Carr, Edward Hallett, *c.*524
Carroll, Kevin M., 380*n.*
Carroll, Lewis, *q.*6, 144, 356, 370
Carthage, 36, 46
Casablanca, *C.*, 1943, 194
"Cash and carry," 136
Cassel, G., *c.*394
Castle, Eugene W., *c.*613
Castro, Fidel, 631
Catherine II, 76, 78
Catroux, Georges, 372
"Caucasian" peoples, 17
Cavour, Conte di, 87
Cecil, Robert, 212
Cecil-Requin, *T.* (1923), *q.*250
Central American Court of Justice, 159
Central Intelligence Agency, 185*n.*
Ceram, C. W., *c.*28, 54
Cervantes, *q.*61
Ceylon, 111, 383, 623
Chadwick, H. Munro, *c.*394
Chaeronea, *B.*, 44
Chalmers, Henry, *c.*394
Châlons-sur-Marne, *B.*, 51
Chamberlain, Houston Stewart, *c.*342
Chamberlain, Lawrence H., *c.*607
Chamberlain, Neville, 476, 504*f.*, 559, 577*ff.*, *d.*579; *q.*223; *c.*587
Chandragupta Maurya, 37
Chandrasekhar, S., *c.*650
Chang, Hsueh-Liang, 530*f.*
Chang Tso Lin, 527, 530
Chang Wen-tien, 537
Chapultepec, Act of, 319
Chargés d'affaires, 168*f.*
Charlemagne, 51*f.*, 59, 468
Charles the Fat, 52
Charles V, 61, 64, 82, 285
Charles VIII, 63
Charles XII, 75
Charter of UN, 227*f.*, 682–702
Chase, Eugene P., *c.*269
Chataigneau, Yves, 199
Château-Thierry, *B.*, 93
Chautemps, Camille, 559, 563
Cheever, D. S., *c.*201, 269
Chen, Stephen, *c.*541
Chen, T. C., *c.*142

Chen Yun, 537
Cherwell, Viscount, *q.*247*n.*
Chevalier, Maurice, 186
Chiang Kai-shek, 111*n.*, 113*n.*, 147, 194*f.*, 230, 242, 438, 530*ff.*, 549*f.*, 599, 601, 604, 642; *c.*541
Chiappe, Jean, 559
Chicago Tribune, 160*n.*
Chicherin, George, 471
Childs, James R., *c.*201
Chile, 154, 631
China: ancient, 16, 38, 526; modern, 147, 186, 194, 196, 225, 327*ff.*, 441, 525*ff.*; 1914*f.*, 92; 1937*f.*, 444, 531*ff.*; 1939*f.*, 96*f.*; Peoples' Republic, 536*ff.*; population, 623; recognition, 113*n.*; and USSR, 534, 543
"China Lobby," 534*f.*
Christendom, 56*f.*
Christianity, 36, 50*f.*
Christina, Queen of Sweden, 167
Chou En-lai, 387, 532*ff.*, 535*f.*, 537*ff.*, 543, 642*f.*, 645; *q.*552, 643
Chowdhuri, R. N., *c.*335
Chu Teh, 537
Chung, Kyung Cha, *c.*269
Churchill, Winston S., 96, 99, 139, 193*ff.*, 265*f.*, 438, 462, 505, 511, 514, 550, 555, 563, 580*ff.*, 595, 598, 660, 663*f.*, 667; *q.*376, 382, 455, 480, 508, 514, 560, 579, 582; *c.*79, 104, 587
Ciano, Galeazzo, 150, 444, 456, 460, 561
Ciano-Perth Accord (1938), 224
Cicero, *q.*127
Cineas, *q.*298
Cipola, Gioacchino, 464
Citizens' Committee for United Nations Reform, 266
City of Flint, 135
Civil War: American, 88, 112, 134, 138; Chinese, 534*ff.*; Russian, 499*ff.*; Spanish, 558*f.*
Civilization, 15*f.*, 19*f.*, 26*f.*
Clark, Grenville, 267
Clark, Grover, *c.*335
Clark, J. Reuben, 319
Clark, Mark, 113*n.*, 451
Clarke, Arthur C., *c.*680
Claude, Inis L., Jr., *c.*269, 394
Claudius, 47
Clausewitz, Carl von, *q.*284; *c.*303
Clay, Lucius, 485, 486*f.*; *c.*496
Clayton, Will L., 266
Clemenceau, Georges, 93; *q.*291
Clement V, 53
Clementis, Vladimir, 551
Clive, Robert, 76

718

Clough, Shepard B., c.28
Cobban, Alfred, c.394
Cobden, Richard, 358
Cobden, T., 358
Coblentz, Stanton A., c.303
Coblenz, Constance G., c.607
Coexistence, 499ff.
Cold War, 99f., 235, 513ff., 516ff., 542ff., 580ff., 594ff., 599ff., 612, 670ff.
Cole, G. D. H., c.587
Cole, W. Sterling, 669f.
Collective Measures Committee of UN, 244
Collective Security, 35, 138, 203f., 232f., 260f.
College of Fetials, 47
Colombia, 171n., 631
Colombo Plan, 626
Colombus, John C., c.142
Columbus, Christopher, 633
Colonialism, 306ff.
Combatants, 129f.
Comecon, 544
Cominform, 413, 514, 544, 550, 554
Comintern, 502, 514, 559
Commager, Henry S., c.104
Commissions of Inquiry, 151f.
Committee to Frame a World Constitution, 267
Committee of National Liberation, French, 563f.; Italian, 462
Communism, 436ff., 498ff. (See also China; USSR; specific names of other States)
Communist Parties, 530ff.; Chinese, 540; French, 564ff.; German, 473, 485ff.; Indian, 635ff.; Italian, 462ff.; Japanese, 451f.; USSR, 512ff.
Compagnie Française de Pétrole, 379
Compromis, arbitral, 125, 153, 155, 156
Compton, Arthur Holly, c.680
Conant, James B., 662
Concert of Europe, 207
Conciliation, 149f.
Condliffe, J. B., c.394
Conferences: international, 191ff.; major international: Aix-la-Chapelle, 168, 206; Asian-African Peoples' Solidarity, 644; Bandung, 641ff.; Berlin (1954), 200, 544; Bermuda (1953), 584; Bretton Woods, 194, 365; Cairo (1943), 194; Casablanca, 194; Coolidge (1927), 253; Constantinople (1888), 147, 408; q.400; Dumbarton Oaks, 194, 232, 265; Geneva (1954), 200, 386f., 544, 569, 601; Geneva, Summit (1955), 101, 201, 492, 544, 603, 670; Genoa (1922), 471; Hague (1899 and 1907), 128, 131, 133n., 135,

154, 156, 158; Laibach, 206; London, Naval (1908–1909), 158 (1930), 253; Munich, 226, 476, 503, 559; Moscow (1943), 194 (1944), 195 (1945), 196, 661 (1955), 200; Pan-American, 319ff., 118n.; Potsdam (1945), 195, 483; Quebec (1944), 194; San Francisco (1945), 227f. (1951), 199; Teheran, 194; Tilsit, 82; Troppeau, 206; Utrecht, 167; Verona, 206; Vienna (1815), 84, 167 (1955), 200, 206; Washington (1921), 253f.; Westphalia, 191; Yalta, 195, 232, 514, 534
Confucianism, 526, 553
Confucius, q.525
Congo, 309
Congress (USA) and foreign affairs, 187ff.
Congress Party (India), 635ff.
Connally, Thomas, 162n.
Conquest as basis of title, 120 (See also Pact of Paris; Paris; Stimson Doctrine)
Consolato del Mare, 58, 62
Constantine the Great, 50
Constantine Paleologus, 61
Constantinople Convention of 1888, 400ff.
Constitutional Convention of 1787 (USA), 261f.
Constitutions: Chinese, 539; French, 564; Indian, 635; Italian, 462f.; USA, 187f.
Consulate (Roman), 45f.
Consuls, 178f.
"Continuous voyage," 135
Contraband of war, 131, 134f.
Conventions, 125 (See also Treaties)
Cook, Fred J., c.602n.
Cook, Robert C., c.650
Cook, Thomas I., c.303
Coolidge, Calvin, 253, 588; q.341
Coolidge, C. (1927), 253
Coon, Carleton S., c.28
Cooper, R. M., c.202
Copernicus, 81
Corbett, P. E., c.164
Cordova, Roberto, 162n.
Corfu, 146, 163, 218, 459
Corn laws, 358
Corridor, Polish, 94
Cortines, Adolfo Ruiz, 630
Corwin, E. S., c.202
Cossack, 135
Costa Rica, 159, 631
Coty, René, 569; c.574
Coughlin, Father, q.160n.
Coulondre, Robert, 561; q.560
Council of Europe, 266

INDEX

Council of Foreign Ministers, 191, 195*ff.*, 486, 544

Council on Foreign Relations, *c.*607

Counts, George S., 266

Coupland, R., *c.*394

Courts (in international relations), 189*ff.* (*See also* specific names of cases)

Cousins, Norman, 267; *c.*680

Covenant of Human Rights, 355

Covenant of League of Nations, 213*f.*; *q.*328, 703*ff.*

Cowles, Virginia, *c.*587

Cox, Edmund C., *q.*282*n.*

Craig, Gordon A., *c.*202, 496

Crankshaw, Edward, *c.*524, 553

Cranston, Alan, 267

Cremona, P., *c.*467

Cressey, George B., *c.*541

Crete (ancient), 39

Cretzianu, Alexandre, *c.*553

Crimean War, 86*f.*, 499

Cripps, Stafford, 382, 508

Croesus, 37; *q.*272

Cromagnon man, 14*f.*

Cromwell, Oliver, 81, 152

Crow, John A., *c.*650

Crucé, Emeric, 204

Crum, Bartley C., *q.*325*n.*

Crusade for Freedom, 413

Crusades, 58, 60

Cuba, 88, 310, 319, 631

Culbertson, Ely, 266

Cultures, 15*f.*

Cumberland, C. C., *c.*650

Curie, Marie, 655

Curtis, H. J., 660

Curtis, John Shelton, *c.*524

Curtis, Lionel, 267; *c.*269

Curzon, Lord, 329

Curzon Line, 195, 514

Cushing, Caleb, 327   [109*ff.*

Custom (as source of international law),

Customs unions, 364*f.*

Cynoscephalae, *B.*, 46

Cyprus, 407, 410*f.*, 419, 611*f.*

Cyrankiewicz, Josef, 413

Cyrus, King, 36*f.*, 272

Czechoslovakia, 93, 111, 226, 475*f.*, 550*f.*, 556, 558*f.*

D'Abernon, Viscount, *c.*578*n.*

Dahl, Robert A., *c.*202

Dairen, 195, 543, 550

Dakin, Edwin Franden, *c.*19*n.*, 28

Daladier, Edouard, 559*ff.*, 561*ff.*; *q.*560; *c.*574

Dallin, David J., *c.*553

Dangerfield, R. I., *c.*202

Dante Alighieri, *q.*49, 53, 204

Danube, 399*ff.*; European Commission, 207, 400*f.*

Danzig, 213, 215, 251

Dardanelles, 479

Darius I, 37, 39

Darwin, Charles, *c.*12, 28

Daughters of the American Revolution, 268

Davies, John, 533

Davies, John Paton, Jr., 181

Davis, Garry, 267

Davis, Helen Miller, *c.*431

D'Avraux, Count, 167

Dawes Plan, 362

Dawson, Charles, 13

Day, Clarence, *q.*1

Dayan, Moshe, 417

Deak, Francis, *c.*142

Dean, Gordon, 670, *c.*680

Dean, Vera Micheles, *c.*524, 607

De Bono, Emilio, *c.*467

Debs, Eugene V., 588

Declaration of war, 188 (*See also* Wars)

Declarations, 125 (*See also* Treaties)

De Gaulle, Charles, 194, 299, 562*ff.*, 566*f.*; *c.*574

De Lattre, Jean, 483

Delbos, Yvon, 558

De Martinie, Raymond, *c.*164

Democracy, 435*ff.*, 555*ff.* (*See also* specific democratic States)

Demosthenes, 44

Denmark, 85, 96*f.*, 477

Dennett, Raymond, *c.*524

Dennis, Eugene, 551

Dennis, Lawrence, *c.*369*n.*, 607, 616*n.*

Dennison, Eleanor E., *c.*202

Dertinger, Georg, 494

De Russett, Alan, *c.*269

Desborough, Lady, 578*n.*

Descola, Jean, *c.*79

Deterrence, 282*f.*, 302*f.*, 604*f.*

Deutsch, Karl W., *c.*394

Deutsche Wehr, *q.*286*n.*

Deutscher, Isaac, *c.*524, 553

De Visscher, Charles, 142

DEW-line, 673*f.*

Dexter, Lewis A., *q.*340*n.*

Dhahram, 375

Diaspora, 36, 350

Diefenbaker, John, 611

Diehl, Charles, *c.*54

Dienbienphu, *B.*, 386, 569

INDEX

Dies, Martin, 588, *q*.284*n*., 508
Dillon, Douglas C., 176
Diocletian, 50
Diplomacy: 148*f*., 166*f*., 279*f*.; ancient, Greek, 42; Papal, 56*f*.; Roman, 47; modern, "dollar," 312, 360*n*., 380; origins of, 62*f*.
Diplomatic missions, 169*f*.
Diplomatic privileges, 170*f*.
Diplomatic recognition (*see* Recognition)
Diplomatic ruptures, 145*f*.
Dirksen, Herbert von, *c*.496
Disarmament, 252*f*., 257*f*., 672*ff*.
Discovery and occupation, 119
Disengagement, 258*f*., 489*f*., 495, 606
Disraeli, Benjamin, 400*f*.
Dixon, Owen, 240
Djang Chu, *c*.541
Djilas, Milovan, *c*.553
Djuanda, 390*f*.
Dobb, Maurice, *c*.524
Dobriansky, L. E., 600*n*.
Dodd, Martha, *c*.202
Dodd, William E., *q*.172
Dodd, William E., Jr., *c*.202
Dodecanese Islands, 457
Doenitz, Karl, 140*n*., 483; *q*.482
Dogger Bank affair, 151
Doihara, Kenji, 141*n*.
Dollar diplomacy, 312, 360*n*., 380
Dollfuss, Engelbert, 459
Dombrowski, Roman, *c*.467
Domestic jurisdiction, 139
Dominican Republic, 632
Donne, John, *q*.628
Donovan, Robert J., *c*.607
Donovan, William J., *c*.266*n*.
Dooley, Mr., *q*.172
Doolittle, Jimmy, 448
Doriot, Jacques, 557, 559
Dorls, Fritz, 485
Dorn, Walter L., *c*.79
Douglas, William O., 267, 627; *c*.613
Douhet, Giulio, 299
Downing Street, 183
Draper, Theodore, *c*.553, 574
Draper, William N., Jr., 485
Drummond, Donald L., *c*.607
Drummond, Eric, 215
Druse tribesmen, 322
Dryopithecus, 12
Dual Alliance (1894), 89
Dubois, Eugene, 13
Dubois, Pierre, 204
Du Bois, W. E. Burghardt, *c*.650
Duclos, Jacques, 564
Due diligence, 116, 134

Dulles, Foster Rhea, *c*.607
Dulles, John Foster, 147, 162*n*., 181, 183, 187, 230, 259, 404*ff*., 423*ff*., 430*f*., 451*f*., 465, 488, 490, 493, 544, 570, 598, 601, 603*ff*., 609*ff*., 644, 645; *q*.175, 246*n*., 409, 414, 424, 598, 604, 670
Dumbarton Oaks, C., 194, 232, 265
Duncan, Ronald, *c*.335
Dunkirk, 477
Dunn, F. S., *c*.202, 269
Dunn, James C., 463
Dutra, E. G., 146

Eagleton, Clyde, *c*.228*n*., 269
Earle, Edward Meade, *c*.304, 574
Earle, George H., 482
Earth, 2*f*. (*See also* Satellites)
East Africa, 328
East Prussia, 195
Eastern question, 207 (*See also* Ottoman Empire; Turkey)
Eban, Abba, 417; *c*.431
Ebenstein, William, *c*.28, 496
Eberstadt, Ferdinand, 662
Eckstein, Alexander, *c*.553
Economic and Financial Organization (L. of N.), 216
Economic and Social Council (UN), 228, 233
Ecuador, 631
EDC, 488*ff*., 569, 570
Eden, Anthony, 194*f*., 201, 223, 258, 404*ff*., 412, 544, 572, 580*ff*., 584*ff*.; *q*.661
Edward VIII, 575
Edwin, King of Northumbria, 4
Eghbal, Manouchehr, 380*n*.
Ego, 25, 339*f*.
Egypt: ancient, 16, 33*f*., 36; modern, 147, 316*f*., 324*f*., 374, 399*ff*., 460; 1956*f*., 399*ff*., 585
Ehrenburg, Ilya, *q*.341; *c*.574
Ehrmann, Henry W., *c*.574
Einaudi, Luigi, 462, 465
Einstein, Albert, 655*f*., 660, *d*.671
Einzig, Paul, *c*.394
Eisenhower, Dwight D., 97, 101, 201, 230, 245, 246, 258, 266, 379, 386, 404*ff*., 428*ff*., 452, 466, 483, 488, 511, 524, 544, 570, 584, 598, 600*n*., 603, 606, 616*n*., 622*n*., 632, 644, 645, 647, 670; *q*.259, 303, 411, 419, 422, 424, 544, 601, 604; *c*.104
Eisenhower Doctrine, 246, 428*ff*., 466
Ekirch, Arthur A., Jr., *c*.304
El Alamein, *B*., 97
El Salvador, 159

INDEX

Elam, 36
Elites, 22f.
Elizabeth II, 573, 575, 584f., 639
Elliot, William Y., c.202, 587, 607
Ellis, Howard S., c.394, 613
Ellis, I. Ethan, c.607
Ellsworth, P. T., c.394
Embargo, 145f.
Embree, John P., c.454
Emergency Committee of Atomic Scientists, q.666
Emerson, Rupert, c.613
Emmanuel, Victor (see Victor Emmanuel)
Engels, Friedrich, 549, 619; q.498
Engholm, Carl, 425
England (18th Century), 75, 78 (See also United Kingdom)
Eniwetok, 658, 669
Enosis, 612
Entente cordiale, 89
Envoys extraordinary and ministers plenipotentiary, 168f.
Eoanthropus dawsoni, 13
Equality, right of, 116f.
Erhard, Ludwig, 491
Ernst, Karl, 474
Estonia, 93, 113n., 251, 502, 506f.
Ethiopia, 219f., 252, 321, 327, 457, 558, 646; conquest of, 221f., 459
Etorofu Island, 446
Etruscans, 45
Eugénie, Empress, 400
Eupen, 345
Euratom, 366
Euripides, 44
Europa publications, c.587
European Commission of the Danube, 207, 400f.
European Movement, 266
European Payments Union, 365
European Union of Federalists, 266
Evans, Trevor, c.587
Executive agreements, 125f., 188
Exequaturs, 112, 178
Explorer, 673n.
Extradition, 35, 123
Extraterritoriality, 124, 178, 449, 530, 533; c.79
Eyre, Edward, c.79

Fabres, Donnedieu de, 140
Fainsod, Merle, c.524
Fairbank, John King, c.541
Falkenhorst, Nicholas von, 508
Falkland Islands, 120
Fall, Bernard B., c.394

Fanfani, Amintore, 466
FAO, 234
Far Eastern Commission, 196, 449
Farmer, Fyke, 267
Farouk, King, 316f., 324, 402
Farrand, Max, c.262n.
Fascism, 434ff., 457ff., 556f.
Fast, Howard, q.551
Faubus, Orval, 647
Faure, Edgar, 201, 258, 544, 566, 571
Fay, Sidney B., c.104
Fearey, Robert A., c.454
Federal Union, Inc., 265f., 267
Federalism, 264f.
Federalist, The, q.263
Feiling, Keith, c.587
Feis, Herbert, 547; c.454, 541
Feisal II, 375
Fenelon, 71
Feng Yu-hsiang, 527, 530f.
Fenwick, Charles G., c.142
Ferdinand, Francis, 91
Ferdinand III, 167
Ferrell, Robert H., c.269
Fermi, Enrico, 655
Fernau, Friedrich Wilhelm, c.431
Field, Carter, c.662n.
Fifield, Russell H., c.304
"Fifth Columnists," 287
Figl, Leopold, 200, 544
Fignole, Pierre, 631
Figueres, José, 631
Finer, Herman, c.104, 269, 467
Finkelstein, Lawrence S., c.332n.
Finland, 85, 93, 362, 516, 545, 561; W. with USSR (1939), 96f., 226, 499, 507; T. (1947), 198
Finletter, Thomas K., c.304
Fischer, John, c.607
Fischer, Louis, c.335, 471n., 524, 547
Fisher, Admiral, q.282n.
Fisher, Harold H., c.524
Five Power T. (1922), 253
Five Year Plans (see India; USSR)
Flandin, Pierre-Etienne, 559, 563; q.560
Fleckamore, Christopher, 166
Fleming, Denna Frank, c.165, 269
Fletcher, Admiral, 97
Fleury, André de, q.205
Florence, 63f.
Floridas, 85
Foch, Ferdinand, 93, 299
Folger, John C., 176
Folsom man, 17n.
Foo Ping-sheung, 194
Foot, Michael, c.431
Ford, Alan W., c.394

Foreign Offices, 182*f.*, 184*f.*, 187*f.*
Foreign Services, 175*f.*, 179*f.*, 182
Formosa, 124*n.*, 147, 199, 441, 537*f.*, 540, 596, 601, 603, 610, 642; *T.* with USA (1954), 602*f.*
Formosa Resolution, 603
Fortunate Dragon, 671
Fosdick, Dorothy, *c.*304
Foster, John W., *q.*175
Foster, William Z., *c.*524
Four Freedoms, 592
Fox, William T. R., *c.*228*n.*, 304, 666*n.*
France: 555*ff.*; 18th Century, 74*f.*, 78; Napoleonic, 82; 1870*f.*, 88; 1914*f.*, 91*f.*; 1939*f.*, 96*f.*; 1956*f.*, 399*ff.*; colonial empire, 309; Constitution (1946), 189; *q.*189*n.*; foreign affairs, 184, 188; German rearmament, 490; nonaggression *T.*, Germany, 476, 560; *T.*, Czechoslovakia (1935), 557; *T.*, Turkey (1939), 560; *T.*, UK (1947), 567; *T.*, USA (1778), 112, 589*f.*; *T.*, USSR (1935), 557; *T.*, USSR (1944), 567; *W.*, Franco-Prussian, 87*f.*, 207*f.*; *W.*, French-Indian, 76; World War I, 91*f.*; World War II, 96*f.*
Francis of Austria, 206
Francis I of France, 70; *q.*285
Francis, David R., 169*f.*
Franco, Francisco, 95, 114, 371, 563, 604
Frank, Hans, 140*n.*
Frank, Tenney, *c.*54
Frank, Waldo, *c.*431
Frankel, Charles, *c.*28
Franklin, Benjamin, 172
Franks, 51
Frazer, James, *c.*26*n.*, 28
Frederick the Great, 71, 78, 338, 475, 495; *q.*76
Frederick William of Prussia, 206
Fredland, J. R., *c.*304
Free trade, 358*ff.*
Freedom of the seas, 135*f.*
Freeman, Harrop, *c.*262*n.*
Freidin, Seymour, *c.*496
Frenay, Henry, 266
French Yellow Book of 1914, *q.*289*n.*
Freud, Sigmund, 25; *c.*26*n.*, 54
Frick, Wilhelm, 140*n.*
Fried, John H. E., *c.*496
Friedeburg, 468
Friedrich, Carl J., *c.*79
Frischauer, Willi, *c.*496
Fritzsche, Hans, 140*n.*
Fuchs, Klaus, 667*n.*
Fulbright, J. William, 407
Fuller, J. F. C., *c.*104, 304

Functionalists, 209*f.*
Funk, Walter, 140*n.*
Furniss, Edgar S., Jr., *c.*574, 607
Furnivall, J. S., *c.*335
Furtseva, Ekaterina, 520

Gaevernitz, Gero V. S., *c.*292*n.*
Gaillard, Felix, 573
Gaitskell, Hugh, 547, 584
Galaxies, 2
Galbraith, John Kenneth, *c.*104
Galileo, 81
Galindez, Jesus de, 632
Gama, Vasco da, 75
Gamelin, Maurice, 299, 557*ff.*
Gandhi, Mohandas, 381*ff.*, *d.*384, 635
Garcia-Mora, Manuel R., *c.*165
Gardner, Richard N., *c.*587
Garibaldi, Giuseppe, 87
Gasperi, Alcide de, 266, 462*ff.*, 465
Gatzke, Hans W., *c.*496
Gauls, 45
Gaus, John, *c.*337*n.*
Gayn, Mark, *c.*454
Gaza Strip, 419*ff.*, 423*f.*
Gbedemah, Kimla Agbell, 646
Gedye, G. E. R., *c.*587
Geer v. Conn., 189*n.*
General Agreement on Trade and Tariffs (GATT), 365, 366*f.*
Genet, "Citizen," 113
Geneva: Arbitration Tribunal, 134; *C.* (1954), 200*f.*, 386*f.*, 544, 569, 601; Convention (1949), 132; Protocol of 1924, *q.*250; Summit *C.* (1955), 201
Genoa, *C.* (1922), 471
Genocide Convention, 132, 353
Gentilis, Albericus, 68
Geopolitics, 299*f.*
George V, 575
George VI, 575
Gerard, James W., 169
Gerig, B., *c.*335
German Confederation, 85
German Democratic Republic, 412, 487*ff.*, 493
German Federal Republic, 487*ff.*
Germany: 467*ff.*, 1914*f.*, 91*f.*; 1939*f.*, 96*f.*; Anti-Comintern Pact (1936), *q.*443; Anti-Semitism, 350*ff.*; Belgium (1914), 115; Constitution (1949), *q.*189*n.*, 487; disarmament, 253*f.*; Jugoslavia, 146; L. of N., 215, 218, 254; Naval Pact (1935), 255, 475*f.*; nonaggression pacts, 475, 476, 560; occupation zones, 195; reparations (1947*f.*), 198; *T.*,

INDEX

Italy (1939), 460; *T.* of Peace (1945*f.*), 198; *T.*, Rapallo (1922), 471; *T.*, USA (1923), *q.*364*n.*; *T.* of Versailles, 213, 254; Triplice Pacts, 444, 460, 477, 479, 481; unification of, 87*f.*; *W.*, Franco-Prussian, 87*f.*, 207*f.*; *W.* of Liberation, 475; *W.*, Seven Weeks', 87; *W.*, Seven Years', 77; *W.*, Thirty Years', 67; withdrawal from disarmament *C.*, 254; withdrawal from L. of N., 254; World War I, 91*f.*; World War II, 96*f.*, 487*ff.*

Gero, Erno, 414*f.*

Gerschenkron, Alexander, *c.*496

Gerson, Louis L., *c.*607

Geyl, Pieter, *c.*28

Ghalibbin Ali, 430

Ghana, 111, 230, 637, 646

Ghavam, Ahmed, 236, 379

Ghent, *T.*, 85, 145

Ghibellines, 53

Ghulam Mohammed, 384

Gianninni, Guglielmo, 463

Giap, Gen., 386

Gibb, H. A. R., *c.*335

Gibbon, Edward, 49, 50; *q.*78

Gibson, Hugh, *c.*467

Gilbert, Allan H., *c.*79

Gilbert, Prentiss B., 218

Giolitti, Giovanni, 457

Girard, William S., 124*n.*, 194

Gleason, D. Everett, *c.*607

Glubb, John Bagot, 406

Gluck, Maxwell H., 176

Goa, 645

Gobineau, Arthur de, *c.*342

Godfrey, E. Drexel, Jr., *c.*574

Goebbels, Paul J., 140*n.*, 288*n.*, 290, *d.*468, 485, 581; *q.*289*n.*, 468

Goerdeler, Karl, 482

Goering, Hermann, 140*n.*, 351*n.*, 469; *q.*473

Goerlitz, Walter, *c.*496

Goitein, S. D., *c.*431

Gold, Harry, 667*n.*

Gold Coast, 637

Gold standard, 361*f.*

Goldman, Eric F., *c.*607

Gomulka, Wladyslaw, 413, 551*f.*, 604

"Good Neighbor" policy, 118*n.*, 319*f.*

Good Offices Committee (UN), 149, 245

Goodrich, Leland M., *c.*269

Gordon, Morton, *c.*607

Gottschalk, Louis R., *c.*104

Gourevitch, Boris, *c.*269

Graf Spee, 121, 136

Graham, Frank P., 240

"Grand Design" of Henry IV, 204

Grandi, Dino, 460

Great Britain (*see* United Kingdom)

Great Depression, 95, 362*f.*, 472, 622

Greece: 460; ancient, 38*f.*; 1939*f.*, 96*f.*; 1944*f.*, 514; Cyprus, 612; independence, 86*f.*, 111, 207; invasion and conquest of (1941), 477

Greene, Fred, *c.*539*n.*, 636*n.*

Greenglass, David, 667*n.*

Grew, Joseph C., *q.*173; *c.*454

Grey, Edward, *q.*91; *c.*104

Grindrod, Muriel, *c.*467

Grodzins, Morton, *c.*394

Groesz, Bishop, 416

Gromyko, Andrei, 236, 520, 666; *q.*665

Gronchi, Giovanni, 465, 466

Grotewohl, Otto, 485, 487*f.*, 494*f.*, 545

Gross, Leo, *c.*425*n.*

Grotius, Hugo, 68*f.*, 132, 167, 204; *q.*67, 108, 119, 125

Groves, Leslie R., 662, 655; *q.*660

Grow, Robert W., *q.*283*n.*

Groza, Petru, 514

Gruliow, Leo, *c.*553

Guardia, Ernesto de la, Jr., 631

Guatemala, 118, 159, 632

Guderian, Heinz, *c.*496

Guelfs, 53

Guerrero, José Gustavo, 162

Guerrillas, 130

Guest, Edgar, 588

Guidi, Rachele, 456

Guizado, José Ramon, 631

Gunther, John, *c.*650

Gupta Empire, 38

Gurney, Henry, 389

Guzman, Jacobo Arbenz, 118, 632

H-bomb, 658*ff.*, 669*ff.*

Haber, Fritz, 351*n.*

Habomoi, 454, 545

Habicht, Max, *c.*165

Hachiya, Michihiko, *c.*680

Hackworth, Green H., 162; *c.*142

Hadrian, 49

Haeckel, Ernst, 13

Hague *C.* (1899, 1907), 128, 131, 133*n.*, 135, 154, 156, 158

Hague Conventions: (1899, 1907), 131, 133*n.*, 135, 156, 158 (1907), 128, 154; *q.*149, 151, 152

Hahn, Emily, *c.*541

Haines, C. Grove, *c.*431, 650

Haiti, 310, 319, 631

Haj Amin el Husseini, 323

Hale, O. J., *c.*202

724

INDEX

Halifax, Lord, 150, 225, 459, 505, 561, 579; *q*.224; *c*.587
Hall, H. Duncan, *c*.587
Hall, W. E., *c*.116*n*., 142
Halle, Louis J., *c*.304, 422*n*.
Halperin, S. William, *c*.467
Hamaguchi, Yuko, *d*.443
Hambro, Carl, *q*.226
Hambro, Edvard, 163
Hamilton, Alexander, 299, 590; *q*.263
Hammarskjold, Dag, 231, 406, 423*f*.; *q*.237
Hammer, Ellen J., *c*.394
Hammond, Mason, *c*.54
Hammurabi, 33, 37
Hancock, John, 662
Handlin, Oscar, *c*.394
Hango, 507
Hannibal, 46
Hapsburgs, 52, 74, 93, 468*f*.
Harahap, Bernanuddin, 390
Harding, Warren G., 253
Hare, Raymond A., 407
Haring, Douglas G., *c*.454
Harlow, Ralph S., *q*.325*n*.
Haroun-al-Raschid, 59
Harper, Samuel N., *c*.337*n*., 524
Harriman, Averill, 196, 377, 508
Harrington, Donald, 267, 598
Hart, B. H. Liddell, 299, 490; *c*.304, 524
Hart, The, 135*n*.
Harvey, Heather, *c*.587
Harvey, William, 81
Harwell, William A., 267
Hashem, Ibrahim, 429
Haskins, Caryl P., *c*.28
Hassan al Atassi, 375
Hassell, Ulrich von, 482
Hatay, 560
Hatoyama, Ichiro, 450*ff*., 454
Hatta, Mohammed, 390
Hattushilish III, 34*f*.
Haushofer, Albrecht, 301, 482
Haushofer, Heinz, 301
Haushofer, Karl, 300*f*., 474
Haviland, H. Field, Jr., *c*.269
Hawaiian Islands, 88, 334
Hawariati, Tecla, 221
Hawtrey, R. G., *q*.284; *c*.304
Hay, John, 188; *q*.327; *c*.280*n*.
Haya de la Torre, Victor Raul, 170–171*n*.
Hayari, Ali, *q*.429
Hayes, C. J. H., *c*.104, 337*n*., 340*n*., 394
Hayman, Robert, *q*.272
Hazard, John N., *c*.553
Hearst press, 160*n*.
Heath, Donald R., *c*.169
Hebrews, 36

Hegedus, Andras, 415
Hegel, Georg, *q*.66
Heidelberg man, 13
Heilperin, Michael A., *c*.394
Heimatrecht, 355
Helldorf, W. von, 482
Hellenes, 39*f*.
Hemleben, Sylvester John, *c*.269
Henderson, Arthur, *d*.254, 561
Henderson, Loy W., 410*ff*., 430
Henderson, Neville, *c*.587
Hendry, James Macleod, *c*.202
Henriques, Robert, *c*.431
Henry the Fowler, 52
Henry IV, Emperor, 224
Henry IV, King of France, 204
Henry VII, Emperor, 53
Henry VIII, King of England, 70
Herder, Gottfried, *q*.338
Herring, Hubert, *c*.650
Herriot, Edouard, 204, *d*.573; *q*.565
Hersey, John, *c*.662*n*., 680
Hershey, A. S., *c*.142
Herter, Christian, 181*n*.; *q*.186
Hertz, Frederick, *c*.394
Hertzler, J. C., *c*.650
Herzl, Theodore, *q*.351
Hess, Rudolph, 140*n*., 300, 469, 477
Heuss, Theodore, 487, 492
Hexner, Ervin, *c*.394
Higashi-Kuni, Naruhiko, 440
Higgins, A. P., *c*.142
High seas, 121
Higham, John, *c*.394
Hilaili Pasha, 402
Hilger, Gustav, *c*.496
Hill, David Jayne, *q*.52*n*.; *c*.54, 63*n*., 167*n*.
Hill, Norman, *c*.142, 202, 269
Hill, Russell, *c*.496
Hilton, James, *q*.678*n*.
Himmler, Heinrich, 140*n*., 468
Hindenburg, Paul von, 139, 472*f*., *d*.474
Hinduism, 37
Hinterland doctrine, 120
Hiranuma, Kiichiro, 141*n*.
Hirohito, Emperor, 446; *q*.440, 449
Hiroshima, 99, 132, 440, 657
Hirota, Koki, 141*n*., *d*.443
Hiss, Alger, 180, 602; *c*.602*n*.
Hitler, Adolf, 95*f*., 98*f*., 139, 150, 254*f*., 300, 351, 563, 444*f*., 468*ff*., 507, 523, 556, 558, 560*f*.; *q*.292*n*., 470, 474, 479, 480, 492, 509; *c*.280, 496
Hitler, Alois, 469
Hittites, 34*f*.
Ho Chi Minh, 114, 385, 387, 545, 569
Hoa Hoa, 387

INDEX

Hoare, Samuel, 223, 255, 459; q.220
Hoare-Laval Plan (1935), 221
Hobbes, Thomas, 16, 67; q.32, 68, 271
Hodgkin, Thomas, c.394
Hodgson, J. G., c.394
Hoepner, Ernest, 482
Hogan, Willard N., c.269; 332n.
Hohenstaufens, 52, 468f.
Hohenzollerns, 93, 468f.
Holborn, Hajo, c.104, 496
Holiday, W. T., 267
Holland, 78 (See also Netherlands)
Holmes, Oliver Wendell, Jr., 189n., 588
Holt, Hamilton, q.264
Holy Alliance, 206f.
Holy Roman Empire, 52f., 85
Homer, 39
Homma, Masaharu, 140n.
Homo, Leon P., c.54
Homo neanderthalensis, 13
Homo sapiens, 3f., 12f., 24f., 103f.
Honduras, 159
Hook, Sidney, 266
Hoot, J. Weldon, c.395
Hooton, Earnest A., c.28
Hoover, Herbert C., 25
Hoover, Herbert C., Jr., 379
Hoover Commission, 179; q.185n.
Hopkins, Harry, 195, 508
Horne, Alistair, c.496
Horthy, Nicholas, 415
Hot pursuit, 121
Houghton, Amory, 176
House, E. M., 212
Houston, John A., c.650
How, Julie Lien-ying, c.542
Howe, Quincy, c.104
Howells, William, c.13n., 28
Howley, Frank L., q.283n.
Hrozny, Bedrich, c.54
Hubertusburg, T., 77
Hudson, Manley O., 160n., c.161n., 165
Hugenberg, Alfred, 472f.
Hughes, Charles Evans, 161n.
Hughes, H. Stuart, c.28, 467
Hukbalahaps, 319
Hull, Cordell, 96, 183, 194, 254, 445f.; q.227, 280nf., 306; c.607
Hull, W. I., c.165
Humber, Robert Lee, 268
Hume, David, 71
Hungary: 60, 96f., 399ff.; revolution, 101, 118, 413ff.; T. (1947), 198; T. Trianon, 213
Huns, 38, 51
Hunter, Edward, c.541
Hurewitz, J. C., c.79

Hurley, Patrick, 533f.
Hurst, Cecil, 212; c.142
Hussein, Emir, 322
Hussein, King, 375, 406, 427ff.; q.429
Hussein Ala, 380n.
Hutchins, Robert M., 267, 660; q.268
Hutchinson, Keith, c.587
Hutheesing, Raja, c.541
Huzar, Elias, c.304
Hyde, Charles Cheney, c.142; q.152
Hyderabad, 118, 240

Ibanez, Carlos, 631
Ibn-Saud, 317, 324, 375
Ibrahim Awal, 419
Iceland, 111n.
Id, 25
Idris I, 374
Ifni, 372
Ignatiev, N. G., 520n.
Ike, Nobutaka, c.454
Ikhnaton, 30, 34
Imam Yahyah, 322
Immigrants (USA), 621f.
Imperial Rule Assistance Association, 448
Imperialism, 306ff.
Incas, 16, 37
Independence, right of, 116
India: 380ff., 570, 612, 633ff.; ancient, 37f., 277; independence, 111; National Congress, 381ff.; population, 318, 623; Tibet, 540; UN, 240
Indo-China: 96, 101, 335, 385f., 569f., 601; armistice agreement, 200; independence, 111; W., 385f.
Indonesia: 123, 309, 318, 389ff., 641ff., 645; independence, 111; UN, 238
Industrial Revolution, 81f., 358f., 619
Ingram, Kenneth, c.547
Innocent passage, 121, 134
Inonu, Ismet, 194
Institute of Pacific Relations, 525n.
Insurgents, 114
Intellectual Cooperation Organization of League of Nations, 216
Intercontinental Ballistic Missile (ICBM), 259, 260, 647, 671ff.
Interhandel, 157
Internal Security Act (USA), 622
International Atomic Energy Agency, 670
International Bank for Reconstruction and Development, 194, 234, 365, 406
International Bureau of Weights and Measures, 209
International Civil Aviation Organization, 234

726

International Court of Justice, 121, 161*f.*, 162, 171*n.*
International Development Advisory Board, 626
International Geophysical Year (1957–1958), 2
International Institute of Agriculture, 209
International Labor Organization: 160*n.*, 216, 218, 234, 329; conventions, 217
International law: 108*ff.*; ancient Greek, 42; Korean war, 136; origins, 68*f.*; private, 108; Roman, 47; sources, 109 (*See also* specific concepts and principles)
International Monetary Fund, 194, 234, 365
International Opium Commission, 209
International organizations: private, 209; public, 209*ff.*
International Prize Court, 158
International Radio Telegraphic Union, 208
International Red Cross, 209
International Refugee Organization, 234, 354
International relations, "science" of, 9*f.*, 396*ff.*
International Telegraphic Union, 207
International Trade Organization, 365, 366
International Union for the Publication of Customs Tariffs, 209
Intervention, 117*f.*, 146*f.*
Inukai, K. T., *d.*443
Investments: colonial, 312; foreign, 359*n.*
Iran, 163, 236, 316, 377*ff.*
Iraq, 323, 375
Ireland, 576
Irian, 389, 644*f.*
Iron Curtain, 186, 512, 550, 581, 595
Irredentas, 353*f.*
Irredentism, 345*f.*
Irving, Washington, *q.*191
Isaacs, Harold R., *c.*541
Isaiah, *q.*107, 315
Isard, Walter, *c.*680
Ishibashi, Tanzan, 452
Islam, 36, 58*f.*, 321*f.*
Ismael el Azhri, 374
Ismail, Khedive, 399*f.*
Ismailia, *B.*, 402
Isolationism (USA), 589*ff.*
Israel: 147, 163, 168, 238, 375*ff.*, 399, 407*ff.*; ancient, 36; independence, 111; *W.* (1948), 238
Ita, Eyo, 267
Itagaki, Seishiro, 141*n.*
Italy: 455*ff.*; 1914*f.*, 91*f.*; 218; 1935*f.*, 219; Irredenta, 87, 89, 345*f.*; sanctions, 221*f.*; Tirol, 346; *T.*, Germany (1939), 460; *T.* (1947), 197, 463; Triplice Pact, 481; Trusteeship Council, 332; unification, 87; World War I, 457; World War II, 460*ff.*
Ivan the Terrible, 54
Iwo Jima, *B.*, 99
IWW, 588
Izzeddin, Nejla, *c.*431

Jackson, Andrew, *q.*183
Jackson, J. Hampden, 547
Jackson, Robert H., 136, 140; *q.*141; *c.*142
Jacoby, Annalee, *c.*542
James, David H., *c.*454
Janowsky, Oscar I., *c.*394
Japan: 88, 95, 195, 437*ff.*; 1914*f.*, 92; 1931*f.*, 218; 1939*f.*, 96*f.*; Allied Council, 196; constitution (1946), *q.*450; L. of N., 226; M-F-N treatment, 367; "neutralism," 454; population problems, 311, 624; Stimson Doctrine, 252; *T.*, Anti-Comintern, *q.*443; *T.*, Peace (1951), 199, 452; *T.*, Triplice, 481; *T.*, USA, 200, 596; *T.*, USSR (1941), 444; *T.*, USSR (1956), 454, 545; *W.*, China (1894), 441; *W.*, China (1937*f.*), 444*f.*; *W.*, Russia (1904), 88, 149, 441*f.*; *W.*, USSR (1945), 534; World War I, 441*f.*; World War II, 444*ff.*
Jarman, T. L., *c.*496
Jarvis, H. Wood, *c.*431
Jaszi, Oscar, *c.*337*n.*
Javits, Jacob K., 427
Jay *T.* (1794), 152*f.*
Jebb, Gladwyn, 244
Jefferson, Thomas, 113, 589, 598
Jellinek, Frank, *c.*574
Jenghis Khan, 60
Jenner, William E., 534; *q.*292
Jennings, Ivor, *c.*394
Jessup, Phillip C., 142
Jesus of Nazareth, 381
Jews, 139, 350*ff.*, 355, 376*ff.*, 392 (*See also* Anti-Semitism; Israel; Palestine)
Jhering, von, *c.*342
Jiminez, Marcoș Perez, 632
Jinnah, Mohammed Ali, 382, *d.*384
Jodl, Alfred, 140*n.*, 468
John, Otto, 492
Johnson, Alan Campbell, *c.*587
Johnson, Hewlett, 186
Johnson, Hiram, 362
Johnson, Joseph E., *c.*524
Johnson, Julia Emily, *c.*269

INDEX

Johnson, Samuel, *q.*289
Jones v. U.S., 112*n.*
Jones, F. C., *c.*454
Jones, Joseph M., *c.*607
Jones, Mervyn, *c.*431
Jordan, 111, 375, 401*ff.*, 427*ff.*, 429
Jorrin, Miguel, *c.*650
Judah, 36
Judaism, 36
Judd, Walter, 534
Jugoslavia, 93, 96*f.*, 146, 195, 199, 465, 477, 516*ff.*, 556*f.*, 648
Julius II, 63
Jupiter-C missile, 673*n.*
Jurisdiction: 119*f.*; aerial and spatial, 121*n.*; exemptions from, 123*f.*; maritime, 121*ff.*
Jus gentium, 47, 57, 68
Jus naturae, 68
Jus sanguinis, 123
Jus soli, 123
Justinian, 51
Jutland, *B.*, 93

Kadar, Janos, 401, 415, 420
Kafka, Franz, *q.*171
Kaganovich, Lazar, 413, 518, 520*f.*
Kahin, George McTurnam, *c.*394, 650
Kahler, Erich, *c.*28
Kalijarvi, Thorsten V., *c.*608
Kalinin, Mikhail, 508
Kamikaze aviators, 448
Kang Sheng, 537
Kant, Emmanuel, 206
Kao Kang, 537
Kaplan, Morton A., *c.*607
Kardiner, Abram, *c.*24*n.*, 28
Karelian Isthmus, 507
Karikal, 570
Karnataka, 635
Kars, 502, 544
Karunakaran, K. P., *c.*394
Kashmir, 118, 240, 383*f.*, 612, 645
Katayama, Tetsu, 450*f.*
Kato, Masuo, *c.*454
Katyn massacre, 288*n.f.*
Kaufman, Irving R., 667*n.*
Kaufman, William W., *c.*304
Kautilya, *q.*277
Kee-Connally Act (1946), 179
Keenan, Joseph B., 139
Keeton, George W., *c.*541
Keightly, Charles, 419
Keitel, Wilhelm, 140*n.*, 468
Kellogg, Frank B., 161*n.*, 250
Kellogg-Briand Pact, 250*f.*

Kelly, Alfred H., *c.*607
Kelson, Hans, *c.*142, 165, 269
Kennan, George F., 176, 533; *q.*281*n.*, 287*n.*, 598*n.*; *c.*xi, 524, 595, 607
Kennedy, Malcolm, *c.*553
Kenny, George C., *q.*652
Kenya, 460, 638
Kenyatta, Jomo, 638
Kepler, Johannes, 81
Kerala, 501, 635*f.*
Kerensky, Alexander, 499
Kerr, Clark, 196
Kersten, Charles J., *q.*600*n.*
Kertesz, Stephen D., *c.*431
Keynes, John Maynard, 358, 615; *c.*104
Khalidi, Hussein Fakhari, 429
Khama, Seretse, 349
Khrushchev, Nikita S., 259, 413*f.*, 430, 518*ff.*, 520, 545, 551*ff.*; *q.*521, 652
Kianga, 329
Kiaochow, 441
Kibbutz Galuyoth, 377
Kikuyu, 638
Killby, J. Keith, 266, 257
Kim, The, 135*n.*
Kim Il-sung, 242
Kim Koo, 241
Kimmel, H. E., 446
Kimura, Heitaro, 141*n.*
Kindleberger, Charles P., *c.*394
King, John Kerry, *c.*650
King, Mackenzie, 660
Kipling, Rudyard, *q.*101, 306, 325
Kirichenko, Alexei I., 520*n.*
Kirk, Alan G., 600*n.*
Kirk, George, *c.*393*n.*, 432
Kish, 33
Kishi, Nobusuke, 452
Kissinger, Henry A., *c.*680
Kjellen, Rudolf, 300
Klaestad, Helge, 162*n.*
Klagenfurt, 345
Klausener, Erich, 474
Knappen, Marshall, *c.*607
Knight, B. W., *c.*304
Knight, Frances, 186
Knorr, Klaus E., *c.*304, 646*n.*
Knox, Philander, 155
Koenig, Louis W., *c.*607
Koenigswald, G. H. Ralph von, 13; *c.*28
Kogan, Norman, *c.*467
Kohlberg, Alfred, 534
Kohn, Hans, *q.*333; *c.*395
Koiso, Kuniaki, 141*n.*, 448
Kolnai, Aurel, *c.*496
Konev, Ivan, 544

INDEX

Konoye, Fumimaro, 141n., d.440, 444f.
Korbel, Josef, c.613
Korea: 101, 194, 196, 199, 441, 453, 538, 540, 583, 596, 598, 601; armistice (1953), 200, 245; W. (1950f.), 132, 133n., 136, 240ff.
Kosok, Paul, c.337n.
Kossovo, B., 60
Kossuth, Louis, 415
Kotelawala, John, 642
Kozhevnikov, Fedor Ivanovich, 162n.
Kozlov, F. R., 520n.
Kravchenko, Victor, 182
Kreisky, Bruno, 200
Krieger, Seymour, c.496
Kris, Ernst, c.304
Krishnamashari, T. T., 637
Krutch, Joseph Wood, c.28
Krupp von Bohlen und Halbach, Alfred, 483n.
Kubitschek, Juscelino, 630
Kubla Khan, 523
Kulski, W. W., c.524
Kun, Bela, 415
Kundra, J. C., c.650
Kung, H. H., 532
Kuniaki, Koiso, 141n.
Kuomintang, 527ff.
Kurenberg, Joachim von, c.496
Kuril Islands, 195, 199, 453f., 514
Kurusu, Saburo, 444ff.
Kuusinen, Otto, 507
Kuwait Oil Company, 317
Kuwatly, Shukru, 427, 545
Kuznets, Simon, c.650

LaCoste, Robert, 372
Lagash, 33
Laibach, C. (1821), 206
Laika, 673n.
Lamb, Harold, c.54
Landau, Rom, c.395
Langer, Paul, c.455
Langer, William L., c.104, 607
Language, 342f.
Laniel, Joseph, 569, 584
Lansing, Robert, 169
Lansing-Ishii Agreement (1917), 327
Lao-tse, q.525
Laos, 111, 200, 386f., 544, 610
Lapp, Ralph E., 671; c.680
Laqueur, Walter Z., c.432
Larrazabal, Wolfgang, 632
Larsen, J. A. O., c.54
Lasker, Bruno, c.650
Laski, Harold, c.79

Lasky, Melvin J., c.432
Lasswell, Harold D., c.28, 304
Latin America, 85, 88, 316, 319f., 611, 629ff., 632 (See also specific names of States)
Latourette, Kenneth Scott, c.454
Lattimore, Owen, 525n., 533; c.454, 541, 602n.
Latvia, 93, 113n., 251, 502, 506f.
Lausanne, T., 94, 215
Lauterpacht, Hersch, 162n.; c.142
Laval, Pierre, 459, 557ff., 559, 563, d.564; q.220
Lawrence, Lord Justice, 140
Lawrence, T. E., c.395
Lawrence, William L., c.680
Lawton, L., q.578n.
League to Enforce Peace, 211
League of Nations: 94, 211f.; Assembly, 214; budget, 214; Covenant, 213f.; Disarmament Conference, 253f.; Economic and Financial Organization, 216; end of, 226; ILO, 216f.; Intellectual Cooperation Organization, 216; membership, 241f.; minority treaties, 348; nonmembers, 214; Permanent Mandates Commission, 216, 328ff., 376; Secretariat, 215f.; WHO, 216; withdrawals, 217; World Court, 160f.; Austria, 225; China; 225; Germany, 215, 218, 254; Italy, sanctions, 221f.; Japan, 226; Russia, expulsion, 226; USSR, 503
Leaseholds, 120
Lebanon, 111, 324, 375
Lebrun, Albert, 563
Lee, Dwight E., c.104
Lee Bum Suk, 251
Leeb, Wilhelm von, 508
Leipzig, B., 83
Leiss, Amelia C., c.202
Lemkin, Raphael, 132
Lenczowski, George, c.432
Lend-Lease Act (USA), 136, 194, 508, 580, 592
Lenin, V. I. (Ulianov, Vladimir Ilitch), 499ff., 549, 553; q.542; c.335
Leningrad, B., 48, 511
Leo the Isaurian, 59
Leo III, 51f.
Leonard, L. Larry, c.269, 332n., 607
Leonidas the Spartan, 39
Leopold II of Belgium, 150, 309
Lepanto, B., 61
Lerner, Daniel, c.28, 304
Lerner, Max, q.64; c.607
Lesseps, Ferdinand de, 399
Letters of marque and reprisal, 131, 146

Leuthen, *B.*, 76
Levi, Werner, *c.*269
Ley, Robert, 140*n.*, 473
Leyson, Burr W., *c.*680
Li Chien-nung, *c.*541
Li Tsung-jen, 536
Liaotung Peninsula, 441
Liberia, 321, 646
Libya, 111, 373*f.*, 457
Lichfield, Edward H., *c.*496
Lie, F. F., *c.*541
Lie, Trygve, 228*f.*, 231, 245; *q.*237, 246*n.*, 257, 667; *c.*269
Liechtenstein, 111*n.*
Lilienthal, David, 662, 665*f.*
Lilienthal-Acheson proposals, 662*f.*
Lima, Declaration of, *q.*118*n.*
Lin Piao, 537
Lin Yutang, *c.*525
Lincoln, Abraham, *d.*594; *q.*433
Linebarger, Paul, *c.*54
Lippmann, Walter, *q.*7, 235*n.*, 261, 665*n.*; *c.*607, 613
Lips, Julius E., *c.*28
Lissitzyn, Oliver J., *c.*165
List, Frederick, 299
Lithuania, 93, 113*n.*, 251, 502, 506
Little Entente, 94, 556
Little Rock, Ark., 647
Litvinoff, Barnet, *c.*432
Litvinov, Maxim, 194, 223, 250, 256, 503*f.*, 509, 511, 559; *q.*225
Litvinov Protocol, 251
Liu Chi-jin, 124*n.*
Liu Shao-chi, 537
Lloyd, Selwyn, 404*ff.*, 584, 610, 644; *q.*586
Lloyd George, David, 93, 505; *q.*226, 267
Locarno, *T.*, 249, 250, 252, 254, 476, 558
Lockwood, William W., *c.*455
Lodge, Henry Cabot, Jr., 230; *q.*419
Lodger, Benjamin T. C., *q.*157
Loewenstein, Karl, *c.*266*n.*
London, Jack, 588
London, Kurt, *c.*202
London: Naval *C.* (1908–1909), 158; Naval *C.* (1930), 253; Naval *T.* (1930), 254; Naval *T.* (1936), 255
Londonderry, Marquess of, *q.*578*n.*
Lorimer, Frank, *c.*650
Lorwin, Val R., *c.*574
Lothian, Lord, 261
Loucks, William N., *c.*395
Louis the Pious, 52
Louis XI, 166; *q.*66
Louis, XII, 63
Louis XIII, 69
Louis, XIV, 70, 74*f.*, 82, 577; *q.*110

Louis XV, 76*f.*
Louis XVIII, 84
Louisiana, 85
Lowdermilk, Walter Clay, *q.*325*n.*
Lowie, Robert H., *c.*18*n.*, 28
Loyalty Review Board (USA), 181
Luce, Clare Booth, 176, 464
Ludendorf, Erich von, *c.*304
Luethy, Herbert, *c.*574
Lugal-Zaggisi, 33
Lukacs, John A., *c.*432
Lumby, E. W. R., *c.*395
Luther, Hans, 492
Luxembourg, 96*f.*, 111*n.*, 477
Lysander of Sparta, 40
Lytton Commission, 218
Lyuh Woong Hyung, 241

MacArthur, Douglas, 140, 141*n.*, 244*f.*, 440, 449*ff.*, 534, 582, 596; *q.*xi, 132, 369*n.*, 451
Macartney, M. H. H., *c.*467
McCamy, James L., *c.*202
McCarran, Patrick, *q.*525*n.*, 622*n.*
McCarran-Walter Immigration Act (USA), 186, 622
McCarthy, Joseph, 180, 525*n.*, 534, 588, 602; *q.*292
McCarthyism, 601*f.*
McCloy, John J., 483*n.*, 487, 662
McCrae, John, 93
McCune, George M., *c.*269
MacDonald, Austin F., *c.*650
McDonald, James G., 352; *q.*325*n.*; *c.*335
McDonald, John, *c.*304
Macedonia, 43*f.*
McGovern, William M., *c.*496
Machiavelli, Niccolo, 63*f.*, 166, 286, 398, 459, 467; *q.*64, 65, 291, 293*n.*; *c.*79, 396
MacIver, Robert M., *c.*18*n.*, 28
McKay, Donald D., *c.*574
McKay, Vernon, *c.* 324*n.*
MacKellar, Kenneth, *q.*665
MacKinder, Halford S., *q.*300; *c.*304
McKinley, William, *q.*310
McKnight, John P., *c.*467
Maclaurin, John, *c.*269
MacLean, Donald, 182
McLeod, Scott, 176
MacLeod, W. C., *c.*18*n.*
MacMahon, Arthur W., *c.*202, 269
McMahon, Brian, 626, 658
Macmillan, Harold, 427, 493, 544, 584, 586
McMillan, James M., 182
McNeill, William Hardy, 547

McReynolds, George E., *c*.454
Madden, Ray J., 288*n*.
Madison, James, 598; *q*.262, 263
Madras, 635
Magellan, Ferdinand, 75
Maginot Line, 299, 557, 562
Magloire, Paul E., 631
Magyars, 60 (*See also* Hungary)
Mahan, Alfred Thayer, 299
Mahasabha (India), 635*ff*.
Mahe, 570
Mahoney, Thomas H. D., *c*.454
Main, E., *c*.335
Maine, Henry, 39
Makarios, Archbishop, 612
Maki, John M., *c*.455
Makin, Norman J. O., 229, *q*.242*n*.
Malan, Daniel F., 349, 639
Malaya, 111, 230, 316, 387*f*.
Malenkov, Georgi, 508, 513, 518*ff*., 520*f*., 544*f*., 670
Malik, Charles, 424
Malik, Jacob, 242; *q*.257
Malinovsky, Rodion V., 521
Malinowski, Bronislaw, *c*.26*n*.
Mallon, Paul, *q*.284*n*.
Malmédy, 345
Malthus, Thomas, 619*f*., 622
Manchu Dynasty, 526*f*.
Manchukuo, 218, 252
Manchuria, 95, 195, 218, 311, 441, 443, 453, 531, 534, 536, 540, 550, 583
Mandate system, 213, 215*f*., 328*ff*.
Mandel, Georges, 563
Mander, Linden A., *q*.107, 249; *c*.269
Mangone, Gerard J., *c*.269
Manhattan District, 655
Mann, Thomas, *q*.468
Mannerheim, Gustav, 507*f*.
Mannoni, O., *c*.335
Mansfield, Mike, 610
Manuel, Frank E., *c*.574
Manuilsky, Dmitri, 236
Mao Tse-tung, 532*ff*., 537*ff*., 550, 592; *q*.552; *c*.541
Marathon, *B*., 39
Marburg, Theodore, *c*.270
Marc, Alexandre, 266
Marcus Aurelius, 47, 50
Marder, Arthur J., *c*.304
Marek, Krystyna, *c*.142
Maria, The, 135*n*.
Maria Theresa, 76
Mariana Islands, 333
Marie, André, 566
Marienwerder, 345
Marin, Louis, 563

Mark Twain, *q*.271; *c*.285*n*.
Markets, colonial, 311*f*.
Marne, *B*., 91, 93
Marquet, Adrien, 561
Marriott, John A. P., *c*.270
Mars, 3
Marschak, Jacob, *c*.680
Marsh, F. B., *c*.54
Marshall, Charles Burton, *c*.304
Marshall, George C., 180, 183, 195, 237, 241, 291, 446, 525*n*., 534*f*.; *q*.284*n*., 535; *c*.295*n*.
Marshall Islands, 333
Marshall Plan, 246, 550, 580*f*., 595
Martel, Francis, *c*.574
Martens, Ludwig, 170
Martin, James Stewart, *c*.483*n*.
Martin, John Stuart, *c*.524
Martino, Gaetano, 465*f*.
Marx, Karl, 358, 549, 619; *q*.86, 498, 548
Marxism, 615*ff*.
Masaryk, Thomas Garrigue, *c*.524
Mason, Edward S., *c*.395
Mason, George, *q*.262, 263
Master, Dexter, *c*.680
Matsu Island, 603
Matsui, Iwane, 141*n*.
Matsumoto, Sunichi, 454
Matsuoka, Yosuke, *q*.444
Matthews, Francis, 141; *q*.283*n*.
Matthews, Ronald, *c*.574
Matusow, Harvey, *c*.602*n*.
Mau Mau, 638
Mauretania, 372
Maurras, Charles, *q*.340*n*.
Maximilian, Emperor, 63
May, Arthur J., *c*.104
May, Rollo, *c*.28
Mayas, 16, 37
Mayer, René, 566, 569
Maynard, John, *c*.524
Mazarin, Cardinal, 74
Mazour, Anatole G., *c*.524
Mead, George H., *c*.339*n*.
Meade, J. E., *c*.395, 650
Mediation, 149
Medici, 63
Meerloo, Joost A. M., *c*.304
Megaro, G., *c*.467
Meir, Golda, 409*ff*., 417, 424; *q*.573
Mende, Tibor, *c*.613
Menderes, Adnan, 430
Mendès-France, Pierre, 490, 569*ff*., 572, 574; *q*.387
Menemencioglu, Numan, 194
Menes, 33
Menjou, Adolphe, 588

INDEX

Menon, Krishna, 420, 645
Menon, V. P., c.335
Menthon, François de, 140
Menzies, Robert Gordon, 410ff.; q.247n.
Mercantilism, 357ff.
Merriam, Charles E., c.28, 337n.
Metternich, Klemens von, 84
Mexico, 88, 630
Meyer, Alfred G., c.496
Meyer, Cord, Jr., 267; c.270
Micaud, Charles A., c.574
Michael, King, 196, 514
Michener, James A., c.432
Middle East Command, 402 (*See also*
    Baghdad Pact)
Middleton, Drew, c.304
Middleton, L., c.335
Midway, B., 97, 446
Mikesell, Raymond F., c.607
Mikoyan, Anastas, 413, 415f., 520f., 545
Miksche, F. O., c.680
Miletus, B., 39
Military occupation, 130
Miliukov, Paul, 169
Milky Way, 2f.
Miller, David Hunter, 212; c.270
Miller, Mas, c.342
Millis, Walter, c.285n., 304, 607
Mills, C. Wright, c.607
Mindszenty, Josef, 401ff., 415f.
Ming Dynasty, 526
Minindel (USSR), 183
Ministers Resident, 168f.
Ministries of Foreign Affairs, 184ff. (*See
    also* specific States)
Minorities, T., 347ff.
Minquiers and Ecrehou Islands, 163
Mirandola, Pico Della, q.11, 679
Missouri v. Holland, 189n.
Mitchell, Kate L., c.394
Mitchell, William, 299
Mitterand, François, q.372
Mixed commissions, 151f.
Mohács, B., 61
Mohammed, Prophet, 58
Mohammed, Sultan, 371
Mohammed Ali, 642
Mohammed Riza Pahlevi, 377
Mohammed II, 61
Mollet, Guy, 372, 404, 412, 545, 572ff.;
    q.407
Molotov, Vyacheslav, 115, 194ff., 236, 256,
    387, 413f., 477f., 477n., 485, 504f., 508,
    518, 520, 533, 544; q.438, 479, 505
Moltke, H. von, 299
Monaco, 111n.
Monarchomachs, 67

Mongoloid peoples, 17
Mongols, 60, 498
Monnet, Jean, 366; q.386
Monroe Doctrine, 85, 88, 156, 251, 319, 589
Montcalm, Louis de, 76
Montenegro, 87, 111
Montesquieu, Baron de, 598
Montevideo, C., q.118
Montgomery, Bernard, 97, 483
Montross, Lynn, c.304
Moon, 2f.
Moon, P. T., q.309; c.335
Moore, Hugh, 266
Moore, John Bassett, 155, 161n.; c.143
Moore, Ruth, c.28
Moos, Malcolm, c.303
Moraes, Frank, c.650
Moral principles, 281f.
Morgenthau, Hans J., c.175n., 281n., 304,
    422n.
Morgenthau Plan, 195, 483
Morocco, 90, 111, 163, 230, 322, 334, 371,
    373, 570, 572
Morris, Charles, c.28
Morrison, Herbert, 582f.; q.376
Morse, H. B., c.104
Moscicki, Ignacy, 150
Moscow: B., 96, 480, 509; C., 1943, 194;
    1944, 195; 1945, 196, 661f.; 1955, 200
Moscow Youth Festival, 186
Mosely, Philip E., c.553
Moslem League, 381ff.
Mossadegh, Mohammed, 377f.
Most-favored-nation clause, 199, 327, 333,
    363f.
Mosul dispute, 215
Mott, N. F., q.582
Mountbatten, Louis, 382
Mountbatten, Philip, 575
Moutet, Marius, q.385
Mozambique, 309, 638
Muller, Herbert J., c.28
Mumford, Lewis, q.659
Munich, T. (1938), 226, 476, 503, 559
Münster, T., 74
Munters, Wilhelm, 244
Murphy, Gerald Lester, 632
Murphy, Robert, 409, 427
Murra, John V., c.638n.
Muscat and Oman, 430
Mushakoji, Amb., q.443n.
Mussolini, Benito, 95f., 98f., 150, 221,
    d.456, 458ff., 462, 469, 473, 563; q.128,
    220, 456, 457, 460
Mussolini, Edda, 456
Mustafa Nahas Pasha, 402
Muta, Akira, 141n.

Mutsu Hito, Emperor, 441
Mutual Security Act: 1951 (USA), *q*.600*n*.; 1952 (USA), 367
Mutual Security Agency, 185*n*., 596
Myrdal, Gunnar, *c*.395

Nabulsi, Suleiman, 406, 429
Nagasaki, 99, 132, 440, 658
Naguib, Mohammed, 402
Nagumo, Chuichi, 446, *d*.448
Nagy, Ferenc, 401
Nagy, Imry, 415*ff*.
Namboodiripad, Elamkulam Manakai Sankaran, 636
Napoleon I, 82*f*., 508, 577; *q*.80, 82
Napoleon III, 87*f*., 399*f*.
Naram-Sin, 33
Narkomindel, 183 (*See also* USSR)
Nasser, Gamal Abdel, 118, 147, 402*ff*., 465, 642, 644; *q*.407–409
Nathan, Otto, *c*.496
Nathan, Robert R., *c*.335
National income, comparative, 618
National interest, 281*f*.
National minorities, 346*ff*.
National Planning Associations (USA), *c*.646*n*.
National Security Council (USA), 185*n*.
Nationalism, 336*ff*.; Arab, 321*f*. (*See also* specific States)
Nationality laws, 123
Naughton, James W., *c*.467
Nauru, 331, 332*n*.
Nautilus, 670
Navarino, *B*., 146
Nazi-Soviet Pact, 1939, *q*.476*n.f*., 505
Nazi-Soviet relations (1939–1941), *c*.289*n*.
Nazimuddin, Khwaja, 384
Neanderthal man, 17
Nebuchadnezzar, 36
Nef, John U., *c*.304
Negroes, 355, 639; in USA, 348*f*., 618
Negroid peoples, 17
Nehru, Jawaharlal, 381*ff*., 420, 545, 572, 635, 642*ff*., 668; *q*.384, 695; *c*.335
Nenni, Pietro, 462, 465*ff*.; *q*.551
Neo-Destour, 373
Neomercantilism, 357*ff*.
Nepal, 111*n*.
Nero, 47
Netherlands, 74, 96*f*., 189*n*., 288, 477
Neuilly, *T*., 94, 213
Neumann, Franz, *c*.496
Neurath, Constantine von, 140*n*.
Neutralism, 454, 582, 641*ff*., 647*ff*.

Neutrality, law of, 133*f*.; proclamations, 187; USA, 590*f*.
"New Economic Policy" (USSR), 502
New Guinea, 331
N.Y. Life Insurance Company v. Louise C. Bennion, 129*n*.
New York Times, The, *q*.284
New Zealand, 597, 610
Ngo Dinh Diem, 387
Nicaragua, 159, 319, 631
Nice and Savoy, 87
Nickerson, Hoffman, *c*.304
Nicola, Umberto di, 462
Nicolas II, 499
Nicolson, Harold, *q*.90; *c*.104, 202
Niebuhr, Reinhold, *q*.325*n*.; *c*.304
Nietzsche, Friedrich W., 18; *q*.272
Nigeria, 637
Nikitchenko, I. T., 140
Nimitz, Chester, 240
Nine Power Pact (1922), 127
Nineveh, 36
Nisei, 349
Nixon, Richard M., 631; *q*.646
Nizamudden, Tewfik, 430
Nkrumah, Kwame, 637, 646*f*.; *c*.650
Nomura, Kichisaburo, 445*f*.
Noncombatants, 130
Norman, Herbert E., 181*n*.
Norstad, Lauris, 491; *q*.672
North Atlantic Treaty, 567, 589, 595*ff*.; *q*.609
North Atlantic Treaty Organization, 258, 490, 570
Northern Bukovina, 96
Norway, 85, 96*f*., 135, 477
Nover, Barnet, *c*.664*n*.
Noyes, C. Reinold, *c*.28
NSDAP, 469*ff*. (*See also* Germany; Hitler)
Nuclear tests, 259, 657*ff*.
Numelin, Ragnar, *c*.54
Nunn, Allan May, 667*n*.
Nuremberg, War Crimes trials, 139*f*.
Nuremberg laws, 352
Nuseibeh, Hazem Zaki, *c*.432
Nussbaum, Arthur, *c*.143
Nutting, Anthony, 585
Nyasaland, 639

Oberth, Hermann, *c*.680
O'Connell, D. P., *c*.143
Oder-Niesse line, 195, 485, 489
Odoacer, 51
Oedipus, 25*f*.
Office of War Information (USA), 185*n*.

Ogdai Khan, 60
Ogier, M., q.167
Oil, Middle East, 317f., 403ff.
Okada, Keisuki, 443
Okinawa, B., 99
Olbricht, Friedrich, 482
Oliver, Lunsford, q.288
Olney, Richard, 155
Olympias, 44
Oman, C. W., c.79
O'Neill, H. C., c.104
"Open Door," 326f., 329ff., 589
"Open Skies," 258f.
Opie, Redvers, c.606, 613
Opium wars, 327
Oppen, Beata van, c.496
Oppenheim, L., c.143
Oppenheimer, Ernest, 639
Oppenheimer, Franz, q.18; c.18n., 28
Oppenheimer, J. Robert, 657, 660, 662,
    670ff.
Optional clause, 161, 162, 164
Ording, Aake, 209
Organization of American States, 319f.
Organization for Communications and
    Transit (L. of N.), 216
Original sin, 25
Orkan, 60
Orlando, Vittorio, 93
Orr, Lord Boyd, 267
Orwell, George, 261
Osborn, Frederick H., q.666
Osborne, Henry, 267
Osgood, Robert Endicott, c.304
Osman, 60
Osnabrück, T., 74
Otto, Emperor, 52
Otto, Max, q.81
Ottoman Empire, 61, 78, 86
Outer Mongolia, 195, 220, 521, 537
Oxenstierna, Axel, q.408

Pacific blockades, 146
Pacific Charter, 610
Pact of Paris (1928), 141, 218; q.251
Pacta sunt servanda, 125
Padover, Saul K., c.496
Page, Walter Hines, q.172
Paine, Thomas, 588; q.555
Pakistan, 111, 240, 382ff., 610, 612, 633,
    645
Paléologue, Maurice, q.289n.
Palestine, 36, 239, 351f., 375ff. (See also
    Israel; Jordan)
Pallfy, Gyorgy, 415

Palmer, Robert R., c.104
Panama, 121, 631, 632
Pan-American Union, 319
Pan-Islam Society, 322
Panikkar, K. M., c.613
Panmunjon, C. (1953), 200
Papacy, 50f., 56f. (See also Vatican; spe-
    cific names of Popes)
Papen, Franz von, 140n., 472, 474; c.496
Paquete Habaña, q.109
Paracel Islands, 199
Paranthropus, 12
Parapithecus, 12
Pares, Bernard, c.524
Paris: C. (1919), 167f., 197, 212f., 344ff.;
    Declaration of, 130, 146; q.131; T.
    (1763), 77; T. (1815), 85; T. (1856),
    87; T. (1928), 141, 218, q.251; T.
    (1954), 490
Parkin, Raleigh, c.335, 381n.
Parson, Nels A., Jr., c.680
Partisans of Peace, 290
Passports, 186
Patricians, 45f.
Patterson, Jefferson, 176
Patzinaks, 60
Pauker, Ana, 543
Paullin, Theodore, c.262n.
Paulus, Friedrich von, 97, 481, 494, 509,
    511
Pax Britannica, 80
Pax Ecclesiae, 57
Payne, Robert, c.541
Paz, Alberto Gainza, 631
Peace Observation Commission (UN), 244
Pearcy, G. E., c.304
Pearl Harbor, B., 96, 129, 446, 480
Pearson, Lester, 423f.; q.181n.
Pella, Giuseppe, 465
Peloponnesian War, 40
Peninsular War, 83
Penn, William, q.204
Pennock, J. Roland, c.680
People's Front, 557
People's World Convention, 267
Pericles, q.40, 608
Permanent Court of Arbitral Justice, 158
Permanent Court of Arbitration, 156, 158,
    160
Permanent Court of International Justice,
    159f., 161
Permanent Mandates Commission (L. of
    N.), 216, 329f., 376
Peron, Juan, 321, 630
Perry, Matthew C., 88, 440f.
Persia, 37f., 251 (See also Iran)

Persona non grata, 168
Pertinax, *c.*575
Peru, 171*n.*, 631
Pervukhin, Mikhail G., 520*f.*
Pescadores, 199, 441, 603
Pétain, Henri Philippe, 322, 559, 565*ff.*
Peter the Great, 78
Peter II (Jugoslavia), 557
Peter III, 76
Peterson, Val, *q.*670
Petkov, Nikola, 543
Petropolis, Act of, 122, 319, 595, 608
Petsamo, 507
Pew, Joseph, 588
Pfankuchen, Llewellyn, *c.*143
Pflimlin, Pierre, 573
Phelan, Edward J., 216
Philby, H. St. John, *c.*432
Philip of Macedonia, 43*f.*, 577
Philip II of Spain, 82
Philip V, 71
Philippines, 88, 111, 310, 318*f.*, 596, 612
Philistines, 36
Phillimore, Lord, 212
Phillipson, Coleman, *c.*42*n.*, 54
Phoenicians, 36
Phumiphon Adundet, 385, 611
Physiocrats, 358
Pichon, Charles, *c.*467
Pickles, Dorothy, *c.*575
Pieck, Wilhelm, 485, 487, 493
Pilsudski, Josef, 556, *d.*557
Piltdown man, 13
Pinay, Antoine, 544, 566, 569, 571
Pineau, Christian, 404*ff.*, 545, 572*f.*; *q.*572
Pinilla, Gustavo Rohas, 631
Pinson, Koppel S., *c.*496
"Pious Funds," 156
Pirates, 121, 138
Pirenne, Henri, *c.*79
Pisano, Leonardo, 62
Pithecanthropus erectus, 13
Pithecanthropus pekinensis, 13
Pius XII, 150, 646; *q.*267*n.*
Plataea, *B.*, 39
Plato, *q.*7, 38, 434, 614
Playne, Carolyn E., *c.*395
Plebeians, 45*f.*
Plebiscites, 345
Plessy v. Ferguson, 356
Pleven, René, 566
Pleven Plan, 487, 568
Plischke, Elmer, *c.*202
Plutarch, *q.*25, 30, 298
Plutonium, 655*ff.*
Poincaré, Raymond, 556

Point Four, 595, 625*ff.*
Point Five, 627
Poison gas, 138
Poland: 111, 195, 251, 259, 413*ff.*, 475, 551*f.*; minority *T.*, 350; partitions, 72, 77*f.*, 506; *W.* with Russia (1920), 500*f.*, 506; World War II, 96*f.*, 477*f.*
Polish Corridor, 94
Political questions, doctrine of, 189
Politis Report, 250
Pollock, J. K., *c.*497
Pondichery, 570
Pontecorvo, Bruno, 667*n.*
Pope, Arthur Upham, *c.*524
Popular Fronts, 503, 558
Population, 311, 539, 620*f.*
Porkkala, 545
Port Arthur, 195, 441, 514, 540, 543, 550
Portes, Hélène de, 562*f.*
Portsmouth, *T.* (1905), 441
Portugal, 18, 309, 638
Posnack, Emanuel R., 547
Postgate, Raymond, *c.*587
Potsdam, *C.* (1945), 195, 438, 483
Potter, E. B., *c.*304
Potter, Pitman B., *c.*270
Poujade, Pierre, 571
Powell, Adam Clayton, 643
Poznan, 413, 551
Prasad, Rajendra, 384
Pratt, Fletcher, *q.*284*n.*; *c.*304
Pratt, Julius W., *c.*335, 607
Prawiranegara, Sjafruddin, 391
Prescription, 120
Prestes, Carlo Luis, 630
Prestige, 274*f.*
Preston, Richard A., *c.*304
Price, G. Ward, *q.*578*n.*
Price, M. Phillips, *c.*79
Primates, 12*f.*
Prince of Wales, 446
Privateers, 131, 146
Propaganda war, 290*f.*
Property in wartime, 130*f.*
Propliopithecus, 12
Protectorates, 114
Protocols, 125
Protoplasm, 11
Prussia, 74, 75*f.*, 78 (*See also* Germany)
Psychological Strategy Board, 600*n.*
Pu-yi, Henry, 114
Public International Unions, 207*f.*
Puerto Rico, 88, 319
Puleston, W. D., *c.*304
Punic Wars, 46

INDEX

Pushtunistan, 612
Pyrrhus, King of Epirius, 46; *q.*298

Quadruple Alliance (1815), 206
Quai d'Orsay, 182
Quarles, Donald A., *q.*369*n.*
Quebec, *C.* (1944), 194
Quemoy Island, 603
Queuille, Henri, 566
Quigley, Harold S., *c.*455
Quintana, Lucio Moreno, 162*n.*
Quintuple Alliance (1818), 206

Raab, Julius, 200
Race, 17, 342*f.*
Radek, Karl, *q.*542
Radescu, Nicholas, 514
Radford, Arthur W., 386; *q.*259, 369*n.*
Radio Free Europe, 413
Raeder, Erich, 140*n.*
Rafuse, Robert W., *c.*143
Raijk, Lazlo, 401, 415, 543
Rakosi, Matyas, 401, 415
Ralston, J. H., *c.*56, 165
Rameses II, 34
Ramon, José Antonio, 631
Randolph, Edmund, *q.*262
Rapacki, Adam, 259
Rapallo, *T.* (1922), 471, 477
Rapoport, Anatol, *c.*680
Rappard, William E., 329; *c.*270
Rathenau, Walter, 299, 351*n.,* 471, 474, 495
Ratzel, Friedrich, 300
Rauschning, Hermann, 479, *c.*497
Raw materials, 312
Read, John E., 162*n.*
Read el Sulh, 375
Rebus sic stantibus, 127
Reciprocal Trade Agreement Act, 365, 367
Recognition: *de facto* theory, 112, 114; *de jure* theory, 113, 114; diplomatic, 110*f.,* 112*f.*; premature, 112, 114
Redfield, Robert, 268; *c.*12*n.*
Reformation, 73
Reifzel, William, *c.*607
Reinsch, Paul, *c.*209
Reischauer, Edwin O., *c.*455, *c.*607
Remarque, Erich Maria, *q.*293, 294*n.*
Remington, William, 602
Reparations, 199, 362
Repatriation of prisoners, 245
Reprisal, 146
Republic of the South Moluccas, 645
Repulse, 446
Reves, Emery, *c.*270

Reshetar, John S., Jr., *c.*524
Reston, James, 652
Retortion, 145
Reuben, William A., *c.*602*n.*
Reuther, Walter, 626
Revolutions: American, 77*f.,* 133; anti-colonial, 101*f.*; Chinese, 527*ff.*; French, 82*ff.*; Hungarian, 547, 551; Mexican, 630; racial, 101*f.*; 1830, 207; 1848, 207; Russian, 436, 498*ff.*
Reynaud, Paul, 265, 562*f.,* 569; *q.*561; *c.*270
Reynolds, Robert G., 124*n.*
Rhee, Syngman, 241, 604
Rhineland, 254, 476, 484
Rhodes, Cecil, 80, 457; *q.*280*n.*
Rhodesia, 639
Ribbentrop, Joachim von, 115, 140*n.,* 444, 472, 477*n.,* 478*f.,* 505*f.,* 560*f.*; *q.*443*n.*
Ricardo, David, 615
Richards, James P., 428*f.*
Richardson, William, *c.*496
Richthofen, Erich von, 351*n.*
Ridgway, Matthew, 451
Riencourt, Amoury de, *c.*28
Right of asylum, 170
Ripka, Hubert, *c.*553
River boundaries, 122
Robbins, Richard, *c.*650
Roberts, Frank, 199
Roberts, Henry L., *c.*524
Roberts, Henry R., *c.*553
Roberts, Owen I., 266; *q.*137
Robertson, A. H., *c.*270
Robertson, Priscilla, *c.*79
Robinson, Joel, *c.*404*n.*
Rockefeller, Nelson, 626
Rockefeller Report, *c.*305
Rockets: 294; Explorer, 673*n.*; Jupiter, 673*n.*; *Sputnik,* 3, 121*n.,* 673; Vanguard, 673*n.*
Rocque, François de la, 537
Rodgers, James Grafton, *c.*202
Rogers Act, 179
Röhm, Ernst, 469, 474
Rokossovsky, Konstantin, 413, 511
Roman law, 49
Rome (ancient), 45*ff.*
Rommel, Erwin, 97, 482
Romulo, Carlos P., 643; *c.*650
Romulus and Remus, 45
Romulus Augustulus, 51
Roosevelt, Franklin D., 96, 118*n.,* 150, 183, 193*ff.,* 254, 265, 446, 508, 511, 514, 516, 591, *d.*594, 655; *q.*319, 460, 514, 592, 678*n.*

INDEX

Roosevelt, Theodore, 80, 139, 441; *q*.155, 211
Root, Elihu, 155, 159, 160*n*.; *q*.158
Root-Takahira Agreement (1908), 327
Rosebury, Theodor, *c*.680
Rosenberg, Alfred, 140*n*., 469
Rosenberg, Ethel, 601, 667*n*.
Rosenberg, Julius, 601, 667*n*.
Ross, Charles G., 664*n*.
Rossbach, *B.*, 76
Rossi, A., *c*.497
Rossinger, Lawrence K., *c*.650
Rostovtzeff, M., *c*.54
Rostow, W. W., *c*.524, 541
Rotary International, 588
Rougement, Denis de, 266
Rousseau, Jean Jacques, 16, 205; *q*.203
Rovere, Richard H., *c*.607
Rowe, David Nelson, *d*.541
Roxanna, 44
Royal Dutch Shell, 379
Royal Institute of International Affairs, *c*.607
Ruanda-Urundi, 328, 331
Rudenko, R. A., 140
Ruhr, 146, 469, 484, 486
Rumania, 87, 91*f.*, 96*f.*, 111, 196, 198, 251, 477, 514, 556
Rundstedt, Gerd von, 482, 508
Runes, Dagobert D., *c*.54
Russell, Bertrand, 668
Russell, E. John, *c*.650
Russell, Frank M., *c*.104, 575
Russell, Lord, of Liverpool, *c*.497
Russia: 59, 60, 78, 83, 85*f.*, 91*ff.*, 498*ff.*; *W*. Japan (1904*f.*), 88, 149, 441*f.*; *W*. Turkey, 86*f.* (*See also* USSR)
Rydz-Smigly, Edward, 557
Ryukyu Islands, 199

Saar Valley, 94, 213, 215, 345, 475. 487, 677*f.*
Saavedra Lamas Anti-War Treaty, *q*.152
Saburov, Maxim Z., 520*f.*
Sachar, Abram L., *c*.395
Sachs, Alexander, 655
Said bin Taimor, 430
Said Pasha, 399
St. Augustine, 50
St. Germain, *T.*, 94, 213
St. Isidore, 57
St. Laurent, Louis, 611
Saint-Pierre, Abbé, 205
Saito, Hirosi, 254, *d*.443
Sakai, Naka, 124*n*.

Sakhalin, 195, 199, 441, 444*f.*, 453, 479, 514
Sakiet-Sidi-Youssef, 373
Salahben Youssef, 373
Salamis, *B.*, 39
Salandra, Antonio, 218
Salisbury, Lord, 155
Salomon, Ernst von, *c*.497
Salvemini, Gaetano, *c*.467
Samoa, 326, 331, 332
Samuel, Maurice, *c*.28, 393*n*.
San Francisco: *C.* (1945), 227*f.*; *C.* (1951), 199
San Marino, 111*n*., 501
Sanctions, 138, 221*ff.*
Sandys, Duncan, *c*.586
Sanger, Richard H., *c*.432
Sansom, G. B., *c*.455
Santayana, George, *c*.28
Saracens, 51, 58*f.*
Saragat, Giuseppe, 462, 465*f.*
Sarajevo, 91
Sarasin, Pote, 385, 611
Sardinia, 87
Sargent, William, *c*.305
Sargon of Akkad, 33
Sargon II, 36
Sarrazac, Robert, 267
Sastroamidjojo, Ali, 390, 642
Satellites, earth, 3, 121*n*., 259, 673
Sato, Naotake, 438
Satow, Sir Ernest, *q*.166; *c*.202
Sauckel, Fritz, 140*n*.
Saud, King, 426*f.*
Saudi Arabia: 322, 375, 406*ff.*, 426*ff.*; USA *T.* (1957), 427
Savonarola, 63
Sayre, Francis B., 332
Scalapino, Robert A., *c*.455
Scelba, Mario, 465
Schacht, Hjalmar, 140*n*.
Schaefer, Karl, 485
Schaeffer, Fritz, 491
Schaerf, Adolf, 200
Schattschneider, E. E., *c*.395
Schechtman, Joseph B., *c*.650
Schiffer, Walter, *c*.143
Schiklgruber, Maria, 469
Schiller, A. Arthur, *c*.395
Schirach, Baldur von, 140*n*.
Schlabrendorff, Fabian von, *c*.292*n*.
Schleicher, Kurt von, 472, 474
Schlesinger, Arthur M., Jr., *c*.607
Schleswig, 345
Schlieffen, Alfred von, 299
Schlieffen Plan, 91
Schmitt, Bernadotte E., *c*.104

737

Schoenbrun, David, c.575
Schoetensach, Otto, 13
Schrecklichkeit, 129
Schrödinger, Erwin, c.11n.
Schroeder, Kurt von, 472
Schubert, Jack, c.680
Schulenberg, Friedrich Werner von der, 482
Schumacher, Kurt, 485, d.488
Schuman, F. L. (other publications cited), c.21n., 104, 105, 260n., 265n., 266n., 270, 281n., 289n., 393n., 404n., 422n., 478n., 491, 517n., 524, 616n., 648n.
Schuman, Robert, 366, 564, 566f.
Schuman Plan, 266, 366, 487, 568
Schumpeter, Joseph A., c.335, 395
Schurr, Sam H., c.680
Schuschnigg, Kurt, 459; c.497
Schuster, M., c.335
Schwartz, Benjamin I., c.541, 553
Schwartz, Harry, c.525
Schwarz, Paul, c.497
Schwarzenberger, Georg, 143; c.305
Schwebel, Stephen M., c.270
Schweitzer, Albert, 668
Scott, John, c.305, 525
Scullard, H. H., c.54
Scythians, 37
Seabury, Paul, c.202
Searles, Fred, 662
Secret diplomacy, 192
Security risks, 180
Segni, Antonio, 465, 466
Segregation, racial, 639
Segregation cases, 356
Selassie, Haile, 220, 646; q.222ff.
Self-determination, 343ff.
Self-preservation, right of, 115
Seljuk (clan of Turks), 60
Sennacherib, 36
Sepoy Rebellion, 381
Serbia, 86, 87, 91, 111 (See also Jugoslavia)
Serov, Ivan A., 545
Serraj, Abdul Hamid, 430
Service, John Stewart, 181, 533
Servien, Abel, 167
Sevastopol, B., 480
Seven Weeks' War, 87
Seven Years' War, 77
Seversky, Alexander de, 299
Sèvres, T., 94, 213
Seyss-Inquart, Arthur, 140n.
Sforza, Carlo, q.462; c.467
Sforza, Caterina, 63
Shafer, Boyd C., c.395
Shakespeare, William, q.24, 555, 575

Shanghai, 147; B. (1932), 218, 254
Shantung, 441
Sharm el Sheik, 419ff., 423ff.
Shaw, G. B., q.336
Shawcross, Hartley, 140; q.226
Shcherbakov, Alexander S., 517
Shea, Donald R., c.165
Shepherd, Gordon, 547
Shepilov, Dmitri T., 406f., 413ff., 428, 520f., 545
Sherman, William T., q.128
Sherwood, Robert E., 267; c.607
Shidehara, Kijuro, 440, 449f.
Shigemitsu, Mamoru, 141, 440, 453f.
Shih-Huang-Ti, 38
Shiites, 58, 321
Shikotan, 454
Shils, Edward A., c.273n.
Shinto, 448f.
Shipley, Ruth, 186
Shirer, William L., c.497
Shishakly, Adib, 375
Short, W. C., 446
Shub, David, c.525
Shugg, Rodger W., c.105
Shute, Nevile, c.678n.
Shvernik, Nikolai M., 520n.
Shwadran, Benjamin, c.432
Si Bekkai, 371
Siam, 385 (See also Thailand)
Siberia, 441 (See also Russia; USSR)
Sidi Mohammed al-Amin, 373
Sidi Mohammed ben Arafa, 371
Simmons, Ernest J., c.525
Simon, John, 218, 254, 579
Simpson, J. L., c.496
Sinai, W. (1956f.), 417ff.
Singapore, 387f.
Sirry Pasha, 402
Skilling, Gordon H., c.202
Slansky, Rudolf, 543, 550
Slessor, John, c.305
Smith, Adam, c.358, 615, 619
Smith, Alexander, 610
Smith, Dale O., c.305
Smith, Elliott, 16n.
Smith, Howard K., 547
Smith, Louis, c.305, 607
Smith, T. Lynn, c.650
Smith, Walter Bedell, 199
Smith, Wilbur M., c.680
Smith Act (USA), 181
Smolenski Boulevard, 183
Smuts, Jan, 212
Smyth, Henry deWolf, 657; c.680
Snell, H. Gordon, c.202
Snow, Edgar, c.541

Snyder, Louis L., *c.*395, 497
Snyder, Richard Carlton, *c.*395, 607
Sobell, Martin, 667*n.*
Sobolev, Arkady, 230
Socialist parties: French, 564*ff.*; German, 473, 485*ff.*; Indian, 635*ff.*; Italian, 462*ff.*; Japanese, 450*ff.*
Socony-Vacuum, 379
Sohn, Louis B., *c.*270
Sokolsky, George E., *q.*284*n.*
Solomon, 36
Somaliland, 332, 374, 460
Somervell, D. C., 21, *c.*587
Somme, *B.*, 92
Somoza, Anastasio, *q.*631
Songgram, Pibul, 385, 611
Sontag, James, *c.*289*n.*
Soong, Ai-ling, 532
Soong, Charlie, 532
Soong, Ching-ling, 532
Soong, Mei-ling, 532
Soong, T. V., 532
South Africa, 163, 164, 637, 639*f.*
South-West Africa, 328, 332
Southeast Asia Treaty Organization (SEATO), 383, 385, 584, 609*ff.*, 644
Sovereignty, 66*f.*
Spaak, Paul Henri, 228, 266
Spaatz, Carl, 468
Spain: 78, 88, 225, 229, 609; Civil *W.*, 459, 558*f.*; *W.*, Succession, 75; *W.*, USA, 88, 109; World War II, 480
Sparta, 39*f.*
Spear, T. G., *c.*335
Speer, Albert, 140*n.*
Speidel, Hans, 491
Speier, Hans, *c.*304
Spellman, Cardinal, 464
Spencer, Herbert, 358
Spender, Percy, 626
Spengler, Oswald, 19*f.*, 653; *q.*20, 55, 278; *c.*28
Spheres of influence, 326*f.*
Spies, 130, 138
Spiro, Melford E., *c.*335
Spratly Islands, 199
Sprout, Harold, *c.*305
Sprout, Margaret, *c.*305
Spruance, R., 97
Sputniks, 3, 121*n.*, 673
Spychalski, Marian, 413
Spykman, Nicolas J., 301; *c.*300*n.*, 305
Squires, Richard, *c.*283*n.*
Staley, Eugene, *c.*395, 650
Stalin, J. V., 99, 101, 115, 139, 195, 414, 438, 463, 469, 474, 502*ff.*, 505*ff.*, 508*ff.*, *d.*517*f.*, 523, 533, 542, 549, 553, 592,

664; *q.*503*f.*, 509, 511, 513, 550, 659; *c.*280
Stalingrad, *B.*, 97, 481, 509*f.*
Standard Oil of California, 379
Standard Oil of New Jersey, 379
Stassen, Harold E., 259, 265
State: as legal person, 110*ff.*; origin of, 17*f.*, System, 23*ff.*
State Department (USA), 183*ff.* (*See also* specific secretaries of state)
Status-of-forces agreements, 124
Stauffenberg, Claus von, 482
Steed, Wickham, 267
Stephan, Heinrich von, 208
Stereotypes, 8
Sterling bloc, 361
Stettinius, Edward R., Jr., 183, 195, 236; *c.*608
Stevens, Edmund, *c.*395
Stevens, Wallace, *q.*2
Stevenson, Adlai E., 570, 598, 671; *q.*233*n.*, 246*n.*; *c.*608
Stillman, Calvin W., *c.*650
Stilwell, Joseph W., *q.*533
Stimson, Henry L., 446, 660; *q.*141, 283*n.*; *c.*455, 608
Stimson Doctrine, 120, 218, 224, 252
Stone, I. F., *c.*270
Stoph, Willi, 494
Straits (in international law), 122 (*See also* specific straits)
Strang, Lord, *c.*202
Strasser, Gregor, 474
Strategic areas, 332*n.*, 333
Strauss, Franz Josef, 493
Strauss, J. G. N., 639
Strauss, Lewis L., 670*ff.*; *q.*670
Strausz-Hupé, Robert, *c.*613, 680
Streicher, Julius, 140*n.*
Streit, Clarence K., 265, 266; *c.*270
Stresemann, Gustav, 254
Strong, Corrin L., 176
Strontium 90, 668
Strydom, Johannes G., *q.*639
Stuart, Graham H., *c.*202, 650
Stuart, J. Leighton, 535; *c.*541
Stumpf, Felix B., 369*n.*, 468
Suarez, Francisco, 68
Sudan, 111, 230, 326, 374, 402, 460, 646
Sudetendeutsche, 354
Sudetenland, 476
Suez Canal, 122, 147, 399*ff.*
Suez Canal Users Association, 410*ff.*
Sukarno, Achmed, 389*f.*, 545; *q.*389, 390, 643, 644
Suleiman the Magnificent, 61
Sully, Duc de, 204

INDEX

Sulzberger, Cyrus L., 609; c.432
Sumerians, 16, 32f.
Summit Conference (Geneva, 1955), 101, 238, 492, 544, 603, 670
Sun, 2f.
Sun Yat-sen, 527, 532, d.530
Sun Yat-sen, Mme., 530, 537
SUNFED, 625
Sung Dynasty, 526
Sunnites, 58, 321
Super-Ego, 25
Supreme Command, Allied Powers (SCAP), 449ff.
Suslov, Mikhail A., 416, 520n.
Suwirjo, 390
Suzerainties, 114
Suzuki, Kantoro, 438
Suzuki, Teiishi, q.445
Svarlien, Oscar, c.143
Swain, James Edgar, c.79
Swaraj, 381
Swearingen, Rodger, c.455
Sweden, 85, 516, 648
Sweezy, Paul M., c.20n.
Swing, Raymond, 267
Switzerland, 74, 157, 230, 647
Swope, Bayard, 662
Sykes-Picot Agreement (1916), 322
Syria, 111, 324, 375, 399ff., 406ff., 427, 430, 606n.
Syrkin, Marie, c.393n.
Szalai, Andras, 415
Szoenyi, Tibor, 415

Tachen Islands, 603
Taft, Ronald R., c.650
Taft, William Howard, 211; q.155, 360n.
Tahmassebi, Khalil, 377
Taine, Hippolyte Adolphe, q.336
Taiping rebellion, 526
Takahashi, Korekayo, d.443
Takeuchi, Sterling, c.455
Talal, King, 375, 429
Talib bin Ali, 430
Tamerlane, 60
Tanaka Memorial, 280; q.438
Tanganyika, 331, 332
Tangier, 326, 371
Tannenbaum, Frank, c.305
Tannenberg, B., 91
Tannu Tuva, 514
Tansill, C. C., c.608
Tardieu, André, 204
Tariffs, 358ff., 364f.
Tate, Merze, c.270
Taylor, A. J. P., c.105

Taylor, Myron C., 169n.
Taylor, O. R., c.575
Taylor, Phillip B., Jr., c.118n.
Taylor, Robert Louis, c.587
Taylor, Telford, 140; c.487
Tedder, Arthur, 468
Teheran, C. (1943), 194
Tengku Abdul Rahman, 389
Tennessee Valley Authority, 663
Tertius Gaudens, 282
Teutoburger Wald, B., 468
Thailand, 385, 610f.
Thakin Nu, 385
Thalweg, 122
Thami el Glaoui, 371
Thanarat, Sarit, 385, 611
Thayer, Charles W., c.497
Thayer, Philip W., c.650
Themistocles, 39
Theodosius, 50
Thermopylae, B., 39
Theseus, 39
Thirty Years' War, 67, 73, 167
Thomas, A. J., Jr., c.165
Thomas, Ann Van Wymen, c.165
Thomas, Charles A., 662
Thomas, Elbert, 332n.
Thomas, Homer, c.497
Thomas, M. Albert, 216
Thomas, Norman, 266
Thompson, Dorothy, 266
Thompson, Llewellyn E., Jr., 176
Thompson, Ronald, c.524
Thompson, Warren S., c.650
Thomson, David, c.105, 575
Thomson, George, c.680
Thoreau, David, 381ff.
Thorez, Maurice, 564
Thothmes III, 34, 38
Threats of force, 145
3-mile limit, 121
Thucydides, q.40, 608
Thyssen, Fritz, 472
Tiberius, 47
Tibet, 540
Tiglath Pileser I, 36
Tilsit, C., 82
Timoshenko, Semyon K., 508
Tiran, Strait, 419ff.
Tirol, 346
Tito, Josip Broz, 195, 199, 413ff., 463, 520f., 550f., 604, 644
Titoism, 414ff., 452, 463
Tocqueville, Alexis de, q.177, 587, 617
Tod, Marcus N., c.54
Togliatti, Palmiro, 414, 462, 465f., 551
Togo, Shigenori, 141n., 445; c.455

Togoland, 328*f.*, 331, 332
Tojo, Hideki, 141, 445; *q.*448
Tokyo War Crimes trials, 139*f.*
Tolstoy, Leo, 381
Toltec-Aztec culture, 16
Tonelli, Giovanni, 464
Torgau, 483
Totalitarianism, 435*ff.*
Tours, *B.*, 51, 59
Towle, Lawrence W., *c.*395
Towster, Julian, *c.*525
Toynbee, Arnold J., 17, 19*f.*, 547, 653, 671; *q.*20, 21, 291, 297*f.*, 391*f.*, 582; *c.*28, 293*n.*, 305
Toynbee, Veronica M., 547
Trajan, 47
Trans-Jordan, 324 (*See also* Jordan)
Transylvania, 345
Trasimene, *B.*, 46
Treaties (major modern) and other international acts, arranged chronologically and paragraphed by centuries and, more recently, by decades: (*See also* list of treaties following Contents)
Westphalia, 73, 74, 167; Utrecht, 71, 75; Hubertusburg and Paris, 77; USA-France, 589*ff.*; Jay, 152*f.*
Louisiana Purchase, 85; Ghent, 85, 145; Paris, 85; Aix-la-Chapelle, 76; Paris, 87; Cobden, 358; Berlin, 87; Dual Alliance, 89; Hague Conventions, 128, 131, 133*n.*, 135, 154, 156, 158; *q.*149, 151, 152
Portsmouth, 441; Root-Takahira, 327; Bryan-Chamorro, 159; Sykes-Picot, 322; Lansing-Ishii, 327; Versailles, 93*f.*, 130, 138, 146, 328, 475; St. Germain, 94, 213; Neuilly, 94, 213; Trianon, 94, 213; Sèvres, 94, 213; Minority, 350
Five Power, 253; Nine Power, 127; Rapallo, 471; Cecil-Requin, *q.*250; Lausanne, 94, 215; USA-Germany, *q.*364*n.*; Anglo-Soviet, 188; Locarno, 249, 250, 252, 476; Pact of Paris, 141, 218, 250*f.*, *q.*251; London Naval, 254, 255
Argentine Anti-war, 120; *q.*152; Germany-Poland, 475*f.*; Anglo-German Naval, 255, 475*f.*; USSR-France, 503, 557; Czechoslovakia-France, 557; USSR-Czechoslovakia, 503; Anti-Comintern, 95, 476; *q.*443; Ciano-Perth, 224; Munich, 226, 476, 503, 559; Anglo-German nonaggression, 476; French-German nonaggression, 476, 560; German-Italian, 460; Soviet-German nonaggression, *q.*475*f.*, 505; French-Turkish, 560
Triplice, 479, 481; USSR-Japan, 441, 444; Anglo-Soviet, 194, *q.*581; French-Soviet, 567; Sino-Soviet, 534; Peace (1947), 197*f.*, 463; USA-Philippines, 319; Anglo-French, 567; Brussels, 567, 570; NATO, 567, 589, 597*ff.*; *q.*609; Geneva, 132; Genocide, 132
Sino-Soviet, 543; Japan, 199, 452; USA-Japan, 200, 596; USA-Philippines, 597; USA-New Zealand, 597; USA-Australia, 597; USA-German, 598; USA-Formosa, 602*f.*, Baghdad Pact, 383, 405*ff.*, 426, 427, 431, 609; Paris (1954), 490; Warsaw Pact, 494, 544, 554; Austria (1955), 168, 198, 200, 603; USSR-Japan, 454, 545; Tunisia-Morocco, 373; USA-Saudi Arabia, 427
Treaty making: 32*f.*, 109, 125*f.*; arbitration, 154*f.*; commercial, 327, 363*ff.*; "cooling off," 152; Greek, 41*f.*; Roman, 47; U.K., 188; USA, 187
Treitschke, Heinrich von, *q.*72
Trevor-Roper, H. R., *c.*497
Trianon, *T.*, 94, 213
Trieste, 464, 465
Triple Alliance (1882), 89
Triple Entente, 89
Triplice Pacts, 96, 444, 460, 477, 479
"Trojan Horsemen," 287
Troppeau, *C.* (1820), 206
Trotsky, Leon, 503; *c.*525
Troy, 39
Truce of God, 57
Trujillo, Rafael L., 632
Truman, Harry S., 101, 180, 195, 257, 333, 438, 452, 550, 582, 596, 658, 660, 662*ff.*; *q.*367, 535, 595, 622*n.*, 625*f.*, 658*ff.*, 670; *c.*608
Truman Doctrine, 246, 427, 550, 581, 595
Trusteeship Council, 331*f.*
Tsiang, T. S., 230
Tubman, William V. S., 646
Tugwell, Rexford G., 267
Tunisia, 89; independence, 111, 334, 372*f.*, 570, 572
Turkey, 60, 92, 96*f.*, 251, 430*f.*, 606*n.*; and Cyprus, 612; *T.*, France, 560; *T.*, Sèvres, 213; and USSR, 507
Turner, Ralph E., *c.*54

U Nu, 642
Uganda, 638, 646
Ughet, Serge, 170
Ukraine, 185 (*See also* USSR)

Ulam, Adam B., *c*.432
Ulbricht, Walter, 485, 487, 494
Ulianov, Vladimir Ilych (*see* Lenin)
Ultimate destination, 135
Umberto, King, 462
Umezh, Yoshijiro, 440
Umma, 33
UNAEC, 666*ff*.
UNCOK, 241*f*., 244
UNCURK, 244
UNESCO, 234; *c*.10*n*., *c*.273*n*.
Union of International Associations, 209
Union of South Africa, 349*f*.
Union of Soviet Socialist Republics: 195,
  498*ff*.; 1939*f*., 96*f*., 1956*f*., 399*ff*.;
  atomic weapons, 668*ff*.; "backward"
  areas, 645; Berlin blockade (1948*f*.),
  199; diplomatic ruptures, 145*f*.; disarmament, 256*f*.; foreign service, 182;
  and Germany, 485*ff*.; and Iran (1946),
  236; Ministry of Foreign Affairs, 185;
  and national minorities, 349*f*.; nonrecognition, 169*f*.; population, 623*f*.;
  recognition, 113*n*.; and UN, 229*f*.;
  and USA, 521*f*.
  major treaties (chronologically): Rapallo, 471; U.K. (1924), 188; Pact
  of Paris, 251; Czechoslovakia (1935),
  503; France (1935), 503; Germany
  (1939), 476; Japan (1941), 444;
  U.K. (1942), 194; *q*.581; France
  (1944), 534; China (1945), 534;
  China (1950), 543; Japan (1956),
  454, 545
  major wars (chronologically): USA and
  Allies, 500*f*.; Poland, 501*f*.; Finland
  (1939*f*.), 226, 499, 507; World War
  II, 507–512; Cold War, 514*ff*.
Union for the Suppression of African Slave
  Trade, 209
United Arab Republic, 431
United Fruit Company, 316
United Kingdom: 575*ff*., 582; 1815*f*., 85*f*.;
  1914*f*., 91*f*.; 1939*f*., 96*f*.; 1956*f*., 399*ff*.;
  atomic warfare, 669*ff*.; Battle of Brit-
  ain, 478; diplomatic rupture, USSR,
  145*f*.; Empire, 309; foreign affairs,
  188; Foreign Office, 184; foreign serv-
  ice, 182; German Naval Pact (1935),
  225, 475*f*.; optional clause, 164; Par-
  liament, 188; Treaty making, 188 (*See
  also* Treaties; Wars)
United Nations: 96, 227*ff*.; budget, 231;
  Charter, 227*f*., 247, 256, *q*.681*ff*.;
  China, 230, 244; Cold War, 235;
  Collective Measures Committee, 244;
  Committee for Conventional Arma-

  ments, 256; Covenant of Human
  Rights, 355; Declaration of Human
  Rights, 355; *q*.193; disarmament,
  257*f*.; Economic and Social Council,
  228, 233; Emergency Force, 423*f*.;
  Food and Agriculture Organization,
  234; General Assembly, 228*f*., 233*f*.,
  247; Good Offices Committee, 245;
  India, 240; Indonesia, 238; Iran
  (1946), 236; Japan, 230; Kashmir,
  240; Korean *W*., 132, 133*n*., 136,
  242*f*.; "Little Assembly," 237; Malaya, 230; membership, 229*f*.; Military Staff Committee, 232; 1956*ff*.,
  399*ff*.; Outer Mongolia, 220; Pakistan,
  240; Palestine, 238*f*.; Secretariat, 231;
  Secretary-General, 163, 215, 229*f*., 231;
  Security Council, 228*f*., 231*f*.; Spain,
  229; Switzerland, 230; Trusteeship
  Council, 330*ff*., UNRRA, 535; USA,
  229*f*.; USSR, 229*f*.; vetoes, 229*f*.,
  233*n*.; War Crimes, 139; *c*.270, 432
United States of America: 88, 145, 587*ff*.;
  arbitration, 154*f*.; atomic warfare,
  669*ff*.; "backward" areas, 646; China,
  186, 533*ff*.; Constitution of 1787,
  187*f*., 261*f*.; *q*.189, 264; Department
  of State, 183*f*.; *c*.202; disarmament,
  256*f*.; foreign affairs, 188; foreign
  trade, 363, 367*ff*., Foreign Service,
  179*f*.; Germany, 485*ff*., Japan, 445*ff*.,
  minorities, 348; neutrality laws, 136;
  1956, 399*ff*., 405*ff*.; optional clause,
  164; recognition policy, 113*n*., 169*f*.;
  Senate and foreign affairs, 187; Supreme Court, 181 (*See also* specific
  cases); tariff policy, 365*ff*.; travel,
  186; trusteeship, 333; UN, 229*f*.,
  USSR, 521*f*.; World Court, 160*n*., 162
  major treaties: 85, 112, 187, 589*ff*., 598,
  602*f*. (*See also* NATO; SEATO;
  Treaties)
  major wars (chronologically): American Revolution, 77*f*., 133; 1812, 85,
  145, 149, 590; Civil, 88, 112, 134,
  138; Spanish-American, 88, 109;
  World War I, 91*f*., World War II,
  96*f*., 592*ff*.; Korea, 132, 133*n*., 136
U.S. v. Curtis-Wright Export Corporation,
  q.188*n*.
U.S. v. McCullagh, 190*n*.
U.S. v. Shauver, 189–190*n*.
United World Federalists, 267
Uniting for Peace resolution, 244
Universal Postal Union, 208*f*., 234
Unneutral service, 134
UNTCOK, 241

INDEX

Upper Silesia, 94, 345
Uranium, 655*ff.*
Urban II, 57
Utley, Freda, 534, 541
Utrecht, *C.* and *T.*, 71, 75, 167

V-2, 294
Vagts, Alfred, *c.*305
Valens, 50
Valentin, Veit, *c.*497
Van Alstyne, Richard W., *c.*608
Vandals, 51
Vandenberg, Arthur, 162*n.*, 662
Vandenberg resolution, 595, 609
Vandenbosch, Amry, *c.*270, 332*n.*
Vanguard, 673*n.*
Vanzetti, Bartolomeo, *q.*268
Vargas, Getulio, 630
Vatican, 113*n.*, 169*n.*, 463, 464, 473
Vatican City, 111*n.*
Vattel, Emeric de, *q.*71, 115
Vatutin, Nikolai, 511
Vayo, Alvarez del, 225
Veblen, Thorstein, *c.*285*n.*
Venezuela, 632
Venice, Republic of, 62
Venus, 3
Veracruz, 146
Verdi, Giuseppe, 400
Verdun, *B.*, 92
Vergil, 45
Vermeil, Edmond, *c.*496
Vernadsky, George, *c.*525
Verona (1823), *C.*, 206
Versailles, *T.*, 93*f.*, 130, 138, 146, 213, 218, 328, 475
Vespucci, Amerigo, 633
Veterans of Foreign Wars, 268
Victor Emmanuel, 87, 150, 456, 460, 462
Videla, Gabriel Gonzalez, 145
Vienna: *C.* (1814*f.*), 84, 167; *C.* (1955), 200, 206
Vietnam, 111, 114, 200, 387, 540, 544, 569*f.*, 610
Vikings, 59*f.*, 498
Villard, Henry Serrano, *c.*395
Villari, Luigi, *c.*467
Vinacke, Harold M., *c.*105, 455, 541
Vincent, John Carter, 181, 533
Vinci, Leonardo da, 81
Vines, Kenneth N., *c.*607
Virginius, 116*n.*
Vishinsky, Andrei Y., 195*f.*, 236, 241, 514, 543; *q.*237, 257, 658
Vittoria, 68
Vladivostok, 122

Voegelin, Eric, *c.*29
Voice of America, 185*n.*, 413
Volstead, Andrew, 588
Voronov, N. N., 511
Voroshilov, K. E., 505, 508, 520*n.*
Voznesensky, Nikolai A., 520

Waddy, Lawrence, *q.*45; *c.*54
Wagner, Robert, *q.*426
Waithayakon, Wan, 386, 610
Wales, Nym, *c.*541
Walker, Eric A., *c.*587
Walker, Richard L., *c.*541
Wallace, Henry A., 265, 311, 533, 626, 660, 665; *q.*595
Walpole, Robert, *q.*71
Walsingham, Francis, *q.*272
Waltari, Mika, *q.*30
Walter, Gerard, *c.*54
Walters, F. P., *c.*270
Wambaugh, Sarah, *c.*395
Wang Ching-wei, 114, 532
Wang Shih Chieh, 196
War: 144, 272*f.*, 284*f.*; costs, 295*f.*, crimes, 138*f.*; declarations, 128*f.*; debts, 362; law of, 127*f.*; nationalism, 338*f.*; outlawry, 249*f.*
Warburg, James P., *c.*497, 608
Ward, Lester, *c.*18*n.*
Ward, Barbara, *c.*613
Warne, William E., *c.*650
Warren, Earl, 588
Wars (major, chronologically): Peloponnesian, 40; Punic, 46; Wars of Religion, 73; Thirty Years', 67, 73, 167; Spanish Succession, 75; Austrian Succession, 76; Seven Years', 77; French and Indian, 76; American Revolution, 77*f.*, 133; French Revolution, 82*f.*; Peninsular, 83; 1812, 85, 145, 149, 590; Liberation (German), 475; Crimean, 86*f.*, 499; American Civil, 88, 112, 134, 138; Seven Weeks', 87; Franco-Prussian, 87*f.*, 207*f.*; Russo-Turkish, 86*f.*; China (1894), 441; Spanish-American, 88, 109; Russo-Japanese (1904), 88, 149, 441*f.*; Balkan, 87
World War I, 91*f.*, 132; costs, 295*f.* (*See also* names of belligerent States); economic consequences, 361*f.*; Russo-Polish (1920), 500*f.*; Spanish Civil, 558*f.*; China (1937*f.*), 444*f.*
World War II, 96*f.*, 132, 136, 444*ff.*, 460*ff.*, 480, 506*ff.*, 525*ff.*, 531*ff.*, 561*ff.*, 579, 592*ff.*; costs, 295*f.*; economic con-

743

sequences, 362*f.*; USSR-Finland, 226, 499, 507 (*See also* specific belligerent States); "Cold War," 99*f.* (*See also* USA, USSR); Palestine (1948*f.*), 238, 377; Indochina, 385*f.*; Korean, 132, 133*n.*, 136; Hungarian Revolution, 101, 118, 413*ff.*; Algeria, 322, 334, 372, 407, 509, 570*ff.*, 612, 637

World War III, xii, 101, 132, 495, 583, 600, 670*ff.*

Warsaw, *B.*, 502

Warsaw ghetto, *B.*, 353

Warsaw Pact, 258, 494, 544, 554

Washington, George, 589*f.*; *q.*641

Washington Conference (1921*f.*), 253*f.*

Washington Post, *q.*525*n.*

Watanobe, Jotaro, *d.*443

Waterloo, *B.*, 84

Waters, M. Ter, *q.*223

Watt, James, 81

Way, Katharine, *c.*680

Webb, Walter Prescott, *c.*79

Webb, William, 140

Weber, Elizabeth, *c.*337*n.*

Webster, Daniel, 118; *q.*116

Wecter, Dixon, *c.*105

Wedemeyer, Albert, 533*f.*; *q.*536

Weigert, Hans W., *c.*305

Weis, P., *c.*143

Weizmann, Chaim, 351, 375, *d.*377

Weldon, T. D., *c.*29

Welles, Sumner, 508

Wellington, Duke of, 83

Wellington Koo, V. K., 162*n.*; *q.*226

Wells, H. G., *c.*678*n.*

Wendt, Gerald, *q.*294; *c.*680

Wendt, Herbert, *c.*29

Werner, Max, *c.*305

Werth, Alexander, *c.*575

Wertheim, W. F., *c.*395

Westerfield, H. Bradford, *c.*608

Western European Union, 570

Westlake, John, *c.*143

Westphalia, *C.*, 73*f.*, 167, 191

Weygand, Karl von, *q.*284*n.*

Weygand, Maxime, 559, 561; *q.*563

Weymar, Paul, *c.*497

Wheeler-Bennett, J. W., *c.*491

Whitaker, Arthur P., *c.*650

White, Lyman Cromwell, *c.*270

White, Lynn, Jr., *c.*29

White, Theodore H., *c.*105, 542

White, William Allen, 591

White Armies (Russian Civil War), 502

Whitehall, 183

Whitman, Walt, 588

Whitney, Courtney, *c.*270

Whitney, John Hay, 175

Whitney, Vincent, *c.*680

Wilbur, Martin C., *c.*542

Wilcox, Francis O., *c.*270, 608

Wild, P. S., Jr., *c.*165

Wilgus, A. Curtis, *c.*650

Wilhelm II, 80, 138, 475

Wilhelmina, Queen, 150

Wilhelmstrasse, 182

Willcox, William B., *c.*587

Williams, Francis, *c.*587

Williams, Harold F., *c.*651

Williams, Philip, 575

Williams, William Appleman, *c.*525

Williams v. Suffolk Insurance Co., 112*n.*

Willkie, Wendell, 265; *c.*105

Wilmot, Chester, 547; *c.*289*n.*

Wilson, Brewster A., 380*n.*

Wilson, G. G., *q.*117; *c.*165

Wilson, Robert, 660

Wilson, Robert Renbert, *c.*143

Wilson, Woodrow, 113*f.*, 159, 160, 169, 183, 217; *q.*93, 137, 191, 211*ff.*, 344

Winant, John G., 216

Windrich, Elaine, *c.*587

Winfield, Gerald F., *c.*542

Winiarski, Bohdan, 162*n.*

Winne, Harry A., 662

Winslow, E. M., *c.*335

Wiskemann, Elizabeth, *c.*497

Wittfogel, Karl A., *c.*542

Witzleben, Erwin von, 482

Wolfe, Bertram D., *c.*525

Wolfe, James, 76

Wolfe, Thomas, *q.*1

Wolfers, Arnold, *c.*587

Wolff, Theodor, *c.*105

Wolsey, Cardinal, 70

Wood, Robert, 591

Woodman, Dorothy, *c.*395

Woolbert, Robert Gale, *c.*105

Wooton, Barbara, 267

World Court, 160*f.*, 163, 218 (*See also* International Court of Justice; Permanent Court of International Justice)

World federation, 265*ff.*

World Health Organization, 234

World Movement for World Federal Government, 267

World Revolution, 499, 523, 548*ff.*

Wotton, Henry, *q.*166

Woytinsky, W. S., *c.*395, 651

Wrangel, Peter, 114

Wright, Quincy, *q.*329*n.*; *c.*29, 143, 202, 252*n.*, 270, 285*n.*, 305, 335, 680

Wright, Richard, *c.*651

INDEX

Wu, Aitchen K., c.542
Wu, Yuan-li, c.542
Wu Hsiu-chuan, 244
Wu-Pei-fu, 527
Wynner, Edith, c.270
Wyszynski, Stefan Cardinal, 413

Xenophon, 37
Xerxes, 39

Yalta, C., 99f., 195, 232, 514, 534, 595
Yamashita, Tomoyuki, 140n.
Yanaon, 570
Yap, 328
Ybarnegary, Jean, 563
Yemen, 322, 406, 430, 431, 536
Yen Hsi-shan, 530f.
Yeremenko, A. I., 511
York, E., c.270

Yoshida, Shigeru, 450ff.
Young Plan, 362
Yuan Shih Kai, 527

Zafrulla Khan, Muhammad, 162n., 384
Zahedi, Fezollah, 379
Zama, B., 46
Zeeland, Paul van, 223
Zeitzler, Kurt, 482
Zellerback, James P., 176
Zeno, 30
Zhdanov, Andrei, 505, 517
Zhukov, Georgi K., 413, 430, 468, 482f.,
    509, 511, 519ff.
Zilliacus, Koni, c.105
Zinner, Paul E., c.432
Zionism, 238, 324, 350, 351, 375ff., 393
Zoli, Adone, 466
Zoricic, Miloran, 162n.
Zorin, Valerian A., 259

INDEX

Wu, Ch'eng-en, 37
Wu, Tsao-li, 62
Wu Hsu-chang, 244
Wu Pa-in, 521
Wynne, John C., 250
Wyszynski, Stefan Cardinal, 414

Yamataka, 37
Yaran, 20

Yalta Conference, 102, 213, 511, 541, 595
Yenan blacks, Little, ...
Yangtze, 250
Yap, 522
Yoshigami, Isao, 70
Yunan, 278, 400, 402, 403, 500
Yen, Hsi-shan, 290
Yremenko, A. I., 271
Yeh, K., 570

Zabihi, Sukarno, 438
Zumin, Djoku, 62
Zorin shun Dai, 52

Zahedi, Khan Mohammad, 192, 331
Zahuri, Fazullah, 79
Zana, 46
Zeeland, Paul Van, 224
Zander, Kurt, 482
Zukerman, Harry S., 176
Zenn, 20
Zeum, Julius, 267, 511
Zhukov, Georg K., 113, 130, 860, 962, 360, 511, 1109
Zillmann, Anna, 1106
Zunns, Paul E., 155
Zunma, MD, 221, 266, 324, 327, 531
Zoli, Adone, 809
Zorzin, Mikojan, 936
Zorlu, Fatin Rustu, 329